West's Law School Advisory Board

CASES AND MATERIALS ON

INSURANCE LAW

Fifth Edition

By

Leo P. Martinez
Professor of Law
University of California, Hastings College of the Law

John W. Whelan
Professor of Law, Emeritus
University of California, Hastings College of the Law

AMERICAN CASEBOOK SERIES®

THOMSON
WEST

Mat # 40411661

610 Opperman Drive
P.O. Box 64526
St. Paul, MN 55164–0526
1–800–328–9352

ISBN–13: 978–0–314–16342–4
ISBN–10: 0–314–16342–5

TEXT IS PRINTED ON 10% POST CONSUMER RECYCLED PAPER

This edition is dedicated to my girls, Sharon, Jennifer, and Elizabeth. Their collective intellect, dedication, and work ethic is an inspiration.

LEO P. MARTINEZ

*

Preface to the Fifth Edition

We continued to be fascinated by the currents that flow through insurance law. From the seemingly mundane definition of "occurrence" that has multi-billion dollar consequences to resolving the question of whether hurricane winds allow recovery in the face of flood exclusions, insurance law continues to challenge human ingenuity in the crafting, interpretation, and results of insurance policy language. While we have attempted to keep pace with most developments, the rate of change is sometimes overwhelming. Thus, our aim is to acquaint the student with an array of information that can serve as a base of knowledge from which to further delve into an arcane subject.

We are grateful for the constructive suggestions we have received for the improvement of the text over the past years. In that spirit we continue to solicit input. Any colloquy can be directed to martinez@uchastings.edu.

LEO P. MARTINEZ
JOHN W. WHELAN

*

Acknowledgments

The authors wish to acknowledge the following:

Tom McCarthy, Director of Scholarly Publications at the University of California, Hastings College of the Law, for his editorial skills and for his keen eye.

Simone Katz, a student at the University of California, Hastings College of the Law, and Cate Paskoff Chang, a student at Columbia University School of Law, for their insights and for their diligent and able research assistance.

The Insurance Services Office, Inc. (ISO) and Ms. Ellen B. Soliwoda of the ISO for providing the license to use the ISO forms that appear in the Appendix.

*

Editors' Note

In editing cases and materials we have deleted some citations and footnotes without any indication. Otherwise, the remaining footnotes are numbered consecutively within chapters and, in most cases, do not correlate with the original footnote number. Block deletions are indicated by three asterisks.

*

Summary of Contents

Page

Table of Contents

APPENDIX

Table of Cases

The principal cases are in bold type. Cases cited or discussed in the text are roman type. References are to pages. Cases cited in principal cases and within other quoted materials are not included.

CASES AND MATERIALS ON

INSURANCE LAW

Fifth Edition

*

INTRODUCTION

Insurance law is a unique vehicle for the study of the legal and political processes. It combines substantive doctrine with the pull me/push you hurly-burly of regulation and its politics. Moreover, because we all have some passing familiarity with insurance—whether by virtue of having an auto insurance policy, a health plan or being the owner or beneficiary of a life insurance policy—it is a subject that has personal consequences.

To start, insurance is an arcane subject with a language of its own. As a result, law students facing problems of understanding the insurance industry and interpretation of insurance contracts for the first time will encounter unfamiliar terms. Some of these terms are unique to insurance law, others have a more common legal coinage. To avoid confusion, the glossary at the end of the text offers definitions for some of the most commonly used insurance words or terms. Even then, some crucial terms, such as "occurrence," "bodily injury," and "property damage" must be gleaned from insurance policies themselves or be determined by a court.

At the outset it bears mention that ignorance of insurance issues can exact a high price. Although the New York lawyers in the case below avoided liability, they learned a valuable lesson.

DARBY & DARBY v. VSI INTERNATIONAL, INC.

Supreme Court, Appellate Division, First Department, New York, 2000.
701 N.Y.S.2d 50, 268 A.D.2d 270.

MEMORANDUM DECISION.

Orders, Supreme Court, New York County (Franklin Weissberg, J.), entered on or about September 1, 1998 and on or about March 23, 1999, which, in an action to recover a legal fee, inter alia, denied plaintiff law firm's motion for summary judgment on its cause of action for account stated, denied such motion insofar as it sought dismissal of defendants clients' counterclaims for malpractice alleging a failure to advise about the possibility of certain insurance coverage, and granted such motion insofar as it sought dismissal of defendants' counterclaim for malpractice alleging a failure to advise about the potential liability and costs associated with the use of certain products, unanimously modified, on the law, so as to grant those branches of plaintiff's motion seeking dismissal of the counterclaim for malpractice based upon the alleged failure to advise about the possibility of insurance coverage, and summary judgment on its cause of action for an account stated and, as so modified, affirmed, without costs.

The branch of plaintiff's motion challenging defendants' counterclaims alleging attorney malpractice and breach of fiduciary duty was brought pursuant to CPLR 3211. Accordingly, in addressing that application, the court will accept as true the allegations of the counterclaim, and consider whether they state a cause of action upon which relief may be granted.

These counterclaims allege that defendants retained plaintiff law firm to provide legal services in connection with defending them in an intellectual property infringement matter brought against defendant VSI International by Al–Site Corporation. It is asserted, in essence, that plaintiff committed both malpractice and a breach of its fiduciary duty, by failing to either inquire into defendants' insurance coverage, or to inform defendants of the possibility that their comprehensive general liability insurance coverage might cover the intellectual property infringement claim brought against them.

We conclude that the allegations contained in the defendants' answer are insufficient to support findings of either professional malpractice or breach of fiduciary duty. In the absence of a factual assertion that the scope of the task for which counsel was retained specifically included inquiry into the nature and extent of its insurance coverage and whether it was applicable to the claim, the retention of counsel for the defense of such an action simply does not include any responsibility for assisting the client in determining whether sources exist from which to pay for that defense and any ultimate liability finding.

There may be particular circumstances, such as personal injury actions arising out of automobile collisions, in which an attorney who is retained to defend an action has an obligation to bring to the client's attention the possible existence of an insurance policy applicable to the claim (see, Campagnola v. Mulholland, Minion & Roe, 148 A.D.2d 155, 543 N.Y.S.2d 516, affd. 76 N.Y.2d 38, 556 N.Y.S.2d 239, 555 N.E.2d 611). However, we find no support for the proposition that an attorney who was retained to defend a business client in intellectual property litigation has a duty to inquire into the existence, nature and scope of insurance policies previously procured by the client, and to determine whether any such policy provides the client with any entitlement in relation to the claim being litigated.

Nor does a lawyer's duty to advise his client as to all available causes of action or avenues of defense (see, Greenwich v. Markhoff, 234 A.D.2d 112, 650 N.Y.S.2d 704) translate into a broad duty to inquire into all the client's insurance coverage.

Defendants can point to no case in which a claim of attorney malpractice has been sustained based upon an alleged failure to advise a client to make a claim under an insurance policy, when the attorney was neither provided with the policy nor asked for advice as to the scope of its coverage. The one case in which such a claim was made, relied upon by the IAS court, Jordache Enters. v. Brobeck Phleger & Harrison, 56 Cal.Rptr.2d 661, revd. 18 Cal.4th 739, 76 Cal.Rptr.2d 749, 958 P.2d 1062, provides no support for imposition of the proposed duty upon counsel. The court's dismissal of the malpractice claim there was based upon Statute of Limitations grounds, so the most that can accurately be said about the case is that the court implicitly assumed the viability of such a claim; there is no indication that its merits were challenged and considered. The existence of this one case simply does not justify imposing upon an attorney in these circumstances the professional duty suggested by defendants.

Nor do we perceive any other justification in law for imposition of such a duty. It was defendants themselves who procured the general liability insurance policy, and they were chargeable with the knowledge of whether that insurance covered the pending litigation (cf., Hartford Fire Ins. Co. v. Baseball Off. of Commr., 236 A.D.2d 334, 654 N.Y.S.2d 21, lv. denied 90 N.Y.2d 803, 661 N.Y.S.2d 179, 683 N.E.2d 1053; Halstead Oil Co. v. Northern Ins. Co., 178 A.D.2d 932, 933, 579 N.Y.S.2d 266).

The existence of cases from various jurisdictions around the nation holding, in the context of declaratory judgment actions against insurers, that general commercial liability insurance policies may cover certain claims of intellectual property infringement does not warrant a different result. The vast majority of that case law developed after the period of plaintiff's representation of defendants; prior to that time, there were only a few decisions on the topic, they did not apply a uniform line of reasoning, and, given the jurisdictions in which they arose, there was no reason to suppose they were controlling over the claim against defendants.

The IAS court found it germane that successor counsel immediately pursued the question of insurance coverage with successful results. However, this Court will not impose an obligation upon a law firm not otherwise imposed by law, based upon the tasks performed by successor counsel.

However, we agree with the IAS court to the extent that, upon reargument, it dismissed as time-barred the counterclaim for malpractice first asserted in a motion for leave to serve an amended answer. That counterclaim's allegation that defendants retained plaintiff prior to the Al–Site action, for general patent and trademark advice regarding the use of the hanger tags, concerns conduct prior to, separate and different from the retainer alleged in defendants' original answer to defend the trademark litigation. Therefore, it is not saved by CPLR 203(f).

Finally, plaintiff is entitled to summary judgment on its cause of action for an account stated. There is no indication that any protest was made to the regularly issued invoices, aside from the bare assertion of oral protest contained in the unsupported affidavit of defendant Olinsky, and the excuse offered for the absence of any written objection to the bills is similarly vague and conclusory (see, Ruskin, Moscou, Evans & Faltischek, P.C. v. FGH Realty Credit Corp., 228 A.D.2d 294, 644 N.Y.S.2d 206).

Notes

1. Lawyers in other states have faced similar inquiries. California's experience is referred to in the principal case. See Jordache Enterprises, Inc. v. Brobeck, Phleger & Harrison, 18 Cal.4th 739, 76 Cal.Rptr.2d 749, 958 P.2d 1062 (1998) (dismissing the insured's legal malpractice claim based on the statute of limitations). While the lawyers in the *Jordache* case were saved by the statute of limitations, other lawyers have not been so fortunate. See Third Eye Blind, Inc. v. Near North Entertainment Insurance Services, LLC, 127 Cal.App.4th 1311, 1321–23, 26 Cal.Rptr.3d 452 (2005) (lawyer's failure to ascertain insurance coverage exposed them to liability for the resulting harm).

2. A good discussion of the principal case and the underlying issues is contained in article by Professor A. Samuel Oddi. Professor Oddi expresses a healthy skepticism about the result in the case and he suggests that the lawyers may have been fortunate to have escaped liability. A. Samuel Oddi, *Patent Attorney Malpractice: An Oxymoron No More*, 2004 U.Ill.J.L.Tech. & Pol'y 1, 15–19.

WHAT IS INSURANCE?

The foregoing begins with the underlying assumption that we each have an intuitive idea as to what insurance is. As the following cases illustrate, however, the definition is surprisingly elusive and intuition is not a safe guide.

It is an axiom of insurance law that coverage is available for risk of loss. Despite the idea that insurance necessarily deals with risk as a fundamental concept that there exists a high degree of uncertainty as to the boundaries of risk.[1] This uncertainty has been probed and examined as a matter of business strategy by several prominent studies and by experts who have catalogued the development of human thought regarding risk.[2] Still, risk finds itself imperfectly expressed in statute, case law, and policy language.

The events that form from our daily activities are by no means absolute. In even the most seemingly trivial rituals, there may be an underlying element of uncertainty. This aspect of uncertainty surfaces within the meaning of "risk," a fundamental element in any general definition of "insurance." In a standard automobile insurance contract, for example, the insurance company's agreement to pay sums of money to an insured person involved in an accident is contingent upon the accident actually occurring sometime in the future; the insurance company acknowledges the risk of a

1. Richard V. Ericson and Aaron Doyle, Uncertain Business: Risk Insurance and the Limits of Knowledge 5(2004).

2. *Id.*; Peter L. Bernstein, Against the Gods (1996)(aptly subtitled *The Remarkable Story of Risk*).

possible accident. Humankind's ability to master these and other kinds of risk defines, for many, what are modern times.[3]

Although state legislators have explained the individual intricacies relating to the concept of insurance in differing ways, the general meaning attached to each definition is similar. Connecticut General Statute § 38a–1 (1999), for example, defines insurance as "any agreement to pay a sum of money, provide services or any other thing of value on the happening of a particular event or contingency or to provide indemnity for loss in respect to a specified subject by specified perils in return for a consideration." California Insurance Code § 22 (2000) reflects the same meaning in a more concise explication: "Insurance is a contract whereby one undertakes to indemnify another against loss, damage, or liability arising from a contingent or unknown event." Finally, New York Consolidated Laws Services Ins. § 1101 (1999) explains an insurance contract as "any agreement or other transaction whereby one party, the 'insurer,' is obligated to confer benefit of pecuniary value upon the happening of a fortuitous event in which the 'insured' or 'beneficiary' has, or is expected to have at the time of such happening, a material interest which will be adversely affected by the happening of such event."

Each of the foregoing definitions, although phrased uniquely, shares two significant requirements. The first, as mentioned above, is a risk of loss, described as a "contingent or unknown event" or a "fortuitous event." These events are assumed to be substantially beyond the control of the contracting parties. Risk, in this context, is defined as "the degree of hazard or danger upon which the premiums of insurance are calculated."[4] The ultimate effect of an insurance contract is to allocate the risk of loss or damage to another party (the insurance company). The second condition essential to insurance involves a distribution of the risk among similarly situated persons.[5] However, these two requirements, alone, do not necessarily fit a contract within the broad insurance spectrum. Two further inquiries must be made: How do the specific transactions involve one or more of the evils at which the regulatory statutes are aimed, and are the "risk" elements essential or merely incidental to the other elements involved?[6] The following cases explore these questions in more detail.

GRIFFIN SYSTEMS, INC. v. OHIO DEPARTMENT OF INSURANCE

Supreme Court of Ohio, 1991.
61 Ohio St.3d 552, 575 N.E.2d 803.

SWEENEY, JUSTICE.

The determinative issue presented in this appeal is whether appellant's vehicle protection plans are contracts "substantially amounting to insurance" within the meaning of R.C. 3905.42. For the reasons that

3. *Id.* at 1.

4. People ex rel. Daily Credit Service Corp. v. May, 162 A.D. 215, 147 N.Y.S. 487, 489 (1914).

5. Metropolitan Life Insurance Co. v. State Board of Equalization, 32 Cal.3d 649, 654, 652 P.2d 426, 186 Cal.Rptr. 578 (1982).

6. Truta v. Avis Rent A Car System, Inc., 193 Cal.App.3d 802, 238 Cal.Rptr. 806 (1st Dist.1987).

follow, we answer such inquiry in the negative, and therefore reverse the judgment of the court of appeals and reinstate the trial court's judgment.

R.C. 3905.42 provides as follows:

> "No company, corporation, or association, whether organized in this state or elsewhere, shall engage either directly or indirectly in this state in the business of insurance, or enter into any contracts substantially amounting to insurance, * * * unless it is expressly authorized by the laws of this state, and the laws regulating it and applicable thereto, have been complied with."

Appellee ODI argues that the vehicle protection plans offered and sold by appellant are "contracts substantially amounting to insurance," and, thus, should be subject to the full array of insurance regulations within R.C. Title 39. ODI contends, and the court of appeals below agreed, that the key element that subjects appellant's protection plans to insurance laws and regulations is that appellant is neither the seller nor the manufacturer of the product it purports to warrant. ODI essentially asserts that extended warranties offered by sellers and manufacturers are part of the inducement process of making the product more desirable to the prospective buyer. Since appellant is an independent third party to the transaction, ODI submits that the claimed warranty appellant offers and sells is in reality a contract "substantially amounting to insurance."

The appellant, on the other hand, citing State, ex rel. Duffy v. Western Auto Supply Co. (1938), 134 Ohio St. 163, 11 O.O. 583, 16 N.E.2d 256, and State, ex rel. Herbert v. Standard Oil Co. (1941), 138 Ohio St. 376, 20 O.O. 460, 35 N.E.2d 437, contends that since its vehicle protection plans cover only those repairs necessitated by mechanical breakdown of defective parts, the protection plans constitute warranties and not contracts of insurance. Appellant relies on *Duffy*, supra, and argues that the instant vehicle protection plans limit reimbursement to loss due to defects in the product, and do not promise to reimburse loss or damage resulting from perils outside of and unrelated to defects in the product itself. Appellant submits that the issue of whether the seller or manufacturer (as opposed to an independent third party) offers or sells the type of contract in issue is wholly irrelevant.

In *Duffy*, supra, this court was asked to determine whether written guarantees issued by Western Auto covering tires it sold constituted contracts "substantially amounting to insurance" under G.C. 665. The language of one of the Western Auto guarantees stated that it protected the tires " 'against blowouts, cuts, bruises, rim-cuts, under-inflation, wheels out of alignment, faulty brakes or other road hazards that may render the tire unfit for further service (except fire and theft).' It then provided that 'In the event that the tire becomes unserviceable from the above conditions, we will (at our option) repair it free of charge, or replace it with a new tire of the same make at any of our stores, charging ..... th [sic] of our current price for each month which has elapsed since the date of purchase. The new tire will be fully covered by our regular guarantee in effect at time of adjustment. Furthermore: every tire is guaranteed against defects in material or workmanship without limit as to time, mileage or service.' " Id., at 165, 11 O.O. at 584, 16 N.E.2d at 257.

In finding that the Western Auto guarantees were contracts substantially amounting to insurance, this court held in *Duffy*, supra, at paragraphs three and four of the syllabus:

> "A warranty promises indemnity against defects in an article sold, while insurance indemnifies against loss or damage resulting from perils outside of and unrelated to defects in the article itself."
>
> "A contract whereby the vendor of automobile tires undertakes to guarantee the tires sold against defects in material or workmanship without limit as to time, mileage or service, and further expressly guarantees them for a specified period against 'blowouts, cuts, bruises, rim-cuts, under-inflation, wheels out of alignment, faulty brakes or other road hazards that may render the tire unfit for further service (except fire or theft),' or contracts to indemnify the purchaser 'should the tire fail within the replacement period' specified, without limitation as to cause of such 'failure,' is a contract 'substantially amounting to insurance' within the provisions of Section 665, General Code, which requires such guarantor or insurer to comply with the laws of the state authorizing and regulating the business of insurance."

The foregoing syllabus language clearly indicates that the "guarantees" in *Duffy* were found to be contracts substantially amounting to insurance because such guarantees promised to indemnify for losses or damages to the product outside of and unrelated to defects inherent in the product itself. Several years later, in *Herbert*, supra, this court was faced with another tire warranty/guarantee that was challenged by the Attorney General of Ohio. Therein, the tire warranty offered by Standard Oil promised repair or replacement for a limited period under certain conditions and provided in pertinent part:

> "This Warranty and Adjustment Agreement does not cover punctures, tires ruined in running flat, tires injured or destroyed by fire, wrecks or collisions, tires cut by chains, or by obstruction on vehicle, theft, clincher tires, tubes used in any form, or tires used in taxicab or common carrier bus service.
>
> " 'This Warranty and Adjustment Agreement does not cover consequential damages.' " Id., 138 Ohio St. at 378, 20 O.O. at 461, 35 N.E.2d at 439.

In finding that the Standard Oil tire warranty was indeed a warranty, and not a contract substantially amounting to insurance, this court held in paragraphs four and five of the syllabus as follows:

> "A warranty or guaranty issued to a purchaser in connection with the sale of goods containing an agreement to indemnify against loss or damage resulting from perils outside of and unrelated to inherent

weaknesses in the goods themselves, constitutes a contract substantially amounting to insurance within the purview of Section 665, General Code. (State, ex rel. Duffy, Atty. Genl. v. Western Auto Supply Co., 134 Ohio St., 163 [11 O.O. 583, 16 N.E.2d 256], followed.")

"A written warranty delivered to a purchaser, representing that the articles sold are so well and carefully manufactured that they will give satisfactory service under ordinary usage for a specified length of time, and providing for an adjustment in the event of failure from faulty construction or materials, but expressly excluding happenings not connected with imperfections in the articles themselves, is not a contract substantially amounting to insurance within the meaning of Section 665, General Code."

In summarizing the law enunciated in both *Duffy* and *Herbert* it is readily apparent that a contract "substantially amounting to insurance" in this context is one that promises to cover losses or damages over and above, or unrelated to, defects within the product itself.

A careful review of the instant vehicle protection plans indicates that losses or damages sustained by the purchaser of the product which are unrelated to defects within the product itself are specifically excluded from coverage. Thus, it would appear that under both *Duffy* and *Herbert*, the instant vehicle protection plans are indeed warranties, and are not contracts substantially amounting to insurance.

However, as mentioned before, ODI asserts that the crucial distinction, as noted by the court of appeals below, is that warranties not sold by either the vendor or manufacturer of the product are not made to induce a purchase of the product, and therefore constitute contracts substantially amounting to insurance. While the foregoing assertion may appear to be facially valid, we find it to be unpersuasive. Obviously, the distinction made in this vein was of no apparent consequence in *Duffy*, supra, inasmuch as it was the seller of the product therein who issued the "warranty" that this court found to be a contract substantially amounting to insurance.

In our view, the crucial factor in determining whether a contract is a warranty or something substantially amounting to insurance is not the status of the party offering or selling the warranty, but rather the type of coverage promised within the four corners of the contract itself. Under the rule of law announced in both *Duffy* and *Herbert*, it is clear that warranties that cover only defects within the product itself are properly characterized as warranties (as was the case in *Herbert*, supra), whereas warranties promising to cover damages or losses unrelated to defects within the product itself are, by definition, contracts substantially amounting to insurance (as was the case in *Duffy*, supra).

The fact that appellant herein is not the manufacturer, supplier, or seller of the products it purports to warrant is, in our view, of little or no consequence in determining whether its protection plans are subject to R.C. Title 39. Common experience in today's marketplace indicates that a large number of consumer products carry a short-term warranty, but that agreements that extend the warranty beyond the period of time offered by the manufacturer may often be purchased for additional consideration. Certainly, it can be safely surmised that most people are not induced to buy a specific product based upon an extended warranty agreement that may be purchased at an extra cost. Carrying ODI's arguments to their logical extreme, however, a seller of consumer products can offer such extended warranties to cover losses or damages, while independent third parties would be subject to insurance regulations even if the extended warranties specifically exclude losses or damages unrelated to defects in the product. Under such circumstances, we reject the status-determinative approach urged by ODI and adopted by the appellate court below, in favor of the substance-of-the-contract approach urged by appellant. Such a substance-of-the-contract approach was implemented by the court in Mein v. United States Car Testing Co. (1961), 115 Ohio App. 145, 20 O.O.2d 242, 184 N.E.2d 489, and is abundantly more consonant with the law and analysis set forth in both *Duffy*, supra, and *Herbert*, supra.

Therefore, based on all the foregoing, we hold that a motor vehicle service agreement which promises to compensate the promisee for repairs necessitated by mechanical breakdown resulting exclusively from failure due to defects in the motor vehicle parts does not constitute a contract "substantially amounting to insurance" within the purview of R.C. 3905.42. Accordingly, the judgment of the court of appeals is hereby reversed.

Judgment reversed.

DOUGLAS, HERBERT R. BROWN and RESNICK, JJ., concur.

MOYER, C.J., and HOLMES and WRIGHT, JJ., dissent.

WRIGHT, JUSTICE, dissenting.

* * *

In this instance, Griffin had no relationship with the consumer whatsoever until after the consumer had purchased the automobile, at which point Griffin directly solicited the consumer by mail for sale of its VPP. Having signed up the consumer, Griffin reinsured its business with the Great Plains Insurance Company, a Nebraska corporation, which is a wholly owned subsidiary of Griffin and is unlicensed to sell insurance in the state of Ohio. Therefore, without considering whether the VPPs before us here insure against contingencies other than product defects, we have a contract that is totally distinguishable from the warranty we found in *Herbert*. It is perfectly apparent that the VPP is not a warranty proposed by a manufacturer-seller and used for the purpose of inducing or increasing sales of the product in question. In a word, we have a case of first impression here which is certainly not controlled by either *Herbert* or State ex rel. Duffy v. Western Auto Supply Co. (1938), 134 Ohio St. 163, 11 O.O. 583, 16 N.E.2d 256. Indeed, the *Duffy* case seems to directly support the holding of the court of appeals.

Griffin has argued and the majority has inexplicably found that the VPPs involved here do not constitute contracts "substantially amounting to insurance" pursuant to R.C. 3905.42 and, thus, the superintendent has no authority to order a halt to these sundry violations of law. I must vigorously disagree. The majority appears to overlook the difference between the contract sold by Griffin and the warranty described in the *Herbert* case. Here, Griffin is not the warrantor of a product it has manufactured or sold but is rather the insurer of the performance of component parts in a product manufactured and sold by a third party. The *Herbert* case certainly did not exclude all warranties or guarantees from control by ODI but only those warranties guaranteeing "satisfactory service under ordinary usage" of products being sold to a purchaser by the manufacturer or seller of that product. Id. at paragraph five of the syllabus.

The Ohio General Assembly has given ODI the broadest authority to regulate all forms of insurance by way of R.C. 3905.42, which states in pertinent part: "No company * * * shall engage * * * in the business of insurance, or enter into any contracts substantially amounting to insurance, or in any manner aid therein, or engage in the business of guaranteeing against liability, loss, or damage, * * * unless it is expressly authorized by the laws of this state, and the laws regulating it and applicable thereto, have been complied with." In the *Duffy* case, we " '[b]roadly defined insurance * * * [as] a contract by which one party, for a compensation called the premium, assumes particular risks of the other party and promises to pay to him or his nominee a certain or ascertainable sum of money on a specified contingency. As regards property and liability insurance, it is a contract by which one party promises on a consideration to compensate or reimburse the other if he shall suffer loss from a specified cause, or to guarantee or indemnify or secure him against loss from that cause.' * * * " Id. at 168, 11 O.O. at 585, 16 N.E.2d at 258–259. In my view, the VPPs offered by Griffin are within this definition.

The appellee herein cites Vance, The Law of Insurance (3 Ed.1951) 2, Section 1, which lists the following five elements as distinguishing characteristics of insurance: (1) the insured possesses an insurable interest; (2) the insured is subject to loss through the destruction or impairment of that interest by the happening of some designated peril; (3) the insurer assumes the risk of loss; (4) such assumption is part of the general scheme to distribute actual losses among a large group of persons bearing similar risks; and (5) the insured pays a premium as consideration for the promise. There is no question that each of the above-described elements is present under Griffin's VPP.

Griffin can hardly be likened to a manufacturer, supplier or seller offering an extended warranty on one of its products. As stated above, Griffin is clearly not involved in the manufacture or sale of automobiles, and has no control over the risk of defects in those products. It is an independent, for-profit entity offering a contract insuring against the risk of mechanical breakdown of a motor vehicle—an insurable interest.

Griffin, for consideration of a stated premium from the policyholder, assumes the risk of certain specified losses and presumably distributes that risk among a larger group of persons bearing similar risks. This case does not involve a warranty because a warranty is a statement or representation made by the seller or manufacturer of goods contemporaneously with and as a part of the contract of sale.

Appellee has drawn our attention to opinions from out of state and under federal law in support of its position. Griffin Systems, Inc. v. Washburn (1987), 153 Ill.App.3d 113, 106 Ill.Dec. 330, 505 N.E.2d 1121, examined the same VPPs at issue in this case and concluded that they are insurance contracts. That opinion distinguished Griffin's VPPs from a warranty or service contract. The court stated, "* * * the distinguishing feature which sets * * * [manufacturer's or seller's service contracts and warranties] apart from an insurance policy is the fact that the respective compan[ies] manufacture or sell the products which they agreed to repair or replace. No third parties are involved nor is there a risk accepted which the company, because of its expertise, is unaware of. * * *" (Emphasis sic.) Id. at 117–118, 106 Ill.Dec. at 333, 505 N.E.2d at 1124.

As further evidence that Griffin's VPP is insurance and not a warranty, appellee cites a Federal Trade Commission ("F.T.C.") regulation, Section 700.11, Title 16, C.F.R., promulgated pursuant to the authority granted to the F.T.C. to enact rules implementing the Magnuson–Moss Warranty Act, Sections 2301 et seq., Title 15, U.S.Code. See Sections 2309 and 2312(c), Title 15, U.S.Code. The rule is relevant to the issue before us today in that it determines that VPPs such as the ones offered by Griffin are policies of insurance. Part (a) of the rule reads as follows:

> "The [Magnuson–Moss Warranty] Act recognizes two types of agreements which may provide similar coverage of consumer products, the written warranty, and the service contract. In addition, other agreements may meet the statutory definitions of either 'written warranty' or 'service contract,' but are sold and regulated under state law as contracts of insurance. One example is the automobile breakdown insurance policies sold in many jurisdictions and regulated by the state as a form of casualty insurance. The McCarran–Ferguson Act, 15 U.S.C. 1011 et seq., precludes jurisdiction under federal law over 'the business of insurance' to the extent an agreement is regulated by state law as insurance. Thus, such agreements are subject to the Magnuson–Moss Warranty Act only to the extent they are not regulated in a particular state as the business of insurance." (Emphasis added.) Thus, the F.T.C. considers such contracts ripe for insurance regulation.

Griffin urges this court to focus on whether it would "make sense" to apply the insurance statutes and regulations to its VPPs. The real issue, however, is whether each VPP contains the requisite elements of insurance such that it is a contract that "substantially amount[s] to insurance." See Mein v. United States Car Testing Co. (1961), 115 Ohio App. 145, 20 O.O.2d 242, 184 N.E.2d 489. As shown above, Griffin's VPP contains those elements and is, therefore, insurance. Because it is insurance, under R.C. 3905.42, ODI has the authority to regulate it.[7]

Accordingly, I strongly dissent.

Notes

1. Note the varying importance of assumption of risk and risk distribution in determining whether an arrangement between two parties constitutes insurance. The level of importance a court places on risk and the respective roles of the parties involved can lead to inconsistent outcomes. Compare, for example, the Illinois courts' response to a "Griffin Systems" case arising within its borders. In *Griffin Systems v. Washburn*, 153 Ill. App.3d 113, 106 Ill.Dec. 330, 505 N.E.2d 1121 (1987), an Illinois Appellate Court held the same agreement considered in the Ohio case above contained the four required elements "characterizing" insurance:

> 1. a contract or agreement between an insurer and an insured which exists for a specific period of time;
>
> 2. an insurable interest (usually property) possessed by the insured;
>
> 3. consideration in the form of a premium paid by the insured to the insurer; and
>
> 4. the assumption of risk by the insurer whereby the insurer agrees to indemnify the insured for potential pecuniary loss to the insured's property resulting from certain specified perils.

Thus, the Illinois Court held that the Griffin plan constituted insurance subject to state insurance regulation. The Illinois common law definition of insurance is similar to the definition used in the Ohio Department of Insurance's argument rejected by the Ohio Supreme Court majority, but

7. I offer yet further support for the appellee's position. Webster's defines "insurance" in part as "coverage by contract whereby for a stipulated consideration one party undertakes to indemnify or guarantee another against loss by a specified contingency or peril[.]" Webster's Third New International Dictionary (1986) 1173. Black's defines "insurance" similarly: "A contract whereby, for a stipulated consideration, one party undertakes to compensate the other for loss on a specified subject by specified perils. * * * " Black's Law Dictionary (6 Ed.1990) 802. All forms of warranties and guarantees meet this definition on some level. A simple manufacturer's limited warranty that comes with the product protects a purchaser from a specified loss (usually the value of the product) from a specified contingency or peril (usually a manufacturing defect). In fact, looking at Black's definition of "insurance," I am sure an accountant with the relevant actuarial and financial data could specify the amount of the product's price traceable to the warranty. At the same time, however, a manufacturer's warranty included in the price of the product is also a refinement of the manufactured product purchased: you do not just purchase a toaster, but rather you purchase a toaster that works, and a breach of the warranty means the product you received was not the product for which you contracted. I subscribe to this latter view of manufacturers' warranties where they are received as part of the product price; they are not contracts "substantially amounting to insurance." However, any and all warranties sold apart from a product seem to fall into the definition of "insurance." This is particularly apparent under the "modus operandi" before us. This form of insurance is ripe for abuse by the less than scrupulous and, as such, is ripe for regulation by ODI. The record in this case surely supports this premise.

relied on in the dissenting opinion. The Illinois Appellate Court further distinguished the plan from both a service contract and a warranty, based on the allocation of risk. In a service contract or warranty, the manufacturer or seller is responsible for repair or replacement of a defective product, whereas in an insurance agreement, a third party assumes the risk of a consumers potential loss and provides indemnification to the consumer for that loss.

2. Suppose you represent Griffin Systems in another state. What is your advice to Griffin Systems regarding its business practices and its contracts?

3. Clearly, risk plays a significant part. This is exemplified by the "known loss" rule. When a loss is known (i.e., reduced to judgement) *before* the insurance policy is issued, there is no coverage because no risk has been assumed. Montrose Chemical Corp. v. Admiral Ins. Co., 10 Cal.4th 645, 689–90, 42 Cal.Rptr.2d 324, 350, 913 P.2d 878, 904 (1995).

TRUTA v. AVIS RENT A CAR SYSTEM, INC.

Court of Appeal, First District, Division 2, 1987.
193 Cal.App.3d 802, 238 Cal.Rptr. 806.

BENSON, ASSOCIATE JUSTICE.

This is an appeal from a judgment of dismissal entered after a demurrer to the complaint of Marianne Truta (plaintiff) was sustained without leave to amend. Plaintiff instituted this action for herself personally and on behalf of a class of persons similarly situated. The defendants in whose favor judgment was rendered are Avis Rent A Car System, Inc., The Hertz Corporation, Budget Rent A Car Corporation, and National Car Rental System, Inc.

The substance of plaintiff's six-count complaint is that within the four years preceding the filing of the action, plaintiff and other California residents had rented automobiles from the various defendants. Incidental to the rental of these automobiles, plaintiff and the class she purportedly represents agreed to pay an additional fee to defendants for a "collision damage waiver" (hereafter "CDW").[8] The CDW, which plaintiff alleges to be essentially uniform for all car rentals in California, provided that for a fee of $6 per day defendants agreed to assume responsibility (subject to certain terms and conditions) for the term of one day for collision or upset damage or loss to the vehicle in an amount up to $1,000. * * * The pertinent provision of that contract states:

> "LOSS OR DAMAGE TO THE CAR. I'll pay you for all loss of and damage to the car regardless of who is at fault. My responsibility for accidental collision or upset damage won't exceed the amount shown in box 38 [the amount shown was $1,000] on the other side of this agreement. If I've accepted the 'collision damage waiver' option, I won't have to pay anything. But I will be responsible for the full amount of the damage if I violate any of the terms of this agreement

8. Although plaintiff consistently refers to collision damage waiver as "the insurance contract" we will refer to the provision with the same language used in the agreement.

or if I abuse the car or drive it recklessly or while under the influence of alcohol or drugs. I won't have to pay for accidental loss or damage from fire, theft, or other causes that are normally covered by a standard comprehensive physical damage insurance policy. I will report the loss of or any damage to the vehicle promptly by calling the phone number listed on the other side of this agreement."

The first cause of action of the complaint alleges that defendants are engaged in the business of insurance in violation of Insurance Code section 700 in that none of the defendants has been admitted to transact any class of insurance in California.[9] * * *

The second cause of action alleges that because defendants are charging excessive rates for insurance in violation of section 1852 of the Insurance Code, they are consequently engaged in unlawful business practices. * * *

The fifth cause of action alleges that the CDW is unconscionable for five reasons which we summarize as follows: 1) the provision provides no protection for most circumstances, a fact which defendants concealed; 2) its cost is excessive within the meaning of the California Insurance Code and far in excess of a price that would be determined in a competitive business environment; 3) the language of the provision is misleading; 4) the manner in which the rental contracts are printed, worded, packaged and presented disguises the existence of a major portion of the contractual provisions; and 5) defendants obtained unfair advantage by use of their superior bargaining position. * * *

[I]n support of defendants' demurrer to plaintiff's complaint, defendants submitted exhibits of four superior court decisions from foreign jurisdictions dismissing similar actions on the grounds that the CDW is not insurance.[10] Additional exhibits included five opinions from attorneys general or insurance departments in other states.[11] Each document opined that the CDW was not insurance.

After plaintiff filed her points and authorities in opposition to defendants' demurrer, defendants filed a request that the court take judicial notice of a memorandum, dated October 23, 1968, rendered by

9. Section 700 of the Insurance Code provides: "(a) A person shall not transact any class of insurance business in this state without first being admitted for such class. Such admission is secured by procuring a certificate of authority from the commissioner. Such certificate shall not be granted until the applicant conforms to the requirements of this code and of the laws of this state prerequisite to its issue."

10. The decisions were *Burrell v. Avis* (Fla.Cir.Ct., June 21, 1984) No. 83–6162 C–7; *Russell v. Hertz Co.* (Cir.Ct. Cook, Ill., Feb. 28, 1983) 82 CH 6632; *Korn et al. v. Avis et al.* (Pa.Ct. of Com.Pleas, Philadelphia Co., Feb. 10, 1977) No. 1670; *Klein v. National Car Rental* (N.Y.Supreme Ct., Spec.Term, May 4, 1983) No. 227²⁰⁄₈₂; affd., 100 A.D.2d 987, 474 N.Y.S.2d 160 (1984) leave to appeal den., 63 N.Y.2d 605, 481 N.Y.S.2d 1023, 471 N.E.2d 462 (1984).

11. Opinions from the Florida Attorney General, New York Attorney General, North Carolina Insurance Department, Texas State Board of Insurance and the Insurance Department of Iowa were included. However, a subsequently revised opinion by the New York Attorney General that the CDW is insurance was submitted at oral argument before this court. (See Ops. N.Y.Atty.Gen. 86–F9.)

the California Department of Insurance * * * concerning Ford Rent–A–Car System. According to the memorandum, Ford Rent–A–Car leased automobiles to the public whereby the lessees of the automobiles were liable for the first $100 damages due to fire, theft and collision.[12] If a lessee elected to pay for "collision protection," he was no longer liable for the $100 deductible amount. The author of the Department of Insurance memorandum opined as follows: "No insurance coverage is provided for this $100 amount." Rather, the lessor simply agrees not to hold the individual renting a car liable for either negligence or contractual liability for damage to the vehicle. The question here is whether this provision concerning the $100 deductible is doing an insurance business.

"My conclusion is that the Ford Rent–A–Car System operator is not involved in providing insurance. The subject charge is not accumulated to pay any liabilities or costs incurred by the rentor. Rather, the system operator has simply, by contract, released the lessee from responsibility for any damage to the property of the lessor. This is not a spreading of risk within insurance concepts, but is rather an allocation of risk by contractual agreement. As the parties can contract to place full responsibility for damage on the lessee, it seems no less reasonable that they can contract to place this responsibility on the lessor."

* * *

Without, at this point, determining whether we agree with the Department of Insurance's memorandum, it is clear that the agency has taken a position that a car leasing business may, by contract, relieve a lessee from liability for damage done to the leased vehicle without the agreement constituting insurance. * * *

We next consider the question of whether defendants, by virtue of the CDW provision of the rental agreement, are engaged in the insurance business and therefore in violation of Insurance Code section 700.

Section 22 of the Insurance Code defines insurance as "a contract whereby one undertakes to indemnify another against loss, damage, or liability arising from a contingent or unknown event." Case law has construed the statute as requiring two elements: "(1) a risk of loss to which one party is subject and a shifting of that risk to another party; and (2) distribution of risk among similarly situated persons." (*Metropolitan Life Ins. Co. v. State Bd. of Equalization* (1982) 32 Cal.3d 649, 654, 186 Cal.Rptr. 578, 652 P.2d 426.) While a persuasive argument can be made that the CDW transaction meets this criteria, the mere fact that a

12. The memorandum specifically describes the operation as follows: "The Ford Motor Company has a plan whereby, under separate franchise, they [sic] license any Ford dealer to operate a Ford Rent–A–Car System station. Cars are leased by Ford to the franchise holding dealer, who in turn leases them to members of the public. As part of the agreement between Ford and the dealer, insurance is provided including $100 comprehensive fire, theft and collision. By the separate agreements, the dealer in his lease of cars from Ford agrees to be liable for all damage, and in turn the dealer extracts the same agreement from lessees from him. Since the above insurance exists, this liability extends only to the $100 deductible amount. What is named 'collision protection' is sold by the lessor to cover the $100 deductible."

contract contains these two elements does not necessarily mean that the agreement constitutes an insurance contract for purposes of statutory regulation.

"A statute designed to regulate the business of insurance * * * is not intended to apply to all organizations having some element of risk assumption or distribution in their operations. The question of whether an arrangement is one of insurance may turn, not on whether a risk is involved or assumed, but on whether that or something else to which it is related in the particular plan is its principal object and purpose." (12 Appleman, Insurance Law and Practice (1981) § 7002, p. 14, footnotes omitted.) This is because "insurance regulatory laws are not properly construed as aimed at an absolute prohibition against the inclusion of any risk-transferring-and-distributing provisions in contracts for services or for the sale or rental of goods. In short, the presence of a small element of insurance, if one wishes to call it that, closely associated with the predominant element of the transaction—the element that gives the transaction its distinctive character—does not conclusively demonstrate that the transaction is within the reach of insurance regulatory laws." (Keeton, Insurance Law (1971) § 8.2(c), p. 552.)

In analyzing whether a contract constitutes insurance it is advised that two inquiries be made: "To what extent, in each case, did the specific transactions or the general line of business at issue involve one or more of the evils at which the regulatory statutes were aimed? And were the elements of risk transference and risk distribution, characteristic of transactions at which the regulatory statutes were aimed, a central and relatively important element of the transactions or instead merely incidental to other elements that gave the transactions their distinctive character?" (*Keeton, op. cit. supra.*)

A review of the California appellate decisions concerned with the question of whether a particular entity was engaged in the business of insurance within the meaning of the regulatory statutes of this state reveals that the analytical approach mentioned in Keeton has been utilized in this state. For instance, in *California Physicians' Service v. Garrison* (1946) 28 Cal.2d 790, 172 P.2d 4, professional medical services were rendered to low income patients who paid monthly membership dues to a non-profit corporation. Payment for these services was made through a fund created by the dues received by the non-profit corporation. In affirming the trial court's determination that the organization was not involved in the insurance business the Supreme Court stated: "Absence or presence of assumption of risk or peril is not the sole test to be applied in determining [the corporation's] status. The question, more broadly, is whether, looking at the plan of operation as a whole, 'service' rather than 'indemnity' is its principal object and purpose." (*Id.* at p. 809, 172 P.2d 4.) The *Garrison* court in reaching its conclusion also looked to the purpose and nature of the regulatory provisions arising under the Insurance Code, " * * * particularly those relating to the maintenance of reserves and to the regulation of investments and financial operations," and observed: "The extensive insurance regulations ... are designed to protect the insured, or the public, from the insurer. [Citation.] Such regulations become important only if the insurer has assumed definite obligations. Conversely, it is evident that they are not intended to apply where no risk is assumed and no default can exist. * * * "

Similar reasoning was employed in *Transportation Guar. Co. v. Jellins* (1946) 29 Cal.2d 242, 174 P.2d 625. In *Jellins,* the court was called upon to determine whether two truck maintenance contracts containing provisions that the contractor agreed to insure the vehicles for the owner in an authorized insurance company constituted insurance contracts. Recognizing that nearly every business venture entails some assumption of risk, the high court stated: "We are satisfied that a sound jurisprudence does not suggest the extension, by judicial construction, of the insurance laws to govern every contract involving an assumption of risk or indemnification of loss; that when the question arises each contract must be tested by its own terms as they are written, as they are understood by the parties, and as they are applied under the particular circumstances involved." * * *

After reviewing the entire contract, the *Jellins* court concluded that the major purpose of the underlying agreement was to supply labor. The court then stated: "Plaintiff's obligations (with their reciprocal contractual rights) to make repairs, to maintain the truck in good running order, and to keep a truck constantly available to the owner except for reasonable service periods, do not in our opinion, make the plaintiff an insurer. Such obligations are similar to those ordinarily undertaken by a lessor of motor vehicles and, unless we are prepared to hold that any lessor of such vehicles, entering into such a contract, is in the insurance business, then we should not hold that plaintiff is, on that account, in such business." * * *

The principal object and purpose of the transaction before us, the element which gives the transaction its distinctive character, is the rental of an automobile. Peripheral to that primary object is an option, available to the lessee for additional consideration, to reallocate the risk of loss (up to the sum of $1,000) to the lessor in the event the vehicle sustains damage during the rental term. Thus, as in *Jellins,* after reviewing the entire contract we are satisfied that this tangential risk allocation provision should not have the effect of converting the defendants as contracting lessors into insurers subject to statutory regulation.

We also give deference to the Department of Insurance's interpretation of the Insurance Code [citations omitted] and we find a clear expression that the CDW transaction does not lend itself to the insurance regulatory statutes. As previously stated, the Department's analysis of Ford Rent–A–Car System where the lessor had, by contract, released the lessee from responsibility for any damage to the vehicle, opined that * * * "If the situation were such that the lessor was agreeing to pay any monies to third parties, then this conclusion would be different. Such an agreement would be similar to the type of coverage which has been extended by some companies in the past to reimburse for expenses incurred by an individual as a result of a deductible provision. That type of service would clearly be insurance. Here, there is no interest of the public which would be protected by our assuming jurisdiction. Since the lessor is not agreeing to pay anybody anything, but is simply agreeing not to hold the lessee liable, there is no need for accumulating reserves. The solvency or insolvency of the lessor does not affect this contractual provision."

It is obvious from the above that the Department of Insurance does not consider the California Insurance Code as designed to regulate the type of practice contained in the CDW transaction before us. Thus, on the basis of existing case law, legal commentary and the memorandum of the regulatory agency entrusted to enforce this state's insurance statutes, we hold that the CDW provision contained in automobile rental agreements does not constitute an insurance contract for purposes of statutory regulation.

[The court thereupon sustained the demurrer as to the first and second counts of the complaint, but overruled the demurrer to the fifth count that alleged "unconscionability" of the lease agreements pursuant to Cal.Civ.Code § 1670.5—which, parenthetically, is identical with U.C.C. § 2–302. No opinion was expressed as to whether the $6 per day fee for CDW is in fact substantively unconscionable].

* * *

The judgment is reversed and the case remanded for further proceedings on the fifth cause of action.

Notes

1. Courts in other states have similarly held that collision damage waiver (CDW) provisions in automobile rental agreements do not constitute insurance. In *Hertz Corp. v. Corcoran*, 137 Misc.2d 403, 520 N.Y.S.2d 700 (1987), the New York Supreme Court decided that CDW did not fit within New York Insurance Law § 1101(a)'s definition of insurance, in which an insurance contract is defined as any agreement or other transaction whereby one party, the "insurer," is obligated to confer benefit of pecuniary value upon another party, the "insured" or "beneficiary," contingent on the happening of a fortuitous event in which the insured or beneficiary has, or is expected to have at the time of such happening, a material interest which will be adversely affected by the happening of such event. The court reasoned that a daily renter of a car does in fact have the requisite "material" or "insurable interest" in the vehicle. However, the automobile's lessor and owner, Hertz, is indemnifying itself against the loss of its property, and one cannot indemnify oneself against loss. See Chabraja v. Avis Rent A Car System, 192 Ill.App.3d 1074, 140 Ill.Dec. 221, 549 N.E.2d 872 (1989) (a waiver of the lessor's rights is not insurance).

2. Note the unconscionability claim that is made in *Truta*. It is instructive to compute the annual premium rate charged for the CDW to the

potential benefit received. Based on the computation, is CDW unconscionable?

Rate setting is a common function of state insurance commissioners. Courts are generally sympathetic to the idea that insurance commissioners have considerable power to regulate rates. E.g., American Manufacturers Mutual Ins. Co. v. Commissioner of Insurance, 374 Mass. 181, 184, 372 N.E.2d 520 (1978) (upholding retroactive rate setting in the form of required rebates). The threshold question of whether a particular form of doing business constitutes the business of insurance is key.

Recall that the statutory definitions of insurance discussed in the introduction include some characterization of insurance being a contract intended to shift the risk of loss due to an unforeseen event from one party to another. As *Truta* and several other cases show, when applying the definition of insurance found in the California Insurance Code § 22 (2000), the California Supreme Court held that insurance necessarily involves two elements:

(1) A risk of loss to which one party is subject and a shifting of that risk to another party; and

(2) Distribution of risk among similarly situated persons. Metropolitan Life Ins. Co. v. State Board of Equalization, 32 Cal.3d 649, 186 Cal.Rptr. 578, 652 P.2d 426 (1982).

In *Truta*, the statutory definition was embellished to exclude harms that were not intended to be regulated and conduct which only comprised a small part of a business. In *Cates Construction, Inc. v. Talbot Partners*, the California Court of Appeal applied the formula to surety bonds. 53 Cal. App.4th 1420, 62 Cal.Rptr.2d 548 (1997). In the California statutory scheme, Ins. Code § 100 includes surety as a kind of insurance, a definition which is included in Ins. Code § 105. Applying, the *Truta* formulation, the court concluded that the factors which support the regulation of insurance (economic dilemma of the insured, the protection against calamity, the quasi-public nature of the business) supported the classification of surety contracts as insurance. On appeal, the California Supreme court reversed the Court of Appeals decision, noting, as in *Truta*, that meeting the statutory definition is not sufficient. 21 Cal.4th 28, 86 Cal.Rptr.2d 855, 980 P.2d 407 (1999). In reviewing the factors, the court was of the view that insurance is unique and its attributes have not been extended in other areas. *Id.* at 46. The factors supporting the Court of Appeals' characterization of suretyship as insurance were, in the California Supreme Court's opinion, easily cast in the other direction. Surety is primarily a contract in which no additional obligation other than to answer for another's debt is present. No special or fiduciary relation is created and, in the court's view, surety is not quasi public in nature. *Id.* at 54–56. Further, insurance contracts usually involve two parties (the insurer and the insured) whereas surety contracts involve a "tripartite relationship between a surety, principal and an obligee." *Id.* at 46, 58.

Interestingly several other courts which have considered the question have held that surety contracts are insurance. E.g., Transamerica Premier v. Brighton School, 940 P.2d 348 (Colo.1997); Dodge v. Fidelity and Deposit Co. of Maryland, 161 Ariz. 344, 778 P.2d 1240 (1989).

3. A further example of what *does not* constitute insurance presents itself within the medium of self-insurance pools, formed pursuant to a joint powers agreement. In *Orange County Water District v. Association of California Water Agencies–Joint Powers Insurance Authority*, 54 Cal.App.4th 772, 63 Cal.Rptr.2d 182 (1997), the Orange County Water District ("OCWD") entered into a joint powers agreement with other water agencies and created the Association of California Water Agencies–Joint Powers Insurance Authority ("ACWA–JPIA"), which would pool self-insured losses, jointly purchase excess insurance, and share administrative and other claims-related services. The court applied a literal interpretation of both California Insurance Code § 22 and the legislative intent behind California Government Code § 990.8, subdivision (c) and concluded that a self-insurance pool, arranged through a joint powers agreement, did not constitute "insurance." Reasoning that insurance is defined as "a contract which undertakes to indemnify the insured against loss, damage, or liability," the court concluded that "a self-insurer does not contract to indemnify another."

4. *Classification of Insurance.* Couch on Insurance 2d between § 1.17 and § 1.117 lists approximately 80 (give or take a dozen or so) specific types of insurance policies. This is a traditional method of classification which the California Ins. Code § 100, for instance, has reduced to about 20 slots including such items as boiler insurance, team and vehicle insurance as well as the ever useful "miscellaneous" insurance category.

In this book, insurance is divided into three general categories: (1) insurance covering liability; (2) insurance covering property and economic losses; and (3) insurance covering personal concerns including life and disability. Among the most common form of insurance policies now issued are auto and homeowners' policies which may actually incorporate all three categories. In fact, these two varieties of policies could be treated as the basis for a classification of insurance at least as useful as the framework adopted here.

5. *Life Insurance.* Do any of the definitions of insurance in the foregoing cases cover life insurance? What would be a proper definition? As in other types, a "little bit" of life insurance may escape regulation as long as it is not the dominant element in the situation or there is no need for the accumulation of reserves. For example a merchant may promote the installment sale of furniture by promising to cancel the balance due upon the death of the customer. A bit of credit life insurance, which is on an advanced level of commercial development, would deserve, and receive, some regulation.

In some cases a local service club may automatically assess its members a fee to create a fund for the spouse of any member who dies. At this level, the life insurance aspect may be overlooked, but herein is the forerunner of the fraternal benefit insurance societies (The Royal Neighbors, The Woodmen of the World, etc.), who have a respectable share of the life insurance business and are duly regulated. See Hellner, *The Scope of Insurance Regulation: What Is Insurance for Purposes of Regulation?*, 12 Am.J. of Comparative Law 494 (1963).

6. *Automobile Insurance.* Automobile insurance, perhaps more than any other form of insurance, seems to come to the attention of the public-at-large in many intricate ways. The traditional automobile policy has been issued within the framework of what has been called the "fault" system. The basic meaning of this is that the insurer will pay within the policy limits for amounts which the insured (usually the policy owner) is held liable to pay third parties injured by him. Automobile policies were not confined to protection against liability; as they evolved, they expanded to feature other coverages including collision coverage (the insurer's agreement to reimburse the insured for loss to his motor vehicle), comprehensive, medical payments, and other varieties of coverage.

So many personal interests are affected by American automobiles that their freewheeling operation on the streets and highways has led to an immense amount of legislation and regulation. Particularly important are the laws and regulations dealing with the liabilities of owners and operators of automobiles for injuries to persons and property. Of major relevance to such liability laws are interlocking and related laws and regulations dealing with automobile insurance.

Many states have laws, often called "Owners Financial Responsibility Acts," which require demonstration of financial responsibility after certain events involving the automobile have occurred, i.e., an accident. Demonstration of ability to meet any ensuing judgment is most frequently accomplished by presenting proof that an insurance policy applies to the potential judgment liability. Other means of making the required demonstration of responsibility are often allowed although less frequently used. For example, a bond, or a deposit of money or other security may be sufficient under a given state's laws to meet the requirement. Statutes also routinely provide for minimum levels of coverage in auto policies. For example, a commonly established minimum level of coverage is "15–30–5," meaning $15,000 coverage for injuries to one claimant, $30,000 for all claimants in a given incident, and $5,000 for property damage. Inflation and jury verdicts being what they are, these minimum figures may be regarded as unrealistic by an automobile owner; motorists very frequently buy policies with much higher liability ceilings.

The obvious gap is that some motorists won't buy liability insurance at all. This fact has led in California and elsewhere to a variety of statutory remedies. For example, a state may require that every car be covered by a policy (or other demonstration of financial responsibility) as a condition of registration of the motor vehicle. See the Massachusetts Compulsory Motor Vehicle Liability Insurance Act, Mass.Gen.Laws, Chapter 90, Sections 34A–34J; Chapter 175, Sections 113A–113H, as amended.

"Uninsured motorists" legislation is another way in which state legislatures have sought to plug this gap. "Uninsured motorist" acts require policies to contain provisions protecting the insured (usually the auto owner and certain other persons) against injuries inflicted on them by motorists without any insurance policies covering the event. Commonly, a ceiling is placed on this coverage by the statute. Some insurers today provide a related coverage against "underinsured" motorists.

7. *"No–Fault" Legislation.* A number of states have attempted a large scale revision of the whole compensation scheme by enacting the so-called "no-fault" laws. A fairly typical "no-fault" statute is that of New York as

described in the following excerpt from *Goodkin v. United States*, 773 F.2d 19, 21–22 (2d Cir.1985).

New York's No–Fault Scheme

> No-fault laws were created to remedy a long recognized and serious problem—the inability of the tort system to rapidly, adequately and fairly compensate victims of automobile accidents. 12A Couch on Insurance 2d § 45:661 (rev. ed. 1981). In *Montgomery v. Daniels,* 38 N.Y.2d 41, 378 N.Y.S.2d 1, 340 N.E.2d 444 (1975), upholding the constitutionality of New York's no-fault law, the New York Court of Appeals enumerated three particular problems that the legislature intended the [no fault law] to address: (1) the excessive and needless expense of the tort system; (2) the unfair and inequitable distribution of compensation among accident victims, including long delays in payment, and (3) the strain placed on the state judicial system by tort litigation. The [no fault law] sought to remedy these problems by, *inter alia,* removing minor claims from the courts, eliminating fault as a required predicate for recovering certain losses from a predicate determination of liability based on fault, requiring payments to be made immediately on accrual of loss and requiring all owners of motor vehicles to carry no-fault insurance. The preeminent purpose of the no-fault law, according to the Court of Appeals, was "to assure the prompt and full reimbursement of the 'economic' losses those injured in automobile accidents may suffer." *Perkins v. Merchants Mutual Insurance Co.,* 41 N.Y.2d 394, 396, 393 N.Y.S.2d 347, 348, 361 N.E.2d 997, 998 (1977).
>
> New York's no-fault legislation provides a plan for compensating victims of automobile accidents without regard to fault. In essence, it is a two-pronged, partial modification of the preexisting system of reparation for personal injuries suffered in automobile accidents under which system liability was grounded in negligence under classic principles of tort law. One prong deals with compensation; the other with limitation of tort actions. Montgomery v. Daniels, 38 N.Y.2d at 46, 378 N.Y.S.2d at 4, 340 N.E.2d at 446. The [no fault law] partially but not completely eliminated the rights of automobile accident victims to recover in tort for their injuries. It replaced what it excised with a relatively simple and straightforward compensation system designed to quickly reimburse injured parties, up to certain limits, for the common, out-of-pocket expenses generated by their injuries.
>
> Under the [no fault law], every owner of a motor vehicle is responsible, regardless of fault, to a specified class of persons for any and all basic economic loss resulting from injuries occasioned by the use or operation of that vehicle. The class of persons includes the owner himself, operators and occupants of his vehicle and pedestrians. By definition, basic economic loss is limited to an aggregate maximum of $50,000 per person and includes the cost of professional health services ascertainable within one year, lost earnings and the cost of substitute services up to $2,000 per month for not more than three years and other expenses up to $25 per day for not more than one year. N.Y. Ins. Law § 5102(a). Reimbursement for basic economic loss minus certain specified deductions constitutes first party benefits, id., N.Y.Ins.Law § 5102(b), which are due and payable when the loss is incurred.

> The [no fault law] imposes two limitations on recovery for personal injuries. By their terms, these limitations apply only to actions between covered persons: "[n]otwithstanding any other law," a covered person cannot recover against another covered person for basic economic loss, and a covered person who has not sustained serious injury as defined in section 5102(d)[13] cannot recover against another covered person for non-economic loss. *Id.* § 5104. Non-economic loss is "pain and suffering and similar non-monetary detriment." *Id.* § 5102(c).
>
> A covered person as defined by the [no fault law] is "any pedestrian injured through the use or operation of, or any owner, operator or occupant of, a motor vehicle which has in effect the financial security required * * * or which [is among the exceptions in N.Y.Veh. & Traf. Law § 321 (McKinney Supp.1984), which includes vehicles owned by the United States] or any other person entitled to first party benefits." N.Y.Ins.Law § 5102(j). With certain exceptions, the motor vehicle owner's liability carrier must pay first party benefits to any person, "other than occupants of another motor vehicle or a motorcycle," whose injury arises out of the use or operation of the owner's vehicle. *Id.* at § 5103(a)(1). It must also pay first party benefits to "[t]he named insured and members of his household, other than occupants of a motorcycle," for injuries arising from the use or operation of any insured vehicle outside of New York but in the United States or Canada or any uninsured vehicle in the United States or Canada. *Id.* § 5103(a)(2). Finally, it must pay first party benefits to any New York resident not otherwise entitled to such benefits whose injury results from the use or operation of the owner's vehicle outside of New York but in the United States or Canada. *Id.* § 5103(a)(3). Everyone not entitled to first party benefits is a noncovered person.
>
> Intended to address only minor personal injury claims, the no-fault law leaves unaffected the right to recover in tort for economic loss in excess of the basic economic loss limitations and the right to recover for non-economic loss associated with serious injury. The [no fault law] by its terms and operation simply eliminates the right of an injured covered person to recover in tort against another covered person for basic economic loss. In most instances, of course, the practical result of this is that covered defendants will not be liable for any amounts attributable to basic economic loss.

One has to consult each state's laws to find the exact dimensions of "no-fault" coverage. A useful discussion can be found in Woodroof, Fonseca, and Squillante, *Automobile Insurance and No–Fault Law* (Lawyers Cooperative Publishing Company, and Bancroft–Whitney Company, 1974). The CCH Automobile Law Reporter ¶ 1941–1987 lists states with no-fault laws.

13. Section 5102(d) provides as follows:

"Serious injury" means a personal injury which results in death; dismemberment; significant disfigurement; a fracture; a loss of a fetus; permanent loss of use of a body organ, member, function or system; permanent consequential limitation of use of a body organ or member; significant limitation of use of a body function or system; or a medically determined injury or impairment of a non-permanent nature which prevents the injured person from performing substantially all of the material acts which constitute such person's usual and customary daily activities for not less than ninety days during the one hundred eighty days immediately following the occurrence of the injury or impairment.

Chapter 1

GOVERNMENTAL REGULATION OF INSURANCE

A. STATE REGULATION

THE PURPOSE OF INSURANCE REGULATION

The purpose of insurance regulation is dictated by social, political and economic values within and without the insurance industry. This theme was promulgated by Professor Spencer L. Kimball in his article, *The Purpose of Insurance Regulation: A Preliminary Inquiry in the Theory of Insurance Law*, 45 MINN. L. REV. 471 (1961). Insurance provides security for policyholders and much regulation is focused on ensuring the continuity of this security. Requirements for levels of paid-in capital, for adequate premium rates, and for permissive investments are directed to the solidity of the company. Prohibitions against discriminatory classifications, excessive premium rates, and unfair distribution practices address questions of equitable treatment of policyholders.

Another purpose of insurance regulation is to satisfy the general goals of society at large. Notions of democracy, liberty, and consumer protection are apparent in requirements for policyholder participation in management (common in the rest of the world, but not yet implemented in the U.S.), and adherence to notice, hearing, and contract rights. Economic values underlie regulations for free access to the market, local protectionism, and use of investment funds. There are many complex and interacting purposes of insurance regulation. As Professor Kimball stated: "Insurance is a small world that reflects the purposes of the larger world outside it."

STATE REGULATION OF INSURERS

The powers of the chief officers (commissioners or superintendents) of state insurance agencies are complex and far-reaching. Some useful discussion will be found in 2 Couch on Insurance 2d § 21:4–§ 21:23; 19 Appleman, Insurance Law and Practice, § 10391 et seq; *see also* Symposium: Insurance Regulation, 1969 Wisc. L. Rev. 1019; Richard S. L.

Roddis, *Limited Omnipotence: The Bases and Limitations of the Powers of Insurance Regulators*, XIII Forum 386 (1978). Professor Susan Randall provides an excellent overview of state regulation. Susan Randall, *Insurance Regulation in the United States: Regulatory Federalism and the National Association of Insurance Commissioners*, 26 Fla. St. U. L. Rev. 625 (1999).

Regulation of companies transacting business in a state is accomplished by a department within the executive branch, with powers delegated by the state's legislature to enforce the state's insurance laws. The department of insurance is headed by a commissioner or superintendent, who is either appointed by the state's governor or, in a few states (including California and Florida), elected directly.[1]

The administration of insurance regulation tends to be similar among states. In California, for example, regulation is accomplished under the Insurance Code, governed by the Insurance Commissioner and the Department of Insurance. The Commissioner also licenses insurers to do business, can withhold or revoke licenses, and can even take over and run an insurance company.

The California Insurance Code contains provisions of varying scope concerning the contents of insurance policies. For example, the terms of the standard fire insurance policy are prescribed by law in Insurance Code § 2071. In the case of automobile insurance, only individual clauses (and not complete policy texts) are mandated. E.g., Insurance Code § 11580.2 (the "uninsured motorist clause"); Insurance Code § 11580.1(b)(4) (the "omnibus" (permissive use) clause). The statutes contain many other provisions that are prescribed in terms of, or mandated to comply with, certain standards. The problem with respect to a given line of insurance is ascertaining all of the statutory requirements in the elaborate but often disjointed Insurance Code.

In New York, the scope of insurance regulation, and the powers of the Superintendent of Insurance and the Department of Insurance are defined in Title 11 of the New York Code of Rules and Regulations. Connecticut's Insurance Commissioner and Department of Insurance enforce the Regulations of Connecticut State Agencies, Title 38a. In Florida, the Department of Insurance, under the supervision of the Insurance Commissioner, is authorized to regulate state insurance companies under Florida Statutes § 112.

OSTRER v. SCHENCK

Court of Appeals of New York, 1977.
41 N.Y.2d 782, 364 N.E.2d 1107, 396 N.Y.S.2d 335.

JASEN, JUDGE.

In June, 1973, the Superintendent of Insurance promulgated regulation 65, which limits to specified maximum levels, adjusted for volume,

1. Susan Randall, *Insurance Regulation in the United States: Regulatory Federalism and the National Association of Insurance Commissioners*, 26 Fla. St. U. L. Rev. 625, 629 (1999).

the commissions an insurance agent may receive for life insurance policies issued on a mass-merchandising basis under plans sponsored by union-management employee welfare funds. The issue on this appeal is whether regulation 65 conflicts with positive provisions of the Insurance Law and is, therefore, a nullity. Or put more concretely, the issue is whether the Superintendent of Insurance may adopt a regulation to control the masking of a group insurance arrangement, subject to close statutory and administrative regulations, under the guise of issuing individual policies by which a salesman of insurance in complicity with a union-management welfare fund may enhance his commissions.

Plaintiff Benjamin Ostrer is a duly licensed life insurance agent who is in the business of soliciting and placing life insurance coverage for members of union-management welfare funds. Ostrer had an agency relationship with the International Life Insurance Company of Buffalo. Under the terms of his agency agreement with the insurance carrier, Ostrer was to receive a commission on each individual life insurance policy he placed with the company equal to 55% of the first-year premium. The rate of commission applicable to the placement of a single policy covering a group of individuals was substantially lower.

In the spring of 1973, plaintiff successfully arranged for the placement with International Life of a life insurance program to be sponsored by the Airline, Aerospace and Affiliated Employees Severance Fund for Local 732. The assets of this union-management welfare fund were contributed pursuant to the terms of a collective bargaining agreement. Instead of providing for a single-group policy to cover all fund members, plaintiff arranged with the trustees of the fund for a program whereby each member would be issued a uniform individual policy with terms prearranged by the trustees of the fund and the insurance carrier. Ostrer was, thus, able to claim the benefits of the higher commission rate applicable to individual policies. Regulation 65, which took effect prior to payment of the commission to Ostrer, limits his commission to no more than 5.2% of the annual premium of each policy. Relying upon the duly promulgated regulation, the insurance carrier refused to pay Ostrer the full commission specified in the agency agreement.

Plaintiff brought an action to invalidate regulation 65. After a trial, Special Term found in favor of the plaintiff and held that regulation 65 conflicted with subdivision 4 of section 213 of the Insurance Law. The Appellate Division affirmed. We conclude that regulation 65 is a valid exercise of powers conferred upon the Superintendent of Insurance by statute, that the regulation does not conflict with any provision of the Insurance Law, and that the order of the Appellate Division should be reversed.

Subdivision 4 of section 213 of the Insurance Law establishes, as a general principle, that the first-year commission on the sale of life insurance may be as great as 55% of the first-year premium. Plaintiff argues that regulation 65 reduces the maximum commission level below the rate established by statute and must, therefore, be invalidated. However, subdivision 11 of section 213 specifically excludes group insurance from the expense limitations provided elsewhere in the statute. Thus, the threshold question is whether it was reasonable for the Superintendent of Insurance to conclude that the mass-merchandising of identical policies to members of a defined group was, in reality, a form of group insurance. If the classification was reasonable, subdivision 4 of section 213 is no bar to the regulation.

Group life insurance is defined by statute to include a policy issued to the trustees of a fund established by two or more employers in the same industry or labor unions to insure employees of the employer or members of the unions. The basic requirements are that the persons eligible for insurance be employees or union members; that the premium be paid by the trustees from fund assets; that the policy include at least 25 persons on the date of issue; and that the amounts of insurance available under the policy be fixed. (Insurance Law, § 204, subd 1, par [d].) We conclude that the Superintendent of Insurance could reasonably exercise his broad regulatory powers to prevent a collusive arrangement between an insurance salesman and the trustees of a union-management welfare fund from masking a group insurance program through the mass issuance of standard individual policies, pursuant to a common plan to fund members.

The superintendent has wide authority to "prescribe, in writing, official regulations, not inconsistent with the provisions of this chapter * * * interpreting the provisions of this chapter." (Insurance Law, § 21.) Further, the superintendent possesses whatever powers may be "reasonably implied" from the statute. (Insurance Law, § 10.) The courts have consistently recognized that these provisions vest the superintendent "with broad power to interpret, clarify, and implement the legislative policy." (*Breen v. Cunard Lines S. S. Co.*, 33 NY2d 508, 511.) Provided that his regulations are not inconsistent with some specific statutory provision, the superintendent may prescribe regulations "to effectuate any of the powers given to him by law" (*Matter of B. & R. Excess Corp. v. Thacher*, 37 Misc 2d 307, 309, affd 18 AD2d 1137), including any powers that the statute reasonably implies.

The function of a reviewing court is a limited one. The challenger of a regulation must establish that the regulation "is so lacking in reason for its promulgation that it is essentially arbitrary." (*Matter of Marburg v. Cole*, 286 NY 202, 212.) The interpretation given a statute by the administering agency "if not irrational or unreasonable, should be upheld." (*Matter of Howard v. Wyman*, 28 NY2d 434, 438.) As was observed in *Mississippi Val. Barge Co. v. United States* (292 U.S. 282, 286–287), "[the] judicial function is exhausted when there is found to be a rational basis for the conclusions approved by the administrative body."

[The court affirms the "conclusion of the superintendent that mass-merchandised, standard individual policies issued to members of a group are the functional equivalent of a single-group policy issued to the representatives of the group."]

* * *

To resolve the case, we need take the analysis only one further step. Granted that mass-merchandised individual policies are group insurance and, thus, maximum commissions are not regulated by statute, it remains for us to consider whether the superintendent acted reasonably in limiting commissions on such standardized policies to a maximum of 5.2% per annual premium. We believe that he did.

The superintendent's regulation affects only mass-merchandised policies issued pursuant to plans sponsored by union-management welfare funds. (11 NYCRR 202.2.) The record discloses that, coincident with the rapid post-World War II expansion of union welfare funds, some insurance companies began to follow unsound and unethical practices in connection with the solicitation and issuance of group insurance contracts covering union welfare plans. During the early 1950's, "the public [was] shocked by the disclosure of excesses which have taken place in the management of the sums contributed by employers to union welfare funds for insurance and pension benefits of employees and their dependents." (NY Legis Ann, 1956, pp 259, 260.) In 1956, the Legislature reacted to the crisis by vesting considerable authority in the Superintendent of Insurance to supervise operations of employee welfare funds. (L 1956, ch 774; *see* Governor's Message of Approval, McKinney's Session Laws of NY [1956], p 1687.) It became declared State policy "that employee welfare funds are of great benefit to employees and their families and that their growth should be encouraged; that the establishment and management of such funds vitally affect the well-being of millions of people and are in the public interest; and that such funds should be supervised by the state to the extent necessary to protect the rights of employees and their families, without imposing burdens upon such funds which might discourage their orderly growth and without duplicating the supervisory responsibilities presently vested in any state agencies." (Insurance Law, § 37.) Subsequently, the superintendent was granted broad authority to "from time to time promulgate appropriate supplementary rules and regulations designed to carry out the express provisions and purposes" of the statutes regulating employee welfare funds. (Insurance Law, § 37–n, subd 1.)

Upon investigation, the superintendent discovered instances where some employee-management welfare funds were induced to purchase individual policies for each employee, rather than a single policy covering all members of the relevant group. The consequence of this method of purchase, as nicely illustrated in the present case, was to permit insurance agents to collect the substantially higher commissions that result from the issuance of individual policies rather than one group policy. In light of the fact that only one true sales effort is involved, the superintendent found that commissions for such "individual" policies were "unconscionably high." * * *

The record establishes that the incentive to earn the excessive commissions associated with individual policies also induced other abuses in the sale of insurance to union-management welfare funds. For example, the Insurance Department discovered that this plaintiff sold a series of individual policies in a situation where a single-group policy would have more appropriately satisfied the particular insurance needs of the welfare fund. Further, under some plans, individual policies would lapse when an employee, covered for only a few years, was laid off for a period in excess of three months. Upon the employee's return to gainful employment, a new individual policy would be issued and another full commission paid. This was a hardship to the employee because he had aged in the interval, resulting in a diminution of coverage. One company reported instances where welfare fund trustees permitted a whole series of individual policies to be periodically transferred from one carrier to another in order to generate the large first-year premiums. In short, the potential for excessive commissions was a factor in the determination of the form of insurance purchases and the best interests of welfare fund members was frequently overlooked or disregarded. Further, the practice of selling individual policies on a mass-merchandising basis had become so widespread that insurance companies developed programs with such practices specifically in mind.

In our view, regulation 65 is a reasonable exercise of the superintendent's broad power to protect the beneficiaries of union-management welfare funds from abuses. Such funds, the Legislature has declared, are to be operated for the benefit of the members. Clearly, the payment of excessive premiums is not in the economic best interests of the membership. The superintendent could reasonably expect that, as a result of a prohibition against the payment of excessive commissions, welfare fund beneficiaries would receive better coverage and greater return for the same or less cost. The record reflects that, because of reduced commissions, at least one insurance company has requested permission to increase the cash value of existing policies. In short, the superintendent had a rational basis for promulgating regulation 65. In sum, we conclude that regulation 65 is not in conflict with any positive provision of the Insurance Law. Instead, we hold that the regulation is a permissible and reasonable exercise of the superintendent's broad statutory authority to regulate fraudulent and collusive insurance practices so as to carry out the legislative policy to protect the beneficiaries of welfare funds. It is well within the proper province of the Superintendent of Insurance, the official responsible for the effective implementation of the Insurance Law, to regulate, control and suppress devised and contrived schemes targeted at the contravention or avoidance of the legislative policy. Indeed, it is most vital and paramount that the superintendent vigorously pursue and thwart disingenuous efforts to evade and detour the legislative design, especially where the Legislature has acted to protect a particular class from the consequences of fraud and overreaching.

Accordingly, the order of the Appellate Division should be reversed and judgment granted in favor of defendant declaring regulation 65 (11 NYCRR Part 202) valid.

Order reversed, with costs, and judgment granted in favor of defendant declaring regulation 65 valid.

Notes

1. The court in *Ostrer* explained that the role of a court in reviewing an agency's legal interpretation of a statute is a limited one—the court is to determine whether the agency's decision was reasonable. Although *Ostrer* was decided in 1977, this type of deference has come to be known as the *Chevron* doctrine, after a 1984 United States Supreme Court case. *See Chevron U.S.A., Inc. v. Natural Resources Defense Council, Inc.*, 467 U.S. 837, 104 S.Ct. 2778, 81 L.Ed.2d 694 (1984) (holding that federal courts are to defer to administrative judgments as to the meaning of a statute so long as the interpretation is based upon a permissible construction). While the *Chevron* doctrine applies to federal agency decisions, the principle has been applied with regard to state agencies as well. *See e.g McCullar v. Universal Underwriters Life Insurance Co.*, 687 So.2d 156 (Ala. 1996) (state agency's interpretation of a statute is entitled to deference by the reviewing court).

2. For cases in which the *Chevron* doctrine has been applied in the context of insurance, *see Barnhart v. Walton*, 535 U.S. 212, 122 S.Ct. 1265, 152 L.Ed.2d 330 (2002) (holding that a federal agency's interpretation of the Social Security Act falls "within the [a]gency's lawful interpretive authority"); *Patton v. Triad Guaranty Insurance*, 277 F.3d 1294 (11th Cir. 2002) (federal agency's interpretation that federal real estate statute "specifically relates" to mortgage insurance is reasonable). For an evolution of the *Chevron* doctrine, *see United States v. Mead Corp.*, 533 U.S. 218, 121 S.Ct. 2164, 150 L.Ed.2d 292 (2001) (reviewing court is only to give full deference to legal interpretation of a statute made by an agency during rule making or formal adjudication); *see also General Dynamics Land Systems, Inc. v. Cline*, 540 U.S. 581, 124 S.Ct. 1236, 157 L.Ed.2d 1094 (2004) (holding that where language of statute is clear, federal agency is not entitled to deference as to legal interpretation of statute).

WILSON v. ALL SERVICE INSURANCE CORP.

Court of Appeal of California, Second District, 1979.
91 Cal.App.3d 793, 153 Cal.Rptr. 121.

LILLIE, ACTING PRESIDING JUSTICE.

Plaintiffs commenced this action for damages allegedly sustained by them as a result of defendant insurance broker's having obtained for them a policy of automobile insurance issued by an insurance carrier which subsequently became insolvent after the occurrence of an accident covered by the policy. Plaintiffs appeal from summary judgment entered in defendant's favor.

* * *

It [is] alleged that on September 3, 1974, while the Transnational policy issued to plaintiffs was in effect, Rona, minor child of plaintiffs Willie and Yvonne Wilson, sustained bodily injuries through the negligence of an uninsured motorist; as a result of such accident plaintiffs Willie and Yvonne Wilson suffered severe emotional distress and physical injuries; following the accident plaintiffs presented to Transnational, pursuant to the uninsured motorist coverage afforded by the policy, a claim of $15,000 on behalf of Rona and a claim of $15,000 on behalf of Willie and Yvonne; on September 4, 1975, while the claims were pending, Transnational was declared insolvent and placed in liquidation by the Insurance Commissioner; in a reasonable, good faith effort to mitigate damages, plaintiffs settled their claims against Transnational for a total of $10,000; this sum was less than the actual value of the claims; but was fair and reasonable in view of Transnational's insolvency and the pending of liquidation proceedings against it; prior to the commencement of such proceedings, plaintiffs placed Transnational on notice that it was acting in bad faith in connection with their claims under the policy; as a result of Transnational's bad faith, each plaintiff was entitled to punitive damages in excess of $50,000.

The first cause of action concluded that as a "direct and proximate" result of defendant's negligence in failing to select a solvent insurance carrier for plaintiffs, they were denied (1) a major portion of the benefits to which they were entitled under the policy's uninsured motorist coverage, namely: $15,000 for Rona and $15,000 for Willie and Yvonne jointly, less the $10,000 received from Transnational, or a net total of $20,000; and (2) damages in the sum of at least $50,000 for each plaintiff arising out of the bad faith conduct of Transnational.

* * *

The complaint discloses the defendant's liability is predicated on a breach of its alleged duty to plaintiffs to investigate Transnational's financial condition before having placed automobile insurance for plaintiffs with that carrier. If no such duty exists, plaintiffs are not entitled to recover the damages sought herein.

* * * In order to determine whether defendant owed plaintiffs a duty to investigate Transnational's financial condition, it is necessary to consider provisions of the Insurance Code governing the financial qualifications of an insurer to conduct business in this state.

Insurance Code section 700 provides in pertinent part: "(a) A person shall not transact any class of insurance business in this state without first being admitted for such class. Such admission is secured by procuring a certificate of authority from the commissioner. Such certificate shall not be granted until the applicant conforms to the requirements of this code and of the laws of this state prerequisite to its issue. * * * [¶](c) After the issuance of a certificate of authority, the holder shall continue to comply with the requirements as to its business set forth in this code and in the other laws of this state."

Prior to admission, each insurer must file with the Insurance Commissioner a certified copy of its last annual statement or a verified financial statement disclosing its condition and affairs. (Ins.Code, § 706.) Before an incorporated insurer may lawfully transact business in this state, it must meet specified requirements as to paid-in capital. (Id., § 700.01.) In addition to the paid-in capital requirements certain requirements as to surplus must be met before an insurer will be issued a certificate of authority. (Id., § 700.02.) The Insurance Commissioner is required to examine the business and affairs of a domestic insurer before issuing to it an original certificate of authority. (Id., § 730.) In the case of a foreign insurer, the Commissioner may examine its affairs and business, or he may authorize such an investigation to be made by the insurance authorities of the state in which the insurer is organized. (Id., § 731.) The Commissioner may also examine the business and affairs of any admitted insurer whenever he deems it necessary, or when he is requested to do so by verified petition showing that the insurer is insolvent signed by 25 persons interested as shareholders, policyholders or creditors of the insurer. (Id., § 730.) In making such examination the Commissioner has free access to all books and papers of the insurer. (Id., § 733.) Every insurer doing business in the state is required to file a detailed financial statement with the Insurance Commissioner on or before March 1, of each year, showing its condition and affairs as of the preceding December 31 (id., §§ 900.900.7), and to publish a synopsis as adjusted by the Commissioner to show the true condition of the insurer (id., § 901). The statement must show the details relative to capital stock or paid-in capital (id., §§ 905, 906), property or assets owned (§ 907), liabilities (§ 908), income (§ 909), expenditures (§ 910), and amount of premiums on insurance on subject matter in this state (§ 911). The Insurance Commissioner may suspend or revoke the certificate of authority of an insurer which knowingly files a false financial statement. (Id., § 900.8.) Whenever the Commissioner finds that the investments of an admitted insurer are not so made as to make available within a reasonable time sufficient moneys to meet promptly any demand which might in the ordinary course of business be properly made against the insurer, he may order it to cease to effect new contracts of insurance until its financial circumstances have changed sufficiently to remove such condition. If the insurer fails to comply with such order, the Commissioner may suspend or revoke its certificate of authority. (Id., § 706.5.)

Thus, the Insurance Code prescribes financial requirements both for the issuance of a certificate of authority admitting an insurer to transact business in this state, and for an admitted insurer's right to continue conducting business pursuant to its certificate. The code imposes on the Insurance Commissioner the continuing duty to oversee the financial condition of an insurer holding a certificate of authority, and gives the Commissioner the power necessary to execute such duty. It would be superfluous, and would create a conflict with the regulatory scheme outlined in the Insurance Code, to impose upon an insurance broker a similar duty to ascertain the financial soundness of an insurer. Moreover, the imposition of such a duty would be meaningless inasmuch as a broker has no power to compel an insurer to divulge information regarding its financial condition. Accordingly, we hold that an insurance broker, such as defendant, owes no duty to its clients to investigate the financial condition of an insurer before placing insurance with it on their behalf. If a broker places insurance with an insurer conducting business pursuant to a certificate of authority, the broker has fulfilled its duty to its clients.

In support of its motion for summary judgment, defendant submitted the declaration of Joe Morton, Deputy Insurance Commissioner, in which the declarant stated that a certificate of authority to conduct business as an insurer was issued to Transnational on November 2, 1956, and remained in effect until September 4, 1975, when the Insurance Commissioner was appointed liquidator of Transnational by order of the court. Thus, Transnational was authorized to conduct business on August 18, 1974, when it allegedly issued its policy of automobile insurance to plaintiffs.

The judgment is affirmed.

Notes

1. The California Insurance Code (§§ 700.01, 700.02, 706, 706.5, 730, 731, 733, 900, 900.7, 900.8, 901, 905–911) states that before an insurer can transact business in California, the Commissioner must examine the business and affairs of all certificate applicants: insurers must submit their financial statements to the Commissioner, and they must meet specified, paid-in capital and surplus requirements. The Commissioner also has the authority to examine the business affairs of any admitted insurer whenever he deems necessary, or when the insurer's stockholders, creditors or policy holders petition the Commissioner to do so. The Code then provides the Commissioner free access to all of the insurer's "papers and books." Additionally, every insurer must file detailed annual financial statements, and the Commissioner has the power to revoke the certificate of an insurer who knowingly files a false financial statement. Furthermore, if the Commissioner finds that an insurer's investments are inadequate to meet any demand that might be made against the insurer, the Commissioner can order the insurer to stop issuing new insurance contracts until its financial condition has improved.

2. Because they are grounded in public policy considerations, state legislation and regulation have significantly affected the terms of automobile policies. One requirement for automobile insurance policies commonly mandated by state law is the so-called "omnibus" or "permission" clause. When a state legislature has required such a provision and defined what it is supposed to cover, what should be done with a clause that differs from the requirements? In *Metz v. Universal Underwriters Ins. Co.*, 10 Cal.3d 45, 109 Cal. Rptr. 698, 513 P.2d 922 (1973), the court rested its decision on the basis that "the entire automobile financial responsibility law must be liberally construed to foster its main objective of giving 'monetary protection to that

ever changing and tragically large group of persons who while lawfully using the highways themselves suffer grave injury through the negligent use of those highways by others'." Accordingly, it held invalid a clause in an insurance policy that purported to exclude a class of permissive users.

Populism and Insurance Regulation

Many states in the late–19th and early–20th centuries incorporated initiative, referendum and recall measures which allocated power directly to the voters. The "Progressives," an influential political group, were the principal sponsors of these measures. States adopted either all or some of these procedures; in 1911, California adopted all three under the leadership of Governor Hiram Johnson, a Progressive.

The initiative allows California voters to petition for inclusion of constitutional or statutory provisions on an election ballot. This can be done without the consent or approval of the governor or legislature. If the initiative is approved by a majority of the people voting, it goes into effect on the day after the election. Article II of the California Constitution (as in effect from 1976) contains the present statement of the initiative, referendum, and recall powers.

The use of the initiative has affected insurance regulation in California. The movement for "tort reform" had become very significant by the November 8, 1988, California general election. It was clear that one of the principal fuels of the tort system was the presence of insurance, particularly in auto liability cases. The legislature had proven incapable of addressing the problem and various protagonists set about putting initiatives on the ballot that would deal with insurance reform and other issues (despite the fact that the California State Constitution restricts each initiative to "one subject"). There were five initiatives aimed at insurance regulation, including Proposition 103, whose leading advocates included Ralph Nader, Harvey Rosenfield and their aptly-named group, "Voter Revolt to Cut Insurance Rates." Nearly $100 million was spent in support of, and in opposition to, all five initiatives. The only initiative statute that passed, however, was Proposition 103, which passed by a mere 51 percent–49 percent.

Proposition 103 had a variety of provisions, among them: (a) it provided for an immediate roll back of property and casualty insurance rates, including but not limited to auto insurance rates; (b) it called for a system of "good driver" discounts; (c) it mandated advance approval by the Insurance Commissioner of (future) rates; (d) it set up new standards for rates; (e) it subjected the business of insurance (*see* the McCarran–Ferguson Act) to the Unruh Civil Rights Act and to the antitrust and unfair business practice laws of California; (f) it placed new restrictions on the cancellation and non-renewal of auto insurance policies; (g) it provided for public participation in the rate-making process; and (h) it provided that the Insurance Commissioner should be elected.

Given the acrimonious climate surrounding Proposition 103, a court test was inevitable. The day after the election, interested parties went immediately to the Supreme Court of California to challenge the new law. The Court, exercising its original jurisdiction, granted a stay of enforcement of Proposition 103 on November 10, 1988.

After continuous legal maneuvering, the eventual decision, *Calfarm Insurance Co. v. Deukmejian*, 48 Cal.3d 805, 258 Cal.Rptr. 161, 771 P.2d 1247 (1989), had the important effect of declaring that rate-making could not be "confiscatory" and may not deny a "fair return." Additionally, the Court upheld the right of the state to legislate against nonrenewals of existing insurance policies as well as those not yet made. The Court also held that Proposition 103 did not violate the "one subject" rule.[2] This astonished legal professionals and academics, although it should be noted that the California Supreme Court seems to follow a broad and tolerant approach to the meaning of "one subject." A year later, in another Proposition 103 case, the Court also recognized the right of insurers to withdraw from doing business in the state, subject to the somewhat stringent requirements of the California Insurance Code.[3] Finally, in 1994, the Court upheld the validity of Proposition 103 against a broad based "takings" challenge in *20th Century Ins. Co. v. Garamendi*, 8 Cal.4th 216, 32 Cal.Rptr.2d 807, 878 P.2d 566 (1994).

Despite these decisions, Proposition 103 issues still abound. Near the end of 2000, the California Court of Appeal addressed some of Proposition 103's details. California Insurance Code § 1861.02(a), a result of Proposition 103, requires insurers to base automobile insurance rates on driving records, miles driven and years of driving experience. This appeared to conflict with Insurance Code §§ 2632.1, et seq., which precludes insurers from using rating factors that do not bear a substantial relationship to loss. According to the insurers, geography, represented by Zip code ratings, apparently correlates most to loss. Faced with the conflict between the statutes, the court allowed the redlining approach with its reliance on Zip codes to continue in *Spanish Speaking Citizens' Foundation, Inc. v. Low*, 85 Cal.App.4th 1179, 103 Cal.Rptr.2d 75 (2000).

In 2004, the California Supreme Court, in *State Farm Mutual Automobile Ins. Co. v. Garamendi*, 32 Cal.4th 1029, 12 Cal.Rptr.3d 343, 88 P.3d 71 (2004), focused on another aspect of Proposition 103: the data disclosure mandate of California Insurance Code § 1861.07 and the availability of the insurer's statement to the public under California Code of Regulations, title 10, § 2646.6(b). The Insurance Commissioner, under the authority of statutes enacted as part of Proposition 103, had promulgated a regulation requiring that insurers "writing in excess of ten million dollars in" certain "lines of insurance" file a Community Service Statement. Included in the information required of insurers is statistical data and "total earned exposures and total earned premiums

2. Article II, § 8 of the California Constitution states in subdivision (d) that "[an] initiative measure embracing more than one subject may not be submitted to the electors or have any effect." *Calfarm Insurance Co. v. Deukmejian*, 48 Cal.3d at 835.

3. *See Travelers Indemnity Co. v. Gillespie*, 50 Cal.3d 82, 266 Cal.Rptr. 117, 785 P.2d 500 (1990).

* * * for each line of insurance." Under another section of the California Insurance Code, all data provided to the Insurance Commissioner must be made available to the public.

When the insurers challenged the public availability of information they deemed to be trade secrets, the California Supreme Court held that the State's Insurance Commissioner did not exceed his statutory authority by promulgating Regulation 2646.6(c) and that there is no trade secret exemption to the public disclosure mandate of California Insurance Code § 1861.07. *State Farm Mutual Automobile Ins. Co. v. Garamendi*, 32 Cal.4th at 1042, 1047, 12 Cal.Rptr.3d 343, 88 P.3d 71 (noting that the Court's interpretation of § 1861.07, which was enacted by Proposition 103, is "wholly consistent with * * * Proposition 103's goal of fostering consumer participation in the rate-setting process."). It is safe to say that court challenges with respect to Proposition 103 will live on.[4]

A more recent incarnation of populism—Professor Neil Netanel refers to it as "cyberpopulism"[5]—the internet appears to be another mechanism that has limited the efficacy of insurance regulation in California. Because the Internet operates in a more indirect manner, its effects may be less pronounced than that of the initiative movement. For example, California enacted Insurance Code § 703, governing advertising by non-admitted insurers in California. Section 703.1(b) prohibits non-admitted insurers not on the Insurance Commissioner's list of eligible "surplus lines" insurers from advertising in California media that are targeted primarily at California residents. Surplus lines insurance is a way by which would-be policyholders can buy coverage from insurers not licensed to sell policies in their state ("non-admitted insurers"). Surplus lines insurance most often consists of hard-to-place coverage not provided by licensed insurers that are admitted to do business in the state. Buyers of surplus lines insurance are generally sophisticated, understand their insurance needs, and are able to evaluate insurance products adequately, thus they do not need the protection afforded by the regulated, admitted insurance market.

Purveyors of non-eligible surplus lines insurance will be the prime beneficiaries of § 703.1(a). While the statute appears to effectively prohibit advertising in traditional media outlets, it does not reach the Internet because the Internet is not geographically limited. Consequently, the Internet will be a prime advertising outlet for non-eligible, non-admitted insurers seeking California customers. Section 703.1(a) further imposes advertising restrictions on both eligible and ineligible non-admitted insurers, such as requiring disclosure of the insurer's unli-

4. For those seeking good background on the initiative process in California and other states, *see* David B. Magleby, *Governing by Initiative: Let the Voters Decide? An Assessment of the Initiative and Referendum Process*, 66 Col. L. Rev. 13 (1995); Douglas C. Michael, *Preelection Judicial Review: Taking the Initiative in Voter Protection*, 71 Cal. L. Rev. 1216 (1983).

5. Neil Weinstock Netanel, *Cyberspace Self-Governance: A Skeptical View from Liberal Democratic Theory*, 88 Cal. L. Rev. 395, 404 (2000).

censed status, explicitly prohibiting deceptive advertising, and prohibiting the provision of information on insurance rates and specific products.

B. FEDERAL REGULATION

The wide-ranging reach of federal legislation extends to many industries, and the business of insurance is no exception. Tax legislation, for example, can change the fortunes of the insurance industry, which currently benefits from favorable treatment under the Internal Revenue Code.[6] Further, Congress has enacted legislation which circumscribes an individual state's ability to regulate the business of insurance.

FEDERAL INVOLVEMENT IN STATE INSURANCE REGULATION

Pursuant to the McCarran–Ferguson Act, Congress has delegated broad authority to state legislatures in defining the scope and subject-matter of state insurance regulation. For example, a legislature may pass a statute requiring insurance companies to issue premium rebates because the premiums charged under a competitive system were deemed "too high."[7] The result of this kind of legislation might be in the public interest, but such a statute affects the solvency of insurers.

Even with congressional delegation of authority to the states over the scope and subject-matter of state insurance regulation, the McCarran–Ferguson Act supersedes state authority in regulating the insurance industry if the federal law specifically relates to the "business of insurance." The business of insurance encompasses a variety of activities, but has been defined to address the relationship between the insurer and the insured, the type of policy that can be issued, and the liability, interpretation and enforcement of the policy.[8] The business of insurance is conducted by many companies on an interstate basis, and insureds, particularly drivers, move within and without state lines. In this context, Congress' use of its Commerce Clause powers to regulate insurance companies is reasonable—and sometimes desirable.

In the late 1970s, a little known but extremely influential agency of Congress, the United States General Accounting Office (GAO), issued a report to Congress.[9] The report reviewed state regulation, and examined financial and trade practice regulation, price regulation of automobile insurance, regulation of automobile risk classification, insurance availability (to consumers), and organizational issues. Comments of state

6. *E.g. Atlantic Mutual Ins. Co. v. Commissioner*, 523 U.S. 382, 118 S.Ct. 1413, 140 L.Ed.2d 542 (1998) (regulations pertaining to "reserve strengthening" construed to reduce loss reserve deduction).

7. *See e.g., American Manufacturers Mutual Insurance Co. v. Commissioner of Insurance*, 374 Mass. 181, 372 N.E.2d 520 (1978) (Massachusetts Supreme Court held that state legislature could pass such a statute).

8. 116 A.L.R. Fed. 163.

9. *Issues and Needed Improvements in State Regulation of the Insurance Business*, PAD 7972, October 9, 1979.

insurance officials were noted. Without making any specific recommendations for federal legislation, the GAO report stated in its digest:

> There are serious shortcomings in State laws and regulatory activities with respect to protecting the interests of insurance consumers in the United States. In particular, most State insurance departments do not have systematic procedures to determine whether insurance consumers are being treated properly with respect to such matters as claims payments, rate setting, and protection from unfair discrimination.

Question

Consider the *Ostrer* and *Wilson* cases in light of the GAO's comments. Would you conclude that state legislative measures adequately protect the interests of insurance consumers?

THE McCARRAN–FERGUSON ACT

The United States Supreme Court in 1868, said that the making of a contract or policy of insurance was not a "transaction of commerce." *Paul v. Virginia*, 75 U.S. (8 Wall.) 168, 19 L.Ed. 357 (1868). This led to a wide-spread conviction that congressional regulation of the business of insurance was constitutionally improper. More than 75 years later, however, in *United States v. South–Eastern Underwriters Association*, 322 U.S. 533, 64 S.Ct. 1162, 88 L.Ed. 1440 (1944), the Court held that insurance was subject to regulation by Congress and its anti-trust laws. Congress enacted the following piece of legislation in response:

The McCarran–Ferguson Act

59 Stat. 33 (1945) as amended 15 U.S.C.A. §§ 1011–15.

§ 1011. Declaration of policy

Congress declares that the continued regulation and taxation by the several States of the business of insurance is in the public interest, and that silence on the part of the Congress shall not be construed to impose any barrier to the regulation or taxation of such business by the several States.

§ 1012. Regulation by State law; Federal law relating specifically to insurance; applicability of certain Federal laws after June 30, 1948

(a) The business of insurance, and every person engaged therein, shall be subject to the laws of the several States which relate to the regulation or taxation of such business.

(b) No Act of Congress shall be construed to invalidate, impair, or supersede any law enacted by any State for the purpose of regulating the business of insurance, or which imposes a fee or tax upon such business, unless such Act specifically relates to the business of insurance: Provided, That after June 30, 1948, the Act of July 2, 1890, as amended, known as the Sherman Act, and the Act of October 15, 1914, as amended, known as the Clayton Act, and the Act of September 26, 1914, known as the Federal Trade

Commission Act, as amended, shall be applicable to the business of insurance to the extent that such business is not regulated by State law.

§ 1014. Applicability of National Labor Relations Act and Fair Labor Standards Act of 1938

Nothing contained in this chapter shall be construed to affect in any manner the application to the business of insurance of the Act of July 5, 1935, as amended, known as the National Labor Relations Act, or the Act of June 25, 1938, as amended, known as the Fair Labor Standards Act of 1938, or the Act of June 5, 1920, known as the Merchant Marine Act, 1920.

Notes

1. The McCarran–Ferguson Act has generated litigation in various contexts. In *Hartford Fire Insurance Co. v. California*, 509 U.S. 764, 113 S.Ct. 2891, 125 L.Ed.2d 612 (1993), certain domestic and foreign insurers attempted to pressure the Insurance Services Office (ISO), a trade association, to issue its standard comprehensive general liability form policies with a "claims made" provision. According to the Court, the insurers either refused or tried to persuade others to refuse to reinsure policies written on the ISO forms until the desired changes were made. In an opinion by Justice Souter, the Supreme Court held that the McCarran–Ferguson Act did not bar state anti-trust prosecution of the insurers' conduct.

Despite the initial thrust of the opinion, a majority of the court, not including Justice Souter, held that while the McCarran–Ferguson's anti-trust exemption does not apply to "boycotts," the Act's concept of boycott was a narrow one. It remains to be seen whether the initial restriction of the anti-trust exemption will be undone by the Court's narrowing of the boycott definition.

2. More recently, in *Humana Inc. v. Forsyth*, 525 U.S. 299, 119 S.Ct. 710, 142 L.Ed.2d 753 (1999), the Supreme Court held that the McCarran–Ferguson Act does not preclude the application of the Racketeer Influenced and Corrupt Organizations Act (RICO) unless there is a direct conflict with state regulation, state policy is frustrated, or there is interference with a state's administrative scheme. Finding no such conflict, frustration or interference, the Court affirmed the application of RICO against Humana.

Questions

Conceding that the McCarran–Ferguson Act applies to the "business of insurance" but does not provide total immunity from federal regulation:

(a) Can the SEC disapprove a merger of two insurance companies approved by a state? See Securities & Exchange Commission v. National Securities, Inc., 393 U.S. 453, 89 S.Ct. 564, 21 L.Ed.2d 668 (1969) (because the Arizona state law was compatible with the McCarran–Ferguson Act, undoing the state's approval of the merger was an adequate remedy).

(b) Does the federal "Truth in Lending" Act, 15 U.S.C.A. § 1601 et seq., apply to credit financing of auto insurance premiums when insurance rates and premium financing are regulated by state law? See Lowe v. Aarco–American, Inc., 536 F.2d 1160 (7th Cir. 1976) (credit sale of insurance policies by an insurance broker and a premium finance company constitutes the "business of insurance" under the McCarran–Ferguson Act and is beyond the reach of the Truth in Lending Act); cf. King v. Central Bank, 18 Cal.3d 840, 135 Cal.Rptr. 771, 558 P.2d 857 (1977) (credit sale of automobile insurance falls within the Truth in Lending Act).

(c) Would a private treble damage action under the federal antitrust laws be precluded where damages are sought for a nationwide violation of such laws on the ground that Missouri insurance laws provide antitrust remedies? See Seasongood v. K & K Insurance Agency, 548 F.2d 729 (8th Cir. 1977) (possibly yes because "a state regulatory scheme operating essentially extraterritorially is not the kind of regulation contemplated by the McCarran–Ferguson Act").

(d) Is an agreement between a health insurer and pharmacies under which drugs would be furnished to health insurance subscribers within the "business of insurance" exemption or can it be said to be a part of the "business of insurers" which is not protected from the antitrust laws by the exemption? The question cannot be summarily dismissed as hair splitting. See Group Life & Health Insurance Co. v. Royal Drug Co., 440 U.S. 205, 99 S.Ct. 1067, 59 L.Ed.2d 261 (1979) (such agreements are not the "business of insurance").

CIVIL RIGHTS LAWS

Race, color, creed, ethnicity, sex, age, and disability theoretically may discriminatorily affect insurance premiums and the terms of insurance coverage. There may be, on occasion, sound economic grounds for such discrimination. For example, a longer life expectancy would justify different premium calculations for men and women based on easily determinable and verifiable differences in life expectancy. At the same time, there may also be a very good social and political basis for refusing to enforce discriminatory schemes in computing premiums or providing coverage. Not surprisingly, the Civil Rights Acts cast a long shadow on any such area. One early example was *Spirt v. Teachers Insurance and Annuity Association (TIAA), and College Retirement Equities Fund (CREF)*, 475 F.Supp. 1298 (S.D.N.Y.1979), in which the court distinguished between "insurance" and "annuity" for the purposes of deciding whether the McCarran–Ferguson Act exempted either insurance (TIAA) or annuities (CREF) from application of Title VII of the Civil Rights Act of 1964. It held that TIAA was controlled by the state law in fixing premiums (the New York Insurance Law had nondiscrimination provisions of its own) but that CREF was not.

Other similar cases were also making their way through the courts. The case selected for the ultimate decision by the U.S. Supreme Court was *Arizona Governing Committee, etc. v. Norris*, 463 U.S. 1073, 103 S.Ct. 3492, 77 L.Ed.2d 1236 (1983). *Norris* concerned a proposed pension plan for employees of the state of Arizona. The proposal, which was put up for bids from insurance companies, would have required men and women of the same age to pay into the plan in equal monthly installments, but the monthly pay-outs after retirement would have been less for women than for men because actuarially they live longer. The state's female employees contended that such a pay-out practice would constitute employment discrimination against women in violation of Title VII of the Civil Rights Act of 1964. Again, as in *Spirt*, the role of the McCarran–Ferguson Act as a shield against federal regulation of the insurance industry was brought into question.

The majority (5 justices) in *Norris* took the McCarran–Ferguson Act out of the disposition of the case by stating in a footnote that it had not been treated in the briefs, but added:

> All that is in issue in this case is *an employment practice*: the practice of offering a male employee the opportunity to obtain greater monthly annuity benefits than could be obtained by a similarly situated female employee. It is this conduct of the employer that is prohibited by Title VII. By its own terms, the McCarran–Ferguson Act applies only to the business of insurance and has no application to employment practices. Arizona plainly is not itself involved in the business of insurance, since it has not underwritten any risks. * * * Because the application of Title VII in this case does not supersede any state law governing the business of insurance * * * we need not decide whether Title VII 'specifically relates to the business of insurance' within the meaning of the McCarran–Ferguson Act.[10]

The minority (4 justices) in *Norris* asserted that McCarran–Ferguson did indeed constitute a bar to applying Title VII unless Congress expressly intended Title VII to preempt state insurance legislation. But, Justice Powell said, "Nothing in the language of Title VII supports this preemption of state jurisdiction." The dissenters' position on the effect of McCarran–Ferguson is also detailed in a footnote:

> The majority argues * * * that the McCarran–Ferguson Act is inapposite because Title VII will not supersede any state regulation. Because Title VII applies to employers rather than insurance carriers, the majority asserts * * * Title VII will not affect the business of insurance. * * * This formalistic distinction ignores self-evident facts. State insurance laws such as Arizona's, allow employers to purchase sex-based annuities for their employees. * * * It begs reality to say that a federal law that * * * denies the right to do what state insurance law allows does not 'invalidate, impair or supersede' state law.[11]

Having removed the McCarran–Ferguson Act from the picture, the majority in the *Norris* case proceeded to the issue of whether group annuity sales, calculated on the known fact that women live longer than

10. 463 U.S. at 1087 n.17, 103 S.Ct. at 3501 [emphasis in original].

11. 463 U.S. at 1100 n.6, 103 S.Ct. at 3508.

men, is *sex-based* discrimination as applied to employee pension plans. A precedent decision was *City of Los Angeles, Dept. of Water and Power v. Manhart*, 435 U.S. 702, 98 S.Ct. 1370, 55 L.Ed.2d 657 (1978) (holding that an annuity plan that required women employees to pay more monthly into the plan, but get only the same monthly pension pay-out, was discriminatory compensation in employment and invalid). The *Norris* majority applied the *Manhart* reasoning and determined that sex-based discrimination likewise would arise where the pay-in is the same, but the pay-out is less. The minority, in contrast, posited that the mortality tables in use actually reflect longevity, which is a nondiscriminatory factor, and because of this well-established phenomenon, the average male and female pensioner would in the long run have equal benefits.

Given the Court's holding in *Norris*, employers have been left with the task of removing the sex-based discrimination which the *Norris* majority rejected. One solution is to have the same pay-in to the deferred compensation plans by both men and women employees, to be followed by a single lump sum pay-out on retirement—a method of pay-out that most retirees do not prefer, and is, perhaps, socially undesirable as defeating the long-term goal of a disciplined lifelong support system for the aged.

The other alternative that has found favor is the adoption of the so-called *unisex* mortality tables, which are no more than a blending of the existing separate male and female tables. This may be objected to in the annuity cases as substituting a fair system for an unfair one: one that requires males to subsidize enhanced benefits accruing to females (all in the name of eliminating discrimination according to sex). This "fairness" argument was anticipated and rejected by Justice Stevens in the *Manhart* case:

> [W]hen insurance risks are grouped, the better risks always subsidize the poorer risks. Healthy persons subsidize medical benefits for the less healthy; unmarried workers subsidize the pensions of married workers; persons who eat, drink or smoke to excess may subsidize pension benefits for persons whose habits are more temperate. Treating different classes as risks as though they were the same for purposes of group insurance is a common practice which has never been considered as inherently unfair.[12]

Therefore, according to Justice Stevens' reasoning, it is not unfair that shorter-lived men subsidize longer-lived women annuitants.

Query: Age discrimination is now the target of much prohibitory legislation. Must a 45-year-old person hired as an employee at the same time as a 20-year-old be legally entitled to subsidization of his or her annuity by the 20-year-old by using mortality tables that eliminate any longevity factors?

12. 435 U.S. 702 at 710, 98 S.Ct. at 1376.

The required use of *unisex* mortality tables in effecting annuity programs cuts both ways. As applied to conventional life insurance, men benefit at the expense of longer-lived women and the unfairness thus created falls upon women. The foregoing decisions arise from congressionally mandated non-sexist employment compensation programs and the funding of such programs by group insurance. Remove this special context and a sharp and discomforting fact appears. The pursuit of absolute equality with regard to sex, age, or other forms of discrimination in insurance rate regulation automatically creates patent unfairness and other socially undesirable results. In weighing the considerations, states have implemented approaches at both ends of the spectrum, either by administrative fiat, legislative enactment, or judicial inclination.

In *Hartford Accident and Indemnity Co. v. Insurance Commissioner*, 505 Pa. 571, 482 A.2d 542 (1984) the Hartford Company filed a rate classification plan with differential charges applied to young male drivers as compared to female drivers. The Commissioner approved; whereupon a 26 year-old male questioned the validity of charging him a $360 premium, while charging a female $212 with no difference between the two policyholders other than gender. The Commissioner changed his mind and disapproved the insurer's rating plan. The matter wound up in court, the male policyholder taking the position that the sex-based distinction violated his constitutional rights. The court sustained his position and the authority of the Commissioner (supported by the Equal Rights Amendment incorporated into the Pennsylvania State Constitution in 1971) to disapprove such gender-based rate plans.

At the other end of the spectrum is a statute such as West's Annotated California Insurance Code § 790.03:

> The following are hereby defined as unfair methods of competition and unfair and deceptive acts or practices in the business of insurance.
>
> * * *
>
> (f) Making or permitting any unfair discrimination between individuals of the same class and equal expectation of life in rates charged for any contract of life insurance or of life annuity or in the dividends or other benefits payable thereon * * *.
>
> This subdivision shall be interpreted, for any contract of *ordinary* life insurance or *individual* life annuity * * * to *require* differentials based on the sex of the *individual* insured or annuitant in the rates or dividends or benefits, or any combination thereof. [emphasis added] * * *

As a gesture toward the *Norris* decision, a 1983 amendment to the above section states that sex-based differentials in rates or dividends shall *not* be required for group life insurance or annuities as to terms, conditions or privileges of employment as such terms are used in Title VII of the Civil Rights Act of 1964.

As an example of modern anti-discrimination legislation affecting insurance, *see* West's Annotated California Insurance Code § 10140, as amended in 1990, which reads:

> (a) No admitted insurer, licensed to issue life or disability insurance, shall fail or refuse to accept an application for that insurance, to issue that insurance to an applicant therefor, or issue or cancel that insurance, under conditions less favorable to the insured than in other comparable cases, except for reasons applicable alike to persons of every race, color, religion, national origin, ancestry, or sexual orientation. Race, color, religion, national origin, ancestry, or sexual orientation shall not, of itself, constitute a condition or risk for which a higher rate, premium, or charge may be required of the insured for that insurance.
>
> (b) It shall be deemed a violation of subdivision (a) for any insurer to consider sexual orientation in its underwriting criteria or to utilize marital status, living arrangements, occupation, gender, beneficiary designation, zip codes or other territorial classification within this state, or any combination thereof for the purpose of establishing sexual orientation or determining whether to require a test for the presence of the human immunodeficiency virus or antibodies to that virus, where that testing is otherwise permitted by law. Nothing in this section shall be construed to alter, expand, or limit in any manner the existing law respecting the authority of insurers to conduct tests for the presence of human immunodeficiency virus or evidence thereof.
>
> (c) Any insurer that knowingly violates this section shall for each violation be assessed a civil penalty in an amount not less than one thousand dollars ($1,000) and not more than five thousand dollars ($5,000) plus court costs, as determined by the court.
>
> (d) This section shall not be construed to limit the authority of the commissioner to adopt regulations prohibiting discrimination because of sex, marital status, or sexual orientation or to enforce these regulations, whether adopted before or on or after January 1, 1991.

As a final note, the Americans with Disabilities Act (ADA) has not yet affected the insurance coverage of those with disabilities. Thus far, the few courts addressing ADA concerns in connection with insurance products have sided with insurers on the basis that the content of policies is not a matter of public accommodation within the meaning of the ADA. *Chabner v. United of Omaha Life Ins. Co.*, 225 F.3d 1042 (9th Cir. 2000) (differential life insurance rates do not violate the ADA though state rate making regulation might provide remedy); *Doe v. Mutual of Omaha Ins. Co.*, 179 F.3d 557 (7th Cir. 1999) (insurer's practice of imposing lifetime caps on AIDS related conditions did not violate the ADA); *Parker v. Metropolitan Life Ins. Co.*, 121 F.3d 1006 (6th Cir. 1997), cert. denied 522 U.S. 1084, 118 S.Ct. 871, 139 L.Ed.2d 768 (1998) (insurer's practice of providing longer disability benefits to those with physical, as opposed to mental, disabilities did not violate the ADA); *but see Pallozzi v. Allstate Life Ins. Co.*, 204 F.3d 392 (2d Cir. 2000) (insurer cannot deny coverage where denial is a subterfuge to evade the purposes of the ADA).[13]

ERISA

The Employee Retirement Income Security Act (ERISA) was enacted in 1974, to protect the rights of employees and their beneficiaries in employee benefit plans. ERISA also serves another purpose: it provides for *preemption* of state law remedies when an employee seek redress under a benefit plan. A state law, as Laurence Tribe explains, may be preempted because it "intrudes jurisdictionally upon a field that Congress has validly reserved for exclusively federal regulation."[14]

Employee Retirement Income Security Program

Protection of Employee Benefit Rights

29 U.S.C.A. § 1144 (2004).

§ 1144. Other laws

(a) Supersedure; effective date. Except as provided in subsection (b) of this section, the provisions of this subchapter and subchapter III of this chapter shall supersede any and all State laws insofar as they may now or hereafter relate to any employee benefit plan described in section 1003(a) of this title and not exempt under section 1003(b) of this title. This section shall take effect on January 1, 1975.

(b) Construction and application.

* * *

(2)(A) Except as provided in subparagraph (B), nothing in this subchapter shall be construed to exempt or relieve any person from any law of any State which regulates insurance, banking, or securities.

[(2)](B) Neither an employee benefit plan described in section 1003(a) of this title, which is not exempt under section 1003(b) of this title (other than a plan established primarily for the purpose of providing death benefits), nor any trust established under such a plan, shall be deemed to be an insurance company or other insurer, bank, trust company, or investment company or to be engaged in the business of insurance or banking for purposes of any law of any State purporting to regulate insurance companies, insurance contracts, banks, trust companies, or investment companies.

In the following opinion written by Justice O'Connor, the Supreme Court explored the implications of these ERISA provisions, while analyzing the impact of ERISA upon the state common law rights of an employee to sue for "bad faith" in the first-party context. Professor

13. For an economic overview of insurance classification, *see*, Leah Wortham, *The Economics of Insurance Classification, etc.*, 47 Ohio St. L.J. 835 (1986).

14. Laurence H. Tribe, American Constitutional Law vol. 1, § 6–28, 1177 (3d ed., Found. Press 2000).

Jeffrey Stempel and Nadia von Magdenko have written an excellent article on ERISA in the context of insurance law principles that provides a comprehensive background of the history of ERISA as well as a discussion of the *Pilot Life* case. Jeffrey W. Stempel & Nadia von Magdenko, *Doctors, HMOs, ERISA, and the Public Interest after Pegram v. Herdrich*, 36 Tort & Ins. L.J 687, 694–710 (2001). As the article notes, *Pilot Life* was criticized for its overbroad reading of ERISA which was, in turn, seen as unduly favoring employer and insurer interests. *Id.* at 702. Keep this admonition in mind when reading the case law developments spelled out in the notes following the case.

PILOT LIFE INSURANCE CO. v. DEDEAUX

Supreme Court of the United States, 1987.
481 U.S. 41, 107 S.Ct. 1549, 95 L.Ed.2d 39.

Justice O'Connor delivered the opinion of the Court.

* * *

[After a 1975 accident related to his employment for Entex, Inc., Dedeaux claimed permanent disability benefits under a group disability policy from Pilot Life Insurance Co. obtained by his employer. Pilot, however, terminated his benefits after two years. For the next three years, Dedeaux's benefits were reinstated and terminated several times. Dedeaux sued in 1980, seeking damages for failure to pay benefits, damages for mental and emotional distress, and punitive damages. Pilot argued that ERISA preempted Dedeaux's common law claim for failure to pay benefits on the group insurance policy.]

At the close of discovery [at the district court level], Pilot Life moved for summary judgment, arguing that ERISA pre-empted Dedeaux's common law claim for failure to pay benefits on the group insurance policy. The District Court granted Pilot Life summary judgment, finding all Dedeaux's claims pre-empted.

The Court of Appeals for the Fifth Circuit reversed, primarily on the basis of this Court's decision in *Metropolitan Life Ins. Co.* v. *Massachusetts, 471 U.S. 724 (1985).* We granted certiorari, and now reverse.

II

In ERISA, Congress set out to "protect . . . participants in employee benefit plans and their beneficiaries * * *." [citing 29 U.S.C. § 1001(b)]

ERISA comprehensively regulates, among other things, employee welfare benefit plans that, "through the purchase of insurance or otherwise," provide medical, surgical, or hospital care, or benefits in the event of sickness, accident, disability or death. § 3(1), 29 U.S.C. § 1002(1).

Congress capped off the massive undertaking of ERISA with three provisions relating to the pre-emptive effect of the federal legislation:

"Except as provided in subsection (b) of this section [the saving clause], the provisions of this subchapter and subchapter III of this chapter shall supersede any and all State laws insofar as they may now or hereafter relate to any employee benefit plan...." § 514(a), as set forth in 29 U.S.C. § 1144(a) (pre-emption clause).

"Except as provided in subparagraph (B) [the deemer clause], nothing in this subchapter shall be construed to exempt or relieve any person from any law of any State which regulates insurance, banking, or securities." § 514(b)(2)(A), as set forth in 29 U.S.C. § 1144(b)(2)(A) (saving clause).

"Neither an employee benefit plan ... nor any trust established under such a plan, shall be deemed to be an insurance company or other insurer, bank, trust company, or investment company or to be engaged in the business of insurance or banking for purposes of any law of any State purporting to regulate insurance companies, insurance contracts, banks, trust companies, or investment companies." Section 514(b)(2)(B), 29 U.S.C. § 1144(b)(2)(B) (deemer clause).

To summarize the pure mechanics of the provisions quoted above: If a state law "relate[s] to ... employee benefit plan[s]," it is pre-empted. § 514(a). The saving clause excepts from the pre-emption clause laws that "regulat[e] insurance." § 514(b)(2)(A). The deemer clause makes clear that a state law that "purport[s] to regulate insurance" cannot deem an employee benefit plan to be an insurance company. § 514(b)(2)(B).

* * *

III

There is no dispute that the common law causes of action asserted in Dedeaux's complaint "relate to" an employee benefit plan and therefore fall under ERISA's express pre-emption clause, § 514(a). * * *

Unless these common law causes of action fall under an exception to § 514(a), therefore, they are expressly pre-empted. Although Dedeaux's complaint pleaded several state common law causes of action, before this Court Dedeaux has described only one of the three counts—called "tortious breach of contract" in the complaint, and "the Mississippi law of bad faith" in respondent's brief—as protected from the pre-emptive effect of § 514(a). The Mississippi law of bad faith, Dedeaux argues, is a law "which regulates insurance," and thus is saved from pre-emption by § 514(b)(2)(A).

In *Metropolitan Life*, we were guided by several considerations in determining whether a state law falls under the saving clause. First, we took what guidance was available from a "common sense view" of the language of the saving clause itself. 471 U.S., at 740. Second, we made use of the case law interpreting the phrase "business of insurance" under the McCarran–Ferguson Act, 15 U.S.C. § 1011 et seq., in interpreting the saving clause. Three criteria have been used to determine whether a practice falls under the "business of insurance" for purposes of the McCarran–Ferguson Act:

"[F]irst, whether the practice has the effect of transferring or spreading a policyholder's risk; *second*, whether the practice is an integral part of the policy relationship between the insurer and the insured; and *third*, whether the practice is limited to entities within the insurance industry." *Union Labor Life Ins. Co. v. Pireno*, 458 U.S. 119, 129 (1982) (emphasis in original).

In the present case, the considerations weighed in *Metropolitan Life* argue against the assertion that the Mississippi law of bad faith is a state law that "regulates insurance."

* * *

Certainly a common sense understanding of the phrase "regulates insurance" does not support the argument that the Mississippi law of bad faith falls under the saving clause. A common sense view of the word "regulates" would lead to the conclusion that in order to regulate insurance, a law must not just have an impact on the insurance industry, but be specifically directed toward that industry. Even though the Mississippi Supreme Court has identified its law of bad faith with the insurance industry, the roots of this law are firmly planted in the general principles of Mississippi tort and contract law. Any breach of contract, and not merely breach of an insurance contract, may lead to liability for punitive damages under Mississippi law.

Neither do the McCarran–Ferguson Act factors support the assertion that the Mississippi law of bad faith "regulates insurance." Unlike the mandated benefits law at issue in *Metropolitan Life*, the Mississippi common law of bad faith does not effect a spreading of policyholder risk. The state common law of bad faith may be said to concern "the policy relationship between the insurer and the insured." The connection to the insurer-insured relationship is attenuated at best, however. In contrast to the mandated benefits law in Metropolitan Life, the common law of bad faith does not define the terms of the relationship between the insurer and the insured; it declares only that, whatever terms have been agreed upon in the insurance contract, a breach of that contract may in certain circumstances allow the policyholder to obtain punitive damages. The state common law of bad faith is therefore no more "integral" to the insurer-insured relationship than any state's general contract law is integral to a contract made in that state. Finally, as we have just noted, Mississippi's law of bad faith, even if associated with the insurance industry, has developed from general principles of tort and contract law available in any Mississippi breach of contract case.

* * *

Considering the common-sense understanding of the saving clause, the McCarran–Ferguson Act factors defining the business of insurance, and, most importantly, the clear expression of congressional intent that ERISA's civil enforcement scheme be exclusive, we conclude that Dedeaux's state law suit asserting improper processing of a claim for benefits under an ERISA-regulated plan is not saved by § 514(b)(2)(A), and therefore is pre-empted by § 514(a). Accordingly, the judgment of the Court of Appeals is *Reversed*.

Notes

1. Even health insurance coverage requirements have been preempted by ERISA. See District of Columbia v. Greater Washington Board of Trade, 506 U.S. 125, 113 S.Ct. 580, 121 L.Ed.2d 513 (1992). In *Greater Washington Board of Trade*, the Court grappled with section 2(c)(2) of the District of Columbia Workers' Compensation Equity Amendment Act of 1990, which required employers who provide health insurance for their employees to provide equivalent health insurance coverage for injured employees eligible for workers' compensation benefits. *See id.* at 127. Workers' compensation plans are among those exempted from ERISA coverage under 29 U.S.C. § 1003(b). *Id.*

In the opinion by Justice Thomas, the Court held that ERISA preempted section 2(c)(2). Id. Justice Thomas explained that a law "relate[s] to a covered employee benefit plan for purposes of § 514(a) if it has a connection with or reference to such a plan." Id. at 129 (internal quotations omitted). Moreover, the Court explained, "ERISA pre-empts any [such] state law * * * even if the law is not specifically designed to affect such plans, or the effect is only indirect." Id. at 129–30 (internal quotations omitted).

Justice Thomas went on to state:

> Section 2(c)(2) of the District's Equity Amendment Act specifically refers to welfare benefit plans regulated by ERISA and on that basis alone is pre-empted. The health insurance coverage that § 2(c)(2) requires employers to provide for eligible employees is measured by reference to 'the existing health insurance coverage' * * * [which] is a welfare benefit plan under ERISA § 3(*l*).
>
> * * *
>
> It makes no difference that § 2(c)(2)'s requirements * * * also "relate to" ERISA-exempt workers' compensation plans. The exemptions from ERISA coverage * * * do not limit the pre-emptive sweep of § 514 once it is determined that a law relates to a covered plan. *See Alessi v. Raybestos–Manhattan, Inc.*, 451 U.S. 504, 525 (1981).* * *

Relying on *Metropolitan Life Ins. Co. v. Massachusetts*, 471 U.S. 724, 105 S.Ct. 2380, 85 L.Ed.2d 728 (1985), the petitioners tried to establish that § 514(a) requires a two-part analysis under which a state law relating to an ERISA-covered plan would survive preemption if employers could comply with the law through separately administered exempt plans. See id. at 132. Justice Thomas was quick to dismiss this assertion. Justice Thomas reasoned that *Metropolitan Life* did not intend to add "any further gloss on § 514(a). * * * [Therefore, the Court] cannot engraft a two-step analysis onto a one-step statute." Id. at 133.

2. In *UNUM Life Ins. Co. v. Ward*, 526 U.S. 358, 119 S.Ct. 1380, 143 L.Ed.2d 462 (1999), the Court held that ERISA's savings clause exempts state insurance regulations from preemption. The Court opined that California's notice-prejudice common law rule, which bars an insurer from avoiding

liability where a claim is "untimely," absent a showing of prejudice, strictly regulates insurance and, thus, was not preempted by ERISA. Id. at 364, 373. The *UNUM Life* opinion then turned to the reasoning in *New York State Conference of Blue Cross & Blue Shield Plans v. Travelers Ins. Co.*, 514 U.S. 645, 115 S.Ct. 1671, 131 L.Ed.2d 695 (1995), in which the Court held that ERISA does not preempt state health care regulations that are administrative in nature (e.g., bookkeeping obligation regarding to whom benefits checks must be sent). UNUM Life, 526 U.S. at 379. However, where a regulation bleeds into anything substantive, e.g., "mandat[ing] employee benefit structures," the regulation is preempted. Id. at 378–79.

3. Perhaps the most fertile ground of new law involving ERISA deals with health maintenance organizations (HMOs) and how HMOs are administered. An HMO receives a fixed fee from each enrolled member, and in return contracts to provide specified health care to its members if needed. Consequently, an HMO assumes the financial risk of providing promised benefits to its members. While HMOs may argue that they are health care providers (rather than insurers), case law has generally regarded H.M.O.s as risk-bearing organizations and typically treats HMOs as insurers. See e.g. Rush Prudential HMO, Inc. v. Moran, 536 U.S. 355, 122 S.Ct. 2151, 153 L.Ed.2d 375 (2002) (an HMO is both an insurer and a health care provider); Pegram v. Herdrich, 530 U.S. 211, 218, 120 S.Ct. 2143, 147 L.Ed.2d 164 (2000) (comparing HMOs as risk-bearing organizations to insurers); Washington Physicians Service Association v. Gregoire, 147 F.3d 1039, 1046 (9th Cir. 1998) (reasoning that HMOs "function the same way as a traditional health insurer").

4. *Pegram v. Herdrich*, 530 U.S. 211, 120 S.Ct. 2143, 147 L.Ed.2d 164 (2000), illustrates an example of a claim in this area that does is not preempted by ERISA. In *Pegram*, the Supreme Court unanimously ruled that treatment decisions made by an HMO, acting through its physician employees, were not fiduciary acts within the meaning of ERISA (under which fiduciaries are to discharge their duties solely in the interest of the participants/beneficiaries). "A fiduciary within the meaning of ERISA must be someone acting in the capacity of manager, administrator or financial adviser to a 'plan,' see 29 U.S.C. §§ 1002(21)(A)(i)-(iii)." Pegram v. Herdrich, 530 U.S. 211, 222, 120 S.Ct. 2143, 147 L.Ed.2d 164 (2000).

The case was triggered by the decision of petitioner Lori Pegram, a physician connected to an HMO, to delay her patient's (respondent Cynthia Herdrich) ultrasound for eight days, during which time respondent's appendix burst. Respondent sued in state court, claiming medical malpractice and fraud. Petitioners removed to federal court, at which point respondent amended her claim to allege that the HMO breached its fiduciary duty (under ERISA) by giving the physicians a share of the end-of-year profits through an express provision in the HMO's plan. The amended complaint argued that this created an incentive for the HMO's physicians to make decisions in their own self-interests, as opposed to the participants' interests. Justice Souter, writing for the Court, rejected this argument, explaining that in such an action, the issue is whether the provider was actually acting as a fiduciary (and not whether the provider, acting through its physicians, adversely affected a beneficiary's interest). He rationalized that the payout provision of the plan could be freely adopted without breaching any fiduciary duty under ERISA. Because respondent's claims of breach of a fiduciary duty were nothing more than mixed eligibility and treatment decisions ("physicians' conclusions about when to use diagnostic tests; about proper standards of care"), these determinations were not fiduciary decisions within the meaning of ERISA.

By not implicating a breach of fiduciary duty under ERISA, *Pegram* has a positive effect on the continued operation of HMOs' physician profit-sharing scheme. At the same time, one of ERISA's original aims was to protect employees and their beneficiaries' rights in employee benefit plans. Does *Pegram* undermine this aim by concentrating on whether or not the provider acted as a fiduciary, rather than examining whether or not the employee's interests under the benefit plan were adversely affected by the provider's actions? Does *Pegram* suggest that the limitation of ERISA preemption articulated in *UNUM Life* will continue? This decision seems to be consistent with the *UNUM Life* opinion's reliance on the reasoning found in *New York State Conference of Blue Cross & Blue Shield Plans v. Travelers Ins. Co.*, 514 U.S. 645, 115 S.Ct. 1671, 131 L.Ed.2d 695: so long as a regulation is found to be purely "administrative," it will not be preempted by ERISA.

5. The U.S. Supreme Court weighed in on this debate in *Rush Prudential HMO, Inc. v. Moran*, 536 U.S. 355, 122 S.Ct. 2151, 153 L.Ed.2d 375 (2002). According to the Seventh Circuit, Debra Moran visited her primary care physician, a Rush Prudential HMO-affiliated doctor, when she began experiencing pain and loss of mobility in her right shoulder. Because traditional treatments were failing, both Moran and her primary care physician requested to see an out-of-network surgeon who specialized in providing unconventional treatment for Moran's condition. Despite numerous appeals, Rush denied the request on the grounds that the procedure was not "medically necessary." Moran then invoked an Illinois law that required that an HMO's decision to deny benefits be subjected to a binding independent medical review. Rush and Moran agreed on an expert who reviewed the case and determined that the unconventional surgery Moran sought was "medically necessary;" however, Rush still refused to cover the treatment, arguing that the statute was preempted by ERISA. Despite Rush's decision, on her own accord Moran received the treatment from the independent surgeon anyway; she then sought reimbursement for the treatment in state court pursuant to the Illinois law.

The U.S. Supreme Court held that ERISA did not preempt the Illinois statute mandating independent medical review of Rush's decision to deny benefits. The Court reasoned that the state statute was saved because it regulated insurance, provided no new cause of action, authorized no new form of relief, and therefore did not "fall within Pilot Life's categorical preemption." Id. at 380. Furthermore, the Court seems to have foreclosed any further litigation attempting to limit the breadth of the saving clause. Although the Court had recognized a limited exception from the saving clause for alternative causes of action and alternative remedies (See e.g. Pilot Life, Ingersoll–Rand), in *Moran* the Justices declared they would be unlikely to hear any more cases that limit insurance regulation based on a cause of action that purports to be preserved by ERISA.

6. In contrast, the U.S. Supreme Court determined that a cause of action brought under a Texas statute, the Texas Health Care Liability Act (THCLA), that allowed an individual to sue his or her HMO for alleged failures to exercise ordinary care in the handling of coverage decisions was preempted by ERISA. Aetna Health Inc. v. Davila, 542 U.S. 200, 124 S.Ct. 2488, 159 L.Ed.2d 312 (2004). Two individuals, Juan Davila and Ruby Calad, brought separate suits in Texas state court against their respective HMOs, Aetna Health Inc and CIGNA Healthcare of Texas, for alleged injuries they had suffered as results of Aetna's and CIGNA's decisions not to provide coverage for certain treatment and services recommended by their treating physicians. Both HMOs removed the cases to federal district courts arguing that Davila and Calad's causes of action fit within the scope of ERISA § 502(a) and were therefore completely preempted by it. The district courts agreed and refused to remand the cases to state court. Both Davila and Calad appealed the district courts' refusals to remand to state court and the Fifth Circuit consolidated their cases. Applying the rationale from *Pegram v. Herdrich,* 530 U.S. 211, 120 S.Ct. 2143, 147 L.Ed.2d 164 (2002), the Court of Appeals determined that Davila and Calad were suing their HMOs for mixed eligibility and treatment decisions that were not fiduciary in nature and thus their claims did not fall under ERISA § 502(a)(2). Additionally, the Fifth Circuit held that the claims did not fall within the scope of ERISA § 502(a)(1)(B) because THCLA did not duplicate the cause of action provided for in § 502(a)(1)(B) that allows recovery for wrongfully denied benefits.

The U.S. Supreme Court reversed the Fifth Circuit and determined that the state causes of action were preempted by ERISA. The Court rejected Davila and Calad's argument that their causes of action arose independently of ERISA or the terms of their employee benefit plans because Davila and Calad brought suit "only to rectify a wrongful denial of benefits promised under ERISA-regulated plans" and did not "attempt to remedy any violation of a legal duty independent of ERISA." Id. at 214. Justice Thomas, writing for a unanimous court, reasoned that "any state-law cause of action that duplicates, supplements, or supplants the ERISA civil enforcement remedy conflicts with the clear congressional intent to make the ERISA remedy exclusive and is therefore pre-empted." Id. at 209. Because ERISA's purpose is to provide uniform regulation of employee benefit plans, ERISA includes expansive preemption provisions (*see e.g.* ERISA § 514) which are intended to ensure that employee benefit plan regulation is an exclusive federal concern. Id. at 208 (citing Alessi v. Raybestos–Manhattan, Inc., 451 U.S. 504, 523, 101 S.Ct. 1895, 68 L.Ed.2d 402 (1981)).

Justice Thomas, responding to the Courts of Appeals' interpretation of *Pegram*, distinguished *Pegram* from the case before the Court in *Davila*:

> *Pegram* cannot be read so broadly. In *Pegram*, the plaintiff sued her physician-owned-and-operated HMO (which provided medical coverage through plaintiff's employer pursuant to an ERISA-regulated benefit plan) and her treating physician, both for medical malpractice and for a breach of an ERISA fiduciary duty. * * * The plaintiff's treating physician was also the person charged with administering plaintiff's benefits; it was she who decided whether certain treatments were covered. * * *

We reasoned that the physician's "eligibility decision and the treatment decision were inextricably mixed."

* * *

Since administrators making benefits determinations, even determinations based extensively on medical judgments, are ordinarily acting as plan fiduciaries, it was essential to *Pegram*'s conclusion that the decisions challenged there were truly "mixed eligibility and treatment decisions," * * * *i.e.*, medical necessity decisions made by the plaintiff's treating physician *qua* treating physician and *qua* benefits administrator. Put another way, the reasoning of *Pegram* "only makes sense where the underlying negligence also plausibly constitutes medical maltreatment by a party who can be deemed to be a treating physician or such a physician's employer." * * * Here, however, petitioners are neither respondents' treating physicians nor the employers of respondents' treating physicians. Petitioners' coverage decisions, then, are pure eligibility decisions, and *Pegram* is not implicated. Id. at 218–221.

Justice Ginsburg, though concurring in the opinion, wrote separately to "join 'the rising judicial chorus urging that Congress and [this] Court revisit what is an unjust and increasingly tangled ERISA regime.' " Id. at 222. It will be interesting to see how—or even whether—Congress responds to the *Davila* opinion and Justice Ginsburg's charge.

7. For a general discussion of ERISA's preemption within health care legislation, *see* Mark Alan Edwards, *Comment, Protections for ERISA Self-Insured Employee Welfare Benefit Plan Participants: New Possibilities for State Action in the Event of Plan Failure*, 1997 WISC. L. REV. 351; Jesselyn Alicia Brown, *ERISA and State Health Care Reform: Roadblock or Scapegoat?*, 13 YALE L. & POLICY REV. 339 (1995); *see also* Troy Paredes, *Stop-Loss Insurance, State Regulation, and ERISA: Defining the Scope of Federal Preemption*, 34 HARV. J. LEGIS. 233, 236–38 (1997).

8. For a recent discussion of ERISA's preemption including a discussion of *Rush Prudential*, *see* Lorraine Schmall and Brenda Stephens, *ERISA Preemption: A Move Towards Defederalizing Claims for Patients' Rights*, 42 BRANDEIS L.J. 529 (2004). *See also* David L. Trueman, *Will the Supreme Court Finally Eliminate ERISA Preemption?*, 13 ANNALS HEALTH L. 427 (2004), for an analysis of the cases leading up to *Davila*. For a critique of ERISA preemption, *see* Elaine Gareri Kennedy, *Comment: For the Sake of Your Health: ERISA's Preemption Provisions, HMO Accountability, and Consumer Access to State Law Remedies*, 38 U.S.F.L. REV. 361 (2004); Russell Korobkin, *The Failed Jurisprudence of Managed Care, and How to Fix It: Reinterpreting ERISA Preemption*, 51 U.C.L.A. L. REV. 457 (2003).

FINANCIAL SERVICES REFORM

On November 12, 1999, President Bill Clinton signed into law the Gramm–Leach–Bliley Financial Modernization Act (the "Act").[15] The goal of the Act was to break down the regulatory barriers that prevented the entry of banking, insurance, and securities firms into the others'

15. 106 P.L. 102, 113 Stat. 1338.

industries.[16] A major impetus for this legislation was the creation of Citigroup: in 1998, Citicorp, whose primary subsidiary, Citibank, was a bank, merged with the Travelers Group, whose subsidiaries included the Travelers Insurance company and the Salomon Smith Barney securities firm. Under prior law, the merger would not have been allowed. Indeed, prior to the Act's passage, the Federal Reserve Board required Citigroup to sell off its insurance underwriting businesses as a condition of merger approval.[17]

The breakdown of barriers and regulatory reform is not all encompassing. For instance, banks and their direct subsidiaries are still prohibited from underwriting insurance.[18] Financial holding companies must be created in order to allow banks to affiliate with insurance companies.[19] The insurance activities of such financial holding companies will still be regulated by the states, as they were before the Act's passage.[20]

At the same time, the Act has brought about significant change. The Act preempts state laws that prevent such affiliation of banks with insurance companies.[21] Prior to the Act, in order to offer a non-traditional banking service, a bank had to persuade the government that the service was "incidental to banking," whereas the Act has liberalized that standard to be anything "financial in nature."[22] The Act has also relaxed the requirement that banks base their insurance agency activities in towns with a population of less than 5,000, thus giving banks greater leeway in locating their insurance operations.[23]

On the other hand, a new layer of regulation is added to businesses which combine financial services. For example, insurance companies which want to create a financial holding company to enter banking will have to deal with the Federal Reserve Board's oversight of parts of their operations.[24] In that regard, a financial holding company's capital requirements will be determined by the size of the bank, not by the size of the insurance business.[25]

16. Joseph A. Smith, *Retail Delivery of Financial Services After the Gramm–Leach–Bliley Act: How Will Public Policy Shape the "Financial Services Supermarket"?*, 4 N.C. Banking Inst. 39 (April 2000).

17. Michelle Heller, *In Brief: Citi Gets More Time to Make Divestitures*, The American Banker, Oct. 10, 2000, § Washington, at 6.

18. James A. Cain & John J. Fahey, *Survey: Banks & Insurance Companies—Together in the New Millennium*, 55 Bus. Law. 1409 (May 2000).

19. *Id.*

20. *Id. See also* 4 N.C. Banking Inst. at 49–50.

21. James A. Cain & John J. Fahey, *Survey: Banks & Insurance Companies—Together in the New Millennium*, 55 Bus. Law. 1409 (May 2000).

22. Barbara A. Rehm, *Commerce, A Reform Gem, In Fed's Hands*, The American Banker, Nov. 9, 2000, § Washington, at 1.

23. *See e.g.* James A. Cain & John J. Fahey, *Survey: Banks & Insurance Companies—Together in the New Millennium*, 55 Bus. Law. 1409 (May 2000); Steve Cocheo, *Financial Holding Companies Debut—And They're Not All Giants*, A.B.A. Banking Journal, June 2000, § Briefing, at 7; Barbara A. Rehm, *No Merger Wave, But Money Saved*, The American Banker, Nov. 7, 2000, § Washington, at 1.

24. Barbara A. Rehm, *Reform Law Leaves Some Doubters*; *Fed Oversight of Financial Holding Companies is a Stumbling Block*, The American Banker, Nov. 8, 2000, § Washington, at 1.

25. *Id.*

Additionally, insurance companies may now be subjected to Community Reinvestment Act (CRA) requirements.[26] The CRA was created to prod banks into meeting the credit needs of communities often underserved by banks, and was typically invoked when banks merged. However, the Act now extends the CRA's reach to the activities of the new types of financial holding companies authorized under the Act. Thus, when a bank creates a holding company to acquire an insurer, that acquisition will be scrutinized to see if CRA requirements are met. Thus, not only will a bank's extension of loans and other credit to underserved communities be reviewed, so will an insurance company's extension of insurance to those same communities.

While the Act was intended to spur the creation of financial services conglomerates, few such companies have been created thus far.[27] Banks have been reluctant to buy insurance companies because they would have to tie up significant capital at low returns.[28] Banks are also concerned with the unpredictability of insurance underwriting, especially in the areas of property and casualty insurance.[29] Many insurance companies cannot afford to buy a bank big enough to provide a national network of outlets to sell their insurance products.[30] Those insurance companies that can afford a big enough bank might be reluctant to do so because banking profits can be less predictable than those from insurance activities.[31] In addition, such factors as low stock prices for financial services companies and consolidation within the banking and insurance sectors have discouraged cross-sector mergers.[32]

Despite these obstacles, a large number of companies became financial holding companies shortly after enactment of CRA.[33] The most notable, of course, is the creation of Citigroup, and insurer MetLife's plan to become a force in retail banking through its first step of

26. 4 N.C. BANKING INST. at 54.

27. *See e.g.,* Bill Streeter, *An Insurer Talks About Banks in Insurance*, A.B.A. Banking Journal, Mar. 2000, § Briefing, at 7; *It's Been More Effective Than People Think*, The American Banker, Nov. 7, 2000, § News, at 1; Barbara A. Rehm, *No Merger Wave, But Money Saved*, The American Banker, Nov. 7, 2000, § Washington, at 1; Joseph B. Treaster, *INTERNATIONAL BUSINESS: A Dutch Behemoth Invades America; ING Group Makes Its Move in Virtual Banking and Insurance*, N.Y. Times, Aug. 26, 2000, at C1.

28. *See e.g.,* Bill Streeter, *Insurance Aftermath*; *Financial Modernization*; *Gramm Leach Blilely Act*; *Putting it Together*, A.B.A. Banking Journal, Feb. 2000, § Features, at 24; Joseph B. Treaster, *INTERNATIONAL BUSINESS: A Dutch Behemoth Invades America; ING Group Makes Its Move in Virtual Banking and Insurance*, N.Y. Times, Aug. 26, 2000, at C1.

29. *See e.g.*, Bill Streeter, *Insurance Aftermath*; *Financial Modernization*; *Gramm Leach Blilely Act*; *Putting it Together*, A.B.A. Banking Journal, Feb. 2000, § Features, at 24; Bill Streeter, *An Insurer Talks About Banks in Insurance*, A.B.A. Banking Journal, Mar. 2000, § Briefing, at 7.

30. Joseph B. Treaster, *INTERNATIONAL BUSINESS: A Dutch Behemoth Invades America*; *ING Group Makes Its Move in Virtual Banking and Insurance*, N.Y. Times, Aug. 26, 2000, at C1.

31. *Id.*

32. Barbara A. Rehm, *Reform Law Leaves Some Doubters*; *Fed Oversight of Financial Holding Companies is a Stumbling Block*, The American Banker, Nov. 8, 2000, § Washington, at 1.

33. *Id.*

acquiring a small New Jersey bank.[34] Many of these have occurred on a small scale, such as the acquisition of local insurance agencies by small community banks.[35] From Europe, where banking and insurance combinations have operated for a decade, a Dutch company plans to come to the U.S. and operate an internet bank which will eventually sell insurance.[36] The relative ease of setting up on-line operations, compared to creating bricks-and-mortar outlets may further encourage the formation of financial holding companies.[37] With the foregoing, it is likely that the Act will spur the creation of more financial holding companies that combine banking and insurance. In fact, the central theme of the Act is convergence: the recognition that banks, insurance companies and securities firms have been evolving towards a new, all-encompassing financial services paradigm that, at least from the consumers' perspective, eliminates many of the traditional distinctions between these different types of firms.[38]

Finally, the North American Free Trade Agreement (NAFTA), creating a free market between the United States, Mexico, and Canada, resulted in the liberalization of Mexico's insurance laws. As of the year 2000, several limits on foreign ownership of Mexican insurance companies and limits on foreign companies' share of the Mexican insurance market were lifted.[39] The liberalization of Mexico's economy, the continued acquisition of material goods by Mexican consumers, and the relatively small numbers of Mexicans with any kind of insurance in their earthquake-prone country is beginning to create a need for liability, life, and property and casualty insurance, posing an opportunity for U.S. and Canadian insurance companies in particular.[40] In addition, Texas has passed legislation permitting Mexican insurance companies to sell insurance in Texas, thereby allowing such companies to take advantage of selling liability coverage to the growing numbers of trucking companies

34. Barbara A. Rehm, *No Merger Wave, But Money Saved*, The American Banker, Nov. 7, 2000, § Washington, at 1.

35. Steve Cocheo, *Financial Holding Companies Debut–and They're Not All Giants*, A.B.A. BANKING JOURNAL, June 2000, § Briefing, at 7.

36. Joseph B. Treaster, *INTERNATIONAL BUSINESS: A Dutch Behemoth Invades America; ING Group Makes Its Move in Virtual Banking and Insurance*, N.Y. Times, Aug. 26, 2000, at C1.

37. *See e.g.* Jerry M. Markham, *Banking Regulation: Its History and Future*, 4 N.C. BANKING INST. 221, 275 (April 2000).

38. Douglas P. Faucette, *The Impact of Convergence and the Gramm–Leach–Bliley Act on the Insurance Industry*, 8 GEO. MASON L. REV. 623, 624 (Summer 2000).

39. *See e.g.* Margo D. Beller, *U.S. Insurers Find Restrictions Limit Access to Mexican Market*, J. Commerce, June 27, 1994, § Specials, at 7A; Paul Dykewicz, *Insurers Put a Premium on Mexican Market*, J. Commerce, Dec. 3, 1992 § Specials, at 2C; Kevin G. Hall, *Deregulation Reshapes Insurance in Mexico*, J. Commerce, Nov. 7, 1994, § Front, at 1A.

40. *See e.g.* Margo D. Beller, *U.S. Insurers Find Restrictions Limit Access to Mexican Market*, J. Commerce, June 27, 1994, § Specials, at 7A; Paul Dykewicz, *Insurers Put a Premium on Mexican Market*, J. Commerce, Dec. 3, 1992 § Specials, at 2C; Kevin G. Hall, *Deregulation Reshapes Insurance in Mexico*, J. Commerce, Nov. 7, 1994, § Front, at 1A; George F.W. Telfer, *Insurance Needs are Expanding in Mexico, Executives Say*, J. Commerce, Apr. 22, 1994, § Insurance, at 9A.

operating between Mexico and the U.S. due to increased trade resulting from NAFTA.[41]

TERRORISM RISK INSURANCE

In the aftermath of September 11, Congress enacted the Terrorism Risk Insurance Act of 2002 (TRIA) which was signed into law by President George W. Bush on November 26, 2002.[42] TRIA creates a program under which the federal government will share with private insurers the coverage of losses attributable to acts of terrorism. TRIA requires the Secretary of the Treasury, with the concurrence of the Secretary of State and the Attorney General, to certify that a particular act of terrorism falls within the ACT.[43] Under TRIA, the federal government is responsible for 90 percent of losses attributable to certified acts of terrorism after an insurer's exposure exceeds 15 percent (in 2005) of its commercial premiums.[44] The program is capped at $100 billion in each year.[45] Significantly, TRIA preempts and nullifies insurance policy terrorism exclusions and it preempts state causes of action.[46] TRIA was to expire on December 31, 2005, however in December 2005 Congress passed a bill that extended the statute through 2007 and President Bush signed the bill into law on December 22, 2005.

This area has spawned an interesting array of commentary. Professor Jeffrey Thomas notes that the insurance industry is expected to pay about $50 billion in claims as a result of September 11. In a comprehensive article he suggests that the transaction costs associated with the exclusion for terrorism losses may well outweigh the benefits of the exclusion.[47] Professor Thomas posits that the certification by the Secretary of the Treasury of terrorism acts that fall within TRIA will be a significant step in limiting transaction costs.[48]

Professor Robert J. Rhee takes the stance that government has a number of roles to play both in terrorism-caused catastrophes and natural disasters.[49] He presents a very readable but sophisticated financial view of the broad effects of insurance disasters can have on the U.S. and global economies and ultimately concludes that the government should facilitate a capital market solution to increase insurance capacity for catastrophic terrorism risk.[50] Others take a skeptical view of the federal government's intrusion into the insurance marketplace as repre-

41. Kevin G. Hall, *Mexican Firm Wins Right to Sell Insurance in Texas*, J. Commerce, Apr. 25, 1994, § Insurance, at 9A.

42. Pub. L. No. 107–297, 116 Stat. 2322 (2002).

43. Terrorism Risk Insurance Act § 101.

44. Terrorism Risk Insurance Act § 103(e)(6).

45. Terrorism Risk Insurance Act § 103(e).

46. Terrorism Risk Insurance Act §§ 105(a), 107(a). An insurer can reinstate such exclusion with the written authorization of its insured. Terrorism Risk Insurance Act § 105 (c).

47. Jeffrey E. Thomas, *Exclusion of Terrorist–Related Harms from Insurance Coverage: Do the Costs Justify the Benefits?*, 36 Ind. L. Rev. 397 (2003).

48. Id. at 423.

49. Robert J. Rhee, *Terrorism Risk in a Post–9/11 Economy: the Convergence of Capital Markets, Insurance, and Government Action*, 37 Ariz. St. L.J. 435 (2005).

50. *Id.* at 529.

sented by TRIA. For example, Professor Michelle Boardman makes a persuasive case that a government role in this context is not required because government can compensate victims apart from the system of insurance, because the pricing is hugely uncertain, and because government presence tends to dissuade entry into the market.[51]

As the foregoing illustrates, the insurance industry faces a number of cross-currents which will affect how the business of insurance is conducted. While it is too soon to describe the eventual landscape, it will be fascinating to watch the future unfold.

51. Michelle Boardman, *Known Unknowns; The Illusion of Terrorism Insurance,* 93 GEORGETOWN L.J. 783, 836 (2005); see also Anne Fron & Alan O. Dykes, *Terrorism and Insurance Markets: A Role for the Government as Insurer?,* 36 IND. L. REV. 447 (2003).

Chapter 2

FORMING AND NEGOTIATING THE INSURANCE CONTRACT

A. FORMALITIES OF CONTRACT MAKING

Courts of late have been keen to emphasize that an insurance policy is, fundamentally, a contract. Montrose Chemical Corporation of California v. Admiral Insurance Company, 10 Cal.4th 645, 666, 42 Cal.Rptr.2d 324, 913 P.2d 878 (1995); J.A. Brundage Plumbing and Roto–Rooter, Inc. v. Massachusetts Bay Ins. Co., 818 F.Supp. 553, 556 (W.D.N.Y.1993). The tacit message is that, as contracts, insurance policies should be treated under the general rubric of contract law.

Despite case law admonitions to the contrary, insurance policies differ from traditional contracts. With a typical bilateral contract, the parties exchange performances and receive the benefits of performance simultaneously, and a breach is generally easily identifiable. With insurance policies, on the other hand, the insured tenders performance in the form of payments of premiums and the insurer is obligated to perform only if some event identified in the policy triggers the performance—recall the concept of a condition precedent. Further, the insured typically does not assume an active role in negotiating or drafting the terms memorialized in the policy document itself. Greater detail on the process is provided below.

STEPS IN THE NEGOTIATION OF INDIVIDUAL POLICIES

For the purposes of early familiarization, a rough outline of important steps in the negotiation of an insurance contract and some examples of the papers used to make a record thereof are useful. More detailed coverage may be found in the portions of this book dealing with insurance of the person, property insurance, and liability insurance.

(1) *Application*. An application (sometimes "the app") is generally made by the prospective insured on a form supplied by the prospective insurer. Prior to this, it's likely that there will have been some solicitation by an agent of the insurer. Applications are normally in writing and

contain representations by the prospective insured, which may later surface as alleged misrepresentations. The agent may also make the entries on a form application for the applicant or he may inform the prospective insured about the meaning of requests for information contained in the form. The agent may also say the information is unimportant. This may later surface in the form of an asserted "waiver and estoppel." Applications yield litigation in most lines of insurance but perhaps no more colorfully than in life insurance cases.

(2) *Binder.* Often the insurer or an agent will provide the prospective insured with a "binder." The agent may have the power or appear to have the power to bind the insurer immediately upon application to a policy obligation although the formal papers constituting the policy are to follow at a later date. This may leave room for speculation as to what the policy provisions were intended to be. The binder may be oral or evidenced by a memorandum sent by the agent to the insured. In life insurance cases under so-called "conditional receipts," some special problems arise. In the excerpt from the *World Trade Center Properties* case below, the binder played a large role in one of the largest casualty losses ever experienced.

(3) *Evaluation.* When the effectiveness of the policy is conditioned in any way on insurer "headquarters" approval, the company has an opportunity to check the application and use such means as it has to validate it. That may include an applicant's driving record (auto liability insurance), condition or use of the property (property insurance), and medical history (life and health insurance). Available information extrinsic to the application (including public records, computer data banks) may be of assistance to the insurer.

(4) *Issuance.* The day of issuance or "effective date" is sometimes hard to ascertain (see the materials on insurance of the person, infra), but whatever the precise date, issuance of the policy means its establishment as an obligation of the insurer. The *documents evidencing the insurer's obligation* are complex and prolix and contain a great deal of fine print ("what the front page giveth, the back page taketh away"). Most of these documents are forms. The discussion of their terms and conditions will be a major part of the insurance law course based on this or any book.

Methods of Marketing Insurance

Insurance is variously solicited or sold by mail, by direct sales by employees of the insurance company, through independent agents, through brokers, or even machines. The legal problems associated with the negotiation and consummation of the insurance transaction necessarily center upon the actual or ostensible authority of the person at the point of contact with the customer. Some such persons can conclude the contract and bind the company on the spot. Others may only be authorized to wrangle an offer out of the applicant which will be transmitted upward to, say, vice presidents specifically authorized to countersign the acceptance. The legal rules of Agency are necessary for purposes of dealing with the principles of "waiver" and "estoppel" (or "election"), which in turn require a general comprehension of methods of marketing various forms of insurance. A standard textbook[2] on the general subject affords illuminating information:

> **Property and Liability Insurance.** Most types of property and liability insurance are regularly sold through general insurance agents. * * *
>
> A general insurance agent usually has authority, within specified limits, to make and modify contracts of insurance and to receive notices on behalf of his principal, and he may be given authority, formally or informally, to settle losses of small amounts.
>
> Typically, the general insurance agent handles all financial transactions with the insured, billing and collecting premiums and extending credit. He reports monthly to his insurers, who have no direct contact with the insured except, but not always, in the adjustment of losses. Following the success of many direct writers and exclusive-agency insurers whose representatives serve mostly to make the original sale, an increasing number of independent-agency insurers have turned to policy writing by the insurer and to *direct billing* and *automatic renewal,* with the insurer taking over the financial relationship, crediting the agent with commission at a lower rate than formerly. Insurers are seeking economy and identification by these practices; agents have tended to oppose these changes because of the expected weakening of their personal relationship with the insured with these practices.
>
> **Life Insurance.** In life insurance the agent is primarily a salesman equipped with a rate book showing the rates, surrender values, and other features of policies issued by his company, as well as sample policies and application blanks. These correspond, respectively, to the price lists, samples, and order blanks of a merchandise salesman. The agent is expected diligently to canvass his field for his insurer, usually devoting his entire time to it, and canvassing only the type of person covered by his instructions. He is paid by a commission on the premiums for policies issued upon applications secured by him. The policy is sent to him for delivery, and his powers are limited to securing the application, delivering the policy, and collecting the premium. He cannot bind the company on the acceptance of risks or the settlement of losses. However, if the insured pays the premium at the time he submits his application, the agent can issue the binding receipt [described in *Washington National Insurance Co. v. Strickland* reprinted in this text below].
>
> While his primary function is that of salesman, the life-insurance agent is becoming more and more an adviser to his clients. Many life-insurance companies insist on full-time exclusive representation and will accept business only from agents who conform to this requirement. Others accept business freely from general insurance agents and brokers

2. Mowbray, Blanchard and Williams, *Insurance, Its Theory and Practice in the United States,* 6th ed., 1979. Reprint edition. Printed and Published by Robert E. Krieger Publishing Co. Inc., New York. Copyright © McGraw–Hill, Inc. [The above extracts have been abridged and the sequence slightly changed. Reprinted with permission.]

doing a general business, who for this purpose are generally licensed as agents.

Health Insurance. Health insurance is sold by specializing agents, by general insurance agents, by life-insurance agents, and, to a considerable extent, by mail. With life-insurance companies increasing their activities in this field, greater interest in it is being shown by their agents. Life insurance and health insurance are complementary, since both are primarily concerned with the problems of the individual and his family.

Group–Insurance Marketing. Group life and health insurance underwritten by commercial insurers is sold by commissioned agents and brokers, with agents selling the most contracts and brokers accounting for the most premium dollars because they tend to specialize in large accounts. These agents and brokers, however, receive considerable technical assistance from salaried insurer group representatives and other specialists in selling, installing, and servicing the plan. * * * Blue Cross plans, Blue Shield plans, and most independent plans are usually marketed by salaried employees.

Group property and liability insurance * * * currently accounts for considerably less than 10 per cent of the total property-and-liability-insurance premium volume and it has only recently become a topic of major concern. In a recent comprehensive study of group property and liability insurance, Dr. James Chastain cited several reasons why the group concept has developed much less rapidly in this field than in life and health insurance.[3] Because the employer is the source of income payments interrupted by poor health, death, or retirement, he feels obligated to provide some protection against these perils, but he feels no similar obligation with respect to potential property or liability losses. Pressures to compete with the expanding social-insurance system have likewise been limited to potential losses caused by poor health, death, or retirement. Until recently property-and-liability insurers have had much less need for alternative marketing channels, primarily because it is easier to sell the need for adequate property and liability insurance than for life and health insurance. Agents selling individual insurance are more prone to resist group property and liability insurance than group life and health insurance[4] because the market for property and liability insurance is more nearly saturated and because group coverages are more likely to eliminate the need for any individual coverages. Because of this near saturation, public pressures for a new marketing channel are also small. Post-sales servicing needs are greater

3. James J. Chastain, "An Evaluation of Group Property Insurance." See also J.J. Chastain, "Group Property and Liability Insurance," chap. 39 in R.D. Eilers and R.M. Crowe (eds.), "Group Insurance Handbook."

4. Group life and health insurance, however, was also violently opposed by several groups before it became commonplace. Its extension beyond certain limits is still opposed, particularly by agents selling individual insurance, but also by others who are concerned about possible unsound underwriting.

under property and liability insurance because of more difficult loss adjustments and changing exposures. In addition to other effects, this post-sales servicing makes the choice of the insurer more important to the group member and may reduce his interest in a particular group. The tighter rate regulation applicable to property and liability insurance has also been a retarding factor. Most state insurance departments are opposed in principle to group property and liability insurance because, among other things, they believe that it discriminates unfairly against nongroup members and the higher-quality members of the group, threatens the present marketing system. The destruction of which would be against the public interest because it would create a chaotic rating system and lead to insolvencies. Finally, the tax incentives that have made group life and health insurance an attractive fringe benefit are not applicable to group property and liability insurance.

Nevertheless, ways have been found to write group property and liability insurance or related plans, and the demand for this coverage has increased. Intense competition in recent years has increased insurer interest in alternative marketing channels.

* * *

LLOYD'S OF LONDON

Most people interested in insurance law sooner or later become interested in "Lloyd's of London" and the way brokers conduct business in the venerable institution.

[Editors' note. The following is based on material from Edinburgh Assurance Co. v. R.L. Burns Corp., 479 F.Supp. 138, 144–46 (C.D. Cal. 1979) as supplemented by Monograph, National Association of Insurance Commissioner, Lloyd's: a Review by U.S. State Insurance Regulators (1998); Monograph, National Association of Insurance Commissioner, Lloyd's: a Follow-up Review by U.S. State Insurance Regulators (1999). The material has been abridged, edited for clarity and the sequence of subjects has been changed.]

Overview. Lloyd's of London is not an insurer; it is a market where members write insurance. The Members can consist of individual Members (names) and corporate Members. Members write insurance by joining syndicates who underwrite insurance or reinsurance. Lloyd's is the fifth largest global reinsurer and the second largest commercial lines insurer. At the beginning of 1998, Lloyd's had 6,825 individual and 435 corporate Members, 19 Member's Agents (who provide guidance to the Members on selecting syndicates and perform administrative functions on their behalf), and 155 main syndicates (groups of Members, which are formed annually and pledge unlimited liability and deposit capital with the Lloyd's market in the form of assets held in trust investments). Most insurance policies are placed with several syndicates. The syndicates are managed by designated Managing Agents (66 as of 1998), who appoint and employ an active underwriter and other staff to function on behalf of the syndicates. Lloyd's brokers are the middlemen between the clients and the Lloyd's market, bringing almost all the insurance business that Lloyd's undertakes. In 1998, Lloyd's employed 187 brokers worldwide.

History. The concept that is now known as Lloyd's began in the 17th century in a coffee shop owned by Edward Lloyd. Affluent marine merchants would share the risk of loss of ship voyages by accepting a specific amount of risk on a line and writing their names underneath (i.e., underwriter). Non-marine policies were introduced in the late 19th century. As Lloyd's evolved structurally throughout the 20th century, it began allowing foreigners and women to become Members, as long as the wealth requirement was met.

Problems. During the 1970s, Lloyd's experienced a decrease in real capital. That, coupled with a surprising chain of events beginning in the late 1980s, illuminated increasing problems in the Lloyd's market. These problems included: (1) the London Market Excess of Loss Spiral, in which large risks were underwritten and reinsured and retroceded within only a few syndicates; (2) major catastrophes from 1988 to 1992, which included the Exxon Valdez disaster and Hurricane Hugo; (3) large-scale environmentally based injuries, such as asbestos and pollution; and (4) inadequate capital requirements, whereby some members did not have the means to take on the extraordinary levels or risk that they did. These problems resulted in a series of unexpected losses, about $461,000 per Member. Many Members' losses exceeded their capacity to pay, and some of these Members concluded that the underwriting practices of Lloyd's were negligent and took legal action.

Reconstruction and Renewal. In 1995, following acknowledgement of this serious crisis, Lloyd's initiated the Reconstruction and Renewal Program (R & R) to reinsure all pre–1992 liabilities under one reinsurance contract and cede them to a new venture, Equitas Reinsurance Limited (ERL), which in turn would cede all these liabilities to its wholly owned subsidiary Equitas Limited (EL). The R & R programs intended to fulfill three major objectives: (1) to determine the appropriate level of reserves for all Lloyd's liabilities for 1992 and before; (2) to formulate a market settlement that would enable Lloyd's to settle outstanding litigation with the Members; (3) to reform Lloyd's internal operations, governance and regulation. The R & R program was successfully completed in the fall of 1996.

Recent Changes. According to a 1999 report, two major shifts have occurred at Lloyd's. First, corporate Members have increased in number, accounting for a much larger percentage of the capital and underwriting capacity in the market, while the numbers of individual Members have decreased. In 1998, for example, the individual Members consisted of 40.4 percent of total members, down from 56.4 percent in 1997. In 1999, this percentage dropped again to 27.4 percent. By contrast, corporate Members have increased from 43.6 percent in 1997 to almost 73 percent in 1999. Second, the number of brokers and syndicates have decreased, as consolidations have occurred. The functions of each component of the organization (as discussed below) remains the same.

Organization. Lloyd's has its own Acts of Parliament (the Lloyd's Acts), which delegate governance of Lloyd's to the Council of Lloyd's. The Council is made up of nineteen members, thirteen elected and six nominated or non-executives approved by the Governor of the Bank of England. Since 1982, the Council has had control over the management and regulation of Lloyd's affairs and the power to make bylaws for this purpose.

The second subset of organization consists of the Boards, a Regulatory Board (LRB) and a Market Board (LMB). The LRB operates a regulatory structure for the market's business. A nominated member of the Council chairs it. The LMB focuses on business leadership and the Chairman of Lloyd's heads this.

Lastly, the Corporation of Lloyd's functions to provide services to the myriad of market participants and is directed by the Chairman of Lloyd's.

Business Functions. The business processes of Lloyd's are unique and rather intricate. For example, the placing of a risk involves several interrelated steps. First, a customer approaches a Lloyd's broker with details of a risk. The Lloyd's broker then approaches an underwriter who specializes in the class of business involved. If the underwriter is able to accept such a risk, then the broker negotiates the premium terms and policy conditions with the underwriter. Following negotiations, the broker consults the customer through the brokering chain. If the customer is satisfied, then the broker can place a firm order.

The broker prepares an underwriting slip, which sets out the nature of the risk, the premium, and the terms and conditions. The broker presents the slip to the underwriter, who confirms his acceptance of the terms and conditions and puts down his line on the bottom. A contract now exists between the customer and the Members. The underwriter accepting the risk becomes the lead underwriter.

The broker then consults several other underwriters (following underwriters), who review the risk and decide whether or not to accept a portion of it on behalf of their syndicate. The following underwriters rely entirely on the lead underwriter's decisions. Once the slip is finalized, the Lloyd's broker presents it to the Lloyd's Policy Signing Office (LPSO) for checking and processing. The LPSO prepares, signs, and embosses the policy before sending it to the client through the brokering chain. The LPSO is responsible for ensuring that the policy meets the risk requirements set forth in the terms and conditions, and that the policy language meets regulatory requirements. Once this is completed, the broker retains the slip for his files.

The Lloyd's Central Accounting (LCA) system handles all settlements of premiums. Once the underwriter determines the premium, the broker collects the premium from the insured. The customer or an intermediary broker then deducts any brokerage due and pays the premium to a Lloyd's broker. The Lloyd's broker submits a Premium Advice Note to the LPSO. The LPSO records the details of any premiums due and any terms governing the settlement date of those premiums. The premium is settled within three days of the LPSO signing. The LCA system handles all premium processing, claims, and adjustment amounts as a daily bulk settlement.

All claims processes are carried out by the Lloyd's Claims Office (LCO), which provides central claims authorization and processing services on behalf of Lloyd's syndicates. The LCO is also responsible for setting up letters of credit on behalf of the underwriting Members. Claims processing is also a multi-step procedure. First, the claims are reported from the insured through the brokering chain to the Lloyd's broker in London. The broker prepares a claims file and reports the details to the lead underwriter and the LCO. The LCO acts for the other underwriters on the risk (the following market) and works with the lead underwriter to handle claims efficiently. Once claims payment is agreed upon, the decisions of the lead underwriter and the LCO are binding. The LCO then creates a settlement record on its computer system. Once settlement is confirmed, the details of payment are sent to LCA. When payment is due, the LCA debits the relevant share from participating syndicates and pays the total amount to the Lloyd's broker, who then transfers the amount to the insured.

Despite Lloyd's ups and downs, it continues to promote its long-standing underwriting practices with even-handed stability.

Note

Jeremy A. Herschaft's article, *Not your average coffee shop: Lloyd's of London—a Twenty–First–Century Primer on the History, Structure, and Future of the Backbone of Marine Insurance*, 29 Tul. Mar. L.J. 169 (2005), provides a history of Lloyds with a recent gloss on the financial troubles it has faced with losses and the departure of members (or "names").

B. NEGOTIATION, AGENCY, AND BINDERS: INSURERS' PROBLEMS

WASHINGTON NATIONAL INSURANCE COMPANY v. STRICKLAND

Supreme Court of Alabama, 1985.
491 So.2d 872.

Houston, Justice.

* * * On January 15, 1981, Bruce Palmer met with Carol Strickland and members of her family to discuss medical insurance. Mrs. Strickland was five feet, two inches tall, and weighed 180 pounds. Palmer described plans for medical insurance with four different companies, including a plan with Washington National which Mrs. Strickland and her husband

chose. She completed a Washington National application for insurance; Palmer tore from the application a detachable form called a "conditional receipt" and gave it to Mrs. Strickland. He took a check from Mrs. Strickland for $100. The receipt stated that the effective date of coverage was January 15, 1981.

Mrs. Strickland and members of her family testified that Palmer told them at the meeting that Strickland's insurance coverage would be effective as of that date, January 15, 1981, and that she would be covered if she had an accident going home from that meeting. As a result of these assurances, Mrs. Strickland cancelled an application for hospitalization insurance with another company. Palmer testified, to the contrary, that he told Strickland she would be covered as of that date only "if everything was in order." The application for insurance and a statement in the conditional receipt given to Mrs. Strickland provided that no agent was authorized to make or modify contracts, to waive any of the company's rights or requirements, or to bind the company by making or receiving representations.

Four days after the meeting with Palmer, Mrs. Strickland fell and hurt her ankle. At the time of the accident, Palmer had not yet submitted Mrs. Strickland's application for medical insurance to Washington National. Palmer testified that he submitted the application to John Martin, a general agent for Washington National, on January 22, 1981. Following subsequent underwriting review, Washington National declined to issue a policy of coverage for Mrs. Strickland on grounds that she was physically unfit.

Palmer testified that his authority with Washington National was limited to the solicitation of applications and the collection of initial premiums. Martin testified that Palmer could solicit applications, but had no authority to bind Washington National to coverage. He stated that Palmer was a broker for Mutual of New York, and was not an agent for Washington National. The record shows, however, that Bruce Palmer was a licensed agent for Washington National in the State of Alabama. * * *

Mrs. Strickland sued Washington National and Bruce Palmer for fraud and misrepresentation. The jury awarded Mrs. Strickland $22,500. The parties had stipulated that the amount of compensatory damages involved in the case was $1,369.14, so $21,130.86 of the verdict constituted punitive damages. * * *

The first issue before this Court is whether Washington National could properly be found liable for the misrepresentation by Palmer that Mrs. Strickland had insurance coverage as of January 15, 1981. This would depend upon whether Palmer was acting as a general or soliciting agent for Washington National or as an independent agent or broker. If Palmer were a general or soliciting agent, Washington National would be liable. If Palmer were an independent agent or broker, Washington National would not be liable. A discussion of the distinctions between brokers, agents, and soliciting agents will go far to allay any initial confusion.

A "general agent" is one who has authority to transact all of the business of the principal, of a particular kind, or in a particular case. *Southern States Fire Insurance Co. v. Kronenberg,* 199 Ala. 164, 170–71, 74 So. 63, 67 (1917). The powers of such an agent are coextensive with the business entrusted to his care, authorizing him to act for the principal in all matters coming within the usual and ordinary scope and character of such business. *Id.,* 199 Ala. at 171, 74 So. at 67. A general agent has full power to bind the insurer to the agent's contract of insurance or to issue policies or to accept risks. *McGhee v. Paramount Life Insurance Co.,* 385 So.2d 969 (Ala.1980). In fact, a general agent "stands in the shoes" of the principal for the purpose of transacting business entrusted to him. Since a general agent's powers are coextensive with the business entrusted to him, his fraudulent act is the fraudulent act of his insurer principal as well.

An insurance company also has the right to employ agents with limited authority. [Citation omitted.] A "special agent," as distinguished from a "general agent," is authorized to act for the principal only in a particular transaction, or in a particular way. [Citation omitted.] In the insurance context, the most prevalent type of special agent is the "soliciting agent." A soliciting agent is different from a general agent in that he has no power to bind his insurer principal in contract. [Citation omitted.] However, when a soliciting agent commits a fraud upon one who seeks insurance coverage, his insurer principal will be liable for that fraud, if the fraud was perpetrated by the agent within the scope of his employment. The liability of an insurer for the fraudulent acts of its soliciting agents is grounded in the doctrine of "respondeat superior," and not the doctrine of agency. *National States Insurance Co. v. Jones,* 393 So.2d 1361 (Ala.1980). Since a soliciting agent is regarded as the "servant" of the insurer "master," the insurer has the full right of control over the agent's actions. A general agent, however, stands in the shoes of the principal; his actions are regarded as those of the principal. The law deems the principal to have "participated" in the fraud of its general agent, and so subjects the principal to direct liability. Where a soliciting agent commits fraud the insurer's liability is vicarious, and the principal is liable in spite of the fact that he did not participate in the fraud, or even forbade it. [Citation omitted.]

An independent agent or broker is usually not an agent for the insurer at all; rather, he is the agent of the insured. See Code 1975, § 27–7–1. For example, this Court has held that when an independent agent or broker fails in his duty to obtain insurance coverage, the principal may sue either for a breach of contract, or, in tort, for breach of duty imposed on the agent or broker to [show] reasonable skill, care, and diligence in obtaining insurance. *Highlands Underwriters Insurance Co. v. Eleganté Inns,* 361 So.2d 1060 (Ala.1978). In *Highlands,* the principal was the insured.

Washington National contends that Palmer was an independent agent or broker and that it was not liable for Palmer's misrepresentation. It cites *Northington v. Dairyland Insurance Co.,* 445 So.2d 283 (Ala.1984). In the *Northington* case, it was undisputed that the person committing the fraud was an independent agent and broker. But the court properly analyzed Dairyland Insurance Company's liability for the fraud of the independent agent/broker in terms of actual and apparent authority, because the issue was whether the agent/broker, normally an agent of the insured, was also acting as an agent for Dairyland.

Although an independent agent or broker is normally an agent for the insured, for some purposes he may at the same time be an agent for the insurer as well. See *Mobile Insurance, Inc. v. Smith,* 441 So.2d 894 (Ala.1983). In such cases, if the insurer principal authorizes the agent to make representations, and the agent makes those representations within the scope of his authority to make them, the principal will be liable if those representations are false. In other words, an insurer's liability for the fraud of an independent agent or broker is predicated upon actual or apparent authority conferred upon the agent/broker by the insurer to make representations on the insurer's behalf. The doctrine of respondeat superior does not apply in the independent agent or broker situation because the insurance company does not exert sufficient control over the activities of the agent/broker to put him in the same position as a company employee. An independent agent or broker can never impose liability upon his principal for representations that are not authorized by the principal.

In the instant case, appellant Washington National relies upon the *Northington* case for the proposition that it is not liable for Palmer's misrepresentation to Mrs. Strickland. But whereas in *Northington* it was clear that the person committing the fraud was an independent agent and broker, in the instant case Palmer's status is the subject of dispute. The issue is whether the jury could properly have found Palmer to be a general or soliciting agent for Washington National so that Washington National would be liable for Palmer's misrepresentation to Mrs. Strickland. The evidence clearly shows that Palmer had no actual or apparent authority to make the representations, so if Palmer had been an independent agent or broker, Washington National would not be liable for the fraud. * * *

There is sufficient evidence in the record to support the jury verdict in favor of Mrs. Strickland. Even though Martin testified that Palmer was a broker, and even though the record shows that Palmer offered four different companies' policies to Mrs. Strickland for her consideration, there is evidence indicating that Palmer was a licensed agent for Washington National. Copies of Palmer's Alabama Department of Insurance license and license application were introduced at trial. The license application gives the applicant a choice of describing himself as "agent," or "broker," or "solicitor." Palmer was designated as "agent" in the license application. Although the application was dated November 16, 1981, ten months after Palmer's meeting with Mrs. Strickland and her family, it was admitted into evidence without objection. The license itself purports to cover the years 1980, 1981, and 1982, so it described Palmer's past, present, and future status with Washington National, including his status at the time he took Mrs. Strickland's application. Martin notarized Palmer's signature on the license application. Likewise, Washington National provided Palmer with applications, sales literature, and instructions. Martin knew that persons purchasing Washington National insurance from Palmer would be relying on Palmer's representations about insurance coverage. In order to hold Washington National liable for Palmer's misrepresentation, the jury must have found that Palmer was either a general agent, thereby subjecting Washington National to direct liability, or that he was a soliciting agent, thereby subjecting Washington National to vicarious liability under the doctrine of respondeat superior. There is sufficient evidence in the record to support either finding by the jury. * * *

In this case, the evidence, when viewed in the light most favorable to the nonmoving party, shows that an award of punitive damages by the jury was proper. The evidence of fraud in this case consists of Palmer's verbal statement to Mrs. Strickland that coverage would be effective as of January 15, 1981, and Palmer's handwritten notation on the conditional receipt, to wit: "coverage effective 15 January 81 on Carol and children." These representations were obviously ineffective for contract purposes in light of the following language found in the conditional receipt:

> "This Conditional Receipt does not create any temporary or interim insurance and does not provide any coverage except as expressly provided herein. This payment is received subject to the agreements contained in part 1 of the application and to the following terms and conditions:
>
> > "1. If the Company shall be satisfied that on the date of the application or the date of the last of any required medical examinations, whichever is the later date, the person or persons proposed for insurance were insurable under the Company's rules governing the acceptance of risks at the classification and for the amount and plan of insurance applied for, and
> >
> > "2. if the amount paid with the application equals or exceeds a monthly premium for the insurance premium for the insurance applied for, then insurance under the terms of the policy applied for shall take effect on the latest of the following dates: (a) the date of the application, (b) the date of the last of any required medical examinations or (c) the policy date, if any, requested in the application.
>
> "Unless all of the preceding conditions are met, there shall be no liability on the part of the Company except to return this payment."

From the evidence introduced, the jury could reasonably have inferred that Palmer knew that Mrs. Strickland's height and weight were such that a medical examination was likely to be required before Washington National would determine whether or not to assume the risk of coverage; that Mrs. Strickland was relying on Palmer's representation that she was insured as of that moment and so cancelled her application for hospital insurance with another insurer based upon Palmer's representation; and that Palmer made the representation in order to make a sale, without concern for whether Mrs. Strickland received insurance coverage as of that moment as promised. All this constitutes sufficient evidence from which a jury could reasonably have inferred that the fraud was committed with an intent to deceive or defraud. Consequently, the jury's award of punitive damages was proper. * * *

Note

Douglas Richmond, a prolific author and insurance company executive, has written an excellent summary of the various agency distinctions. Douglas R. Richmond, *Insurance Agent and Broker Liability*, 40 TORT & INS. L.J. 1, 3–7 (2004). Of note is Richmond's clear articulation of "broker" status. He writes:

> An insurance broker is not a salaried insurance company employee or otherwise identified with a single insurer but, rather, is an independent middleman. A broker typically has contracts with a number of insurers and is compensated by way of commissions paid by the insurers with which he places coverage. Brokers are sometimes referred to as independent agents and are generally considered to be the insured's agent.
>
> Brokers actually fall into two categories: retail and wholesale. It is common for one broker to approach another in an attempt to procure specialized insurance for a client, or to secure insurance after several insurers have declined to accept the risk being shopped. A broker's need for assistance in procuring coverage is particularly acute in the surplus lines market. The broker with whom the insured deals is the retail broker. The broker to whom the retail broker looks for assistance in placing coverage is the wholesale broker.
>
> Wholesale brokers consider their clients to be the retail brokers who seek their assistance. Wholesale brokers are exceptionally reluctant to interact with any insured. They generally will not communicate with an insured unless asked to do so by the retail broker. Wholesale brokers' customer bases of retail brokers would dwindle if they were perceived to be involved in retail insurance transactions. Although it is possible a wholesale broker may be deemed to be an agent of the insured on the right facts, such a finding is unlikely. Even more unlikely is the possibility a wholesale broker could be held vicariously liable for a retail broker's negligence. A wholesale broker essentially functions as a conduit between a retail broker and an insurer without which the retail broker would not otherwise be able to do business. Wholesale brokers do not control retail brokers' businesses or operations.
>
> A related issue is whether a retail broker can be deemed to be an agent of the insurer with which a wholesale broker places coverage. In a word, no. Given the respective roles of retail and wholesale brokers,

there simply is no factual basis on which to premise an agency relationship between a retailer and an insurer where a wholesale broker is involved.

Finally, the description or designation of an intermediary as a producer merits some attention. The term "producer" has no special meaning in insurance law. It can refer to either an agent or a broker. An insurer often will designate a producer on a policy's declarations page to identify the intermediary that it deems to have placed the coverage with the company. An insurer's designation of an intermediary as a producer typically reflects the carrier's view as to whom it owes a commission, especially where multiple intermediaries are involved in a transaction. Within an insurance agency or brokerage, the term may refer to someone who is responsible for attracting clients, ultimately earning commission income for the firm. In short, the meaning of the term "producer" depends on the context in which it is used. (footnotes omitted).

TALBOT v. COUNTRY LIFE INSURANCE CO.

Appellate Court of Illinois, Third District, 1973.
8 Ill.App.3d 1062, 291 N.E.2d 830.

DIXON, JUSTICE.

This is an appeal from a judgment of the Circuit Court of Rock Island County dismissing, for failure to state a cause of action, an amended complaint filed by Suzanne Talbot, the plaintiff, against Country Life Insurance Company, the defendant in Count I and against Roy Melody, the defendant in Count II.

Count I of the amended complaint alleges in substance that: on September 13, 1969 Larry L. Talbot the husband of plaintiff applied in writing to the company's agent, Roy Melody for a life insurance policy in the amount of $15,000.00 on his own life, designating plaintiff as beneficiary; a first premium was then and there paid; on Feb. 19, 1970 Larry Talbot died; defendant retained the first premium and made no attempt to return it until Feb. 21, 1970; between the time of application and death Larry L. Talbot was in good health, his life was an insurable risk; he would have been able to obtain and would have obtained a policy from another company if it had not been for the representations of defendant; that defendant failed to take action on the application within a reasonable time; failed to issue a policy in accordance with the application and; failed to give notice of the action, if any, taken on the application and; that as a direct and proximate result the plaintiff was damaged.

One of the steps necessary to effecting an insurance policy is the filing of an application by the prospective insured; the application, being a mere offer or proposal for a contract of insurance, is not a contract. The existence of a contractual relationship between the parties (absent a binder) depends upon the acceptance by the insurer of the application. In the instant case the appellant concedes that she has no action ex contractu (the original complaint was on that theory). Neither the application nor the premium receipt provisions, if any, were pleaded, no binder is claimed; so the issue (Count I) is whether an insurer may be liable in tort for damage resulting from unreasonable delay in passing on an application for insurance.

There are divergent views on the question. On the one hand, it has been said that the failure of an insurer to act upon an application for insurance within a reasonable time, with resultant damage is a breach of the insurer's duty subjecting the company to liability for negligence. On the other hand, it has been said that an application for insurance is a mere offer and the insurer is under no duty to act on the offer. 43 Am.Jur.2d Insurance, Secs. 214, 215; 14 Am.Jur.Pl. and Pr.Forms (Rev.) Form 111; Couch on Insurance 2d, Sec. 7:29; 44 C.J.S. Insurance § 232(c)bb., page 986.

* * *

This court in Wille v. Farmers Equitable Ins. Co., 89 Ill.App.2d 377, 232 N.E.2d 468 recognized unreasonable delay and quoted Appleman, Insurance Law and Practice, vol. 12, Sec. 7226 where the author states, "The more liberal, and probably the better rule, is to the effect that an insurance company obtaining an application for insurance is under a duty to accept it or reject it within a reasonable time."

Appleman also states in Sec. 7232, "The better rule is to the effect that where application was made for a life policy with a beneficiary being designated to receive the proceeds, a cause of action lodges in such beneficiary, upon the applicant's death, for unreasonable delay on the part of the insurer, in accepting or rejecting such application."

Count II charges the agent Roy Melody with having failed to take action on said application within a reasonable time and failing to give notice of any action taken on the application. The complaint clearly alleges that Roy Melody was the agent of Country Life Insurance Company (as distinguished from being a broker). Brokers as distinguished from soliciting agents have long been held liable in tort, 22 I.L.P. Insurance Sec. 77, page 123. The agent here is not the agent of the applicant. He is the agent of the company and his primary responsibility is to the company.

It has been suggested that the duty of an agent to use care in dealing with the application may be based on the principle, familiar in negligence cases, that one who enters upon an affirmative undertaking, to perform a service for another, is required to exercise reasonable care in performing it, to avoid injury to the beneficiary of the undertaking. Insurance agents who take applications, particularly where they receive premiums, may be said to have entered definitely upon a course of affirmative conduct, and be liable for misfeasance if they unreasonably delay. Prosser, Delay in Acting on an Application for Insurance, 3 University of Chicago Law Review 39 (1935). This appears to us to be a salutary rule. The thought it stands for is that the agent or company owes an applicant for insurance what amounts to be a legal obligation to act with reasonable promptness on the application, either by providing the desirable coverage or by notifying the applicant of the rejection of the risk so that he may not be lulled into a feeling of security or put to prejudicial delay in seeking protection elsewhere. Coffey v. Polimeni, 9 Cir., 188 F.2d 539; 43 Am.Jur.2d Insurance, Sec. 175; Annotation 29 A.L.R.2d 171.

Those engaged in the insurance business understand perfectly the peculiar urgency of the need for prompt attention in these matters, and in fact many premium receipts provide for delay by inserting an express provision that if the application is not accepted within a definite time it shall be deemed to have been rejected; others provide for a definite termination date (where conditional insurance is expressly given from the date of the application provided the applicant is then insurable for the plan and amount and at the premium rate applied for). Meyer, Life and Health Insurance Law, p. 121.

* * *

Reversed.

A Note on Binder

In reading the next few cases, keep in mind Professor Peter Swisher's definition of binders:

> A binder is a temporary contract of insurance, consisting of an insurer's acknowledgment that it will temporarily protect the insured against a specified loss at an agreed premium until a formal policy is issued. Binders are for the convenience of the applicant, to protect the insured from a risk of loss during the period between the completion of the insurance application and the acceptance of risk by the underwriter, when the formal policy is issued (or until the rejection of the risk by the insurer). A binder can be sketchy, informal, and temporary, but it is nevertheless an enforceable insurance contract.[1]

MARYLAND CASUALTY CO. v. J.M. FOSTER

Supreme Court of New Mexico, 1966.
76 N.M. 310, 414 P.2d 672.

MOISE, JUSTICE.

The facts of the case are generally undisputed and not complicated. Some time prior to July 2, 1962, Poynor's White Stores, Inc., hereinafter referred to as "Poynor's," had appellant Foster write all of their insurance. At that time appellant sent all Poynor's old policies to someone in Albuquerque, but the workmen's compensation policy was not included. On July 2, Poynor's informed appellant of two minor accidents involving their employees, and it was at that time that appellant first became aware that no workmen's compensation insurance had been written.

1. Peter Nash Swisher, *Insurance Binders Revisited,* 39 Tort Trial & Ins. L.J. 1011, 1013 (2004).

Upon advising Poynor's of this fact, at some time before noon on July 2, appellant was told to "cover" them immediately, and appellant responded that he would and that they were covered. No particular insurance company was designated by Poynor's. Neither did appellant name the company that he would have issue the policy. The Poynors were told that they should check and give appellant the approximate amount of the payroll. Appellant returned to his office and picked up the phone to call Whyburn and Company, general agents for appellee, Maryland Casualty Company, in El Paso, but decided to wait for the payroll figures, and so hung up before completing the call. Appellant was then interrupted by a man who came to his office, and with whom he went out of the office. While out of the office, appellant met with an accident and, as a consequence, never completed the call. The next morning, July 3, appellant received a call from Poynor's and was told that the payroll was $25,000.00 and, at the same time, that a man had been seriously injured. Thereupon, appellant called Whyburn and Company and explained the situation to a Mr. Connell of that company who said he would determine if they "were on the risk or not."

Appellant had an agency contract with appellee which allowed him to bind appellee as a workmen's compensation insurer. He also was agent for three other companies for which he had similar authority. Prior to July 2, 1962, he had written only four workmen's compensation policies, all of which were with appellee. In each instance, it had been his practice to call the general agent and place the insurance. He had not actually written the policies himself. It was his intention to phone the general agent and place the insurance when he started to call on July 2. It was his purpose to have the insurance issued by appellee, but there was no statement made or disclosure of this fact.

This action was commenced by J.W. Mason, an employee of defendant Poynor's who was injured in the July 3rd accident. He brought suit against his employer and against appellee as his employer's workmen's compensation insurer. Pursuant to permission granted by the court, appellee was permitted to file a third-party complaint against appellant and the three other insurance companies for whom he was agent.

* * * [W]e are impressed that the only real question involved is whether an insurance company can be bound by an oral agreement of its agent to insure when that agent represents several other companies and has not outwardly indicated his intention to act for the particular company.

Since the decision in Harden v. St. Paul Fire & Marine Ins. Co., 51 N.M. 55, 178 P.2d 578, there can be no question that oral contracts of insurance are recognized in this state. This is in accord with the general rule. See note, 15 A.L.R. 995, 69 A.L.R. 559, 92 A.L.R. 232. In that case, it was said that an oral contract of insurance is effected when the parties have agreed upon "(1) the subject matter; (2) the risk insured against; (3) the duration of the risk; (4) the amount of insurance; (5) the rate of premium paid or agreed to be paid; and (6) the identity of the parties."

No question is here raised concerning any of these elements except "(6) the identity of the parties." The trial court concluded that appellant's secret intention to write the insurance in appellee company was not effective to bind appellee company, particularly in view of the fact that appellant was agent for other companies.

There can be no question that the trial court's holding is in accord with the great majority of decisions in cases involving undisclosed intention to place insurance with a particular company. Grimes v. Virginia Fire & Marine Ins. Co. (Tex.Civ.App.1920) 218 S.W. 810, is such a case. We quote the following therefrom:

> "The controlling question in the case is whether or not the evidence was sufficient to show that a parol contract of insurance was made. The question must be answered in the negative. That a parol contract of insurance is ordinarily valid and enforceable seems to be well settled. But an agreement by a fire insurance agent to furnish insurance to a property owner in some company to be selected by the agent from a number of companies represented by him is not enforceable against a particular company in the absence of proof that such agent before the fire properly designated such company as the insurer. In other words, a parol contract of insurance, made with an insurance agent representing several companies—the company to take the risk not being specified—is not enforceable. * * * "

The following additional cases support the rule: [citing cases from Kentucky, Texas, Michigan, South Carolina, Washington and Mississippi]

* * * [W]e are in entire accord with the statement in Fire Ins. Co., Philadelphia County v. Sinsabaugh, 101 Ill.App. 55, 57, to the following effect:

> " * * * The observation and experience of business men are that where applications for insurance are made, and officers or agents, with authority to issue the policies of several companies, have promised to issue the same, it is frequently left to the agent to write the policy in such company as he chooses, and it is not the intention of either party that the representatives of these companies shall be considered the agent of the insured for any purpose. If an insurance company will make a person agent for it, who at the same time holds commissions from other companies, they must be held to know, from general observation, that it is the practice of such agencies to make selections of the insurer who is to assume a particular risk, and after loss they can not be heard to deny that such agent had authority to do so. * * * "

In that case, the agent had written but had not delivered the policy and it was the court's conclusion that the agent had effectively bound the principal. See also Milwaukee Bedding Co. v. Graebner, 182 Wis. 171, 196 N.W. 533. * * * If appellant at any time before the loss had, by the slightest act, indicated that he was placing the insurance with appellee, a different result might have followed.

* * *

It follows from what has been said that the judgment appealed from is free from reversible error. It is, accordingly, affirmed.

It is so ordered.

Note

Compare the *Foster* decision with *Julien v. Spring Lake Park Agency*, 283 Minn. 101, 166 N.W.2d 355 (1969). In *Julien*, plaintiff, a contractor, secured builder's risk policies from defendant. The agency retained the policies so plaintiff had no way of knowing what insurance companies had assumed the risk. On one occasion, the plaintiff made a request to defendant's president that two new builder's risk policies be written for houses under construction. Plaintiff explained that he wanted the same coverage as that of a third house ($12,000, insured by Ohio Farmers Insurance Company). Although the president assured that the buildings were covered, the Quincy Street property was, in fact, not covered when a tornado struck the house and caused substantial damage. The court held Ohio Farmers Insurance Company liable, since defendant was acting within the scope of its authority granted by Ohio. The court reasoned that when Spring Lake Park Agency specified that the policy to be written on Quincy Street was to contain the same coverage as another specified property and the president intended that the same company write the policy, these actions satisfied the rule requiring designation of an insurance company before a valid insurance contract is created.

Under *Julien*, the insurance company is liable. However, in *Foster*, the agent, not the insurance company is liable, when that agent represents other companies and does not expressly indicate his intention to write the insurance with a particular company. Any affirmative act regarding this intention, however slight, could have bound the company as well as the agent.

Applying the theory of the *Foster* decision to the *Julien* facts, are both the agent *and* the insurance company free from liability?

SOUTHEASTERN COLORADO HOMELESS CENTER v. WEST

Colorado Court of Appeals, Div. I, 1992.
843 P.2d 117, certiorari denied Jan. 4, 1993.

Opinion by JUDGE HUME.

Willard West and his employer, The Southeastern Colorado Homeless Center, seek review of the final order of the Industrial Claim Appeals Panel, which ruled that the Colorado Compensation Insurance Authority was not liable to pay workers' compensation benefits to West because the Center's insurance coverage had lapsed before the industrial accident in which he was injured. We set aside the order.

The facts are undisputed. The Center applied to the Authority for workers' compensation insurance coverage in a letter received by the Authority on May 15, 1989. In a letter dated May 25, 1989, the Authority advised the Center that a binder had been issued in accordance with the Workers' Compensation Act and that the premium was due by June 12 for coverage to be effective from May 16. The letter further stated that if the Authority received payment after June 12, coverage would be effective the day after receipt of the premium. The Authority and the Center later agreed on payment of the premium in quarterly installments, but did not otherwise alter the terms of the May 25 letter.

The Authority received the payment on June 16, and issued a policy effective June 17. West, however, was injured in a job related accident on June 15.

The administrative law judge ruled that coverage began on May 16 and did not lapse because the Center paid the premium within the 30–day grace period provided by § 8–45–113, C.R.S. (1991 Cum.Supp.). The Panel reversed, concluding that the grace period did not apply to binders.

Section 8–45–112, C.R.S. (1991 Cum.Supp.) provides in part that: "No contract of insurance between the Colorado compensation insurance authority and any employer shall be in effect until a policy or binder has been actually issued by the board and the premium therefor paid as and when required by this article." (emphasis added)

Section 8–45–113 provides in relevant part that: If any employer is in arrears for more than thirty days in any payment or wage report required to be made by said employer to the Colorado compensation insurance authority as provided in articles 40 to 47 of this title for advance premium, deposit premium, additional audited premium, or periodic premium, the employer shall by virtue of such arrearage be in default of such payment or reporting and any policy issued to such employer by said authority shall thereupon be cancelled without notice as of the effective or renewal date in the case of a new or renewal policy or as of the due date in the case of an existing policy. (emphasis added)

The Panel based its conclusion that § 8–45–113 was inapplicable on the absence therein of a reference to binders following the express reference to both policies and binders in § 8–45–112. We reject the Panel's approach and agree with West and the Center that a binder is a policy within the scope of § 8–45–113.

The term, "any policy," is ambiguous. There is no statutory definition of "policy" or "binder," and the common law definitions are ambiguous. Depending on the definitions used, a binder may be a temporary policy, or it may be a contract preliminary to a policy.

Although technically the term, "insurance policy," means the formal written instrument evidencing a contract of insurance, it is often used interchangeably with the term, "contract of insurance." See 1 G. Couch, Cyclopedia of Insurance Law § 3:1 (R. Anderson rev. 2d ed. 1984);

United Benefit Life Insurance Co. v. McCrory, 414 F.2d 928 (8th Cir. 1969), cert. denied, 396 U.S. 1039, 90 S.Ct. 687, 24 L.Ed.2d 684 (1970).

A binder has been defined as a temporary or preliminary contract of insurance that protects the insured until issuance of a formal policy or as a written memorandum evidencing the existence of such a contract. See 1 G. Couch, supra, § 3:2; 2 G. Couch, supra, § 14:26.

In the absence of an express agreement to the contrary, a binder generally incorporates the terms of the contemplated policy. See 2 G. Couch, supra, § 14:35. A binder is therefore sometimes described as a temporary policy. See Great American Insurance Co. v. Fireman's Fund Insurance Co., 481 F.2d 948 (2d Cir.1973); Turner v. Worth Insurance Co., 106 Ariz. 132, 472 P.2d 1 (1970).

In light of these varied and overlapping meanings, inasmuch as § 8–45–113 does not expressly exclude binders, the specific mention of both policies and binders in § 8–45–112, but only of policies in § 8–45–113 does not resolve the ambiguity inherent in the statutory reference to "any policy."

On the other hand, since § 8–45–113 expressly includes new policies, the grace period provided therein applies to the first premium. Therefore, since binders are commonly issued in connection with payment of the first premium for a new contract of insurance, application of the grace period to the first payment due under a binder would give effect to the express application of the statute to new policies.

Moreover, § 8–44–102, C.R.S. (1991 Cum.Supp.) provides that: "Every contract for the insurance of compensation and benefits" is "subject to all the provisions" of the Workers' Compensation Act. Thus, since, under a broad definition, a binder is a contract of insurance, § 8–44–102 would make the grace period of § 8–45–113 applicable to binders. Also, § 8–45–113 is intended to protect employers as well as employees from lapses in coverage resulting from late payment of premiums, including first premiums for new policies. Construing the statute broadly to include binders will serve that purpose. See B.B. v. People, 785 P.2d 132 (Colo.1990) (construction of ambiguous statute should give effect to its underlying purpose).

Furthermore, the ultimate object of compensation insurance is to assure payment of benefits to injured employees. 4 A. Larson, Workmen's Compensation Law §§ 92.00, 92.20 (1990). See § 8–44–101(1), C.R.S. (1991 Cum.Supp.); Travelers Insurance Co. v. Savio, 706 P.2d 1258 (Colo.1985).

That purpose is served if the statutory requirements for the cancellation of workers' compensation insurance policies is applied to binders, and such construction of the statute is consistent with holdings in other jurisdictions. See Ives v. Sunfish Sign Co., 275 N.W.2d 41 (Minn.1979); Moore v. Adams Electric Co., 264 N.C. 667, 142 S.E.2d 659 (1965). See also Red Cab Co. v. St. Paul Mercury Indemnity Co., 98 F.2d 189 (7th Cir.), cert. denied, 305 U.S. 646, 59 S.Ct. 148, 83 L.Ed. 417 (1938); T.H.

Mastin & Co. v. Russell, 214 Miss. 700, 59 So.2d 321 (1952). Accordingly, we conclude that "any policy" in § 8–45–113 includes binders as well as formal policies. Thus, since the premium was paid within the 30–day grace period, coverage did not lapse, and West was entitled to receive benefits under the policy.

The order is set aside, and the cause is remanded with directions to reinstate the order of the administrative law judge.

PIERCE and ROTHENBERG, JJ., concur.

Note

Georgia Code § 56–2420(1) states: "Binders or other contracts for temporary insurance may be made orally or in writing and shall be deemed to include all the usual terms of the policy as to which the binder was given * * * except as superseded by the clear and expressed terms of the binder." Insured held an automobile policy "limiting coverage to events taking place within 300 miles radius of the [insured's] place of business." The policy also contained a paragraph: "Changes: Notice to any agent * * * shall not effect a waiver or a change in any part of this policy or estop the company from asserting any right under the terms of this policy; *nor shall the terms of this policy be waived or changed except by endorsement issued to form a part of this policy.*" [Emphasis added].

On May 18th, the insured requested the soliciting agent to remove the mileage limitation. Apparently the soliciting agent orally agreed. The soliciting agent, however, also notified the general agent, which issued the requested endorsement effective May 31 at 5:05 p.m. At 3:05 p.m. on that date a covered auto was involved in a collision more than 300 miles from insured's place of business. A federal district court in *Canal Insurance Co. v. Aldrich,* 489 F.Supp. 157 (S.D.Ga.1980), held for the insurer in a declaratory judgment suit: "[the soliciting agent] had no power to orally modify the terms of the policy * * *. The courts have no more right or power to extend coverage of a policy or to make it more beneficial to the insured than they do to rewrite the contract and insurance coverage."

If the agent can orally bind why is she not able to orally modify, as long as the modification produces a policy which he could have bound in the first place?

WORLD TRADE CENTER PROPERTIES, L.L.C. v. THE TRAVELERS INDEMNITY CO.

United States Court of Appeals for the Second Circuit, 2003.
345 F.3d 154.

[The facts in this case are set forth in greater detail in Chapter 3 below. The case involves the property loss policy for the World Trade Center. The building had just changed ownership before September 11 and the final policies had not yet been issued prior to the disaster. The case contains a useful discussion of the role that binders play in the process.]

As an initial matter, the parties dispute which contract governs the present dispute. The Silverstein Parties [the new owners] argue that the final Travelers policy issued on September 14th governs Travelers' obligations for the events of September 11th. They premise this claim on the fact that the Travelers policy that issued on September 14 specified an effective period of July 19, 2001 to July 18, 2002, and on the legal contention that under New York law, the terms of the insurance policy that is ultimately issued govern coverage during the binder period. However, the case that the Silverstein Parties assert establishes this rule, Employers Commercial Union, 45 N.Y.2d 608, 384 N.E.2d 668, 412 N.Y.S.2d 121, is inapposite. There, the court sought to determine whether there was insurance coverage at the time a loss occurred, which was after a binder had been given but before the final policy was issued. In response to plaintiff's argument that "its ... coverage was not in place" at the time of the loss, the court stated, "We reject any notion that the [insurer's] policy was not in force" at the time of loss. Id. at 669–70. The Silverstein Parties seize on this language as support for the proposition that the later-issued policy was the instrument governing the insurer's obligations. The language is taken out of context, however. As the rest of the opinion makes plain, the court's use of the word "policy" here is a reference to "insurance coverage" generally, and not to the later-issued formal policy. See id.; see also id. at 671 (stating in consecutive sentences, "[the Insurer's] insurance was in effect" and "[the Insurer's] policy was in effect"). The court's conclusion that insurance coverage was in place at the time of the loss rested in part on the fact that the final policy, although issued after the loss had occurred, specified coverage during the period in question. Id. at 669–70. But the relevance of this fact to the court's reasoning was not that the final policy terms therefore governed coverage, but simply that they demonstrated that the insurer had done "nothing to repudiate its coverage" after the loss occurred. Indeed, the court rejected the insurer's claim that the binder had not created an enforceable contract, observing that daily, important affairs and rights in our society are made to depend upon [binders]. It is a common and necessary practice in the world of insurance, where speed often is of the essence, for the agent to use this quick and informal device to record the giving of protection pending the execution and delivery of a more conventionally detailed policy of insurance. Courts, recognizing that the cryptic nature of binders is born of necessity and that many policy clauses are either stereotypes or mandated by public regulations, are not loath to infer that conditions and limitations usual to the contemplated coverage were intended to be part of the parties' contract during the binder period.Id. at 670.

We do not read Employers Commercial Union to stand for the proposition that a final policy that is issued after a loss is the relevant contract governing the loss. In fact, as we have explained earlier in this opinion, New York law is quite to the contrary. See, e.g., Springer, 731 N.E.2d at 1108 (noting that binder and final policy are "two distinct agreements"); Rosenblatt, 594 N.Y.S.2d at 459 (holding in case where loss occurred prior to the issuance of final policy, that "the dispositive issue ... concerns the risks covered under the binder agreement ..., and this is unaffected by any changes regarding insurance policies issued subsequent to the loss"); Del Bello, 585 N.Y.S.2d at 918–19 (holding that because binder identified plaintiff as an insured, it was covered for fire damage even though plaintiff was not so listed in policy that issued post-loss). Thus, as we held in connection with the Rule 54(b) appeal, it is the Travelers binder, not the September 14 Travelers policy that applies to determine Travelers' obligations.

* * *

Notes

1. Why does the court hold that the binder trumps the more detailed insurance policy that will be issued? Is this reasoning persuasive?

2. What arguments does the insured make with respect to avoiding enforceability of the binder? Are these arguments persuasive?

3. Professor Peter Nash Swisher's article, *Insurance Binders Revisited,* 39 TORT TRIAL & INS. L.J. 1011 (2004), provides a comprehensive discussion on binders. He notes that while the need for binders is unquestioned, there are differences in the treatment of binders depending on the context in which they are used.

4. For a thorough discussion of oral binders, see *Granco Steel, Inc. v. Workmen's Compensation Appeals Board*, 68 Cal.2d 191, 65 Cal.Rptr. 287, 436 P.2d 287 (1968). In *Granco*, plaintiff had made arrangements regarding various insurance policies, including a workmen's compensation policy, with a general agent representing Hartford Accident and Indemnity Company (Hartford). Id. at 193. The agent provided oral binders to allow for immediate coverage. Id. Since Granco had not yet hired any employees, it requested that the workmen's compensation policy be cancelled, to recommence when employees were hired. Id. at 194. When Granco began to hire employees, its president telephoned the agent's office, reached his employee and requested that the workmen's compensation coverage be recommenced. Id. at 195. Some months later, one of Granco's employees was severely injured, at which point the agent informed Granco's vice-president that Granco was not covered by workmen's compensation insurance. Id.

The California State Supreme Court acknowledged the existence of oral binders (preliminary parol contracts entered into to issue new policies, renew existing policies, or to transfer existing insurance that may be effected on behalf of an insurer by any agent possessing the authority to bind the company by contracts of insurance generally), noting that the identity of the insurer must be established in order to hold the insurer liable. Id. at 197–198. Although the Court conceded that identity of the insurer in the instant case seemed unclear because the agent represented several insurance companies and could have placed the Granco risk with any one company, the Court recognized several circumstances in which the prior acts of an insurer or agent were sufficient to estop the insurer from denying coverage. Reasoning that, in the instant case, Hartford had engaged in prior dealings with the insured regarding workmen's compensation insurance, the court concluded that Granco's officers had a right to believe that coverage would be resumed with the original carrier when the need arose. Id. at 204. The court held that Hartford should not be permitted to deny coverage, in light of the present relationships among the agent, the insured, and Hartford. Id. at 205.

CRITERION LEASING GROUP v. GULF COAST PLASTERING & DRYWALL

District Court of Appeal of Florida, First District, 1991.
582 So.2d 799.

PER CURIAM.

This cause is before us on appeal from a final order determining appellants' responsibility for compensation benefits. For the following reasons, we affirm.

On July 7, 1989, Robert Bruce was injured in a work-related accident when he tripped and suffered a broken coccyx bone. The incident occurred while working for Evans & Blount Stucco (hereinafter Evans Blount) at a construction project known as the Crescent Beach Club.

Sea Coast Towers Construction (hereinafter Sea Coast) was the general contractor on the Crescent Beach Club project. Gulf Coast Plastering & Drywall (hereinafter Gulf Coast) subcontracted with Sea Coast to provide plastering and drywall.[5] Thereafter, Gulf Coast subcontracted the stucco work to Evans Blount. Evans Blount provided proof of workers' compensation coverage which showed the coinsureds as Criterion Leasing Corporation (hereinafter Criterion) and Evans Blount.[6]

Criterion acts as a large personnel department for a number of small companies. Criterion handled the workers' compensation coverage and payroll for Evans Blount. On April 13, 1989, all personnel who had formerly been employees of Evans Blount were then considered employees of Criterion. However, new employees of Evans Blount did not become employees of Criterion until after Criterion was notified that a new employee had been hired. Criterion was unaware that Evans Blount had hired claimant.

Gulf Coast and its carrier, Continental Loss Adjusting, accepted the claim as compensable but reserved its right to seek reimbursement from Criterion, Evans Blount, and Hartford.[7] After hearing [sic], the judge of compensation claims (JCC) found that Hartford issued a certificate of insurance indicating that Evans Blount employees were covered. Gulf Coast and Continental relied on this certificate and were detrimentally damaged by this reliance. The JCC found all the elements of equitable

5. Gulf Coast provided Sea Coast with a current certificate of workers' compensation coverage.

6. Gulf Coast requires subcontractors to provide proof of workers' compensation coverage. When a subcontractor does not have coverage, Gulf Coast provides coverage and pays the premium with a portion of the draw paid to the subcontractor.

7. Hartford issued the workers' compensation policy listing Evans Blount and Criterion as coinsureds.

estoppel had been established, and therefore Evans Blount, Criterion, and Hartford were estopped from denying coverage.

Initially, we determine that the JCC erred in finding that "all of the elements of equitable estoppel have been satisfied." (emphasis added). Equitable estoppel may not be used to affirmatively create or extend insurance coverage. However, "[a]n exception to the general rule is the doctrine of promissory estoppel, a qualified form of equitable estoppel which applies to representations relating to a future act of the promisor rather than to an existing fact." Crown Life Ins. Co. v. McBride, 517 So.2d 660, 661 (Fla.1987) (citations omitted). Because the JCC found the elements of promissory estoppel present and followed the dictates of Masonry v. Miller Construction, 558 So.2d 433 (Fla. 1st DCA 1990), we affirm.

A party will be estopped from denying liability under the principle of promissory estoppel when the party makes "[a] promise which the promisor should reasonably expect to induce action or forbearance of a definite and substantial character on the part of the promisee and which does induce such action or forbearance ... [and] injustice can be avoided only by enforcement of the promise." Coral Way Properties, Ltd. v. Roses, 565 So.2d 372, 374 (Fla. 3d DCA 1990), citing 1 Restatement of the Law Second, Contracts 2d § 90 at 242 (1987).

We find that it was foreseeable to Hartford that Evans Blount would use the certificate of insurance as proof of workers' compensation coverage. First, Hartford provided workers' compensation coverage to Criterion Leasing. The certificate of insurance listed both Criterion and Evans Blount as coinsureds. The certificate was presented to Gulf Coast as proof of workers' compensation coverage. If Evans Blount did not present proof of insurance, Gulf Coast would have obtained a policy providing workers' compensation coverage prior to Evans Blount's employment. Therefore, Hartford's promise to provide workers' compensation coverage to the coinsureds (Criterion and Evans Blount) induced Gulf Coast to allow Evans Blount to begin working at the job site. Claimant's injury constituted the detrimental result that followed Gulf Coast's reliance.

Second, Section 440.10(1), Florida Statutes, requires a general contractor to provide workers' compensation coverage for a subcontractor's employees except when the subcontractor already has obtained coverage. Therefore, Hartford should have reasonably expected that Gulf Coast would rely on the certificate of insurance naming Evans Blount as a coinsured. This promise of coverage induced Gulf Coast to subcontract with Evans Blount.

Accordingly, we affirm the order under the principle of promissory estoppel.

Notes

1. In *Tate v. Charles Aguillard Ins. & Real Estate*, 508 So.2d 1371 (La.1987), Tate, the insured, owned a horse named British Colonial, which was insured for $100,000 for one year beginning October 30, 1980 for a $4,500 premium subject to the condition that British Colonial be in good health on the date of the policy. It was undisputed that the condition was not met. The horse had become sick before October 30, 1980, and was destroyed December 25, 1981.

Tate's claim was that failure to deny coverage promptly prevented him from seeking alternative coverage and that he delayed destruction of British Colonial thereby missing the coverage period under a prior policy. Although Tate was successful in avoiding the "waiving into coverage" restriction, he was unable to show that the insurer had waived the condition of the policy. The Louisiana court noted that Tate could not show reliance because no other insurer would have insured British Colonial due to the existing illness and because the prior insurer would not have allowed destruction of the horse inasmuch as the horse's health was not hopeless until November when that policy lapsed.

2. Insured (now deceased) indicated to insurer's agent when applying for a life policy that he had driven "60/45 zone" [presumably 60 miles per hour in a 45 miles per hour zone] and disclosed that he had other driving offenses although he was not clear on all the details. Insurer's agent indicated that the disclosure was sufficient and that insured's record would be checked with the Department of Motor Vehicles. Insured's application form disclosed only the "60/45 zone" offense. The insured dies in an auto accident. Is the insurer charged with knowledge of the other driving offenses so that it cannot disclaim liability for payment under the policy? See Willetts v. Integon Life Insurance Corp., 45 N.C.App. 424, 263 S.E.2d 300 (1980) (yes, because agent's knowledge of insured's driving record was imputed to the insurer).

3. Agent accepted insured's application for an all-risk policy on his boat, knowing that insurance company refuses to provide coverage for boats of that value and age without a survey. Without a survey, agent stated to insured that the boat was covered. It does not appear that insured knew anything about insurance company's refusal of coverage for boats like his. Naturally, the boat sank. Can insured recover against *both* agent and insurance company? If insured recovers from insurance company can it recover "over" against agent? Crawford v. DiMicco, 216 So.2d 769 (Fla.App. 1968) (holding yes to the former question and further holding the agent liable to the insurance company for acting without the insurance company's authority).

4. The preceding cases have addressed the question whether an insurer is justified in withholding payment under the policy based on its perception of the insured's conduct where the conduct relates to the terms of the policy. In *Spindle v. Travelers Ins. Cos.*, 66 Cal.App.3d 951, 136 Cal.Rptr. 404 (1977), the California Court of Appeal addressed the unique question of whether an insurer is justified in cancelling a policy for conduct not related

directly to the terms of the policy. In finding for the insured, the court held that the insurer's unilateral right to cancel under the policy was bounded by its obligation of good faith and fair dealing. Accordingly, the insured's allegation that the cancellation stemmed from the insured's activism against the insurer in obtaining a favorable group medical malpractice policy was sufficient to survive a demurrer. See Eric G. Anderson, *Good Faith in the Enforcement of Contracts*, 73 Iowa L. Rev. 299 (1988) (general discussion of vindictive conduct by insurers).

5. In *Murphy v. Seed–Roberts Agency, Inc.*, 79 Mich.App. 1, 261 N.W.2d 198, 99 A.L.R.3d 457 (1977), the court held that an issue of fact remained as to whether an insurer's right to cancellation was exercised in good faith despite an apparently unilateral right to cancel. For a general discussion of insurer's liability for canceling policies as a breach of the implied covenant of good faith and fair dealing, see Wrongful Cancellation of Medical Malpractice Insurance, 99 A.L.R.3d 469 (1990).

6. Does an insurance agent have standing to seek reformation of the insurance contract between the insurer and the insured? B (insured) asked R (agent) to add coverage of a new piece of heavy construction equipment to B's existing policy with W (insurer). R never informed W of the request for coverage. B sued R and W. W settled with B and R asked that the policy be reformed to include the requested coverage. Biondo v. Ridgemont Insurance Agency, Inc., 104 Mich.App. 209, 304 N.W.2d 534 (1981). Why would an agent *want* reformation?

C. THE LAW OF MISREPRESENTATION: AN APPLICANT'S PROBLEM IN NEGOTIATION

The subjects of misrepresentation, concealment and fraud will also arise in subsequent portions of this book. We felt that some substantial treatment of the subject was warranted here, because misrepresentation, fraud and concealment cut across the law of insurance contracts. The reader, having the courses in Contracts and Torts fresh in mind, might ask:

(a) What remedies are available for misrepresentation, concealment, mistake?

(b) Is a remedy available in case of an innocent misrepresentation?

(c) What remedies are available in the case of fraudulent misrepresentation?

MERCHANTS FIRE ASSURANCE CORP. v. LATTIMORE

United States Court of Appeals, Ninth Circuit, 1959.
263 F.2d 232.

HAMLEY, CIRCUIT JUDGE.

In this action, Miss Ann E. Lattimore, the insured under a policy of personal property insurance, recovered judgment against the insurer in the sum of $17,034. Of this sum $7,084 was for loss in connection with the disappearance of, or damage to, scheduled fine arts. The remaining $9,950 was for loss due to the disappearance of, or damage to, unscheduled personal property covered by a personal property floater provision of the policy.

Appealing to this court, defendant, Merchants Fire Assurance Corporation, contends that with regard to the scheduled fine arts the trial court should have found the loss to be $4,339.45 instead of $7,084. Concerning the $9,950 loss relating to unscheduled personal property, the company contends that it should have been relieved from all liability on its defense of concealment and misrepresentation of a material fact.[8]

* * *

The material concealment or misrepresentation upon which appellant relies has to do with the declarations which Miss Lattimore made in paragraph 4 of the policy concerning "the unscheduled personal property." Appellant argues that in this paragraph the insured was called upon to declare the approximate value of all the unscheduled personal property which she owned.

The value which she declared in this paragraph under five of the fifteen listed categories of property was $9,950.[9] At the trial it was

8. The first paragraph of the policy under the heading "Conditions" reads: "This policy shall be void if the Assured has concealed or misrepresented any material fact or circumstance concerning this insurance or the subject thereof or in case of any fraud, attempted fraud or false swearing by the Assured touching any matter relating to this insurance or the subject thereof, whether before or after a loss."

This provision in effect carries into the insurance contract the applicable sections of the West's Ann.California Insurance Code referred to in this opinion. Section 331 of that code provides: "Concealment, whether intentional or unintentional, entitles the injured party to rescind insurance."

9. The pertinent part of paragraph 4 as filled in reads as follows:

"4. The following are the approximate values of the unscheduled personal property, other than jewelry, watches and furs, as estimated by the Assured, at the time of issuance of this policy:

Wherever Located

(a) Silverware and pewter	$3,000.00
(b) Linens (including dining room and bedroom)	$ 500.00
(c) Clothing (Men's, Women's, Children's)	$5,000.00
(d) Rugs (including floor coverings) and draperies	$ Nil
(e) Books	$ Nil
(f) Musical Instruments (including pianos)	$ Nil
(g) Television sets, radios, record players and records	$ Nil
(h) China & Glassware (including bric-a-brac)	$ Nil
(i) Camera & Photographic equipment	$ Nil
(j) Golf, hunting, fishing and other sports & hobby equipment	$ Nil
(k) Paintings, etchings, pictures and other objects of art	$1,000.00
(*l*) Refrigerators, washing machines, stoves, electrical appliances and other kitchen equipment	$ Nil
(m) Bedding (including blankets, comforters, covers, pillows, mattresses, and springs)	$ Nil
(n) Furniture (including tables, chairs, sofas, desks, beds, chests, lamps, mirrors, clocks)	$ Nil
(*o*) All other personal property (including wines, liquors, foodstuff, garden and lawn tools and equipment, trunks, traveling bags, children's playthings, miscellaneous articles in basement and attic) and professional equipment, if any, covered under paragraph 7(b)	$ 450.00
Total	$9,950.00"

stipulated that when the policy was issued, and for many years prior thereto, the actual value of the unscheduled property was at least $36,500. The insured thus failed to disclose that, in addition to the property declared in paragraph 4, she owned unscheduled personal property of the approximate value of $27,000.

In determining whether the failure to disclose this information constitutes the kind of "concealment" which warrants avoidance of liability, we turn first to the West's Ann.California Insurance Code. Under § 330 of that code, "neglect to communicate that which a party knows, and ought to communicate, is concealment."

Miss Lattimore either had personal knowledge of the approximate value of all the unscheduled personal property owned by her, or is charged therewith by reason of the knowledge of her agents Langman and Raymond Armsby. She is consequently presumed to know the approximate value of the portion thereof which was not declared in paragraph 4. It remains to be determined whether, within the meaning of § 330, this was information which appellee "ought" to have communicated to the company.

A party to an insurance contract "ought" to communicate to the other at least such information as he is under a statutory duty to communicate. Section 332 of the West's Ann.California Insurance Code requires the parties to such a contract to disclose certain facts. The section reads:

> "Each party to a contract of insurance shall communicate to the other, in good faith, all facts within his knowledge which are or which he believes to be material to the contract. * * * "

As we have already indicated, the facts concerning the approximate total value of all unscheduled personal property owned by Miss Lattimore were within her knowledge, or that of her agents. Miss Lattimore, who testified at the trial, did not explicitly state whether at the time the contract was entered into she believed that information as to the value of all her unscheduled personal property was material to the contract. Nor did the trial court make an express finding of fact as to this. But the court noted in its findings that the policy conveyed no explicit information as to the materiality of the declaration to be made in paragraph 4.

These and other more general findings of fact may have been intended to reflect an implicit finding that when the contract was negotiated Miss Lattimore had no reason to believe that this information was material to the contract. We will so assume.

Belief in the materiality of the withheld facts, as referred to in § 332, is satisfied, however, if an authorized agent of the contracting party held such belief. This follows from the general rule which charges an insured with the knowledge and acts of his agent. See Gelb v. Automobile Insurance Co., 2 Cir., 168 F.2d 774. Armsby testified, without contradiction, that he was aware of the facts and circumstances which made such information material to the contract. In view of her broker's awareness of the materiality of the information in question, Miss Lattimore had a duty under § 332 to communicate that information to appellant.

But even if it be supposed that Armsby was not aware of the materiality of these facts, the same result must be reached. Section 332 placed upon Miss Lattimore the duty to communicate material facts to appellant regardless of whether she or her broker believed them to be material. This is made clear by the disjunctive "or" in the phrase of § 332 reading "* * * which *are* or which he believes to be material to the contract * * *." (Emphasis supplied.)

Application of this alternative provision, which does not require belief as to materiality, is dependent upon whether the undisclosed facts as to value were in fact material to the contract. There are three tests which the courts employ to determine the materiality of undisclosed facts. The test most frequently applied is whether a fact is regarded as material by all similar insurers. A second test is what a reasonable and prudent insurer would regard as material.[10]

The third test is whether the particular individual insurer regarded the undisclosed facts as material to the contract. This test looks only to the evidence concerning the attitude or practice of the insurance company involved in the suit. The courts of California have determined that under § 334 of the West's Ann.California Insurance Code[11] they are required to adopt this third test in determining the materiality of concealed or misrepresented facts.

The trial court made no finding as to whether the fact of total approximate value of the unscheduled personal property owned by Miss Lattimore was material to the contract. Appellant, however, submitted considerable evidence to the effect that under its practice, and also under the practice of similar insurers, this fact was material. Thus, appellant produced evidence which, under either the stringent California rule or the more generally used first test mentioned above, tended to show materiality.

According to this testimony, the reason why the fact of total approximate value of all such property owned by the insured is material is that it definitely affects the risk assumed. As the witnesses giving this testimony explained it, most losses under a personal property floater are partial rather than total, but the risk of partial loss increases with the total value and amount of property owned. The chance of a $2,000 loss

10. Standard Accident Ins. Co. v. Walker, 127 Va. 140, 102 S.E. 585. Both of these tests reflect the rule of contract law that the materiality of facts which are misrepresented depends on whether the misrepresentation would affect the conduct of a reasonable man. See Restatement, Contracts, § 470.

11. Section 334 reads as follows: "Materiality is to be determined not by the event, but solely by the probable and reasonable influence of the facts upon the party to whom the communication is due, in forming his estimate of the disadvantages of the proposed contract, or in making his inquiries."

occurring is thus much greater in the case of a person who owns $50,000 worth of property than in the case of one who owns only $2,000 worth.[12]

Because of this, it was uniformly testified, it is customary for companies writing such insurance, and appellant in particular, to ask that the insurance coverage be not less than eighty per cent of the total value of the property owned. Hence, had it been disclosed to appellant that the approximate value of all unscheduled personal property owned by Miss Lattimore was $36,500, appellant would have insisted on a coverage of at least $29,200. The premium on such a coverage would have been $548.02, instead of the actual premium of $316.89.

As against this evidence of materiality, appellee calls attention to other evidence which, in her view, shows that the undisclosed fact was not material. One such item of evidence relates to a letter which appellee's broker wrote to appellant's issuing agent in July 1950. In this letter it was stated that certain personal property was stored in a named warehouse. Among the items of property referred to was "household furniture." Appellee argues that this letter put appellant on notice that Miss Lattimore owned some furniture—hence knew that the declaration of "nil" for furniture in the policy then in effect was wrong. In spite of this knowledge, the company entered into the contract, thereby indicating, so appellee contends, that the total value of property owned was not considered to be a material fact.

The fact is, however, that the policy then in effect had no separate item declared as value of furniture. It follows that the 1950 letter did not show any inaccuracy whatever in the 1949 declarations. In the 1950 form, used after this letter was sent, a category of furniture was added for the first time. It was contained in the 1952 form involved in this suit. It is apparently appellee's view that the 1950 letter should have put the company on notice in 1952 that Miss Lattimore had some furniture.

We do not believe that either lack of materiality or estoppel can be shown by a process of reasoning as speculative as this. Moreover, appellee or her broker had been in possession of the 1952 policy for three years and had never advised appellant that the "nil" declaration on furniture was erroneous. Appellee thereby adopted and confirmed the declarations just as if she had personally repeated them to the insurer. Telford v. New York Life Ins. Co., 9 Cal.2d 103, 69 P.2d 835.

12. There was testimony to the effect, and appellant concedes, that a declaration of value is not to be regarded as a warranty. An insurance man, called as a witness by appellant, testified that "companies generally like to get about eighty per cent insurance to value." It is true that he further testified: "* * * I have seen any number of cases where the declaration, for example, might show $2,000 estimated value for clothing, and when loss finally overtakes the assured there might be $3,000 [or] $4,000 in value of clothing. Now, if that $4,000 falls within the limit of liability for the unscheduled items there is no question of the company not paying the loss." This testimony did not relate to any practice of appellant. In any event, the decision of a company to be lenient, once a loss has occurred, does not mean that it would have entered into the contract on the terms stated had it known the facts which were concealed.

Another item of evidence upon which appellee relies to show that the fact of total value was not material has to do with a clothing loss in 1950. This was a loss of $2,800, at a time when the declaration in the 1949–52 policy stated only $2,000 for clothing. Despite this declaration, the full claim of $2,800 was paid.

At the time of this incident, the total value declared was $6,950, and the unscheduled insurance was $5,578. After paying the loss, appellant's agent suggested to Miss Lattimore's broker that perhaps the values and the insurance were too low. As a consequence, the declaration on clothing value was increased from $2,000 to $5,000. It therefore appears that when an under-declaration came to the attention of appellant, the insured was requested to raise the declaration, and this was done. We find nothing in this incident to indicate that appellant did not regard the declaration of total value material.

* * *

It would therefore appear that, either because of Armsby's belief that such information was material or because, in any event, it was material, appellee had a statutory duty under § 332 to communicate this information to appellant. Her neglect to do so, unless otherwise excused, was therefore "concealment" within the meaning of § 330. This, under the terms of the contract and of § 331 of the West's Ann. California Insurance Code (see footnote 52) would seem to void the policy.

But appellee contends that she is to be excused for failing to disclose total value of property owned because, in her view, the declaration form contained in paragraph 4 of the policy did not plainly call for a statement of approximate value of all unscheduled personal property owned by Miss Lattimore. In this connection it is pointed out that there was not, in that paragraph or elsewhere in the policy, any reference to the company's eighty per cent practice referred to above. It is argued that it was reasonable for her to believe that all that was called for by this provision was a declaration as to that part of her total property which she desired to have protected by insurance. Appellee contends that it was pursuant to this belief that a declaration of $9,950 was entered in paragraph 4.

The trial court did not enter an express finding to the effect that Miss Lattimore or her broker understood that paragraph 4 called only for a declaration of the value of property sought to be protected by insurance. If such a finding is implicit in other general findings, it is clearly erroneous. Miss Lattimore did not so testify. As a matter of fact, she testified that when in 1946 she examined a predecessor policy containing a similar paragraph of declaration, "I thought it covered whatever belongings I had." In any event, her then broker, Armsby, made it clear that he knew that all property owned was to be declared. The fact that the policy makes no reference to the company's eighty per cent practice is immaterial, since appellee's broker was aware of that practice.

That appellee, or at least her broker, did not so construe the declaration provision is also indicated by the fact that her claim against the company is not limited to the categories of property for which she declared a value. See footnote 5. She had no clothing loss, and only $525 was claimed on silverware and pewter. Adding this figure to the valuations declared on three other categories, only $2,475 insurance coverage would be available to satisfy appellee's claim. Yet her claim was for $9,950, the full amount.

A claim in this amount would be justified only if the $9,950 coverage specified in paragraph 3(a) on "unscheduled personal property" meant coverage to this extent on all the personal property which Miss Lattimore owned. But if those words had that meaning in paragraph 3(a), they must also have had that meaning in paragraph 4.

* * *

This is not a case where the company had conducted an independent investigation by reason of which it became aware of some falsity. DiPasqua v. California Western States Life Ins. Co., 106 Cal.App.2d 281, 235 P.2d 64. In California an insured may not escape the consequences of his deception by placing on the insurer the burden of investigating his verified statements. Robinson v. Occidental Life Ins. Co., 131 Cal.App.2d 581, 281 P.2d 39.

One of the essential elements of estoppel or waiver in an insurance case is knowledge of the pertinent facts. Rizzuto v. National Reserve Ins. Co., 92 Cal.App.2d 143, 206 P.2d 431. A waiver cannot be established by a consent given under a mistake regarding essential facts, or in ignorance of the facts the effect of which is claimed to have been waived. * * * Mere cause for suspicion is not a substitute for knowledge. * * *

It is our conclusion that, both as a matter of fact and law, appellant established the defense of concealment, entitling it to void the personal property floater provision of the policy. This being the case, it is unnecessary to discuss the facts and law relative to appellant's defense based on asserted misrepresentation of a material fact.

The judgment is reversed and the cause is remanded with directions to enter judgment for appellee in the sum of $7,084, with interest, and costs, as provided in the original judgment, additionally increased in a sum equal to the premium paid for the personal property floater, with interest thereon. Appellant will recover its costs on this appeal.

Notes

1. The Dean of Educational Administration at an Illinois college was an art collector. In applying for coverage for his collection from Lloyds of London, he submitted an appraisal signed by X stating the value to be $275,800. The collection was stolen and a claim for the appraised amount was submitted. The insurers refused payment, having discovered that the insured had purchased the stuff from X for $19,800 and that the appraisal

was made contemporaneously with the purchase. The court ruled that the concealment of this information was grounds for rescinding the coverage. Stone v. Those Certain Underwriters at Lloyds, London, Subscribing to Cover Note No. SL 10001, 81 Ill.App.3d 333, 36 Ill.Dec. 781, 401 N.E.2d 622 (1980). Was the court justified in holding that the concealed information was material?

2. *The Standard for Testing the Materiality of a Non-deliberate Misrepresented Fact.* For a subjective standard see Vance, 3d ed. 1951 at p. 407:

> "* * * Any statement is material which in any wise induced the issuer to make a contract which he otherwise would not have made or would have made only on different terms."

For an objective standard see Couch, Cyclopedia of Insurance Law, 2d ed., § 69.121:

> "The question of the materiality to the risk of statements by the insured in an application for reinstatement is not to be determined by the jury on the basis of what the applicant may think as to materiality, but upon the basis of what those engaged in the life insurance business, acting reasonably and naturally, in accordance with the practice usual among such companies, under similar circumstances, would do. Otherwise stated, the test * * * depends not upon what the insurer or the insured may think about the materiality or the importance of the false information given or the true information withheld, but upon what those engaged in the insurance business, acting reasonably and naturally in accordance with the usual practice among insurance companies under such circumstances, would have done had they known the truth; that is to say, whether reasonably careful and intelligent men would have regarded the facts stated as substantially increasing the chances of the happening of the event insured against so as to cause a rejection of the application."

Numerous case citations are made available for both propositions. The objective standard espoused by Couch more clearly tracks the general rule applicable outside of insurance cases. See § 538 Restatement of Torts, 2d adopting the reasonable man standard (the qualification in that section is not adaptable to the insurance situation). See also § 162 Restatement of Contracts (2d). A major objection to the subjective test (i.e., did *this* insurer consider the fact material) is that it duplicates the requirement that the insurer prove it was induced to issue the policy in *reliance* upon the misrepresentation, which is obviously also a purely subjective matter.

3. *Deliberate misrepresentations of non-material facts.* Generally, rescission and restitution may be had by an aggrieved party who was induced to enter into a contract as a result of deliberate misrepresentation regardless of materiality. See Restatement of Restitution § 9, comment b; e.g., § 186 Mass.Gen.Laws. However it will be a rare case when a large insurance company is able to convince a trier of fact that it justifiably relied and was victimized by an immaterial misrepresentation.

4. *Materiality and Causation.* Suppose X on his insurance application has misrepresented his history of drug abuse, but his untimely death is from an accidental gunshot wound. Obviously there is no relationship between the

fact misrepresented and his untimely death, so why should the insurer not pay? In *Howard v. Aid Association for Lutherans*, 272 N.W.2d 910 (Minn. 1978), the court summarized the situation:

> In general, we have held that an insurer has the option to void an insurance contract once it discovers that the insured has wilfully made a false representation which is material and which increases the contractual risk undertaken by the insurer. Minn.St. 61A.11.[13] * * * Shaughnessy v. New York Life Ins. Co., 163 Minn. 134, 203 N.W. 600 (1925); * * *.
>
> A review of authorities analyzing the effect of an insured's misrepresentation upon the insurer's coverage obligation reveals two distinct approaches to materiality. Plaintiff urges our adoption of the minority position that coverage may only be defeated when the facts misrepresented specifically relate to the cause of death. See, e.g., Central National Life Ins. Co. v. Peterson, 23 Ariz.App. 4, 529 P.2d 1213 (1975), and National Old Line Ins. Co. v. People, 256 Ark. 137, 506 S.W.2d 128 (1974). He asserts that since there exists no causal connection between a failure to disclose a history of drug abuse and an accidental shooting death, it is consistent with public policy to enforce the terms of the insurance contract.
>
> However, a majority of jurisdictions, including this court, has measured the materiality of a misrepresentation by the extent to which the disclosure influenced the insurer's decision to initially assure the risk of coverage, not by the degree of causal connection between the false statement and the loss protected by the policy. Neither decisional nor statutory authority in this state requires more than that an insured wilfully misstate necessary information or intentionally mislead the insurer into issuing a policy for coverage. Minn.St. 61A.11. In Shaughnessy v. New York Life Ins. Co., supra, we concluded that false responses to insurance application inquiries precluded recovery under the policy. The facts presented indicated that the deceased insured failed to disclose conditions of anemia and headaches, the latter having been diagnosed as related to syphilis. We held that while the insured's death was caused by a brain tumor and had no relationship to the matters concealed, the insured was obliged to truthfully detail her medical condition. A breach of that fundamental obligation affects the very essence of the insurer's decision to offer coverage and was therefore held material.

5. A common statutory provision addresses the materiality-causation problem—e.g., Kansas Stat. Ann.:

> **40–418. Materiality of misrepresentation in obtaining policy.** No misrepresentation made in obtaining or securing a policy of insurance on the

13. Minn.St. 61A.11 provides: "In any claim upon a policy issued in this state without previous medical examination, or without the knowledge or consent of the insured, or, in case of a minor, without the consent of his parent, guardian, or other person having his legal custody, the statements made in the application as to the age, physical condition, and family history of the insured shall be valid and binding upon the company, unless *willfully false or intentionally misleading.*" (Emphasis supplied.)

life or lives of any person or persons, citizens of this state, shall be deemed material or render the policy void unless the matter misrepresented shall have actually contributed to the contingency or event on which the policy is to become due and payable. (see also, R.S.Mo. (1968) § 376.580)

Query: Why does the statute single out life insurance?

6. Although the subjects of misrepresentation, concealment, and fraud come up frequently enough in connection with claims under insurance policies, more of the decisions seem to deal with applications for policies. Considerable legislative attention has been attracted from time to time because a good deal of money and important personal and public interests are at stake. There are large variations among the statutes, a fact that does not help clarification at the casebook level. Sometimes the statutes are not received with the utmost hospitality by the learned writers. See Patterson, *Some Contracts Provisions of the California Insurance Code*, 32 So. Cal. L. Rev. 227 (1959). Nonetheless we have reproduced the following sections to illustrate legislative attention to the subject.

CALIFORNIA (California Insurance Code)

§ 330. Definition

Neglect to communicate that which a party knows, and ought to communicate, is concealment.

§ 331. Effect

Concealment, whether intentional or unintentional, entitles the injured party to rescind insurance.

§ 332. Required disclosures

Each party to a contract of insurance shall communicate to the other, in good faith, all facts within his knowledge which are or which he believes to be material to the contract and as to which he makes no warranty, and which the other has not the means of ascertaining.

§ 333. Matters not required to be disclosed except upon inquiry

Neither party to a contract of insurance is bound to communicate information of the matters following, except in answer to the inquiries of the other:

1. Those which the other knows.

2. Those which, in the exercise of ordinary care, the other ought to know, and of which the party has no reason to suppose him ignorant.

3. Those of which the other waives communication.

4. Those which prove or tend to prove the existence of a risk excluded by a warranty, and which are not otherwise material.

5. Those which relate to a risk excepted from insurance, and which are not otherwise material.

§ 334. Determination of materiality

Materiality is to be determined not by the event, but solely by the probable and reasonable influence of the facts upon the party to whom the communication is due, in forming his estimate of the disadvantages of the proposed contract, or in making his inquiries.

§ 335. Presumed knowledge

Each party to a contract of insurance is bound to know:

(a) All the general causes which are open to his inquiry equally with that of the other, and which may affect either the political or material perils contemplated.

(b) All the general usages of trade.

§ 336. Waiver of right to information

The right to information of material facts may be waived, either (a) by the terms of insurance of (b) by neglect to make inquiries as to such facts, where they are distinctly implied in other facts of which information is communicated.

§ 337. Nature and amount of insured's interest

Information of the nature or amount of the interest of one insured need not be communicated unless in answer to an inquiry, except as prescribed by section 381, or by the provisions of the insurance contract if such provisions are prescribed by this code as part of a standard form.

§ 339. Information of party's own judgment

Neither party to a contract of insurance is bound to communicate, even upon inquiry, information of his own judgment upon the matters in question.

§ 350. Nature

A representation may be oral or written.

§ 351. Time of making

A representation may be made at the time of, or before, issuance of the policy.

§ 353. As to future

A representation as to the future is a promise, unless it is merely a statement of a belief or an expectation.

§ 354. Effect upon policy

A representation cannot qualify an express provision in a contract of insurance; but it may qualify an implied warranty.

§ 355. Alteration or withdrawal

A representation may be altered or withdrawn before the insurance is effected, but not afterwards.

§ 356. Time referred to

The completion of the contract of insurance is the same to which a representation must be presumed to refer.

§ 357. Information of others

When an insured has no personal knowledge of a fact, he may nevertheless repeat information which he has upon the subject, and which he believes to be true, with the explanation that he does so on the information of others; or he may submit the information, in its whole extent, to the insurer. In neither case is he responsible for its truth, unless it proceeds from an agent of the insured, whose duty it is to give the information.

§ 358. Falsity defined

A representation is false when the facts fail to correspond with its assertions or stipulations.

§ 359. Effect of falsity

If a representation is false in a material point, whether affirmative or promissory, the injured party is entitled to rescind the contract from the time the representation becomes false.

§ 360. Materiality

The materiality of a representation is determined by the same rule as the materiality of a concealment.

NEW YORK (New York Insurance Law)

§ 3105. Representations by the Insured

(a) A representation is a statement as to past or present fact, made to the insurer by or by the authority of the applicant for insurance or the prospective insured, at or before the making of the insurance contract as an inducement to the making thereof. A misrepresentation is a false representation, and the facts misrepresented are those facts which make the representation false.

(b) No misrepresentation shall avoid any contract of insurance or defeat recovery thereunder unless such misrepresentation was material. No misrepresentation shall be deemed material unless knowledge by the insurer of the facts misrepresented would have led to a refusal by the insurer to make such contract.

(c) In determining the question of materiality, evidence of the practice of the insurer which made such contract with respect to the acceptance or rejection of similar risks shall be admissible.

(d) A misrepresentation that an applicant for life, accident or health insurance has not had previous medical treatment, consultation or observation, or has not had previous treatment or care in a hospital or other like institution, shall be deemed, for the purpose of determining its materiality, a misrepresentation that the applicant has not had the disease, ailment or other medical impairment for which such treatment or care was given or which was discovered by any licensed medical practitioner as a result of such consultation or observation. If in any action to rescind any such contract or to recover thereon, any such misrepresentation is proved by the insurer, and the insured or any other person having or claiming a right under such contract shall prevent full disclosure and proof of the nature of such medical impairment, such misrepresentation shall be presumed to have been material.

FUNCHESS v. UNITED STATES LIFE INSURANCE CO.

Supreme Court of New York, Appellate Division, 1980.
77 A.D.2d 516, 430 N.Y.S.2d 77.

Memorandum Decision

* * * The decedent met his end at the point of a gun. So far as is pertinent to this appeal, two affirmative defenses sought rescission, upon tendered refund of premiums, because of misrepresentation of age, the age of thirty-seven having been stated in the application instead of forty-seven. The difference between the two, claimed defendant, was material because the actual age would have, under the company's rules, required a physical examination. Materiality of representation to provide a basis for rescission was not proven. There was no showing that coverage would have been refused had the truth been told, or that the insured suffered at any time from any condition whatever which would have increased the carrier's risk, nor was any reason whatever assigned for the misstatement. Certainly, it was not demonstrated that the incorrect information had anything whatever to do with the actual cause of death or that its happening was thereby accelerated. In the circumstances, the trial court properly invoked section 155(1)(d) of the Insurance Law, requiring a provision in every policy—and found in the subject contract—that, if the age of an insured has been misstated, the benefit payable would be limited to such as the premium would have bought at the proper age. * * *

All concur.

Notes

1. Why the special treatment given to misrepresentations of age in life insurance policies? Why not allow the insured in all cases of misrepresentation to avoid rescission by paying the difference between the premium paid and the premium which the insurer would otherwise have charged particularly where there is no causal connection between the misrepresentation and the cause of loss?

2. *Meaning of the word "concealment."* In ordinary contract cases, the word "concealment" means an active intentional endeavor to prevent the other party from discovering the truth—e.g., papering over the hole in the wall in a house offered for sale. In this sense "concealment" is a form of fraudulent misrepresentation (complete with scienter) so that both rescission and damages are remedies available to the aggrieved party. Mere silence with regard to material facts unknown to the other party is, in the usual contract, characterized as "non-disclosure" which is remediable by rescission only under limited circumstances. In other words, mere "non-disclosure" is basically privileged conduct unless a special obligation to disclose exists. The

Restatement of Contracts 2d § 161 lists the standard instances in which such an obligation arises. Insurance law uses not only its own rules but its own nomenclature—i.e., "concealment" in insurance law includes the "non-disclosure" of ordinary contract law.

3. *The Effect of concealment.* Originally concealment, with or without intent to deceive, was sufficient to avoid the policy. As with many other quirks in insurance law, this has been attributed to the realities of maritime risks which comprised the bulk of British underwriting in the developing days of insurance. Risks in precarious water, thousands of miles away and virtually beyond the communication means of the times, could not be inspected, and their fair evaluation necessarily depended upon honest disclosure of all material information by the applicants. Reliance could be had on little else. The traditional description of a contract of insurance as a contract "uberrimae fidei"—the utmost good faith—became both a label and a legal guide.

Yet it was not necessarily the good faith of the applicant alone which was determinative but the materiality of the information; and that was a matter for the underwriter to determine.

This rigorous rule as to concealment is still said to prevail in all branches of insurance in England. Horne v. Poland, [1922] 2 K.B. 364. In the United States, it is applied to marine risks, but has been widely relaxed in other areas (even so-called inland marine or floater policies) so that a good faith, unintentional non-disclosure even of a material fact will not avoid the policy. The relaxation no doubt is influenced by the comparative ease with which an underwriter can investigate a risk should it be considered important in this modern age of data storage and retrieval, and also by a tendency to assume that the failure of the insurer to make inquiry as to a specific facet of a risk suggests that it did not regard the information as material.

Nevertheless there are still echoes to be found in American law of the strict application of the concealment rule in non-marine cases. In California, for instance, this is discernable from the preceding statutes.

THOMPSON v. OCCIDENTAL LIFE INSURANCE CO.

Supreme Court of California, 1973.
9 Cal.3d 904, 109 Cal.Rptr. 473, 513 P.2d 353.

[The *Thompson* case covered a number of important issues including the effect of a conditional receipt and agent's authority. The excerpt below is comprised only of the facts and the portion of the case dealing with the effect of alleged misrepresentation. Particularly relevant are the circumstances relating to medical examination. The decision went for Thompson, 4–3.]

BURKE, JUSTICE.

We are asked to decide whether, under the particular facts of this case, a contract of life insurance existed between plaintiff's deceased spouse and defendant insurance company, and if so, whether decedent's alleged misrepresentations regarding the state of his health and past medical history rendered that contract void and unenforceable. The trial court, aided by an advisory jury, found in plaintiff's favor and awarded her $200,000, plus interest. Defendant appeals. We have concluded that the judgment should be affirmed.

Donald L. Thompson, husband of plaintiff Ruth M. Thompson, was insured by defendant Occidental Life Insurance Company of California ("Occidental") under a $15,000 life insurance policy which provided for double indemnity for accidental death. Concerned about the adequacy of his medical and life insurance, Thompson contacted John Kelly, the Oakland manager of Occidental, for the purpose of increasing his insurance coverage. Kelly then met with Thompson's accountant to determine what type of policy Thompson should purchase and decided upon a five-year convertible term policy for $100,000 with double indemnity for accidental death. On August 5, 1964, Thompson signed an application for the recommended policy and on August 11 submitted to a medical examination.

* * *

Thompson's application was received by Occidental's underwriters on August 17. The underwriters decided to require an additional medical examination. On August 24, before he was informed of this decision, Thompson sustained an accident (falling into his bathtub and nearly suffocating) which resulted in his death four days later. Occidental determined that Thompson's death was accidental and paid plaintiff, as beneficiary, $30,000 as double indemnity under the $15,000 life insurance policy. However, Occidental notified plaintiff on September 4 that it would neither issue nor make payment under the $100,000 life insurance policy because the additional medical examination had not been completed. Thereafter, Occidental returned to plaintiff the first premium by a check drawn on its own account. Plaintiff retained the check and sued to recover $200,000 as double indemnity under the $100,000 policy and, as indicated above, judgment was entered awarding plaintiff $200,000 and $82,108.60 as interest. Defendant appeals.

* * *

2. Misrepresentation

Occidental's second contention is that, even if a contract of insurance were formed, it was rendered unenforceable by reason of misrepresentations by Thompson concerning his medical history. It is true that under certain circumstances material misrepresentations regarding the medical history of an applicant may justify the rescission of a life insurance contract. * * * In the instant case, however, both the advisory jury, answering a special interrogatory, and the trial judge, exercising his independent judgment, found that Thompson did not misrepresent or conceal the state of his health and past medical history to Occidental. That finding is supported by substantial evidence.

The alleged misrepresentations occurred during the insurance medical examination on August 11, 1964, and pertain to matters set forth in

Thompson's insurance application. The record discloses that Thompson did not fill out the application himself; instead, his oral responses were recorded by the examining physician, Dr. Epstein, a private practitioner on Occidental's "approved" list of physicians, who, by prior arrangement with Occidental, performed medical examinations of insurance applicants. Dr. Epstein read the questions on the application to Thompson during a Friday afternoon session which included both a physical examination and completion of the questionnaire; since Epstein could perform three or four such examinations in an hour, Thompson's session may have lasted only 15 to 20 minutes. Occidental contends that Thompson misrepresented or concealed the answers to questions 5 and 6. Question 5 asked:

"During the past five years have you:

"A. Consulted, been examined or been treated by any physician or practitioner?

"B. Had an X-ray, electrocardiogram or any laboratory test or study?

"C. Had observation or treatment at a clinic, hospital, or sanitarium?

"D. Had or been advised to have a surgical operation?"

Dr. Epstein entered an affirmative answer to each portion of question 5 and noted the following on the portion of the application which requested details of affirmative answers: "5 ABCD—Vein ligation—Hernia, Providence Hosp. Oakland, 1963, M.C. Green MD 330 Elm St., Oakland, Cal." The "vein ligation" was a surgical operation involving the tying of the patient's veins; evidently, Thompson suffered from varicose veins, and the ligation was necessary to relieve this condition.

The pertinent portions of question 6 asked:

"Have you ever had or been told you had: * * *

"B. * * * pain or pressure in the chest, or any disorder of the heart, blood or blood vessels?"

"C. * * * any disorder of the lungs, bronchial tubes, throat or respiratory systems?"

* * *

"I. Any disease, condition or disorder not indicated above?"

Epstein entered negative answers to each of these questions.

The alleged misrepresentations consist of Thompson's apparent failure to report to Epstein approximately 10 medical consultations he had at Kaiser Hospital with five different doctors which commenced on June 3, 1964, two months before the insurance medical examination, and ended only the day before the examination took place. During these consultations he (1) had complained of chest pain, (2) had an electrocardiogram performed, (3) was treated for "phlebitis" (vein inflammation), (4) was advised to keep off his feet to avoid the possibility that a clot in a leg vein might break off and travel to his lungs, (5) had his legs X-rayed for "intermittent claudication" (leg pain), and (6) was advised to undergo a "chemical sympathectomy" (injection of local anesthetic) to relieve the foregoing leg pain.

We first review the rules of law applicable in appraising a claim of misrepresentation in procuring insurance. It is generally held that an insurer has a right to know all that the applicant for insurance knows regarding the state of his health and medical history. * * * Material misrepresentation or concealment of such facts are grounds for rescission of the policy, and an actual intent to deceive need not be shown. * * * Materiality is determined solely by the probable and reasonable effect which truthful answers would have had upon the insurer. * * * The fact that the insurer has demanded answers to specific questions in an application for insurance is in itself usually sufficient to establish materiality as a matter of law. * * *

On the other hand, if the applicant for insurance had no present knowledge of the facts sought, or failed to appreciate the significance of information related to him, his incorrect or incomplete responses would not constitute grounds for rescission. * * * Moreover, "Questions concerning illness or disease do not relate to minor indispositions but are to be construed as referring to serious ailments which undermine the general health." * * * Finally, as the misrepresentation must be a material one, "An incorrect answer on an insurance application does not give rise to the defense of fraud where the true facts, if known, would not have made the contract less desirable to the insurer. [Citations.]" * * * And the trier of fact is not required to believe the "post mortem" testimony of an insurer's agents that insurance would have been refused had the true facts been disclosed. * * *

Although there are several items on Occidental's list of alleged "misrepresentations," many items appear to relate to the ailment which Thompson affirmatively disclosed in answering question 5, namely, his varicose vein problem which led to the vein ligation surgery. As we shall see, the remaining items seemingly pertained to minor matters likely to have been of no interest to Occidental. Since Thompson disclosed his basic problems with his veins and circulation, the trial court might have concluded that it was the responsibility of the examining doctor to elicit additional details as to causes, consultations, treatments, diagnosis and prognosis.

It is suggested by the dissent, however, that Thompson knowingly concealed from Occidental that he suffered from *two* major problems, namely, varicose veins and arteriosclerosis, that the two conditions were unrelated, and that the latter condition had substantially reduced Thompson's life expectancy. Yet this theory (which was not raised in defendant's briefs in this case) finds no support in the record. The dissent relies primarily upon testimony by one of defendant's witnesses, Dr. Thompson, who never examined decedent Thompson during his life, and who consequently never discussed the arteriosclerosis condition with him. Contrary to the suggestion in the dissenting opinion (Circ. opn., p. 486), none of the physicians with whom decedent consulted testified that decedent was ever advised that he had arteriosclerosis, that this condition was unrelated to the past varicose vein problem disclosed to Dr. Epstein, or that this new "malady ... would shorten his life span by one-half to two-thirds." (Circ. opn., p. 490.) In fact, with respect to the intermittent claudication (leg pain) which Thompson was experiencing, Dr. Pellegrin told Thompson merely that it had "something to do with circulation * * *." According to Dr. Pellegrin, "You don't want to get somebody all wound up and alarmed and concerned about themselves and find out it isn't bad at all, and they are tense and anxious for no reason at all." From this testimony, the judge and jury could reasonably conclude that Thompson believed that he had a single leg circulation problem, related to his varicose vein condition. Accordingly, the finding that Thompson did not misrepresent his medical condition is supported by the evidence and the reasonable inferences which could be drawn from that evidence. As we have often stated, our reviewing power begins and ends with the determination whether there is any substantial evidence to support the trial court's findings. (E.g., Green Trees Enterprises, Inc. v. Palm Springs Alpine Estates, Inc., 66 Cal.2d 782, 784, 59 Cal.Rptr. 141, 427 P.2d 805.) On the present record, we cannot say that the trial court's finding is wholly unsupported by substantial evidence when viewed in the light of the foregoing legal principles.

There are at least four additional possible bases to support the finding that Thompson did not misrepresent or conceal the facts. (1) The court may have found that, in addition to disclosing his leg vein problems and surgery, Thompson also mentioned to Dr. Epstein the additional consultations regarding vein inflammation and leg pain but Epstein, in the course of hurrying to complete the brief examination, intentionally or inadvertently failed to record the information.[14] (See Rutherford v.

14. Dr. Epstein could not recall what information Thompson in fact disclosed, although Epstein did testify that he customarily recorded all information furnished by the applicant in response to the questionnaire. The latter testimony may have been questioned by the trial court, for the record discloses that Epstein entered a negative response to the question calling for "evidence of past or present diseases or disorders of the * * * blood vessels," even though Thompson's legs bore visible scars of the vein ligation. Epstein also failed to indicate whether there was evidence of varicose veins, despite Thompson's disclosure of that problem to Epstein.

It is true that Thompson signed the application himself, thereby certifying to the accuracy of the questionnaire. Although some cases have emphasized that applicants for insurance must read the application and report any misstatements or omissions (see Telford v. New York Life Ins. Co., 9 Cal.2d 103, 107–108, 69 P.2d 835), other cases have indicated that even if the applicant has signed the application, his omissions may be excused if it can be inferred that the examining doctor gave him the impression that additional written responses were unnecessary (see Rutherford v. Prudential Ins. Co., 234 Cal.App.2d 719, 728, 44 Cal.Rptr. 697; Boggio v. Cal.-Western States Life Ins. Co., 108 Cal.App.2d 597, 239 P.2d 144). Moreover, the fact that Thompson signed the application does not foreclose the argument that the information was immaterial to Occidental, or pertained to minor indispositions, or that Thompson failed to recall the facts or appreciate their significance.

Occidental's officer, Mr. Ryan, testified that Occidental would have declined to issue a policy had Thompson fully disclosed his medical history. Ordinarily, "the direct evidence of one witness who is entitled to full credit is sufficient for proof of any

Prudential Ins. Co., 234 Cal.App.2d 719, 726–729, 44 Cal.Rptr. 697.) (2) The court may have believed that Thompson, as an ordinary layman, failed to recollect or appreciate the significance of the subject matter of the various Kaiser consultations. For example, the terms "phlebitis," "intermittent claudication," and "chemical sympathectomy" might well have been meaningless jargon to him. (3) Next, the court may have found that most of Thompson's undisclosed problems related to "minor indispositions" rather than serious ailments undermining the general health. For example, the chest pain of which he had complained was diagnosed as mild pneumonia and pleurisy caused by the pneumonia from which Thompson recovered in a single day following office treatment by a doctor. The electrocardiogram performed on Thompson showed no significant or abnormal tracings, and the X-rays of Thompson's legs were likewise negative. (4) Finally, the court may have determined that the subject matter of the Kaiser consultations would not have affected Occidental's decision to issue a policy; the court was not required to accept the contrary testimony of Occidental's officer.

Occidental asserts that there is no substantial evidence in the record to explain the incomplete responses on the insurance application. Yet we must remember that Thompson himself was unavailable for direct interrogation, and Dr. Epstein, who recorded Thompson's responses, was unable to remember the substance of their conversation. Under such circumstances, were the burden of proof upon them, the insured's beneficiaries would have a nearly insurmountable proof problem in establishing a satisfactory explanation for the various omissions in decedent's application for insurance. Yet under the authorities, the burden of proving misrepresentation rests upon the insurer. * * * Some cases have even assumed that fraud must be proven by "clear and convincing" evidence. * * * [preponderance of evidence sufficient]. Thus, the burden was on Occidental to negate to the satisfaction of the trier of fact the various plausible explanations for the incomplete answers on Thompson's application.

Under the facts in this case, it is conceivable the court could have found that Thompson withheld pertinent information and to that extent misrepresented the facts. Yet, as we have pointed out, the court was entitled to find to the contrary based upon its appraisal of the testimony, the credibility (or lack thereof) of Occidental's witnesses, and the fair

fact." (Evid.Code, § 411; see Hicks v. Reis, 21 Cal.2d 654, 659–660, 134 P.2d 788; Camp v. Ortega, 209 Cal.App.2d 275, 281–285, 25 Cal.Rptr. 873; Krause v. Apodaca, 186 Cal.App.2d 413, 417–419, 9 Cal.Rptr. 10.) Yet the trial court was entitled to withhold "full credit" from Ryan's testimony, either on the basis of his relationship with Occidental (see Witkin, Cal.Evidence, § 1113), or his manner of testifying (id., § 1115). (See McAuliffe v. John Hancock Mut. Life Ins. Co., supra, 245 Cal.App.2d 855, 858, 54 Cal.Rptr. 288; Hicks v. Reis, supra, 21 Cal.2d, p. 660, 134 P.2d 788.) This same reasoning could apply to Dr. Epstein's testimony; in addition, that testimony was not "direct evidence" (see Evid.Code, § 410) of Thompson's misrepresentation. Since Epstein could not recall Thompson's words, the court would have been required to infer that Epstein correctly and completely recorded Thompson's responses, an inference which the court could refuse to draw.

inferences arising from the evidence. It is not our function to second guess the trier of fact in such matters.

Notes

1. What is the test of materiality stated in *Thompson*?

2. Would the result in *Thompson* have been different in New York under its statutory scheme?

3. In *Life Insurance Company of North America v. Capps*, 660 F.2d 392 (9th Cir.1981), Mrs. Capps answered "no" to the question on her application:

> "Have you * * * ever had heart trouble, high blood pressure, chest pains * * * or other health impairments?"

In fact Mrs. Capps had within recent years suffered symptoms of a heart condition of which she was aware. She had consulted cardiologists and had been in a hospital coronary care unit on an emergency basis within the past year. None of this was revealed in response to another question as to whether she had consulted a physician. She died of heart failure within six months of the issuance of the policy. The beneficiaries, relying on *Thompson* supra, argued that Mrs. Capp's physician and husband misled her about the seriousness of her condition and that she believed it was insubstantial. The trial court granted summary judgment for the insurance company. Based on *Thompson* how would you have decided the appeal?

LETTIERI v. EQUITABLE LIFE ASSURANCE SOCIETY OF UNITED STATES

United States Court of Appeals, Ninth Circuit, 1980.
627 F.2d 930.

GOODWIN, CIRCUIT JUDGE.

California beneficiaries of a life insurance policy appeal a judgment in favor of the insurer. The district court ruled that the substantive law of New York, rather than that of California, governed the questions of the enforceability of the policy. Because the plaintiffs had no legal theory upon which to proceed under New York law, they saved their objection to the choice-of-law ruling and judgment was entered.

The decedent, Alfredo Lettieri, a resident of New Jersey, while in poor health, bought a $400,000 five-year term life insurance policy from an agent Alfredo met in a New York City bar. Alfredo named his estate and his son Anthony, a California resident, as beneficiaries. His wife Becky later was substituted for the estate.

Alfredo obtained his required medical examination in New York City from a Dr. Martin, a physician on the insurer's approved medical examiner list. Neither Alfredo's medical history nor medical examination reports, which were completed and signed by Dr. Martin, revealed Alfredo's current or past ailments (save for an early appendectomy). Alfredo had been addicted to heroin as a youth, had been hospitalized for alcohol-related treatment, was at the time of the examination suffering from liver disease and alcoholism, and had other abnormalities that should have been obvious to a medical examiner.

The company issued the insurance policy in reliance upon Alfredo's application, which included the medical reports. Alfredo's signature certified the truthfulness of the application's contents. Within four months, Alfredo died of a bleeding ulcer in part caused by excessive use of alcohol. The insurer conducted an investigation of the claim and uncovered the falsehoods and omissions in the insurance application. The insurer then denied liability on the policy, asserting a right to rescind the policy upon discovery of the concealment or misrepresentation of material fact by the insured with respect to his medical history and state of his health when he applied for the policy. The beneficiaries brought this action in California where the choice of law appeared to be more favorable than that of other possible venues.

Under the substantive laws of both California and New York, an insurer may avoid liability on a policy procured through material misrepresentations by the insured. Where the laws arguably differ is in the method by which the factual issues are determined.[15]

Under New York law the insurer has an absolute right to rescind a life insurance policy if the application, signed by the insured and attached to the policy, contains false statements or omissions about medical history which the insured failed to correct. Under New York law, then false statements or omissions about health are conclusively presumed to be material misrepresentations. Minsker v. John Hancock Mut. Life Ins. Co., 254 N.Y. 333, 173 N.E. 4 (1930). See John Hancock Life Ins. Co. v. Yates, 299 U.S. 178, 180, 57 S.Ct. 129, 130–131, 81 L.Ed. 106 (1936). Thus, the district court's choice of New York law effectively precluded plaintiffs from pursuing their theory that the decedent had in fact disclosed the whole truth to Dr. Martin, and that Dr. Martin, or one of his employees, acting as the insurer's agent, or the company itself, had negligently or otherwise kept Alfredo's true medical history from reaching the insurer's files.[16]

15. We are not concerned with proof of materiality. In this case, the omissions and misstatements in the insurance application were material. The only triable questions are whether Alfredo in fact misrepresented his health history and under what substantive law that issue should be determined.

16. Plaintiffs' theory was that Alfredo had disclosed his health history but had wished to hide it—particularly his earlier heroin addiction and present alcoholism—from his family. They then surmise that Alfredo had requested that the attached report not reveal his actual history and condition, but that a second confidential and accurate report be forwarded separately to the insurer. No such confidential report is in the file. Plaintiffs assert that this failure is due to the negligence of either the doctor or the insurer. The ultimate credibility of this theory is not before us. Alfredo had obvious physical abnormalities at the time of his medical examination but none were noted on the report. Dr. Martin testified that although he could recall nothing about Alfredo or the examination, he signed the reports; therefore, he assumed that he must have conducted the examination as he normally did. He stated that if those abnormalities were present, he would have detected them. He further testified, consistently in part with plaintiffs' theory, on how he might have handled a request for a confidential report.

As we have already noted, California law also permits the insurer to avoid liability on a life insurance policy issued to an applicant who made material misrepresentations about health history. However, the parties disagree over whether the question of misrepresentation under that state's law remains one for the trier of fact even in the face of untrue statements or omissions in an application. Plaintiffs maintain that California law permits them to offer a plausible explanation for the falsehoods appearing in the insurance application, an explanation which the insurer then may rebut in order to avoid liability on the policy. They cite Thompson v. Occidental Life Ins. Co., 9 Cal.3d 904, 109 Cal.Rptr. 473, 513 P.2d 353 (1973), to support this position. The defendant, on the other hand, argues that *Thompson* is limited to its peculiar facts, and that California would apply a conclusive presumption similar to New York's in the instant situation. The insurer relies on the old case of Telford v. Occidental Ins. Co., 9 Cal.2d 103, 69 P.2d 835 (1937).

We agree with plaintiffs' interpretation of California substantive law. In *Thompson,* the California Supreme Court upheld the trial court's finding that the insurer was liable on a life insurance policy despite obvious misstatements and omissions concerning the insured's medical history in the signed application. The court reached this result through a broad willingness to engage in speculation concerning plausible reasons—other than actual misrepresentations by the insured—for the falsehoods, speculations for which as the dissent in *Thompson* points out, there was little supporting evidence in the record. Although the insured in that case had answered truthfully about his basic medical problem, the court indicated that misstatements or nondisclosures could be excused even absent some minimal disclosure. For example, the court suggested that the trial court may have concluded that the insured forgot or did not appreciate the significance of the undisclosed facts, or that he did, in fact, disclose the truth to the medical examiner but that the latter inadvertently or intentionally failed to record it. The court went on to hold that, in order to avoid liability based on material misrepresentation, the insurer must negate, to the trier's satisfaction, the plausible explanations offered by the beneficiary-plaintiff for the false or incomplete answers in the application. Although the case represents a departure from the earlier ruling of *Telford,* which was similar to current New York law, *Thompson* states the most recent California law on the issue to be resolved here. Because California case law differs from that of New York, we must address the choice of law question raised on appeal.

A federal court applies the choice of law rules of the state in which it sits, here California, to determine the substantive law to apply in a diversity action. Klaxon Co. v. Stentor Co., 313 U.S. 487, 496, 61 S.Ct. 1020, 1021–1022, 85 L.Ed. 1477 (1941). The parties agree that California uses governmental interest analysis as its choice of law rule, supplemented by the doctrine of comparative impairment in cases posing a true conflict. Travelers Ins. Co. v. Workmen's Comp. App. Bd., 68 Cal.2d 7, 11–15, 434 P.2d 992 (1967); Bernhard v. Harrah's Club, 16 Cal.3d 313,

128 Cal.Rptr. 215, 546 P.2d 719 (1976). They disagree, however, on the result that application of these rules yields in the present case.

New York law and California law implement competing governmental interests in the context of this case. The defendant is a New York insurer. New York has an interest in protecting its resident insurance companies from fraudulent claims and is also interested in regulating the conduct of parties forming insurance contracts within its borders. California has an interest in the rights of local plaintiffs, and while California law does not purport to demand for its resident-beneficiaries an absolute right to collect proceeds in the face of actual misrepresentation or fraud against insurers, it has economic, and, as the forum, judicial interests, in protecting its residents from an erroneous denial of insurance proceeds. Plaintiffs' theory here is that their claims are, in fact, valid despite what appear to be errors, omissions, or misstatements in the decedent's application. Without the opportunity that California law provides its residents to pursue such a theory, these residents might become an economic burden to the state.

Competing interests of two interested states direct the next inquiry, therefore, thus: As between California and New York, "whose interest would be the more impaired if its law were not applied"? Bernhard v. Harrah's Club, supra, 16 Cal.3d at 320, 128 Cal.Rptr. at 219, 546 P.2d at 723.

If California law is applied, the New York insurer still receives some protection against fraud, although at the additional cost of having to submit the issue of the insured's misrepresentation to the hazards of local triers of fact.

Assuming, as we must, that triers do their work impartially, and can discern fraudulent claims from those which are only apparently fraudulent, the insurer has all the protection insurers in interstate business are entitled to expect. The extra litigation expense occurs only when the beneficiaries reside in, or move to, a jurisdiction like California. That additional economic burden can be spread actuarially among policy purchasers across the nation as a cost of doing business nationwide. Thus, even if New York has an interest in protecting its resident insurers from those litigation costs, even that interest is not unreasonably impaired by application of California law. In theory, truly culpable conduct will still be deterred. The effect of the California rule will be to protect the legitimate claims of local beneficiaries while permitting the insurer to prevail if the decedent's conduct was as culpable as the paper record on its face tends to prove.

We conclude that New York interests would not be greatly impaired if California law were applied in this case. On the other hand, some significant California policy or interest would be impaired if New York law were applied. By virtue of their position, beneficiaries cannot protect their own interests at the insurance contract formation stage. Thus, if they are to be denied proceeds because of fraud at the time the insurance contract is entered into, beneficiaries have a strong need for protection from an erroneous denial—that is, denial when in fact the insured did not withhold material facts from the insurer. California affords its resident beneficiaries greater protection than does New York by leaving the question of actual misrepresentation to the trier rather than by resorting to a conclusive presumption. If New York law were to govern, then some California beneficiaries with valid claims might be denied the policy proceeds without any concomitant furtherance of New York's interests in protecting its insurers against invalid or fraudulent claims. Application of the doctrine of comparative impairment in this case, then, should lead to the adoption of California law.

The insurer seeks to avoid this result by arguing, among other things, that denial of the force of New York law would lead to forum shopping and nonuniformity of result on the same policy if beneficiaries should reside in different jurisdictions. Neither of these possibilities is present under the facts of this case. The insurer knew from the time the policy was issued that one beneficiary was a California resident. It thus had notice that a claim might arise from that state and the insurer could have protected itself better at the onset by conducting an investigation appropriate to the risk being underwritten. Both individual plaintiffs here are bona fide residents of the same state. There is no evidence that Becky Lettieri took up her residence for the purpose of forum shopping, and we express no opinion on the effect of such evidence if it were present.

The judgment is vacated and the case is remanded for further proceedings under the guidance of California law to the extent that it applies in federal diversity litigation within the district.

Remanded.

Notes

1. (a) An agent reads the questions propounded in the insurance application to the applicant who truthfully answers the questions. Because such answers would preclude the issuance of the policy (and mean the loss of a commission by the agent), the agent enters a false answer. Is the insurance company estopped from denying liability under the policy on the grounds of false statements in the application? Does it matter which State's law applies? (Bear in mind the *Minsker* rule cited in the main case.)

(b) Suppose the applicant read the "doctored" application containing the false entries before signing the application. Is the insurer estopped?

(c) Suppose the agent tells the applicant that his truthful answers will mean he can't get insurance whereupon the applicant changes his truthful answers. Is the insurer estopped?

2. Variations on this situation are common. *Liberty National Life Insurance Co. v. Houk*, 248 Ga. 111, 281 S.E.2d 583 (1981), is a typical (and divided) decision. In *Houk*, an insurer was denied summary judgment for the non-disclosure of a preexisting condition, where the agent completed the application and the insured signed it. A majority held that the insurer was

estopped from denying coverage because of the agent's fraud or negligence. The dissent would deny coverage on the basis of the false answers where the insured read and signed the application.

3. X applied for life insurance and was examined and interviewed by the insurer's doctor who asked a series of questions set forth in a form entitled "Declarations to Medical Examiner" and wrote down X's answers. One question (#44) asked the applicant to identify any attending physicians consulted in the last 5 years and the results of the examination. X had mentioned only his regular physician for a routine physical in response to another question. No answer was entered as to question #44. In fact X had had several medical examinations during the past 5 years for gonorrhea of the throat, swollen lymph glands, etc. X signed the "Declaration" and the policy was issued with it attached. X died of AIDS within a year. The beneficiary asserts that the examining doctor failed to ask X question #44 and it may be assumed this is true. Does the insurer have to pay (1) under New York law? (2) under California law? See Zachary Trading Inc. v. Northwestern Mut. Life Ins. Co., 668 F.Supp. 343 (S.D.N.Y.1987) (held for insurer).

Chapter 3

INTERPRETATION OF INSURANCE CONTRACTS

A. GENERAL PRINCIPLES

PRELIMINARY NOTE—INTERPRETATION OF INSURANCE POLICIES

The nature of the "formation" process involved in arriving at an insurance agreement is what gives rise to the range of possible approaches a court may take when called upon to interpret contested terms in the policy. In an article in the Drake Law Review, Professor Jeffrey Stempel discusses the "adhesion contract" nature of insurance policies:[1]

> A contract of adhesion is one in which the drafter offers the terms on a "take it or leave it" basis, with no negotiation or revision of contract language. Although the term is popularly associated with Professor Friedrich Kessler's famous article, it was first seen in American legal literature in describing an insurance policy. Insurance policies might even be termed "super-adhesive" contracts because their language is more rigid than many other standardized contracts. First, insurance policies are, as previously noted, not ordinarily read and discussed prior to their issuance (particularly in consumer lines). Second, the insurance sales force usually lacks any authority to alter terms or coverages. Third, insurance contract language is drafted either by ISO [Insurance Services Office] (in property/casualty lines) or adopted through industry-wide convention (in life/health lines), making individual insurers reluctant to alter policy text, even if inclined to at the request of highly sought clients. Fourth, the usefulness of replicable standard form policy language in assessing risk makes it unlikely insurers will want to customize contract language, even for the largest accounts. Even when a policy is tailored to a large commercial client, insurers generally accomplish this through mixing and matching various

1. Jeffrey Stempel, *Reassessing the 'Sophisticated Policyholder' Defense*, 42 Drake L. Rev. 807, 829–30 (1993), reprinted with permission.

standardized language endorsements, working with the policyholder's broker, rather than through freshly drafted language.

In a typical adhesion contract, the parties do negotiate, or at least discuss, price, quantity, duration, and possibly factors such as warranty or delivery. Measured against this comparison, insurance contracts might also be termed super-adhesive because insurers typically will not alter premiums per $1000 of coverage or alter their customary policies regarding the contracting process, even for the most valued customers. The essence of insurance—risk spreading—makes individualized pricing hazardous with even the most seemingly secure risks. Insurance policies are also super-adhesive in terms of length and complexity. * * *

Of course, the super-adhesive nature of insurance policies does not make them "bad" or legally suspect. Standardized adhesion contracts are probably the majority of contracts in use today and are widely enforced. Courts view standardization as an inevitable consequence of a mass contracting, consumer-driven, market-oriented economy. Standardization reduces the time and money spent on contracting and courts generally are receptive to enforcing them so these savings can be realized, so long as the adhesive terms are not unfair. When dealing with insurance policies, courts and commentators are even more solicitous of the benefits derived from standardized terms and adhesion marketing, because they not only lower transaction costs but facilitate risk spreading through developing a risk pool of policyholders all subject to the same contract language. When focused on these aspects of adhesion, courts construing insurance policies are generally solicitous of insurers.

The flip side of the inquiry often leads courts to focus on the policyholder's dependence on coverage that hinges on an adhesion contract term the policyholder never read, probably could not understand or did not expect, and contained in a document he or she received long after making the insurance commitment. When focused on these traits, courts are more likely to make liberal use of doctrines such as contra proferentum and reasonable expectations and find for policyholders. This tendency is, as expected, more pronounced in close cases and those involving consumer insureds.[2]

With this background, we can probe in greater detail the interpretive techniques used by courts in construing and interpreting the arcane language of insurance policies. Courts have shown an inclination to interpret insurance policies as simply variations of typical contracts, with some notable exceptions. The following excerpts from recent New York and California cases demonstrate these ideas.

2. *Id.*

J.A. BRUNDAGE PLUMBING AND ROTO-ROOTER, INC. v. MASSACHUSETTS BAY INS. CO.

United States District Court, Western District, New York, 1993.
818 F.Supp. 553, vacated by settlement, 153 F.R.D. 36 (1994).

HECKMAN, UNITED STATES MAGISTRATE JUDGE.

* * *

Insurance policies are contracts to which the ordinary rules of contractual interpretation apply. The goal of contract interpretation is to give effect to the intention of the parties. If the contract language is clear and explicit, it governs. If it is ambiguous, the court must interpret the language in context with regard to its intended function in the policy to give effect to the reasonable expectation of the insured. Murray Oil Products v. Royal Exchange Assurance Co., supra, 21 N.Y.2d at 445, 288 N.Y.S.2d 618, 235 N.E.2d 762; A. Meyers & Sons Corp. v. Zurich American Insurance Group, 74 N.Y.2d 298, 302–03 (1989).

Furthermore, terms which are not defined in the policy are to be given the meaning ascribed to those terms in the common law or as they ordinarily would be understood by laypersons. Ruder & Finn, Inc. v. Seaboard Surety Co., 52 N.Y.2d 663, 671, 439 N.Y.S.2d 858, 422 N.E.2d 518 (1981). If this rule does not resolve the ambiguity, the Court must then resolve it against the insurer. See, e.g., Id. at 671, 439 N.Y.S.2d 858, 422 N.E.2d 518. The complaint must be liberally construed to "protect against poorly or incompletely pleaded cases as well as those artfully drafted." Id. at 669, 439 N.Y.S.2d 858, 422 N.E.2d 518.

* * *

MONTROSE CHEMICAL CORPORATION OF CALIFORNIA v. ADMIRAL INSURANCE COMPANY

Supreme Court of California, En Banc, 1995.
10 Cal.4th 645, 42 Cal.Rptr.2d 324, 913 P.2d 878.

LUCAS, CHIEF JUSTICE.

* * *

Insurance policies are contracts and, therefore, are governed in the first instance by the rules of construction applicable to contracts. Under statutory rules of contract interpretation, the mutual intention of the parties at the time the contract is formed governs its interpretation. (Civ.Code, § 1636.) Such intent is to be inferred, if possible, solely from the written provisions of the contract. (Id., § 1639.) The "clear and explicit" meaning of these provisions, interpreted in their "ordinary and popular sense," controls judicial interpretation unless "used by the parties in a technical sense, or unless a special meaning is given to them by usage." (Id., §§ 1638, 1644.) If the meaning a layperson would ascribe to the language of a contract of insurance is clear and unambiguous, a court will apply that meaning. [citations omitted]

In contrast, "[i]f there is ambiguity . . . it is resolved by interpreting the ambiguous provisions in the sense the promisor (i.e., the insurer) believed the promisee understood them at the time of formation. (Civ. Code, § 1649.) If application of this rule does not eliminate the ambiguity, ambiguous language is construed against the party who caused the uncertainty to exist. (Id., § 1654.)" (AIU, supra, 51 Cal.3d at p. 822, 274 Cal.Rptr. 820, 799 P.2d 1253.) "This rule, as applied to a promise of coverage in an insurance policy, protects not the subjective beliefs of the insurer but, rather, 'the objectively reasonable expectations of the insured.' " (AIU, supra, at p. 822 [274 Cal.Rptr. 820, 799 P.2d 1253].) Only if this rule does not resolve the ambiguity do we then resolve it against the insurer. [citations omitted]

We explained further in AIU, supra, 51 Cal.3d at page 822, 274 Cal.Rptr. 820, 799 P.2d 1253, that "[i]n the insurance context, we generally resolve ambiguities in favor of coverage. [citations omitted] Similarly, we generally interpret the coverage clauses of insurance policies broadly, in order to protect the objectively reasonable expectations of the insured. [citations omitted] These rules stem from the fact that the insurer typically drafts policy language, leaving the insured little or no meaningful opportunity or ability to bargain for modifications. [citations omitted] Because the insurer writes the policy, it is held 'responsible' for ambiguous policy language, which is therefore construed in favor of coverage." (Fn. omitted) [citation omitted]

* * *

Despite case law that states insurance policies are contracts, we have observed that there are notable exceptions. Thus, a caution is appropriate against the temptation to apply ordinary contract interpretation principles in this context. First, any area of the law has its own conventions that affect the substantive law. For example, real estate sales contracts contain language unique to real estate. Insurance law is not immune from this phenomenon. Professor Hazel Beh echoes this caution by observing that the contra proferentum doctrine and the reasonable expectations doctrine are examples of context specific differences in interpretative principles.[3] According to Professor Beh, contra proferentum exceeds the role of tiebreaker in insurance law and is a substantive law principle.[4] In the same way, Professor Beh observes that the doctrine of reasonable expectations finds itself in a heightened role in insurance law.[5]

3. Hazel Glenn Beh, *Reassessing the Sophisticated Insured Exception*, 39 Tort & Ins. L.J. 85, 90–92 (2003).

4. *Id.* at 90.

5. Id. at 92.

A COMMENT ON THE METHODS OF JUDICIAL INTERPRETATION

Contract Construction

Application of the rules governing contract interpretation has led to a range of approaches courts apply when interpreting the terms of an insurance policy. A court may apply the conservative option provided by a strict application of the general rule of contract construction or take a judicially active role by applying the doctrine of reasonable expectations to determine what a typical insured person would expect by purchasing a policy, or elect an option in between.

As a starting point, courts will first look to the general rule governing contract interpretation: when a contract term has plain meaning, the plain meaning of the term applies regardless of the extrinsic circumstances surrounding the agreement. This approach assumes that the parties have equal bargaining power and their intentions are accurately reflected in the agreement. A consistent application of this approach in the insurance law setting almost immediately leads to challenges based on fairness to the insured. Hence, courts rarely apply the "Four Corners" approach to interpret insurance policy terms.[6]

Doctrine of contra proferentum

An approach that tends to be more favorable to the insured is embodied in Restatement, Contracts (2d) § 206,[7] also known by the Latin "contra proferentum:"

> In choosing among the reasonable meanings of a promise or agreement or a term thereof, that meaning is generally preferred which operates against the party who supplies the words or from whom a writing otherwise proceeds.

The Comment to the section points out the reasons for the rule: that the party choosing terms is likely to protect his own interests first, that he is more likely to know about uncertainties in the words chosen, and that he may have deliberately left meanings obscure. The result ought to be that, when there is doubt, and other factors do not prevail, the meaning attached to the words by the *other* party ought to be the one employed in interpreting the contract. Very commonly the rule is said to apply when the contract or one of its provisions is "ambiguous." The rule has a special application in case of standardized contracts where the drafting party has the stronger economic position, "contracts of adhesion"; and the principle sometimes resembles that of "unconscionability." It has found especially wide interpretation in insurance contracts.

6. See Jeffrey Stempel, *Reassessing the 'Sophisticated Policyholder' Defense*, 42 DRAKE L. REV. 807, 810–11 (1993).

7. Copyright 1981 by the American Law Institute. Reprinted with the permission of the American Law Institute.

Comment (b) is specifically pertinent to insurance policies:

> *b. Compulsory contract or term.* The rule that language is interpreted against the party who chose it has no direct application to cases where the language is prescribed by law, as is sometimes true with respect to insurance policies, bills of lading and other standardized documents. In some cases, however, the statute or regulation adopts language which was previously used without compulsion and was interpreted against the drafting party, and there is normally no intention to change the established meaning. Moreover, insurers are more likely than insureds to participate in drafting prescribed forms and to review them carefully before putting them into use.

Application of this doctrine is almost a natural choice when the court begins with the assumption that an insurance agreement is essentially a contract of adhesion. However, as Professor Stempel notes:

> [s]cholars have found contra proferentum suspect because (1) the doctrine is only partially effective in protecting policyholders (a very clear but oppressive policy term will not run afoul of contra proferentum), (2) courts are pressured by interests of fairness, and contra proferentum's failure to easily achieve it, to stretch the concept of ambiguity out of shape, and (3) the doctrine relies on legal fictions about "freedom of contract, mutual assent, and the parties' mutual intent" that are hopelessly divorced from modern insurance contracting reality.
>
> * * *
>
> [Nevertheless,] Contra proferentum continues to have force when applied to many coverage questions because most policyholders are nondrafters who have nothing to say about the language of the contract. Consequently, if someone has to lose a contract dispute, one can make a good case it should not be the nondrafting policyholder.[8]

Professor Michael Rappaport has taken the unconventional view that resolution of contract ambiguities in favor of the insured is a mistake.[9] He argues persuasively and simply that the costs of the approach outweigh its benefits. Notwithstanding the insurers role in drafting an insurance policy, Professor Rappaport believes that the approach increases costs by making policies impossibly technical and long (causing collateral difficulties as well), by increasing the uncertainty by which courts construe policies, and by dissuading the insurance industry from using untested language that judges might find ambiguous.[10] Ultimately, Professor Rappaport finds that all would be better served by a more conventional contracts approach that looks to the intent of the parties. According to Professor Rappaport, the ordinary process of contract interpretation (as opposed to confra proferentum)

8. Jeffrey Stempel, *Reassessing the 'Sophisticated Policyholder' Defense*, 42 DRAKE L. REV. 807, 824–25, 826.

9. Michael B. Rappaport, *The Ambiguity Rule and Insurance Law: Why Insurance Contracts Should not be Construed Against the Drafter*, 30 GEORGIA L. REV. 171 (1995).

10. *Id.* at 175.

leads to more efficient results in ambiguous cases. Under the ordinary process, courts attempt to figure out what would have made sense to the parties ex ante—which is often the efficient result. Under the ambiguity rule, the courts simply decide for the insured. While Professor Rappaport's ideas have not held sway in the courts, his views are worth considering as we review conventional insurance law interpretation.

Reasonable Expectations Doctrine

The doctrine of contra proferentum has evolved or expanded to include the doctrine of reasonable expectations, which offers an even more liberal approach to interpreting ambiguous policy terms and construing exclusions narrowly. Again, we refer to Professor Stempel:

> Although the underlying concept of contract construction to accord with the intent of the parties is of long standing, modern insurance law, particularly in the consumer context, is uncomfortable with the degree of interpretative divergence between the understandings of insurers and policyholders. Modern insurance law also recognizes the potential unfairness of adopting an objective theory of the meaning of contract terms in situations when the policyholder never read the contract in question or when the contracting involved an adhesion agreement with no real negotiation and bargaining. Consequently, one subcurrent of the contra proferentum line of cases had explicitly stated or implied that ambiguities should be resolved to accord with the reasonable interpretation given the challenged provision by the policyholder or even the reasonable expectations of the policyholder.
>
> In 1970, Robert E. Keeton, then a law professor and now a federal judge, synthesized and expanded upon these developments in his famous article *Insurance Law Rights at Variance with Policy Provisions.* Keeton's insight, in its most direct nutshell formulation, stated, "The objectively reasonable expectations of applicants and intended beneficiaries regarding the terms of insurance contracts will be honored even though painstaking study of the policy provisions would have negated those expectations." For courts that embraced this more express formulation of what, according to Judge Keeton, they had been doing tacitly, the duty to read contracts became largely irrelevant, at least for unsophisticated policyholders, in cases when the policyholder had a sufficiently reasonable understanding of the term in dispute and the insurer had done nothing to dispel that objectively reasonable understanding of the policyholder.
>
> Approximately fifteen states have adopted a strong or broad version of the reasonable expectations concept and have invoked the doctrine to find in favor of policyholders, despite clear policy language, when the language is insufficiently apparent and not drawn to the policyholder's attention. Some reasonable expectations states appear to have moved from the Keeton-stated formula to a more narrow view in which the degree of the policyholder's reasonableness, reliance, and damage is weighed against the clarity of the policy,

insurer conduct, and disclosure in light of the overall equities of the situation. A similarly sized group of states has rejected the reasonable expectations doctrine in more or less explicit terms.

Another third of the states appear receptive to the underlying notion of vindicating the reasonable expectations of the policyholder but stop short of treating the notion as a distinct doctrine or principle for decision. Instead, these courts introduce reasonable expectations thinking into their opinions, often combining it with the ambiguity doctrine and relatively broad notions of promissory and equitable estoppel, waiver, unconscionability, and public policy review, but stop short of using the policyholders' expectations, however reasonable, to override policy language viewed as clear. Despite the general retreat from reasonable expectations shown by courts in the 1980s, some jurisdictions appear to have moved toward the Keeton concept. In general, however, the reasonable expectations approach, like strong forms of the ambiguity approach, appears to have receded in use during the past decade. This inconsistency and eclecticism of the states (including a good deal of intra-state divergence between the states) results from changing court composition, different courts and majority opinion writers, and different focuses and equities.[11]

David Goodwin, a partner in San Francisco's Heller, Ehrman, White & McAuliffe law firm notes:[12]

> [Because] contra proferentum, including the reasonable expectations doctrine, has been adopted explicitly or implicitly in most jurisdictions, albeit with variations from state to state, and even within the same state [it is worth noting the way courts generally apply the rules of policy interpretation].
>
> * * *
>
> *First*, courts applying contra proferentum will construe coverage provisions in an insurance policy as broadly as possible and will read exclusions from coverage narrowly. Thus, when a carrier describes a policy as "all risk" or "comprehensive," many courts will find coverage under the policy for risks that the carrier argues the specific language of the insuring agreement was not intended to cover. Likewise, exclusions in a policy must be both clearly written and reasonably prominent to be effective. *Second*, language in an insurance policy will be given its plain meaning. Undefined words in the policy will be read in their ordinary and popular sense, and not according to a legal or technical meaning. Courts often ascertain the ordinary and popular sense of undefined words in an insurance policy by consulting a dictionary. *Webster's Dictionary, Random House, American Heritage*, and *Funk & Wagnall's* have become essential tools for any insurance coverage attorney. *Third*, if policy

11. Stempel, supra, 42 DRAKE L. REV. at 827–28.

12. David Goodwin, *Disputing Insurance Coverage Disputes*, 43 STANFORD L. REV. 779, 783–85 (1991), reprinted with permission.

language is capable of two or more reasonable constructions, the language will be construed against the carrier and in favor of coverage. *Fourth*, the insured's private views as to the meaning of policy language are irrelevant since the insured's "reasonable expectations" are judged against an objective standard. *Finally*, whenever it is appropriate for courts to consider extrinsic evidence in interpreting standard form policy language, it normally should be a "heads I win tails I win" matter for the insured. In many jurisdictions, extrinsic evidence is not admissible to alter the language of a document unless the document is ambiguous, but if language in an insurance policy is ambiguous, the insured wins and there should be no reason to look at the extrinsic evidence. In other jurisdictions, extrinsic evidence is admissible to show that seemingly unambiguous language in the policy is in fact ambiguous. Once again, if the policy language is ambiguous, the insured wins. In contrast, extrinsic evidence favoring the insurer-drafter of a standard form policy usually is inadmissible because it is fundamentally unfair to allow an insurer to draft a form contract and then seek to introduce extrinsic evidence to show that the terms of the contract mean something else. Moreover, the carrier's previously undisclosed intent in drafting the form language reflects neither the mutual intent of the parties nor, usually, the insured's reasonable expectations of coverage.

Further complicating the situation is the fact that the terms of many insurance policies are mandated by statute or are the result of the uniformity in policy language facilitated by the Insurance Services Office. The Insurance Services Office (ISO), successor organization to the National Bureau of Casualty Underwriters and the Mutual Insurance Rating Board, is a non-profit trade association that provides rating, statistical, and actuarial policy forms and related drafting services to approximately 3,000 nationwide property or casualty insurers. Policy forms developed by ISO are approved by its constituent insurance carriers and then submitted to state agencies for review. Most carriers use the basic ISO forms, at least as the starting point for their general liability policies.[13] In reading the following cases, ask whether the existence of standard contracts affects the interpretive approach and whether the standardization is a desirable end.

Note

A thorough discussion of the doctrine of contra proferentum is found in Kenneth S. Abraham, *A Theory of Insurance Policy Interpretation*, 95 Mich. L. Rev. 531 (1996).

13. Montrose Chemical Corp. v. Admiral Ins. Co., 10 Cal.4th 645, 42 Cal.Rptr.2d 324, 913 P.2d 878 (1995), *citing* New Castle County v. Hartford Acc. and Indem. Co., 933 F.2d 1162, 1181 (3d Cir.1991).

STEVEN v. FIDELITY AND CASUALTY COMPANY OF NEW YORK

Supreme Court of California, In Bank, 1962.
58 Cal.2d 862, 27 Cal.Rptr. 172, 377 P.2d 284.

TOBRINER, JUSTICE.

* * *

On March 3, 1957, Mr. George A. Steven purchased at Los Angeles, California, a round-trip airplane ticket to Dayton, Ohio. As part of the return trip Mr. Steven's itinerary included a flight from Terre Haute, Indiana, to Chicago, Illinois. Mr. Steven simultaneously purchased for a premium of $2.50 a $62,500 life insurance policy which named his wife, appellant, as the beneficiary.

Mr. Steven bought the policy by means of a vending machine. The policy set out across the top the following specifications: "DO NOT PURCHASE MORE THAN A TOTAL OF $62,500 PRINCIPAL SUM NOR FOR TRAVEL ON OTHER THAN SCHEDULED AIR CARRIERS. THIS POLICY COVERS ON ONE-WAY TRIP ONLY UNLESS ROUND TRIP TICKET IS PURCHASED BEFORE DEPARTURE." Below this printed statement a box form provided for the insertion on appropriate lines of the insured's name, the name and address of the beneficiary, the point of departure and destination, the extent of the trip as on a one-way or round-trip ticket, the date, the principal sum of insurance ($62,500), the amount of the premium ($2.50), and the insured's signature. The evidence does not clearly show whether at the time of purchase the aperture of the vending machine disclosed the entire top portion of the policy, including the printed warning as to amount and coverage for travel on "scheduled air carriers," or merely the form for the personal data and flight information to be furnished by the purchaser. After obtaining the policy, Mr. Steven, using the envelope provided by the machine, mailed it to his wife.

On March 6, 1957, on his return trip from Dayton, Mr. Steven, according to his original plan, stopped off at Terre Haute. He arrived there between 7 and 8 o'clock in the morning. His round-trip ticket scheduled him to take a Lake Central Airlines plane to Chicago at noon that day. At about that time the public address system at the airport announced that the Lake Central plane had been grounded in Indianapolis and that there would be some delay. After several further announcements of repeated delays, the scheduled Lake Central flight to Chicago was finally cancelled at 4:30 p.m.

The agent of Lake Central Airlines then attempted to arrange for Mr. Steven and three other men substitute means of transportation to Chicago. The agent phoned railroads, bus lines and even an automobile rental company. After concluding that he could not thereby arrange a connection with the scheduled Chicago flight to Los Angeles, the agent took Mr. Steven and the other three men to the office of the Turner Aviation Corporation (hereinafter designated Turner) at the Terre Haute airport and introduced them to the agent there in charge. The Lake Central agent indicated that a flight on a Turner plane provided the only means for Mr. Steven to make his scheduled connection with the Chicago plane, a connection which Mr. Steven particularly desired because an essential work project awaited him in Los Angeles the next morning. Turner agreed to fly the men to Chicago for $36 per person, or, if two more passengers could be obtained, for $21 a person. Two additional passengers were obtained and accordingly Mr. Steven and each of the other passengers paid Turner $21 for his ticket.

Mr. Steven boarded the Turner aircraft, a Piper Tri–Pacer airplane, which took off from the Terre Haute airfield at 5:55 p.m. Some time around 7 p.m. on March 6, 1957, near Grant Park, Illinois, the plane crashed. Mr. Steven suffered fatal injuries.

* * * The plane trip on which the accident occurred was not a regular and scheduled flight of Turner.

The trial court found that the deceased at the time of the accident "was not riding as a passenger on an aircraft operated by a scheduled air carrier, as defined in (the) policy, and further * * * that he was riding a charter plane from Terre Haute, Indiana, to Chicago, Illinois," and concluded that appellant could not recover on the policy.

The purpose and intent of the insured in taking out the insurance was to obtain insurance protection for the trip. The insured could fairly believe that the policy would cover a reasonable emergency substitution necessitated by the exigencies of the situation. Since weather conditions and mechanical failure upon not infrequent occasions require such substitution, the insured would not ordinarily expect that his insurance would fail in the event of these foreseeable contingencies. Since his contract covered the trip, he would not contemplate a hiatus in coverage; he bargained for protection for the whole, not part of, the trip.

A reasonable person, having bought his ticket for a fixed itinerary, and thus having at the moment of purchase of the policy gained insurance protection for the whole trip, would normally expect that if a flight were interrupted by breakdown or other causes, his coverage would apply to substitute transportation for the same flight. If, for instance, the scheduled plane crashlanded, he would certainly assume that the policy covered the emergency relief plane whether or not it were a scheduled air liner. The same normal expectation would apply to the substitution of an alternate plane because the scheduled one had been grounded by mechanical failure.

The risk of injury on the substitute conveyance in many cases will be no greater than the risk on the scheduled flight; in all cases it will be less than if the scheduled air line attempts to fly the scheduled flight despite bad weather or mechanical difficulty. Thus, both in the terms of occurrence and magnitude of risk, substitute emergency transportation falls well within the obligation undertaken by the insurer.

The language of the policy does not specifically exclude the expected coverage for the substituted flight. Neither the insuring clause, the definitions of a scheduled air carrier nor section 3(b) infra negates, without ambiguity, protection for the emergency substitute flight.

The insuring clause alludes to a loss occurring "during the first one-way or round airline trip taken by the Insured after the purchase of this policy on Aircraft Operated by a Scheduled Air Carrier as defined below * * *" and does not mention the subject of substitution of another carrier in the event of breakdown. Section 4, which defines "aircraft operated by a scheduled air carrier" differentiates between the scheduled and nonscheduled carriers but likewise does not describe the accorded coverage if an emergency causes the use of a nonscheduled carrier. These sections provide that the policy applies, as the heading in the box states, to the "round trip ticket * * * purchased before departure." Mr. Steven complied with these requirements: he purchased the round trip ticket on the scheduled airliner, and, when initially ensconced upon his plane, enjoyed the protection of his policy.

The only allusion to substituted transportation in the policy, contained in clause 3(b), does not in and of itself exclude coverage for the Turner flight. This provision affirmatively extends coverage to injuries sustained "while riding in or on a land conveyance provided or arranged for, directly or indirectly, by such scheduled air carrier * * * for the transportation of passengers necessitated by an interruption or temporary suspension of such scheduled air carrier's service. * * *" It thus makes clear that, at least in some cases, substitute emergency transportation will be included in the policy, and that, despite the narrowing of the insuring clause of the policy to "Aircraft Operated by a Scheduled Air Carrier," coverage may be extended to a nonscheduled nonflying vehicle not operated by an air carrier.

The crucial issue resolves into whether the limitation of that extension to "land conveyances" sufficiently overcomes the normal expectation that coverage would extend to any reasonable form of substitute conveyance. The clause clearly does not specifically exclude substitute emergency aircraft; it does not mention nonland conveyances at all. An inference of such noncoverage could arise only with the aid of the rule of construction expressio unius est exclusio alterius; i.e., that mention of one matter implies the exclusion of all others.

We do not believe the application of the maxim can resolve the present case. The maxim serves as an aid to resolve the ambiguities of a contract. If we invoke the expressio unius approach, we must necessarily thereby recognize the ambiguity of the contract; in that event other legal techniques for the resolution of ambiguities, including the rule that they should be interpreted against the draftsman, also come into play. Thus McNee v. Harold Hensgen & Associates (1960) 178 Cal.App.2d 881, 3 Cal.Rptr. 377, holds that if the applicability of a contract provision can be determined only by use of the maxim expressio unius, the contract is ambiguous, and extrinsic evidence is therefore admissible to prove the intent of the parties.

The rule of resolving ambiguities against the insurer does not serve as a mere tie-breaker; it rests upon fundamental considerations of policy. In view of the somewhat fictional nature of intent in standardized contracts, the considerations which support the rule that ambiguities in the policy are to be interpreted against the insurer are more compelling that those which prompt the application of the mechanical expressio unius maxim. We do not believe the maxim should serve to defeat the basic rule that the insurance contract should be interpreted against the draftsman.

In any event, the maxim of expressio unius, which is surely a legalistic concept, hardly enters into the thinking of the reasonable layman. As we have stated, we interpret an insurance contract in the light of that understanding. We could not logically conclude that when Mr. Steven, unversed in legal abstractions, boarded the Turner plane at Terre Haute, he invoked this maxim of interpretation.

The facts of this case buttress the above conclusion. Mr. Steven planned a round trip entirely on scheduled air carriers; he purchased his policy with the expectation that it would provide insurance against death or injury in such contingencies as might arise in the course of such a trip. In Terre Haute, Mr. Steven, upon learning that the Lake Central flight had been cancelled, exhausted all the possibilities of obtaining substitute land transportation. He could complete his original itinerary only by the Turner flight. Indeed, the Lake Central agent suggested the Turner substitution, took him over to the Turner office and introduced him to the Turner agent. While the policy specified coverage for injuries suffered in a land conveyance provided by the scheduled carrier, it contains no statement whatsoever as to such substituted air conveyance. We do not see how such verbal vacuity can serve as clear and plain notice to the insured of noncoverage.

We therefore conclude that section 3(b) should not be interpreted to restrict coverage exclusively to land conveyances. The policy did not clearly notify Mr. Steven that in spite of his expectation, and in view of the intention of the parties in entering into the contract, the coverage did not extend to a substitute flight in the event of emergency. The provision for substitute transportation did not clearly overcome the normal expectation that coverage would extend to any reasonable form of substitute conveyance.

Turning to the second aspect of the policy which affects the substituted Turner flight, that is, the definition of scheduled air carrier, we find that it, too, created an ambiguity and failed to apprise Mr. Steven of the asserted noncoverage. * * *

Since Turner did not file and publish regular schedules, nor possess a certificate of public convenience and necessity, Turner does not fall under the literal affirmative definition of scheduled air carrier in the policy. Neither does Turner qualify under the exclusionary language in the last sentence of clause 4; it was not a military airline and was not designated by government regulations as an irregular carrier. Thus the negative definition of the term in the exclusionary phrase may serve to extend coverage to all types of air transport except the two that were specifically excluded.

In summary, the air-taxi carrier constitutes a third category of aircraft under the federal regulations; the air-taxi is neither a scheduled carrier nor a non-scheduled carrier. So regarded, air-taxi carriers are neither included in, nor excluded from, the coverage for the policy; clause 4 creates an ambiguity. "(T)he burden in such a case as this is on the defendant to establish that the words and expressions used not only are susceptible of the construction sought by defendant but that it is the only construction which may fairly be placed on them." (Lachs v. Fidelity & Cas. Co., supra, 118 N.E.2d at p. 555; emphasis added.) This burden has not been met.

If the classic rules of interpretation lead to the conclusion that the policy afforded coverage here, we must point out additionally that they apply with special force in the circumstances of this case. We do not deal here with the orthodox insurance policy sold in the protective aura of the insurer's explanation and discussion of its terms. The vending machine emitted a complex stereotyped document, which, because of the short time elapsing before the start of Mr. Steven's flight, hardly afforded him an opportunity even to read the policy. The mass-made contract, sold by the machine under such conditions, symbolizes the kind of transaction that lends to the accepted rules a special gloss of interpretation. As we shall explain in more detail, the cases have held that in such contracts the expected coverage of the policy can only be defeated by a provision for limitation which has been plainly brought to the attention of the insured.

Nothing in the instant contract or transaction apprised the insured that the protection of the policy would not extend to the substituted emergency flight. The manner of sale of the policy negated any possibility of such notice. The inanimate machine told the purchaser nothing, and even if he had wanted to ask about the coverage in the event of emergency, the box could not have answered. While the testimony leaves us in some doubt as to whether Mr. Steven saw the words in the window of the machine stating "Nor for travel on other than Scheduled Air Carriers," we know that if he did see them, he could neither have read the definition of "scheduled air carrier" nor the clause concerning substitute emergency transportation on "land conveyances." These clauses lay hidden behind the mechanized face of the vendor. Even after Mr. Steven purchased the policy he would only have found such clauses among the many complexities of the instrument. They were inconspicuous clauses, and, as we have stated, they were unclear.

To assume that Mr. Steven read the provisions, or conceivably understood them, is to rest upon hypothesis rather than fact. The insurer instructed the purchaser to mail the policy to the beneficiary and provided envelopes for this purpose. Like most purchasers, Mr. Steven, before boarding the plane at the very commencement of the trip, did mail the policy to the beneficiary. The company provided no duplicate. Thus, when Mr. Steven found it necessary at Terre Haute to take the Turner flight he could not have consulted the policy to determine its applicability. Instead, even assuming that three days earlier he had read it carefully, he would have been compelled to rely upon his memory. The policy is about 2,000 words long. It is so tightly drawn that if Mr. Steven had forgotten a single word in clause 3(b) or a short phrase in clause 4 he might well have concluded that the policy covered the Turner trip.

Even upon the highly unrealistic assumption that Mr. Steven surmounted all of these obstacles, the policy still would not have notified him that he was not covered. The policy, in defining scheduled airlines, refers to an airline possessing certificates of public convenience and necessity and filing schedules. Later it attempts to exclude lines designated in government regulations as irregular or nonscheduled. These facts, important in determining whether the Turner flight were covered, obviously do not compose the facts a passenger typically knows. "(T)he average man * * * is (not) expected to carry the Civil Aeronautics Act or the Code of Federal Regulations when taking a plane." (Lachs v. Fidelity & Cas. Co., supra, 118 N.E.2d at p. 558.) Neither can he generally be expected to inquire into the nature of the certification of the airline.

The company so arranged this transaction that Mr. Steven could not possibly read the policy before purchase and could not practically consult the policy after purchase. The language of the policy in itself was insufficient to afford the necessary notice of non-coverage. The facts of the case foreclose any contention of the company that it afforded Mr. Steven plain warning of non-coverage of the Turner flight. While the insurer has every right to sell insurance policies by methods of mechanization, and present-day economic conditions may well justify such distribution, the insurer cannot then rely upon esoteric provisions to limit coverage. If it deals with the public upon a mass basis, the notice of non-coverage of the policy, in a situation in which the public may reasonably expect coverage, must be conspicuous, plain and clear.

Finally, the one provision that deals with substitution of transportation in the event of emergency, section 3(b) of the policy, was not only hidden beneath the machine before purchase, and, subject after purchase, to obscurity and ambiguity, but literally applied, tended toward the harsh and unconscionable. The section states that coverage for "the transportation of passengers necessitated by an interruption or temporary suspension of such scheduled air carrier's service before arrival at destination" is limited to "riding in or on a land conveyance provided or arranged for, directly or indirectly, by such scheduled air carrier" (emphasis added). Yet innumerable flights traverse bodies of water; if a plane were forced down at such point and the scheduled carrier arranged for conveyance by water, the language would not apply. Indeed, if the plane were forced down upon land or water and relief was afforded by a chartered non-scheduled carrier, which, of course, is a very likely contingency, the language again would not apply. Does not such a provision approach a trap for the unwary purchasing public?

In standardized contracts, such as the instant one, which are made by parties of unequal bargaining strength, the California courts have long been disinclined to effectuate clauses of limitation of liability which are unclear, unexpected, inconspicuous or unconscionable. The attitude of the courts has been manifested in many areas of contract.

* * *

The approach of the California courts to the exculpatory or exclusionary clause of the standardized contract finds a reflection in cases of other states and in the writings of the commentators. Indeed, some legal authorities categorize the instant contract and comparable agreements under the term "contract of adhesion" to give it a more definite place in the law and to emphasize the need for the strict judicial scrutiny of its terms. The term refers to a standardized contract prepared entirely by one party to the transaction for the acceptance of the other; such a contract, due to the disparity in bargaining power between the draftsman and the second party, must be accepted or rejected by the second party on a "take it or leave it" basis, without opportunity for bargaining and under such conditions that the "adherer" cannot obtain the desired product or service save by acquiescing in the form agreement.

In an exhaustive analysis of such contracts the New Jersey Supreme Court in the recent case of Henningsen v. Bloomfield Motors, Inc., (1960) 32 N.J. 358, 161 A.2d 69, 75 A.L.R.2d 1, held void as against public policy an exculpatory provision of an express warranty that excluded claims against a dealer or manufacturer for personal injuries resulting from a defective car. The court stated the rationale of its ruling in these words: "The task of the judiciary is to administer the spirit as well as the letter of the law. On issues such as the present one, part of that burden is to protect the ordinary man against the loss of important rights through what, in effect, is the unilateral act of the manufacturer. * * * From the standpoint of the purchaser, there can be no arms length negotiating on the subject. Because his capacity for bargaining is too grossly unequal, the inexorable conclusion which follows is that he is not permitted to bargain at all. * * * " (161 A.2d p. 94.) The court emphasizes the requirement for an *understanding consent* of the consumer to any limitation of liability. "Basically, the reason a contracting party offering services of a public or *quasi*-public nature has been held to the requirements of fair dealing, and, when it attempts to limit its liability, of securing the understanding consent of the patron or consumer, is because members of the public generally have no other means of fulfilling the specific need represented by the contract. * * * "(161 A.2d p. 92.)

The instant contract presents an even stronger case than Henningsen for the requirement that the exclusionary clause of the contract should not be enforced in the absence of plain and clear notification to the public. The disparity in bargaining power between the insured and the insurer here is so tremendous that the insurer had adopted a means of selling policies which makes bargaining totally impossible. The purchaser lacks any opportunity to clarify ambiguous terms or to discover inconspicuous or concealed ones. He must purchase the policy before he even knows its provisions.

Because of the special dangers inherent in the mechanized selling of air travel insurance, the New York Court of Appeals has insisted that the burden of giving clear notice of non-coverage rests with the insurer. In Lachs v. Fidelity & Casualty Co. of New York (1954) supra, 306 N.Y. 357, 118 N.E.2d 555, an "Airline Trip Insurance" vending machine stood near a ticket counter for sales of nonscheduled flights in the airport; a smaller placard limited coverage to "any scheduled airline"; the printed policy provided for coverage for "Civilian Scheduled Airlines." As in the instant case the insurer provided envelopes for the immediate mailing of the policy to the beneficiary. Unlike the passenger in the instant case the New York purchaser arranged for her trip to Miami on a nonscheduled flight, which subsequently crashed. The Court of Appeals held that the trial court properly denied the insurer's motion for summary judgment. The court points to the ambiguity of the term "Civilian Scheduled Airline" and to the ambiguity of the situation itself. It holds "* * * (T)he burden in such a case as this is on the defendant to establish that the words and expressions used not only are susceptible of the construction sought by defendant but that it is the only construction which may fairly be placed on them. The defendant in its large illuminated lettering and in its application could have added proper, unambiguous words or a definition or could have avoided allowing its vending machine to be placed in front of the ticket counter 'utilized by all nonscheduled airlines operating out of the Newark Airport', thus removing the ambiguity or equivocal character of the invitation to insure, of the application for insurance and the contract of insurance itself. * * * (118 N.E.2d p. 559)."

We must view the instant claim in the composite of its special and unique circumstances. To equate the bargaining table, where each clause is the subject of debate, to an automatic vending machine, which issues a policy before it can even be read, is to ignore basic distinctions. The proposition that the precedents must be viewed in the light of the imperatives of the age of the machine has become almost axiomatic. Here the age of the machine is no mere abstraction; it presents itself in the shape of an instrument for the mass distribution of standard contracts. The exclusionary clause of that contract, upon which the insurance company relies, is an unexpected one. Its application in some circumstances would be unconscionable. It is placed in an inconspicuous position of the document. In view of all these characteristics its rigid application would cast an unexpected burden upon the travelling public and would prefer formality of phrase to the reality of the transaction.

The judgment is reversed, and the cause is remanded to the trial court with directions to enter judgment for the plaintiff.

Notes

1. "The objectively reasonable expectations of applicants and intended beneficiaries regarding the terms of insurance contracts will be honored even though painstaking study of the policy provisions would have negated those expectations." This description of the doctrine of reasonable expectations was first put forth by Professor Robert Keeton in his important article, *Insurance Law Rights at Variance with Policy Provisions*, 83 HARV. L. REV. 961, 967 (1970). Professor Stempel also argues that the principle of reasonable expectations is useful to "overcome clear text violative of the insured's reasonable expectations but also to sever as a check on absurd hyperliteral interpretations of policy text." Jeffrey Stempel, *Unmet Expectations: Undue Restriction of the Reasonable Expectations Approach and the Misleading Mythology of Judicial Role*, 5 CONN. INS. L.J. 181, 184 (1998). Professor Stempel recognizes seven variants of the reasonable expectations approach, with a pure Keeton approach at one end of the spectrum where policyholder expectations may overcome clear text in the policy to rejection of any role for policyholder expectations on the other end of the spectrum. *Id.* at 192–193.

2. As the *Steven* case (decided in 1962) illustrates, judicial recognition of the principles underlying the reasonable expectation doctrine was evident prior to Professor Keeton's articulation of the doctrine in 1970. In fact, "reasonable expectations" is often considered to be an extension of the general contract principal which mandates interpretation of ambiguities within the contract against the drafter. However, the unique formulation of insurance contracts (boilerplate, contracts of adhesion) and the unequal bargaining power between the insured and the insurer calls for a more strict application of this principle. Professor Rahdert notes that "[a]lthough the law of contracts generally supports the notion that ambiguities in contract language should be resolved against the drafter, the search for and resolution of ambiguity attains a new dimension in the law of insurance. There, the ambiguity principle is transformed from a last resort interpretive "tie breaker" into a tool of substantive policy that is intended systematically to favor the weaker party in the transaction." Mark C. Rahdert, *Reasonable Expectations Reconsidered*, 18 CONN. L. REV. 323, 328 (1986).

3. Two other cases often considered by casebooks addressing the doctrine of reasonable expectations are *C & J Fertilizer v. Allied Mutual Insurance Co.*, 227 N.W.2d 169 (Iowa 1975) and *Atwater Creamery Co. v. Western National Mutual Insurance Co.*, 366 N.W.2d 271 (Minn.1985). These cases involve similar facts which revolve around an insured who tries to collect on an insurance policy following a burglary. The burglaries in question each were done by skilled burglars who left no marks (destroyed doors, etc.), yet it was clear that both businesses had been burgled. In both cases, the policies contained language which required visible marks of entry or evidence of force in order for coverage to be triggered. The rationale behind this requirement for coverage seems to be an effort on the part of insurers to avoid fraudulent claims. The courts in both cases found that the policyholders could have reasonably expected that any type of burglary would be covered, despite the technical definition contained within the policy. In the courts' view, the technical definitions of burglary were outside

of the common understanding of burglary, and the courts allowed the insureds to collect on the policies.

The authors acknowledge Professor Stempel's close reading of this text commenting that ours is the only text which does not contain either *C & J Fertilizer* or *Atwater Creamery*, the "paradigmatic example[s] of the Keeton reasonable expectation doctrine in action." Jeffrey Stempel, *Unmet Expectations: Undue Restriction of the Reasonable Expectations Approach and the Misleading Mythology of Judicial Role*, 5 Conn. Ins. L.J. 181, 200 (1998). This is not an accident on our part. We view the *Steven* case as an early and influential example of the reasonable expectations doctrine cited by Professor Keeton. Robert Keeton, *Insurance Law Rights at Variance with Policy Provisions*, 83 Harv. L. Rev. 961, 969 n.10 (1970).

4. As noted earlier, California, like many states, recognizes that insurance policies are contracts to be governed by contact law principles. See e.g. Bank of the West v. Superior Court, 2 Cal.4th 1254, 10 Cal.Rptr.2d 538, 833 P.2d 545 (1992); AIU Ins. Co. v. Superior Court, 51 Cal.3d 807, 274 Cal.Rptr. 820, 799 P.2d 1253 (1990). At the same time, as the introductory note indicates, there is an explicit recognition that the unique context of insurance policies as contracts demands attention to the area in which insurance sets itself apart, hence the *Steven* case.

California has subtly limited the reach of *Steven* or at least the reach of the *contra proferentum* doctrine. In *Bank of the West v. Superior Court,* the court notes that the doctrine of reasonable expectations is to be used as a tool which does not necessarily result in an interpretation of the contract in the insured's favor. 2 Cal.4th at 1264–65, 10 Cal.Rptr.2d at 544–45, 833 P.2d at 551–52. According to this formulation then, only if the doctrine of reasonable expectations does not resolve ambiguity does the *contra proferentum* principle apply. See John L. Romaker & Virgil B. Prieto, *Expectations Lost: Bank of the West v. Superior Court Places the Fox in Charge of the Henhouse,* 29 Cal. W.L. Rev. 83, 125 n. 326 (1992).

Two cases which have applied the rules of *AIU* and *Bank of the West* to resolve policy ambiguity issues are *Old Republic Insurance Co. v. Superior Court*, 66 Cal.App.4th 128, 77 Cal.Rptr.2d 642 (1998) and *Mez Industries, Inc. v. Pacific National Insurance Co.*, 76 Cal.App.4th 856, 90 Cal.Rptr.2d 721 (1999). In *Old Republic* an insurer sought contribution and indemnity from three other insurance companies because it had been found liable for coverage to a common insured. The contract between the insured and each of the four insurance companies contained essentially identical policy language regarding coverage under the policies. The three companies who opposed contribution claimed that no coverage existed under the policies, and so the primary task of the *Old Republic* court was to interpret the policy language to determine if coverage was triggered. *Mez Industries* involves the issue of whether a liability insurer providing coverage for "advertising injury" was required to defend its insured in an action charging patent infringement inducement. Both cases cite *AIU* for the proposition that "the interpretation of an insurance policy is no different than the interpretation of contracts generally." *Mez Industries* at 867, *Old Republic* at 142. Also, both cases quote *Bank of the West* to summarize the principles propounded by it and *AIU*: "if the terms of a promise are in any respect ambiguous or uncertain, it must be interpreted in the sense in which the promisor believed, at the time of making it, that the promisee understood it.... This rule ... protects ... the objectively reasonable expectations of the insured.... Only if this rule does not resolve the ambiguity do we then resolve it against the insurer." *Mez Industries* at 868, *Old Republic* at 142–143.

The *Old Republic* court, however, found that no ambiguities existed and concluded that coverage was excluded. See *Old Republic* at 146. The *Mez Industries* court concluded that, after reading the questioned insurance provisions "in the context of the entire policy, the general circumstances of this case, and simple common sense," the provisions didn't extend to patent infringement. Furthermore, *Mez Industries* could not have had an objectively reasonable expectation of coverage for a claim of willful patent infringement inducement, even if the policy language was found to be somewhat ambiguous. *Mez Industries* at 874. The apparent lesson is that the courts have reemphasized the role of context and objectivity in construing insurance policies. The California courts are not alone in adopting this view. E.g., Amerada Hess Corp. v. Zurich Insurance Co., 51 F.Supp.2d 642, 648 (D.V.I. 1999) (language is ambiguous if reasonably intelligent persons considering language in context would differ honestly as to meaning). The cases explicitly recognize that the liberality of the interpretive regime prior to *AIU* has been circumscribed. *Old Republic* at 143 n. 17.

5. At least one court has followed the approach in *Bank of the West*. In *American Family Mutual Insurance Group v. Kostaneski*, the court noted that the doctrine of reasonable expectations does not apply unless there is an ambiguity in the policy language. 688 N.W.2d 410, 414 (S.Dak. 2004).

6. Professor Peter Swisher argues for a middle ground of judicial interpretation that strikes a balance between textualism and functionalism. Peter N. Swisher, *Judicial Interpretations of Insurance Contract Disputes: Toward a Realistic Middle Ground Approach*, 57 Ohio St. L.J. 544 (1996).

7. Courts have noted the reasonable expectation that coverage under a "Comprehensive General Liability" policy be comprehensive and that an "all risks" property policy cover all risks. Insurers now title these policies "Commercial General Liability" and "Special" form property coverage.

FEDERAL INSURANCE CO. v. STROH BREWING CO.

United States Court of Appeals, Seventh Circuit, 1997.
127 F.3d 563.

Before CUDAHY, FLAUM and ROVNER, Circuit Judges.

CUDAHY, Circuit Judge.

Say "discrimination" today and those around you may think of race or sex discrimination, usually in connection with a school or work setting. But that has not always been the case. Time was, "discrimination" might have brought immediately to mind charging one person more than another for the same product. That definition, although perhaps less in public consciousness, remains just as valid today.

G. Heileman Brewery Company, Inc. (Heileman) purchased an umbrella business liability insurance policy from Federal Insurance

Company (Federal). In June of 1994 Calumet (a wholesale beer distributor in Indiana) sued Heileman for discrimination allegedly based on Heileman's pricing practices. In March of 1995, Heileman turned this lawsuit over to its insurer, Federal, and requested both that Federal defend it against Calumet and that Federal cover any losses Heileman might incur as a result of the suit. Not until August of 1995 (with trial set for November 6 of the same year) did Federal alert Heileman that it was declining both coverage and the duty to defend. Heileman spent $650,000 defending itself and then settled for an additional $850,000. Heileman then sued Federal, seeking coverage, and Federal countersued, seeking a declaratory judgment of no coverage. The district court entered summary judgment in favor of Federal, denying coverage. We review a summary judgment de novo, and will affirm only if no genuine issue of material fact remains to be resolved and if Federal is entitled to judgment as a matter of law. See Alexander v. City of Chicago, 994 F.2d 333, 335 (7th Cir.1993). We reverse.

We must determine the extent of Federal's duty to defend and duty to indemnify. Whether Federal had a duty to defend Heileman depends on whether Calumet's complaint alleged facts giving rise to liability. Calumet's suit accused Heileman of engaging in price discrimination. Heileman offered a staggered price discount based on the volume purchased. Calumet sued; it believed that Heileman's pricing structure discriminated against smaller wholesalers unable to purchase large amounts of beer on a monthly basis. Only one wholesaler, Central Distributing, was able consistently to purchase enough beer to qualify for the largest discount. Calumet thus believed Heileman favored Central Distributing over other wholesalers. Calumet sought relief under the Clayton Act, the Robinson–Patman Act and Indiana beverage laws.

Heileman's policy covers, among other personal injuries, "discrimination." Calumet repeatedly alleged discrimination in its complaint: "Heileman is now and has been discriminating in price between different purchasers of commodities of like grade and quality, that is, Heileman is selling and has sold beer, a commodity, of identical grade and quantity at the same time at different prices to different customers." Calumet Complaint at 17 (internal quotation marks omitted). "The sales by Heileman to Central Distributing, Heileman's favored purchaser, and Calumet, Heileman's disfavored purchaser, are a discrimination in commerce." Id. "The effect of such discrimination not only may be to substantially lessen competition but has, in fact, already substantially lessened competition in the sale of Heileman beer in Northwest Indiana." Id. "The effect of such discrimination by Heileman has also been to injure, destroy or prevent competition with any person who either grants or knowingly receives the benefit of such discrimination, or with customers of either of them." Id. "This discrimination is not because of any due allowance for difference in the cost of manufacture, sale, or delivery." Id. at 18 (internal quotation marks omitted). "This discrimination is not in response to changing conditions." Id. Thus, if discrimination in price is covered by the policy, Federal had a duty to defend Heileman.

Heileman argues that Calumet's complaint falls within the plain language of the policy and that Federal's duty to defend is correspondingly clear. Federal believes "price discrimination" to be a term of art describing conduct not included in coverage for "discrimination." The district court agreed with Federal and gave two alternative reasons for denying coverage. First, that the term "discrimination" was unambiguous and had only one meaning which did not include "price discrimination." Second, that, even if "price discrimination" were properly understood as part of "discrimination," the policy contained an exclusion which applied to the facts as alleged by Calumet. Because we find that "price discrimination" is simply a particular form of discrimination, and because we find that, even if the exclusion does apply, Federal is estopped from asserting it, we reverse.

I. Duty to Defend

* * *

[W]e examine the policy issued by Federal and the complaint filed by Calumet to determine if Federal had a duty to defend Heileman in the Calumet litigation. Heileman's umbrella policy contained two forms of coverage, of which only Coverage B is at issue here. Coverage B promised that Federal would pay on Heileman's behalf any damages resulting from "personal injury" or "advertising injury" if caused by an offense committed during the policy period and no primary insurance applied. We are concerned only with the "personal injury" coverage in the present case. Personal injury is defined by the policy, in part, as "humiliation or discrimination EXCEPT: (1) when arising out of the willful violation of a statute; (2) when committed by or with knowledge or consent of the insured." The term "discrimination" within this definition is not defined in the policy. Nevertheless, to determine if Calumet's allegations are properly considered discrimination under the policy we must look to the meaning of "discrimination" as used in the policy.

Federal defends its denial of coverage with the argument that "price discrimination" is a term of art, not covered by the policy under the designation "discrimination." Heileman argues both that Calumet's complaint alleges discrimination, pure and simple, and that "price discrimination" is merely a label for the particular form of discrimination alleged by Calumet. Further, because the policy at issue is an "umbrella" policy, drafted by Federal, Heileman argues that the language should be interpreted broadly and against the insurer. See Commercial Union Ins. Co. v. Walbrook Ins. Co., 7 F.3d 1047, 1053 (1st Cir.1993) ("Umbrella policies differ from standard excess insurance policies in that they are designed to fill gaps in coverage both vertically (by providing excess coverage) and horizontally (by providing primary coverage).... Moreover, this interpretation is consonant with the broader function served by umbrella policies—extending coverage even to unanticipated 'gaps.'

As one authority has explained, umbrella policies effectively shift away from the insured the burden of choosing the risks to which the insured remains exposed.") (citations omitted) (emphasis supplied).

In Indiana, the clear and unambiguous language of an insurance policy must be given its plain and ordinary meaning. See American States Ins. Co. v. Kiger, 662 N.E.2d 945, 947 (Ind.1996); City of Muncie v. United Nat'l Ins. Co., 564 N.E.2d 979, 982 (Ind.Ct.App.1991). However, when there is ambiguity, "insurance policies are to be construed strictly against the insurer." Kiger, 662 N.E.2d at 947. Further, an "intelligent layperson['s]" view is the standard used to interpret insurance terms. Id. at 948 n. 2. A term is ambiguous if reasonable persons could "honestly differ as to the meaning of the policy language," Eli Lilly & Co. v. Home Ins. Co., 482 N.E.2d 467, 470 (Ind.1985), or whenever the language has two or more reasonable meanings. See Wood v. Allstate Ins. Co., 21 F.3d 741, 744 (7th Cir.1994); see also Ramirez v. American Family Mut. Ins. Co., 652 N.E.2d 511, 514 (Ind.Ct.App.1995). "Price discrimination" is not merely a sui generis term of art, but also describes a form of the more general term, "discrimination." Discrimination "simply means differential treatment." Indiana Wholesale Wine & Liquor Co., Inc. v. State ex rel. Indiana Alcoholic Beverage Comm'n, 662 N.E.2d 950, 960 (Ind.Ct.App.1996). Whether that differential treatment takes the form of not receiving a promotion to which one is entitled or of being required to pay a higher price for beer does not make it any the less "discrimination." See, e.g., Oregon Waste Systems, Inc. v. Department of Envtl. Quality, 511 U.S. 93, 114 S.Ct. 1345, 128 L.Ed.2d 13 (1994) ("discrimination simply means differential treatment of in-state and out-of-state economic interests that benefits the former and burdens the latter."); Texas & Pac. Ry. Co. v. Abilene Cotton Oil Co., 204 U.S. 426, 27 S.Ct. 350, 51 L.Ed. 553, seriatim, 447–48 (1907) (discussing price differentials in rail fares as discrimination and referring to law making it "a misdemeanor to offer, grant, give, solicit, accept, or receive any rebate from published rates or other concession or discrimination."); Richmond, Fredericksburg & Potomac R.R. Co. v. Department of Taxation, 762 F.2d 375, 380 n. 4 (4th Cir.1985) ("In essence, discrimination is a 'failure to treat all persons equally where no reasonable distinction can be found between those favored and those not favored.' "); Hocking Valley Ry. Co. v. United States, 210 F. 735, 738 (6th Cir.1914) (describing "discrimination" as the giving of an advantage). As these cases show, courts frequently define discrimination as differential treatment.

Heileman offers a number of dictionary definitions as well; we note one, from Black's Law Dictionary. That dictionary has been approvingly cited by the Indiana Supreme Court as the type of resource an "intelligent layperson" might consult. Kiger, 662 N.E.2d at 948 n. 2. A portion of Black's "discrimination" definition reads: "With reference to common carriers, a breach of the carrier's duty to treat all shippers alike, and afford them equal opportunities to market their product. A carrier's failure to treat all alike under substantially similar conditions.... See also . . . Price discrimination." BLACK'S LAW DICTIONARY 467 (6th ed.1990). Black's defines "price discrimination" thus:

> Exists when a buyer pays a price that is different from the price paid by another buyer for an identical product or service. Price discrimination is prohibited if the effect of this discrimination may be to lessen substantially or injure competition, except where it was implemented to dispose of perishable or obsolete goods, was the result of differences in costs incurred, or was given in good faith to meet an equally low price of a competitor.

Id. at 1189. The second sentence of Black's definition of "price discrimination" parallels the language of the Robinson–Patman Act. This may lend some weight to Federal's argument that "price discrimination" is a term of art under that Act. However, this tracking of the Act does not show that "price discrimination" is not a form of generic discrimination.

The Robinson–Patman Act has been interpreted by courts to prohibit discrimination, not just "price discrimination." See Falls City Indus., Inc. v. Vanco Beverage, Inc., 460 U.S. 428, 436, 103 S.Ct. 1282, 1289, 75 L.Ed.2d 174 (1983) ("the Act 'is of general applicability and prohibits discriminations generally' "); Jones v. Metzger Dairies, Inc., 334 F.2d 919, 924 (5th Cir.1964) ("The evil at which the Robinson–Patman Act is aimed is discrimination between different competing purchasers where the effect of such discrimination may be substantially to lessen competition or tend toward a monopoly in commerce.") (quoting Hartley & Parker, Inc. v. Florida Beverage Corp., 307 F.2d 916 (5th Cir.1962)). The Supreme Court has said that discrimination in price means "selling the same kind of goods cheaper to one purchaser than to another." Federal Trade Comm'n v. Anheuser–Busch, Inc., 363 U.S. 536, 549, 80 S.Ct. 1267, 1274, 4 L.Ed.2d 1385 (1960); Federal Trade Comm'n v. Cement Inst., 333 U.S. 683, 721, 68 S.Ct. 793, 813, 92 L.Ed. 1010 (1948). Further, the Robinson–Patman Act has long been recognized to forbid discrimination in a variety of forms. In Centex–Winston Corp. v. Edward Hines Lumber Co., 447 F.2d 585, 587 (7th Cir.1971), we noted that the Act "is directed against discriminatory treatment of purchasers engaged in the resale of the seller's goods." (Citations omitted.) Federal concedes that discrimination can be defined as differential treatment. Federal Br. at 14. Federal insists, however, that "price discrimination" is a term of art, not a designation of a particular form of discrimination. We do not agree with Federal's position, but even if we did, we would find that the term "discrimination" as used in the Heileman policy is ambiguous. Thus, we must interpret the term in favor of coverage and against Federal. "Discrimination," as used in the policy, encompasses Calumet's allegations. Federal had a duty to defend.

This duty may be supported further by examining the parties' expectations when the policy was written and purchased. See Wood, 21 F.3d at 743 ("Insurance policies are contractual agreements, and in divining their terms the starting point is of course the intent of the parties.") (citing Evans v. National Life Accident Ins. Co., 467 N.E.2d 1216, 1219 (Ind.Ct.App.1984)). Because the term "discrimination" is not defined in the policy and because price discrimination suits such as Calumet's are common in the beer industry, it is not objectively unreasonable for Heileman to have believed that it was purchasing coverage for just such a suit as Calumet's. See, e.g., Vanco Beverage, 460 U.S. 428, 103 S.Ct. 1282, 75 L.Ed.2d 174 (price discrimination suit); Anheuser–Busch, 363 U.S. 536, 80 S.Ct. 1267, 4 L.Ed.2d 1385 (same); Lake County Beverage Co., Inc. v. 21st Amendment, Inc., 441 N.E.2d 1008 (Ind.Ct. App.1982) (same). This may be the case even though in the present day "discrimination" might bring first to mind differences in personal treatment.

The district court is mistaken in its conclusion that to allow coverage in this case would have the effect of encouraging Heileman to engage in the illegal activity of price discrimination. Unlike the apparent belief of the district court that all price discounts are discriminatory in some way, quantity discounts are legal so long as they are cost justified. Vanco Beverage, 460 U.S. at 435, 103 S.Ct. at 1288–89. In fact, the district court's concern would be equally appropriate with respect to insurance covering any intentional acts. Whether the policy insures for personal discrimination (e.g., age or sex) and price discrimination or for only personal discrimination, the policy "encourages" discrimination in either case.

II. Policy Exclusion

The district court held that, even if price discrimination is covered by the policy, the facts alleged by Calumet fit an exception, thus removing the coverage. The policy language reads:

c. humiliation or discrimination EXCEPT:

(1) when arising out of the willful violation of a statute;

(2) when committed by or with knowledge or consent of the insured.

The district court held that the exceptions contained in clauses (1) and (2) are "mutually exclusive." Memo. Op. at 12. It reached this conclusion on the grounds that "the policy states two separate exceptions which are made textually clear by the division of the exceptions into two subparagraphs and are made syntactically clear by the use of a semicolon." Id. Because "the pricing of a product is a conscious, carefully considered business decision ... not ... done arbitrarily or by accident" the court determined that clause (2) applied and would exclude coverage. Id. Just as general policy language must be clear to be enforced, so must the language of any policy exceptions. Doubts and ambiguities should be construed against the drafter, see Allstate Ins. Co. v. United Farm Bureau Mut. Ins. Co., 618 N.E.2d 31, 33 (Ind.Ct.App.1993), particularly where the policy language purports to exclude coverage. See Kiger, 662 N.E.2d at 947.

Heileman argues that the exclusion is not to be read in the disjunctive as the district court held, but in the conjunctive, as if the semicolon represented an "and." Heileman relies on a grammatical construction, supported by several policy arguments, to interpret the exclusion in its favor. Heileman, in its grammatical argument, notes first that the two branches of the exclusion are separated by a semicolon and second, that throughout the policy, when an alphabetic provision is followed by numbered subparts (as in this exclusion), the semicolon between the numeric (but not necessarily the alphabetic) subparts is either followed by the word "or" or is not followed by any word.[14] In the three cases where the semicolon is standing alone, substituting the word "and" makes sense in every case. Heileman concedes that in the present exclusion either "or" or "and" can be read and still make grammatical sense.

But, Heileman argues, an "or" does not make sense in terms of the policy's purpose and the parties' intent. Further, if the exclusion is in the conjunctive, it is a standard type of exclusion. See, e.g., Ethicon, Inc. v. Aetna Cas. & Sur. Co., 737 F.Supp. 1320, 1326 (S.D.N.Y.1990) ("The policy goes on to state that it does not apply 'to injury arising out of the wilful violation of a penal statute or ordinance [and] committed by or with the knowledge or consent of any insured.' "). On the other hand, if the exclusion is disjunctive, then an insurance policy purporting to cover intentional acts no longer does so. In addition, Heileman argues that to interpret the exclusion as has the district court eliminates all coverage for any kind of discrimination from the policy. Finally, Heileman argues that when one interpretation favors the insured and the opposite interpretation favors the insurer, the rules of insurance policy interpretation dictate that the insured be favored. Especially is this true in a case such as this one, where the Calumet lawsuit is of a type common in the industry and thus, reasonably foreseeable by both Heileman and Federal. See Anheuser–Busch, 363 U.S. 536, 80 S.Ct. 1267, 4 L.Ed.2d 1385; Lake County Beverage, 441 N.E.2d 1008.

Federal sees no pattern in the use of the semicolon in place of "and" or "or" and believes that viewing the policy as a whole dictates that the semicolon be read as if it were an "or." Federal also notes that each subpart begins with the word "when" and argues that this indicates each is an independent condition. If the subparts were conjunctive, Federal argues, the "when" would have immediately followed "except." Finally, Federal argues that there are other places in the policy where a semicolon must be read as "or" for the policy to make sense and that this fact refutes Heileman's argument. For example, the "personal injury" definition contains the alphabetic subparts separated by semicolons. Each semicolon must act as an "or" for the policy to make sense. Otherwise coverage for personal injury would require the allegation of three forms of injury in every claim (e.g., false arrest and libel and

14. Federal responds by pointing to the occasions when the policy follows a semicolon with "and" "at the ends of paragraphs and within sentences." This is not the construction Heileman is arguing. In no way does Heileman assert that every semicolon in the policy is followed either by an "or" or nothing. Heileman merely points out that in a particular type of construction (alphabetic lists with subparts of numeric lists) the semicolon use is consistent and meaningful.

humiliation). Federal also believes that the exclusion applies to the acts alleged in Calumet's suit because those allegations presume Heileman's intent to discriminate through its pricing structure, and the setting of prices is necessarily a conscious decision which must take place with Heileman's knowledge and consent.

But we need not consider Federal's arguments in detail because, as drafter of the policy, Federal chose what punctuation to use in this exclusion. Had Federal intended to definitively establish two independent exclusions it could have done so through the use of a period or an "or." Instead, Federal used a lone semicolon. The semicolon can be read as an "or" or as an "and," in both cases creating a grammatically logical sentence. This ambiguity alone is sufficient to support a conclusion that the semicolon should be construed to operate as an "and." We therefore decline to examine further the parties' grammatical and usage arguments with respect to semicolon placement.

Even were the exclusion not ambiguous, however, we could not find that it applies. Acts done with "knowledge and consent" are intentional. Yet the coverage for discrimination is coverage for Heileman's intentional acts. If Federal's interpretation of the exclusion were correct, the policy would simultaneously promise to cover and to refuse to cover Heileman's intentional discrimination.

The policy limits "occurrences" of "bodily injury" and "property damage" to those injuries "neither expected nor intended from the standpoint of the insured." Policy at 17. The policy does not similarly limit "personal injury" caused by an "offense." "Personal injury" and "advertising injury" policies regularly cover intentional acts. See, e.g., Indiana Ins. Co. v. North Vermillion Community Sch. Corp., 665 N.E.2d 630, 634 (Ind.Ct.App.1996) (suit alleging intentional libel or slander generated duty to defend under personal injury policy). Thus the "personal injury" coverage includes intentional acts. If subpart (2) of the exclusion were interpreted to operate independently, all coverage for intentional acts is extinguished. The exclusion reads "discrimination EXCEPT: ... (2) when committed by or with knowledge or consent of the insured." Policy at 18. This could be re-written: coverage for

"discrimination EXCEPT: ...

when committed by [the insured] or with knowledge [of the insured] or consent of the insured."

Thus stated, no intentional action of the insured would remain covered by the policy. Therefore, the semicolon in question must be interpreted as an "and."

We now consider whether reliance on the exclusion must be rejected on other grounds as well. Heileman argues that because Federal delayed six months before notifying Heileman of its wrongful decision to decline to defend, Federal now should be barred from denying coverage based on an exclusion. See Indiana Ins. Co. v. Ivetich, 445 N.E.2d 110, 112 (Ind.Ct.App.1983) ("when an insurer induces the insured to effect self-help to protect himself, it cannot then hide behind the language of the insurance policy to avoid its duty to defend or insure.") (citing American Family Mut. Ins. Co. v. Kivela, 408 N.E.2d 805 (Ind.Ct.App.1980)). In Ivetich the insurance company refused to pay a claim on the grounds that the claims alleged were not covered. Similarly, in Kivela the insurer denied both coverage and a duty to defend. Because the insurance companies in both cases wrongfully denied coverage, the Indiana courts held that the insurer could not then "hide behind the language of the contract in an attempt to avoid its duty to insure." Id. In other words, choosing to deny coverage based on non-coverage by the insuring clause, thus leaving the insured to fend for itself, bars the insurer from recourse to its exclusions. Thus, regardless of whether the exclusion would apply in another circumstance, Federal may not now rely on it.

The grant of summary judgment is

REVERSED.

[The dissenting opinion of Judge Flaum is omitted.]

Note

Judge Flaum's dissenting opinion contains the following statement:

I [cannot] agree with the majority that finding coverage for antitrust claims under this provision is in accord with the reasonable expectations of the parties. The majority reasons that, because price discrimination claims are common within the beer industry, Heileman would have reasonably believed that it was purchasing coverage for this type of claim. I submit that the more plausible assumption, given that these claims are not uncommon, is that the parties would have addressed the issue of antitrust coverage in a more direct manner if they had in fact intended to do so. One would expect recurring claims to be addressed with a certain degree of precision and clarity. Relying upon the placement of the phrase "humiliation or discrimination" in the "Personal Injury" section of the policy is a highly unusual, if not obtuse, means of indemnifying one's company against antitrust suits of this nature.

Is Judge Flaum correct?

WORLD TRADE CENTER PROPERTIES, L.L.C. v. THE TRAVELERS INDEMNITY CO.

United States Court of Appeals for the Second Circuit, 2003.
345 F.3d 154.

Before: WALKER, Chief Judge, CABRANES and POOLER, Circuit Judges.

* * *

BACKGROUND

As a condition of its 99–year lease of the WTC, Silverstein Properties was required to obtain first-party property insurance on the property. Silverstein Properties engaged Willis of New York ("Willis"), an insurance broker, to set up a multi-layered insurance program, which consisted of a primary insurance layer and 11 excess insurance layers providing a total of approximately $3.5 billion insurance on a "per occurrence" basis. In soliciting insurers for the program, Willis circulated a Property Underwriting Submission (the "Underwriting Submission") containing information regarding the proposed placement, including descriptions of the property and the insureds, desired coverage terms and conditions, estimated property values, engineering information, and a property loss history. With respect to at least the four insurers involved in these appeals, the Underwriting Submission also included a specimen copy of Willis's own "broker" form (the "WilProp form").[17] Section VIII of the Underwriting Submission states:

> Policy Form and Contract between Silverstein and the [Port Authority] are attached. DRAFT WilProp for Real Estate Risks is attached. We anticipate that this form will ultimately require amendment to comply with the Contract between Silverstein Properties, Inc. and the [Port Authority]. In the meantime, we provide this document as a starting point.

Of the four insurers in these appeals, Travelers was the only insurer to submit its own specimen policy form (the "Travelers form") during the course of negotiating the terms of coverage.[18] Whereas the Travelers form did not define the term "occurrence, "the WilProp form defined occurrence as follows:

> "Occurrence" shall mean all losses or damages that are attributable directly or indirectly to one cause or to one series of similar causes. All such losses will be added together and the total amount of such losses will be treated as one occurrence irrespective of the period of time or area over which such losses occur. SR Int'l Bus. Ins. Co. v. World Trade Ctr. Props. LLC, 222 F. Supp. 2d 385, 398 (S.D.N.Y. 2002)

As we will explain in greater detail, each of the appellees negotiated separately with Willis concerning its participation in the insurance program and all had bound coverage on various layers as of July 20, 2001. During the course of the next several weeks, Willis negotiated with Travelers over the terms of its final policy, but the Silverstein Parties have presented no evidence to indicate that any of the other appellees participated in or were aware of the details of those negotiations. As of September 11, 2001, none of the appellee-insurers had issued a final

17. The parties have indicated that some insurers did not receive a specimen copy of the WilProp form. We do not address the possible consequences that failure to receive the form may have for those insurers because any such consequences are not relevant to the present appeal.

18. We note, however, that Industrial Risk Insurers ("IRI") issued a binder that expressly bound on the basis of its own policy form, "Standard Fire Policy and Comprehensive All Risk Form C–AR."

policy form, nor had Willis issued the WilProp form as a final policy form, although at least one other participating insurer, Allianz Insurance Company ("Allianz"), had issued a final policy. SR Int'l Bus. Ins. Co. v. World Trade Ctr. Props. LLC, 2002 U.S. Dist. LEXIS 9966, No. 01 Civ. 9291 (JSM), 2002 WL 1163577, at *2 & n.3 (S.D.N.Y. June 3, 2002); see also SR Int'l Bus. Ins. Co. v. World Trade Ctr. Props. LLC, 2003 U.S. Dist. LEXIS 1103, No. 01 Civ. 9291 (JSM), 2003 WL 192487, at *4 (S.D.N.Y. Jan. 29, 2003). On September 14, 2001, three days after the WTC was destroyed, following discussions between Willis and Travelers, Travelers issued its final policy form.

DISCUSSION

[part I discussing diversity and statutory jurisdiction and part II discussing the standard of review for summary judgment are omitted]

III. SECTION 1292(B) APPEAL—TRAVELERS

The Silverstein Parties' appeal from the denial of their motion for summary judgment against Travelers raises a different set of issues from those just discussed. This motion was based chiefly on the argument that where an insurance policy uses the term "occurrence" without defining the term, then, as a matter of law, the term's meaning is not ambiguous and must be decided by reference to well established New York legal precedent. The Silverstein Parties further argue that under the definition of "occurrence" established by New York law, the events of September 11th constituted two occurrences as a matter of law.

As was the case with the Rule 54(b) appeal, we review the district court's denial of the Silverstein Parties' motion for summary judgment against Travelers de novo. See Gibbs–Alfano, 281 F.3d at 18 ("We review the ... denial of summary judgment de novo.") (internal quotation marks omitted). However, whereas in the Rule 54(b) appeal, we construed the evidence in the light most favorable to the Silverstein Parties, in this 1292(b) appeal, we must construe the evidence in the light most favorable to non-movant Travelers. See Anderson, 477 U.S. at 255; Maguire, 147 F.3d at 235. Before turning to the Silverstein Parties' arguments, we briefly review the history of the Travelers binder and its treatment by the district court.

A. Willis' Negotiations With Travelers

On June 7, 2001, Boyd sent an e-mail to James B. Coyle, III, an underwriter at Travelers, that included both the Underwriting Submission for the WTC and the WilProp form. In an affidavit submitted in opposition to the Silverstein Parties' motion, Coyle attested that he responded to Boyd's offer by stating that if Travelers were to participate in the primary layer, it would insist on using its own form, but that Travelers would agree to the use of the WilProp form if Travelers participated only in the excess layers. At deposition, Boyd testified that he told Coyle that if Travelers would permit changes to its form to meet the Silverstein Properties' needs, Silverstein Properties would accept the Travelers form. On July 9, Coyle e-mailed to Boyd an authorization for coverage, to which he attached Travelers' specimen excess policy. Two days later, on July 11, Coyle e-mailed Boyd again setting forth a revised authorization for coverage and attaching Travelers' specimen primary policy. On July 17, Boyd e-mailed Coyle, stating that Willis was "pleased to bind [Travelers'] participation." Coyle's colleague Robert Malm confirmed Travelers' coverage by e-mail on July 18. On July 20, Boyd e-mailed to Travelers a binder similar to the one he had sent to Hartford and Royal, stating, "Attached is Binder to be used with Marketplace. We are aware of use of Travelers Form requirement and are reviewing same to make sure we and you agree where we can amend if need be. In the meantime, went out with specs as binder." Although Travelers never returned a signed copy of the binder, the parties agree that Travelers had bound coverage as of July 18.

After July 18, Boyd and Fenn Harvey, also of Willis, reviewed the WilProp and Travelers forms to identify the areas of difference between the two forms. Boyd then submitted a list of more than 76 differences to Travelers as a starting point for negotiating the terms of the final policy form. The list did not identify the presence or absence of a definition of "occurrence" as a point of difference between the two. During the next several weeks, the parties met to negotiate policy terms and exchanged drafts of the policy. By September 11th, however, the parties had not agreed to a final policy form. Following the destruction of the WTC, on either September 12 or 13, Boyd asked Coyle for a copy of the policy incorporating the changes that had been agreed to as of September 10, 2001. Boyd stated at deposition that he and Coyle agreed to freeze the draft as of that date. On September 14, 2001, Coyle issued the Travelers Policy for final review and approval by Silverstein Properties.

B. The District Court Decision

On June 3, 2002, the district court denied the Silverstein Parties' motion for summary judgment against Travelers. See SR Int'l Bus. Ins. Co. v. World Trade Ctr. Props. LLC, 2002 U.S. Dist. LEXIS 9966, 2002 WL 1163577 (S.D.N.Y. June 3, 2002) ("Travelers Dec."). In construing Travelers' binder, which incorporated by reference the Travelers form, the district court found

> that the dispositive issue on this motion is whether the term "occurrence" has such a clear and unambiguous meaning that the trier of fact should be barred from considering the available extrinsic evidence concerning the meaning that the parties gave to that term when they were negotiating the insurance coverage for the World Trade Center. 2002 U.S. Dist. LEXIS 9966, [WL] at *3.

The district court then cited to Curry Road Ltd. v. K Mart Corp., 893 F.2d 509 (2d Cir. 1990), for its enunciation of the standard for determining whether a contract term is ambiguous:

> A term is ambiguous when it is capable of more than one meaning when viewed objectively by a reasonably intelligent person who has examined the context of the entire integrated agreement and who is cognizant of the customs, practices, usages and terminology as

generally understood in the particular trade or business. Travelers Dec., 2002 U.S. Dist. LEXIS 9966, 2002 WL 1163577, at *4 (quoting Curry Road, 893 F.2d at 511) (internal quotation marks omitted).

Applying the Curry Road test, the district court found that the meaning of "occurrence" to be incorporated into the Travelers binder was ambiguous given the history of litigation over the term, the fact that the term has been variously defined in different insurance policies, and the varying treatment of the term in different cases. 2002 U.S. Dist. LEXIS 9966, [WL] at *5–*6. The district court rejected the Silverstein Parties' argument that there is a single generally accepted meaning of "occurrence" under New York law. Id. The district court also found that the fact that Willis had circulated a policy that defined "occurrence" lent further support for a finding that the term as used in the Travelers binder was ambiguous. 2002 U.S. Dist. LEXIS 9966, [WL] at *5.

Accordingly, the court held that summary judgment had to be denied and that what the parties intended to be the meaning of "occurrence" would have to be determined by reference to extrinsic evidence, including

> the specific definition of the term occurrence circulated by the insurance agent for the [insureds], testimony and documents relating to the negotiations prior to September 11th and the overall structure of the insurance program from the World Trade Center, and testimony and documentary evidence concerning statements made after September 11th by those who had been involved in negotiating the insurance contracts, in which they expressed their views on the question of whether there had been one or two occurrences.2002 U.S. Dist. LEXIS 9966, [WL] at *6.

On October 22, 2002, the district court amended the Opinion and Order to include a certification pursuant to 28 U.S.C. 1292(b), thereby permitting the Silverstein Parties to seek leave to immediately appeal the denial of the summary judgment motion against Travelers together with the Rule 54(b) grants of summary judgment in favor of Hartford, St. Paul, and Royal.

C. [The discussion of the enforceability of the binder is contained in Chapter 2 above]

D. Is the Binder Ambiguous?

The Silverstein Parties argue that the meaning of "occurrence" as used in the Travelers insurance coverage is not ambiguous and, therefore, that resort to extrinsic evidence to construe it is both unnecessary and improper. Because nothing in the documents that constitute the Travelers binder defined "occurrence," we must decide whether the undefined term "occurrence" when used in a first-party property damage contract is ambiguous.

Applying New York law, we have held that

> the cardinal principle for the construction and interpretation of insurance contracts—as with all contracts—is that the intentions of

the parties should control. Unless otherwise indicated, words should be given the meanings ordinarily ascribed to them and absurd results should be avoided. As we have stated before, the meaning of particular language found in insurance policies should be examined "in light of the business purposes sought to be achieved by the parties and the plain meaning of the words chosen by them to effect those purposes." Newmont Mines Ltd. v. Hanover Ins. Co., 784 F.2d 127, 135 (2d Cir. 1986) (internal citations omitted).

Whether a contract is ambiguous is a question of law for a court to determine as a threshold matter. As noted by the district court, an ambiguity exists where a contract term "could suggest 'more than one meaning when viewed objectively by a reasonably intelligent person who has examined the context of the entire integrated agreement and who is cognizant of the customs, practices, usages and terminology as generally understood in the particular trade or business.' " Morgan Stanley Group Inc. v. New England Ins. Co., 225 F.3d 270, 275 (2d Cir. 2000) (internal quotation marks omitted). Moreover, "a contract may be ambiguous when applied to one set of facts but not another. Therefore, ambiguity is detected claim by claim." Id. at 278.

Once a court finds that a contract is ambiguous, it may look to extrinsic evidence to determine the parties' intended meaning. See id. at 275–76. If factfinding is necessary to determine the parties' intent, however, the matter must be submitted to the finder of fact. See id. at 279.

1. Applicability of Extrinsic Evidence

The first argument made by the Silverstein Parties invokes the doctrine that "whether an ambiguity exists must be ascertained from the face of an agreement without regard to extrinsic evidence," Reiss v. Fin. Performance Corp., 97 N.Y.2d 195, 764 N.E.2d 958, 961, 738 N.Y.S.2d 658 (N.Y. 2001) (internal quotation marks); see also Md. Cas. Co. v. W.R. Grace & Co., 23 F.3d 617, 625 (2d Cir. 1993) ("Interpretation of unambiguous contract language does not bring extrinsic evidence into play."). This argument fails because it is based on the faulty premise that the September 14 Travelers policy rather than the Travelers binder governs the parties' obligations. While New York law is clear that extrinsic evidence may not be used to contradict clearly unambiguous language contained in an insurance binder, see Am. Sur. Co. v. Patriotic Assurance Co., 242 N.Y. 54, 150 N.E. 599, 601 (N.Y. 1926) (holding that it was error to admit extrinsic evidence to contradict unambiguous description of location in insurance binder), it is just as well settled in New York that extrinsic evidence is admissible to determine the parties' intentions with respect to the incomplete and unintegrated terms of a binder. See, e.g., Underwood v. Greenwich Ins. Co., 161 N.Y. 413, 55 N.E. 936, 938–39 (N.Y. 1900) (holding that because binder was not "in and of itself, . . . such a complete and perfect instrument that it embodied all the mutual stipulations of the parties . . . [it] was open to explanation by parol proof as to the intention of the parties, and the established custom of the business''); see also Thomas v. Scutt, 127 N.Y. 133, 27 N.E. 961, 962–63 (N.Y. 1891) (noting that exception to general rule that parol evidence is inadmissible to contradict a written contract is where ''the written instrument, [though] existing and valid, . . . [is] incomplete, either obviously, or at least possibly, and . . . parol evidence [is admitted], not to contradict or vary, but to complete, the entire agreement, of which the writing is only a part''). Indeed, the Silverstein Parties have relied on this exception to the parol evidence rule in the context of their disputes with other insurers. See, e.g., SR Int'l Bus. Ins. Co. v. World Trade Ctr. Props. LLC, 2003 U.S. Dist. LEXIS 1843, 2003 WL 289600, at *1 (S.D.N.Y. Feb 11, 2003) (agreeing with the Silverstein Parties that question of whether defendant-insurer Zurich's binder ''provided coverage on a 'per occurrence' basis [could] not be resolved without resort to extrinsic evidence''); Appellants' Rule 54(b) Br. at 2–3 (arguing that due to the fact that ''binders are a species of temporary, unintegrated contracts,'' a court must resort to extrinsic evidence of industry usage and custom to discern the expectations of the parties, particularly where, as here, the binders are ''not remotely unambiguous''). In fact, in their brief appealing the district court's grants of summary judgment in the Rule 54(b) appeal, the Silverstein Parties take the clear position that the parol evidence rule does not come into play at all when dealing with unintegrated contracts, such as appellees' binders. Rather, extrinsic evidence is ''admissible to supply the terms that the parties intended to incorporate into their agreement.'' Saxon Capital v. Wilvin Assocs., 195 A.D.2d 429, 600 N.Y.S.2d 708, 709 (1st Dep't 1993); see also Bourne v. Walt Disney, 68 F.3d 621, 627–28 (2d Cir. 1995). And, in such circumstances, ''summary judgment does not lie'' unless the extrinsic evidence itself is so one-sided as to negate the existence of a triable issue of fact. Lowell v. Twin Disc, 527 F.2d 767, 770 (2d Cir. 1975); see also Saxon Capital, 600 N.Y.S.2d at 709.

Appellants' Rule 54(b) Br. at 77. We agree with this statement of the law, which fully applies to the Travelers binder.

2. Custom and Usage

The Silverstein Parties' next contention, that the undefined term ''occurrence'' is not ambiguous because it is typical for insurance policies not to define ''occurrence'' and, further, that the WilProp definition is ''atypically broad,'' is undercut by the policy forms of the two other WTC insurers who provided their own forms for coverage, each of which defined occurrence. IRI issued a binder expressly incorporating its own policy form, which defines ''loss arising out of one Occurrence'' as ''the sum total of all loss or damage insured against arising out of or caused by one event.'' Allianz, in the only final policy to issue before September 11, 2001, defined occurrence in language similar to the WilProp definition: ''any one loss, disaster or casualty, or series of losses, disasters or casualties arising out of one event.''

In addition, in order to demonstrate the ambiguity of the undefined term ''occurrence,'' Travelers has proffered evidence of industry custom and usage concerning the meaning of occurrence that differs from the definition asserted by the Silverstein Parties. For example, a Willis forms specialist testified that she did not believe that the WilProp form definition of an occurrence as, inter alia, losses attributable to "one series of similar causes" deviated from the commonly understood meaning of "occurrence." Similarly, Daniel McCrudden, an underwriter at Travelers, testified that "it's recognized that multiple causes of loss can be involved in a single occurrence, and it's recognized that all loss arising out of an overriding cause or group of causes is considered a single occurrence. It's never been a question."

Although the Silverstein Parties argue that it was improper for the district court to consider such evidence of custom and usage in deciding whether the policy is ambiguous, we have specifically instructed courts to consider the "customs, practices, usages and terminology as generally understood in the particular trade or business" in identifying ambiguity within a contract. Int'l Multifoods Corp. v. Commercial Union Ins. Co., 309 F.3d 76, 83 (2d Cir. 2002) (quoting Morgan Stanley Group, 225 F.3d at 275). And New York courts have long held that such evidence is admissible for purposes of construing an insurance binder. See, e.g., Underwood, 55 N.E. at 937 (holding that binder "was open to explanation by parol proof as to ... the established custom of the business").

3. Meaning of Occurrence under New York Law

Finally, the Silverstein Parties assert that the mere fact that the word "occurrence" was not defined in the binder is not enough to render it ambiguous. They contend that in the absence of a definition in the binder, a court seeking to construe the meaning of "occurrence" must first turn to well established New York precedent. If there is a clear and uniform meaning of the term under the law, they argue, then a court must reject a claim of ambiguity and apply that definition. This argument fails because its underlying premise—that there is a uniform meaning of "occurrence" under New York law—is erroneous.

The Silverstein Parties maintain that under New York law, there is but one meaning of "occurrence," which is the direct, physical cause of a loss and not more remote causes. This definition is so accepted and well settled, they contend, that it must be implied into the Travelers binder as a matter of law. Applying this definition to the facts of this case, it follows that because the destruction of the WTC was the result of two physical impacts from two separate planes, there were two occurrences as a matter of law.

To support their argument, the Silverstein Parties rely on a string of authorities beginning with Arthur A. Johnson Corp. v. Indem. Ins. Co., 7 N.Y.2d 222, 164 N.E.2d 704, 196 N.Y.S.2d 678 (N.Y. 1959). In Arthur A. Johnson, the court considered whether there was one or two accidents within the meaning of a third-party liability insurance policy where two separate walls constructed by the same insured contractors in two adjacent buildings collapsed 50 minutes apart during the course of an unusually heavy rainfall and caused flooding within the buildings. The insurer argued that there was only one occurrence because all the damage was ultimately caused by the heavy rainfall. In rejecting this argument, the court started from the premise that in determining the number of accidents, it must consider "the 'reasonable expectation and purpose of the ordinary business man when making an ordinary business contract.' " Id. at 706 (quoting Bird v. St. Paul Fire & Marine Ins. Co., 224 N.Y. 47, 120 N.E. 86, 87 (N.Y. 1918)). The court then held that "the term [accident] is to be used in its common sense of an event of an unfortunate character that takes place without one's foresight or expectation . . . that is, an unexpected, unfortunate occurrence." Id. at 707 (internal quotation marks and emphasis omitted). Reviewing the facts before it, the court concluded that there had been two separate accidents on the rationale that the walls that collapsed belonged to separate buildings, there was no indication that the flooding in the first building would have caused the flooding in the second building in the absence of a second defective wall, and the two walls collapsed almost an hour apart. Id. at 708.

Because Arthur A. Johnson and nearly all of the other cases relied on by the Silverstein Parties to provide the definition of "occurrence" are third-party liability insurance cases, however, they involve different interests, both public and private, than first-party property insurance cases such as the instant case. See generally Great N. Ins. Co. v. Mount Vernon Fire Ins. Co., 92 N.Y.2d 682, 708 N.E.2d 167, 170, 685 N.Y.S.2d 411 (N.Y. 1999) ("Wholly different interests are protected by first-party coverage and third-party coverage."); see also Port Auth. v. Affiliated FM Ins. Co., 311 F.3d 226, 233 (3d Cir. 2002) (finding third-party definitions of contract terms unhelpful in first-party context because of "the fundamental differences between liability policies and first-party contracts"). For example, for third-party liability policies, there is no reason to look any further back in the chain of causation than to the insured's acts of negligence, because it is the insured's negligence that triggers liability. See, e.g., In re Prudential Lines Inc., 158 F.3d 65, 80–81 (2d Cir. 1998) (holding, in third-party liability context, that "courts should look to the event for which the insured is held liable," regardless of whether it is the physical impact closest in time) (internal quotation marks and emphasis omitted); Stonewall Ins. Co. v. Asbestos Claims Mgmt. Corp., 73 F.3d 1178, 1213–14 (2d Cir. 1995) (same), modified on other grounds, 85 F.3d 49 (2d Cir. 1996). Thus, the approach taken by courts reviewing the number of occurrences in the context of third-party liability—such as the court's focus in Arthur A. Johnson on the separate wall collapses rather than the rain—makes sense for such policies because the insured is held liable only for its own negligence and not for the act of nature that may have been the initiating cause. See Arthur A. Johnson, 164 N.E.2d at 708 ("Here the proximate cause cannot be said to be the heavy rainfall but separate negligent acts of preparing and constructing separate walls which, for all we know, may have been built at separate times by separate groups of workmen.").

In addition, construction of the term "occurrence" in a liability insurance context is influenced by the public policy concern of ensuring adequate compensation for injured third-parties who are not parties to the insurance contract, and, perforce, played no role in negotiating its terms. See Affiliated FM Ins. Co., 311 F.3d at 233. It is no surprise, therefore, that a salient characteristic of the third-party liability cases relied on by the Silverstein Parties is that each one involved multiple liability claims filed against the insured by multiple parties. See, e.g., In re Prudential Lines, 158 F.3d at 68 (liability on multiple asbestos claims); Stonewall Ins., 73 F.3d at 1187 (liability on thousands of asbestos claims); Travelers Cas. & Sur. Co. v. Certain Underwriters at Lloyd's of London, 96 N.Y.2d 583, 760 N.E.2d 319, 322, 734 N.Y.S.2d 531 (N.Y. 2001) (liability claims involving decades of commercial activities at numerous industrial and waste disposal sites); Hartford Accident & Indem. Co. v. Wesolowski, 33 N.Y.2d 169, 305 N.E.2d 907, 908, 350 N.Y.S.2d 895 (N.Y. 1973) (car liability insurance where insured struck two different cars); Arthur A. Johnson, 164 N.E.2d at 704 (liability for destruction of retaining walls of two buildings owned by different owners). And the "test" that the Silverstein Parties argues is universally applicable in all insurance contexts was described by the Arthur A. Johnson court as applying "in a given set of circumstances when the damage is to several persons." Arthur A. Johnson, 164 N.E.2d at 706 (emphasis added). In such cases, of course, a finding of a separate occurrence as to each claimant ensures compensation for the injured third parties. See Affiliated FM Ins. Co., 311 F.3d at 233.

In a first-party property case, by contrast, the insured's negligence is not at issue; rather, the policy insures against external perils such as fires, floods, and intentional acts that cause damage to the insured's property, and against which a property interest holder can take adequate measures to protect his investment in advance of any loss. See Newmont Mines, 784 F.2d at 136 ("The goal of such a [first-party] policy, simply stated, is to provide financial protection against damage to property."). As a result of these differences, a court's construction of the undefined term "occurrence," or the synonymous term "accident," as intended by the parties for use in the third-party context is not necessarily applicable in the context of first-party property insurance.

We also find it noteworthy that while the Silverstein Parties assert that Arthur A. Johnson "provides the applicable legal test for determining number of occurrences," they do not try to apply that case's definition to the facts of this case. Instead, they assert that "the governing test under 'well-established precedent' under New York law is to look to the immediate, efficient, physical cause of the loss, and not to some indirect or remote cause of causes." The Silverstein Parties' source for this rule appears to be some New York cases that have applied a similar rule to determine causation in the context of whether an exclusionary clause applies to a loss. See, e.g., Album Realty Corp. v. Am. Home Assurance Co., 80 N.Y.2d 1008, 607 N.E.2d 804, 805, 592 N.Y.S.2d 657 (N.Y. 1992) (applying "proximate, efficient and dominant cause" test to hold that covered risk of water damage, which was caused by frozen pipes, rather than excluded risk of freezing, was cause of loss); but see Tonkin v. Cal. Ins. Co., 294 N.Y. 326, 62 N.E.2d 215, 216–17 (N.Y. 1945) (applying proximate cause test to hold that covered risk of fire, rather than excluded risk of collision was cause of loss, where blinding smoke from fire caused driver to collide with another car). But no New York case of which we are aware has set forth such a test for purposes of determining the number of occurrences that comprise a loss.

The test actually enunciated by Johnson and its progeny in the third-party liability context is considerably more nuanced:

> We have expressed the rule of these cases as follows: "In determining the number of occurrences for deductible purposes, New York inquires whether multiple claims result from 'an event of an unfortunate character that takes place without one's foresight or expectation.' ... Although a single 'occurrence' may give rise to multiple claims, courts should look to the event for which the insured is held liable, not some point further back in the causal chain." In re Prudential Lines, 158 F.3d at 80 (quoting Stonewall Ins., 73 F.3d at 1213).

Even if we were to accept the Silverstein Parties' contention that this statement sets forth the uniform and well settled definition of "occurrence" under New York law, its application to the facts before us would not establish as a matter of law whether the events of September 11th were one or two occurrences. For example, what, precisely, is the "event" here for which insurance coverage is being sought? In the context of third-party liability insurance—the type of insurance at issue in Arthur A. Johnson—the "event" is the insured's negligence. According to the Silverstein Parties, under the insurance with Travelers, "the 'event' that triggers coverage ... is 'direct physical loss or damage' to property." This wording traces the language contained in the Travelers form upon which the Travelers binder was issued, which provides that

> the Company will pay for direct physical loss or damage to Covered Property at premises ..., caused by or resulting from a Covered Cause of Loss. Covered Cause of Loss means risks of direct physical loss unless the loss is excluded in Section D., Exclusions; limited in Section E., Limitations; or excluded or limited in the Supplemental Coverage Declarations or by endorsements.

A jury construing this language, however, could reasonably conclude that the "event" that triggers coverage is the Covered Cause of Loss, rather than the damage itself. It also could find that the cause of the destruction of the WTC was either the individual impacts caused by each plane or a single coordinated terrorist attack. The latter cause, Travelers argues in its opposition to summary judgment, was a Covered Cause of Loss expressly specified in the Underwriting Submission and, thus, intended by the parties to be covered by the policy. In fact, a jury could find that the words "direct physical loss or damage" does not refer to the "event" that triggers coverage at all, but rather sets forth the scope of the damage resulting from the "event" that the insurer will pay for, namely, direct physical damage as distinct from remote or incidental damage.

In any event, we are not called upon here to decide whether there was one occurrence or two in this case, only whether the district court properly concluded that because there is no well settled definition of the term "occurrence" under New York law, the Travelers binder was sufficiently ambiguous to preclude summary judgment and to permit the factfinder to consider extrinsic evidence of the parties' intent.

We think the case most directly on point is our decision in Newmont Mines, the only first-party property insurance case cited by the Silverstein Parties that addresses the meaning of "occurrence." 784 F.2d at 135–37. In that case, we were "not persuaded ... [by defendants] that the term 'occurrence' has obtained any ... specialized or singular meaning in the context of property insurance," and we interpreted both Arthur A. Johnson and Wesolowski as "rejecting any single definition of occurrence." Id. at 136. Our conclusion, at bottom, was that "the meaning of 'occurrence' must be interpreted in the context of the specific policy and facts of the case." Id. at 136 n.9.

In Newmont Mines, a heavy accumulation of snow caused two separate parts of a roof to collapse several days apart, requiring two independent repairs. Id. at 129–31. We held that there was sufficient evidence to support the jury's verdict that the two partial losses constituted two occurrences under the policies. Id. at 137. We also upheld the instruction given to the jury on the meaning of occurrence:

> it is for you to decide whether or not the losses which are alleged to have occurred or the loss that's alleged to have occurred in this case was the result of a single, continuous event or incident, or whether or not it was the result of two separate incidents. If you find that the collapse of the two sections of the roof was a single, continuous event or incident, then the collapse constituted a single occurrence—and there would be only one loss. If, on the other hand, you find that the collapse of the two sections of the roof constituted separate events or incidents that were not causally related, then of course you would have two separate losses. Id. at 134.

We held that the instruction was proper on the rationale that given the goals of first-party property insurance, "the parties ... must have intended to provide coverage for property damage each time it occurred unexpectedly and without design, unless the damage occurring at one point in time was merely part of a single, continuous event that already had caused other damage." Id. at 136.

Notwithstanding the express statements to the contrary in our decision, see id. at 135–36 & n.8. (rejecting any one definition of "occurrence" and stating that "the meaning of 'occurrence' must be interpreted in the context of the specific policy and facts of the case"), the Silverstein Parties contend that Newmont Mines sets forth "the rule of law" with respect to the meaning of "occurrence" in the context of first-party property insurance, and that this rule favors them. However, even if we were to agree with the Silverstein Parties that the approved jury instruction and our separate definition of "occurrence" are applicable to this case (a question we need not and do not reach), the one thing Newmont Mines makes certain is that the question of how many occurrences the events of September 11th constituted is a question properly left to the fact-finder. To be sure, a jury could find two occurrences in this case, as it did in Newmont Mines, or it could find that the terrorist attack, although manifested in two separate airplane crashes, was a single, continuous, planned event causing a continuum of damage that resulted in the total destruction of the WTC, and, thus, was a single occurrence. Instead of supporting the Silverstein Parties' argument that New York law mandates a finding of two occurrences under the Travelers binder as a matter of law, Newmont Mines confirms our belief that in a first-party property insurance case, the meaning of the undefined term "occurrence" is an open question as to which reasonable finders of fact could reach different conclusions.

Accordingly, we conclude that given the significant distinction between first-party and third-party insurance policies, the fact-specific nature of the inquiry, and the fact that it is the parties' intent that controls, the district court properly concluded that the meaning of "occurrence" in the Travelers binder is sufficiently ambiguous under New York law to preclude summary judgment and to warrant consideration by the fact finder of extrinsic evidence to determine the parties' intentions. We therefore affirm the denial of summary judgment against Travelers.

CONCLUSION

For the foregoing reasons, we affirm the judgments of the district court.

Notes

1. Should doctrines such as *contra proferentum* and reasonable expectations that protect powerless policyholders also apply to sophisticated insureds which have a great deal of bargaining power vis-a-vis insurance agencies? Courts have often rejected or substantially modified the ambiguity principle when the insured was a sophisticated party. See Jeffrey Stempel, *Reassessing the "Sophisticated" Policyholder Defense in Insurance Coverage Litigation*, 42 DRAKE L. REV. 807, 832 (1993). Professor Stempel cites several cases in which courts both reject and uphold an ambiguity analysis (see Eagle Leasing Corp. v. Hartford Fire Ins. Co., 540 F.2d 1257, 1261 (5th Cir.1976): "We do not feel compelled to apply ... the general rule that an insurance policy is construed against the insurer in the commercial insurance field when the insured is not an innocent but a corporation of immense size.... "; but see General Ins. Co. v. City of Belvedere, 582 F.Supp. 88, 89–90 (N.D.Cal. 1984), ruling in favor of the policyholder's claim that the exclusion clause was ambiguous and rejecting the insurer's invitation to

apply a variant of the sophisticated policyholder defense: "Language in the policy is to be construed as a layman would read it, not as an attorney or insurance agent might read it.... [The insurer's] further contention that ... the City of Belvedere should be held to a higher standard of knowledge or sophistication concerning interpretation of terms in insurance policies is unsupported by California case law.... ").

Professor Stempel takes a more moderate view regarding the application of the sophisticated policyholder's defense. He rejects an unwavering focus on the sophistication, wealth, or other attributes of the policyholder and encourages courts to consider several other factors in determining what variation of contract law should control an insurance coverage dispute. These include: a determination as to whether the sophisticated policyholder is merely adhering to a contract of adhesion or is a co-drafter of the policy, the presence and activity of a broker and/or attorney, examination of actual ambiguity in the disputed term (placing the sophisticated policyholder on a higher pedestal than a consumer policyholder), and the presence of any objectively reasonable expectations of or reasonable reliance upon coverage. See Stempel, 42 DRAKE L. REV. at 853.

2. Despite the hue and cry regarding an insured's lack of bargaining power in defining the terms of insurance policies, standardization of policies is an important consideration. See Wondie Russell, Barry S. Levin & Celia M. Jackson, *Insurance Policy Construction and the Non Sequitur of the "Sophisticated Insured,"* 3 ENVIRONMENTAL CLAIMS J. 3 (1990).

3. In *Ponder v. Blue Cross of Southern California*, 145 Cal.App.3d 709, 193 Cal.Rptr. 632 (1983), Mrs. Ponder purchased a "High Option Performance Plan" insurance policy that specifically excluded coverage for "temporo-mandibular joint syndrome," which the policy listed under a dental care exclusion. Mrs. Ponder was diagnosed with the syndrome, but not by a dentist.

Without finding it necessary to determine if temporo-mandibular joint syndrome was ambiguous, the court held that "understandability" was required. Relying on the adhesive nature of the relationship, the court focused on whether the language of the exclusion was (1) conspicuous, (2) plain and clear, and (3) whether the exclusion would disappoint the reasonable expectations of the insured.

The court concluded that the exclusion would not apply to Mrs. Ponder. It found that the term was not conspicuous because it was not in a section with a highlighted or bold-faced heading, and the ordinary meaning of the "dental" heading would not encompass the condition in the exclusion. The court further found that the term was not plain and clear, in part because it was not part of the ordinary vocabulary of laypersons and because Blue Cross chose to provide plain language translations for other technical medical terms but not for temporo-mandibular joint syndrome. Given that the policy implied all-inclusive coverage, the court also noted that Mrs. Ponder would have an expectation that a condition like temporo-mandibular joint syndrome would be covered.

4. *A duty to explain?* In the course of the *Ponder* opinion it is stated that "there is nothing in the record * * * indicating that anyone from Blue Cross attempted to explain the plain language meaning of temporo-mandibu-

lar joint syndrome to appellant or her husband before they accepted the contract." Is this a suggestion that an insurer has an affirmative duty to sit down and explain the existence and meaning of all coverage provisions that might conceivably escape the comprehension of the applicant? Such a proposal appears from time to time in the cases and at least on one occasion has received short-lived judicial approval. In 1974, an intermediate appellate court laid down the following rule in *Hionis v. Northern Mutual Ins. Co.*, 230 Pa.Super. 511, 327 A.2d 363:

> "Even where a policy is written in unambiguous terms, the burden of establishing the applicability of the exclusion or limitation involves proof that the insured was aware of the exclusion or limitation and that the effect thereof was explained to him."

However, reservations and doubts also began surfacing as to the practical application and the unfairness of imposing an essentially unsustainable burden of proof—although the "Hionis Rule" did allow two exceptions: (1) where the parties were of equal bargaining power and (2) where the facts demonstrated that the insured clearly understood the terms of the exclusion independent of any explanation offered by the insurer.

The doubts were articulated in *Standard Venetian Blind Co. v. American Empire Insurance Co.*, 503 Pa. 300, 469 A.2d 563 (1983), in which the Pennsylvania Supreme Court said:

> "Venetian maintains that this Court should adopt this language [of *Hionis*] as a rule of insurance law, as the Superior Court has done here and in other cases decided since *Hionis*. [citations omitted]
>
> "We believe that the burden imposed by *Hionis* fails to accord proper significance to the written contract, which has historically been the true test of parties' intentions. By focusing on what was and was not said at the time of contract formation rather than on the parties' writing, *Hionis* makes the question of the scope of insurance coverage in any given case depend upon how a factfinder resolves questions of credibility.... Thus, *Hionis,* which would permit an insured to avoid the application of a clear and unambiguous limitation clause in an insurance contract, is not to be followed." 503 Pa. 300, 306, 469 A.2d 563, 566–67.

But see *Tonkovic v. State Farm Mutual Automobile Insurance Co.*, 513 Pa. 445, 521 A.2d 920 (1987) a 5–2 decision in which the dissenters objected, in effect, to the limitation of *Standard Venetian*.

5. *A duty to explain?—another view.* The late Professor Alan Widiss believed that insurers are obligated to inform insureds about all coverages which afford an insured a right of indemnification, actions needed to preserve rights, and collateral rights. He justified this obligation on the basis of contract, good faith and fair dealing, reasonable expectations, and the avoidance of fraud. Alan I. Widiss, *Obligating Insurers to Inform Insureds About the Existence of Rights and Duties Regarding Coverage for Losses*, 1 CONN. INS. L.J. 67 (1995).

6. "Plain and clear" meaning problems are not limited to technical or medical language. Consider whether the use of the word "nil" in a policy plainly and clearly meant that certain medical expense coverage was omitted. See Read v. Western Farm Bureau Mutual Insurance Co., 90 N.M. 369,

563 P.2d 1162 (App.1977). If "nil" fails the "plain and clear" test because it is a word not ordinarily used in common speech, then does it follow *a fortiori* that "discrimination" fails the test?

7. Notwithstanding an insurer's diligent attempts to achieve clarity in the writing of policies, ambiguities, or at least uncertainties, will arise. For example, the New Mexico Supreme Court consolidated on appeal two cases involving contract language that modified the colloquial definitions of "spouse" in one case and "relative" in the other, based on where such a person "lived with" the insured. In each case, the same insurer interpreted "lived with" differently to deny coverage, thus providing the best evidence that the language was ambiguous. Loya v. State Farm Mutual Insurance Company and Smyth v. State Farm Mutual Automobile Insurance Company, 119 N.M. 1, 3, 7, 888 P.2d 447 (1994).

In the *Loya* case, the insured married couple had purchased uninsured motorist coverage for the two cars they owned. After the policy had been issued, the couple separated and Mr. Loya moved out of the marital residence. A few months later, at a meeting to discuss the divorce, Mrs. Loya ran over Mr. Loya with one of the insured cars, seriously injuring him. Mr. Loya sought to recover on the policy on his wife's car, arguing that he was covered because he was a "spouse" of the named insured (Mrs. Loya).

State Farm denied coverage, arguing that Mr. Loya was not a "spouse" because he didn't currently "live with" the insured, even though he slept with and ate meals with his wife during the separation period. In finding for Mr. Loya the court held that Mr. Loya "had a reasonable expectation of coverage during the whole policy period ... [and] the policy did not contain any warnings that separation could result in forfeiture of coverage.... " *Id.* at 5–6.

In the *Smyth* case, Mr. Smyth purchased liability and uninsured motorist coverage. An "Amendatory Endorsement" separate from the policy stated that "relative" was defined in part as one who "lives with you". Id. at 7. Mr. Smyth shared legal and physical custody of his son Sean with his ex-wife. While Sean was temporarily living with his mother, he was seriously injured in a car accident, and the family sought to recover on Mr. Smyth's policy.

State Farm denied coverage, saying that Sean did not meet the policy definition of "relative" because he no longer lived with Mr. Smyth. The court held that Sean was covered under the policy in part because the word "relative" has a common and generally understood meaning. Id. at 8. The court also noted that the terms "spouse" and "relative" were ambiguous because in both cases the unique definitions were located on separate pages and required "a party seeking insurance to untangle a web of provisions and related definitions in order to determine who the policy actually covers." Id. at 8.

Summing up the two cases, the court stated "State Farm argues that in the Loya policy, 'while living with' means that the individual must be actually and currently living in fact with the named insured on a daily basis [yet] ... [i]t argues that in the Smyth policy, however, the phrase 'who lives with' means only that the individual must provide some 'indication that he resides with his father at all.' Because State Farm has used language that may be ambiguously applied, it is able to argue both ways. It is exactly this kind of uncertainty of coverage that our rules requiring strict construction against the insurer and in favor of coverage are intended to guard against." Id. at 9.

Human imperfections in communication make it unlikely that arguments relating to the meaning of expression will ever cease. E.g., McHugh v. United Service Automobile Assn., 164 F.3d 451 (9th Cir.1999) (a saturated soil mass was a covered "mudslide" and not an excluded "landslide").

8. *A Duty to Read?* In *Morta v. Korea*, 840 F.2d 1452 (9th Cir.1988), the court considered whether a release signed by the plaintiff bars recovery for injuries discovered after the release was signed. Plaintiff, who was injured in a car accident in Guam, signed an agreement releasing the other driver's insurance company from further liability in exchange for $900. After he was given the proposed settlement agreement but before he signed the agreement, Morta consulted a lawyer who told him that he was unlikely to recover much more than that amount. Morta signed the agreement, and within a week discovered further injuries (dizziness, etc.) which he believed were related to the accident. Morta filed suit against the insurance company and challenged the validity of the release. At the close of the trial, the defendant insurer's motion for a directed verdict was denied and the jury returned a verdict for Morta finding that the release was invalid. The verdict was affirmed by the Appellate Division of the District of Guam, and the insurer appealed to the Ninth Circuit.

In the opinion, written by Judge Kozinski, the Ninth Circuit found that no evidence presented at trial supported Morta's theories of fraud, mistake, or undue influence. The court found that the Superior Court erred in not directing a verdict for the insurer. The court discussed the sanctity of contract and the freedom of the parties to make a bad bargain before stating: "[p]arties can never be sure about what the future will bring; they sign contracts for the very purpose of guarding against unforeseen contingencies. Morta freely entered into a settlement that specifically released unknown claims for latent or progressive personal injuries." Id. at p. 1460. Therefore, there was no duty on the part of the insurance company to discuss with Morta all the implications of signing the release.

Compare *Casey v. Proctor*, 59 Cal.2d 97, 28 Cal.Rptr. 307, 378 P.2d 579 (1963), which held that a "general" release of an insurance company from liability in a car accident did not bar a later claim for personal injuries resulting from the accident, because there was no negotiation surrounding the signing of the release and the injuries were unknown at the time the releaser signed the release.

B. WAIVER, ESTOPPEL AND OTHER THEORIES

FOREMOST INSURANCE CO. v. PUTZIER [INCLUDING EVEL KNIEVEL]

Supreme Court of Idaho, 1980.
100 Idaho 883, 606 P.2d 987.

DONALDSON, CHIEF JUSTICE.

This action arose in connection with the events surrounding the September 9, 1974 attempt by Robert C. Knievel, a/k/a Evel Knievel, to jump the Snake River Canyon near Twin Falls, Idaho on a jet powered motorcycle. As a prerequisite to his use of the land required for the event, Knievel and Snake River Enterprises, Inc. (the entity by which Knievel undertook the event) were required to secure a land use permit from the State of Idaho and a license from Twin Falls County.

* * *

[Both the State and the County permits required Knievel to obtain liability insurance under which the State and County would receive protection.]

* * *

For the purpose of obtaining the insurance required by the permit and license, Knievel's attorneys entered into negotiations with one Cardell Smith, a vice-president of the Fidelity Marketing Corporation insurance brokerage. * * * These negotiations culminated in the issuance by Foremost Insurance Company to Knievel and Enterprises of an insurance policy, which policy was later superseded by a second policy, effective August 28, 1974. Attached near the middle of the 29 separate pages of the second policy was an exclusion designated G332 which provided:

> "It is agreed that the insurance does not apply to bodily injury or property damage arising out of riot, civil commotion or mob action or out of any act or omission in connection with the prevention or suppression of any of the foregoing."

There was conflicting testimony as to whether this was read by or discussed with Knievel's attorneys.

Knievel attempted the jump September 4, 1974. During the preceding day or two, numerous unknown individuals damaged or destroyed the goods and equipment of Harold Putzier and Bob Crandall, each of whom was a concessionaire at the time. Putzier and Crandall filed an action against Knievel and Enterprises to recover compensation for their damages. [Foremost responded with a suit for declaratory judgment that the exclusion barred recovery on the policy.] The trial court held the exclusion valid in all respects; that the damage sustained by Putzier and Crandall fell within the exclusion, thereby relieving Foremost of liability for the damage. * * * We affirm.

The first issue presented is whether the trial court erred in finding the exclusion valid and applicable, thereby defeating appellants' claim of policy coverage. Appellants initially contend the parties entered into a valid contract for comprehensive general liability coverage prior to the issuance of the policy itself. In their view, the exclusion in the subsequently issued policy was at variance with the contract earlier negotiated, and therefore constituted a modification to which there was no agreement. Respondent Foremost agrees that a contract for liability coverage was negotiated by its agent and Knievel's attorneys. However, the parties are in sharp disagreement on the question whether the riot exclusion was at odds with the coverage for which Knievel bargained. Foremost contends, and the trial court found, that before August 28, 1979 [sic] (the effective date of the coverage), all exclusions, including the riot exclusion, were read to Knievel's attorney over the telephone and a general discussion was had concerning the athletic, medical malpractice, and pollution exclusions. A week later, a meeting was had between Foremost's agent and Knievel's attorneys. At this meeting, the insurance agent inquired of one of Knievel's attorneys whether he was familiar with the policy and whether there were any questions concerning it. Knievel's attorney advised that the policy had been reviewed and that he had no questions about it. Discussion was then had on the procedures to be used in processing claims covered by the policy. No dissatisfaction with the policy was expressed until after the event. Foremost's agent testified that the riot exclusion was common to comprehensive general liability policies written for special events, and that removal of the exclusion could be had only upon payment of an additional premium. Knievel's insurance expert testified on direct examination that a standard comprehensive general liability policy would not contain such an exclusion. However, it was brought out on cross-examination that he had never written such a policy and did not deal in the type of coverage involved here. Based on the evidence before it, the trial court concluded the written policy, together with the four exclusions attached thereto, accurately reflected the agreement of the parties. Nothing in the record compels a different conclusion here.

Appellants next attack the validity of the exclusion on the ground it was in contravention of the public policy of this state. They contend that by requiring Knievel to maintain "comprehensive public liability insurance" as a condition precedent to the validity of the temporary land use permit issued to him, the State of Idaho, through the Department of Lands, has articulated a policy which precludes recognition of the riot exclusion. We disagree. An agreement voluntarily made between competent persons is not lightly to be set aside on public policy grounds. Whether the contract is against public policy is to be determined from all the facts and circumstances of each case. Stearns v. Williams, 72 Idaho 276, 240 P.2d 833 (1952). In our view, the requirement of the land use permit that Knievel carry comprehensive public liability coverage falls far short of any declaration of public policy against exclusions for damage occasioned by riot, civil commotion, or mob action. Nor do we find the exclusion inimical to any articulable public interest. Accordingly, we decline to hold the exclusion void as against public policy.

It is next argued the doctrine of estoppel should be applied to prevent Foremost from raising the exclusion at all. However, the purpose of the doctrine in insurance cases is to enforce the contract as originally agreed upon by the parties, and not to write a new contract. Lewis v. Continental Life and Accident Co., 93 Idaho 348, 461 P.2d 243 (1969). As we pointed out above, the trial court found, on substantial and competent evidence, that Knievel's attorneys were made aware of the exclusion before the effective date of coverage, and made no comment or inquiry concerning it. From this, it was proper for the court to conclude the policy, with the exclusions, represented the agreement of the parties. The doctrine of estoppel is inapplicable here.

In a related argument, appellants contend the doctrine of reformation should be applied to write the exclusion out of the policy. However, reformation is inapplicable where, as here, the writing is a true expression of the parties' agreement. See Bilbao v. Krettinger, 91 Idaho 69, 415 P.2d 712 (1966).

Appellants also urge application of the doctrine of reasonable expectations. The thorn of Corgatelli v. Globe Life & Accident Ins. Co., 96 Idaho 616, 533 P.2d 737 (1975), which made the adoption of that doctrine in Idaho a debatable question, was recently removed from the side of our jurisprudence. Casey v. Highlands, 100 Idaho 505, 600 P.2d 1387 (1979), decided after this appeal was brought, expressly rejected the doctrine of reasonable expectations in favor of traditional contract rules of construction. We therefore reject appellants' contention that the doctrine of reasonable expectations should be applied here.

Appellants next contend the exclusion must fall because it was inconspicuous and ambiguous. Both contentions are without merit. We need not discuss the question whether the exclusion was inconspicuous, and if it was what effect such a determination would have, because Knievel's attorneys were expressly made aware of its existence prior to the effective date of the coverage. Nor do we find any basis for the contention that the language used in the exclusion is subject to more than a single, plain meaning.

Finally appellants contend respondent Foremost failed to carry its burden of proving the damage sustained was caused by activity specified in the exclusion. We disagree. In the absence of ambiguity, the words used in an insurance policy are to be given their plain, ordinary and popular meaning. * * * The trial court entered the following findings of fact concerning the activities here involved:

> "12. An estimated ten to fifteen thousand people congested at the jump site on September 7, 1975, and sometime after dark some of the people present knocked down a number of temporary toilets or 'outhouses' and others, riding motorcycles, jumped over the downed toilets. At about the same time several hundred of the people present surrounded a large semi-trailer, and members of the crowd broke into it and removed its contents, consisting of cases of beer, which was distributed and drunk by a great number of those present.
>
> "13. Shortly after the beer was removed from the semi-trailer referred [to] in Finding [12], the crowd moved over to another large semi-trailer, surrounded it, and members of the crowd broke a hole through its roof and removed its contents, consisting of beer, water-

melons, cantaloupes and meat, which was distributed to the people congregated thereabouts."

* * * [W]e conclude, as did the trial court, that the damages sustained by appellants Putzier and Crandall were caused by persons who formed or were part of a mob and arose out of civil commotion or mob action.

* * *

The judgment of the trial court is affirmed. Costs to respondent.

[Author's note—the following case makes a distinction between first party insurance and third party insurance. An explanation of the distinction appears at the beginning of Chapter 4.]

FOREMOST INSURANCE CO. v. PUTZIER [INCLUDING ANTONIO GUANCHE]

Supreme Court of Idaho, 1981.
102 Idaho 138, 627 P.2d 317.

BISTLINE, JUSTICE.

Antonio Guanche was named as a defendant in Civil Action No. 27353, Fifth Judicial District of the State of Idaho, which action produced two other appeals in addition to this. Those other two appeals, which were consolidated, were decided in Foremost Insurance Co. v. Putzier, 100 Idaho 883, 606 P.2d 987 (1980). In that opinion this Court upheld the trial court's determination as to the extent of *liability* coverage under the Foremost policy.

This appeal was taken by Foremost from the trial court's decision that Foremost is liable to Antonio Guanche, as a first party insured. The relationship of Foremost and Guanche is well stated in the trial court's findings of fact:

"Insofar as the issues framed by the complaint and defendant Guanche's answer to that complaint are involved in these proceedings, the following additional findings and conclusions are made.

"14. The defendant Antonio R. Guanche speaks English in a heavy French–Italian dialect, which makes communication in the English language difficult between Guanche and third parties. At all times material to this proceeding he was engaged as a chef and entrepreneur. He had permission of the defendant Snake River Canyon Enterprises to erect a food stand on the premises to be used in selling food and drink to the spectators attending the public spectacle. He was told by one Veccio, an agent of the defendants Knievel and Snake River Canyon Enterprises, that he was required to have insurance before he began the operation of his food concession, and that it was obtainable through the plaintiff. [Foremost]

"15. Sometime prior to August 28, 1977 [sic], the defendant Guanche delivered his check in the amount of $300 to Cardell W. Smith in return for insurance coverage. Guanche's $300 was accepted by Smith on behalf of the plaintiff, and Smith told Guanche that he was 'covered.' The record will not support any finding that Guanche ever advised plaintiff of the type or kind of insurance he desired, nor will it support a find [sic] that Guanche was ever advised by plaintiff as to the specific insurance coverage his $300 was purchasing. He has never been provided with any insurance policy. He has not read any insurance policy purporting to evidence his insurance contract with the plaintiff. He simply paid his money and was told that he was 'covered.'

"16. *The defendant Guanche intended to insure his property against loss caused by theft* or the elements, *and* at all times material to this action *believed that* upon payment of $300 to the plaintiff *the property* located at the jump site in which he had an interest *was insured* by plaintiff *against loss by theft,* fire or other calamity. *This belief was a reasonable belief under the facts in this case.*

"17. Sometime prior to September 7, 1974, the defendant Guanche had purchased, and had delivered to the jump site, a large truckload of provisions consisting of beer, melons, meat and ice cream. The activity described in Finding 13 involved property owned by the defendant Guanche.[19]" (Emphasis added.)

The trial court entered the following conclusions of law:

"F When the plaintiff accepted a premium from Guanche, it had a duty to provide him with the insurance policy or advise Guanche in detail of the risks it was assuming in return for the premium. Failure to do so makes Guanche's intentions and expectations paramount in interpreting the terms of any insurance contract existing between Guanche and the plaintiff.

"G *Under the theories expounded in* Corgatelli v. Globe Insurance, 96 Idaho 616 [533 P.2d 737], *a valid contract of insurance existed* between the plaintiff and the defendant Guanche, supported by ample consideration, *which provided Guanche with first party coverage* for loss of and damage to property in which Guanche had an interest, and which was located at the jump site between August 28, 1974 and September 10, 1974." (Emphasis added) * * *

"It is, therefore, ORDERED, ADJUDGED and DECREED that the defendant Antonio R. Guanche recover from the plaintiff Foremost Insurance Company $29,979.63 damages, together with his costs taxed at $3,746.10, and that the claims of Foremost against Guanche and Guanche against Foremost be severed from this action and the remainder of the case be proceeded with according to law."

* * *

19. Finding No. 13:

"Shortly after the beer was removed from the semi-trailer referred to in Finding 11, the crowd moved over to another large semi-trailer, surrounded it, and members of the crowd broke a hole through its roof and removed its contents, consisting of beer, watermelons, cantaloupes and meat, which was distributed to the people congregated thereabouts."

On appeal Foremost challenges (1) the finding of the trial court that Guanche intended to and believed he had purchased first party coverage, and that this belief was reasonable, and (2) the legal theory of the doctrine of reasonable expectations, thought to have been utilized by the trial court.

We note at the outset that the doctrine of reasonable expectations has since been declared not to be the law in Idaho. Foremost Insurance Co. v. Putzier, 100 Idaho 883, 606 P.2d 987 (1980); Casey v. Highlands Insurance Co., 100 Idaho 505, 600 P.2d 1387 (1979). Rather, where there is an ambiguity in an insurance contract, special rules of construction apply to protect the insured. Casey v. Highlands, supra. Under these special rules, insurance policies are to be construed most liberally in favor of recovery, with all ambiguities being resolved in favor of the insured. Abbie Uriguen Oldsmobile Buick, Inc. v. United States Fire Insurance Co., 95 Idaho 501, 511 P.2d 783 (1973). "Where language may be given two meanings, one of which permits recovery and the other does not, it is to be given the construction most favorable to the insured." Shields v. Hiram C. Gardner, Inc., 92 Idaho 423, 427, 444 P.2d 38, 42 (1968). Accord, Erikson v. Nationwide Mutual Insurance Co., 97 Idaho 288, 543 P.2d 841 (1975).

Moreover, although the doctrine of reasonable expectations is not the law in Idaho, there is the closely analogous rule of contract construction pointed out by Justice Donaldson in his opinion in Corgatelli v. Globe Life & Accident Co., 96 Idaho 616, 533 P.2d 737 (1975)[20] wherein, citing Shields v. Hiram C. Gardner, Inc., supra, he wrote:

> "*[t]he doctrine of probability or reasonableness has long been a rule of construction geared toward ascertaining intent in situations of ambiguity. The standard to be applied is what a reasonable person* in the position of the insured *would have understood* the language to mean." 96 Idaho at 622, 533 P.2d at 743. (Donaldson, J., dissenting.) (Emphasis added.)

Under this rule of construction, which utilizes an objective standard and which is used in the case of ambiguously written insurance policies, to effectuate the intent of the parties, the test is what a reasonable person in the position of the insured would have understood the language of the contract to mean. This test is not necessarily conclusive as to the intent of the parties, but is only one rule of construction to be considered in construing an ambiguous contract. This standard is, of course, in accord with the general rule of construing insurance contracts against those who write them. See, e.g., Dunford v. United of Omaha, 95 Idaho 282, 506 P.2d 1355 (1973).[21]

20. The rationale of this opinion was adopted by the Court in Casey v. Highlands, 100 Idaho 505, 600 P.2d 1387 (1979).

21. Under the doctrine of reasonable expectations, on the other hand, the controlling test is a purely subjective one as to what the insured believed he was purchasing, with the only restraint being that that belief be reasonable.

In the present case, however, we are faced with the unusual situation where Guanche was never given a policy at all; he had an insurance transaction wherein he was simply told by an agent of Foremost that, in exchange for $300, he was "covered." This is not a case where the insured challenges the terms of the written policy as being ambiguous, but rather a case where he relies upon the oral binder or contract made by the agent. Under these unique facts, we must recognize this transaction as creating a patently ambiguous oral contract of insurance. It was Foremost's responsibility to provide Guanche with a copy of the policy which it believed it was selling to him, I.C. § 41–1824. By not delivering that contract or informing Guanche of its terms Foremost must be bound by the terms of the oral contract. We simply apply the above rules of construction to this oral transaction without regard to the terms of the actual written policy.

This Court was faced with an analogous problem in Toevs v. Western Farm Bureau Life Insurance Co., 94 Idaho 151, 483 P.2d 682 (1971). In that case, a purchaser paid the initial premium on a life insurance policy but died before having had the required physical examination. His widow testified, and the court so found, that there was no discussion as to the date the policy would become effective, and that she expected that it was effective immediately.

> "In view of this finding [that the agent did not explain or discuss the effective date of the policy], the unequal bargaining power of the two parties, the complex legalistic and ambiguous phrasing used throughout the contract, and the use by the insurance company of the procedure or device known as 'conditional premium receipt,' this Court holds that a contract of insurance was in existence on the date that the insured died. By this holding the Supreme Court of Idaho is subscribing to the theory known as a 'temporary contract of insurance.' The conditional premium receipt created a temporary contract of insurance subject to a condition, i.e., rejection of Toevs' application by the insurance company. Since rejection did not occur prior to Toevs' death, the company is liable." 94 Idaho at 155, 483 P.2d at 686.

In that case, the fact that the agent did not tell the purchaser that he would not be covered until he had undergone the physical exam was one of the factors considered by the Court in holding that the insured was covered in spite of the provision in the policy to the contrary.

In the present case, as in *Toevs,* the agent did not tell Guanche of any limitations in his coverage. Further, there could be no more unequal bargaining situation than the present one where Foremost took Guanche's money and never even told (or asked) him what he had purchased. Foremost could easily have told Guanche what he was purchasing, but it did not. As stated in Roeske v. Diefenbach, 75 Wis.2d 253, 249 N.W.2d 555, 559 (1977), in regard to an oral contract of insurance, "[i]f insurers desire to incorporate the provisions of their usual policies that are in derogation of the rights of the insured, such provisions must be specifically brought to the attention of the person seeking insurance at the time of the oral agreement." It is the duty of the insurer to inform the insured of what he is obtaining; it is not the duty of the insured to seek out exclusions and limitations not revealed to him. Where an insurance company, or its agent, accepts a premium as was done here, without explaining at all what was being sold, the company does so at the risk of being bound by what a reasonable person in the position of the insured would have understood. We will not look to the terms of an unmentioned, undelivered written policy to defeat coverage in the absence of any attempt by the insurer at explaining to the insured the coverage with which he was being provided.

* * *

[W]e find it unnecessary on our part to pin down with exactitude which of the many theories, all of which have application to varying degrees, brought the trial court to its ultimate conclusion. This Court has many times stated that it will affirm on a correct legal theory utilizing the trial court's findings where those findings are substantiated. * * * Applying the standard rules of construction for insurance contracts (to which we add insurance transactions) that all ambiguities are to be resolved against the insurer, and that what a reasonable person in the position of the insured would have believed to be the meaning of the language used is the standard to be used in resolving ambiguities—we are not persuaded that the trial court erred in concluding that Guanche had first party coverage protecting him against the losses which he sustained.

The judgment is affirmed, with costs, including I.C. § 41–1839 attorney fees, to respondent.

* * *

BAKES, CHIEF JUSTICE, dissenting:

* * *

The majority fails to discuss some of the more salient facts of this case. State and county licensing authorities had required Knievel and Snake River Canyon Enterprises to obtain liability insurance covering the event in question. First party coverage was not required. Representatives of Foremost, Knievel and Snake River Canyon Enterprises then negotiated the same insurance policy at issue in both this appeal and in Foremost Insurance Co. v. Putzier, 100 Idaho 883, 606 P.2d 987 (1980). Foremost was informed that some of Knievel's concessionaires might be added as additional insureds on the policy.

Representatives of Knievel and Snake River Canyon Enterprises in turn informed Guanche that he, too, would need insurance. There is no indication that Guanche would have purchased any insurance but for the fact that Snake River Canyon Enterprises required it. Guanche testified that he was too busy to "take care of insurance," and that he thought representatives of Knievel and Snake River Canyon Enterprises would "take care" of him. They did. He was made an additional insured on Snake River Canyon Enterprises' liability policy.

Guanche's testimony does demonstrate that he thought he was "fully" covered. When asked who had informed him that he had "full" coverage, he answered that it was the representatives of Knievel and Snake River Canyon Enterprises, and not any agent of Foremost. Guanche did testify that Foremost's agent informed him that he was "covered," although Guanche never asked the agent what for.

The entire transaction is summarized neatly in Guanche's amended counterclaim.

> "Guanche contracted with Snake River Canyon Enterprises, Inc., to provide food and beverage concessions * * * and as a part of said contract, *was required to maintain certain liability insurance in force. Guanche contacted Foremost Insurance Company and asked to have the required insurance coverage provided.* Foremost agreed to provide the coverage and merely added Guanche's name as an additional named insured to the policy of insurance described in the Complaint." (Emphasis added.)

Finally, it is clear, although the majority refuses to recognize it, that the court below based its decision squarely upon the now discredited doctrine of reasonable expectations.[22] In Finding of Fact 16, the trial court stated that Guanche "intended" to insure his property; that he "believed" he had first party coverage; and that such belief was "reasonable * * * under the facts in this case." On the basis of these "facts" and the "theories expounded in Corgatelli v. Globe Insurance," the trial court concluded that there did indeed exist a contract for first party coverage between Foremost and Guanche. In so concluding the trial court held as a matter of law that "Guanche's intentions and expectations [are] paramount in interpreting the terms of any insurance contract existing between Guanche and [Foremost]."

The above legal conclusion was erroneous, the doctrine of reasonable expectations having been "expressly rejected * * * in favor of traditional contract rules of construction." Foremost Ins. Co. v. Putzier, 100 Idaho at 888, 606 P.2d at 992. That being the case, we ought to reverse and remand the case for a new trial in order to give the lower court an opportunity to correct its legal error. But in no event should this Court decide the case on a legal theory not even asserted by Guanche, and then

22. The majority quotes some language from the *Corgatelli* dissent in support of its assertion that an ambiguous insurance contract should be construed in accordance with the understandings of a reasonable person in the position of the insured. The majority failed to quote the preceding sentence in the *Corgatelli* dissent. "If the meaning of the contract is in doubt, it must be construed in the sense in which the insurer believed, at the time of making, the insured understood the terms." Corgatelli v. Globe Life & Accident Co., 96 Idaho 616, 622, 533 P.2d 737, 743 (1975) (Donaldson, J., dissenting). If that standard were applied to the instant case, there could be no doubt as to the end result. In Guanche's case, Foremost was merely adding an additional insured to a negotiated special policy of liability coverage. Any reasonable insurance agent would be mildly astonished to discover that Guanche's unexpressed desires would ripen into first party coverage.

make an appellate finding of fact that there was an oral contract of first party insurance. There is no evidence to sustain such an appellate finding, and it is directly contrary to the trial court's express finding that Guanche never "advised [Foremost] of the type or kind of insurance he desired * * *." I would reverse.

Notes

1. In the second *Putzier* case, Chief Justice Bakes neatly places his objections to the result in a footnote:

> What are, I wonder, the outer limits of Guanche's oral contract for insurance "coverage"? If a Mrs. Guanche was blessed with a child during Knievel's jump, could Guanche recover maternity benefits? How about life insurance for any children, or Guanche's horse? I think the limits of Guanche's coverage should be established, not by his secret and unexpressed desires, but by the context in which the insurance was obtained. Thus, the trial court should consider the probability that Guanche intended to procure, and Foremost intended to sell, only that coverage which satisfied the county's requirements, which did *not* include [the property loss].

Is Chief Justice Bakes correct? Does he overstate the case?

These cases raise real difficulty where the express language of the policy contradicts, without ambiguity, the representations of the agent. The temptation is great for courts to find a basis for coverage—essentially holding that the misrepresentation trumps the policy language. Even in those cases where an insurer survives the main point, it might still face exposure on other fronts. E.g. Cooper v. Berkshire Life Insurance Co., 148 Md.App. 41, 810 A.2d 1045 (2002) (holding that an insurer is not liable for an agent's misrepresentations that contradict the policy language but that the insurer could be liable for fraud).

2. The doctrine of reasonable expectations has not been without its detractors. See Jeffrey Stempel, *Unmet Expectations: Undue Restriction of the Reasonable Expectations Approach and the Misleading Mythology of Judicial Role*, 5 Conn. Ins. L.J. 181 (1998). A symposium issue of the Connecticut Insurance Law Journal devoted to the doctrine surfaced considerable criticism. Some scholars feel the doctrine casts courts in the unusual role of displacing the measure of control normally held by insurers. See Mark Rahdert, *Reasonable Expectations Revisited*, 5 Conn. Ins. L.J. 107, 147–50; Susan Popik and C. Quackenbos, *Reasonable Expectations after Thirty Years: A Failed Doctrine*, 5 Conn. Ins. L.J. 425 (1998).

3. According to Ostrager and Newman, Handbook on Insurance Coverage Disputes, 9th Edition, 1998, 38 states recognize at least "some variation" of the reasonable expectation approach. Included among the states who employ this approach are California (AIU Insurance Co. v. Superior Court, 51 Cal.3d 807, 274 Cal.Rptr. 820, 799 P.2d 1253 (1990)), New Jersey (Meier v. New Jersey Life Ins. Co., 101 N.J. 597, 503 A.2d 862 (1986); McNeilab, Inc. v. North River Ins. Co., 645 F.Supp. 525 (1986)), Texas (Fritz v. Old American Ins. Co., 354 F.Supp. 514 (S.D.Tex.1973)), New York (Fried v. North River Ins. Co., 710 F.2d 1022 (4th Cir.1983)), and Connecticut

(Hansen v. Ohio Casualty Ins. Co., 239 Conn. 537, 544, 687 A.2d 1262 (1996)). *Id.*, § 102(b)(2)(B) at p. 23–26. States which have rejected the reasonable expectations approach to insurance contract interpretation include Florida, Utah, Ohio, South Carolina, Washington, Illinois, and Idaho. *Id.* § 102(b)(2)(C) at 27–8. However, Ostrager notes that in the states which have rejected the reasonable expectations approach "[t]he courts . . . apply contra-insurer rules of construction to resolve ambiguous policy language in favor of the insured". *Id.* Consider this distinction in connection with the two *Foremost* cases *supra*.

4. Interpretation is, of course, an enduring problem. Possibly the last generation's choice of words, thought then to be clear and simple, pass before the eyes of this generation's judges in muddy swirls. Despite the futility of the task, "readability" ought to be promoted. Rudolph Franz Flesch sought to help with his book *Testing Readability* (1951). See Skarlat commenting on readability in 21 For the Defense (1980).

Massachusetts General Laws Annotated

Chapter 175.

§ 2B. Readability of policy form; definition; approval; actions based on language

1. No policy form of insurance shall be delivered or issued for delivery to more than fifty policyholders in the commonwealth until a copy of the policy form has been on file for thirty days with the commissioner, unless before the expiration of said thirty days the commissioner shall have approved the form of the policy in writing as complying with this section; nor shall any such policy be delivered or issued for delivery if the commissioner notifies the company in writing within said thirty days that in his opinion the form of said policy does not comply with the provisions of this section, specifying the reasons for his opinion, provided that such action of the commissioner shall be subject to review by the supreme judicial court, but during any such review the form shall not be delivered or issued for delivery in the commonwealth; nor shall any such policy form be so delivered or issued for delivery unless:

(a) The text achieves a minimum Flesch scale readability score of fifty;

(b) It is printed, except for tables, in not less than ten point type, one point leaded.

(c) The style, arrangement and overall appearance of the policy give no undue prominence to any portion of the text of the policy and any endorsements or riders;

(d) It contains a table of contents or an alphabetical subject index;

(e) The width of margins and ink to paper contrast do not unreasonably interfere with the readability of the form; and

(f) The organization of the content of the policy and the summary of the policy is conducive to understandability of the form.

Nothing in this section shall be construed to require the affirmative approval of the commissioner before issuance of a policy form which has been on file for at least thirty days.

For the purposes of this section, a Flesch scale readability score shall be measured as hereinafter provided:

(1) For policy forms containing ten thousand words or less of text, the entire form shall be analyzed. For policy forms containing more than ten thousand words, the readability of two two hundred word samples per page may be analyzed in lieu of the entire form. The samples shall be separated by at least twenty printed lines.

(2)(a)(i) The number of words and sentences in the text shall be counted and the total number of words divided by the total number of sentences. The figure obtained shall be multiplied by a factor of 1.015.

(ii) The total number of syllables shall be counted and divided by the total number of words. The figure obtained shall be multiplied by a factor of 84.6.

(iii) The sum of the figures computed under subclause (i) and subclause (ii) subtracted from 206.835 equals the Flesch scale readability score for the policy form.

(b) For the purposes of clause (a) the following procedures shall be used:

(i) A contraction, hyphenated word, or numbers and letters, when separated by spaces, shall be counted as one word;

(ii) A unit of words ending with a period, semicolon, or colon, but excluding headings and captions shall be counted as a sentence; and

(iii) A syllable means a unit of spoken language consisting of one or more letters of a word as divided by an accepted dictionary. Where the dictionary shows two or more equally acceptable pronunciations of a word, the pronunciation containing fewer syllables may be used.

Every policy form filed with the commissioner under this section shall be accompanied by a certificate stating the Flesch scale readability score achieved by such form.

The term "text" as used in this section shall include all printed matter except the name and address of the insurer, name or title of the policy, the brief description if any, captions and subcaptions, and schedule pages and tables.

The commissioner may, after notice and hearing, designate other readability tests as acceptable alternative tests to the Flesch scale readability analysis if he finds that any other such tests are equivalent in function, result and understandability. This section shall apply to any domestic or foreign company, whether licensed or unlicensed by the commissioner to do business in the commonwealth.

* * *

Promoting "readability" to a statutory mandate ought to do the job, ought it not? Does the Massachusetts statute epitomize a certain irony?

REPUBLIC INSURANCE CO. v. SILVERTON ELEVATORS, INC.

Supreme Court of Texas, 1973.
493 S.W.2d 748, 91 A.L.R.3d 500.

DANIEL, JUSTICE.

This suit was brought by Respondents, Silverton Elevators, Inc. and Carl L. Tidwell, against Petitioner, Republic Insurance Company, to recover under a Texas Standard Fire Policy issued to Silverton Elevators by Republic covering a residential dwelling and household goods contained therein. In a non-jury trial, Silverton was awarded $3,000 "for the use and benefit" of Carl L. Tidwell for the loss of the household goods. The Court of Civil Appeals affirmed. 477 S.W.2d 336. We affirm.

Carl L. Tidwell was at all times material to this controversy, an officer, director and the general manager of Silverton Elevators, Inc. Silverton owned and furnished to Tidwell a house near its elevators, together with the insurance on the house and on Tidwell's household goods, as part of his compensation as general manager. Since 1964, Republic's local agent had issued and renewed insurance policies in the name of Silverton covering the dwelling and its household goods. It is undisputed that the local agent, who had authority to issue the policies and receive the premiums, knew that the household goods belonged to Tidwell and that Silverton was carrying the insurance for the benefit of Tidwell. On April 17, 1970, a tornado destroyed the house and the household goods.

On the date of the tornado there was in effect a Texas Standard Fire Policy with Extended Coverage on DWELLING & HOUSEHOLD GOODS in the sum of $10,000 issued by Republic to Silverton for the period of April 20, 1969 to April 20, 1972, insuring against loss from windstorm the specifically described "occupied dwelling" for $7,000 and "household goods * * * while in the described building" for $3,000.00. It is undisputed that Silverton paid the $227.00 premium, and the local agent admitted that at the time he issued the policy he knew the facts heretofore mentioned with respect to actual ownership of the insured property. He testified that he wrote the policy to cover Tidwell's household goods located in the dwelling which Tidwell and his family occupied; that he knew Silverton was carrying the policy on the household goods for the benefit of Tidwell; that when he issued the policy he did not think it made any difference that it was in the name of Silverton because "they were paying the premium"; and that he told Tidwell that the policy covered his household goods both before and after the tornado.

Republic acknowledged coverage on the house and paid Silverton $7,000 for its damage, but it denied any liability to Silverton or Tidwell on the household goods. Thereupon, Silverton and Tidwell brought this suit against Republic claiming coverage to the limit of the policy ($3,000) on the household goods owned by Tidwell. Republic defended on the grounds that Silverton had no ownership and therefore no insurable interest in the household goods and that the policy as written was limited by its terms to household goods owned by Silverton Elevators, Inc., the named insured.

Silverton and Tidwell's pleadings asserted that they both had insurable interests; that the insurance was purchased by Silverton and extended to Tidwell as part of his compensation as manager and as "a legal representative of Silverton Elevators, Inc."; and that when Republic issued its policy and accepted premiums with full knowledge of the true ownership and relations between Silverton and Tidwell, it waived the right to complain about any lack of ownership or insurable interest of the named insured and was estopped from denying coverage on behalf of Tidwell. As heretofore indicated, the trial court awarded Silverton Elevators $3,000 "for the use and benefit of Carl L. Tidwell."

Since the policy refers to and clearly purports to cover the household goods located in the specifically described dwelling, we agree with the Court of Civil Appeals that the knowledge of Tidwell's ownership of the household goods by Republic's local agent and his actions with respect thereto were imputed to and binding upon Republic. Issuance of the policy and collection of the premiums with such knowledge operates as a waiver of any requirement that the named insured own or possess a beneficial interest in the insured property. [citations].

In the above cases, the named insureds were not the owners or sole owners of the insured properties. In each case, the true owner was known to the insurance agent and was allowed direct recovery, or recovery for his benefit, on the grounds that the insurance company had waived warranties of sole ownership or lack of insurable interest. There is no conflict between the above cases and those which hold that waiver and estoppel cannot operate to bring within the terms of a policy liabilities or benefits which were expressly excepted therefrom, such as liability from injuries due to gunshot wounds in Washington Nat. Ins. Co. v. Craddock, 130 Tex. 251, 109 S.W.2d 165 (1937); loss for injuries while in military service in time of war, as in Ruddock v. Detroit Life Ins. Co., 209 Mich. 638, 177 N.W. 242 (1920); or payment of benefits beyond a specified termination date at age 65, as in Great American Reserve Ins. Co. v. Mitchell, 335 S.W.2d 707 (Tex.Civ.App.1960, writ ref.). The latter cases recognize that waiver and estoppel may operate to avoid forfeiture of coverage and benefits stated in the policy, but not to add specifically excluded risks or to enlarge the benefits or risks therein set forth. In the present case, plaintiffs seek to recover only on the risk assumed by Republic under the terms of the written policy. Republic's policy insured against the destruction of precisely the same household goods identified in its policy and for which it collected its premiums. There is no evidence that its risk was enlarged because the household goods were owned by Tidwell rather than Silverton.

* * *

[A portion of the opinion dealing with policy construction has been omitted.]

It has been suggested, but not by Republic, that the building item provision contained in the "Mortgage or Trustee" clause at the bottom of the face of the policy, and particularly the last sentence thereof, limits liability for compensation to the "interest of the insured," and that this applies to personal property. Even though the provision does not speak of "named insured," and for all practical purposes Tidwell was the "insured" because the policy as to household goods was written for his benefit, there are other more compelling reasons why this provision is inapplicable to the personal property involved in this case. Clearly, the entire clause refers to loss on "building items," their value at the time of loss less depreciation, repair, replacement and reconstruction, etc. None of the language refers to personal property. Furthermore, the last sentence begins with the words, "Subject to Article 6.13 of the Texas Insurance Code," and this Article contains the specific provision that: "The provisions of this article shall not apply to personal property."

The above clause has been a part of the Texas Standard Fire Policy form prescribed by the Insurance Commission since 1943. * * *

Whether applicable to personal property or not, we hold that the portion of the clause relating to limitation of liability to "the interest of the insured" falls within the category of ownership provisions which may be waived; the insurer may be estopped from denying liability to the true owner on policies issued in the names of third parties covering the risks on identified property with full knowledge by the company that the property is actually owned by the one for whose benefit the policy was written or maintained. * * *

Republic insists that reformation of the policy is the only proper remedy, if any, for recovery by Silverton on behalf of Tidwell, because of failure of the written policy to identify the household goods as belonging to Tidwell. We disagree. As heretofore indicated, under the undisputed facts, the household goods described in the policy belonged to Tidwell and were insured by Silverton for his benefit in a policy drawn by Republic's agent for such purpose, with assurances from the agent that it would cover Tidwell's furniture. If this was a mistake, it was made by Republic's agent, and it was mutual, because Tidwell and Silverton took the agent's word that it expressed the true agreement. With this evidence being fully developed in the present record, there is no reason to require another trial for reformation of the written policy. It has been held that even without a plea for reformation, when the facts show the true agreement intended and a mutual mistake, or mistake of the agent, in preparing the written policy, the agreement intended will be enforced without going through the formal proceedings of reformation. Aetna Ins. Co. v. Brannon, 99 Tex. 391, 89 S.W. 1057; Aetna Ins. Co. v. Brannon, 53 Tex.Civ.App. 242, 116 S.W. 116 (Tex.Civ.App.1909, no writ). See also 25 A.L.R.3d 589 § 3; 25 A.L.R.3d 1239 § 3; and 32 A.L.R.3d 677 § 3.

Silverton and Tidwell made every proof in this case that would entitle recovery on the policy as written. Under the above cited authorities, the trial court and Court of Civil Appeals have properly held that Silverton is entitled to recover for the benefit of Tidwell on the written policy without seeking a reformation thereof.

Accordingly, the judgments of the lower courts are affirmed.

* * *

WALKER, JUSTICE (dissenting).

* * *

The net effect of the majority holding is to extend the policy coverage and create an entirely different contract by waiver or estoppel. That is contrary, of course, to the established rule in Texas and most other jurisdictions. * * *

> * * * Waiver and estoppel may operate to avoid a forfeiture of a policy, but they have consistently been denied operative force to change, re-write and enlarge the risks covered by a policy. In other words, waiver and estoppel can not create a new and different contract with respect to risks covered by the policy. This has been the settled law in Texas since the decision in Washington Nat. Ins. Co. v. Craddock, 130 Tex. 251, 109 S.W.2d 165, 113 A.L.R. 854.

None of the cases cited in support of the waiver holding is pertinent here. Most of them involved the so-called sole and unconditional ownership clause, which provided that the entire policy would be void if the interest of the insured was other than sole and unconditional ownership. Others involved a stipulation that the policy would be void in case of a change of ownership unless otherwise provided by agreement endorsed on the policy. The policy in Old Colony Insurance Co. v. Messer, Tex.Civ.App., 328 S.W.2d 335 covered the dwelling that was damaged by fire, but it contained a provision limiting liability to the interest of the insured and another making the policy void if the insured had concealed any material fact. These provisions as well as lack of insurable interest were pled by the insurance company in bar. Although the jury made findings tending to support an estoppel theory, the Court of Civil Appeals affirmed the trial court's judgment in favor of the true owner on the basis of its holding that the provisions in question had been waived by issuance of the policy and acceptance of the premiums with knowledge of the ownership of the property. Be that as it may, there was no question of coverage in the case, and the decision does not stand for the proposition that the limitation of liability may be waived out of the policy for the purpose of determining coverage.

* * *

It is my opinion that respondents are not entitled to recover on the policy as written, and that is all they have attempted to do thus far. Tidwell may show his right to recover by offering evidence and obtaining findings that establish mutual mistake and the terms of the true agreement. See Aetna Ins. Co. v. Brannon, 99 Tex. 391, 89 S.W. 1057. The trial court would then be in position to enter a judgment based on the coverage actually agreed upon and intended by the parties. It would also be in position to insure that petitioner receives the appropriate premium for the risk actually assumed. I would reverse the judgments of the courts below and remand the cause in the interest of justice.

Notes

1. "Waiver," "estoppel" and "waiver and estoppel" occur with some frequency in insurance decisions because of the conduct of agents. A good analysis is found in Crais, W.C. *Comment Note: Doctrine of Estoppel or Waiver As Available to Bring Within Coverage of Insurance Policy Risks Not Covered By Its Terms or Expressly Excluded Therefrom*, 1 A.L.R. 3d 1139 (2000). A succinct statement of doctrine is found in *Salloum Foods & Liquor, Inc. v. Parliament Insurance Co.*, 69 Ill.App.3d 422, 26 Ill.Dec. 399, 388 N.E.2d 23, 27–28 (1979): [Citations omitted]

> An insurance company can waive the limitation provision of an insurance contract, or, by its conduct, become estopped from invoking the provision as a defense to an action on the policy. * * *
>
> In the context of insurance law, and especially with regard to limitation provisions in insurance policies, the terms "waiver" and "estoppel" have often been used without careful distinction, and thereby abused and confused. * * * This doctrinal confusion, epitomized by the frequently echoed phrase "waiver by estoppel," is so deeply rooted some courts have suggested that the term waiver, as applied in Illinois to insurance cases, is simply another name for estoppel. * * *
>
> Notwithstanding the confusion already engendered by many of these cases, it is elementary that waiver and estoppel are two separate and distinct doctrines. * * * The fact that these doctrines are closely akin and often may coexist does not mean they are identical in connotation.
>
> Waiver encompasses either an express or an implied * * * voluntary and intentional relinquishment of a known and existing right * * *.
>
> Waiver is essentially unilateral in character, focusing only upon the acts and conduct of the insurer. Prejudice to, or detrimental reliance by the insured is *not* required. * * *
>
> Equitable estoppel, on the other hand, generally is based upon an insurance carrier's conduct and/or representations which mislead an insured to his detriment. * * * Thus, if an insurance carrier's investigation and/or negotiation of a policy claim reasonably induces within the insured a false sense of security—namely, that the claim will be settled without suit—and the insured, in reliance thereon, foregoes filing suit during the policy's limitation period, the insurance carrier is estopped from later raising the limitation provision as a defense to an action on the policy. * * *
>
> It is not necessary that the insurer intentionally mislead or deceive the insured, or even intend by its conduct to induce delay. * * * All that is

necessary is that the insured reasonably relies on the insurer's representations or conduct in forbearing suit.

2. Another word that purports to have conceptual significance in this context is "election," referred to in texts and used occasionally in the cases. It is defined as "a cross between waiver and estoppel," and described as a "difficult concept to cope with, even when dealt with candidly." See R. Keeton, Basic Insurance Law § 6.1 for a full discussion of the doctrine. Presumably the opportunity to use it is when the insurer, in a position to keep the benefit of the deal or to take advantage of an opportunity to get out, waffles unnecessarily. That's why—when the company has collected a premium while an agent is aware of a breach of condition—the application of the doctrine does not require detrimental reliance or voluntary relinquishment of a right, and obviously is related to the necessary choice of substantive rights which accompanies the rescission of contracts in general.

In truth, the doctrine is rarely made the basis for decisions in recent times, and the use of the word is as a tag along ("the conduct of the insurer constitutes waiver, estoppel or election") without any significance.

3. A father applied for a homeowners' policy on a house he and his wife owned but which was occupied by his son. The agent was told of the actual state of ownership, and he suggested that the homeowners' policy be issued in the son's name as the insured; this was done and father and mother were listed as mortgagees. The father paid the premiums and the taxes as well as the cost of improvements. Title never changed hands. The house and its contents were destroyed by fire after the son had occupied it for several years. Putting aside the question of whether the son might have an insurable interest (a topic we will visit later), is it possible to dispose of the case on the basis that the Insurance Company is *estopped* to deny liability? See McGehee v. Farmers Insurance Company, 734 F.2d 1422, 1424–25 (10th Cir.1984) (insurer estopped from denying liability).

4. The common assurances by insurance salespersons or by marketing brochures that the applicant is getting "full coverage" is an open invitation to claim estoppel against the insurance carrier when gaps in coverage later appear. The problem is that the fairly well entrenched principle of "no estoppel into coverage" is obviously being challenged. A frequently cited case is *Harr v. Allstate Ins. Co.*, 54 N.J. 287, 255 A.2d 208 (1969). Harr owned a house and contents, and held a homeowner's (HO) policy covering a broad range of risks including water damage. He also carried on a small business in the basement and realized that the HO policy would not apply to property used for business pursuits. Before leaving on a trip to Florida he contacted an agent of Allstate, which had issued the HO policy, for appropriate coverage. The agent orally assured him that the business property was "fully covered," and urged him to enjoy his trip. Thereafter the house was flooded and it was then discovered that the policy while indeed containing very broad coverage of business risks, had an exclusion for water damage. The court, on several grounds including a mention of reasonable expectations, held the exclusion unenforceable. The primary basis for the holding was estoppel, adopted deliberately by the court while recognizing that this meant estoppel into coverage. But see Harmon v. American Interinsurance Exchange Co., 39 Mich.App. 145, 197 N.W.2d 307 (1972) (representation of "full coverage" held unenforceable).

Chapter 4

EXTRA-CONTRACTUAL LIABILITY: THE COVENANT OF GOOD FAITH AND FAIR DEALING

A. DISTINGUISHING FIRST PARTY AND THIRD PARTY INSURANCE

Insurance students should distinguish two situations: (a) *first-party claims,* where the insured person alleges failure of good faith and fair dealing by the insurer in handling the insured's claims under the policy (e.g., to disability benefits), and (b) *third party claims,* where the insurer fails to practice good faith and fair dealing in discharging his obligations to the insured with respect to claimants against the insured (e.g., fails to defend or to negotiate a settlement when a third party claims the insured is liable to the third party and the insured can claim that his insurance applies). The following excerpt is instructive in differentiating between the two types of claims and the requirements to establish a cause of action.

MONTROSE CHEMICAL CORP. OF CALIFORNIA v. ADMIRAL INS. CO.

Supreme Court of California, In Bank, 1995.
10 Cal.4th 645, 42 Cal.Rptr.2d 324, 913 P.2d 878.

LUCAS, Chief Justice.

[A summary of the facts in this complex case was provided above. The following excerpt pertains to the distinction between first party insurance and third party insurance.]

* * *

[A] first party insurance policy provides coverage for loss or damage sustained directly by the insured (e.g., life, disability, health, fire, theft and casualty insurance). A third party liability policy, in contrast, provides coverage for liability of the insured to a "third party" (e.g., a CGL [Commercial General Liability] policy, a directors' and officers' liability policy, or an errors and omissions policy). In the usual first party policy, the insurer promises to pay money to the insured upon the happening of an event, the risk of which has been insured against. In the typical third party liability policy, the carrier assumes a contractual duty to pay judgments the insured becomes legally obligated to pay as damages because of bodily injury or property damage caused by the insured.

The difference in the nature of the risks insured against under first party property policies and third party liability policies is also reflected in the differing causation analyses that must be undertaken to determine coverage under each type of policy. " 'Property insurance ... is an agreement, a contract, in which the insurer agrees to indemnify the insured in the event that the insured property suffers a covered loss. Coverage, in turn, is commonly provided by reference to causation, e.g., 'loss caused by ...' certain enumerated perils. The term 'perils' in traditional property insurance parlance refers to fortuitous, active, physical forces such as lightning, wind, and explosion, which bring about the loss.' " In contrast, " 'the 'cause' of loss in the context of a property insurance contract is totally different from that in a liability policy.' " [*citing* Garvey v. State Farm Fire and Casualty Co., 48 Cal.3d 395, 406, 257 Cal.Rptr. 292, 770 P.2d 704 (1989).] "[T]he right to coverage in the third party liability insurance context draws on traditional tort concepts of fault, proximate cause and duty. This liability analysis differs substantially from the coverage analysis in the property insurance context, which draws on the relationship between perils that are either covered or excluded in the contract. In liability insurance, by insuring for personal liability, and agreeing to cover the insured for his own negligence, the insurer agrees to cover the insured for a broader spectrum of risks." [*Id.* at 407.]

The parties' expectations may also differ depending upon the type of coverage sought. First party property coverage is typically purchased in an amount sufficient to cover the insured's maximum potential loss (e.g., fire insurance typically covers the value of the property insured). Hence, there is no reason for a first party insured to look to more than one policy in the event of loss (the policy in effect at the time of the fire). Third party liability coverage differs substantially. As the Court of Appeal below observed, "at best, the insured makes an educated guess about its potential exposure to third parties. At worst, the insured's best guess falls far short of the mark."

Yet another distinction between the two types of insurance coverage is that third party CGL policies do not impose, as a condition of coverage, a requirement that the damage or injury be discovered at any particular point in time. Instead, they provide coverage for injuries and damage caused by an "occurrence," and typically define "occurrence" as an accident (or sometimes a "loss"), including a "continuous or repeated exposure to conditions," that results in bodily injury or property damage during the policy period. The standardized CGL policy language (like the language in Admiral's policies) will be reviewed in greater detail below.

As will be seen, nothing about this language suggests a manifestation or discovery requirement as a prerequisite for triggering coverage.

Another important difference between first and third party policies is that first party insurance policies require the insured to bring any action against the insurer within 12 months after "inception of the loss." Before an action is filed under such a policy, there must be a dispute between the insured and insurer. Before there can be a dispute, the insured must (or reasonably should) know it has suffered a "loss." By contrast, third party liability policies do not include a 12–month limitations period in which the insured must bring an action against the insurer (although the policies may contain express notification requirements). It is the damaged or injured third party who initiates the action against the insured. If coverage is ultimately established, it is the insurer that in turn must indemnify the insured for "all sums which the insured shall become legally obligated to pay." Hence, there is no "inception of the loss" language in a standard CGL policy, and, as will become apparent, no corollary need to apply the definition of "inception of the loss" that this court articulated in Prudential–LMI.

Unfortunately, some courts have failed to draw these critical distinctions when discussing coverage issues under first and third party insurance policies. In the third party liability insurance context, some reported cases have muddied the waters by seemingly failing to distinguish between disputes arising between an insured and insurer, and actions among several CGL carriers that seek a judicial declaration allocating a loss already paid out to the insured under one or more such policies. In suits between an insured and an insurer to determine coverage, interpretation of the policy language and, in the case of ambiguous policy language, the expectations of the parties, will typically take precedence. The existence of excess or "secondary insurance" policies, "other insurance" clauses, or similar policy language decreeing the manner of apportionment of liability under multiple policies may also factor into the coverage analysis.

In contrast, where two or more CGL carriers turn to the courts to allocate the cost of indemnity for a paid loss, different contractual and policy considerations may come into play in the effort to apportion such costs among the insurers.

* * *

B. THE COVENANT OF GOOD FAITH AND FAIR DEALING

The Restatement, Contracts, (2d) § 205[1] states:

"Every contract imposes upon each party a duty of good faith and fair dealing in its performance and its enforcement."

1. Copyright 1981 by the American Law Institute. Reprinted with the permission of the American Law Institute.

The comments following the section provide some enlightenment for interpretation:

> "*d. Good faith performance.* Subterfuges and evasions violate the obligation of good faith in performance even though the actor believes his conduct to be justified. * * * A complete catalogue of types of bad faith is impossible, but the following types are among those which have been recognized in judicial decisions: evasion of the spirit of the bargain, lack of diligence and slacking off, willful rendering of imperfect performance, abuse of a power to specify terms, and interference with or failure to cooperate in the other party's performance."
>
> "*e. Good faith in enforcement.* The obligation of good faith and fair dealing extends to the assertion, settlement and litigation of contract claims and defenses. * * * The obligation is violated by dishonest conduct such as conjuring up a pretended dispute, asserting an interpretation contrary to one's own understanding, or falsification of facts. It also extends to dealing which is candid but unfair, * * *. Other types of violation have been recognized in judicial decisions: harassing demands for assurances of performance, rejection of performance for unstated reasons, willful failure to mitigate damages, and abuse of a power to determine compliance or to terminate the contract. * * * "

PPG INDUSTRIES, INC. v. TRANSAMERICA INS. CO.

Supreme Court of California, 1999.
20 Cal.4th 310, 84 Cal.Rptr.2d 455, 975 P.2d 652.

KENNARD, J.

* * * Implied in every contract is a covenant of good faith and fair dealing that neither party will injure the right of the other to receive the benefits of the agreement. (Comunale v. Traders & General Ins. Co. (1958) 50 Cal.2d 654, 658, 328 P.2d 198.) This covenant imposes a number of obligations upon insurance companies, including an obligation to accept a reasonable offer of settlement. (Murphy v. Allstate Ins. Co. (1976) 17 Cal.3d 937, 941, 132 Cal.Rptr. 424, 553 P.2d 584; Crisci v. Security Ins. Co. (1967) 66 Cal.2d 425, 430, 58 Cal.Rptr. 13, 426 P.2d 173.) An insurer's breach of the implied covenant of good faith and fair dealing "will provide the basis for an action in tort." (Foley v. Interactive Data Corp. (1988) 47 Cal.3d 654, 684, 254 Cal.Rptr. 211, 765 P.2d 373.) Because breach of the implied covenant is actionable as a tort, the measure of damages for tort actions applies and the insurance company generally is liable for "any damages which are the proximate result of that breach."

* * *

Keep these comments in mind as you read the following cases, focusing particularly on the performance of the insurer.

C. CONSTITUTIONAL LIMITATIONS

Douglas R. Richmond states the substantive law in this area succinctly. He writes "In most jurisdictions an insurer that breaches its duty of good faith and fair dealing commits the tort of bad faith." Douglas R. Richmond, *Bad Insurance Bad Faith Law*, 39 TORT TRIAL & INS. PRACTICE L.J. 1, 4 (2003). This simple statement forms the core of the remainder of this chapter.

The United States Court has taken up a number of punitive damage cases in the last several years the most recent relevant one of which appears below. Other cases are discussed in the notes following the case. The cases represent a significant limitation to the deference given by appellate courts to jury awarded damages. In reading the case, keep in mind that the case is a third party case.

STATE FARM MUTUAL AUTOMOBILE INS. CO. v. CAMPBELL

Supreme Court of the United States, 2003.
538 U.S. 408, 123 S.Ct. 1513, 155 L.Ed.2d 585.

JUSTICE KENNEDY delivered the opinion of the Court.

We address once again the measure of punishment, by means of punitive damages, a State may impose upon a defendant in a civil case. The question is whether, in the circumstances we shall recount, an award of $145 million in punitive damages, where full compensatory damages are $1 million, is excessive and in violation of the Due Process Clause of the Fourteenth Amendment to the Constitution of the United States.

I

In 1981, Curtis Campbell (Campbell) was driving with his wife, Inez Preece Campbell, in Cache County, Utah. He decided to pass six vans traveling ahead of them on a two-lane highway. Todd Ospital was driving a small car approaching from the opposite direction. To avoid a head-on collision with Campbell, who by then was driving on the wrong side of the highway and toward oncoming traffic, Ospital swerved onto the shoulder, lost control of his automobile, and collided with a vehicle driven by Robert G. Slusher. Ospital was killed, and Slusher was rendered permanently disabled. The Campbells escaped unscathed.

In the ensuing wrongful death and tort action, Campbell insisted he was not at fault. Early investigations did support differing conclusions as to who caused the accident, but "a consensus was reached early on by the investigators and witnesses that Mr. Campbell's unsafe pass had indeed caused the crash." 2001 UT 89, 65 P.3d 1134, 2001 Utah LEXIS 170, 2001 WL 1246676, (Utah, Oct. 19, 2001). Campbell's insurance company, petitioner State Farm Mutual Automobile Insurance Company (State Farm), nonetheless decided to contest liability and declined offers by Slusher and Ospital's estate (Ospital) to settle the claims for the policy limit of $50,000 ($25,000 per claimant). State Farm also ignored the advice of one of its own investigators and took the case to trial, assuring the Campbells that "their assets were safe, that they had no liability for the accident, that [State Farm] would represent their interests, and that they did not need to procure separate counsel." *Id.* at 1142. To the contrary, a jury determined that Campbell was 100 percent at fault, and a judgment was returned for $185,849, far more than the amount offered in settlement.

At first State Farm refused to cover the $135,849 in excess liability. Its counsel made this clear to the Campbells: " 'You may want to put for sale signs on your property to get things moving.' " Ibid. Nor was State Farm willing to post a supersedeas bond to allow Campbell to appeal the judgment against him. Campbell obtained his own counsel to appeal the verdict. During the pendency of the appeal, in late 1984, Slusher, Ospital, and the Campbells reached an agreement whereby Slusher and Ospital agreed not to seek satisfaction of their claims against the Campbells. In exchange the Campbells agreed to pursue a bad faith action against State Farm and to be represented by Slusher's and Ospital's attorneys. The Campbells also agreed that Slusher and Ospital would have a right to play a part in all major decisions concerning the bad faith action. No settlement could be concluded without Slusher's and Ospital's approval, and Slusher and Ospital would receive 90 percent of any verdict against State Farm.

In 1989, the Utah Supreme Court denied Campbell's appeal in the wrongful death and tort actions. Slusher v. Ospital, 777 P.2d 437. State Farm then paid the entire judgment, including the amounts in excess of the policy limits. The Campbells nonetheless filed a complaint against State Farm alleging bad faith, fraud, and intentional infliction of emotional distress. The trial court initially granted State Farm's motion for summary judgment because State Farm had paid the excess verdict, but that ruling was reversed on appeal. 840 P.2d 130 (Utah App. 1992). On remand State Farm moved in limine to exclude evidence of alleged conduct that occurred in unrelated cases outside of Utah, but the trial court denied the motion. At State Farm's request the trial court bifurcated the trial into two phases conducted before different juries. In the first phase the jury determined that State Farm's decision not to settle was unreasonable because there was a substantial likelihood of an excess verdict.

Before the second phase of the action against State Farm we decided BMW of North America, Inc. v. Gore, 517 U.S. 559, 134 L. Ed. 2d 809, 116 S. Ct. 1589 (1996), and refused to sustain a $2 million punitive damages award which accompanied a verdict of only $4,000 in compensatory damages. Based on that decision, State Farm again moved for the exclusion of evidence of dissimilar out-of-state conduct. App. to Pet. for Cert. 168a–172a. The trial court denied State Farm's motion. Id., at 189a.

The second phase addressed State Farm's liability for fraud and intentional infliction of emotional distress, as well as compensatory and punitive damages. The Utah Supreme Court aptly characterized this phase of the trial:

> "State Farm argued during phase II that its decision to take the case to trial was an 'honest mistake' that did not warrant punitive damages. In contrast, the Campbells introduced evidence that State Farm's decision to take the case to trial was a result of a national scheme to meet corporate fiscal goals by capping payouts on claims company wide. This scheme was referred to as State Farm's 'Performance, Planning and Review,' or PP & R, policy. To prove the existence of this scheme, the trial court allowed the Campbells to introduce extensive expert testimony regarding fraudulent practices by State Farm in its nation-wide operations. Although State Farm moved prior to phase II of the trial for the exclusion of such evidence and continued to object to it at trial, the trial court ruled that such evidence was admissible to determine whether State Farm's conduct in the Campbell case was indeed intentional and sufficiently egregious to warrant punitive damages." 65 P. 3d, at 1143.

Evidence pertaining to the PP & R policy concerned State Farm's business practices for over 20 years in numerous States. Most of these practices bore no relation to third-party automobile insurance claims, the type of claim underlying the Campbells' complaint against the company. The jury awarded the Campbells $2.6 million in compensatory damages and $145 million in punitive damages, which the trial court reduced to $1 million and $25 million respectively. Both parties appealed.

The Utah Supreme Court sought to apply the three guideposts we identified in Gore, supra, at 574–575, and it reinstated the $145 million punitive damages award. Relying in large part on the extensive evidence concerning the PP & R policy, the court concluded State Farm's conduct was reprehensible. The court also relied upon State Farm's "massive wealth" and on testimony indicating that "State Farm's actions, because of their clandestine nature, will be punished at most in one out of every 50,000 cases as a matter of statistical probability," 65 P. 3d, at 1153, and concluded that the ratio between punitive and compensatory damages was not unwarranted. Finally, the court noted that the punitive damages award was not excessive when compared to various civil and criminal penalties State Farm could have faced, including $10,000 for each act of fraud, the suspension of its license to conduct business in Utah, the disgorgement of profits, and imprisonment. 65 P.3d at 1154–1155. We granted certiorari. 535 U.S. 1111 (2002).

II

We recognized in Cooper Industries, Inc. v. Leatherman Tool Group, Inc., 532 U.S. 424, 149 L. Ed. 2d 674, 121 S. Ct. 1678 (2001), that in our judicial system compensatory and punitive damages, although usually awarded at the same time by the same decisionmaker, serve different purposes. Id. at 432. Compensatory damages "are intended to redress the concrete loss that the plaintiff has suffered by reason of the defendant's wrongful conduct." Ibid. (citing Restatement (Second) of Torts 903, pp. 453–454 (1979)). By contrast, punitive damages serve a broader function; they are aimed at deterrence and retribution. Cooper Industries, supra, at 432; see also Gore, supra, at 568 ("Punitive damages may properly be imposed to further a State's legitimate interests in punishing unlawful conduct and deterring its repetition"); Pacific Mut. Life Ins. Co. v. Haslip, 499 U.S. 1, 19, 113 L. Ed. 2d 1, 111 S. Ct. 1032 (1991) ("Punitive damages are imposed for purposes of retribution and deterrence").

While States possess discretion over the imposition of punitive damages, it is well established that there are procedural and substantive constitutional limitations on these awards. Cooper Industries, supra; Gore, 517 U.S., at 559; Honda Motor Co. v. Oberg, 512 U.S. 415, 129 L. Ed. 2d 336, 114 S. Ct. 2331 (1994); TXO Production Corp. v. Alliance Resources Corp., 509 U.S. 443, 125 L. Ed. 2d 366, 113 S. Ct. 2711 (1993); Haslip, supra. 499 U.S. 1 The Due Process Clause of the Fourteenth Amendment prohibits the imposition of grossly excessive or arbitrary punishments on a tortfeasor. Cooper Industries, supra, at 433; Gore, 517 U.S., at 562; see also id., at 587 (BREYER, J., concurring) ("This constitutional concern, itself harkening back to the Magna Carta, arises out of the basic unfairness of depriving citizens of life, liberty, or property, through the application, not of law and legal processes, but of arbitrary coercion"). The reason is that "elementary notions of fairness enshrined in our constitutional jurisprudence dictate that a person receive fair notice not only of the conduct that will subject him to punishment, but also of the severity of the penalty that a State may impose." Id., at 574; Cooper Industries, supra, at 433 ("Despite the broad discretion that States possess with respect to the imposition of criminal penalties and punitive damages, the Due Process Clause of the Fourteenth Amendment to the Federal Constitution imposes substantive limits on that discretion"). To the extent an award is grossly excessive, it furthers no legitimate purpose and constitutes an arbitrary deprivation of property. Haslip, supra, at 42 (O'CONNOR, J., dissenting) ("Punitive damages are a powerful weapon. Imposed wisely and with restraint, they have the potential to advance legitimate state interests. Imposed indiscriminately, however, they have a devastating potential for harm. Regrettably, common-law procedures for awarding punitive damages fall into the latter category").

Although these awards serve the same purposes as criminal penalties, defendants subjected to punitive damages in civil cases have not been accorded the protections applicable in a criminal proceeding. This increases our concerns over the imprecise manner in which punitive damages systems are administered. We have admonished that "punitive damages pose an acute danger of arbitrary deprivation of property. Jury instructions typically leave the jury with wide discretion in choosing amounts, and the presentation of evidence of a defendant's net worth creates the potential that juries will use their verdicts to express biases against big businesses, particularly those without strong local presences." Honda Motor, supra, at 432; see also Haslip, supra, at 59 (O'CONNOR, J., dissenting) ("The Due Process Clause does not permit a State to classify arbitrariness as a virtue. Indeed, the point of due process—of the law in general—is to allow citizens to order their behavior. A State can have no legitimate interest in deliberately making the law so arbitrary that citizens will be unable to avoid punishment based solely upon bias or whim"). Our concerns are heightened when the decisionmaker is presented, as we shall discuss, with evidence that has little bearing as to the amount of punitive damages that should be awarded. Vague instructions, or those that merely inform the jury to avoid "passion or prejudice," App. to Pet. for Cert. 108a–109a, do little to aid the decisionmaker in its task of assigning appropriate weight to evidence that is relevant and evidence that is tangential or only inflammatory.

In light of these concerns, in Gore supra, 517 U.S. 559, we instructed courts reviewing punitive damages to consider three guideposts: (1) the degree of reprehensibility of the defendant's misconduct; (2) the disparity between the actual or potential harm suffered by the plaintiff and the punitive damages award; and (3) the difference between the punitive damages awarded by the jury and the civil penalties authorized or imposed in comparable cases. Id., at 575. We reiterated the importance of these three guideposts in Cooper Industries and mandated appellate courts to conduct de novo review of a trial court's application of them to the jury's award. 532 U.S., at 424. Exacting appellate review ensures that an award of punitive damages is based upon an " 'application of law, rather than a decisionmaker's caprice.' " Id., at 436 (quoting Gore, supra, at 587 (BREYER, J., concurring)).

III

Under the principles outlined in BMW of North America, Inc. v. Gore, this case is neither close nor difficult. It was error to reinstate the jury's $145 million punitive damages award. We address each guidepost of Gore in some detail.

A

"The most important indicium of the reasonableness of a punitive damages award is the degree of reprehensibility of the defendant's conduct." Gore, supra, at 575. We have instructed courts to determine the reprehensibility of a defendant by considering whether: the harm caused was physical as opposed to economic; the tortious conduct evinced an indifference to or a reckless disregard of the health or safety of others; the target of the conduct had financial vulnerability; the conduct involved repeated actions or was an isolated incident; and the harm was the result of intentional malice, trickery, or deceit, or mere accident. 517

U.S., at 576–577. The existence of any one of these factors weighing in favor of a plaintiff may not be sufficient to sustain a punitive damages award; and the absence of all of them renders any award suspect. It should be presumed a plaintiff has been made whole for his injuries by compensatory damages, so punitive damages should only be awarded if the defendant's culpability, after having paid compensatory damages, is so reprehensible as to warrant the imposition of further sanctions to achieve punishment or deterrence. Id., at 575.

Applying these factors in the instant case, we must acknowledge that State Farm's handling of the claims against the Campbells merits no praise. The trial court found that State Farm's employees altered the company's records to make Campbell appear less culpable. State Farm disregarded the overwhelming likelihood of liability and the near-certain probability that, by taking the case to trial, a judgment in excess of the policy limits would be awarded. State Farm amplified the harm by at first assuring the Campbells their assets would be safe from any verdict and by later telling them, postjudgment, to put a for-sale sign on their house. While we do not suggest there was error in awarding punitive damages based upon State Farm's conduct toward the Campbells, a more modest punishment for this reprehensible conduct could have satisfied the State's legitimate objectives, and the Utah courts should have gone no further.

This case, instead, was used as a platform to expose, and punish, the perceived deficiencies of State Farm's operations throughout the country. The Utah Supreme Court's opinion makes explicit that State Farm was being condemned for its nationwide policies rather than for the conduct direct toward the Campbells. 65 P. 3d, at 1143 ("The Campbells introduced evidence that State Farm's decision to take the case to trial was a result of a national scheme to meet corporate fiscal goals by capping payouts on claims company wide"). This was, as well, an explicit rationale of the trial court's decision in approving the award, though reduced from $145 million to $25 million. App. to Pet. for Cert. 120a ("The Campbells demonstrated, through the testimony of State Farm employees who had worked outside of Utah, and through expert testimony, that this pattern of claims adjustment under the PP & R program was not a local anomaly, but was a consistent, nationwide feature of State Farm's business operations, orchestrated from the highest levels of corporate management").

The Campbells contend that State Farm has only itself to blame for the reliance upon dissimilar and out-of-state conduct evidence. The record does not support this contention. From their opening statements onward the Campbells framed this case as a chance to rebuke State Farm for its nationwide activities. App. 208 ("You're going to hear evidence that even the insurance commission in Utah and around the country are unwilling or inept at protecting people against abuses"); id., at 242 ("This is a very important case.... It transcends the Campbell file. It involves a nationwide practice. And you, here, are going to be evaluating and assessing, and hopefully requiring State Farm to stand accountable for what it's doing across the country, which is the purpose of punitive damages"). This was a position maintained throughout the litigation. In opposing State Farm's motion to exclude such evidence under Gore, the Campbells' counsel convinced the trial court that there was no limitation on the scope of evidence that could be considered under our precedents. App. to Pet. for Cert. 172a ("As I read the case [Gore], I was struck with the fact that a clear message in the case ... seems to be that courts in punitive damages cases should receive more evidence, not less. And that the court seems to be inviting an even broader area of evidence than the current rulings of the court would indicate"); id., at 189a (trial court ruling).

A State cannot punish a defendant for conduct that may have been lawful where it occurred. Gore, supra, at 572; Bigelow v. Virginia, 421 U.S. 809, 824, 44 L. Ed. 2d 600, 95 S. Ct. 2222 (1975) ("A State does not acquire power or supervision over the internal affairs of another State merely because the welfare and health of its own citizens may be affected when they travel to that State"); New York Life Ins. Co. v. Head, 234 U.S. 149, 161, 58 L. Ed. 1259, 34 S. Ct. 879 (1914) ("It would be impossible to permit the statutes of Missouri to operate beyond the jurisdiction of that State ... without throwing down the constitutional barriers by which all the States are restricted within the orbits of their lawful authority and upon the preservation of which the Government under the Constitution depends. This is so obviously the necessary result of the Constitution that it has rarely been called in question and hence authorities directly dealing with it do not abound"); Huntington v. Attrill, 146 U.S. 657, 669, 36 L. Ed. 1123, 13 S. Ct. 224 (1892) ("Laws have no force of themselves beyond the jurisdiction of the State which enacts them, and can have extra-territorial effect only by the comity of other States"). Nor, as a general rule, does a State have a legitimate concern in imposing punitive damages to punish a defendant for unlawful acts committed outside of the State's jurisdiction. Any proper adjudication of conduct that occurred outside Utah to other persons would require their inclusion, and, to those parties, the Utah courts, in the usual case, would need to apply the laws of their relevant jurisdiction. Phillips Petroleum Co. v. Shutts, 472 U.S. 797, 821–822, 86 L. Ed. 2d 628, 105 S. Ct. 2965 (1985).

Here, the Campbells do not dispute that much of the out-of-state conduct was lawful where it occurred. They argue, however, that such evidence was not the primary basis for the punitive damages award and was relevant to the extent it demonstrated, in a general sense, State Farm's motive against its insured. Brief for Respondents 46–47 ("Even if the practices described by State Farm were not malum in se or malum prohibitum, they became relevant to punitive damages to the extent they were used as tools to implement State Farm's wrongful PP & R policy"). This argument misses the mark. Lawful out-of-state conduct may be probative when it demonstrates the deliberateness and culpability of the defendant's action in the State where it is tortious, but that conduct must have a nexus to the specific harm suffered by the plaintiff. A jury must be instructed, furthermore, that it may not use evidence of out-of-state conduct to punish a defendant for action that was lawful in the jurisdiction where it occurred. Gore, 517 U.S., at 572–573 (noting that a State "does not have the power . . . to punish [a defendant] for conduct that was lawful where it occurred and that had no impact on [the State] or its residents"). A basic principle of federalism is that each State may make its own reasoned judgment about what conduct is permitted or proscribed within its borders, and each State alone can determine what measure of punishment, if any, to impose on a defendant who acts within its jurisdiction. Id., at 569 ("The States need not, and in fact do not, provide such protection in a uniform manner").

For a more fundamental reason, however, the Utah courts erred in relying upon this and other evidence: The courts awarded punitive damages to punish and deter conduct that bore no relation to the Campbells' harm. A defendant's dissimilar acts, independent from the acts upon which liability was premised, may not serve as the basis for punitive damages. A defendant should be punished for the conduct that harmed the plaintiff, not for being an unsavory individual or business. Due process does not permit courts, in the calculation of punitive damages, to adjudicate the merits of other parties' hypothetical claims against a defendant under the guise of the reprehensibility analysis, but we have no doubt the Utah Supreme Court did that here. 65 P. 3d, at 1149 ("Even if the harm to the Campbells can be appropriately characterized as minimal, the trial court's assessment of the situation is on target: 'The harm is minor to the individual but massive in the aggregate' "). Punishment on these bases creates the possibility of multiple punitive damages awards for the same conduct; for in the usual case nonparties are not bound by the judgment some other plaintiff obtains. supra, at 593 (BREYER, J., concurring) ("Larger damages might also 'double count' by including in the punitive damages award some of the compensatory, or punitive, damages that subsequent plaintiffs would also recover").

The same reasons lead us to conclude the Utah Supreme Court's decision cannot be justified on the grounds that State Farm was a recidivist. Although "our holdings that a recidivist may be punished more severely than a first offender recognize that repeated misconduct is more reprehensible than an individual instance of malfeasance," Gore, supra, at 577, in the context of civil actions courts must ensure the conduct in question replicates the prior transgressions. TXO, 509 U.S., at 462, n. 28 (noting that courts should look to " 'the existence and frequency of similar past conduct' ") (quoting Haslip, 499 U.S., at 21–2).

The Campbells have identified scant evidence of repeated misconduct of the sort that injured them. Nor does our review of the Utah courts' decisions convince us that State Farm was only punished for its actions toward the Campbells. Although evidence of other acts need not be identical to have relevance in the calculation of punitive damages, the Utah court erred here because evidence pertaining to claims that had nothing to do with a third-party lawsuit was introduced at length. Other evidence concerning reprehensibility was even more tangential. For example, the Utah Supreme Court criticized State Farm's investigation into the personal life of one of its employees and, in a broader approach, the manner in which State Farm's policies corrupted its employees. 65 P. 3d, at 1148, 1150. The Campbells attempt to justify the courts' reliance upon this unrelated testimony on the theory that each dollar of profit made by underpaying a third-party claimant is the same as a dollar made by underpaying a first-party one. Brief for Respondents 45; see also 65 P. 3d, at 1150 ("State Farm's continuing illicit practice created market disadvantages for other honest insurance companies because these practices increased profits. As plaintiffs' expert witnesses established, such wrongfully obtained competitive advantages have the potential to pressure other companies to adopt similar fraudulent tactics, or to force them out of business. Thus, such actions cause distortions throughout the insurance market and ultimately hurt all consumers"). For the reasons already stated, this argument is unconvincing. The reprehensibility guidepost does not permit courts to expand the scope of the case so that a defendant may be punished for any malfeasance, which in this case extended for a 20–year period. In this case, because the Campbells have shown no conduct by State Farm similar to that which harmed them, the conduct that harmed them is the only conduct relevant to the reprehensibility analysis.

B

Turning to the second Gore guidepost, we have been reluctant to identify concrete constitutional limits on the ratio between harm, or potential harm, to the plaintiff and the punitive damages award. Gore, supra, at 582 ("We have consistently rejected the notion that the constitutional line is marked by a simple mathematical formula, even one that compares actual and potential damages to the punitive award"); TXO, supra, at 458. We decline again to impose a bright-line ratio which a punitive damages award cannot exceed. Our jurisprudence and the principles it has now established demonstrate, however, that, in practice, few awards exceeding a single-digit ratio between punitive and compensatory damages, to a significant degree, will satisfy due process. In Haslip, in upholding a punitive damages award, we concluded that an award of more than four times the amount of compensatory damages might be close to the line of constitutional impropriety. 499 U.S., at 23–24. We cited that 4–to–1 ratio again in Gore. 517 U.S., at 581. The Court further referenced a long legislative history, dating back over 700 years and going forward to today, providing for sanctions of double, treble, or quadruple damages to deter and punish. Id., at 581, and n. 33. While these ratios are not binding, they are instructive. They demonstrate what should be obvious: Single-digit multipliers are more likely to comport with due process, while still achieving the State's goals of deterrence and retribution, than awards with ratios in range of 500 to 1, id., at 582, or, in this case, of 145 to 1.

Nonetheless, because there are no rigid benchmarks that a punitive damages award may not surpass, ratios greater than those we have previously upheld may comport with due process where "a particularly egregious act has resulted in only a small amount of economic damages." Ibid.; see also ibid. (positing that a higher ratio might be necessary where "the injury is hard to detect or the monetary value of noneconomic harm might have been difficult to determine"). The converse is also true, however. When compensatory damages are substantial, then a lesser ratio, perhaps only equal to compensatory damages, can reach the outermost limit of the due process guarantee. The precise award in any case, of course, must be based upon the facts and circumstances of the defendant's conduct and the harm to the plaintiff.

In sum, courts must ensure that the measure of punishment is both reasonable and proportionate to the amount of harm to the plaintiff and to the general damages recovered. In the context of this case, we have no doubt that there is a presumption against an award that has a 145–to–1 ratio. The compensatory award in this case was substantial; the Campbells were awarded $1 million for a year and a half of emotional distress. This was complete compensation. The harm arose from a transaction in the economic realm, not from some physical assault or trauma; there were no physical injuries; and State Farm paid the excess verdict before the complaint was filed, so the Campbells suffered only minor economic injuries for the 18–month period in which State Farm refused to resolve the claim against them. The compensatory damages for the injury suffered here, moreover, likely were based on a component which was duplicated in the punitive award. Much of the distress was caused by the outrage and humiliation the Campbells suffered at the actions of their insurer; and it is a major role of punitive damages to condemn such conduct. Compensatory damages, however, already contain this punitive element. See Restatement (Second) of Torts 908, Comment c, p. 466 (1977) ("In many cases in which compensatory damages include an amount for emotional distress, such as humiliation or indignation aroused by the defendant's act, there is no clear line of demarcation between punishment and compensation and a verdict for a specified amount frequently includes elements of both").

The Utah Supreme Court sought to justify the massive award by pointing to State Farm's purported failure to report a prior $100 million punitive damages award in Texas to its corporate headquarters; the fact that State Farm's policies have affected numerous Utah consumers; the fact that State Farm will only be punished in one out of every 50,000 cases as a matter of statistical probability; and State Farm's enormous wealth. 65 P. 3d, at 1153. Since the Supreme Court of Utah discussed the Texas award when applying the ratio guidepost, we discuss it here. The Texas award, however, should have been analyzed in the context of the reprehensibility guidepost only. The failure of the company to report the Texas award is out-of-state conduct that, if the conduct were similar, might have had some bearing on the degree of reprehensibility, subject to the limitations we have described. Here, it was dissimilar, and of such marginal relevance that it should have been accorded little or no weight. The award was rendered in a first-party lawsuit; no judgment was entered in the case; and it was later settled for a fraction of the verdict. With respect to the Utah Supreme Court's second justification, the Campbells' inability to direct us to testimony demonstrating harm to the people of Utah (other than those directly involved in this case) indicates that the adverse effect on the State's general population was in fact minor.

The remaining premises for the Utah Supreme Court's decision bear no relation to the award's reasonableness or proportionality to the harm. They are, rather, arguments that seek to defend a departure from well-established constraints on punitive damages. While States enjoy considerable discretion in deducing when punitive damages are warranted, each award must comport with the principles set forth in Gore. Here the argument that State Farm will be punished in only the rare case, coupled with reference to its assets (which, of course, are what other insured parties in Utah and other States must rely upon for payment of claims) had little to do with the actual harm sustained by the Campbells. The wealth of a defendant cannot justify an otherwise unconstitutional punitive damages award. Gore, 517 U.S., at 585 ("The fact that BMW is a large corporation rather than an impecunious individual does not diminish its entitlement to fair notice of the demands that the several States impose on the conduct of its business"); see also id., at 591 (BREYER, J., concurring) ("[Wealth] provides an open-ended basis for inflating awards when the defendant is wealthy.... That does not make its use unlawful or inappropriate; it simply means that this factor cannot make up for the failure of other factors, such as 'reprehensibility,' to constrain significantly an award that purports to punish a defendant's conduct"). The principles set forth in Gore must be implemented with care, to ensure both reasonableness and proportionality.

C

The third guidepost in Gore is the disparity between the punitive damages award and the "civil penalties authorized or imposed in comparable cases." Id., at 575. We note that, in the past, we have also looked to criminal penalties that could be imposed. Id., at 583; Haslip, 499 U.S., at 23. The existence of a criminal penalty does have bearing on the seriousness with which a State views the wrongful action. When used to determine the dollar amount of the award, however, the criminal penalty has less utility. Great care must be taken to avoid use of the civil process to assess criminal penalties that can be imposed only after the heightened protections of a criminal trial have been observed, including, of course, its higher standards of proof. Punitive damages are not a substitute for the criminal process, and the remote possibility of a criminal sanction does not automatically sustain a punitive damages award.

Here, we need not dwell long on this guidepost. The most relevant civil sanction under Utah state law for the wrong done to the Campbells appears to be a $10,000 fine for an act of fraud, 65 P. 3d, at 1154, an amount dwarfed by the $145 million punitive damages award. The Supreme Court of Utah speculated about the loss of State Farm's business license, the disgorgement of profits, and possible imprisonment, but here again its references were to the broad fraudulent scheme drawn from evidence of out-of-state and dissimilar conduct. This analysis was insufficient to justify the award.

IV

An application of the Gore guideposts to the facts of this case, especially in light of the substantial compensatory damages awarded (a portion of which contained a punitive element), likely would justify a punitive damages award at or near the amount of compensatory damages. The punitive award of $145 million, therefore, was neither reasonable nor proportionate to the wrong committed, and it was an irrational and arbitrary deprivation of the property of the defendant. The proper calculation of punitive damages under the principles we have discussed should be resolved, in the first instance, by the Utah courts.

The judgment of the Utah Supreme Court is reversed, and the case is remanded for proceedings not inconsistent with this opinion.

It is so ordered.

DISSENT:

JUSTICE SCALIA, dissenting.

I adhere to the view expressed in my dissenting opinion in BMW of North America, Inc. v. Gore, 517 U.S. 559, 598–99, 134 L. Ed. 2d 809, 116 S. Ct. 1589 (1996), that the Due Process Clause provides no substantive protections against "excessive" or " 'unreasonable' " awards of punitive damages. I am also of the view that the punitive damages jurisprudence which has sprung forth from BMW v. Gore is insusceptible of principled application; accordingly, I do not feel justified in giving the case stare decisis effect. See id., at 599. I would affirm the judgment of the Utah Supreme Court.

JUSTICE THOMAS, dissenting.

I would affirm the judgment below because "I continue to believe that the Constitution does not constrain the size of punitive damages awards." Cooper Industries, Inc. v. Leatherman Tool Group, Inc., 532 U.S. 424, 443, 149 L. Ed. 2d 674, 121 S. Ct. 1678 (2001) (THOMAS, J., concurring) (citing BMW of North America, Inc. v. Gore, 517 U.S. 559, 599, 134 L. Ed. 2d 809, 116 S. Ct. 1589 (1996) (SCALIA, J., joined by THOMAS, J., dissenting)). Accordingly, I respectfully dissent.

JUSTICE GINSBURG, dissenting.

Not long ago, this Court was hesitant to impose a federal check on state-court judgments awarding punitive damages. In Browning–Ferris Industries of Vt., Inc. v. Kelco Disposal, Inc., 492 U.S. 257, 106 L. Ed. 2d 219, 109 S. Ct. 2909 (1989), the Court held that neither the Excessive

Fines Clause of the Eighth Amendment nor federal common law circumscribed awards of punitive damages in civil cases between private parties. Id., at 262–276, 277–280. Two years later, in Pacific Mut. Life Ins. Co. v. Haslip, 499 U.S. 1, 113 L. Ed. 2d 1, 111 S. Ct. 1032 (1991), the Court observed that "unlimited jury [or judicial] discretion . . . in the fixing of punitive damages may invite extreme results that jar one's constitutional sensibilities," id., at 18; the Due Process Clause, the Court suggested, would attend to those sensibilities and guard against unreasonable awards, id., at 17–24. Nevertheless, the Court upheld a punitive damages award in Haslip "more than 4 times the amount of compensatory damages, . . . more than 200 times [the plaintiff's] out-of-pocket expenses," and "much in excess of the fine that could be imposed." Id., at 23. And in TXO Production Corp. v. Alliance Resources Corp., 509 U.S. 443, 125 L. Ed. 2d 366, 113 S. Ct. 2711 (1993), the Court affirmed a state-court award "526 times greater than the actual damages awarded by the jury." Id., at 453;[2] cf. Browning–Ferris, 492 U.S., at 262 (ratio of punitive to compensatory damages over 100 to 1).

It was not until 1996, in BMW of North America, Inc. v. Gore, 517 U.S. 559, 134 L. Ed. 2d 809, 116 S. Ct. 1589 (1996), that the Court, for the first time, invalidated a state-court punitive damages assessment as unreasonably large. See id., at 599 (SCALIA, J., dissenting). If our activity in this domain is now "well-established," see ante, at 5, 17, it takes place on ground not long held.

In Gore, I stated why I resisted the Court's foray into punitive damages "territory traditionally within the States' domain." 517 U.S., at 612 (dissenting opinion). I adhere to those views, and note again that, unlike federal habeas corpus review of state-court convictions under 28 U.S.C. 2254, the Court "works at this business [of checking state courts] alone," unaided by the participation of federal district courts and courts of appeals. 517 U.S., at 613. It was once recognized that "the laws of the particular State must suffice [to superintend punitive damages awards] until judges or legislators authorized to do so initiate system-wide change." Haslip, 499 U.S., at 42 (KENNEDY, J., concurring in judgment). I would adhere to that traditional view.

I

The large size of the award upheld by the Utah Supreme Court in this case indicates why damage-capping legislation may be altogether fitting and proper. Neither the amount of the award nor the trial record, however, justifies this Court's substitution of its judgment for that of Utah's competent decisionmakers. In this regard, I count it significant that, on the key criterion "reprehensibility," there is a good deal more to the story than the Court's abbreviated account tells.

2. By switching the focus from the ratio of punitive to compensatory damages to the potential loss to the plaintiffs had the defendant succeeded in its illicit scheme, the Court could describe the relevant ratio in *TXO* as 10 to 1. See *BMW of North America, Inc. v. Gore*, 517 U.S. 559, 581, 134 L. Ed. 2d 809, 116 S. Ct. 1589, and n. 34 (1996).

Ample evidence allowed the jury to find that State Farm's treatment of the Campbells typified its "Performance, Planning and Review" (PP & R) program; implemented by top management in 1979, the program had "the explicit objective of using the claims-adjustment process as a profit center." App. to Pet. for Cert. 116a. "The Campbells presented considerable evidence," the trial court noted, documenting "that the PP & R program ... has functioned, and continues to function, as an unlawful scheme ... to deny benefits owed consumers by paying out less than fair value in order to meet preset, arbitrary payout targets designed to enhance corporate profits." Id., at 118a–119a. That policy, the trial court observed, was encompassing in scope; it "applied equally to the handling of both third-party and first-party claims." Id., at 119a. But cf. ante, at 13, 17 (suggesting that State Farm's handling of first-party claims has "nothing to do with a third-party lawsuit").

Evidence the jury could credit demonstrated that the PP & R program regularly and adversely affected Utah residents. Ray Summers, "the adjuster who handled the Campbell case and who was a State Farm employee in Utah for almost twenty years," described several methods used by State Farm to deny claimants fair benefits, for example, "falsifying or withholding of evidence in claim files." Id., at 121a. A common tactic, Summers recounted, was to "unjustly attack the character, reputation and credibility of a claimant and make notations to that effect in the claim file to create prejudice in the event the claim ever came before a jury." Id., at 130a (internal quotation marks omitted). State Farm manager Bob Noxon, Summers testified, resorted to a tactic of this order in the Campbell case when he "instructed Summers to write in the file that Todd Ospital (who was killed in the accident) was speeding because he was on his way to see a pregnant girlfriend." Ibid. In truth, "there was no pregnant girlfriend." Ibid. Expert testimony noted by the trial court described these tactics as "completely improper." Ibid.

The trial court also noted the testimony of two Utah State Farm employees, Felix Jensen and Samantha Bird, both of whom recalled "intolerable" and "recurrent" pressure to reduce payouts below fair value. Id., at 119a (internal quotation marks omitted). When Jensen complained to top managers, he was told to "get out of the kitchen" if he could not take the heat; Bird was told she should be "more of a team player." Ibid. (internal quotation marks omitted). At times, Bird said, she "was forced to commit dishonest acts and to knowingly underpay claims." Id., at 120a. Eventually, Bird quit. Ibid. Utah managers superior to Bird, the evidence indicated, were improperly influenced by the PP & R program to encourage insurance underpayments. For example, several documents evaluating the performance of managers Noxon and Brown "contained explicit preset average payout goals." Ibid.

Regarding liability for verdicts in excess of policy limits, the trial court referred to a State Farm document titled the "Excess Liability Handbook"; written before the Campbell accident, the handbook instructed adjusters to pad files with "self-serving" documents, and to leave critical items out of files, for example, evaluations of the insured's exposure. Id., at 127a–128a (internal quotation marks omitted). Divisional superintendent Bill Brown used the handbook to train Utah employees. Id., at 134a. While overseeing the Campbell case, Brown ordered adjuster Summers to change the portions of his report indicating that Mr. Campbell was likely at fault and that the settlement cost was correspondingly high. Id., at 3a. The Campbells' case, according to expert testimony the trial court recited, "was a classic example of State Farm's application of the improper practices taught in the Excess Liability Handbook." Id., at 128a.

The trial court further determined that the jury could find State Farm's policy "deliberately crafted" to prey on consumers who would be unlikely to defend themselves. Id., at 122a. In this regard, the trial court noted the testimony of several former State Farm employees affirming that they were trained to target "the weakest of the herd"—"the elderly, the poor, and other consumers who are least knowledgeable about their rights and thus most vulnerable to trickery or deceit, or who have little money and hence have no real alternative but to accept an inadequate offer to settle a claim at much less than fair value." Ibid. (internal quotation marks omitted).

The Campbells themselves could be placed within the "weakest of the herd" category. The couple appeared economically vulnerable and emotionally fragile. App. 3360a–3361a (Order Denying State Farm's Motion for Judgment NOV and New Trial Regarding Intentional Infliction of Emotional Distress). At the time of State Farm's wrongful conduct, "Mr. Campbell had residuary effects from a stroke and Parkinson's disease." Id., at 3360a.

To further insulate itself from liability, trial evidence indicated, State Farm made "systematic" efforts to destroy internal company documents that might reveal its scheme, App. to Pet. for Cert. 123a, efforts that directly affected the Campbells, id., at 124a. For example, State Farm had "a special historical department that contained a copy of all past manuals on claim-handling practices and the dates on which each section of each manual was changed." Ibid. Yet in discovery proceedings, State Farm failed to produce any claim-handling practice manuals for the years relevant to the Campbells' bad-faith case. Id., at 124a-125a.

State Farm's inability to produce the manuals, it appeared from the evidence, was not accidental. Documents retained by former State Farm employee Samantha Bird, as well as Bird's testimony, showed that while the Campbells' case was pending, Janet Cammack, "an in-house attorney sent by top State Farm management, conducted a meeting ... in Utah during which she instructed Utah claims management to search their offices and destroy a wide range of material of the sort that had proved damaging in bad-faith litigation in the past—in particular, old claim-handling manuals, memos, claim school notes, procedure guides and other similar documents." Id., at 125a. "These orders were followed even though at least one meeting participant, Paul Short, was personally aware that these kinds of materials had been requested by the Campbells in this very case." Ibid.

Consistent with Bird's testimony, State Farm admitted that it destroyed every single copy of claim-handling manuals on file in its historical department as of 1988, even though these documents could have been preserved at minimal expense. Ibid. Fortuitously, the Campbells obtained a copy of the 1979 PP & R manual by subpoena from a former employee. Id., at 132a. Although that manual has been requested in other cases, State Farm has never itself produced the document. Ibid.

"As a final, related tactic," the trial court stated, the jury could reasonably find that "in recent years State Farm has gone to extraordinary lengths to stop damaging documents from being created in the first place." Id., at 126a. State Farm kept no records at all on excess verdicts in third-party cases, or on bad-faith claims or attendant verdicts. Ibid. State Farm alleged "that it has no record of its punitive damage payments, even though such payments must be reported to the [Internal Revenue Service] and in some states may not be used to justify rate increases." Ibid. Regional Vice President Buck Moskalski testified that "he would not report a punitive damage verdict in [the Campbells'] case to higher management, as such reporting was not set out as part of State Farm's management practices." Ibid.

State Farm's "wrongful profit and evasion schemes," the trial court underscored, were directly relevant to the Campbells' case, id., at 132a:

"The record fully supports the conclusion that the bad-faith claim handling that exposed the Campbells to an excess verdict in 1983, and resulted in severe damages to them, was a product of the unlawful profit scheme that had been put in place by top management at State Farm years earlier. The Campbells presented substantial evidence showing how State Farm's improper insistence on claims-handling employees' reducing their claim payouts ... regardless of the merits of each claim, manifested itself ... in the Utah claims operations during the period when the decisions were made not to offer to settle the Campbell case for the $50,000 policy limits—indeed, not to make any offer to settle at a lower amount. This evidence established that high-level manager Bill Brown was under heavy pressure from the PP & R scheme to control indemnity payouts during the time period in question. In particular, when Brown declined to pay the excess verdict against Curtis Campbell, or even post a bond, he had a special need to keep his year-end numbers down, since the State Farm incentive scheme meant that keeping those numbers down was important to helping Brown get a much-desired transfer to Colorado.... There was ample evidence that the concepts taught in the Excess Liability Handbook, including the dishonest alteration and manipulation of claim files and the policy against posting any supersedeas bond for the full amount of an excess verdict, were dutifully carried out in this case.... There was ample basis for the jury to find that everything that had happened to the Campbells—when State Farm repeatedly refused in bad-faith to settle for the $50,000 policy limits and went to trial, and then failed to pay the 'excess' verdict, or at least post a bond, after trial—was a direct application of State Farm's overall profit scheme, operating through Brown and others." Id., at 133a–134a.

State Farm's "policies and practices," the trial evidence thus bore out, were "responsible for the injuries suffered by the Campbells," and the means used to implement those policies could be found "callous, clandestine, fraudulent, and dishonest." Id., at 136a; see id., at 113a (finding "ample evidence" that State Farm's reprehensible corporate policies were responsible for injuring "many other Utah consumers during the past two decades"). The Utah Supreme Court, relying on the trial court's record-based recitations, understandably characterized State Farm's behavior as "egregious and malicious." Id., at 18a.

II

The Court dismisses the evidence describing and documenting State Farm's PP & R policy and practices as essentially irrelevant, bearing "no relation to the Campbells' harm." Ante, at 12; see ante, at 14 ("conduct that harmed [the Campbells] is the only conduct relevant to the reprehensibility analysis"). It is hardly apparent why that should be so. What is infirm about the Campbells' theory that their experience with State Farm exemplifies and reflects an overarching underpayment scheme, one that caused "repeated misconduct of the sort that injured them," ante, at 13? The Court's silence on that score is revealing: Once one recognizes that the Campbells did show "conduct by State Farm similar to that which harmed them," ante, at 14, it becomes impossible to shrink the reprehensibility analysis to this sole case, or to maintain, at odds with the determination of the trial court, see App. to Pet. for Cert. 113a, that "the adverse effect on the State's general population was in fact minor," ante, at 17.

Evidence of out-of-state conduct, the Court acknowledges, may be "probative [even if the conduct is lawful in the state where it occurred] when it demonstrates the deliberateness and culpability of the defendant's action in the State where it is tortious.... " Ante, at 11; cf. ante, at 8 (reiterating this Court's instruction that trial courts assess whether "the harm was the result of intentional malice, trickery, or deceit, or mere accident"). "Other acts" evidence concerning practices both in and out of State was introduced in this case to show just such "deliberateness" and "culpability." The evidence was admissible, the trial court ruled: (1) to document State Farm's "reprehensible" PP & R program; and (2) to "rebut [State Farm's] assertion that [its] actions toward the Campbells were inadvertent errors or mistakes in judgment." App. 3329a (Order Denying Various Motions of State Farm to Exclude Plaintiffs' Evidence). Viewed in this light, there surely was "a nexus" between much of the "other acts" evidence and "the specific harm suffered by [the Campbells]." Ante, at 11.

III

When the Court first ventured to override state-court punitive damages awards, it did so moderately. The Court recalled that "in our federal system, States necessarily have considerable flexibility in determining the level of punitive damages that they will allow in different classes of cases and in any particular case." Gore, 517 U.S., at 568. Today's decision exhibits no such respect and restraint. No longer content to accord state-court judgments "a strong presumption of validity," TXO, 509 U.S., at 457, the Court announces that "few awards exceeding a single-digit ratio between punitive and compensatory damages, to a significant degree, will satisfy due process." Ante, at 14.[3] Moreover, the Court adds, when compensatory damages are substantial, doubling those damages "can reach the outermost limit of the due process guarantee." Ante, at 15; see ante, at 18–19 ("facts of this case . . . likely would justify a punitive damages award at or near the amount of compensatory damages"). In a legislative scheme or a state high court's design to cap punitive damages, the handiwork in setting single-digit and 1–to–1 benchmarks could hardly be questioned; in a judicial decree imposed on the States by this Court under the banner of substantive due process, the numerical controls today's decision installs seem to me boldly out of order.

* * *

I remain of the view that this Court has no warrant to reform state law governing awards of punitive damages. Gore, 517 U.S., at 607 (GINSBURG, J., dissenting). Even if I were prepared to accept the flexible guides prescribed in Gore, I would not join the Court's swift conversion of those guides into instructions that begin to resemble marching orders. For the reasons stated, I would leave the judgment of the Utah Supreme Court undisturbed.

Notes

1. Despite the limitations imposed on the award of punitive damages by *State Farm v. Campbell*, the United States Supreme Court clearly affirms the constitutionality of punitive damage awards. See TXO Production Corp. v. Alliance Resources Corp., 509 U.S. 443, 113 S.Ct. 2711, 125 L.Ed.2d 366 (1993); Pacific Mutual Life Insurance Company v. Haslip, 499 U.S. 1, 111 S.Ct. 1032, 113 L.Ed.2d 1 (1991).

In *BMW of North America v. Gore,* 517 U.S. 559, 116 S.Ct. 1589, 134 L.Ed.2d 809 (1996), discussed within the *State Farm v. Campbell* case, BMW adopted a nationwide policy that damaged cars would be repaired and sold as new without disclosing that prior repairs were made, as long as repair costs did not exceed 3 percent of the suggested retail price. Gore bought a BMW in Alabama for approximately $40,000, which had been partially repainted at a cost of $601.37, 1.5 percent of the suggested retail price. Nine months later, at an auto detailing shop, Gore discovered the car had been repainted. Gore

3. TXO Production Corp. v. Alliance Resources Corp., 509 U.S. 443, 462, n. 8, 125 L. Ed. 2d 366, 113 S. Ct. 2711 (1993), noted that "under well-settled law," a defendant's "wrongdoing in other parts of the country" and its "impressive net worth" are factors "typically considered in assessing punitive damages." It remains to be seen whether, or the extent to which, today's decision will unsettle that law.

brought an action in Alabama state court alleging BMW's failure to disclose a material fact and claimed actual damages of $4000 (10 percent of value of a new car), and punitive damages of $4 million, which the jury awarded. The case went to the Alabama Supreme Court, which rejected BMW's claim that the award exceeded the constitutionally permissible amount, but found that the jury improperly computed the amount of punitive damages, held that "a constitutionally reasonable award was $2 million" and ordered a remittitur in that amount. The United States Supreme Court granted certiorari and, in an opinion written by Justice Stevens, affirmed the rule that punitive damages may properly be imposed to further a State's legitimate interests in punishing unlawful conduct and deterring its repetition. However, a State may not impose economic sanctions on violators with the intent of changing tortfeasors' lawful conduct in other states. The Court held that the $2 million punitive damages award was grossly excessive for three reasons: first, none of the aggravating factors associated with particularly reprehensible conduct was present; second, the award was 500 times the amount of Gore's actual harm, and there was no proof of additional potential harm by the distributor's non-disclosure policy; and third, the sanction imposed was substantially greater than the statutory fines available in Alabama and elsewhere.

2. On remand, the Utah Supreme Court reduced the punitive damage award to $9 million for a 9 to 1 ratio of punitive damages to compensatory damages. Post *State Farm v. Campbell* cases have generally adhered to the single digit ratio. E.g., Romo v. Ford Motor, Co., 11 Cal.App.4th 738, 6 Cal.Rptr.3d 793 (2003)(5 to 1); Bocci v. Key Pharmaceuticals, Inc., 189 Ore.App. 349, 76 P.3d 669 (2003)(7 to 1).

3. In an influential article written before *State Farm v. Campbell*, Professor William Dodge takes a unique position regarding the use of punitive damages for breach of contract. See William Dodge, *The Case for Punitive Damages in Contracts*. 48 Duke L.J. 629 (1999). He explains:

> The traditional rule, adopted by the Restatement (Second) of Contracts and followed by a majority of states, does not allow punitive damages in the absence of an independent tort, even if the breach is opportunistic [the breaching party attempts to get more than he bargained for at the expense of the nonbreaching party]. Judge Posner approves of punitive damages in the absence of an independent tort, but not for efficient ones. * * * I go further and argue that punitive damages should be available to all willful breaches of contract, even those that are "efficient." *Id.* at 653–54.

Professor Dodge contends that, in terms of efficiency, allowing a party to breach and pay expectation damages is not as effective as threatening that party with punitive damages and forcing a negotiation with the other party for a release of the contract. *See id.* at 663. Relying on prior analytical approaches, he differentiates between "property rules," which require negotiation between the parties, and "liability rules," which excuse nonperformance upon payment of a court-determined amount. *Id.* at 634. In a contractual context, expectation damages act as a liability rule, while punitive damages operate as property rules. *Id.* Because of high costs associated with litigation and errors of judgment resulting from contract breaches, Professor Dodge argues that protecting contractual obligations with expectation damages is less efficient than protecting them with punitive damages, because the threat of punitive damages for willful breach will push the party who wants to avoid the contract to negotiate a release of her obligations, a less expensive alternative to litigation. *See id.* at 675.

Is Professor Dodge's position altered by *State Farm v. Campbell*?

4. *Punitive Damages.* The lure of punitive damages unquestionably provides the impetus to inflate the breach of an implied contract promise of fair dealing into a full fledged "tort" of bad faith. The "tort" thus created usually causes moderate actual economic damages and only problematical emotional or physical distress. It is one which leaves behind no shattered bodies, no destroyed reputations or environmental pollution. But by computing the deterrent and factors of the award as a minuscule fraction of the extraordinary "gross (or net) worth" of insurance companies—even those with cash flow difficulties—a sensational guaranteed funded prize is offered. Bitter controversy is also generated, and in the overall commotion about tort reform, the punitive awards against insurers for bad faith have provided a major disturbing element. Only a few cases from a mountain of material are needed to highlight the ongoing debate.

In Mississippi, Mr. Crenshaw lost his leg, whether by accident as he claimed or by pre-existing disease as his accident insurer contended. A jury sided with Mr. Crenshaw and awarded $20,000 in actual damages plus $1,600,000 punitive damages for bad faith handling of the claim. The Supreme Court of Mississippi affirmed the award in *Bankers Life and Cas. Co. v. Crenshaw*, 483 So.2d 254 (Miss.1985) and, in a pre-*State Farm v. Campbell* world, it survived before the U.S. Supreme Court on a constitutional challenge to punitive damages as such. Bankers Life and Casualty Co. v. Crenshaw, 486 U.S. 71, 108 S.Ct. 1645, 100 L.Ed.2d 62 (1988).

One prominent aspect of tort reform is to place a cap on punitive damages. In Montana in 1985 a statute was passed to tighten up on the proof required for punitive damages and to put a limit of $25,000 or 1 percent of the defendant's net worth which ever is greater (except in cases of actual fraud or actual malice). Consider how little effect such a law has on the potential liability of an insurance company the size of Allstate. In *Safeco Ins. Co. v. Ellinghouse*, 223 Mont. 239, 725 P.2d 217 (1986), a trial court awarded $25,000 in economic damages, $200,000 emotional damages and $5 million in punitive damages for the mishandling of the defense in a third party case. A remittitur of $4 million was ordered. The above statute was not yet in effect, but it will be observed that even the $5 million award would probably have been under the statutory cap when Safeco had "amassed assets" of $3.4 billion.

An empirical study that covers over two thousand claims in 38 jurisdictions, verifies the intuition that the existence of a bad-faith cause of action has the result of producing higher settlements—even in cases in which the insured party is not represented by an attorney. Mark J. Browne, Ellen S. Pryor & Bob Puelz, *The Effect of Bad-Faith Laws on First-Party Insurance Claims Decisions,* 33 J. LEGAL STUDIES 355 (2004).

5. Many cases using the rationale of "good faith and fair dealing" to aid the insured will be encountered in the course of this book, and assuredly

in the advance sheets of newly published opinions in the years ahead. The parameters of the doctrine are not yet set, and some of the applications may seem rather extraordinary. Consider, for example, *Davis v. Blue Cross of Northern California*, 25 Cal.3d 418, 158 Cal.Rptr. 828, 600 P.2d 1060 (1979), involving claims made against Blue Cross, a health insurer. Blue Cross' policies contained an unambiguous (but not particularly conspicuous) provision that if the subscriber (the insured) did not agree with Blue Cross' determination not to pay, "then such determination shall be made by arbitration under the laws of the State of California" [California has a strong public policy in favor of arbitration]. Certain subscribers initiated a class action suit against Blue Cross, which invoked the arbitration clause. In a 4–3 decision, the California State Supreme Court held that the failure to make the arbitration clause more conspicuous or to advise the subscribers when a claim was filed that arbitration was to be used was a breach of the duty of good faith. Therefore, Blue Cross had waived the arbitration provision and could not now compel arbitration.

In what possible way were the subscribers harmed by this "breach" of the duty of good faith and fair dealing? What about the public policy favoring arbitration? How are cases like this affected by *State Farm v. Campbell*?

6. Generally in an action for breach of contract, the measure of damages is "the amount which will compensate the party aggrieved for all the detriment proximately caused thereby, or which, in the ordinary course of things, would be likely to result therefrom" (Cal. Civ. Code, § 3300), provided the damages are "clearly ascertainable in both their nature and origin" (Cal. Civ. Code, § 3301). In other words, the damages available to parties in a breach of contract action are limited to compensatory damages and punitive damages are generally not awarded. This comports with Justice Holmes' observation that breach of contract is a morally neutral act, and that there is no morality in contract law. Further, it has been said that "[t]his limitation on available damages serves to encourage contractual relations and commercial activity by enabling parties to estimate in advance the financial risks of their enterprise." Applied Equipment Corp. v. Litton Saudi Arabia Ltd., 7 Cal.4th 503, 515, 28 Cal.Rptr.2d 475, 869 P.2d 454 (1994).

7. To be sure, an insured's action against an insurer is not a task undertaken lightly. One problem in such actions is the insurer's resort to the attorney-client privilege and to the work-product doctrine in resisting discovery by an insured. Some courts have been liberal in allowing discovery of a claims file—at least for the time before the action is brought—despite the insurer's attempt to rely on the attorney client privilege. Boone v. Vanliner Ins. Co., 91 Ohio St.3d 209, 744 N.E.2d 154 (2001); State Farm Mutual Auto. Ins. Co. v. Lee, 199 Ariz. 52, 13 P.3d 1169 (2000). Other courts have not been so generous to insureds who sue their insurers. E.g., Hartford Fin. Servs. Group, Inc. v. Lake County Park & Recreation Board, 717 N.E.2d 1232 (Ind. App. 1999) (attorney-client relationship must be protected under our legal system).

Douglas R. Richmond's article, *Advice of Counsel and Insurance Bad Faith*, 73 Miss. L.J. 95 (2003), contains an excellent discussion of the problems faced by insurers in bad faith cases. In criticizing the *Vanliner* and

Lee cases cited immediately above, he argues for a narrowing of an insured's rights of discovery. Id. at 133.

8. *Coverage for punitive damages.* California has declined to allow coverage for punitive damages. In *PPG Industries, Inc. v. Transamerica Ins. Co.*, 20 Cal.4th 310, 84 Cal.Rptr.2d 455, 975 P.2d 652 (1999), the California Supreme Court concluded that to allow coverage for punitive damages would be to (1) violate public policy by allowing the negligence of one party to offset the liability for intentional wrongdoing of another, (2) defeat the deterrence and punishment goals of punitive damages, and (3) would violate public policy against indemnification for intentional wrongdoing.

The moral and legal arguments against permitting a person to insure against his or her liability for punitive damages, quite similar to those against allowing insurance for the consequences of intentional acts, need no belaboring here. Many jurisdictions are adamantly opposed to insurance coverage for punitive damages. (Even in these states, however, the insurer may have to defend a claim which includes punitive damages. Ohio Cas. Ins. Co. v. Hubbard, 162 Cal.App.3d 939, 208 Cal.Rptr. 806 (1984)).

Unlike the California experience, some jurisdictions find no objection to the practice, it being considered a matter of contract—if an insurer is willing to accept the consequences of such risky underwriting. Other states are tolerant of insurance for punitive damages imposed for vicarious acts, where the moral argument is of less weight. The cases have mainly arisen in the context of policies (usually CGL policies) that simply did not refer to punitive damages at all. No one argues that coverage of punitive damage cannot be expressly excluded.

Professor Tom Baker argues persuasively that there is little evidence of a need for judicial regulation in the form of dissallowing insurance coverage for punitive damages. Tom Baker, *Reconsidering Insurance for Punitive Damages*, 1998 Wisc. L. Rev. 101. A table of the various jurisdictional holdings is found in Schumaier and McKinsey, 72 A.B.A.J. 69 (March 1986). It has been updated with information from the treatise by Richard L. Blatt, Robert W. Hammesfahr and Lori S. Nugent, Punitive Damages, §§ 8.2–8.3 (West 1991).

D. THE ORIGINS: THIRD PARTY CASES

CRISCI v. SECURITY INSURANCE COMPANY

Supreme Court of California, In Bank, 1967.
66 Cal.2d 425, 58 Cal.Rptr. 13, 426 P.2d 173.

PETERS, JUSTICE.

In an action against The Security Insurance Company of New Haven, Connecticut, the trial court awarded Rosina Crisci $91,000 (plus interest) because she suffered a judgment in a personal injury action after Security, her insurer, refused to settle the claim. Mrs. Crisci was also awarded $25,000 for mental suffering. Security has appealed.

June DiMare and her husband were tenants in an apartment building owned by Rosina Crisci. Mrs. DiMare was descending the apartment's outside wooden staircase when a tread gave way. She fell through the resulting opening up to her waist and was left hanging 15 feet above the ground. Mrs. DiMare suffered physical injuries and developed a very severe psychosis. In a suit brought against Mrs. Crisci the DiMares alleged that the step broke because Mrs. Crisci was negligent in inspecting and maintaining the stairs. They contended that Mrs. DiMare's mental condition was caused by the accident, and they asked for $400,000 as compensation for physical and mental injuries and medical expenses.

Mrs. Crisci had $10,000 of insurance coverage under a general liability policy issued by Security. The policy obligated Security to defend the suit against Mrs. Crisci and authorized the company to make any settlement it deemed expedient.[4] Security hired an experienced lawyer, Mr. Healy, to handle the case. Both he and defendant's claims manager believed that unless evidence was discovered showing that Mrs. DiMare had a prior mental illness, a jury would probably find that the accident precipitated Mrs. DiMare's psychosis. And both men believed that if the jury felt that the fall triggered the psychosis, a verdict of not less than $100,000 would be returned.

An extensive search turned up no evidence that Mrs. DiMare had any prior mental abnormality. As a teenager Mrs. DiMare had been in a Washington mental hospital, but only to have an abortion. Both Mrs. DiMare and Mrs. Crisci found psychiatrists who would testify that the accident caused Mrs. DiMare's illness, and the insurance company knew of this testimony. Among those who felt the psychosis was not related to the accident were the doctors at the state mental hospital where Mrs. DiMare had been committed following the accident. All the psychiatrists agreed, however, that a psychosis could be triggered by a sudden fear of falling to one's death.

The exact chronology of settlement offers is not established by the record. However, by the time the DiMares' attorney reduced his settlement demands to $10,000, Security had doctors prepared to support its position and was only willing to pay $3,000 for Mrs. DiMare's physical injuries. Security was unwilling to pay one cent for the possibility of a plaintiff's verdict on the mental illness issue. This conclusion was based on the assumption that the jury would believe all of the defendant's psychiatric evidence and none of the plaintiff's. Security also rejected a $9,000 settlement demand at a time when Mrs. Crisci offered to pay $2,500 of the settlement.

A jury awarded Mrs. DiMare $100,000 and her husband $1,000. After an appeal (DiMare v. Cresci,[5] 58 Cal.2d 292, 23 Cal.Rptr. 772, 373 P.2d 860) the insurance company paid $10,000 of this amount, the amount of its policy. The DiMares then sought to collect the balance

4. Mrs. Crisci's own attorney, Mr. Pardini, was consulted by the counsel for the insurance company, but Mr. Pardini did not direct or control either settlement negotiations or the defense of Mrs. DiMare's suit.

5. In the prior litigation plaintiff was sued as "Rosina Cresci."

from Mrs. Crisci. A settlement was arranged by which the DiMares received $22,000, a 40 percent interest in Mrs. Crisci's claim to a particular piece of property, and an assignment of Mrs. Crisci's cause of action against Security. Mrs. Crisci, an immigrant widow of 70, became indigent. She worked as a babysitter, and her grandchildren paid her rent. The change in her financial condition was accompanied by a decline in physical health, hysteria, and suicide attempts. Mrs. Crisci then brought this action.

The liability of an insurer in excess of its policy limits for failure to accept a settlement offer within those limits was considered by this court in Comunale v. Traders & General Ins. Co., 50 Cal.2d 654, 328 P.2d 198, 68 A.L.R.2d 883. It was there reasoned that in every contract, including policies of insurance, there is an implied covenant of good faith and fair dealing that neither party will do anything which will injure the right of the other to receive the benefits of the agreement; that it is common knowledge that one of the usual methods by which an insured receives protection under a liability insurance policy is by settlement of claims without litigation; that the implied obligation of good faith and fair dealing requires the insurer to settle in an appropriate case although the express terms of the policy do not impose the duty; that in determining whether to settle the insurer must give the interests of the insured at least as much consideration as it gives to its own interests; and that when "there is great risk of a recovery beyond the policy limits so that the most reasonable manner of disposing of the claim is a settlement which can be made within those limits, a consideration in good faith of the insured's interest requires the insurer to settle the claim." (50 Cal.2d at p. 659, 328 P.2d at p. 201.)

In determining whether an insurer has given consideration to the interests of the insured, the test is whether a prudent insurer without policy limits would have accepted the settlement offer.

Several cases, in considering the liability of the insurer, contain language to the effect that bad faith is the equivalent of dishonesty, fraud, and concealment. Obviously a showing that the insurer has been guilty of actual dishonesty, fraud, or concealment is relevant to the determination whether it has given consideration to the insured's interest in considering a settlement offer within the policy limits. The language used in the cases, however, should not be understood as meaning that in the absence of evidence establishing actual dishonesty, fraud, or concealment no recovery may be had for a judgment in excess of the policy limits. Comunale v. Traders & General Ins. Co., supra, 50 Cal.2d 654, 658–659, 328 P.2d 198, makes it clear that liability based or an implied covenant exists whenever the insurer refuses to settle in an appropriate case and that liability may exist when the insurer unwarrantedly refuses an offered settlement where the most reasonable manner of disposing of the claim is by accepting the settlement. Liability is imposed not for a bad faith breach of the contract but for failure to meet the duty to accept reasonable settlements, a duty included within the implied covenant of good faith and fair dealing. Moreover, examination of the balance of the Palmer, Critz, and Davy opinions makes it abundantly clear that recovery may be based on unwarranted rejection of a reasonable settlement offer and that the absence of evidence, circumstantial or direct, showing actual dishonesty, fraud, or concealment is not fatal to the cause of action.

Amicus curiae argues that, whenever an insurer receives an offer to settle within the policy limits and rejects it, the insurer should be liable in every case for the amount of any final judgment whether or not within the policy limits. As we have seen, the duty of the insurer to consider the insured's interest in settlement offers within the policy limits arises from an implied covenant in the contract, and ordinarily contract duties are strictly enforced and not subject to a standard of reasonableness. Obviously, it will always be in the insured's interest to settle within the policy limits when there is any danger, however slight, of a judgment in excess of those limits. Accordingly the rejection of a settlement within the limits where there is any danger of a judgment in excess of the limits can be justified, if at all, only on the basis of interests of the insurer, and, in light of the common knowledge that settlement is one of the usual methods by which an insured receives protection under a liability policy, it may not be unreasonable for an insured who purchases a policy with limits to believe that a sum of money equal to the limits is available and will be used so as to avoid liability on his part with regard to any covered accident. In view of such expectation an insurer should not be permitted to further its own interests by rejecting opportunities to settle within the policy limits unless it is also willing to absorb losses which may result from its failure to settle.

The proposed rule is a simple one to apply and avoids the burdens of a determination whether a settlement offer within the policy limits was reasonable. The proposed rule would also eliminate the danger that an insurer, faced with a settlement offer at or near the policy limits, will reject it and gamble with the insured's money to further its own interests. Moreover, it is not entirely clear that the proposed rule would place a burden on insurers substantially greater than that which is present under existing law. The size of the judgment recovered in the personal injury action when it exceeds the policy limits, although not conclusive, furnishes an inference that the value of the claim is the equivalent of the amount of the judgment and that acceptance of an offer within those limits was the most reasonable method of dealing with the claim.

Finally, and most importantly, there is more than a small amount of elementary justice in a rule that would require that, in this situation where the insurer's and insured's interests necessarily conflict, the insurer, which may reap the benefits of its determination not to settle, should also suffer the detriments of its decision. On the basis of these and other considerations, a number of commentators have urged that the insurer should be liable for any resulting judgment where it refuses to settle within the policy limits. (Note (1966) 18 Stan.L.Rev. 475, 482–

485; Note (1951) 60 Yale L.J. 1037, 1041–1042; Comment (1949) 48 Mich.L.Rev. 95, 102; Note (1945) 13 U.Chi.L.Rev. 105, 109.)

We need not, however, here determine whether there might be some countervailing considerations precluding adoption of the proposed rule because, under Comunale v. Traders & General Ins. Co., supra, 50 Cal.2d 654, 328 P.2d 198, and the cases following it, the evidence is clearly sufficient to support the determination that Security breached its duty to consider the interests of Mrs. Crisci in proposed settlements. Both Security's attorney and its claims manager agreed that if Mrs. DiMare won an award for her psychosis, that award would be at least $100,000. Security attempts to justify its rejection of a settlement by contending that it believed Mrs. DiMare had no chance of winning on the mental suffering issue. That belief in the circumstances present could be found to be unreasonable. Security was putting blind faith in the power of its psychiatrists to convince the jury when it knew that the accident could have caused the psychosis, that its agents had told it that without evidence of prior mental defects a jury was likely to believe the fall precipitated the psychosis, and that Mrs. DiMare had reputable psychiatrists on her side. Further, the company had been told by a psychiatrist that in a group of 24 psychiatrists, 12 could be found to support each side.

The trial court found that defendant "knew that there was a considerable risk of substantial recovery beyond said policy limits" and that "the defendant did not give as much consideration to the financial interests of its said insured as it gave to its own interests." That is all that was required. The award of $91,000 must therefore be affirmed.

We must next determine the propriety of the award of Mrs. Crisci of $25,000 for her mental suffering. In Comunale v. Traders & General Ins. Co., supra, 50 Cal.2d 654, 663, 328 P.2d 198, 203, it was held that an action of the type involved here sounds in both contract and tort and that "where a case sounds both in contract and tort the plaintiff will ordinarily have freedom of election between an action of tort and one of contract. Eads v. Marks, 39 Cal.2d 807, 811, 249 P.2d 257. An exception to this rule is made in suits for personal injury caused by negligence, where the tort character of the action is considered to prevail (citations), but no such exception is applied in cases, like the present one, which relate to financial damage (citations)."[6] Although this rule was applied in Comunale with regard to a statute of limitations, the rule is also applicable in determining liability. Insofar as language in Critz v. Farmers Ins. Group, supra, 230 Cal.App.2d 788, 799, 41 Cal.Rptr. 401, might

6. Comunale v. Traders & General Ins. Co., supra, 50 Cal.2d 654, 328 P.2d 198, was mainly concerned with the contract aspect of the action. This may be due to the facts that the tort duty is ordinarily based on the insurer's assumption of the defense and of settlement negotiations (see Keeton, Liability Insurance and Responsibility for Settlement (1954) 67 Harv.L.Rev. 1136, 1138–1139; Note (1966), supra, 18 Stan.L.Rev. 475), and that in Comunale the insurer did not undertake defense or settlement but denied coverage. In any event Comunale expressly recognizes that "wrongful refusal to settle has generally been treated as a tort." (50 Cal.2d at p. 663, 328 P.2d at p. 203.)

be interpreted as providing that the action for wrongful refusal to settle sounds solely in contract, it is disapproved.

Fundamental in our jurisprudence is the principle that for every wrong there is a remedy and that an injured party should be compensated for all damage proximately caused by the wrongdoer. Although we recognize exceptions from these fundamental principles, no departure should be sanctioned unless there is a strong necessity therefor.

The general rule of damages in tort is that the injured party may recover for all detriment caused whether it could have been anticipated or not. (Civ.Code, § 3333; see Hunt Bros. Co. v. San Lorenzo etc. Co., 150 Cal. 51, 56, 87 P. 1093, 7 L.R.A., N.S., 913.) In accordance with the general rule, it is settled in this state that mental suffering constitutes an aggravation of damages when it naturally ensues from the act complained of, and in this connection mental suffering includes nervousness, grief, anxiety, worry, shock, humiliation and indignity as well as physical pain. The commonest example of the award of damages for mental suffering in addition to other damages is probably where the plaintiff suffers personal injuries in addition to mental distress as a result of either negligent or intentional misconduct by the defendant. Such awards are not confined to cases where the mental suffering award was in addition to an award for personal injuries; damages for mental distress have also been awarded in cases where the tortious conduct was an interference with property rights without any personal injuries apart from the mental distress.

We are satisfied that a plaintiff who as a result of a defendant's tortious conduct loses his property and suffers mental distress may recover not only for the pecuniary loss but also for his mental distress. No substantial reason exists to distinguish the cases which have permitted recovery for mental distress in actions for invasion of property rights. The principal reason for limiting recovery of damages for mental distress is that to permit recovery of such damages would open the door to fictitious claims, to recovery for mere bad manners, and to litigation in the field of trivialities. (Prosser, Torts (3d ed. 1964) § 11, p. 43.) Obviously, where, as here, the claim is actionable and has resulted in substantial damages apart from those due to mental distress, the danger of fictitious claims is reduced, and we are not here concerned with mere bad manners or trivialities but tortious conduct resulting in substantial invasions of clearly protected interests.[7]

Recovery of damages for mental suffering in the instant case does not mean that in every case of breach of contract the injured party may recover such damages. Here the breach also constitutes a tort. Moreover, plaintiff did not seek by the contract involved here to obtain a commercial advantage but to protect herself against the risks of accidental losses, including the mental distress which might follow from the losses.

7. Nor are we here concerned with the problem whether invasion of the plaintiff's right to be free from emotional disturbance is actionable where there is no injury to person or property rights in addition to the inflicted mental distress.

Among the considerations in purchasing liability insurance, as insurers are well aware, is the peace of mind and security it will provide in the event of an accidental loss, and recovery of damages for mental suffering has been permitted for breach of contracts which directly concern the comfort, happiness or personal esteem of one of the parties. (Chelini v. Nieri, 32 Cal.2d 480, 482, 196 P.2d 915.)

It is not claimed that plaintiff's mental distress was not caused by defendant's refusal to settle or that the damages awarded were excessive in the light of plaintiff's substantial suffering.

The judgment is affirmed.

Notes

1. In *Comunale v. Traders & General Ins. Co.,* 50 Cal.2d 654, 328 P.2d 198 (1958), cited in *Crisci,* plaintiffs were struck in a marked pedestrian crosswalk by a truck driven by Percy Sloan, who was insured by Traders & General Insurance. Sloan's policy provided for maximum liability of $10,000 for each person injured and $20,000 for each accident, but when Sloan notified Traders of the accident, he was told that the policy did not provide coverage because he was driving a truck that did not belong to him. Traders repeatedly refused to defend Sloan against a suit brought by plaintiffs, despite being informed that a judgment was likely to exceed the policy limits, and it refused to accept an offer of settlement within the policy limits. A judgment in excess of the policy limits was subsequently entered. Plaintiff obtained an assignment of Sloan's rights against Traders and commenced an action against Traders to recover the portion of the judgment that was in excess of the policy limits.

The California State Supreme Court stated that "[t]here is an implied covenant of good faith and fair dealing in every contract that neither party will do anything which will injure the right of the other to receive the benefits of the agreement. This principle is applicable to insurance." The court further stated that the implied obligation of good faith and fair dealing requires the insurer to settle in an appropriate case even though the express terms of the policy do not impose such a duty. When there is a great risk of recovery in excess of the policy limits, a consideration in good faith of the insured's interest requires the insurer to settle the claim. "The insurer, in deciding whether a claim should be compromised, must take into account the interest of the insured and give it at least as much consideration as it does its own interest." Finally, the court held that "an insurer, who wrongfully declines to defend and who refuses to accept a reasonable settlement within the policy limits in violation of its duty to consider in good faith the interest of the insured in the settlement, is liable for the entire judgment against the insured even if its exceeds the policy limits."

In analyzing whether the duty of good faith and fair dealing was a contract or a tort action, the court stated "[a]n action for damages in excess of the policy limits based on an insurer's wrongful failure to settle is assignable whether the action is considered as sounding in tort or in contract." In dealing with a statute of limitations issue, the court indicated that "where a case sounds both in contract and tort the plaintiff will ordinarily have freedom of election between an action of tort and one of contract."

2. Note the mechanics of the transaction in the *Crisci* case. Crisci assigned the proceeds of her lawsuit against her insurer to the plaintiff. Track this aspect of the next several cases.

3. About ten years ago, two influential commentators saw a decline of tort actions for breach of the covenant of good faith and fair dealing because they saw the area as having matured and because the deterrent effect of punitive damages might be having some effect. Kenneth S. Abraham, *The Natural History of the Insurer's Liability for Bad Faith*, 72 TEX. L. REV. 1295 (1994); Robert H. Jerry, II, *The Wrong Side of the Mountain: A Comment on Bad Faith's Unnatural History*, 72 TEX. L. REV. 1317 (1994). Douglas R. Richmond, a prolific writer of many perceptive insurance related articles, observes that the demise of tort actions (what he labels bad faith actions) in this area has not come about. Douglas R. Richmond, *Bad Insurance Bad Faith Law*, 39 TORT TRIAL & INS. PRACTICE L.J. 1 (2003). Richmond notes that while bad faith law has matured, the size and number of bad faith verdicts has increased. Id. at 2–3. Perhaps anticipating the *State Farm v. Campbell* case, Richmond also notes that this increase has occurred despite the susceptibility of large bad faith awards to reduction or reversal on appeal. Id.

4. Over the past years, there has been some curtailing of bad faith actions. For example, in *Freeman & Mills Inc. v. Belcher Oil Co.*, 11 Cal.4th 85, 44 Cal.Rptr.2d 420, 900 P.2d 669 (1995), the California State Supreme Court overruled an earlier case, *Seaman's Direct Buying Service, Inc. v. Standard Oil Co.*, 36 Cal.3d 752, 206 Cal.Rptr. 354, 686 P.2d 1158 (1984), which held that an action in tort may lie when a defendant seeks to defend himself from liability by denying, in bad faith, the existence of a contract between the parties. The Freeman court held that, in the general commercial context, a tort action would not lie for bad faith denial of contract. However, the court explicitly noted that "nothing in this opinion should be read as affecting the existing precedent governing enforcement of the implied covenant [of good faith and fair dealing] in insurance cases." *Id.* at 103. This precedent is based on the "special relationship" between the insured and the insurer, which is based on elements of adhesion, public interest, and fiduciary responsibility.

BETTS v. ALLSTATE INSURANCE COMPANY

Court of Appeal of California, Fourth District, 1984.
154 Cal.App.3d 688, 201 Cal.Rptr. 528.

[Ed. Note: A good part of the elaborate statement of facts by the Court has been summarized. Summarized portions are placed in brackets.]

STANIFORTH, ASSOCIATE JUSTICE.

In an earlier (underlying) lawsuit for damages arising out of an automobile intersection accident (*Gallucci v. Betts*), Anne E. Gallucci obtained a jury verdict-judgment against Debra Betts for damages of $450,000, $350,000 in excess of Betts' automobile insurance policy issued by Allstate Insurance Company (Allstate). Allstate assumed the Betts defense, furnished the law firm of Ruston and Nance (Ruston) to represent Betts in the underlying lawsuit, but flatly denied liability and adamantly refused during the entire course of litigation and up to and including the motion for new trial to accept Gallucci's offer to accept its policy limits in settlement.

In the present action Betts sued Allstate, alleging breach of covenant to deal fairly and in good faith. She charges a "bad faith" refusal to accept a settlement offer within the policy limits. Betts alleges Ruston was negligent in conducting the defense of her lawsuit. A jury returned special verdicts awarding (1) compensatory damages against Allstate of $500,000 (to which the trial court added prejudgment interest and costs) and (2) punitive damages of $3,000,000. The jury found Ruston was also negligent and awarded $500,000 jointly and severally against the lawyers and Allstate for emotional distress. A motion for new trial was conditionally granted as to the latter $500,000 award of damages unless Betts accepted a reduction of the award of $500,000 to $50,000. Betts accepted that condition and a new trial was denied in its entirety. Allstate and Ruston appeal the respective portions of the judgment against them. Betts cross-appeals the order which conditionally granted the partial new trial.

[It appears Gallucci, the victim, was also insured by Allstate. After the accident, Allstate made several estimates of liability, at one point concluding that the case was 95–5 against liability. Because the accident involved two cars colliding in an intersection, Allstate hired Truesdale Laboratories, an accident reconstruction firm, to investigate and report. Truesdale filed three reports serially, each meeting with dissatisfaction at Allstate, (201 Cal.Rptr. at 534): "Thereafter from Allstate's head office to the district level the hiding of the Truesdale reports became a focus of activity." It was suggested at one juncture that the reports be put in the hands of a law firm where, after deletion of references to Allstate, the firm could assert the attorney's work product privilege. The Ruston firm refused to cooperate. Allstate obtained from another of its District offices Gallucci's medical records (held there because she had filed her claim for medical payments under her own Allstate policy) and relabelled it to indicate that it had originated in connection with Gallucci's claim against Betts. One of the witnesses to the accident (Pamela Thayer) seemed initially favorable to Betts but later revised her version of the collision which at first had Gallucci at fault. Allstate came to regard her as "flaky" and "unreliable" and unable to substantiate Betts' version of the accident.

Allstate's appointed lawyers (the Ruston firm acting through attorney Powers) did not report an initial settlement offer at the policy limits to Betts, but did report a succeeding pre-trial offer by Gallucis lawyer (the "Bahan demand") to her. Strowmatt, an Allstate employee, notified her of this and she was subsequently summoned to a conference at the Ruston office where: (201 Cal.Rptr. at 536)]

* * *

Nineteen-year-old Betts went to Ruston's office to participate in the meeting concerning Bahan's demand. Betts said she relied entirely on Dragonette, Allstate's trial attorney. She had no reason to doubt that he was advising her or making a decision other than in her best interest. She did not understand the reference to a *settlement* conference nor did she understand what was meant by the Strowmatt letter saying that *her policy limits were being demanded.* At that meeting there was no discussion of a possible conflict of interest arising because of the settlement demand. *Betts was told nothing about the known liability problems arising from the Truesdale findings, Gallucci's employment of a specialist on traffic signals, or Thayer's dismissal,* not as a favorable witness, but *as "a flake."* Betts was not informed of the settlement recommendation of Dragonette and Strowmatt.

The jury could draw a rational inference the lawyers assured Betts she would win at trial. Typical of the statements made to her were: "You had a green light and you got to give that a try. You shouldn't have someone else in the wrong get the money. They're trying to get the money and you had a green light and you should try it. We can win. While we admire you Ms. Betts there is not too many people like you who stand behind what they say and feel the right and take action upon it." Myers recounted Betts and her father had met with the defense attorneys and they "both tell us to try the case." Betts maintained she had done nothing wrong and should *the verdict exceed the limits she would "just file bankruptcy."*

Dragonette signed a letter to the insurance company (actually written by Strowmatt) asserting Betts was *virtually judgment proof.* He noted *her understanding that should the jury not believe her and should a substantial verdict result she would file bankruptcy to discharge the obligation.* Most important to the lawyer was this: Betts was positive she had the green light and the other party was entirely at fault. He stated Betts understood the law of comparative negligence but simply did not feel the accident was one percent her fault.

Pursuant to instructions from Allstate's office, Dragonette's response (August 4, 1977) to Bahan's demands was to continue the "deny/defend" posture of the insured.

A judicial settlement conference was held on August 10, 1977; Allstate refused to *pay one cent in settlement.* The conference occurred without any notice to Betts. Strowmatt was present and the court questioned him at the outset as to any offer. He stated that he had "zilch" or "zip" (no money) to offer. Thereupon the court terminated the conference.

[Apparently evidence began to point more strongly toward liability on Betts' part. Gallucci's attorney, Trotter, hired a specialist in accident reconstruction, Krueper, who after a study concluded that Betts had run a red light at the intersection. At the trial, the defense made no effective rebuttal of evidence pointing to liability. Defense counsel refused to stipulate Gallucci's incompetence (she was diagnosed as having a brain stem injury with coma) and Trotter brought her into the courtroom where an Allstate employee said that she was one of the "most pathetic pieces of humanity" he had observed. Nonetheless, Allstate continued to refuse to pay and rejected all offers from Gallucci's side to settle within the policy limits.]

[At the end of the trial (Dragonette representing Betts) the jury returned a verdict for Gallucci in the amount of $450,000.]

* * *

Immediately after the excess verdict a senior claims attorney for Allstate, Wathen, took over active control of the case from Ruston. Allstate's posture, however, remained the same regarding settlement. At this late date Ruston engaged in a series of acts (which will be explored later in connection with the negligence claim against the Ruston firm), in failing to look after Betts' obligation arising from the excess verdict. For example, Trotter wished, in exchange for an assignment of Betts' rights, to release her from personal liability. Powers advised her not to assign; Trotter was described as the "enemy."

Allstate filed a motion for new trial. Pending its hearing, Allstate failed to explore the possibility of paying the $100,000 limits immediately in exchange for an offer of a full satisfaction. Although initially authorizing $100,000 for that purpose Allstate lawyer Wathen reversed himself. Wathen feared the money, if offered, would be irretrievably lost in the event the motion for new trial was granted or Allstate prevailed on appeal.[8] At no time during this period was Betts ever advised by anyone she might have to sue Allstate. Moreover, there was an attempted manipulation of Betts to keep her from seeking independent counsel. *Only after Betts was examined at a debtor's examination by Trotter and his offer to pay the cost of such consultation with an independent attorney did Dragonette give Betts the name of a lawyer to consult.*

In the post-judgment period Allstate attempted to change its files by the inclusion of a suggestion had Allstate known of Krueper's testimony in time the matter would have been settled, but *the opposition's tactics had prevented such knowledge.* After the judgment, Ruston continued to cooperate with Allstate. Powers wrote to Allstate: The verdict was "not supported by the evidence."

Discussion

Allstate Appeal

A.

In addition to the duties imposed upon the parties to a contract by the express terms of their agreement the law implies in every contract a covenant of good faith and fair dealing. * * * The implied promise requires each contracting party to refrain from doing anything to impair

8. The good faith of this position may be questioned. An appeal was not seriously considered because a bond would be necessary; in the event of affirmance Trotter would be able to obtain a full satisfaction of judgment without a bad faith lawsuit.

the right of the other to receive the benefits of the agreement. * * * And as was pointed out in Egan v. Mutual of Omaha Ins. Co., supra, 24 Cal.3d at 818, 169 Cal.Rptr. 691, 620 P.2d 141: "The precise nature and extent of the duties imposed by such implied promise will depend upon the contractual purposes."

The California Supreme Court in Comunale v. Traders & General Ins. Co., [50 Cal.2d 654, 328 P.2d 198] addressed the nature and extent of duties imposed by this implied covenant in liability insurance policies. There the Supreme Court held an insurer in determining whether to settle a claim must give at least as much consideration to the welfare of the insured as it gives to its own interest. The governing standard is whether a prudent insurer would have accepted the settlement offer if it alone were to be liable for the entire judgment. * * * An insurer may be held liable for a judgment against the insured in excess of its policy limits where it has breached the implied covenant of good faith and fair dealing by unreasonably refusing to accept a settlement offer within the policy limits. * * * Allstate's argument that liability for an excess judgment is not imposed unless there is a "bad faith" breach of the contract is unsound. Liability is imposed "for failure to meet the duty to accept reasonable settlements, a duty included within the implied covenant of good faith and fair dealing." (Crisci v. Security Ins. Co., 66 Cal.2d 425, 430, 58 Cal.Rptr. 13, 426 P.2d 173.) "[R]ecovery may be based on an unwarranted rejection of a reasonable settlement offer and * * * *the absence of evidence, circumstantial or direct, showing actual dishonesty, fraud, or concealment is not fatal to the cause of action.*" (Ibid.; italics added; see also Gruenberg v. Aetna Ins. Co., 9 Cal.3d 566, 573, 108 Cal.Rptr. 480, 510 P.2d 1032.)

The duty to deal in good faith with the other party to the contract of insurance "*is a duty imposed by law, not one arising by the terms of the contract itself.*" (Gruenberg v. Aetna Ins. Co., supra, at p. 574, 108 Cal.Rptr. 480, 510 P.2d 1032; italics added.) In other words this duty of dealing fairly and in good faith is nonconsensual in origin rather than consensual.

The obligation of good faith and fair dealing requires the insurer to settle a claim in an appropriate case although the express terms of the policy do not impose such a duty. (Murphy v. Allstate Ins. Co., supra, 17 Cal.3d at p. 941, 132 Cal.Rptr. 424, 553 P.2d 584.) *The insurer must settle "within policy limits where there is a substantial likelihood of recovery in excess of those limits."* (Ibid. italics added.) This duty to settle is implied in law to protect the insured from exposure to liability in excess of coverage as a result of the insured's gamble on which only the insured might lose. (Ibid.; Shapero v. Allstate Ins. Co., 14 Cal.App.3d 433, 92 Cal.Rptr. 244.) "[I]n deciding whether or not to compromise the claim, the insurer must conduct itself as though it alone were liable for the entire amount of the judgment." (Johansen v. California State Auto. Assn. Inter–Ins. Bureau, supra, 15 Cal.3d at p. 16, 123 Cal.Rptr. 288, 538 P.2d 744.)

Thus, the permissible considerations in evaluating the reasonableness of the settlement offer are whether in light of the victim's injury and the probable liability of the insured the ultimate judgment is likely to exceed the amount of the settlement offer. Such factors as the limits imposed by the policy, a desire to reduce the amount of future settlements, or a belief that the policy does not provide coverage do not affect a decision as to whether the settlement offer in question is a reasonable one.

B.

A key factual question put to the jury was: Were the repeated offers made by the Trotter firm reasonable in the light of all of the circumstances of this case? If reasonable, their rejection by Allstate became unreasonable, therefore imposing on Allstate responsibility for the excess judgment.

The judgment was four and one-half times the offer of settlement. It is a rational inference the value of Gallucci's claim was the equivalent of the amount of the judgment. An acceptance of an offer within the policy limits was a most reasonable method of dealing with her claim.

These conclusions do not just arise by hindsight. There is uncontradicted evidence Allstate, whether blindly or purposefully, accepted the statement of the 17–year–old Debra Betts and upon that basis and that basis alone proclaimed its "no pay/defend stance" and refused to make any offer whatsoever. There was a mountain of available evidence which put Allstate on notice that this was a case of enormous liability. The findings of the Truesdale expert are the most significant. They demonstrate the Allstate prediction of 95–5 exposure had no rational basis.

Allstate failed to question the accuracy and soundness of its own client's conclusion. Gallucci's expert was able to take Betts' exact words and make out a prima facie case for Betts' liability. Betts' first account, if *facts* not conclusions, are the measure, would support at least an offer of the policy limits once the enormous Gallucci damages were known. These facts warrant the rational inference of either a willful or negligent failure by Allstate to investigate the facts surrounding Betts' liability.

In Egan v. Mutual of Omaha Ins. Co., supra, 24 Cal.3d 809, 817, 169 Cal.Rptr. 691, 620 P.2d 141, it was held an insurer may breach the covenant of good faith and fair dealing by failing to properly investigate its insured's claim. By equal parity of reasoning a failure to investigate and fairly appraise the third party's claim against the insured would breach the covenant of good faith and fair dealing. (Ibid.) Allstate's figurative hiding its head in the sand (or hiding adverse reports) is not a law-sanctioned approach to reasonable investigation and performance of its duty.

There is more than substantial evidence to support the jury's conclusion Allstate unreasonably rejected the policy limits offer made on several occasions by Gallucci's attorney. The compensatory money award, the excess over the policy limits plus interest, is affirmed.[9]

C.

The next question is: Was Allstate's breach of duty accompanied by oppression, fraud and/or malice warranting exemplary damages? In an action for breach of an obligation not arising from contract, Civil Code section 3294, subdivision (a), provides for sanctions by way of exemplary damages "where the defendant has been guilty of oppression, fraud, or malice." The plaintiff, in addition to the actual damages, "may recover damages for the sake of example and by way of punishing the defendant." (Civil Code § 3294, subd. (a).)

Under subdivision (c)(1) of the same section, "malice" means "conduct which is intended by the defendant to cause injury to the plaintiff or conduct which is carried on by the defendant with a conscious disregard of the rights or safety of others." The term "oppression" means "subjecting a person to cruel and unjust hardship in conscious disregard for that person's rights" (Civil Code § 3294, subd. (c)(2)) and the term "fraud" means "an intentional misrepresentation, deceit, or concealment of a material fact known to the defendant with the intention on the part of the defendant of thereby depriving a person of property or legal rights or otherwise causing injury." (Civil Code § 3294, subd. (c)(3); see Johns, California Damages (2d ed. 1977) at pp. 394–395.) Thus an insurer's bad faith may not only breach the implied covenant of good faith and fair dealing but also can be treated for tort purposes as a basis for exemplary damages where it occurs in a context of malice, fraud or oppression. * * *

As summarized above, there was more than substantial evidence before the jury to support a finding Allstate had breached its duty to deal reasonably and in good faith with Betts, rendering Allstate liable to pay compensatory damages for all detriments caused by the breach. However, such a determination does not in itself establish Allstate acted with the quality of intent which is requisite to an award of punitive damages. * * *

To find the requisite intent for an award of punitive damages, it is necessary to search beyond the facts of (un)reasonable response to those adducing motive and intent. * * * There must be substantial evidence of an intent to vex, injure and annoy, a conscious disregard of the plaintiff's rights, before punitive damages may be awarded. (Silberg v. California Life Ins. Co., 11 Cal.3d 452, 462, 113 Cal.Rptr. 711, 521 P.2d 1103.)

A brief highlighting of the evidence demonstrates the substantial evidence that warranted the jury in making a finding Allstate's intended

9. Allstate now challenges the sufficiency, competency, adequacy of the Gallucci offers. Allstate summarily rejected these offers without any attempt to seek clarification—it felt them ambiguous or incomplete. Allstate cannot now in good conscience use its own failure to explore the settlement offer as a defense of its own breach of duty to tender the policy limits—exactly what the Gallucci attorneys were willing to accept.

to vex, injure, and annoy. From almost the day of commencement of its duty to represent, defend and indemnify Betts, Allstate adopted an objectively unreasonable "no liability/no pay/defend" stance. This obstinate attitude-intent grew in strength in face of evidence piled upon evidence pointing to liability and ultimately to a verdict far in excess of policy limits.

There is much more here than Allstate's unwillingness to accept its responsibility to defend its insureds. Evidence abounds of an irrational refusal to face up to adverse evidence. The Truesdale reports disclosed Betts liability. The jury could draw a rational inference that Allstate deliberately concealed these adverse reports, not only from the other side but from their own insured.

Attorney Dragonette's failure for some unknown reason to pursue the cross examination of Gallucci's expert to determine his opinion and its fact basis gives rise to a whole series of rational adverse inferences suggesting Allstate's attorneys, as well as Allstate were unwilling to develop a record which would require abandonment of their "no liability/no pay/defend" policy.

The highly questionable practice of Allstate not putting adverse facts in writing—the "use the telephone" directive—indicates a lack of good faith in dealing with, an intent to vex, injure, and annoy, their client. Allstate's disreputable practice of violating its duty to one insured by "backdooring"—examining into the cross-file of another—suggests an intent to defraud or oppress its own clients.

The jury could reasonably conclude Allstate wilfully manipulated its own client through the process of coaching, encouraging a patently unreasonable belief in 17–year–old Betts that she had not run the red light—contrary to a whole series of developing facts. It is a further reasonable inference that Allstate, through its counsel, attempted to instill in Betts the determination, if there was an excess judgment, to go bankrupt. The post-trial manipulation of Betts again evidences an intent to vex, injure, and annoy. The moment of the excess verdict (if not before) there arose a duty to offer Betts independent counsel. Ruston, the Allstate–hired law firm, was at that moment placed in a position of open conflict of interest. Yet neither Allstate nor its attorneys bothered to inform the client. It was not until Betts was examined by opposing counsel, Trotter, at the debtor's examination, that she was advised of the necessity of and thereafter tendered independent counsel.

The foregoing evidence supports a conclusion of callous indifference to, an intent to vex, injure and annoy its insured. Allstate's counsel, even on this appeal, seek to minimize the disturbing practice by Allstate claiming "only by a handful of disgruntled former employees" does this evidence appear.

Many of the actions by Allstate could be, with myopic charity, described as negligent failures to investigate the claim against their insured. However, from these same facts a more sinister conclusion appears—an intent to vex, injure, and annoy Betts.

Finally, the almost irrational refusal to authorize any settlement even after an excess judgment and denial of a motion for new trial is hard evidence of malice, a willful intent to vex, injure, and annoy Betts.

The Supreme Court in Egan v. Mutual of Omaha Ins. Co., supra, 24 Cal.3d 809, 820, 169 Cal.Rptr. 691, 620 P.2d 141, shed light on the duties owed to an insured in context of a claim of exemplary damages:

> " '[A]s a supplier of a public service rather than a manufactured product, the obligations of insurers go beyond meeting reasonable expectations of coverage. *The obligations of good faith and fair dealing encompass qualities of decency and humanity inherent in the responsibilities of a fiduciary. Insurers hold themselves out as fiduciaries, and with the public's trust must go private responsibility consonant with that trust.' [Citation.] Furthermore, the relationship of insurer and insured is inherently unbalanced;* the adhesive nature of insurance contracts places the insurer in a superior bargaining position. *The availability of punitive damages is thus compatible with recognition of insurers' underlying public obligations and reflects an attempt to restore balance in the contractual relationship.* [Citation.]" (Italics added.)

More than substantial evidence warrants the conclusion that Allstate was guilty of oppression and malice and acted with an intent to vex, injure, and annoy and with a conscious disregard of Betts' rights. * * *

The judgment in all respects is affirmed.

Notes

1. Suppose you represented the insurer on appeal. Would you advise Allstate to appeal the trial court's decision? What is at stake for the parties?

2. The facts in *Betts* state that the insured was advised that she could avoid liability by filing bankruptcy. Suppose a third party is injured by an automobile driven by an insured. The third party offers to settle for the policy limits but the insurer refuses the offer. The third party then executes a release of the insured from any liability for damages above the policy limits and takes an assignment of the insured's cause of action for bad faith failure to settle against the insurer. What will the third party get under the assignment? Apparently nothing. Because the insured can no longer be hurt by an excess judgment because of the release, the assignment is valueless. See Clement v. Prudential Property & Cas. Ins. Co., 790 F.2d 1545 (11th Cir.1986) (if an injured third party releases the insured from liability, any bad faith claim ceases to exist because the insured is no longer exposed to any excess damages); Camp v. St. Paul Fire and Marine Insurance, 958 F.2d 340 (11th Cir.1992) (insurer no longer liable because insured's bankruptcy precluded further claims); Romano v. American Casualty Co., 834 F.2d 968 (11th Cir.1987) (no bad faith claim lies if a plaintiff is not exposed to any liability). What tactical lessons in insurance practice are to be learned here?

E. LIMITING THIRD PARTY CLAIMS

Although courts will extend the implication of the covenant of good faith and fair dealing to reach insurance cases examining an insurer's failure to settle a claim, this extension is limited to claims brought by the insured only. As the next case illustrates, courts normally disallow a third party's claim that an insurer breached its duty to settle. The rationale is that the covenant of good faith and fair dealing is intended to benefit the insured, not the injured party; therefore, regardless of whether the insurer treated the injured claimant badly or not, the latter has no grounds for recovery.

MURPHY v. ALLSTATE INSURANCE COMPANY

Supreme Court of California, 1976.
17 Cal.3d 937, 132 Cal.Rptr. 424, 553 P.2d 584.

CLARK, JUSTICE.

* * *

The complaint alleges plaintiff sued Pollard—insured by Allstate Insurance Company—for wrongful death of her nine-year-old son. Allstate rejected settlement demands of $23,500 and $25,000, the latter being the maximum coverage provided by Pollard's policy. Plaintiff thereafter received a verdict of $85,000, but on motion for new trial, accepted a reduction in judgment to $42,000.

Subsequent to entry of judgment, Allstate advised it would pay the policy limit of $25,000 and, if that were rejected, would appeal. The offer was rejected, and Allstate appealed contending the award was excessive. As Allstate posted no bond on appeal, plaintiff obtained writ of execution ordering immediate payment by Pollard of the judgment plus interest. In supplemental proceedings pursuant to Code of Civil Procedure section 717, Allstate denied obligation owing to either Pollard or to plaintiff.

Plaintiff brought the present action against Allstate alleging breach of the duty of good faith to its insured by having refused to settle within policy limits. There is no allegation Pollard has assigned any cause of action.

In her first cause of action, plaintiff seeks recovery under Insurance Code section 11580, subdivision (b)(2) authorizing direct action against the insurance company by a judgment creditor. In her second, plaintiff alleges direct action is permitted by Code of Civil Procedure section 720 by creditors' suit. Allstate moved for judgment on the pleadings, first on the ground there is no allegation Pollard assigned to plaintiff his cause of action for failure to settle and, secondly that Allstate is not indebted to Pollard within the meaning of section 720.[10] The motion was granted.

10. Plaintiff's memorandum of points and authorities in opposition to the motion for judgment on the pleadings recites Allstate has paid Murphy $27,464.77 (policy limits plus interests and costs).

THE DUTY TO SETTLE

* * * "[T]he implied obligation of good faith and fair dealing requires the insurer to settle in an appropriate case although the express terms of the policy do not impose such a duty" (*Comunale v. Traders & General Ins. Co.* (1958) 50 Cal.2d 654, 659, 328 P.2d 198, 201).

More specifically, the insurer must settle within policy limits when there is substantial likelihood of recovery in excess of those limits. [citations omitted]

The duty to settle is implied in law to protect the insured from exposure to liability in excess of coverage as a result of the insurer's gamble—on which only the insured might lose. * * *

The insurer's duty to settle does not directly benefit the injured claimant. In fact, he usually benefits from the duty's breach. Instead of receiving an award near policy limits, he stands to obtain judgment exceeding policy coverage. For instance, in the present case plaintiff has already received an amount equal to her highest settlement demand, holding an unsatisfied judgment for an additional $17,500.

The insurer's duty to settle—running to the insured and not to the injured claimant—is also demonstrated by *Shapero v. Allstate Insurance Co.,* 14 Cal.App.3d 433, 92 Cal.Rptr. 244. The insured died leaving no asset other than the insurance policy. Thus, a judgment in excess of policy limits presenting no risk to the insured or to his heirs, the insurer had no duty to settle within policy limits.

When the carrier does breach its duty to settle, the insured has been allowed to recover excess award over policy limits (*Comunale v. Traders & General Ins. Co., supra,* economic loss, physical impairment, emotional distress and punitive damage).[11] [citations omitted]

The insured may assign his cause of action for breach of the duty to settle without consent of the insurance carrier, even when the policy provisions provide the contrary. (*Comunale v. Traders & General Ins. Co., supra.*) However, part of the damage arises from the personal tort aspect of the bad faith cause of action. * * * And because a purely personal tort cause of action is not assignable in California, it must be concluded that damage for emotional distress is not assignable. (See *Reichert v. General Insurance Company of America* (1968) 68 Cal.2d 822, 834, 69 Cal.Rptr. 321, 442 P.2d 377; 7 Cal.Jur.3d, Assignments, § 5 at pp. 12–13.) The same is true of a claim for punitive damage. * * *

In *Purcell v. Colonial Ins. Co.* (1971), 20 Cal.App.3d 807, 814, 97 Cal.Rptr. 874, an insured assigned his cause of action for breach of the

11. Unlike other damages listed in the text, punitive damage may not be recovered for mere breach of the covenant without more: "While we have concluded that defendant violated its duty of good faith and fair dealing, this alone does not necessarily establish that defendant acted with the requisite intent to injure plaintiff." (*Silberg v. California Life Ins. Co.,* 11 Cal.3d at 462–463, 113 Cal.Rptr. at 718, 521 P.2d at 1110.) Defendant must act with intent to vex, injure or annoy, or with a conscious disregard of plaintiff's rights. (*Id.*)

duty to settle, the assignee suing on the assignment. Subsequently, the insured sued for mental distress. The second action was held to violate the rule against splitting a cause of action. The court suggested the insured should have brought a single action in his own name for all damage, agreeing to pay part of the recovery to the assignee.

INSURANCE CODE SECTION 11580, SUBDIVISION (B)

Insurance Code section 11580 lists provisions to be included in every liability insurance policy issued or delivered in this state. Subdivision (b), subpart (1) provides insolvency or bankruptcy of the insured will not release the insurer from payment, and subpart (2) of the subdivision permits the judgment creditor of the insured to maintain an action "against the insurer on the policy and subject to its terms and limitations * * * to recover on the judgment."

Subpart (2) makes the judgment creditor a third party beneficiary of the insurance contract between the insurer and the insured. * * *

A third party beneficiary may enforce a contract expressly made for his benefit. (Civ.Code, § 1559.) And although the contract may not have been made to benefit him alone, he may enforce those promises directly made for him. * * *

A third party should not [however] be permitted to enforce covenants made not for his benefit, but rather for others. He is not a contracting party; his right to performance is predicated on the contracting parties' intent to benefit him. * * * As to any provision made not for his benefit but for the benefit of the contracting parties or for other third parties, he becomes an intermeddler. Permitting a third party to enforce a covenant made solely to benefit others would lead to the anomaly of granting him a bonus after his receiving all intended benefit. Because, as we have seen, the duty to settle is intended to benefit the insured and not the injured claimant, third party beneficiary doctrine does not furnish a basis for the latter to recover. Moreover, Allstate having paid plaintiff the policy limits, she has already received all benefit contemplated by the policy.

Next, the Financial Responsibility Law does not require plaintiff be permitted to sue for breach of the duty to settle. Again, the duty is based not on the Financial Responsibility Law but rather on the implied covenant of good faith and fair dealing found in every contract. Unlike a failure to investigate the representations of the insured, a breach of the duty to settle does not involve the risk that a person injured by a negligent motorist will fail to receive the compensation called for by that law. Breach of the duty to settle will, if anything, allow the injured party to recover the amount of the offered settlement, perhaps an additional sum to the extent of the policy limits, and sums in excess of those limits from the negligent motorist. Because an insurer's refusal to accept a reasonable settlement does not diminish the injured claimant's recovery, the policy of compensating persons injured by negligent motorists is not frustrated.

Having concluded section 11580 does not authorize plaintiff to proceed against Allstate for the excess of the judgment over policy limits, we next consider whether Code of Civil Procedure section 720 permits plaintiff to proceed by way of creditors' suit.

CODE OF CIVIL PROCEDURE SECTION 720

A cause of action is not subject to levy and execution sale. * * * Code of Civil Procedure sections 714–723 provide for supplemental proceedings for a judgment creditor when his writ of execution against the judgment debtor has been returned unsatisfied.

Section 719 states that in supplemental proceedings, property of the judgment debtor may be ordered applied toward satisfaction of the judgment provided that no such order may be made as to property or money in the hands of another who also claims an interest in the property adverse to the judgment debtor or who denies the debt.

When the judgment debtor's alleged debtor denies owing the judgment debtor or denies holding property in which the judgment debtor claims an interest, the judgment creditor must proceed by creditors' suit under section 720. (*Bond v. Bulgheroni* (1932) 215 Cal. 7, 10, 8 P.2d 130.) * * *

"Whether choses in action founded upon torts are subject to creditors' suit must depend upon whether they are, by the law of the state, assignable. If they are not, then they are not subject to such suits, otherwise they are so subject." (Freeman, Executions (3d ed. 1900) § 425 at pp. 2290–2291.) Because causes of action for tort committed to property are assignable (Code Civ.Proc., § 954), they may be reached by proceedings under section 720. On the other hand, section 720 should not be applied so as to render the nonassignable assignable. And nonassignable tort actions may not be reached in proceedings pursuant to section 720. The language of the section referring to "debt" and "interest in property," reinforces this conclusion.

We are confronted with a hybrid cause of action, assignable—yes—but comprising potential damage unassignable and unrecoverable in section 720 proceedings.

No case has been cited or found determining whether a hybrid cause of action may be enforced in proceedings under section 720. Even assuming other hybrid causes of action might be subject to section 720 proceedings, the policy reflected by the cases establishing the duty to settle and the direct action statute (Ins.Code, § 11580), compels us to conclude the cause of action before us may not be reached under section 720. As we have seen, in view of the potential conflicts among injured party, insured and insurer, the courts imposed the duty to settle to protect the insured—not the injured party. Permitting the injured party to proceed under section 720 would substantially defeat the very purpose of the cause of action and again, because it may not be split, the insured could be deprived of substantial recovery.

Requiring assignment before the claimant may proceed would of course insure notice to the insured that the claimant wished to proceed against the insurer. At that point the insured would have the choice of partially assigning and then joining in the action, or of bargaining for a release from liability in excess of coverage. The release would permit the insured to protect himself from continued exposure to personal liability. Further, because the judgment creditor would then both own and control the cause of action against the insurer, he could attempt to satisfy his judgment thereby. Finally, the insured could protect his right to nonassignable claims for punitive, emotional and personal injury damage.

The judgment is affirmed.

Notes

1. Professor Francis J. Mootz III argues that third parties should be able to have some recourse as a result of bad faith litigation tactics. Francis J. Mootz III, *Holding Liability Insurers Accountable for Bad Faith Litigation Tactics with the tort of Abuse of Process*, 9 Conn. Ins. L.J. 467 (2003). His comprehensive article contains an excellent background of the doctrine underpinning cases like *Murphy*. Id. at 470–74. He discusses the countervailing policy considerations for providing third party remedies and, in a *tour de force*, his provocative suggestion is that the tort of abuse of process might be a suitable vehicle for redress. Id. at 474–88, 488–525. This follows his earlier work in which he constructs a hypothetical opinion allowing third party relief. Francis J. Mootz III, *The Sounds of Silence: Waiting for Courts to Acknowledge that Public Policy Justifies Awarding Damages to Third Party Claimants when Liability Insurers Deal with Them in Bad Faith,* 2 Nev. L.J. 443–88 (2002).

2. May a court *order* an insured to assign his bad faith claim to his judgment creditor? See Bergen v. F/V St. Patrick, 686 F.Supp. 786, 788 (D.Alaska 1988) ("In states where [bad faith] causes of action are assignable and where the question has arisen, it has almost universally been held that involuntary transfer to a judgment creditor is also possible.").

3. If bad faith failure to settle is a hybrid "contort," which statute of limitation should apply? Suppose the tort statute has run? May the action be continued under the contract statute?

The majority rule on this issue appears to hold that the statute of limitations that governs an action for breach of the covenant of good faith and fair dealing against a liability insurer for failure to settle a claim against the insured is the normally longer statute of limitations applicable to actions founded on a written contract. See Insurance Bad Faith Litigation, § 20.07(3). Matthew Bender & Company, Inc., 2000. The leading case illustrating this view is *Comunale v. Traders & General Ins. Co.*, 50 Cal.2d 654, 328 P.2d 198 (1958), in which the California Supreme Court, while conceding that the wrongful refusal to settle is normally treated as a tort, the plaintiff, in a hybrid case, is free to elect between an action in tort and one in contract. *Id. citing* Eads v. Marks, 39 Cal.2d 807, 811, 249 P.2d 257 (1952). Conversely, in *Wolfe v. Continental Cas. Co.*, 647 F.2d 705 (6th Cir.1981), the court, unwilling to apply different statutes of limitation to identical claims, held that the (shorter) tort statute of limitations applied, reasoning that because the purpose of the action was to recover damages for injury to plaintiff's rights, the cause of action was one of bad faith.

F. THE FIRST PARTY PROBLEM

BECK v. FARMERS INSURANCE EXCHANGE

Supreme Court of Utah, 1985.
701 P.2d 795.

ZIMMERMAN, JUSTICE:

Beck injured his knee in a hit-and-run accident on January 16, 1982, when his car was struck by a car owned by Ann Kirkland. Ms. Kirkland asserted that her car had been stolen and denied any knowledge of or responsibility for the accident. Beck filed a claim with Kirkland's insurer, but liability was denied on April 20, 1982.

At the time of the accident, Beck carried automobile insurance with Farmers. Under that policy, Beck was provided with both no-fault and uninsured motorist insurance benefits. On February 23, 1982, while his claim against Kirkland was pending, Beck filed a claim with Farmers for no-fault benefits. Sometime prior to May 26, 1982, Farmers paid Beck $5,000 for medical expenses (the no-fault policy limit) and $1,299.43 for lost wages.

On June 23, 1982, Beck's counsel filed a claim with Farmers for uninsured motorist benefits, demanding the policy limit, $20,000, for general damages suffered as a result of the accident. His counsel alleges that the brochure documenting Beck's damages, submitted to Farmers with the June 23rd settlement offer, established that his claim was worth substantially more than $20,000. Farmers' adjuster rejected the settlement offer without explanation on July 1, 1982.

Beck filed this lawsuit one month later, on August 2, 1982, alleging three causes of action: first, that by refusing to pay his uninsured motorist claim, Farmers had breached its contract of insurance with him; second, that by acting in bad faith in refusing to investigate the claim, bargain with Beck, or settle the claim, Farmers had breached an implied covenant of good faith and fair dealing; and third, that Farmers had acted oppressively and maliciously toward Beck with the intention of, or in reckless disregard of the likelihood of, causing emotional distress. Under the first claim, Beck sought damages for breach of contract in the amount of the policy limits; under the second, he asked for compensatory damages in excess of the policy limits for additional injuries, including mental anguish; and under the third, he sought punitive damages of $500,000.

Sometime in August of 1982, Beck's counsel contacted Farmers' counsel and offered to settle the whole matter for $20,000. This offer was rejected. Farmers filed an answer on September 1, 1982, and at the same time, moved to strike the prayer for punitive damages on the ground that they were unavailable for a breach of contract. Farmers' motion was granted. On September 29th, the trial court bifurcated the case and agreed to try the claim for failure to pay uninsured motorist benefits independent of Beck's claim alleging breach of an implied covenant of good faith and fair dealing.

Immediately after the trial judge bifurcated the case, Beck's counsel expressly revoked the previously rejected offer to settle the whole matter for $20,000. Instead, Beck offered to settle only the failure to pay the uninsured motorist benefits claim for $20,000, reserving the implied covenant or "bad faith" claim for separate resolution.

On October 20, 1982, Farmers apparently counteroffered. Negotiations proceeded, and sometime in late November, the parties agreed to settle the uninsured motorist claim for $15,000. On December 6, 1982, the parties stipulated to dismissal of that claim and specifically reserved the bad faith claim for later disposition.

In mid-December, Farmers moved to dismiss the reserved bad faith claim on two theories. First, Farmers asserted that under *Lyon v. Hartford Accident and Indemnity Co.,* 25 Utah 2d 311, 480 P.2d 739 (1971), it "had no duty to bargain with or settle plaintiff's uninsured motorist claim and, therefore, [could not] be held liable" for breach of contract or bad faith. Second, Farmers argued that even if it had some duty to bargain or to settle the claim, the facts set forth in the pleadings on file did not establish that it had breached the duty. No memoranda or factual affidavits supported this motion.

Farmers' motion was opposed by affidavits of Beck, his counsel, and a former insurance adjuster who worked for Beck's counsel as a paralegal. In his affidavit, Beck's counsel recited the dates and terms of the various settlement offers and the fact that they had been rejected without counteroffer. Beck's affidavit stated that he had accepted the $15,000 offer only because of financial pressures caused by the substantial expenses he had incurred in the ten months since the accident. The paralegal's affidavit stated that he had been an insurance adjuster for 19 years and that he had reviewed the settlement documentation submitted to Farmers in June when the claim was first filed. He expressed the opinion that a reasonable and prudent insurance company would have valued the claim at between $30,000 and $40,000 and attempted to settle the matter within weeks after the initial offer. The paralegal charged that the "only reason for such a substantial delay in settling this claim would be to put Mr. Beck in a situation of financial need and stress so that he would accept the first settlement offer," a tactic he characterized as acting in bad faith. Farmers filed no rebuttal affidavits, and the trial court granted Farmers' motion without specifying the basis for its holding.

Beck asks this Court to overrule *Lyon* and permit an insured to sue for an insurer's bad faith refusal to bargain or settle. * * *

Our ruling in *Lyon* left an insured without any effective remedy against an insurer that refuses to bargain or settle in good faith with the insured. An insured who has suffered a loss and is pressed financially is at a marked disadvantage when bargaining with an insurer over payment for that loss. Failure to accept a proffered settlement, although less than fair, can lead to catastrophic consequences for an insured who, as a direct consequence of the loss, may be peculiarly vulnerable, both economically and emotionally. The temptation for an insurer to delay settlement while pressures build on the insured is great, especially if the insurer's exposure cannot exceed the policy limits. *See Lawton v. Great Southwest Fire Insurance Co.,* 118 N.H. 607, 392 A.2d 576, 579 (1978); Harvey & Wiseman, *First Party Bad Faith: Common Law Remedies and a Proposed Legislative Solution,* 72 Ky.L.J. 141, 146, 167–69 (1983–84) (hereinafter cited as "First Party Bad Faith"); Note, *The Availability of Excess Damages for Wrongful Refusal to Honor First Party Insurance Claims—An Emerging Trend,* 45 Fordham L.Rev. 164, 164–67 (Oct. 1976) (hereinafter cited as "Availability of Excess Damages").

In light of these considerations, we now conclude that an insured should be provided with a remedy. However, we do not agree with plaintiff that a tort action is appropriate. Instead, we hold that the good faith duty to bargain or settle under an insurance contract is only one aspect of the duty of good faith and fair dealing implied in all contracts and that a violation of that duty gives rise to a claim for breach of contract.[12] In addition, we do not adopt the limitation suggested by Farmers, but hold that the refusal to bargain or settle, standing alone, may, under appropriate circumstances, be sufficient to prove a breach.

We recognize that a majority of states permit an insured to institute a tort action against an insurer who fails to bargain in good faith in a "first-party" situation, adopting the approach first announced by the California Supreme Court in *Gruenberg v. Aetna Insurance Co.,* 9 Cal.3d 566, 510 P.2d 1032, 108 Cal.Rptr. 480 (1973). *See, e.g., Bibeault v. Hanover Insurance Co.,* R.I., 417 A.2d 313 (1980); *Craft v. Economy Fire & Casualty Co.,* 572 F.2d 565 (7th Cir.1978) (applying Indiana law); *MFA Mutual Insurance Co. v. Flint,* Tenn., 574 S.W.2d 718 (1978). Apparently, these courts have taken this step as a matter of policy in order to provide what they perceive to be an adequate remedy for an insured wronged by an insurer's recalcitrance. These courts have reasoned that under contract law principles, an insurer who improperly refuses to settle a first-party claim may be liable only for damages measured by the maximum dollar amount of the insurance provided by the policy, and such a damage measure provides little or no incentive to an insurer to promptly and faithfully fulfill its contractual obligations. Accordingly, these courts have adopted a tort approach in order to allow an insured to recover extensive consequential and punitive damages, which they consider to be unavailable in an action based solely on a breach of contract. *See Availability of Excess Damages, supra,* at 168–77; *First Party Bad Faith, supra,* at 158.

12. The Court in *Lyon* considered only the question of whether a claim of bad faith gave rise to a tort cause of action; however, to the extent that *Lyon* is philosophically inconsistent with our recognition today of a cause of action in contract, it is overruled.

We conclude that the tort approach adopted by these courts is without a sound theoretical foundation and has the potential for distorting well-established principles of contract law. Moreover, the practical end of providing a strong incentive for insurers to fulfill their contractual obligations can be accomplished as well through a contract cause of action, without the analytical straining necessitated by the tort approach and with far less potential for unforeseen consequences to the law of contracts.

The analytical weaknesses of the tort approach are easily seen. In *Gruenberg,* the California court held that an insurer has a duty to deal in good faith with its insured and that an insured can bring an action in tort, rather than contract, for breach of that duty because the duty is imposed by law and, being nonconsensual, does not arise out of the contract. Glossing over any distinctions between first-and third-party situations, the court concluded that the duty imposed upon the insurer when bargaining with its insured in a first-party situation is merely another aspect of the fiduciary duty owed in the third-party context. *Gruenberg v. Aetna Insurance Co.,* 9 Cal.3d at 573–74, 510 P.2d at 1037, 108 Cal.Rptr. at 485.

Although this Court, in *Ammerman v. Farmer's Insurance Exchange,* 19 Utah 2d 261, 430 P.2d 576 (1967), recognized a tort cause of action for breach of an insurer's obligation to bargain in a third-party context, we cannot agree with the *Gruenberg* court that the considerations which compel the recognition of a tort cause of action in a third-party context are present in the first-party situation. In *Ammerman,* we stated that because a third-party insurance contract obligates the insurer to defend the insured, the insurer incurs a fiduciary duty to its insured to protect the insured's interests as zealously as it would its own; consequently, a tort cause of action is recognized to remedy a violation of that duty.

However, in *Lyon v. Hartford Accident and Indemnity Co.,* we held that a tort cause of action did not arise in a first-party insurance contract situation because the relationship between the insurer and its insured is fundamentally different than in a third-party context:

> In the [third-party] situation, the insurer must act in good faith and be as zealous in protecting the interests of the insured as it would be in regard to its own. In the [first-party] situation, the insured and the insurer are, in effect and practically speaking, adversaries.

* * *

This distinction is of no small consequence. In a third-party situation, the insurer controls the disposition of claims against its insured, who relinquishes any right to negotiate on his own behalf. * * * An insurer's failure to act in good faith exposes its insured to a judgment and personal liability in excess of the policy limits. * * * In essence, the contract itself creates a fiduciary relationship because of the trust and reliance placed in the insurer by its insured. * * * The insured is wholly dependent upon the insurer to see that, in dealing with claims by third parties, the insured's best interests are protected. In addition, when dealing with third parties, the insurer acts as an agent for the insured with respect to the disputed claim. Wholly apart from the contractual obligations undertaken by the parties, the law imposes upon all agents a fiduciary obligation to their principals with respect to matters falling within the scope of their agency. * * *

In the first-party situation, on the other hand, the reasons for finding a fiduciary relationship and imposing a corresponding duty are absent. No relationship of trust and reliance is created by the contract; it simply obligates the insurer to pay claims submitted by the insured in accordance with the contract. *Santilli v. State Farm Life Insurance Co.*, 278 Or. at 61–62, 562 P.2d at 969. Furthermore, none of the indicia of agency are present. * * *

Clearly, then, it is difficult to find a theoretically sound basis for analogizing the duty owed in a third-party context to that owed in a first-party context. And wholly apart from any theoretical problems, tailoring the tort analysis to first-party insurance contract cases has proven difficult. The pragmatic reason for adopting the tort approach is that it exposes insurers to consequential and punitive damages awards in excess of the policy limits. However, the courts appear to have had difficulty in developing a sound rationale for limiting the tort approach to insurance contract cases. This may be because there is no sound theoretical difference between a first-party insurance contract and any other contract, at least no difference that justifies permitting punitive damages for the breach of one and not the other. In any event, the tort approach and the accompanying punitive damages have moved rather quickly into areas far afield from insurance. *See, e.g., Seaman's Direct Buying Service, Inc. v. Standard Oil Co.*, 36 Cal.3d 752, 686 P.2d 1158, 1166–67, 206 Cal.Rptr. 354, 362–63 (1984); *Wallis v. Superior Court,* 160 Cal.App.3d 1109, 207 Cal.Rptr. 123, 127–29 (1984); *Gates v. Life of Montana Insurance Co.,* Mont., 668 P.2d 213, 214–16 (1983).

Furthermore, the courts adopting the tort approach have had some difficulty in determining what degree of bad faith is necessary to sustain a claim. *E.g., Anderson v. Continental Insurance Co.,* 85 Wis.2d 675, 692–94, 271 N.W.2d 368, 376–77 (1978). From a practical standpoint, the state of mind of the insurer is irrelevant; even an inadvertent breach of the covenant of good faith implied in an insurance contract can substantially harm the insured and warrants a remedy.

We therefore hold that in a first-party relationship between an insurer and its insured, the duties and obligations of the parties are contractual rather than fiduciary. Without more, a breach of those implied or express duties can give rise only to a cause of action in contract, not one in tort.[13] This position has not been widely adopted by

13. We recognize that in some cases the acts constituting a breach of contract may also result in breaches of duty that are independent of the contract and may give rise to causes of action in tort. *Hal Taylor Assoc. v. UnionAmerica,* 657 P.2d at 750;

other courts, although a "respectable body of authority" is developing. *See Duncan v. Andrew County Mutual Insurance Co.,* 665 S.W.2d at 18–19, and cases cited therein; *Lawton v. Great Southwest Fire Insurance Co.,* 118 N.H. 607, 392 A.2d 576 (1978); *Kewin v. Massachusetts Mutual Life Insurance Co.,* 409 Mich. 401, 295 N.W.2d 50 (1980); *Availability of Excess Damages, supra* p. 4, at 168–71. We further hold that as parties to a contract, the insured and the insurer have parallel obligations to perform the contract in good faith, obligations that inhere in every contractual relationship. *State Automobile & Casualty Underwriters v. Salisbury,* 27 Utah 2d 229, 232, 494 P.2d 529, 531 (1972); *Leigh Furniture & Carpet Co. v. Isom,* Utah, 657 P.2d 293, 306 (1982).[14]

Few cases define the implied contractual obligation to perform a first-party insurance contract in good faith. However, because the considerations are similar, we freely look to the tort cases that have described the incidents of the duty of good faith in the context of first-party insurance contracts. From those cases and from our own analysis of the obligations undertaken by the parties, we conclude that the implied obligation of good faith performance contemplates, at the very least, that the insurer will diligently investigate the facts to enable it to determine whether a claim is valid, will fairly evaluate the claim, and will thereafter act promptly and reasonably in rejecting or settling the claim. *See Anderson v. Continental Insurance Co.,* 85 Wis.2d at 692–93, 271 N.W.2d at 377; *Egan v. Mutual of Omaha Insurance Co.,* 24 Cal.3d 809, 818–19, 620 P.2d 141, 145–46, 169 Cal.Rptr. 691, 695–96 (1979). The duty of good faith also requires the insurer to "deal with laymen as laymen and not as experts in the subtleties of law and underwriting" and to refrain from actions that will injure the insured's ability to obtain the benefits of the contract. * * * These performances are the essence of what the insured has bargained and paid for, and the insurer has the obligation to perform them. When an insurer has breached this duty, it is liable for damages suffered in consequence of that breach.

In adopting the contract approach, we are not ignoring the principal reason for the adoption of the tort approach—to provide damage exposure in excess of the policy limits and thus remove any incentive for breaching the duty of good faith. Despite what some courts have suggested, *e.g., Santilli v. State Farm Insurance Co.,* 562 P.2d at 969, and what some commentators have asserted, *e.g.,* J. Appleman, *Insurance Law &*

Lawton v. Great Southwest Fire Ins. Co., 392 A.2d at 580. For example, the law of this state recognizes a duty to refrain from intentionally causing severe emotional distress to others. *Samms v. Eccles,* 11 Utah 2d 289, 358 P.2d 344 (1961). Thus, intentional and outrageous conduct by an insurer against an insured, coupled with a failure to bargain, could conceivably result in tort liability independent of (and concurrent with) liability for breach of contract. Additionally, the facts that give rise to a breach of the duty to bargain in good faith could also amount to fraudulent activity, rendering an insurer independently liable for damages flowing from the fraud. *See Wetherbee v. United Ins. Co.,* 265 Cal.App.2d 921, 71 Cal.Rptr. 764 (1968). Also, under various unfair practices acts, there may be statutory requirements that give rise to independent causes of action. *E.g.,* U.C.A., 1953, §§ 31–27–1 to–24.

14. The duty to perform the contract in good faith cannot, by definition, be waived by either party to the agreement.

Practice § 8878.15 at 424–26 (1981), there is no reason to limit damages recoverable for breach of a duty to investigate, bargain, and settle claims in good faith to the amount specified in the insurance policy.[15] Nothing inherent in the contract law approach mandates this narrow definition of recoverable damages. Although the policy limits define the amount for which the insurer may be held responsible in performing the contract, they do not define the amount for which it may be liable upon a breach. * * *

Damages recoverable for breach of contract include both general damages, *i.e.,* those flowing naturally from the breach, and consequential damages, *i.e.,* those reasonably within the contemplation of, or reasonably foreseeable by, the parties at the time the contract was made. *Pacific Coast Title Insurance Co. v. Hartford Accident & Indemnity Co.,* 7 Utah 2d 377, 379, 325 P.2d 906, 907 (1958), *citing Hadley v. Baxendale,* 9 Exch. 341, 156 Eng.Rep. 145 (1854). We have repeatedly recognized that consequential damages for breach of contract may reach beyond the bare contract terms. *See, e.g., Pacific Coast Title Insurance Co. v. Hartford Accident & Indemnity,* 7 Utah 2d at 379, 325 P.2d at 908 (attorney fees incurred for settling and defending claims were foreseeable result of contractor's default); *Bevan v. J.H. Construction Co.,* Utah, 669 P.2d 442, 444 (1983) (home purchasers entitled to damages for loss of favorable mortgage interest rate resulting from builder's breach of contract).

In an action for breach of a duty to bargain in good faith, a broad range of recoverable damages is conceivable, particularly given the unique nature and purpose of an insurance contract. An insured frequently faces catastrophic consequences if funds are not available within a reasonable period of time to cover an insured loss; damages for losses well in excess of the policy limits, such as for a home or a business, may therefore be foreseeable and provable. *See, e.g., Reichert v. General Insurance Co.,* 59 Cal.Rptr. 724, 728, 428 P.2d 860, 864 (1967), *vacated on other grounds,* 68 Cal.2d 822, 442 P.2d 377, 69 Cal.Rptr. 321 (1968) (because bankruptcy was a foreseeable consequence of fire insurer's failure to pay, insurer was liable for consequential damages flowing from bankruptcy). Furthermore, it is axiomatic that insurance frequently is purchased not only to provide funds in case of loss, but to provide peace of mind for the insured or his beneficiaries. Therefore, although other courts adopting the contract approach have been reluctant to allow such an award, *Lawton v. Great Southwest Fire Insurance Co.,* 392 A.2d at 581–82, we find no difficulty with the proposition that, in unusual cases, damages for mental anguish might be provable.[16] *See Kewin v. Massachusetts Mutual Life Insurance Co.,* 409 Mich. at 440–55, 295 N.W.2d at

15. In *Ammerman,* we suggested in dicta that in an action for breach of an insurance policy, the damages could not exceed the policy limits. 19 Utah 2d at 264, 430 P.2d at 578. We expressly disavow this dicta.

16. Clearly, damages will not be available for the mere disappointment, frustration, or anxiety normally experienced in the process of filing an insurance claim and negotiating a settlement with an insurer.

64–72 (Williams, J., dissenting). * * * The foreseeability of any such damages will always hinge upon the nature and language of the contract and the reasonable expectations of the parties. * * *

With the foregoing principles in mind, we return to a consideration of the present case. * * *

Under [the] circumstances and resolving all doubts in Beck's favor, we cannot say that a jury could not find that Farmers breached its duty of good faith in rejecting Beck's claim without explanation and in failing to further investigate the matter. Therefore, we remand the matter to the trial court for further proceedings.

Affirmed.

Notes

1. In *Gruenberg v. Aetna Ins. Co.,* 9 Cal.3d 566, 108 Cal.Rptr. 480, 510 P.2d 1032 (1973), decided after *Crisci,* the court recognized the insurer's duty of good faith and fair dealing toward its insured (*Comunale* and *Crisci* both considered the duty of the insurer to act in good faith in handling the claims of third persons). In *Gruenberg,* the plaintiff owned a restaurant which was destroyed by fire. Plaintiff was charged with arson and defrauding an insurer, both charges of which were dismissed at a preliminary hearing. Plaintiff alleged that the defendant insurer acted to falsely imply that plaintiff had motive to burn down his place of business. Further, when plaintiff refused to appear at an examination conducted by defendant on the advice of his attorney (pending the outcome of the criminal charges), defendant denied liability.

In its analysis, the court cited *Comunale* and *Crisci,* stating that an insurer has a duty to deal fairly and in good faith with its insured, a duty which sounds in both contract and tort and is imposed because there is an implied covenant of good faith and fair dealing in every contract. The duty not to unreasonably withhold payment due an insured are "merely two different aspects of the same duty."

"An insurer owes to its insured an implied-in-law duty of good faith and fair dealing that it will do nothing to deprive the insured of the benefits of the policy." The court went on to say that, as in *Crisci,* the violation of that duty sounds in tort notwithstanding that it also constitutes a breach of contract. The court concluded that "it is manifest that a common legal principle underlies all of the foregoing decisions; namely that in every insurance contract there is an implied covenant of good faith and fair dealing." This duty applies equally whether the insurer is dealing with the claims of third persons against the insured or with the claims of the insured. "Accordingly, when the insurer unreasonably and in bad faith withholds payment of the claim of its insured, it is subject to liability in tort."

2. *Beck* raises interesting questions. One must ask whether the interests of the insured are well served if the appropriate remedy for violation of the covenant of good faith and fair dealing lies in contract and not in tort in the face of egregious conduct by an insurer. An illustrative case is *State Farm Fire and Cas. Co. v. Superior Court*, 54 Cal.App.4th 625, 62 Cal.

Rptr.2d 834 (1997), in which the insureds sued the insurer alleging wrongful acts, including fraudulent and negligent misrepresentations, breach of contract and bad faith. The intriguing facts of the case, set forth in the opinion, also included excerpts of the deposition testimony of one of State Farm's claims specialists, in which she evaded several questions as to whether she signed and sent letters to the insureds regarding their insurance claims. The specialist even went so far as to deny recognition of her own voice on a tape-recorded message, stating, "Oh, I don't know if it's my voice or not. I don't know how I sound to other people." Additionally, the case indicates that one of the insurer's agents forged the insured's signature on the original declarations page of the application for insurance, that the insurer adopted a policy of destroying potentially relevant documents to avoid production in bad faith actions, and that the insurer manufactured evidence in relation to the claim. It did not bode well for the insurer when the court began its opinion with the statement, "At issue in this case is the preservation of public trust in the scrupulous administration of justice and the integrity of the bar."

3. The *State Farm* case cited above is not an isolated incident nor is questionable conduct confined to the borders of California. Douglas R. Richmond, in explaining that an insurer's refusal to settle a claim without prior investigation may show that the insurer breached the implied covenant of good faith and fair dealing, refers to *Republic Ins. Co. v. Stoker*, 867 S.W.2d 74 (Tex.Ct.App.1993). Douglas R. Richmond, *An Overview of Insurance Bad Faith Law and Litigation*, 25 SETON HALL L. REV. 74 (1994). In *Stoker*, a first-party case, the insurer denied the plaintiff insured's auto accident claim even though the adjuster ignored the police report of the accident, failed to visit the site of the accident, did not to interview the insured and three witnesses, and failed to obtain photographs other than those of the insured. *Id.* at 79. With these facts, the *Stoker* court had little difficulty in concluding that the plaintiff stated a bad faith claim.

4. *Standards for Establishing "Bad Faith." First Party Compared to Third Party Cases.* Extracts from Travelers Ins. Co. v. Savio, 706 P.2d 1258 at 1274–1276 (Colo.1985):

> Courts in California, the first jurisdiction to recognize the existence of a bad faith tort action in a first-party insurer context, have long recognized significant differences between first-party and third-party cases. *See, e.g., Austero v. National Casualty Co. of Detroit, Michigan,* 84 Cal.App.3d 1, 148 Cal.Rptr. 653 (1978). In defining the standard of care applicable in a first-party context, these distinctions should not be ignored. *See Employers Equitable Life Insurance Co. v. Williams,* 282 Ark. 29, 665 S.W.2d 873 (1984) (standard of care in third-party insurance tort action is negligence, while first-party cause of action requires "dishonest, malicious, or oppressive conduct").
>
> In *Anderson v. Continental Insurance Co.,* 85 Wis.2d 675, 271 N.W.2d 368 (1978), the Supreme Court of Wisconsin recognized the peculiar characteristics of first-party insurance claims and concluded that the appropriate standard for determining the presence or absence of bad faith dealing by an insurer with regard to a claim of its insured consisted of two parts: "the absence of a reasonable basis for denying benefits of the policy and the defendant's knowledge or reckless disre-

gard of the lack of a reasonable basis for denying the claim." The court made the following observations concerning the applicability of this standard in first-party cases:

> It is appropriate, in applying the test, to determine whether a claim was properly investigated and whether the results of the investigation were subjected to a reasonable evaluation and review. * * *
>
> While we have stated above that, for proof of bad faith, there must be an absence of a reasonable basis for denial of policy benefits *and* the knowledge or reckless disregard of a reasonable basis for a denial, implicit in that test is our conclusion that the knowledge of the lack of a reasonable basis may be inferred and imputed to an insurance company where there is a reckless disregard of a lack of a reasonable basis for denial or a reckless indifference to facts or to proofs submitted by the insured.
>
> Under these tests of the tort of bad faith, an insurance company, however, may challenge claims which are fairly debatable and will be found liable only where it has intentionally denied (or failed to process or pay) a claim without a reasonable basis.
>
> * * *
>
> The first element of this test—unreasonable conduct—was recognized in *Trimble* [Farmers Group, Inc. v. Trimble, 691 P.2d 1138 (Colo.1984)] as the sole standard for the tort of bad faith dealing by an insurance carrier with its insured in a third-party setting. Whether an insurer has acted reasonably in denying or delaying approval of a claim will be determined on an objective basis, requiring proof of the standards of conduct in the industry. The second element of the test reflects a reasonable balance between the right of an insurance carrier to reject a non-compensable claim submitted by its insured and the obligation of such carrier to investigate and ultimately approve a valid claim of its insured. If an insurer does not know that its denial of or delay in processing a claim filed by its insured is unreasonable, and does not act with reckless disregard of a valid claim, the insurer's conduct would be based upon a permissible, albeit mistaken, belief that the claim is not compensable. While the distinction is subtle, recognition of the permissible scope of an insurer's right to refuse invalid claims requires the conclusion that in the context of a first-party claim the insured must establish the insurer's knowledge or reckless disregard of the fact that a valid claim has been submitted. * * * The conclusion of the Court of Appeals that the tort of bad faith conduct by an insurer in a first-party context requires proof only of simple negligence is erroneous.
>
> [See also deVries v. St. Paul Fire & Marine Ins. Co., 716 F.2d 939 (1st Cir.1983)].

5. Decisions as to "bad faith" in first party cases continue to range across a broad spectrum. A representative tabulation of opinions may be found in the *Savio* case (note 5 above), 706 P.2d 1258 at 1273, and in *Caruso v. Republic Ins. Co.*, 558 F.Supp. 430 (D.Md.1983). Some jurisdictions continue to join the so-called "majority" in recognizing the tort of "bad faith." See Justin v. Guardian Ins. Co., 670 F.Supp. 614 (D.V.I.1987). Others

approach it but back away. E.g. Federal Kemper Ins. Co. v. Hornback, 711 S.W.2d 844, 845 (Ky.1986) (overruling a prior Kentucky decision to allow tort recovery for an insurer's breach of the covenant of good faith and fair dealing). Others may hold fast to a conservative position. E.g., Northwestern National Ins. Co. v. Pope, 791 F.2d 649, 651 (8th Cir.1986) (following Iowa law which does not recognize an independent tort action for an insurer's bad faith failure to settle a first party claim).

Even in the many jurisdictions that judicially reject the tort of bad faith, the effect is softened by the rather open encouragement of consequential contract damages and other side benefits. The main case is an example. Another is *Murphy v. Cincinnati Ins. Co.*, 772 F.2d 273 (6th Cir.1985), applying Michigan law, and extending the reach of consequential damages under *Hadley v. Baxendale* to the insured's attorneys' fee. Indiana claims to not need a tort of bad faith because it offers special contractual remedies (including punitive damages). Liberty Mut. Ins. Co. v. Parkinson, 487 N.E.2d 162 (Ind.App.1985). Of course, if the "bad faith" consists in a cognizable tort, the punitive damages, are to be expected if allowed in the jurisdiction.

G. REVERSE BAD FAITH

There is a measure of ironic consistency in the fact that the state in which bad faith first reached full flower is also the point of origin of cases suggesting the counter use of the doctrine. In *California Casualty General Ins. Co. v. Superior Court*, 173 Cal.App.3d 274, 218 Cal.Rptr. 817 (1985), the insured sued for bad faith in the handling of her uninsured motorist claim. During the proceedings the insurer moved to amend its answer to assert the theory of "comparative" bad faith based on the manner in which the insured and her attorney prosecuted, handled, and managed her first party claim. The insured protested that this was a "disfavored" defense because it had never before been recognized. The trial court refused to allow the amendment and the insurer appealed. In issuing a mandate to the lower court to vacate its order the appellate court stated:

> "[A] duty of good faith and fair dealing in an insurance policy is a two-way street, running from the insured to his insurer as well as vice versa [citation]." * * * The specific content of each party's duty "is dependent upon the nature of the bargain struck between the insurer and the insured and the legitimate expectations of the parties which arise from the contract." * * *
>
> There can be little question but that an insurer which provides uninsured motorist coverage has a reasonable expectation that if the insured suffers a loss claimed to be covered under the uninsured motorist provisions of the policy, the insured will promptly and accurately furnish it with all the information and evidence pertinent to the claim that is known to the insured. If a failure of the insured to do so results in delaying or impeding the investigation of the claim by the insurer or delays or makes improvident the insurer's payment of the claim, any economic loss and emotional distress

caused the insured by virtue of any such nonpayment or delay in investigation or payment will have been caused either wholly or in part by the conduct of the insured. We perceive no sound reason, nor is any suggested, why the doctrine of comparative fault enunciated and applied to negligent conduct by the California Supreme Court in *Li v. Yellow Cab Co.* (1975) 13 Cal.3d 804, 119 Cal.Rptr. 858, 532 P.2d 1226, and later applied as between a strictly liable defendant and a negligent plaintiff (*Daly v. General Motors Corp.* (1978) 20 Cal.3d 725, 144 Cal.Rptr. 380, 575 P.2d 1162) and as between two tortfeasors one of whose liability was based on strict products liability and the other on negligence (*Safeway Stores, Inc. v. Nest–Kart* (1978) 21 Cal.3d 322, 146 Cal.Rptr. 550, 579 P.2d 441) should not be applicable to bad faith cases. While the duty of good faith and fair dealing arises out of a contractual relationship between the parties, breach of the duty and ensuing damages are governed by tort principles.

In a later case, *Handel v. United States Fidelity & Guaranty Co.*, 192 Cal.App.3d 684, 237 Cal.Rptr. 667 (1987) the insurer cross-complained in a fire loss case, alleging fraud and false swearing on the part of the insured and requesting punitive damages. These were awarded at trial. The Appellate Court reversed because of failure to prove reliance—a necessary element in a common law deceit action. By dicta, however, the court recognized the existence of an independent "reverse bad faith" cause of action, but avoided the issue because it was neither pleaded nor tried in the case.

In theory an insurer has always been entitled (in addition to avoiding the policy) to sue its patrons for damages for common law fraud plus punitive damages, but this is rarely done. However to categorize as "bad faith torts" the breach of contractual conditions by the insured (or his or her attorney) such as "non-cooperation" or "failure to give prompt notice of a claim" or "false swearing as to the value of destroyed property" (to be dealt with shortly in this book) would open new vistas in tort and contract law in general, and require a reappraisal of commonly employed legal strategies. And what about an affirmative defense asserting that an insured's tactical moves to "set up" a bad faith claim against the insurer constitutes "reverse" bad faith? See Shipstead and Thomas, *Comparative and Reverse Bad Faith, etc.*, 28 Tort & Ins.L.J. 215 (1987). In the same vein, Douglas Richmond also explains that an insured has a duty to cooperate (discussed in Chapter 5 in this text) with regard to an insurance claim, a duty he views a stringent as the insurer's duty to defend (also discussed in Chapter 5 in this text). Douglas Richmond, *An Overview of Insurance Bad Faith Law and Litigation*, 25 Seton Hall L. Rev. 74 (1994).

Notwithstanding the foregoing, the California Supreme Court seems to have retreated from the theory of reverse bad faith. In *Kransco v. American Empire Surplus Lines Ins. Co.*, 23 Cal.4th 390, 97 Cal.Rptr.2d 151, 2 P.3d 1 (2000), the court held that an insured is not subject to a comparative fault offset of a bad faith claim. The court noted that an insurer is held to a higher duty and the insured's conduct sounds in contract in which the insurer is limited to contract remedies. The court went on to explicitly disapprove of *California Casualty* in this respect. *Kransco* follows the reasoning of an earlier opinion. Agricultural Ins. Co. v. Superior Court, 70 Cal.App.4th 385, 82 Cal.Rptr.2d 594 (1999) (an insured's conduct sounds in contract). For an excellent pre-*Kransco* treatment of the subject cited by the majority, see Ellen Smith Pryor, *Comparative Fault and Insurance Bad Faith*, 72 Tex. L. Rev. 1505 (1994).

Justice Kennard, in her *Kransco* dissent, cites another Richmond article the title of which neatly summarizes their views. Douglas Richmond, *The Two-Way Street of Insurance Good Faith: Under Construction, But Not Yet Open*, 28 Loy. U. Chi. L.J. 95 (1996).

H. THE LEGISLATIVE RESPONSE

THE UNFAIR PRACTICES ACT

The Unfair Practices Act, a version of which is the subject of interpretation in the following case, was originally formulated by the National Association of Insurance Commissioners. The California version of the Act is found in the Insurance Code beginning at § 790. California adopted the Act in 1959; it has been amended several times. But one thing stands out: the Act was adopted to make up for the regulatory powers renounced by Congress in the McCarran–Ferguson Act. Ins. Code § 790 makes explicit reference to McCarran–Ferguson (using the Public Law citation). Of all the sections of the Unfair Practices Act, § 790.03 seems to have attracted the most interest in recent times. This section provides in part:

> The following are hereby defined as unfair methods of competition and unfair and deceptive acts or practices in the business of insurance, * * *
>
> "(h) Knowingly committing or performing with such frequency as to indicate a general business practice any of the following unfair claims settlement practices:
>
> "(1) Misrepresenting to claimants pertinent facts of insurance policy provisions relating to any coverages at issue.
>
> "(2) Failing to acknowledge and act reasonably promptly upon communications with respect to claims arising under insurance policies.
>
> "(3) Failing to adopt and implement reasonable standards for the prompt investigation and processing of claims arising under insurance policies.
>
> "(4) Failing to affirm or deny coverage of claims within a reasonable time after proof of loss requirements have been completed and submitted by the insured.
>
> "(5) Not attempting in good faith to effectuate prompt, fair, and equitable settlements of claims in which liability has become reasonably clear.

"(6) Compelling insureds to institute litigation to recover amounts due under an insurance policy by offering substantially less than the amounts ultimately recovered in actions brought by the insureds, when the insureds have made claims for amounts reasonably similar to the amounts ultimately recovered.

"(7) Attempting to settle a claim by an insured for less than the amount to which a reasonable man would have believed he was entitled by reference to written or printed advertising material accompanying or made part of an application.

"(8) Attempting to settle claims on the basis of an application which was altered without notice to, or knowledge or consent of, the insured, his representative, agent, or broker.

"(9) Failing, after payment of a claim, to inform insureds or beneficiaries, upon request by them, of the coverage under which payment has been made.

"(10) Making known to insureds or claimants a practice of the insurer of appealing from arbitration awards in favor of insureds or claimants for the purpose of compelling them to accept settlements or compromises less than the amount awarded in arbitration.

"(11) Delaying the investigation or payment of claims by requiring an insured, claimant, or the physician of either, to submit a preliminary claim report, and then requiring the subsequent submission of formal proof of loss forms, both of which submissions contain substantially the same information.

"(12) Failing to settle claims promptly, where liability has become apparent, under one portion of the insurance policy coverage in order to influence settlements under other portions of the insurance policy coverage.

"(13) Failing to provide promptly a reasonable explanation of the basis relied on in the insurance policy, in relation to the facts or applicable law, for the denial of a claim or for the offer of a compromise settlement.

"(14) Directly advising a claimant not to obtain the services of an attorney.

"(15) Misleading a claimant as to the applicable statute of limitations.

"(16) Delaying the payment or provision of hospital, medical, or surgical benefits for services provided with respect to acquired immune deficiency syndrome or AIDS–related complex for more than 60 days after the insurer has received a claim for those benefits, where the delay in claim payment is for the purpose of investigating whether the condition preexisted the coverage. However, this 60–day period shall not include any time during which the insurer is awaiting a response for relevant medical information from a health care provider."

Other provisions of the Act prohibit unfair practices (§ 790.02), grant authority to the Commissioner of Insurance to fix a penalty not exceeding $5,000 for negligent violations, and $10,000 for willful violations (§ 790.035), prohibit advertising of insurance not available (§ 790.036), provide for investigation by the commissioner (§ 790.04), authorize cease and desist orders and court orders against unfair practices (§§ 790.05, 790.06), suspend or revoke the violator's license (§ 790.07), establish that action taken under the Act does not affect an insurer's liability to other administrative action or to civil liability or to criminal penalty under the laws of California. The purpose of the Act is "to regulate trade practices in the business of insurance in accordance with the intent of Congress" as expressed in the McCarran–Ferguson Act, 15 U.S.C.A. §§ 1011–1015.

STATE FARM MUTUAL AUTOMOBILE INSURANCE COMPANY v. REEDER

Supreme Court of Kentucky, 1988.
763 S.W.2d 116.

WINTERSHEIMER, JUSTICE.

This appeal is from a decision of the Court of Appeals which reversed the circuit court and held that KRS 304.12–230, the Unfair Claims Settlement Practices Act, creates a private right of action against an insurance company by third-party claimants. The Court of Appeals affirmed the denial by the circuit court of prejudgment interest because it was based on unliquidated damages.

The principal issue is the enforceability of a private cause of action under the unfair claims settlement practices statute.

Reeder and the parents of Paul Hampton are next door neighbors and share a common driveway. While visiting his parents, Hampton accidentally drove his car into the support for the Reeder carport which collapsed. The impact damaged the roof, the home and demolished a ladder and boat in the carport. Hampton's parents were insured by State Farm and the company was promptly notified. State Farm obtained an estimate of repair for $8,471. The lowest estimate Reeder obtained was $13,392. Having declined the insurance company's subsequent offer of $8,961, Reeder sued for the amount he claimed for property damage and expenses, plus $15,000 for his attorney fees as well as $250,000 for violation of KRS 304.12–230. The circuit judge dismissed the unfair practice claim but the remainder of the case was tried by a jury which returned an $11,000 verdict which has been satisfied.

On appeal, Reeder argued a violation of KRS 304.12–230, and also sought prejudgment interest which had been denied by the circuit court. State Farm contends that the statute does not create a private right of action, but only gives the Commissioner of Insurance authority to perform a regulatory function. They claim the statute applies to a frequency of incidences indicating a general practice and that the statute lists 14 types of unfair claims settlement practices. They also argue that the Commissioner of Insurance may take action to prevent unfair practices when they are performed with such frequency as to indicate a general business practice.

KRS 304.12–230 does not specifically provide that any individual may maintain a claim for damages for violation of the act. However, the statute does not state that a violation of its terms is enforceable only by the insurance commissioner, and it does not prohibit a claim by an individual for damages for its breach. In our view, a person may maintain an action for damages resulting from the commission of such unfair practices only as a result of KRS 446.070. The right of a private citizen to maintain an action for violation of the Unfair Claims Settlement Practices Act is clearly supported by KRS 446.070 which provides: A person injured by the violation of any statute may recover from the offender such damages as he sustained by reason of the violation although a penalty or forfeiture is imposed for such violation.

Grzyb v. Evans, Ky., 700 S.W.2d 399 (1985) held that "Where the statute both declares the unlawful act and specifies the civil remedy available to the aggrieved party, the aggrieved party is limited to the remedy provided by the statute." Id. at 401. Here there was not only a contractual dispute over the amount of damages, for which the plaintiff has been awarded damages, but there is also a claim of a violation under the Unfair Claims Settlement Practices Act. This statute does not provide the aggrieved party with a civil remedy and therefore KRS 446.070 applies to such a violation. Reeder belongs to the class intended to be protected by the Insurance Code. Although the Insurance Code prescribes the remedy for its enforcement by the Insurance Commissioner, it does not provide a remedy for those individuals intended to be protected by the act.

This statute is very old; it was cited in City of Henderson v. Clayton, Ky., 57 S.W. 1, 22 K.L.R. 283 (1900). It has been part of the statutory law of Kentucky for at least 88 years. It has been frequently cited by this Court. See Hackney v. Fordson Coal Co., 230 Ky. 362, 19 S.W.2d 989 (1929). There is no reason why it should not be applied to third party claims. It creates a private right of action for the violation of any statute so long as the plaintiff belongs to the class intended to be protected by the statute.

It can be assumed that the General Assembly was aware of the existence of this statute when it enacted KRS 304.12–230. See Haven Point Enterprises, Inc. v. United Kentucky Bank, Inc., Ky., 690 S.W.2d 393 (1985). It can easily be harmonized with the unfair claims act. We find no reason to excuse this matter because it is brought by a third party claimant. The action results from the bad faith in adjusting the claim. If a first-party carrier can be sued for bad faith, there is no reason why a third party carrier cannot also be sued.

The Kentucky Unfair Claims Settlement Practices Act enumerates 14 specific practices which, if performed with such frequency as to indicate a general business practice, can amount to unfair claims settlement practices. It should be noted that this statute has been amended, effective July 15, 1988, so as to eliminate the requirement that the prohibited conduct be performed "with such frequency as to indicate a general business practice * * *." This amendment was after this cause of action accrued and so on remand Reeder must prove frequency of acts.

The Kentucky law is similar to those adopted by thirty-eight other states and is based on the 1971 amendment that the National Association of Insurance Commissioners made to its model "act relating to unfair methods of competition and unfair and deceptive acts and practices in the business of insurance." This statute is intended to protect the public from unfair trade practices and fraud. It should be liberally construed so as to effectuate its purpose. KRS 446.080; DeHart v. Gray, Ky., 245 S.W.2d 434 (1952).

There is a substantial split in authority among other states as to whether individuals can maintain an action under their respective state laws. Whether other states permit private individuals to maintain claims is based upon their particular statutory system and is of no consequence here. Our decision must be based on the language of the Kentucky law.

There is no common law cause of action in Kentucky for first party bad faith. Federal Kemper Ins. Co. v. Hornback, Ky., 711 S.W.2d 844 (1986). However, the legislature can enact a law creating a cause of action where none existed at common law. The act in question indicates a definite intention to prohibit unfair claims settlement practices and constitutes the public policy of Kentucky.

It is the holding of this Court that private citizens are not specifically excluded by the statute from maintaining a private right of action against an insurer by third party claimants. KRS 446.070 and KRS 304.12–230 read together create a statutory bad faith cause of action.

[The court added that prejudgment interest may be awarded on a claim, or portion thereof, that consists of an uncontested "liquidated" amount, even if litigation is pending. The court reasoned that a defendant should pay interest on an item of damages if the amount is fixed or ascertainable with reasonable certainty and if the defendant fails to pay in a timely manner.]

Therefore, this matter is remanded to the circuit court to award interest at the statutory rate on the admitted amount of $8,471.14 from June 30, 1985.

The decision of the Court of Appeals is affirmed in regard to the private right of action under the Unfair Claims Settlement Practices Act but reversed in regard to the question of prejudgment interest.

The case is remanded to the trial court for further proceedings consistent with this opinion.

Notes

1. In 1979 the California State Supreme Court announced that West's Annotated California Insurance Code § 790.03, prohibiting unfair claims practices, created a private right of action that could be used by insureds and by third parties. In *Royal Globe Insurance Co. v. Superior Court,* 23 Cal.3d

880, 153 Cal.Rptr. 842, 592 P.2d 329 (1979), the plaintiff filed an action for personal injuries sustained when she slipped at a food market. She joined as defendants the Royal Globe Insurance Company, which had issued a policy of liability insurance to the market. The plaintiff claimed that defendant had violated subdivision (h)(5) of section 790.03 of the Insurance Code, a provision of the Unfair Practices Act that requires insurers to attempt in good faith to effectuate prompt settlement of claims when liability is reasonably clear.

The court first held that a private litigant may bring an action to impose civil liability for violation of § 790.03. In making this decision, the court focused on the language of the Act "Section 790.03 provides that a cease and desist order issued by the commissioner * * * shall not absolve an insurer from 'civil liability or criminal penalty under the laws of this State arising out of the methods, acts or practices found unfair or deceptive.' " The court reasoned that "[t]his provision appears to afford to private litigants a cause of action against insurers which commit the unfair acts or practices defined in subdivision (h)." The court concluded that the fair construction of that language is that a person to whom the civil liability runs has the right to enforce an action against the insurer.

The court further held that the insurer's duty runs not only to the insured, but also to third party claimants. The court analyzed the language of the statute and the legislative history to conclude that creating a distinction between insureds and third party claimants would be contrary to the law's purpose, which is the prevention of unfair claims practices by insurers.

Nine years after *Royal Globe,* the California State Supreme Court reversed itself in *Moradi–Shalal v. Fireman's Fund Insurance Companies,* 46 Cal.3d 287, 250 Cal.Rptr. 116, 758 P.2d 58 (1988). In *Moradi–Shalal,* the court held that "the Royal Globe court incorrectly evaluated the legislative intent underlying the passage of section 790.03, subdivision (h), and that accordingly *Royal Globe* should be overruled." In concluding that there is no private cause against insurers engaging in unfair practice, the court used the following factors to support its decision: stare decisis, the rejection of *Royal Globe* by other state courts, scholarly criticism, the 1980 report of the National Association of Insurance Commissioners, additional legislative history, adverse social and economic consequences resulting from the *Royal Globe* decision and analytical difficulties caused by the insufficient guidance provided by the *Royal Globe* court.

2. Although some version of the Unfair Insurance Practices Act (UPA) is in place in all jurisdictions (save perhaps the District of Columbia), few states have held that the Act creates a private cause of Action. See *Pekular v. Eich*, 355 Pa.Super. 276, 513 A.2d 427 (1986) which holds that a private cause of action can be brought according to consumer and fair trade laws, but no private cause of action exists under the state's UPA. Some states such as South Dakota and Tennessee have passed statutes specifically prohibiting such private causes of action.

On the other hand even fewer states have held that their version of the Act preempts common law bad faith actions that might otherwise exist. Kinney v. St. Paul Mercury Ins. Co., 120 Ill.App.3d 294, 75 Ill.Dec. 911, 458 N.E.2d 79 (1983); but see Calcagno v. Personalcare Health Management,

Inc., 207 Ill.App.3d 493, 499, 152 Ill.Dec. 412, 419, 565 N.E.2d 1330, 1337 (1991) (questioning the holding in Kinney and limiting preemption to punitive damages); see also Emerson v. American Bankers Ins. Co. of Florida, 223 Ill.App.3d 929, 166 Ill.Dec. 293, 298, 585 N.E.2d 1315, 1320 (1992) (criticizing the holding in Kinney).

Some states have held that a private cause of action can be implied though unfair trade practices statutes rather than through unfair insurance practices. See Mead v. Burns, 199 Conn. 651, 509 A.2d 11 (1986) holding that a private cause of action exists through the Connecticut Unfair Trade Practices Act to enforce violation of the Connecticut Unfair Insurance Practices Act, but that there is no private cause of action under the latter act.

Meanwhile, a few states have passed laws specifically creating a statutory bad faith cause of action. See Jones v. Continental Ins. Co., 670 F.Supp. 937 (S.D.Fla.1987) (upholding the constitutionality of such a statute in Florida); Russell v. Protective Ins. Co., 107 N.M. 9, 751 P.2d 693 (1988) (discussing a new act which specifically grants a private cause of action).

A thorough compendium of the cases appears in Theisin, *Recent Developments in Private Rights of Action Under the Unfair Claims Settlement Act*, 28 Tort & Ins. L.J. (1987).

3. *"Final determination of liability."* Nationwide Ins. Co. issued a $25,000 auto liability policy to Ms. Johnson. Ms. Calzada was injured in an accident in which Ms. Johnson was the other driver. A jury returned a verdict of $93,000 against Ms. Johnson in a personal injury action. Ms. Johnson appealed from the ensuing judgment. While the appeal was pending, Ms. Calzado sued Nationwide under West's Ann.Cal.Ins. Code § 790.03 for bad faith in failing to negotiate a settlement within the policy limit. Nationwide demurred and moved for judgment on the pleading. The appellate court ruled the trial court erred in not sustaining the demurrer and granting the motion, stating that *Royal Globe* holds "the injured third party may not institute [a direct] action [under the statute] until a judgment establishing liability of the insured has been secured. * * * When a court speaks of final judgment of liability it has reference to a judgment that is final for res judicata purposes, not for purpose of appeal." Nationwide Insurance Co. v. Superior Court for County of San Bernardino, 128 Cal.App.3d 711, 180 Cal.Rptr. 464 (1982).

Bodenhamer Jewelers was burglarized. Lost in the burglary were items of jewelry belonging to customers of the store. Bodenhamer's insurer, St. Paul Fire & Marine Ins. Co., despite advice of counsel that it was liable under its policy, delayed payments for a substantial time and advised Bodenhamer's customers who had lost property that its position was that the policy provided no coverage. Nonetheless, more than three years after the burglary most (but not all) of the customers' claims had been paid by St. Paul. Bodenhamer alleged that it had lost customers due to ill will developed during and on account of the delays in payment of claims. Bodenhamer sued asserting both violations of the general law principles of good and fair dealing and of Ins. Code 790.03(h). The Superior Court granted St. Paul's motion for a summary adjudication of issues adverse to Bodenhamer explaining that neither the general law claim nor the 790.03(h) claim could be asserted absent a determination of liability against Bodenhamer by the third party (customer) claimants. Is this the right result? See Bodenhamer v. Superior Court, 192 Cal.App.3d 1472, 238 Cal.Rptr. 177 (1987).

4. *Statutory Controls on Insurance Company Settlement Practices.* The question arises as to whether or not a statutory schedule of penalty payments (if stiff enough) to the insured for dilatoriness in handling his or her claim might not be as effective, and at the same time easier to enforce, than the somewhat ad hoc punishment meted out in the name of "good faith and fair dealing" at the whim of a particular jury.

A number of states do have such statutes usually providing for additional interest payments on the award plus attorneys' fees (see, Vance, 3d ed. p. 46). A notable example is Louisiana (L.S.A.–R.S.) which imposes an 8 percent penalty for failure to pay within 60 days "without just cause" on a life policy (§ 656); or 100 percent penalty on health and accident contracts where payment is not made within 30 days "unless just and reasonable grounds, such as would put a reasonable and prudent businessman on his guard" are shown (§ 657); and the greater of 10 percent or $1,000 "damages" for failure to pay other types of insurance claims (25 percent "damages" in case of fire or theft of an auto) within 60 days "when such failure is found to be 'arbitrary, capricious or without probable cause' " (§ 658). See, Lombard v. Manchester Life Insurance Co., 406 So.2d 742 (La.App.1981) (determining which category a claim under a "Student Accident Insurance" policy should fall).

Where the Louisiana statute, in common with most other states, makes allowance for nonpayment on reasonable grounds, the Arkansas statute (§ 23–79–208 Ark.Stat.Rev.) imposes flat 12 percent "damages" together with attorneys' fees upon the amount of the loss in all cases of delay in payment beyond the time stipulated in the policy even though refusal is in good faith and on reasonable grounds. This statute withstood constitutional attack in *Life and Casualty Insurance Co. v. McCray*, 291 U.S. 566, 54 S.Ct. 482, 78 L.Ed. 987 (1934). However, a 1991 addition to this statute deters an insured's unreasonable failure to settle a claim, providing, "(d) Recovery of less than the amount demanded by the person entitled to recover under the policy shall not defeat the right to the twelve percent (12%) damages and attorneys' fees provided for in this section if the amount recovered for the loss is within twenty percent (20%) of the amount demanded or which is sought in the suit."

5. The California Vehicle Code § 16053 allows any person who is the registered owner of 25 or more vehicles to qualify as a self-insurer by obtaining a certificate of self insurance from the Department of Motor Vehicles. Should such a self insurer be subject to the Unfair Claims Practice Act (Ins.Code § 790.03(b)) when conducting settlement negotiations? See Nathanson v. Hertz Corp., 183 Cal.App.3d 78, 85 n. 9, 227 Cal.Rptr. 799 (1986) (holding that Veh. Code § 16053 does not exempt self-insurers from the requirements of Ins. Code § 790.03(b)). Should an uninsured motorist who balks at settling a tort claim against him be subject to the act?

6. For a general discussion of ambiguous practices within insurance law, see Thomas J. Holdych, *Standards for Establishing Deceptive Conduct*

Under State Deceptive Trade Practices Statutes That Impose Punitive Remedies, 73 ORE. L. REV. 235 (1994).

I. A POSTSCRIPT

Many courts have been reluctant to embrace the California approach. In Hawaii, for example, the Federal District Court held (in the absence of a Hawaii state court's pronouncement on the subject) that while a contract action can sound in tort and justify the imposition of non-contract damages, the imposition of punitive damages requires egregious or outrageous conduct. Genovia v. Jackson National Life Ins. Co., 795 F.Supp. 1036 (Hi. Dist. 1992). In 1996, Hawaii explicitly adopted California's *Gruenberg* approach to first party actions holding that punitive damages might be justifiable in a first party action for breach of the covenant of good faith and fair dealing. The Best Place, Inc. v. Penn America Ins. Co., 82 Hawai'i 120, 920 P.2d 334 (1996). *The Best Place* case contains a good summary of the law in various jurisdictions in this area.

Other jurisdictions have refused to recognize an underlying tort action within a claim for breach of the duty to settle an insurance claim. E.g., Glenn v. Fleming, 247 Kan. 296, 799 P.2d 79 (1990) (holding that a wrongful failure to settle arises from the insurer's contractual obligation to defend and such an action enforcing that obligation is based on breach of contract). In *Glenn*, however, the Kansas Supreme Court acknowledged the problems inherent in this blurring of the boundaries between tort and contract actions:

> We have adopted ... the principle that the insurer's duties are contractually based and then approved a tort standard of care for determining when the contract duty has been breached. Perhaps this contract/tort relationship has contributed to the confusion arising from our efforts to describe the duty of good faith and to identify the situations involving bad faith/negligent duty to settle and to defend. 799 P.2d at 90.

Scholars have mirrored this mixed view. In *The Wrong Side of the Mountain: A Comment on Bad Faith's Unnatural History*, 72 TEXAS L. REV. 1317 (1994), Dean Robert Jerry posits that courts have ignored bad faith's contractual heritage and have undermined contract law's ability to respond to insurer misconduct. He focuses on bad faith claims in the insurance context, restating the position of the majority of jurisdictions in the early 1980s: That an insurer's breach of duty to defend, duty to settle, or duty to pay proceeds constituted bad faith, and this bad faith performance of the contracts constituted a tort. The rationale is that insurance policies are different from ordinary commercial contracts and contract remedies are inadequate to properly balance insurer/insured interests. However, Dean Jerry illustrates a flaw in this assumption: There is no current data to demonstrate that traditional contract law principles are unable to deter misconduct and fairly compensate wronged insureds. He explains that contract law *can* award consequential damages as necessary, reasoning that any excess judgment resulting from an insurer's failure to defend or settle a claim is a natural and foreseeable consequence of the breach. Contract law also provides the insured with a remedy for loss of bargain, along with a remedy for emotional distress resulting from an insurer's nonperformance. He concludes by stating that treating insurer bad faith as a contract breach involving contract remedies may give insurers more certainty about outcomes, thereby reducing system-wide costs.

Douglas R. Richmond, in his article *Trust Me: Insurers Are Not Fiduciaries to Their Insureds*, 88 Ky. L.J. 1 (1999), takes much same approach in observing that the one area of the law which has traditionally been free of fiduciary relationships is contract law. According to him, insurance law should be no exception. Richmond argues that a fiduciary relationship deprives the insurer of the ability to protect its own interests. Richmond asserts that the duty owed by an insurer in either the first or third party context is that of good faith and fair dealing. An insurer does not owe the insured undivided loyalty, as the insurer has a contractual right to exercise its own discretion on whether or not to litigate or settle a claim. Because this may go against the stated wishes of the insured, the insurer retains the duty to appoint independent counsel to protect the insured's interests. In the first party insurance context, Richmond argues that an insurer has no duty to pay its insured on demand, and retains a right to examine claims and verify the loss. This allows insurance companies to keep premium costs down and to preserve the right to investigate claims is important to combat insurance fraud.

Richmond continues by noting that in recognition of the special relationship between the insured and the insurer, courts have fashioned a tort remedy for breach of this duty in the insurance context. He feels this remedy is sufficient as a deterrent to unscrupulous insurers, and should not elevate the relationship to a fiduciary one. The danger of incorrect nomenclature, warns Richmond, is that it is the nomenclature of the relationship that defines the rights and duties of the parties, and it is therefore important not to mischaracterize the relationship. Treating the insurer-insured relationship as a special one, but not fiduciary, is enough to provide a predictable basis for deciding disputes.

A distinctly contrary view is expressed by Professor Roger Baron in *When Insurance Companies Do Bad Things: The Evolution of the "Bad Faith" Causes of Action in South Dakota*, 44 S. Dak. L. Rev. 471 (1999). Professor Baron notes that the development of first and third party bad faith claims in South Dakota has been "a measured response [to indignities perpetuated by insurance companies]—a response which is warranted an justified." Id. at 492. He sums up by concluding that not all insurers need to worry about bad faith claims against them; "[t]hroughout the evolution of the bad faith causes of action, there has been at least one constant theme—insurers who do operate in *good faith* need not be concerned [emphasis in original]." Id. at 493.

Chapter 5

LIABILITY INSURANCE

A. INTRODUCTION—THE UNDERTAKING

PRELIMINARY NOTE

Liability insurance introduces a new twist to the contractual relationship between the insurer and the insured. The underlying contractual relationship between the insurer and the insured in both first and third party insurance agreements is essentially the same: in exchange for the payment of premiums, the insurer agrees to indemnify the insured against potential financial loss. However, with a liability insurance contract, the insurer's responsibility to pay for an injury or loss, should a specified event occur, runs both to the insured and to an injured third party. The introduction of responsibilities to third parties presents an expansion of the insurer's responsibilities to the insured, as well as adding to the complexity of insurance law.

Persons who purchase liability insurance which they hope will protect them against liability to third persons want two things: (a) the insurer's promise to pay (within the policy limit) any amount adjudged against the insured and (b) the insurer's promise to defend the insured in an action to have such liability adjudged. Insurers are, of course, willing to sell such promises. The terms in which such promises are clothed are, after decades of judicial interpretation, less than simple. A fairly ordinary set of clauses (slightly adapted from ones in use) bearing on the insurer's liability to pay and to defend in an automobile liability policy would include:

> (a) Insurer will pay on behalf of an insured all damages which the insured shall be legally obligated to pay because of bodily injury sustained by any person, and injury to or destruction of property arising out of the ownership or use of the owned automobile. The Insurer will defend any lawsuit, however groundless, false or fraudulent, against any insured for such damages as are payable under this policy but the Insurer may make such settlement of any claim or suit as it thinks appropriate.

(b) No action shall lie against the Insurer until after full compliance with the terms of the policy and until the amount of the insured's obligation to pay shall have been finally determined by judgment against the insured or written agreement of settlement among the insured, the claimant and the Insurer.

(c) The insured shall cooperate with the Insurer by disclosing all pertinent facts known to him or her, and upon Insurer's request shall attend hearings and trials, shall assist in obtaining evidence and the attendance of witnesses and shall participate in effecting settlements and conducting suits.

Other policy terms will clearly be involved in determining when the insurer's promise to pay and promise to defend are to be performed. E.g., the terms of the policy concerning the extent and the amount of coverage, the meaning of "insured" under the policy, and clauses (or state statutes) prohibiting coverage of willful injuries inflicted by an insured. But the ones outlined above are thicket enough, e.g.: (a) who has real control over a lawsuit against the insured, (b) can the insurer refuse to defend the lawsuit if the insurer believes that the policy does not cover the underlying liability, (c) does the insurer breach its duties when it refuses to make a settlement on behalf of the insured within the policy limits and the settlement offer was a reasonable one, (d) when, if at all, do third parties have the right to sue the insurer directly, (e) what is the responsibility of the insurer when it has breached either its duty to pay or its duty to defend, (f) is the insurer's duty to defend conditional on the insured complying with his duty to cooperate, and (g) in any case of breach of duty, what is the measure of damages?

The following case provides a brief introduction to the basic relationship.

AEROJET–GENERAL CORP. v. TRANSPORT INDEMNITY CO.

Supreme Court of California, 1997.
17 Cal.4th 38, 70 Cal.Rptr.2d 118, 948 P.2d 909.

* * *

Standard comprehensive or commercial general liability insurance policies are contracts between an insurer and an insured: In each, the insurer makes promises, and the insured pays premiums, the one in consideration for the other, against the risk of loss. (E.g., Buss v. Superior Court (1997) 16 Cal.4th 35, 44–45, 65 Cal.Rptr.2d 366, 939 P.2d 766.)

In pertinent part, standard comprehensive or commercial general liability insurance policies provide that the insurer has a duty to indemnify the insured for those sums that the insured becomes legally obligated to pay as damages for a covered claim. (E.g., Buss v. Superior Court, supra, 16 Cal.4th at p. 45, 65 Cal.Rptr.2d 366, 939 P.2d 766.) By definition, this duty entails the payment of money (e.g., id. at p. 46, 65

Cal.Rptr.2d 366, 939 P.2d 766), which is expressly limited in amount (see Croskey et al., Cal. Practice Guide: Insurance Litigation 2, supra, P 7:354, p. 7A–76), in order to resolve liability (e.g., Buss v. Superior Court, supra, 16 Cal.4th at p. 46, 65 Cal.Rptr.2d 366, 939 P.2d 766). It is not narrowly confined to money that the insured must give under law as compensation to third parties, but may also include money that the insured must itself expend in equity in order to provide relief of the same sort. (AIU Ins. Co. v. Superior Court, supra, 51 Cal.3d at pp. 818–843, 274 Cal.Rptr. 820, 799 P.2d 1253.) It runs to claims that are actually covered, in light of the facts proved. (E.g., Buss v. Superior Court, supra, 16 Cal.4th at pp. 45–46, 65 Cal.Rptr.2d 366, 939 P.2d 766.) It arises only after liability is established and as a result thereof. (E.g., id. at p. 46, 65 Cal.Rptr.2d 366, 939 P.2d 766; see Montrose Chemical Corp. v. Admiral Ins. Co., supra, 10 Cal.4th at p. 659, fn. 9, 42 Cal.Rptr.2d 324, 913 P.2d 878.) It is triggered if specified harm is caused by an included occurrence,[1] so long as at least some such harm results within the policy period. (Montrose Chemical Corp. v. Admiral Ins. Co., supra, 10 Cal.4th at pp. 669–673, 42 Cal.Rptr.2d 324, 913 P.2d 878.) It extends to all specified harm caused by an included occurrence, even if some such harm results beyond the policy period. (See id. at p. 686, 42 Cal.Rptr.2d 324, 913 P.2d 878.) In other words, if specified harm is caused by an included occurrence and results, at least in part, within the policy period, it perdures to all points of time at which some such harm results thereafter. To illustrate by a hypothetical similar to the present case: Insurer has a duty to indemnify Insured for those sums that Insured becomes legally obligated to pay as damages for property damage caused by its discharge of hazardous substances, up to a limit of $1 million. Insured discharges such a substance. It thereby causes property damage to Neighbor's land, in the amount of $100,000 (determined by the cost of returning the soil to its original condition), within the policy period of year 1. It causes further damage of this sort as the substance spreads under the surface, in the amount of $100,000 annually, in year two through year thirty. Insured must pay Neighbor $3 million in damages under judgment. Insurer must pay Insured the limit of $1 million for indemnification.

Standard comprehensive or commercial general liability insurance policies also provide that the insurer has a duty to defend the insured in any action brought against the insured seeking damages for a covered claim. (E.g., Buss v. Superior Court, supra, 16 Cal.4th at p. 45, 65 Cal.Rptr.2d 366, 939 P.2d 766.) By definition, the duty entails the rendering of a service, viz., the mounting and funding of a defense (e.g., id. at p. 46, 65 Cal.Rptr.2d 366, 939 P.2d 766), which is not limited, expressly or otherwise (see Travelers Ins. Co. v. Lesher (1986) 187

1. As stated, prior to 1966, in its insuring clause the standard comprehensive general liability insurance policy covered specified harm, such as bodily injury or property damage, caused by "accident" rather than by an "occurrence." (Croskey et al., Cal. Practice Guide: Insurance Litigation 2, supra, P 7:26, p. 7A–8.) As pertinent here, the difference in words does not reflect any difference in substance. (See id., PP 7:25 to 7:32, pp. 7A–8 to 7A–10.)

Cal.App.3d 169, 191, 231 Cal.Rptr. 791, disapproved on other points, Buss v. Superior Court, supra, 16 Cal.4th at pp. 50, fn. 12, & 52, fn. 14, 65 Cal.Rptr.2d 366, 939 P.2d 766; cf. Croskey et al., Cal. Practice Guide: Insurance Litigation 2, supra, P 7:647, p. 7B–32 [speaking generally and without specific reference to such policies]), in order to avoid or at least minimize liability (see Gray v. Zurich Insurance Co. (1966) 65 Cal.2d 263, 279, 54 Cal.Rptr. 104, 419 P.2d 168). As such, it requires the undertaking of reasonable and necessary efforts for that purpose (see ibid.), including investigation (see Pacific Indem. Co. v. Universal etc. Ins. Co. (1965) 232 Cal.App.2d 541, 543–544, 43 Cal.Rptr. 26). It also requires the incurring of reasonable and necessary costs to that end (see Travelers Ins. Co. v. Lesher, supra, 187 Cal.App.3d at p. 191, 231 Cal.Rptr. 791), including investigative expenses (see Pacific Indem. Co. v. Universal etc. Ins. Co., supra, 232 Cal.App.2d at pp. 543–544). It runs to claims that are merely potentially covered, in light of facts alleged or otherwise disclosed. (E.g., Buss v. Superior Court, supra, 16 Cal.4th at p. 46, 65 Cal.Rptr.2d 366, 939 P.2d 766.) It arises as soon as tender is made (e.g., ibid.), before liability is established and apart therefrom (e.g., Montrose Chemical Corp. v. Admiral Ins. Co., supra, 10 Cal.4th at p. 659, fn. 9, 42 Cal.Rptr.2d 324, 913 P.2d 878). It is discharged when the action is concluded. (E.g., Buss v. Superior Court, supra, 16 Cal.4th at p. 46, 65 Cal.Rptr.2d 366, 939 P.2d 766.) It may be extinguished earlier, if it is shown that no claim can in fact be covered. (E.g., ibid.) If it is so extinguished, however, it is extinguished only prospectively and not retroactively: Before, the insurer had a duty to defend; after, it does not have a duty to defend further. (E.g., ibid.) It is triggered if specified harm may possibly have been caused by an included occurrence, so long as at least some such harm may possibly have resulted within the policy period. (Cf. Montrose Chemical Corp. v. Admiral Ins. Co., supra, 10 Cal.4th at pp. 669–673, 42 Cal.Rptr.2d 324, 913 P.2d 878 [holding to such effect as to the duty to indemnify].) It extends to all specified harm that may possibly have been caused by an included occurrence, even if some such harm may possibly have resulted beyond the policy period. (Cf. id. at p. 686, 42 Cal.Rptr.2d 324, 913 P.2d 878 [holding to such effect as to the duty to indemnify].) In other words, if specified harm may possibly have been caused by an included occurrence and may possibly have resulted, at least in part, within the policy period, it perdures to all points of time at which some such harm may possibly have resulted thereafter. To illustrate again by a hypothetical: Insurer has a duty to defend Insured as to a claim for damages for property damage caused by its discharge of hazardous substances brought by Neighbor. Insured may possibly have discharged such a substance. It thereby may possibly have caused property damage to Neighbor's land within the policy period of year one. It may possibly have caused further damage as the substance may possibly have spread under the surface in year two through year thirty. Insurer must defend Insured as to the claim in its entirety.

It is plain that the insurer's duty to defend is broader than its duty to indemnify. (E.g., Buss v. Superior Court, supra, 16 Cal.4th at p. 46, 65

Cal.Rptr.2d 366, 939 P.2d 766.) But it is also plain that it is not unlimited. (E.g., ibid.) It extends beyond claims that are actually covered to those that are merely potentially so, but no further. (E.g., ibid.) Thus, in an action wherein all the claims are at least potentially covered because they may possibly embrace some triggering harm of the specified sort within the policy period caused by an included occurrence, the insurer has a duty to defend. (Buss v. Superior Court, supra, 16 Cal.4th at pp. 46–47, 65 Cal.Rptr.2d 366, 939 P.2d 766.) "This obligation is express in the policy's language. It rests on the fact that the insurer has been paid premiums by the insured for a defense. 'The rule is grounded in basic principles of contract law.' [Citation.] The duty to defend is contractual. [Citations.] 'An insurer contracts to pay the entire cost of defending . . . claim[s]' that are at least potentially covered." (Id. at p. 47, 65 Cal.Rptr.2d 366, 939 P.2d 766.)

* * *

B. THE INSURER'S UNDERTAKING

1. The Duty to Indemnify

An insured is generally entitled to compensation for covered losses during the policy period. Coverage under an insurance policy is determined by focusing on the terms of the policy itself taking into account the scope and the limitations of the insurer's undertaking.[2] As one court has noted: "[t]o establish coverage under an insurance policy, the insured must show that the occurrence on which the claim is based falls within the scope of basic coverage."[3] Thus, the determination of coverage often implicates the interpretation doctrines discussed earlier in this text.

In determining coverage, the starting point is the insuring clause—that portion of the policy under which an insurer promises to "pay on behalf of the insured all sums that the insured shall become legally obligated to pay as damages because of . . . property damage . . . caused by an occurrence. . . . "[4] A court or a lawyer advising a client must first determine, using applicable principles of interpretation, whether a claim falls within the terms of a policy. Even more fundamentally, courts have grappled with the threshold question of whether costs required to be expended by an administrative agency are "damages." Many courts have found such sums are not within the reach of the duty to indemnify.[5]

2. Springdale Donuts, Inc. v. Aetna Casualty & Surety Co., 247 Conn. 801, 805–09, 724 A.2d 1117, 1119–21 (1999); Northwest Pump & Equipment Co. v. American States Ins. Co., 144 Ore. App. 222, 227, 925 P.2d 1241, 1243 (1996); Chantel Associates v. Mount Vernon Fire Ins. Co., 338 Md. 131, 142, 656 A.2d 779, 784 (1995).

3. Aydin Corp. v. First State Ins. Co., 18 Cal.4th 1183, 77 Cal.Rptr.2d 537 (1998), *citing* Weil v. Federal Kemper Life Assurance Co., 7 Cal.4th 125, 148, 27 Cal.Rptr.2d 316, 866 P.2d 774 (1994); Searle v. Allstate Life Ins. Co., 38 Cal.3d 425, 438, 212 Cal. Rptr. 466, 696 P.2d 1308 (1985).

4. Old Republic Insurance Co. v. Superior Court, 66 Cal.App.4th 128, 144, 77 Cal. Rptr.2d 642. 651 (1998).

5. Certain Underwriters at Lloyd's, London v. Superior Court, 24 Cal.4th 945, 103 Cal.Rptr.2d 672, 16 P.3d 94 (2001).

Important to note is that the duty to indemnify and the duty to defend are independent and are governed by different standards.[6] Accordingly and as the cases below make plain, each is given separate treatment.

Liability insurers may (and commonly do) seek to avoid paying the more esoteric varieties of personal injury and to limit coverage to "bodily" or "physical" injuries. For example, a standard homeowners insurance policy covers bodily injury which it cautiously defines as "bodily harm, sickness or disease." This language may be given literal effect to eliminate noneconomic damages such as emotional suffering from coverage.[7] At the other end of the spectrum, a court by liberal and expansive use of the canons of insurance policy interpretation may stretch "bodily injury" to embrace loss of consortium damages sustained by the spouse of a person injured in an auto accident.[8]

The interplay of these different interpretive philosophies and the attempts by insurers to make the ambiguous clearer further complicate the picture. For example, many policies employ the new or simplified ["plain, easy to understand English"] in defining terms and the scope of coverage. The phraseology below is common:

> "What do we mean by an accident or incident? Anything that causes property damage, personal injury or death without your expecting or intending it. If you could've expected the result you're not covered."
>
> * * *
>
> "What do we mean by personal injury? Bodily injury, of course. But also injuries to a person's feelings or reputation. Like mental injury. Mental anguish. Shock. Wrongful eviction. Libel. Slander. Defamation of character. Invasion of privacy. False arrest."

Despite attempts to clarify, there remain uncertainties. Suppose the insured is sued for alienation of affections—and justifiably so. Is there coverage? How about false arrest? Can there be false arrest without intention or expectation of the result? How about malicious prosecution, etc.? Some insight on such issues appears in *Smith v. St. Paul Guardian Ins. Co.*, 622 F.Supp. 867 (W.D.Ark.1985). The *Smith* court concluded that defendant insurer had a duty to defend Smith in an action alleging the tort of alienation of affections. The court found a duty to defend under two policies: a "plain language" policy, reasoning that the alleged injury constitutes a personal injury as defined in the policy, which the plaintiff may not have intended; and an umbrella policy, because the injury is a personal injury as defined in that policy as well, and the policy does not exclude coverage for other such injuries even if intentionally caused.

6. Northwest Pump & Equipment Co. v. American States Ins. Co., 144 Ore. App. 222, 227, 925 P.2d 1241, 1243 (1996); EDO Corp. v. Newark Ins. Co., 898 F.Supp. 952, 955 (D.Conn.1995).

7. E.g., St. Paul Fire and Marine Ins. Co. v. Campbell County School Dist. No. 1, 612 F.Supp. 285 (D.Wyo.1985).

8. E.g., Abellon v. Hartford Ins. Co., 167 Cal.App.3d 21, 212 Cal.Rptr. 852 (1985).

Notes

1. Although we tend to speak of liability in the context of CGL policies in tort terms, the California Supreme Court has held the phrase in the insuring clause, "legally obligated to pay as damages," can include contract damages as well. Vandenberg v. Superior Court, 21 Cal.4th 815, 88 Cal. Rptr.2d 366, 982 P.2d 229 (1999) ("Coverage under a CGL insurance policy is not based upon the fortuity of the form of action chosen by the injured party.").

2. As a general proposition, an insured has the burden of proving that damage for which it seeks indemnification falls within the scope of a policy's coverage. Consolidated Edison Co. of New York, Inc. v. Allstate Ins. Co., 98 N.Y.2d 208, 218, 746 N.Y.S.2d 622, 774 N.E.2d 687, 690 (2002); Transamerica Leasing, Inc. v. Inst. Of London Underwriters, 267 F.3d 1303, 1310 (11th Cir. 2001); Insurance Co. of North America v. Forty–Eight Insulations, 633 F.2d 1212, 1225 (6th Cir. 1980); Aydin Corp. v. First State Ins. Co., 18 Cal.4th 1183, 1203, 959 P.2d 1213, 1224, 77 Cal.Rptr.2d 537, 548 (1998) (holding that once the insurer proves that a pollution exclusion clause applies, the insured must prove that its claim falls within the "sudden and accidental" exception to the exclusion clause).

2. The Duty to Defend

The more often litigated undertaking by the insurer is its duty to defend. As the preceding has stated, this duty is broadly defined. The material on breach of the covenant of good faith and fair dealing serves to illustrate the consequences of an insurer's failure to meet its obligations. Those desiring a more comprehensive discussion of the issues can find them in two separate articles. Susan Randall, *Redefining the Insurer's Duty to Defend*, 3 Conn. Ins. L.J. 221 (1997); Ellen Smith Pryor, *The Tort Liability Regime and the Duty to Defend*, 58 Md. L. Rev. 1 (1999).

GRAY v. ZURICH INSURANCE CO.

Supreme Court of California, 1966.
65 Cal.2d 263, 54 Cal.Rptr. 104, 419 P.2d 168.

TOBRINER, JUSTICE.

This is an action by an insured against his insurer for failure to defend an action filed against him which stemmed from a complaint alleging that he had committed an assault. The main issue turns on the argument of the insurer that an exclusionary clause of the policy excuses its defense of an action in which a plaintiff alleges that the insured intentionally caused the bodily injury. Yet the language of the policy does not clearly define the application of the exclusionary clause to the duty to defend. Since in that event we test the meaning of the policy according to the insured's reasonable expectation of coverage and since the language of the policy would lead the insured here to expect defense of the third party suit, we cannot exonerate the carrier from the rendition of such protection.

Plaintiff, Dr. Vernon D. Gray, is the named insured under an insurance policy issued by defendant. A "Comprehensive Personal Liability Endorsement" in the policy states, under a paragraph designated "Coverage L," that the insurer agrees "(T)o pay on behalf of the insured all sums which the insured shall become legally obligated to pay as damages because of bodily injury or property damage, and the company shall defend any suit against the insured alleging such bodily injury or property damage and seeking damages which are payable under the terms of this endorsement, even if any of the allegations are groundless, false or fraudulent; but the company may make such investigation and settlement of any claim or suit as it deems expedient." The policy contains a provision that "(T)his endorsement does not apply" to a series of specified exclusions set forth under separate headings, including a paragraph (c) which reads, "under coverages L and M, to bodily injury or property damages caused intentionally by or at the direction of the insured."

The suit which Dr. Gray contends Zurich should have defended arose out of an altercation between him and a Mr. John R. Jones.[9] Jones filed a complaint in Missouri alleging that Dr. Gray "wilfully, maliciously, brutally and intentionally assaulted" him; he prayed for actual damages of $50,000 and punitive damages of $50,000. Dr. Gray notified defendant of the suit, stating that he had acted in self-defense, and requested that the company defend. Defendant refused on the ground that the complaint alleged an intentional tort which fell outside the coverage of the policy. Dr. Gray thereafter unsuccessfully defended on the theory of self-defense; he suffered a judgment of $6,000 actual damages although the jury refused to award punitive damages.

Dr. Gray then filed the instant action charging defendant with breach of its duty to defend. Defendant answered, admitting the execution of the policy but denying any such obligation. The record on appeal has been augmented to include an offer of proof, presented by plaintiff and rejected by the trial court, which detailed the circumstances surrounding the altercation. The augmented record also includes exhibits introduced at the trial, consisting of copies of the pleadings and verdict in the Missouri suit and a copy of the subject insurance policy. The parties waived written findings of fact and conclusions of law; the court rendered judgment in favor of defendant. We must decide whether or not defendant bore the obligation to defend plaintiff in the Missouri action.

Defendant argues that it need not defend an action in which the complaint reveals on its face that the claimed bodily injury does not fall within the indemnification coverage; that here the Jones complaint

9. Immediately preceding the altercation Dr. Gray had been driving an automobile on a residential street when another automobile narrowly missed colliding with his car. Jones, the driver of the other car, left his vehicle, approached Dr. Gray's car in a menacing manner and jerked open the door. At that point Dr. Gray, fearing physical harm to himself and his passengers, rose from his seat and struck Jones.

alleged that the insured committed an assault, which fell outside such coverage. Defendant urges, as a second answer to plaintiff's contention, that the contract, if construed to require defense of the insured, would violate the public policy of the state and that, indeed, the judgment in the third party suit upholding the claim of an intentional bodily injury operates to estop the insured from recovery. Defendant thirdly contends that any requirement that it defend the Jones suit would embroil it in a hopeless conflict of interest. Finally it submits that, even if it should have defended the third party suit, the damages against it should encompass only the insured's expenses of defense and not the judgment against him.

We shall explain our reasons for concluding that defendant was obligated to defend the Jones suit, and our grounds for rejecting defendant's remaining propositions. Since the policy sets forth the duty to defend as a primary one and since the insurer attempts to avoid it only by an unclear exclusionary clause, the insured would reasonably expect, and is legally entitled to, such protection. As an alternative but secondary ground for our ruling we accept, for purposes of argument, defendant's contention that the duty to defend arises only if the third party suit involves a liability for which the insurer would be required to indemnify the insured, and, even upon this basis, we find a duty to defend.

In interpreting an insurance policy we apply the general principle that doubts as to meaning must be resolved against the insurer and that any exception to the performance of the basic underlying obligation must be so stated as clearly to apprise the insured of its effect.

* * *

Thus we held in Steven v. Fidelity & Casualty Co., 58 Cal.2d 862, 27 Cal.Rptr. 172, 377 P.2d 284, that we would not enforce an exclusionary clause in an insurance contract which was unclear, saying: "If (the insurer) deals with the public upon a mass basis, the notice of non-coverage of the policy, in a situation in which the public may reasonably expect coverage, must be conspicuous, plain and clear." (P. 878, 27 Cal.Rptr. p. 182, 377 P.2d p. 294.)

When we test the instant policy by these principles we find that its provisions as to the obligation to defend are uncertain and undefined; in the light of the reasonable expectation of the insured, they require the performance of that duty. At the threshold we note that the nature of the obligation to defend is itself necessarily uncertain. Although insurers have often insisted that the duty arises only if the insurer is bound to indemnify the insured, this very contention creates a dilemma. No one can determine whether the third party suit does or does not fall within the indemnification coverage of the policy until that suit is resolved; in the instant case, the determination of whether the insured engaged in intentional, negligent or even wrongful conduct depended upon the judgment in the Jones suit, and, indeed, even after that judgment, no one could be positive whether it rested upon a finding of plaintiff's negligent or his intentional conduct. The carrier's obligation to indemnify inevitably will not be defined until the adjudication of the very action which it should have defended. Hence the policy contains its own seeds of uncertainty; the insurer has held out a promise that by its very nature is ambiguous.

Although this uncertainty in the performance of the duty to defend could have been clarified by the language of the policy we find no such specificity here. An examination of the policy discloses that the broadly stated promise to defend is not conspicuously or clearly conditioned solely on a nonintentional bodily injury; instead, the insured could reasonably expect such protection.

The policy is a "comprehensive personal liability" contract; the designation in itself connotes general protection for alleged bodily injury caused by the insured. The insurer makes two wide promises: "(1.) To pay on behalf of the insured all sums which the insured shall become legally obligated to pay as damages because of bodily injury or property damage, and (2.) the company shall defend any suit against the insured alleging such bodily injury or property damage and seeking damages which are payable under the terms of this endorsement, even if any of the allegations of the suit are groundless, false, or fraudulent": clearly these promises, without further clarification, would lead the insured reasonably to expect the insurer to defend him against suits seeking damages for bodily injury, whatever the alleged cause of the injury, whether intentional or inadvertent.

But the insurer argues that the third party suit must seek "damages which are payable under the terms of this endorsement"; it contends that this limitation *modifies* the general duty to defend by confining the duty only to actions seeking damages within the primary coverage of the policy. Under "Exclusions" the policy provides that it "does not apply * * * under coverage L and M to bodily injury * * * caused intentionally by * * * the insured."

The very first paragraph as to coverage, however, provides that "the company shall defend any such suit against the insured alleging such bodily injury" although the allegations of the suit are groundless, false or fraudulent. This language, in its broad sweep, would lead the insured reasonably to expect defense of *any* suit regardless of merit or cause. The relation of the exclusionary clause to this basic promise is anything but clear. The basic promise would support the insured's reasonable expectation that he had bought the rendition of legal services to defend against a suit for bodily injury which alleged he had caused it, negligently, nonintentionally, intentionally or in any other manner. The doctrines and cases we have set forth tell us that the exclusionary clause must be "conspicuous, plain and clear." (Steven v. Fidelity & Casualty Co., supra, 58 Cal.2d 862, 878, 27 Cal.Rptr. 172, 377 P.2d 284.) This clause is not "conspicuous" since it appears only after a long and complicated page of fine print, and is itself in fine print; its relation to the remaining clauses of the policy and its effect is surely not "plain and clear."

A further uncertainty lurks in the exclusionary clause itself. It alludes to damage caused "intentionally by or at the direction of the insured." Yet an act of the insured may carry out his "intention" and also cause unintended harm. When set next to the words "at the direction of the insured" the word "intentionally" might mean to the layman collusive, wilful or planned action beyond the classical notion of intentional tort. This built-in ambiguity has caused debate and refined definition in many courts; in any event, the word surely cannot be "plain and clear" to the layman.

The insured is unhappily surrounded by concentric circles of uncertainty: the first, the unascertainable nature of the insurer's duty to defend; the second, the unknown effect of the provision that the insurer must defend even a groundless, false or fraudulent claim; the third, the uncertain extent of the indemnification coverage. Since we must resolve uncertainties in favor of the insured and interpret the policy provisions according to the layman's reasonable expectations, and since the effect of the exclusionary clause is neither conspicuous, plain nor clear, we hold that in the present case the policy provides for an obligation to defend and that such obligation is independent of the indemnification coverage.

The insurer counters with the contention that this position would compel an insurer "issuing a policy covering liability of the insured for maintenance, use or operation of an automobile * * * to defend the insured in an action for damages for negligently maintaining a stairway and thereby allegedly causing injury to another—because the insured claims that the suit for damages was false or groundless." The "groundless, false, or fraudulent" clause, however, does not extend the obligation to defend without limits; it includes only defense to those actions of the nature and kind covered by the policy. Here the policy insures against "damages because of bodily injury." As we have pointed out, in view of the language of the policy, the insured would reasonably expect protection in an action involving alleged bodily injury. On the other hand the insured could not reasonably expect protection under an automobile insurance policy for injury which occurs from defect in a stairway. Similarly an insured would not expect a defense for an injury involving an automobile under a general comprehensive policy which excluded automobile coverage. We look to the nature and kind of risk covered by the policy as a limitation upon the duty to defend; we cannot absolve the carrier from the duty to defend an insured for loss of the nature and kind against which it insured.

Our holding that the insurer bore the obligation to defend because the policy led plaintiff reasonably to expect such defense, and because the insurer's exclusionary clause did not exonerate it, cuts across defendant's answering contention that the duty arises only if the pleadings disclose a cause of action for which the insurer must indemnify the insured. Defendant would equate the duty to defend with the complaint that pleaded a liability for which the insurer was bound to indemnify the insured. Yet even if we accept defendant's premises, and define the duty to defend by measuring the allegations in the Jones case against the carrier's liability to indemnify, defendant's position still fails. We proceed to discuss this alternative ground of liability of the insurer, accepting for such purpose the insurer's argument that we must test the third party suit against the indemnification coverage of the policy. We point out that the carrier must defend a suit which *potentially* seeks damages within the coverage of the policy; the Jones action was such a suit.

Defendant cannot construct a formal fortress of the third party's pleadings and retreat behind its walls. The pleadings are malleable, changeable and amendable. Although an earlier decision reads: "In determining whether or not the appellant was bound to defend * * * the language of its contract must first be looked to, and next the allegations of the complaints * * * " (Lamb v. Belt Casualty Co., 3 Cal.App.2d 624, 630, 40 P.2d 311, 314), courts do not examine only the pleaded word but the potential liability created by the suit. Since the instant action presented the potentiality of a judgment based upon nonintentional conduct, and since liability for such conduct would fall within the indemnification coverage, the duty to defend became manifest at the outset.

To restrict the defense obligation of the insurer to the precise language of the pleading would not only ignore the thrust of the cases but would create an anomaly for the insured. Obviously, as Ritchie v. Anchor Casualty Co., 135 Cal.App.2d 245, 286 P.2d 1000, points out, the complainant in the third party action drafts his complaint in the broadest terms; he may very well stretch the action which lies in only nonintentional conduct to the dramatic complaint that alleges intentional misconduct. In light of the likely overstatement of the complaint and of the plasticity of modern pleading, we should hardly designate the third party as the arbiter of the policy's coverage.

Since modern procedural rules focus on the facts of a case rather than the theory of recovery in the complaint, the duty to defend should be fixed by the facts which the insurer learns from the complaint, the insured, or other sources. An insurer, therefore, bears a duty to defend its insured whenever it ascertains facts which give rise to the potential of liability under the policy. In the instant case the complaint itself, as well as the facts known to the insurer, sufficiently apprised the insurer of these possibilities; hence we need not set out when and upon what other occasions the duty of the insurer to ascertain such possibilities otherwise arises.

Jones' complaint clearly presented the possibility that he might obtain damages that were covered by the indemnity provisions of the policy. Even conduct that is traditionally classified as "intentional" or "wilful" has been held to fall within indemnification coverage. Moreover, despite Jones' pleading of intentional and wilful conduct, he could have amended his complaint to allege merely negligent conduct. Further, plaintiff might have been able to show that in physically defending himself, even if he exceeded the reasonable bounds of self-defense, he did not commit wilful and intended injury, but engaged only in nonintentional tortious conduct. Thus, even accepting the insurer's premise that it had no obligation to defend actions seeking damages not within the indemnification coverage, we find, upon proper measurement of the third party action against the insurer's liability to indemnify, it should have defended because the loss could have fallen within that liability.

We turn to the insurer's second major contention that the contract cannot be read to require the insurer to defend an action seeking damages for an intentional wrong because such an obligation would violate public policy. In support of this argument it relies upon Insurance Code section 533, and Civil Code section 1668.[10]

The contention fails on two grounds. In the first place, the statutes forbid only contracts which indemnify for "*loss*" or "*responsibility*" resulting from wilful wrong-doing. Here we deal with a contract which provides for *legal defense* against an action charging such conduct; the contract does not call for indemnification of the insured if the third party plaintiff prevails. In the second place, as we pointed out in Tomerlin v. Canadian Indemnity Co. (1964) 61 Cal.2d 638, 648, 39 Cal.Rptr. 731, 737, 394 P.2d 571, 577, the statutes "establish a public policy to prevent insurance coverage from encouragement of wilful tort." Thus Tomerlin held that if an insurer's obligation to pay a judgment based on wilful conduct results from an estoppel *after* the conduct, the obligation could not have previously encouraged the conduct. Similarly, the present contract does not offend the statute; a contract to defend an assured upon mere accusation of a wilful tort does not encourage such wilful conduct.

Nor can we accept defendant's argument that the duty to defend dissolves simply because the insured is unsuccessful in his defense and because the injured party recovers on the basis of a finding of the assured's wilful conduct. Citing Abbott v. Western Nat. Indem. Co. (1958) 165 Cal.App.2d 302, 331 P.2d 997, the insurer urges that if the judgment in a third party suit goes against the insured it operates as "res judicata or collateral estoppel in the insured's action or proceeding against the insurer."

We have explained that the insured would reasonably expect a defense by the insurer in all personal injury actions against him. If he is to be required to finance his own defense and then, only if successful, hold the insurer to its promise by means of a second suit for reimbursement, we defeat the basic reason for the purchase of the insurance. In purchasing his insurance the insured would reasonably expect that he would stand a better chance of vindication if supported by the resources and expertise of his insurer than if compelled to handle and finance the

10. Insurance Code section 533 provides: "An insurer is not liable for a loss caused by the wilful act of the insured; but he is not exonerated by the negligence of the insured, or of the insured's agents or others."

Civil Code section 1668 provides, in relevant part: "All contracts which have for their object, directly or indirectly, to exempt anyone from responsibility for his own * * * willful injury to the person or property of another * * * are against the policy of the law."

presentation of his case. He would, moreover, expect to be able to avoid the time, uncertainty and capital outlay in finding and retaining an attorney of his own. "The courts will not sanction a construction of the insurer's language that will defeat the very purpose or object of the insurance." (Ritchie v. Anchor Casualty Co., supra, 135 Cal.App.2d 245, 257, 286 P.2d 1000, 1007.)

Similarly, we find no merit in the insurer's third contention that our holding will embroil it in a conflict of interests. According to the insurer our ruling will require defense of an action in which the interests of insurer and insured are so opposed as to nullify the insurer's fulfillment of its duty of defense and of the protection of its own interests. For example, the argument goes, if defendant had defended against the Jones suit it would have sought to establish either that the insured was free from any liability or that such liability rested on intentional conduct. The insured, of course, would also seek a verdict holding him not liable but, if found liable, would attempt to obtain a ruling that such liability emanated from the nonintentional conduct within his insurance coverage. Thus, defendant contends, an insurer, if obligated to defend in this situation, faces an insoluble ethical problem.

Since, however, the court in the third party suit does not adjudicate the issue of coverage, the insurer's argument collapses. The only question there litigated is the insured's *liability.* The alleged victim does not concern himself with the theory of *liability;* he desires only the largest possible judgment. Similarly, the insured and insurer seek only to avoid, or at least to minimize, the judgment. As we have noted, modern procedural rules focus on whether, on a given set of facts, the plaintiff, regardless of the theory, may recover. Thus the question of whether or not the insured engaged in intentional conduct does not normally formulate an issue which is resolved in that litigation.[11]

In any event, if the insurer adequately reserves its right to assert the noncoverage defense later, it will not be bound by the judgment. If the injured party prevails, that party or the insured will assert his claim against the insurer.[12] At this time the insurer can raise the noncoverage defense previously reserved. In this manner the interests of insured and insurer in defending against the injured party's primary suit will be identical; the insurer will not face the suggested dilemma.

Finally, defendant urges that our holding should require only the reimbursement of the insured's expenses in defending the third party action but not the payment of the judgment. Defendant acknowledges the general rule that an insurer that wrongfully refuses to defend is

11. In rare cases the issue of punitive damages or a special verdict might present a potential conflict of interests, but such a possibility does not outweigh the advantages of the general rule. Even in such cases, however, the insurer will still be bound, ethically and legally, to litigate in the interests of the insured.

12. Insurance Code section 11580, subdivision (b)(2) provides that "whenever judgment is secured against the insured * * * in an action based upon bodily injury, death, or property damage, then an action may be brought against the insurer on the policy and subject to its terms and limitations, by such judgment creditor to recover on the judgment."

liable on the judgment against the insured. (Arenson v. Nat. Automobile & Cas. Ins. Co. (1955) 45 Cal.2d 81, 84, 286 P.2d 816; Civ.Code, § 2778.) Defendant argues, however, that the instant situation should be distinguished from that case because here the judgment has not necessarily been rendered on a theory within the policy coverage. Thus defendant would limit the insured's recovery to the expenses of the third party suit.

We rejected a similar proposal in Tomerlin v. Canadian Indemnity Co., supra, 61 Cal.2d 638, 649–650, 39 Cal.Rptr. 731, 394 P.2d 571. In that case, as we have noted, the insurer's obligation to defend arose out of estoppel. The insurer contended that we should apply a "tort" theory of damages to its wrongful refusal to defend. Such a theory, we explained, would impose upon the insured "the impossible burden" of proving the extent of the loss caused by the insurer's breach. As this court said in an analogous situation in Arenson v. National Auto. & Cas. Ins. Co. (1957) 48 Cal.2d 528, 539, 310 P.2d 961, 968: "Having defaulted such agreement the company is manifestly bound to reimburse its insured for the full amount of any obligation reasonably incurred by him. It will not be allowed to defeat or whittle down its obligation on the theory that plaintiff himself was of such limited financial ability that he could not afford to employ able counsel, or to present every reasonable defense, or to carry his cause to the highest court having jurisdiction, * * *. Sustaining such a theory * * * would tend * * * to encourage insurance companies to similar disavowals of responsibility with everything to gain and nothing to lose."

In summary, the individual consumer in the highly organized and integrated society of today must necessarily rely upon institutions devoted to the public service to perform the basic functions which they undertake. At the same time the consumer does not occupy a sufficiently strong economic position to bargain with such institutions as to specific clauses of their contracts of performance, and, in any event, piecemeal negotiation would sacrifice the advantage of uniformity. Hence the courts in the field of insurance contracts have tended to require that the insurer render the basic insurance protection which it has held out to the insured. This obligation becomes especially manifest in the case in which the insurer has attempted to limit the principal coverage by an unclear exclusionary clause. We test the alleged limitation in the light of the insured's reasonable expectation of coverage; that test compels the indicated outcome of the present litigation.

The judgment is reversed and the trial court instructed to take evidence solely on the issue of damages alleged in plaintiff's complaint including the amount of the judgment in the Jones suit, and the costs, expenses and attorney's fees incurred in defending such suit.

TRAYNOR, C.J., and PETERS, PEEK, MOSK and BURKE, JJ., concur. The dissenting opinion of McCOMB, J. is omitted.

Notes

1. California extends its duty to defend to cases in which an insured—as plaintiff—brings an action in which affirmative defenses are asserted. Construction Protective Services, Inc. v. TIG Specialty Ins. Co., 90 Cal. App.4th 149, 108 Cal.Rptr.2d 282 (2001). In light of the caution to prospective lawyers to be aware of insurance coverage matters in the introduction to this text, this case adds a layer of knowledge.

2. An insurer must act promptly with respect to providing a defense. Insurer delay in declining a defense that results in prejudice to the insured may give rise to an estoppel. Bluestein & Sander v. Chicago Ins. Co., 276 Fed.3d 119 (2d Cir. 2002). An element of the insured's reasonable belief in coverage seems to permeate this field. Ringler Associates Inc. v. Maryland Casualty Co., 80 Cal.App.4th 1165, 96 Cal.Rptr.2d 136 (2000); Greenberg & Covitz v. National Union Fire Ins. Co., 711 A.2d 909, 312 N.J.Super. 251 (1998).

FITZPATRICK v. AMERICAN HONDA MOTOR CO., INC.

Court of Appeals of New York, 1991.
78 N.Y.2d 61, 571 N.Y.S.2d 672, 575 N.E.2d 90.

Opinion of the Court, Titone, J.

It is well established that a liability insurer has a duty to defend its insured in a pending lawsuit if the pleadings allege a covered occurrence, even though facts outside the four corners of those pleadings indicate that the claim may be meritless or not covered (see, e.g., Ruder & Finn v. Seaboard Sur. Co., 52 N.Y.2d 663, 669–670, 439 N.Y.S.2d 858, 422 N.E.2d 518). The issue in this appeal is whether the insurer has a duty to defend in the opposite circumstance, i.e., where the pleadings do not allege a covered occurrence but the insurer has actual knowledge of facts demonstrating that the lawsuit does involve such an occurrence. Under these facts, we hold that the insurer cannot use a third party's pleadings as a shield to avoid its contractual duty to defend its insured.

The plaintiff in the main action, Linda Fitzpatrick, sought recovery for the wrongful death of her husband, John Fitzpatrick, who died on October 31, 1985 while operating a three-wheel all-terrain vehicle. The complaint alleged that the vehicle in question was owned by defendant Frank Moramarco and that Moramarco had given Fitzpatrick permission to use it in connection with the performance of certain yardwork and household chores. According to the complaint, codefendant Cherrywood Property Owners Association (CPOA), the owner of the property on which the accident occurred, had retained Moramarco, and Moramarco, acting as CPOA's agent, had in turn hired Fitzpatrick as an "independent contractor."

In fact, Moramarco was an officer, shareholder and director of an independent concern called Cherrywood Landscaping, Inc. (CLI), which had been retained by CPOA to do landscaping work on CPOA's property.

The vehicle involved in Fitzpatrick's accident had been purchased by Moramarco on behalf of CLI for use in its landscaping and gardening business. CLI had also purchased a liability insurance policy from National Casualty Co. (National), which indemnified the corporation against having to pay damages for bodily injury and property damage arising out of its business. While the policy was not an "owner's policy" and Moramarco was not a specifically named insured, the terms of the policy included as "insured persons" "any executive officer, director or stockholder [of the named insured (i.e., CLI)] while acting within the scope of his duties as such."

Shortly after Moramarco was served with papers in the main action, he notified National and requested that the insurer provide him with a defense. National, however, refused, stating that the policy it had issued to CLI did not appear to cover the claim against Moramarco. In subsequent correspondence, Moramarco advised the insurer that the vehicle involved in the Fitzpatrick accident was "owned for and * * * used exclusively for landscaping operations" and that the claims asserted against him in the main action all arose out of activities he undertook for CLI, the named insured. The same circumstances were brought to the insurer's attention in a letter from its own agent in which the company was urged to reconsider its prior decision. Nonetheless, National maintained that it was not required to provide a defense because the complaint did not name CLI, and Moramarco, the named defendant, was not insured as an individual.

Moramarco thereafter commenced a third-party action against National seeking payment of his legal fees in the main action, as well as "judgment over" for any judgment entered against him in the main action. National promptly moved, pursuant to CPLR 3211(a)(1) and (7), to dismiss the third-party complaint. Relying wholly on the absence of allegations in the Fitzpatrick complaint suggesting that the claim against Moramarco arose in connection with his activities as an officer, shareholder or director of the insured CLI, National argued that it had no duty to defend or indemnify Moramarco under the terms of the policy. In response, Moramarco submitted proof to show that, despite the complaint's inaccuracies, the Fitzpatrick claim actually did involve a covered event.

The Supreme Court denied National's dismissal motion, holding that the question of whether its policy covered the Fitzpatrick accident "must await a plenary trial." The Appellate Division, 159 A.D.2d 548, 552 N.Y.S.2d 413, however, reversed and dismissed the third-party complaint. The court held that the allegations in the complaint are the determinative factor in resolving whether the provisions of an insurance policy have been "activated" in a particular action. Since the Fitzpatrick complaint named Moramarco only in his individual capacity and the insured, CLI, was never even mentioned, the Appellate Division concluded that the existing documentary evidence, i.e., the Fitzpatrick complaint and the National policy, was sufficient to warrant dismissal of Moramarco's third-party claim (see, CPLR 3211[a][1]). This Court granted Moramarco leave to appeal from the Appellate Division order. We now reverse.

This Court has repeatedly held that an insurer's duty to defend its insured arises whenever the allegations in a complaint state a cause of action that gives rise to the reasonable possibility of recovery under the policy (see, e.g., Technicon Elecs. Corp. v. American Home Assur. Co., 74 N.Y.2d 66, 73, 544 N.Y.S.2d 531, 542 N.E.2d 1048; Meyers & Sons Corp. v. Zurich Am. Ins. Group, 74 N.Y.2d 298, 302, 546 N.Y.S.2d 818, 545 N.E.2d 1206; see, Servidone Constr. Corp. v. Security Ins. Co., 64 N.Y.2d 419, 424, 488 N.Y.S.2d 139, 477 N.E.2d 441). In the present appeal, National asks this Court to hold that the converse is also true. According to National, the complaint allegations are, in all cases, the *sole* determining consideration and, consequently, an insurer is relieved of the duty to defend whenever the complaint allegations do not on their face set forth a covered cause of action. However, the position National advocates is neither compelled by our prior case law nor consistent with sound legal principles and policies. Accordingly, we reject it.

The rationale underlying the cases in which the "four corners of the complaint" rule was delineated and applied (see, e.g., Meyers & Sons Corp. v. Zurich Am. Ins. Group, supra; International Paper Co. v. Continental Cas. Co., 35 N.Y.2d 322, 361 N.Y.S.2d 873, 320 N.E.2d 619; Goldberg v. Lumber Mut. Cas. Ins. Co., 297 N.Y. 148, 77 N.E.2d 131), is based on the oft-stated principle that the duty to defend is broader than the duty to indemnify (see, e.g., Ruder & Finn v. Seaboard Sur. Co., 52 N.Y.2d 663, 669–670, 439 N.Y.S.2d 858, 422 N.E.2d 518, supra). In other words, as the rule has developed, an insurer may be contractually bound to defend even though it may not ultimately be bound to pay, either because its insured is not factually or legally liable or because the occurrence is later proven to be outside the policy's coverage.

It follows logically from this principle that an insurer's duty to defend is called into play whenever the pleadings allege an act or omission within the policy's coverage. Even where there exist extrinsic facts suggesting that the claim may ultimately prove meritless or outside the policy's coverage, the insurer cannot avoid its commitment to provide a defense, since "[a] complaint subject to defeat because of debatable theories * * * must [nevertheless] be defended by the insured." (International Paper Co. v. Continental Cas. Co., supra, 35 N.Y.2d at 326, 361 N.Y.S.2d 873, 320 N.E.2d 619.) Accordingly, the courts of this State have refused to permit insurers to look beyond the complaint's allegations to avoid their obligation to defend and have held that the duty to defend exists "[i]f the complaint contains any facts or allegations which bring the claim even potentially within the protection purchased" (Technicon Elecs. Corp. v. American Home Assur. Co., supra, 74 N.Y.2d at 73, 544 N.Y.S.2d 531, 542 N.E.2d 1048). The holdings thus clearly establish that an insurer's duty to defend is at least broad enough to apply when the "four corners of the complaint" suggest the reasonable possibility of coverage.

However, to say that the duty to defend is *at least* broad enough to apply to actions in which the complaint alleges a covered occurrence is a far cry from saying that the complaint allegations are the *sole* criteria for measuring the scope of that duty. Indeed, in these circumstances, where the insurer is attempting to shield itself from the responsibility to defend despite its actual knowledge that the lawsuit involves a covered event, wooden application of the "four corners of the complaint" rule would render the duty to defend narrower than the duty to indemnify—clearly an unacceptable result. For that reason, courts and commentators have indicated that the insurer must provide a defense if it has knowledge of facts which potentially bring the claim within the policy's indemnity coverage. [citations omitted]

We agree with these authorities and hold that, rather than mechanically applying only the "four corners of the complaint" rule in these circumstances, the sounder approach is to require the insurer to provide a defense when it has actual knowledge of facts establishing a reasonable possibility of coverage. This holding fits easily and appropriately within the existing rules governing coverage disputes, which certainly do not require us to extend the "four corners of the complaint" rule to a situation such as this one, where it has not been applied before and, in fact, has no apparent value. Although it has been argued that the "four corners of the complaint" rule has the advantage of certainty (see, dissenting opn., at 73, at 679 of 571 N.Y.S.2d, at 97 of 575 N.E.2d), there is no reason to believe that the rule we adopt here will engender any more litigation.

The conclusion we reach here flows naturally from the fact that the duty to defend derives, in the first instance, not from the complaint drafted by a third party, but rather from the insurer's own contract with the insured. While the allegations in the complaint may provide the significant and usual touchstone for determining whether the insurer is contractually bound to provide a defense, the contract itself must always remain a primary point of reference (see also, Technicon Elecs. Corp. v. American Home Assur. Co., supra, 74 N.Y.2d at 73, 544 N.Y.S.2d 531, 542 N.E.2d 1048 [duty to defend arises from complaint and insurance contract]). Indeed, a contrary rule making the terms of the complaint controlling "would allow the insurer to construct a formal fortress of the third party's pleadings * * * thereby successfully ignoring true but unpleaded facts within its knowledge that require it * * * to conduct the * * * insured's defense" (Associated Indem. Co. v. Insurance Co., 68 Ill.App.3d 807, 816–817, 25 Ill.Dec. 258, 265, 386 N.E.2d 529, 536). Further, an insured's right to a defense should not depend solely on the allegations a third party chooses to put in the complaint. This is particularly so because the drafter of the pleading may be unaware of the true underlying facts or the nuances that may affect the defendant's coverage and it might not be in the insured's (or the insurer's) interest to reveal them.

The principle that an insurer may not rely on the pleadings to narrow the scope of its duty to defend also finds support in the practical realities that prevail under modern pleading rules. As one commentator has observed, "considering the plasticity of modern pleadings, in many cases no one can determine whether the third party suit does or does not fall within the indemnification coverage of the policy until the suit itself is resolved" (7C Appleman, op. cit., § 4684, at 83). This observation is particularly apt in the context of New York's liberal pleading rules, which permit the pleadings to be amended to conform to the proof *at any time*, provided that no prejudice is shown (see, CPLR 3025[a]).

The facts in this case—where the complaint on its face did not state a covered claim but the underlying facts made known to the insurer by its insured unquestionably involved a covered event—present a clear example. The insurer here refused to defend Frank Moramarco because he was sued, albeit mistakenly, as an employee of CPOA and the owner of the injury-causing vehicle. Had the complaint correctly identified Moramarco as an officer and/or shareholder of the insured CLI, he would have unquestionably been covered for this lawsuit, since the policy provided that "any executive officer, director or stockholder [of CLI] while acting within the scope of his duties as such" was an additional "insured person" under the policy. Further, the insurer promised to "defend any suit against the insured seeking damages on account of * * * bodily injury or property damage" arising out of CLI's landscaping and gardening business—a condition plainly satisfied here. To deny Moramarco an insurance-company sponsored defense under these circumstances merely because the attorney for the plaintiff in the main action accidentally mischaracterized Moramarco's role would be to afford the insurer an undeserved windfall at the expense of its insured.

Indeed, relieving the insurer of its duty to defend is particularly imprudent and counterproductive where, as here, the inaccuracies in the plaintiff's pleadings are likely to become apparent when the true facts are developed on the record and the role of the insured in the incident is fully exposed. At that point, the trial court could well grant a request by the plaintiff to conform the pleadings to the proof (see, CPLR 3025[c]), in which event the insurer's core policy obligation to defend Frank Moramarco as an additional insured would unquestionably be triggered. Moramarco should not be required to wait until that point is reached before obtaining an insurance-company sponsored defense, since a "provision for defense of suits is useless and meaningless unless it is offered when the suit arises" (7C Appleman, op. cit., § 4684, at 83).

In sum, application of the "four corners of the complaint" rule in these circumstances is not required by our prior cases and is not even supported by the rationale usually offered in support of the rule. Further, invocation of the rule here and in analogous cases leads to an unjust result, since it exalts form over substance and denies an insured party the benefit of the "litigation insurance" for which it has paid. These factors militate in favor of a rule requiring the insurer to provide a defense where, notwithstanding the complaint allegations, underlying facts made known to the insurer create a "reasonable possibility that the insured may be held liable for some act or omission covered by the policy" (Meyers & Sons Corp. v. Zurich Am. Ins. Group, supra, 74 N.Y.2d at 302, 546 N.Y.S.2d 818, 545 N.E.2d 1206). We therefore hold that National cannot ignore the facts made known to it by its insured and rely instead on the Fitzpatrick complaint alone to assess its duty to defend Moramarco. The third-party complaint by Moramarco seeking payment of his attorney's fees and indemnification in the event that a judgment was entered against him should not have been dismissed. Accordingly, the order of the Appellate Division should be reversed, with costs, and the motion to dismiss the third-party complaint denied.

ALEXANDER, JUDGE (dissenting).

Because the majority today discards a rule of long standing and, in my view, does so without justification and under circumstances not warranting such a drastic departure from settled precedent, I respectfully dissent.

It is axiomatic that the obligations of a liability insurance carrier to its insured are governed by the terms of the contract of insurance between them and it is only by examining the terms and conditions of that policy that those obligations can be determined with certainty. Obviously, where an insured has been found liable to a third party in respect to a risk covered by the policy, the carrier is obligated to indemnify its insured. Additionally, where the policy so provides, the carrier is obligated to defend its insured against claims asserting risks covered by the policy. Indeed the rule is firmly established that the duty to defend is broader than the duty to indemnify (Ruder & Finn v. Seaboard Sur. Co., 52 N.Y.2d 663, 669–670, 439 N.Y.S.2d 858, 422 N.E.2d 518; Servidone Constr. Corp. v. Security Ins. Co., 64 N.Y.2d 419, 424, 488 N.Y.S.2d 139, 477 N.E.2d 441). When the policy contains the insurer's promise to defend the insured, the "liability insurance" is in fact "litigation insurance" as well (Seaboard Sur. Co. v. Gillette Co., 64 N.Y.2d 304, 486 N.Y.S.2d 873, 476 N.E.2d 272; International Paper Co. v. Continental Cas. Co., 35 N.Y.2d 322, 326, 361 N.Y.S.2d 873, 320 N.E.2d 619).

However, this Court has repeatedly held, in a long line of cases, unbroken until now, that the duty of a liability insurer to defend an action brought against an insured is determined by the allegations in the complaint pursuant to which the insured's liability is asserted (see, Meyers & Sons Corp. v. Zurich Am. Ins. Group, 74 N.Y.2d 298, 546 N.Y.S.2d 818, 545 N.E.2d 1206; Technicon Elecs. Corp. v. American Home Assur. Co., 74 N.Y.2d 66, 544 N.Y.S.2d 531, 542 N.E.2d 1048; Servidone Constr. Corp. v. Security Ins. Co., 64 N.Y.2d 419, 488 N.Y.S.2d 139, 477 N.E.2d 441, supra; Seaboard Sur. Co. v. Gillette Co., 64 N.Y.2d 304, 486 N.Y.S.2d 873, 476 N.E.2d 272, supra; International Paper Co. v. Continental Cas. Co., 35 N.Y.2d 322, 361 N.Y.S.2d 873, 320 N.E.2d 619, supra; Goldberg v. Lumber Mut. Cas. Ins. Co., 297 N.Y. 148, 77 N.E.2d 131). "If the facts alleged [in the complaint] raise a reasonable possibility that the insured may be held liable for some act or omission covered by the policy, then the insurer must defend" (Meyers & Sons Corp. v.

Zurich Am. Ins. Group, 74 N.Y.2d 298, 302, 546 N.Y.S.2d 818, 545 N.E.2d 1206, supra).

In determining whether there is a duty to defend however, the Court must compare the allegations of the complaint with the terms of the policy (see, Lionel Freedman, Inc. v. Glens Falls Ins. Co., 27 N.Y.2d 364, 367, 318 N.Y.S.2d 303, 267 N.E.2d 93). If those allegations, on their face, are within the compass of the risk covered by the insurance policy, the insurer is obligated to assume the defense of the action (Goldberg v. Lumber Mut. Cas. Ins. Co., supra; International Paper Co. v. Continental Cas. Co., 35 N.Y.2d 322, 361 N.Y.S.2d 873, 320 N.E.2d 619, supra). Conversely, it logically follows, that if that comparison demonstrates that those allegations are not within the coverage of the policy, the insurance company's duty to defend does not arise (see, Goldberg v. Lumber Mut. Cas. Ins. Co., 297 N.Y. 148, 77 N.E.2d 131). Indeed where it can be determined "that no basis for recovery within the coverage of the policy is stated in the complaint * * * defendant's refusal to defend [may be sustained]." (Lionel Freedman, Inc. v. Glens Falls Ins. Co., 27 N.Y.2d 364, 368, 318 N.Y.S.2d 303, 267 N.E.2d 93, rearg. denied 28 N.Y.2d 859, 322 N.Y.S.2d 1029, 271 N.E.2d 236; Sucrest Corp. v. Fisher Governor Co., 83 Misc.2d 394, 400, 371 N.Y.S.2d 927.)

* * *

Deviating from these settled rules, the majority concludes that notwithstanding that the Fitzpatrick complaint, when compared to the terms of the policy, fails to demonstrate the existence of a covered event, "the insurer must provide a defense if it has knowledge of facts which potentially bring the claim within the policy's indemnity coverage" (majority opn., at 66, at 674 of 571 N.Y.S.2d, at 92 of 575 N.E.2d). It should be noted that to support this proposition the majority relies upon cases from other jurisdictions which impose an obligation upon the insurance company to investigate the claim before declining to defend—a requirement that this Court has never before imposed.

The rule which until now has prevailed in this jurisdiction provides certainty in this area of law and is easily applied. By changing the rule, the majority has supplanted certainty with uncertainty; an insurer now will be less clear as to what, if any, investigation it must make into a demand to defend and when it is permissible to decline representation. Concomitantly, the new rule presumably will increase collateral proceedings such as this, to determine whether an insurer in fact has a duty to defend. These collateral proceedings will be made more complicated because courts now will be obligated to look beyond the allegations in the complaint to discover the "actual" facts, or at a minimum whether the insurer "knew" or perhaps even "should have known" of such "actual facts". The rule could also place the insured in the position of dictating the theory of the action, conceivably requiring the carrier to defend a claim the plaintiff has no intention of asserting merely because allegedly there are "facts" which support such a claim.

The majority posits this new rule as being corollary to the established rule that where the allegations of the complaint state a claim within the coverage of the policy, the "insurers [may not] look beyond the complaint's allegations to avoid their obligation to defend" (majority opn., at 66, at 674 of 571 N.Y.S.2d, at 92 of 575 N.E.2d). The fact is, however, that under the rule cited by the majority, "the insurance company's duty to defend came into being when it appeared from the allegations in the negligence action that the injury was within the coverage of the policy, and it persisted despite the advice [from the insured] pointing [to] a contrary conclusion" (Goldberg v. Lumber Mut. Cas. Ins. Co., 297 N.Y. 148, 154, 77 N.E.2d 131, supra).

Thus it is clear that under that established rule it is the allegations of the complaint, compared to the policy provisions, that trigger the duty to defend, a duty which persists notwithstanding that liability may ultimately be shown not to exist. This rule gives certainty to the inception of the carrier's duty to defend and is entirely consistent with its obligations under its policy. No satisfactory reason for altering this rule is shown to exist here; thus the order granting summary judgment to the third-party defendant National Casualty Co. should be affirmed.

WACHTLER, C.J., and KAYE and BELLACOSA, JJ., concur with TITONE, J.

ALEXANDER, J., dissents and votes to affirm in a separate opinion in which SIMONS and HANCOCK, JJ., concur.

Order reversed, etc.

NORTHFIELD INSURANCE CO. v. LOVING HOME CARE, INC.

United States Court of Appeals, Fifth Circuit, 2004.
363 F.3d 523.

DeMOSS, Circuit Judge:

* * *

BACKGROUND

This appeal stems from a dispute about the duty of an insurer to defend its insured in an underlying negligence suit in Texas state court. The Daniels ran LHC, a business that provided nannies for in-home child care. Celia Giral ("Giral") was employed by LHC and worked as a nanny for the Barrows. On October 13, 1997,Giral was caring for the Barrows' baby daughter, Bianca, when Bianca was fatally injured. Bianca died at the hospital on the evening of October 14, 1997. The Harris County coroner ruled Bianca's death a homicide, as the autopsy findings noted that Bianca's injuries included multiple skull fractures, brain hemorrhages, and blood behind the eyes. The cause of death listed was "cranio-cerebral injuries due to blunt force trauma of the head." On May 22, 1998, a Texas state court jury found Giral guilty of first-degree felony injury to a child in the death of Bianca Barrows; Giral was sentenced to seven years in prison.

The Barrows filed the underlying suit against several parties, including LHC and the Daniels. The Barrows' Third–Amended Petition, * * * remove[d] all allegations relating to Giral's criminal conviction and the intentional nature of her behavior. At the time of Bianca's death, LHC was covered by a two-part insurance policy (including both commercial general liability, "CGL," and CPL coverage) issued by Northfield. Under the terms of the policy, LHC and the Daniels requested defense and indemnification from Northfield in the underlying action.

Northfield defended under a reservation of rights, filing a declaratory judgment action in district court against LHC, the Daniels, and others. In the course of the declaratory judgment action, Northfield argued that it was not obligated to defend or indemnify LHC and the Daniels in the underlying action because of various exclusions in the policy. In particular, in Northfield's motion for summary judgment, it argued it had no duty to defend or indemnify LHC and the Daniels under the CGL part of the policy because the "designated professional services" exclusion barred coverage for damages "due to the rendering or failure to render any professional service." Northfield also argued that it had no duty to defend or indemnify LHC and the Daniels under the CPL part of the policy, which provided coverage for damages "because of a negligent act, error or omission in the rendering of or failure to render professional services," because of two exclusions relating to "criminal acts" and "physical/sexual abuse." The criminal acts exclusion stated that coverage would not apply to "[a]ny damages arising out of any dishonest, fraudulent, criminal or malicious act or omission of any insured or 'employee.' " The physical/sexual abuse exclusion stated that coverage would not apply to "any damages arising out of" the following:

1. The actual, alleged, or threatened physical abuse, sexual abuse or molestation by anyone.

2. The investigation, hiring, training, placement, supervision, or retention of anyone who engages or has engaged in physical abuse, sexual abuse or molestation. This endorsement applies whether damages arise from an act or failure to act.

3. The reporting of or failure to report to authorities any physical abuse, sexual abuse, or molestation.

The district court initially granted Northfield's motion for summary judgment in its entirety, ruling that the professional services exclusion applied so as to preclude coverage under both parts of the policy. LHC, the Daniels, and the Barrows then filed motions for reconsideration of the summary judgment, pointing out that the professional services exclusion only applied to the CGL part of the policy. The district court recognized its error and granted the motions for reconsideration as to the CPL part of the policy but affirmed its ruling as to Northfield having no duties under the CGL part. The district court ultimately determined that the criminal acts and physical/sexual abuse exclusions did not apply so as to preclude coverage and a duty to defend under the CPL part. The court entered its declaratory judgment on October 8, 2002, which ordered that Northfield has a duty to defend LHC and the Daniels. The Barrows then filed a motion to amend the judgment, requesting the district court delete the phrase "This is a final judgment" because the duty-to-indemnify issue was still before the court. The district court denied the motion and dismissed the duty-to-indemnify issue without prejudice. Northfield timely appealed, and the Barrows cross-appealed.

DISCUSSION

This Court reviews whether an insurer has a duty to defend its insured in an underlying suit as a de novo question of law. Guar. Nat'l Ins. Co. v. Vic Mfg. Co., 143 F.3d 192, 193 (5th Cir.1998). Under Texas law, which the parties agree governs this diversity case, the duty to defend and the duty to indemnify are distinct and separate duties. See King v. Dallas Fire Ins.Co., 85 S.W.3d 185, 187 (Tex.2002) (citation omitted). The duty to defend is broader than the duty to indemnify. Am. States Ins. Co. v. Bailey, 133 F.3d 363, 368 (5th Cir.1998) (applying Texas law).

The Texas Supreme Court recently restated in King that: An insurer's duty to defend is determined solely by the allegations in the pleadings and the language of the insurance policy. This is the "eight corners" or "complaint allegation rule." If a petition does not allege facts within the scope of coverage, an insurer is not legally required to defend a suit against its insured. But we resolve all doubts regarding the duty to defend in favor of the duty. 85 S.W.3d at 187 (quotations and footnotes omitted); see also Nat'l Union Fire Ins. Co. v. Merchs. Fast Motor Lines, Inc., 939 S.W.2d 139, 141 (Tex.1997) (noting that courts give the petition's allegations a liberal interpretation). Thus, the duty to defend arises only when the facts alleged in the complaint, if taken as true, would potentially state a cause of action falling within the terms of the policy. Canutillo Indep. Sch. Dist. v. Nat'l Union Fire Ins. Co., 99 F.3d 695, 701 (5th Cir.1996) (applying Texas law) (citation omitted). The insured bears the initial burden of establishing that a claim against it is potentially within the policy's coverage. Id. (citation omitted). The insurer is obligated to defend the insured, provided that the petition or complaint alleges at least one cause of action potentially within the policy's coverage. Id. (citation omitted).

The duty to defend is determined by consulting the latest amended pleading. Id. (citation omitted); see also Guar. Nat'l, 143 F.3d at 194. The focus of the inquiry is on the alleged facts, not on the asserted legal theories. St. Paul Fire & Marine Ins. Co. v. Green Tree Fin. Corp.—Tex., 249 F.3d 389, 392 (5th Cir.2001) (applying Texas law). "[I]n case of doubt as to whether or not the allegations of a complaint against the insured state a cause of action within the coverage of a liability policy sufficient to compel the insurer to defend the action, such doubt will be resolved in insured's favor." Merchants, 939 S.W.2d at 141 (citation omitted). If the petition only alleges facts excluded by the policy, however, the insurer is not required to defend. Fid. & Guar. Ins. Underwriters, Inc. v. McManus, 633 S.W.2d 787, 788 (Tex.1982). Facts ascertained before suit, developed in the process of litigation, or determined by the ultimate outcome of the suit do not affect the duty to defend. Trinity Universal Ins. Co. v. Cowan, 945 S.W.2d 819, 829 (Tex.1997) (citation omitted).

After the insured meets his burden to show that the alleged facts in the petition state a potential claim against him, to defeat the duty to defend, the insurer bears the burden of showing that the plain language of a policy exclusion or limitation allows the insurer to avoid coverage of all claims, also within the confines of the eight corners rule. See Tex. Ins.Code Ann. art. 21.58(b) (Vernon Supp.1997); Calderon v. Mid–Century Ins. Co. of Tex., No. 03–97–00735–CV, 1998 WL 898471, at *2 (Tex.App.—Austin Dec. 29, 1998, pet. denied) (not designated for publication) (citing E & L Chipping Co. v. Hanover Ins. Co., 962 S.W.2d 272, 274 (Tex.App.—Beaumont 1998, no pet.)); Butler & Binion v. Hartford Lloyd's Ins. Co., 957 S.W.2d 566, 568 (Tex.App.-Houston [14th Dist.] 1995, writ denied).

In contrast, "the duty to indemnify is not based on the third party's allegations, but upon the actual facts that underlie the cause of action and result in liability." Canutillo, 99 F.3d at 701 (citations omitted); see also Tesoro Pet. Corp. v. Nabors Drilling USA, Inc., 106 S.W.3d 118, 125 (Tex.App.-Houston [1st Dist.] 2002, pet. denied) ("Facts, however, not allegations, determine an indemnitor's duty to indemnify."). If any ambiguity exists, exceptions and limitations in a policy are construed strictly against the insurer. Canutillo, 99 F.3d at 701 (citations omitted). Thus, courts "adopt the construction of an exclusionary clause urged by the insured as long as that construction is not itself unreasonable, even if the construction urged by the insurer appears to be more reasonable or a more accurate reflection of the parties' intent." Id. (quoting Barnett v. Aetna Life Ins. Co., 723 S.W.2d 663, 666 (Tex.1987)). Generally, Texas law only considers the duty-to-indemnify question justiciable after the underlying suit is concluded, unless "the same reasons that negate the duty to defend likewise negate any possibility the insurer will ever have a duty to indemnify." Farmers Tex. County Mut. Ins. Co. v. Griffin, 955 S.W.2d 81, 84 (Tex.1997).

Whether there is an exception to the strict eight corners rule in Texas.

The Texas Supreme Court has never recognized any exception to the strict eight corners rule that would allow courts to examine extrinsic evidence when determining an insurer's duty to defend. Landmark Chevrolet Corp. v. Universal Underwriters Ins. Co., 121 S.W.3d 886, 890 (Tex.App.—Houston [1st Dist.] 2003, pet. filed). However, as the district court in Westport Insurance Corp. v. Atchley, Russell, Waldrop & Hlavinka, L.L.P., 267 F.Supp.2d 601, 611–22 (E.D.Tex.2003), extensively examined, certain Texas appellate courts, this Court, and district courts in this Circuit have appeared to recognize a narrow exception. The most recent Texas appellate court case to apply an exception to the eight corners rule is State Farm Fire & Casualty Co. v. Wade, 827 S.W.2d 448 (Tex.App.—Corpus Christi 1992, writ denied), which was decided in

1992. There, an appeals court found that in the absence of any factual allegation concerning how the boat which was the subject of the policy was used, because the court could not determine whether or not the personal boat owner's private liability policy possibly provided coverage even by reading the underlying petition broadly, extrinsic evidence could be considered. Id. at 453. The court found that how the boat in question was used at the time of the accident—whether the use was commercial or private—was an essential fact of coverage that did not question the truth or falsity of any facts alleged in the underlying petition. Id.

However, in making an Erie [R.R. Co. v. Tompkins] guess about what the current Texas Supreme Court would say about the existence and application of such an exception, the court in Westport noted that no Texas appellate decision has ever both cited and applied this Wade line of cases. 267 F.Supp.2d at 618–19 ("[E]ven the court that announced the decision on which the Wade line of cases depends has retreated.... "); see also Tri–Coastal Contractors, Inc. v. Hartford Underwriters Ins. Co., 981 S.W.2d 861, 863–64 (Tex.App.-Houston [1st Dist.] 1998, pet. denied) (applying the strict eight corners approach to reverse the trial court's use of extrinsic evidence and noting how no other Texas appellate court has ever applied Wade).

In Tri–Coastal, the appellate court declined to follow Wade and refused to consider extrinsic evidence, even though the petition did not contain sufficient facts to determine the application of a worker's compensation exclusion, which indisputably would have applied to bar the duties to defend and indemnify if such evidence had been considered. 981 S.W.2d at 863–64. The court found the petition did allege facts regarding the negligence of the insured sufficient to state a potentially covered cause of action. Id. at 864. The court also concluded that the issue of whether an injured employee of the insured collected worker's compensation benefits went to the merits of his lawsuit; extrinsic evidence could not be considered even if the court were to "craft an exception to the general rule." Id. Most recently in December 2003, in light of the consideration and rejection of any exception to the strict eight corners rule by the Texas appellate court in Tri–Coastal, the appeals court in Landmark Chevrolet again declined to apply any Wade-type exception to supplement insufficient pleadings that, even given a liberal interpretation, did not state even a possibly covered truth-in-lending claim. 121 S.W.3d at 890–91.

The Westport court thus came to the conclusion that only in very limited circumstances is extrinsic evidence admissible in deciding the duty to defend—where fundamental policy coverage questions can be resolved by readily determined facts that do not engage the truth or falsity of the allegations in the underlying petition, or overlap with the merits of the underlying suit. 267 F.Supp.2d at 621 (quotations and citation omitted). Fundamental coverage issues have been defined to include: (1) whether the person sued has been specifically excluded by name or description from any coverage, (2) whether the property in suit is included in or has been expressly excluded from any coverage, and (3) whether the policy exists. Id.; see also Calderon, 1998 WL 898471, at *4; Tri–Coastal, 981 S.W.2d at 863 n. 1.

As mentioned above, this Court has previously relied on the Wade line of Texas appellate cases to recognize a narrow exception to Texas's strict eight corners rule. For example, in Western Heritage, we determined that extrinsic evidence could be used in an insurance dispute where the underlying amended petition did not allege or provide any factual explanation for how the restaurant patron involved had arrived at such an impaired state that he could not operate a vehicle. 998 F.2d at 313–15. There, because the facts alleged were not specific enough, even interpreted in the light most favorable to the insured, to possibly bring the claim within the negligence coverage of the policy, which specifically excluded damages stemming from the sale of alcoholic beverages to an intoxicated person, extrinsic evidence was allowed to determine the insured's duty to defend. Id. Likewise, in John Deere Insurance Co. v. Truckin' U.S.A., 122 F.3d 270, 272–73 (5th Cir.1997), we determined that extrinsic evidence could be considered in an insurance dispute where the underlying petition only alleged that the tractor trailer rig involved in an accident had been furnished to the defendants or that defendants had a working relationship with the insured trucking company. There, because the facts alleged were insufficient, even if taken as true, to state a cause of action under the policy, extrinsic evidence was allowed to show whether the rig was a "covered auto" such that insurer had a duty to defend. Id.

In light of the Texas appellate courts' unwavering unwillingness to apply and recent repudiations of the Wade type of exception, this Court makes its Erie guess that the current Texas Supreme Court would not recognize any exception to the strict eight corners rule. That is, if the four corners of the petition allege facts stating a cause of action which potentially falls within the four corners of the policy's scope of coverage, resolving all doubts in favor of the insured, the insurer has a duty to defend. If all the facts alleged in the underlying petition fall outside the scope of coverage, then there is no duty to defend. However, in the unlikely situation that the Texas Supreme Court were to recognize an exception to the strict eight corners rule, we conclude any exception would only apply in very limited circumstances: when it is initially impossible to discern whether coverage is potentially implicated and when the extrinsic evidence goes solely to a fundamental issue of coverage which does not overlap with the merits of or engage the truth or falsity of any facts alleged in the underlying case.

Whether the district court erred in determining that Northfield had a duty to defend LHC and the Daniels in the underlying tort suit.

On appeal, Northfield only challenges the district court's refusal to look to extrinsic evidence to determine "whether Bianca Barrows' death resulted from a criminal act' by Celia Giral" or arose from physical abuse by Giral. Northfield points to the Barrows' petition and labels all the so-called factual allegations—such as the negligent dropping and/or shaking of Bianca by Giral and the negligent hiring, training, and supervising of Giral by LHC—as legal theories that do not determine the duty to defend. Thus, Northfield asserts that Texas law allows courts to consider extrinsic evidence when the petition in the underlying suit does not allege facts sufficient to enable the court to determine whether the criminal acts and physical exclusions apply. Northfield relies on three cases for this proposition: Guaranty National, 143 F.3d at 194 (applying Western Heritage); John Deere, 122 F.3d at 272 (applying Wade); and Matagorda Ventures, Inc. v. Travelers Lloyds Insurance Co., 203 F.Supp.2d 704, 714 (S.D.Tex.2000) (citing but not applying Wade). Northfield thus argues that Giral's criminal conviction and the autopsy report on Bianca's injuries establish as a matter of law that all the damages suffered by the Barrows arise from a criminal act and/or physical abuse; thus, no duty to defend or to indemnify LHC and the Daniels can be imposed on Northfield.

Northfield maintains that although the general rule under Texas law is that where the complaint does not allege facts sufficient to bring it clearly within the scope of coverage, the insurer is obligated to defend if there is potentially a case falling within coverage, the exception applies when the petition labels conduct as negligent, where the true nature of the conduct has been found criminal. Northfield relies on a North Dakota Supreme Court case, Ohio Casualty Insurance Co. v. Clark, 583 N.W.2d 377, 380 (N.D.1998), which held that an insurer had no duty to defend based on extrinsic evidence of criminal conviction that established that "intentional injury" exclusion applied, even where the underlying petition alleged negligence.

Northfield also contends that Texas law under the Wade line of cases permits exceptions to the eight corners rule, such as in Western Heritage. There, the district court concluded that based on extrinsic evidence establishing that a "liquor liability" exclusion applied, there was no duty to defend the insured restaurant, even where all references to alcohol and intoxication had been deleted in the amended complaint. 998 F.2d at 313, 315.[13] In essence, Northfield argues the Barrows are perpetuating a fraud upon the court by artfully pleading facts to bring excluded claims within coverage; courts can look to extrinsic evidence when the petition omits or misrepresents material facts that clearly would have excluded coverage, such as the Barrows have done here. Finally, Northfield argues that the fundamental coverage caveat to the eight corners exception is either wrong, or is not limited to the three definitions laid out in case law. That is, if the caveat applies, the question of the application of the criminal acts and physical abuse exclusions is one of fundamental coverage.

13. What fully distinguishes this case from Western Heritage is that the Barrows' petition did not fail to explain what factually had happened to Bianca to result in her death at all. Moreover, the facts alleged clearly indicated LHC and its employees had a duty toward the Barrows and Bianca. In Western Heritage, the petition did not factually explain at all how the patron involved had arrived at such an impaired state that he could not operate a vehicle such that any possible duty owed by the restaurant to the patron might have arisen. 998 F.2d at 313.

The Barrows, LHC, and the Daniels argue that because this is a duty-to-defend inquiry only, the district court properly applied Texas law, which is clear that extrinsic evidence is not to be considered under any exception. The Barrows' third-amended petition clearly alleged negligent dropping and/or shaking behavior by Giral toward Bianca, not intentional acts of physical abuse; and these facts, if properly assumed to be true, unambiguously stated at least one negligence claim facially within the policy's coverage. See Lafarge Corp. v. Hartford Cas. Ins. Co., 61 F.3d 389, 394 (5th Cir.1995), overruled on other grounds by Grapevine Excavation, Inc. v. Maryland Lloyds, 35 S.W.3d 1, 5 (Tex.2000) (noting that the complaint as amended to include facts alleging negligence was clearly not a case where it was impossible to discern whether coverage was potentially indicated). The Barrows, LHC, and the Daniels contend that any uncertainties as to whether allegations in a petition state a covered cause are to be resolved in favor of the insured. See Tri–Coastal, 981 S.W.2d at 863. In Tri–Coastal, the Texas appeals court refused to consider extrinsic evidence, even though the petition did not contain sufficient facts to determine the application of a worker's compensation exclusion, where the employee's underlying petition alleged facts indicating negligence potentially covered by the employer's liability policy. Id. at 862–64. Likewise, here, without such extrinsic evidence, Northfield cannot and did not demonstrate that any exclusion applied to all the Barrows' claims against LHC and the Daniels.

The Barrows, LHC, and the Daniels assert that even if an exception to the eight corners rule does exist, it does not apply here because the Barrows' petition properly alleged facts sufficient, if taken as true, to potentially state at least one cause of action falling within the policy; namely, negligence on the part of Giral in dropping and/or shaking Bianca. This is a separate, alternative allegation from that claiming Giral's behavior was criminally negligent under Texas Penal Code Section 6.03. Likewise, the allegation of Giral's negligent behavior, criminal or not, does not constitute the kind of culpable mental state to which the physical abuse exclusion would apply. This is clearly what the district court found, and what Northfield did and does not contest: the Barrows' petition alleged facts sufficient to state a claim of negligence potentially falling within Northfield's policy with LHC.

The Barrows attack the cases relied on by Northfield for its proposition that extrinsic evidence may be considered when a petition does not state sufficient facts to determine the applicability of an exclusion. Guaranty National did not address this issue because in that case there was no doubt a pollution exclusion applied; extrinsic evidence was necessary because sufficient facts were not alleged to meet the insured's burden of showing a sudden and accidental exception to the exclusion applied. 143 F.3d at 195. The Barrows' case is distinguished because LHC has already carried its initial burden of showing that the claims against it fall potentially within the scope of coverage, and Northfield has failed to meet its burden of showing an exclusion plainly applied to exclude all the Barrows' claims. The Barrows also argue against any exception applying here to use extrinsic evidence to trigger an exclusion because such evidence would not pertain only to coverage, but to liability as well, Gonzales v. American States Insurance Co., 628 S.W.2d 184, 186–87 (Tex.App.—Corpus Christi 1982, no writ), and because such evidence would tend to contradict allegations pertaining to Giral's neglectful dropping and/or shaking behavior in the Barrows' petition, id. at 187.

The Barrows emphasize that the Wade rationale applied by Western Heritage has never been followed by other Texas courts and should be rejected. And even if such limited exception exists, it does not apply here because the extrinsic evidence would engage the truth or falsity of the Barrows' alleged facts. Wade, 827 S.W.2d at 453. That is, evidence of the intentional actions of Giral would place the accidental nature of the dropping and/or shaking allegations in the Barrows' petition in question.[14] Unlike the petition in John Deere, which did not sufficiently allege that the rig involved in the accident was a vehicle covered by the policy, 122 F.3d at 272, the Barrows' petition clearly did trigger the negligence coverage provision of the CPL part of the policy. Likewise, Matagorda Ventures is inapposite because the court's statement that an exception applies when the petition does not state facts sufficient to determine the applicability of an exclusion is dicta and has never been applied in practice, 203 F.Supp.2d at 714–15. Finally, the Barrows argue that if any exception applies to the eight corners rule, it solely concerns the determination of fundamental coverage questions, which does not encompass whether any criminal act or physical abuse exclusion applies here.

Here, the district court correctly looked to the strict eight corners rule to determine the duty to defend. It properly focused on the alleged facts in the Barrows' petition about Bianca and Giral's behavior toward her, not legal theories, and that they should be construed in the insured's favor. Contrary to what may have been implied by Northfield, the district court did not refuse to acknowledge that any exception to the eight corners rule might exist. In fact, the district court cited John Deere for the proposition that Texas law would allow extrinsic evidence if the petition did not allege facts sufficient to trigger coverage. 122 F.3d at 272 (citation omitted). The district court properly placed the initial burden on LHC and the Daniels to establish that at least one claim against them was potentially within the scope of coverage and then shifted the burden to Northfield to establish that an exclusion plainly applied to all claims to defeat coverage. The district court correctly determined that the Barrows' complaint asserted a claim of negligence within the policy's scope of coverage—properly construing in LHC's favor the Barrows' factual allegations pertaining to Giral's dropping and/or shaking behavior. This determination was not challenged by Northfield.

14. Giral was convicted of first-degree felony injury to a child, which means the jury had to find that she acted intentionally or knowingly. Tex. Pen.Code Ann. <section> 2.04(a)(1), (e) (West 1996).

What Northfield did challenge was that the policy's exclusions vitiated any duties to defend and indemnify LHC based on the Barrows' original complaint, which referenced Giral's criminal conviction. LHC, the Daniels, and the Barrows responded that the live, third-amended petition's alleged facts only supported a cause of action for negligence. The district court properly refused to read extrinsic facts into the pleadings and followed the strict eight corners rule, finding no exception to apply. Although Northfield makes arguments that stress the artful pleading by the Barrows to keep the criminal and intentional allegations out, the latest pronouncement on the eight corners rule by the Texas Supreme Court in King reemphasized the strictness of the rule. Once the Barrows alleged facts that stated a cause of action that potentially fell within the scope of CPL coverage, no matter what facts the previous versions of their petition alleged, the burden shifted to Northfield to show that the plain language of the policy exclusions when compared against the facts alleged in the underlying petition precluded coverage. Northfield did not meet this burden under the duty to defend's eight corners inquiry.

And even in the unlikely event that the Texas Supreme Court were to allow for a limited exception, whether the criminal acts and physical abuse exclusions bar the duty to defend in this case would not fit such narrow exception. First, it is clearly possible to discern whether coverage is potentially implicated here, as distinguished from all the cases Northfield relies on, including Wade and Western Heritage. In fact, Northfield did not even raise this argument before the district court. Second, there is no case in Texas or this Circuit that has ever applied any exception to allow extrinsic evidence where the insurer submits the petition in the underlying suit that does not allege facts sufficient to enable the court to determine whether certain exclusions apply, as distinct from and after the initial inquiry to determine whether coverage is potentially implicated. Third, even if Texas law permitted extrinsic evidence during the initial duty-to-defend determination of potential coverage, the possible application of these specific exclusions does not constitute a fundamental issue of coverage. It is at least a step removed from any inquiry about express inclusions or exclusions of specific property or persons, or if the policy exists. There is no express exclusion in the policy specific to Giral as a covered employee or to injuries to Bianca as covered property, such as could be resolved by any readily determined fact.

Finally, even if the application of these exclusions were considered a fundamental coverage issue that could be answered by looking to extrinsic evidence, the extrinsic evidence here (Giral's conviction and the autopsy report on Bianca) would be barred by the prohibition that such evidence cannot put the truth of the dropping and/or shaking facts alleged in the Barrows' petition into question. Such evidence clearly overlaps with the merits of the Barrows' underlying negligence suit. Thus, the district court properly used Texas's strict eight corners rule in determining Northfield had a duty to defend LHC and the Daniels in the underlying tort suit filed against them by the Barrows.

[The discussion of the Fifth Circuit's power to review whether the district court properly refused to decide the issue of Northfield's duty to indemnify LHC and the Daniels is omitted.]

CONCLUSION

Having carefully reviewed the record of this case, the parties' respective briefing and arguments, and for the reasons set forth above, we AFFIRM the district court's decisions as to Northfield's duty to defend LHC and the Daniels in the underlying tort suit filed against them by the Barrows and as to the present nonjusticiability of Northfield's duty to indemnify LHC and the Daniels.

AFFIRMED.

Notes

1. The court's decision in *Fitzpatrick* to not limit the analysis of insurance coverage to allegations of the "four corners of the complaint" has had particular significance in the defense of environmental litigation. See Employers Ins. of Wausau v. Duplan Corp., 899 F.Supp. 1112, 1123 (1995) (finding that per *Fitzpatrick*, an insurer is required to provide a defense if it has knowledge of facts that not included in the third party complaint that would bring the claim within the boundaries of the insurance policy); Incorporated Village of Cedarhurst v. Hanover Insurance Co., 89 N.Y.2d 293, 675 N.E.2d 822, 653 N.Y.S.2d 68 (1996). In addition, courts have turned to the broad holding of *Fitzpatrick* in defense of asbestos litigation. See Frontier Insulation Contractors v. Merchants Mut. Ins. Co., 91 N.Y.2d 169, 667 N.Y.S.2d 982, 690 N.E.2d 866 (1997).

2. The preceding cases form a nice triangulation of geography and substance. In each case the court found grounds to enforce the duty to defend. It is useful take a moment to compare the approaches of each court. Is one approach better than the others? How do the courts deal with the duty to indemnify?

3. Of the three cases, *Gray v. Zurich* is the broadest. Is this breadth defensible? Does this breadth result in intolerable transaction costs? Whatever the answer, *Gray v. Zurich* has been an influenial case. One of the authors has written on the influence of *Gray v. Zurich* in other jurisdictions and its use as a pedagogical tool. Leo P. Martinez, *Classic Insurance Law in a Postmodern World*, 2 Nevada L.J. 403 (2002).

4. For a broad interpretation of an insurer's duty to defend, see *Vann v. Travelers Companies*, 39 Cal.App.4th 1610, 46 Cal.Rptr.2d 617 (1995). In the case, the plaintiff Vann owned an auto body repair business and rented the property from one Henry Williamson, who filed suit against Vann in 1991, alleging that Vann improperly handled and disposed of certain substances, thereby contaminating the property. Travelers, which had issued liability policies to Vann that covered damages caused by accidents and resulting from garage operations, refused to defend Vann, claiming that a pollution exclusion clause relieved Travelers from its duty to defend. The court held that because Travelers had not refuted every possibility that the

insurance policy covered at least a portion of the alleged damage, Travelers did not satisfy its burden of proof that there was no potential for coverage, and thus summary judgment was inappropriate.

5. *Civil Procedure and the Duty to Defend.* The courts of California and other states have had difficulty defining the boundaries of the *Gray* doctrine. In a typical coverage dispute, the carrier or insured seeks a judicial determination of the duty to defend in a separate action for declaratory relief. What evidence should be available, and what should be the burden of proof for each party's routine motion for summary judgement? The California Supreme Court addressed this issue in the thorny context of a massive CERCLA litigation. Montrose Chemical Corp. of California v. Superior Court, 6 Cal.4th 287, 24 Cal.Rptr.2d 467, 861 P.2d 1153 (1993). Montrose Chemical Corp. produced DDT at a Southern California location from 1947 to 1982. The federal government ordered Montrose to participate in the cleanup of the now infamous Stringfellow disposal site and the Los Angeles Harbor. Seven carriers who wrote CGL coverage for Montrose over the period refused or severely limited tender of defense for various reasons, among them that the dumpings were intentional acts. The court held that in proceedings for summary judgement: (1) both the insured and insurer could look to facts outside the third party's complaint to determine the coverage question, (2) the insured must make a *prima facie* showing of the *potential* for coverage, and (3) the insurer must show as a matter of law that there is no coverage under the policy. The insurer, however, is limited to reliance on *undisputed or extrinsic facts* in making its showing so that the insured is not prejudiced by the prospect of having an adverse finding in the declaratory relief action. The court did not decide whether a carrier could demand reimbursement of defense costs under a prior reservation of rights if the third party action is later found to be outside the scope of coverage, but it seems unlikely in light of the continuing vitality of *Gray*. *Montrose* is involved in other court actions which bear watching by students of insurance and environmental law, and the courts's decision bears resemblance to *Fitzpatrick* and the responsibility imposed on the insurer to defend regardless of the breadth of third party claims.

6. The California courts have grappled with the meaning of the word "suit" in analyzing an insurer's duty to defend. In *Foster–Gardner Inc. v. National Union Fire Ins. Co.,* 56 Cal.App.4th 204, 65 Cal.Rptr.2d 127 (1997), the California Court of Appeal followed the "functional equivalent" approach of prior case law and held that "suit" could refer to something other than a traditional court proceeding, including an administrative "claim," concluding that an insurer had a duty to defend such a claim. However, in the same year *Foster–Gardner* was decided, the Court reached the opposite conclusion in a case with indistinguishable facts. In *Fireman's Fund Ins. Co. v. Superior Court,* 65 Cal.App.4th 1205, 78 Cal.Rptr.2d 418 (1997), the insured received notice from the Regional Water Quality Control Board (RWQCB) and the Environmental Protection Agency (EPA) that it was potentially liable for the investigation and remediation of soil and groundwater contamination at its facility. However, neither the RWQCB nor the EPA filed suit against the insured. When the insured contacted its insurer, Fireman's Fund, Fireman's denied any duty to defend, arguing that these demands were not suits under the insured's CGL insurance policies. The

Court of Appeal agreed with Fireman's argument, reasoning that there was no ambiguity in the word "suit" and a notification letter by a state agency does not trigger an insurer's duty to defend because such a notice does not have the attributes of a suit. The court cited several problems with the reasoning in *Foster–Gardner*, including a lack of discussion about the policy language and possible ambiguity, and a failure to consider the plain meaning of "suit" and "claim." The court asserted that Fireman's consistently treated the two words differently to limit its obligations under the policy. Further, it cited the settled rule that ambiguity will not be found unless a policy provision is capable of two or more reasonable constructions. Defining "suit" as a formal proceeding initiated in a court of law under established procedures, tried before a judge or jury under traditional rules of evidence, resulting in a formal judgment, and "claim" as any number of things, none of which rise to the formal level of a suit, the court concluded that there was no other reasonable construction of the terms. Finding no ambiguity, the court interpreted the word "suit" according to its plain and ordinary meaning—as an action or proceeding pursued in a court of law—and held that Fireman's had no duty to defend its insured in an administrative action.

Ultimately, the California Supreme Court resolved the conflict by siding with the *Fireman's Fund* court holding that an environmental cleanup order was not a "suit" which triggered the duty to defend. Foster–Gardner, Inc. v. National Union Fire Insurance Co., 18 Cal.4th 857, 77 Cal.Rptr.2d 107, 959 P.2d 265 (1998); see Janet E. Bender, *No Duty to Defend CERCLA Environmental Protection Agency Administrative Proceedings Under the Comprehensive General Liability Policy in California*, 30 McGeorge L. Rev. 1461 (1999) (discussing the *Foster–Gardner* case).

BUSS v. SUPERIOR COURT

Supreme Court of California, 1997.
16 Cal.4th 35, 65 Cal.Rptr.2d 366, 939 P.2d 766

MOSK, JUSTICE.

* * *

H & H Sports, Incorporated, brought an action against Buss and others in the superior court. In the final amended form of its complaint, it alleged, in pertinent part, as follows: Buss owned and operated the Los Angeles Lakers, a professional basketball team, the Los Angeles Lazers, a professional indoor soccer team, and the Los Angeles Kings, a professional hockey team; through one entity, Buss owned and operated the Great Western Forum indoor sports arena in the City of Inglewood; through another entity, Buss leased the facility and presented athletic competitions, including professional basketball, indoor soccer, and hockey, and also entertainment events, and in addition subleased the facility to others who presented similar competitions and events; Buss owned and operated, at least indirectly and in part, certain cable television broadcasting networks, including the Forum Entertainment Network, Box Seat, and Prime Ticket Network; Buss entered into various contracts with H & H Sports, including certain modifications and extensions, under which H & H Sports provided, and Buss obtained, advertising and other services; for a time, Buss and H & H Sports performed under the contracts; subsequently, however, H & H Sports continued but Buss did not, with Buss unilaterally terminating his relationship with H & H Sports. H & H Sports asserted 27 causes of action (up from 12 originally), with most but not all against Buss and Buss–related persons and entities. . . .

Buss tendered defense of the H & H Sports action to his insurers. With the exception of Transamerica, each refused, denying coverage.

Transamerica had issued Buss two comprehensive or commercial general liability insurance policies pertinent to the H & H Sports action.

* * *

Transamerica accepted the defense of the H & H Sports action as tendered by Buss, ultimately under both its comprehensive and commercial general liability insurance policies. As noted above, out of the 27 causes of action in the final amended form of the complaint, there was a single one for defamation against Buss: it was alleged that Buss made statements to third persons about H & H Sports that were "false and slanderous *per se,*" and were "understood . . . to mean that [it] had overcharged its customers and lacked integrity." (Italics added in place of underscoring in original.) It was in light of such allegations that Transamerica agreed to defend Buss, ultimately taking the position that the defamation cause of action, and only the defamation cause of action, was at least potentially covered. But it reserved all its rights, including to deny that any cause of action was actually covered, and, "[w]ith respect to defense costs incurred or to be incurred in the future, . . . to be reimbursed and/or [to obtain] an allocation of attorney's fees and expenses in this action if it is determined that there is no coverage. . . . " Because of its reservation of rights and the conflict of interests arising therefrom, Transamerica agreed to pay on Buss's behalf the cost of independent "Cumis" counsel—so called after the eponymous decision of San Diego Federal Credit Union v. Cumis Ins. Society, Inc. (1984) 162 Cal.App.3d 358, 208 Cal.Rptr. 494—in accordance with Civil Code section 2860. Buss acknowledged Transamerica's reservation of rights with a reservation of rights of his own. Later, Buss and Transamerica entered into an agreement supported by consideration that provided, among other things, that "[i]f a court . . . orders that defense costs be shared pro rata by . . . Buss . . . and Transamerica, . . . Buss . . . shall reimburse Transamerica for the appropriate pro rata share of the fees and costs paid to that date."

In due course, Buss settled the H & H Sports action, paying H & H Sports $8.5 million. Altogether, Transamerica paid Buss's independent counsel a sum stated variously as $1,066,000 and $1,004,018.11—with an amount ranging between $21,720 and $55,767.50, according to an expert retained by Transamerica, being the cost of defending the defamation cause of action. Buss had requested contribution to the settlement by Transamerica, but had been refused.

Buss brought the underlying action against Transamerica, among others, in the superior court. In the final amended form of his complaint, he alleged, in pertinent part, that Transamerica denied any duty to defend the H & H Sports action in its entirety, and also denied any duty to contribute to the settlement thereof. He asserted causes of action entitled declaratory relief, breach of contract, and breach of the implied covenant of good faith and fair dealing. He prayed for relief including a declaration that Transamerica did indeed have a duty to defend and a duty to contribute, and an award of damages by way of compensation according to proof.

In a cross-complaint, Transamerica alleged, in pertinent part, that Buss denied its right to obtain reimbursement for the costs it expended to defend the H & H Sports action other than as to the defamation cause of action, and also denied its right not to contribute to the settlement thereof. It asserted causes of action, among others, entitled declaratory relief and declaratory relief and reimbursement. It prayed for relief including a declaration that it did indeed have a right to obtain reimbursement, and an order therefor in an amount to be proved at trial, and also a declaration that it did indeed have a right not to contribute to the settlement.

Transamerica moved the superior court for summary judgment against Buss on his complaint. The court granted the motion. Determining, among other things, that there was no "reasonable basis for Transamerica to join in the settlement" as to the defamation cause of action, it concluded in substance that there was no triable issue of material fact and that Transamerica was entitled to judgment as a matter of law.

Buss then moved the superior court for summary judgment against Transamerica on its cross-complaint for reimbursement for defense costs.... [T]he court denied the motion.

It was against the superior court and its denial of his summary judgment motion that Buss filed his petition for writ of mandate in the Court of Appeal. He also submitted a request for a stay of proceedings in the superior court pending determination thereof.

Evidently without a stay, the Court of Appeal ordered the parties to show cause why a peremptory writ of mandate should not issue. Transamerica filed opposition to Buss's petition. Buss filed a reply to Transamerica's opposition. The superior court did not appear.

In an opinion certified for publication, the Court of Appeal discharged the order to show cause and denied a peremptory writ. It determined that the superior court's denial of Buss's summary judgment motion was subject to independent review. After such review, it found no error.

* * *

On Buss's petition and request, we granted review and stayed proceedings in the superior court pending determination thereof.

II

Before we address the four questions relating to standard comprehensive or commercial general liability insurance policies stated at the outset, we must explicate the law that stands behind and beneath the answers we shall give.

A

* * *

The insurer's duty to indemnify runs to claims that are actually covered, in light of the facts proved. By definition, it entails the payment of money in order to resolve liability. It arises only after liability is established.

By contrast, the insurer's duty to defend runs to claims that are merely potentially covered, in light of facts alleged or otherwise disclosed. It entails the rendering of a service, viz., the mounting and funding of a defense in order to avoid or at least minimize liability. It arises as soon as tender is made. It is discharged when the action is concluded. It may be extinguished earlier, if it is shown that no claim can in fact be covered. If it is so extinguished, however, it is extinguished only prospectively and not retroactively: before, the insurer had a duty to defend; after, it does not have a duty to defend further.

Obviously, the insurer's duty to defend is broader than its duty to indemnify. But, just as obviously, it is not unlimited. It extends beyond claims that are actually covered to those that are merely potentially so—but no further.

Thus, in an action wherein all the claims are at least potentially covered, the insurer has a duty to defend. (Hogan v. Midland National Ins. Co., supra, 3 Cal.3d at p. 563, 91 Cal.Rptr. 153, 476 P.2d 825 [semble]; see, e.g., Horace Mann Ins. Co. v. Barbara B., supra, 4 Cal.4th at pp. 1081–1087, 17 Cal.Rptr.2d 210, 846 P.2d 792 [holding that the insurer has a duty to defend when only one of several claims is at least potentially covered].) This obligation is express in the policy's language. It rests on the fact that the insurer has been paid premiums by the insured for a defense. "The rule is grounded in basic principles of contract law." (SL Industries v. American Motorists (1992) 128 N.J. 188, 215, 607 A.2d 1266 [applying N.J. law, but speaking generally].) The duty to defend is contractual. (E.g., McMillin Scripps North Partnership v. Royal Ins. Co. (1993) 19 Cal.App.4th 1215, 1220–1221, 23 Cal.Rptr.2d 243; Ins. Co. North America v. Forty–Eight Insulations (6th Cir.1980) 633 F.2d 1212, 1224, rehg. granted and opn. mod. in part not pertinent here and den. in part not pertinent here sub nom. Ins. Co. of N.A. v. Forty–Eight Insulations (1981) 657 F.2d 814 [applying Ill. and N.J. law, but speaking generally]; SL Industries v. American Motorists, supra, 128 N.J. at p. 215, 607 A.2d 1266 [applying N.J. law, but speaking generally].) "An insurer contracts to pay the entire cost of defending ... claim[s]" that are at least potentially covered. (Ins. Co. North America v. Forty–Eight Insulations, supra, 633 F.2d at p. 1224 [applying Ill. and

N.J. law, but speaking generally]; accord, SL Industries v. American Motorists, supra, 128 N.J. at p. 215, 607 A.2d 1266 [applying N.J. law, but speaking generally].)

Conversely, in an action wherein none of the claims is even potentially covered, the insurer does not have a duty to defend. (E.g., Waller v. Truck Ins. Exchange, Inc., supra, 11 Cal.4th at p. 29, 44 Cal.Rptr.2d 370, 900 P.2d 619; Gray v. Zurich Insurance Co., supra, 65 Cal.2d at p. 276, fn. 15, 54 Cal.Rptr. 104, 419 P.2d 168.) This freedom is implied in the policy's language. It rests on the fact that the insurer has not been paid premiums by the insured for a defense. This "rule" too "is grounded in basic principles of contract law." (SL Industries v. American Motorists, supra, 128 N.J. at p. 215, 607 A.2d 1266 [applying N.J. law, but speaking generally].) As stated, the duty to defend is contractual. "The insurer has not contracted to pay defense costs" for claims that are not even potentially covered. (Ins. Co. North America v. Forty–Eight Insulations, supra, 633 F.2d at pp. 1224–1225 [applying Ill. and N.J. law, but speaking generally]; accord, SL Industries v. American Motorists, supra, 128 N.J. at p. 215, 607 A.2d 1266 [applying N.J. law, but speaking generally].)

It follows that, in a "mixed" action, in which some of the claims are at least potentially covered and the others are not, the insurer has a duty to defend as to the claims that are at least potentially covered, having been paid premiums by the insured therefor, but does not have a duty to defend as to those that are not, having not been paid therefor. This conclusion is in line with the "general rule" that "[w]hen a complaint in an action ... states different causes of action ... against the insured, one of which is within ... coverage ... and others of which may not be, the insurer is bound to defend with respect to those which, if proved, would be within ... coverage." (Annot.(1955) 41 A.L.R.2d 434, 435, italics added and boldface omitted; accord, 14 Couch on Insurance (2d ed.1982) s 51:47, p. 482.) As we ourselves have held more than once over the years (see Waller v. Truck Ins. Exchange, Inc., supra, 11 Cal.4th at p. 19, 44 Cal.Rptr.2d 370, 900 P.2d 619; Gray v. Zurich Insurance Co., supra, 65 Cal.2d at p. 275, 54 Cal.Rptr. 104, 419 P.2d 168), "the duty to defend, although broad, is not unlimited; it is measured by the nature and kinds of risks covered" (Waller v. Truck Ins. Exchange, Inc., supra, 11 Cal.4th at p. 19, 44 Cal.Rptr.2d 370, 900 P.2d 619; accord, Gray v. Zurich Insurance Co., supra, 65 Cal.2d at p. 275, 54 Cal.Rptr. 104, 419 P.2d 168).

Despite the forgoing, we have nevertheless held that, in a "mixed" action, the insurer has a duty to defend the action in its entirety. (Horace Mann Ins. Co. v. Barbara B., supra, 4 Cal.4th at p. 1081, 17 Cal.Rptr.2d 210, 846 P.2d 792; see Hogan v. Midland National Ins. Co., supra, 3 Cal.3d at p. 563, 91 Cal.Rptr. 153, 476 P.2d 825.) This holding is rooted in Hogan. (See Horace Mann Ins. Co. v. Barbara B., supra, 4 Cal.4th at p. 1081, 17 Cal.Rptr.2d 210, 846 P.2d 792; California Union Ins. Co. v. Club Aquarius (1980) 113 Cal.App.3d 243, 247–248, 169

Cal.Rptr. 685.) But it is not explained in that decision or in any of its progeny.

We cannot justify the insurer's duty to defend the entire "mixed" action contractually, as an obligation arising out of the policy, and have never even attempted to do so. To purport to make such a justification would be to hold what we cannot—that the duty to defend exists, as it were, in the air, without regard to whether or not the claims are at least potentially covered. (See Waller v. Truck Ins. Exchange, Inc., supra, 11 Cal.4th at p. 19, 44 Cal.Rptr.2d 370, 900 P.2d 619; Gray v. Zurich Insurance Co., supra, 65 Cal.2d at p. 275, 54 Cal.Rptr. 104, 419 P.2d 168.) As stated, the duty to defend goes to any action seeking damages for any covered claim. If it went to an action simpliciter, it could perhaps be taken to reach the action in its entirety. But it does not. Rather, it goes to an action seeking damages for a covered claim. It must therefore be read to embrace the action to the extent that it seeks such damages. So read, it accords with the general rule, set out above, that the insurer has a duty to defend as to the claims that are at least potentially covered, but not as to those that are not. (See 14 Couch on Insurance, supra, s 51:47, p. 482; Annot., supra, 41 A.L.R.2d at p. 435.) Even if the policy's language were unclear, the hypothetical insured could not have an objectively reasonable expectation otherwise.

That being said, we can, and do, justify the insurer's duty to defend the entire "mixed" action prophylactically, as an obligation imposed by law in support of the policy. To defend meaningfully, the insurer must defend immediately. (Montrose Chemical Corp. v. Superior Court, supra, 6 Cal.4th at p. 295, 24 Cal.Rptr.2d 467, 861 P.2d 1153.) To defend immediately, it must defend entirely. It cannot parse the claims, dividing those that are at least potentially covered from those that are not. To do so would be time consuming. It might also be futile: the "plasticity of modern pleading" (Gray v. Zurich Insurance Co., supra, 65 Cal.2d at p. 276, 54 Cal.Rptr. 104, 419 P.2d 168) allows the transformation of claims that are at least potentially covered into claims that are not, and vice versa. The fact remains: As to the claims that are at least potentially covered, the insurer gives, and the insured gets, just what they bargained for, namely, the mounting and funding of a defense. But as to the claims that are not, the insurer may give, and the insured may get, more than they agreed, depending on whether defense of these claims necessitates any additional costs.

B

We now turn to the first question—In a "mixed" action, may the insurer seek reimbursement from the insured for defense costs?

The answer is as follows.

As to the claims that are at least potentially covered, the insurer may not seek reimbursement for defense costs. Apparently, none of the decisional law considering such claims in and of themselves suggests otherwise.

The reason is this. Under the policy, the insurer has a duty to defend the insured as to the claims that are at least potentially covered. With regard to defense costs for these claims, the insurer has been paid premiums by the insured. It bargained to bear these costs. To attempt to shift them would upset the arrangement. (See Val's Painting & Drywall, Inc. v. Allstate Ins. Co. (1975) 53 Cal.App.3d 576, 582–585, 126 Cal.Rptr. 267.) This would not be the case if the policy itself provided for reimbursement: such a policy would qualify itself. It would also not be the case if there were a separate contract supported by separate consideration: such a contract would supersede the policy pro tanto. Otherwise, however, the insurer may not seek reimbursement. Surely, it does not have a right of reimbursement implied in fact in the policy, having bargained to bear the costs in question. Neither does it have such a right implied in law. Under the law of restitution, a right of this sort runs against the person who benefits from "unjust enrichment" and in favor of the person who suffers loss thereby. (See Rest., Restitution s 1, coms. a, c, & d, at pp. 12 & 13; accord, Rest.2d Restitution (Tent. Draft No. 1, Apr. 5, 1983) s 1, pp. 8–9.) Any "enrichment" of the insured by the insurer through the insurer's bearing of bargained-for defense costs is consistent with the insurer's obligation under the policy and therefore cannot be deemed "unjust." It follows a fortiori that the insurer may not proceed by means of a "reservation" of its "right" of reimbursement. It simply has no such "right" to "reserve." That is true even if the insured agrees to the "reservation." The creation of a right of reimbursement would amount to a pro tanto supersession of the policy—which would require a separate contract supported by separate consideration. (Reliance Ins. Co. v. Alan (1990) 222 Cal.App.3d 702, 710, fn. 4, 272 Cal.Rptr. 65.)

As to the claims that are not even potentially covered, however, the insurer may indeed seek reimbursement for defense costs. Apparently, all the decisional law considering such claims in and of themselves so assumes. So has it been held: "California law clearly allows insurers to be reimbursed for attorney's fees" and other expenses "paid in defending insureds against claims for which there was no obligation to defend."

The reason is this. Under the policy, the insurer does not have a duty to defend the insured as to the claims that are not even potentially covered. With regard to defense costs for these claims, the insurer has not been paid premiums by the insured. It did not bargain to bear these costs. To attempt to shift them would not upset the arrangement. (See Ins. Co. North America v. Forty–Eight Insulations, supra, 633 F.2d at pp. 1224–1225 [applying Ill. and N.J. law, but speaking generally].) The insurer therefore has a right of reimbursement that is implied in law as quasi-contractual, whether or not it has one that is implied in fact in the policy as contractual. As stated, under the law of restitution such a right runs against the person who benefits from "unjust enrichment" and in favor of the person who suffers loss thereby. The "enrichment" of the insured by the insurer through the insurer's bearing of unbargained-for defense costs is inconsistent with the insurer's freedom under the policy and therefore must be deemed "unjust." It is like the case of A and B. A has a contractual duty to pay B $50. He has only a $100 bill. He may be held to have a prophylactic duty to tender the note. But he surely has a right, implied in law if not in fact, to get back $50. Even if the policy's language were unclear, the hypothetical insured could not have an objectively reasonable expectation that it was entitled to what would in fact be a windfall. (See Morgan, Lewis & Bockius LLP v. Hanover Ins. Co. (D.N.J.1996) 929 F.Supp. 764, 771 [applying N.J. law, but speaking generally]; see also E.E.O.C. v. Southern Pub. Co. (5th Cir.1990) 894 F.2d 785, 791 [apparently applying Miss. law, but speaking generally].) Whatever hopes such an insured may have had based on the decisional law's imposition on the insurer of a duty to defend the entire "mixed" action would have been dispelled by that same law's assumption that the insurer may seek reimbursement for the kind of costs identified above. (Cf. Johansen v. California State Auto. Assn. Inter–Ins. Bureau (1975) 15 Cal.3d 9, 19, 123 Cal.Rptr. 288, 538 P.2d 744 [stating that "[i]f, having reserved" "its right to assert a defense of noncoverage" and "having accepted a reasonable [settlement] offer, the insurer subsequently establishes the noncoverage of its policy, it would be free to seek reimbursement of the settlement payment from its insured"]; Maryland Casualty Co. v. Imperial Contracting Co. (1989) 212 Cal.App.3d 712, 720–722, 260 Cal.Rptr. 797 [concluding to that effect].)

Not only is it good law that the insurer may seek reimbursement for defense costs as to the claims that are not even potentially covered, but it also makes good sense. Without a right of reimbursement, an insurer might be tempted to refuse to defend an action in any part—especially an action with many claims that are not even potentially covered and only a few that are—lest the insurer give, and the insured get, more than they agreed. With such a right, the insurer would not be so tempted, knowing that, if defense of the claims that are not even potentially covered should necessitate any additional costs, it would be able to seek reimbursement.

C

The second question, which follows from the first, is this: In a "mixed" action, for what specific defense costs may the insurer obtain reimbursement from the insured?

The answer is: Defense costs that can be allocated solely to the claims that are not even potentially covered.

The reason is this. It is as to defense costs that can be allocated solely to the claims that are not even potentially covered that the insurer has not been paid premiums by the insured. By contrast, the insurer has in fact been paid as to costs that can be allocated solely to the claims that are at least potentially covered. So too as to costs that can be allocated jointly to the claims that are at least potentially covered and to those that are not—by definition, these costs are fully attributable to the former as well as the latter.

* * *

[In subparts D and E, the Court held that in a mixed action the insurer has the burden of proof by a preponderance of the evidence standard. It reasoned that Evidence Code section 500 provides that a party desiring relief must carry the burden of proof thereon and declared its unwillingness to create an exception for an insurer seeking reimbursement for defense costs.]

III

* * *

On the merits, the Court of Appeal found the superior court's denial of Buss's summary judgment motion to be free from error. It was right here as well. Considered in their full context, as disclosed by the motion's supporting papers, Transamerica's comprehensive and commercial general liability insurance policies did not either one of them provide that Transamerica had a contractual duty to defend Buss in a "mixed" action in its entirety. The policies' language is clear. The duty to defend did not exist in the air, without regard to whether or not the claims were at least potentially covered. To be sure, as to the claims that were at least potentially covered, Transamerica had been paid premiums by Buss for a defense. But as to those that were not, it had not. Even if the policies' language were not clear, there is no appreciable evidence that, at formation, Transamerica believed that Buss understood the words to state or imply a duty to defend an entire "mixed" action, or that Buss had objectively reasonable expectations that they did. Of course, the law imposed a prophylactic duty on Transamerica to defend Buss in a "mixed" action in its entirety. And, in the H & H Sports action, Transamerica did so. As to the defamation cause of action against Buss, which was at least potentially covered, Transamerica gave, and Buss got, just what they bargained for, the mounting and funding of a defense. But as to all or at least most of the others, which were not, Transamerica may have given, and Buss may have gotten, more than they agreed, depending on whether defense of these causes of action necessitated any additional costs. Even if the language of the policies were unclear, Buss could not have had a reasonable expectation that he was entitled to what would in fact be a windfall. Whether Transamerica will be able to carry its burden of proof by a preponderance of the evidence that specific costs can be allocated solely to the causes of action that were not even potentially covered is far from plain. But there is at least a triable issue of material fact that it can. It must be allowed the attempt.

IV

For the reasons stated above, we conclude that we must affirm the judgment of the Court of Appeal. It is so ordered.

GEORGE, C.J., and BAXTER, WERDEGAR, CHIN and BROWN, JJ., concur.

[The dissenting opinion of Justice Kennard is omitted.]

Notes

1. The court holds that an insurer seeking reimbursement of defense costs bears the burden of proof. Is it an impossible burden? Does the case encourage a further layer of litigation that was viewed with disapproval in *Gray v. Zurich*?

2. *Buss* deals with an insurer who provides defense. How would a California court decide a case with the *Gray v. Zurich* facts in which no defense is provided? Would this court still hold an insurer liable for defense costs not within coverage? What about indemnity for acts not within coverage where the insurer provides no defense?

3. How does an insurer go about establishing a plausible allocation?

4. Justice Kennard, in a forceful dissent, expressly disagreed with the majority's holding that an insurer may require the insured to reimburse the carrier for defense costs despite the absence of any such agreement made between the carrier and the insured. She argues that this holding suggests that the insurer is only contractually obligated to defend specific claims and not entire actions, a reasoning incompatible with the language in the policy itself. Kennard refutes the majority's general rule by arguing that there is no stated source of legal authority that justifies the court's adoption of the rule and that general rules of construction are subdued by express policy language to the contrary:

> Here, the insurer expressly agreed to defend not merely individual covered claims, but any suit seeking damages covered by the policies. Once an insurer has made such an agreement, it is obligated to honor it, regardless of how costly this may prove in a particular instance. Buss v. Superior Court, 16 Cal.4th 35, 65 (1997) (Kennard, J., dissenting).

Justice Kennard echoes the minority view described in the note below.

5. The efficacy of the reservation of rights letter depends on the jurisdiction. A minority of jurisdictions refuse to permit an insurer to recover defense costs pursuant to a reservation of rights absent an express provision to that effect in the insurance contract between the parties—even in cases where it is later determined that there is no coverage. General Agents Ins. Co. of Am., Inc. v. Midwest Sporting Goods Co., 215 Ill.2d 146, 293 Ill.Dec. 594, 828 N.E.2d 1092 (2005); Terra Nova Insurance Co. v. 900 Bar, Inc., 887 F.2d 1213 (3d Cir. 1989)(applying Pennsylvania law). According to this view

> A rule permitting such recovery would be inconsistent with the legal principles that induce an insurer's offer to defend under reservation of rights. Faced with uncertainty as to its duty to indemnify, an insurer offers a defense under reservation of rights to avoid the risks that an inept or lackadaisical defense of the underlying action may expose it to if it turns out there is a duty to indemnify. [footnote omitted]. At the same time, the insurer wishes to preserve its right to contest the duty to indemnify if the defense is unsuccessful. Thus, such an offer is made at least as much for the insurer's own benefit as for the insured's. If the insurer could recover defense costs, the insured would be required to

pay for the insurer's action in protecting itself against the estoppel to deny coverage that would be implied if it undertook the defense without reservation. Terra Nova Insurance Co., 887 F.2d at 1219–20.

In most jurisdictions, however, it is generally unquestioned that a reservation of rights letter will be enforced where it is subsequently found that no duty to defend exists and where the letter is clear and unambiguous. United Nat'l Ins. Co. v. SST Fitness Corp., 309 F.3d 914, 917–19 (6th Cir. 2002) (includes survey of other jurisdictions).

6. It seems well settled that an insurer cannot terminate its duty to defend by the simple expedient of tendering the policy limits to the insured. Gross v. Lloyds of London Ins. Co., 121 Wis.2d 78, 358 N.W.2d 266 (1984)(recognizing the duty of defense is a separate and distinct obligation).

7. Could the insurer in *Buss* have withdrawn if the single covered claim had been dismissed? Professor Hazel Beh has directed us to decisions that considered the question before *Buss* that precluded the insurer's withdrawal. Meadowbrook, Inc. v. Tower Ins. Co., Inc., 559 N.W.2d 411 (Minn. 1997)(duty to defend is not terminated until rights of appeal are exhausted); Commerce & Industry Ins. Co. v. Bank of Hawaii, 73 Haw. 322, 832 P.2d 733 (1992)(duty to defend is not terminated until appeal period of dismissal expires or final judgment is rendered). Even with the advantage of the *Buss* opinion, courts have been reluctant to lessen the insurer's duty to defend. Texas Association of Counties County Gov't Risk Management Pool v. Matagorda County, 52 S.W.3d 128 (Tex.S.Ct.2000) (insurer's claim for reimbursement denied in a mixed action); Shoshone First Bank v. Pacific Employers Ins. Co., 2 P.3d 510, 515–16 (Wy. 2000)(insurer required to defend entire action under a standard CGL insurance policy).

The Duty to Defend—a Postscript

Because of the ever-increasing costs of litigation, insurers have attempted to limit their responsibilities for paying attorney bills for defending the insured by including a clause limiting the insurer's obligation to defend the insured to a set amount of litigation expenses. This is known as "defense within limits" and this clause essentially provides the insurer the ability to stop defending the insured in the midst of an ongoing litigation once the policy limits have been exhausted. While one may raise an eyebrow and question the ethics of such an abandonment of a client, it is perfectly legitimate, as the insured is aware of the financial limitation available for litigation costs when he enters into the insurance contract. The insured is notified that he is reaching the limits of the policy and he has the option to maintain the attorneys currently on his case at his own expense or to hire private counsel. The attorneys hired by the insurer essentially stand behind the right to withdraw from further defense based on the policy limits.

Allowing an insurer to withdraw from litigation once the policy limits are exhausted is not a trivial concern. While policy language may literally allow an insurer to withdraw from litigation once policy limits are exhausted, other factors will affect the withdrawal. For example, the unfortunate insured who finds herself in this predicament may well be represented by a lawyer who is also in a quandary over her obligations in this regard. Clearly, litigation strategy will be affected by lawyers mindful that funds are being dissipated.

In the few cases that have arisen, the courts have tended to find in favor of insureds based largely on perceived ambiguities in policy language. E.g., Brown v. Lumbermens Mutual Casualty Co., 326 N.C. 387, 390 S.E.2d 150 (1990). There is not, however, a decidedly pro-insured bias in this area. For example, two Illinois cases decided five years apart yielded contrary results. Conway v. Country Casualty Ins. Co., 92 Ill.2d 388, 65 Ill.Dec. 934, 442 N.E.2d 245 (1982) (finding that the duty to defend continued after policy limits are exhausted); Zurich Ins. Co. v. Raymark Indus., 118 Ill.2d 23, 112 Ill.Dec. 684, 514 N.E.2d 150 (1987) (finding that the duty to defend terminated upon exhaustion of policy limits); see Christine J. Wichers, *Brown v. Lumbermans Mutual Casualty Co.: When Does Exhaustion of Policy Limits Terminate an Insurer's Duty to Defend?*, 69 N.C.L. Rev. 1660 (1991).

A yet more recent Illinois case has tangentially addressed whether or not it was proper for the insurer to withdraw from the defense. Douglas v. Allied American Insurance, 312 Ill.App.3d 535, 727 N.E.2d 376, 245 Ill.Dec. 123 (2000). In *Douglas*, the insurer paid the policy's maximum coverage to the court in an ongoing litigation without obtaining a release or settlement and withdrew representation of its insured. The court, citing public policy concerns, stated that the insurer cannot simply pay the limit and leave the insured to defend for himself. *Id.* at 383. Although the court cited the *Brown* and *Conway* cases with approval, the court did not address whether or not walking away from the defense would be proper if the policy expressly limited the costs of defense for which the insurer is responsible. Assuming there was such a clause, would the courts in these cases find that the insurer was free to walk away from an on-going case? How does the freedom to contract come into play or should it?

While California makes clear that an insurer cannot avoid its duty to defend an insured once trial has begun, it is also clear that an insurer may withdraw once an insured is otherwise free of liability. Heredia v. Farmers Insurance Exchange, 228 Cal.App.3d 1345, 279 Cal.Rptr. 511 (1991) (plaintiff wanted to force insurer to continue defense beyond release of insurer and tender of limits to avoid an "empty chair defense" by remaining defendants); Johnson v. Continental Insurance Companies, 202 Cal.App.3d 477, 248 Cal.Rptr. 412 (1988) (claims against plaintiff insured had been settled at limits, insured named in cross-complaint in a later action). While *Heredia* cites *Gross* with apparent disapproval, as of the date of this edition of the text, no California case has arisen which addresses squarely the question of whether an insurer can withdraw from a case in which the policy includes defense costs within the policy limits and those policy limits are exhausted.

California courts have addressed the ability of an insurer to withdraw its defense during ongoing litigation when the insured has reached the set liability amount in complex litigations involving many parties and multiple settlements. In *Hartford Acc. & Indem. Co. v. Superior Court of the City and County of San Francisco*, 23 Cal.App.4th 1774, 29 Cal.Rptr.2d 32 (1994), the issue before the court was whether or not a primary insurer's duty to defend continued after a dispute arose over exhaustion of policy limits, but before the insurer has established in court that its coverage limits have been exhausted. The insured was sued by more than 2,500 plaintiffs in 66 private causes of actions and by the United States and the state of Missouri for massive environmental contamination. Hartford, the insurer, defended the insured for a number of years, paying litigation expenses and settlements of $4.1 million before withdrawing from its defense relying on the fact that the insured had exhausted its policy limits. *Id.* at 1777. The court, applying the reasoning contained in *Montrose* addressing the duty to defend, held that the insurer improperly withdrew from defending the insured because there was no final judgment or summary judgment determining whether or not the policy limits had in fact been exhausted. *Id.* at 1781. The court noted that the insurer remains obligated to defend during the determination of coverage, and the insurer is free to seek reimbursement for expenses once it proves that the limit has been reached. *Id.* at 1174.

This decision only indicates that an insurer cannot prematurely terminate its duty to defend, which leaves open the idea that as long as there is a clear determination that a policy's coverage, be it payments to third parties or defense costs, has been reached, then the duty to defend is satisfied.

Consider the position of a company that insured an asbestos manufacturer against liability for one year in the early 1960s under a pre–1967 CGL policy. For some time it has shared in the defense of the manufacturer in a jurisdiction that adheres to the continuing exposure (or triple trigger) theory of liability. The jurisdiction also follows the line of cases holding that pre–1967 policies do not allow discharge from the duty to defend upon exhaustion of policy limits, whereas post–1967 policies do. The insurer would very much like to pay its policy limits and be done with it—as the insurers under the post–1967 policies are doing—but instead appears to be faced with the prospect of increasing defense costs. What would be your advice to insureds or insurers regarding their legal posture? What risks do you take?

3. The Duty to Negotiate and to Effect Settlements

GRAY v. GRAIN DEALERS MUTUAL INSURANCE CO.

United States Court of Appeals, D.C. Circuit, 1989.
276 U.S. App. D.C. 388, 871 F.2d 1128.

SILBERMAN, CIRCUIT JUDGE:

Following a personal injury claim filed against Windell Speed by Vernon Gray, a pedestrian Speed hit while driving his car, Grain Dealers Mutual Insurance Company breached its duty to settle on behalf of its insured, Speed. In doing so, Grain Dealers exposed itself to liability in excess of Speed's policy limits for consequential damages resulting from its breach. Speed assigned to Gray Speed's chose in action against Grain Dealers in exchange for Gray's release of Speed from liability to pay a default judgment of $334,000 entered against him. The district court awarded Gray $334,000, 684 F.Supp. 1108, and we affirm that result.

I.

This case comes to us primarily on stipulated facts. The district court, however, made certain findings, apparently not in dispute, which supplement the stipulations. In 1985, Grain Dealers Mutual Insurance Company, an Indiana corporation, issued an automobile liability insurance policy to Windell Speed, then a North Carolina resident. The contract, mailed to Speed at his North Carolina address, lists a North Carolina agent for Grain Dealers. Subsequently, Speed moved to Washington, D.C. and in August 1985, while driving his car in Washington, D.C., struck and seriously injured Vernon Gray, a pedestrian. Speed timely reported the accident to Grain Dealers, which referred Speed to its agent in Northern Virginia, R.W. Parker. In September 1985, Gray filed suit against Speed seeking $2 million in damages. The insurance contract included a standard "duty-to-defend clause" obligating the insurer to provide legal counsel to defend or settle on behalf of Speed in the event of a lawsuit arising out of an insured risk. Speed accordingly mailed the complaint to Parker who assured Speed that he would take care of the lawsuit. Gray's attorney made several attempts to contact Parker and discuss settlement of the case. In a letter dated January 7, 1986, Gray's attorney offered to settle the case for $25,000—the policy limit. Parker did not respond to the letter.

In light of Parker's silence, Gray's attorney sought and gained a default judgment against Speed at the end of January 1986. The next month, when the district court held a hearing to ascertain Gray's damages, no one appeared for Speed. After hearing evidence on Gray's injuries and medical expenses, the court awarded him $334,000. Several months later, in April 1986, Parker sent Gray's January 7 settlement offer to Grain Dealers.

In June, Speed agreed to assign his claim against the insurance company to Gray in exchange for Gray's releasing Speed of any obligation to pay the judgment. Shortly thereafter Gray sued Grain Dealers and R.W. Parker to recover the amount of the judgment. After Gray filed his suit against Grain Dealers and Parker, Grain Dealers filed, in its own name, a "motion for relief from judgment" in the previous suit that Gray had filed against Speed. The court granted Gray's responsive motion to strike Grain Dealers' motion, on the grounds that Grain Dealers was not a party to that suit, and that the assignment released Speed from any obligation under the suit. In response to the suit filed against it, Grain Dealers asserted that it was only liable under the policy to indemnify Speed and by reason of the assignment, Speed's liability to Gray—and any liability of Grain Dealers to Speed or Gray—was extinguished. Alternatively, the company claimed it could not be held liable under North Carolina law in excess of its policy limits for only negligence, to which the company had stipulated. On cross motions for summary judgment, the district court awarded Gray the full amount of the default judgment against Grain Dealers, notwithstanding its recognition that the result was "harsh."

II.

[Part II of the opinion holding that North Carolina law applied to the case is omitted.]

III.

We therefore examine first Grain Dealers' contention that under North Carolina law, it is not liable in excess of policy limits for ordinary negligence in handling Gray's claim against Speed. If appellant is correct, then Speed had no claim in excess of policy limits against the company that could have been assigned to Gray, and the assignment would be, at least in part, a nullity.

Although North Carolina law is by no means crystal clear on the point, we think appellee has the better argument. It may well be that in North Carolina, if the insurance company actively assumes the defense of an insured, it is not liable for mere negligence in failing to gain the best settlement for the insured. In that event, a showing of bad faith may be required to recover in excess of policy limits. Coca–Cola Bottling Co. v. Maryland Casualty Co., 325 F.Supp. 204, 206 (W.D.N.C.1971).

Still, the Supreme Court of North Carolina and lower courts have described the insurer's settlement duty as "to act diligently and in good faith." Alford v. Textile Ins. Co., 248 N.C. 224, 103 S.E.2d 8, 12 (1958) (emphasis added); Coca–Cola Bottling Co., 325 F.Supp. at 206; Abernethy v. Utica Mut. Ins. Co., 373 F.2d 565, 568 (4th Cir.1967). It is surely impossible to characterize the company's conduct in this case as diligent. Although the North Carolina courts may wish to insulate insurance companies from liability for "honest mistakes of judgment" Coca–Cola, 325 F.Supp. at 206 (which might be characterized as negligent), we detect no solicitude for the insurance company that negligently fails to exercise any judgment at all. Indeed, Grain Dealers' stipulated negligence in this case may even be indistinguishable from bad faith under North Carolina law. In Abernethy, the Fourth Circuit heard an appeal from summary judgment granted in "a case of a flat refusal to negotiate under circumstances that * * * gave rise to an obligation to engage with bona fides in settlement negotiations." 373 F.2d at 569. Deciding that a jury question was presented, the court found that "the flat refusal to negotiate, under the circumstances of substantial exposure to liability, a demonstrated receptive climate for settlement and limited insurance coverage, *could have been found to show lack of good faith* in [the insurer's] exercise of its exclusive power to settle." Id. at 570 (emphasis added).

Even assuming it could be liable in excess of policy limits as a result of its behavior, Grain Dealers further argues that it is not liable to Gray because the judgment against Speed was not paid or shown to be payable. Appellant contends that in order to recover against the insurance company, Gray must prove that Speed would have paid the judgment against Gray, otherwise the insurance company is liable for more than its insured's true damage. Grain Dealers argues that the value of Speed's claim against the insurance company should be modified by his ability to pay the judgment to Gray. If the modification is not made, then, through the assignment-release, a silk purse has been made out of a sow's ear. Although no direct evidence was presented by either party as to Speed's net worth, his earnings, or his intention to attempt to pay the judgment prior to the assignment and release, we could infer from the record that Speed was a man of modest means.

Under circumstances such as this, where the insured has not yet paid any of the judgment, there is a split of authority among the states as to the extent of an insurance company's liability to the assignee of its insured for a claim above the policy limit. The majority of jurisdictions adheres to the judgment rule:[15] "an entry of judgment in excess [of policy limits] alone is sufficient damage to sustain a recovery from an insurer for its breach of duty." Carter v. Pioneer Mut. Casualty Co., 67 Ohio St.2d 146, 423 N.E.2d 188, 190 (1981). To be sure, not all of the states following the judgment rule have considered the case of an insolvent or bankrupt insured, which presents the most difficult challenge to the integrity of the judgment rule.[16] (But, of course, Speed was never found to be insolvent.)[17] The minority, concerned about collusion between the insured and the assignee, follows the payment rule and limits the insurance company's liability to that portion of the judgment that equals "the amount of [the insured's] assets not exempt from legal process."[18]

15. Those states supporting the judgment rule are: Alabama, Arizona, Arkansas, California, Delaware, Florida, Georgia, Illinois, Indiana, Iowa, Kansas, Kentucky, Louisiana, Maryland, Massachusetts, Minnesota, Missouri, Montana, New Hampshire, New Mexico, Ohio, Oregon, Pennsylvania, South Carolina, Tennessee, Texas, and Utah. Annotation, Liability Insurer's Failure to Settle, 63 A.L.R.3d 630, 641–69 (1975 & Supp.1986); Torrez v. State Farm Mut. Auto. Ins. Co., 705 F.2d 1192, 1197–1201 (10th Cir.1982).

16. The following states have applied the judgment rule where the insured (or his estate) was insolvent or even bankrupt: California, Florida, Indiana, Iowa, Kansas, Louisiana, Maryland, Minnesota, Montana, New Mexico, Ohio, South Carolina, and Tennessee; but see n. 8. Although not squarely presented with an insolvent or bankrupt insured, courts in Alabama, Delaware, Georgia, Illinois, Massachusetts, New Hampshire, Pennsylvania, Texas, and Utah have written dicta indicating that the judgment rule would be followed in those states under such circumstances. Arizona, Arkansas, Kentucky, Missouri, and Oregon endorse the judgment rule without discussing the solvency of the insured. Annotation, Liability Insurer's Failure to Settle, 63 A.L.R.3d 630, 641–69 (1975 & Supp.1986).

17. In any event, even if Speed were to have been found insolvent, Grain Dealers would be disadvantaged by the language of the contract: "Bankruptcy or insolvency of the *covered person* shall not relieve us of any obligations under this policy."

18. In addition to Michigan, California, Connecticut and New York have endorsed the payment rule noting that where an insured (or his estate) is insolvent or bankrupt no damage is shown to have harmed him. Annotation, Liability Insurer's Failure to Settle, 63 A.L.R.3d 630, 641–69 (1975). The California courts distinguish between the case of an insured who dies penniless

Stockdale v. Jamison, 416 Mich. 217, 330 N.W.2d 389, 390–91 (1982). If the insurance company were to be obliged to pay more than the insured was capable of paying at the time of the assignment and release, the insurance company, it has been thought, would be charged punitive damages. Gordon v. Nationwide Mut. Ins. Co., 30 N.Y.2d 427, 334 N.Y.S.2d 601, 611, 285 N.E.2d 849 (1972) (Fuld, C.J., concurring), cert. denied, 410 U.S. 931, 93 S.Ct. 1374, 35 L.Ed.2d 593 (1973). Although it is never fully articulated, a somewhat different perception of normal behavior underlies these rules. The courts appear to be in fundamental disagreement over the issue of whether or not it is proper to presume that a person will attempt to pay his debts, and therefore that a judgment against an insured, in itself, can be assumed to be good for full value.

Unfortunately, North Carolina courts have not been obliged to choose which line of authority they prefer. A court of appeals has held that an insurance company was not liable where an insured and a plaintiff (injured party) entered into a consent judgment which, by its terms, provided that it was not enforceable against the insured. Huffman v. Peerless Ins. Co., 17 N.C.App. 292, 193 S.E.2d 773, 774, cert. denied, 283 N.C. 257, 195 S.E.2d 689 (1973). The Supreme Court, however, in Alford v. Textile Ins. Co., 248 N.C. 224, 103 S.E.2d 8 (1958), said: "If the insurer had failed to make these settlements, and judgments for greater amounts had been obtained against its insured; it would * * * be liable to [the tortfeasor/insured] for such amounts as the judgments exceeded the amounts for which the insurer could have settled * * *. *The liability imposed on the insurer would not * * * be affected or diminished by the question of solvency or insolvency of its insured.*" Id. 103 S.E.2d at 12. (citations omitted and emphasis added). Although dictum, that passage suggests sympathy with the policies underlying the judgment rule. Therefore we think we would be safe in concluding that, under North Carolina law, introduction of the judgment is at least prima facie evidence that the insured was obligated, willing, and capable of paying the judgment. It may be open to the insurer to challenge that evidence or even to show collusion but Grain Dealers produced no such evidence here.

We note, moreover, that the insurance contract states that Grain Dealers "will pay damages for bodily injury or property damage for which any covered person becomes *legally responsible* because of an auto accident." It seems rather clear to us that after the judgment but before

and then has a judgment levied against his estate (payment rule applies) and an insured who is forced into bankruptcy by a judgment (judgment rule applies). In New York, the rule varies according to the circumstances in which it is applied: "1) where the assured pays part of the judgment or is solvent enough to do so at the time of the excess judgment, the judgment rule applies and he is entitled to the full amount of the excess as his damages; 2) where he was insolvent before the judgment and obtained a bankruptcy discharge after it, he is not damaged and may not recover for it; and 3) where he was insolvent or nearly insolvent prior to the judgment the jury must consider his past, his prospects, and other economic factors and assess his damages." Levantino v. Insurance Co. of N. Am., 102 Misc.2d 77, 422 N.Y.S.2d 995, 1002 (1979).

the assignment and release, Speed was legally responsible to pay the judgment, whether or not he ever intended to pay. So we conclude under North Carolina law Grain Dealers could be made liable for the whole judgment.

IV.

That brings us to question whether or not the assignment and release were self-contradicting. According to the insurance company, the release nullified the assignment of the claim because the release extinguished the basis for the assignment. If so, that which Speed assigned to Gray was worthless upon transfer. This somewhat metaphysical contention is to be tested first according to D.C. law because it depends on a construction of the agreement reached between the two parties in the District. We note somewhat ruefully that there are no cases in the District squarely on point. However, many other jurisdictions have considered similar transactions and the majority of them have allowed the transfer.[19] A few courts have taken the path urged by the appellant, and have held that a similar transaction was ineffective in passing the claim against the insurance company to the assignee. It is apparent that underlying the construction of the assignment and release made by those courts declining to uphold them is the concern—discussed in the previous portion of the opinion—about collusion between the insured and the assignee. See, e.g., Freeman v. Schmidt Real Estate & Ins., 755 F.2d 135, 138–39 (8th Cir.1985) (where insurer, like insured, is no longer "legally obligated to pay" court cites fear of collusion as policy rationale for declining to give effect to assignment/release); Bendall v. White, 511 F.Supp. 793, 794–95 (N.D.Ala.1981) (same).[20] That policy rationale arises not so much out of a construction of the assignment and release, but rather stems from an evaluation of the insurance company's liability under the insurance policy. As we have already concluded, North Carolina law determines liability under the insurance policy. We think it would be quite artificial therefore to allow these policy considerations to enter into our interpretation of the assignment and release. That would be so even if D.C. law reflected these anti-collusion considerations—

19. Steedly v. London & Lancashire Ins. Co., 416 F.2d 259, 262 (6th Cir.1969) (assignment/release did not free insurer from liability; if insured "had satisfied judgment by making full payment * * * in return for the release, [insurer] agrees that he could have then brought an action against it or have assigned this right"); LaRotunda v. Royal Globe Ins. Co., 87 Ill.App.3d 446, 42 Ill.Dec. 219, 408 N.E.2d 928 (1980) (agreement not to collect against insured given in exchange for assignment of rights against insurer evidenced no collusion); Metcalf v. Hartford Accident & Indem. Co., 176 Neb. 468, 126 N.W.2d 471, 475–76 (1964) (rejecting insurer's contention that consent judgment created no legal obligation to pay); Zander v. Casualty Ins. Co., 259 Cal.App.2d 793, 66 Cal.Rptr. 561, 568 (1968) (settlement with insured does not release insurer because to do so penalizes insured for attempt to minimize damages); Critz v. Farmers Ins. Group, 230 Cal.App.2d 788, 41 Cal. Rptr. 401, 404 (1964) (assignment of chose of action in exchange for release from liability before judgment entered against insured not void against public policy because assignment's value is determined by bad faith of insurer).

20. See also Steil v. Florida Physicians' Ins. Reciprocal, 448 So.2d 589, 592 (Fla. Dist.Ct.App.1984) (suspicion of collusion and fraud led court to deny effect to settlement agreement/assignment but, in dictum, court indicated that such an agreement may be upheld where free from taint).

which it does not—because the *effect* of the assignment on the insurance company must be governed by North Carolina law. See Fox–Greenwald Sheet Metal Co. v. Markowitz Bros., 452 F.2d 1346, 1354 (D.C.Cir.1971).

Accordingly, we see no reason why, under D.C. and North Carolina law, we should not construe the assignment and release to give full effect to its terms. After all, if the release of Speed extinguished the claim Speed had against the insurance company simultaneously with the assignment of the claim, that would also be true of that part of the claim Speed had against the insurance company within the policy limits. As appellee points out, appellant's argument reduces to an absurd conclusion: if the insured were to have paid the judgment in full and obtained a release from the injured party, he would have no right to proceed against the insurer for indemnification. We think appellant's self-destruct interpretation of the document can only be adopted for policy reasons quite apart from appropriate legal methods of document construction, and therefore the judgment of the district court is

Affirmed.

Notes

1. See Annotation, Bankruptcy or insolvency of insured as affecting right of person injured to proceeds of indemnity insurance, in absence of provision in policy in that regard 59 A.L.R. 1123 (1929).

2. Michigan statutes provide that liability policies, with certain exemptions, contain "a provision that the insolvency or bankruptcy of the person insured shall not release the insurer from the payment of damages for injury sustained or loss occasioned * * *." M.C.L.A. §§ 500.3004, 500.3006. Upon the return unsatisfied of an execution on the insured, an action in the nature of a writ of garnishment may be maintained against the insurer "under the terms of the policy for the amount of the judgment in the said action not exceeding the amount of the policy." M.C.L.A. § 500.3006.

3. California has a statutory provision similar to the first of those quoted above: West's Ann. Cal. Insurance Code § 11580, which provides:

§ 11580. Insolvency, bankruptcy, or death of insured

A policy insuring against losses set forth in subdivision (a) shall not be issued or delivered to any person in this state unless it contains the provisions set forth in subdivision (b). * * *

(b) * * *

(1) A provision that the insolvency or bankruptcy of the insured will not release the insurer from the payment of damages for injury sustained or loss occasioned during the life of such policy.

(2) A provision that whenever judgment is secured against the insured or the executor or administrator of a deceased insured in an action based upon bodily injury, death, or property damage, then an action may be brought against the insurer on the policy and subject to its terms and limitations, by such judgment creditor to recover on the judgment.

Subsection 11580(b)(2) "makes the judgment creditor a third party beneficiary of the insurance contract between the insurer and the insured." Murphy v. Allstate Insurance Company, 17 Cal.3d 937, 943, 132 Cal.Rptr. 424, 428, 553 P.2d 584, 588 (1976).

4. Recall *Crisci v. Security Insurance Co.* discussed within the context of an implied covenant of good faith and fair dealing in Chapter 4. *Crisci* demonstrates that the duty to settle is inherently linked to the insurer's duty to act in good faith toward the insured's interests when a third party claim is raised. While neither of these duties is included as an express term in an insurance contract, courts have readily affirmed judgments in excess of an insured's policy limits when the facts indicated that the insurer acted in bad faith or rejected the opportunity to settle the case prior to judgment. Another important element to recall from the *Crisci* case is that a bad faith-based failure to settle can give rise to a claim of the insurer in both contract and tort theories of liability. Thus, the insurer can be liable not only for the third party's judgment in excess of the insured's policy limits, but also for punitive or exemplary damages to the insured because of a tort claim of mental distress.

5. Dean Kent Syverud has written a comprehensive discussion on the insurer's duty to settle. Kent D. Syverud, *The Duty to Settle*, 76 Va. L. Rev. 1113 (1990).

C. THE INSURED'S UNDERTAKING

The contract alluded to in the *Aerojet–General v. Transport Indemnity* case above is not entirely one-sided. In return for the insurer's undertaking, the insured is required to supply consideration in the form of premiums. Additionally, the insured is subject to a number of obligations required as part of the policy or required as a matter of substantive law.

1. Notice Requirements for Liability Claims

SECURITY MUTUAL INSURANCE CO. OF NEW YORK v. ACKER–FITZSIMONS CORP.

Court of Appeals of New York, 1972.
31 N.Y.2d 436, 340 N.Y.S.2d 902, 293 N.E.2d 76.

Jasen, Judge.

The issue on this appeal is whether the insured complied with a liability insurance policy provision requiring notice to the insurer "as soon as practicable" after the "occurrence".[21]

On November 29, 1964, Security Mutual Insurance Company of New York (Security Mutual) issued its Owner's, Landlords' and Tenants' Liability Policy to Fernley Realty Corp. (Fernley) insuring it against liability for personal injuries arising from the operation of certain

21. An occurrence is defined in the policy as "an event, or continuous or repeated exposure to conditions, which unexpectedly causes injury during the policy period."

premises located at 2–10 East 196 Street, Bronx, New York. In addition to the named insured, the policy covered Norman Levy, president of Fernley, and Acker–Fitzsimons Corp. (Acker–Fitzsimons), managing agents of the property.

On May 23, 1965, a major fire occurred on the insured premises and three days later the New York City Department of Buildings lodged certain structural violations against them. The buildings were again swept by fire on October 4, 1965, during the course of which three firemen, defendants Adams, Harrington and Manning, were allegedly injured. The buildings were subsequently demolished.

Levy evidently learned of the second fire (but not the personal injuries) on the afternoon of its occurrence. On November 9, 1965, he heard "rumors"[22] that certain unnamed firemen had been injured in the October 4 fire. He then telephoned this information to James Kannar, Fernley's insurance broker, and followed up with a letter, also dated November 9, instructing him to notify the insurer of the claimed injuries. Kannar was of the view that until a more concrete claim was made, there was no obligation to report the incident to the insurer. He also opined that since firemen go at their own risk, there was no liability anyway.

In ordinary course, the plaintiff issued a renewal policy for the premises. But on November 15, 1965, before the effective date of the renewal policy, Kannar wrote to Security Mutual advising it of the contemplated demolition of the premises. Telephone conversations followed on November 16 between Kannar and Theodore Moschitta, an employee of Security Mutual, during which Moschitta was advised of the fire of October 4, but no mention was made of any personal injuries. The policy was subsequently canceled on January 6, 1966.

On December 19, 1965, the *Sunday News* reported that two firemen (Adams and Manning) had filed a claim for $1,500,000 against the City of New York for injuries allegedly sustained in the fire of October 4. Mention was also made of alleged liability of the owners and operators of the premises. The article was brought to Levy's attention, who, on December 27, 1965, forwarded a copy to Kannar, together with a letter stating that he believed it should be forwarded to the liability carrier. Kannar took no action, apparently believing that, absent some more substantial basis, there was nothing to report to the carrier.

In October, 1966, the firemen, Adams and Manning, now joined by Harrington, commenced the prime action by serving a summons and complaint on the City of New York only. Service upon Fernley and Acker–Fitzsimons was effected by service upon the Secretary of State on April 28, 1967. Levy was personally served on June 23, 1967. Upon receiving the summons, the defendant Acker–Fitzsimons promptly notified Security Mutual of the pendency of the action—some 19 months after the actual occurrence.

22. The "rumors" consisted of a phone call to Levy from an unnamed person.

Notice provisions in insurance policies afford the insurer an opportunity to protect itself, and the giving of the required notice is a condition to the insurer's liability. (Rushing v. Commercial Cas. Ins. Co., 251 N.Y. 302, 167 N.E. 450.) Absent a valid excuse, a failure to satisfy the notice requirement vitiates the policy (Deso v. London & Lancashire Ind. Co., 3 N.Y.2d 127, 164 N.Y.S.2d 689, 143 N.E.2d 889; Insurance Law, Consol.Laws, c. 28, § 167, subd. 1, par. [d]), and the insurer need not show prejudice before it can assert the defense of noncompliance. (31 N.Y.Jur., Insurance, § 1262.)

There may be circumstances, such as lack of knowledge that an accident has occurred, that will explain or excuse delay in giving notice and show it to be reasonable. (Rushing v. Commercial Cas. Co., 251 N.Y. 302, 167 N.E. 450, supra; Woolverton v. Fidelity & Cas. Co. of N.Y., 190 N.Y. 41, 82 N.E. 745.) But the insured has the burden of proof thereon. (Rushing v. Commercial Cas. Co., 251 N.Y. 302, 167 N.E. 450, supra.) Moreover, he must exercise reasonable care and diligence to keep himself informed of accidents out of which claims for damages may arise.

Then, too, a good-faith belief of nonliability may excuse or explain a seeming failure to give timely notice. (875 Forest Ave. Corp. v. Aetna Cas. & Sur. Co., 37 A.D.2d 11, 322 N.Y.S.2d 53, affd. 30 N.Y.2d 726, 332 N.Y.S.2d 896, 283 N.E.2d 768; Woolverton v. Fidelity & Cas. Co. of N.Y., 190 N.Y. 41, 82 N.E. 745, supra; 31 N.Y.Jur., Insurance, § 1281.) But the insured's belief must be reasonable under all the circumstances, and it may be relevant on the issue of reasonableness, whether and to what extent, the insured has inquired into the circumstances of the accident or occurrence. Haas Tobacco Co. v. American Fid. Co., 226 N.Y. 343, 123 N.E. 755, * * *

Finally, a provision that notice be given "as soon as practicable" after an accident or occurrence, merely requires that notice be given within a reasonable time under all the circumstances. Deso v. London & Lancashire Ind. Co., 3 N.Y.2d 127, 164 N.Y.S.2d 689, 143 N.E.2d 889. * * *

The Appellate Division, 39 A.D.2d 34, 330 N.Y.S.2d 865, was of the view that the insureds had no direct knowledge that injuries had resulted from the fire of October 4, 1965, and that the insureds' belief of nonliability was reasonable. The majority concluded that the notice given upon receiving the summons in the prime action (some 19 months after the occurrence) was, therefore, given as soon as practicable. We disagree.

On December 19, the *Sunday News* reported that two firemen had filed claims against the City of New York for injuries allegedly sustained in the October 4 fire. Mention was also made in the article of the possible liability of the owners and operators of the premises. This article was brought to the attention of the insureds, Levy and Acker–Fitzsimons, in late December. While this information was, in our view, sufficient to apprise the insureds of the occurrence, of itself, it probably was not a sufficient predicate for giving immediate notice. However, it seems to us that such information would cause a reasonable and prudent person to investigate the circumstances, ascertain the facts, and evaluate his potential liability, particularly where there were, at the time of the alleged injuries, existent violations against the premises involving structural deficiencies caused by the first fire (May 23, 1965). Similarly, although the belief that firemen go at their own risk generally accords with the law, (see, e.g., McGee v. Adams Paper & Twine Co., 26 A.D.2d 186, 271 N.Y.S.2d 698, affd. 20 N.Y.2d 921, 286 N.Y.S.2d 274, 233 N.E.2d 289), under these circumstances, and absent an investigation of the facts, the insured's bare reliance on that belief would appear to be unreasonable.[23]

The recent case of 875 Forest Ave. Corp. v. Aetna Cas. Corp. (37 A.D.2d 11, 322 N.Y.S.2d 53, affd. 30 N.Y.2d 726, 332 N.Y.S.2d 896, 283 N.E.2d 768, supra), relied upon by the majority at the Appellate Division, is distinguishable. In that case a three-year-old child fell from a fourth floor apartment window and was killed. It was held that delayed notice of the accident did not breach the notice provision where the insured, acting as a reasonable and prudent person, believed he was not liable. That accident, however, simply was not one which would lead a reasonable person to envision any possible liability on the part of the insured corporate owner of the building. In fact, the circumstances (of which the insured apprised itself) indicated negligence on the part of the child's mother. Here, the insureds had information (the newspaper article) about personal injuries arising from a fire at their building against which certain structural violations had been posted—yet they failed to pursue the facts or reasonably evaluate their potential liability.

In sum, we conclude that the insureds failed to exercise reasonable care and diligence in ascertaining the facts about the alleged accident and in evaluating their potential liability. Thus, the otherwise unreasonable delay of 19 months in giving notice may not be excused or explained on the basis of "lack of knowledge" or a "belief of nonliability".

For the reasons stated, the order of the Appellate Division should be reversed and the judgment of the Supreme Court, Bronx County, reinstated.

Notes

1. In 1981 North Carolina reversed a long line of decisions to the effect that the requirement of notice by the insured "as soon as practicable" was a condition precedent to coverage under a liability policy so that it was immaterial whether the insurer was prejudiced by delay. With the holding in *Great American Insurance Co. v. C.G. Tate Construction Co.*, 303 N.C. 387, 279 S.E.2d 769 (1981), that a showing of prejudice was required, the court then proceeded to the question of which party should have the burden of proof on the issue of prejudice.

23. As we have previously noted, Levy was sufficiently concerned about the alleged injuries that he instructed his insurance broker to inform the carrier. But this did not constitute the notice contemplated by the policy since a broker is normally the agent of the insured and notice to the ordinary insurance broker is not notice to the liability carrier.

The authorities are split on this issue. Some hold that because the insured is seeking relief from the literal meaning of the terms of the contract, he should bear the burden of showing that his delay has not materially prejudiced the insurer. E.g., Hartford Accident & Indemnity Co. v. Lochmandy Buick Sales, Inc., 302 F.2d 565 (7th Cir.1962); Dairyland Insurance Co. v. Cunningham, 360 F.Supp. 139 (D.Colo.1973). Other jurisdictions have reasoned that the burden of showing prejudice should be on the insurer because it is seeking to escape its obligation to defend and indemnify, the very thing which it is paid to do. E.g., State Farm Mutual Automobile Insurance Co. v. Milam, 438 F.Supp. 227; Cooper v. Government Employees Insurance Co., 51 N.J. 86, 237 A.2d 870. "[A]lthough the policy may speak in terms of 'condition precedent' * * *, nonetheless what is involved is a forfeiture, for the carrier seeks, on account of a breach of that provision, to deny the insured the very thing paid for." Id. at 93–94, 237 A.2d at 873.

We believe the sounder rule to be that requiring the insurer to prove that it has been materially prejudiced by the delay. If the insurer has the burden of proving prejudice, then when it receives a delayed notification the rule will encourage the insurer to make a prompt preliminary investigation of the claim to protect its interests. An investigation may reveal that the delay has materially prejudiced the insurer, and, in that event, the insurer may deny coverage and either wait for a suit against it or file suit for declaratory relief. If, on the other hand, the preliminary investigation reveals that the ability of the insurer to investigate and defend has not been materially prejudiced, the insurer, presumably, will proceed with the claim and the question of coverage will never reach the courts. Additionally, the insurer, because it is an expert in investigation of accidents, is in a much better position to know what factors are relevant to its ability to investigate and to recognize prejudice. An insured would be in a far less enviable position if he had the burden of showing an absence of prejudice. Indeed, the insured would be forced to prove a negative. Placing the burden of showing prejudice on the insurer encourages an adequate investigation by the qualified party at the earliest possible time. These factors lead us to conclude that the burden of proof on the issue of prejudice is properly placed on the insurer.

* * *

The rule which we adopt today amounts to a reversal of a long line of previous cases upon which insurers have justifiably relied. Lest this decision be perceived as encouraging dilatory tactics in the notification of the insurer and, thus, as being unfair to insurers, we also now impose the requirement that any period of delay beyond the limits of timeliness be shown *by the insured* to have been in good faith. Anyone who knows that he may be at fault or that others have claimed he is at fault and who purposefully and knowingly fails to notify ought not to recover even if no prejudice results. Equity dictates that a bad faith delay in notifying an insurer, even though no material prejudice results, should bar the insured from enforcing the policy. This requirement is in accord with the common law principle that implicit in every contract is the obligation of each party to act in good faith.

The effect of this decision is to create a three-step test for determining whether the insurer is obliged to defend. When faced with a claim that notice was not timely given, the trier of fact must first decide whether the notice was given as soon as practicable. If not, the trier of fact must decide whether the insured has shown that he acted in good faith, e.g., that he had no actual knowledge that a claim might be filed against him. If the good faith test is met the burden then shifts to the insurer to show that its ability to investigate and defend was materially prejudiced by the delay.

2. In contrast to the New York rule described in *Security Mutual*, California's "notice-prejudice" rule operates to bar insurers from denying coverage on the basis of lack of timely notice unless the insurance company can show actual prejudice from the delay in providing notice to the insurer of a potential trigger for coverage. Prejudice may not be presumed from delayed notice alone. The notice provisions in insurance contracts are intended to aid the insurer in investigating, settling, and defending claims. See Truck Ins. Exchange v. Unigard Ins. Co., 79 Cal.App.4th 966, 975, 94 Cal.Rptr.2d 516 (2000); Shell Oil Co. v. Winterthur Swiss Insurance Co., 12 Cal.App.4th 715, 15 Cal.Rptr.2d 815 (1993).

3. *"Reinsurance" policies.* In *Unigard Sec. Ins. Co. v. North River Ins. Co.*, 79 N.Y.2d 576, 584 N.Y.S.2d 290, 594 N.E.2d 571 (1992), the plaintiff company issued a "facultative reinsurance" policy to North River Ins. Co. A facultative reinsurance policy is typically held by a small insurance company, (the "primary insurer") by which it is able to minimize its exposure to large risks by contracting with a larger insurance company (the "reinsurer") who will indemnify the primary insurer in the event of a large judgement for which it would otherwise be liable. This allows the primary insurer (in this case, North River) to reduce the amount of required reserves for the protection of policyholders and increase the company's ability to underwrite more policies. The reinsurer does not assume liability for losses paid, it merely agrees to indemnify the primary insurer. In *Unigard,* North River found, as a result of massive asbestos litigation involving its insureds, its reinsurance policy with Unigard would be implicated. Unigard denied coverage based on late notice by North River, and cited *Security Mutual* for the proposition that the reinsurer need not show prejudice to successfully deny coverage on the policy. However, the New York Court of Appeal disagreed, and found that the "no prejudice" rule did not apply to reinsurance contracts. The court reasoned that reinsurance contracts are distinguishable from primary insurance contracts, in that the only obligation of the reinsurer is to indemnify the primary insurer; the duty of the reinsurer does not extend to providing a defense, for investigating a claim, or for conducting settlement negotiations. Therefore, the requirement of notice in the reinsurance context is of much less significance to a reinsurer than to a primary insurer. Further, the court found that the reinsurer and the primary insurer have similar interests in the outcome of the case, unlike the relationship between the primary insurer and its insured in which the interests of the parties are often adverse. The court concluded that "* * * the reinsurer must demonstrate how it was prejudicial and may not rely on the presumption of prejudice that applies in the late notice disputes between primary insurers and their insureds." *Id.* at 584.

4. In 2002, the New York Court of Appeal seemed to signal a concern with the notice prejudice rule noting that it was in the distinct minority of

jurisdictions that adhere to the rule. Brandon v. Nationwide Mut. Ins. Co., 97 N.Y.2d 491, 495–96, 769 N.E.2d 810, 813, 743 N.Y.S.2d 53, 56 (2002)(observing that New York was in the minority but that the case didn't reasonably raise the issue). In a recent memorandum opinion, however, the New York Court of Appeal still cited *Acker–Fitzsimons* as controlling authority on validity of the notice prejudice rule. Great Canal Realty Corp. v. Seneca Ins. Co., 5 N.Y.3d 742, 743, 833 N.E.2d 1196, 1197, 800 N.Y.S.2d 521, 522 (2005).

2. The Insured's Duty of Cooperation

OGUNSUADA v. GENERAL ACCIDENT INS. CO. OF AMERICA

Supreme Court of Rhode Island, 1997.
695 A.2d 996.

Before WEISBERGER, C.J., and LEDERBERG, BOURCIER, FLANDERS, and GOLDBERG, JJ.

OPINION

BOURCIER, JUSTICE.

This matter comes before us on the appeal of the plaintiff, Olajide Ogunsuada (plaintiff), from a final judgment entered in favor of the defendant, General Accident Insurance Company of America (General Accident), on General Accident's motion for summary judgment filed in the Superior Court.

On December 31, 1987, Philip Guilbeault (Guilbeault) was involved in a motor-vehicle accident with the plaintiff in Providence, Rhode Island. At the time of the accident Guilbeault was insured by General Accident under a Massachusetts policy.

General Accident was notified of the accident on January 21, 1988, through General Accident's counsel. General Accident acknowledged receipt of the claim on February 1, 1988. After attempts at negotiating a settlement failed, the plaintiff filed suit against Guilbeault on July 2, 1990. Guilbeault was served with notice of that action through the Registrar of Motor Vehicles and by certified mail mailed to his resident address at 25 County Street in Blackstone, Massachusetts. The return receipt for the certified mail was signed, but the signature was unintelligible.

A copy of the summons and complaint was also sent to General Accident. In response, General Accident assigned defense counsel to the case. On July 26, 1990, General Accident sent a letter to Guilbeault acknowledging receipt of the complaint. By that letter General Accident also informed Guilbeault of the name, address, and telephone number of defense counsel and indicated that it was necessary for Guilbeault to advise General Accident of any changes in his address. On August 10, 1990, defense counsel for General Accident entered his appearance on behalf of Guilbeault.

In September 1990, the plaintiff served Guilbeault with interrogatories, which were forwarded to Guilbeault on September 17, 1990, by General Accident's defense counsel. Those interrogatories were sent to the 25 County Street address. After receiving no response to the interrogatories, General Accident sent two additional letters by certified mail to Guilbeault on October 10 and October 24, 1990. The return receipt for the October 24 letter, in which General Accident reminded Guilbeault of the provision in his policy requiring that he cooperate with General Accident in the defense of his action or risk losing his coverage, was signed by a "Richard Guilbeault," apparently a relative of Guilbeault's. No response to those letters, however, was ever received by General Accident.

On March 12, 1991, General Accident sent Guilbeault yet another letter that requested him to contact defense counsel immediately regarding his then-pending interrogatories. That letter was returned to General Accident with a notation indicating a forwarding address of 165 Main Street, Blackstone, Massachusetts. The letter was remailed to that Main Street address, but still no response was received.

On October 7, 1991, the plaintiff's complaint was the subject of court-annexed arbitration. Liability was contested by General Accident, but Guilbeault, still not reached, did not appear or testify. As a result, the defense to the plaintiff's claim was presented solely through documents prepared by General Accident's claim investigators and counsel's argument. Notwithstanding Guilbeault's absence, judgment was entered for the defendant. The plaintiff rejected the arbitrator's decision and appealed to the Superior Court.

In May 1992, General Accident hired Diamond Skip Tracing (Diamond) in order to definitively locate Guilbeault. Diamond confirmed the Main Street address. General Accident again sent a letter by certified mail to that address, informing Guilbeault that he was in danger of being defaulted in the pending civil action for failure to answer plaintiff's interrogatories. He was further reminded that his failure to cooperate with General Accident would result in a voiding of the policy. The certified letter was returned as unclaimed and remailed by General Accident by general mail to that same address. Another letter giving Guilbeault seven days to respond before General Accident discontinued its defense of the action was sent on June 5, 1992.

A final letter was sent on July 27, 1992, to Guilbeault and requested that he respond within seven days. On September 10, 1992, after receiving no response to the July 27 letter, a claims representative from General Accident called the telephone number he had for Guilbeault and was informed by a child who answered the telephone call that Guilbeault had moved to Florida.

Counsel for General Accident then filed his motion to withdraw as counsel for Guilbeault and forwarded a copy thereof to Guilbeault at his County Street address on September 10, 1992. The return receipt for the letter was signed "M. Guilbeault." The motion, when called for hearing on September 30, 1992, was passed. A new motion to withdraw was filed on October 5 and assigned to be heard on October 14, 1992.[24] The plaintiff objected to defense counsel's motion to withdraw but did not press that objection at the time of the hearing on the motion. The motion was granted by the trial justice sitting on the formal and special cause calendar. A copy of the resulting order was sent to Guilbeault at the 25 County Street address on October 15, 1992. No appeal was taken therefrom.

Some eighteen months later, on April 21, 1994, the plaintiff recovered a default judgment in the Superior Court against Guilbeault in the amount of $22,937.75 plus interest and costs. In an attempt to collect that judgment, the plaintiff filed the present action against General Accident, allegedly pursuant to G.L. 1956 § 27–7–2. General Accident moved for summary judgment on the basis of Guilbeault's lack of cooperation that, General Accident contended, voided the policy. General Accident asserted further that pursuant to § 27–7–2 the plaintiff had no rights against General Accident other than those rights that were derivative of Guilbeault's rights under the policy. General Accident took the position that because the policy was voided, which eliminated Guilbeault's rights under the policy, the plaintiff stood in no better position under the policy than did Guilbeault. The plaintiff asserted in response to General Accident's voiding-of-policy contention that the policy was ambiguous concerning the effect of Guilbeault's failure to cooperate and that that ambiguity created a question of fact that should not be decided on a motion for summary judgment. After hearing the arguments of counsel, the trial justice granted summary judgment in favor of General Accident. We conclude that the trial justice's determination was correct and that the plaintiff has no right of recovery against General Accident pursuant to the insurance policy that had existed between General Accident and Guilbeault but had been voided by Guilbeault's failure to cooperate.

In the policy provision insuring Guilbeault that is entitled "Our Agreement," General Accident agreed "to provide the insurance protection [Guilbeault] purchased for accidents which happen while this policy is in force." In that same section Guilbeault, in return for General Accident's insurance protection, agreed "to pay premiums and any Merit Rating surcharges when due and to cooperate with us in case of accidents or claims." Another policy section entitled "When There Is An Accident Or Loss" provided that "after an accident or loss, you or anyone else covered under this policy must cooperate with us in the investigation, settlement and defense of any claim or lawsuit. We must be sent copies of all legal documents in connection with the accident or loss." Those two provisions clearly and unambiguously set forth the mandate that Guilbeault was requested to cooperate with General Accident in the defense of any claim brought against Guilbeault.

24. There is no evidence in the record indicating that Guilbeault was ever sent notice of the hearing date for the second motion to withdraw.

Ordinarily an insured's failure to cooperate with the insurer after an occurrence giving rise to a claim against the insured creates a question of fact about whether the insurer has been so prejudiced by the insured's noncooperation as to permit the insurer to void the policy of insurance. See, e.g., American Guarantee and Liability Insurance Co. v. Chandler Manufacturing Co., 467 N.W.2d 226 (Iowa 1991). When, as in this case, a plaintiff is a judgment creditor of the insured, Guilbeault, "the burden of going forward with the evidence on the issue" of Guilbeault's noncooperation was upon defendant insurer. (citations omitted)

There exists, however, a notable minority view that an insured's unexcused or unexplained failure to cooperate is itself sufficient to void the policy and relieve the insurer of its liability without a showing of prejudice to the insurer. 9 A.L.R.4th at 236–56.

In Marley v. Bankers' Indemnity Insurance Co., 53 R.I. 289, 292, 166 A. 350, 351 (1933), we concluded that a cooperation provision was "not a covenant but a condition which if not complied with gives the insurer the right to terminate the policy."

In that case, Marley, the plaintiff, had obtained a judgment after trial against the defendant's insured and then proceeded on that judgment against the defendant insurer in a separate action. The insurer, Bankers Indemnity Insurance Co., interposed as one of its defenses the failure of its insured to cooperate. The trial justice, in the plaintiff's direct action against the insurer, concluded that the insurer failed to present sufficient evidence of the insured's alleged failure to cooperate, treating that defense as a question of fact, and found that the insurer could not avoid its liability on its policy.

Marley, it appears, finds itself in accord with what can be said to be the majority view that cooperation clauses in automobile liability policies are regarded as conditions precedent,[25] "so that no rights would accrue under the policy until they were satisfied." 8 Appleman, § 4771 at 214–15. Any alleged breach of a cooperation clause, however, has to be substantial as well as material in order to relieve the insurer of its liability under the policy, and a mere technical or inconsequential lack of cooperation would be insufficient to void the policy and the liability of the insurer. 8 Appleman, at § 4773; 14 Rhodes, at § 51:190.

In this case, the plaintiff is a judgment creditor seeking to recover against a judgment debtor's insurer under the debtor's automobile liability insurance policy. In such a situation we recognize the clear rule that the plaintiff stands in the shoes of the defendant's insured and is subject to any defenses that the insurer would have against its insured. When as here, the dispute and the defense involved concern an alleged breach of an insurance policy cooperation clause that is a condition

25. Other courts have construed cooperation clauses as a condition subsequent necessitating proof by the insurer of facts sufficient to relieve the insurer of liability. See, e.g., Anderson v. Slayton, 662 S.W.2d 575, 577 (Mo.Ct.App.1983); 7A Am.Jur.2d, Automobile Insurance § 463 (1980); Romualdo P. Eclavea, Annotation, Liability Insurance: Failure or Refusal of Insured to Attend Trial or to Testify as Breach of Co–Operation Clause, 9 A.L.R.4th 218, 236 (1981).

precedent to the insurer's liability, we believe that we should adopt the majority rule and reasoning recently expressed by the Supreme Court of Iowa in American Guarantee and Liability Insurance Co., supra.[26] There the Iowa court held that in order for a party claiming entitlement to recovery under a tort-feasor insured's policy, he or she must prove compliance by the insured with the cooperation clause policy by showing (1) that the insured substantially complied with the condition precedent cooperation clause, (2) that the insured's failure to cooperate was excused or waived, or (3) that the insured's failure to comply was not prejudicial to the insurer. In adopting that three-pronged rule, we note with similar approval the Iowa court's statement that the insurer's and the insured's obligations under an insurance policy's cooperation clause are reciprocal and require the insured to cooperate in good faith with the insurer and the insurer in good faith to use reasonable diligence in obtaining the insured's cooperation. 467 N.W.2d at 229. See also 9 A.L.R.4th at 256.

Applying the rules we have outlined to the facts in the record before us, we conclude that the plaintiff bore the burden of proving that Guilbeault had substantially complied with the cooperation provision in his liability insurance contract, that any failure on his part to do so was either excused or waived, or that his failure to comply was not prejudicial to the defendant insurer.

The record discloses that the plaintiff failed to meet his burden of proof in resisting the defendant's motion for summary judgment. If the motion record is viewed in the light most favorable to him, there is no evidence in that record by way of affidavit or pleading that could even remotely suggest to the motion justice that Guilbeault, despite diligent effort by General Accident for him to do so, had ever made any attempt to cooperate with General Accident in the defense of the plaintiff's action. On facts similar to those reflected in the record before us, the Massachusetts court in Polito v. Galluzzo, 337 Mass. 360, 149 N.E.2d 375 (1958), denied recovery against an insurer. See also Foshee v. Insurance Company of North America, 359 Mass. 471, 269 N.E.2d 677 (1971).

In Marley, we concluded that "when a question of cooperation is raised it usually has to be determined as a question of fact." Marley, 53 R.I. at 292, 166 A. at 352. Therefore, although the factual question of cooperation should not ordinarily be decided on a summary judgment motion, here all facts suggest only one conclusion, namely, that Guilbeault did not cooperate with General Accident in the defense of his case. The trial justice accordingly did not err in granting General Accident's motion for summary judgment. See DeNardo v. Fairmount Foundries Cranston, Inc., 121 R.I. 440, 448, 399 A.2d 1229, 1234 (1979) ("'where

26. The Iowa decision reflects what is generally considered the prevailing rule to be applied in breach-of-cooperation clause cases. See 8 John Alan Appleman et al., Insurance Law and Practice, §§ 4771–4773 (1981); 14 Mark S. Rhodes, Couch Cyclopedia of Insurance Law, §§ 51:189–51:195 (rev.2d ed.1982).

the facts suggest only one reasonable inference, the trial justice may properly treat the question as a matter of law' ").

The plaintiff contends that despite Guilbeault's unexplained absence § 27–7–2 permits him to file a direct action against General Accident because Guilbeault could not be located by him or General Accident. The plaintiff fails to recognize, however, that although § 27–7–2 permits a direct action against an insurer in a situation in which the individual insured cannot be located, the plaintiff in such an action merely " 'succeed[s] to the insured's rights against the insurer' " and does not, through such an action, "enlarge the liability of the insurer beyond the limits stated in the policy." Barber v. Canela, 570 A.2d 670, 671 (R.I.1990). See also Polito, 149 N.E.2d at 377; Muzichuk v. Liberty Mutual Insurance Co., 2 Mass.App.Ct. 266, 311 N.E.2d 558, 561–62 (1974). Thus, "the right of the claimant is merely derivative * * * and is therefore dependent upon the existence of liability of the insurer to the insured under the contract of insurance." Barber, 570 A.2d at 671. Since Guilbeault was not entitled to continued coverage under the policy because he failed to cooperate with General Accident in the preparation of his defense, the plaintiff, as successor to Guilbeault's rights under the policy agreement, was not entitled to any greater right of coverage and thus could not recover against General Accident directly pursuant to § 27–7–2. Muzichuk, 311 N.E.2d at 561–62.

The plaintiff also posits that the language of the policy between General Accident and Guilbeault was ambiguous concerning whether there would be coverage following Guilbeault's failure to cooperate with General Accident in the defense of the plaintiff's claim. The plaintiff focuses on that section of the policy setting forth the terms of Massachusetts's compulsory insurance. That policy section provided that "we [General Accident] must pay their claims even if false statements were made when applying for this policy or your auto registration. We must also pay even if you or the legally responsible person fails to cooperate with us after the accident." The plaintiff's contention in this regard is without merit. That quoted policy language is preceded by the specific limitation that "[t]he law [that is, the Massachusetts compulsory insurance law] provides a special protection for anyone entitled to damages under this Part." (Emphasis added.) Thus, it is clear that the provisions of the policy providing for coverage in the absence of cooperation applied only to accidents covered by that part of the policy providing for Massachusetts's compulsory insurance and not to the part of that policy providing for the optional insurance, which is the part that covered the accident involving the plaintiff. That optional insurance, since it was contained in a part of the insurance policy that was completely separate and distinct from the Massachusetts compulsory insurance policy section, was subject to the general cooperation provisions noted and quoted earlier.

Accordingly, for all the foregoing reasons, the plaintiff's appeal is denied and dismissed. The final judgment appealed from is affirmed, and the papers in this case are remanded to the Superior Court.

GOLDBERG, J., not participating.

Notes

1. Whose economic interests are at risk in *Ogunsuada*? Should this influence the approach taken by the court?

2. As noted in the principal case, generally an insured's breach of the duty to cooperate must be material and substantial, significantly prejudicing the interests of the insurer and its ability to defend a claim before the insurer is able to disclaim coverage. In *Darcy v. Hartford Insurance Co.* 407 Mass. 481, 554 N.E.2d 28 (1990), Royal Globe Insurance Company provided comprehensive commercial liability insurance with personal injury coverage to United Building Maintenance, Inc., a subcontractor providing janitorial services at the John F. Kennedy Federal Building in Boston. While cleaning an office, a United employee caused an accident injuring two individuals working in the building. The accident occurred in 1979, and the individuals sued United in 1981. United failed to appear and failed to notify its insurer, Royal Globe. Judgment was entered against United on September 23, 1983. The injured parties then sued the Hartford Insurance Company, the principal contractor's insurer, in order to recover damages. In January 1985, Hartford filed a third-party claim against Royal Globe, providing Royal Globe with the first and only notice of the 1979 accident.

In response the this claim, Royal Globe began an attempt to track down United's principals, using an investigative bureau. Royal Globe limited the investigation to a phone book search, a public records search, and contacting the attorney of record on United's articles of incorporation. After finding one principal who turned out to be the improper individual to receive notice, Royal Globe sent him the notice of its intent to disclaim coverage because United had breached its duty to cooperate. The Massachusetts Supreme Court held that an insured's forfeiture of insurance coverage for failure to notify the insurer would only be justified if the insurer can show actual prejudice to its interests. Thus, even though there was a five-year delay in Royal Globe receiving notice of the action against United, it could not disclaim coverage unless it had exercised "diligence and good faith" in obtaining cooperation. In this case, Royal Globe's efforts to track down the appropriate United representatives were not sufficient to relieve them of liability for the injuries caused by its insured.

Does the court's approach in Darcy turn the insured's duty of cooperation on its head? Is it likely that contacting the insured's principals would have made any evidence less stale?

3. In *Earle v. State Farm Fire & Casualty Co.*, 935 F.Supp. 1076 (N.D.Cal.1996), plaintiffs sued State Farm to recover attorney's fees and a portion of a judgment against them that was covered by an insurance policy issued by State Farm. The initial action that resulted in the judgment against the plaintiff in July 1994 was begun in April 1993. The court held that because the plaintiffs notified State Farm *after* a judgment was entered against them, State Farm's interests were adversely affected as a matter of law. The court reasoned that State Farm was not allowed the opportunity to defend against the claim, nor was it able to select counsel. Thus, the

plaintiffs' failure to involve the insurer at the outset of the underlying claim against them relieved the insurer of any liability including the payments of the plaintiffs' attorney's fees in the underlying action.

4. The line between failure to give prompt notice and breach of cooperation clause may be vague, and the consequences equally detrimental to the insured and the third party. A practical distinction was made in *Miller v. Dilts*, 463 N.E.2d 257 (Ind.1984), which held that prompt notice is a condition precedent and the insurer need not show prejudice to invoke its lack; whereas the duty to co-operate is a condition subsequent and the insurer must show prejudice for its breach. The same distinction is drawn in *Illinois Insurance Guaranty Fund v. Lockhart*, 152 Ill.App.3d 603, 105 Ill.Dec. 572, 504 N.E.2d 857 (1987). It remains preserved in Indiana. Frankenmuth Mutual Ins. Co. v. Williams, 645 N.E.2d 605, 608 (1995) *rehearing*, 690 N.E.2d 675 (1997).

3. Intentional Injury

PACHUCKI v. REPUBLIC INSURANCE CO.

Supreme Court of Wisconsin, 1979.
89 Wis.2d 703, 278 N.W.2d 898.

COFFEY, JUSTICE.

This is an appeal taken from interlocutory judgments entered in favor of the defendant-respondents Underwriters Insurance Company (hereinafter Underwriters) and Republic Insurance Co. (hereinafter Republic.) Judgment was granted dismissing the plaintiff-appellant, Gary Pachucki's complaint and the cross-complaints against Underwriters and Republic after a bifurcated trial to the court on the issue of insurance coverage.

The plaintiff-appellant, Gary Pachucki, commenced this action seeking to recover damages for personal injuries suffered during an incident at work on September 10, 1972 when he was struck in the right eye. On the date of the accident, the plaintiff was employed as a printer at Steins Garden Center of Milwaukee. At approximately 5:30 p.m., co-employees and the defendants in this action, Dale Boschke, Bernard Halas and Anthony Anderson, entered the room where Pachucki was working and started a "greening pin war." A greening pin war is described as being comparable to the shooting of paper clips with rubber bands. The flying metal object that caused an injury to the cornea of the plaintiff's right eye was a greening pin, similar in size and weight to a bobby pin.

The plaintiff's complaint also named as defendants in this action Republic and Underwriters insurance companies. At the time of the accident, Republic had in full force and effect policies of homeowners insurance covering the parents of Dale Boeschke and Anthony Anderson, with their children named as additional insureds. Similarly, Underwriters had issued a homeowners policy to the parents of Bernard Halas, naming him as an additional insured. The original answers filed by the insurance companies were subsequently amended to allege certain defenses in coverage relying upon the "business pursuit" and the "intentional tort" policy exclusions. Each policy contained the following language in the coverage exclusionary provisions:

"THIS POLICY DOES NOT APPLY:

"1. Under Coverage E—Personal Liability and Coverage F—Medical Payments to Others: * * *

"(d) to bodily injury or property damage arising out of business pursuits of any insured except activities therein which are ordinarily incident to non-business pursuits; * * *

"(f) to bodily injury or property damage which is either expected or intended from the standpoint of the insured."

Republic and Underwriters moved for summary judgments of dismissal upon the above recited policy exclusions. In the alternative, the insurers requested a bifurcated trial with respect to the issue of policy coverage in the event that the motions for summary judgment were denied. The trial court denied the respective summary judgment motions but granted Republic's and Underwriter's requests for a separate trial on the issue of coverage.

At the trial on the issue of coverage, the defendant Boeschke stated that he did not mean to hit or hurt the plaintiff as he was taking haphazard aim. However, on cross-examination, Boeschke contradicted this testimony stating that although he had no intention of hitting the plaintiff in the eye, he had intended to strike Pachucki's body with the rubber band-propelled projectile. In his testimony, Boeschke stated "You do not have too much control" when shooting a greening pin; and admitted that the plaintiff could be hit in the eye because of the lack of control over the flying object's course of travel. Boeschke personally realized the danger of the flying object, testifying that on one occasion he had bled after being struck with a greening pin.

The defendant, Bernard Halas, testified that he was aiming in the plaintiff's general direction but was not trying to hit any particular part of his body. He explained that since a flying greening pin could strike anywhere on a person's body he realized there was a possibility that the pin could hit Pachucki in the face. The Defendants, as well as the plaintiff, stated that the "war" game was spontaneous and not the result of any provocation or animosity. During the 3–5 minute "game of war" the plaintiff and the defendants fired approximately 30 greening pins with only one other pin striking the plaintiff in the leg. It is undisputed in the record that the plaintiff returned the defendants' volleys and that Boeschke was standing about 6 feet away when he fired the pin into the plaintiff's eye.

After trial, the court granted judgment in favor of the insurance companies and made the following pertinent findings of fact:

"21. That the shooting of greening pins is an activity ordinarily associated with non-business pursuits.

"22. That the defendants were shooting greening pins with the intent of hitting the plaintiff, although they had no intent to hit plaintiff in the eye and cause the specific injury which occurred.

"23. That it was a substantial certainty that the plaintiff would sustain some kind of damage.

"24. That from the standpoint of the actors, the shooting of the greening pins was an intentional act of the kind and character exempted from coverage pursuant to the exclusion contained in each of the three policies."

ISSUE:

Whether pursuant to the language contained in a homeowners insurance policy excluding coverage for bodily injury or property damage which is either expected or intended from the standpoint of the insured is coverage excluded only upon adequate proof that the insured specifically intended the resulting injury?

* * *

The appellant's principal argument is that the policy provision excluding coverage for " * * * bodily injury * * * which is either expected or intended from the standpoint of the insured" should be construed as requiring proof of a specific intent to cause injury. The appellant maintains that under this construction of the intentional tort exclusion, insurance coverage should be provided as it is virtually undisputed that none of the defendant co-employees intended to inflict injury to the plaintiff's eye.

To the contrary, the respondents support the trial court's analysis of the policy exclusion interpreting the provision to mean: where the insured intends to strike or hit a third party, the intent to injure may be inferred by the nature of the act as well as the reasonable foreseeability of the resulting harm, even though the actual injury is different in character or magnitude.

Home Insurance v. Neilsen, (Ind.App.1975), 332 N.E.2d 240 outlines three general rules that have emerged with respect to the construction of an intentional tort exclusion:

(1) The minority view follows the classic tort doctrine of looking to the natural and probable consequences of the insured's act;

(2) The majority view is that the insured must have intended the act *and* to cause some kind of bodily injury;

(3) A third view is that the insured must have had the specific intent to cause the type of injury suffered.[27]

The trial court denied coverage in the instant case with application of the majority view. The majority position is summarized in the following:

27. See: Annotation: Liability Insurance: Specific Exclusions of Liability Intentionally Caused by the Insured, 2 A.L.R.3d 1238 (1965).

(1) it is necessary that the insured intend both the act as well as intending to cause bodily injury in order for the exclusion to apply; (2) intent may be actual or may be inferred by the nature of the act and the accompanying reasonable foreseeability of harm; (3) once it is found that harm was intended, it is immaterial that the actual harm caused is of a different character or magnitude than that intended. See: Butler v. Behaeghe, 37 Colo.App. 282, 548 P.2d 934 (1976); Clark v. Allstate Ins. Co., 22 Ariz.App. 601, 529 P.2d 1195 (1975).

To date, there is no Wisconsin case law that has squarely met the issue of determining the interpretation of "* * * bodily injury or property damage which is either expected or intended from the standpoint of the insured." In Peterson v. Western Cas. & Surety Co., 5 Wis.2d 535, 93 N.W.2d 433 (1958) the court construed the phrase excluding coverage for "* * * injury * * * caused intentionally by * * * the insured" and affirmed the trial court's finding of coverage. Peterson was injured while standing next to the insured's open car door and was struck as the car moved away from its parked position. The court concluded that although the insured may have acted intentionally in an effort to escape from the police as he rapidly backed up his auto, his intentional acts were not directed toward the plaintiff. This court stated in regard to the trial court's finding that the insured's acts constituted gross negligence:

> "The law may treat gross negligence as equivalent to intentional wrongdoing for some purposes, but not for the purpose of excluding liability for gross negligence from the coverage of a liability insurance policy." Supra at 542, 93 N.W.2d at 437.

Thus *Peterson* is interpreted as requiring proof of an intent to inflict harm in addition to an intentional act before coverage will be denied.

In Falk v. Whitewater, 65 Wis.2d 83, 221 N.W.2d 915 (1974) the court again pointed out that an intentional act is a separate legal consideration and must be distinguished from the intent to cause injury. In *Falk,* the defendants contended that a cause of action in negligence had not been stated as the plaintiff alleged the defendant intentionally made a fist and negligently struck him in the face. The defense argued "because the making of a fist in and of itself is an intentional act, * * * any further act resulting therefrom is likewise intentionally done." In rejecting this argument, the court stated:

> "Even assuming that the making of a fist is necessarily an intentional act, to reason that the striking of someone with that fist is therefore necessarily likewise intentional is a *non sequitur.* Almost all negligent conduct is composed of individual intentional components; to constitute an intentional tort, however, the actor must intend the consequences of his acts, or believe that they are substantially certain to follow. Restatement, 1 *Torts* 2d, p. 15, sec. 8A. While a driver may intentionally step on the accelerator and intentionally steer his car into the passing lane, a resulting collision with an oncoming car is not ipso facto intentional on the driver's part. . . . "

The language in *Falk* defining intentional conduct as contrasted to negligent behavior is similar to the criteria set forth in Prosser, Law of Torts, 4th ed. (1971) and cited by the trial court. Professor Prosser, in defining the meaning of intent, stated:

> "The intent with which tort liability is concerned is not necessarily a hostile intent, or a desire to do any harm. Rather it is an intent to bring about a result which will invade the interests of another in a way that the law will not sanction. The defendant may be liable although he has meant nothing more than a good-natured practical joke, * * *
>
> * * *
>
> "Intent, however, is broader than a desire to bring about physical results. It must extend not only to those consequences which are desired, but also to those which the actor believes are substantially certain to follow from what he does. * * * The man who fires a bullet into a dense crowd may fervently pray that he will hit no one, but since he must believe and know that he cannot avoid doing so, he intends it. The practical application of this principle has meant that where a reasonable man in the defendant's position would believe that a particular result was substantially certain to follow, he will be dealt with by the jury, or even by the court, as though he had intended it. * * * " Id. at 31–32.

Thus, we note that in each case of this type, the intent to inflict injury is a question of fact, Peterson v. Western Cas. Ins. Co., supra, 5 Wis.2d at 541–43, 93 N.W.2d 433, and therefore the applicability of this decision is limited to the policy language and the facts presently before us. As the intent to cause injury is a question of fact, the test to be applied to the trial court's determination relating to the question of intent is whether or not the finding of intent is contrary to the great and clear preponderance of the evidence. Ehlers v. Colonial Penn Ins. Co., 81 Wis.2d 64, 259 N.W.2d 718 (1977).

In the instant case, there is no dispute from the record that the defendants intentionally fired the greening pins. Despite some statements to the contrary, each of the defendants admitted to attempting to hit the plaintiff but not in the eye, and they further testified it is almost impossible to obtain any degree of accuracy when shooting a greening pin. We note there is no direct evidence that the defendants were intending to inflict any harm other than to "sting" the plaintiff.

Upon this evidence, the trial court found that none of the defendants specifically intended to inflict injury to the plaintiff's eye. * * *

The trial court's finding that the intent to inflict injury could be inferred from the nature of the defendants' intentional acts is not contrary to the great weight and clear preponderance of the evidence in the record. There was testimony supporting the fact that each of the defendants had prior knowledge that being struck with a greening pin will result in injury. Boeschke stated on one occasion after being hit by a greening pin he suffered an injury and bled.

In support of the trial court's finding, we examine Clark v. Allstate Insurance Co., supra. In that case, Clark struck another student in the face with his fist causing severe injuries. Allstate had issued a policy of homeowners insurance to Clark's parents and had denied coverage, interpreting similar contract language as contained in this exclusionary clause. Clark maintained that he never intended to hurt the other student even though he did intend to hit him in the face with a "short jab." Concluding that the injuries herein were intentionally caused, the court stated:

> "* * * an act may be so certain to cause a particular harm that it can be said that a person who performed such an act intended the harm." Id. 529 P.2d at 1196.

Some courts might characterize the defendants' conduct in this case as "horseplay" as there was no specific intent to do harm. However, the boys' actual knowledge based upon prior experience that a greening pin will cause harm when it strikes, especially when fired at the close range of six feet, distinguishes this appeal from the classic "horseplay" case of Morrill v. Gallagher, 370 Mich. 578, 122 N.W.2d 687 (1963). In *Morrill* the defendant Gallagher threw a cherry bomb into the plaintiff's office attempting to scare him but the result was a serious hearing impairment. The insurer, in its defense of the case, relied in part upon the intentional tort exclusion. The court rejected the defense position and stated:

> "There is nothing in this case to justify [the] conclusion that [the insured] intended to cause any physical harm to the plaintiff." Id., 122 N.W.2d at 691.

In *Morrill* the remote possibility of harm cannot be equated with the substantial certainty that harm would result under the facts of this case.

The present case is properly similar to Butler v. Behaeghe, supra, wherein the defendant's insurer refused to defend based on an identical exclusionary clause. The plaintiff and the insured got into an argument after an altercation between their two teen-aged sons. The insured ordered the plaintiff off his property and when the plaintiff refused to leave, the insured procured a steel pipe. Although he intended to strike the plaintiff in the stomach, he hit the plaintiff on the head and an injury ensued. Finding that the insured's conduct fell within the exclusionary provision, the court concluded:

> "Where coverage is excluded if bodily injury is 'intended or expected' by the insured, such exclusion is inapplicable if and only if the insured acts without any intent or any expectation of causing any injury, however slight. And conversely, such exclusion is applicable [quotation corrected to conform to source] if the insured acts with the intent or expectation that bodily injury will result even

though the bodily injury that does result is different either in character or magnitude from the injury that was intended." Id. 548 P.2d at 938.

Thus, we hold the applicable case law supports the trial court's findings that the facts and circumstances of this case bar recovery pursuant to the language contained in the intentional tort exclusionary sections in the respective policies. We affirm the trial court's finding that the defendants' intent to inflict injury to the plaintiff can be inferred from the evidence and circumstances in this case.

Judgments affirmed.

Notes

1. The policy reasons for allowing an insurer to avoid the duty to indemnify when the insured is held liable for an intentionally wrongful act seem clear. Like many states, California Insurance Code § 533 provides:

> An insurer is not liable for a loss caused by the wilful act of the insured; but he is not exonerated by the negligence of the insured, or of the insured's agents or others.

California Civil Code § 1668 provides:

> All contracts which have for their object, directly or indirectly, to exempt anyone from responsibility for his own fraud, or willful injury to the person or property of another, or violation of law, whether willful or negligent, are against the policy of the law.

South Dakota Codified Laws § 53–9–3 (2006) provides nearly identically:

> All contracts which have for their object, directly or indirectly, to exempt anyone from responsibility for his own fraud or willful injury to the person or property of another or from violation of law whether willful or negligent, are against the policy of the law.

2. Is the "BB gun game" by juveniles which causes eye injury to be looked at in the same way as the "greening pin war?" See Allstate Insurance Co. v. Steinemer, 723 F.2d 873 (11th Cir.1984) (the intentional act exclusion does not apply if the 19 year old insured's intentional act causes harm when his intent was to cause no harm); but see Bell v. Tilton, 234 Kan. 461, 674 P.2d 468 (1983) (the intentional act exclusion applies if the 11 year old insured knew the consequences were substantially certain to result from his act).

3. Messrs. W., L., and B. were each convicted on several (fraud) counts of violating the Federal securities laws. They belonged to an accounting firm which maintained a professional liability policy with St. Paul Fire & Marine Ins. Co. Civil suits for damages were filed against W., L., and B., some of these suits being based on negligence. St. Paul asks the court to declare that it need not provide W., L., and B. with a defense. It refers to clauses in the professional liability policy excluding liability for "dishonesty, misrepresentation, or fraud," to the statutes quoted above, and to "collateral estoppel." What result? See St. Paul Fire & Marine Insurance Co. v. Weiner, 606 F.2d 864 (9th Cir.1979) (reversing summary judgment in favor of the insurer because (1) the policy's ambiguous exclusionary should be construed in favor

of the insured based on the insured's reasonable expectations, and (2) collateral estoppel was improperly applied by the district court because, "[d]espite the defendants' criminal convictions, the possibility remained that St. Paul had a duty to defend the civil action brought against the defendants"). The criminal case is United States v. Weiner, 578 F.2d 757 (9th Cir.1978), certiorari denied 439 U.S. 981, 99 S.Ct. 568, 58 L.Ed.2d 651 (1978).

4. Because society and the law are not static, new issues regularly arise. A legislative enactment may produce a new body of law to be applied, as Congress did with passage of the Americans with Disabilities Act of 1990 (42 U.S.C.A. § 12101 *et seq.*). Beyond legislation, the changing attitudes of modern society have developed a new source of litigation with respect to intentional acts—sexual misconduct. While reading the cases that follow, keep in mind the policies embodied in prior contexts. Perhaps the questions presented are not as novel as they first appear.

5. The duty to indemnify in the context of intentional conduct was explored by the California Supreme Court in *Gray v. Zurich Ins.* Co., 65 Cal.2d 263, 54 Cal.Rptr. 104, 419 P.2d 168 (1966). As discussed above, *Gray* involved an insured (Gray) who was sued for assault. Gray held a policy with Zurich which included a "Comprehensive Personal Liability Endorsement" provision, which provided that Zurich would defend Gray in a suit alleging bodily injury and would indemnify Gray in the event that Gray was found liable for personal injury to another. The policy, of course, contained a clause which excluded coverage for intentional acts committed by Gray. Zurich refused to defend Gray in the assault suit, claiming that the alleged conduct was an intentional tort and that coverage for intentional torts was excluded by the policy. After judgment was entered against Gray in the amount of $6,000, Gray filed suit against Zurich alleging breach of its duty to defend. Examining the language of the exclusionary provision in the policy and the applicability of said provision to the assault suit, the court stated,

> "No one can determine whether the third party suit does or does not fall within the indemnification coverage of the policy until that suit is resolved; in the instant case, the determination of whether the insured engaged in intentional, negligent or even wrongful conduct depended upon the judgment in the [assault] suit, and, indeed, even after that judgment, no one could be positive whether it rested upon a finding of plaintiffs negligent or his intentional conduct. The carrier's obligation to indemnify inevitably will not be defined until the adjudication of the very action which it should have defended." *Id.* at 271–72.

The court, therefore, found the exclusionary provision ambiguous and, applying principles of interpretations with which the student is now familiar, construed the ambiguity in the language against Zurich. The court found that Gray could have reasonably expected coverage in the assault suit, and that Zurich therefore breached its duty to defend. The court noted, however, that the insurer may reserve its right to contest coverage after judgment is entered, and that the insurer may then litigate the issue of coverage.

6. The recent spate of cases dealing with allegations of corporate wrongdoing have raised significant duty to defend issues. Directors and officers liability insurance policies typically contain exclusions for fraud.

Where there is an allegation of fraud, insurers may try to avoid the considerable costs of providing a defense. So far, courts have not been receptive such attempts and have insisted on enforcing the insurer's duty to defend absent an adjudication of wrongdoing. Associated Elec. & Gas Ins. Svcs. V. Rigas, 382 F.Supp.2d 685, 695 (E.D.Pa. 2004), *citing* Little v. MGIC Indemnity Corp., 836 F.2d 789, 792–93 (3d Cir. 1987) (insurer not permitted to rescind policy and avoid duty to defend in Adelphia Communications case); Federal Ins. Co. v. Kozlowski, 792 N.Y.S.2d 397, 401, 18 A.D.3d 33 (2005)(insurer required to defend in the face of fraud allegation in Tyco International case). In one case, the court cited a criminal defendant's presumption of innocence as a public policy support for its decision. Associated Elec. & Gas Ins. Svcs. v. Rigas, 382 F.Supp.2d 685, 701 (E.D.Pa. 2004). It also advanced the argument that it is unfair to allow an insurer to collect premiums and then attempt to avoid its duty to defend by the expedient of rescission of the policy. Id. at 701.

7. It is tempting for a court to find that coverage is not precluded in cases involving intentional conduct because of the perceived need to make victims whole. E.g., Young v. Brown, 658 So.2d 750, 753 (La.App. 1995)(victim compensation is an important public policy consideration). Still these cases tend to be rare and the weight of authority is to the contrary. E.g., Littlefield v. Acadia Ins. Co. 392 F.3d 1, 10–11 (1st Cir. 2004) (criticizing the victim compensation orientation).

D. PROBLEMS OF MULTIPLE COVERAGE

The material following combines the knottiest aspects of insurance coverage when multiple insurers are involved. We start with the problem of "when" insurance coverage applies. We then deal with the various aspects of multiple coverage including; the "stacking" of coverage, the apportionment of coverage, and the problem of conflicting coverage. Before we begin, an overview of these four areas is useful to understand the scope of the problem.

The "when" of insurance coverage matters in cases where injury occurs over time, specifically over many years and where many different insurance policies can come into play. This problem has been dealt with by the selection of various "triggers" of coverage. While the term "trigger" of coverage is not found in policy language and while the application of a particular trigger depends both on the context of loss and the jurisdiction, the range of judicially crafted triggers is manageable. A footnote in a well-known California case states the issue plainly:

> In the third party liability insurance context, "trigger of coverage" has been used by insureds and insurers alike to denote the circumstances that activate the insurer's defense and indemnity obligations under the policy. * * * The word "trigger" is not found in the CGL policies themselves, nor does the Insurance Code enumerate or define "trigger of coverage." Instead, "trigger of coverage" is a term of convenience used to describe that which, under the specific terms of an insurance policy, must happen in the policy period in order for

the potential of coverage to arise. The issue is largely one of timing—what must take place within the policy's effective dates for the potential of coverage to be "triggered"? Whether coverage is ultimately established in any given case may depend on the consideration of many additional factors, including the existence of express conditions or exclusions in the particular contract of insurance under scrutiny, the availability of certain defenses that might defeat coverage, and a determination of whether the facts of the case will support a finding of coverage. Montrose Chemical Corp. v. Admiral Ins. Co., 10 Cal.4th at 645, 655 n.2, 42 Cal.Rptr.2d 324, 326, 913 P.2d 878, 881 (1995).

"[S]tacking policy limits means that when more than one policy is triggered by an occurrence, each policy can be called upon to respond to the claim up to the full limits of the policy." Ostrager & Newman, *Insurance Coverage Disputes*, (6th ed. 1993) § 9.04 (c) p. 342. The California Supreme Court, in *Wagner v. State Farm Mutual Auto Insurance Company*, defined stacking to mean "the ability of the insured, when covered by more than one insurance policy, to obtain benefits from a second policy on the same claim when recovery from the first policy would alone be inadequate." 40 Cal.3d 460, 463 n.2, 220 Cal.Rptr. 659, 709 P.2d 462 (1985). Put another way, "stacking" raises the issue of whether the policies are aggregated or not in the event multiple policies cover a loss that occurs over time. For example, if a loss occurs over two years and the insured is covered in the first year by Insurance Company A for $1 million and in the second year by Insurance Company B for $2 million, the principle of stacking would allow the insured coverage totaling $3 million. Whether stacking is allowed depends largely on the jurisdiction in which the loss occurs.

Whether stacking is allowed or not, a loss over number of years with multiple insurers raises the question of the amount of exposure of each insurer. For example, in the simple loss over two years described above suppose the loss totals $800,000. How should the insurers share the liability? Should it be based on premiums paid, on policy limits, or other methods? Should an insured bear some proportion of the loss for periods of no coverage and how, if at all, should retained limits be addressed? Finally, how should excess insurers share in all of this? These are the matters addressed under the rubric of apportionment.

Finally, how should conflicting coverages be resolved? At the simplest level, can two insurers who would otherwise be liable for loss escape by the expedient of policy language that provides for no liability if another insurer is involved? Can an insured who has faithfully paid premiums in such a situation be left without recourse? These and other questions are addressed if not fully answered in the materials that follow.

1. Concurrent Policies: Coverage Triggers

In beginning a comprehensive look at this subject, it is worth emphasizing that the application of the appropriate trigger is very much a matter of context and jurisdiction. As the California Supreme Court cautions in the following case, "[t]he term "trigger of coverage" should not be misunderstood as a doctrine to be automatically invoked by a court to conclusively establish coverage in certain categories of cases, or under certain types of policies." Montrose Chemical Corp. v. Admiral Ins. Co., 10 Cal.4th at 645, 655 n.2, 42 Cal.Rptr.2d 324, 326, 913 P.2d 878, 881 (1995).

MONTROSE CHEMICAL CORP. v. ADMIRAL INS. CO.

Supreme Court of California, In Bank, 1995.
10 Cal. 4th 645, 42 Cal. Rptr. 2d 324, 913 P.2d 878.

* * *

The issue of trigger of coverage in continuous injury or damage cases has been explored by many courts. (See Annot. (1993) 14 A.L.R. 5th 695.) Courts have recognized several "triggers" as a means of identifying the nature and timing of damage or injury that will give rise to liability coverage under an occurrence-based CGL policy. The courts have generally viewed the timing of damage or injury under occurrence-based CGL policies in four ways: at the date of exposure to the injurious or damage-causing event or conditions; at the date of the first occurrence of "injury in fact"; at the date of manifestation or discovery of the damage or injury; and over the continuous period from exposure through manifestation and beyond, where the damage or injury is ongoing, continuous, or progressively deteriorating throughout a policy period or successive policy periods. At this point it will be helpful to briefly outline the various trigger theories formulated by the courts.

The exposure (or continuous exposure) trigger. This trigger of coverage theory, first applied in cases involving asbestos-related bodily injuries, focuses on the date on which the injury-producing agent first contacts the body. The exposure theory apportions the cost of indemnity among those insurers whose policies were in effect from that point in time onward. In effect, under this theory, damage or injury is deemed to commence from the first contact of the injury-producing agent with the injured party. The leading case espousing this trigger of coverage analysis is the Sixth Circuit's decision in Ins. Co. of North America v. Forty–Eight Insulations (6th Cir.1980) 633 F.2d 1212, clarified (1981) 657 F.2d 814, cert. den. (1981) 454 U.S. 1109, 102 S.Ct. 686, 70 L.Ed.2d 650 (Forty–Eight Insulations.) The court in Forty–Eight Insulations found that the covered occurrence of injury commenced with the immediate contact of an asbestos fiber with the lungs, even though the progressive disease typically took some 20 years to develop. (633 F.2d at pp. 1215, 1218–1220.) The court reasoned that because of the cumulative and progressively deteriorating nature of the disease, it had to be distinguished from the ordinary accident or injury situation, and further, that because the injury is a continuing one, the insurers who furnished comprehensive general liability policies would expect the scope of their policies' coverage to parallel the applicable theory of liability.

The manifestation (or manifestation of loss) trigger. This trigger of coverage, which, as already explained, was adopted by this court in the first party property insurance context in Prudential–LMI, supra, 51 Cal.3d 674, 274 Cal.Rptr. 387, 798 P.2d 1230, holds the insurer insuring the property at the time appreciable property damage first becomes manifest solely responsible for indemnification to the insured. For purposes of applying the rule, the time at which the property damage becomes manifest (also the point of "inception of the loss") is "that point in time when appreciable damage occurs and is or should be known to the insured, such that a reasonable insured would be aware that his notification duty under the policy had been triggered." (Id. at p. 699, 274 Cal.Rptr. 387, 798 P.2d 1230.)

In Prudential–LMI, supra, 51 Cal.3d 674, 274 Cal.Rptr. 387, 798 P.2d 1230, we identified three reasons supporting the application of the manifestation theory in the first party property insurance context. First, application of that trigger of coverage meets the reasonable expectations of the insureds who, in seeking to insure against perils to their property, would normally look to their present carrier for coverage. (Id. at p. 699, 274 Cal.Rptr. 387, 798 P.2d 1230.) Second, "the underwriting practices of the insurer can be made predictable because the insurer is not liable for a loss once its contract with the insured ends unless the manifestation of loss occurred during its contract term." (Ibid.) Third, since the insured is required under a standard first party property insurance policy to file suit against the insurer within 12 months after "inception of the loss," and since inception of the loss is the date on which appreciable damage occurs and is or should be known to the insured, the definition of manifestation of loss and inception of the loss must be one and the same, that is to say, "that point in time when appreciable damage occurs and is or should be known to the insured, such that a reasonable insured would be aware that his notification duty under the policy had been triggered." (Prudential–LMI, supra, 51 Cal.3d at pp. 686–687, 699, 274 Cal.Rptr. 387, 798 P.2d 1230.) These policy reasons led us to conclude, "in conformity with the loss-in-progress rule, [that first party property] insurers whose policy terms commence after initial manifestation of the loss are not responsible for any potential claim...." (Id. at p. 699, 274 Cal.Rptr. 387, 798 P.2d 1230.)[2]

2. We are aware of only one appellate court decision that has adopted the manifestation trigger of coverage for bodily injuries in the context of third party liability insurance. In Eagle–Picher Industries v. Liberty Mut. Ins. Co. (1st Cir.1982) 682 F.2d 12, the United States Court of Appeals for the First Circuit concluded on the evidence before it that the injury resulting from inhalation of asbestos fibers did not "occur" until the symptoms of the disease asbestosis had manifested themselves. The asbestos manufacturer had no insurance prior to 1968, the period when most of the exposure took place. The manufacturer's CGL insurance coverage began when the number of claims began accelerating. As was the case in Forty–Eight Insulations, supra, 633 F.2d 1212, the court in Eagle–Picher, in adopting the manifestation trigger, made clear its intention to interpret the policies in a manner that would afford and maximize coverage on the particular facts of that case. (682 F.2d at p. 23.) The Eagle–Picher case therefore stands as somewhat of an aberration.

The continuous injury (or multiple) trigger. Under this trigger of coverage theory, bodily injuries and property damage that are continuous or progressively deteriorating throughout successive policy periods are covered by all policies in effect during those periods. The timing of the accident, event, or conditions causing the bodily injury or property damage, e.g., an insured's negligent act, is largely immaterial to establishing coverage; it can occur before or during the policy period. Neither is the date of discovery of the damage or injury controlling: it might or might not be contemporaneous with the causal event. It is only the effect—the occurrence of bodily injury or property damage during the policy period, resulting from a sudden accidental event or the "continuous or repeated exposure to conditions"—that triggers potential liability coverage. The appellate cases in which this trigger of coverage was developed are discussed in greater detail below.

The injury-in-fact trigger. Under an injury-in-fact trigger, coverage is first triggered at that point in time at which an actual injury can be shown, retrospectively, to have been first suffered. This rationale places the injury-in-fact somewhere between the exposure, which is considered the initiating cause of the disease or bodily injury, and the manifestation of symptoms, which, logically, is only possible when an injury already exists. (See Abex Corp. v. Maryland Cas. Co. (D.C.Cir.1986) 790 F.2d 119 [asbestos]; American Home Products Corp. v. Liberty Mut. Ins. Co. (2d Cir.1984) 748 F.2d 760 [pharmaceuticals].) In the context of continuous or progressively deteriorating injuries, the injury-in-fact trigger, like the continuous injury trigger, affords coverage for continuing or progressive injuries occurring during successive policy periods subsequent to the established date of the initial injury-in-fact. However, the injury-in-fact trigger, unlike the exposure trigger, when applied in asbestos cases excludes from coverage the period from initial exposure to the date on which the injury-in-fact was first suffered.[3]

3. The injury-in-fact trigger has been applied in actions involving asbestos-related disease because symptoms of the disease often will not manifest themselves until decades after actual inhalation of asbestos fibers. Like the manifestation and continuous injury theories, the injury-in-fact theory assumes as a predicate that mere exposure to asbestos during the policy period is not enough to trigger coverage: "The plain language of the definition of 'occurrence' used in the CGL policy requires exposure that 'results, during the policy period, in bodily injury' in order for an insurer to be obligated to indemnify the insured. The unambiguous meaning of these words is that an injury—and not mere exposure—must result during the policy period. The CGL policies expressly distinguish exposure from injury; to equate the two ... is to ignore this distinction. Any argument that mere exposure—without injury—triggers liability is simply unsound linguistically." (Abex Corp. v. Maryland Cas. Co., supra, 790 F.2d at p. 127, italics in original; see also American Home Products Corp. v. Liberty Mut. Ins. Co., supra, 748 F.2d at p. 764.) Unlike the manifestation trigger, however, the injury-in-fact trigger acknowledges that actual injury may "occur" before it has become manifest or been discovered. Under the injury-in-fact approach, coverage is triggered by " 'a real but undiscovered injury, proved in retrospect to have existed at the relevant time ... irrespective of the time the injury became [diagnosable].' " (American Home Products Corp. v. Liberty Mut. Ins. Co., supra, 748 F.2d at p. 766.) That is, after an injury has been diagnosed, it may be inferred, from evidence establishing the "gestation period" and the stage to which the illness has advanced, that the harm or "injury-in-fact" actually began sometime earlier. (Id. at p. 765.) The injury-in-fact trigger therefore affords coverage for any ensuing continuing or progressively deteriorating

Notes

1. The leading case on the "Manifestation Theory: Reasonable Date of Diagnosis" is cited as *Eagle–Picher Indus., Inc. v. Liberty Mut. Ins. Co.*, 682 F.2d 12 (1st Cir.1982); see also James Pest Control, Inc. v. Scottsdale Ins. Co., 765 So.2d 485 (La.App.2000) (termite infestation did not become "damage" until discovered, i.e. manifested). Exactly when does a disease become "reasonably capable of medical diagnosis"? This question came back to the First Circuit in the same case five years later. See *Eagle–Picher Indus., Inc. v. Liberty Mut. Ins. Co.*, 829 F.2d 227 (1st Cir.1987), which resulted in a further remand. Observe how the court in the next main case disposed of the "diagnosable" test.

2. The 9th Circuit espoused the "exposure" test in *Hancock Laboratories, Inc. v. Admiral Ins. Co.*, 777 F.2d 520 (9th Cir.1985); see Guaranty Nat'l Ins. Co. v. Azrock Indus., 211 F.3d 239 (5th Cir.2000) (adopting exposure theory as Texas law in an *Erie* case).

3. Policies issued after 1973 cover three items under the term "bodily injury"—bodily injury itself/sickness/disease. Should not a different trigger be applied to each? In *Zurich Ins. Co. v. Raymark Industries, Inc.*, 118 Ill.2d 23, 112 Ill.Dec. 684, 514 N.E.2d 150 (1987), the court held that separate triggers should be used because "under the plain and unambiguous language of the policies at issue, the insurer must provide coverage of asbestos-related claims if the claimant in the underlying action suffered "bodily injury," "sickness" or "disease" during the policy period. "Bodily injury" takes place at or shortly after the time a claimant is exposed to asbestos and continues throughout a claimant's exposure to asbestos. * * * "Disease" takes place when it is reasonably capable of clinical detection and diagnosis. * * * "Sickness" takes place at any time during which the claimant "suffers from a disordered, weakened or unsound condition" before the clinical manifestation of a disease." *Id.* at 47.

4. While the preceding excerpt remains a viable reference, commentators have continued to discuss coverage triggers. Michael G. Doherty, *Allo-*

injury that can be shown to have occurred during a successive policy period, regardless of whether such injury manifested itself or was discovered during that period. In Armstrong World Industries, Inc. v. Aetna Casualty & Surety Co. (Cal.App.) (rev. granted Jan. 27, 1994, S023768, briefing deferred) (Armstrong), the First District Court of Appeal affirmed a trial court's decision applying a "continuous injury" trigger to asbestos claims for which coverage was being sought under various CGL policies. The Armstrong court observed, however, that "[t]he trial court's continuous trigger decision ... [was] based upon factual findings that for asbestos claimants an injury-in-fact took place during each triggered policy period, even though the injury was not diagnosable and compensable during the policy period." (Italics added.) Indeed, the Armstrong court carefully noted that the trial court had "relied upon medical evidence to make factual findings on the physiological processes that actually occur upon inhalation of asbestos fibers and continue until death.... " in determining to apply a "continuous injury" trigger in that case. Although the Armstrong court's trigger of coverage discussion appears largely consistent with our analysis of the applicable principles of third party CGL coverage in the present case, because we do not here face the unique facts of asbestos-related bodily injury claims, we deem it appropriate that trigger of coverage questions specifically involving asbestos claims be left for decision, in the first instance, on an appropriate record in a case in which they are squarely presented.

cating Progressive Injury Liability Among Successive Insurance Policies, 64 U. Chi. L. Rev. 257 (1997); James M. Fischer, *Insurance Coverage for Mass Exposure Tort Claims: The Debate Over the Appropriate Trigger Rule*, 45 Drake L. Rev. 625 (1997); Thomas M. Jones and Jon D. Hurwitz, *An Introduction to Insurance Allocation issues in Multiple–Trigger Cases*, 10 Vill. Envtl. L.J. 25 (1999); Jeffrey W. Stempel, *Domtar Baby: Misplaced Notions of Equitable Apportionment Create a Thicket of Potential Unfairness for Insurance Policyholders*, 25 William Mitchell L. Rev. 769 (1999).

5. One consequence of the various trigger theories, with the exception of perhaps the actual injury theory, is that CGL policies have long "tails." That is, the insurer is at risk long after the policy period. One effort to limit this exposure is the resort to "claims-made" policies in which the insured must make the claim within the policy period. See, James F. Hogg, *The Tail of a Tail*, 24 Wm. Mitchell L. Rev. 515 (1998); Charles R. McGuire, Kathleen A. McCullough, George B. Flanigan, *Exposure Triggers and Allocation Methods: Learning Lessons From Prior Court Rulings*, 7 Risk Mgt. & Ins. Rev 1, 73 (2004). A claims-made policy limits claims to those made during the policy period; thus, if no claim is made during the policy period, the insurer is no longer liable for harm occurring during that policy period.

AMERICAN HOME PRODUCTS CORPORATION v. LIBERTY MUTUAL INSURANCE COMPANY

United States Court of Appeals, Second Circuit, 1984.
748 F.2d 760.

Kearse, Circuit Judge:

* * *

A. The Insurance Policies

The policies at issue here were the product of negotiation between AHP and Liberty and are variants of the Comprehensive General Liability Policy ("CGL"), a standard-form policy for liability coverage introduced by the insurance industry in the mid–1960's to deal with the problem of liability for injuries caused over a period of time. The question is what event triggers coverage.

During the relevant period, Article I of AHP's policies provided liability coverage for occurrences that result in "personal injury, sickness or disease, including death at any time resulting therefrom, sustained by any person." Article IV of the policy provided that "[t]his policy applies only to (1) personal injury, sickness or disease including death resulting therefrom * * * which occurs during the policy period." Effective in 1968, AHP's policies also contained a proviso ("Proviso") that "[t]he policy does not apply to such injury, death or destruction caused by such continuous or repeated exposure any part of which occurs after the termination of the policy."

B. The Proceedings Below

AHP, a manufacturer of drugs, foods, and household products, has been named a defendant in the 54 Underlying Suits which arose from its manufacture and sale of six pharmaceuticals: Ovral and L/Ovral (oral contraceptives), DES (Diethylstilbestrol), Mysoline (an anticonvulsant used to treat epileptic seizures), Atromid–S (an antilipidemic used to treat high levels of blood cholesterol), Premarin (used in estrogen replacement therapy), and Anacin (a nonprescription analgesic). In each suit, the injury complained of did not manifest itself until after termination of Liberty's insurance coverage on November 1, 1976. In each case, AHP requested that Liberty defend it; Liberty refused to defend and denied coverage. AHP then initiated this suit seeking a judgment declaring that Liberty is obligated under the policies to defend and indemnify it in each of the Underlying Suits.

After a period of discovery, AHP moved for summary judgment. It contended that the policies should be read as providing either (a) that coverage was triggered if exposure, or injury, or manifestation occurred during the policy period, or (b) that regardless of when the injuries occurred or became manifest, coverage was triggered if exposure occurred during the policy period. It argued, *inter alia,* that the policy language was ambiguous, that discovery had revealed no conclusive evidence of the parties' intent at the time the language was drafted, and that New York law therefore required the application of the doctrine of *contra proferentem,* which requires that all ambiguities in contract language be resolved against the drafter of the language.

Liberty opposed AHP's motion, arguing that the trigger-of-coverage clause was unambiguous and provided coverage only when an injury became manifest within the policy period. Liberty also moved for partial summary judgment on the ground that the Proviso unambiguously excluded coverage for all cases in which exposure to the allegedly injurious substance continued after the termination of Liberty's coverage on November 1, 1976, regardless of when the injury occurred or manifested itself.

The district court rejected both parties' interpretations of the policies. It found that the trigger-of-coverage clause was unambiguous; that it did not support either AHP's continuous trigger theory, or its exposure theory, or Liberty's manifestation theory; and that, construed "as * * * written," the clause plainly called for coverage upon the occurrence of an injury in fact during the policy period. The court stated that the policies required

> a showing of actual injury, sickness or disease occurring during the policy period, based upon the facts proved in each particular case. Thus, an occurrence of "personal injury, sickness, or disease" is read to mean any point in time at which a finder of fact determines that the effects of exposure to a drug actually resulted in a diagnosable and compensable injury.

565 F.Supp. at 1489. The court elaborated as follows:

> The most basic demand of the policy language is that to establish Liberty's liability the insured must prove that an "occurrence"—injury, sickness, or disease—arose during the policy period.

> The plain language demands that the insured prove the cause of the occurrence (accident or exposure), the result (injury, sickness, or disease), and that the result occurred during the policy period. An exposure that does not result in injury during coverage would not satisfy the policy's terms. On the other hand, a real but undiscovered injury, proved in retrospect to have existed at the relevant time, would establish coverage, irrespective of the time the injury became manifest.

Id. at 1497.

The court also rejected Liberty's interpretation of the Proviso as unsupported by any evidence or by any reasonable reading of the policy as a whole. Rather, the court found that the plain language of the Proviso supported its view of the plain meaning of the trigger-of-coverage clause:

> Liberty argues correctly that the provision is unambiguous, but its meaning is not the one Liberty suggests. Rather, on its face the provision removes from coverage only injury, death, or destruction that is caused by continuous or repeated exposure occurring in part after November 1, 1976, the date AHP terminated the policy. It does not remove from coverage harm caused wholly by exposure occurring prior to November 1, 1976. Nothing in the language of the provision takes such harm out of the policy simply because exposure to the same products continued after November 1, 1976, or indeed because further harm may have occurred from such continued exposure. If, in a particular case, pre-November 1, 1976 exposure is found to have caused a particular harm, no exposure after November 1, 1976 would be a cause of that particular harm; such harm is not "caused by * * * exposure any part of which" occurred after November 1, 1976, because all of that harm-causing exposure occurred before that date.

Id. at 1498–99.

Finally, the court ruled that the policies' broad language concerning Liberty's duty to defend requires that Liberty defend AHP in every suit in which the complaint permits proof of facts establishing coverage, until Liberty is able to exclude the possibility of any recovery for which it provided insurance. *Id.* at 1499–1500. The court declined, however, to determine Liberty's actual duty in any given Underlying Suit to defend and indemnify AHP because it concluded that those questions depended on the particular facts of each case, including what injury was alleged and what drug was alleged to have caused it. The court therefore concluded that a determination of whether the complaint in each of the Underlying Suits permitted proof of a recovery for which Liberty would be liable under the policies was an issue inappropriate for resolution in an action for a declaratory judgment.[49] These appeals followed.

49. The final judgment declared, in pertinent part, as follows:

1. Liberty is required by the provisions of its above policies to pay all sums which

DISCUSSION

* * *

We agree with the district court's conclusion, substantially for the reasons stated in its opinion, that the trigger-of-coverage clause unambiguously provides for coverage based upon the occurrence during the policy period of an injury in fact. We reject only so much of the court's decision as holds that "injury in fact" means an injury that was "diagnosable" or "compensable" during the policy period.

A. *Coverage in General*

We agree with the district court that the plain language of the policies is quite inconsistent with any of the interpretations put forth by the parties. The provision that the policies give coverage for occurrences that cause injury, read with the provision that the policies apply only to "personal injury, sickness or disease * * * which occurs during the policy period," clearly supports the court's conclusion that coverage is triggered by injury in fact. Liberty's construction of "injury" as "manifestation of injury" is inconsistent with this language. Some types of injury to the body occur prior to the appearance of any symptoms; thus, the manifestation of the injury may well occur after the injury itself. There is no language in the policies that purports to limit coverage only to injuries that become apparent during the policy period, regardless of when the injury actually occurred. Therefore, we agree with the district court that Liberty's manifestation interpretation is not reasonable.

AHP's contentions that exposure alone is sufficient to trigger coverage are likewise contrary to the plain language of the policies. Injury cannot be read as the equivalent of exposure, because the policy contemplates injury caused by exposure; since a cause normally precedes its effect, it is plain that an injury could occur during the policy period although the exposure that caused it preceded that period. AHP's interpretations urging that exposure alone could trigger coverage are thus also not reasonable.

The same recognition of the sequence of cause and effect supports the court's rejection of Liberty's interpretation of the Proviso as elimi-

AHP has become, is, or becomes liable to pay by reason of liability of AHP for damages arising from the use of AHP products, insofar as such damages result from diagnosable and compensable injury, sickness, or disease to a claimant during the coverage period of such a policy; no such indemnification is required, however, with respect to any injury, sickness, or disease which Liberty can establish resulted solely from the use of AHP product after November 1, 1976.

2. Liberty shall bear the costs of defense of each lawsuit against AHP in which [ ] the complaint could be read to permit proof, or does not exclude the possibility, of the existence of any diagnosable, compensable injury, sickness or disease during any policy period. Liberty shall enter and defend, and shall bear the costs of defense, in every case brought against AHP for damages caused by any of the drugs at issue, from the time each case is brought, until and unless Liberty confines a particular plaintiff's claim so as to exclude the possibility of a recovery for which Liberty has provided insurance. Whether Liberty has so confined any particular claim shall be determined by the Court before which each such case is brought, based upon the facts developed in each litigation.

nating its responsibility for injury that occurred during the policy period where exposure that commenced prior to or during that period continued thereafter. An effect never precedes its cause. The policies plainly give coverage for injury that occurred during the policy period and was caused by exposure to AHP products; injury occurring during the policy period could not have been caused by an exposure that occurred thereafter.

* * *

We find no basis, however, for a ruling that "injury in fact" means injury that is "diagnosable" or "compensable" during the policy period. First, no clause in the policies uses either of those terms or any equivalents. Second, compensability is a legal concept that is not material to the determination of whether an injury has in fact occurred. As the district court ruled, that determination must be made according to the facts of the particular case based on medical evidence as to which drug was used and what type of injury is claimed.

Finally, the requirement that the injury be diagnosable during the policy period, like Liberty's contention for a requirement that it be manifested during that period, presents the potential for imposing an unwarranted limitation on the injury-in-fact concept. *See generally* Dykhouse & Falik, *Trigger of Coverage: The Business Context, the Plain Language and American Home Products*, 16 Conn.L.Rev. 497, 504–12 (1984). For example, a person may suffer an injury or illness that does not become diagnosable until after some period of gestation; it may be possible after diagnosis to infer that the harm must have begun some time prior to diagnosability because of the stage of the illness at the time it is diagnosed and the fact that the type of illness that is diagnosed does not occur without a gestation period. Thus, diagnosability need not coincide with the actual occurrence of injury; to add the requirement that an injury be diagnosable limits the scope of the "injury-in-fact" trigger-of-coverage clause in a way that is not justified by the policies' language. To paraphrase the district court's analysis rejecting the manifestation theory, "a real but undiscovered injury, proved in retrospect to have existed at the relevant time, would establish coverage, irrespective of the time the injury became [diagnosable]." 565 F.Supp. at 1497.

Accordingly, we modify the district court's judgment, *see* note 1 *supra,* to eliminate from paragraphs 1 and 2 thereof the words "diagnosable" and "compensable."

B. *Coverage in the 54 Underlying Suits*

We affirm the district court's refusal to issue a declaratory judgment as to the question of Liberty's duty to defend and indemnify AHP in the Underlying Suits. The issuance of declaratory relief is a matter committed to the discretion of the trial court; it is not a matter of right of the litigants. We see no basis for concluding that the court abused its discretion here.

* * *

The judgment of the district court is modified to eliminate the terms "diagnosable" and "compensable"; as modified, the judgment is affirmed.

Notes

1. What does the case hold? How is "injury in fact" defined? Must the injury in fact be either diagnosable or compensable?

2. *American Home Products* has become the exemplar of the "injury in fact" approach to determining *when* the liability policy coverage is triggered. See also Aetna Cas. & Surety Company v. Abbott Laboratories, Inc., 636 F.Supp. 546 (D.Conn.1986); Spartan Petroleum Co. v. Federated Mutual Ins. Co., 162 F.3d 805 (4th Cir.1998) (injury in fact theory applies in South Carolina).

3. The diversity of theories in the federal courts is attributable in part to the necessity of applying state law in an area where the latter is likewise divergent, opaque, or nonexistent. For example, New York law is the purported authority for the "injury in fact" theory set forth here.

In *Keene Corp. v. Insurance Co. of North America*, 667 F.2d 1034 (D.C. Cir. 1981), the D.C. Circuit, without authoritative guidance by state law developed the widely approved triple-trigger, continuous injury theory. Yet in *Abex Corp. v. Maryland Casualty Co.*, 790 F.2d 119 (D.C.Cir.1986), the same court, obligated by the *Erie* doctrine, applied the New York "injury in fact" approach of the main case and produced an opinion virtually, if not literally, in antithesis to *Keene.*

MONTROSE CHEMICAL CORP. v. ADMIRAL INS. CO.

Supreme Court of California, In Bank, 1995.
10 Cal.4th 645, 42 Cal.Rptr.2d 324, 913 P.2d 878.

LUCAS, CHIEF JUSTICE.

* * *

In this case we ... must determine whether four comprehensive general liability (CGL) policies issued by defendant and respondent Admiral Insurance Company (Admiral) to plaintiff and appellant Montrose Chemical Corporation of California (Montrose) obligate Admiral to defend Montrose in lawsuits seeking damages for continuous or progressively deteriorating bodily injury and property damage that occurred during the successive policy periods. These losses, it is alleged, were caused by Montrose's disposal of hazardous wastes at times predating the commencement of Admiral's policy periods.

As explained below, we conclude that the standard CGL policy language, such as was incorporated into Admiral's policies in issue in this case, provides coverage for bodily injury and property damage that occurs during the policy period. In the case of successive policies,[50] bodily

50. Throughout this opinion, any reference to "successive" policies is intended to also include policies or policy periods which are temporally separated from one another by gaps or lapses in the coverage periods.

injury and property damage that is continuous or progressively deteriorating throughout several policy periods is potentially covered by all policies in effect during those periods. Stated in the insurance industry's parlance, we conclude the "continuous injury" trigger of coverage should be adopted for third party liability insurance cases involving continuous or progressively deteriorating losses. In this case, because the potential of coverage arose under Admiral's policies, so too did its duty to defend Montrose in the underlying lawsuits.

* * *

We shall therefore affirm the judgment of the Court of Appeal reversing the summary judgment granted in favor of Admiral.

* * *

[T]he Court of Appeal reversed the [trial court's] summary judgment order. The appellate court rejected a "manifestation of loss" or "discovery" trigger of coverage analysis (as employed in the first party insurance context), finding it incompatible with the language of Admiral's third party CGL policies. It held that, because the underlying Levin Metals actions allege that continuous or progressively deteriorating property damage "occurred" throughout the period Admiral's policies were in effect, potential coverage under those policies was triggered, at least for purposes of the duty to defend. The court further held that the loss-in-progress rule did not bar coverage in the Stringfellow cases. It reasoned that Montrose's potential liability to third parties for the progressive property damage alleged to have "occurred" throughout the period of Admiral's policies was still "contingent," and thus insurable, under section 250, even if damage as defined in the Admiral policies was inevitable, and notwithstanding Montrose's earlier receipt of the PRP letter. The Court of Appeal remanded Admiral's affirmative defense—that Montrose had concealed material facts prior to purchasing the CGL policies from Admiral—and further declined to address the insurer's argument, not raised in the trial court, that coverage for progressive damage at the Stringfellow site is also barred under specific policy exclusions because Montrose "expected or intended" the progressive damage that occurred during Admiral's policy periods.

We granted Admiral's petition for review to consider the complex and important issue of when potential coverage is triggered under a CGL policy where the underlying third party claims involve continuous or progressively deteriorating damage or injury, and how the loss-in-progress rule applies to such policies.

II

TRIGGER OF COVERAGE IN THIRD PARTY PROGRESSIVE LOSS CASES

As noted, Admiral moved for summary judgment in the trial court on grounds that it had no duty to defend or indemnify Montrose in the Levin Metals cases because the circumstances which trigger coverage, within the meaning of the coverage clauses in its policies, did not occur during the policy periods, and that it had no duty to defend or indemnify Montrose in the Stringfellow cases because the contamination alleged in those actions was an uninsurable loss-in-progress prior to the effective date of the first policy it issued to Montrose. Having convinced the trial court, but not the Court of Appeal, Admiral seeks to renew these claims. Admiral asserts in its brief on the merits that "the fact that the Stringfellow CERCLA action alleges continuing or progressive contamination does not establish there was an occurrence while Admiral's policies were in effect." Admiral asserts that an "occurrence," as defined in its policies, is the precipitating act or event which gave rise to the contamination, or, as Admiral phrases it in the context of the Stringfellow litigation, "the same general conditions that had already resulted in damage ... before the policy [commenced]." Admiral submits that "all damage was caused by a single occurrence outside (i.e., prior to commencement of) Admiral's policy period," and urges that any determination that continuous or progressive damage or injury occurring during its ensuing policy periods can itself trigger coverage, "ignore[s] the policy language and confuse[s] the consequences of the occurrence with the occurrence itself, i.e., the event that 'resulted' in damage." In short, Admiral asserts that coverage under its CGL policies is established at the time of the "occurrence," i.e., the precipitating act or event which first gives rise to the damage or injury.

* * *

As already indicated, in the case before us, Montrose urges our adoption of a continuous injury trigger of coverage. Admiral in turn, in its briefs, urges us to apply a manifestation trigger of coverage. At oral argument, however, counsel for Admiral appeared to deviate from this position, arguing instead that an injury-in-fact trigger, and not a manifestation trigger, should be applied. We shall give Admiral the benefit of the doubt and consider which, if any, of the recognized trigger of coverage theories should be applied here. The precise question, of course, is what result follows under the language of the policies of insurance to which the parties agreed, including the standardized definitions that were incorporated into those policies. As will be seen, most courts that have analyzed the issue have found the continuous injury trigger of coverage applicable to the standard occurrence-based CGL policy.

One of the first cases to apply a continuing injury theory of loss allocation in the context of progressive property damage was Gruol Construction Co. v. Insurance Co. of North America (1974) 11 Wash.App. 632 [524 P.2d 427] (Gruol). In that case, a contractor prevailed in an action against his insurer who had failed to defend him under his general liability policy in a third party construction defect suit for recovery of dry rot damage to a building. The contractor's improper piling of dirt against the building had caused the dry rot. The court held that the injury was a continuous process which began at the time of the negligent construction and continued through the manifestation of the dry rot damage, " 'even though there [was] a lapse of time between the initial negligent act and the occurrence of the ultimate damage.... ' " (Id. at p. 636 [524 P.2d at p. 430].) Thus the holding of Gruol was that, when warranted by the facts, property damage should be deemed to occur over the entire process of the continuing injury. An insurer would become liable at any point in the process for the entire loss up to the policy limits, even though the continuing injury or progressively deteriorating damage may extend over several policy periods.

The first reported California case to discuss the triggering of potential coverage under third party liability insurance policies, where continuous or progressively deteriorating property damage was involved, was California Union Ins. Co. v. Landmark Ins. Co., supra, 145 Cal.App.3d 462, 193 Cal.Rptr. 461 (California Union). That case involved a gradual leak of water from a swimming pool which caused damage to adjoining property. The parties stipulated that the pool began to leak in June 1979, and that a crack in the pool was the sole cause of the ensuing property damage. Damage to the adjoining property occurred between July 1979 and November 1980. Landmark Insurance Company (Landmark) was on the risk from July 1978 to July 1980. California Union Insurance Company (Cal Union) provided liability coverage from July 1980 to July 1981. (Id. at pp. 467–469, 193 Cal.Rptr. 461.)

The source of the leakage damage in California Union was discovered during an inspection of the pool in October 1980, at a point in time following expiration of the Landmark policy and during the term of the successive Cal Union policy. At trial, the two carriers contested liability for the damage that occurred between October 1980 (discovery of the leak) and November 1980 (repair of the source of the damage). Landmark had undertaken repairs prior to the expiration of its policy in July 1980, but apparently repaired only the damage to the slopes of the adjoining property, and not the as-yet undiscovered source of the damage: the leaking pool. Landmark contended that the post-discovery damage (that which occurred after October 1980) constituted a separate occurrence within the definition of that term in the Cal Union policy, and was therefore Cal Union's sole responsibility. Cal Union in turn argued the damage was a continuation of a single occurrence that began during the period of coverage provided by the Landmark policies, and was thus the sole responsibility of Landmark. (California Union, supra, 145 Cal.App.3d at p. 468, 193 Cal.Rptr. 461.)

The trial court held that each manifestation of damage should be treated as a separate occurrence under the policies, rejecting Cal Union's position that separate incidents of manifestation of damage which are attributable to the same underlying cause are merely manifestations of the same continuous "occurrence" of damage. (California Union, supra, 145 Cal.App.3d at p. 469, 193 Cal.Rptr. 461.) The Court of Appeal reversed, concluding that the trial court's ruling contravened the express language of each insurer's policies. (Ibid.)

On appeal, both insurers in California Union readily acknowledged that under the rule of Remmer, supra, 140 Cal.App.2d 84, 295 P.2d 19 (ante, at pp. 336–337 of 42 Cal.Rptr.2d, pp. 13–14 of 897 P.2d), a coverable "occurrence" arose under their policy language at the point at which the complaining party was actually damaged, not the time at which the initial damage-causing act or conditions transpired. (California Union, supra, 145 Cal.App.3d at p. 470, 193 Cal.Rptr. 461.) The California Union court agreed, pointing out that the precise facts of Remmer were distinguishable from those in the case before it. Observing that the dangerous condition in Remmer (a defectively graded lot) had failed to manifest any damage for a period of five years, the California Union court noted that in the case before it the leaking pool was a "continuous active force at work" during the 18 months between the time of the "wrongful act" (the crack in the pool that first gave rise to the water damage to the adjoining property) and the manifestation of the actual loss. (Id. at p. 473, 193 Cal.Rptr. 461.) Focusing on the identical "one occurrence" language in Cal Union's and Landmark's CGL policies (" 'all ... property damage arising out of continuous or repeated exposure to substantially the same general conditions shall be considered as arising out of one occurrence' "), the California Union court concluded that, given the continuing and progressively deteriorating nature of the pool leakage damage, the trial court's determination that each manifestation of damage was a separate occurrence conflicted with the "one occurrence" policy language in each insurer's policies. (Id. at p. 469, 193 Cal.Rptr. 461.)

The California Union court next surveyed several California appellate decisions which, up to that time, had attempted to set, for definitional purposes, the timing of occurrences of damage or injury transpiring prior to, during, or after the effective periods of successive third party liability insurance policies. (California Union, supra, 145 Cal.App.3d at pp. 471–472, 474, 193 Cal.Rptr. 461, and cases cited.) Although each such case "[w]ithout exception ... involved delays in varying periods of time between the wrongful act and [manifestation of] the actual loss," the California Union court observed that none had involved actual continuous or progressively deteriorating damage or injury. (Id. at p. 473, 193 Cal.Rptr. 461.) The court also took note of the settled authorities holding that an insurer's obligation to indemnify an insured for manifested losses may continue even after the term of the policy expires. (Ibid.) Even in the third party liability insurance context, an insurer's liability for a still insured and continuing event is not terminated by the expiration of the policy term. (California Union, supra, 145 Cal.App.3d at p. 475, 193 Cal.Rptr. 461; accord, Harman v. American Casualty Co. of Reading, Pa. (C.D.Cal.1957) 155 F.Supp. 612.) As stated in California Union: "[I]n a 'one occurrence' case involving continuous, progressive and deteriorating damage, the carrier in whose policy period the damage first becomes apparent remains on the risk until the damage is finally and totally complete, notwithstanding a policy provision which purports to limit the coverage solely to those accidents/occurrences within the time parameters of the stated policy term." (California Union, supra, 145 Cal.App.3d at p. 476, 193 Cal.Rptr. 461.)

Having found under settled principles of law that insurer Landmark remained obligated to indemnify the insured for the pool leakage damage which commenced prior to, but continued to progressively deteriorate after, expiration of Landmark's policy, the California Union court then turned to the unsettled question of whether the successive insurer, Cal Union, was also on the risk for the damage occurring during its successive policy period. Although it was true that the force producing the continuing pool leakage was already set in motion when Cal Union came on the risk with the initiation of its successive policy, that damage-causing force continued into the period of Cal Union's policy, further damage occurred during that policy period, and substantial corrective procedures were necessary and performed after the October–November 1980 damage manifested itself during the period of Cal Union's policy. (California Union, supra, 145 Cal.App.3d at p. 476, 193 Cal.Rptr. 461.)

The California Union court concluded Cal Union was on the risk to indemnify the insured for the continuous property damage occurring through its successive policy period. The court placed primary reliance on three cases. The first was Gruol, supra, 11 Wash.App. 632 [524 P.2d 427]. Gruol, as noted above (ante, at pp. 341–342 of 42 Cal.Rptr.2d, pp. 18–19 of 897 P.2d), held that progressive property damage should be deemed to occur over the entire process of the continuing injury, with a CGL carrier liable at any point in the process for the entire loss up to the policy limits, even though the continuous or progressively deteriorating damage extends over successive policy periods. (11 Wash.App. at p. 636 [524 P.2d at pp. 430–431].)

The second case relied on by the California Union court was the Sixth Circuit Court of Appeals' decision in Forty–Eight Insulations, supra, 633 F.2d 1212. As noted above, Forty–Eight Insulations was the leading case on the exposure theory of coverage, holding that due to the continuing and cumulative nature of asbestos-related diseases, insurers providing CGL coverage commencing at the time of the worker's initial exposure to asbestos particles would be held potentially liable to defend and indemnify the insured manufacturer of asbestos products in underlying third party actions alleging bodily injury claims against the insured. (Ante, at p. 339 of 42 Cal.Rptr.2d, p. 16 of 897 P.2d.) Recognizing that Forty–Eight Insulations was an asbestos products liability case, the California Union court nonetheless concluded that because the Sixth Circuit Court of Appeals' decision involved a CGL policy covering "single accident/occurrence, continuing damage claims," the basic rationale of that decision was applicable to the continuous injury trigger analysis being invoked for the ongoing property damage at issue in California Union. (California Union, supra, 145 Cal.App.3d at p. 478, 193 Cal.Rptr. 461.)

The third case relied on by the California Union court was Keene Corp. v. Insurance Co. of North America (D.C.Cir.1981) 667 F.2d 1034. Like Forty–Eight Insulations, Keene was a products liability case in which the manufacturer of insulation products containing asbestos brought an action for a declaratory judgment seeking a determination of the obligations of four liability insurance carriers to defend and indemnify it in pending products liability litigation. Holding that the "occurrence" which caused the bodily injury took place substantially before the manifestation of the ultimate injury (asbestosis), the District of Columbia Circuit Court of Appeals found each insurer on the risk between the initial exposure and the manifestation of disease to be potentially liable for indemnification and defense costs. (667 F.2d at pp. 1046–1047; California Union, supra, 145 Cal.App.3d at p. 478, 193 Cal.Rptr. 461.)

The Keene court based its rationale primarily on the expectations of the parties and the ambiguities it perceived as inherent in the standard CGL policy language. Applying the presumption requiring ambiguities to be construed in favor of the insured, the Keene court reasoned that Keene Corporation (the insured) could have reasonably expected that it was covered for future liabilities: "A latent injury, unknown and unknowable to Keene at the time it purchased [liability] insurance, must, at least, be covered by an insurer on the risk at the time it manifests itself." (Keene, supra, 667 F.2d at p. 1044.) In the context of a progressive disease like asbestosis, where the medical evidence indicates that the disease can develop or manifest as late as 20 or more years after exposure, the continuous injury trigger of potential coverage adopted in Keene, consistent with the expectations of the insured, fixes the timing of the injury at the point of initial exposure of the injured third party to the injury-causing agent, at the time of manifestation of symptoms of bodily injury, and during the development and progression of the disease in between those points in time. The Keene court also broadly interpreted bodily injury to mean "any part of the single injurious process that asbestos-related diseases entail." (Id. at p. 1047.)

Fireman's Fund Ins. Co. v. Aetna Casualty & Surety Co., supra, 223 Cal.App.3d 1621, 273 Cal.Rptr. 431 (Fireman's Fund) was the next California appellate decision postdating California Union to directly address the question of coverage for continuous property damage or losses under successive third party CGL policies. In Fireman's Fund, two liability carriers insured a contractor that had undertaken the restoration of the exterior facade of a hotel. The first carrier (Fireman's Fund) was on the risk when construction defects (spalling and cracking of the restored facade) were first discovered; the second carrier (Aetna) was on the risk when the defects progressed and when their cause became known. (Fireman's Fund, supra, 223 Cal.App.3d at p. 1623, 273 Cal.Rptr. 431.) On cross-motions for summary judgment, based upon stipulated facts and purporting to rely on the rationale of Home Ins. Co. v. Landmark Ins. Co. (1988) 205 Cal.App.3d 1388, 253 Cal.Rptr. 277 (Home) (a first party property insurance case holding that only the first of two successive insurers, the carrier on the risk on the date of first manifestation of the property damage, was liable for the entire claim), the trial court determined Fireman's Fund was solely responsible to indemnify the contractor for an arbitration award returned against it. The Fourth District Court of Appeal (the same court that decided Home) affirmed the trial court's order, rejecting Fireman's Fund's argument that the analysis of Home was inapposite because that case involved first party property insurance coverage, not third party general liability insurance. (Fireman's Fund, supra, 223 Cal.App.3d at pp. 1623–1624, 273 Cal.Rptr. 431.)

Although the Fireman's Fund court was construing standardized third party CGL policies, the court refused to apply the continuous injury trigger of coverage analysis adopted for third party liability insurance policies in California Union, supra, 145 Cal.App.3d 462, 193 Cal.Rptr. 461. The Fireman's Fund court observed that it had already considered and rejected the reasoning of California Union in Home, supra, 205 Cal.App.3d 1388, 253 Cal.Rptr. 277, and opined that coverage under successive third party CGL policies, in essence, should require no different analysis than that which was applied in the first party property insurance context in Home. In short, the Fireman's Fund court applied the manifestation trigger of coverage which it had earlier adopted in Home. (Fireman's Fund, supra, 223 Cal.App.3d at pp. 1626–1627, 273 Cal.Rptr. 431.) The court indicated that "[t]o the extent Home's rationale rests on the loss-in-progress rule, it, too, is fully applicable to a third party claim." (Id. at p. 1627, 273 Cal.Rptr. 431, fn. omitted.) And the Fireman's Fund court reasoned further that, "[l]ike the situation in Home, here the issues arise in a context where the claimant [i.e., the insured] has been fully satisfied and the case involves allocating loss between insurers. Home is, therefore, dispositive. Contrary to Fireman's Fund's contention, Garvey, supra, 48 Cal.3d 395, [257 Cal.Rptr. 292, 770 P.2d 704] does not change the result." (Id. at p. 1628, 273 Cal.Rptr. 431.)

The Fireman's Fund court made clear in its opinion that our admonishments in Garvey, respecting the differences between first party property and third party liability insurance, had little impact on that court's determination to apply its earlier trigger of coverage analysis in Home to the third party liability insurance case before it. The Fireman's Fund court suggested: "In Garvey, the Supreme Court held it is 'important to separate the causation analysis necessary in a first party property loss case from that which must be undertaken in a third party tort liability case.' (Garvey, supra, 48 Cal.3d at p. 406 [257 Cal.Rptr. 292, 770 P.2d 704], italics added.) However, although there are important differences between property damage insurance and liability insurance—not the least of which is causation analysis—the issues here do not even remotely involve causation. Garvey neither holds nor suggests that all legal principles developed in first party cases are inapplicable in third party cases. Thus, even if Home's rationale was solely based upon first party insurance provisions (which it is not), Garvey does not prohibit its application to liability coverage." (Fireman's Fund, supra, 223 Cal. App.3d at p. 1628, 273 Cal.Rptr. 431, italics in original.)

The Fireman's Fund court failed to engage in any meaningful discussion of what factors set first party property insurance policies apart from third party comprehensive liability insurance policies. Nor did the court set forth in its opinion, or make any attempt to analyze, the standard definition of "occurrence" found in the standard form CGL policy. Finally, apparently satisfied with its earlier observation in Home that, "[b]y its terms, section 22 [the codified loss-in-progress rule] applies to both first-party [property insurance] and third-party [liability insurance] cases" (Home, supra, 205 Cal.App.3d at p. 1395, 253 Cal.Rptr. 277, fn. 4), the Fireman's Fund court made no further effort to analyze how application of the loss-in-progress rule might differ in the third party liability insurance context.

Only one reported California decision followed Fireman's Fund in holding the manifestation trigger of coverage applicable in cases of continuous or progressively deteriorating damage or injury under successive third party CGL policies. In Pines of La Jolla Homeowners Assn. v. Industrial Indemnity (1992) 5 Cal.App.4th 714, 7 Cal.Rptr.2d 53, the Fourth District Court of Appeal once again, relying on its earlier holding in Fireman's Fund, supra, 223 Cal.App.3d 1621, 273 Cal.Rptr. 431, concluded that a manifestation theory should be applied in determining the trigger of potential coverage applicable under several CGL policies for continuous property damage resulting from construction defects. (5 Cal.App.4th at pp. 721–722, 7 Cal.Rptr.2d 53.)

Most recently, the Fourth District Court of Appeal decided Zurich Ins. Co. v. Transamerica Ins. Co. (Cal.App.) (1995), 38 Cal.Rptr.2d 345, 889 P.2d 539 (Zurich). Zurich involved a declaratory relief action, brought by one of four liability insurers who provided successive periods of coverage to a construction company, to determine the respective defense and indemnity obligations of each insurer with regard to three underlying construction defect actions against the company pertaining to a condominium project.

The Fourth District Court of Appeal in Zurich repudiated the rationale of its earlier decision in Fireman's Fund, supra, 223 Cal.App.3d 1621, 273 Cal.Rptr. 431. The court acknowledged that "[t]he manifestation rule developed in the first party context is not appropriately applied across the board," and that "[i]nstead, in this [third party] liability context, a 'continuing injury' trigger should be used, because property damage occurred ... and continued ... [over a period of several years]." The court "[n]oted that the manifestation rule presupposes that the first party insured will be on site to observe the damage; it is in the nature of a discovery rule. However, third party liability policies do not contain in their occurrence sections any discovery requirement or a policy limitations period for the filing of an action after manifestation of a defect." The Zurich court also retreated from the "rather narrow definition of contingency" espoused in Fireman's Fund in connection with that opinion's discussion of the loss-in-progress rule, and reached new conclusions regarding the applicability of that rule in third party liability insurance cases, consistent with the conclusions we reach today respecting the applicability of that rule to this case. (Post, at pp. 350–352 of 42 Cal.Rptr.2d, pp. 904–905 of 913 P.2d.)

Accordingly, to the extent the decisions in Fireman's Fund, supra, 223 Cal.App.3d 1621, 273 Cal.Rptr. 431, and Pines of La Jolla Homeowners Assn. v. Industrial Indemnity, supra, 5 Cal.App.4th 714, 7 Cal.Rptr.2d 53, are inconsistent with the principles discussed herein, those decisions are hereby disapproved.

5. Various practical and policy considerations further support adoption of the continuous injury trigger of coverage for the third party claims of continuous or progressively deteriorating damage or injury brought under the CGL policies in this case.

Our foregoing review of the standard CGL policy language, as incorporated into Admiral's policies, as well as the relevant cases and authorities that have construed that language, leads us to conclude that the continuous injury trigger of coverage should be adopted for claims of continuous or progressively deteriorating damage or injury under the third party CGL policies in issue in this case.

We have shown why Admiral's express policy language supports application of the continuous injury trigger of coverage. We have explained that, contrary to Admiral's arguments in its briefs, it has long been understood that the standard form CGL policy provides liability coverage for damage or injury occurring during the policy period which results from an accident, or from continuous or repeated exposure to injurious conditions. There is no requirement that the sudden, accidental damage-causing act or event, or the conditions giving rise to the damage or injury, themselves occur within the policy period in order for potential liability coverage to arise. We have also explained how retention of the term "accident" within the standard definition of occurrence in the "occurrence-based" policies drafted after 1966 was intended to serve the one-occurrence rule, and was never intended to impose a requirement that the damage-causing accident, event, or conditions occur within the policy period. We have noted the settled rule that an insurer on the risk when continuous or progressively deteriorating damage or injury first manifests itself remains obligated to indemnify the insured for the entirety of the ensuing damage or injury. And we have reviewed the rationale of California Union, supra, 145 Cal.App.3d 462, 193 Cal.Rptr. 461, and the decisions cited and relied on therein, which, together with the weight of more recent authorities,[53] conclude that where successive

53. Decisions of the highest courts of other states which are consistent with the conclusions we reach today—rejecting a manifestation trigger and adopting the continuous injury trigger of coverage for claims of continuing or progressively deteriorating bodily injury or property damage arising under third party CGL policies—include Owens–Illinois, Inc. v. United Ins. Co. (1994) 138 N.J. 437, 650 A.2d 974, 990, 995 [New Jersey Supreme Court unanimously adopts continuous injury trigger in a case involving CGL coverage for asbestos claims relating to both bodily injury and property damage]; Trustees of Tufts Univ. v. Commercial Union Ins. Co. (1993) 415 Mass. 844, 616 N.E.2d 68, 74 [Massachusetts Supreme Judicial Court unanimously rejects manifestation trigger in environmental property damage case involving claims under occurrence-based CGL policies, explaining, "Nothing in the language of the poli-

CGL policies have been purchased, bodily injury and property damage that is continuing or progressively deteriorating throughout more than one policy period is potentially covered by all policies in effect during those periods.

Lastly, we have explained how first party insurance differs from third party liability insurance in many fundamental respects, and why the rationale of our holding in Prudential–LMI, supra, 51 Cal.3d 674, 274 Cal.Rptr. 387, 798 P.2d 1230, adopting the manifestation trigger of coverage for first party cases, would be inapposite if applied in the context of third party liability insurance coverage.

Our conclusion that the continuous injury trigger of coverage should be applied to the third party CGL policies in this case is also in conformity with several important policy considerations. In Prudential–LMI, supra, 51 Cal.3d at page 699, 274 Cal.Rptr. 387, 798 P.2d 1230, we observed, as one policy reason favoring adoption of the manifestation trigger of coverage in first party property insurance cases, that "the underwriting practices of the insurer can be made predictable because the insurer is not liable for a loss once its contract with the insured ends unless the manifestation of loss occurred during its contract term." Admiral here suggests that the general policy favoring the predictability of underwriting practices and reserves will be negatively affected by adoption of a continuous injury trigger in the third party CGL insurance context. We disagree. A number of factors undercut Admiral's concerns.

First, leaving aside the availability of excess (multiple) policies or "other insurance" clauses, and absent express policy language decreeing the manner of apportionment of contribution among successive liability insurers, the courts will generally apply equitable considerations to

cies requires that the claimed property damage be discovered or manifested during the policy period. The inquiry instead is whether property damage, as defined in the policies, 'occurred' within the policy period and within the meaning of the word 'occurrence.' [Citation.] Indeed, the very nature of an 'occurrence' as opposed to a 'claims-made' policy is to provide coverage for property damage that occurred during the policy period whenever that liability is imposed."]; J.H. France Refractories Co. v. Allstate Ins. Co. (1993) 534 Pa. 29, 626 A.2d 502, 507 [Pennsylvania Supreme Court unanimously adopts continuous injury or "multiple" trigger for asbestos-related bodily injury claims brought under CGL policies, noting, "Rather than selecting one or another of the phases [exposure, manifestation, discovery, etc.] as the exclusive trigger of liability, it seems more accurate to regard all stages of the disease process as bodily injury sufficient to trigger the insurers' obligation to indemnify, as all phases independently meet the policy definition of bodily injury."]; Harford County v. Harford Mutual Ins. Co. (1992) 327 Md. 418, 610 A.2d 286, 294–295 [Maryland Court of Appeals rejects manifestation trigger in environmental pollution case]; see also Sentinel Ins. Co. v. First Ins. Co. (1994) 76 Hawaii 277, 875 P.2d 894, 917 [Hawaii Supreme Court unanimously adopts injury-in-fact trigger in construction defect case alleging claims for property losses under CGL policies, but explains that "where injury-in-fact occurs continuously over a period covered by different insurers or policies, and actual apportionment of the injury is difficult or impossible to determine, the continuous injury trigger may be employed to equitably apportion liability among insurers."]. Other courts which have recently applied a continuous injury trigger in environmental property damage cases for which coverage was claimed under standardized occurrence-based CGL policies include the Oregon Court of Appeals (St. Paul Fire & Marine Ins. Co. v. McCormick & Baxter Creosoting Co. (1994) 126 Or.App. 689, 870 P.2d 260, 264–265), and the United States District Court for the District of Delaware (Harleysville Mut. Ins. Co. v. Sussex County (D.Del.1993) 831 F.Supp. 1111, 1124 [applying Delaware law]).

spread the cost among the several policies and insurers. (See, e.g., CNA Casualty of California v. Seaboard Surety Co. (1986) 176 Cal.App.3d 598, 619–620, 222 Cal.Rptr. 276; Olympic Ins. Co. v. Employers Surplus Lines Ins. Co. (1981) 126 Cal.App.3d 593, 601–602, 178 Cal.Rptr. 908.)

Second, in establishing reserves for the standard form occurrence-based CGL policies which replaced accident-based policies in 1966, the insurance industry, as we have shown, was fully aware of the intended scope of coverage of the new policies, coupled with the specific provision providing coverage for continuous or repeated exposure to conditions causing property damage or bodily injury. Indeed, the drafting history of the standard occurrence-based CGL policy reflects that not only did the drafters understand the term occurrence to mean an accident or exposure to injurious conditions resulting in the occurrence of damage or injury during the policy period, they specifically considered and rejected the suggestion that language establishing a manifestation or discovery trigger of coverage be incorporated into the standard form CGL policy. Among the reasons relied on for rejecting the incorporation of such limitations into the standard definitions in the coverage clauses were several stated equitable concerns: the difficulty of applying such limitations or requirements in cases of continuing damage or injury over the course of successive policy periods, the uncertainty of who would bear the burden of a discovery requirement (i.e., the insured or third party claimants), the arbitrariness, from the carrier's perspective, of telescoping all damage in a continuing injury case into a single policy period, and the fear that policyholders could be disadvantaged by such an approach. (See American Home Prod. v. Liberty Mut. Ins. Co., supra, 565 F.Supp. 1485, 1501–1502, affd. as mod., supra, 748 F.2d 760 [surveying joint committee hearings and drafting materials].) In short, the insurance industry is on record as itself having identified several sound policy considerations favoring adoption of a continuous injury trigger of coverage in the third party liability insurance context.

Finally, we agree with Montrose that application of a manifestation trigger of coverage to an occurrence-based CGL policy would unduly transform it into a "claims made" policy. Claims made policies were specifically developed to limit an insurer's risk by restricting coverage to the single policy in effect at the time a claim was asserted against the insured, without regard to the timing of the damage or injury, thus permitting the carrier to establish reserves without regard to possibilities of inflation, upward-spiraling jury awards, or enlargements of tort liability after the policy period.[54] The insurance industry's introduction

54. "Claims made" policies beneficially permit insurers more accurately to predict the limits of their exposure and the premium needed to accommodate the risk undertaken, resulting in lower premiums than are charged for an occurrence-based policy. (See, e.g., Pacific Employers Ins. Co. v. Superior Court (1990) 221 Cal.App.3d 1348, 1359–1360, 270 Cal.Rptr. 779.) Another name for a "claims made" policy is a "discovery" policy. (VTN Consol., Inc. v. Northbrook Ins. Co. (1979) 92 Cal.App.3d 888, 891, 155 Cal.Rptr. 172.) "Claims made" coverage arose more than 20 years ago, initially in the field of professional liability insurance, because underwriters were concerned that occurrence-based coverage was adversely affecting the underwriting proof "claims made" policies into the area of comprehensive liability insurance itself attests to the industry's understanding that the standard occurrence-based CGL policy provides coverage for injury or damage that may not be discovered or manifested until after expiration of the policy period. That understanding is clearly reflected in the higher premiums that must be paid for occurrence-based coverage to offset the increased exposure. (Pacific Employers Ins. Co. v. Superior Court, supra, 221 Cal.App.3d at pp. 1359–1360, 270 Cal.Rptr. 779.) We agree with the conclusion of the Court of Appeal below that to apply a manifestation trigger of coverage to Admiral's occurrence-based CGL policies would be to effectively rewrite Admiral's contracts of insurance with Montrose, transforming the broader and more expensive occurrence-based CGL policy into a claims made policy. (Accord, Harford County v. Harford Mut. Ins., supra, 610 A.2d at pp. 294–295.)

We therefore conclude that the continuous injury trigger of coverage should be applied to the underlying third party claims of continuous or progressively deteriorating damage or injury alleged to have occurred during Admiral's policy periods. Where, as here, successive CGL policy periods are implicated, bodily injury and property damage which is continuous or progressively deteriorating throughout several policy periods is potentially covered by all policies in effect during those periods.

Notes

1. The physical injury (as well as legal) ramifications of the asbestosis phenomenon were not clearly apparent to the insurers of the manufacturers, product handlers, etc. of the material at the various periods during which the so-called CGL policies, under which coverage is asserted, were in use. These fairly standardized policies are drafted and periodically revised by joint committees within the industry. Over the course of years there have been changes in the policy language defining the insured event, and in reading the cases wherein there are multiple successive insurers, one becomes aware that the policies may not be exactly the same. As a rough guide:

(a) pre–1967 policies provide for coverage with respect to bodily injury or property damage resulting from an "occurrence" which is defined as "an event or continuous exposure to conditions, which unexpectedly caused injury during the policy period;"

(b) from 1967 to 1973 the definition of occurrence was changed to: "an accident, including injurious exposure to conditions, which results, dur-

cess. Because the injury and negligence giving rise to a malpractice claim is often not discoverable until years after the negligent act or omission, professional liability insurance carriers, in an effort to reduce their exposure to an unpredictable and lengthy "tail" of lawsuits, shifted to the "claims made" policy. (Pacific Employers Ins. Co. v. Superior Court, supra, 221 Cal.App.3d at p. 1358, 270 Cal.Rptr. 779; see also Keeton & Widiss (1988) Insurance Law: A Guide to Fundamental Principles, Legal Doctrines, and Commercial Practices, s 5.10(d), at p. 598.) The "claims made" concept was subsequently extended into the field of general liability coverage, and in 1986 ISO issued both a revised standard form occurrence-based CGL policy (now referred to as a commercial general liability policy) and a new standard form CGL "claims made" policy.

ing the policy period, in bodily injury, property damage neither expected nor intended from the standpoint of the insured;"

(c) after 1973 the policies cover "bodily injury," meaning "bodily injury, sickness or disease, which occurs during the policy period."

The court in *Keene Corp. v. Insurance Co. of North America*, 667 F.2d 1034 (D.C.Cir.1981), which as the text notes is the primary example of the continuous injury (or "triple trigger") approach, has an elaborate appendix on the differences in policy language of the various insurers at risk, but concludes that none of the differences warrant different interpretation. 667 F.2d at 1039.

Is it not possible (even likely), however, that the language of the pre–1967 policies might lead a court to the conclusion that "exposure" is *the* trigger of coverage?

2. With the continuous trigger, when does coverage begin? When does it end?

3. Is a real estate encroachment a "continuous injury?" In *Borg v. Transamerica Ins. Co.*, 47 Cal.App.4th 448, 54 Cal.Rptr.2d 811 (1996), George Borg bought residential property in 1971 that contained a redwood deck, three wooden planter boxes, and a concrete pad for a garage, all of which extended past his property line onto the vacant lot next door. In October 1991, the owner of the adjacent vacant lot filed a lawsuit against Borg, seeking damages and a permanent injunction to force Borg to remove the encroaching structures. However, Borg's homeowners insurance policy with Transamerica contained comprehensive general liability coverage as was in effect from February 8, 1991 to February 8, 1992. He tendered the defense to Transamerica on December 27, 1991. On January 6, 1992, Transamerica refused to defend Borg, stating that the encroachments were constructed prior to the commencement of the policy period. The encroachment lawsuit ultimately was resolved in Borg's favor, with the court finding that he had acquired the right to retain his encroachments based on a prescriptive easement by adverse possession theory. Borg sued Transamerica for breach of contract and breach of the implied covenant of good faith and fair dealing for its refusal to defend his lawsuit. Noting that the California Supreme Court had adopted the "continuous injury" trigger in *Montrose*, the appeals court held that "continuous injury" is not limited to hazardous waste cases or cases involving progressively worsening exposure to injury-causing substances. The court concluded that the encroachment was a continuous injury and that Transamerica had a duty to defend Borg.

4. California courts have also applied the continuous trigger theory to construction defect actions. Pepperell v. Scottsdale Ins. Co., 62 Cal.App.4th 1045, 73 Cal.Rptr.2d 164 (1998).

5. *Montrose* notes the states that have adopted the continuous trigger approach. 10 Cal.4th 687 & n. 22 (Hawaii, Maryland, Massachusetts, New Jersey, Pennsylvania, Oregon, and Delaware). Despite the suggestion in *Montrose* to the contrary, only a handful of states have adopted the continuous trigger approach. Including the seven states cited in *Montrose*, plus *Montrose* itself, a total of eleven states have adopted the continuous trigger theory. The other three are Illinois, Minnesota and Wisconsin. United States

Gypsum Co. v. Admiral Ins. Co., 268 Ill.App.3d 598, 205 Ill.Dec. 619, 643 N.E.2d 1226 (1994); Northern States Power Co. v. Fidelity & Casualty Co., 523 N.W.2d 657 (Minn.1994); Society Insurance v. Town of Franklin, 233 Wis.2d 207, 607 N.W.2d 342, 2000 WI App 35 (2000).

6. Michigan has explicitly declined to follow *Montrose* in adopting the continuous trigger theory. American Bumper and Mfg. Co. v. Hartford Fire Ins. Co., 452 Mich. 440, 550 N.W.2d 475 (1996).

7. A difficulty exacerbated by the continuous trigger theory, and other trigger theories that occur over time, is that many policies may be implicated over an extended period of time and it is not inconceivable that one or more policies can be lost. In one case that has considered the problem, an insured was able to meet its burden of proving coverage through the testimony of the insurer's agent. Dart Industries v. Commercial Union Insurance Co., 28 Cal.4th 1059, 1070–71, 52 P.3d 79, 86–87, 124 Cal.Rptr.2d 142, 151–52 (2002)(secondary evidence allowed to prove contents of lost policy).

2. Stacking of Coverage

The following discussion proceeds on the assumption that the insurance policies under consideration contain no anti-stacking provisions. The problem of enforcement of anti-stacking provisions is contained in the notes following the succeeding cases.

EMPLOYERS INSURANCE OF WAUSAU v. GRANITE STATE INSURANCE CO.

United States Court of Appeals, Ninth Circuit, 2003
330 F.3d 1214

HALL, Circuit Judge:

* * *

FACTS

Wausau issued five general liability insurance policies to CWS [California Water services] during the five-year period from January 1, 1980 to January 1, 1985. Granite issued five excess policies covering the same time period. The parties stipulated to the following characterization of their insurance policies:

1) "Each of the Wausau policies contained a per year limit of liability of $2 million for each occurrence and a $2 million aggregate limit of liability."

2) "The Granite State policies were first layer excess policies over the Wausau policies, and each of the Granite State policies contained a $5 million limit of liability for each occurrence and a $5 million aggregate limit of liability."

Beginning in 1980, a group of homeowners experienced property damage caused by a landslide that was activated, in part, by ruptures in CWS's underground waterlines. Thirty-two homeowners subsequently brought suit against CWS. Wausau defended CWS, and ultimately settled the homeowners' claims for a total of $7,752,070.

Wausau filed the instant subrogation action against Granite on January 21, 1992, seeking $5 million. At Granite's request, on March 22, 1993, the district court stayed the action pending resolution of several potentially relevant California cases. On March 31, 1993, during the stay, Granite filed a motion for summary judgment, asserting that Wausau's action was barred by a two-year statute of limitations. The district court denied the motion, holding that the case was governed by *California Code of Civil Procedure § 337*, which provides for a four-year statute of limitations in actions based on insurance policies and other written instruments.

On February 23, 2000, Granite filed an unsuccessful motion to dismiss for failure to prosecute. Thereafter, the parties filed cross-motions for summary judgment. On March 15, 2001, the district court granted Wausau's motion and denied Granite's motion. On August 23, 2001, Granite filed a timely motion for reconsideration. The district court granted Granite's motion, concluding that its prior decisions had erroneously applied a four-year statute of limitations. The court held that Wausau's action was not founded on a written instrument, and thus was barred by the two-year statute of limitations provided for in California Code of Civil Procedure *§ 339*. Accordingly, the district court vacated its earlier judgment in favor of Wausau, and entered judgment in favor of Granite. The parties filed timely Notices of Appeal and Cross–Appeal. [The discussion of the standard of review and the statute of limitation is omitted.]

WAUSAU'S POLICY LIMITS

Granite cross-appeals the district court's interpretation of the Wausau insurance policy, which limited Wausau's total liability to $2 million, thus exposing Granite's policy to its $5 million annual limit. The district court held that the individual limits of Wausau's five policies could not be "stacked" to create coverage greater than one annual "per occurrence" limit. Granite disputes this interpretation of the Wausau policy, contending that because the "occurrence" giving rise to the CWS settlement took place over a five-year period, during which five separate policies with $2 million annual limits were in effect, Wausau's policies provided a total of $10 million in coverage.

Wausau and Granite do not dispute that the property damage giving rise to the CWS settlement arose from a single occurrence, and that continuous damage occurred proportionately throughout five policy periods. Through a joint stipulation, the parties also agreed that each of Wausau's five insurance policies limited Wausau's annual liability to $2 million, per occurrence and in the aggregate. Similarly, the parties do not dispute that Wausau's policy limit is properly characterized as a "per occurrence per year" limit. Thus, the narrow issue before the court is whether a primary insurer's total exposure can be greater than its annual policy limit, where a single occurrence caused damage during multiple years in which annual "per occurrence, per year" policies were in effect.

Stonewall Ins. Co. v. City of Palos Verdes Estates, 46 Cal.App.4th 1810, 54 Cal.Rptr.2d 176 (1996), answers this question in the affirmative. Like the instant appeal, *Stonewall* was an insurance dispute arising out of a suit alleging negligence on the part of an insured party. *Stonewall, 46 Cal.App.4th at 1823*. Several of the policies in effect during the time that the insured's negligence caused property damage had definitions of "occurrence" that were similar in breadth to the definition in Wausau's policy. *See id. at 1849* ("all damage arising from continuous and repeated exposure is deemed a single occurrence"). One such policy provided $300,000 in "per occurrence" coverage for each of three policy periods. *Id.* Under these circumstances, the insurer argued that its liability should be limited to $300,000. *Id.* The California Court of Appeal, however, held that the policy provided up to $900,000 in coverage for one occurrence that spanned the three-year period of coverage. *Id.*

Our present inquiry is virtually indistinguishable from the situation addressed by *Stonewall*. Like the instant case, *Stone-wall* involved a continuing injury that was deemed a single "occurrence." *See id. at 1825* (noting that the case involved "a continuous 'occurrence,' using the language of the policies ... throughout the period from the beginning of the damage ... until that damage became complete"). Moreover, *Stonewall*'s decision was based, in part, on a stipulation that the policy limit was "per occurrence per year." *Id. at 1849*. Similarly, Wausau has expressly stipulated that its policy "contained a per year limit of liability of $2 million for each occurrence." In addition, Wausau has repeatedly characterized its policy limit as "per occurrence per year." For these reasons, we conclude that, under *Stonewall*, Wausau's policy limits may be "stacked" to create coverage in excess of $2 million.

Wausau, however, argues that *Stonewall* is in conflict with another recent decision from the California Court of Appeal. In *FMC Corp. v. Plaisted and Cos., 61 Cal.App.4th 1132, 72 Cal.Rptr.2d 467 (1998)*, another California Court of Appeal panel held that, where "coverage is ultimately keyed to and limited by the concept of 'occurrence,'" an insured may recover an amount no greater than the policy limit for one policy period. *FMC, 61 Cal.App.4th at 1191*. The court reasoned that allowing the insured to "stack" policy limits would give the insured more coverage for any given occurrence than the parties had bargained for. *Id. at 1189*.

Wausau contends that *FMC*, in connection with several cases rejecting stacking in the "self insured retention" (SIR) context, indicates that California courts have adopted a broad rule against stacking insurance policy limits. Wausau over-states the impact of these decisions. Whether or not SIRs may be stacked is not relevant to our present inquiry, which involves a primary insurer. *See Montgomery Ward & Co. v. Imperial Cas.*

& Indem., 81 Cal.App.4th 356, 369, 97 Cal.Rptr.2d 44 (2000) ("SIR's may not be deemed primary insurance."); *Cal. Pac. Homes, Inc. v. Scottsdale Ins. Co., 70 Cal.App.4th 1187, 1194–95, 83 Cal.Rptr.2d 328 (1999)* (declining to apply *Stonewall* in a dispute involving SIRs, and emphasizing the inapplicability of precedent involving primary insurers to the SIR setting).

FMC is also distinguishable from both *Stonewall* and the instant case. The *FMC* court expressly distinguished *Stone-wall* by noting that it addresses a situation involving a "per occurrence, per year" stipulation. *FMC, 61 Cal.App.4th at 1190.* As we have noted, the Wausau policy contained a virtu-ally indistinguishable stipulation. *FMC*, therefore, neither conflicts with *Stonewall* nor requires us to limit Wausau's liability to one "per occurrence" limit.

We conclude that California courts have not broadly rejected "stacking" in the primary insurer context. To the contrary, California courts have expressly approved stacking successive "per occurrence per year" policy limits where, as here, a single occurrence extends through more than one policy period. *See Stonewall, 46 Cal.App.4th at 1849* (stacking three "per occurrence per year" limits). Here, Wausau's policy provides $2 million in coverage *per year*. The parties have stipulated that $7,752,070 in damage occurred proportionately during the five policy periods. Per the parties' stipulation, we must conclude that $1,550,414 of damages occurred during each policy period. Because Wausau's policy provided up to $2 million in coverage per year, Wausau is responsible for the entire settlement paid on behalf of CWS.

Finally, Wausau argues that allowing an insured to recover more than one policy limit would render Granite's excess coverage illusory. The only basis provided for this argument is the fact that, *as applied to this case*, Granite's theory does not trigger the excess policy. This does not render Granite's coverage illusory. Clearly, if damages had exceeded Wausau's $2 million limit during any given year, Granite would be liable for the excess. Under a principle commonly termed the "horizontal exhaustion" rule, in California, "liability under a secondary [excess] policy will not attach until all primary insurance is exhausted, even if the total amount of primary insurance exceeds the amount contemplated in the secondary policy." *Stonewall, 46 Cal.App.4th at 1850* (citing cases). Granite's argument is consistent with this rule. We conclude that the district court erred by limiting Wausau's liability to $2 million.

CONCLUSION

We REVERSE the district court's decision to dismiss the action as time-barred, REVERSE the district court's decision that Granite's excess policy was triggered, and REMAND with instructions to enter judgment in favor of Granite.

[Circuit Judge Thompson's dissent is omitted]

FMC CORP. v. PLAISTED & COS.

Court of Appeal of California, Sixth District, 1998.
61 Cal.App.4th 1132, 72 Cal.Rptr.2d 467 as modified in denial of rehearing, March 27, 1998 hearing denied, May 27, 1998.

BAMATTRE-MANOUKIAN, J.

These eight appeals arise from a single superior court action, and address specific aspects of the duty of a general liability insurer to indemnify its insured for the cost of reimbursing government agencies and of complying with orders for investigation and remediation of toxic contamination to soil, surface water, and groundwater beneath the surface of the soil.

The general liability insurance policies, issued by London insurers, are of the type known in American insurance practice as comprehensive or commercial general liability (or CGL) policies. The policies contain indemnification provisions similar to those of standard form CGL policies but omit the explicit duty-to-defend provisions commonly included in CGL policies. The policies' indemnification provisions require, in pertinent part and subject to many qualifications, that the insurer indemnify the insured for all sums the insured shall be obligated to pay by reason of liability for property damage as defined. In a writ proceeding arising out of this action the Supreme Court has established as general propositions, and insofar as applicable to these policies, that contamination of the environment is property damage and, in essence, that amounts the insured is required to pay to reimburse government agencies and to comply with government orders under statutes such as the Comprehensive Environmental Response, Compensation, and Liability Act of 1980 (CERCLA) (42 U.S.C. 9601 et seq.) and similar statutes, once hazardous wastes have been released, are sums the insured is obligated to pay by reason of liability for property damage. (AIU Ins. Co. v. Superior Court (1990) 51 Cal.3d 807, 824–843 [274 Cal.Rptr. 820, 799 P.2d 1253].) These appeals call upon us to resolve additional coverage issues, as well as procedural and evidentiary questions which arose in the course of trial.

FMC Corporation, a diversified manufacturer of equipment and chemical compounds, acknowledges that over a period of many years its commercial activities, and the activities of others at sites for which FMC was or became responsible under environmental laws, caused toxic contamination to soil and groundwater at and near many sites throughout the country. Beginning as early as 1959, FMC spent substantial sums to investigate the nature and extent of the contamination, to undertake measures of its own to remediate the contamination, to reimburse government agencies for their remediation work, and to comply with related orders of state and federal agencies.

Throughout the relevant period FMC had purchased and maintained extensive general liability insurance. Liberty Mutual Insurance Company provided FMC's primary coverage to limits of $10 million. FMC also bought umbrella and excess coverage provided by a number of insurers including certain underwriters at Lloyds of London and certain London insurance companies. We shall refer to these London underwriters and insurance companies, including one company that engaged separate counsel in the course of the proceedings, as "the London insurers" or "the London defendants," and to the umbrella and excess policies they issued as "the London policies." Many other insurers were involved in the proceedings below, but of all of FMC's insurers only the London defendants are now before this court. Exhaustion of FMC's primary coverage (cf. Community Redevelopment Agency v. Aetna Casualty & Surety Co. (1996) 50 Cal.App.4th 329, 337–340 [57 Cal.Rptr.2d 755]) is not an issue on these appeals.

[In the course of nine trials, the jury found that FMC was entitled to insurance coverage for claims arising out of several locations. The Court of Appeal eventually addressed whether FMC could "stack" its coverage.]

The concepts of "stacking" and "anti-stacking" warrant brief introduction.

"Stacking policy limits means that when more than one policy is triggered by an occurrence, each policy can be called upon to respond to the claim up to the full limits of the policy. Under the concept of stacking . . . the limits of every policy triggered by an 'occurrence' are added together to determine the amount of coverage available for the particular claim. Thus, for example, if an insured could establish that each of four consecutive $10 million policies were triggered by a particular claim, the insured could recover $40 million for a single occurrence, rather than the $10 million available under any single policy." (Ostrager & Newman, Insurance Coverage Disputes (9th ed. 1998) Trigger and Scope of Coverage, 9.04[c], p. 464.)

The "stacking" concept could apply in the circumstances of this case. London policy Nos. K 79446 and CX2062 each provided, subject to certain specific exceptions, limits of $1 million (over and above underlying coverages where appropriate) for each "occurrence" and also "in the aggregate for each annual period where applicable." Policy No. K 79446 declared six annual policy periods (the first being the short period from August 5 to October 1, 1964), and policy No. CX2062 was in effect for only the policy year ending October 1, 1970 (the effective date of the first pollution exclusion). Characteristically there was only one "occurrence," based on "a continuous or repeated exposure to conditions," at any particular site. But by application of the continuous injury trigger identified and approved in Montrose II, that single occurrence could be deemed (depending on the facts) to have triggered coverage in more than one, or all, of the policy periods. By application of the "stacking" concept, at any particular site FMC might have aggregated up to $7 million in liability coverage (over and above underlying coverages), for a single occurrence, under London policies which specified a $1 million per-occurrence limit.

This kind of "stacking" of the limits of an insurer's policies for consecutive policy periods has been criticized as affording the insured substantially more coverage, for liability attributable to any particular single occurrence, than the insured bargained or paid for. (Cf., e.g., Ins. Co. North America v. Forty–Eight Insulations (6th Cir.1980) 633 F.2d 1212, 1226, fn. 28 [a variant of "stacking" "amounts to giving [the insured] much more insurance than it paid for"]; Uniroyal, Inc. v. Home Ins. Co. (E.D.N.Y.1988) 707 F.Supp. 1368, 1392 ["stacking in this manner makes the aggregate limits and the separately negotiated premiums for each policy illusory by expanding coverage to the sum of both policies"].)

Insurers sometimes include "anti-stacking" provisions in their policies to avoid just this kind of result. Where, as in this action, there is no anti-stacking provision, there is precedent, characteristically in asbestos cases, for judicial intervention.

Thus in Ins. Co. North America v. Forty–Eight Insulations, supra, 633 F.2d 1212, the federal court of appeals agreed with the district court that " '[i]n any event, no insurer should be held liable in any one case to indemnify Forty–Eight for judgment liability for more than the highest single yearly limit in a policy that existed during the period of the claimant's exposure for which judgment was obtained.' * * * The initial exposure to asbestos fibers in any given year triggers coverage. However, under the terms of the policies, additional exposure to asbestos fibers is treated as arising out of the same occurrence. Thus, on its face, the liability of each insurer is limited to maximum amount 'per occurrence' provided by each policy. We have no problem with the district court's extending the policy language so that each insurer would face no more liability per claim than the maximum limit it wrote during any applicable year of coverage." (633 F.2d at p. 1226, fn. 28.)

Keene Corp. v. Ins. Co. of North America, supra, 667 F.2d 1034, citing Forty–Eight Insulations, dealt similarly with the stacking issue: "Keene claims that it is entitled to full indemnity for each injury up to the sum of the limits provided by the applicable policies. We do not agree. The principle of indemnity implicit in the policies requires that successive policies cover single asbestos-related injuries. That principle, however, does not require that Keene be entitled to 'stack' applicable policies' limits of liability. To the extent possible, we have tried to construe the policies in such a way that the insurers' contractual obligations for asbestos-related diseases are the same as their obligations for other injuries. Keene is entitled to nothing more. Therefore, we hold that only one policy's limits can apply to each injury. Keene may select the policy under which it is to be indemnified." (667 F.2d at pp. 1049–1050.)

Armstrong World Industries touched on stacking only in the footnote from which we have previously quoted, noting that the trial court had adopted Keene's approach and that "[t]he policyholders have not challenged this ruling." (45 Cal.App.4th at p. 50, fn. 15.)

FMC cites Community Redevelopment Agency v. Aetna Casualty & Surety Co., supra, 50 Cal.App.4th at page 340, and Stonewall Ins. Co. v.

City of Palos Verdes Estates (1996) 46 Cal.App.4th 1810, 1849 [54 Cal.Rptr.2d 176], for the proposition that "any implied 'anti-stacking' rule is contrary to California law," and Cole v. Celotex Corp. (La.1992) 599 So.2d 1058 and J.H. France Refractories v. Allstate (1993) 534 Pa. 29 [626 A.2d 502] for the proposition that the "anti-stacking" rule of Forty–Eight Insulations and Keene "has been rejected by a number of courts applying multiple triggers of coverage." None of these cases is dispositive. Community Redevelopment Agency is essentially a duty-to-defend case which does not address stacking or anti-stacking. Stonewall does not analyze the issue and appears to base its conclusion at least in part on a stipulation between the parties. Cole expresses support for a generalized concept of "stacking," but undertakes to distinguish Keene and acknowledges that Louisiana's approach to the issue is perceived to be sui generis. (599 So.2d at p. 1077, fn. 56; cf. Ostrager & Newman, Insurance Coverage Disputes, supra, Trigger and Scope of Coverage, 9.04[c], p. 467 ["Louisiana appears to be the only jurisdiction that permits stacking in the context of cumulative injury tort cases"].) And J.H. France Refractories deals with the distinct issue of allocation of coverage among multiple insurers.

In proceedings to settle the fifth trial "judgment" in this action, the trial court indicated a strong belief that the anti-stacking rule was integral to Armstrong World Industries' all-sums holding, but the trial court's only formal ruling on the point was that implied by the fifth trial "judgment" the court subsequently filed and from which we have quoted.

Although we disagree with the trial court's perception that the anti-stacking rule was integral to Armstrong World Industries, we agree with the sense of its conclusion that Keene's statement of such a rule is appropriate in the circumstances of this case for reasons well articulated in Keene and cognate cases. Because in the case before us coverage is ultimately keyed to and limited by the concept of "occurrence," and because the London defendants provided multiple layers of coverage, with varying effective dates, in each policy period, application of Keene's rule in this case is relatively complex. For clarity we shall modify the judgment herein to substitute for the trial court's references to "the anti-stacking qualifications of . . . Armstrong and Keene" a provision that only the policy limits of London umbrella and excess policies in effect as of July 1 in one of the policy periods in which coverage is triggered for a single occurrence can apply to property damage attributable to that occurrence, but that if coverage for that occurrence is triggered in more than one policy period FMC may select the policy period in which the policy limits are to be fixed.

* * *

Notes

1. As the *Wausau* case observes, *Plaisted* is inconsistent with several other California cases. With the exception of its definition of stacking, the case may be more significant for what it doesn't say than for its limited holding. Both *Armstrong World Industries* and *Stonewall* adopt a stack and allocate approach. While *Plaisted* may be bypassed, the inconsistency remains in the California case law. The case is useful for its survey of other approaches.

2. *Armstrong World Industries v. Aetna Casualty and Surety Co.*, 45 Cal.App.4th 1, 52 Cal.Rptr.2d 690 (1996), held that all insurers on the risk were liable to the limits of the policy subject only to the actual loss suffered and the method of apportionment among the insurers on the risk. *Id.* at 51–52. Implicit in the opinion is that policies would be stacked. See Stonewall Ins. Co. v. City of Palos Verdes Estates, 46 Cal.App.4th 1810, 54 Cal.Rptr.2d 176 (1996).

3. The problems of "stacking" of insurance policies in first-party insurance cases in the context of uninsured motorist coverage is also a troublesome area. In *North River Insurance Co. v. Tabor*, 934 F.2d 461 (3d Cir.1991), decided the same year as the principal case, the court refused to differentiate between uninsured and underinsured motorist coverage with regard to "stacking" coverage to exceed liability. As the underlying issue in the policy was an express offset provision entitling the insurer to reduce the underinsured motorist benefits owing under its own policy by the liability coverage amounts previously paid by other companies, North River argued that its liability for underinsured benefits could not exceed $50,000 ($300,000 in stacked underinsured motorist coverage less a $250,000 set-off previously paid by another insurer). The court disagreed with this logic, reading the applicable statute as reflecting a legislative intent in favor of "excess" underinsured motorist protection. Further, the court noted that the insured is entitled to believe that he had multiple coverage if he has paid multiple premiums. The court analogized the set-off provisions to the unfairness of anti-stacking provisions that have been previously condemned, holding that Tabor's estate was entitled to stack underinsured motorist coverage in excess of liability coverage. See West American Ins. Co. v. Park, 933 F.2d 1236 (3d Cir. 1991)(in accord).

4. For a further discussion of "stacking," see Kirsch v. Nationwide Ins. Co., 532 F.Supp. 766 (E.D.Pa.1982) (holding that "stacking" of no-fault benefits is not allowed under the Pennsylvania No–Fault Act). The *Kirsch* court distinguished the No–Fault Act from the Uninsured Motorist Act, explaining that the latter was enacted specifically to provide coverage to innocent victims of negligent acts of uninsured third parties and places no statutory maximum on the amount of coverage an individual insured can obtain. The No Fault Act does contain a statutory maximum of possible recovery indicating a legislative intent to limit recovery. Subsequent to *Kirsch* the Pennsylvania No Fault Act was repealed and replaced by an auto insurance system featuring certain mandatory first party benefits for accident victims with no restrictions on the right to sue.

5. Insurers have argued for the stacking of uninsured retentions. The *Owens–Illinois* case below suggests that retained limits require contribution by the insured. Other jurisdictions are in accord. Atchison, Topeka & Santa Fe Railway Co. v. Stonewall Insurance Co., 275 Kan. 698, 71 P.3d 1097 (2003) (exhaustion of retentions is required). This is not unfair if the insured consciously retained some risk and thereby obtained some premium benefit in the bargain. However, in California, policies which are on the risk may be available to indemnify the insured for other years in which the insured had retained limits. The Vons Companies v. United States Fire Ins. Co., 78 Cal.App.4th 52, 92 Cal.Rptr.2d 597 (2000). The rationale for this is the CGL language in which the insurer agrees to indemnify for "all loss."

6. The insurance industry has begun to use "non-cumulation" clauses to prevent the stacking of successive policies triggered by a single occurrence. John K. DiMungo and Paul E.B. Glad, *California Insurance Law Handbook*, Chapter 44, § 44:16 (2004). The language of non-cumulation provisions provides that if a loss covered under a policy is also covered under an earlier policy, the limit of liability in the latter policy is reduced by the amount due to the insured for the loss under the prior insurance. Id. The Umbrella Book, a source designed for use by insurance agents and brokers, notes that "the effect of the provision is clear: a "prior insurance" condition in a policy reduces its limits of liability ... by the amount available to the insured under any applicable insurance in effect prior to the subject policy's inception date." Id., *quoting*, The Umbrella Book, Vol. 1 at CNPNC–1 (Griffin Communications 1993).

Courts outside of California have held non-cumulation clauses to be unambiguous and enforceable, though no reported California decision has addressed the issue. *Id.* Non-cumulation clauses have been interpreted to prevent stacking of per occurrence limits of policies. Id., *quoting* In re Asbestos Insurance Coverage Cases, Judicial Council Coordination Proceeding No. 1072 (Cal. Supp. Ct. 1988) 1998 Litigation Reporter 17, 621 (reprint ed in Mealey's Litigation Reports: Insurance, slip op. at 34–34). Thus, non-cumulation clauses present insurers with the option of writing a valid anti-stacking provision into their insurance contracts.

3. Apportioning Liability

It is well-settled law in the insurance industry that apportionment of liability among multiple insurers is allowed when multiple policies are triggered on a single claim. The following case is one of the early cases to deal with the apportionment of liability among multiple insurers.

OWENS–ILLINOIS, INC. v. UNITED INSURANCE CO.

Supreme Court of New Jersey, 1994.
138 N.J. 437, 650 A.2d 974.

The opinion of the Court was delivered by O'Hern, J.

This appeal involves two aspects of a dispute between a manufacturer of an asbestos product and its insurers concerning the coverage afforded to the manufacturer under its liability insurance policies. First is the "trigger of coverage" issue, a shorthand expression for identifying the events that must occur during a policy period to require coverage for losses sustained by the policyholder. Second is the "allocation issue," which involves the scope of coverage afforded under a triggered policy. One question, for example, in the case of gradually-inflicted injury or property damage triggering a number of successive policies is whether the policyholder may recover the sum of all the policies or some allocated portion of each policy. The case is complicated by the fact that the plaintiff-manufacturer used a "captive insurance company" to manage its risks and to acquire the subject policies. That captive company, a wholly-owned subsidiary of the manufacturer, was in form a shell that reinsured the risks with the various defendant insurance companies.

* * *

In an early phase of the proceedings, Judge Keefe, then sitting as a Chancery Division judge, concluded that an "injury in fact" triggering coverage under the insurance policies occurs on the inhalation of asbestos fibers and continues up to and including manifestation of an asbestos-related disease. Following discovery, Judge Conley reaffirmed Judge Keefe's ruling and held all insurers whose policies were triggered to be jointly and severally liable to O–I to the extent of the policy limits. In addition, the court held that the continuous trigger should apply to claims for property damage.

* * *

The economic realities of this litigation are stark. By 1991, when O–I filed its Appellate Division briefs, it had settled 43,000 bodily-injury lawsuits. More than 90,000 bodily-injury and sixty-three property-damage cases were pending in all states and some territories. With bodily-injury lawsuits accumulating at the rate of 1700 per month, O–I's unreimbursed costs of defending and settling those cases had by then exceeded $95 million. O–I had already spent close to $10 million in defense and settlement costs associated with the property-damage cases. The questions raised here concern which of the insurance policies issued from 1977 to 1985 provide indemnity to O–I and to what extent.

Our grant of certification, 135 N.J. 301 (1994), was limited to two issues: (1) the application of the "continuous trigger" theory, and (2) any consequent apportionment of liability.

[The court's discussion of the inability of the policy language to address problem and its adoption of the continuous trigger of coverage theory is omitted.]

The conceptual model employed by the Keene court [667 F.2d 1034 (D.C. Cir. 1981)] is that of a pleated accordion surrounding the entire "occurrence" and representing the time span from exposure to manifestation. Its solution to the problem of indivisible injury was to collapse the injuries in the accordion into a single year. It wrote:

> The principle of indemnity implicit in the policies requires that successive policies cover single asbestos-related injuries. That princi-

ple, however, does not require that Keene be entitled to "stack" applicable policies' limits of liability. To the extent possible, we have tried to construe the policies in such a way that the insurers' contractual obligations for asbestos-related diseases are the same as their obligations for other injuries. Keene is entitled to nothing more. Therefore, we hold that only one policy's limits can apply to each injury. Keene may select the policy under which it is to be indemnified. 667 F.2d at 1049–50.

That theory is sometimes referred to as one of joint-and-several allocation. The Keene court explained that it did not mean that a single insurer will be saddled with full liability for any injury. Keene held that when more than one policy applies to a loss, the "other insurance" provisions of each policy provide a scheme by which the insurer's liability is to be apportioned. Id. at 1050.[57] The Appellate Division adopted the Keene theory of joint-and-several allocation.

* * *

If the Keene court's concern was that the insurance companies' liability for long-term exposure to injury be the same as their obligations for other types of losses, only one policy's limits would seem to apply to all claims arising out of the same occurrence, as would have been the case had an asbestos-laden steam pipe exploded in the fourth year of our illustration, causing immediate injury to thirty of the building occupants. We surmise, however, that the Keene court's holding is that one policy's limits apply to each claim of injury.... The cross-indemnity among the policies would neutralize the effect of contribution on policy limits. In Air Products and Chemicals, Inc. v. Hartford Accident and Indemnity Co., 707 F. Supp. 762 (E.D.Pa.1989), aff'd in part, vacated in part, 25 F.3d 177 (3d Cir.1994), the district court applied a per-claim analysis to triggered policies but did not permit the policyholder the discretion to select the policy for coverage. Following Pennsylvania law, that court directed that "liability among triggered policies 'should be apportioned chronologically and seriatim.'" 707 F. Supp. at 769 (quoting J.H. France Refractories Co. v. Allstate Ins. Co., No. 3933 (Phila. Ct. C.P. Apr. 18, 1986), vacated on other grounds, 539 A.2d 1345 (Pa.Super.1988), rev'd, 555 A.2d 797 (Pa.1989), on remand, 578 A.2d 468 (Pa.Super.1990), aff'd in part rev'd in part, 626 A.2d 502 (Pa.1993)). The Third Circuit Court of Appeals in Air Products and Chemicals citing the Pennsylvania Supreme Court decision on this subject in the J.H. France litigation, 626 A.2d at 508, supra, rejected the lower court's apportionment method in favor of joint-and-several allocation allowing the insured to select the policy under which it is to be indemnified. 25 F.2d at 181.

One anomaly in the Keene court's analysis is that a single claim for the cost of cure of a long-term release of contaminants that polluted a

57. Because no specific allocation was made in Keene, the District Court held on remand that a company whose policy was triggered was to make a claim against the other insurance companies without participation or involvement by Keene. Marcy L. Kahn, The "Other Insurance" Clause, 19 Forum 591, 612 (1984).

city water supply would be limited to one policy's limits, whereas if 300 residential wells were affected, the limits of multiple policies would be available, though the occurrence (cause) was the same. Another anomaly is that although the opinion's premise is that all damages can be claimed in any one of the years, it nonetheless calls for contribution from other policies. By definition, if all damages occurred in one of the years (in the sense of that year's injury establishing the damages), none of the other policies would be triggered.

B.

Pro–Rata Allocation

Several courts selecting multi-year triggers of coverage have held that "triggered policies must respond to a claim on a prorated basis and that a policyholder is responsible for a portion of indemnification and defense obligations as a result of periods of time when it was uninsured or self-insured." Steuber, supra, at *60. The leading case for that proposition is Insurance Co. of North America v. Forty–Eight Insulations, Inc., 633 F.2d 1212 (6th Cir.1980), clarified, 657 F.2d 814 (6th Cir.), cert. denied, 454 U.S. 1109, 102 S. Ct. 686, 70 L. Ed. 2d 650 (1981). Courts taking the same allocation approach as Forty–Eight Insulations include Gulf Chemical & Metallurgical Corp. v. Associated Metals & Minerals Corp., 1 F.3d 365, 372 (5th Cir.1993) (apportioning cost of policyholder's defense among insurers on risk; policyholder must bear its share of defense costs determined by fraction of time it lacked coverage) (applying Texas law); Fireman's Fund Insurance Cos. v. Ex–Cell–O Corp., 685 F. Supp. 621, 626 (E.D.Mich.1987) (holding insurer on risk during period of alleged exposure liable for policyholder's defense in proportion that period on risk bears to total period of alleged exposure; policyholder must bear pro-rata share of costs for uninsured periods); and Northern States Power, supra, 523 N.W.2d at 662 (allocating damages to insurers in proportion to time on risk; policyholder carrying only excess insurance must assume retained limit with respect to each policy).

Forty–Eight Insulations concluded that a reasonable means of allocating costs among the triggered policies was available based on the number of years of exposure. 633 F.2d at 1225. (The policyholder disputed only the allocation of defense costs in the Court of Appeals in Forty–Eight Insulations.) In Uniroyal, supra, 707 F.Supp. 1368, Judge Weinstein applied a different formula because evidence was available to differentiate between the various periods of coverage. He applied a pro-rata method under which the loss would be allocated to each policy according to the portion of injuries triggering that policy. Id. at 1393. He resolved that portion by the quantity of the substance released during the policy periods. Id. at 1393–94. He appeared to reject the Keene theory of joint-and-several liability

> because for one period the manufacturer had had no insurance, and the Keene court viewed its mission as ensuring that the manufacturer received complete indemnity for all its asbestos-related losses. A

> firm that fails to purchase insurance for a period, however, is self-insuring for all the risk incurred in that period; otherwise it would be receiving coverage for a period for which it paid no premium. Self-insurance is called "going bare" for a reason. [Id. at 1392 (citation omitted).]

In Diamond Shamrock Chemicals Co. v. Aetna Casualty & Surety Co., 258 N.J. Super. 167, 222–23, 609 A.2d 440 (App.Div.1992), certif. denied, 134 N.J. 481 (1993), the Appellate Division, applying New York law, let stand a similar allocation among policies covering liabilities for dispersal of Agent Orange.

[The court's discussion of the failure of the policy language to resolve the allocation issue is omitted.]

The theory of insurance is that of transferring risks. Insurance companies accept risks from manufacturers and either retain the risks or spread the risks through reinsurance. John A. Appleman & Jean Appleman, 13A Insurance Law and Practice 7681 (1976). Because insurance companies can spread costs throughout an industry and thus achieve cost efficiency, the law should, at a minimum, not provide disincentives to parties to acquire insurance when available to cover their risks. Spreading the risk is conceptually more efficient.

Almost all such insurance controversies are retrospective, and to reflect now on what might have been done if the parties had contemplated today's problem is almost fatuous. Our job, however, is not just to solve today's problems but to create incentives that will tend to minimize their recurrence. "To send the correct signals to the economic system, a judge must appreciate the consequences of legal decisions on future behavior." Hallett & Berney, supra, at *15. Future actors would know that if they do not transfer to insurance companies the risk of their activities that cause continuous and progressive injury, they may bear that untransferred risk.

* * *

The Remedy That We Propose

The final question that we must address, however, is whether our proposed solution will be an efficient response to the problem of insurance coverage for long-term environmental damage. The court in Forty–Eight Insulations, aptly described the challenge:

> The only thing on which all parties agree is that there is a need for us to arrive at an administratively manageable interpretation of the insurance policies—one that can be applied with minimal need for litigation. Reaching such a beneficial result is certainly desirable, but it greatly complicates our task. In the real world, there are few Solomonian possibilities. [Id. at 1218.]

One thing is certain: The present system is inefficient. " 'The largest transaction cost today is money being spent by insurance companies and industry making claims. [The cost is estimated] at about $500 million annually. These are the litigation costs between insured and insurers.' " Hallett & Berney, supra, at *21–22 (quoting testimony of Doctor Joel Hirschhorn before a Congressional Subcommittee). "The legal costs of environmental coverage litigation today may run as high as 70 percent of total cleanup costs." Eugene R. Anderson & Giovanni Rodriguez, Settling Environmental Coverage Disputes: What You Know About Your Enemy Cannot Hurt You in Environmental and Toxic Tort Claims: Insurance Coverage in 1991 and Beyond 383 (PLI Comm. Law & Practice Course Handbook Series No. 579, 1991), available in Westlaw, PLI–COMM Database, *3. Concededly, legal disputes have necessarily preceded the cleanup work under new and complex laws like CERCLA, and once the rules are settled, litigation costs may decline. Hallett & Berney, supra, at *22. Still, the present rules do not seem to be working.

We will not attempt a universal resolution of all issues of coverage for gradual release of pollutants or toxins. At least in the context of asbestos-related personal injury and property damage, the rules that we adopt will attempt to relate the theory of a continuous trigger causing indivisible injury to the degree of risk transferred or retained in each of the years of repeated exposure to injurious conditions. In the absence of a satisfactory measure of allocation (as in the Uniroyal (Agent Orange) case, supra, 707 F.Supp. at 1391–93), we believe that straight annual progression is not an appropriate measure of allocation. The degree of risk transferred or retained in the early years of an enterprise like O–I's obviously was not at all comparable to that sought to be insured in later years. Hence, any allocation should be in proportion to the degree of the risks transferred or retained during the years of exposure. We believe that measure of allocation is more consistent with the economic realities of risk retention or risk transfer. That later insurers might need to respond to pre-policy occurrences is not unfair. "These are 'occurrence' policies which, by their nature, provide coverage for pre-policy occurrences (acts) which cause injury or damage during the policy period." Montrose Chem. Corp. of California v. Admiral Ins. Co., 3 Cal.App.4th 1511, 5 Cal.Rptr.2d 358, 367 (Ct. App.), review granted, 24 Cal.Rptr.2d 661 (1992). In this case, the year-by-year increase in policy limits must have reflected an increasing awareness of the escalating nature of the risks sought to be transferred. We believe that a better formula (putting aside for a moment the problem of periods of self-insurance) is that developed in California. In Armstrong World Industries, supra, 26 Cal. Rptr. 2d at 57, the court allocated the losses among the carriers on the basis of the extent of the risk assumed, i.e., proration on the basis of policy limits, multiplied by years of coverage.

* * *

We realize that many complexities encumber the solution that we suggest involving, as it does, proration by time and degree of risk assumed—for example, determining how primary and excess coverage is to be taken into account or the order in which policies are triggered. See Hickman & DeYoung, supra, at 310–11; Roger Westendorf and Ronald R.

Robinson, Insurance Coverage for Environmental Claims Under the Comprehensive General Liability Policy, in Pollution Liability: Managing the Challenges of Coverage and Defense in 1991, at 57 (ALI–ABA Video Law Review Study, Q205, 1991), available in Westlaw, ALI–ABA Database, *54–57 (each discussing various theories of horizontal and vertical stacking and relationship to excess coverage issues). The parties did not focus on those issues. Still, we do not believe that the issues are unmanageable. Constructing the model for analysis of the self-insurance portion of the risk assumed by O–I is difficult but not impossible. We recognize the difficulties of apportioning costs with any scientific certainty. However, the legal system "frequently resolves issues involving considerable uncertainty." SL Indus., Inc. v. American Motorists Ins. Co., 128 N.J. 188, 216, 607 A.2d 1266 (1992).

This case is undoubtedly more difficult to manage than most because of the great number of claims involved. On the other hand, the record is reasonably well-developed on the measure of risk assumed or transferred, at least since 1963. To extrapolate back from 1963 to establish a rough measure of the risk assumed or retained in the years from 1948 to 1963 should not be difficult. A rough measure is all that we can achieve in this imperfect resolution of these issues. Moreover, we do not have a sense of the extent to which exposures date back to 1948 or to other periods before 1963.

In addition, we are informed that Aetna has paid its policy limits for the years 1963 to 1977, so that Aetna's policy proceeds will not be called on for future contribution. If that be so, rather than go back to revisit Aetna's contributions, we shall start forward and treat pending matters from the perspective of one having a long view of the entire occurrence (the extended accordion). Because of the large number of claims of asbestos exposure, the net effect of proration may simply be to cover more cases with partial indemnity in each case, rather than to cover fewer cases with full indemnity.

On remand, coincident with resolving the other coverage issues, the court shall appoint a master, one skilled in the economics of insurance, to create a model for allocating the claims. Above all, the master should develop a workable system for efficient assignment and administration of the claims. Because the defendants refused to involve themselves in the defense of the claims as presented, they should be bound by the facts set forth in the plaintiff's own records with respect to the dates of exposure and with respect to the amounts of settlements and defense costs. See Kahn, supra, at 612 (describing the remand procedure in Keene). Those losses for indemnity and defense costs should be allocated promptly among the companies in accordance with the mathematical model developed, subject to policy limits and exclusions. We stress that there can be no relitigation of those settled claims. Exact dates of exposure may not now be available. Available data should enable the master to grasp the generality of the underlying claims and the exposures involved. (Even under the Keene formula exposure dates were necessary to determine contribution.)

These cases, like the underlying environmental cases to which they are related, demand special attention, such as the use of special case calendars, management conferences, monitoring, alternative methods of dispute resolution, or other specialized treatment. Some techniques and specifics of such case management are set forth in the Report of the Supreme Court Committee on Environmental Litigation, March 23, 1990, at 11–32, 36–38. And management can do more to resolve those issues itself. A case history of such an effort by Champion International Corp. to resolve disputes with sixty-three of its insurance carriers is in John H. Gross, Strategic Considerations in Coverage Litigation, in 11th Annual Insurance, Excess, and Reinsurance Coverage Disputes 7 (PLI Litig. & Admin. Practice Course Handbook Series No. 494, 1994), available in WESTLAW PLI–LIT Database. "The settlement was reasonable and the parties saved millions of dollars in litigation expense and thousands of hours of management time." Id. at *2.

In future cases, insurers aware of their responsibility under the continuing-trigger theory might minimize their costs by assuming responsibility for or involving themselves in the defense of the actions with the ultimate allocation of costs to be determined in accordance with the same general formulas. See R. 4:42–9a(6) (allowing counsel fees in actions on indemnity policies). If, after experience, we are convinced that our solution is inefficient or unrealistic, we will not hesitate to revisit the issue. "We do not expect that this case will be the 'last word' in this area. Environmental liability insurance law, like any other area of law, will have to develop over time and trial courts must be flexible in responding to new fact situations." Northern States Power Co., supra, 523 N.W.2d at 665.

VII

To recapitulate, we hold that when progressive indivisible injury or damage results from exposure to injurious conditions for which civil liability may be imposed, courts may reasonably treat the progressive injury or damage as an occurrence within each of the years of a CGL policy. That is the continuous-trigger theory for activating the insurers' obligation to respond under the policies.

Although the use of a continuous trigger for property damage attributable to long-term embedding of contaminants is more problematic (for example, the "property damage" may be attributable only to third-party intervention, as in the form of a government order to rip out material previously thought not to be defective), the latent nature of such property damage, at least in the case of asbestos products, is sufficiently analogous to that in personal injury to warrant use of a continuous trigger under the terms we have outlined. We need not resolve in these cases exactly when the continuum ends in the contexts of bodily injury and property damage.

Because multiple policies of insurance are triggered under the continuous-trigger theory, it becomes necessary to determine the extent to which each triggered policy shall provide indemnity. "Other insurance" clauses in standard CGL policies were not intended to resolve that question. A fair method of allocation appears to be one that is related to both the time on the risk and the degree of risk assumed. When periods of no insurance reflect a decision by an actor to assume or retain a risk, as opposed to periods when coverage for a risk is not available, to expect the risk-bearer to share in the allocation is reasonable. Estimating the degree of risk assumed is difficult but not impossible. Insurers whose policies are triggered by an injury during a policy period must respond to any claims presented to them and, if they deny full coverage, must initiate proceedings to determine the portion allocable for defense and indemnity costs. For failure to provide coverage, a policyholder may recover costs incurred under the provisions of Rule 4:42–9(a)(6). Policyholders must cooperate in furnishing information concerning coverage. Courts must take an active role in the management and resolution of such coverage controversies. A trial court may repose a large measure of discretion in a special master to aid the court in developing a formula for allocation of the costs of defense and indemnity. R.4:41–2. Masters should use specialized procedures to resolve the issues. Ultimately, insurance companies are in the best position to hold down their costs. They are the most skilled in claims management and claims disposition. Data in the record suggest that in some years defense costs exceeded claims paid. Courts cannot simplify issues that are intrinsically complex. We can, however, narrow the range of disputes and provide procedures better to resolve the disputes that remain. If we can accomplish that much, we can better channel the available resources into remediation of environmental harms.

VIII

The judgment of the Appellate Division is reversed insofar as it allocated none of the costs of indemnity or defense to periods of no-insurance and otherwise directed contribution under the "other insurance" clauses of the policies. The matter is remanded to the Chancery Division for further proceedings in accordance with this opinion.

JUSTICES CLIFFORD, HANDLER, POLLOCK, GARIBALDI, and STEIN join in this opinion. CHIEF JUSTICE WILENTZ did not participate.

Notes

1. *Stonewall Ins. Co. v. City of Palos Verdes Estates*, 46 Cal.App.4th 1810, 54 Cal.Rptr.2d 176 (1996), decided in the same year as *Armstrong World Industries v. Aetna Casualty and Surety Company*, constructed a more detailed analysis of possibilities of apportionment. After concluding that liability should rest upon the primary carriers up to the respective policy limits and that each primary carrier should bear some proportion of the ultimate burden of that liability, the court listed several methods of apportionment. These methods included: Apportionment based upon the relative policy limits of each primary policy, apportionment based upon the relative

duration of each primary policy in relation to the overall period of "occurrences" (the "time on the risk" method), apportionment based on the relative durations and multiplied by the amount of the respective limits of the primary policies, apportionment based on premiums paid, and apportionment among each carrier in equal shares. The court rejected all approaches save the "time on the risk" method, reasoning this approach would deliver in most equitable results. However, to cloud the situation further, the court conceded that situations might arise in which another approach is more qualified and accordingly directed the trial court to use the rule only in the absence of another more equitable approach.

2. A recent case followed the analyses of both *Armstrong* and *Stonewall* in concluding that once an insured's ultimate net loss resulting from a damages settlement exceeds the insured's retained limit, the insurer must provide coverage up to the policy limits. See California Pacific Homes v. Scottsdale Ins. Co., 70 Cal.App.4th 1187, 83 Cal.Rptr.2d 328 (1999). In *California Pacific Homes*, the insurers argued that the insured was required to satisfy the settlement in an aggregate amount equal to its retained limit ($250,000) for each of the five successive policies ($1.25 million). The court disagreed, explaining that stacking of retained limits would have the inequitable result of affording the insured far less coverage than what was purchased. The court cited *Armstrong* and noted that once coverage is triggered, an insurance policy obligates the insurer to indemnify for the insured's entire loss up to the policy limits. Further, the court observed that *Stonewall* granted the trial court discretion to select the method of apportionment that would generate the fairest results.

3. A good comparison of the joint and several allocation method with the pro rata method is found in Joren S. Bass, *The Montrose Decision and Long–Tail Environmental Liability*, 5 Hastings West–Northwest J. of Envtl. L. & Pol'y 209, 214–22 (1998/1999).

4. According to *Armstrong World Industries v. Aetna Casualty and Surety Co.,* 45 Cal.App.4th 1, 52 Cal.Rptr.2d 690 (1996), the period of no coverage does not require the insured to contribute. According to *Armstrong* "[O]nce a policy is triggered, the policy obligates the insurer to pay 'all sums' which the insurer shall become liable to pay . . . [T]he insured need not pay a pro rata share for periods during which it had no insurance." *Id.* at 105, 52 Cal.Rptr.2d at 742. The court reasoned that apportionment among multiple insurers does not affect the insurer's duties to the policyholder to cover the full extent of the policyholder's liability (up to the policy limits). The *Armstrong* result is consistent with other California cases. See Aerojet–General v. Transport Indemnity, 17 Cal.4th 38, 70 Cal.Rptr.2d 118, 948 P.2d 909 (1997); Truck Insurance Exchange v. Amoco Corp., 35 Cal.App.4th 814, 814, 41 Cal.Rptr.2d 551 (1995).

5. *Owens–Illinois* suggests that an insured must contribute to account for periods of no coverage. See also, In re Wallace & Gale, 385 F.3d 820, 832–33 (4th Cir. 2004) (insured responsible for a share during periods in which it was uninsured where pro rata time-on-the-risk applies). How, should this be accomplished? Is the insured to be assigned an arbitrary level of risk assumption?

4. Overlapping and Conflicting Liability Insurance Coverage

PRELIMINARY NOTE

Where more than one insurer covers a loss or liability, difficult questions arise as to the distribution of the obligation to pay among the insurers. These distribution questions raise a slightly different kind of allocation issue than those discussed above.

If Policy A (Insurer A) and Policy B (Insurer B) apply to cover the same loss or liability and *neither* policy contains a provision indicating how losses or liabilities are to be shared with other insurers, presumably the insured can recover no more than the extent of his loss or liability in the light of the principle of indemnity. Double recovery should not be permitted and, if Insurer A pays the whole loss or liability, A ought somehow to receive contribution from Insurer B on the basis of a fair prorating of responsibility. And if the amount of the loss or liability is greater than the amount of Policies A and B, then the insured should receive the face amount of Policies A and B. See 15 Couch on Insurance, 3d §§ 217.1, 217.9.

Of course, insurers have given thought to this problem and want to have their responsibilities as clearly delineated as they may be. For this reason, Policy A and Policy B may (especially if they are property or liability policies) contain provisions, referred to as "other insurance" provisions, to the following effect:

(a) Policy A and/or Policy B may state that it will only share proportionally in covering the loss or liability ("pro rata" clause); or

(b) Policy A and/or Policy B may state that if there is other valid insurance then Policy A or Policy B will be invalid ("escape" clause); or

(c) Policy A and/or Policy B may state that it will be "primary" or "excess" insurance. That is, if Policy A is primary it will pay up to its face value for any loss or liability incurred by the insured; if Policy B is excess it will cover only the amount of loss or liability over that paid by Insurer A and then only to B's face value. Obviously critical difficulties will arise if *both* Policy A and B say that they are "excess;" or

(d) Various combinations of (a), (b), or (c).

(e) In addition, we should take careful note, primary and excess provisions will be found in liability insurance where insurers may desire to arrange for a contingent sharing of the insured's liability. E.g., Insurer A may "cover" the first $1,000,000 and Insurer B may cover anything over that sum. This sort of planned "primary" and "excess" structure should be allowed to operate as planned.

It seems obvious that legislatures will be tempted or prompted to intervene. In California, Insurance Code 11580.9 provides a careful scheme for identifying "primary" and "excess" auto insurers depending on the type of vehicle, its use, and certain other factors. The section includes a "catch all" provision stating:

> "(d) Except as provided in subdivisions (a), (b), and (c) * * *, where two or more policies affording valid and collectible liability insurance apply to the same motor vehicle in an occurrence out of which a liability loss shall arise, it shall be conclusively presumed that the insurance afforded by that policy in which such motor vehicle is described or rated as an owned automobile shall be primary and the insurance afforded by any other policy or any other policies shall be excess."

The presumption stated in the subsection quoted, and presumptions in other subsections of Insurance Code 11580.9, are permitted by the statute to be modified or amended only by written agreement signed by all insurers who have issued a policy or policies applicable to the loss and all named insureds under such policies.

The problems of "primary" and "excess" as well as "escape" provisions reach throughout the field of insurance. It is certainly a substantial problem in property and casualty insurance, but the strikingly complicated illustrations seem today to be found in the area of automobile liability insurance. John P. Kurtock, Jr., in an article in 25 Federation of Insurance Counsel Quarterly 45 (Fall, 1974) comments extensively on the subject. Kurtock says:

> Duplication of coverage is common. In automobile insurance it is not impossible for a person driving the automobile of another with permission to receive protection for the same loss under insurance contracts issued to:
>
> (1) himself, on his personal automobile temporary substitute;
>
> (2) the owner of the borrowed automobile (omnibus coverage);
>
> (3) his employer, under a nonowned automobile cover; and
>
> (4) his employer, under a general liability policy for an on premises automobile loss.
>
> Overlapping coverages can result from a number of combinations of insurance contracts, such as:
>
> (1) the omnibus coverage of an auto owner's personal automobile liability policy and the nonowned automobile coverage of the driver's automobile liability policy;
>
> (2) the temporary substitute or nonowned automobile coverage of the driver's personal automobile policy and the omnibus or leased car coverage under a garage liability policy;
>
> (3) an employee's personal automobile policy, and his employer's comprehensive general liability policy covering business use of the employee's automobile;
>
> (4) two concurrent liability policies on the same automobile;

(5) a lessor's policy with provisions as to leased vehicles and a lessee's policy with provisions as to hired vehicles;

(6) a driver's nonowned automobile coverage of his personal automobile liability policy while using a leased vehicle and the omnibus coverage provided by the lessor;

(7) a comprehensive general liability policy covering an employee who is assisting in loading or unloading a motor vehicle and a motor vehicle liability policy.

8A Appleman, Insurance Law and Practice, 4906, suggests some additional overlapping coverages.

The effect (on the overlapping coverages described by Kurtock) of the three types of "other insurance" clauses described previously in this note (that is the "pro rata," the "excess" and the "escape" clauses) is obviously going to raise perplexing questions. What if Policy A contains an "excess" clause and Policy B contains a "pro rata" clause? Many courts impose primary liability on the policy containing the pro rata clause and hold that the "excess clause" policy provides only excess insurance. See R.J. Robertson, Jr., *"Other Insurance" Clauses in Illinois*, 20 S. Ill. U.L.J. 403 (1996). Professor Robertson criticizes this result, however, because the courts provide little justification for the decision. Further, Robertson claims that the courts' implied reasoning for the decisions, to effectuate the intent of the parties according to the policy language, is flawed. Instead of ascertaining the "intent of the parties," Robertson contends, Illinois courts are simply classifying "other insurance" clauses by type and then applying a perfunctory rule that one type of clause prevails over another type (for example, in a conflict between a pro rata clause and an excess clause, the policy containing the pro rata clause is deemed "primary" and the excess clause applies as excess coverage). Robertson concludes by arguing in favor of adoption of the Lamb–Weston approach (cited in the principal case below). He asserts it is the "soul of simplicity" and will yield several desirable results, most notable a reduction in the tremendous amount of litigation on "other insurance" clauses.

RICHARDSON v. LUDWIG

Court of Appeals of Minnesota, 1993.
495 N.W.2d 869.

SCHUMACHER, J.

* * *

Appellant Jermike Corporation, a Domino's Pizza franchisee, operated two pizza delivery franchises. Jermike employed approximately 30 drivers, who delivered about 10,000 pizzas per month. Jermike required its drivers to have liability coverage on their delivery vehicles.

Respondent Debra L. Richardson commenced a negligence action as a result of injuries sustained in an October 21, 1988 automobile accident.

Richardson's automobile was rear-ended by an automobile driven by respondent Richard Byron Ludwig and owned by respondent Elizabeth Couture, Ludwig's stepmother. At the time of the accident, Ludwig was returning from delivering a pizza for Jermike.

The vehicle Ludwig used for making pizza deliveries was owned by Couture and insured by State Farm, which provided liability coverage through a personal automobile policy. As a permissive user of Couture's vehicle and as a resident relative of the named insured, Ludwig was insured under the State Farm policy.

Jermike was insured under a business automobile policy issued by U.S. Fire. Under the U.S. Fire policy, liability coverage was afforded only for hired autos or non-owned autos. Non-owned autos were defined as: "Only those 'autos' you do not own, lease, hire, rent or borrow that are used in connection with your business. This includes 'autos' owned by your employees or partners or members of their households but only while used in your business or your personal affairs." Richardson sued Ludwig, Couture, Jermike, and Domino's Pizza. Ludwig and Couture cross-claimed against Jermike and Domino's; Jermike and Domino's cross-claimed against Ludwig and Couture.

U.S. Fire, through its insured, Jermike, moved for summary judgment, claiming Ludwig was not an insured under its policy and, even if he were, the State Farm policy was primary. State Farm, through its insureds, Ludwig and Couture, brought a cross motion for summary judgment, asserting the U.S. Fire policy was primary. The trial court denied U.S. Fire's motion and granted State Farm's motion, finding the U.S. Fire policy to be primary.

Subsequently, U.S. Fire settled Richardson's claims. The settlement agreement reserves U.S. Fire's right to seek indemnity from State Farm. After settling, U.S. Fire moved for reconsideration of the trial court's prior order. * * * Jermike appeals.

* * *

[The court concluded that Ludwig was not an insured within the meaning of the U.S. Fire policy.]

The Minnesota Supreme Court has stated, with respect to situations in which two or more insurance companies may be liable for the same loss:

> Often two or more companies would be fully liable for a loss but for their respective other insurance clauses, and many times those clauses conflict in their provisions. When it is clear that two or more companies are among themselves liable to the insured for his loss but the apportionment among the companies cannot be made without violating the other insurance clause of at least one company, then the courts must look outside the policies for rules of apportionment. One approach, known as the Lamb–Weston doctrine, is to require, when "other insurance" clauses conflict, that the loss be prorated among the insurers on the basis of their respective limits of

> liability. Lamb–Weston, Inc. v. Oregon Auto. Ins. Co., 219 Or. 110, 341 P.2d 110 (1959).
>
> The approach of the Minnesota court has traditionally been more complex than the Lamb–Weston doctrine. In Federal Ins. Co. v. Prestemon, 278 Minn. 218, 231, 153 N.W.2d 429, 437 (1967), we stated that the better approach is to allocate respective policy coverages in light of the total policy insuring intent, as determined by the primary policy risks upon which each policy's premiums were based and as determined by the primary function of each policy. * * *
>
> The nub of the Minnesota doctrine is that coverages of a given risk shall be "stacked" for payment in the order of their closeness to the risk. That is, the insurer whose coverage was effected for the primary purpose of insuring that risk will be liable first for payment, and the insurer whose coverage of the risk was the most incidental to the basic purpose of its insuring intent will be liable last. Integrity Mut. Ins. Co. v. State Auto. & Casualty Underwriters Ins. Co., 307 Minn. 173, 174–76, 239 N.W.2d 445, 446–47 (1976).

In Prestemon, the supreme court noted certain criteria for determining the primary and secondary liability of insurers of the same risk. Among the criteria noted were which policy was intended to cover the activity out of which the accident arose; which company specifically described the involved automobile in its policy; which company charged a premium reflecting a greater contemplated exposure; and which company apparently issued a policy designed to cover the particular car and the risks inherent in using that particular car. Prestemon, 278 Minn. at 229–30, 153 N.W.2d at 436–37, cited in Auto Owners Ins. Co. v. Northstar Mut. Ins. Co., 281 N.W.2d 700, 704 (Minn.1979).

Until 1988, the law in Minnesota was that, when two insurers insured against the same risk, the priority of applicability of coverage was to be determined by examining the total policy insuring intent of the policies; this intent was to be determined by using three or four nonexclusive criteria. It was essentially a balancing test, in which the court was to consider all of the circumstances surrounding the policies.

In 1988, indications began to appear that this singular test was, in fact, two separate tests. See Interstate Fire & Casualty Co. v. Auto–Owners Ins. Co., 433 N.W.2d 82, 86 (Minn.1988). In that case, the dispute was whether a homeowner's policy covering a student or an umbrella liability policy issued to a school district was primarily liable for injuries inflicted on another student occurring on school property. In determining that the umbrella policy issued to the school district was primarily liable, the Minnesota Supreme Court stated: "It appears to us that, in this case, rather than applying the three-part 'closest-to-the-risk' test, it is more helpful to use the broader approach set out in Integrity of allocating respective policy coverages in light of the total policy insuring intent, as determined by the primary policy risks and the primary function of each policy." Id. Subsequently, the Minnesota Supreme

Court apparently reaffirmed the existence of two separate tests, the "broader" test of Integrity Mutual and the three-part test of Auto Owners. Garrick v. Northland Ins. Co., 469 N.W.2d 709, 712 (Minn. 1991).

This court has stated that the "broader" analysis of Interstate Fire and Garrick applies when the policies were intended to cover risks differing in kind and in size. Illinois Farmers Ins. Co. v. Depositors Ins. Co., 480 N.W.2d 657, 661 (Minn.App.1992). The analysis of Garrick and Interstate Fire, however, is "broader" only in the sense that it involves more than a mechanical application of the three factors set out in Auto Owners. The earlier cases, particularly Integrity Mutual and Prestemon, indicate that an analysis of all relevant factors must be made in every case involving overlapping coverage of the same risk.

U.S. Fire contends the other insurance clauses of the two policies can be reconciled and these clauses determine which policy is primary. The Minnesota Supreme Court has stated, however, that the language of the other insurance clauses—or even the existence of such a clause—is not dispositive. Garrick, 469 N.W.2d at 712. In addition, where, as in this case, one policy contains an excess clause and the other policy contains a pro rata clause, the clauses conflict. Integrity, 307 Minn. at 176–77, 239 N.W.2d at 447.

Specific Description

State Farm's policy covered the specific vehicle involved. State Farm agrees that its policy was intended to cover Couture and permissive drivers, including Ludwig, while using the car for business or pleasure. The U.S. Fire policy's declarations page does not specifically describe any vehicle; instead, it states that it covers nonowned autos.

Premium

Jermike paid a $46 annual premium for its business auto coverage. The premium paid for the State Farm policy is not in the record. The U.S. Fire policy provided only liability coverage; the State Farm policy also provided all the coverages required by the No–Fault Act.

Primary/Incidental Coverage

The State Farm policy was intended to cover Couture, Couture's vehicle, and permissive drivers of that vehicle. The U.S. Fire policy, on the other hand, provided liability coverage to Jermike for its vicarious liability arising out of automobiles it did not own. The State Farm policy provided coverage for business or pleasure use; the U.S. Fire policy provided coverage only for business use of nonowned autos.

Other Relevant Factors

Although Ludwig was using Couture's vehicle for business purposes, this is not a case similar to Garrick, in which an automobile insurer had been held primarily liable for an accident involving a commercial truck. State Farm, in fact, specifically agreed to provide coverage for business use. By its very nature, pizza delivery is the sort of use of a personal automobile that an individual's insurer ought to anticipate.

We conclude the trial court erred in finding the U.S. Fire policy primary. The State Farm policy was intended to provide coverage for precisely what occurred in this case. The U.S. Fire policy was not intended to provide primary liability coverage for Jermike's driver employees.

DECISION

Ludwig was not an insured under the U.S. Fire policy and, even if the U.S. Fire policy provided coverage, it would be secondary to State Farm's coverage.

Reversed.

EMPLOYERS REINSURANCE v. MISSION EQUITIES CORP.

Court of Appeal of California, First District, 1977.
74 Cal.App.3d 826, 141 Cal.Rptr. 727.

FEINBERG, ACTING PRESIDING JUSTICE.

We are asked in this appeal to decide which of two insurance companies must bear a loss occasioned by a claim of negligence on the part of an attorney.

There is no dispute as to the relevant facts. Mission Equities Corporation (hereinafter Mission) issued its malpractice policy to a firm of attorneys (hereinafter Attorneys) effective January 1, 1968 to January 1, 1969. Employers Reinsurance Corporation (hereinafter Employers) issued its policy to the Attorneys effective January 2, 1969 through January 2, 1970. On February 22, 1971, at which time the Employers' insurance policy was in effect through renewal, a malpractice action was filed against the Attorneys. The action alleged that the Attorneys filed an action on August 6, 1963, and that as a result of Attorneys' failure to prosecute the action in a timely fashion, the case was dismissed on September 20, 1968, pursuant to Code of Civil Procedure section 583. Employers defended the action and settled the case for $13,000. Mission was given notice of the suit by a letter from Attorneys but did not participate in the defense. On May 29, 1974, Employers filed suit against Mission, requesting a declaration that Mission afforded primary coverage for the alleged negligence and that Mission shall pay Employers $13,000 plus interest, attorney's fees and for costs of the suit. Both Employers and Mission filed motions for summary judgment. Employers' motion was granted on the issue of liability. A subsequent trial on the issue of damages resulted in a judgment against Mission in the amount of $15,580.17 plus costs. Mission appeals from that judgment.

Did Mission's policy cover the malpractice action where the cause of action for malpractice arose during the life of the policy but the action was not begun until after the policy had expired?

The operative clause of the Mission policy at issue here has been interpreted in two previous California cases. The clause reads as follows: "This insurance is to indemnify * * * against any claim or claims for breach of professional duty as Lawyers *which may be made against them* during the period set forth in the Certificate by reason of any negligent act, error or omission * * *." (Emphasis added.) In Gyler v. Mission Ins. Co. (1973) 10 Cal.3d 216, 219, 110 Cal.Rptr. 139, 140, 514 P.2d 1219, 1220, the court considered identical language and held that the term "which may be made against them" should be construed to require indemnity "for claims maturing during the policy period whether or not the claim is actually asserted during that period." The court reached this result by first finding that the term "may" created an ambiguity. It then enunciated the rules that "(t)he meaning of an insurance policy is determined by the insured's reasonable expectation of coverage" and that "(a)ny uncertainty or ambiguity in the peril insured against will be resolved in favor of imposing liability." (Id.) (Parenthetically, we note that Gyler, too, involved a policy of legal malpractice insurance issued by the same company that is appellant herein.)

Appellant argues that the holding of Gyler is inapposite here because Gyler should apply only to disputes between an insurance company and the insured because the purpose of the holding was to protect the reasonable expectation of the insured. This same contention, however, was argued by this same appellant and decided adversely to appellant by Division Two of this court in Chamberlin v. Smith (1977) 72 Cal.App.3d 835, 140 Cal.Rptr. 493. We agree with the decision in Chamberlin.

Who must provide primary coverage for the claim here?

Both appellant's and respondent's policies have provisions concerning the effect of other insurance upon its coverage. The Mission policy provides: "There shall be no liability hereunder in respect of any claim for which the Firm are entitled to any indemnity under any other insurance." Employers' policy provides: "If, but for the insurance afforded by this policy, the assured would have other insurance against a loss otherwise covered hereby, the insurance afforded by this policy shall be excess over such other insurance."

The question arises how to reconcile Mission's escape clause with Employers' excess clause, which, on their faces, seem irreconcilable. The particular fact situation of a pure excess clause conflicting with a pure escape clause does not appear to have been addressed hitherto. This case does not involve a conflict between a composite excess-escape clause and a pro rata clause (Peerless Cas. Co. v. Continental Cas. Co. (1956) 144 Cal.App.2d 617, 301 P.2d 602), or an escape clause specifically authorized by statute (Argonaut Ins. Co. v. Transport Indem. Co. (1972) 6 Cal.3d 496, 99 Cal.Rptr. 617, 492 P.2d 673), or a composite escape and excess clause reconcilable with a pure excess clause (Underground Constr. Co. v. Pacific Indemnity Co. (1975) 49 Cal.App.3d 62, 122 Cal.Rptr. 330), or a conflict between an escape clause and a clause excepting certain acts, errors or omissions from coverage (Chamberlin v. Smith, supra, 72

Cal.App.3d 835, 140 Cal.Rptr. 493.) In addition to the absence of direct authority on the question whether an excess clause should be given preference over an escape clause, there exists no clear trend from other jurisdictions as to a resolution of this question.[58]

Absent direct authority from California cases and a clear trend from other jurisdictions, we must rest our decision here on analogy to related cases and considerations of policy. Both of these considerations dictate that the excess clause be given preference over the escape clause. California decisions demonstrate a preference for excess clauses. Where one policy contains a pro rata clause and the other contains an excess clause, for example, the excess clause will be given effect and the carrier with the pro rata clause will become the primary insurer. (See Fireman's Fund etc. Ins. Companies v. State Farm etc. Ins. Co. (1969) 273 Cal. App.2d 445, 78 Cal.Rptr. 38, followed in Donahue Constr. Co. v. Transport Indem. Co. (1970) 7 Cal.App.3d 291, 301–303, 86 Cal.Rptr. 632, and Owens Pacific Marine, Inc. v. Insurance Co. of North America (1970) 12 Cal.App.3d 661, 668–669, 90 Cal.Rptr. 826.) This is true even where it is clear that there will be no excess and the excess clause therefore operates much like an escape clause. (Owens Pacific Marine, Inc. v. Insurance Co. of North America, supra, at pp. 668–669, 90 Cal.Rptr. 826.) Consistency in the judicial interpretation of "other insurance" clause thus demands that the excess clause be preferred over the escape clause.

More importantly, it is well established that an escape clause is less favored under the law than a pro rata or excess clause. [citations omitted] The trial court, thus, correctly concluded that Mission's escape provision was disfavored because of its potential for leaving the insured without coverage.

The final argument on behalf of Mission is that the court here should follow the "Oregon rule," disregarding both of these irreconcilable provisions and mandating proration. This rule, however, is the minority rule and has not been adopted in California. (See Peerless Cas. Co. v. Continental Cas. Co., supra, at p. 623, 301 P.2d 602; Note, Conflicts Between "Other Insurance" Clauses in Automobile Liability Insurance Policies (1969) 20 Hastings L.J. 1292, 1305–1306.)

* * *

The judgment is affirmed.

58. Most courts have given effect to the "excess" provision and imposed full liability for the loss upon the other policy involved despite the "escape" (no liability) provision contained therein. [citations omitted] A number of courts, however, have given effect to the "escape" clause and imposed full liability for the loss upon the other policy involved despite the excess provision contained therein. [citations omitted] Other courts have refused to recognize either "other insurance" clause and have prorated the loss between the insurance companies. This position is known as the "Oregon rule" because the leading case espousing proration is Oregon Auto. Insurance Co. v. United States Fidelity & Guar. Co. (9th Cir.1952) 195 F.2d 958.

Notes

1. In the case of conflicting excess coverages, the California courts have declined to follow the main case on the basis that the escape provisions are strongly disfavored while there is no basis for choice of one excess policy or another. Continental Casualty Co. v. Pacific Indemnity Co., 134 Cal.App.3d 389, 184 Cal.Rptr. 583 (1982); see Peerless Insurance v. Vermont Mutual Insurance Co., 151 N.H. 71, 849 A.2d 100 (2004) (insurers liable on pro rata basis in case of mutually repugnant other insurance clauses).

2. An example of the California treatment is *Commerce & Industry Ins. Co. v. Chubb Custom Ins. Co.*, 75 Cal.App.4th 739, 89 Cal.Rptr.2d 415 (1999). According to the facts, fire destroyed a New Orleans warehouse causing millions of dollars in damage. The property was covered by insurance policies issued by Commerce & Industry Ins. Co. and by Chubb Customs Inc. Both policies had "other insurance" clauses—Commerce's provision contained an "excess only" clause, while Chubb's provision included a hybrid "pro rata/escape" clause. Commerce initiated an action for equitable contribution, equitable indemnity and declaratory relief, complaining that Chubb paid nothing while Commerce was required to contribute more than 40 percent of total loss. The trial court granted Chubb's motion for summary judgment, reasoning that Commerce and Chubb were not co-insurers of the same loss.

On appeal, the court established that both insurers should be treated as primary insurers and held that the amount of loss should be prorated between the two. Chubb argued that its policy only provided contingent (excess) coverage and not primary coverage; therefore Chubb should avoid responsibility. The court disagreed, reasoning that the policy language was too clear and explicit to fit any such interpretation—the policy met the definition of primary coverage because the insurer's liability arose immediately upon occurrence of a covered loss. The court held that Commerce was entitled to the pro rata allocation it requested, explaining that this result "will most accurately reflect the equities."

CARRIERS INSURANCE CO. v. AMERICAN POLICYHOLDERS' INSURANCE CO.

Supreme Judicial Court of Maine, 1979.
404 A.2d 216.

DELAHANTY, JUSTICE.

This action was brought in the Superior Court, Kennebec County, by the plaintiff, Carriers Insurance Company (Carriers), seeking contribution from the defendant, American Policyholders' Insurance Co. (American). The parties joined issue upon whether and to what extent American was required to contribute to a settlement made by the plaintiff. Upon an agreed statement of facts, the presiding Justice found for Carriers, and American has appealed. We deny the appeal.

During April of 1963, Cummings Bros. (Cummings) entered into a contractual agreement with Merrill's Rental Service, Inc. (Merrill's) whereby it leased certain motor vehicles from Merrill's. Pursuant to the lease and for Cummings' benefit, Merrill's agreed to provide insurance coverage—both personal injury and property damage—for its vehicles while they were being operated by Cummings' employees. In 1971, this personal injury liability coverage which Merrill's obtained through Carriers stood at approximately $3,000,000 with $500,000 of property damage coverage. In the meantime, Cummings independently procured $250,000 of liability insurance through the defendant, American.

In March of 1972, one of Cummings' employees, while negligently driving a vehicle leased from Merrill's, collided with a Lincoln Continental killing the driver and extensively damaging his automobile. Carriers, acting in good faith and in the best interests of its insured, settled a wrongful death claim for $200,000 and a property damage claim for approximately $8,000. Both prior and subsequent to the settlement, American refused Carriers' demand for contribution. Thereafter, Carriers instituted the present action and received a judgment against the defendant for approximately $104,000. Both Carriers and American had "other insurance" clauses in their insurance policies. Carriers' contract stated:

> OTHER INSURANCE
>
> If there is other insurance against an occurrence covered by this policy, the insurance afforded by this policy shall be deemed *excess insurance* over and above the applicable limits of all such other insurance. (emphasis supplied.)

American's policy contained an endorsement specifically covering "hired automobiles" which provided:

> OTHER INSURANCE
>
> This insurance shall be *excess insurance* over any other valid and collectible insurance for Bodily Injury Liability, for Property Damage Liability and for Automobile Medical Payments. (emphasis supplied.)

Faced with these competing clauses, the presiding Justice disregarded them as "mutually repugnant." American assigns this as error and insists that its clause should be given preference over Carriers'.

I

We begin our discussion by acknowledging the utter confusion that pervades the entire realm of "other insurance" clauses. See Insurance Company of Texas v. Employers Liability Assurance Corp., 163 F.Supp. 143, 145 (S.D.Cal.1958). Originating in the property insurance field, these clauses were designed to prevent fraudulent claims induced by overinsuring. With automobiles, however, the fear of death or injury was in itself sufficient to deter specious accidents. The original purpose of other insurance clauses has little relevance, therefore, to automobile liability insurance other than to limit, reduce, or avoid an insurer's loss in those cases where there is multiple coverage. See Comment, "Other Insurance" Clauses: The Lamb–Weston Doctrine, 47 Or.L.Rev. 430 (1968); Note, Concurrent Coverage in Automobile Liability Insurance, 65 Colum.L.Rev. 319 (1965). However, these clauses violate no public policy and in the absence of a statute to the contrary they will be given effect, even if the insured is unaware of the existence of the other insurance. 8 D. Blashfield, Automobile Law and Practice § 345.10 (3rd ed. 1966).

There are three basic types of other insurance clauses which regulate how liability is to be divided when multiple coverage exists. The first, a "pro-rata" clause, limits the liability of an insurer to a proportion of the total loss. The second, an "escape" clause, seeks to avoid all liability. The third, an "excess" clause, the provision used in the present case, provides that the insurance will only be excess. See 8 J. Appleman, Insurance Law and Practice § 4911 (Cum.Supp.1973); 7 Am.Jur.2d *Automobile Insurance* §§ 200–202 (2d ed. 1963).

No problems arise as long as only one policy contains an other insurance clause since the particular provision can be given effect as written. Complications and conflicts occur where more than one applicable policy contains an other insurance clause. In that situation, the court is faced with a battle of the clauses.[59]

In the case at bar, each policy, in virtually identical language, states that it will be excess over any other valid and collectible insurance. Any attempt at a literal reconciliation of the clauses involves hopeless circular reasoning. One clause cannot be given effect as "excess" unless the other is considered "primary." Since both claim to be excess, neither could operate as primary and hence neither could take effect as excess. Taken to its *reductio ad absurdum* conclusion, even though each insurer concedes that its policy would have covered the loss in the absence of the other, where there is double coverage both would escape liability, a result which neither party advocates. As well stated in State Farm Mutual Insurance Co. v. Travelers Insurance Co., 184 So.2d 750, 753–54 (La.App.1966) (Tate, J., concurring),

> [i]ndeed, there is actually no way by logic or word-sense to reconcile two such clauses, where each policy by itself can apply as a primary insurer, but where the clause in each policy nevertheless attempts to make its own liability secondary to that of any other policy issued by a similar primary insurer: For then the primary and (attempted) secondary liability of each policy chase the other through infinity, something like trying to answer the question: Which came first, the chicken or the egg?

Faced with this logical logjam, a number of different and conflicting methods have at various times been used to determine which policy is primary and hence which should bear the brunt of the loss. Thus, it has been stated that the primary policy is the one: covering the tortfeasor, Employers Mutual Liability Insurance Company of Wisconsin v. Pacific Indemnity Company, 167 Cal.App.2d 369, 334 P.2d 658 (1959); issued

59. Some of the more common interchanges have been commented upon: excess clause v. pro-rata clause, see Annot., 76 A.L.R.2d 502 (1961); escape clause v. pro-rata clause, see Annot., 46 A.L.R.2d 1163, 1167 (1956); excess clause v. excess clause, see Annot., 69 A.L.R.2d 1122 (1960); excess clause v. escape clause, see 46 A.L.R.2d, supra at 1165. See Union Ins. Co. (Mut.) v. Iowa Hardware Mut. Ins. Co., 175 N.W.2d 413, 415 (Iowa 1970).

prior in time, Automobile Insurance Company of Hartford v. Springfield Dyeing Company, 109 F.2d 533 (3d Cir.1940); insuring the vehicle's owner, Farm Bureau Mut. Automobile Ins. Co. v. Preferred Acc. Ins. Co., 78 F.Supp. 561 (W.D.Va.1948); whose policy covered the particular loss more specifically, Trinity Universal Insurance Co. v. General Accident, Fire & Life Assurance Corp., 138 Ohio St. 488, 35 N.E.2d 836 (1941); or whose other insurance clause is written in more general terms, Zurich General Accident & Liability Insurance Co. v. Clamor, 124 F.2d 717 (7th Cir.1941).

Seizing on one of these approaches, American argues that Carriers' policy should be construed as primary based upon minute differences in the language of the excess insurance clauses. We prefer not to engage in such semantic microscopy. "It [merely] encourages the continuing draftsmanship battle by which insurers seek still more specific policy terms, and the end is not in sight." Note, Concurrent Coverage in Automobile Liability Insurance, supra at 322. Fairly read, each insurer, through its excess clause, seeks to place the initial loss on any other applicable insurance, saving for itself a role as secondary insurer.

As an alternative argument, American asserts that the intent of the underlying parties should be given effect. Merrill's, for valuable consideration, contractually agreed to insure Cummings.[60] Merrill's insurance should therefore be considered primary.

We disagree.

American's argument would be well taken were this suit simply one for breach of contract between Cummings and Merrill's. We fail, however, to see the relevance in this case of the lease agreement to which the insurers were neither parties nor beneficiaries. The only appropriate considerations are the two insurance policies through which the respective insurers and insureds manifested their contractual intent. See Farm Bureau Mutual Insurance Co. v. Waugh, 159 Me. 115, 188 A.2d 889 (1963). An examination of the policies issued is the single criteria for analyzing an insurer's obligations which can neither be enlarged nor diminished beyond the terms employed. Limberis v. Aetna Casualty & Surety Co., Me., 263 A.2d 83 (1970). A determination of the primary

60. In pertinent part, the lease provided:

F. INSURANCE COVERAGE AND LIABILITY

Subject to the following conditions, MERRILL shall provide, at its expense, insurance coverage for its benefit and the benefit of CUMMINGS and the drivers and/or operators of CUMMINGS.

1. All rental units described in Schedule A including any emergency spares or other vehicles or trailers of MERRILL's used by CUMMINGS under the terms hereof will be covered, for the benefit of CUMMINGS and its operating and driving personnel:

(a) Personal injury, [$2,990,000.00].

(b) Property damage, $500,000.00.

2. CUMMINGS shall not be liable to MERRILL for any damages or injuries sustained to the rental units described in Schedule A while being used by CUMMINGS under the terms hereof if occasioned by:

(a) The negligent operation of CUMMINGS' drivers or operators while operating or driving said rental units in the scope of their employment with CUMMINGS.

insurer must turn, therefore, upon a construction of the insurance contracts and not upon a collateral agreement between an insured and a third party.

We perceive no methodology which is neither arbitrary nor utterly mechanical by which we could rationally resolve the enigma of which policy should be given effect over the other. Both clauses attempt to occupy the same legal status. Any construction this Court renders should attempt to maintain this status quo. This goal can be achieved only by abandoning the search for the mythical "primary" insurer and insisting instead that both insurers share in the loss. Such an approach best carries out the intent of the insurers which was to reduce or limit their liability.

There are additional benefits to adopting this rule. It would introduce certainty and uniformity into the insurance industry, discourage litigation between insurers, and enable underwriters to predict the losses of the insurers more accurately. Note, Conflicts Between "Other Insurance" Clauses in Automobile Liability Insurance Policies, 20 Hastings L.J. 1292, 1304 (1969). We hold that where there are conflicting excess insurance clause provisions they are to be disregarded as mutually repugnant thus rendering applicable the general coverage of each policy. This, we note, is the clear majority rule [citations].

[In part II the court explained the three possible proration methods: prorating liability according to each policy's limits; prorating on the basis of the paid premiums; and prorating the loss equally up to the limits of the lower policy. The court chose this last option, the "minority rule", reasoning it was easier to administer and did not lend itself to unfair discrimination.]

* * *

Judgment affirmed.

Notes

1. The Washington Supreme Court has overruled *Pacific Indemnity Co. v. Federated American Insurance Co.*, 82 Wn.2d 412, 511 P.2d 56 (1973) (the majority rule) to adopt the "minority" rule of apportionment as espoused in the principal case. Mission Insurance Co. v. Allendale Mutual Insurance Co., 95 Wn.2d 464, 626 P.2d 505 (1981).

2. For a further discussion of a court's treatment of excess insurance clauses that are repugnant, see *York Mut. Ins. Co. v. Continental Ins. Co.*, 560 A.2d 571 (1989) (holding that each insurance company must contribute equally until the limit of the smaller policy is exhausted, at which point any remaining loss shall be paid from the larger policy up to its limits).

3. Can an excess surety be subrogated to the insured's claim against the primary insurer for breach of the duty of good faith? See Continental Casualty Co. v. Reserve Insurance Co., 307 Minn. 5, 238 N.W.2d 862 (1976) (holding "yes").

4. May an excess carrier bring an equitable subrogation action against the primary insurer? Some jurisdictions allow such an action. See *American Centennial Insurance Co. v. Canal Insurance Co.*, 843 S.W.2d 480 (Tex.1992), in which the court extended the well-settled rule that the insured may sue the primary carrier for wrongful refusal to settle a claim. The court also allowed the action against defense counsel for alleged mishandling of the claim, reasoning that such an action would not interfere with the attorney-client relationship and would simply permit the insurance company to "enforce existing duties of defense counsel to the insured." The court reiterated that neither the primary carrier nor the defense counsel is relieved of the duty to protect the insured's interest simply because the insured contracted separately for excess coverage.

5. The majority method of apportionment calls for prorating "according to the limits in each policy." Suppose two auto policies contain irreconcilable or mutually repugnant "other insurance" clauses. Policy A (issued by company Y) states a single limit of $50,000 per occurrence; Policy B (issued by company Z) states a limit of $15,000, per person, $30,000 (that is for all persons injured in one occurrence) and $5,000 for property damages. This is usually referred to as "15/30/5." Both policies A and B cover Jones in an accident in which Jones is responsible for injuries to two persons in the total amount of $29,000 and for property damage of $2,500. How would you pro rate between the insurers? See Forest Industries Ins. Exchange v. Viking Ins. Co., 82 Or.App. 615, 728 P.2d 943 (1986) (holding that the per accident limits of both contributing insurance policies should be used, and allocating to Policy B one-eleventh of the total property damage and three-eighths of the total bodily injury settlement).

6. Some sense to this area is imparted in Susan Randall, *Coordinating Liability Insurance*, 1995 Wisc. L. Rev. 1339.

5. A Problem

The principles of the preceding cases can be neatly applied in the following deceptively simple problem.

In October 2000, Goodwin Industries lost a $10 million judgment in a liability case in which the plaintiff suffered progressive bodily injury for three years following an accident which occurred in 1996. The suit was commenced in 1999.

In 1996, Goodwin Industries had $1 million in primary CGL coverage and $4 million in excess CGL coverage. In 1997, Goodwin Industries changed its insurers and again had $1 million in primary CGL coverage subject to a retained limit of $100,000, and $6 million in excess CGL coverage. All of the four different insurers in the first and second years have admitted coverage for the judgment. Goodwin Industries had no insurance coverage in 1998. In 1999, Goodwin Industries once again obtained insurance coverage. This time it obtained $1 million in primary CGL coverage subject to a retained limit of $100,000 from AAA Mutual Insurance Company (AAA), and $6 million in excess coverage from ZZZ Casualty Company (ZZZ).

AAA and ZZZ have denied coverage on the sole ground that the plaintiff sued Goodwin Industries shortly before their insurance policies took effect. As noted above, final judgment was entered in October 2000.

All of the insurance policies have an "excess other insurance" clause ("this policy shall be excess of any other insurance that covers this loss"). Assuming California law applies, please answer the following questions.

1. Are AAA and ZZZ justified in denying coverage? Discuss.

2. How should the judgment be allocated among the various insurers and how much of the judgment, if any, must Goodwin Industries bear? Discuss. This is not a math exercise. It is the methodological approach that is important.

E. WAIVER AGREEMENTS, RESERVATIONS OF RIGHTS, AND LAWYER'S OBLIGATIONS

The cases in this section highlight the difficulty of balancing the duties and relationships of insurance defense counsel. The insurance contract does not alter the primary attorney-client relationship. However, it does introduce potentially conflicting objectives between the insurer and the insured, especially where an insurer's "House" counsel is assigned. A defense attorney may lose the ability to objectively manage settlement and litigation when a long term relationship with an insurer is contrasted with a transitory claim file. As the cases show, there may be divergent interests when a claim rests on alternative theories, or when a claim is partially covered. Consider the effect on settlement and litigation strategy when defense expenses are included within the policy limits (Professional Liability–Appendix F) or are unlimited (Commercial GL–Appendix E).

The American Bar Association addressed the inherent conflict of the tripartite relationship in the Model Rules of Professional Conduct. Rule 1.8(f) requires that the attorney assess any conflicts and explain them to the client as well as maintain confidentiality. Courts and counsel alike have been unable to formulate a satisfactory bright-line test.

There are a number of excellent treatments on the ethical and malpractice considerations of insurance law practice. A few of them are cited here. Robert E. Keeton, *Taking Professional Risks*, 4 Conn. Ins. L.J. 405 (1997–98); Tom Baker, *Liability Insurance Conflicts and Defense Lawyers; From Triangles to Tetrahedrons*, 4 Conn. Ins. L.J. 101 (1997–98); Douglas R. Richmond, *Lost in the Eternal Triangle of Insurance defense Ethics*, 9 Geo. J. Legal Ethics, 475 (1996); Charles Silver & Kent Syverud, *The Professional Responsibilities of Insurance Defense Lawyers*, 45 Duke L.J. 255 (1995); Robert E. O'Malley, *Ethics Principles for the Insurer, the Insured, and Defense Counsel: The Eternal Triangle Reformed*, 66 Tul. L. Rev. 511 (1991); William C. Carpenter, *Note: Reserva-*

tion of Rights in Insurance Contracts, 32 Ariz. L. Rev. 387 (1990); 2 Ronald E. Mallen and Jeffrey M. Smith, *Legal Malpractice* § 23 (3rd ed. 1989), Keeton and Widiss, *Insurance Law,* § 7.6(c) (1988); Stanley, *Can We Defend Both: A Defense Counsel's Dilemma*, 22 Tort & Ins. L.J. 59 (Fall 1986); Sharpe and Shaffer, *The Parameters of the Insurer's Duty to Defend*, XIX Forum 555 (1984); Dondanville, *Defense Counsel Beware: The Perils of Conflicts of Interest*, XVIII Forum 62 (1982); Revere and Chapman, *Insurer's Duty to Defend*, 13 Pac. L.J. 889 (1982).

CHI OF ALASKA, INC. v. EMPLOYERS REINSURANCE CORP.

Supreme Court of Alaska, 1993.
844 P.2d 1113.

MATTHEWS, J.

A seaman aboard a vessel owned by Oceanic Research Services, Inc. (Oceanic) accidentally sustained serious injuries. Oceanic believed it was insured against the loss by a $500,000 bodily injury insurance policy it purchased through CHI of Alaska, Inc. (CHI). That policy, however, actually had a bodily injury limit of only $100,000. Oceanic sued CHI, asserting contract and negligent tort claims, as well as a claim that CHI had intentionally misrepresented that the policy coverage was $500,000. Oceanic sought compensatory and punitive damages.

CHI tendered the defense of this suit to its liability insurer, Employers Reinsurance Corporation (Employers). Employers agreed to defend CHI, conditional on reserving its rights to disclaim coverage with respect to Oceanic's claim of intentional misconduct. Employers claimed that intentional misconduct would be excluded under the policy if such misconduct was ratified by CHI.

CHI objected, noting that the reservation of rights created a conflict of interest between Employers and CHI, and demanded independent counsel paid for by Employers and selected by CHI. CHI stated that it wanted its personal attorney Brett von Gemmingen to defend it. Employers expressed reservations about von Gemmingen's experience in handling claims of this nature and suggested that CHI provide the names of other attorneys with more experience who might be retained by Employers to defend CHI. This was not acceptable to CHI. Next Employers offered to pay von Gemmingen to defend that portion of the lawsuit pertaining to the intentional misconduct claim while retaining the law firm of Hughes, Thorsness, Gantz, Powell & Brundin to act as co-counsel for CHI with responsibility for the defense of all claims. CHI declined this offer. CHI then brought the present action for declaratory relief, seeking vindication of its position that it is entitled to select independent counsel. In the meanwhile, the Oceanic case has been jointly defended by Hughes Thorsness and von Gemmingen.

CHI and Employers each moved for summary judgment in the present case. CHI contended that there was necessarily a conflict of interest between CHI and Employers respecting the defense of Oceanic's claim because Employers could win either by defeating all claims of liability or by establishing that CHI is liable for intentional misconduct. Given this conflict of interest, CHI contended that Employers should have no role in the selection of defense counsel because any attorney selected by an insurance company "will attempt to help his real client, the insurance company, at the expense of the insured." CHI argued that the retention of von Gemmingen "to defend claims as they are pushed outside the policy coverage does not resolve the conflict." Instead, dual representation, according to CHI, would still permit the attorney hired by the insurance company to work against the interests of the insured and in addition would cause confusion concerning who is to control various litigation decisions. In response and in support of its motion for summary judgment, Employers argued that potential conflicts were eliminated by allowing CHI to have its personal attorney handle the non-covered claim at Employers' expense.

The superior court granted Employers' motion for summary judgment. The court ruled that Employers' offer to allow CHI to retain counsel of its choice to defend it on the intentional tort claim adequately resolved potential conflicts of interest. In addition, the court stated that if CHI contends at the conclusion of the Oceanic lawsuit "that a conflict existed despite Employers' action in allowing it to retain its own counsel to defend uncovered claims, then it can raise this issue at the coverage trial." Following the order granting Employers' motion for summary judgment, a final judgment was entered which contained no explicit declaration. CHI has appealed from this judgment.

There are three issues on appeal: 1. Did Employers' reservation of rights to disclaim coverage give CHI a right to retain independent counsel? 2. Does the two-counsel scheme proposed by Employers and approved by the superior court satisfy CHI's right to independent counsel? 3. Does CHI have the unilateral right to select independent counsel? We turn to a discussion of these issues.

1. *Did Employers' reservation of rights to disclaim coverage give CHI a right to retain independent counsel?*

We answer this question in the affirmative.

Liability insurers have separate duties to defend and to indemnify their insureds. In order to discharge their duty to defend, insurers hire counsel to conduct the defense of their insureds. Often there is no conflict of interest between the interests of the insurers and the interests of the insureds. Both wish to successfully defend and, if that is not possible, minimize damages.

Sometimes, however, the insurer claims that the policy has been breached by the insured. These are so-called policy defenses of which the insured's failure to give notice or to cooperate are typical examples. The insurer may wish to preserve its policy defenses and still provide a defense to the insured. By doing so it may be able to avoid paying the underlying claim either by succeeding in its defense of the insured or, failing that, by successfully asserting its policy defense. The insurer can preserve these options by defending the insured under a reservation of rights to later disclaim coverage if the reservation of rights is acquiesced in by the insured. Continental Ins. Co. v. Bayless & Roberts, Inc., 608 P.2d 281, 288 (Alaska 1980).

Similarly, the insurer may claim that although no condition of the policy has been breached by the insured, a particular claim made by the plaintiff does not come within the coverage of the policy. Such defenses are called coverage defenses. The most typical example is the coverage defense in this case where alternative theories of negligent and intentional tort are plead and negligent acts are covered by the policy but intentional acts are not. In such cases the insurer's duty to defend may require it to defend even if the most likely theory of recovery is one for which there is no insurance coverage.[61] The insurer can preserve its coverage defense and fulfill its duty to defend by defending under a reservation of rights to later disclaim coverage if liability is attributable to the excluded theory.

In cases where an insurer asserts either policy or coverage defenses, and defends its insured under a reservation of rights, there are various conflicts of interest between the insurer and the insured. We identified three of these in Continental. First, if the insurer knows that it can later assert non-coverage, or if it thinks that the loss which it is defending will not be covered under the policy, it may only go through the motions of defending: "it may offer only a token defense * * *. [I]t may not be motivated to achieve the lowest possible settlement or in other ways treat the interests of the insured as its own." Id. at 289. Second, if there are several theories of recovery, at least one of which is not covered under the policy, the insurer might conduct the defense in such a manner as to make the likelihood of a plaintiff's verdict greater under the uninsured theory. Id. Third, the insurer might gain access to confidential or privileged information in the process of the defense which it might later use to its advantage in litigation concerning coverage. Id. at 291.

Merely because the insurer and the insured have divergent interests when the insurer seeks to defend under a reservation of rights does not necessarily mean that appointed counsel also has conflicting interests. If appointed counsel makes it clear at the outset of his engagement that he is going to be involved only in the defense of the liability claim, not in coverage issues, and that his client is the insured, not the insurer, conflicts should be rare. A number of authorities hold that this is the appropriate role of appointed counsel. For example, the Arizona Supreme Court held that appointed counsel who in the course of representing the insured gains access to information which may give rise to a policy

61. The duty to defend arises "if the complaint *on its face* alleges facts which, standing alone, give rise to a possible finding of liability covered by the policy," Afcan v. Mutual Fire, Marine & Inland Ins. Co., 595 P.2d 638, 645 (Alaska 1979); or, if the complaint does not contain such allegations, where "the true facts are within, or potentially within, the policy coverage and are known or reasonably ascertainable to the insurer." National Indem. Co. v. Flesher, 469 P.2d 360, 366 (Alaska 1970).

defense is prohibited from communicating that information to the insurance company. Farmers Ins. Co. of Arizona v. Vagnozzi, 138 Ariz. 443, 448, 675 P.2d 703, 708 (1983): "We emphasize that the attorney who represents the insured owes him an undeviating allegiance whether compensated by the insurer or the insured and cannot act as an agent of the insurance company by supplying information detrimental to the insured." Employers agrees with this view, noting that counsel has "an absolute duty of fidelity to the insured over the interests of the insurer."

Other authorities, however, take the view that appointed counsel represents both the insured and the insurer. A former president of the Defense Research Institute has written that appointed counsel has an obligation to disclose to the insurance company information detrimental to the insured. Thomas A. Ford, The Insurance Contract: The Conflicts of Interest it Breeds, Ins.Couns.J. 610, 620 (Oct. 1969): "In order for the attorney to perform his role properly, he must never lose sight of the fact that he is working for two different and distinct parties—the insured and the insurer. He must fully disclose to both parties the information he has obtained as a result of his unique relationship with them." See also Shafer v. Utica Mutual Ins. Co., 248 A.D. 279, 289 N.Y.S. 577, 587 (1936) (appointed attorney acted properly in disclosing to insurer information which enabled insurer to disclaim liability); Alaska Code of Professional Responsibility EC 5–17 (stating that one typically recurring situation involving potentially different interests is dual representation of insured and insurer).

Where there is a conflict between insurer and insured, appointed counsel may tend to favor the interests of the insurer primarily because of the prospect of future employment. United States Fidelity & Guar. Co. v. Louis A. Roser Co., 585 F.2d 932, 938 n. 5 (8th Cir.1978) ("Even the most optimistic view of human nature requires us to realize that an attorney employed by an insurance company will slant his efforts, perhaps unconsciously, in the interest of his real client—the one who is paying his fee and from whom he hopes to receive future business—the insurance company."); San Diego Navy Fed. Credit Union v. Cumis Ins. Soc'y, Inc., 162 Cal.App.3d 358, 208 Cal.Rptr. 494, 498 (1984) ("'A lawyer who does not look out for the carrier's best interest may soon find himself out of work.'" (quoting the trial court)); Michael A. Berch and Rebecca W. Berch, Will the Real Counsel for the Insured Please Rise?, 19 Ariz.St.L.J. 27, 29–30 (1987) ("[T]he attorney's economic interests weigh heavily in favor of the insurer, which, after all, may retain his services in other cases; yet the rules of professional responsibility tip the scales toward the insured."); Arthur P. Berg, Losing Control of the Defense—The Insured's Right to Select His Own Counsel, 26 For the Defense 10, 15 (July 1984) ("Although [some] courts seem to trust the insurer and attorney to act in the best interests of the insured, the more common view is that the longstanding ties that defense counsel has with the insurer will inevitably influence his conduct of the case."); Sampson A. Brown and John L. Romaker, Cumis, Conflicts and the Civil Code: Section 2860 Changes Little, 25 Cal.W.L.Rev. 45, 54 (1988) ("The attorney, wishing to maintain the insurer's business, does not want to aggravate the company.''); Mark A. Saxon, Conflicts of Interest: Insurers' Expanding Duty to Defend and the Impact of "Cumis" Counsel, 23 Idaho L.Rev. 351, 353 (1987) (Insurance counsel's "relationship with the insurer is contractual, usually ongoing, supported by strong financial interests, and often strengthened by sincere friendships."). In recognition of this, most courts hold that in conflict situations the insured has the right to independent counsel to conduct its defense and the insurance company has the obligation to pay the reasonable value of the defense conducted by independent counsel.

In dicta in National Indemnity Co. v. Flesher, 469 P.2d 360, 367 n. 22 (Alaska 1970), we recognized the right of the insured to independent counsel under circumstances involving a coverage defense: "In such circumstances, the insurer must provide the insured with independent counsel." Ten years later in Continental Insurance Co. v. Bayless & Roberts, Inc., 608 P.2d 281 (Alaska 1980), we recognized the right of the insured to independent counsel in cases involving policy defenses. However, we reserved the question whether the insured had the same right in coverage defense cases. Id. at 289.

In Continental the insurer claimed that the insured had breached the cooperation clause of the policy, but offered to defend the insured under a reservation of rights. Id. at 283. The insured rejected the insurer's offer of a conditional defense and demanded a defense without a reservation of rights. Id. at 286. This the insurer refused to do. Id. Subsequently, the insured's personal counsel took over the defense of the case and entered into a settlement which resulted in a consent judgment against the insured. Id. In the ensuing litigation between the insured and the insurer, the insurer contended that the insured had breached the insurance policy by refusing to accept the insurer's offer to defend under a reservation of rights. Id. at 288. We held that the insured did not breach the policy and that it was within its rights to require the insurer to defend unconditionally or withdraw from the defense. Id. at 291. We also affirmed the jury's award which included $4,000 expended by the insured as its defense costs. Id. at 296 n. 28.

In reaching this result, we expressed and adopted in policy defense cases the general rule that the insurer must surrender its right to control the defense to the insured if the insured refuses to accept a defense under a reservation of rights: "[T]he general rule is that, if an insured refuses to accede to the insurer's reservation of rights, the carrier must either accept liability under the policy and defend unconditionally or surrender control of the defense * * *." Id. at 288. We explained in some detail the types of conflicts of interests which arise when the insurer asserts a right to later contest its liability. Id. at 289–90. We noted that these conflicts might be avoided if the insured were offered the right to retain independent counsel: "The possibility of a conflict might be avoided in such cases if the insurance company were to offer its insured the right to retain independent counsel to conduct his defense, and agree to pay all the necessary costs of that defense. In that event, it would seem that the company should be entitled to reserve the right to later litigate an alleged policy defense." Id. at 291 n. 17. As already stated, the holding in Continental was limited to policy defenses; the question as to whether the same rules should apply where coverage defenses are involved was reserved. Id. at 289.

All three general types of conflicts of interests between insurer and insured which we identified in Continental—the insurer may offer mere token defense, the insurer may steer result to judgment under an uninsured theory of recovery, the insurer may gain access to confidential or privileged information which it may later use to its advantage—apply in coverage defense cases. However, the second reason does not apply in policy defense cases. Policy defenses, such as lack of notice or non-cooperation, involve facts which are generally irrelevant to the litigation between the plaintiff and the insured. Therefore, appointed counsel has no opportunity to "covertly frame [a] defense to achieve a verdict based upon [a theory under which no coverage would result] so that [the insurer] could later assert that the defense was not covered * * *." Id. at 289. Thus, the need for independent counsel is, if anything, greater in coverage than in policy defense cases. We conclude that the right to independent counsel recognized in Continental should also apply to cases involving coverage defenses.[62] We thus adhere to the dicta contained in National Indemnity, which we noted above.

2. *Does the two-counsel scheme proposed by Employers and approved by the superior court satisfy CHI's right to independent counsel?*

We answer this question in the negative.

The trial court was of the view that neither CHI nor Employers was bound by any determination of fact made in the underlying tort suit concerning whether CHI's conduct was negligent or intentional. From this the trial court concluded that Employers' two-counsel scheme would solve the conflict of interest between the insurer and the insured. The view that issues determined in the initial action as to which a conflict of interest exists between insurer and insured may be subsequently relitigated appears to be sensible and in accordance with a number of authorities. That view, however, does not resolve all conflicts of interest between insurer and insured. It does not alleviate the access of appointed counsel to information in possession of the insured which may be used against the insured in subsequent coverage litigation: "This solution overlooks the fact that, during the initial litigation, the insured may

62. We have recently recognized the application of the right to independent counsel expressed in Continental in the context of a coverage defense case in Sauer v. The Home Indemnity Co., 841 P.2d 176, 182, 183 (Alaska 1992), where we stated:

> However, if the insured does not consent to a non-waiver agreement, or to a defense under a reservation of rights, then the insurance company must choose whether it wishes to defend unconditionally or pursue other options. One such option is to permit the insured to exercise its right to reject the defense offered by the insurer and to obtain substitute counsel at the insurer's expense. In the event the defense is conducted by substitute counsel, the insurance company retains the right to later contest policy coverage. See Continental Ins. Co. v. Bayless & Roberts, Inc., 608 P.2d 281, 291 n. 17 (Alaska 1980).

transmit information to counsel that the insurer could use in subsequent litigation to the insured's disadvantage. A heavy burden of silence falls on the attorney the insurer selects to defend the insured.'' Berch & Berch, supra, at 32 n. 23. The fact that personal counsel for CHI is acting as co-counsel with counsel appointed by the insurer also does not eliminate this conflict. Appointed counsel has and should have full access to the client so that the defense may be effectively conducted.

Moreover, even where the facts in conflict may be relitigated, the opportunity to direct a case through witness selection, interrogation, and discovery may afford a dispositive advantage in subsequent litigation: ''In such cases, the insured's attorney has the opportunity to develop the facts through discovery and to shape the case for, and present the evidence at, the trial. So even though the insured or the insurer may relitigate the coverage issue in a subsequent proceeding, controlling the defense in the main proceeding could be critical. Testifying under oath in the main proceeding may freeze in the witnesses' minds one version of the facts. Very little latitude may remain in subsequent proceedings to mold the evidence bearing upon coverage.'' Id. at 37–38.

We conclude therefore that the two-counsel solution does not satisfactorily resolve the conflicts which have given rise to the right to independent counsel.

3. *Does CHI have the unilateral right to select independent counsel?*

We answer this question in the affirmative.

Most cases which recognize the right to independent counsel express the view that the insured has the right to select independent counsel of its choice. American Family Life Assur. Co. v. United States Fire Co., 885 F.2d 826, 831 (11th Cir.1989) (if insured had rejected conflicted counsel, insurer ''would have been obligated to pay'' for defense conducted by insured) (interpreting Georgia law); Rhodes v. Chicago Ins. Co., 719 F.2d 116, 120–21 (5th Cir.1983) (''When a reservation of rights is made * * * the insured may * * * pursue his own defense [and the] insurer remains liable for attorneys' fees'') (interpreting Texas law); Previews, Inc. v. California Union Ins. Co., 640 F.2d 1026 (9th Cir.1981) (''the insurer's obligation to defend extends to paying the reasonable value of the legal services and costs performed by independent counsel selected by the insured'') (interpreting California law); San Diego Navy Fed. Credit Union v. Cumis Ins. Soc'y, 162 Cal.App.3d 358, 208 Cal.Rptr. 494, 501–02 (1984) (''the insurer must pay the reasonable cost for hiring independent counsel by the insured''); Maryland Casualty Co. v. Peppers, 64 Ill.2d 187, 355 N.E.2d 24, 31 (1976) (The insured ''has the right to be defended * * * by an attorney of his own choice who shall have the right to control the conduct of the case.''); Illinois Masonic Medical Ctr. v. Turegum Ins. Co., 168 Ill.App.3d 158, 118 Ill.Dec. 941, 943, 522 N.E.2d 611, 613 (1988) (''where a conflict of interest exists the insured, rather than the insurer, is entitled to assume control of the defense of the underlying action; * * * the insurer must underwrite the reasonable costs incurred by the insured in defending the action with counsel of his own choosing."); Prashker v. United States Guar. Co., 1 N.Y.2d 584, 154 N.Y.S.2d 910, 915, 136 N.E.2d 871, 876 (1956) ("the selection of the attorneys to represent the assureds should be made by them rather than by the insurance company, which should remain liable for the reasonable value of the services"); Allstate Ins. Co. v. Noorhassan, 158 A.D.2d 638, 551 N.Y.S.2d 942, 944 (1990) (the insured "should be permitted to select their own attorney [and the insurer] is liable for the reasonable value of the services"); Gorman v. Pattengell, 145 A.D.2d 411, 535 N.Y.S.2d 402, 404 (1988) (the insured "is entitled to retain, at her insurer's expense, an attorney with no business connection to her insurance carrier and who will defend solely her interests"). Under this line of authority the insurance company is obligated to pay the "reasonable cost for hiring independent counsel by the insured." Cumis, 208 Cal.Rptr. at 506.

A recent California case, Center Foundation v. Chicago Insurance Co., 227 Cal.App.3d 547, 278 Cal.Rptr. 13 (1991), has noted that the insured's right to select independent counsel is subject to the implied covenant of good faith and fair dealing. In context, this means that the insured must act reasonably to select an attorney who is capable of presenting an effective defense and who will bill reasonably for his or her services. The court stated: "In our view, the duty of good faith imposed upon an insured includes the obligation to act reasonably in selecting as independent counsel an experienced attorney qualified to present a meaningful defense and willing to engage in ethical billing practices susceptible to review at a standard stricter than that of the marketplace. Conduct arguably acceptable in the ordinary attorney-client relationship where the latter pays the former from his own pocket is not necessarily appropriate in the tripartite context created when independent counsel undertakes to represent the insured at the expense of the insurer." Center Foundation, 278 Cal.Rptr. at 21 (footnote omitted).

A few cases support Employers' argument that it should have the right to approve of CHI's choice for independent counsel. In Employers' Fire Insurance Co. v. Beals, 103 R.I. 623, 240 A.2d 397, 404 (1968), the court approved of the solution suggested in Prashker, that the insured should be allowed to select independent counsel. However, the Beals court added the proviso that counsel selected by the insured should be approved by the insurer and that "[s]uch approval, however, should not be unreasonably withheld." Id. 240 A.2d at 404. Fireman's Fund Insurance Co. v. Waste Management of Wisconsin, 777 F.2d 366 (7th Cir. 1985) (apparently interpreting Wisconsin law), involves an atypical fact pattern. The question whether the insurer should have approval rights for independent counsel was not the issue; however, the case does contain dicta which states that giving the insurer the right to approve or disapprove of independent counsel selected by the insured is "fair, sensible and reasonable." Id. at 370.

We conclude that the insured should have the unilateral right to select independent counsel and that this right should be subject to the implied covenant of good faith and fair dealing. In our view the covenant of good faith and fair dealing in this context requires that the insured select an attorney who is, by experience and training, reasonably thought to be competent to conduct the defense of the insured. Such a result, in our view, fairly balances the interest of the insured—being defended by competent counsel of undivided loyalty—with the interests of the insurer—having the defense of the insured conducted by competent counsel. The insurer is only required to pay the reasonable cost of the defense. See, e.g., Turegum, 118 Ill.Dec. at 943, 522 N.E.2d at 613 ("insurer must underwrite reasonable costs incurred by the insured in defending the action"); Noorhassan, 551 N.Y.S.2d at 944 (same). This provides a measure of protection for insurers against overbilling—and overlitigating—by independent counsel.

In the present case the record is unclear as to whether it is reasonable for CHI to select von Gemmingen as independent counsel. On remand, a hearing should be conducted promptly in order to determine this question. If the trial court finds that von Gemmingen is a reasonable selection, a declaration should be entered that he may conduct the defense of CHI as independent counsel. If the court finds that he is not a reasonable selection, the court should so declare and CHI should proceed to select qualified counsel.

For the above reasons the judgment of the superior court is REVERSED and this case is REMANDED for further proceedings and entry of a declaration in accordance with this opinion.

MOORE, J., concurring in part and dissenting in part.

In its decision today, the court holds that an insured has the right to reject the counsel appointed by the insurer and to unilaterally select replacement counsel whenever dual representation creates a potential conflict of interest. Under the guise of balancing the interests of the insured and the insurer, the court completely abrogates the insurer's right to participate in the insured's defense. Neither existing case law nor sound policy mandates such a drastic curtailment of the insurer's contract rights. Although I agree that the insured is entitled to select independent counsel in conflict of interest situations, I believe the insurer retains the right of reasonable approval. Such a rule accommodates both the important interest of the insured in controlling the litigation and the legitimate interest of the insurer in assuring that the defense will be competently handled by qualified counsel in a cost-effective manner.

Most courts agree that an insured may reject insurer-selected counsel when the insurer assumes the defense under a reservation of rights because of a coverage question. See Ronald E. Mallen, A New Definition of Insurance Defense Counsel, 53 Ins.Couns.J. 108, 113 (Jan. 1986). Most courts also conclude that the presence of a conflict of interest does not relieve an insurer of its obligation to pay defense costs under its duty to defend. See Babcock & Wilcox Co. v. Parsons Corp., 430 F.2d 531, 538 (8th Cir.1970). The critical issue, which few courts have identified, is whether, in this context, an insured has the unilateral right to select replacement counsel when the insurance agreement gives the insurer the right to defend the insured. This is a matter of first impression in Alaska. I would hold that the insurer has the right to approve the counsel selected by the insured, but that the insurer may not unreasonably withhold such approval.

The court simply fails to recognize that Employers has both a contractual right as well as the contractual duty to defend CHI. An insurer's right to control the defense is "a valuable one in that it reserves to the insurer the right to protect itself against unwarranted liability claims and is essential in protecting its financial interest in the outcome of litigation." 7C John A. Appleman, Insurance Law and Practice § 4681 (Walter F. Berdal ed., rev. ed. 1979). Such an important right should not be ignored in the analysis. Although the insurer's right to control the litigation must yield to the insured's right to independent representation when a conflict arises, this does not mean that the insurer's right to defend is completely extinguished.

* * *

Two cases cited by the court, while speaking of a "right to independent counsel," implicitly recognize the right of an insurer to participate in the defense of its insured. The courts in both American Family Life Assur. Co. v. U.S. Fire Co., 885 F.2d 826 (11th Cir.1989), and San Diego Navy Fed. Credit Union v. Cumis Ins. Soc'y, Inc., 162 Cal.App.3d 358, 208 Cal.Rptr. 494 (1984), required an insurer to pay the cost of "independent counsel" selected by the insured to act as co-counsel with an attorney selected by the insurer. Neither case stands for the proposition that an insured has a unilateral right to select exclusive defense counsel when a coverage dispute creates a conflict of interest. In fact, American Family Life includes a partial quote from Appleman which recognizes the right of an insured "to refuse to accept an offer of counsel appointed by the insurer," 885 F.2d at 831 (citing 7C Appleman, supra, § 4685.01), but omits that part of the sentence which recognizes the insurer's right to approve of substitute counsel.

Some courts and commentators recognize that cases permitting an insured to select "independent counsel" do not define what is meant by that term. See, e.g., Federal Ins. Co. v. X–Rite, Inc., 748 F.Supp. 1223, 1228 n. 1 (W.D.Mich.1990) (" 'Independent Counsel' is a term which has not been defined in the case law."); Allan D. Windt, Insurance Claims and Disputes—Representation of Insurance Companies and Insureds § 4.20 at 179 (2d ed. 1988). Courts have used the phrase in a variety of contexts, some of them diametrically opposed. Commentators have stated that "[t]he right to independent counsel means an attorney of the insured's choice." Ronald E. Mallen & Jeffrey M. Smith, Legal Malpractice § 23.16 at 418 (3d ed. 1989). On the other hand, courts have also recognized "a right in the insurer to determine whether to provide independent counsel of its choosing or to reimburse the insured for counsel of its choice." Federal Ins. Co., 748 F.Supp. at 1228 (citing nine cases for this proposition). Because there is disagreement as to what the right to independent counsel entails, and because many cases recognize the insurer's right to select replacement "independent counsel," or at a minimum, to participate in the defense of the insured alongside counsel selected by the insured, it is questionable whether the view espoused by the court represents a "majority view," statements by courts and commentators to that effect notwithstanding.

However, if, as the court apparently believes, an insured's interest in fair representation requires the complete abrogation of an insurer's right to participate in the defense, the insurer's right should at least be addressed in terms of established principles of contract law. In interpreting a contract, a court must give effect to the reasonable expectation of the parties. Peterson v. Wirum, 625 P.2d 866 (Alaska 1981); Fairbanks N. Star Borough v. Tundra Tours, Inc., 719 P.2d 1020 (Alaska 1986) (in order to give effect to the parties' reasonable expectations, a court should look to the contract language, relevant extrinsic evidence and case law interpreting similar provisions). Clearly, the insurance agreement here gave Employers a reasonable expectation that it would have some control over the defense. Even if the right to defend provision is deemed ambiguous and is therefore construed against the insurer, see Puritan Life Ins. Co. v. Guess, 598 P.2d 900 (Alaska 1979), it is not necessary to extinguish the right entirely. Rather, the right to defend provision can and should be interpreted in a way which balances the interests of both the insurer and the insured.

As one court has stated when considering the scope of an insurer's contractual right to defend in conflict situations: "Unless 'right to defend' is to be deemed mere surplusage, * * * it must be viewed as conferring upon [the insurer] some prerogative with respect to the defense beyond simply paying expenses. This prerogative cannot, in a conflict of interest situation, include an absolute right to control the litigation. On the other hand, [the insured's] apparent presumption that the conflict of interest, posing a potential of prejudice to its interests, automatically and completely negated all prerogative, is not reasonable. * * * [The] 'right to defend' can hardly be deemed to contemplate anything less than participation in selection of counsel, which contractual right ought to be enforced unless contrary to public policy." Federal Ins. Co., 748 F.Supp. at 1229; see also New York State Urban Dev. Corp. v. VSL Corp., 738 F.2d 61, 65–66 (2d Cir.1984). Here, Employers' right to participate in CHI's defense should encompass, at a minimum, the right to have a role in the selection of defense counsel.

Courts which have recognized the right of the insurer to participate in the selection of substitute counsel do not agree as to the latitude an insurer should have. In Federal Ins. Co., the court concluded that, under Michigan law, an insurer is entitled to select replacement counsel, but its selection must be made with the utmost of good faith. 748 F.Supp. at 1229. On the other hand, in Employers' Fire Ins. Co. v. Beals, 240 A.2d 397 (R.I.1968), the court held that an insured may elect to choose its own counsel, but that the insurer has a right to approve of the counsel selected by the insured. The Beals court stated: "Because the insurer has a legitimate interest in seeing that any recovery based on finding of negligence on the part of its insured is kept within reasonable bounds, and since the total expense of this defense is to be assumed by the insurer under its promise to defend, we believe that * * * the engagement of an independent counsel to represent the insured should be approved by the insurer. Such approval, however, should not be unreasonably withheld." 240 A.2d at 404; see Fireman's Fund Ins. Co. v. Waste Management of Wis. Inc., 777 F.2d 366, 370 (7th Cir.1985) (approving parties' agreement to allow insured to select replacement counsel subject to insurer's approval as the most "fair, sensible, and reasonable way for both parties to terminate [conflict of interest] dispute and to get on with trial of the [cases against insured] on their merits"). This approach is also recommended by a noted commentator on insurance law who stated: "[W]here a conflict of interest exists between the insurer and the insured in the conduct of the defense of the action brought against the insured, the insured has the right to refuse to accept an offer of the counsel appointed by the insurer and insurer's desire to control the defense must yield to its obligation to defend the policyholder; and where a conflict of interest exists the engagement of independent counsel to represent the insured should be approved by the insurer to assure the employment of competent counsel. Such approval should not be unreasonably withheld." 7C Appleman, supra, § 4685.01 (footnotes omitted).

The majority dismisses these authorities without analysis, summarily concluding that the insurer's interests are sufficiently protected by the implied covenant of good faith and fair dealing inherent in all contracts. Principally relying on a recent California court of appeals decision, Center Found. v. Chicago Ins. Co., 227 Cal.App.3d 547, 278 Cal.Rptr. 13 (1991), the majority observes that the covenant of good faith and fair dealing requires that the insured "select an attorney who is, by experience and training, *reasonably thought to be competent to conduct the defense of the insured.*" (emphasis added) The majority asserts that the implied covenant "provides a measure of protection for insurers against overbilling—and overlitigating—by independent counsel."

Unfortunately, the majority fails to specify by whose standards the competency of replacement counsel should be measured. In the absence of any objective criteria by which to judge whether replacement counsel is "reasonably competent," I believe that this "measure of protection" is both inadequate and unworkable.

* * *

When the insured has selected independent counsel to represent him or her, the insurer may exercise its right to require that the counsel selected by the insured possess certain minimum qualifications which may include that the selected counsel have (1) at least five years of civil litigation practice which includes substantial defense experience in the subject at issue in the litigation, and (2) errors and omissions coverage. While I would not adopt this standard as a per se rule in Alaska, I believe that section 2860(c) provides reasonable guidance as to whether an insurer must approve of its insured's selection of substitute counsel.

Here, it is undisputed that attorney von Gemmingen graduated from law school in May, 1985. When this dispute arose in late 1989, he had been practicing law for approximately four years. Nothing in the record indicates that he had substantial defense experience in the types of disputes at issue in the suit against CHI. For these reasons, I would hold that Employers did not unreasonably withhold its approval of CHI's choice of attorney.

Apparently, the court believes that any participation by the insurer in the appointment of independent counsel automatically taints the outcome. However, it is far from clear that the scope of the conflict of interest problem in the defense context is so broad and the frequency of harm to the insured so great as to warrant such a drastic curtailment of the insurer's contract rights. None of the authorities cited by the court address the prevalence of the problem in quantifiable terms, nor do they address effectiveness of malpractice actions, disciplinary actions, or insurance bad faith actions in remedying the problem. As one commentator has noted, "[t]he validity of the assumption that there exists a severe risk that an insurer will favor its coverage interests over the insured's liability has not been critically examined." Mallen, supra, at 108. The same can be said of the assumption that there is a severe risk that defense attorneys will favor the interests of the insurer over the insured. Assuming without conceding that these risks are great, conflict of interest concerns would be a compelling policy reason for permitting an insured to reject counsel selected by the insurer. They would also be a reason for allowing the insured to select a new attorney at the insurer's expense. But it goes too far to ignore the insurer's contractual right to defend and to hold that these perceived dangers warrant allowing an insured to unilaterally select substitute counsel regardless of the attorney's qualifications.

* * *

The dissent of COMPTON, J. is omitted.

Notes

1. As noted in the *CHI* dissent, in many states the insured does not necessarily have the exclusive right to select its independent defense counsel where a conflict exists. The dissent cites *New York State Urban Development Corp. v. VSL Corp.,* 738 F.2d 61 (2d Cir.1984), in which VSL faced a claim for damages allegedly sustained as a result of its work on the Roosevelt Island tramway. In a separate trial, VSL's professional liability insurer, Northbrook, was ordered to provide a defense. When VSL refused to name or accept any counsel other than the firm which had represented it against Northbrook in the prior action, Northbrook made an appointment. VSL argued that this violated the order, but the court held that, despite the earlier conflict, Northbrook was still able to assert the policy term which

called for payment of, "(1) fees charged by any attorney designated by [Northbrook] * * * (3) fees charged by any attorney designated by [VSL] with the written consent of [Northbrook]." By this term, the insurer would be justified in unilaterally selecting independent counsel provided the power was exercised in good faith. After reviewing the Northbrook's failed attempt to satisfy VSL, the qualifications of the appointed counsel and the insurer's impartial relationship and instructions to counsel, the court found the requisite good faith.

2. In some circumstances, the technique employed by insurers of seeking declaratory relief (a proceeding in which the insurer appears as a party plaintiff perhaps without a jury trial) while a tort action is progressing against its insured has been questioned. Recognizing the dilemma in which the insured is placed, the Colorado State Supreme Court held that it was not an abuse of discretion for the trial court to postpone the declaratory suit until resolution of the tort litigation. Hartford Insurance Group v. District Court, 625 P.2d 1013 (Colo.1981).

3. *San Diego Navy Federal Credit Union v. Cumis Ins. Soc., Inc.*, cited in both the majority and the dissenting opinions of the previous case, spawned such expressions as "Cumis Counsel," "Cumis Provision" and the like. Essentially the case holds that whenever the insurer denies coverage or proceeds under a reservation of rights or there is a conflict of interest (when the insured is sued for damages above the liability coverage), the insured has the right to independent counsel paid by the insurer. The only questionable treatment of the case is in a footnote of *Dynamic Concepts, Inc. v. Truck Insurance Exchange*, 61 Cal.App.4th 999, 1002, 71 Cal.Rptr.2d 882, 887 (1998), in which the court stated California Civil Code § 2860, reprinted below, overruled dicta in Cumis indicating that insurer-appointed defense would only offer token advocacy to claims outside the policy limits or serve to protect only the insurer's interests.

4. Controversy regarding the Cumis counsel approach has ensued centering around such issues as:

a. Whether or not the insurer has in effect lost control of the defense in the underlying tort case?

b. What is the proper standard of conduct for Cumis counsel? What has he or she to lose, since his or her bill will be paid in any event? Is not the Cumis attorney in a basic conflict of interest situation?

c. Excessive Costs? The Cumis lawyer is paid according to an essentially open-ended scale, not according to the fees established between insurance companies and the traditional defense firm specialists. Moreover in cases involving multiple victims, the courtroom may be filled with 25 attorneys of whom 18 or more may be "Cumis."

d. Qualifications? Insurers have complained of having to pay fees of "brothers-in-law who have only been doing drunk driving cases for years."

e. Does not protection of the interests of the victims of torts outweigh all other considerations?

5. The California Legislature responded to some of these concerns by enacting Civil Code § 2860. Among other things, § 2860 purports to limit

fees by using the insurer's practices in the community where the dispute is adjudicated. The California Supreme Court has suggested that the limitations do not apply if the insurer has refused to provide a defense–in such case the fees paid by an insured for defense are presumptively reasonable. Aerojet–General Corp. v. Transport Indemnity Co., 17 Cal.4th 38, 64, 70 Cal.Rptr.2d 118, 948 P.2d 909 (1997).

OBLIGATION TO DEFEND ACTION

§ 2860. Conflict of interest; duty to provide independent counsel; waiver; qualifications of independent counsel; fees; disclosure of information

(a) If the provisions of a policy of insurance impose a duty to defend upon an insurer and a conflict of interest arises which creates a duty on the part of the insurer to provide independent counsel to the insured, the insurer shall provide independent counsel to represent the insured unless, at the time the insured is informed that a possible conflict may arise or does exist, the insured expressly waives, in writing, the right to independent counsel. An insurance contract may contain a provision which sets forth the method of selecting that counsel consistent with this section.

(b) For purposes of this section, a conflict of interest does not exist as to allegations or facts in the litigation for which the insurer denies coverage; however, when an insurer reserves its rights on a given issue and the outcome of that coverage issue can be controlled by counsel first retained by the insurer for the defense of the claim, a conflict of interest may exist. No conflict of interest shall be deemed to exist as to allegations of punitive damages or be deemed to exist solely because an insured is sued for an amount in excess of the insurance policy limits.

(c) When the insured has selected independent counsel to represent him or her, the insurer may exercise its right to require that the counsel selected by the insured possess certain minimum qualifications which may include that the selected counsel have (1) at least five years of civil litigation practice which includes substantial defense experience in the subject at issue in the litigation, and (2) errors and omissions coverage. The insurer's obligation to pay fees to the independent counsel selected by the insured is limited to the rates which are actually paid by the insurer to attorneys retained by it in the ordinary course of business in the defense of similar actions in the community where the claim arose or is being defended. This subdivision does not invalidate other different or additional policy provisions pertaining to attorney's fees or providing for methods of settlement of disputes concerning those fees. Any dispute concerning attorney's fees not resolved by these methods shall be resolved by final and binding arbitration by a single neutral arbitrator selected by the parties to the dispute.

(d) When independent counsel has been selected by the insured, it shall be the duty of that counsel and the insured to disclose to the insurer all information concerning the action except privileged materials relevant to coverage disputes, and timely to inform and consult with the insurer on all matters relating to the action. Any claim of privilege asserted is subject to in camera review in the appropriate law and motion department of the superior court. Any information disclosed by the insured or by independent counsel is not a waiver of the privilege as to any other party.

(e) The insured may waive its right to select independent counsel by signing the following statement: "I have been advised and informed of my right to select independent counsel to represent me in this lawsuit. I have considered this matter fully and freely waive my right to select independent counsel at this time. I authorize my insurer to select a defense attorney to represent me in this lawsuit."

(f) Where the insured selects independent counsel pursuant to the provisions of this section, both the counsel provided by the insurer and independent counsel selected by the insured shall be allowed to participate in all aspects of the litigation. Counsel shall cooperate fully in the exchange of information that is consistent with each counsel's ethical and legal obligation to the insured. Nothing in this section shall relieve the insured of his or her duty to cooperate with the insurer under the terms of the insurance contract.

6. An injured person files a personal injury action against an insured. The liability insurer undertakes the defense under a reservation of rights letter, at the same time advising the insured that it unequivocally disclaims any coverage under the policy. The insured then files suit in another court for declaratory judgment as to whether there is coverage, and for an injunction against the injured party's proceeding with the tort action. Should the declaratory relief be granted? See American Food Management v. Transamerica Insurance Co., 608 S.W.2d 552 (Mo.App.1980).

7. It is usually said that joint tortfeasors are jointly liable, that is, that the injured person may sue both or either (in which case the injured person may recover all his damage against the one he sues), leaving the latter to whatever recourse against his joint tortfeasor the law allows and whatever is practicable. Suing the "deeper pocket" may have its practical aspects.

8. An injured person's suit against joint tortfeasors in a single action can get complicated. We must reflect that, although an insurer will not be able to be sued directly *on the tort,* in many instances one or another tortfeasor may have applicable insurance. Consider the situation in which an injured party and one of several joint tortfeasors enter into an agreement (enforceable in many states) in which the liability on the tortfeasor who is party to the agreement has its liability limited in return for a settlement with the injured party. Booth v. Mary Carter Paint Co., 202 So.2d 8 (Fla.App.1967).

9. Of course, rules on liability and settlements may be modified by statute. To illustrate the rules applicable in one jurisdiction—California—the following statutes are quoted in part. In passing California Civil Code § 1431, the California Legislature provided that any duty or right of several persons is presumptively joint, not several, unless language clearly contradicts the presumption. California Civil Code §§ 1431.1 and 1431.2 were enacted by one of California's "initiatives," Proposition 51

of 1986, and modify the approach. Section 1431.2 provides that liability for non-economic damages are presumptively several. The rationale underlying the approach is specified in § 1431.1.

10. These are not the only statutes which may pertain in cases like the *Mary Carter* case set out above. California Code of Civil Procedure § 877 et seq. sets forth guidelines by which one or more joint tortfeasors may be released from an obligation. The chief California case under § 877 et seq. is *Tech–Bilt, Inc. v. Woodward–Clyde & Associates, Inc.*, 38 Cal.3d 488, 213 Cal.Rptr. 256, 698 P.2d 159 (1985) in which Justice Grodin outlined some tests for the fairness of settlements under the cited sections. His tests were summarized in *Yanez v. United States*, 989 F.2d 323, 328 (9th Cir.1993):

> We agree that whether a settlement is in good faith under Cal.Civ.P.Code § 877 is a finding of fact for the trial court * * *. The district court is advised to apply all the factors enunciated in Tech–Bilt, Inc. v. Woodward–Clyde & Associates, 38 Cal.3d 488, 213 Cal.Rptr. 256, 698 P.2d 159 (1985). It appears that the district court overlooked several of these factors when determining the settlement was not in good faith. The factors are: 1. A rough approximation of plaintiffs' total recovery and the settlors' proportionate liability; 2. The amount paid in settlement; 3. The allocation of settlement proceeds among plaintiffs; 4. A recognition that a settlor should pay less in settlement than he would if he were found liable after trial; 5. The financial conditions and insurance policy limits of settling defendants; and, 6. The existence of collusion, fraud, or tortious conduct aimed to injure the interest of non-settling defendants. Tech–Bilt, 213 Cal.Rptr. at 262–63, 698 P.2d at 166–67.

Texas has also dealt with this issue and the courts seem to take a stance of aggressive policing of what may be seen as collusive agreements. E.g., State Farm Fire & Casualty Co. v. Gandy, 925 S.W.2d 696, 713–15 (Texas 1996) (containing a summary of the approaches in other jurisdictions).

11. One California case has held that an insurer who selects defense lawyers for its insureds is a "client" of those lawyers for purposes of disqualifying conflicts. Accordingly, such lawyers are precluded from representing clients whose interests are adverse to those of the insurer. State Farm Mut. Auto. Ins. Co. v. Federal Ins. Co., 72 Cal.App.4th 1422, 86 Cal.Rptr.2d 20 (1999).

12. A Texas case discusses but rejects the idea that an insurer may be held vicariously liable for the malpractice of lawyers they retain to defend their insureds. State Farm Mutual Automobile Ins. Co. v. Traver, 980 S.W.2d 625 (Tex.1998).

13. A succinct version of a California insurer's power to reserve rights is provided in *Buss v. Superior Court*, 16 Cal.4th 35, 61 n. 27, 65 Cal.Rptr.2d 366, 939 P.2d 766 (1997):

We note that the Court of Appeal assumed that, in order to obtain reimbursement for defense costs, the insurer *must* reserve its right thereto. To the extent that this right is implied in law as quasi-contractual, it must indeed be reserved. (Cf. 1 Witkin, Summary of Cal. Law (9th ed. 1987) Contracts, § 92, p. 123 [stating that, "[i]n an action in quasi-contract . . . , a demand is ordinarily a necessary prerequisite" (italics in original)].) Through reservation, the insurer gives the insured notice of how it will, or at least may, proceed and thereby provides it an opportunity to take any steps that it may deem reasonable or necessary in response—including whether to accept defense at the insurer's hands and under the insurer's control (see fn. 9, ante; see also fns. 2 & 3, ante) or, instead, to defend itself as it chooses. To the extent that this right is implied in fact in the policy as contractual, it should be reserved. Through reservation, the insurer avoids waiver. (See Val's Painting & Drywall, Inc. v. Allstate Ins. Co., supra, 53 Cal.App.3d at pp. 586–587, 126 Cal.Rptr. 267.) Here, Transamerica reserved all its rights, contractual and otherwise.

We also note that the Court of Appeal was evidently of the view that the insurer can reserve its right of reimbursement for defense costs by itself, without the insured's agreement. Such a view is in accord with the "modern trend." (Walbrook Ins. Co. Ltd. v. Goshgarian & Goshgarian, supra, 726 F.Supp. at p. 783.) More important, it is sound. Because the right is the insurer's alone, it may be reserved by it unilaterally. Not only did Transamerica reserve all its rights, contractual and otherwise [sic]. But, receiving consideration, Buss agreed thereto.

F. CONTEXT SPECIFIC APPLICATION

The principles described in this book to this point have not focused on any particular area of insurance law. In order to review a number of disparate ideas in context, we have chosen to highlight three different areas that affect the practice today. These are, in order of coverage, the environment, intellectual property, and employer practice liability.

1. The Environment

During the last quarter-century or so, concerns over the environment and invasive "pollution" (including pollution by toxic material) have grown. Statutes were enacted, regulations under them were promulgated and enforced. It quickly became apparent that industrial and other enterprises would have to bear the brunt of liability for "pollution," as the public purse was not going to pay the entire bill. Naturally, insurance coverage was sought, particularly under the "Commercial General Liability" types of policy (for an example, see the Appendix). The insurance industry became aware of the immense potential for liability and sought to exercise some form of "damage control" by means of various exclusions. The CGL policies generally provided, inter alia, coverage for "bodily injury" or "property damage" arising out of an "occurrence," with various exclusions, e.g.:

> This insurance does not apply: (f) to bodily injury or property damage arising out of the discharge, dispersal, release or escape of smoke, vapors, soot, fumes, acids, alkalis, toxic chemicals, liquids or gases, waste materials or other irritants into or upon land, the atmosphere or any watercourse or body of water; *but this exclusion does not apply if such discharge, dispersal, release or escape is sudden or accidental* (emphasis added).

Such exclusion clauses would appear to have considerable effect on what seems to have been a very common sort of pollution: the gradual escape of pollutants from one property to another. Many courts took the words "sudden or accidental" quite literally. (For an example of "sudden" as importing a strictly temporal condition, see Hybud Equipment Corp. v. Sphere Drake Ins. Co., Ltd., 64 Ohio St.3d 657, 597 N.E.2d 1096 (1992), rehearing denied 65 Ohio St.3d 1445, 600 N.E.2d 686 (1992), cert. denied 507 U.S. 987, 113 S.Ct. 1585, 123 L.Ed.2d 152 (1993)). Other courts perceived ambiguity and held for coverage, see, e.g., Queen City Farms, Inc. v. Central National Ins. Co., 64 Wn.App. 838, 827 P.2d 1024, 1049 (1992), review granted 120 Wash.2d 1025, 847 P.2d 481 (1993). Recall also the discussion in Chapter 2 above in *Montrose Chemical* and the issue of "sudden discharge." Another form of the exclusion reads:

> "We won't cover claims or damage caused by the *continuous or intentional* discharge or release of pollutants such as: Smoke, Vapors, Soot, Fumes, Acids, Alkalis, Toxic Chemicals, Liquids or Gases, Or Waste Materials. But will cover sudden accidents involving pollutants."

This poses the same possibility of ambiguity as the first quotation (i.e., "sudden accidents" and added another, i.e., "intentional"). Another formula may present the latter problem more clearly—injuries are not covered when "neither expected nor intended from the standpoint of the insured." The interaction of these interpretational problems seem realized in the next cases.

CLAUSSEN v. AETNA CASUALTY & SURETY CO.

Supreme Court of Georgia, 1989.
259 Ga. 333, 380 S.E.2d 686.

CLARKE, PRESIDING J.

In this case we are called upon to interpret the meaning of the "pollution exclusion" clause of a comprehensive general liability insurance policy. For the reasons stated below, we hold that the insurance policy at issue does not preclude coverage for liability for environmental contamination caused by the discharge of pollutants over an extended period of time.

Briefly stated, the history of the case is as follows: Since 1966, Henry Claussen has owned, either individually or through corporate entities, fifty-two acres of land known as Picketville. In 1968, the City of Jacksonville, Florida contracted to use the site as a landfill. Beginning in 1971, the City dumped industrial and chemical waste there almost exclusively. The City closed the site in 1977, and returned it to Claussen completely filled, graded and seeded. Claussen claims he had no knowledge that the site was used for dumping hazardous wastes.

In 1985, the Environmental Protection Agency determined that the groundwater beneath the site had been contaminated by the release of hazardous substances. In a list ranking the 115 worst hazardous waste sites in the nation, Love Canal was ranked twenty-fourth, and Picketville was ranked twenty-sixth. The agency informed Claussen, the City and others that they were responsible for taking corrective action.

Henry Claussen then filed an action against Aetna Casualty & Surety Company and others seeking a declaratory judgment that the insurance company is obligated under a "comprehensive general liability" policy for the costs to be incurred in connection with the EPA's demand that the hazardous site be studied and cleaned up. Aetna denied coverage citing exclusion (f), commonly referred to as the "pollution exclusion" which states that coverage is excluded for: "* * * bodily injury or property damage arising out of the discharge, dispersal, or release or escape of smoke, vapors, soot, fumes, acids, alkalis, toxic chemicals, liquids or gases, waste materials or other irritants, contaminants or pollutants into or upon land, the atmosphere or any water course or body of water; but this exclusion does not apply if such discharge, dispersal, release or escape is sudden and accidental * * *."

The federal district court granted Aetna's motion for summary judgment, holding that the exclusion clause precludes coverage for Claussen's environmental liabilities. The court found the clause to be clear and unambiguous and decided that dumping of toxic wastes occurring over several years was not "sudden" within the policy language. Claussen appealed to the Eleventh Circuit Court of Appeals which certified the following question to this court: Whether, as a matter of law, the pollution exclusion clause contained in the comprehensive general liability insurance policy precludes coverage to its insured for liability for costs for liability for the environmental contamination caused by the discharge of pollutants at the site over an extended period of time? To put it another way, does the insurance policy in this case require the insurance company to provide a defense and coverage to the insured for liability for the discharge of pollutants that occurred over an extended period of time?

1. "The construction of a contract is a matter of law for the court." OCGA § 13–2–1. Extrinsic evidence to explain ambiguity in a contract becomes admissible only when a contract remains ambiguous after the pertinent rules of construction have been applied. Holcomb v. Word, 239 Ga. 847, 238 S.E.2d 915 (1977). Under Georgia rules of contract interpretation, words in a contract generally bear their usual and common meaning. OCGA § 13–3–2(2). However, "if the construction is doubtful,

that which goes most strongly against the party executing the instrument or undertaking the obligation is generally to be preferred." OCGA § 13–2–2(5). Georgia courts have long acknowledged that insurance policies are prepared and proposed by insurers. Thus, if an insurance contract is capable of being construed two ways, it will be construed against the insurance company and in favor of the insured. See, e.g., Richards v. Hanover Ins. Co., 250 Ga. 613, 299 S.E.2d 561 (1983); Cincinnati Ins. Co. v. Davis, 153 Ga.App. 291, 265 S.E.2d 102 (1980); American Casualty Co. v. Callaway, 75 Ga.App. 799, 44 S.E.2d 400 (1947); Massachusetts Benefit Life Ass'n v. Robinson, 104 Ga. 256, 30 S.E. 918 (1898).

What is the meaning of the word "sudden" as it is used in the insurance policy? Claussen argues that it means "unexpected"; Aetna asserts that the only possible meaning is "abrupt." This seemingly simple question has spawned a profusion of litigation. The majority of courts considering the issue have adopted the meaning asserted by Claussen. See Developments—Toxic Waste Litigation, 99 Harv. Law Rev. 1458, 1582 (1986). See also cases cited in Claussen v. Aetna Casualty & Surety Co., 865 F.2d 1217, 1218 (11th Cir.1989). Other courts have decided that "sudden" cannot be defined without its temporal connotation. See, e.g. Claussen v. Aetna Casualty & Surety Co., 676 F.Supp. 1571 (S.D.Ga.1987), and cases cited therein.

The primary dictionary definition of the word is "happening without previous notice or with very brief notice; coming or occurring unexpectedly; not foreseen or prepared for." Webster's Third New International Dictionary, at 2284 (1986). See also, Funk and Wagnalls Standard Dictionary, at 808 (1980); Black's Law Dictionary, at 1284 (1979). The definition of the word "sudden" as "abrupt" is also recognized in several dictionaries and is common in the vernacular. Perhaps, the secondary meaning is so common in the vernacular that it is, indeed, difficult to think of "sudden" without a temporal connotation: a sudden flash, a sudden burst of speed, a sudden bang. But, on reflection one realizes that, even in its popular usage, "sudden" does not usually describe the duration of an event, but rather its unexpectedness: a sudden storm, a sudden turn in the road, sudden death. Even when used to describe the onset of an event, the word has an elastic temporal connotation that varies with expectations: Suddenly, it's spring. See also, Oxford English Dictionary, at 96 (1933) (giving usage examples dating back to 1340, e.g., "She heard a sudden step behind her"; and, "A sudden little river crossed my path As unexpected as a serpent comes.") Thus, it appears that "sudden" has more than one reasonable meaning. And, under the pertinent rule of construction the meaning favoring the insured must be applied, that is, "unexpected."

2. Aetna next argues that construing "sudden" to mean "unexpected" violates another pertinent rule of construction, which requires that the contract be read so as to give all parts meaning. The policy states: "The company will pay on behalf of the insured all sums which the insured shall become legally obligated to pay as damages because of

property damage to which this policy applies, caused by an occurrence * * *." The policy goes on to define "occurrence" as "property damage neither expected nor intended from the standpoint of the insured." Aetna contends that if "sudden" is interpreted as "unexpected," it simply restates the definition of "occurrence." We do not agree. The pollution exclusion clause focuses on whether the "*discharge, dispersal or release*" of the pollutants is unexpected and unintended; the definition of occurrence focuses on whether the *property damage* is unexpected and unintended. The pollution exclusion clause therefore has the effect of eliminating coverage for damage resulting from the intentional discharge of pollutants.[66]

3. Aetna also argues that the construction proposed by Claussen violates the cardinal rule of contract interpretation because it is inconsistent with the intention of the parties. They assert that pollution liability is an enormous risk that was not assessed in the process of underwriting this policy.

Sixteen years ago when the policy at issue here went into effect, it is unlikely that either party anticipated the extent of potential liability for pollution damage. "The past two decades have seen an explosion of litigation seeking compensation for damage to the environment and injuries arising from environmental pollution." Note, The Pollution Exclusion Clause Through the Looking Glass, 74 Geo.L.J. 1237 (1986). Moreover, the Federal Superfund Act, passed in 1980, imposed "retroactive strict liability" for the costs of cleaning up hazardous waste storage sites on the generators and transporters of hazardous wastes and on the owners and operators of the sites. Abraham, Environmental Liability and the Limits of Insurance, 88 Colum.L.Rev. 942, 957 (1988). Referring to the decade before CERCLA passed, one commentator noted:

> In the past, insurance was available at prices that did not reflect the full environmental risks of each insured firm. Insurers had little incentive to tailor premiums closely to an individual firm's risk profile, because such tailoring requires the expense of monitoring each firm and because insurers did not expect courts to impose significant waste-related liabilities. Developments—Toxic Waste Litigation, 99 Harv.L.Rev. 1458, 1575 (1986).

If Aetna had been aware of the yawning extent of potential liability, it almost certainly would have drafted its policy differently. However, the fact that it did not, cannot be construed to the detriment of the insured who purchased a "comprehensive general liability" policy. Under Georgia law, the risk of any lack of clarity or ambiguity in an insurance contract must be borne by the insurer. Ranger Ins. Co. v. Culberson, 454 F.2d 857 (5th Cir.1971), cert. denied 407 U.S. 916, 92 S.Ct. 2440, 32 L.Ed.2d 691 (1972).

66. Other Courts have denied coverage under the policy to insureds that actively disposed of toxic or radioactive wastes in the regular course of business activity. See, e.g., American Motorists Ins. Co. v. General Host Corp., 667 F.Supp. 1423 (D.Kan.1987); American States Ins. Co. v. Maryland Casualty Co., 587 F.Supp. 1549 (E.D.Mich.1984); City of Milwaukee v. Allied Smelting Corp., 344 N.W.2d 523 (Wis.Ct.App.1983).

Further, the interpretation of the policy advanced by Claussen is not contrary to the interpretation Aetna gave the clause when it was adopted. Documents presented by the Insurance Rating Board (which represents the industry and on which Aetna participated) to the Insurance Commissioner when the "pollution exclusion" was first adopted suggest that the clause was intended to exclude only intentional polluters. The Insurance Rating Board represented "the impact of the [pollution exclusion clause] on the vast majority of risks would be no change." See, Claussen, 676 F.Supp. at 1573.

4. Finally, Aetna argues that Claussen's proposed interpretation of the policy language contravenes public policy because it encourages the land owner to keep his head in the sand—to remain oblivious to ongoing polluting activities on his land. This argument would be somewhat persuasive, but for the many events that have taken place between the date of this policy and the present lawsuit. "Environmental liability insurance has recently undergone a shift from apparent under-deterrence to apparent over-deterrence of environmental damages." Developments 99 Harv.L.Rev. 1458, 1574 (1986). Federal and state laws now require waste treatment facilities to carry insurance for both short and long term environmental risks or to meet a financial test alternative. See, Georgia Department of Natural Resources, Environmental Protection Division v. Union Timber Corporation, 258 Ga. 873, 375 S.E.2d 856 (1989). Insurance companies have become wary of insuring against environmental risks and have either dropped out of the field or are charging higher premiums. Id. In short, the situation has changed so that our decision is not likely to have any serious impact on prospective behavior.

In sum, we conclude that the pollution exclusion clause is capable of more than one reasonable interpretation. The clause must therefore be construed in favor of the insured to mean "unexpected and unintended."

Question answered.

HUNT, J., dissenting.

I respectfully dissent because in my view the Federal District Court was correct in finding the "pollution exclusion" clear and unambiguous. While "sudden" may have a number of meanings, and, over the years, may have been used in a number of contexts, in this context it clearly means abrupt and unexpected. Certainly, its use within this context does not encompass the gradual dumping of toxic wastes over a period of several years.

Note

One of the more prominent problems of environmental litigation has been caused by the provisions of CERCLA (the Federal "Comprehensive Environmental Response, Compensation and Liability Act of 1980"), as amended, and similar statutes. For example Sec. 107 of CERCLA, 42 U.S.C.A. § 9607, provides in part:

(a) Covered persons; scope; recoverable costs and damages; interest rate; "comparable maturity" date

Notwithstanding any other provision or rule of law, and subject only to the defenses set forth in subsection (b) of this section—

(1) the owner and operator of a vessel or a facility,

(2) any person who at the time of disposal of any hazardous substance owned or operated any facility at which such hazardous substances were disposed of,

(3) any person who by contract, agreement, or otherwise arranged for disposal or treatment, or arranged with a transporter for transport for disposal or treatment, of hazardous substances owned or possessed by such person, by any other party or entity, at any facility or incineration vessel owned or operated by another party or entity and containing such hazardous substances, and

(4) any person who accepts or accepted any hazardous substances for transport to disposal or treatment facilities, incineration vessels or sites selected by such person, from which there is a release, or a threatened release which causes the incurrence of response costs, of a hazardous substance, shall be liable for—

(A) all costs of removal or remedial action incurred by the United States Government or a State or an Indian tribe not inconsistent with the national contingency plan;

(B) any other necessary costs of response incurred by any other person consistent with the national contingency plan;

(C) damages for injury to, destruction of, or loss of natural resources, including the reasonable costs of assessing such injury, destruction, or loss resulting from such a release; and

(D) the costs of any health assessment or health effects study carried out under section 9604(i) of this title.

The amounts recoverable in an action under this section shall include interest on the amounts recoverable under subparagraphs (A) through (D). Such interest shall accrue from the later of (i) the date payment of a specified amount is demanded in writing, or (ii) the date of the expenditure concerned. The rate of interest on the outstanding unpaid balance of the amounts recoverable under this section shall be the same rate as is specified for interest on investments of the Hazardous Substance Superfund established under subchapter A of chapter 98 of Title 26. For purposes of applying such amendments to interest under this subsection, the term "comparable maturity" shall be determined with reference to the date on which interest accruing under this subsection commences.

(b) Defenses

There shall be no liability under subsection (a) of this section for a person otherwise liable who can establish by a preponderance of the evidence that the release or threat of release of a hazardous substance and the damages resulting therefrom were caused solely by—

(1) an act of God;

(2) an act of war;

(3) an act or omission of a third party other than an employee or agent of the defendant, or than one whose act or omission occurs in connection with a contractual relationship, existing directly or indirectly, with the defendant (except where the sole contractual arrangement arises from a published tariff and acceptance for carriage by a common carrier by rail), if the defendant establishes by a preponderance of the evidence that (a) he exercised due care with respect to the hazardous substance concerned, taking into consideration the characteristics of such hazardous substance, in light of all relevant facts and circumstances, and (b) he took precautions against foreseeable acts or omissions of any such third party and the consequences that could foreseeably result from such acts or omissions; or

(4) any combination of the foregoing paragraphs.

(c) Determination of amounts

(1) Except as provided in paragraph (2) of this subsection, the liability under this section of an owner or operator or other responsible person for each release of a hazardous substance or incident involving release of a hazardous substance shall not exceed—

(A) for any vessel, other than an incineration vessel, which carries any hazardous substance as cargo or residue, $300 per gross ton, or $5,000,000, whichever is greater;

(B) for any other vessel, other than an incineration vessel, $300 per gross ton, or $500,000, whichever is greater;

(C) for any motor vehicle, aircraft, pipeline (as defined in the Hazardous Liquid Pipeline Safety Act of 1979 [49 U.S.C.A. § 2001 et seq.]), or rolling stock, $50,000,000 or such lesser amount as the President shall establish by regulation, but in no event less than $5,000,000 (or, for releases of hazardous substances as defined in section 9601(14)(A) of this title into the navigable waters, $8,000,000). Such regulations shall take into account the size, type, location, storage, and handling capacity and other matters relating to the likelihood of release in each such class and to the economic impact of such limits on each such class; or

(D) for any incineration vessel or any facility other than those specified in subparagraph (C) of this paragraph, the total of all costs of response plus $50,000,000 for any damages under this subchapter.

(2) Notwithstanding the limitations in paragraph (1) of this subsection, the liability of an owner or operator or other responsible person under this section shall be the full and total costs of response and damages, if (A)(i) the release or threat of release of a hazardous substance was the result of willful misconduct or willful negligence within the privity or knowledge of such person, or (ii) the primary cause of the release was a violation (within the privity or knowledge of such person) of applicable safety, construction, or operating standards or regulations; or (B) such person fails or refuses to provide all reasonable cooperation and assistance requested by a responsible public official in connection with response activities under the national contingency plan with respect to regulated carriers subject to the provisions of Title 49 or vessels subject

to the provisions of Title 33 or 46, subparagraph (A)(ii) of this paragraph shall be deemed to refer to Federal standards or regulations.

(3) If any person who is liable for a release or threat of release of a hazardous substance fails without sufficient cause to properly provide removal or remedial action upon order of the President pursuant to section 9604 or 9606 of this title, such person may be liable to the United States for punitive damages in an amount at least equal to, and not more than three times, the amount of any costs incurred by the Fund as a result of such failure to take proper action. The President is authorized to commence a civil action against any such person to recover the punitive damages, which shall be in addition to any costs recovered from such person pursuant to section 9612(c) of this title. Any moneys received by the United States pursuant to this subsection shall be deposited in the Fund.

Clearly, these provisions, which are actually only a small part of 42 U.S.C.A. § 9607, pose their own problems of interpretation. At the same time, the statute obviously imposes liability on the insured. For example, the impact of subsec. (a)(4)(A) and (B) making persons subject to the Act liable for "all costs of removal or remedial action" by the U.S., a State, or an Indian tribe and for "any other necessary costs of response" sound minatory in the extreme. Can such costs come within the coverage of a CGL policy?

AIU INSURANCE CO. v. SUPERIOR COURT

Supreme Court of California, 1990.
51 Cal.3d 807, 274 Cal.Rptr. 820, 799 P.2d 1253.

LUCAS, CHIEF JUSTICE.

We are called on to decide whether, under comprehensive general liability (CGL) insurance policies issued by petitioners (insurers) to real party in interest FMC Corporation (FMC), insurers are obligated to provide coverage to FMC for cleanup and other "response" costs incurred pursuant to the Comprehensive Environmental Response and Compensation and Liability Act (CERCLA) (42 U.S.C. § 9601 et seq.) and related state and federal environmental laws. FMC seeks review of the peremptory writ of mandate issued by the Court of Appeal, which directed the superior court to enter summary adjudication on this issue in favor of the insurers.

We reverse the decision of the Court of Appeal. The insurance policies at issue provide coverage to FMC for all sums FMC becomes legally obligated to pay as "damages" (under two policy forms) or "ultimate net loss" (under a third) because of property damage. Under established principles of contract interpretation, we construe policy language according to the mutual intentions of the parties and its "plain and ordinary" meaning, resolving ambiguities in favor of coverage. Applying these rules, we conclude that the policies cover the costs of reimbursing government agencies and complying with injunctions ordering cleanup under CERCLA and similar statutes. Although many of the policies contain exclusions arguably relevant to whether environmental cleanup costs are covered, we do not consider the applicability of exclusions in this case, which comes to us on motion for summary adjudication solely as to the coverage clauses.

I. FACTUAL AND PROCEDURAL BACKGROUND

A. The Insurance Policies

FMC holds over 60 primary and excess CGL policies issued by the insurers. Each policy contains one of three coverage clauses:

1. Policies issued by the Liberty Mutual Insurance Company and others provide coverage to FMC for "all sums which [FMC] shall become legally obligated to pay as damages because of * * * property damage to which this policy applies."

2. Policies issued by the FMC Insurance Company and others provide coverage to FMC for "all sums which [FMC] shall become obligated to pay by reason of the liability * * * imposed upon [FMC] by law * * * for damages on account of * * * property damage * * *."[67]

3. Policies issued by the First State Insurance Company and others provide coverage to FMC for "all sums which [FMC] shall be obligated to pay by reason of the liability * * * imposed upon [FMC] by law * * * for damages, direct or consequential and expenses, all as more fully defined by the term 'ultimate net loss' on account of * * * property damages * * *."

These coverage provisions were adopted verbatim from standard CGL policies used by the insurance industry. (See Mountainspring, Insurance Coverage of CERCLA Response Costs: The Limits of "Damages" in Comprehensive General Liability Policies (1989) 16 Ecology L.Q. 755, 759; Chesler et al., Patterns of Judicial Interpretation of Insurance Coverage for Hazardous Waste Site Liability (1986) 18 Rutgers L.J. 9, 53.) They contain several common elements. Each provision covers only sums that FMC is "legally obligated" or "obligated * * * by law" to pay. They each require that the sums paid be the result of FMC's liability for "property damage[s]." The first two policies limit coverage to sums paid as or for "damages." None of these terms is defined in any of the policies. The only relevant definition contained in any of the policies is of "ultimate net loss" (covered by the third policy), which includes both "damages" and "expenses."

B. The Third Party Suits Against FMC

The United States and local administrative agencies (hereafter agencies) filed suits against FMC, seeking relief for alleged violations of CERCLA, the Resource Conservation and Recovery Act (RCRA) (42 U.S.C. § 6901 et seq.), the Clean Water Act (33 U.S.C. § 1251 et seq.), the Safe Drinking Water Act (42 U.S.C. § 300f et seq.), and California's

67. FMC Insurance Company is a subsidiary of FMC. As such, it is not named as a defendant in this suit, although it issued policies to its parent corporation identical to those under which FMC seeks coverage here.

Hazardous Substance Account Act (Health & Saf.Code, § 25300 et seq.). In sum, the suits allege that FMC is responsible for the contamination of 79 different hazardous waste disposal sites, groundwater beneath the sites, aquifers beneath adjoining property, and surrounding surface waters. The agencies seek two types of relief: (i) injunctions compelling FMC both to terminate disposal of further hazardous waste and to remove contaminants already present on and around the disposal sites, and (ii) reimbursement of their costs of investigating, monitoring, and initiating cleanup of hazardous waste for which FMC allegedly is responsible.

All of the statutes on which the third party suits are based expressly authorize injunctive relief. (See CERCLA, 42 U.S.C. § 9606(a); RCRA, 42 U.S.C. § 6973(a); Clean Water Act, 33 U.S.C. § 1364(a); Safe Drinking Water Act, 42 U.S.C. § 300i(a); Hazardous Substance Account Act, Health & Saf.Code, § 25358.3, subd. (a).) CERCLA and the Hazardous Substance Account Act, however, also authorize government recovery of the costs of removing hazardous waste and restoring affected property, providing the agencies with a choice (subject to judicial approval) of how to proceed with and finance cleanup efforts. (See CERCLA, 42 U.S.C. § 9607(a)(4)(A) [reimbursement of government costs of removal or remedial action]; Hazardous Substance Account Act, Health & Saf.Code, § 25360 [reimbursement of state cleanup expenses.].) In addition, CERCLA authorizes the federal government to recover sums for "damages to natural resources." (42 U.S.C., § 9607(a)(4)(C).) In their present suits against FMC, however, the agencies do not seek recovery under this last provision, although surface and groundwater nominally owned by the state (Wat.Code, § 102) has been damaged at many of the sites where remedial action is sought, and although CERCLA defines "natural resources" to include water and groundwater "belonging to, managed by, held in trust by, appertaining to, or otherwise controlled by" the federal or state government.[68] (See CERCLA, 42 U.S.C. § 9601(16).)

C. The Present Suit

In the present suit, FMC seeks declaratory relief establishing that the CGL policies cover costs it may become obligated to pay as a result of injunctive relief and/or reimbursement ordered in the third party suits. The insurers moved for summary adjudication, asserting that, as a matter of law, the CGL policies do not cover costs of abating and cleaning up hazardous waste and reimbursing governmental agencies for their cleanup efforts. In response, FMC contended that (i) the policy language encompasses all of its costs resulting from the agencies' suits under CERCLA and the other statutes, (ii) the intent of the parties to the policies is a relevant and contested issue of material fact bearing on

68. Because the agencies do not seek recovery under the CERCLA "damages to natural resources" provision, we do not here directly consider whether such recovery would be covered by CGL policies. We note the existence of the provision, however, because the insurers in part rely on its existence to support their argument that recovery of response costs is mutually exclusive from recovery of statutory "damages."

the issue of coverage, and (iii) FMC should be granted preliminary discovery of evidence bearing on such intent.

* * *

We granted review to determine whether the Court of Appeal correctly directed the superior court to enter summary adjudication for the insurers.

II. Discussion

At issue here is whether, as a matter of law, the CGL policies cover either or both of the types of costs that FMC may be required to pay as a result of the third party suits. Specifically, we must determine whether (i) any adverse orders issued in those suits will "legally obligate" FMC to pay such costs, (ii) the costs will constitute "damages" or "ultimate net loss," and (iii) such costs will be incurred because of "property damage." Only if all three conditions are fulfilled will the insurers' duty to provide coverage arise under the policies.

Our task has two distinct parts. First, we must determine, under California law, what rules of insurance policy interpretation apply in this context. Second, we must interpret the CGL policies under applicable principles of insurance coverage. Although one can readily conceive of arguments for and against permitting insurance against the costs of rectifying pollution, at the outset we note that such arguments are not pertinent to either of our inquiries in this case. Both CERCLA and the Hazardous Substance Account Act expressly permit responsible parties to insure against the costs of relief available under the legislation. Thus, because Congress and the Legislature already have made the relevant public policy determinations, the issue before this Court is not whether CGL policies *may* provide the coverage sought, but whether they *do* provide it according to their terms. The answer is to be found solely in the language of the policies, not in public policy considerations.

Numerous state and federal courts have addressed the issue presented in this case. Until the present Court of Appeal decision, nearly every state appellate decision has concluded that cleanup costs incurred under environmental statutes are covered by policies identical to those concerned here.

These decisions have generally held that the costs of reimbursing governments or third parties for their remedial and mitigative efforts are covered, either because such costs are plainly "damages" that the insured is "legally obligated" to pay as a result of "property damage", or because these phrases are ambiguous and therefore must be resolved in favor of coverage under ordinary rules of insurance policy interpretation. We have found only one state appellate decision holding to the contrary. (See Braswell v. United States Fidelity & Guar. Co. (1989) 300 S.C. 338, 387 S.E.2d 707.)

Similarly, state courts have consistently held costs of compliance with environmental injunctions covered, either because such costs fit within a broad definition of "damages", or because a contrary holding would unreasonably make coverage hinge on the "mere fortuity" of which recovery mechanism (injunction, reimbursement, or "damages to natural resources") the government selects in enforcing CERCLA. Again, only one state appellate decision, in dictum, reaches the opposite conclusion.

The federal courts, however, purporting to apply state law, are sharply divided on whether environmental cleanup costs are covered by CGL policies. Several courts have followed the majority of state decisions, concluding that both forms of relief sought by the government in statutory environmental suits constitute "damages" covered under the standard policies. (See, e.g., Avondale Industries, Inc. v. Travelers Indem. Co. (2d Cir.1989) 887 F.2d 1200 [insurers' duty to defend suits seeking reimbursement of response costs]; Intel Corp. v. Hartford Acc. and Indem. Co. (N.D.Cal.1988) 692 F.Supp. 1171, app. pending 9th Cir. (Intel).)

Other courts, however, have ruled that cleanup costs are not covered. These decisions all rely on one or more of four basic arguments. First, looking to the language of CERCLA itself, they often emphasize that because it contains separate provisions for government recovery of "damages" to natural resources (see 42 U.S.C. § 9607(a)(4)(C)) and of "remedial costs" compensating it for cleanup (id., § 9607(a)(4)(A)), the latter form of recovery cannot be classified as "damages," notwithstanding whether state law principles would permit such a characterization in the absence of the statutory distinction.

Second, some courts have held, as the Court of Appeal did in this case, that because the agencies may recover their response costs without having suffered harm to property or resources in which they have a proprietary interest, such recovery is not for "damages," as that term is defined at law.

Third, several decisions conclude that "damages," defined either in lay or legal terms, is an unambiguous term that does not include costs of complying with injunctive relief available under CERCLA and related statutes. Such costs, they reason, are not sums paid to another party to compensate it for wrongs committed by the insured; they are simply "sums which the insured becomes legally obligated to pay because of property damage," failing to fulfill the "as damages" qualifier on coverage under CGL policies. Relying on decisions holding that an insured's costs of complying with mandatory injunctions issued in suits asserting common law claims are not "damages" (see, e.g., Aetna Casualty and Surety Company v. Hanna (5th Cir.1955) 224 F.2d 499 (Hanna)), these courts have held that the costs of compliance with environmental injunctions should be treated no differently.

Fourth, several courts have reasoned that the costs of injunctions and reimbursement are not covered because, in the corporate "insurance context," insureds should not receive the benefit of insurance policy interpretation principles designed to protect unsophisticated, arguably disadvantaged policyholders. Under this view, courts should interpret CGL policies by affording them narrow legal meanings under which the terms "legally obligated" and "damages" exclude the costs of *equitable* relief from coverage. Classifying reimbursement of government cleanup costs as equitable "restitution" and costs of compliance with injunctions as a consequence of equitable relief, several courts have concluded for this reason that neither type of relief is covered.

As these decisions suggest, two general arguments underlie the insurers' position that expenses incurred under CERCLA and similar statutes are not covered by the CGL policies at issue. First, it is argued that established rules of insurance policy interpretation are inapplicable in this context, and that we should apply more restrictive principles that will preclude coverage of environmental response costs under these policies. Second, even under traditional principles of interpretation, the policies should be interpreted to unambiguously exclude coverage of the types of relief sought in the underlying suits. We examine these propositions in turn.

A. *Principles of Insurance Policy Interpretation*

Under statutory rules of contract interpretation, the mutual intention of the parties at the time the contract is formed governs interpretation. (Civ.Code, § 1636.) Such intent is to be inferred, if possible, solely from the written provisions of the contract. (Id., § 1639.) The "clear and explicit" meaning of these provisions, interpreted in their "ordinary and popular sense," unless "used by the parties in a technical sense or a special meaning is given to them by usage" (id., § 1644), controls judicial interpretation. (Id., § 1638.) Thus, if the meaning a layperson would ascribe to contract language is not ambiguous, we apply that meaning. (See, e.g., Reserve Insurance Co. v. Pisciotta (1982) 30 Cal.3d 800, 807, 180 Cal.Rptr. 628, 640 P.2d 764; Crane v. State Farm Fire & Cas. Co. (1971) 5 Cal.3d 112, 115, 95 Cal.Rptr. 513, 485 P.2d 1129.)

If there is ambiguity, however, it is resolved by interpreting the ambiguous provisions in the sense the promisor (i.e., the insurer) believed the promisee understood them at the time of formation. (Civ.Code, § 1649.) If application of this rule does not eliminate the ambiguity, ambiguous language is construed against the party who caused the uncertainty to exist. (Id., § 1654.) In the insurance context, we generally resolve ambiguities in favor of coverage. (See, e.g., State Farm Mut. Auto. Ins. Co. v. Jacober (1973) 10 Cal.3d 193, 197, 110 Cal.Rptr. 1, 514 P.2d 953). Similarly, we generally interpret the coverage clauses of insurance policies broadly, protecting the objectively reasonable expectations of the insured. (See, e.g., Garvey v. State Farm Fire & Casualty Co. (1989) 48 Cal.3d 395, 406, 257 Cal.Rptr. 292, 770 P.2d 704). These rules stem from the fact that the insurer typically drafts policy language, leaving the insured little or no meaningful opportunity or ability to bargain for modifications. (See, e.g., Garcia v. Truck Ins. Exchange (1984) 36 Cal.3d 426, 438, 204 Cal.Rptr. 435, 682 P.2d 1100.) Because the insurer writes the policy, it is held "responsible" for ambiguous policy language, which is therefore construed in favor of coverage.

It follows, however, that where the policyholder does not suffer from lack of legal sophistication or a relative lack of bargaining power, and where it is clear that an insurance policy was actually negotiated and jointly drafted, we need not go so far in protecting the insured from ambiguous or highly technical drafting. (Garcia v. Truck Ins. Exchange, supra, 36 Cal.3d at p. 438, 204 Cal.Rptr. 435, 682 P.2d 1100 [refusing to resolve ambiguity against insurer when insured enjoyed "substantial bargaining power vis-a-vis the carrier," and actually negotiated and joined in drafting terms of coverage].)

FMC unquestionably possesses both legal sophistication and substantial bargaining power. For this reason, the insurers contend, we should neither construe the policy language at issue in this case in the broad sense understood by laypersons (as opposed to a narrower technical sense) nor resolve ambiguities in favor of coverage. There is some force to these arguments, particularly in light of the fact that FMC itself operates a subsidiary that drafts CGL policies identical to those at issue in this case. In the absence of evidence that the parties, at the time they entered into the policies, intended the provisions at issue here to carry technical meanings and implemented this intention by specially crafting policy language, however, we see little reason to depart from ordinary principles of interpretation. Similarly, in the absence of evidence that the insurers had cause to believe, at the time of formation, that FMC understood policy language in any technical or restrictive manner, we decline to depart from the settled rule that ambiguities are resolved against the party responsible for their inclusion in the policies.

We deem this party to be the insurers. They have presented no evidence suggesting that the provisions in question were actually negotiated or jointly drafted. (Compare Garcia v. Truck Ins. Exchange, supra, 36 Cal.3d at p. 434, 204 Cal.Rptr. 435, 682 P.2d 1100.) Indeed, the evidence that is before us reveals that such provisions, drafted by the insurers, are highly uniform in content and wording. For the above reasons, we interpret their contents, if ambiguous, in favor of coverage.

B. Interpretation of CGL Policy Language

The CGL policies at issue in this case cover sums which FMC becomes "legally obligated" to pay as "damages" (or "ultimate net loss") incurred because of "property damage." We next consider whether, as a matter of law, the types of relief at issue in the third party suits satisfy these requirements.

1. "Legally Obligated"

The first requirement for coverage is that FMC be legally obligated to pay the costs at issue. Because it is clear that, if FMC is held liable in the third party suits, it will be "obligated" to pay for whatever relief the courts order, the only remaining question is whether that obligation may be considered "legal" under applicable rules of interpretation. The insurers contend it may not, for the simple reason that whether the courts award injunctive relief or order FMC to reimburse the agencies for their response costs, they will be exercising "equitable" rather than "legal" authority.

Both injunctions and awards of response costs under CERCLA reasonably can be viewed as equitable relief. (See, e.g., United States v. Northeastern Pharmaceutical (8th Cir.1986) 810 F.2d 726, 749, cert. den. (1987) 484 U.S. 848, 108 S.Ct. 146, 98 L.Ed.2d 102 [no right to jury trial in suit seeking reimbursement of response costs].) The mere characterization of relief under federal law, however, is not dispositive of the proper construction of insurance policies under state law. Because California has generally abandoned the traditional distinction between courts of equity and courts of law (see Code Civ.Proc., §§ 24, 30; Aerojet, supra, 211 Cal.App.3d at p. 230, fn. 8, 257 Cal.Rptr. 621, 258 Cal.Rptr. 684), even a legally sophisticated policyholder might not anticipate that the term "legally obligated" precludes coverage of equitably compelled expenses. Because the relief is ordered by a court of law, as that term is used in the modern sense, FMC could reasonably believe that its obligation to pay is legal. As the Court of Appeal noted in Aerojet, supra, 211 Cal.App.3d at page 228, 257 Cal.Rptr. 621, 258 Cal.Rptr. 684: "[P]etitioners would be surprised indeed to learn that coverage depended on whether the proceeding employed to obtain recompense was defined as 'legal' or 'equitable.' * * * It would come as an unexpected, if not incomprehensible, shock to the insureds to discover that their insurance coverage was being denied because the plaintiff chose to frame his complaint in equity rather than in law." Thus, as a matter of plain meaning, the term "legally obligated" covers injunctive relief and recovery of response costs.

Moreover, even if this phrase raises doubts in the minds of legally trained observers about whether a law-equity distinction was intended, it would be unreasonable to conclude that it unambiguously incorporates this sophisticated distinction into the policies. In this respect, whatever ambiguity it possesses in light of a party's legal knowledge is resolved in favor of coverage. Whether the term "legally obligated" is ambiguous or not, therefore, we conclude that it encompasses the types of relief sought in the third party suits.

2. "Damages"

We next consider whether FMC's prospective legal obligation in the third party suits is to pay "damages." Because the CGL policies do not define the word "damages," for interpretation purposes we look to its "ordinary and popular" definition. (Civ.Code, § 1644; Allstate Ins. Co. v. Thompson (1988) 206 Cal.App.3d 933, 938, 254 Cal.Rptr. 84.) Section 3281 of the Civil Code provides: "Every person who suffers detriment from the unlawful act or omission of another, may recover from the person in fault a compensation therefor in money, which is called damages." As our cases have pointed out, this provision is intended to represent the plain and ordinary meaning of the word "damages." Other lay and legal definitions are similar. [discussion of dictionary meanings is omitted]

We note, however, that CERCLA and the Hazardous Substance Account Act authorize alternative remedies—injunction and reimbursement—that are relatively interchangeable in a way perhaps not foreseen by the parties at the time they entered the CGL policies. As we discuss at greater length below, the policies necessarily present some ambiguity in light of statutory schemes that by their very operation tend to eliminate the formal distinction between compensation paid to an aggrieved party and sums expended by the insured under compulsion of injunction. For this reason, although we take the statutory and dictionary definitions described above to be the "ordinary and popular" definition of "damages" for interpretation purposes, we will not apply this definition inflexibly. To the extent that policy language is ambiguous in light of the way environmental statutes authorize relief, our goal remains to protect the objectively reasonable expectations of the insured.

With this background, we now examine whether the basic forms of relief at issue in the underlying suits are "damages."

(a) Reimbursement of government response costs

In numerous CERCLA suits seeking recovery from responsible parties, courts have routinely referred to reimbursement of response costs as "damages," regardless of the nature of the cleanup performed or property interest possessed by the plaintiff. (See, e.g., Pennsylvania v. Union Gas Co. (1989) 491 U.S. 1, 19–20, 109 S.Ct. 2273, 2284–2285, 105 L.Ed.2d 1.) In the insurance context, this view is persuasive. The ordinary, nontechnical meaning of "damages," as stated by statute and dictionaries and used by the courts in related contexts, encompasses reimbursement of response costs. The agencies' expenditure of federal funds to investigate and initiate cleanup of hazardous waste constitutes "loss" or "detriment." Furthermore, reimbursement by responsible parties is monetary "compensation" for such loss.

The first element of the statutory and dictionary definitions of "damages" is fulfilled in this case. The agencies suffer "loss" or "detriment" in two separate ways when they incur response costs under CERCLA and similar statutes. First, release of hazardous waste into groundwater and surface water constitutes actual harm to property in which the state and federal governments have an ownership interest; this harm is "detriment" in statutory terms. (Civ.Code, § 3282; Wat. Code, § 102 ["All water within the State is the property of the people of the State, but the right to the use of water may be acquired by appropriation in the manner provided by law."]) Second, the agencies' out-of-pocket expenses of investigating and removing the waste as required by statute is "loss" incurred as a direct result of harm allegedly created through the unlawful act or omission of FMC.

Viewed in this second context, such expenditure constitutes "loss" or "detriment" even as to agency efforts specifically directed at cleaning up property in which neither the state nor the federal government has an ownership interest. Under statute, the agencies are charged with the duty of removing hazardous waste, whether or not their proprietary interests are harmed or they ultimately are compensated for their efforts. They are not mere contractors who act out of an expectation of recompense for their cleanup work; their expenses are incurred as a matter of public duty rather than hope of private gain. Thus, when they seek reimbursement of their response costs, the basis of the claim is harm done to the public fisc. In ordinary terms, such harm constitutes "loss" or "detriment."

The language of the CGL policies themselves supports this view. The clauses at issue here cover sums expended as damages "because of property damage." If "damages" is construed to include a requirement that the aggrieved party suffered harm to a proprietary interest in the damaged property, the latter phrase becomes redundant. The plain language of the policies therefore supports the conclusion that the agencies' out-of-pocket expenditures, irrespective of the government interest in the property sought to be cleaned up, constitute "loss" or "detriment."

The second element of the statutory and dictionary definitions of "damages" is also fulfilled in this case. FMC's reimbursement of government response costs is monetary "compensation" for the loss suffered by the agencies when they proceed with environmental cleanups. Moreover, because the compensable loss is all remedial out-of-pocket expenditures incurred by the agencies, the "compensation" sought from FMC includes reimbursement for costs of cleaning up existing contamination on and off the disposal site itself, investigating the extent of contamination or the viability of cleanup options, and monitoring the spread of waste from the site. (See, e.g., Intel, supra, 692 F.Supp. at p. 1192.) As long as some "property damage," as defined below, has already taken place, the agencies' expenses for responding constitute loss or detriment, whether or not the expenses are attributable to actual cleanup, mitigation of damage, or investigation and monitoring. When the agencies seek reimbursement of such expenses from the insured under CERCLA, their claim is for compensation for all their expenses, not merely those resulting from actual cleanup efforts on government property. Any other conclusion would be illogical as a matter of the reasonable expectations of the insured.

For three specific reasons not relating to the ordinary meaning of the word "damages," however, the insurers contend that a reasonable interpretation excludes reimbursement of response costs from coverage under the CGL "damages" provision. First, they argue that because CERCLA distinguishes response costs from damages, it mandates the same distinction in the insurance context because the agencies do not seek "damages" as prescribed by statute. Second, the insurers contend that because environmental statutes authorize the agencies to recover response costs even if they suffer no property damage or personal injury, such recovery is "a government-imposed cost of doing business" rather than compensation for loss or detriment. Finally, the insurers contend that reimbursement is best characterized as restitutive relief, the measure and purpose of which is sufficiently different from "damages" to render the two concepts mutually exclusive. None of these arguments is persuasive in the insurance context. [insurers' arguments are omitted]

The insurers' argument contains several flaws. First, recovery of tort damages is not invariably limited by the value of damaged property. The courts have recognized that recovery in excess of such value may be necessary to restore the plaintiff to the position it occupied prior to a defendant's wrongdoing.

Second, even if the courts generally award tort "damages" in an amount limited to the lesser of the value of damaged property or the costs of repair, that does not mandate that a greater recovery authorized by state or federal statute therefore should be held to constitute something other than "damages" in conceptual terms. Even if a court applying common law might not award the full extent of such costs, the excess above what is awarded remains "damages" for insurance policy interpretation purposes. The whole recovery of response costs, not just the amount limited to the value of harmed property, constitutes loss or detriment for harm caused by FMC's allegedly unlawful act or omission.

This brings us to the alternative thrust of the insurers' argument: reimbursement of government response costs is not "damages" because it is a restitutive remedy that is "specific" rather than "substitutive" in character. The United States Supreme Court recently adopted this distinction in discussing whether a state's claim for "reimbursement" of federal Medicaid subsidies is a claim for "money damages" under the terms of the Administrative Procedure Act (APA) (5 U.S.C. § 702). Characterizing such a claim as one for "restitution," the high court held that it was therefore not a claim for money damages: "Our cases have long recognized the distinction between an action at law for damages—which are intended to provide a victim with monetary compensation for an injury to his person, property, or reputation—and an equitable action for specific relief—which may include an order providing * * * for 'the recovery of specific property *or monies* * * *.' " (Bowen v. Massachusetts (1988) 487 U.S. 879, 893, 108 S.Ct. 2722, 2732, 101 L.Ed.2d 749 [citation omitted, italics in original].)

We too have recognized a distinction between restitution and compensatory damages. Reimbursement can reasonably be labelled a restitutive remedy, either because it awards a plaintiff "the very thing to which he was entitled", or because it attempts to compensate a plaintiff for the cost of performing the duty of another (see Rest., Restitution, § 115 [providing that a person who performs the duty of another is entitled to "restitution"]).

This label does not, however, preclude characterization of the amounts in question here as "damages" awarded to compensate a plaintiff for out-of-pocket expenditures. Indeed, restitution, to which the insurers analogize the reimbursement at issue here, is frequently denominated as one type of "damages" for descriptive purposes. Whatever technical distinctions we and other courts have drawn between restitution and compensatory damages in other contexts, in ordinary terms both concepts are within the definition of "damages." For the purposes of interpretation, this fact is dispositive.

Nonetheless, because reimbursement of response costs is restitutive in that it attempts to restore to the governments the value of a benefit constructively conferred on FMC, we consider one further argument. California courts have held that, as a matter of public policy, an insured's payment of certain types of restitution cannot be covered by insurance. (See, e.g., State Farm Fire & Cas. Co. v. Superior Court (1987) 191 Cal.App.3d 74, 236 Cal.Rptr. 216 [insurer has no duty to defend criminal prosecution of insured, because "restitution" to victims of criminal conduct is punitive remedy not coverable as "damages"]; Jaffe v. Cranford Ins. Co., 168 Cal.App.3d 930, 214 Cal.Rptr. 567 [insurer has no duty to defend insured against criminal prosecution for Medicaid fraud, despite fact that state could have sought civil reimbursement of fraudulently procured funds instead of prosecuting; such reimbursement would be "restitution," not "damages"].)

These cases are inapposite. Unlike State Farm Fire & Cas. Co. v. Superior Court, the relief sought in the underlying suits at issue here is not punitive. CERCLA, for example, is a strict liability statute that serves essentially remedial goals, irrespective of fault. Reimbursement of response costs, moreover, is not restitutive in the narrow sense identified by Jaffe as inappropriate for insurance coverage. (See Jaffe v. Cranford Ins. Co., supra, 168 Cal.App.3d at p. 935, 214 Cal.Rptr. 567 ["Although the concept of 'restitution' may have a broader meaning in other contexts, we limit our reference to it here to situations in which the defendant is required to restore to the plaintiff that which was wrongfully acquired."].) In short, we are not persuaded that the relief at issue here is of the narrow type identified by these cases as not a proper subject of coverage by insurance. We conclude that reimbursement of environmental response costs is "damages" under the terms of the insurance policies at issue here, and that public policy does not prevent coverage.

(b) Costs of compliance with injunctions

The statutes on which the third party suits are based provide that, in lieu of remedying contamination and seeking reimbursement, the agencies may obtain injunctions compelling responsible parties to both cease discharging hazardous waste and clean up damage already present. As courts and commentators have recognized, government cleanup efforts are generally considerably more expensive than cleanups performed by the responsible party. (See, e.g., Intel, supra, 692 F.Supp. at p. 1183; Chemical Applications Co. v. Home Indemnity Co. (D.Mass.1977), 425 F.Supp. 777, 778–779; Pendygraft et al., Who Pays for Environmental Damage: Recent Developments in CERCLA Liability and Insurance Coverage Litigation (1988) 21 Ind.L.Rev. 117, 151.) For this reason, federal and state governments generally seek voluntary and involuntary cleanup by the responsible party (pursuant to injunction if necessary) before performing it themselves and seeking reimbursement under CERCLA. We now examine whether any or all of the costs of complying with injunctions issued under CERCLA and similar statutes are "damages" under the CGL policies.

The costs of injunctive relief, whether incurred for prophylactic, mitigative, or remedial purposes, do not readily satisfy the statutory or dictionary definitions of "damages." Because such costs are paid to employees or independent contractors rather than aggrieved parties, they do not directly "compensate" aggrieved persons for "loss" or "detriment." To be sure, in economic terms it may make little difference whether cleanup is performed and paid for directly by the insured pursuant to injunction or undertaken by the agencies (who then seek reimbursement). Nonetheless, it is difficult to construe the two methods of payment as equally covered by the ordinary definition of the word "damages," as we have described it above. If the costs of injunctive relief may be deemed "damages," the "as damages" limitation contained in the policies seems to be rendered meaningless. The costs of injunctions are essentially "sums to which the insured becomes legally obligated to pay * * * because of property damage." Construing them also to be "sums to which the insured becomes legally obligated to pay as damages because of property damage" makes the italicized phrase redundant. Because we are obligated to give effect to every part of an insurance policy (Civ.Code, § 1641), we hesitate to reach this result.

It is unlikely, however, that the parties to CGL policies intended to cover reimbursement of response costs but not the costs of injunctive relief, at least where the latter costs are incurred—generally at a lower total cost—for exactly the same purposes addressed through governmental expenditure of response costs. In this respect, we note that the relationship between the remedies authorized by CERCLA and similar statutes is not the same as that between damages and injunctive remedies traditionally available at common law and in equity. In ordinary tort actions, injunctive relief is generally available only if legal remedies (e.g., monetary compensation) are inadequate. (Code Civ.Proc., § 526; Civ. Code, § 3422; see generally 6 Witkin, Cal.Procedure (3d ed. 1985) Provisional Remedies, § 276, p. 576, and cases cited therein.) Thus, a plaintiff ordinarily may seek to enjoin conduct that constitutes a nuisance, even though the activity complained of does not cause him any cognizable property or personal damage. In such a situation, the defendant's costs of complying with an injunction might not be covered by CGL policies.

In Hanna, supra, 224 F.2d 499, the leading case holding that the cost of complying with mandatory injunctions in tort actions is not "damages" under CGL policies, adjoining property owners brought suit against the insured, alleging trespass by boulders and debris from the insured's property. The owners sought no damages (and there was no evidence that the value of their property had decreased as a result of the encroachment). Instead, they sought, and obtained, an injunction ordering the insured to remove the debris. The Fifth Circuit Court of Appeals held the costs of complying with the injunction not covered under the insured's liability policy, which contained substantially the same coverage clause as those at issue here. Its reasoning, however, focused on the fact that, under Florida law, the owners' potential damages remedy was limited to the diminution in value of their property; injunctive relief, by contrast, required monetary payment whether or not the value of the owners' property had decreased. Because there was no evidence of any decrease in property value, the court reasoned, the costs of complying with the injunction were not "damages."

We need not here decide whether the reasoning of Hanna is persuasive as a matter of California law.[69] Unlike Florida, California does not, as is noted above, absolutely limit damages for trespass to the diminution in value of the plaintiff's property. Moreover, the basic foundation of the Hanna decision—the interplay of legal and equitable remedies in tort actions in which it is entirely speculative whether the plaintiff has suffered compensable harm—differs from the relationship between the various remedies authorized by CERCLA, under which injunctive relief may be available even though legal or restitutive remedies are adequate.

The mere fact that the agencies seek an injunction in an environmental protection action does not indicate an absence of cognizable property damage or personal injury. The prima facie case for injunctive relief is identical to that for reimbursement of response costs, with the single added element of "imminent and substantial endangerment" of public health or welfare or the environment. Moreover, in its remedial aspects, the injunction results in exactly the type of expenditures involved in reimbursement of response costs, whether or not the agencies have an adequate remedy in the form of reimbursement. (See, e.g., United States v. Price (D.N.J.1983) 577 F.Supp. 1103, 1112 [Congress intended injunctive relief under 42 U.S.C. § 9606 to be "a viable alternative or concurrent means of achieving the same goal" as reimbursement under 42 U.S.C. § 9607].)

For these reasons, it would exalt form over substance to interpret CGL policies to cover one remedy but not the other. Given the practical similarity of remedies available under the environmental statutes at issue here, we believe a reasonable insured would expect both remedies to fall within coverage as "damages." Insofar as injunctive relief is an

69. In this respect, we agree with the court in Aerojet, supra, 211 Cal.App.3d at page 234, 257 Cal.Rptr. 621, that Hanna, supra, 224 F.2d 499, is distinguishable from CERCLA cases. We note, however, that the approach taken in Aerojet to resolve the issue presented here may have unintended consequences in distinguishable cases. Because Aerojet applies an extremely broad definition of "damages" (i.e., "any economic outlay compelled by law to rectify and mitigate property damage caused by the insured's pollution"), it implicitly suggests that the costs of mandatory injunctive relief in all contexts, common law as well as statutory, may be covered by CGL policies. (Id. at p. 228, 257 Cal.Rptr. 621.) We find that a more debatable proposition than the limited one—based on the peculiar juxtaposition of injunctive and reimbursement remedies in CERCLA—we endorse here. The precise issue presented in Hanna remains unresolved as a matter of California law.

equivalent substitute for the goal of government remedial action, the distinction relied on by Hanna is inapposite in the CERCLA context.

A majority of courts have also reached this conclusion. Some have reasoned that such costs are "damages" according to the reasonable expectations of the parties, even if they would not be "damages" under technical definitions. Others have stated this conclusion in terms of public policy: costs of compliance must be interpreted as "damages" in the environmental context, because to hold otherwise would make insurance coverage hinge on the "mere fortuity" of the way in which government agencies seek to enforce cleanup requirements, would unreasonably constrain the agencies' choice of cleanup mechanisms, and would introduce substantial inefficiency into the cleanup process.

We agree with the underlying rationale of these decisions. Under CERCLA and similar statutes, injunctive relief and reimbursement of response costs serve substantially the same purpose. For this reason, we find CGL policy language is ambiguous as applied to remedial and mitigative costs incurred pursuant to injunction under CERCLA and similar statutes, and therefore must be construed in favor of coverage to satisfy the reasonable expectations of the insured.

In contrast to our determination, two federal Courts of Appeals have concluded that the costs of injunctive relief under CERCLA and similar statutes are not covered by CGL policies. (See NEPACCO, supra, 842 F.2d at p. 986; Armco, supra, 822 F.2d at p. 1353.) One of these decisions essentially relies on an uncritical adoption of the Hanna result. (NEPACCO, supra, 842 F.2d at p. 986 [stating that "black letter insurance law holds that claims for equitable relief are not claims for 'damages' under liability insurance contracts," while citing four cases supporting the proposition and three challenging it in the environmental context].) The other decision supports its conclusion by referring to the "prophylactic," and therefore uninsurable, nature of injunctive relief. (See, e.g., Armco, supra, 822 F.2d at p. 1353.) Because the reasoning of the Hanna court is not compelling in the CERCLA context, and because it is incorrect to portray injunctive relief under CERCLA and related statutes as wholly prophylactic in nature, we decline to follow these decisions.[70]

It is true that some costs required under environmental injunctions are prophylactic in nature (e.g., altering dumping practices to prevent recurrences of leakage). As we discuss below, these costs are not incurred "because of property damage," and therefore are not covered by CGL policies. Nevertheless, environmental injunctions requiring remedial and mitigative action result in costs that constitute "damages" under CGL policies. Because an insured would reasonably expect equal coverage of

70. We again note that the additional justification offered by these decisions for their result—the fact that coverage of the costs of injunctive relief would render the "as damages" clause of CGL policies meaningless—possesses some merit. For the reasons stated above, however, it is our view that "damages" is ambiguous in the CERCLA context and therefore should be construed in favor of coverage and in accordance with the objectively reasonable expectations of the insured, regardless of any formal or technical difficulties this reading poses.

the costs of equivalent or alternative remedies, the costs of injunctive relief under the statutes in question here are "damages" for CGL purposes.[71]

3. "Because of Property Damage"

Several courts have held that government claims for injunctive relief and reimbursement of costs incurred in cleaning up disposal sites and water surrounding them are not covered by CGL policies, because such claims do not allege "property damage." We disagree. As we note above, these decisions either misperceive the basic character of remedies available under environmental statutes or apply an unduly narrow definition of "property damage." CGL policies cover sums expended as damages not only because of "harm to human or animal life" (Armco, supra, 822 F.2d at p. 1354), but more generally because of "property" damage. Contamination of the environment satisfies this requirement.

We also hold that reimbursement of response costs and the costs of injunctive relief under CERCLA and related statutes are incurred "because of" property damage. As discussed above, the mere fact that the governments may seek reimbursement of response costs or injunctive relief without themselves having suffered any tangible harm to a proprietary interest does not exclude the recovery of cleanup costs from coverage under the "damages" provision of CGL policies. For similar reasons, in plain and ordinary terms such recovery is "because of" property damage. It is immaterial whether motivations other than protection of property—for example, protection of the health of persons living near hazardous waste sites—also contribute to the agencies' pursuit of statutory relief. The Court of Appeal's emphasis on the fact that the agencies' objectives may be regulatory rather than proprietary is misplaced. Whatever their dominant motive, the event precipitating their legal action is contamination of property. The costs that result from such action are therefore incurred "because of" property damage.

This is true, moreover, whether the cleanup at issue in the underlying suits takes place on property owned by FMC, the state or federal government, or third parties. The provisions at issue here do not specify that coverage hinges on the nature or location of property damage. We therefore construe them to encompass damages because of property damage in general, regardless of by whom it is suffered.

We do agree that prophylactic costs—incurred to pay for measures taken in advance of any release of hazardous waste—are not incurred

71. Our conclusion—that the costs of injunctive relief as well as reimbursement of government response costs constitute "damages"—applies equally to the policies covering "ultimate net loss." As defined by the policies, "ultimate net loss" includes "the *total sum* which [FMC] * * * becomes obligated to pay by reason of * * * property damage," including "expenses" as well as "damages." (Italics added.) The plain meaning of this definition encompasses reimbursement of response costs and the costs of compliance with injunctions ordering FMC to clean up hazardous waste. For this reason, such costs are "ultimate net loss" within the meaning of these policies, as we are compelled to interpret them. (Civ. Code, § 1638 ["The language of a contract is to govern its interpretation, if the language is clear and explicit, and does not involve an absurdity."].)

"because of property damage." Until such damage has occurred, whether on the waste site itself or elsewhere, there can be no coverage under CGL policies. Beyond this limited circumstance, however, and because the agencies in this suit allege that the waste sites themselves and water on and surrounding the sites have already been contaminated by hazardous waste, we conclude that the reimbursement and the costs of injunctive relief sought here at least in part constitute "damages because of property damage."

III. Conclusion

For the foregoing reasons, we conclude that the Court of Appeal erred in directing the superior court to enter summary adjudication in favor of the insurers. It is not clear, as a matter of law, that all of the relief for which FMC is potentially liable in the underlying suits cannot be deemed sums which it will be "legally obligated to pay as damages because of property damage." Although the costs of compliance with injunctions ordering FMC to undertake prophylactic measures are not covered by CGL policies covering payment of damages "because of property damage," the remaining remedies sought by the agencies in the underlying suits are not precluded from coverage as a matter of law; such relief satisfies the plain and ordinary meanings of the phrases "legally obligated," "damages," "ultimate net loss," and "because of property damage." Accordingly, we reverse the decision of the Court of Appeal and vacate its order issuing a writ of mandate, and direct the Court of Appeal to remand this case to the superior court for further proceedings consistent with this opinion.

Notes

1. As the *AIU* case makes clear, the federal courts have not provided consistent treatment of coverage for "damages." An illustrative case is *Maryland Casualty Co. v. Armco*, 822 F.2d 1348 (4th Cir.1987), in which Armco made claims against its insurer for coverage and defense of claims for injunctive relief and reimbursement of environmental damage caused by Armco. As in *AIU*, the policy provided coverage suits for injury seeking "damages." Noting that it is black letter law that damages are legal not equitable, the court held that the insurer has no duty to defend unless there is a possibility of recovery under the policy. Without an allegation of legal injury there is no coverage for the purely equitable claim.

2. The California State Supreme Court has held that "damages" do not include expenses required by an administrative agency under the aegis of an environmental statute. Certain Underwriters at Lloyd's, London v. Superior Court (Powerine Oil Co., Inc.), 24 Cal.4th 945, 103 Cal.Rptr.2d 672, 16 P.3d 94 (2001)). The court distinguished *AIU* on the basis that *AIU* did not consider other than money ordered by a court. *Id.* at 966.

3. One insured's odyssey with respect to coverage and the duty to defend an environmental case is described in *Vann v. Travelers Companies*, 39 Cal.App.4th 1610, 46 Cal.Rptr.2d 617 (1995).

2. Intellectual Property

An Intellectual Property Primer

The United States Constitution specifically authorizes Congress to provide authors and inventors rights of exclusive ownership and control of their creations, to the extent that doing so promotes "the Progress of Science and useful Arts."[72] It is this protection to which we refer to as "intellectual property."

Today, federal intellectual property rights are divided into three primary categories: patents, trademarks, and copyrights.[73] Patents are granted through an application process, whereby the applicant must show that he or she has developed a new, useful and non-obvious process or product.[74] Trademarks are words or symbols that distinguish the product or service of one person or entity from those of others. Prime examples are the Nike swoosh or the word "Pepsi." Trademarks may be registered, but whether registered or not, the trademark claimant must show that the mark is distinctive and non-functional, and that the claimant uses it in commerce.[75] Copyrights provide exclusive rights in original forms of expression that have been recorded in some tangible form. Examples include works of literature, musical compositions, and works of fine art. Copyrights arise automatically when the author's original expression is fixed in a permanent or concrete form.[76]

Intellectual property law has gained greater importance and visibility in recent years. In addition to becoming a more valuable commodity, intellectual property has also become more vulnerable to infringement. Infringement of intellectual property occurs when another person or entity makes an unauthorized copy or use of the protected creation. Importantly for our purposes, except for some trademark disputes, intent is not a required element of infringement claims although intent may affect the amount or type of damage award.[77]

The increasing popularity of the Internet has made it easier both to infringe intellectual property rights, and to be caught for such infringement.[78] Between 1992 and 1996, there was a 20% increase in the number of infringement suits filed in the federal court system.[79] Moreover, the economic consequences of infringement are generally greater, and more immediate; thus, the potential liability for the offenders has increased.

72. *See* U.S. Const., Art. 1, § 8, cl. 8.

73. As a technical matter, trademark law is authorized by the Commerce Clause and not by Article 1, § 8, cl. 8. There are additionally a number of state intellectual property doctrines including trade secrets and publicity rights.

74. 35 U.S.C.A. §§ 101, 102, 103.

75. 15 U.S.C.A. § 1051.

76. There is an optional registration process, and it is important to note that the owner of a copyright cannot make a legal claim against an infringer unless the work in dispute has been registered. 17 U.S.C.A. § 411(a).

77. 17 U.S.C.A. § 504; 35 U.S.C.A. § 284; 35 U.S.C.A. § 1117.

78. See generally Alfred C. Yen, *Internet Service Provider Liability for Subscriber Copyright Infringement, Enterprise Liability, and the First Amendment*, 88 Georgetown L.J. 1833 (2000).

79. Melvin Simensky and Eric C. Osterberg, *Insurance and Management of Intellectual Property Risks*, 16 SUM. Ent. & Sports Law 3 (Summer 1998).

As a result, more and more businesses are turning to insurance to recoup the costs of litigation and damage awards. There are essentially two sources of insurance coverage for alleged infringement: the advertising clause of the Commercial General Liability Policy, and the very recently created "patent infringement" policies.

This section provides an overview of the existing judicial interpretations of coverage for intellectual property. At present, there is not a uniform approach to, or understanding of the issues, and it will be fascinating to watch this new area of insurance law unfold.[80]

We begin by looking at disputes over the duty to defend and indemnify CGL policy-holders who are accused of infringement. We continue by examining the texts of an entirely new breed of insurance—first and third-party coverage for patents. We conclude with the cautionary malpractice tale of attorneys who neglected to consider the potential for coverage under CGL policies.

Throughout the chapter, keep in mind the higher level of sophistication and bargaining power held by the insureds in these cases. Consider also the fact that much of the existing case law comes from the decisions of federal courts, which have considerably less experience in resolving insurance disputes. This is true because most intellectual property claims are brought under federal law. Might coverage issues encourage venue-shopping in intellectual property cases? Another factor to consider is the extent to which the actual content of the plaintiff's complaint can affect a claim for coverage. Finally, consider the issue of intent, and whether exclusions for intentional acts might bar coverage. Intent is not usually an element of a complaint for infringement of intellectual property rights. If the complaint contains no allegations of intentional conduct, how might that affect the decisions of the defendant's insurers?

(a) Copyright Infringement

The majority of courts which have addressed the issue of coverage for copyright infringement have come down in favor of the insured. Coverage is held to exist under the CGL's "advertising clause," which explicitly defines coverage as including copyright infringement.

BEN BERGER & SON, INC. v. AMERICAN MOTORIST INS. CO.

United States District Court, S.D. New York, 1995.
36 U.S.P.Q.2d 1105.

CHIN, DISTRICT JUDGE.

In this insurance coverage case, the parties have cross-moved for summary judgment. For the reasons stated below, plaintiff's motion is granted in part and denied in part; defendant's motion is denied.

80. *See* Bradford P. Lyerla and Manual A. Abascal, *Insurance Coverage for Intellectual Property Claims: The California v/s the New York Approach*, 19 AIPLA Q.J. 189 (1991). Though useful starting point, this article is already somewhat dated.

FACTS

Plaintiff Ben Berger & Son, Inc. ("Berger") is engaged in the design and manufacture of adult clothing. In 1984, Berger entered into a licensing agreement with Cynthia McKinney, a children's clothing designer, pursuant to which Ms. McKinney was to design a line of adult clothing accessories, including gloves and socks, that would be sold by Berger and advertised in Berger's catalogue. Ms. McKinney's designs were unique in that her gloves and socks each contained an embroidered "whimsical figure," often containing a microchip that played music suitable to the season (for example, her Christmas line featured socks that played Christmas carols). Ms. McKinney also created a "Toe Sock" that had applique designs on each of the toes. Prior to her licensing agreement with Berger, Ms. McKinney sold her items through the Neiman Marcus department store.

Ms. McKinney's designs were first displayed in Berger's catalogues in 1985 and 1986. In 1987, at Ms. McKinney's request, Berger's catalogues expressly stated that Ms. McKinney's designs were copyrighted. The McKinney line was then advertised in Berger's 1987, 1989, 1990 and 1992 catalogues.

In 1992, Berger began manufacturing a sock that was similar to Ms. McKinney's design items and advertising it in his catalogue. At Berger's insistence, however, these socks were not subject to the licensing agreement between Ms. McKinney and Berger. In January 1993, Ms. McKinney terminated her licensing relationship with Berger and began marketing her designs through another company. She later learned that Berger had manufactured a Christmas line of gloves and socks that was nearly identical to her line. Ms. McKinney then sued Berger in November 1993, alleging unlawful use of trade dress (Lanham Act violation), false advertising (Lanham Act), copyright infringement, deceptive acts and practices, dilution, common law unfair competition, and breach of contract (the "McKinney action"). Ms. McKinney essentially complained that Berger's continued manufacture and marketing of clothing accessories that were identical or similar in design to her own injured her business reputation, caused consumer confusion and diminished her sales.

Prior to the commencement of the McKinney lawsuit, plaintiff had purchased a Commercial General Liability Insurance Policy, effective April 5, 1993 to April 5, 1994 (the "Policy"), from defendant American Motorist Insurance Co. ("American"). The Policy required American to "pay those sums that the insured becomes legally obligated to pay as damages" because of, among other things, advertising injury caused by plaintiff's advertising its goods, products or services. The Policy also imposed on American the "duty to defend any 'suit' seeking those damages." "Advertising injury" was defined in the Policy as an injury arising out of "certain offenses," the relevant ones for this case being "[m]isappropriation of advertising ideas or style of doing business," or "[i]nfringement of copyright, title or slogan."[81]

Pursuant to the terms of the Policy, Berger timely notified American of McKinney's lawsuit and requested coverage. American, however, disclaimed coverage in a letter dated January 12, 1994, maintaining that Berger's infringing activities did not fall within the policy definition of "advertising injury."

Plaintiff later settled with McKinney for $135,000 and then commenced this action against American. Both parties have moved for summary judgment. Defendant argues that it is not obligated to reimburse Berger for Berger's defense costs and settlement payment because McKinney did not sue plaintiff for his advertising activities, but rather for the manufacture and sale of clothing accessories that infringed on McKinney's design and copyright. Plaintiff replies that each of the claims in McKinney's complaint fell within the scope of the insurance contract because, among other things, plaintiff's allegedly infringing products were advertised in plaintiff's catalogue.

DISCUSSION

The standards applicable to motions for summary judgment are well settled. A court may grant summary judgment only where there is no genuine issue of material fact and the moving party is therefore entitled to judgment as a matter of law. See Fed.R.Civ.P. 56(c). Accordingly, the court's task is not to "weigh the evidence and determine the truth of the matter but [to] determine whether there is a genuine issue for trial." Anderson v. Liberty Lobby, Inc., 477 U.S. 242, 249, 106 S.Ct. 2505, 2511 (1986).

Here, the parties agree that there are no issues of material fact with regard to the issue of coverage; rather, the only issues are legal issues concerning the meaning of the Policy.

I. DUTY TO DEFEND

[The court's discussion of the duty to defend and the applicable interpretive scheme is omitted].

Because the Policy applies exclusively to certain injuries that arise from Berger's advertising its goods, American's duty to defend is triggered only if: 1) the McKinney action alleges an injury that occurred in the course of plaintiff's advertising its goods, and 2) that injury emanated from one of the enumerated offenses. Reviewing the McKinney complaint together with the Policy, and keeping in mind that the insurer's duty to defend must be broadly construed and that that duty is triggered if even a single claim falls within the Policy, I conclude that defendant had a duty to defend plaintiff.

81. Since the insurance policy does not define "misappropriation of advertising ideas or style of doing business" or "infringement of copyright," I will give these terms their common, ordinary meaning. See J.A. Brundage Plumbing v. Massachusetts Bay Insurance Co., 818 F.Supp. 553 (W.D.N.Y.1993) (citing Ruder & Finn Inc. v. Seaboard Surety Co., 52 N.Y.2d 663, 671, 439 N.Y.S.2d 858 (1981)).

A. Lanham Act Claims

Ms. McKinney's first two claims alleged violations of the Lanham Act, specifically, infringement of trade dress and false advertising. With respect to her trade dress claim, Ms. McKinney alleged that her style and design was a "fanciful and arbitrary trade dress" identifying her as the designer. She claimed that Berger violated her trade dress because he "used and is continuing to use words, terms, names, designs and devices in connection with the promotion of its Christmas gloves and socks, which are likely to cause confusion, or to cause mistake, ... and has continued to use that trade dress on gloves and socks, and in advertising, and by so doing, has continued to represent to the public that it is an authorized distributor of Cynthia McKinney products." (Cmplt. PP 43, 47) (emphasis added). The crux of Ms. McKinney's false advertising claim is that Berger marketed socks and gloves that were "confusingly similar" to her design. Ms. McKinney further alleged that Berger's catalogue was "used as a commercial advertisement by Ben Berger," by which he "deceived the recipients of the catalog into believing that these items are being offered as result of its previous license agreement with Cynthia McKinney." (Cmplt. PP 58–59).

Plaintiff argues that McKinney's Lanham Act claims allege injuries that occurred from its misappropriation of McKinney's advertising ideas and style of doing business and thus required American to defend.[82] I agree. Berger copied McKinney's "style of doing business" because it manufactured gloves and socks that were startlingly similar to McKinney's. The injury caused by Berger's infringement of McKinney's trade dress is an advertising injury because it was Berger's advertising its similar products in its catalogue, in which McKinney's own products had previously been advertised, that diluted McKinney's distinctive trade dress and caused confusion as to the source of the products. See generally Milstein v. Greger, Lawlor, Roth, Inc., 1995 U.S.App. LEXIS 15539 (2d Cir. June 19, 1995) ("trade dress" "includes the design and appearance of the product as well as that of the container and all elements making up the total visual image by which the product is presented to customers") (emphasis added).

B. Copyright Infringement

The third claim is for copyright infringement. McKinney alleged that certain of her Christmas designs were copyrighted and that Berger infringed on her copyright by copying those designs for its own use. In addition, Berger allegedly marketed the infringing designs in its catalogue. (Cmplt. PP 66, 70, 72). This claim clearly falls within the scope of the Policy since one of the enumerated offenses that would trigger American's duty to defend is advertising injury caused by copyright infringement. See Policy, Section V(1)(d).

82. Since those terms are not defined, they will be given their common, everyday meaning. "Advertising" is action intended to make something known to the public or to call public attention to something by emphasizing its desirable qualities so as to arouse a desire to buy. With respect to "style of doing business," that term's common meaning clearly encompasses trade dress as concepts, ideas and styles.

C. State Law Claims

Ms. McKinney alleged four state and common law claims: deceptive acts and practices, dilution of trade dress, unfair competition and breach of contract. With the exception of the breach of contract claim, these claims are also covered by the Policy and trigger defendant's duty to defend.

McKinney's deceptive acts and practices, dilution of trade dress and unfair competition claims are substantively similar to her trade dress and false advertising claims. In her claim for deceptive acts and practices, McKinney alleged that by Berger's "continued misrepresentations and use of the Cynthia McKinney trade dress on its gloves and socks and, in advertising, Berger has engaged in deceptive trade practices and false advertising." (Cmplt. P 76) (emphasis added). With respect to the dilution claim, McKinney alleged that "Berger has willfully, knowingly and with predatory intent marketed its infringing line of gloves and socks with the intent to associate its products with those of plaintiffs." (Cmplt. P 86). Finally, the unfair competition claim stated that Berger's actions were an "unlawful misappropriation of . . . McKinney's valuable property rights and goodwill in the trade dress" and that Berger acted "for the purpose of associating its products with those of plaintiffs." (Cmplt. P 90). Thus, these claims are covered by the Policy for the same reasons that McKinney's Lanham Act claims are covered: McKinney was complaining that she had a distinctive trade dress or style of doing business in her designs that Berger misappropriated and that, because of Berger's advertising its similar products, her trade dress, or style, was diluted.[83]

Finally, McKinney's breach of contract claim is not covered under the express terms of the Policy. The "Exclusions" section of the Policy plainly states "This insurance does not apply to: . . . (b) 'Advertising injury' arising out of 1) Breach of contract, other than misappropriation of advertising ideas under an implied contract." See Village of Sylvan Beach, New York v. Travelers Indemnity Co., 1995 WL 314728 (2d Cir.1995) (insurer has no duty to defend if insured's claim is unambiguously excluded from the policy); Jakobson Shipyard v. Aetna Casualty & Surety, 775 F.Supp. 606, 614 (S.D.N.Y.1991) (same). Notwithstanding this exclusion, defendant still had a duty to defend the entire case because the other claims asserted in the McKinney case were covered by the Policy.

II. Duty to Indemnify

An insurer's duty to indemnify is construed more narrowly than the duty to defend and is determined by whether the insured is, in actuality,

83. Defendant's argument that the Policy does not apply to this case because McKinney complained of Berger's "ripping off" her socks and gloves, and not her advertising, is unavailing. (Def.Mem. at 17). The fact of the matter is that McKinney complained of both—both that her advertising and her products were "ripped off." Clearly, an important focus of the complaint was Berger's alleged misappropriation of the concepts, ideas and styles used by McKinney to arouse the public into purchasing her products.

liable to a third party. See Servidone Construction Corp. v. Security Insurance Company of Hartford, 64 N.Y.2d 419, 424, 488 N.Y.S.2d 139, 142 (1985). Neither of the parties discuss this duty in more than a cursory fashion, and based upon the present submissions I cannot determine the issue of plaintiff's liability in the McKinney action or the extent thereof. See id. at 143 (where insured settled underlying action before determination could be made as to insured's liability, and then sued insurer for allegedly failing to indemnify, summary judgment deemed inappropriate and case remanded to trial court for further proceedings to determine insured's liability in underlying action).

Accordingly, summary judgment is denied as to plaintiff's claim for breach of the duty to indemnify.

CONCLUSION

Plaintiff's motion for summary judgment is granted with respect to defendant's duty to defend and denied as to defendant's duty to indemnify. Defendant's motion for summary judgment is denied. The parties shall appear on August 7, 1995 at 3:00 p.m. in Courtroom 11A at 500 Pearl Street for a conference to discuss: 1) the appropriate method to determine whether plaintiff was in fact liable to McKinney for conduct covered under the Policy; and 2) any allocation issues.

SO ORDERED.

Notes

1. While coverage for copyright infringement is not open to much dispute, the issue of causation can result in the denial of coverage. The California State Supreme Court, in interpreting the advertising clause, has held that there must be causal connection between advertising activities, and the underlying injury alleged by plaintiff. Bank of the West v. Superior Court, 2 Cal.4th 1254, 1275–77, 10 Cal.Rptr.2d 538, 552–53, 833 P.2d 545, 559–60 (1992). California is not the only state to require such a connection. Other state courts have required a similar causal connection. See Fluoroware v. Chubb Group of Ins. Cos., 545 N.W.2d 678 (Minn.Ct.App.1996). This concept is also included in trademark infringement cases as well. See J.A. Brundage Plumbing and Roto–Rooter, Inc. v. Massachusetts Bay Ins. Co., 818 F.Supp. 553 (W.D.N.Y.1993), vacated by settlement, 153 F.R.D. 36 (1994).

2. What is the meaning and scope of "advertising?" How much is enough? A Minnesota court has held that even one letter to a single customer can constitute advertising. John Deere Insurance Company v. Shamrock Industries, Inc., 696 F.Supp. 434 (D.Minn.1988).

3. Isn't the insured's conduct in the *Berger* case intentional? Could the insurer have avoided liability on the basis that the injury was intentional?

(b) Trademark Infringement

Many courts have found coverage for trademark infringement under the CGL's advertising clause. The terms "title" and "slogan" in the advertising clause may be interpreted as including trademarks, but this result will vary from state to state.

LEBAS FASHION IMPORTS OF USA, INC. v. ITT HARTFORD INS. GROUP

Court of Appeal of California, Second Appellate District, Division Three, 1996.
50 Cal.App.4th 548, 59 Cal.Rptr.2d 36.

Croskey, Associate Justice.

Lebas Fashion Imports of USA, Inc. ("Lebas"), appeals from a summary judgment granted in favor of ITT Hartford Insurance Group ("Hartford") on Lebas' first amended complaint for breach of an insurance contract and breach of the implied covenant of good faith. After Lebas had been sued in federal court for trademark infringement, Hartford, which had issued a commercial general liability ("CGL") policy to Lebas, denied coverage and refused to provide Lebas with a defense on the ground that the policy did not provide coverage for a claim based on trademark infringement. Lebas thereafter defended and settled the federal suit and then commenced this action.

We agree with Lebas that the "advertising injury" coverage provided under Hartford's CGL policy does extend to a claim for trademark infringement. This is so because the applicable advertising injury offense set out in Hartford's policy is ambiguous and, in the context of the entire policy and all of the relevant circumstances, Lebas had an objectively reasonable expectation of coverage. This requires us to resolve that ambiguity in Lebas's favor. As a result, based on the allegations of the underlying federal action, a potential for coverage existed and Hartford owed Lebas a duty to defend that action. We therefore reverse the judgment and remand for further proceedings.

Factual and Procedural Background

Lebas is an importer and wholesaler of men's clothing in Los Angeles and sells and distributes goods under different brand names. Lebas had obtained a CGL policy from Hartford which was effective during the period October 15, 1991 through October 15, 1992.

On June 15, 1992, Parfums Guy Laroche, a Societe Anonyme (similar to a United States corporation, but organized under the laws of the Republic of France) and Cosmair, Inc., a Delaware Corporation (collectively, "Guy Laroche") filed an action in the United States District Court for the Central District of California in which Lebas was named as the defendant. In this action, Guy Laroche alleged that it was engaged in the manufacture, distribution and sale (on a worldwide basis) of high fashion perfumes and cosmetic products under its trade name and trademarks, "DRAKKAR" and "DRAKKAR NOIR." It was also alleged that prior to June 15, 1992, Lebas had adopted and commenced to use the name "DRAKKAR" on its clothing products, including men's suits, and to advertise those clothing products under the name(s) "DRAKKAR" and "DRAKKAR NOIR." In addition, it was alleged that Lebas had filed an application with the United States Patent and Trademark Office to register the name "DRAKKAR" as its own (an application to which Guy Laroche had filed opposition).

Lebas tendered defense of this action to Hartford. After concluding that the claims asserted against Lebas were not potentially covered under its CGL policy, Hartford denied coverage and refused a defense. The relevant portion of the CGL policy with which we are concerned is that which provides coverage for "advertising injury."

Under its policy, Hartford promised to "pay those sums that [Lebas] becomes legally obligated to pay as damages because of ... 'advertising injury' ... "; and the policy also stated that Hartford would "have the right and duty to defend any 'suit' seeking those damages." In addition, the policy provided that the "advertising injury" to which it applied was limited to "an offense committed in the course of advertising [Lebas'] goods, products or services." The term "advertising injury" was defined to mean an "injury arising out of one or more of the following offenses: a ..... [¶] c. Misappropriation of advertising ideas or style of doing business; or [¶] d. Infringement of copyright, title or slogan." (Italics added.) There is no claim by Hartford that any exclusion contained in the policy has any application to the coverage issue. Thus, the insuring clause provisions quoted above are the only portions of the policy with which we are concerned.

After Hartford refused to provide a defense, Lebas undertook to and did settle the underlying action with Guy Laroche. Lebas entered into a stipulated consent judgment which required the payment of monetary damages and an injunction restraining any future use of the name "DRAKKAR." Lebas then filed this action against Hartford for its breach of contract and bad faith refusal to defend Lebas in the underlying action. Hartford moved for summary judgment, claiming that there never was any potential for coverage under the policy and therefore no duty to defend had ever arisen. Lebas opposed the motion, arguing that coverage was available under the "advertising injury" provisions of the policy.

On February 17, 1994, the trial court granted Hartford's motion after it concluded that the relevant policy provisions were clear and unambiguous and that no coverage was provided for a trademark infringement. Judgment was entered on March 3, 1994 and this timely appeal by Lebas followed.

Issue Presented

The sole question before us is whether an alleged trademark infringement is potentially covered by policy language promising coverage for (1) the misappropriation of advertising ideas or style of doing business or (2) the infringement of copyright, title or slogan. This is an issue which has not heretofore been directly addressed by any California court and involves the construction and application of relatively new standard policy language contained in many post–1986 CGL policies.

DISCUSSION

* * *

3. General Principles of Trademark Infringement.

A trademark is defined under the relevant federal statute (15 U.S.C. § 1127) as "any word, name, symbol or device or any combination thereof [¶] (1) used by a person, or [¶] (2) which a person has a bona fide intention to use in commerce and applies to register on the principal register ... to identify and distinguish his or her goods, including a unique product, from those manufactured or sold by others and to indicate the source of the goods, even if that source is unknown."

An infringement of a trademark is defined as an act committed by any person who, without the consent of the registrant shall: "(a) use in commerce any reproduction, counterfeit, copy, or colorable imitation of a registered mark in connection with the sale, offering for sale, distribution, or advertising of any goods or services on or in connection with which such use is likely to cause confusion, or to cause mistake, or to deceive; or [¶] (b) reproduce, counterfeit, copy, or colorably imitate a registered mark and apply such reproduction, counterfeit, copy, or colorable imitation to labels, signs, prints, packages, wrappers, receptacles or advertisements intended to be used in commerce upon or in connection with the sale, offering for sale, distribution, or advertising of goods or services on or in connection with which such use is likely to cause confusion, or to cause mistake, or to deceive." (15 U.S.C. § 1114.)

"A trademark serves three distinct and separate purposes: (1) It identifies a product's origin, (2) it guarantees the product's unchanged quality, and (3) it advertises the product. Injury to the trademark in any of its offices as an identifying, guaranteeing or advertising device should suffice to constitute an infringement thereof." (Callmann, The Law of Unfair Competition, Trademarks and Monopolies (4th ed. 1994) § 21.06, at p. 41, italics added, fn. omitted.) As one court has stated, "A trademark is but a species of advertising, its purpose being to fix the identity of the article and the name of the producer in the minds of people who see the advertisement, so that they may afterwards use the knowledge themselves and carry it to others having like desires and needs for such article." (Northam Warren Corp. v. Universal Cosmetic Co. (7th Cir.1927) 18 F.2d 774, 774.) Moreover, as the trademark statute itself makes clear, the advertising of a good or service is one of the ways in which an act of infringement can occur.

Contrary to cases involving patent infringement, where the infringing activity usually involves the making, using or selling of the patented invention, and thus may not occur in the course of the insured's advertising activities (see, e.g., Iolab Corp. v. Seaboard Sur. Co. (9th Cir.1994) 15 F.3d 1500, 1506; National Union Fire Ins. Co. v. Siliconix, Inc. (N.D.Cal.1989) 729 F.Supp. 77, 79), a trademark infringement by the insured can and often does occur in the course of the insured's act of advertising its products. Thus, we do not have the problem, presented in other circumstances (see e.g., Bank of the West v. Superior Court (1992) 2 Cal.4th 1254, 1275, 10 Cal.Rptr.2d 538, 833 P.2d 545), of determining whether a nexus exists between the insured's advertising activity and the alleged infringement. We will, at least for the purposes of this opinion, accept as true the proposition that Lebas' alleged trademark infringement occurred in the course of its advertising activities and that the required nexus existed. However, that still requires us to resolve the question as to whether Lebas's infringing acts constituted an "advertising injury" as defined in the Hartford policy.

4. Trademark Infringement Is Covered By Hartford's "Advertising Injury" Policy Provisions.

Prior to 1986, coverage for advertising injury was defined differently than it is under Hartford's policy. The 1973 standard Insurance Services Office ("ISO") form defined "advertising injury" to include: "Injury arising out of an offense committed during the policy period occurring in the course of the named insured's advertising activities, if such injury arises out of libel, slander, defamation, violation of right of privacy, piracy, unfair competition, or infringement of copyright, title or slogan." (Italics added.) Coverage for trademark infringement was expressly excluded.

In 1986, this definition was modified significantly. Advertising injury is now defined under the relevant portion of Hartford's policy as an injury arising from either (1) "misappropriation of an advertising idea or style of doing business" or (2) "infringement of copyright, title or slogan." The offenses of unfair competition and piracy have been deleted, as has the exclusion for trademark infringement. While the fact of these changes is consistent with the proposition that a potential for coverage of a claimed trademark infringement might now exist, it is hardly determinative. The terms "misappropriation," "advertising idea" and "style of doing business" are not defined.

Lebas relies on such lack of definition to argue that the terms are ambiguous and that they should therefore be construed in its favor because its expectation of a defense was objectively reasonable. Hartford, on the other hand, contends that the term "misappropriation," as used in the policy, refers only to the common law tort and not to federal statutory trademark protection. It further contends that the misappropriation of an "advertising idea" which is covered by the policy is limited to the circumstance where one party is presented with an idea or plan for an advertising campaign or promotion by another, who has a protectable property interest in that idea, and the first party uses the idea without compensation to its creator. Similarly, Hartford argues that misappropriation of a "style of doing business," as that term is used in its policy, refers solely to a company's manner of operating its business or, to put it simply, its "trade dress." (See, e.g., St. Paul Fire & Marine v. Advanced Interventional (E.D.Va.1993) 824 F.Supp. 583, 585, affd. (1994) 21 F.3d 424 [applying California substantive law to conclude that a patent infringement did not amount to the misappropriation of a "style of doing business"].)

It is settled that the absence from the policy of a definition of particular terms does not necessarily establish that such terms are ambiguous (Bay Cities Paving & Grading Inc. v. Lawyers' Mutual Ins. Co. (1993) 5 Cal.4th 854, 866, 21 Cal.Rptr.2d 691, 855 P.2d 1263); however, that circumstance can certainly lead to the kind of dispute which is now before us. It is also clear that we are required, in interpreting a policy, to read the disputed terms as " 'a layman would read [them] and not as [they] might be analyzed by an attorney or an insurance expert.' [Citation.]" (Delgado v. Heritage Life Ins. Co. (1984) 157 Cal.App.3d 262, 271, 203 Cal.Rptr. 672; see also Lunsford v. American Guarantee & Liability Ins. Co. (9th Cir.1994) 18 F.3d 653, 655; American Star Ins. Co. v. Insurance Co. of the West (1991) 232 Cal. App.3d 1320, 1330–1331, 284 Cal.Rptr. 45; Cal–Farm Ins. Co. v. TAC Exterminators, Inc. (1985) 172 Cal.App.3d 564, 578, 218 Cal.Rptr. 407.) As we now explain, applying this principle, as well as settled rules of policy construction, causes us to conclude that these terms are indeed ambiguous .....

What this requires us to do first is to try and determine the parties' mutual intention solely from the words used. As there is no evidence that the parties intended any technical or special meaning for the relevant policy provisions, we must examine the words used in "their ordinary or popular sense." (AIU Ins. Co. v. Superior Court (1990) 51 Cal.3d 807, 822, 274 Cal.Rptr. 820, 799 P.2d 1253.) If two or more constructions of a word or phrase are reasonable, then an ambiguity exists. (Bay Cities Paving & Grading Inc. v. Lawyers' Mutual Ins. Co., supra, 5 Cal.4th at p. 867, 21 Cal.Rptr.2d 691, 855 P.2d 1263.) While we cannot adopt a strained construction of any term in order to create an ambiguity and we must read the policy language in the context of the instrument as a whole (ibid.), we cannot but conclude, after applying these well settled principles of policy construction, that Lebas is correct in its assertion that the policy terms "misappropriation," "advertising idea" and "style of doing business" do not have a single, plain and clear meaning. Hartford insists that the ordinary and popular usage of the terms "misappropriation," "advertising idea" and "style of doing business" suggests only one meaning, thus precluding a conclusion of ambiguity. We disagree. Although general dictionary definitions of the relevant policy terms would reflect many popular meanings, any one of which might be reasonable in the abstract, we recognize that discovery of an ambiguity is not a matter of "abstract philology." (Bank of the West v. Superior Court, supra, 2 Cal.4th at p. 1265, 10 Cal.Rptr.2d 538, 833 P.2d 545.) We must evaluate and apply the ordinary and popular sense of the words in the context of their use in the policy.

Thus, we look at these words not in isolation but rather as part of the disjunctive phrases which are actually used in the policy: "misappropriation of an advertising idea" and "[misappropriation] of [a] style of doing business." We also examine these phrases through the eyes of a layman rather than an attorney or insurance expert. Using that approach, we inquire whether those phrases have a single "clear and explicit" meaning or are they subject to two or more reasonable constructions which can be placed on them without engaging in a strained interpretation. (Shell Oil Co. v. Winterthur Swiss Ins. Co. (1993) 12 Cal.App.4th 715, 737, 15 Cal.Rptr.2d 815.)

As already noted, Hartford contends that the term misappropriation has a single plain and clear meaning which can only refer to the common law tort of misappropriation. Hartford primarily relies on the now vacated and superseded (sub. opn. [N.D.Cal.1994] 900 F.Supp. 1246) decision in American Economy Ins. Co. v. Reboans, Inc. (N.D.Cal.1994) 852 F.Supp. 875 ("Reboans I"), where the court first noted that common law misappropriation has three elements, none of which involves the confusion of source element required for a trademark infringement claim. Those three elements are: (1) the plaintiff "has made a substantial investment of time, effort and money into creating the thing misappropriated such that the court can characterize that 'thing' as a kind of property right," (2) the defendant "has appropriated the 'thing' at little or no cost, such that the court can characterize defendant's actions as 'reaping where it has not sown' " and (3) the defendant "has injured plaintiff by the misappropriation." (Id. at p. 879, citing J. Thomas McCarthy, McCarthy on Trademarks and Unfair Competition (3d ed.1992) § 10.25.)

In Reboans I, the court went on to state that while a viable trademark infringement claim depends upon a showing of consumer confusion, "Common law misappropriation is different. Its sole purpose is to create quasi-property rights, and Congress has stated that a person has a property right in a word or style—things that would otherwise be subject to a First Amendment challenge—only if the word or style is distinctive and another's use of it would likely cause consumer confusion. 'If there can be such a thing as "misappropriation" of another's trademark, irrespective of distinctiveness and likelihood of buyer confusion, then a big step has been taken to wipe out the law of trademarks.' [Citations.] Recognizing a property right in an advertising idea or style of doing business that would not be protected under the Lanham Act would undermine the 'purposes and objectives of Congress.' [Citations.] Accordingly, it cannot be done." (Id. at pp. 880–881.) The court then concluded, "Until 1986, the standard ISO CGL form included 'unfair competition' as a covered class of advertising injuries, and explicitly excluded injuries resulting from trademark, service mark, and trade name infringement. In 1986, ISO revised the standard form: unfair competition was eliminated in favor of misappropriation of advertising ideas and style of doing business, and the trademark, service mark and tradename exclusion was eliminated. As [the insurer points out], the trademark infringement exclusion had been necessary when the policy insured unfair competition claims, because 'unfair competition' includes counterfeiting and trademark infringement. After unfair competition was replaced with misappropriation of advertising ideas and style of doing business, however, the exclusion was redundant, because one could not misappropriate a trademark." (Reboans I, supra, 852 F.Supp. at p. 882.) Hartford presses this same argument here.

In our view, however, it is equally reasonable, for example, to ascribe to the term misappropriation the more general meaning of "to take wrongfully" as it is to limit it to its technical common law sense. (See, e.g., Dogloo, Inc. v. Northern Ins. Co. of New York (C.D.Cal.1995) 907 F.Supp. 1383, 1388–1389.) Similarly, while the misappropriation of an "advertising idea" certainly would include the theft of an advertising plan from its creator without payment, it is also reasonable to apply it to wrongful taking of the manner or means by which another advertises its goods or services. As we have already explained, one of the basic functions of a trademark is to advertise the product or services of the registrant. For the same reason, a trademark could reasonably be considered an integral part of an entity's "style of doing business." One need look no further than today's current crop of expensive television commercials advertising high fashion jeans, heavily endorsed athletic shoes or distinctively styled fast food restaurants to know the truth of that statement.

Given these multiple reasonable meanings and connotations which may be given to the new policy language defining one of the advertising injury offenses, we conclude that an ambiguity exists. Applying the analytical approach outlined in Bank of the West, we must next attempt to resolve that ambiguity by interpreting the language used in the sense in which Hartford believed that Lebas must have understood it at the time of policy issuance; or, to put it another way, we must look to the objectively reasonable expectations of Lebas. We do this by examining the language in the context of its apparently intended function in the policy and with due consideration to the circumstances in this case. (Bank of the West v. Superior Court, supra, 2 Cal.4th at p. 1265, 10 Cal.Rptr.2d 538, 833 P.2d 545.)

The policy expressly provides coverage for advertising injury claims. While it is true that the language we consider was adopted contemporaneously with the deletion of the offense of "unfair competition," it does not follow that trademark infringement was likewise eliminated as a covered act.[84] Trademark infringement is an act of unfair competition

84. We recognize that drafting history documents may provide some evidence of a contrary intent on the part of those responsible for drafting the 1986 ISO policy changes. However, whatever use may properly be made of drafting history (see e.g., Montrose Chemical Corp. v. Admiral Ins. Co. (1995) 10 Cal.4th 645, 673, 42 Cal. Rptr.2d 324, 913 P.2d 878), it may not be considered to defeat an insured's objectively reasonable expectations of coverage arising from the policy language utilized by the insurance industry draftsmen. (See, e.g., American Star Ins. Co. v. Insurance Co. of the West, supra, 232 Cal.App.3d at pp. 1330–1332, fns. 8 and 9, 284 Cal.Rptr. 45; see also Prudential–LMI Commercial Ins. Co. v. Reliance Ins. Co. (1994) 22 Cal. App.4th 1508, 1513, 27 Cal.Rptr.2d 841.) Those draftsmen had it within their power to make clear the full scope of the coverage offered as well as any limitations they wished to place thereon. Their failure to do so cannot justify our rejection of an insured's objectively reasonable expectations as to coverage which arise from the words chosen by the drafters. (Union Insurance Co. v. The Knife Co., Inc. (W.D.Ark.1995) 897 F.Supp. 1213, 1216.)

(Curtis–Universal v. Sheboygan E.M.S., Inc. (7th Cir.1994) 43 F.3d 1119, 1124 ["The traditional trademark infringer gets sales unfairly from a competitor by leading consumers to think that the infringer's product or service is of higher quality than it is."]); it amounts to the wrongful taking of another's identifying mark. In other words, trademark infringement involves a very specific kind of unfair competition.

Hartford's contention that the phrase "misappropriation of an advertising idea or style of doing business" is necessarily limited to a common law tort, which excludes a claim for trademark infringement, depends upon an unreasonably narrow construction of the single word, "misappropriation." But even if examined in isolation, as the court stated in Reboans I, supra, 852 F.Supp. 875, the three elements of the common law tort of misappropriation require that: (1) a plaintiff must have "invested substantial time and money" in developing a property, (2) the defendant must have appropriated the property at little or no cost, and (3) the plaintiff was injured by the defendant's conduct. (Id. at p. 879; see also, Balboa Ins. Co. v. Trans Global Equities (1990) 218 Cal.App.3d 1327, 1342, 267 Cal.Rptr. 787, cert. denied, sub nom., Collateral Protection Ins. Services v. Balboa Ins. Co. (1990) 498 U.S. 940, 111 S.Ct. 347, 112 L.Ed.2d 311.) A trademark infringement would arguably include all of these elements, but also would require a showing which satisfied the additional statutory elements of a trademark claim including evidence that the unauthorized use was "likely to cause confusion, or to cause mistake, or to deceive." (15 U.S.C. § 1114.) This additional element, necessary to the assertion of the statutory claim, does not preclude the conclusion that a wrongful taking has occurred. If, as we have already concluded, a trademark could reasonably be considered to be part of an advertising idea or a style of doing business, then certainly the objectively reasonable expectations of Lebas could have included the possibility that a trademark infringement was covered. In other words, contrary to Hartford's argument, "misappropriation of an advertising idea or style of doing business" and trademark infringement are not mutually exclusive....

It appears to us, reading the policy as a layman would, that an objectively reasonable purpose of the phrase "misappropriation" of either an "advertising idea" or a "style of doing business" is an attempt to restrict or more narrowly focus the broader coverage potentially encompassed by the general term, "unfair competition" which was utilized in the earlier policy language. When read in light of the fact that a trademark infringement could reasonably be considered as one example of a misappropriation, and taking into account that a trademark could reasonably be considered to be part of either an advertising idea or a style of doing business, it would appear objectively reasonable that "advertising injury" coverage could now extend to the infringement of a trademark.

In addition, it is not obvious that elimination of the trademark infringement exclusion was because it was no longer needed in light of the deletion of unfair competition as a covered offense. In the mind's eye of an objectively reasonable insured, that elimination could well represent a conscious recognition of trademark infringement as an offense subject to advertising injury coverage. Indeed, the fact that the trademark exclusion was dropped from the policy could contribute to the objectively reasonable expectation that a trademark infringement was now a covered act under the advertising injury clause. Such a result is entirely consistent with a significant number of federal cases which have decided, albeit without much analysis, that a trademark is both an "advertising idea" and a "style of doing business" and its misappropriation is an advertising injury offense. (Dogloo Inc. v. Northern Ins. Co. of New York, supra, 907 F.Supp. at pp. 1389–1390;) Union Ins. Co. v. The Knife Co., Inc., supra, 897 F.Supp. at p. 1216; Poof Toy Products, Inc. v. U.S. Fid. & Guar. Co. (E.D.Mich.1995) 891 F.Supp. 1228, 1234; Advance Watch Co., Ltd. v. Kemper Nat. Ins. Co. (E.D.Mich.1995) 878 F.Supp. 1034, 1039; P.J. Noyes Co. v. American Motorists Ins. Co. (D.N.H.1994) 855 F.Supp. 492, 494–495; J.A. Brundage [50 Cal.App.4th 567] Plumbing v. Massachusetts Bay Ins. (W.D.N.Y.1993) 818 F.Supp. 553, 557, vacated after settlement, 153 F.R.D. 36, 38 (W.D.N.Y.1994.)

We therefore conclude that the allegations of Guy Laroche's complaint charging Lebas with trademark infringement were sufficient to charge the commission of an act potentially covered under the policy. This was enough to establish Hartford's duty to provide Lebas with a defense to the underlying federal action. It was thus error for the trial court to enter summary judgment in Hartford's favor.

DISPOSITION

The judgment is reversed. The matter is remanded for further proceedings consistent with the views expressed herein. Lebas shall recover its costs on appeal.

KLEIN, P.J., AND KITCHING, J., concur.

(c) Patent Infringement

Coverage for patents is less common, and may very well depend on whether the CGL policy at issue is pre– or post–1986. Prior to 1986, CGL policies defined "advertising injury" as

> injury arising out of an offense committed during the policy period occurring in the course of the named insured's advertising activities, if the injury arises out of libel, slander, defamation, violation of right of privacy, piracy, unfair competition or infringement of copyright, title or slogan.

In 1986, the advertising clause was revised, and coverage for unfair competition and piracy was eliminated. Also, the term defamation received more specific explanation. The new language reads:

> This insurance applies to: "advertising injury" caused by an offense committed in the course of advertising your goods, products or services.... "Advertising injury" means injury arising out of one or more of the following offenses: Oral or written publication of material that slanders or libels a person or organization or disparages a person's or organization's goods, products or services oral or written publication of material that violates a person's right of privacy misappropriation of advertising ideas or style of doing business or infringement of copyright, title or slogan.

The cases that follow illustrate the importance of the currently omitted terms "piracy" and "unfair competition."

AETNA CASUALTY & SURETY CO. v. SUPERIOR COURT

Court of Appeal of California, Fourth Appellate District, Division Three, 1993.
19 Cal.App.4th 320, 23 Cal.Rptr.2d 442.

MOORE, ASSOCIATE JUSTICE.

The primary issue in this case is whether a standard comprehensive general liability policy (CGL) which includes coverage for "advertising injury" potentially affords coverage for inducing or contributing to patent infringement so as to trigger an insurer's duty to defend.

FACTS AND PROCEDURAL BACKGROUND

Aetna Casualty and Surety Company and Industrial Indemnity Company issued standard CGL policies to Watercloud Bed Co., Inc. and its President, Richard LaBianco (collectively Watercloud). The policies provide the insurers will pay "all sums which the insured shall become legally obligated to pay as damages because of ... advertising injury to which this policy applies ... and the company shall have the right and duty to defend any suit against the insured seeking damages on account of such injury." Advertising injury is defined as "injury arising out of an offense committed during the policy period occurring in the course of the named insured's advertising activities, if such injury arises out of libel, slander, defamation, violation of the right of privacy, piracy, unfair competition, or infringement of copyright title or slogan." In Bank of the West v. Superior Court (1992) 2 Cal.4th 1254, 10 Cal.Rptr.2d 538, 833 P.2d 545 (hereafter Bank of the West), our Supreme Court interpreted this standard language to cover only injuries caused by an advertisement. (Id. at p. 1263, 10 Cal.Rptr.2d 538, 833 P.2d 545; see also Chatton v. National Union Fire Ins. Co. (1992) 10 Cal.App.4th 846, 863, 13 Cal.Rptr.2d 318; Standard Fire Ins. Co. v. Peoples Church of Fresno (9th Cir.1993) 985 F.2d 446, 449.)

In April 1987, Somma Mattress Company sued Watercloud in federal court. Somma contended it had patented a water mattress and that Watercloud had sought a license under the patent to manufacture and sell such mattresses. When Somma denied the request, "Watercloud began to manufacture, use, offer for sale and sell ... , in direct competition with Somma, copies of Somma's patented mattress...." Somma's complaint alleged Watercloud "infringed and ... actively induced ... others to infringe, and ... contributed to ... the infringement of [Somma's] patent ... by manufacturing, using and selling, without authority or license ..., products which infringe [the] patent.... " The infringements were alleged to have been "willful and deliberate, and with full knowledge of [Somma's] patent...." The complaint alleged Watercloud's actions were in violation of the United States patent laws. (35 U.S.C. § 271.) No cause of action or theory was asserted for unfair competition or under any state law theory of recovery.

Watercloud tendered defense of the lawsuit to Aetna and Industrial Indemnity. Aetna sent Watercloud a letter agreeing to defend, but reserving its rights to deny coverage, to refuse to pay for the defense, and to seek reimbursement in the event it was determined that its policy did not cover Watercloud's liability. Initially, Industrial Indemnity denied coverage, but later it agreed to defend and indemnify Watercloud for any damages incurred for slander of title, but reserved all of its rights under the policy.

Ultimately, both Aetna and Industrial Indemnity concluded no defense was owed under their policies. In March 1988, Industrial Indemnity withdrew its defense.

The Somma action was settled without payment of money or a judgment being entered. Nevertheless, Watercloud brought the present action in state court against Aetna and Industrial Indemnity, asserting causes of action for breach of the implied covenant of good faith and fair dealing, breach of contract, intentional and negligent infliction of emotional distress, and breach of fiduciary duty, and seeking a declaration that Aetna and Industrial Indemnity were liable to indemnify Watercloud for the total amount of the fees billed by Watercloud's attorneys.

Watercloud filed motions for summary adjudication against the insurers on the duty to defend. When the motions were ultimately heard, the trial court held that direct infringement of a patent was not covered under the subject policies and any other basis for liability against Watercloud would require proof that it knowingly and intentionally induced the infringement. Nevertheless, the court found there was the potential for coverage and therefore a duty to defend triggered by Somma's claim for inducing infringement and for contributory infringement because "the allegations in the Somma action trigger the possibility or potential for liability...."

In March 1992, the insurers filed petitions for writs of mandate which were denied by this court. Thereafter, the Supreme Court granted the insurers' petitions for review, then transferred the matter to this court with directions to hear them. Accordingly, this court issued an alternative writ of mandate. We now consider the matter in light of Bank of the West.

DISCUSSION

In Bank of the West, the Supreme Court considered the scope of coverage afforded by standard CGL policy language and held that a CGL does not cover claims for advertising injury arising under the Unfair Business Practices Act. (Bus. & Prof.Code, § 17200 et seq.) The court noted that CGL policies generally include coverage for " 'advertising injury' which applies to 'damages' the insured must pay for injury arising out of 'unfair competition' occurring in the course of the insured's 'advertising activities.' " (Bank of the West, supra, 2 Cal.4th at p. 1258, 10 Cal.Rptr.2d 538, 833 P.2d 545.)

The duty to defend is of course much broader than the duty to indemnify, and an insurer must defend a case which potentially seeks damages within the coverage of the policy. (Gray v. Zurich Ins. Co. (1966) 65 Cal.2d 263, 275, 54 Cal.Rptr. 104, 419 P.2d 168.) However, if there is no potential liability for covered damages as a matter of law, there cannot be the potential for indemnification, nor can there be a duty to defend. (See, e.g., Royal Globe Ins. Co. v. Whitaker (1986) 181 Cal.App.3d 532, 537, 226 Cal.Rptr. 435; see also Safeco Ins. Co. of America v. Andrews (9th Cir.1990) 915 F.2d 500, 502; Allstate Ins. Co. v. Miller (N.D.Cal.1990) 743 F.Supp. 723, 729.) Here, the patent infringement allegations against Watercloud create no potential recovery of covered damages because the alleged infringement could not occur "in the course of the named insured's advertising activities." (National Union Fire Ins. Co. v. Siliconix, Inc. (N.D.Cal.1989) 729 F.Supp. 77, 79; see also Bank of the West, supra, 2 Cal.4th at p. 1275, 10 Cal.Rptr.2d 538, 833 P.2d 545.)

The trial court held that unfair competition could include inducing patent infringement. That holding was before Bank of the West, supra, 2 Cal.4th 1254, 10 Cal.Rptr.2d 538, 833 P.2d 545, in which the Supreme Court held that the language used in the policies referred to the common law tort of unfair competition. That tort refers to the passing off of one's goods as those of another. (Id. at p. 1263, 10 Cal.Rptr.2d 538, 833 P.2d 545; see also Chatton v. National Union Fire Ins. Co., supra, 10 Cal. App.4th at p. 863, 13 Cal.Rptr.2d 318; Standard Fire Ins. Co. v. Peoples Church of Fresno, supra, 985 F.2d at p. 449.)

Watercloud argues there is evidence that it was passing off its goods as being those of Somma. Not so. The sole example of such "evidence" is a brief passage from the deposition testimony of Somma's president, who testified a Somma customer told him another retailer had sold a mattress and wrote "Somma mattress" on a sale's receipt. Even if that were true, it would not provide a basis for coverage. The CGLs cover only unfair competition occurring in connection with Watercloud's advertising activity, not that of another retailer. Moreover, in connection with its own advertising activity, the evidence indicated that far from passing off its goods as those of Somma, Watercloud touted itself as "the flotation industry's pioneer in the engineering of soft-sided waterbeds" and stated it had created "a new way of sleeping" and "we are proud to put the

Watercloud name upon it." Thus, there was no basis for coverage under the unfair competition clause.

Patent infringement is a separate and distinct area of the law. The grant of a patent is the grant of a statutory monopoly and is an express exception to laws prohibiting monopolies. (Sears, Roebuck & Co. v. Stiffel Co. (1964) 376 U.S. 225, 229, 84 S.Ct. 784, 788–789, 11 L.Ed.2d 661.) Patent infringement therefore concerns the unauthorized manufacture, use or sale of a device or process containing an invention reserved exclusively to the patent holder. (35 U.S.C. § 271(a); see also 4 Chisum, Patents, (1991) § 1.04(6), § 10.1 et seq.)

One who makes, uses or sells a product incorporating a patented invention is guilty of direct patent infringement. (35 U.S.C. § 271(a).) One who aids or abets infringement of a patent by intentionally inducing infringement is as liable as a direct infringer. (35 U.S.C. § 271(b); see also 4 Chisum, Patents, supra, § 17.04(1).)

Patent infringement cannot be committed in the course of advertising activities. (Bank of the West, supra, 2 Cal.4th at p. 1277, 10 Cal.Rptr.2d 538, 833 P.2d 545; see also National Union Fire Ins. Co. v. Siliconix Inc., supra, 729 F.Supp. at p. 80.) The patentee is not injured because a product incorporating its invention is advertised, but because the infringer, without consent, used or sold a product utilizing a protected invention. Accordingly, patent infringement cannot be covered under the subject policies.

Watercloud contends, however, that aiding and abetting a third party's patent infringement can be covered. We disagree. A direct infringer—one who makes, uses or sells another's patent invention—cannot be liable for inducing or contributing to patent infringement. (See Self v. Fisher Controls Co., Inc. (9th Cir.1977) 566 F.2d 62, 64, hereafter Self.) In Aro Mfg. Co. v. Convertible Top Replacement Co. (1961) 365 U.S. 336, 81 S.Ct. 599, 5 L.Ed.2d 592, the United States Supreme Court held that under 35 United States Code section 271(c) there could be no contributory infringement in the absence of direct infringement. (Id. at pp. 341–342, 81 S.Ct. at pp. 602–603.)

With the enactment of the Patent Act of 1952, the concept of contributory infringement was divided between "active inducement" and "contributory inducement." (35 U.S.C. § 271(b), (c); see also Hewlett–Packard Co. v. Bausch & Lomb Inc. (Fed.Cir.1990) 909 F.2d 1464 at p. 1469.) However, the legislative history indicates no change in the scope of what constituted "contributory infringement" was intended by the enactment of the Act. (Aro Mfg. Co. v. Convertible Top Replacement Co. (1964) 377 U.S. 476, 485–486, 84 S.Ct. 1526, 1531–1532, 12 L.Ed.2d 457.) Thus, contributory infringement will not lie against one who is a direct infringer.

As stated in Self, supra, 566 F.2d at p. 64, the doctrine of contributory infringement is "limited to situations where defendant itself has not directly infringed the patent by making, using, or selling the invention, ... but has induced someone else to infringe the patent." (Emphasis added; see also MAGICorp. v. Kinetic Presentations, Inc. (D.N.J.1989) 718 F.Supp. 334, 346, fn. 8; Picker Intern., Inc. v. Varian Associates Inc. (N.D.Ohio 1987) 661 F.Supp. 347, 350.) Thus, a patent infringement plaintiff can recover from a direct infringer for all damages caused by the infringing product, including damages caused by a purchaser's use of the product, but the defendant may not be required to pay additional sums as a result of allegedly inducing others to infringe. (Aro Mfg. Co. v. Convertible Top Replacement Co. (1964) 377 U.S. 476, 508, 84 S.Ct. 1526, 1543, 12 L.Ed.2d 457.)

Here, it is undisputed that Watercloud made and sold the products it is accused of infringing. Its alleged inducement to infringe or contributory infringement is, therefore, merely a part of the direct infringement for which it would be liable because of its manufacturing and sale of the product. As a result, if it is found liable at all, Watercloud would be liable for direct infringement, not for inducing infringement or contributory infringement. (Self, supra, 566 F.2d at p. 64; Aro Mfg. Co. v. Convertible Top Replacement Co., supra, 365 U.S. 336, 341–342, 81 S.Ct. 599, 602–603.) Inasmuch as there is no potential liability on the allegation of inducement of infringement or contributory infringement, there is no potential recovery of covered damages and therefore no duty to defend. (See B & E Convalescent Center v. State Compensation Ins. Fund (1992) 8 Cal.App.4th 78, 100, 9 Cal.Rptr.2d 894; Safeco Ins. Co. of America v. Andrews (9th Cir.1990) 915 F.2d 500, 501–502.)

Watercloud contends it could be found to have induced infringement because it "also separately sold water mattresses without any bladder, but [19 Cal.App.4th 330] included instructions and advertisements on how to insert any of the available bladders into the mattress for proper use including the tube or cylinder bladders to which Somma claimed a patent. These materials taught a retailer or consumer how to set up a Watercloud soft-sided mattress with a tube-style bladder.... Only when Watercloud's mattress was combined with tube bladders did Somma contend that it was infringing. Thus, without instructions or advertisements directing the use of tube bladders, sale of the Watercloud mattress would not infringe Somma's patent. Therefore, Watercloud's advertising and instructions are claimed to be the operative fact that induced these retailers and consumers to infringe Somma's patent." There is no citation to the record to support this assertion. Small wonder, since there were no facts or evidence adduced below to substantiate this contention. Furthermore, the Somma complaint alleges it was a codefendant, American National Watermattress Corp., not Watercloud, that sold the individual water cylinders.

In addition, even if Watercloud could be liable for inducement of the patent infringement, there would still be no duty to defend. It is against public policy for an insurer to provide coverage for willful conduct. (See Tomerlin v. Canadian Indemnity Co. (1964) 61 Cal.2d 638, 648, 39 Cal.Rptr. 731, 394 P.2d 571; see also Civ.Code, § 1668.) California Insurance Code section 533 provides, in pertinent part: "An insurer is not liable for a loss caused by the willful act of the insured...." The purpose of these statutory proscriptions is to discourage the commission of willful conduct by withholding insurance coverage for the conduct. (See J.C. Penney Casualty Ins. Co. v. M.K. (1991) 52 Cal.3d 1009, 1021, 278 Cal.Rptr. 64, 804 P.2d 689; Tomerlin v. Canadian Indemnity Co., supra, 61 Cal.2d at p. 648, 39 Cal.Rptr. 731, 394 P.2d 571.)

To be liable for inducing infringement, a party must have the specific intent to induce another to infringe. (Manville Sales Corp. v. Paramount Sys., Inc. (Fed.Cir.1990) 917 F.2d 544, 553.) Accordingly, it must be shown "the defendant possessed specific intent to encourage another's infringement and not merely that the defendant had knowledge of the acts alleged to constitute inducement." (Id. at p. 553, emphasis added.)

In Clemmer v. Hartford Ins. Co. (1978) 22 Cal.3d 865, 151 Cal.Rptr. 285, 587 P.2d 1098, the Supreme Court addressed what constitutes a "willful act" under Insurance Code section 533, and held that "even an act which is 'intentional' or 'willful' within the meaning of traditional tort principles will not exonerate the insurer from liability under Insurance Code section 533 unless it is done with a 'preconceived design to inflict injury.' " (Id. at p. 887, 151 Cal.Rptr. 285, 587 P.2d 1098.) Recently, in J.C. Penney Casualty Ins. Co. v. M.K., supra, 52 Cal.3d 1009, 278 Cal.Rptr. 64, 804 P.2d 689, the court clarified that "Clemmer does [19 Cal.App.4th 331] not require a showing by the insurer of its insured's 'preconceived design to inflict harm' when the insured seeks coverage for an intentional and wrongful act if the harm is inherent in the act itself." (Id. at p. 1025, 278 Cal.Rptr. 64, 804 P.2d 689, emphasis added.) After being denied a license to manufacture and sell the patented water mattresses, Watercloud began to manufacture, use, and sell copies of Somma's mattresses. Such acts are inherently harmful.

It is not necessary to analyze the subjective intent of the insured where the act itself is wrongful. (State Farm Fire & Cas. Co. v. Ezrin (N.D.Cal.1991) 764 F.Supp. 153, 156.) Rather, the insured's motive "is relevant only to the issue of whether his conduct was wrongful in the first instance." (Fire Ins. Exchange v. Altieri (1991) 235 Cal.App.3d 1352, 1359, 1 Cal.Rptr.2d 360; accord B & E Convalescent Center v. State Compensation Ins. Fund, supra, 8 Cal.App.4th at p. 96, 9 Cal. Rptr.2d 894.) Thus, the question is not whether the insured subjectively intended to cause harm, but whether the conduct was intentional and inherently harmful.

Case law is clear that an act that is not inherently harmful in the abstract may nevertheless be so if the insured is aware of the potential harm. So, in Aetna Cas. & Sur. Co. v. Sheft (C.D.Cal.1990) 756 F.Supp. 449, the plaintiff alleged the insured had engaged in high-risk sex while intentionally concealing the fact that he had AIDS. (Id. at p. 451.) The court focused on the wrongfulness of the act rather than the intent to harm, and held the insured's acts were willful under Insurance Code section 533. (Id. at p. 451.) By contrast, in State Farm Fire & Cas. Co. v. Eddy (1990) 218 Cal.App.3d 958, 267 Cal.Rptr. 379, the court held that transmission of herpes was not willful because the insured believed he did not have the disease. (Id. at pp. 969–972, 267 Cal.Rptr. 379.) In both cases there was intentional sexual activity which led to the transmission of a disease. The only difference was that in Sheft the insured knew he had the disease, while in Eddy the insured did not know. The act itself was intentional in both cases, but Insurance Code section 533 applied only in Sheft, where the insured was aware of the harm inherent in the act.

Liability for inducing patent infringement can only be imposed where the defendant "knowingly" induced the infringement. As a result, any acts by Watercloud for which inducement liability could be imposed would have to be intentionally performed with knowledge of their harmful nature. Coverage for such damages is barred by Insurance Code section 533 and Civil Code section 1668. Because as a matter of law there is no potential for recovery of covered damages for inducement of infringement in the absence of a showing that the insured acted with specific intent to induce the infringement, there is no potential for coverage in this case and therefore no duty to defend.

Watercloud argues Insurance Code section 533 does not apply. It cites 35 U.S.C. section 284, which provides for the enhancement of damages, and argues that section presupposes that an infringing act can be committed in a manner which is not willful. However, that section merely provides the court with the discretion to award treble damages if necessary to adequately compensate the plaintiff for the infringement.

Watercloud seeks to rely on Westvaco Corp. v. International Paper Co. (Fed.Cir.1993) 991 F.2d 735 and Minnesota Mining and Mfg. v. Johnson & Johnson Orthopaedics, Inc. (Fed.Cir.1992) 976 F.2d 1559 for the proposition that not all infringements are willful and that reliance upon advice of counsel can militate against a finding of willfulness. However, those cases are inapposite inasmuch as both dealt with the question of willfulness in the context of the propriety of assessing treble damages. (35 U.S.C. § 284.) Advice of counsel may be a relevant factor for the court to consider on the issue of whether to impose treble damages. (See, e.g., Wilden Pump & Engineering Co. v. Pressed & Welded Products Co. (9th Cir.1981) 655 F.2d 984.) However, to be liable for inducing infringement, the party must have the specific intent to induce another to infringe. (Manville Sales Corp. v. Paramount Sys., Inc., supra, 917 F.2d at p. 553.) . . . .

Here, however, because the gravamen of Somma's action is that Watercloud either directly infringed the patent or intentionally induced infringement, there can be no potential for coverage and therefore no duty to defend.

DISPOSITION

Let a preemptory writ of mandate issue directing the respondent superior court to set aside and vacate its order granting real parties' motion for summary adjudication of the duty to defend issue.

SILLS, P.J., and SONENSHINE, J., concur.

Notes

1. A difficulty with these cases is that state courts have little experience with patent law.

2. Note that the court finds conduct sufficient to preclude not only indemnity but also defense under Cal. Insurance Code § 533. Is this approach consistent with *Gray v. Zurich*? The holding of *Aetna Casualty* was affirmed in *Mez Industries, Inc. v. Pacific National Ins. Co.*, 76 Cal.App.4th, 856, 90 Cal.Rptr.2d 721 (1999). While *Mez* holds that patent infringement is not covered in the post–1986 CGL policy, it also suggests that patent infringement itself requires specific intent and thus is barred from coverage.

IOLAB CORP. v. SEABOARD SURETY CO.

United States Court of Appeals, Ninth Circuit, 1994.
15 F.3d 1500.

D.W. Nelson, Circuit Judge:

* * *

Factual and Procedural Background

Iolab is a wholly owned subsidiary of Johnson & Johnson. From 1980 to 1990, Iolab manufactured and sold an intraocular lens designed to replace the natural lens. In 1986 Dr. Ronald P. Jensen, who owned the patent for the optical device, brought suit against Iolab alleging that Iolab was infringing his patent. The trial was bifurcated between liability and damages. In August of 1990, the district court for the Central District of California found Iolab liable for patent infringement. See Jensen v. Iolab Corp., CV–86–4384 (C.D. Cal. 1990). Although at that time the Jensen court did not determine the amount of the damages, it held that the measure of damages should be a reasonable royalty, estimated at 3.5%, of Iolab's net sales for the period from 1980 to the date of the judgment in 1990, and that, with the addition of a penalty, Iolab should pay a total of one and one-half times the sum of the royalties. According to Iolab, based on the district court's measure of damages, Iolab would have had to pay in excess of $33 million to Jensen.

Before reaching the damages portion of the trial, however, Iolab raised the defense that, under 35 U.S.C. § 271(e)(1), Iolab was authorized to sell the patented product because its sales were "solely for uses reasonably related to the development and submission of information." 35 U.S.C. § 271(e)(1) (1988). In response to Iolab's section 271(e)(1) defense, Jensen argued that Iolab was not entitled to a section 271(e)(1) exemption because Iolab sold the intraocular lens for economic gain rather than for research and to obtain FDA approval. Jensen pointed to the extensive marketing techniques, including advertising, employed by Iolab to maximize sales as evidence that Iolab's motive for selling the patented product was financial, and contended that the sales thus did not fall within the section 271(e)(1) exemption. Subsequently, the parties settled and Iolab agreed to pay $13.5 million to Dr. Jensen. In the present action, Iolab seeks indemnification from its insurers for $13.5 million together with costs estimated at $1 million, a total of $14.5 million. Iolab contends that the Jensen loss is covered by clauses in the insurance policies (the "policies") providing coverage for piracy arising out of or committed in advertising.[85]

Iolab brought suit against fifteen insurance companies (collectively the "insurers"), four of which are primary insurers and eleven of which are excess insurers. Specifically, the primary insurers are Seaboard Surety Company, American Motorists Insurance Company, Lumbermens Mutual Casualty Company, and Employers Reinsurance Corporation; the excess insurers are National Union Fire Insurance Company, Granite State Insurance Company, Stonewall Insurance Company, North River Insurance Company, Insurance Company of North America, Republic Insurance Company, Allstate Insurance Company, Hartford Casualty Insurance Company, Twin City Fire Insurance Company, Lexington Insurance Company, and Employers Insurance of Wausau. Iolab's aggregate primary coverage between 1980 and 1990 amounted to $36 million; Seaboard provided eight years of coverage at $1 million per year, Employers Reinsurance provided three years of coverage at $1 million per year, American provided four years of coverage at $5 million per year, and Lumbermens provided one year of coverage at $5 million per year. The excess policies specifically provide that their liability does not attach until the underlying insurers have paid or have been held liable to pay.

The district court dismissed on the pleadings the actions against four insurers, dismissed a fifth based on the complaint alone, and granted summary judgment dismissing the remaining ten. Iolab appealed.

[The discussion of jurisdiction and the standard of review for summary judgment is omitted.]

DISCUSSION

The insurers raise several defenses in response to Iolab's claim against them. We limit our discussion to the two grounds on which we affirm. This is not to suggest, however, that other defenses raised by defendants-appellees may also have merit.

[The discussion finding the excess insurers not liable for coverage is omitted.]

85. The wording in the policies varies slightly. For example, the policy issued by Seaboard Surety Company provides in relevant part that it will indemnify the insured for "piracy, plagiarism, or unfair competition or idea misappropriation committed or ... arising out of the insured's advertising activities;" Lumbermens Mutual Casualty Company's policy provides coverage for damages caused by injuries "arising out of ... [piracy, unfair competition, idea misappropriation, plagiarism] ... committed ... in any advertisement."

B. THE PRIMARY INSURERS

The district court dismissed or granted summary judgment in favor of the primary insurers. We affirm the district court on the ground that the Jensen loss was not covered under the policies.

The provisions of the policies at issue provide coverage for piracy arising out of or committed in advertising.[86] Under California law, we must decide whether Iolab had a reasonable expectation that the policies, which promised indemnification for advertising injuries, provided coverage for the liability resulting from Iolab's infringement of Dr. Jensen's patent. See, e.g., AIU Ins. Co. v. Superior Court, 51 Cal.3d 807, 822, 274 Cal.Rptr. 820, 799 P.2d 1253 (1990). We conclude that Iolab's infringement of Dr. Jensen's patent was not an act of piracy arising out of or committed in advertising and thus was not covered by the policies.

In Bank of the West v. Superior Court, 2 Cal.4th 1254, 10 Cal. Rptr.2d 538, 833 P.2d 545 (1992), the California Supreme Court considered the scope of coverage afforded by insurance covering for liability arising out of advertising. In its decision, the court held that " 'advertising injury' must have a causal connection with the insured's 'advertising activities' before there can be coverage," Id. at 1277, 10 Cal.Rptr.2d 538, 833 P.2d 545. The Bank of The West court explained that "a claim of patent infringement does not 'occur in the course ... of advertising activities' within the meaning of the policy even though the insured advertises the infringing product, if the claim of infringement is based on the sale or importation of the product rather than its advertisement." Id. at 1275, 10 Cal.Rptr.2d 538, 833 P.2d 545 (citing National Union Fire Ins. Co. v. Siliconix Inc., 729 F.Supp. 77, 80 (N.D.Cal.1989)). Thus, under Bank of the West, unless Dr. Jensen's claim was that Iolab infringed his patent in its advertising, in a manner independent of its sale of the intraocular lens, the Jensen loss is not a form of piracy arising out of or committed in advertising and is not covered under the policies.

In Siliconix, the court held that "even if piracy is construed to encompass patent infringement, patent infringement does not occur in the course of advertising, and is not covered as a type of advertising injury." Siliconix, 729 F.Supp. at 80. According to the Siliconix court, patent infringement cannot constitute an advertising injury because,

86. Iolab argues that variations in wording in different policies provide a basis for distinguishing this case from Bank of the West v. The Superior Court of Contra Costa County, 2 Cal.4th 1254, 10 Cal. Rptr.2d 538, 833 P.2d 545 (1992), which our holding relies on. According to Iolab, a crucial difference between the policy involved in Bank of the West and the policies in the present case, is that none of the policies in question include the sentence "in the course of" or "advertising injury" but refer instead to offenses "arising out of advertising." We are not persuaded by Iolab's argument. We see no reason to distinguish the policies in question from the one considered in Bank of the West. We think that the Bank of the West court did not intend its holding to be limited to insurance policies that include the term "in the course of advertising injury" but rather to apply to a broader category of policies including the ones considered here. See Bank of the West, 2 Cal.4th at 1273–74, 10 Cal. Rptr.2d 538, 833 P.2d 545 ("[O]ther questions about the scope of coverage for 'advertising injury' continue to have substantial importance. For that reason we shall address, ... the parties' arguments about the requisite connection between 'advertising activities' and 'advertising injury.' ").

under 35 U.S.C. § 271, a patent is infringed by making, using or selling a patented invention, not by advertising it. Id. at 79. Similarly, the California Court of Appeals has recently held that "[p]atent infringement cannot be committed in the course of advertising activities." Aetna Casualty & Surety Co. v. Superior Court, 19 Cal.App.4th 320, 23 Cal. Rptr.2d 442, 446 (1993) (interpreting Bank of the West). The Aetna court explained that, in patent infringement cases, "the patentee is not injured because a product incorporating its invention is advertised, but because the infringer, without consent, used or sold a product utilizing a patented invention." Id.

In response, Iolab argues that, under Bank of the West, if we determine that the Jensen loss was causally connected to Iolab's advertising, we must hold that Iolab's infringing activities constituted piracy arising out of or committed in advertising. Iolab further argues that it incurred legal liability not simply by selling the product—an activity which, according to Iolab would have been immunized under section 271(e)(1)—but by advertising it. Through its advertising, Iolab claims, it thrust itself into a purely commercial realm unrelated to FDA approval activities and beyond the protection of the statute. Thus, according to Iolab, the Jensen loss was caused by the advertising. Neither argument is persuasive. First, regardless of the causal connection between advertising the intraocular lens and the Jensen loss, Iolab's patent infringement cannot reasonably be considered an act of piracy arising out of or committed in advertising. Second, we do not agree with Iolab's contention that there existed a causal nexus between its advertising of the intraocular lens and the Jensen loss.

In the context of policies written to protect against claims of advertising injury, "piracy" means misappropriation or plagiarism found in the elements of the advertisement itself—in its text form, logo, or pictures—rather than in the product being advertised. Iolab's claim of piracy arising out of advertising has no basis because Dr. Jensen's claim was based on Iolab's infringement of his patent for the intraocular lens itself rather than on an element of Iolab's advertising of the lens.

While patent infringement can be piracy of the advertised product, generally it is not piracy of the elements of the advertisement itself. The policies in question seem designed to cover two types of injury which might occur in the course of advertising: First, dignitary injuries such as defamation, libel, and invasion of privacy and, second, various kinds of misappropriation and passing off which might occur in the text, words, or form of an advertisement. Iolab's infringement of Dr. Jensen's patent does not fit into either of these categories. Iolab was held liable for patent infringement based on its for-profit sales of the intraocular lens, not on piracy of elements of Dr. Jensen's advertising. Had Iolab merely advertised the intraocular lens but not sold the product, Dr. Jensen could not have accused Iolab of infringing his patent. Since Iolab's advertising of the intraocular lens was not an element of Dr. Jensen's claim, Iolab could not reasonably have expected insurance coverage for its infringement. Moreover, although in Bank of the West, the California

Supreme Court appears to leave open the possibility that in some cases, a patent infringement claim may be "based on ... the advertisement," Bank of the West, 2 Cal.4th at 1275, 10 Cal.Rptr.2d 538, 833 P.2d 545, we hold that Dr. Jensen's claim against Iolab was not based on the advertising of the intraocular lens.

Iolab's claim with regard to the relationship between its advertising activities and the Jensen loss does not establish the causal nexus required by Bank of the West. First, under Bank of the West, Iolab would have to show its advertising caused the patent infringement, not the liability. Second, Iolab fails to show that the Jensen loss was caused by its advertising rather than its infringement of Dr. Jensen's patent. The fact that Dr. Jensen produced evidence of Iolab's extensive advertising activities in response to Iolab's attempt to raise a section 271(e)(1) defense, does not establish that the advertising caused the infringement. The advertising was merely evidence of the commercial nature of Iolab's infringing activities. Iolab infringed Dr. Jensen's patent because it sold the intraocular lens, and did so for commercial gain rather than for research. Iolab's advertising activities did not cause the infringement, but merely helped to establish that Iolab's interest in the Jensen patent was for profit and not for research or to obtain FDA approval. Consequently, the Jensen loss was caused by Iolab's patent infringement not by its advertising activities.

Accordingly, the Jensen loss was not covered under the policies in question and the grant of the motions to dismiss and summary judgment was appropriate.

CONCLUSION

With respect to the excess insurers, we affirm the district court on the ground that under California law, primary coverage must be exhausted before liability attaches to the excess insurers. Iolab did not exhaust its primary coverage and did not establish that the Jensen loss would ever trigger excess coverage and thus the district court properly dismissed Iolab's claim against the excess insurers. With respect to the primary insurers, we affirm the district court on the ground that Iolab's infringing activities did not constitute "piracy arising out of advertising activities" and, thus, as a matter of law, Iolab cannot show that the Jensen loss was covered by the insurance policies. Consequently, the district court properly dismissed the claims against or granted summary judgment in favor of each of the primary and excess insurers.

AFFIRMED.

Note

Obviously, the content of the plaintiff's complaint matters. If the plaintiff alleges covered offenses, such as misappropriation of trade secrets, as well as patent infringement, the insurer may be required to cover defense costs for the entire action. See John Deere Insurance Company v. Shamrock Industries, Inc., 696 F.Supp. 434 (D.Minn.1988).

(d) Specialty Policies

With uncertainty of coverage for patents (and perhaps other intellectual property disputes) under CGL policies, there has been a recent trend in the insurance industry. Several new policies are being offered, including first-and third-party coverage exclusively for patents. Given the increase in applications for patents, this trend is both predictable and necessary. Between 1997 and 1998, there was a 25.7 percent increase in patents issued; of those patents, there was a 44.9 percent increase in computer-related patents, and a 234 percent increase in Internet-related patents.[87]

In 1994, AIG began offering patent infringement insurance and others have followed suit.[88] There have also emerged policies that may reimburse the costs of bringing an infringement suit in addition to the defense of counterclaims.[89] These policies recognize that an insured's business viability may very well depend on its ability to enforce its intellectually property rights against others.[90] However, such policies have not yet been tested by the courts and, as it is inevitable, the scope of the coverage under these policies has yet to be determined definitively.[91]

While the creation of the new policies sorts itself out, the insurance industry still faces the difficult question of setting fair rates. How does one value any one item of intellectual property? After all, the degree of profit that will derive from the actualization of an idea is purely speculative. Intellectual property is by nature not the same as other types of property. Unlike items such as land, or a painting, or a diamond, there is (usually) not an existing market or system of appraisal. How does one assess the risks and cost of infringement especially in these days when the germ of an, as yet unprofitable idea, can send a nascent company's stock soaring?

3. Employment Practices Liability

The succeeding area has shown explosive growth in the past several years. A preliminary inquiry about insurance coverage in this area is the question of the exclusion for intentional conduct. If sexual harassment or age discrimination is an intentional act, how is coverage afforded? The answer is found from the unique facts of each case as well as by application of principles described earlier in this test. For example, an

87. John T. Aquino, *Patently Permissive*, 85 A.B.A.J. 30 (May 1999).

88. 6 No. 3 J. Proprietary Rts. 27 (1994); *First-of-its-Kind Patent Infringement Insurance Offers Comprehensive Protection for the Insured*, 6 Intellectual Property Today 2 (Feb. 1999).

89. Jason A. Reyes, *Patents and Insurance: Who will Pay for Infringement?*, 1 B.U.J. Sci. & Tech. 3, 34 (1995); *Coverage for Pursuit of Infringers*, Texas Lawyer, December 1997, at p. 24.

90. Melvin Simensky and Eric C. Osterberg, *The Insurance and Management of Intellectual Property Risks*, 17 Cardozo Arts & Ent. L.J 321, 337 (1999).

91. *Dan Goodin,* Is IP Insurance Worth It?, *Intellectual Property Magazine (Apr. 1997); David M. Fried,* A Policy of Infringement, *Intellectual Property Magazine (May 1998).*

employer who employs a sexual harasser may be guilty of negligent supervision which can be a covered act. Moreover, the aspect of intentionality does not necessarily preclude a defense as in *Gray v. Zurich.* Finally, it is always possible that a trial will reveal that the conduct was not in fact intentional.

The increase in discrimination suits brought against employers has made risk management of discrimination liabilities particularly important. In a comprehensive article on the subject Professor Francis J. Mootz, III, suggests that employment practices liability insurance may have a greater regulative effect than the underlying discrimination statutes. He attributes this to the twin effects of premium payment and insurer mandated preventative measures. Francis J. Mootz, III, *Insurance Coverage of Employment Discrimination Claims*, 52 Miami L. Rev. 1 (1997). A good discussion of insurance disputes relating to employment can be found in *Symposium: Insurance Coverage of Employment Disputes*, 18 W. New Eng. L. Rev. 1 (1996). A more recent useful compendium is found in Barbara A. O'Donnell, *The First Wave of Decisions Interpreting Employment Practices Liability Policies*, 35 The Brief 39 (Fall 2005).

We begin with a case that deals with statutory rights and we conclude with a sordid case of sexual harassment.

ANDOVER NEWTON THEOLOGICAL SCHOOL, INC. v. CONTINENTAL CASUALTY CO.

United States Court of Appeals, First Circuit, 1991.
930 F.2d 89.

Coffin, Senior Circuit Judge.

In 1987, a jury found that Andover Newton Theological School, Inc. (Andover) both violated the Age Discrimination in Employment Act (ADEA), 29 U.S.C. §§ 621–634, and breached an employment contract when it terminated a tenured professor. This court affirmed the jury's verdict in Linn v. Andover Newton Theological School, Inc., 874 F.2d 1 (1st Cir.1989). Andover thereafter made a claim on its insurance carrier, Continental Casualty Co. (Continental). When Continental refused to pay the claim, Andover filed suit, alleging breach of insurance contract and unfair and deceptive trade practices. The district court held that Continental was not obligated under the policy to reimburse Andover for damages arising from the Linn case because Massachusetts law precluded an insurance company from insuring a willful violation of the ADEA. See Mass.Gen.L. ch. 175, § 47 Sixth (b). The court also held that the policy language unambiguously excluded payments for amounts due under the terms of a contractual obligation. The court held, however, that the policy permitted recovery of costs associated with the defense of the Linn case, and awarded $102,748.85 for that loss.

On appeal, Andover challenges * * * the district court's determination that a willful violation of the ADEA fell within the public policy proscriptions of Mass.Gen.L. ch. 175, § 47 Sixth (b) * * *. Continental, in turn, appeals the award of litigation costs.

After hearing oral argument, this court concluded that a critical issue in this case turned on a question of Massachusetts law on which we could find no controlling precedent. We therefore certified a single question to the Massachusetts Supreme Judicial Court in accordance with Mass.S.J.C. Rule 1:03: "Does a finding of willfulness under the Age Discrimination in Employment Act (ADEA), if based on a finding of 'reckless disregard as to whether [defendant's] conduct is prohibited by federal law,' constitute 'deliberate or intentional * * * wrongdoing' such as to preclude indemnification by an insurer under the public policy of Massachusetts as codified at Mass.Gen.L. ch. 175, § 47 Sixth (b)?" Andover Newton Theological School, Inc. v. Continental Casualty Co., 901 F.2d 1, 3 (1st Cir.1990). The SJC answered that it did not. Andover Newton Theological School, Inc. v. Continental Casualty Co., 409 Mass. 350, 566 N.E.2d 1117 (1991). With that answer in hand, we now address the parties' contentions on appeal. Concluding that the district court erred, we reverse and remand the case for further proceedings consistent with this opinion.

I. The ADEA Claim

Andover was insured by Continental for losses arising out of wrongful acts. The scope of the insured loss specifically was limited by policy language stating that: "such subject of loss shall not include * * * matters which shall be deemed uninsurable under the law pursuant to which this policy shall be construed."

In the underlying action, Andover was found by a jury to have violated the ADEA by discharging Dr. Edmund Linn from his tenured faculty position when he was 62 years of age. The jury also found Andover's conduct to have been willful under the ADEA. The jury's finding of willfulness was based on an instruction that "[a] defendant acts willfully if it knows its conduct was prohibited by federal law or if it acts in reckless disregard as to whether its conduct is prohibited by federal law. 'Prohibited' being age discrimination in this case."

The district court granted summary judgment to Continental, holding that the United States Supreme Court had defined "willful" under the ADEA to mean "voluntary," "deliberate" or "intentional" in McLaughlin v. Richland Shoe Co., 486 U.S. 128, 133, 108 S.Ct. 1677, 1681, 100 L.Ed.2d 115 (1988). The court then concluded that "willful" conduct was within the meaning of the Massachusetts provision precluding insurance coverage for "deliberate or intentional * * * wrongdoing."

The district court's reliance on this language from McLaughlin was misplaced. First, the controlling definition by the Supreme Court of the word "willful" in the liquidated damages provision of the ADEA, 29 U.S.C. § 626(b), appears in Trans World Airlines, Inc. v. Thurston, 469 U.S. 111, 128, 105 S.Ct. 613, 625, 83 L.Ed.2d 523 (1985), where the Court held that "a violation is 'willful' if 'the employer either knew or showed reckless disregard for the matter of whether its conduct was prohibited by the ADEA.' " Second, the language from McLaughlin quoted by the district court was preliminary discussion; the McLaughlin Court ultimately adopted the Thurston standard. Finally, regardless of the standard enunciated by the Supreme Court, what is significant here is the standard actually applied by the jury in reaching its finding of willfulness—knowing or reckless disregard of whether conduct is proscribed by federal law. And, answering our certified question, the SJC has held that an action taken in reckless disregard of the ADEA is not conduct uninsurable under Massachusetts law. It would seem, therefore, that Continental is obligated under the policy to reimburse Andover for the loss if the jury's finding of willfulness rested on a finding of recklessness.

Continental, however, advances one further reason why Andover's conduct falls within the Massachusetts statute's proscription. It argues that, in an individual disparate treatment case, a finding of liability constitutes a finding of intentional discrimination. See, e.g., Menzel v. Western Auto Supply Co., 848 F.2d 327, 329 (1st Cir.1988) ("finding of pretext is the equivalent of a finding that the employer intentionally discriminated"). Therefore, Continental suggests, once the jury found liability, coverage was illegal under the Massachusetts statute, and the finding of willfulness was unnecessary.

Continental relies for this argument on cases from other circuits adopting a standard of willfulness higher than the Thurston standard in actions alleging individual disparate treatment because, in such cases, a finding of liability requires a finding of intentional discrimination, and therefore willfulness will almost always be present. Those courts concluded that a more stringent willfulness standard must be applied in such cases to respond to the Thurston Court's understanding that "willfulness" was not intended to be interpreted so as to result in double damages in almost every case. See Thurston, 469 U.S. at 128, 105 S.Ct. at 625. But these cases do not state that every finding of liability in an individual disparate treatment case necessarily requires a finding of willfulness under the Thurston standard. More importantly, these cases do not even come close to suggesting that the standard for liability in individual disparate treatment cases is higher than the Thurston standard for willfulness—in other words, that a finding of discrimination precludes the employer's conduct from being merely reckless with regard to the Act—as defendant argues here.

In addition, the SJC's opinion expressly rejects the defendant's loose understanding of the word "intentional." As the court says, "[t]he fact that a wrongful act was committed intentionally * * * does not alone bar coverage. That bar arises only if an intentionally committed, wrongful act was also done deliberately or intentionally, in the sense that the actor knew that the act was wrongful." Andover Newton, 409 Mass. at 352, 566 N.E.2d 1117.[92]

92. In other words, Massachusetts law only proscribes coverage of acts committed with the specific intent to do something the law forbids. Cf. Loeb v. Textron, Inc., 600 F.2d 1003, 1020 n. 27 (1st Cir.1979) (" 'An act is done "willfully" if done voluntarily

There is no indication in this case that the jury made a determination about Andover's state of mind other than in its conclusion that Andover had acted willfully—a finding that would bar recovery only if the jury based its determination on a conclusion that Andover knew its actions were wrongful. Instead, the jury was asked to determine whether "age was a motivating factor in [Linn's] discharge in the sense that but for defendant's motive to discriminate against him because of his age he would not have been discharged." And the judge specifically instructed the jury that Andover legally could not consider the availability of a pension to Linn or make assumptions about the productivity of older persons in deciding which faculty member to terminate. The jury could have found that Andover considered these factors—and therefore discriminated—without consciously appreciating the illegality of its act. See Burlew, 869 F.2d at 1066 (" '[A]ge discrimination may simply arise from an unconscious application of stereotyped notions of ability rather than from a deliberate desire to remove older employees from the workforce * * *.' ") (quoting Syvock v. Milwaukee Boiler Mfg. Co., 665 F.2d 149, 154–55 (7th Cir.1981), overruled in part by Coston v. Plitt Theatres, Inc., 860 F.2d 834 (7th Cir.1988) (emphasis in original)). There is simply nothing inherent in the finding of age discrimination or in the instructions given the jury here that rendered a finding of willfulness superfluous.

We therefore conclude that Massachusetts public policy does not bar insurance coverage of an employment action solely because it is found to violate the ADEA in an individual disparate treatment case. Nor, according to the SJC, does a jury's determination that the violation was willful bar coverage, if the jury based that determination on a finding of recklessness. The district court therefore erred in granting summary judgment to Continental on this issue.

* * *

III. Defense Litigation Costs

Continental argues that the district court erred in determining that it was liable under the policy to reimburse Andover for defense costs incurred in the Linn action. Continental asserted below that coverage for defense costs is limited to those situations in which there is underlying policy coverage for the act. The district court determined that, notwithstanding the fact that liability coverage was unavailable for willful discrimination under the ADEA, the policy failed to exclude coverage for defense costs associated with those claims. We agree.

The Continental policy covers losses the assured becomes legally obligated to pay, and "loss" is defined as: "any amount which the Assureds are legally obligated to pay * * * for a claim or claims made

and intentionally, and with the specific intent to do something the law forbids; that is to say, with bad purpose either to disobey or to disregard the law.' ") (quoting E. Devitt & C. Blackmar, Federal Jury Practice and Instructions § 14.06, at 384 (3d ed. 1977)).

against the Assureds for a Wrongful Act and shall include but not be limited to damages, judgments, settlements and costs, cost of investigation and defense of legal actions, (excluding from such costs of investigation and defense, salaries of officers or employees of the School District or any other governmental body) claims or proceedings and appeals therefrom, * * * provided always, however, such subject of loss shall not include * * * matters which shall be deemed uninsurable under the law pursuant to which this policy shall be construed." Continental does not deny that discriminatory acts are "wrongful acts" within the meaning of the policy. Coverage for wrongful acts, however, is limited by a specific exclusion of those "subjects of loss" deemed uninsurable under Massachusetts law. The exclusion of defense costs therefore is dependent on whether Massachusetts would consider such costs uninsurable.

As we have discussed, Massachusetts law precludes an insurance company from insuring "any person against legal liability for causing injury, other than bodily injury, by his deliberate or intentional crime or wrongdoing." Mass.Gen.L. ch. 175, § 47, Sixth (b). As we read this language, while public policy proscribes insuring against *legal liability* for intentional wrongdoing, the language of the public policy prohibition expresses no intent with respect to insurance coverage for the costs of defending against such liability. Although an argument can be made that a public policy is to some extent subverted by insurance against defense costs, the basic fact is that this is not insurance against liability. Continental points to no authority for extending the public policy bar to these claims. Where the SJC has declined to interpret the scope of the public policy provision expansively, see Andover Newton, 409 Mass. 350, 566 N.E.2d 1117, we also are loath to do so.

As we have noted, exclusions must state clearly what items are to be excluded, see American Home Assur., 786 F.2d at 26. Continental, while it could have done so, made no attempt to exclude defense costs associated with uninsurable claims. The policy therefore allows such coverage. See Starkville Mun. Separate School Dist. v. Continental Casualty Co., 772 F.2d 168, 170 (5th Cir.1985) ("While punitive damages themselves may be uninsurable for reasons of public policy, that same public policy does not apply to costs and attorney's fees incurred in a defense against a plea for punitive damages * * *. If CNA intended to exclude these other costs from the policy's coverage, it needed to do so more explicitly * * *.").[93]

Continental, however, relies on an unpublished district court case, Continental Casualty Co. v. McAllen Indep. School Dist., No. B–86–007 (S.D.Tex. May 19, 1987), holding that with a reimbursement policy such as the one in this case, the reimbursement coverage obligation is limited to losses incurred with respect to "covered claims." But even were this decision of precedential value here, see Loc.R.App.P. 36.2 (citation to

93. Continental attempts to distinguish Starkville because the defense of the punitive damages claim in that case ultimately was successful, unlike in this case. But the Starkville court, while noting that this factor was an additional reason supporting coverage, did not rest its analysis on the distinction. * * *

unpublished decisions limited to related cases), the case is inapposite. McAllen decided that the underlying acts did not fall within the scope of covered acts under the policy. It is therefore reasonable for reimbursement for defense costs to extend only as far as coverage for the acts. In this case, as we have observed, there is no dispute that the policy covers "wrongful acts" of the type that occurred here. It is only the scope of the *exclusion* that is at issue, and the exclusion language is narrow.

We therefore conclude that Continental is liable for defense costs incurred in the Linn action, regardless of whether the termination ultimately is found to have been taken in knowing violation of federal law. Continental does not dispute that defense costs associated with the contract action are recoverable if the ADEA defense costs are covered. Andover therefore is entitled to reimbursement for its defense costs associated with all claims.

* * *

COIT DRAPERY CLEANERS, INC. v. SEQUOIA INSURANCE CO.

Court of Appeal of California, First District, 1993.
14 Cal.App.4th 1595, 18 Cal.Rptr.2d 692.

PETERSON, PRESIDING JUSTICE.

* * *

I. FACTS AND PROCEDURAL HISTORY

We summarize the claims and evidence before the trial court as follows.

A. *Sexual Harassment*

During 1987, Linda Seahorn, who was about 28 at the time, interviewed for a telephone dispatcher and management trainee position at Coit Drapery Cleaners, Inc. She was interviewed by Dr. Louis J. Kearn, who had founded the company more than 40 years ago and was its president, a major stockholder, and chairman of the board of directors.

Kearn relished his reputation around the company as "a dirty old man." The evidence disclosed Kearn had a long history of sexually harassing young women employees, which was "common knowledge" at Coit. "[A]ny female employee who wanted to remain in Coit's employment, and particularly if she wanted to advance, * * * had to make herself available in some way to Lou Kearn. * * * Lou was very free to put his hands on the female employees." He invited female employees to share his bedroom on trips to Mexico, made sexual advances to female employees in his office, sexually fondled and groped female employees on the job, and offered to pay female employees thousands of dollars from corporate funds for sex. There was also evidence that Coit employees, including Dr. Kearn, jokingly referred to the corporate name Coit as short for "coitus."

If a female employee did not accede to Kearn's demands, she would be fired.

When Seahorn was interviewed by Kearn, he did not dwell upon her qualifications for the job or other business-related inquiries. Instead, he followed his usual practice in interviewing women applicants, by inquiring as to her attitudes toward sex, telling her that he took business trips with female employees and stayed in the same hotel room with them, asked if she had a boyfriend or was unattached, and inquired whether she would be willing to go to bed with prospective clients.

When Seahorn asked another Coit management employee, Sandra Park, whether such highly personal inquiries were "normal," Park told Seahorn not to " 'worry' " about Kearn, that he was " 'just a dirty old man.' "Park told Seahorn that Kearn, despite his sexual insinuations, was harmless. Although Seahorn felt Kearn's behavior in the interview was bizarre and upsetting, she very much needed the job and felt she could handle the situation for the 90 days she would be in Coit's California offices, near Kearn, before her promised position as a Coit manager in Chicago came through.

Seahorn testified Kearn made numerous unwelcome advances and propositions to her during the approximately two months she worked for Coit, before she was terminated for rejecting his advances. He tried to involve her in a game of strip poker, asked about her underwear, and tried to get her into a hot tub—with the aid of Park, who acted as Kearn's procuress in these efforts, and suggested to Seahorn that she should have sex with Kearn.

On one occasion, Kearn invited Seahorn into his private office during business hours—which was strange since there was no business reason requiring the president of the company to confer with a telephone dispatcher, who was separated from him by intermediate supervisors. Kearn asked Seahorn to pour him a drink, and she did so. He asked her to give him a hug, and she gave him a non-passionate hug. He asked for a passionate hug, and squeezed her tighter. He then pulled her into his office bathroom, put her hand inside his pants on his penis, and put his hand under her skirt and panties. He tried to push her down to the carpeted floor and demanded sex; but Seahorn resisted, pulled away, and left the office. Seahorn was afraid she would lose her job since she did not comply with Kearn's sexual demands.

Shortly thereafter, Kearn had Seahorn fired under the pretext of a reduction in force due to adverse economic conditions. However, the economic conditions in question had been the same two months previously when Seahorn was hired. Thereafter, Kearn called Seahorn on numerous occasions, offered her money, and tried to keep her quiet and away from lawyers.

Kearn's sexual harassment and termination of Seahorn caused her to suffer lost wages and serious psychiatric problems, including depression, chemical dependency, and suicidal thoughts.

B. Seahorn's Lawsuit and Its Tender to an Insurer

Seahorn brought an action against Coit, Kearn, and Park, alleging theories of sexual harassment in violation of Government Code section 12940 et seq., invasion of privacy, wrongful termination, breach of public policy, infliction of emotional distress, fraud, and battery, with demands for punitive damages.

Several months later, Coit sought to tender defense of the Seahorn lawsuit to its insurer, respondent Sequoia Insurance Company, which had in force a policy of general liability coverage for Coit's dry cleaning business.

Sequoia referred the matter to its counsel for investigation and, on the advice of counsel, declined to accept the tender of the defense. Sequoia relied on the fact that, inter alia, the claimed sexual harassment and wrongful termination of Seahorn could not constitute an "occurrence" under its policy, since these events were expected or intended by the insured.

In March 1990, the action was settled by Seahorn and the defendants, without the participation of Sequoia, for slightly more than $1 million. The settlement agreement contains a number of rather unusual features designed to force respondent insurer Sequoia to pay the bulk of the settlement, despite its refusal to admit coverage for intentional acts of sexual harassment and wrongful termination. For instance, the total amount of the settlement was $1,055,000 ($750,000 plus costs and attorney fees of $305,000) of which Coit was to ultimately pay only $350,000, with nothing contributed by Kearn or Park, who were allegedly the actual wrongdoers. The settling parties agreed among themselves that Sequoia would have to pay the almost two-thirds of the settlement which was remaining—$705,000. Seahorn made an uncontested motion to determine that this settlement was in "good faith," and the trial court granted the unopposed motion. No judgment of dismissal was ever filed, so technically the Seahorn action is still pending.

C. Suit Against the Insurer

Coit, Kearn, and Park then filed this action against respondent insurer Sequoia, alleging breach of contract and of the covenant of good faith and fair dealing for Sequoia's refusal to defend or indemnify against Seahorn's sexual harassment and wrongful termination claims under its general liability policy.

* * *

II. DISCUSSION

We affirm the trial court's ruling that the acts of sexual harassment and wrongful termination claimed here were intentional acts, for which coverage was excluded by the language of the relevant insurance policy and by Insurance Code section 533 (section 533). * * *

A. Section 533 Bars Coverage for Sexual Harassment

California law and applicable precedents do not allow the recharacterization of such clearly intentional and willful sexual misconduct as merely negligent or nonwillful, so as to trigger insurance coverage. In the lead case of J.C. Penney Casualty Ins. Co. v. M.K. (1991) 52 Cal.3d 1009, 1020–1021, 278 Cal.Rptr. 64, 804 P.2d 689, our Supreme Court clarified the applicable legal principles by holding that section 533 bars recovery on an insurance policy for the "wilful act" of sexually molesting a child. In Fire Ins. Exchange v. Altieri (1991) 235 Cal.App.3d 1352, 1359–1360, 1 Cal.Rptr.2d 360, the Sixth District held that section 533 bars insurance recovery for an intentional battery, such as the one Seahorn allegedly suffered as a result of Kearn's attack on her in his office. In Studley v. Benicia Unified Sch. Dist. (1991) 230 Cal.App.3d 454, 281 Cal.Rptr. 631, Division One of this district held that section 533 bars insurance recovery for the death of a victim during an assault by her estranged boyfriend. In B & E Convalescent Center v. State Compensation Ins. Fund (1992) 8 Cal.App.4th 78, 9 Cal.Rptr.2d 894, the Second District held that section 533 bars insurance recovery for an employer's willful act in wrongfully discharging an employee.

* * *

"Section 533 is an implied exclusionary clause statutorily read into all insurance policies. (J.C. Penney [supra, 52 Cal.3d at p. 1019, 278 Cal.Rptr. 64, 804 P.2d 689.]) It is subject to the rules of *statutory* construction, *not* to the rules governing contract interpretation, and must be construed in order to effect its purpose. [Citations.]" (California Casualty Management Co. v. Martocchio, supra, 11 Cal.App.4th at p. 1531, 15 Cal.Rptr.2d 277, emphasis in original.)

Quite apart from the plain meaning of section 533, and its obvious application to claims of intentional wrongdoing such as those in issue here, the purpose and public policy represented by the section, and the public and statutory policy of this state against sexual harassment of employees, would not be well served by a ruling which would exonerate a perpetrator from payment of damages for his own willful act of sexual gratification, by shifting such liability to an insurer. (See Bank of the West v. Superior Court (1992) 2 Cal.4th 1254, 1267, 10 Cal.Rptr.2d 538, 833 P.2d 545.) "If insurance coverage were available for monetary awards under the Unfair Business Practices Act, a person found to have violated the act would simply shift the loss to his insurer * * *." (Ibid.)

B. The Unavailability of Coverage As to Coit

We understand, but reject, the various arguments appellants make in an attempt to secure insurance coverage for these intentional and willful acts of its high managerial agents and policy makers.

1. Defamation

First, appellants claim coverage might be available, at least to the extent of creating a duty to defend, if a claim for defamation had been made against defendants. However, as the trial court aptly noted, no such claim for defamation was made, nor do the facts alleged in the complaint or put before the trial court support the existence of such a claim.

* * *

Further, we note that, after the parties to the Seahorn lawsuit did begin to discuss a potential claim for defamation, Sequoia agreed to defend the lawsuit, despite its objections. The Coit defendants refused that offer of a defense, because they had already decided to settle the case. These events do not support a claim of bad faith breach of covenant by an insurer for failure to defend a potential claim of defamation—rather the reverse.

2. Negligence

Moreover, despite the Coit defendants' latter-day contention that a claim for "negligent supervision" of the sex life of its president and chairman of the board might have somehow been covered, Seahorn never made such a claim in her complaint, and in fact disavowed any such claim. In her counsel's words: "This is not an action involving negligent supervision * * *." Review of the complaint confirms the truth of this statement: There are, in fact, no allegations at all of negligent supervision.

* * *

Our conclusion as to the duty to defend is consistent with that reached recently by our Supreme Court in Horace Mann Ins. Co. v. Barbara B. (1993) 4 Cal.4th 1076, 17 Cal.Rptr.2d 210, 846 P.2d 792. Horace Mann dealt with an unusual situation, in which a junior high school band teacher had had apparently nonforcible sexual contact with a 13–year–old student. The student alleged she was harmed by both the teacher's intentional conduct in carrying on his affair with a minor, and by his negligent conduct in publicly embarrassing her with the fact of the affair, through his inept statements and conduct in front of other students. (Id. at p. 1079, 17 Cal.Rptr.2d 210, 846 P.2d 792.) As to the sexual contact with the minor, our Supreme Court held there clearly was no duty to defend. (Id. at p. 1083, 17 Cal.Rptr.2d 210, 846 P.2d 792.)

The Supreme Court also recognized that the claimed negligent conduct could lie outside the scope of the duty to defend, if the alleged instances of negligent conduct "occurred in such close temporal and spatial proximity to the molestation as to *compel* the conclusion that they are inseparable from it for purposes of determining whether [the insurer] owed a duty to defend [the insured]." (Horace Mann Ins. Co. v. Barbara B., supra, 4 Cal.4th at p. 1084, 17 Cal.Rptr.2d 210, 846 P.2d 792, emphasis in original.) While rather unclear, we take the language "temporal and spatial proximity to the molestation" to mean that certain alleged conduct can be "inseparable" from intentional wrongful conduct and, therefore, not subject to any duty to defend, even where such conduct might have triggered such a duty when standing alone. For instance, if in the course of inseparably intentional sexual molestation or harassment of the victim, the wrongdoer so negligently behaved as to cause the victim additional physical or emotional harm, there is no duty to defend, even though mere negligence not occurring during an inseparable course of intentional conduct might theoretically be covered. (See ibid.)

However, as the Supreme Court noted in Horace Mann, it was dealing with the case "in somewhat of a factual vacuum." (4 Cal.4th at p. 1084, 17 Cal.Rptr.2d 210, 846 P.2d 792.) There were "unresolved factual disputes" concerning whether certain conduct, which the Court of Appeal and Supreme Court called " 'parasexual' " (hugging, kissing, and dandling the victim in front of other students) was either intentional or inseparable from intentional conduct; therefore, the duty to defend might still exist. (Id. at pp. 1083, 1084–1085, 17 Cal.Rptr.2d 210, 846 P.2d 792.) One might question the assumption that a teacher may unintentionally kiss, hug, and fondle a young student with whom the teacher is intentionally having an illicit affair. (See id. at p. 1088, 17 Cal.Rptr.2d 210, 846 P.2d 792 (conc. opn. of Baxter, J).) "On this record, that conclusion strains common sense." (Ibid.) However, our Supreme Court, dealing with the case in a "vacuum," apparently entertained this as at least a theoretical possibility.

In the present case, of course, the conduct of the defendants was inseparably intentional. It was part of a consistent course of sexual harassment of an unconsenting victim, in an employment setting. All of this conduct was harmful and wrongful, as a matter of law; there are no unresolved factual issues as to the intentionality of Kearn's harassing conduct, as appellants conceded at oral argument. There was no duty to defend. (See Horace Mann Ins. Co. v. Barbara B., supra, 4 Cal.4th at pp. 1083–1084, 17 Cal.Rptr.2d 210, 846 P.2d 792.)

In the present case, no claim for negligent supervision was made in the complaint and none was supportable by the facts; and the sexual abuse of female employees by Kearn was so widespread, well-known, and so ratified by the corporation as to constitute intentional corporate policy, which cannot be the subject of insurance coverage. (Loyola Marymount University v. Hartford Accident & Indemnity Co. (1990) 219 Cal.App.3d 1217, 1225, 271 Cal.Rptr. 528 [No coverage for damages caused by university's allegedly discriminatory policy of discharging married priests, despite claims that the university might have been merely negligent in failing to comply with federal anti-discrimination laws, because "an intentional discharge or application of an employment policy does not become an accidental occurrence even if it has only an unintended federally prohibited discriminatory effect."]) * * *. Here, the trial court found Coit, its managers, and board of directors were well aware of, and ratified and condoned, the sexual harassment of female employees as a way to satisfy Kearn's urges for sexual domination of females. Coit should not receive insurance coverage for the liability it, thus, intentionally created.

For the same reasons, it is unavailing for appellants to suggest Coit was merely negligent in failing to enact and enforce corporate policies against sexual harassment, so as to prevent its president and major shareholder from attacking female employees. Coverage cannot be created by claimed negligence in failing to dissuade oneself from committing an intentional act, otherwise every intentional act would be covered and section 533 would have no meaning. (See J.C. Penney Casualty Ins. Co. v. M.K., supra, 52 Cal.3d at pp. 1019–1021, 278 Cal.Rptr. 64, 804 P.2d 689.) We are required to interpret section 533 so as to give effect and meaning to all its provisions; just as we cannot allow insurers to recharacterize negligent conduct as intentional, we cannot allow the insured to recast intentional conduct as merely negligent. (See ibid.)

* * *

Although we also believe the acts claimed in the Seahorn lawsuit would not in any event constitute an "occurrence" under the terms of the policy—since they were not unexpected or unintended from the standpoint of the insured, we base our holding more directly upon the statutory mandate of section 533 since, as our Supreme Court held in J.C. Penney, supra, section 533 forms part of the policy by operation of law, and the parties to an insurance contract cannot in any event agree, intend, or expect to create coverage which violates section 533.

* * *

4. The Public Policy Against Sexual Harassment Must Be Harmonized with Section 533

In light of the strong public policy against sexual discrimination and harassment in employment, as embodied in Government Code section 12940 et seq., we seriously question whether section 533 would ever permit insurance coverage for any intentional course of conduct, as evidenced by this record, consisting of a long pattern of behavior of sexual discrimination and sexual harassment by a corporation's high managerial agents which have been known, ratified, and condoned by the corporation. As Justice Croskey observed in B & E Convalescent Center, when considering the public policy against unlawful employment discrimination in light of the mandates of section 533: "Under any reasonable criterion, a termination in violation of such public policies must be held *wrongful as a matter of law.* As we have pointed out, such claim[s] can *only* be established by evidence of an employer's motive and intent to violate and frustrate the law(s) declaring or establishing fundamental public policy. It would be unreasonable, mischievous and improper if section 533, which reflects the 'fundamental public policy of denying coverage for willful wrongs' (J.C. Penney, supra, 52 Cal.3d at pp. 1019–1020, fn. 8 [278 Cal.Rptr. 64, 804 P.2d 689]), were construed in any way other than to deny insurance coverage in the most certain and unambiguous terms for willful and intentional acts that contravene 'fundamental policies that are delineated in constitutional or statutory provisions' (Gantt, supra, 1 Cal.4th at p. 1095 [4 Cal.Rptr.2d 874, 824 P.2d 680])." (8 Cal.App.4th at p. 99, 9 Cal.Rptr.2d 894, emphasis in original.)

In order to effectuate this public policy, corporate employers have been made liable for the acts of sexual harassment by their managerial agents in the workplace of which the corporation was aware and which it ratified or condoned; theories of negligent supervision are no longer even necessary to establish corporate liability for the intentional acts of managerial agents in this context. (See Fisher v. San Pedro Peninsula Hospital (1989) 214 Cal.App.3d 590, 608, fn. 6, 262 Cal.Rptr. 842.)

We are concerned here, however, not with corporate liability but with an insurer's responsibilities to defend and indemnify the corporation it insures when such intentional acts occur under the circumstances of this case. The sexual harassment complained of here occurred in the context of a policy of quid pro quo, where corporate funds, employment, and advancement were used or withheld, as a matter of common knowledge and routine, to coerce sexual favors for a high managerial employee. The corporation here, in allowing, condoning, and ratifying such intentional conduct as a matter of corporate policy, triggered the prohibition against insurance coverage for such intentional wrongful conduct embodied in section 533. Thus, the insurer had no duty to defend.

In words which our Supreme Court applied in denying insurance coverage under section 533 for sexual molestation of a child, and which are equally applicable to the actions of the insured corporation in the sexual harassment in issue here: "Section 533 precludes coverage in this case because [the wrongful act] is *always* intentional, it is *always* wrongful, and it is *always* harmful." (J.C. Penney Casualty Ins. Co. v. M.K., supra, 52 Cal.3d at p. 1025, 278 Cal.Rptr. 64, 804 P.2d 689, emphasis in original.)

III. Disposition

The judgment of dismissal is affirmed. Costs are awarded to Sequoia.

Notes

1. In a modification to the principal case on May 12, 1993, the court addressed the contention that though insurance coverage for intentional sexual harassment is barred by section 533 and by public policy, there is no statute or public policy directly forbidding an insurer's provision of a defense to its insured for intentional acts. Despite the absence of legislation regarding the duty to defend, the court noted that "it is well established, however, that where * * * both statute and public policy bar any possibility of indemnity for conduct which is inseparably intentional, there is also no duty to defend. Otherwise, an insurer would have a duty to defend actions alleging only intentional wrongful conduct outside the scope of any potential for coverage provided by the insurance policy itself or permitted by statute."

2. The victim in cases like *Coit* is faced with a dilemma. By arguing the intentional injury aspect of the case, the victim may well be left without economic compensation if the tortfeasor is otherwise insolvent. For these reasons, the Fifth Circuit in *American Home Assurance Co. v. Stephens*, 130

F.3d 123 (5th Cir.1997), held that an insurer's limitation of $25,000 for sexual misconduct in the context of a policy which otherwise contained a $1 million limit for professional liability was void for public policy reasons. According to the court, the effect of the provision would be to chill the victim's enthusiasm for reporting sexual misconduct. Upon rehearing the Fifth Circuit certified the question to the Texas Supreme Court as to whether the insurer's two tiered system of liability would be against public policy. Receiving a negative answer, the Fifth Circuit affirmed the District Court's initial decision for the insurer. *American Home Assurance Co. v. Stephens*, 164 F.3d 956 (5th Cir.1999).

3. A number of cases arise out of sex contact situations where the contact was intended but the intent to harm is denied by the actor. For example, in *Horace Mann Ins. Co. v. Independent School District No. 656*, 355 N.W.2d 413 (Minn.1984), an adult school teacher-counselor engaged in sexual contact with a minor student. The court held that intent to cause "bodily injury" may be inferred as a matter of law despite the teacher-counselor's protestations to the contrary. See Grange Ins. Ass'n v. Authier, 45 Wn.App. 383, 725 P.2d 642 (1986) (in accord). Even a minor boy (the insured) who engages in sex with minor girls is subject to the inference. See Illinois Farmers Ins. Co. v. Judith G., 379 N.W.2d 638 (Minn.App.1986); State Auto Mut. Ins. Co. v. McIntyre, 652 F.Supp. 1177 (N.D.Ala.1987).

Yet a different approach is demonstrated by the characterization of allegations of sexual misconduct as slander. Bradley Corp. v. Zurich Insurance Co., 984 F.Supp. 1193 (E.D.Wi.1997) (claimant's allegations were sufficient to trigger duty to defend on the basis of slander).

4. At times an insurer may be relieved of its duties even when the acts of the insured are not illegal. After Hollywood–star Rock Hudson's death from an AIDS–related illness, his partner prevailed in a lawsuit for damages in which the jury found that Hudson had concealed his HIV status and continued to have high risk sex. The jury awarded $14.5 million in compensatory damages. The estate administrator sued Hudson's liability insurer for coverage, but the court held that high risk sex is an intentional act which is inherently harmful and therefore uninsurable. *Aetna Casualty and Surety Co. v. Sheft,* 989 F.2d 1105 (9th Cir.1993).

The position adopted by the Supreme Court of Wisconsin may differ with that of California. In *Loveridge v. Chartier,* 161 Wis.2d 150, 468 N.W.2d 146 (1991), the court held in part that statutory rape of a consenting 16 year-old female was not harmful as a matter of law, and that allowing insurance coverage for *negligent* transmission of a sexually transmitted disease would not violate public policy. In response to the nationwide increase in similar claims, many homeowners policies now include an "STD" exclusion.

5. Can the rule on insurability of intentional acts applied in *Coit* be reconciled with the position adopted by the Massachusetts Supreme Judicial Court in *Andover Newton?* The *Andover* opinion noted that the jury was free to find recklessness in committing an intentional act that violated a statute/public policy. Consequently, the insurer would be bound to defend for a seemingly intentional act.

6. *Lack of capacity to have intent.* Many policies exclude coverage for events caused "intentionally by or at the direction of the insured." Steven H. was an additional insured under his parents' homeowners policy providing comprehensive personal liability coverage. He set fire to a wastebasket in a classroom of the synagogue he attended and the resulting fire caused property damage of nearly $50,000. Steven was under a psychiatrist's care prior to the fire and the issue of his mental capacity to cause damage intentionally was involved in litigation initiated to establish the responsibility of the homeowners policy insurer for the fire loss. The policy contained the language quoted at the beginning of the paragraph. Is Steven's conduct not intentional only if he could be deemed legally insane for purposes of criminal responsibility? In *Congregation of Rodef Sholom v. American Motorists Insurance Co.*, 91 Cal.App.3d 690, 154 Cal.Rptr. 348 (1979), the court noted: "If Steven was suffering from a mental disease or defect which deprived him of capacity to intend to set the fire and cause the damage complained of, or which deprived him of the capacity to govern his conduct in accordance with reason, then he did not act intentionally as that word is used in the exclusionary clause.... " See American Family Mutual Ins. Co. v. Mueller, 570 F.Supp. 348 (E.D.Mo.1983) (intentional act exclusion does not apply to insured suffering psychotic depression, as well as a pain in his foot, who shot his doctor in the legs).

Voluntary drunkenness may reach the stage that insured lacks the requisite intent and the exclusion becomes inoperative. MacKinnon v. Hanover Ins. Co., 124 N.H. 456, 471 A.2d 1166, 1169 (1984); but see American Family Mut. Ins. Co. v. Peterson, 405 N.W.2d 418 (Minn.1987) (contra).

Self-defense may bar application of the exclusion. Western Fire Ins. Co. v. Persons, 393 N.W.2d 234 (Minn.App.1986).

7. *Collateral estoppel.* In *Clemmer v. Hartford Insurance Co.*, 22 Cal.3d 865, 151 Cal.Rptr. 285, 587 P.2d 1098 (1978), Dr. Lovelace killed Dr. Clemmer and was convicted of second degree murder after withdrawing a plea of not guilty by reason of insanity. The widow Clemmer obtained a judgment against Lovelace for wrongful death. In an action against Lovelace's comprehensive liability insurer, the widow was not to be estopped, said the Supreme Court, from litigating the issue of wilfulness because she lacked the requisite privity to Lovelace's criminal defense. The insurer had the burden of proving wilfulness. Similarly, a plea of guilty to voluntary manslaughter does not appear to collaterally estop the insured from escaping the exclusion in a civil case. See St. Paul Fire and Marine Ins. Co. v. Weiner, 606 F.2d 864 (9th Cir.1979); Country Mut. Ins. Co. v. Duncan, 794 F.2d 1211 (7th Cir.1986).

Alternatively, if the insured has been found not guilty of criminal conduct in a battery charge because of mental disease, the insurer is not precluded from litigating the intent issue in a civil case brought by victim against the insured. See Rajspic v. Nationwide Mutual Ins. Co., 110 Idaho 729, 718 P.2d 1167 (1986); State Farm Fire and Cas. Co. v. Poomaihealani, 667 F.Supp. 705 (D.Hawai'i 1987).

8. In *State Farm Fire & Casualty Co. v. Drasin*, 152 Cal.App.3d 864, 199 Cal.Rptr. 749 (1984), the defendants in an action for malicious prosecution tendered defense to their homeowners policy insurer. The court held that the insurer could enforce the intentional acts exclusion by showing the nature of the alleged tort has an element of intentional wrongdoing.

Chapter 6

PROPERTY INSURANCE

A. BASIC PRINCIPLES

COVERAGE DEFINED IN PROPERTY INSURANCE

There are two ways of describing what the insured thinks of as coverage and what the insurance company thinks of as exposure.

1. *Specific designation of risks* with "add ons" or "wrap arounds" to extend coverage as desired. The obvious example in property insurance is the STANDARD FIRE POLICY which simply insures against "loss by fire, lightning and other perils insured against in this policy including removal from premises endangered by the perils insured against in this policy.... " Additional coverage is obtainable for other risks, such as windstorm, earthquake, flood, vandalism, etc. by endorsements or separate policies—for additional premiums. Depending upon the special circumstances of the property owner, this approach can result in a policy tailored to need and pocketbook.

Drawbacks to this method of coverage definition lie in the requirement that the insured has the burden of proving that the event specified in the insurance policy has occurred—or in other words, that a specifically designated risk, e.g. fire, was the actual cause of the loss.

2. *"All risks"* or *"all physical loss"* (APL) or *"special causes of loss"* policies with listed exclusions or exceptions or excepted causes.

This approach can be traced to the ancient policy form memorialized in the British Marine Insurance Act 1906:

> "Touching the adventures and perils which we the assurers are contented to bear and do take upon us in this voyage: they are of the seas, men of war, fire, enemies, pirates, rovers, thieves, jettisons, letters of mart and countermart, surprisals, takings at sea, arrests, restraints, and detainments of all kings, princes, and people, of what nation, condition, or quality so ever, barratry of the master and mariners, and of all other perils, losses, and misfortunes, that have or shall come to the hurt, detriment, or damage of the said goods and merchandises, and ship, etc., or any part thereof, without prejudice to this insurance."

Thus the form first appears to elevate the insured's expectations of complete security, followed by the insurer's limitation of this broad coverage by exclusions, exceptions, and "this policy does not cover" paragraphs. These exclusions, exceptions, and the rest are unfortunately too often relegated to the nether regions of the policy. This method of defining coverage has the advantage to the insured of merely requiring proof of the casualty, with the burden shifting to the company to effect an escape via an applicable exclusion.

An instructive case on the interpretation of "all risks" policies is *Pan American World Airways v. Aetna Casualty & Surety Co.*, 505 F.2d 989 (2d Cir.1974). In *Pan Am Airways*, the court relies heavily on the principle of *contra proferentum* discussed in Chapter 3. It also serves as a template for discussing the issues raised by the events of September 11, 2001.

On September 6, 1970, Pan American Flight 093, while on a regularly scheduled flight from Brussels to New York, was hijacked in the sky over London about 45 minutes after it had taken off from an intermediate stop in Amsterdam. Two men, Diop and Gueye, acting for the Popular Front for the Liberation of Palestine (the "PFLP"), forced the crew of the aircraft to fly to Beirut, where a demolitions expert and explosives were put on board. The aircraft, a Boeing 747, was then flown to Egypt still under PFLP control. In Cairo, after the passengers were evacuated, the aircraft was totally destroyed.

Pan American obtained policies from a number of companies each insuring against all physical loss of or damage to the aircraft save for any loss "due to or resulting from 'certain exclusions.'" These exclusions included damage by military or usurped power, war, warlike operations, insurrection, strikes, civil commotion or riot. Perhaps such disasters at one time encompassed the known range of human villainy, but "hijacking" is only in more current lexicons. Hence the issue evolves: (a) do the carriers have the burden of bringing hijacking within the scope of the named exclusions; and, if so, (2) can this burden be actually carried off—in other words can hijacking, by any stretch of argument, be equated with a war, insurrection, riot, etc.? The Second Circuit, in affirming judgment against the insurers, stated:

> The all risk insurers, if they were to prevail, had the burden of proving that the proximate cause of the loss of the 747 was included within one of the terms of exclusion. The all risk insurers' task is made even more difficult by the rule that exclusions will be given the interpretation which is most beneficial to the insured. * * *
>
> In the district court the insured had the burden of proving the existence of the all risk policies, and the loss of the covered property. Neither of these elements is disputed. Thus Pan American began the action with a prima facie case for recovery which the all risk insurers could meet only by proving that the cause of the loss came under one of the terms of exclusion.

[Relying on the principle of contra proferentum as a rule of interpretation, the court found that hijacking was not so far-removed or remote that the insurers could not have included it in the policy exclusions, if such a thing was intended to be excluded.]

The current practice of packaging diverse insurance coverages in a single policy naturally produces a mixture of the above basic approaches to coverage definition. The homeowners (HO) policy is an example at hand—using the language of a standard fire policy at one point, and that of an "all risks" plus exclusions at another point. Homeowners' policies are of recent development (roughly in the last 50 years) and the differences in language composition may have been influenced by the type of insurance that the underwriter was accustomed to marketing when the decision was made to branch out into multiple risks coverage. Thus the regular fire insurers (of fixed objects) would tend to build their HOs with basic plus specific extended coverages. Alternatively, those whose business had been primarily in the writing of inland marine or floater policies would be likely to produce a predominantly "all risks" HO form.

A final observation is in order. Many cases proceed on the assumption that courts should err on the side of coverage. Without arguing the point, this is not a costless decision. As the California State Supreme Court has stated: "[W]e are also cognizant that judicially created insurance coverage leaves 'ordinary insureds to bear the expense of increased premiums necessitated by the erroneous expansion of their insurers' potential liabilities'."[1]

1. Notice of Loss

GARDNER DENVER CO. v. DIC–UNDERHILL CONSTRUCTION CO.

United States District Court, Southern District of New York, 1976.
416 F.Supp. 934.

MOTLEY, DISTRICT JUDGE.

Plaintiff in this diversity action seeks to recover from defendants the value of an air compressor which it allegedly rented to defendants Dic–Underhill on or about August 3, 1973 for their use on the construction site of the World Trade Center in New York, owned by defendant Port Authority. This compressor was not returned to plaintiff, according to defendants, because it was stolen from the construction site. Defendants, in turn, seek indemnity for any possible loss in this action from Dic–Underhill's insurer, St. Paul, with the Port Authority basing its claim upon a subrogation clause in the contract between itself and Dic–Underhill. In response, St. Paul has moved for summary judgment pursuant to Rule 56, Fed.R.Civ.P., and the court grants this motion.

1. Foster–Gardner, Inc. v. National Union Fire Ins. Co., 18 Cal.4th 857, 887, 77 Cal.Rptr.2d 107, 128, 959 P.2d 265, 286 (1998) *citing* Garvey v. State Farm Fire & Casualty Co. (1989) 48 Cal.3d 395, 408, 257 Cal.Rptr. 292, 770 P.2d 704.

The facts are not disputed. Dic Concrete Corp. and Underhill Construction Corp. were parties to a contract with the Port Authority for the performance of concrete construction in connection with the construction of the World Trade Center. Prior to the date of the alleged theft, St. Paul issued to defendants Dic–Underhill a Contractors' Equipment insurance policy, numbered 365 JD 4974, insuring certain portable equipment[2] against "all risks of [p]hysical loss or damage from any external cause", with certain enumerated exceptions.

On or about August 16, 1973, the mobile compressor was allegedly stolen from the World Trade Center jobsite and was never returned. By letter of the same date, Dic–Underhill Joint Venture notified Armitage & Co., Inc. of the loss, since Armitage was the agent for American Home Assurance Co., the insurance carrier of the Port Authority and its contractor, Dic–Underhill, for all work at the World Trade Center. Subsequently, on August 20, 1973, Armitage forwarded the claim to Edward D. Weinstock, Inc. for adjustment.

From August 16, 1973 until March 31, 1975, Dic–Underhill and the Port Authority believed in good faith that the claim would be covered by American Home Assurance Co. However, by letter dated March 27, 1975 and received March 31, 1975, Dic–Underhill was informed by the Weinstock firm that the loss of the compressor was outside the scope of property covered under defendant's policy of builder's risk insurance, and that the claim would therefore be disallowed.

On April 29, 1975, Dic–Underhill Joint Venture notified its own insurance broker, John C. Vorbach Company, of the loss. By letter dated April 30, 1975, the Vorbach Company notified St. Paul's agent, The Maloy Agency, Inc., and the agent forwarded the letter of notification to St. Paul, which received it on May 3, 1975.

On September 2, 1975, St. Paul wrote to Dic–Underhill Joint Venture and informed them that "after careful consideration", St. Paul had concluded that the loss did not fall within the protection of the policy. Finally, on December 2, 1975, the instant suit was commenced by Gardner–Denver.

On the basis of the above chronology, St. Paul moved for summary judgment, arguing that defendants (Dic–Underhill, as the insured, and the Port Authority, as subrogee) have failed to comply with that provision of their insurance contract which requires that the insured notify St. Paul of any loss "as soon as practicable."[3] On the authority of a number of New York cases, St. Paul contends that the interval between

2. The contract of insurance provides coverage for "contractor's equipment, as listed below, the property of the Insured or the property of others in the custody or control of the Insured, for which they may be liable." An attached endorsement indicates that the coverage included, *inter alia,* "all portable equipment usual to Insured's concrete construction operations, [etc.]"

3. "Notice of Loss. The Insured shall as soon as practicable report in writing to the Company or its agent every loss, damage or occurrence which may give rise to a claim under this Policy and shall also file with the Company or its agent within ninety (90) days from the date of discovery of such loss, damage or occurrence, a detailed sworn proof of loss."

the alleged theft in August of 1973 and the notification given to its agent in April of 1975 is unreasonable and amounts to a contractual violation as a matter of law.[4]

It is established New York law that compliance with the notice provision of an insurance contract is a condition precedent to an insurer's liability, and that an insurer need not show prejudice before it can assert the defense of noncompliance. Security Mutual Insurance Company of New York v. Acker–Fitzsimons Corp., 31 N.Y.2d 436, 340 N.Y.S.2d 902, 293 N.E.2d 76 (Ct.App.1972). Absent a valid excuse, a failure to satisfy the notice requirement vitiates the policy. Id. at 905, 293 N.E.2d at 78. A provision that notice be given "as soon as practicable" after an occurrence merely requires that notice be given within a reasonable time under all the circumstances. * * *

Since it is not disputed that St. Paul's agent did not receive notice until April 30, 1975, the question is whether this delay of some twenty months after the date of the theft is unreasonable as a matter of law.

Absent some excuse or mitigating circumstances, courts have passed judgment on the insured's compliance with notice provisions, and have found much shorter delays to be unreasonable. (51 days, Deso, supra; 27 days, Reina v. United States Casualty Co., 228 App.Div. 108, 239 N.Y.S. 196 (App.Div., 1st Dept. 1930), aff'd 256 N.Y. 537, 177 N.E. 130 (1931); 30 days, Mason v. Allstate Insurance Co., 12 A.D.2d 138, 209 N.Y.S.2d 104 (App.Div., 2d Dept. 1960)). However, "[m]itigating circumstances may arise if the insured lacks, or is incapable of acquiring, knowledge of the occurrence; or the insured is out of the state; or in good faith reasonably believes there is no policy coverage or that the insured was not liable on the main action. [citations omitted]." Kason v. City of New York, 83 Misc.2d 810, 373 N.Y.S.2d 456, 459 (Sup.Ct., N.Y.Cty.1975). Where these excuses are asserted by the insured in mitigation of his failure to provide prompt notice to the insurer, the New York courts have apparently allowed the jury to evaluate the reasonableness of the insured's conduct. * * *

However, defendants do not rely on any of these accepted mitigating theories. Rather, they argue that their twenty-month delay in notifying St. Paul is excused by their good faith belief that their loss would be reimbursed by the American Home Assurance Company. Although it appears possible that there might be a serious question as to the reasonableness of their delay from the end of March, 1975 to the end of April, 1975 which could properly be entrusted to a jury for decision, defendants have cited no case, nor has the court's research discovered any case, in which notification of the "wrong" insurer has excused a failure to promptly notify the insurer being sued.

4. Dic–Underhill and the Port Authority do not appear to question that the time for purposes of judging the reasonableness of the notification, is to be measured from the date of the alleged theft. They only argue that such notification was "as soon as practicable", in view of the circumstances. They specifically do not argue that they are not, even yet, obliged to give notice, since the "occurrence" upon which their claim would be based is an adjudication of their liability to plaintiff in the instant suit.

As a matter of fact, the law in New York seems to be that timely notification to another insurer does not excuse failure to notify the insurer being sued as soon as practicable. Mason, supra; Reina, supra. In *Mason,* the insured had inadvertently notified the wrong insurer concerning an automobile accident, and the proper insurer was not notified until a substantially later time. After reviewing the circumstances which may be legally sufficient to excuse a failure to promptly notify the proper insurer, the Appellate Division found "no extenuating circumstances in the instant case." "[N]egligence in notifying the wrong insurer does not excuse failure to give notice to the proper one." 209 N.Y.S.2d at 113.

The facts of this suit seem to present an even stronger case for application of the principle established by *Mason* and *Reina.* In this case, there seems to be no doubt that the defendants knew that they had a policy of insurance with St. Paul and suspected that they might be held liable for the compressor's loss. Their decision to look to American Home Assurance for reimbursement was apparently not based on any confusion as to the identity of the insurer, but rather reflected an election between those insurers whose policies might arguably cover the loss. No circumstance has been brought to the attention of the court which would have prevented defendants from notifying St. Paul at the time of loss in order that that insurer might investigate the occurrence—whether or not a claim might later be filed.[5]

Accordingly, the court finds that Dic–Underhill failed to notify St. Paul "as soon as practicable" after discovery of the loss of the compressor, and that that failure constitutes a breach of a material condition precedent to St. Paul's liability under its contract of insurance. Accordingly, both Dic–Underhill and its subrogee, the Port Authority, are contractually barred from recovery against St. Paul.

The only remaining question is whether St. Paul waived its defense to Dic–Underhill's claim by considering the claim after it was finally filed,[6] and by rejecting the claim in its letter dated September 2, 1975.[7] In support of their argument that St. Paul waived its policy defense based on lack of timely notice, Dic–Underhill and the Port Authority merely note that over four months elapsed between filing of the claim and final rejection, and that, during that period, St. Paul did not indicate to any representative of the insured that the claim was improper for failure to give the requisite notice. In these circumstances, the court finds neither that "manifested intention to release a right" necessary to infer a waiver, nor any legal prejudice to the insured necessary for a

5. The contract of insurance does, after all, require notification of any "loss, damage or occurrence" which "*may* give rise to a claim." (emphasis added)

6. Counsel for Dic–Underhill and the Port Authority has not vigorously advanced the waiver argument. No authorities are cited in support of the argument. Moreover, counsel at one point in argument withdrew the waiver point entirely, but then decided to stand by his assertion of waiver.

7. The entire text of that letter is as follows:

> "We have completed our investigation in connection with the above captioned claim and after careful consideration we feel that this loss does not fall within the protection of the policy."

finding of estoppel against the insurer. See Allstate Insurance Company v. Gross, 27 N.Y.2d 263, 317 N.Y.S.2d 309, 314, 265 N.E.2d 736, 739 (Ct.App.1970); 31 N.Y.Jur., Insurance § 1589[8] (1963). The letter from St. Paul disallowing the claim is by no means an unequivocal statement that the loss at issue simply was not covered by the policy; it is also susceptible of a construction whereby the claim was disallowed due to lack of timely notice. Had the letter based the disallowance on some other ground, then there might be some basis for inferring that the insurer had chosen to waive the defense of improper notice. However, such does not appear to be the case here.

* * *

The motion for summary judgment is granted.

Notes

1. Here Dic–Underhill held two policies. The loss fell under a bailee's policy whereas a claim was made under a builder's risk policy. Whether or not bailees' policies cover bailed goods "for which they may be liable" is not an easy question to answer as will be seen in cases on the point later in this Part. E.g.: Was Dic–Underhill "liable" for the theft of the compressor? Did the policy apply to the compressor simply because Dic–Underhill was generally "liable" as a bailee? That issue, in fact, actually underlies the basic action here.

Isn't it natural for laymen to put in a claim under the builder's risk policy? The contractors for one of the biggest buildings in the world as well as the directors of the Port Authority of New York, neither one exactly innocents in the industrial arena, mistakenly thought so. Shouldn't the insured at least have the opportunity to prove that its mistaken delay did not cause any detriment to the insurer?

Could an insurance company ever be held estopped to deny a claim which has been filed late? What sort of conduct would have to be shown? As to a claimed waiver, would not additional consideration be necessary to re-establish the coverage? See Petrice v. Federal Kemper Insurance Co., 163 W.Va. 737, 260 S.E.2d 276 (1979) (insured's claim not barred by provision requiring sworn proof of loss where insurer tendered settlement check without requiring the sworn proof).

Should a distinction be made between ignorance of a cause of loss and ignorance of the fact that a loss has occurred for the purpose of excusing the

8. "In general, to operate as a waiver by the company of, or an estoppel to assert, a condition in the policy limiting the time in which suit shall be brought after the loss, the act or declaration relied upon must be done or made during the running of the period of limitation, or at least commenced during such period, since acts taking place entirely after the expiration of the period cannot be said to have induced the insured not to bring action within the period." While this quotation pertains most directly to provisions, such as that in the instant policy, which require that suit be brought within a specified time after discovery of the loss or occurrence giving rise to the claim, the rationale is equally applicable to provisions requiring notification to the insurer "as soon as practicable". In this case, the claim itself was filed with St. Paul long after the expiration of a "reasonable time" after the loss, and any action or inaction by St. Paul could not have prevented the insured from correcting that fact.

filing of a late claim? The opinion in *USLIFE Savings and Loan Association v. National Surety Corp.*, 115 Cal.App.3d 336, 171 Cal.Rptr. 393, 398 (1981) says so, but why? Which type of ignorance was it in the principal case?

2. *The prejudice to the insurer requirement.* Note the statement in the principal case as to the necessity of showing prejudice with the flat assertion that "California law does not require strict compliance with insurance notice clauses, unless the insurer can show actual prejudice." Fidelity Savings & Loan Association v. Aetna Life & Casualty Co., 647 F.2d 933 (9th Cir.1981).

3. *A step-by-step judicial rewrite of the notice requirements of the standard fire policy. The Rhode Island gambit.* Back in 1917 the rule was declared in *Sherwood Ice Co. v. United States Casualty*, 40 R.I. 268, 100 A. 572 (1917), that whether an insurer was prejudiced by the insured's neglect to give the notice required in the policy was wholly immaterial.

In 1971 the plaintiff, holding an automobile policy, filed a late notice and proof of a claim against an uninsured motorist. Employing the "contract of adhesion" rationale the Rhode Island Supreme Court rejected the *Sherwood* holding and adopted the rule that "an insurer could not rely on the so-called 'notice' provision of its policy unless it could demonstrate that it had been prejudiced by lack of notice." Pickering v. American Employers Insurance Co., 109 R.I. 143, 282 A.2d 584 (1971).

In 1980 it was decided that the same rule would apply to the legislatively mandated 60–day notice provision in the standard fire policy. Naturally, the company questions its applicability to a policy not characterized as a contract of adhesion. The answer according to the court is simple: Failure to give notice as required results in a forfeiture and the legislature would not intend to mandate a forfeiture. Q.E.D. the standard policy is not changed—only interpreted. Siravo v. Great American Insurance Co., 122 R.I. 538, 410 A.2d 116 (1980).

4. Where property insurance (crime, flood, etc.) is obtained from a federal agency, the applicant should be aware that there is little or no give in the procedural requirements of notice and proof of loss. Cohen v. Federal Insurance Administration, 654 F.Supp. 824 (E.D.N.Y.1986); Spratlin v. Federal Crop Ins. Corp., 662 F.Supp. 870 (E.D.Ark.1987). Why?

5. *Failure to give notice and breach of the cooperation clause.* Failure to give notice, according to the Florida Supreme Court in *Bankers Insurance Co. v. Macias*, 475 So.2d 1216 (1985), is a condition precedent with a rebuttable presumption of prejudice, a position the court admits may be out of step with the modern trend. On the other hand, the failure to cooperate in a P.I.P. case is a condition subsequent, and the burden is on the insurer to show prejudice. An intermediate appellate court decision confusing the two was reversed. Is the distinction really all that clear?

SCHREIBER v. PENNSYLVANIA LUMBERMAN'S MUTUAL INSURANCE COMPANY

Supreme Court of Pennsylvania, 1982.
498 Pa. 21, 444 A.2d 647.

ROBERTS, JUSTICE.

* * * Appellants' sole contention throughout these proceedings has been that the one-year limitation of suit provision contained in their

policy of fire insurance should not bar appellants from bringing suit on the policy over two years and two months after their alleged loss unless appellee insurance company can demonstrate that it has been prejudiced by appellants' delay. We find this contention to be without merit and, accordingly, affirm. * * *

In Brakeman v. Potomac Insurance Co., 472 Pa. 66, 371 A.2d 193 (1977), this Court held that a policyholder's failure to abide by a provision in an automobile insurance contract requiring timely notice of claims would not bar suit on the policy absent a showing of prejudice by the insurer. Appellants argue that *Brakeman* mandates a similar conclusion with regard to the statutory limitation of suit provision at issue here.

Contrary to appellants' assertion, the rationale of our decision in *Brakeman* is not applicable to the present case. In *Brakeman,* the insurer had chosen to include in its automobile insurance policy a provision requiring that,

> "[i]n the event of an accident, occurrence or loss, written notice * * * shall be given by or for the insured to the company or any of its authorized agents as soon as practicable."

* * *

* * * Because the above provision requiring notice "as soon as practicable" was included at the exclusive discretion of the insurer, this Court found the provision to be in the nature of a contract of adhesion. Thus this Court departed from precedent and held that an insurer must prove that it has been prejudiced by an insured's late notice before it can successfully invoke such a provision as a defense to a claim.

In contrast, the limitation of suit provision in appellants' fire insurance policy was not "dictated by the insurance company to the insured." Rather, the Legislature has mandated that every policy of fire insurance issued in this Commonwealth shall contain the proviso that

> "[n]o suit or action on this policy for the recovery of any claim shall be sustainable in any court of law or equity * * * unless commenced within twelve months next after inception of the loss."

* * * Such a statutory requirement can hardly be termed a "contract of adhesion," imposed unfairly by the stronger party upon the weaker. Rather, it represents a legislative determination of a reasonable period within which suits must be brought, a careful balancing of the interests of both insurers and insured. The validity of this statutorily mandated limitation of suit provision has been consistently upheld. See, e.g., General State Authority v. Planet Insurance Co., 464 Pa. 162, 346 A.2d 265 (1975); Lardas v. Underwriters Insurance Co., 426 Pa. 47, 231 A.2d 740 (1967).

We have recognized that in certain circumstances, a limitation of suit provision will not be permitted to bar a delayed suit: "a provision of this nature may be extended or waived where the actions of the insurer lead the insured to believe the contractual limitation period will not be enforced." General State Authority v. Planet Insurance Co., supra, 464 Pa. at 165 n. 6, 346 A.2d at 267 n. 6. * * * Here, however, despite ample opportunity to do so, appellants have at no time alleged that any conduct of appellee, either active or passive, was in any way responsible for appellants' delay of over two years in commencing their action on the policy. In these circumstances, the court of common pleas properly granted appellee's motion for judgment on the pleadings, and the Superior Court properly affirmed. * * *

Order affirmed.

Notes

1. In *Plant v. Illinois Employers Insurance of Wausau*, 20 Ohio App.3d 236, 485 N.E.2d 773 (1984), the court held that the 12–month limitation on bringing suit on the policy will bar the breach of contract claim but not a tort claim based on the insurer's duty to act in good faith, as the claim is independent of the insurance policy. Cf. Hearn v. Rickenbacker, 428 Mich. 32, 400 N.W.2d 90 (1987).

2. In California law, the 12–month limitation is tolled between the time the claim is made and the time the claim is denied. Prudential–LMI Com. Ins. v. Superior Court, 51 Cal.3d 674, 693, 274 Cal.Rptr. 387, 798 P.2d 1230 (1990).

2. Proof of Loss

NAGEL–TAYLOR AUTOMOTIVE SUPPLIES, INC. v. AETNA CASUALTY & SURETY CO.

Appellate Court of Illinois, Fourth District, 1980.
81 Ill.App.3d 607, 37 Ill.Dec. 412, 402 N.E.2d 302.

GREEN, JUSTICE:

The principal issue in this case is whether under the evidence a jury could properly find that coverage under a fire insurance policy had not been voided by fraud and false swearing when the insured submitted a verified proof of loss containing an unreasonably high estimate of its business interruption loss.

The suit was brought in the circuit court of Sangamon County by plaintiffs Marvin C. Taylor (Taylor) and Nagel–Taylor Automotive Supplies, Inc., a corporation of which Taylor was the sole owner and principal officer. It was brought against defendant Aetna Casualty & Surety Company of Illinois to recover for a fire loss occurring on May 13, 1976, when a building near Litchfield, owned and operated by plaintiffs as a nightclub, burned. After a trial by jury a verdict was returned for plaintiff allowing $125,000 for damage to the building, $50,000 for damages to its contents and nothing for business interruption loss.

The trial court granted defendant's motion for judgment n.o.v. ruling that defendant had proved as a matter of law that plaintiffs had committed fraud and false swearing in the proof of loss statement. * * *

Plaintiffs appeal and defendant has filed notice of cross appeal.

Defendant's affirmative defense of fraud and false swearing was based on a policy provision which stated:

> "*Concealment, fraud.* This entire policy shall be void if, whether before or after a loss, the insured has willfully concealed or misrepresented any material fact or circumstance concerning this insurance or the subject thereof, or the interest of the insured therein, or in case of any fraud or false swearing by the insured relating thereto."

Under the terms of the policy plaintiffs were insured for actual business interruption losses such that they would be reimbursed for the amount by which their profits decreased (or losses increased) during the interruption, "but not exceeding the reduction in gross earning less charges and expenses which do not necessarily continue during the interruption of business * * *." The policy limited payment for this type of loss to the sum of $50,000. A written proof of loss verified by Taylor and timely mailed to defendant stated, "Gross earnings—estimated loss in excess of $100,000 for twelve month period."

The insured property was located on U.S. Route 66 south of Litchfield, a municipality of some 7,000 population. Prior to its purchase and remodeling by plaintiffs, the building had been used as a fast food franchise restaurant. The evidence indicated that the location became undesirable for that purpose when Interstate Route 55, passing Litchfield farther to the west, was opened to traffic. The strongest evidence in support of the affirmative defense of fraud and false swearing were the financial records of the operation. They indicated a deficit exceeding $17,000 to have accumulated in the eight months of the club's operation on total receipts of about $95,000. The cost of goods sold was about $14,000.

Charles T. Baker, a certified public accountant specializing in business interruption claims testified on behalf of defendant concerning his examination of the club's records. He described the business as being "in very poor financial condition" and stated that liabilities exceeded current assets by 16 to 1 but he did not state the seemingly more important ratio of current liabilities to current assets. He described the records as somewhat unreliable but concluded from his examination of them that no business interruption loss was sustained.

Taylor testified, attempting to justify his optimistic expectations by explaining how entertainment expenses had been drastically cut prior to the fire. He described how previously he had hired expensive entertainers such as those used in expensive Las Vegas nightclubs but due to small weeknight crowds he had recently begun to hire cheaper performers who would appeal to younger crowds.

Taylor presented a profit and loss statement for nine months, the figures for the last month having been lost. When this statement was compared with the records for the eight months as contained in the books it was shown that a profit of $4,500 would have had to have been made in the last month in order for the statement to reconcile with the books. Taylor apparently obtained the results shown on the statement by crediting expense accounts which previously listed as expense, rent theoretically owed, but not paid by the corporation to Taylor or vice versa. The business was run and the records kept in such a way that one could not readily tell the respective functions of Taylor and the corporation.

We consider Taylor's estimate to be unreasonably high, but in determining whether the jury could have properly determined that fraud and false swearing did not exist we deem it important that the estimate contained no assertion of an existing fact nor even an opinion concerning the quality or value of an existing object. It was merely a projection of future earnings.

* * * [T]he most analogous fraud and false swearing cases are those involving proof of loss claims which greatly overestimate the value of physical objects. In Tenore v. American and Foreign Insurance Co. of N.Y. (7th Cir.1958), 256 F.2d 791, cert. denied 358 U.S. 880, 79 S.Ct. 119, 3 L.Ed.2d 110, an insured had submitted a proof of loss statement claiming $78,000 for a destroyed gun collection. At the trial undisputed evidence showed many guns were old and missing parts. The insured's own expert testified to the collection being worth no more than $20,000. Similarly in Saks & Co. v. Continental Ins. Co. (1968), 23 N.Y.2d 161, 295 N.Y.S.2d 668, 242 N.E.2d 833, an insured's proof of loss statement that clothing destroyed by fire had been worth $985,000 was held to be false swearing as a matter of law. The holding was based largely upon the jury's having found the actual value to have been only $104,316 and plaintiffs having shown no explanation for this great disparity. The court noted that the insured was an expert in the clothing field and reasoned that the gross disparity caused an unrebutted presumption of fraud. In American Home Fire Assurance Co. v. Juneau Store Co. (7th Cir.1935), 78 F.2d 1001, a disparity between a proof of loss valuation estimate of $73,000 for certain goods and a subsequent jury determination that they were only worth $33,000 was held sufficient to make the proof of loss estimate fraudulent as a matter of law. The court concluded that the disparity showed that claim was made for goods that had not in fact been destroyed because no dispute existed as to the value of individual items.

In other cases where fraud and false swearing have been held to exist as a matter of law additional factors have been present. In Kavooras v. The Insurance Company of Illinois (1912), 167 Ill.App. 220, an insured's proof of loss statement claimed that destroyed groceries had a value of $4,114. However, the insured admitted that these groceries consisted of $714 worth recently salvaged from a fire and $450 worth recently purchased. In Folk v. National Ben Franklin Ins. Co. (1976), 45 Ill.App.3d 595, 4 Ill.Dec. 104, 359 N.E.2d 1056, plaintiff's proof of loss statement included items he had sold after the fire. In Harold J. Warren, Inc. v. Federal Mutual Ins. Co. (1st Cir. 1961), 386 F.2d 579, uncontradicted evidence showed that the contractor engaged to repair damaged air conditioning units had told the insured that only $3000 worth needed to be replaced because of the fire but nevertheless the insured submitted an $8750 proof of loss statement which included replacement of undamaged air conditioning units. Although holding fraud to have been proved as a matter of law there, the court stated:

> "Intent to defraud is not to be presumed and the trier of facts should make all reasonable allowance for lack of knowledge or sound judgment or for honest mistake on the part of the insured as well as for the tendency to believe that which is to one's own interest * * *." 386 F.2d 579, 581.

Reviewing courts have refused to find fraud or false swearing despite substantial discrepancies between the amount claimed in the proof of loss and the jury's verdict in Commercial Insurance Company of California v. J. Friedlander (1895), 156 Ill. 595, 41 N.E. 183 ($9,840 vs. $1,278); Badger Mutual Ins. Co. v. Morgan (1963), 313 F.2d 783 ($95,000 v. $35,400); and C–Suzanne's Beauty Salon, Ltd. v. General Ins. Co. (2nd Cir.1978), 574 F.2d 106. * * * See also Annot., 16 A.L.R.3d 774, "Insurance—Over-valuation of Loss" (1967).

Even in regard to the making of estimates of *existing* values of personal property, the court in *Harold J. Warren, Inc.* warned of the necessity for courts to make "reasonable allowances for lack of knowledge or sound judgment" on the part of the insured. That is even more applicable when applied to the making of *future* projections of earnings in a relatively new establishment in a volatile type of business. Many such businesses lose for a while and then become profitable. Taylor indicated an intention to change his method of operation. The jury could have believed that he thought that he could start operating at a substantial profit. Defendant points to the club's poor location and lack of surrounding population to support it. But these factors existed from the beginning, and the jury could have concluded that Taylor originally thought he could succeed because he was an overly optimistic person and this, rather than fraudulent design, accounted for his inflated proof of loss claim. This is especially true when we consider the dictum of *Harold J. Warren, Inc.* which noted that natural tendency "to believe that which is to one's own interest."

* * * We consider the inherently speculative nature of future profits to account for the lack of precedent. The more speculative an estimate is, the more difficult it becomes to find fraud or false swearing as a matter of law, especially where the estimate is made by a nonexpert.

Even though the jury rejected plaintiff's claimed business interruption loss and, even though Taylor's estimate of the loss was clearly unreasonable, neither prevented the jury from being able to properly conclude that Taylor actually had such an unrealistic view of the future. The jury's verdict was neither wrong as a matter of law nor contrary to the manifest weight of the evidence.

Defendant has properly called to our attention the damage to society resulting from fraud, false swearing, and arson by insureds. We recognize the seriousness of the problem but we do not think that our decision here, which may have the effect of permitting insureds to be imprecise in estimates of future earnings, will enlarge the problem. We recognize that an insurer need not be defrauded in order for the defense of false swearing to be established (16 A.L.R.3d 774, 798, sec. 10[b]), but we deem it appropriate to note that insurers are unlikely to give any significant weight to an assertion by an insured, as speculative as the instant one, without an examination of facts upon which it might be based.

As we now turn to the arson issue, we also note that defendant has stated that we should consider the evidence of arson as bearing upon the proof of fraud and false swearing. We consider the evidence of arson to have some probative value as to plaintiff's *modus operandi* and intent. But, whether plaintiff committed arson was a question of fact. * * *

Defendant's theory that the fire was caused by plaintiff's arson is based upon the strong and unrefuted testimony of two experts in the fire and arson investigation field which would indicate that someone purposefully set the building on fire by use of gasoline. Taylor testified, by way of alibi, that he spent the night of the fire in a motel in Jacksonville with his girlfriend while on a business trip. This testimony was supported by strong corroboration but there was also substantial circumstantial evidence that the fire was set at his direction. He had the obvious motive to set the fire to recoup his investment in a failing business. Evidence also showed that at the time of the fire all of the keys to enter the building were in Taylor's possession or that of those friendly to him. Firemen arriving on the scene found the building locked. Thus it could have been difficult for anyone else to have gotten into the building to set the fire. The jury could also have inferred that by controlling all of the known sets of keys, Taylor hoped that firemen answering the fire call would be impeded in getting in the building to put it out.

Other circumstantial evidence also inferred Taylor's complicity. He had left very little liquor in the store at the time of the fire and had recently moved out several pinball and cigarette machines. The alibi testimony could have been considered to be so perfect as to be likely contrived. Taylor had obtained a very detailed receipt from the motel. Nevertheless, the evidence was all circumstantial and, in view of the alibi testimony, did no more than to create a question of fact which the jury resolved in plaintiff's favor.

The result of our determination is that the jury verdict should be reinstated.

Notes

1. The principal case took considerable pains to distinguish a 1979 Seventh Circuit opinion applying Illinois law, *Lykos v. American Home Insurance Co.*, 609 F.2d 314 (7th Cir.1979). Factually the cases are somewhat similar—a restaurant-bar burned by arsonists, and a jury verdict for the insureds overturned by the trial judge n.o.v.

Lykos, the insured, employed a public insurance adjuster at a fee of 10 percent of the total recovery. Together the two came up with demonstrably inflated figures for damage to the building and for the food, liquor, and equipment (e.g., a clock that cost $200 was claimed as damaged to the extent of $2,200). A modest sum of $39,703 for business interruption was claimed—an amount apparently so low that the court of appeals did not bother to consider the special problem of evaluating business interruption losses. The over-valuations on the tangible items sufficed to defeat *all* claims. Some observations from the *Lykos* opinion are notable:

> "The plaintiffs not only claimed a loss $395,805 in their sworn statement in proof of loss, but later brought suit for the entire amount. It is clear * * * that the plaintiffs submitted the claim with the intent of receiving the entire amount." * * *
>
> "The plaintiffs attempt to dismiss some of the misrepresentations as mere estimates for purposes of negotiation, and they suggest that the exaggerated claims would have been ironed out had the insurance company been willing to negotiate. They contend that the evidence, therefore, does not establish the requisite intent to defraud. Even assuming that the plaintiffs did not intend to recover more than their actual losses and merely exaggerated the extent of loss with an eye to settling, we think the proper rule is that
>
> > 'a design on the part of the insured to gain a position of advantage in the settlement of the loss through false representations is a fraudulent design and the making of such representations knowingly for that purpose is an attempt to defraud * * *, even though the insured may not have expected or intended ultimately to obtain more than compensation for actual loss.'
>
> 14 Couch on Insurance 2d § 49:556 (1965).
>
> "This court has previously stated that the insured, if he suffers a loss, must honestly state, under oath, the extent of his loss and give this information to the insurer. He must not make false proofs of loss with intent to defraud the insurer. Although the penalty is heavy and seemingly harsh, it is one way of stopping the presentation of false, fictitious or inflated claims. False and exaggerated claims seemingly go hand in hand with incendiarism. The court should therefore unhesitatingly act to prevent attempted frauds on the part of the insured."

Relying upon the abbreviated outline of *Lykos* are the distinctions between the cases to be found in the facts or the basic attitudes of the opinion writers? What practical lessons in settlement negotiations of property claims can be extracted here?

2. *Criminalizing Lies.* State legislatures have captured the sentiment expressed in the preceding cases, essentially criminalizing civil fraud. Below is the California Legislature's treatment of the issue in the Penal Code.

California Penal Code

§ 550. False or fraudulent claims; prohibited acts

(a) It is unlawful to do any of the following:

(1) Knowingly present or cause to be presented any false or fraudulent claim for the payment of a loss, including payment of a loss under a contract of insurance.

(2) Knowingly present multiple claims for the same loss or injury, including presentation of multiple claims to more than one insurer, with an intent to defraud.

(3) Knowingly cause or participate in a vehicular collision, or any other vehicular accident, for the purpose of presenting any false or fraudulent claim.

(4) Knowingly present a false or fraudulent claim for the payments of a loss for theft, destruction, damage, or conversion of a motor vehicle, a motor vehicle part, or contents of a motor vehicle.

(5) Knowingly prepare, make, or subscribe any writing, with the intent to present or use it, or to allow it to be presented in support of any false or fraudulent claim.

(6) Knowingly assist, abet, solicit, or conspire with (A) any person who knowingly presents any false or fraudulent claim for the payment of a loss, including payment of a loss under a contract of insurance; (B) any person who knowingly presents multiple claims for the same loss or injury, including presentation of multiple claims to more than one insurer, with an intent to defraud; (C) any person who knowingly causes or participates in a vehicular collision, or any other vehicular accident, for the purpose of presenting any false or fraudulent claim; and (D) any person who knowingly prepares, makes, or subscribes any writing, with the intent to present or use it, or to allow it to be presented in support on any claim.

(7) Knowingly make or cause to be made any false or fraudulent claim for payment of a health care benefit.

(8) Knowingly submit a claim for a health care benefit which was not used by, or on behalf of, the claimant.

(9) Knowingly present multiple claims for payment of the same health care benefit with an intent to defraud.

(10) Knowingly present for payment any undercharges for health care benefits on behalf of a specific claimant unless any known overcharges for health care benefits for that claimant are presented for reconciliation at that same time.

3. *Arson and False Swearing.* Arson, of course, is an implicitly excluded risk, but it may be hard to prove even with the most suggestive circumstantial evidence as the principal case would indicate. However, arsonists have a tendency to lie when presenting proofs of loss and this may avoid the necessity of proving the arson defense. For example, in *Duke v.*

Hartford Fire Insurance Co., 617 F.2d 509 (8th Cir.1980), the insurer received a directed verdict, not on proof of arson, but because the insured admitted misrepresenting that he had no knowledge of the cause of the fire, that he was on a trip when the fire occurred, and that he had received no medical treatment for burns.

Insurance companies are said to be wary of undertaking arson investigations and defenses because of the prospect of exposure to extra-contractual damages where such investigations have been flubbed or simply failed to support the original suspicions with admissible evidence. See Chavers v. National Security Fire & Cas. Co., 405 So.2d 1 (Ala.1981), reversed, 456 So.2d 293 (1984); Dempsey v. Auto Owners Ins. Co., 717 F.2d 556 (11th Cir.1983); deVries v. St. Paul Fire & Marine Ins. Co., 716 F.2d 939 (1st Cir.1983); Gruenberg v. Aetna Ins. Co., 9 Cal.3d 566, 108 Cal.Rptr. 480, 510 P.2d 1032 (1973).

4. Ordinarily false swearing enables the insurer to recover *all* payments not just overpayments. See Northwestern National Ins. Co. v. Barnhart, 713 P.2d 1360 (Colo.App.1985) (insurer paid the claim, then sued for restitution—a precaution against a bad faith claim perhaps?). *Johnson v. South State Ins. Co.*, 288 S.C. 239, 341 S.E.2d 793 (1986), follows the minority position, holding that a fraudulent claim as to personalty did not avoid entire coverage on realty and living expenses.

5. *Refusal to Produce Records.* The Standard Fire Policy requires the insured to produce records relating to claims made. This represents another requirement that may waylay the insured. To recover for the theft of an auto (with jewelry worth, it is said, about $130,000 in it) should the insured be required to submit to interrogation as to his sources of income, whether or not he has been convicted of a crime, and to produce his income tax returns for the last five years? Yes, suggests the Supreme Court of Georgia in response to questions certified by the Eleventh Circuit U.S. Court of Appeals. Halcome v. Cincinnati Ins. Co., 778 F.2d 606 (11th Cir.1985); see also Stover v. Aetna Casualty & Surety Co., 658 F.Supp. 156 (S.D.W.Va.1987); but see Chavis v. State Farm Fire & Cas. Co., 317 N.C. 683, 346 S.E.2d 496 (1986) (reversing a lower court ruling upholding the right of an insurer, suspecting arson, to have the insured produce for examination all his bank records).

On the other hand, does the cooperation clause give the company the right to insist upon the examination of multiple claimants separately and apart from one another? See, United States Fidelity and Guaranty Co. v. Hill, 722 S.W.2d 609 (Mo.App.1986).

FINE v. BELLEFONTE UNDERWRITERS INS. CO.

United States Court of Appeals, Second Circuit, 1984.
725 F.2d 179, cert. denied, 469 U.S. 874, 105 S.Ct. 233, 83 L.Ed.2d 162.

IRVING HILL, SENIOR DISTRICT JUDGE:

In June 1978, Plaintiff, Fine, purchased three contiguous parcels of land in New York City for a total price of $1,300,000. Each parcel had a building on it. Though the buildings had separate addresses (649, 653 and 657 Broadway), they were also contiguous and were operated as a single economic unit. The three buildings had a single heating system which employed a single boiler.

Following the purchase, Fine, through a broker, obtained a policy of fire insurance covering the three buildings (and other properties) from defendant Bellefonte Underwriters Insurance Co. (hereinafter "Bellefonte"). The policy was in the standard New York form.

At the time of Fine's purchase, the buildings were occupied by commercial tenants, some artists, and others who conducted light manufacturing and warehousing businesses. Fine desired to convert the buildings to residential use. Toward that end, after buying the buildings, he did not renew most expiring leases and he engaged in a "freeze-out" policy designed to minimize expenses and discourage tenants from remaining. The heat timer which controlled operation of the boiler, based in part on outside temperature, was set so that it would not start up the heating system until a sub-freezing temperature was reached. Additionally, the superintendent was told to turn off the heating system entirely from 11 a.m. to 2 p.m. each day regardless of the outside temperature. By February 1979, when the fire occurred, only about one-third of the premises remained occupied.

On February 14, 1979, a fire of unknown origin occurred which started in the 649 and 653 Broadway buildings and spread to 657 Broadway. The buildings at 649 and 653 Broadway were totally destroyed except for their facades and the building at 657 Broadway was substantially damaged.

On the night of the fire the sprinkler system in the buildings, which was the main fire protection device, did not operate. The sprinkler system was of the so-called wet pipe constant pressure type. In this type of system, pipes within the building are filled with water which is under pressure from gravity tanks. In addition, there are fittings outside the buildings at street level to enable the Fire Department to pump water from city mains into the system. The trial judge found that on the night of the fire, none of the sprinkler heads in the system worked. The Fire Department was unable to pump water into the system due to blockage in the pipes which the trial court found was "presumably" caused by ice. The trial court found that had the sprinklers functioned normally, the fire could have been controlled.

Fine submitted claims on the policy which Bellefonte, after investigation, denied. Bellefonte based its denial of liability on the assertion that three separate provisions of the policy had been breached, claiming that a breach of any one of the three would relieve it of liability. The three provisions were:

1. The so-called "Protective Maintenance Clause",[12] which is a warranty that "protective systems and warning devices" will be maintained in complete working order and will not be altered.

12. The language of this policy provision is as follows:

Protective Maintenance. It is warranted that the insured shall maintain in complete

2. The so-called "Increased Hazard Clause",[13] which voids coverage if "the hazard is increased by any means within the knowledge of the insured."

3. The so-called "False Swearing Clause",[14] which provides that coverage is voided if, before or after a loss, the insured has willfully concealed or misrepresented any material fact concerning the insurance or the insured property, or in the event of any "fraud or false swearing by the insured" relating to any such material fact.

Fine filed the instant action against the insurer for payment of the loss. After a lengthy court trial, the trial court found in favor of Fine and against the insurance company and awarded a judgment of $1,214,221 for damage to the buildings[15] plus additional sums of $150,000 for loss of rental and $170,446.60 for debris removal. Bellefonte appeals. * * *

We reverse on the ground that Fine violated the false swearing provision of the policy, thus voiding the coverage and the trial court's conclusion to the contrary cannot stand. It is therefore unnecessary for us to reach the other issues raised in connection with the appeal or the cross-appeal.

The False Swearing Issue

The fire occurred during an extended period of extremely cold weather. Outside temperatures averaged 10° Fahrenheit on the day of the fire. Bellefonte quickly learned, as reported by the Fire Department, that the sprinkler system in the buildings had failed to operate during the fire. The rapid spread of the fire and much of the loss was attributed to the non-operation of the sprinklers.

Bellefonte also became aware, early on, of Fine's decision to rid the buildings of the existing commercial tenants and of the tenants' complaints that he had instituted a freeze-out policy. Bellefonte was naturally very interested, not only in what caused the fire, but also whether a freeze-out policy was in effect and, if so, whether Fine's actions in pursuit of the freeze-out might have contributed to the failure of the sprinkler system. An obvious theory suggested itself, i.e., that there had

working order such protective systems and warning devices as existed at time of attachment of this policy, or which the insured has agreed to install, insofar as it is under the insured's control or supervision, and that no change shall be made in the said protective systems and warning devices without the consent in writing of this company.

13. The language of this policy provision is as follows:

Conditions suspending or restricting insurance. Unless otherwise provided in writing added hereto this Company shall not be liable for loss occurring (a) while the hazard is increased by any means within the control or knowledge of the insured. * * *

14. The language of this policy provision is as follows:

Concealment, fraud. This entire policy shall be void if, whether before or after a loss, the insured has wilfully concealed or misrepresented any material fact or circumstance concerning this insurance or the subject thereof, or the interest of the insured therein, or in case of any fraud or false swearing by the insured relating thereto.

15. Four months after the fire the three properties were sold in their fire-damaged condition for $2 million with the sellers apparently retaining all rights to recovery under the policy.

been extremely low temperatures in the buildings before the fire which caused the pipes in the sprinkler system to freeze and that this was the result of conduct by the insured. The facts of which Bellefonte became quickly aware suggested the possibility that further investigation might establish a material breach of the protective maintenance clause or the increased hazard clause, or both.

With this in mind, Bellefonte conducted extensive examinations under oath of Mr. Martin Fine (the one owner, among the group of owners, in charge of operating the buildings), and of Mr. George Peters, managing agent for the owners. The examination of both dealt to a large extent with the instructions given and the provisions made for inspection and maintenance of the boiler heater and the sprinkler system, and particularly with the temperature setting employed on the heat timer that controlled the operation of the boiler.

The district court found that Fine and Peters each answered falsely during examination under oath. Both Fine and Peters stated in the examinations that they had charged the superintendent, a Mr. Aloisio, with the responsibility for inspecting and maintaining the sprinkler systems as he had been charged under the prior ownership. The trial court found such testimony to be false and that Aloisio had not been so charged or instructed.

During his examination, Mr. Fine testified that the nighttime setting for the heat timer controlling the boiler was 40 degrees and Mr. Peters testified that he had instructed superintendent Aloisio to set the heat timer at 40 degrees for nighttime operation. The trial court found that the testimony of both men was false in this respect. The court found that Aloisio had been instructed by Peters personally to set the heat timer at 25 degrees for nighttime and that Aloisio had, despite such instruction, set it for 30 degrees.

Despite the aforesaid findings of falsity, the trial court rendered judgment for Plaintiffs on the false swearing defense on the ground that the false statements were not material.

Under the heading, "Conclusions of Law", the trial court said:

> "Here the statements were not material to the investigation. Given the extreme temperatures during the period from February 5th to February 14 as noted above, whether the heat timer setting was 25 degrees, 30 degrees or 40 degrees would not have affected the operation of the heating system. Further there was no testimony that a 25 degree or 30 degree setting would have constituted a practice which would have reasonably been foreseen to result in a freezing condition, which, in turn would have made the sprinkler system inoperative."
>
> "Similarly with respect to the sprinkler maintenance issue, whether Aloisio was instructed to perform maintenance on the sprinkler system or not, in fact he did take the action necessary to repair the system, and there is no indication in this record that any

failure of record keeping or regular maintenance was in any way responsible for the freeze-up. Since the Fine policy of freeze-out has not been proved to be the cause of the freeze-up, the false statements, viewing them as such, were not material as contemplated under section 168 [of New York Insurance Law]."[16]

* * *

The trial judge regarded the materiality of the false statements as being dependent upon the ultimate determination of the facts concerning the fire as they were finally revealed to the court after a trial lasting many weeks. As the trial judge analyzed it, if it turned out, after a trial, that the sprinkler system would have been inoperative anyway on the night of the fire for reasons unrelated to the subject of the false statements, false statements about the setting of the heat timer and about maintenance and inspection of the sprinkler system made during the company's earlier investigation became immaterial. To make such statements material, the trial judge appears to reason, the insurer would have had to prove at the trial that the setting of the heat timer or a failure of maintenance of the sprinkler system caused the pipes to freeze and the sprinklers to be inoperative on the night of the fire.

In our view, the trial judge's definition of materiality was far too restrictive and not in accordance with long-established case law.

The issue is: Is a false statement material only if it relates to a matter or subject which ultimately proves to be decisive or significant in the ultimate disposition of the claim, or is it sufficient that the false statement concerns a subject reasonably relevant to the insurance company's investigation at the time? The law is clear that the materiality of false statements during an insurance company investigation is not to be judged by what the facts later turn out to have been. The purpose of a provision requiring an insured to submit to an examination under oath is to enable the insurance company to acquire knowledge or information that may aid it in its further investigation or that may otherwise be significant to the company in determining its liability under the policy and the position it should take with respect to a claim. Thus the materiality requirement is satisfied if the false statement concerns a subject relevant and germane to the insurer's investigation as it was then proceeding.

* * *

16. Section 168(6) of the New York Insurance Law prescribes the exact language to be used in a standard fire insurance policy in New York state, including the exact language of the section on false swearing. The statutory language was followed in the instant policy. Insurance statutes in all or nearly all of the states prescribe a standard fire insurance policy including the exact language to be employed therein. R. Keeton, *Basic Text on Insurance Law* 70 (1971). Of those who do, almost all use the New York form, including its exact "False Swearing Clause". Ins.L.Rep. Fire & Casualty Cas. (CCH) pp. 2002 (Dec. 6, 1972), 2003–04 (Nov.1982), 2007–10 (Apr.1982).

> If the plaintiffs knowingly and wilfully, with intent to defraud the defendants, swore falsely in making the proofs of loss, such act amounted to a fraud upon the defendants which avoided the policies, irrespective of the ultimate effect upon the defendants.

Meyer v. Home Insurance Co., 127 Wis. 293, 299–300, 106 N.W. 1087, 1089 (1906).

* * *

It thus appears that materiality of false statements is not determined by whether or not the false answers deal with a subject later determined to be unimportant because the fire and loss were caused by factors other than those with which the statements dealt. False sworn answers are material if they might have affected the attitude and action of the insurer. They are equally material if they may be said to have been calculated either to discourage, mislead or deflect the company's investigation in any area that might seem to the company, at that time, a relevant or productive area to investigate.

* * * Bellefonte was investigating a plausible theory reasonably derived from the available facts, one which would result in the voiding of its coverage. The questions were material to that investigation. It is irrelevant whether Bellefonte was ultimately able to muster sufficient evidence to prove its theory at trial.

* * * The judgment of the district court is therefore REVERSED. The case is remanded to the district court with instructions to enter judgment for the defendant.

Notes

1. Is the standard of "materiality" different when the false statement is made on the proof of loss than when it is made on the application? Should the state statutes as to the effect of "misrepresentations" be also applied to "false swearing" during post loss investigations?

2. The principal case does not address the issues of whether the insured breached a warranty or violated the "increase of the hazard" provision. Using the facts as related, how would you rule on these issues?

B. INSURERS DEFENSES

1. No Insurable Interest—Variations on a Theme

Insurable Interest: A Search for Consistency

[Extracts from the INSURANCE COUNSEL JOURNAL, Jan. 1979, p. 109 by Robert Stuart Pinzur].

Reprinted with permission.

To avoid the evils inherent in wagering contracts of insurance, the concept of insurable interest developed i.e., the insured was required to have an interest in the subject matter, at some time, as a prerequisite for recovery.

Two basic theories arose as guides for application of the insurable interest doctrine. The "legally enforceable right" theory required that the insured have some valid and recognizable property right in the subject matter. In contrast, the "factual expectations" view is based on the notion that the insured must suffer some actual loss or detriment from the damage, loss or destruction to the insured property, and maintain some gain, benefit or advantage from its continued existence. Courts have been inconsistent in the application of these two viewpoints. In fact, courts have created analytical problems by attempting to place an insured loss in one category or the other. The better view encourages courts to return to the underlying rationale and ask whether or not the particular contract of insurance constitutes a wager. The resolution of this controversy is best achieved by the application of the factual expectations approach, with a limitation that the insured be denied recovery to the extent such interest was created as a means to profit by wager.

The major issues regarding the nature of insurable interest were well-represented in *Lucena v. Crauford*,[17] an early nineteenth century English case. *Lucena* arose out of the capture of a foreign ship. Royal commissioners were authorized, in time of war, under a Parliamentary act, to take possession of certain ships and cargo brought into the territory of the United Kingdom. These commissioners procured insurance on several ships and cargo which were subsequently lost by perils of the sea on voyage from the port of seizure, but before reaching the Kingdom's port. The voyage's purpose was to put the ships and cargo in the commissioners' possession. The issue was whether or not the commissioners held an insurable interest in the ships, cargo and anticipated profits from the voyage. The commissioners, eventually, were awarded a verdict at a later trial. Nevertheless, the views of the Justices on the first appeal considerably influenced the development of insurable interest theory.

Lord Eldon spoke for the view that some legally enforceable property right was a prerequisite for an insurable interest and found that the commissioners lacked an insurable interest. Among other matters, he noted that the commissioners did not have good title to the property because the necessary condemnation by the court had not been formalized.

There was no question that an insured required an "interest" in the subject matter pursuant to 19 Geo. II, ch. 37. Lord Eldon believed that such interest had to be a legally enforceable property right because a mere expectation was inadequate.

The fact that the insurer had admitted the interest by issuing the insurance, but subsequently discovered there was no interest, was of no consequence to Eldon.

17. Bos. & Pul. 269, 127 Eng.Rep. 630 (1806).

Lord Eldon cautioned that the Commissioners were not acting in a trustee capacity. A trustee has a legal interest in the trust property and, therefore, has an insurable interest. Furthermore, Eldon recognized that a consignee could insure for the principal's benefit, but such beneficial interest had to be expressed.

Lord Eldon was concerned with the earlier era's equivalent of a "parade of horribles." If the commissioners held an insurable interest, he reasoned, any warehouseman or remotely interested party could insure. Thus, there would be nothing preventing "the West India Dock Company from insuring all the ships and goods which came to their docks". Numerous persons would then be entitled to insure. Here, Lord Eldon was referring to an insured who took the proceeds for his own benefit, rather than on behalf of another. The benefit would include fees and charges for prospective services, or the like, to be rendered along Eldon's horribles' parade. Furthermore, the insurance would be effective prior to the insured's possession.

Lord Eldon's dichotomy between an expectation, though a moral certainty, and a legally enforceable property right was best-illustrated by his own formulation:

> Suppose A. to be possessed of a ship limited to B. in case A. dies without issue; that A. has 20 children, the eldest of whom is 20 years of age; and B. is 90 years of age; it is a moral certainty that B. will never come into possession, yet there is a clear interest. On the other hand, suppose the case of the heir at law of a man who has an estate worth 20,000 £ a-year, who is 90 years of age; upon his death-bed intestate, and incapable from incurable lunacy of making a will, there is no man who will deny that such an heir at law has a moral certainty of succeeding to the estate; yet the law will not allow that he has an interest, or anything more than a mere expectation.

Lord Eldon added that irrespective of the expectation of profit, upon the loss of a ship of cargo, the "expectation is defeated" and no interest ever arose in such unascertained profits, other than a mere expectancy. Nonetheless, Lord Eldon's approach did not limit the insurable interest doctrine to a contract recognizing only one possible named insured for any insurable subject matter. A property interest is an expanding concept. It may be legal or equitable, a present possessory right or future interest, vested or contingent and may exist regardless of the likelihood that its possessor will ever realize and actually enjoy the specific property.

Vance on Insurance also supports the view that an insurable interest is only maintainable when the insured has some legally enforceable relationship to the property.[18] Citing Lord Eldon's *Lucena* opinion, Vance stated his own interpretation:

> While it is not necessary that the person insured shall have any title to the property insured, either legal or equitable, yet an expectation

18. Vance on Insurance 3d at 156.

of benefit, to be derived from its continued existence, however likely and morally certain of realization it may be, will not afford a sufficient insurable interest unless that expectation has a basis of legal right. If such legal basis exists, an expected benefit, however remote, constitutes an insurable interest.

Graham and six others, in *Lucena,* represented a second view of insurable interest—i.e., an expectancy coupled with an interest. First, it was contended that the commissioners were not claiming a beneficial interest for themselves, but as consignees, agents or trustees for others, namely the Crown. Furthermore, upon the ships' arrivals, the commissioners would have acquired a vested right to the whole legal interest, though held in trust.

* * *

It is unclear why an "expectancy coupled with an interest" does not fall within the two major interpretations: a legally enforceable right or a factual expectancy. If the interest is an enforceable property right, the former view would be sufficient. If the interest is less than an enforceable property right, it is an expectancy and, therefore, the latter theory would apply. Presumably, Graham was searching for some middle ground. However, a right is either legally enforceable or an expectancy, and nothing lies between.

Graham admitted that the commissioners' interest was inchoate and revocable, but compared it to a consignee whose interest is subject to alteration or revocation by the consignor. However, alteration of a consignee's interest results in a change of a legal and enforceable property relationship. In contrast, the commissioners did not change any property right or relationship.

Graham distinguished *Lucena* from *LeCras v. Hughes,*[19] the latter being "a case of mere expectations, and the circumstances were not near so strong in favor of the assured". Nevertheless, Graham maintained that some expectations were insurable. Furthermore, he posited that the commissioners might have sold the ships while at sea, subject to a contingency, and "it would then be most extraordinary if they could not insure them". Lord Eldon, presumably, would simply respond that a contract arose at the time of the sale, thereby creating the necessary legal interest.

19. 3 Dougl. 81, 99 Eng.Rep. 549 (1789). *LeCras* is noted for Lord Mansfield's formulation of the factual expectations doctrine. In *LeCras,* part of a ship's cargo was lost at sea. The ship had been seized during war. Insurance had been procured to protect the interests of the Captain, his officers and the crew. The insurer contended that the profits were a "mere expectancy" and, therefore, were not insurable prior to condemnation. Lord Mansfield recognized that some interest was necessary in a contract of indemnity, "but no particular kind of interest" was mandated. The court held that the Captain, officers and crew properly insured their profits, though they were contingent. Id. at 86, 99 Eng.Rep. at 552. Lord Mansfield added that such insurance prevented the risks of neutral claims and guards against a loss arising from the disappointment of an expectation which hitherto has never been disappointed.

Attempting to simplify the issue, Graham said the question must be whether or not the contract was one of gaming. Graham believed that *LeCras* was more likely to violate the policy against wagering contracts, whereas the commissioners, in *Lucena,* had a duty to preserve the property and, therefore, were not just "any number of persons" who might insure the ships.

Vance's view of a legally enforceable property right includes the so-called "expectancy coupled with an interest". He explained that an insurable interest exists if the insured maintains such relations to the subject property that:

> he has a reasonable expectation, resting upon a basis of legal right, of benefit to be derived from its continued existence, or of loss or liability from its destruction.[20]

Vance then specified the type of cases where an insurable interest would be present.

> (a) Where the insured possesses a legal title to the property insured, whether vested or contingent, defeasible or indefeasible.
>
> (b) When he has an equitable title, of whatever character and in whatever manner acquired.
>
> (c) When he possesses a qualified property or possessory right in the subject of the insurance, such as that of a bailee.
>
> (d) When he has mere possession or right of possession.
>
> (e) When he has neither possession of the property, nor any other legal interest in it, but stands in such relation with respect to it that he may suffer, from its destruction, loss of a legal right dependent upon its continued existence.[21]

The primary criticism of Vance's examples are that they are overly broad. Nonetheless, the list comports with Vance's requirement of a legally enforceable relationship. Vance says a mere possessor of property has an insurable interest therein, e.g., a thief or otherwise wrongful possessor. Vance explained that such person

> has a possessory right good as against all the world except the true owner or one having a prior right of possession.

Lawrence, J. spoke for the other major view of insurable interest in *Lucena,* known as the factual expectations doctrine. This theory was first articulated by Lord Mansfield in LeCras v. Hughes, twenty-four years earlier. It is based on the insured's interest in the preservation of the insurance subject matter. That is, the insured will suffer a detriment or loss, of some kind, if the property is lost or destroyed, but receives some benefit, gain or advantage by its continued existence.

20. Vance on Insurance, 124 (2d Ed.1930) (cited as "Vance").

21. Vance 3d at 161.

Following from his definition of insurance, Lawrence stated that it is available to protect persons against uncertain events which may be disadvantageous to them,

> not only those persons to whom positive loss arise by such events, occasioning the deprivation of that which they may possess, but those also who in consequence of such events may have intercepted from them the advantage or profit, which but for such events they would acquire according to the ordinary and probable cause of things.[22]

Lawrence found it obvious that a title owner is harmed by property loss. The property is important to the owner and he is concerned to avoid exposures to its damage. Yet, he admits it may be difficult to prove that the nonoccurrence of the event would have resulted in the realization of advantage. However, this difficulty was not sufficient proof to Lawrence that insurance, as an abstract concept, must be limited to property rights where it is impossible to measure the profitability of gain being intercepted by such risks. Nevertheless, Lawrence admitted that "an interest so uncertain" may not be insurable. The obvious dilemma arises in attempting to distinguish between an insurable interest and one too uncertain. Yet, one must realize that most legal distinctions and standards are inherently vague, but still subject to resolution.[23]

Lawrence was concerned about the moral hazard and enforcement of wagering agreements. However, he found a sufficient interest in the insured, which overcame the wager question, based on an advantage from continued existence or prejudice from nonexistence. Yet, Lawrence did qualify that the advantage or benefit must be morally certain.

Discussing the context of *Lucena,* Lawrence said the commissioners would have "no existing concern" in the property and, therefore, could suffer no loss until their authority and duty as commissioners would attach. Furthermore, Lawrence noted that the commissioners' incapacity to abandon the property, where capable of abandonment, was indicative of a lack of interest at the time of loss.

Patterson also recognized the factual expectations view. He wrote that an insurable interest was not restricted to property rights, but that some "substantial loss or injury" to the insured was necessary.[24] In fact, Patterson suggested the importance of a factual expectancy:

> (I)t is believed that a carefully drawn policy explicitly covering a genuine factual expectation interest, valued by the policy at a fair sum or measured by any fair scale clearly defined, would not be declared unenforceable on the ground of wagering.

* * *

22. 2 Bos. & Pul. at 301, 127 Eng.Rep. at 643.

23. See, e.g., Bird v. St. Paul Fire & Marine Insurance Co., 224 N.Y. 47, 55, 120 N.E. 86, 88 (1918).

24. Patterson, Essentials of Insurance Law 109 (2d Ed.1957).

Notes

1. Almost 30 years later, the Parliament enacted a statute concerning insurable interest in *lives.* 14 Geo. III, c. 48 (1778).

2. The anachronisms of *Lucena* are preserved in California Insurance Code § 282 which declares that an insurable interest in property may consist in an inchoate interest founded on an existing interest or an expectancy coupled with an existing interest in that out of which the expectancy arises.

3. For additional discussion of the development of insurable interest requirements see Robert E. Keeton & Alan I. Widiss, Insurance Law (West, 1988), 3.2–3.5; see also Robert H. Jerry II, Understanding Insurance Law (3d ed. Matthew Bender 2001), Ch. 4.

G.M. BATTERY & BOAT COMPANY v. L.K.N. CORP.

Supreme Court of Missouri, En Banc, 1988.
747 S.W.2d 624.

BLACKMAR, JUDGE.

LKN Corporation (LKN) leased a commercial building from G.M. Battery and Boat Co. (GMB) for a term of two years commencing March 1, 1982 at a rental of $1,500 per month. The lease granted the lessee an option to purchase the property during the term for $145,000 with a credit on the purchase price of one-half of the rental paid during the second year. The lease also contained the following provision: No. 11. Insurance. Tenant agrees to maintain at his expense throughout the term of this Lease an all hazard insurance policy in the amount of $75,000.00 payable to and acceptable to Landlord. Tenant further agrees to deliver to the landlord a certificate of the insuring company certifying that such insurance is in full force and effect. (L.F. 195–196).

LKN did not obtain an insurance policy which complied with the requirements of the lease. It instead purchased a policy from St. Paul Fire and Marine Insurance Co., effective June 1, 1983, covering the building on the leased premises for $125,000 and the contents for $70,000. GMB was not named as a loss payee under this policy, but Mark Twain State Bank, which had lent money secured by inventory, was so named.

On August 23, 1983, the building and contents were totally destroyed by fire. GMB collected $75,000 on a policy which it had obtained on the building from an insurer other than St. Paul. St. Paul denied liability for any part of the building loss, claiming that LKN had no insurable interest in the building. It admitted liability for the contents coverage, subject to determination of the proper claimant, and for business interruption, to the extent that loss could be proved. These latter coverages are not in issue in this phase of the litigation.

GMB filed suit against LKN, St. Paul, and others. It sought $75,000 in damages from LKN for breach of the lease contract in failing to procure insurance on the building. LKN cross-claimed against St. Paul for the entire proceeds of its policy. St. Paul paid the $70,000 contents coverage into court, seeking to interplead possible claimants, and filed an answer denying liability on the building coverage because of LKN's lack of insurable interest. Other claims in the somewhat complicated litigation are not material to this appeal and need not be discussed.

The trial court entered summary judgment for GMB against LKN for $75,000 for failure to provide insurance, and for LKN against St. Paul for $125,000, this being the entire building coverage under its policy. Both of these judgments were declared to be final and appealable as authorized by Rule 81.06. St. Paul appealed, but LKN did not. The court of appeals reversed, finding that LKN did not have an insurable interest in the building. We granted transfer to consider possible conflict with DeWitt v. American Family Insurance Co., 667 S.W.2d 700 (Mo. banc 1984). Taking the case as on initial appeal, we conclude that DeWitt indeed states the proper rule of decision and affirm the judgment of the circuit court. The case comes to the writer on recent reassignment.

St. Paul urges a single point for reversal, as follows: THE TRIAL COURT ERRED IN FINDING THAT THE LESSEE L.K.N. CORP. WAS ENTITLED TO THE PROCEEDS OF THE INSURANCE FOR THE BUILDING FOR THE REASON THAT THE LESSEE WITH ONLY AN UNEXERCISED OPTION TO PURCHASE HAD NO INSURABLE INTEREST IN THE PLAINTIFF OWNER'S BUILDING SUCH THAT IT COULD OBTAIN COVERAGE FOR THE BUILDING AS THE NAMED INSURED.

* * *

The controlling rule, perhaps borrowed from elsewhere, but expounded in numerous Missouri cases, is as follows:

In general, a person has an insurable interest in the subject matter insured where he has such a relation or concern in such subject matter that he will derive pecuniary benefit or advantage from its preservation, or will suffer pecuniary loss or damage from its destruction, termination, or injury by happening of the event insured against. The substance of this rule, interestingly, is set out in Crossman v. American Insurance Co., supra, 164 N.W. at 429. It was emphatically applied in DeWitt, supra, which is the latest pronouncement of our Court on the subject of insurable interest in property. In DeWitt a husband and wife held real property which was awarded to the husband on dissolution of their marriage. The husband then died and his former wife took possession of the property, which she used to make a home for herself and a child of the marriage. She insured the property against fire in her own name. We held that, inasmuch as she was liable on the note secured by a deed of trust on the property, she had an insurable interest in spite of her lack of title, and that, when the property was totally destroyed, she was entitled to recover the entire face amount of the policy.

In Wrausmann v. Kansas City Fire and Marine Insurance Co., 477 S.W.2d 741 (Mo.App.1972), a person liable on a mortgage note, apparently as a "straw party," was held to have an insurable interest in property. A familiar quotation used by the court, reading as follows, is pertinent: It is not necessary, to constitute an insurable interest, that the interest would be such that the event insured against would necessarily subject the insured to loss; it is sufficient that it might do so, and that pecuniary injury would be the natural consequence * * * although a person has no title, legal or equitable, in the property, and neither possession nor a right to possession, yet he has an insurable interest therein if it is primarily charged in either law or equity with a debtor obligation for which he is secondarily liable.

Graves v. Stanton, 621 S.W.2d 524 (Mo.App.1981), involved an insurance policy taken out by the lessee of a trailer. The lessee had an option to purchase, with rental payments to be credited on the option price, and was required by the lease to maintain insurance on the trailer. The court found that the lessee had an insurable interest. St. Paul seeks to distinguish this case on the ground that the lessee had given notice of his intention to exercise the option before the trailer was destroyed. The attempted distinction is not total, for by established law an insurable interest must exist both when the insurance is written and at the time of the loss. The case is inconsistent with the existence of any categorical rule in Missouri that the holder of an unexercised option does not have an insurable interest. The optionholder has an insurable interest if there is potential for loss in the destruction of the subject property.

Other Missouri cases are consistent with our conclusion. In Farmers Mutual Fire & Lightning Co. v. Crowley, 354 Mo. 649, 190 S.W.2d 250 (1945), the court held that a life tenant could insure property for its full value and could collect the entire proceeds to the exclusion of the remainderman if there is a total loss. A holding of the court of appeals that the insurance would redound to the benefit of the remainderman, 187 S.W.2d 346 (Mo.App.1945), was expressly rejected. In M.F.A. Mutual Insurance Co. v. Gulf Insurance Co., 445 S.W.2d 829 (Mo.1969), we held that a building contractor had an insurable interest in an uncompleted house which he was required by contract to complete. The material circumstance in determining insurable interest is not title, but possibility of loss. Our courts make every effort to find insurable interest, and to sustain coverage, when there is any substantial possibility that the insured will suffer loss from the destruction of the property. Other supporting cases are cited in DeWitt.

St. Paul cites Puritan Insurance Co. v. Yarber, 723 S.W.2d 98 (Mo.App.1987). This is the most recent of a line of court of appeals cases holding that nobody but the holder of a certificate of title (or, no doubt, a duly endorsed lienholder) has an insurable interest in a motor vehicle. The result is deemed necessary by reason of § 301.210, RSMo 1986, which establishes a strong policy against informal transfers of title to motor vehicles and provides that any attempted transfer is void unless accompanied by delivery of a duly endorsed certificate of title. Policy reasons attend the titling of motor vehicles which are not present when the insurance covers real property.

Likewise distinguishable is Lumbermens Mutual Insurance Co. v. Edmister, 412 F.2d 351 (8th Cir.1969), applying Missouri law. There the owner of real property sold the property but maintained the existing insurance in force in his own name. He then sought to collect the proceeds when the property was destroyed by fire. The court found that he had misled the insurance company as to the state of his title. This finding is sufficient to support the denial of recovery.

Here it is patent that LKN could suffer loss if the building on the leased premises were destroyed. It had bound itself to furnish insurance payable to GMB, and has actually been held to pay damages for the breach of this covenant. There is no reason why its failure of literal compliance with the lease term should redound to the benefit of St. Paul, by relieving it of a liability which it voluntarily assumed for a loss actually suffered by its insured. LKN also stood to lose the remaining six months of the term of its lease, as well as the utility of the option and the rent credit on the option price. These very real possibilities for loss establish LKN's insurable interest.

Inasmuch as insurable interest is manifest, LKN is entitled to recover the full face amount of the policy for the total loss. The insurer makes no claim of depreciation, and so full recovery is mandated by Section 379.140, RSMo 1986, which places the risk of overinsurance on the insurer rather than on the insured. The insurer may protect itself by strictly defining the interest covered by its policy, or by obtaining representations or warranties about the state of the title, if it deems this information important. What it cannot do is to issue a policy, collect the premiums, and then argue that the value of the insured's insurable interest in the property is less than the coverage it underwrites. See DeWitt v. American Family Insurance Co., supra; Farmers Mutual Fire & Lighting Co. v. Crowley, supra.

Inasmuch as we reject the only point urged by St. Paul for reversal, the judgment appealed from is affirmed and the case is remanded for further proceedings not inconsistent with this opinion.

Notes

1. Determining whether or not one spouse has an "insurable interest" in a property held by title in the name of the other has lead to inconsistent results. In *Silberman v. Royal Insurance Co.*, 184 A.D.2d 562, 584 N.Y.S.2d 625 (1992), the New York Supreme Court held that a husband, who paid for his wife's vehicle and paid the insurance premiums on the vehicle, did not have an insurable interest because his wife was the uncontested "sole owner" of the automobile. Thus, the husband's case to recover for the loss of the automobile was dismissed because he did not have a valid claim.

2. In *DeWitt v. American Family Mutual Insurance Co.*, 667 S.W.2d 700 (Mo.1984), a case discussed in *G.M. Battery*, the court held that the wife

did have an insurable interest in property that was the "sole and separate property" of her ex-husband. *Id.* at 704. As the court in *G.M. Battery* noted, the wife had an insurable interest in the real property because she was responsible for the deed, regardless of the absence of her name on the title. Thus, in some situations making the payments is enough to give a spouse an insurable interest in property, whereas, in other situations, there is no insurable interest unless the claimant's name appears on the title document. Could the different outcomes be deduced to the different nature of the property involved: personal v. real? What would be the outcome in a community property state?

HUNTER v. STATE FARM FIRE AND CASUALTY COMPANY

Supreme Court of Alabama, 1989.
543 So.2d 679.

PER CURIAM.

This is an appeal from a summary judgment in favor of State Farm Fire and Casualty Company ("State Farm") and its agent, Bobby Baker, in an action by Ida Mae Hunter based on breach of contract and negligence. We reverse.

Ida Mae Hunter and her husband, Howard K. Hunter, acquired their house in Fultondale, Alabama, by warranty deed in 1962. Mr. Hunter died in 1969. In 1970, Mrs. Hunter purchased a homeowner's insurance policy from State Farm through its agent Bobby Baker. This policy insured Mrs. Hunter's interest in the home and the personal property in the home. The policy was renewed each year and was in effect on October 7, 1985, when the insured premises was destroyed by fire.

Mrs. Hunter did not live in the house after her hospitalization in 1982. After staying with a daughter and then living in Florida for a short time, Mrs. Hunter, in 1984, established her residence in an apartment complex for senior citizens. Mrs. Hunter informed State Farm of her change of residence in a letter dated June 1984; State Farm forwarded this letter to Baker, who put it in Mrs. Hunter's file. Mrs. Hunter, however, continued to pay the policy premiums when they were due. Mrs. Hunter's son suffered a theft loss at the house in February 1985, and the claim for this loss was paid by State Farm.

State Farm denied Mrs. Hunter's claim for the loss of the house, contending that Mrs. Hunter did not have legal title to the house. State Farm based its conclusion on the fact that in 1982, while hospitalized after a heart attack, Mrs. Hunter had signed a warranty deed transferring legal title to the house to her children. Mrs. Hunter claims, however, that she was misinformed about the nature of the instrument and that she thought the document she signed in the hospital provided that her home would go to her children upon her death. In addition, Mrs. Hunter continued to pay taxes on the home. Her grandson lived in the house and apparently paid her rent "once or twice." He also agreed to keep up the house for her. She kept most of her belongings, other than personal effects, in the house while she lived in the apartment. Part of the reason she moved into the apartment was that it was thought the house had too many stairs for someone in her condition, and it can be inferred that when her health improved the stairs would not be an obstacle. She maintained that she always intended to return to the house and that she had begun fixing it up for her return.

Mrs. Hunter sued her children, seeking a declaration of rights in the subject property, claiming in particular that the children held the property in a constructive trust. Mrs. Hunter sued State Farm for breach of the terms of the contract of homeowner's insurance. She also sued State Farm and its agent, Bobby Baker, for negligently failing to maintain the insurance to protect her interest in the home and the personal property in it. In its answer, State Farm asserted that Mrs. Hunter did not have an insurable interest in the property damaged by the fire and that State Farm was not guilty of negligence. Bobby Baker's answer denied Mrs. Hunter's claim of negligence on his part. The trial court granted Baker's motion for summary judgment.

The trial court also granted State Farm's motion for summary judgment, except as to Mrs. Hunter's claim for the value of her personal property that had been destroyed by the fire. * * *

On appeal, Mrs. Hunter first claims that State Farm was negligent in failing to provide her with insurance coverage for the subject property. The record is clear, however, that the insurance policy that Mrs. Hunter had purchased for her home was in full force and effect at the time the home was destroyed by fire. The question remains, and was raised by Mrs. Hunter as her second issue on appeal, whether State Farm was justified, under the terms of the policy and the law of Alabama, in refusing to honor Mrs. Hunter's claim for loss.

Alabama Code 1975, § 27–14–4, provides:

> "(a) No contract of insurance of property or of any interest in property, or arising from property, shall be enforceable as to the insurance except for the benefit of persons having an insurable interest in the things insured as at the time of the loss.
>
> "(b) 'Insurable interest,' as used in this section, means any actual, lawful and substantial economic interest in the safety or preservation of the subject of the insurance free from loss, destruction or pecuniary damage or impairment.
>
> "(c) The measure of an insurable interest in property is the extent to which the insured might be damnified by loss, injury or impairment thereof."

The statute is a codification of the longstanding rule in Alabama that, in order to receive benefits for a loss under a contract of property insurance, an insured must have an "insurable interest" in the insured property. National Security Fire & Casualty Co. v. Newman, 53 Ala.App. 614, 303 So.2d 113 (1974). This principle of law is also made part of the language of insurance contracts, such as the instant policy, by words to the effect that the "insured" must be the resident of the insured property.

The Court of Civil Appeals in Ex parte Granite State Ins. Co., 362 So.2d 241 (Ala.1978), correctly held that Alabama law recognizes an insurable interest based upon a "factual expectation" theory as opposed to a "legal interest" theory:

> "That view is that an insurable interest exists if the insured will gain economic advantage from the continued existence of the property or will suffer economic disadvantage upon damage to or loss of the property. Harnett & Thornton, Insurable Interest in Property: a Socio–Economic Reevaluation of a Legal Concept, 48 Colum.L.Rev. 1162 (1948); Vukowich, Insurable Interest: When It Must Exist in Property and Life Insurance, 7 Willamette L.J. 1 (1971).
>
> "We believe Alabama by statute and court decision has already espoused the 'factual expectation' theory of insurable interest. "Our supreme court has stated that one can have an insurable interest, although he has no property in the thing insured, but any limited or qualified interest, equitable right or expectation of advantage is sufficient. Put another way, insurable interest exists where insured would suffer a loss from the property's destruction." Id. at 241.
>
> "[S]ince the requirement of an insurable interest arose merely to prevent the use of insurance for illegitimate (gambling) purposes, it should not be extended beyond the reasons for it by an excessively technical construction. And a right of property is not an essential ingredient of insurable interest; any limited or qualified interest, whether legal or equitable, or any expectancy of advantage, is sufficient. It does not matter in what way such benefit arises or the reason loss would occur thereby, limited presumably by dictates or public policy—if such benefit would be lost by destruction of the subject matter, that interest is insurable.
>
> "Thus, it may safely be said that a fee title is clearly not required of the insured, nor even a direct property interest, the test of exposure to financial loss being all important. An equitable title or interest or other qualified property right would clearly be sufficient. And a person who had made himself responsible for property may insure it against loss." 4 Appleman, Insurance Law and Practice § 2123 (1969).

In Luchansky v. Farmers Ins. Co., 357 Pa.Super. 136, 515 A.2d 598 (1986), the court found an insurable interest in a house destroyed by fire, notwithstanding the fact that the insureds had given an unconditional deed of conveyance to their son. The insureds continued to pay taxes, made mortgage payments, collected all or some of the rent, and made repairs.

Mrs. Hunter undertook most of the same activities as the Luchanskys, albeit on a more limited scale. In addition, it is interesting to note, that as in Luchansky, the grantees in this case subsequently reconveyed the property to the insured. This after-the-fact conveyance gives some credence to Mrs. Hunter's claim that the original conveyance was not intended to be an unconditional fee simple transfer.

A mere expectancy that the owner will make a testamentary disposition of the property to the insured is insufficient to establish an insurable interest. Brewton v. Alabama Farm Bureau Mutual Casualty Ins. Co., 474 So.2d 1120 (Ala.1985). However, both the life tenant and the remaindermen have insurable interests. Dickerson v. Stewart, 473 So.2d 1078 (Ala.Civ.App.1985). There is evidence to support Mrs. Hunter's claim that the conveyance was intended to create a life estate in her. "A constructive trust is a creature of equity which prevents unjust enrichment. It will be applied when property has been acquired by fraud or where it would be inequitable to allow it to be retained by him who holds it." Seals v. Seals, 423 So.2d 222 (Ala.1982).

In light of the above and the fact that the trial court's order does not expressly address the viability of Mrs. Hunter's claim that a constructive trust should be established, we hold that summary judgment on the "insurable interest" issue was improperly granted to the defendant.

Reversed and Remanded.

Note

On remand, the trial court found Ms. Hunter had no insurable interest in the property. Hunter v. State Farm Fire & Casualty Co., 577 So.2d 908 (1991).

TUBLITZ v. GLENS FALLS INSURANCE CO.

Superior Court of New Jersey, Law Division, Essex County, 1981.
179 N.J.Super. 275, 431 A.2d 201.

Baime, J.D.C. (temporarily assigned).

This case presents a question of first impression in New Jersey. Defendant is the insurer of three buildings owned by plaintiff. On November 14, 1979 plaintiff entered into a contract for demolition of the buildings. The contract was to be performed within ten days. On November 18, 1979 one of the buildings was destroyed by fire. At issue is whether the accidental destruction of the building is a loss for which defendant must indemnify plaintiff under the fire insurance policy. The carrier has denied coverage on the ground that plaintiff has suffered no loss since it was the latter's intention to demolish the building in any event. Plaintiff maintains that defendant is liable for the actual cash value of the building. Plaintiff now seeks summary judgment as to liability only.

* * *

No New Jersey court has had occasion to determine the effect of impending demolition upon the insurable interest in a building. This issue has been considered in other jurisdictions, however. It is generally held that the existence of an executory contract for demolition of a building does not deprive the owner of an insurable interest in the property. Garcy Corp. v. Home Ins. Co., 496 F.2d 479, 481 (7 Cir.1974); Knuppel v. American Ins. Co., 269 F.2d 163, 166 (7 Cir.1959); Dubin Paper Co. v. Insurance Co. of North America, 361 Pa. 68, 63 A.2d 85, 93 (Sup.Ct.1949); Eagle Square Mfg. Co. v. Vermont Mut. Fire Ins. Co., 125 Vt. 221, 212 A.2d 636, 639 (Sup.Ct.1965).[25]

The mere fact that an executory contract exists for demolition does not render a structure worthless nor deprive it of its value as a matter of law. * * * The existence of such a contract does not deprive the owner of an insurable interest in his building. Gendron v. Pawtucket Mut. Ins. Co., 384 A.2d 694, 697 (Me.Sup.Ct.1978). A finding that an insurable interest in the building no longer exists typically involves a situation in which the demolition work has begun at the time of the fire. Aetna State Bank v. Maryland Cas. Co., 345 F.Supp. 903 (N.D.Ill.1972); Board of Education v. Hartford Fire Ins. Co., 124 W.Va. 163, 19 S.E.2d 448 (Sup.Ct.1942).[26]

The reasonable expectations of the insured must be considered in determining coverage. * * * In this case the fire occurred before any demolition work had begun. Despite the fact that the demolition contract was scheduled to be performed within ten days, it cannot be stated with certainty that it would, in fact, be commenced within that period. Performance of the contract may have been delayed by a number of factors, both within and beyond the control of the parties. So too, plaintiff could have chosen to repudiate the contract prior to demolition. Therefore, it is reasonable to infer from all the surrounding circumstances that plaintiff expected his fire insurance coverage to be in force until demolition was actually begun.

* * * Therefore, partial summary judgment is granted in favor of plaintiff on the issue of liability. An appropriate order should be submitted.[27]

Notes

1. *The Mortgagor–Grantor. Does the Insurable Interest Cease Upon Sale?* According to the court in *Reid v. Hardware Mutual Insurance Co. of the Carolinas*, 252 S.C. 339, 166 S.E.2d 317 (1969):

25. An exception to this rule is recognized in cases where the executory demolition contract is subject to specific performance. See Royal Ins. Co. v. Sisters of the Presentation, 430 F.2d 759 (9 Cir.1970); Lieberman v. Hartford Ins. Co., 6 Ill.App.3d 948, 287 N.E.2d 38 (Ct.App.1972). This exception is inapplicable to the case at bar.

26. An insurable interest has been recognized even in situations where demolition has begun, however. See Eagle Square Mfg. Co., supra, 212 A.2d at 637; Irwin v. Westchester Fire Ins. Co., 58 Misc. 441, 109 N.Y.S. 612 (Sup.Ct.1908).

27. I have no occasion to decide the applicable measure of damages or whether the executory demolition contract will be admissible at a hearing to determine damages. See Elberon Bathing Co. v. Ambassador Ins. Co., 77 N.J. 1, 389 A.2d 439 (1978). Resolution of those issues must await a plenary hearing.

> "Many cases hold that a mortgagor who has sold the premises, being still liable for the mortgage debt, has an insurable interest in the property. Lumbermen's Nat. Bank v. Corrigan, 167 Wis. 82, 166 N.W. 650; Farmers & Merchants Bank v. Hartford Fire Ins. Co., 43 Idaho 222, 253 P. 379; Hanover Fire Ins. Co. v. Bohn, 48 Neb. 743, 67 N.W. 774; American Ins. Co. v. Dean, Mo.App., 243 S.W. 415; Baughman v. Niagara Fire Ins. Co., 163 Minn. 300, 204 N.W. 321. In the Baughman case it was held that because of the plaintiff's liability on the mortgage note to the bank he had an insurable interest in the property, even though his grantee had assumed the mortgage. In the Dean case it was held that where an owner had conveyed the insured premises and was not released from the payment of the mortgage indebtedness thereon he retained an insurable interest in the property conveyed, as a loss thereof would affect his liability on the note."

But see Sander v. Hartford Fire Ins. Co., 637 S.W.2d 793 (Mo.App.1982) (contra).

2. *Insurable Interest in Stolen Property—Generally Automobiles.* Applying the rubric that there can be no *bona fide* purchase from a thief, a number of cases have held that the luckless possessor of stolen property, however personally innocent, cannot recover on a theft policy when, say, an automobile is in turn stolen from him. Such a result is virtually compelled if one follows the analysis of Lord Eldon in the *Lucena* case. However, a number of re-stolen auto cases have been decided the other way. *Reznick v. Home Insurance Co.*, 45 Ill.App.3d 1058, 4 Ill.Dec. 525, 360 N.E.2d 461 (1977), summarizes the situation:

> While some jurisdictions hold a good faith purchaser of a stolen automobile has no insurable interest in such vehicle (Ernie Miller Pontiac, Inc. v. Home Ins. Co., supra; Ins. Co. of N. Am. v. Cliff Pettit Motors, Inc. (Tenn.1974), 513 S.W.2d 785, 787; Herrington v. American Secur. Ins. Co. (1971), 124 Ga.App. 617, 184 S.E.2d 673, 674), others have held that a good faith purchaser has an insurable interest since he has good title against all but the true owner (Scarola v. Ins. Co. of North America (1972), 31 N.Y.2d 411, 340 N.Y.S.2d 630, 292 N.E.2d 776; Barnett v. London Assur. Corp. (1926), 138 Wash. 673, 245 P. 3). Plaintiff is not involved in a dispute with the true owner, but rather with the insurance company which has accepted premium payments by plaintiff in consideration for comprehensive insurance coverage on the Ford. Plaintiff had a right of possession of the car against any contrary assertion, except that of the true owner.
>
> We find that plaintiff has established in his pleadings and his deposition admitted as part of the record that he would have profited by continued possession of the Ford, and that he suffered an economic loss by its confiscation. We agree with those courts which, under similar facts, hold that a good faith purchaser of a stolen automobile has an insurable interest in such vehicle.

Perhaps these auto cases should be viewed narrowly—because of the practice of using state issued certificates of title in connection with auto transfers. These "pink slips" furnish a source for reasonable reliance by purchasers not applicable as to other chattels. In *Horton v. State Farm Fire*

& Casualty Co., 550 S.W.2d 806 (Mo.App.1977), the court found the victimized buyer had no insurable interest because the state's registration statute mandated literal compliance, whereas the application to transfer title to the previously stolen car did not contain the true I.D. number of the auto.

3. Insured was the owner of a building and the franchisor of the retail hardware business conducted on the premises. His fire policy covered both the building and the inventory belonging to the franchisee. The building and inventory were destroyed by fire. The insurer paid for the building but not for the inventory, claiming that the insured had no insurable interest in it. What ruling? See Seals, Inc. v. Tioga County Grange Mut. Ins. Co., 359 Pa.Super. 606, 519 A.2d 951 (1986) (remanded to apply the factual expectation theory because "Seals clearly offered evidence that might lead a jury reasonably to conclude that it had a reasonable expectation of benefit from the preservation of the inventory or, at a minimum, that it might suffer pecuniary loss if the inventory were to be destroyed").

2. There Is No Contract

CHRIST GOSPEL TEMPLE v. LIBERTY MUTUAL INSURANCE CO.

Superior Court of Pennsylvania, 1979.
273 Pa.Super. 302, 417 A.2d 660.

MONTGOMERY, JUDGE:

* * *

The record shows that for many years, the congregation of Westminster Presbyterian Church (hereinafter referred to as "Westminster") owned and occupied a church building at Green and Reily Streets in the City of Harrisburg. In May, 1968, Westminster purchased a fire insurance policy on this building from the Appellee, Liberty Mutual Insurance Co. (hereinafter referred to as "Liberty"). The policy was written for an initial term of three years, and in May, 1971, was renewed for an additional three years. Premiums were paid annually and the last premium was paid by Westminster to cover the period from May, 1972 through May, 1973. Apparently for reasons of declining membership, in August, 1972, Westminster merged into another Presbyterian organization, the Appellant Presbyterian Church of Harrisburg (hereinafter referred to as "Presbyterian"). In the merger, Presbyterian acquired the former Westminster property at Green and Reily Streets. On December 19, 1972, Presbyterian conveyed that property for $9,000 to the Appellant Christ Gospel Temple (hereinafter referred to as "Christ Gospel"). Presbyterian also made a written assignment to Christ Gospel of Westminster's insurance policy with Liberty, for a separate consideration of $750. That amount apparently represented that part of the policy premium paid in advance for the remainder of the annual policy term. In its deed to Christ Gospel, Presbyterian retained an option, for a period of ten years, to repurchase the property for the original sale price if the premises ever ceased to be used for Christian services.

Liberty was not notified by the parties of the merger of Westminster and Presbyterian nor of the sale by Presbyterian of the property to Christ Gospel. Also, Liberty was not notified by the parties of the purported assignment of the fire insurance policy on the property from Presbyterian to Christ Gospel. On February 9, 1973, an agent of Liberty, as a result of a visit to the church, learned of the merger and the later sale of the property and reported these facts to Liberty. Ten days later, on February 19, 1973, fire substantially damaged the church structure.

Liberty denied coverage and Christ Gospel thereafter filed suit against Liberty for the fire loss. * * * Presbyterian, an additional defendant, then filed a cross-claim against Liberty, asserting that if Christ Gospel was not covered under the policy, then Presbyterian could recover for the loss since it claimed a continuing insurable interest in the property.

* * * With respect to the purported assignment of the policy from Presbyterian to Christ Gospel, Liberty relied greatly in its defense upon a clause in the insurance policy which provided that: "Assignment of this policy shall not be valid except with the written consent of this Company."

* * *

We first address the rights of Christ Gospel against Liberty. Although Christ Gospel is an appellant in this action, no real emphasis is directed on this appeal to contentions that Christ Gospel has any arguable basis upon which it can recover against Liberty for any fire loss to the church building. Christ Gospel, if it had any rights against Liberty, would enjoy those rights by virtue of the purported assignment to it by Presbyterian of the latter's rights under the Liberty policy. Even if we assume that Presbyterian held the position of an insured on the policy, after Presbyterian's merger with Westminster, the original insured, we cannot ignore the import of the provision on the front page of the policy which provides that "Assignment of this policy shall not be valid except with the written consent of this Company."

Although the Appellants argue on several grounds, that we must ignore that clear prohibition against assignments without Liberty's consent, we can find no legal basis for doing so. The provision in question is not simply a self-protective clause inserted at the whim of the Appellee, but rather is a legislatively mandated provision, *specifically required* to be included in fire insurance policies such as the one in issue in the instant case. In view of the lack of consent of Liberty to the assignment of the policy by Presbyterian to Christ Gospel, the latter has no rights under the policy.

We find no merit to the proposition that Liberty is estopped from contesting the assignment on the basis that its agent inspected the premises just a few days before the fire and was aware of the sale of the property to another congregation. It is well settled that a fire insurance policy is a *personal* contract of indemnity, and is on the insured's *interest* in the property, *not on the property itself.* Gorman's Estate, 321 Pa. 292, 184 A. 86 (1936). Therefore, we find no basis for the claim asserted by Christ Gospel against Liberty in the instant case.

We reach a similar conclusion with respect to Presbyterian's claim, but on a different rationale. Although Liberty contends that the merger of Westminster into Presbyterian afforded the latter no rights on the policy, since Liberty did not consent to afford coverage on the policy to Presbyterian, for purposes of this appeal we will assume that Presbyterian succeeded to all the legal rights of Westminster on the policy at the time of the fire loss. Even with that assumption in favor of Presbyterian, however, we cannot find that it enjoyed the required *insurable interest* in the property at the time of the fire as to allow it to recover any amount as a result of the fire loss on February 19, 1973.

Presbyterian conveyed the property to Christ Gospel on December 19, 1972. Its only remaining legal interest in the property was an option to repurchase, at the original selling price within a ten year period, in the event that the property was used for purposes other than for the holding of Christian services. Thus, on the date of the fire loss, Presbyterian had a mere possibility of the expectancy that it might exercise its option to repurchase upon the happening of a contingency. Under prevailing law, this does not amount to an insurable interest. An excellent case on point is Van Cure v. Hartford Fire Insurance Co., 435 Pa. 163, 253 A.2d 663 (1969). In *Van Cure* the Court recognized the long-established principle that an insurable interest in the property is demanded prior to recovery for a fire loss in Pennsylvania, and that a mere expectancy of an option to purchase is "* * * insubstantial and incapable of qualifying as an insurable interest." * * * While the *Van Cure* case involved the rights of a condemnee when a fire damaged the insured property after condemnation, we find the rationale directly applicable in our analysis of Presbyterian's claims on this appeal.[28] Plainly, Presbyterian's claim must fail because it lacked a legally required insurable interest in the building on the date of the fire loss. Thus, we can discern no error in the action of the lower court in dismissing the claims of both Appellants.

Notes

1. Who is to blame for the fact that there was no one who could recover for the damages to the church despite a policy that had been duly paid for more than three years? A hint: the professional responsibility insurer for Christ Gospel's lawyer settled the church's claim against the lawyer for $125,000.

2. *Another interpretation of the "no valid assignment without written consent of insurer" clause: Good faith and fair dealing to the rescue.* In

28. In *Van Cure,* supra, the condemnee was still living in the property at the time of the fire, making her claim of an insurable interest much more compelling, on an equitable basis, than that asserted by Presbyterian in this case.

University of Judaism v. Transamerica Insurance Co., 61 Cal.App.3d 937, 132 Cal.Rptr. 907 (1976), the Flegelmans conveyed property to the plaintiff university and assigned the insurance policies, but did not obtain the insurer's endorsement at the time. Because the premises were in a troubled urban area, the insurers apparently were contemplating cancellation. The fire occurred during a riot on February 1. On February 2, defendant notified the Flegelmans' agent of intent to cancel. It was not until February 12 that the insurers were notified of the loss and that the property had been sold and the policies assigned. The defense is grounded upon the same statutorily mandated provision as to assignment set forth in the principal case. The California court however allowed recovery by the grantee, stating:

> The purpose of this provision is apparent. It is "to prevent an increase of risk and hazard of loss by a change of ownership without the knowledge of the insurer." (16 Couch on Insurance (2d ed. 1966) § 63:31, p. 677; fn. omitted.) As stated in Bergson v. Builders' Ins. Co., 38 Cal. 541, 545, "The insurer has a right to know, and an interest in knowing, for whom he stands as insurer. He may be willing to insure one person and unwilling to insure another, while the owner of a particular parcel of property. He may have confidence in the honesty and prudence of the one in protecting the property and thereby lessening the risk, and may have no confidence in the other."
>
> In this case, had notice been promptly given prior to the loss, defendants would have routinely approved the assignment of the policy to plaintiff. There was no change in the nature of the activity carried on at the premises. There is no evidence that the change of ownership in any way increased the risk to defendants. Since the change of ownership did not increase the risk to defendants, and they would have routinely approved the assignment, they cannot claim they suffered any prejudice from the late notice. (See Sly v. American Indemnity Co., 127 Cal.App. 202, 208, 15 P.2d 522 (1932).)
>
> In effect defendants are asserting that even though they would have approved the assignment as a matter of course, they should have the arbitrary right to disapprove it when the only apparent reason for doing so is that an intervening loss has occurred. The arbitrary refusal of consent in such circumstances would be inconsistent with the insurer's duty of good faith. (See Gruenberg v. Aetna Ins. Co., 9 Cal.3d 566, 573, 575, 108 Cal.Rptr. 480, 510 P.2d 1032 (1973).)
>
> The language of the provision is consistent with plaintiff's theory that defendants should be deemed to have consented to the assignment, and that such consent relates back to the time of the assignment. Unlike prior versions of the standard form, which stated that ' * * * this entire policy shall be void * * * if this policy be assigned before a loss', the present provision merely states that assignment shall not be valid 'except with' the written consent of the company. To avoid a forfeiture, plaintiff may, in lieu of express approval, show that the assignment would have been routinely approved.

3. Loss not Caused by Covered Risk

a. *Substantive v. Evidentiary Conditions*

COCHRAN v. MFA MUTUAL INSURANCE CO.

Supreme Court of Nebraska, 1978.
201 Neb. 631, 271 N.W.2d 331.

CLINTON, JUSTICE.

This is an action upon a homeowner's insurance policy to recover the value of certain tools allegedly stolen from the insured's locked motor vehicle. The policy contained the following exclusion: "c. Theft Exclusions applicable to property away from the described premises: This policy does not apply to loss away from the described premises of: * * *

> "(2) property while unattended in or on any motor vehicle or trailer, other than a public conveyance, unless the loss is the result of forcible entry into such vehicle while all doors, windows or other openings thereof are closed and locked, provided there are visible marks of forcible entry upon the exterior of such vehicle or the loss is the result of the theft of such vehicle which is not recovered within 30 days, but property shall not be considered unattended when the Insured is required to surrender the keys of such vehicle to a bailee."

The evidence shows that there were no visible marks of forcible entry on the exterior of the vehicle. The car had been removed from the place where the owner testified he had parked it. The owner reported the vehicle stolen and it was recovered the same afternoon a few miles from the place where it had been parked. The owner testified that the car was locked when he left it and that all windows were closed. When found, tools were missing from the car and a "jiggle" key was found in the ignition switch. The insured, a locksmith and hardwareman by occupation, testified as an expert witness that a jiggle key is a type of key by which entry may be gained into many cars by proper and knowledgeable manipulation of the key. He gave his opinion that entry to and removal of the car had been gained by use of the jiggle key.

The case was tried in the municipal court of the city of Omaha and judgment was rendered for the defendant insurer. On appeal to the District Court the judgment was affirmed.

The defendant pled and relied upon the exclusion earlier set forth. The District Court found that there had been a forcible entry by use of a jiggle key, that there were no "visible marks of forcible entry upon the exterior of the vehicle," and that the defendant was entitled to rely upon the exclusion.

The plaintiff on this appeal urges that forced entry by use of a jiggle key comes within the coverage of the policy and urges that we so construe it.

The plaintiff relies principally upon the case of C & J Fertilizer, Inc. v. Allied Mut. Ins. Co. (Iowa), 227 N.W.2d 169, in which the Iowa court construed similar language in a policy covering losses through burglary. The court held, among other things, that under the particular facts of that case such a provision was unconscionable and would not be enforced where, although there were no marks of forced entry on the exterior of the building, there was other clear evidence of burglary on the interior door of the particular room from which the theft was made. Plaintiff also relies upon a line of cases which hold that such exclusions are ambiguous and establish a mere rule of evidence and that the exclusion will not be literally enforced if it is clear that the burglary is not an inside job. Ferguson v. Phoenix Assurance Co., 189 Kan. 459, 370 P.2d 379; Rosenthal v. American Bonding Co., 124 N.Y.S. 905.

This court has had prior occasion to consider similar exclusions in policies insuring against burglary and we have upheld the exclusion. Only a few years ago, in Hazuka v. Maryland Cas. Co., 183 Neb. 336, 160 N.W.2d 174, we said: "In a policy indemnifying insured for loss by burglary for 'the felonious abstraction of insured property within a vault or safe * * * by a person making felonious entry into such vault or safe * * *, when all doors thereof are duly closed and locked by all combination locks thereon, provided such entry shall be made by actual force and violence, of which force and violence there are visible marks made by tools, explosives, electricity or chemicals upon the exterior of (a) all of said doors of such vault or such safe and any fault containing the safe, if entry is made through such doors, * * *,' such visible marks requirement was intended to be and is a limitation on liability and not an attempt to determine the character of evidence to show liability.

"Such limited liability provision is not ambiguous and there is no room for the rule that insurance contracts will be construed most favorably to the insured."

We hold that [the] theft exclusion * * * is unambiguous and the provision requiring visible marks of forced entry is not unconscionable. We thus adhere to our former opinion in Hazuka v. Maryland Cas. Co., supra.

* * *

AFFIRMED.

Notes

1. A store owner, suspicious that someone was using a pass key, put strips of transparent tape around the door frame. The next day the tape was broken and items were missing from the stock. Was the breaking of the tape "physical damage" so as to allow recovery on a burglary policy? See Hopson v. Southern American Insurance Co., 618 S.W.2d 745 (Tenn.App.1980) ("[P]ulling loose or breaking of the tape does not constitute physical damage caused by actual force and violence to the exterior of the premises.").

2. "Felonious exit" may be an alternative provision to "felonious entrance." In *Norman v. Banasik*, 304 N.C. 341, 283 S.E.2d 489 (1981),

there were no entry marks, but a bolt was removed from inside a window which allowed it to be pushed outward so that property could be removed. The policy required "physical damage to the interior of the premises at the place of such exit." The court allowed recovery stating that extraction of the bolt "damaged" the security system by which intruders were denied entry.

3. Another form of "evidentiary condition" is to be found in policies covering losses by fraudulent or dishonest acts by employees, but "excluding" from that coverage any losses "the proof of which, either as to its factual existence or as to its amount is dependent upon an inventory computation or a profit and loss computation."

4. We noted above in the material on reasonable expectations that other cases contradict *Cochran*. C & J Fertilizer v. Allied Mutual Insurance Co., 227 N.W.2d 169 (Iowa 1975); Atwater Creamery Co. v. Western National Mutual Insurance Co., 366 N.W.2d 271 (Minn.1985). These cases involve facts similar to those in *Cochran*. The courts in both cases found that the policyholders could have reasonably expected that any type of burglary would be covered by their insurance, despite the technical definition contained within the policy. In the courts' view, the policy definition amounted to overly technical definitions of burglary which were outside of the common understanding of burglary. Therefore, the courts allowed the insureds to collect on the policies. Is this a more defensible result?

b. Implied Exceptions

The following case is a good reminder that insurance policies carry with them the considerable baggage of case law. The friendly fire exception is a small example of this baggage that is not even hinted at in the policy.

ENGEL v. REDWOOD COUNTY FARMERS MUTUAL INSURANCE CO.

Supreme Court of Minnesota, 1979.
281 N.W.2d 331.

KELLY, JUSTICE.

* * *

The issue presented on appeal is whether a loss caused by excessive heat from a fire intentionally kindled and wholly confined to the furnace wherein it was intended to burn is covered under an insurance policy providing coverage for all losses or damage by fire.

The facts are not in dispute. The plaintiff was insured under a "Minnesota Standard Township Mutual Fire Insurance Policy" issued by defendant. In 1973, the plaintiff constructed a hog barn on his farm for use in farrowing hogs. The barn was heated by an L.B. White furnace which was located just outside the building and which blew hot air into the barn by means of a fan. The furnace was controlled by a thermostat which could be adjusted to shut off the fan and furnace at a pre-set temperature.

On January 1, 1976, the plaintiff discovered that 15 of the 16 sows then in the hog barn were dead. Subsequent investigation revealed that the sows died from an inadequate supply of oxygen in the hog barn, caused by increased temperature. The high temperatures resulted from a "short" which rendered the thermostat inoperable allowing the furnace to blow hot air into the barn until the high limit control, set at 120°, shut down the furnace. The thermostat was set at 75° and this was normally as high as temperatures inside the building would rise. At all times the fire inside the furnace burned and produced heat at its usual rate and was confined within the furnace causing no damage to the hog barn or to the furnace nor producing any soot or other foreign material.

Defendant refused to compensate plaintiff, claiming that the loss was not recoverable under his policy as it was the result of a so-called "friendly" rather than "hostile" fire.

The hostile fire doctrine is said to have originated in the early English case of Austin v. Drew, 4 Campb. 360 (1815).[29] In that case, sugar being refined in plaintiff's factory was damaged by excessive heat and smoke. The sugar was contained in various rooms of an 8–story building through which ran a flue supplying the heat necessary for the refining process. At the top of the flue was a register which was normally kept open when the fire was high. An employee started the fire without opening the register. As a result, the fire overheated, smoking up the rooms containing the sugar and causing the damage complained of. The court, in denying recovery, stated:

> "I am of the opinion that this action is not maintainable. There was no more fire than always exists when the manufacture is going on. Nothing was consumed by fire. The plaintiff's loss arose from the negligent management of their machinery. The sugars were chiefly damaged by the heat; and what produced that heat? Not any fire against which the company insures, but the fire for heating the pans, which continued all the time to burn without any excess. The servant forgot to open the register by which the smoke ought to have escaped and the heat to have been tempered." 4 Campb. 361.

From this opinion has emerged a rule of law known as the hostile fire doctrine. It is recognized in a majority of jurisdictions where the issue has been raised, 44 Am.Jur.2d, Insurance, § 1348; 5 Appleman, Insurance Law and Practice, § 3082, although it has been criticized by many commentators. See Vance, Friendly Fires, 1 Conn.Bar J. 284; Reis, The Friendly Versus Hostile Fire Dichotomy, 12 Vill.L.Rev. 109; Morrison, Concerning Friendly Fires, 3 Boston C.Indus. & Com.L.Rev. 15. In brief, the rule generally states that a fire which is intentionally kindled and which remains at all times confined to the place where it was intended to be will be characterized as friendly and will not subject the insurer to any liability for the resulting loss. By adopting this doctrine,

29. Although this case is often cited as first originating the hostile fire doctrine, the terms hostile and friendly fire first appeared in the case of Way v. Abington Mutual Fire Ins. Co., 166 Mass. 67, 43 N.E. 1032 (1896).

courts have in effect established a presumption, seemingly irrebuttable, that the parties to the transaction, particularly the prospective insured, were aware of this doctrine and contemplated its inclusion in the policy. Common sense tells us that this is more than likely not the case. When an insured buys a fire insurance policy which "covers all losses or damage by fire" his expectation is that it will cover all unintentional losses from fire, except listed exclusions, regardless of the nature or character of the fire. The doctrine thus seems to protect the insurer at the expense of the unwitting insured.

In Minnesota, this problem is avoided because of the judicially created limitations on friendly fires. In L.L. Freeberg Pie Co. v. St. Paul Mutual Insurance Co., 257 Minn. 244, 100 N.W.2d 753 (1960), we joined a minority of courts which require that a friendly fire, in addition to the elements listed above, be non-excessive. In the *Freeberg* case, the thermostat on a bake oven failed and, as a result, the flame inside the oven continued to build up to such a degree as to seriously warp and damage the oven. The lower court determined that, because the fire in the oven was intentionally kindled and only burned in its intended place, it was a friendly fire and recovery was precluded.

On appeal, we reexamined the *Austin* decision and aligned ourselves with the minority, reasoning as follows:

> "As has been stated, the rule originated with Austin v. Drew, 4 Campb. 360. However, a reading of that case will disclose that Lord Chief Justice Gibbs did not base the distinction between what is now called a 'friendly' fire and a 'hostile' fire only on the locus or the place where the fire was burning. He stated in the opinion (4 Campb. 361):
>
>> "'* * * There was no more fire than always exists * * * which [the fire] continued all the time to burn without any excess. * * *
>>
>> * * *
>>
>> "'* * * Had the fire been brought out of the flue, and any thing had been burnt, the Company would have been liable. But can this be said, where the fire never was at all excessive, and was always confined within its proper limits?'
>
> "The rule as stated in the texts above cited and in the decided cases ignores entirely these references to the nature of the fire in question, that it continued 'to burn without any excess' and 'never was at all excessive.' The excessiveness of the fire, however great and destructive it might be if confined to the place where it was intended to be, has been considered immaterial in determining whether a fire was 'friendly' or 'hostile.' Although the result we are reaching is contrary to the great majority of decided cases, there is a respectable minority supporting it." 257 Minn. at 248, 100 N.W.2d at 755.

Under the *Freeberg* case, a fire may be found to be hostile although it was intentionally kindled and never escaped its confines if it was excessive or uncontrolled. * * *

In the case before us defendant argues that even under the minority rule it should not be held liable because the fire was in no way excessive. In support of this contention, defendant points to the stipulated facts which state:

> "The fire inside the furnace burned and produced heat at its usual rate."

Defendant reasons that if the furnace burned only at its usual rate it could not possibly be excessive. We disagree. A fire which causes damage by burning for a greater length of time than intended is no less uncontrolled merely because it continues to burn at its usual rate. See, generally, Morrison, Concerning Friendly Fires, 3 Boston C.Indus. & Com.L.Rev. 15.

Returning to the facts before us, the malfunctioning thermostat caused the furnace to burn continuously until the temperature reached 120°—well beyond the pre-set temperature of 75°. We do not believe that under these circumstances this fire can be described as controlled. It burned for an excessive period of time resulting in temperatures much greater than those intended, causing the loss complained of. By characterizing this fire as hostile we are in no way departing from our prior decisions. We merely hold that a fire may be hostile although burning at its usual rate if it burns substantially longer or in some fashion other than expected. For the above reasons, we affirm the decision of the trial court.

AFFIRMED.

Notes

1. In *Schulze and Burch Biscuit Co. v. American Protection Insurance Co.*, 96 Ill.App.3d 350, 51 Ill.Dec. 823, 421 N.E.2d 331 (1981), a bakery oven was left on during a shift change without any contents to dissipate the heat. The temperature rose from the normal 450° to 1600° causing nearly $150,000 damage to the oven. The court rejected the hostile/friendly dichotomy and allowed recovery using the ambiguity approach, the adhesion approach, as well as the doctrine of reasonable expectations. It suggested that the implied exclusion could be easily made express.

2. Courts in other jurisdictions have stepped away from the hostile/friendly fire dichotomy discussed in the principle case in favor of the doctrine of reasonable expectations to justify recovery for the insured's implied expectations of coverage. See Sadlowski v. Liberty Mut. Ins., 487 A.2d 1146 (Del.1984). Assuming an inclination to permit the insured to recover, is this technique as justifiable as the one used in the principal case? Are fire insurers in a position to insert express exclusions in statutorily mandated policies as casually as suggested in *Schulze and Burch Biscuit* (cited in note 1 above)? A version of the Standard Fire Policy is reproduced in the Appendix.

3. *Implied Exception—Destruction of Property by Co-insured.* This is an implied exception which seems to be breaking down. An initial step in this process was to hold that when the interests of the co-insureds were several, i.e. partnerships or tenants in common, rather than joint, i.e., co-owners, joint title-holders, the destruction of the property by one would not void the policy as to the interest of the others. Hoyt v. New Hampshire Fire Insurance Co., 92 N.H. 242, 29 A.2d 121, 148 A.L.R. 484 (1942). This still leaves the situation where the interests of the co-insureds are joint—particularly when they are spouses. Here too, there are recent cases refusing to imply the exception. See *DePalma v. Bates County Mutual Insurance Co.*, 923 S.W.2d 385 (1996), in which the husband and wife held the property as tenants by the entirety, and the wife committed arson once the couple split. The court adopted the "innocent spouse" doctrine for Missouri, thus permitting the husband, as the innocent co-owner, to recover under the insurance policy. (The court provides a nice discussion of the "innocent spouse" doctrine [in support of compensating the innocent co-tenant/co-insured when the other co-owner intentionally destroys the common property] and the split in authority on the topic.) But see *Rena Inc. v. Brien*, 310 N.J.Super. 304, 708 A.2d 747 (1998), in which the court held there was no recovery for innocent parties in a joint venture because the express language of the policy barred recovery for all if any one of the joint venture participants committed an intentional act listed as an exclusion.

If the implied exclusion is contrary to public policy it would seem to follow that an express exclusion would also be so. Cf. the arguments of a similar nature in accident cases—e.g., *Wetzel v. Westinghouse Corp.* below in Chapter 7.

4. What if one spouse intentionally destroys insured community property in a community property state? Is the innocent spouse protected? The authority seems fairly certain in allowing recovery for the innocent spouse. *Murphy v. Texas Farmers Insurance Co.*, 982 S.W.2d 79 (Tex.App.1998), held that the innocent co-owner in a community property state is entitled to recover his or her respective share of the insurance proceeds, provided that this innocent person is, indeed innocent. The court emphasized that a spouse should not be entitled to any benefit from his intentional act, and this implied that if property was community property, the wrongdoer would somehow benefit. The court stated that while the property was community property and the husband committed the excluded acts, the couple subsequently divorced and the husband retained no interest in the damaged property. Thus, the wife was entitled to her share of the insurance coverage. Id. at 83. See generally, Joseph W. McKnight, *Family Law: Husband and Wife*, 52 S.M.U.L. Rev. 1143 (1999).

c. *Concurrent Causation*

PAN AMERICAN WORLD AIRWAYS, INC. v. AETNA CASUALTY & SURETY CORP.

United States Court of Appeals, Second Circuit, 1974.
505 F.2d 989 at 1006–1007.

[The Facts are set forth in note 2, subsection A, "Basic Principles, Coverage Defined in Property Insurance" at the beginning of this chapter.]

* * *

B. PROXIMATE CAUSE.

The all risk policies exclude "loss or damage due to or resulting from" the various enumerated perils, a phrase that clearly refers to the proximate cause of the loss. Remote causes of causes are not relevant to the characterization of an insurance loss. In the context of this commercial litigation, the causation inquiry stops at the efficient physical cause of the loss; it does not trace events back to their metaphysical beginnings. The words "due to or resulting from" limit the inquiry to the facts immediately surrounding the loss. Standard Oil Co. v. United States, 340 U.S. 54, 58, 71 S.Ct. 135, 95 L.Ed. 68 (1950); Airlift International, Inc. v. United States, 335 F.Supp. 442, 449 (S.D.Fla.1971), aff'd, 460 F.2d 1065 (5th Cir. 1972) (mem.). Thus, in Queen Insurance Co. v. Globe & Rutgers Fire Insurance Co., 263 U.S. 487, 492, 44 S.Ct. 175, 176, 68 L.Ed. 402 (1924), Mr. Justice Holmes wrote:

> "[T]he common understanding is that in construing these policies we are not to take broad views but generally are to stop our inquiries with the cause nearest to the loss. This is a settled rule of construction, and if it is understood, does not deserve much criticism, since theoretically at least the parties can shape their contract as they like."

New York courts give especially limited scope to the causation inquiry. The leading case is Bird v. St. Paul Fire & Marine Insurance Co., 224 N.Y. 47, 120 N.E. 86 (1918) (Cardozo, J.) [The *Bird* case is described and discussed within the *Continental Insurance Co. v. Arkwright Mutual Insurance Co.* case which follows.]

* * *

Britain S.S. Co. v. The King, [1919] 2 K.B. 670 (C.A.), aff'd, [1921] 1 A.C. 99 (1920), illustrates how this principle has been applied by the English courts in the context of war-related losses. While on a voyage from England to Alexandria in the company and under the orders of a British escort, the *Matiana* went aground and was lost, because the convoy had taken a more northerly route than usual to avoid German submarines. The Court of Appeals held that the loss was due to a marine peril, running aground, rather than to a "warlike operation." It held that the warlike activity of the escorts did not proximately cause the loss: The Crown's naval authorities ordered the ship to take a general course fraught with maritime perils, but they did not actually order the *Matiana* aground. [1919] 2 K.B. at 699–700 (per Atkins, L.J.). The House of Lords agreed. [1921] 1 A.C. at 1121–22 (per Atkinson, L.J.).

Decisions in a variety of other jurisdictions follow the same approach. When the *Linwood* went aground as a result of the Confederates putting out the Hatteras light, the loss was a "consequence" of a marine peril, rather than "hostilities." Ionides v. Universal Marine Insurance Co., 143 Eng.Rep. 445, 456 (C.P.1863) (per Erle, C.J.). When the *John Worthington* collided with a minesweeper that was clearing the channel approaches to New York harbor in 1942, the loss was due to the collision, a marine peril, rather than the warlike reason for the minesweeper's presence in the harbor. Standard Oil v. United States, 340 U.S. 54, 71 S.Ct. 135, 95 L.Ed. 68 (1950). When the *Napoli* was lost in a head-on collision with another ship because it was sailing without running lights under British order, the loss was due to a marine peril, the collision. Queen Insurance Co. v. Globe & Rutgers Fire Insurance Co., 282 F. 976 (2d Cir.1922), aff'd, 263 U.S. 487, 44 S.Ct. 175, 68 L.Ed. 402 (1924). When an insured aircraft was lost over Vietnam in a collision with a military aircraft, the loss was due to an aviation peril, notwithstanding that the two aircraft were flying over Vietnam only because there was a war. Airlift International, Inc. v. United States, 335 F.Supp. 442, 449 (S.D.Fla.1971), aff'd, 460 F.2d 1065 (5th Cir. 1972) (mem.).

These cases establish a mechanical test of proximate causation for insurance cases, a test that looks only to the "causes nearest to the loss." Queen Insurance Co. v. Globe & Rutgers Fire Insurance Co., supra at 492, 44 S.Ct. 175. This rule is adumbrated by the maxim contra proferentem: if the insurer desires to have more remote causes determine the scope of exclusion, he may draft language to effectuate that desire. Id.; Feeney & Meyers v. Empire State Insurance Co., 228 F.2d 770, 771 (10th Cir.1955). In the present case, events drawn from the general history of unrest in the Middle East did not proximately cause the destruction of the 747. Of course, in some attenuated "cause of causes" sense, the loss may have resulted from the Fedayeen or PFLP pattern of military operations against Israel, from the domestic unrest in Jordan, or from the most recent of the three wars which prior to 1970 had convulsed the Middle East. But for insurance purposes, the mechanical cause of the present loss was two men, who by force of arms, diverted Flight 093 from its intended destination.

* * *

Note

In a comprehensive article on the subject, Steven Plitt names four possible insurance policy exclusions that could apply to cases involving terrorism. Steven Plitt, *The changing Face of Global Terrorism and a New Look of War: an analysis of the War–Risk Exclusion in the Wake of the*

Anniversary of September 11, and Beyond, 39 WILLAMETTE L. REV. 31 (2003). He writes:

> The first exclusion, the war exclusion, focuses on the nature of the act and the actors. The remaining potentially relevant exclusions may become involved depending on the weapon or mechanism used to commit the terrorist act. For example, use of a nuclear device or a "dirty bomb" could cause radioactive contamination, which would fall within the nuclear exclusion. The electrical damage exclusion may apply to damage caused by electromagnetic pulses resulting from nuclear detonation. Finally, the pollution exclusion may apply to biochemical and biotoxic weapons such as anthrax.
>
> Id. at 37–38.

CONTINENTAL INSURANCE CO. v. ARKWRIGHT MUTUAL INSURANCE CO.

United States Court of Appeals, First Circuit, 1996.
102 F.3d 30.

CYR, CIRCUIT JUDGE.

Appellants Continental Insurance Company ("Continental") and Hartford Insurance Company ("Hartford") (collectively: "C & H" or "appellants") challenge the district court's summary judgment ruling under New York law that damage from flooding was not covered under the insurance policy issued by Arkwright Mutual Insurance Company ("Arkwright" or "appellee"). As the district court correctly applied New York law, we affirm.

I

BACKGROUND

In 1992, Olympia and York Development Company, L.P. ("Olympia") owned a high-rise office building at 55 Water Street, New York, New York ("Water Street Building"). On December 11th of that year, a severe storm struck New York City, causing the Hudson and East Rivers to overflow their banks. Flood waters entered the basement of the Water Street Building through cracks in its foundation, resulting in more than one million dollars in property damage. Slightly more than half the damage involved energized electrical switching panels which had come into contact with the flood waters. The water immediately caused a phenomenon known as "electrical arcing"—an electrical short circuit, in lay terms—which in turn caused an immediate explosion that blew large holes in the switching panels. C & H appraised the damage to the switching panels at $581,225. Much of the remaining damage, appraised at $445,592, occurred when the flood waters came in contact with non-energized electrical equipment; it involved no electrical arcing.

At the time of the storm, three separate policies provided various coverages for the Water Street Building. Two of the policies—identical "all risk" policies separately issued by appellants Continental and Hartford—insured against "all risks including Flood and Earthquake" up to

$75,000,000 per occurrence for the one-year period beginning March 3, 1992. Each policy underwrote fifty percent of the $75,000,000 "all risk" coverage on identical terms and conditions, and contained a $100,000 deductible for any loss and damage arising out of each covered occurrence. In addition, each "all risk" policy excluded coverage for mechanical or electrical breakdown caused by artificially generated electrical currents.[30]

The third policy, issued by appellee Arkwright, a Massachusetts corporation, afforded $3,000,000,000 in total liability coverage for the three-year period between January 1, 1992 and January 1, 1995, on approximately forty buildings owned by Olympia around the world. As concerns the Water Street Building in particular, the Arkwright policy afforded up to $100,000,000 in covered property loss from flooding, subject to a $75,000,000 deductible. Thus, the Arkwright policy principally served as excess "all risk" coverage above the $75,000,000 liability limit on the two separate "all risk" policies issued by appellants Continental and Hartford.

The Arkwright policy on the Water Street Building included a "Special Deductible Endorsement," which afforded primary insurance coverage for mechanical or electrical breakdown by substituting a $50,000 deductible for the $75,000,000 "all risk" deductible in the Arkwright policy. The $50,000 Special Deductible Endorsement was subject to the following qualifications:

> *In the event of insured loss or damage under the policy to which this endorsement is attached, the Loss or Damage described below shall be subject to the following deductible amount(s) in lieu of any other Policy deductible amount(s) except those for Flood*, Earthquake or Service Interruption *if applicable*:
>
> [$50,000.00]
>
> * * * * * *
>
> 3. *Loss or damage from* mechanical or *electrical breakdown* (except by direct lightning damage) of any equipment, unless physical damage not excluded results, in which event this Special Deductible shall not apply to such resulting damage. (Emphasis added.)

Olympia submitted claims to appellants Continental and Hartford for the total loss sustained at the Water Street Building. It maintained that the entire loss had been caused by flooding and therefore came within the coverage afforded under the two primary "all risk" policies

30. The policies stated, in pertinent part:

8. *Perils Insured Against*

This policy insures against all risk of direct physical loss of or damage to property described herein except as hereinafter excluded.

9. *Perils Excluded*

This policy does not insure:

* * * * * *

c. against electrical injury or disturbance to electrical appliances, devices, or wiring caused by electrical currents artificially generated unless loss or damage from a peril insured ensues and then this policy shall cover for such ensuing loss or damage.

issued by appellants. Continental and Hartford promptly paid $937,557 to Olympia, representing coverage for the entire loss less a $100,000 deductible, then claimed reimbursement from Arkwright for the $581,225 loss to the electrical switching panels allegedly caused by electrical arcing. Arkwright refused to contribute, contending that all damage to the Water Street Building had been caused by, or resulted directly from, flooding. Relying on the Special Deductible Endorsement language—"in lieu of any other Policy deductible amount(s) except those for Flood"—Arkwright insisted that since the damage had been due to flood, the $50,000 deductible in its endorsement did not displace the $75,000,000 deductible in its policy.

Continental and Hartford instituted this diversity proceeding in United States District Court for the District of Massachusetts, seeking a judicial declaration that Arkwright was liable for the portion of the electrical switching panel loss due to electrical arcing. After all parties moved for summary judgment based on their respective interpretations of the applicable New York caselaw, the district court concluded that under the Arkwright insurance contract, including its Special Deductible Endorsement, as viewed by a reasonable business person in the relevant circumstances, see *Bird v. St. Paul Fire & Marine Ins. Co.*, 224 N.Y. 47, 120 N.E. 86 (1918), the damage to the electrical switching panels had been caused by flooding.

The district court determined that in identifying the cause of the storm-related damage to the electrical switching panels, a reasonable business person would not have segregated the flooding from the arcing. The court based its conclusion on the fact that the $50,000 deductible is made inapplicable to flood loss by the express language in the Special Deductible Endorsement excluding electrical breakdown due to flood, as well as the fact that all the damage occurred virtually simultaneously at the same site.

II

Discussion

Appellants Continental and Hartford challenge the district court ruling that the flooding, rather than the electrical arcing, constituted the legal cause of the damage to the electrical switching panels. Their proximate causation analysis focuses upon what point in the "proverbial chain of causation" a particular cause ceases to be remote and becomes the "legal cause" of the damage. See Richard A. Fierce, *Insurance Law–Concurrent Causation: Examination of Alternative Approaches*, 1985 S. Ill. U. L.J. 527, 534 (1986).

1. Causation under New York Law

Appellants first contend that the district court misapplied New York law in ruling that a reasonable business person would consider the switching panels to have been damaged by flood rather than electrical arcing. Under established New York law governing insurance contract interpretation, appellants maintain, the district court was required to identify the most direct, physical cause of the damage, or what is termed "the dominant and proximate cause." *Novick v. United Servs. Auto. Ass'n*, 639 N.Y.S.2d 469, 471 (App.Div.1996). According to appellants, the most direct, physical cause of a loss under New York law "is that which is nearest to the loss because [it] is invariably the most direct and obvious cause."

Appellants predicate their contention principally upon *Home Ins. Co. v. American Ins. Co.*, 147 A.D.2d 353, 537 N.Y.S.2d 516 (1989), where water and steam precipitated electrical arcing which in turn damaged electrical equipment in a high-rise building. There the New York Supreme Court, Appellate Division, held that electrical arcing, not steam, caused the damage, since the steam "merely set the stage" for the subsequent arcing and therefore constituted the remote, rather than the proximate, cause of the loss. *Id.*, 537 N.Y.S.2d at 517 (" '[T]he causation inquiry stops at the efficient physical cause of the loss; it does not trace events back to their metaphysical beginnings.... ' ") (quoting *Pan Am. World Airways, Inc. v. Aetna Cas. & Sur. Co.*, 505 F.2d 989, 1006 (2d Cir.1974)). Similarly, appellants maintain that the efficient, legal cause of the damage to the switching panels in the present case was the electrical arcing, whereas the flooding merely set the stage for the arcing. Consequently, appellants conclude, the district court need have looked no further than the phenomenon of electrical arcing for the legal cause of the damage to the switching panels.

We turn to the language in the Arkwright insurance contract to determine whether the damage to the switching panels was legally caused by flooding or electrical arcing. Under New York law, insurance policies are to be interpreted in accordance with their terms. *See, e.g., Frey v. Aetna Life & Cas.*, 221 A.D.2d 841, 633 N.Y.S.2d 880, 882 (1995).

In cases involving an electrical breakdown not caused by lightning, the Special Deductible Endorsement substitutes a $50,000 deductible for the $75,000,000 deductible in the Arkwright liability policy proper, except in cases where the higher deductible for "Flood" is "applicable." Appellants would have the court interpret the operative provision ("in lieu of any other Policy amount(s) except those for Flood ... if applicable") to mean that the $75,000,000 deductible in the Arkwright liability policy proper applies only if there is a separate, specific policy deductible for flood damage. Absent such a specific deductible for flood damage, appellants say, the exception for loss from flooding found in the $50,000 Special Deductible Endorsement is never triggered; therefore, the electrical breakdown damage to the switching panels comes within the $50,000 Special Deductible Endorsement, displacing the $75,000,000 deductible in the Arkwright policy itself.

Appellants misinterpret the plain language in the Special Deductible Endorsement, which unambiguously indicates that the $50,000 deductible does not apply if another deductible for flooding damage does apply. Furthermore, the "all risk" general liability coverage in the Arkwright policy itself expressly insures against "loss or damage resulting from a single occurrence," including flood. Thus, the plain language employed in both the Special Deductible Endorsement and the Arkwright general liability policy itself, compatibly interpreted in context, means that damage to mechanical or electrical equipment proximately caused by flooding comes within the exception to the $50,000 Special Deductible Endorsement and hence the $75,000,000 deductible in the Arkwright general liability policy applies in such a situation. *See, e.g., Harris v. Allstate Ins. Co.*, 309 N.Y. 72, 127 N.E.2d 816, 817 (1955). . . . ("words of the policy are to be read in context, the language construed fairly and reasonably with an eye to the object and purpose to be achieved by the writing"); *Moshiko, Inc. v. Seiger & Smith, Inc.*, 137 A.D.2d 170, 529 N.Y.S.2d 284, 287 (1988) (policy endorsements to be read in context of general liability provisions). "Where the provisions of the policy are 'clear and unambiguous, they must be given their plain and ordinary meaning. . . .,' "*United States Fidelity & Guar. Co. v. Annunziata*, 67 N.Y.2d 229, 501 N.Y.S.2d 790, 492 N.E.2d 1206, 1207 (1986) (quoting *Government Employees Ins. Co. v. Kligler*, 42 N.Y.2d 863, 864, 397 N.Y.S.2d 777, 366 N.E.2d 865 (1977)).[31]

2. Legal Cause of Loss

Given the plain language in the Arkwright insurance contract, we must determine the proximate or legal cause of the damage to the switching panels, bearing in mind that "[t]he concept of proximate cause when applied to insurance policies is a limited one," especially under New York law. *Great N. Ins. Co. v. Dayco*, 637 F.Supp. 765, 778 (S.D.N.Y.1986).[32] Moreover, in the context of an insurance contract, our inquiry may not proceed beyond the dominant, efficient, physical cause of the loss. Home Insurance, 537 N.Y.S.2d at 517. Ultimate causation—or what the Second Circuit has referred to as the "metaphysical beginnings"—is not our concern. *Pan Am. World Airways, Inc. v. Aetna Cas. & Sur. Co.*, 505 F.2d 989, 1006 (2d Cir.1974).

31. Appellants' interpretation, on the other hand, renders the exception to the Special Deductible Endorsement mere surplusage and therefore is disfavored. *See Technicon Elec. Corp. v. American Home Assur. Co.*, 74 N.Y.2d 66, 544 N.Y.S.2d 531, 533–34, 542 N.E.2d 1048, 1050–51 (1989) (rejecting interpretation which would render exclusion clause meaningless in context); *Utica Mut. Ins. Co. v. Preferred Mut. Ins. Co.*, 180 A.D.2d 195, 583 N.Y.S.2d 986, 987 (1992) (similar). In cases involving an electrical breakdown, the language of the Special Deductible Endorsement triggers the $50,000 deductible "in lieu of any other Policy amount(s) except those for Flood . . . if applicable." As noted above, appellants argue that the phrase "other Policy amounts" should be read to mean other specific deductible amounts not including the $75,000,000 general deductible in the Arkwright general liability policy. But since no other deductible amount for flood exists in the Arkwright policy covering the Water Street Building, and appellants have not been able to demonstrate the existence of any other special flood deductible in the entire Arkwright policy covering Olympia properties in general, their interpretation would mean that the phrase "in lieu of other Policy amounts" is "mere surplusage"—as, indeed, appellants concede in their brief.

32. Arkwright maintained at oral argument that the Special Deductible Endorsement excludes arcing whenever flood is the remote as well as the proximate cause of the damage. Its contention fails, since the required plain language interpretation dictates an end to our inquiry at proximate causation.

That is not to say, as appellants suggest, that the court is constrained to settle upon the cause nearest the loss without regard to other factors.[33] Rather, we are " 'to follow the chain of causation so far, and so far only as the parties meant that we should follow it.' " *Album Realty Corp. v. American Home Assur. Co.*, 80 N.Y.2d 1008, 592 N.Y.S.2d 657, 658, 607 N.E.2d 804, 805 (1992) (quoting *Goldstein v. Standard Acc. Ins. Co.*, 236 N.Y. 178, 183, 140 N.E. 235, 236 (1923)). In its seminal discourse on the "loss causation" inquiry under an insurance contract, the New York Court of Appeals charted the course: "[O]ur guide is the reasonable expectation and purpose of the ordinary business man when making an ordinary business contract. It is his intention, expressed or fairly to be inferred, that counts. There are times when the law permits us to go far back in tracing events to causes." *Bird v. St. Paul Fire & Marine Ins. Co.*, 224 N.Y. 47, 120 N.E. 86, 87 (1918) (Cardozo, J.).[34]

The *Bird* case involved a fire insurance contract on a vessel. Within the policy period, a fire of unknown origin broke out beneath some freight cars loaded with explosives and located at a considerable distance from the pier where the insured vessel was docked. After burning for approximately 30 minutes, the freight cars exploded, causing another fire, which in turn caused a second explosion, the concussion from which damaged the insured vessel located some 1,000 feet from the site of the second explosion. No fire reached the vessel. *Id.*, 120 N.E. at 86. Then–Judge Cardozo, writing for New York's highest court, employed a pragmatic, "commonsense appraisement" of the circumstances, *id.* at 87 (citation and internal quotation marks omitted), in determining as a matter of law that coverage of the concussion damage sustained by the vessel could not be said to have been within the "range of probable expectation" under a policy which protected against fire. *Id.* at 88.

The critical consideration in *Bird* was the "element of proximity in space." *Id.* at 87. As the initiating event—the fire in the freight cars—occurred a great distance from the insured vessel, the court held that "there was never exposure to its direct perils" and that the exposure to its indirect perils—i.e., the concussion from the second explosion—came "only through the presence of extraordinary conditions, the release and intervention of tremendous forces of destruction." Id. Consequently, the

33. Nor does *Pan Am. World Airways, Inc., supra.*, support appellants' position. It held that proximate causation is determined by a "mechanical ... test that looks only to the *causes* nearest to the loss." 565 F.2d at 1007 (emphasis added). Its use of the plural permits more than one cause to be considered. Moreover, even the language used by the district court in *Great N. Ins. Co. v. Dayco* is qualified; *viz.*, "*generally* [we] are to stop our inquiries with the cause nearest to the loss," 637 F.Supp. 765, 778 (S.D.N.Y.1986) (emphasis added), making the rule something less than a mechanical mandate.

34. As appellants acknowledge, *Bird* remains good law to this day, and continues to be cited for its discussions on intent and proximate causation. See R. Dennis Withers, *Proximate Cause and Multiple Causation in First–Party Insurance Cases*, 20 Forum 256, 261 (January 1985) (citing *Atlantic Cement Co., Inc. v. Fidelity & Cas. Co. of N.Y.*, 91 A.D.2d 412, 459 N.Y.S.2d 425 (1983); *Ace Wire & Cable Co. v. Aetna Cas. & Sur. Co.*, 60 N.Y.2d 390, 469 N.Y.S.2d 655, 457 N.E.2d 761 (1983)); *see also Album Realty Corp.*, 607 N.E.2d at 804; *Pan Am. World Airways, Inc.*, 505 F.2d at 1006.

court concluded, reasonable business people would not have expected that an insurance policy affording protection against fire would cover damage to a vessel following successive concussions precipitated by explosions caused by the fire in the distant freightyard. As the Court of Appeals stated:

> The case comes, therefore, to this. *Fire must reach the thing insured, or come within such proximity to it that damage, direct or indirect, is within the compass of reasonable probability. Then only* is it the proximate cause, because then only *may we suppose that it was within the contemplation of the contract. Id.* at 88 (emphasis added).

In sum, absent an explicit policy declaration of the parties' intention, the contemplation of their insurance contract must be inferred by the court from all the circumstances surrounding the loss, including whether a peril insured against came directly or indirectly within such proximity to the property insured that the damage it sustained fairly can be considered "within the compass of reasonable probability." *Id.* Among the factors which must be assessed are the spatial and temporal proximity between the insured peril and the claimed loss. See R. Dennis Withers, *Proximate Cause and Multiple Causation in First—Party Insurance Cases*, 20 Forum 256, 260 (January 1985) (*Bird* considers "proximity of a cause as a judgment to be made upon matters of fact," including "proximity in space.").

Our case involves no spatial or temporal attenuation at all comparable to that present in *Bird.* The flood waters came *directly* in contact with the electrical equipment in the Water Street Building, *instantaneously* precipitating the arcing which in turn caused the *immediate* short-circuiting and explosion that damaged the switching panels.[emphasis in original] At most, mere seconds would have elapsed from the time the flood waters directly contacted the electrical equipment until the electrical switching panels exploded.

Where any spatial and temporal separation between the covered peril and the ensuing loss is so minimal as to be virtually nonexistent, *Bird* clearly contemplates that the loss be considered well within the "compass of reasonable probability" and therefore inferentially within the contemplation of the parties to the insurance contract. *See Bird*, 120 N.E. at 88. Consequently, given the absence of any significant spatial separation or temporal remoteness between the insurgent flood waters, the electrical arcing and the explosion of the switching panels, we believe the district court correctly concluded that flooding proximately caused the loss.

More recent New York caselaw continues implicitly to recognize the significance of what the Court of Appeals in *Bird* called the "element of proximity in space," *see id.* at 87, as well as the temporal element. In Home Insurance, for example, the Court of Appeals recently held electrical arcing to be the proximate cause of damage where arcing had been precipitated by a gradual intrusion of moisture. The court elucidated upon its analysis as follows:

> *There was no flow of water directly onto the bus duct system. Rather,* the *moisture saturated* the duct *insulation* and supports, *which had deteriorated due to age and environment*, resulting in breakdown of the insulation and *permitting an arc to result*.... Upon review of the record before this Court, we find that ... *the steam merely set the stage for the later event. Home Ins. Co.*, 537 N.Y.S.2d at 517 (emphasis added).

This passage distinguishes an intrusion of water and steam into a basement, gradually causing moisture to seep through deteriorating building materials into a duct, from a situation in which water flows directly onto an electrical system, causing immediate arcing and damage to the electrical system. In *Home Insurance*, substantial time and space separated the peril (the water and steam entering the basement) from the eventual electrical damage to the duct system resulting from the moisture gradually generated by the water and steam. Also interposed between the peril and the damage in *Home Insurance* were the deteriorating insulation and supports, which gave rise to a considerably greater spatial separation than occurred here. "There is no use in arguing that distance ought not to count if life and experience tell us that it does." *Bird*, 120 N.E. at 87.

Thus, neither *Bird* nor *Home Insurance* involved circumstances similar to the present, where flood waters flowed directly onto electrical equipment, immediately precipitating in turn the instantaneous electrical arcing, the short-circuiting, and the explosion which damaged the switching panels. Accordingly, as the district court correctly ruled, the insurgent flood waters cannot reasonably be thought simply to have "set the stage" for a remote event, or to have been merely some metaphysical beginning to a succession of temporally remote events.

Temporal remoteness and spatial separation distinguish many recent New York cases cited by appellants.[35] Given the importance placed upon temporal remoteness and spatial separation in *Bird*, 120 N.E. at 88, the wellspring decision under New York law, we conclude that the district court correctly held that the legal cause of the damage to the electrical switching panels was the flooding, not electrical arcing. We therefore hold that a reasonable business person would consider that the damage sustained by the electrical switching panels in the Water Street

35. *See, e.g., Morgan Guar. Trust Co. v. Aetna Cas. & Sur. Co.*, 199 A.D.2d 72, 604 N.Y.S.2d 952, 953 (1993) (microbiologically-induced corrosion occurring over one-year period, rather than remote flooding which initiated corrosion, held proximate cause of damage to electrical duct); *Album Realty Corp.*, 607 N.E.2d at 805 (electrical damage precipitated by water which was emitted by frozen sprinkler and filled basement, held to have been caused not by freezing but by the more proximate flooding). Such temporal and spatial considerations likewise distinguish other New York cases not involving electrical breakdown. *See, e.g., Kosich v. Metropolitan Property & Cas. Ins. Co.*, 214 A.D.2d 992, 626 N.Y.S.2d 618 (1995) (contractor's cutting into vinyl flooring with chain saw merely "set in motion a chain of events that ultimately resulted" in loss from asbestos contamination); *Pan Am. World Airways, Inc.*, 505 F.2d at 1006–07 (in airline hijacking case, general history of unrest throughout Middle East, extending through three wars and several countries, is too remote to be considered cause for loss under "war risk" insurance due to "reasonable expectations of businessmen").

Building, just as any other water damage to the building, was caused by flood. That is to say, as then-Judge Cardozo did, since the flood waters surged onto the site of the loss, a reasonable business person would consider the damage to the electrical switching panels to have been "within the danger zone of ordinary experience," *see id.* at 87, and consequently would expect the Continental and Hartford flood policy coverages, not the Arkwright Special Deductible Endorsement, to afford Olympia indemnification for the loss. Thus, the exception to the Arkwright Special Deductible Endorsement applies.

3. Appropriateness of Summary Judgment

Finally, we turn briefly to appellants' alternate contention. Continental and Hartford argue that the inquiry into the dominant and efficient cause of the loss presents a question of fact inappropriate for summary judgment. Once again, we disagree.

Generally speaking, the determination as to which of two causes was the dominant and efficient cause of a loss is for the factfinder. *See, e.g., Molycorp, Inc. v. Aetna Cas. & Sur. Co.*, 78 A.D.2d 510, 431 N.Y.S.2d 824, 825–26 (1980); Novick, 639 N.Y.S.2d at 471. The trial courts in the cited cases, however, were presented with a factual question as to which of the two perils physically caused the loss. In our case, on the other hand, there is no dispute concerning the physical, as distinguished from the legal, cause of the damage—i.e., what physical phenomenon precipitated the alteration to the electrical switching panels. As the New York Court of Appeals explained in *Bird*: "For the physicist one thing is cause, for the jurist, another." *Bird*, 120 N.E. at 88. Thus, the question before this court, as in *Bird*, is the question of law already resolved above: What would the New York courts determine to have been the legal or proximate cause of the loss? Like the district court, we hold that flood was the legal cause of the loss in this case.

III

CONCLUSION

As the district court correctly applied the controlling New York law, the judgment is affirmed. Costs are awarded to appellee.

SO ORDERED.

Notes

1. *Bird*, cited in *Continental Ins. Co. v. Arkwright Mutual Ins. Co.*, was decided ten years before Judge Cardozo wrote the opinion in the celebrated *Palsgraf v. Long Island R.R. Co.*, 248 N.Y. 339, 162 N.E. 99 (1928).

2. Despite the apparent approval of the *Bird* approach noted in *Continental Ins. Co. v. Arkwright Mutual Ins. Co., Bird* has not been universally accepted. See Fred Meyer, Inc. v. Central Mutual Ins. Co., 235 F.Supp. 540, 543–44 (D.Or.1964) (a majority of jurisdictions have not recognized *Bird's* rejection of proximate cause).

GRAHAM v. PUBLIC EMPLOYEES MUTUAL INSURANCE CO.

Supreme Court of Washington, En Banc, 1983.
98 Wn.2d 533, 656 P.2d 1077.

DORE, JUSTICE.

This appeal arises from a dispute which erupted between two insurance companies and their insureds following the May 18, 1980 explosion of Mt. St. Helens. The early pyroclastic flows from the eruption, along with hot ash and debris, began melting the snow and ice flanking the mountain and the broken glacial ice blocks within the Toutle River valley. This water, combined with torrential rains from the eruption cloud, existing ground water, water displaced from Spirit Lake, and ash and debris, created mudflows which began moving down the valley shortly after the eruption began. * * * Approximately 10 hours after the eruption began, the appellants' homes, 20–25 miles away from Mt. St. Helens, were destroyed by a mudflow or a combination of mudflows preceded by water damage from flooding.

At the time of the eruption, homeowners insurance policies issued by Public Employees Mutual Insurance Company (hereafter PEMCO) to appellants * * * provided in pertinent part as follows:

SECTION 1—EXCLUSIONS

We do not cover loss resulting directly or indirectly from:

* * *

2. Earth Movement. Direct loss by fire, explosion, theft, or breakage of glass or safety glazing materials resulting from earth movement is covered.

3. Water damage, meaning:

    a. flood, * * *

Of the seven exclusions listed in the PEMCO policy, "earth movement" is the only one not specifically defined in the policy.

Prior to March 1980, PEMCO utilized insurance forms containing this exclusionary language:

This policy does not insure against loss:

* * *

2. caused by, resulting from, contributed to or aggravated by any earth movement, including but not limited to earthquake, volcanic eruption, landslide, mudflow, earth sinking, rising or shifting; unless loss by fire, explosion or breakage of glass constituting a part of the building(s) covered hereunder, including glass in storm doors and storm windows, ensures, and this Company shall then be liable only for such ensuing loss, but this exclusion does not apply to loss by theft;

This language was deleted by PEMCO in an overall effort to simplify the policy language.

The homeowners filed claims against the insurance companies under their homeowners policies, but the insurance companies rejected their claims on the basis that the damage was excludable as "earth movement" in the form of mudflows or a combination of earth movement and water damage. * * * [Summary judgment in favor of the insurance company was entered by the trial court].

For the purpose of ruling on the summary judgment motion, the trial court assumed the movement of Mt. St. Helens to be an "explosion" within the terms of the insurance policies. The trial court noted this issue was a factual issue to be determined by a jury. We agree, as the true meaning of "explosion" in each case must be settled by the common experience of jurors. * * * Because direct loss from an explosion resulting from earth movement is not excluded from coverage, the jury must also determine the factual issue of whether the earth movements were caused by the earthquakes and harmonic tremors which preceded the eruption.

If the jury determines the volcanic eruption was an explosion resulting from earth movement, it will then be necessary to reach the issue of whether the loss was a direct result of the eruption. The trial court held that the causation analysis of Bruener v. Twin City Fire Ins. Co., 37 Wash.2d 181, 222 P.2d 833 (1950) precluded the plaintiffs' claims.

In *Bruener,* the insured's vehicle skidded on icy pavement and collided with an embankment. The insurance policy contained a collision exclusion to the comprehensive coverage. This court held that the loss was a "collision" for insurance purposes, reasoning as follows at 183–84, 222 P.2d 833:

> In tort cases, the rules of proximate cause are applied for the single purpose of fixing culpability, with which insurance cases are not concerned. For that purpose, the tort rules of proximate cause reach back of both the injury and the physical cause to fix the blame on those who created the situation in which the physical laws of nature operated. The happening of an accident does not, in itself, establish negligence and tort liability. The question is always, why did the injury occur. Insurance cases are not concerned with why the injury occurred or the question of culpability, but only with the nature of the injury and how it happened.

The *Bruener* court expressly overruled Ploe v. International Indem. Co., 128 Wash. 480, 223 P. 327 (1924), a case involving a driver who lost control of an automobile while rounding a curve on a mountain road. The car left the highway and traveled 25 feet before striking a stump along the road. Holding that the insurer was not liable, the court characterized the proximate cause of the accident to be the skidding of the car and not the collision with the stump. *Ploe,* at 483, 223 P. 327. The court reasoned that the destruction of the car was imminent from the time it left the highway, whether it struck the stump or not. In overruling the *Ploe* decision, the *Bruener* court, 37 Wash.2d at 185, 222 P.2d 833 replaced this proximate cause analysis with one of "direct, violent and efficient cause".

In Dickson v. United States Fidelity & Guar. Co., 77 Wash.2d 785, 466 P.2d 515 (1970), the plaintiff's boom crane was insured under a policy which excluded coverage for latent defects. The boom crane was damaged when earth, collapsing onto an "H" beam that was being removed, caused a sudden stoppage of the hoist. This stoppage put an increase in load on the boom structure, causing a defective weld to break and the boom to collapse. This court affirmed the trial court's ruling that the earth collapse was the external and responsible cause of the failure of the weld and the collapse of the boom, stating at 793, 466 P.2d 515:

> The trial court regarded the collapsing earth as the external and responsible cause of the failure of the weld and the collapse of the boom. He did not thereby rule in contradiction to our rule on insurance causation, as set forth in Bruener v. Twin City Fire Ins. Co., [37 Wash.2d 181, 222 P.2d 833 (1950)] wherein we stated that, for the purposes of insurance litigation, the responsible cause of a loss is that which is the "direct, violent and efficient cause of the damage."

In reviewing the foregoing cases, we conclude the immediate physical cause analysis is no longer appropriate and should be discarded. The *Bruener* rule is an anomaly, inconsistent with the rule in the majority of other jurisdictions.[36] We have defined "proximate cause" as that cause "which, in a natural and continuous sequence, unbroken by any new, independent cause, produces the event, and without which that event would not have occurred". Stoneman v. Wick Constr. Co., 55 Wash.2d 639, 643, 349 P.2d 215 (1960). Where a peril specifically insured against sets other causes in motion which, in an unbroken sequence and connection between the act and final loss, produce the result for which recovery is sought, the insured peril is regarded as the "proximate cause" of the entire loss. * * *

It is the efficient or predominant cause which sets into motion the chain of events producing the loss which is regarded as the proximate cause, not necessarily the last act in a chain of events. * * * The mechanical simplicity of the *Bruener* rule does not allow inquiry into the intent and expectations of the parties to the insurance contract. Sears, Roebuck & Co. v. Hartford Accident & Indem. Co., 50 Wash.2d 443, 313 P.2d 347 (1957). We now specifically overrule the *Bruener* case.[37]

* * *

36. 18 G. Couch, *Insurance* § 74:693 (2d ed. 1968) states the majority rule as:

> "When loss is sustained by the insured it is necessary that the loss be proximately, rather than remotely, caused by the peril insured against."

37. In Frontier Lanes v. Canadian Indem. Co., 26 Wash.App. 342, 346, 613 P.2d 166 (1980), the Court of Appeals read

In the present case, the mudflows which destroyed the appellants' homes would not have occurred without the eruption of Mt. St. Helens. The eruption displaced water from Spirit Lake, and set into motion the melting of the snow and ice flanking the mountain. A jury could reasonably determine the water displacement, melting snow and ice and mudflows were mere manifestations of the eruption, finding that the eruption of Mt. St. Helens was the proximate cause of the damage to appellants' homes. This issue is not a question of law but a question of fact, to be determined by the trier of facts.

CONCLUSION

The *Bruener* decision is hereby overruled. We remand to the trial court for a jury determination of whether the movement of Mt. St. Helens was an "explosion" within the terms of the insurance policies; whether that "explosion" was preceded by earth movement, and whether appellants' damages were proximately caused by the eruption of Mt. St. Helens on May 18, 1980.

BRACHTENBACH, CHIEF JUSTICE (dissenting).

* * *

The obvious flaw in the majority's opinion is that it improperly applies the terms of the policy to the chain of events. The facts of this case reveal the following possible chain of events which should result in a denial of coverage regardless of proximate cause analysis. As suggested by the majority, on May 18, 1980, earthquakes and moving lava caused earth to move, which caused an eruption (explosion?), which caused earth movement in the form of mudflows. The majority concludes that the exclusion operates to exclude the initial earth movement which preceded the eruption but that the exception for explosion contained in the exclusion brings the incident back within the potential terms of the policy. But if that result is correct, the majority neglects a necessary additional inquiry—that is—should the earth movement exclusion be applied a second time to exclude coverage for mudflows? This last question presents strictly a legal issue involving the proper interpretation of policy terms. I submit that the only logical resolution of this issue is that the earth movement exclusion must be considered a second time. This answer requires, unfortunately, that we deny coverage. To do otherwise, however, would be to use proximate cause analysis to circumvent the clear terms of the policy. In addition, the majority appears to stop its inquiry at a point on the causation chain where coverage would be provided.

* * *

Bruener v. Twin City Fire Ins. Co., 37 Wash.2d 181, 222 P.2d 833 (1950) to require that a loss could be attributed to vandalism or malicious mischief only if "the immediate physical cause of that loss was the vandalistic or malicious act itself or an instrumentality employed directly by the wrongdoer to carry out that act". We decline to follow the *Frontier* analysis insofar as it is inconsistent with our holding in the present case.

The interpretation I suggest is necessary to give effect to the expectations that the parties had at the time they contracted for insurance coverage.[38] I would therefore deny coverage and affirm the trial court.

DOLLIVER and DIMMICK, JJ., concur.

Notes

1. *Concurrent Proximate Causes—Earthquakes and Negligence.* Beginning with *State Farm Mutual Auto. Ins. Co. v. Partridge*, 10 Cal.3d 94, 109 Cal.Rptr. 811, 514 P.2d 123 (1973), California courts have applied a rule that where two proximate causes join in causing an injury one of which is insured against, the insurer is liable under the policy irrespective of the eventuality that there is another concurrent proximate cause which constitutes an uncovered risk. In *Partridge,* the insured while driving a car was injured by his negligent discharge of a pistol. He was allowed recovery under a homeowners policy which excluded injuries arising out of the use, etc. of a vehicle. A federal court applied the same principle in *Safeco Ins. Co. v. Guyton*, 692 F.2d 551 (9th Cir.1982), in holding that a homeowners policy excluding flood to nevertheless cover the flooding of the insured's property where the concurrent proximate cause was the negligence of third parties in maintaining flood control facilities. The court observed that it made no difference that neither of the two causes could be characterized as the "prime," "moving," or "efficient" cause. And in a similar vein the owner of a home which slid down the hill along with the hillside itself recovered under an "all risks" policy expressly excluding earth movement because a concurrent cause could be found in a subdrain that had been negligently damaged so that the ground became saturated and moved. Premier Ins. Co. v. Welch, 140 Cal. App.3d 720, 189 Cal.Rptr. 657 (1983). Although the court recognized that the holding could also be based on the existence of a nonexcluded cause setting in motion the immediate excluded cause, it chose to adopt the *concurrent cause* doctrine of the preceding cases.

Although California is an earthquake prone state, only about 5 percent of the property owners carry earthquake coverage. It follows however, that if a negligently constructed building falls down in an earthquake, the *concurrent cause* rationale can be applied. It is reported that after the 1983 Coalinga earthquake, insurers paid out over $10 mission to owners of property whose insurance excluded or otherwise did not cover earthquakes. It is also reported that one insurer refused to pay a $10,000 claim somewhat similar to the *Welch* case, supra, and thereby incurred a trial court judgment of $47,000 in compensatory and $1 million in punitive damages. As a result the insurer revised more than 6 million of its homeowners policies to avoid the negation of "earth moving" exclusions by citing negligent acts or construction as a concurrent cause. Of course, if your well-constructed house collapses in an earthquake it is simply unfortunate. Legislation now requires

38. The fact that the Grahams made a claim and recovered under their Federal Flood Insurance policy for this damage demonstrates that they at least viewed the primary cause of the damage as unrelated to the explosion. Transcript at 43.

insurers in California to advise policy holders of the availability of earthquake insurance.

2. A useful discussion of *Graham* and the *Garvey* case which follows can be found in Lawrence Alan Wans, Comment, *Washington's Invalidation of Unambiguous Exclusion Clauses in Multiple Causation Insurance Cases*, 67 Wash. L. Rev. 215 (1992).

GARVEY v. STATE FARM FIRE AND CASUALTY COMPANY

Supreme Court of California, In Bank, 1989.
48 Cal.3d 395, 257 Cal.Rptr. 292, 770 P.2d 704.

LUCAS, CHIEF JUSTICE.

We granted review to consider the Court of Appeal's reversal of a directed verdict of coverage in favor of Jack and Rita Garvey (hereafter plaintiffs). We sought to resolve some of the confusion that has arisen regarding insurance coverage under the "all-risk" section of a homeowner's insurance policy when loss to an insured's property can be attributed to two causes, one of which is a nonexcluded peril, and the other an excluded peril.

* * *

I.

FACTS

Plaintiffs bought their house in the mid–1970's. In 1977, plaintiffs purchased from State Farm Fire and Casualty Company (hereafter defendant) an "all risk" homeowner's policy of insurance which was in effect at all times relevant. Section I of the policy in question provided coverage for "all risks of physical loss to the property covered" except as otherwise excluded or limited. Losses excluded by this portion of the policy included those "caused by, resulting from, contributed to or aggravated by any earth movement, including but not limited to earthquake, volcanic eruption, landslide, mudflow, earth sinking, rising or shifting," and losses caused "by * * * settling, cracking, shrinkage, bulging or expansion of pavements, patios, foundations, walls, floors, roofs or ceilings * * *."

In August 1978, plaintiffs noticed that a house addition, built in the early 1960's, had begun to pull away from the main structure. They also discovered damage to a deck and garden wall. There ensued numerous phone calls, letters, meetings and investigations as plaintiffs tried to determine from defendant whether the damage was covered by their homeowner's property insurance policy.

In October 1979, after receiving from its counsel an opinion that the loss was not covered, defendant notified plaintiffs by letter that the "policy excludes coverage for the loss herein. Normally, such a denial of coverage would leave you to your remedies. However, because the company wishes to resolve the coverage issue in an atmosphere free from extraneous matters such as bad-faith and class action issues, the company is prepared to advance you the claimed sum of $11,550 subject to a reservation of rights as authorized by Johansen v. CSAA, [1975], 15 Cal.3d 9 [123 Cal.Rptr. 288, 538 P.2d 744] * * *." Under the agreement proposed, defendant would make the advance and file a declaratory relief action on the issue of coverage; plaintiffs would pay back the advance if the court ruled in defendant's favor, would waive "any claim of consequential or punitive damages arising out of any allegation of bad-faith, mental distress, oppression, fraud or insurance-related tort," and would not "institute any class-action against defendant on account of the facts and issues involved in this loss and claim."

After refusing to sign the foregoing agreement, plaintiffs sued, claiming that although their policy excluded coverage for losses caused or aggravated by earth movement, it implicitly provided coverage for losses caused by contractor negligence because negligence was not a specifically excluded peril under the policy. Plaintiffs also argued that defendant denied their claim before adequately investigating the damage to the structure, and that subsequent investigations were undertaken merely to confirm the original denial. In addition, plaintiffs asserted, defendant's denial of coverage constituted a breach of the implied covenant of good faith and fair dealing and violated various provisions of the Insurance Code. Plaintiffs sought as relief (i) policy benefits, (ii) general damages for economic detriment and emotional distress, and (iii) punitive damages. Defendant rested on the 12th day of trial, and the court granted a directed verdict for plaintiffs on the coverage issue. The court informed the parties it was following the decisions in Partridge, supra, 10 Cal.3d 94, 109 Cal.Rptr. 811, 514 P.2d 123, and Sabella, supra, 59 Cal.2d 21, 27 Cal.Rptr. 689, 377 P.2d 889, and that plaintiffs were covered under the policy because negligent construction, a covered risk, was a concurrent proximate cause of the damage. Specifically, the trial court stated: "[The Supreme Court] told me in Sabella that negligent construction can be a proximate cause. They told me in Partridge there may be coverage whenever an insured risk constitutes simply a concurrent proximate cause of the injuries. Now, to me that is crystal clear, putting those two causes together, that if negligent construction is a concurrent proximate cause of the loss, there is coverage." The court continued, "The key witness for the defense, Mr. Nelson, conceded in his testimony, as I heard it and understood it, that the negligent construction was a cause of the room falling away. He did not use the word 'proximate.' He said a causative factor at one time. I don't recall the exact language when he answered a question. In substance, that it was a cause on another occasion. As a matter of law, based upon the evidence, it was a proximate cause."

The jury subsequently found defendant liable for $47,000 in policy benefits and general damages, and $1 million in punitive damages. The court denied defendant's motions for judgment notwithstanding the verdict and for a new trial, and declined to issue a remittitur with respect to the punitive damages award. The court entered judgment in accordance with the verdict. Defendant appealed, and the Court of Appeal reversed the judgment in a divided opinion. Before reviewing the Court of Appeal holding, and in order to provide sufficient background information that will aid in the understanding of this case, we first discuss the development of multiple and concurrent causation insurance analyses, and the important distinction between property and liability policies.

II.

DISCUSSION

A. Development of Multiple Causation Insurance Coverage Analyses

1. The efficient proximate cause standard

Our courts have long struggled to enunciate principles that determine whether coverage exists when excluded and covered perils interact to cause a loss. Initially, the courts attempted to reconcile section 530 (which provides for coverage when a peril insured against was the "proximate cause" of loss) with section 532 (which provides, that "If a peril is specifically excepted in a contract of insurance, and there is a loss which would not have occurred but for such peril, such loss is thereby excepted [from coverage] even though the immediate cause of the loss was a peril which was not excepted").

In our 1963 Sabella decision, supra, 59 Cal.2d 21, 27 Cal.Rptr. 689, 377 P.2d 889, we faced a difficult property loss coverage question arising after a building contractor constructed a house on uncompacted fill and negligently installed a sewer line; negligent installation was a covered peril. Eventually, the sewer line ruptured causing water to saturate the ground surrounding the insureds' house, resulting in subsidence, an excluded peril. The insureds brought a first-party action against their insurer, seeking recovery for property loss under their homeowner's property policy. (Id., at p. 26, 27 Cal.Rptr. 689, 377 P.2d 889.) The trial court found the loss was not covered because subsidence was a specifically excluded peril under the policy. The insureds appealed this ruling and we reversed.

On its face, section 532 would have precluded coverage because the loss would not have occurred "but for" the excluded peril of subsidence. We recognized, however, that such a result would be absurd because it would deny coverage even though an insured peril "proximately" caused the loss simply because a subsequent, excepted peril was also part of the chain of causation. We reasoned that sections 530 and 532 were not intended to deny coverage for losses whenever "an excepted peril operated to any extent in the chain of causation so that the resulting harm would not have occurred 'but for' the excepted peril's operation * * *." (Sabella, supra, 59 Cal.2d at p. 33, 27 Cal.Rptr. 689, 377 P.2d 889.) Rather, we explained that when section 532 is read along with section 530, the "but for" clause of section 532 necessarily refers to a "proximate cause" of the loss, and the "immediate cause" refers to the cause most immediate in time to the damage. (Id., at pp. 33–34, 27 Cal.Rptr. 689, 377 P.2d 889.)

Thus, Sabella held that: " '[I]n determining whether a loss is within an exception in a policy, where there is a concurrence of different causes, the efficient cause—the one that sets others in motion—is the cause to which the loss is to be attributed, though the other causes may follow it, and operate more immediately in producing the disaster.' " (Id., at pp. 31–32, 27 Cal.Rptr. 689, 377 P.2d 889, quoting from Couch on Insurance (1930) § 1466; Houser & Kent, Concurrent Causation in First–Party Insurance Claims: Consumers Cannot Afford Concurrent Causation (1986) Tort & Ins.L.J. 573, 575.)

Furthermore, in characterizing the "but for" clause of section 532 as referring to the efficient proximate cause of the loss, we impliedly recognized that coverage would not exist if the covered risk was simply a remote cause of the loss, or if an excluded risk was the efficient proximate (meaning predominant) cause of the loss. On the other hand, the fact that an excluded risk contributed to the loss would not preclude coverage if such a risk was a remote cause of the loss.

We relied heavily in Sabella, supra, 59 Cal.2d 21, 27 Cal.Rptr. 689, 377 P.2d 889, on our earlier decision in Brooks v. Metropolitan Life Ins. Co. (1945) 27 Cal.2d 305, 163 P.2d 689, in which recovery was allowed on a homeowner's policy insuring against death by accidental means. In Brooks, the insured, who was suffering from incurable cancer, an excluded peril, died in a fire. We held, "recovery may be had even though a diseased or infirm condition appears to actually contribute to cause the death if the accident sets in progress the chain of events leading directly to death, or if it is the prime or moving cause." (Id., at pp. 309–310, 163 P.2d 689.) Brooks thus defined efficient proximate cause in the first-party loss context as the "prime or moving cause." (Ibid.)

The Court of Appeal here replaced the Sabella term "efficient proximate cause" with the term "moving cause." Sabella defined "efficient proximate cause" alternatively as the "one that sets others in motion" (59 Cal.2d at p. 31, 27 Cal.Rptr. 689, 377 P.2d 889), and as "the predominating or moving efficient cause." (Id., at p. 32, 27 Cal.Rptr. 689, 377 P.2d 889.) We use the term "efficient proximate cause" (meaning predominating cause) when referring to the Sabella analysis because we believe the phrase "moving cause" can be misconstrued to deny coverage erroneously, particularly when it is understood literally to mean the "triggering" cause. Indeed, we believe misinterpretation of the Sabella definition of "efficient proximate cause" has added to the confusion in the courts and, in part, is responsible for the erroneous application of Partridge, supra, 10 Cal.3d 94, 109 Cal.Rptr. 811, 514 P.2d 123, to first-party property loss cases.

By relying on Brooks, supra, 27 Cal.2d 305, 163 P.2d 689, and construing sections 530 and 532, Sabella, supra, 59 Cal.2d 21, 27 Cal.Rptr. 689, 377 P.2d 889, set forth a workable rule of coverage that provides a fair result within the reasonable expectations of both the insured and the insurer whenever there exists a causal or dependent relationship between covered and excluded perils. In multiple cause cases, a proximate cause analysis, focusing on the efficient proximate cause, could be employed to determine whether or not the insured was covered for the loss under the property portion of the homeowner's insurance policy. Indeed, for 10 years following Sabella, the Court of Appeal applied the efficient proximate cause analysis in resolving multiple-cause property-coverage questions under all-risk homeowner's property policies. (See, e.g., Gillis v. Sun Ins. Office, Ltd. (1965) 238 Cal. App.2d 408, 415–420, 47 Cal.Rptr. 868 [coverage afforded under policy insuring loss by windstorm but excluding loss from water damage; wind, causing gangway to fall on and sink a dock, was deemed efficient proximate cause of loss]; Sauer v. General Ins. Co. (1964) 225 Cal.App.2d 275, 278–279, 37 Cal.Rptr. 303 [coverage afforded when water leaking from plumbing system (covered peril) was the efficient proximate cause of subsidence damage (excluded peril)].)

2. The doctrine of concurrent causation

In 1973, we were faced with a third-party tort liability situation that presented a "novel question of insurance coverage" and did not fit the Sabella analysis because no single peril could be labeled the predominant cause of the loss. In Partridge, supra, 10 Cal.3d 94, 109 Cal.Rptr. 811, 514 P.2d 123, the insured was covered under both an automobile liability policy and a homeowner's liability policy with comprehensive personal liability coverage. (The latter liability policy excluded losses "arising out of the use" of a motor vehicle.) The insured, after filing the trigger mechanism of his pistol to create a "hair-trigger" action (such negligence was a covered risk under the homeowner's property policy), hunted jackrabbits at night from his vehicle. As he drove over rough terrain while waving the gun in his hand (negligent driving was an excluded risk under homeowner's liability policy), the gun fired and injured a passenger.

First-party property coverage issues were not involved. The case concerned the personal liability of the insured who was sued by his injured passenger. Both policies were issued by the same insurer, which conceded the accident was covered under the automobile liability policy. The parties, however, disputed whether coverage was also afforded under the homeowner's liability policy, which excluded coverage for injuries "arising out of the use of motor vehicles." As in Sabella, supra, 59 Cal.2d 21, 27 Cal.Rptr. 689, 377 P.2d 889, we relied on Brooks, supra, 27 Cal.2d 305, at pages 309–310, 163 P.2d 689, to find coverage under the homeowner's policy. In analyzing the liability coverage, we explicitly recognized, "the 'efficient cause' language [of Sabella] is not very helpful, for here both causes were independent of each other: the filing of the trigger did not 'cause' the careless driving, nor vice versa. Both, however, caused the injury * * *. If committed by separate individuals, both actors would be joint tortfeasors fully liable for the resulting injuries. Moreover, the fact that both acts were committed by a single person does not alter their nature as concurrent proximate causes. (Cf., Flournoy v.

State of California (1969) 275 Cal.App.2d 806, 811 [80 Cal.Rptr. 485].)" (Partridge, supra, 10 Cal.3d at p. 104, fn. 10, 109 Cal.Rptr. 811, 514 P.2d 123.) We concluded by stating, "Although there may be some question whether either of the two causes in the instant case can be properly characterized as the 'prime,' 'moving' or 'efficient' cause of the accident we believe that coverage under a liability insurance policy is equally available to an insured whenever an insured risk constitutes simply a concurrent proximate cause of the injuries." (Id. at pp. 104–105, 109 Cal.Rptr. 811, 514 P.2d 123, fns. omitted, second italics added.)

Because Partridge dealt with causation in the context of third-party liability insurance, we did not address, nor did we contemplate, the application of our decision to the determination of coverage in the first-party property insurance context. Indeed, Partridge asserted only that the "concurrent cause" standard was "consistent with Insurance Code sections 530 and 532, as authoritatively construed in Sabella v. Wisler. . . . " (Partridge, supra, at p. 105, fn. 11, 109 Cal.Rptr. 811, 514 P.2d 123.)

Furthermore, Partridge never considered in what manner concurrent causation could apply in the first-party property insurance context. Rather, by recognizing in Partridge the "novel question" of liability coverage presented because two separate acts of negligence simultaneously joined together to cause an injury, we also impliedly recognized the limited scope of our holding. We did not extend our holding to first-party property insurance cases. Accordingly, we should not apply the decision to such cases merely because it appears to simplify the coverage analysis.

B. The Distinction Between Liability and Property Insurance

As we will demonstrate, the decision of the Court of Appeal, in applying the Partridge concurrent causation analysis to property damage cases, like other recent insurance cases involving all-risk homeowner's policies, failed to differentiate between property loss coverage under a first-party policy and tort liability coverage under a third-party policy of insurance. First-and third-party coverage is today typically provided in a single policy, and under both types of coverage, once the insured shows that an event falls within the scope of basic coverage under the policy, the burden is on the insurer to prove a claim is specifically excluded. (See Clemmer v. Hartford Ins. (1978) 22 Cal.3d 865, 880, 151 Cal.Rptr. 285, 587 P.2d 1098; Royal Globe Ins. Co. v. Whitaker (1986) 181 Cal.App.3d 532, 537, 226 Cal.Rptr. 435; Strubble v. United Services Auto. Assn. (1973) 35 Cal.App.3d 498, 504, 110 Cal.Rptr. 828.) Moreover, exclusionary clauses are interpreted narrowly, whereas clauses identifying coverage are interpreted broadly. (See Reserve Ins. Co. v. Pisciotta (1982) 30 Cal.3d 800, 808, 180 Cal.Rptr. 628, 640 P.2d 764.)

The scope of coverage and the operation of the exclusion clauses, however, are different in the separate policy portions and should be treated as such. As one commentator has recently stated: "Liability and corresponding coverage under a third-party insurance policy must be carefully distinguished from the coverage analysis applied in a first-party property contract. Property insurance, unlike liability insurance, is unconcerned with establishing negligence or otherwise assessing tort liability." (Bragg, Concurrent Causation and the Art of Policy Drafting: New Perils for Property Insurers (1985) 20 Forum 385, 386.)

For these reasons it is important to separate the causation analysis necessary in a first-party property loss case from that which must be undertaken in a third-party tort liability case. The following quotation summarizes the distinction that must be drawn: "Property insurance * * * is an agreement, a contract, in which the insurer agrees to indemnify the insured in the event that the insured property suffers a covered loss. Coverage, in turn, is commonly provided by reference to causation, e.g., 'loss caused by * * *' certain enumerated perils. The term 'perils' in traditional property insurance parlance refers to fortuitous, active, physical forces such as lightning, wind, and explosion, which bring about the loss. Thus, the 'cause' of loss in the context of a property insurance contract is totally different from that in a liability policy. This distinction is critical to the resolution of losses involving multiple causes. Frequently property losses occur which involve more than one peril that might be considered legally significant. If one of the causes (perils) arguably falls within the coverage grant—commonly either because it is specifically insured (as in a named peril policy) or not specifically excepted or excluded (as in an 'all risks' policy)—disputes over coverage can arise. The task becomes one of identifying the most important cause of the loss and attributing the loss to that cause." (Bragg, supra, 20 Forum at pp. 386–387, italics added.)

On the other hand, the right to coverage in the third-party liability insurance context draws on traditional tort concepts of fault, proximate cause and duty. This liability analysis differs substantially from the coverage analysis in the property insurance context, which draws on the relationship between perils that are either covered or excluded in the contract. In liability insurance, by insuring for personal liability, and agreeing to cover the insured for his own negligence, the insurer agrees to cover the insured for a broader spectrum of risks. In order to further demonstrate the differences between property loss and liability coverage, we compare two sections of a typical homeowner's policy—the all-risk property loss coverage section of the policy in this case and the personal liability section at issue in Partridge.

Each policy section is governed by separate exclusions. For example, the all-risk first-party property loss coverage section in this case provides for coverage against "all risk of physical loss" except: losses "caused by * * * settling cracking, shrinkage, bulging or expansion of pavements, patios, foundations, walls, floors, roofs or ceilings * * *." In comparison, in Partridge, "The coverage clause of the 'Personal Liability' section of the 'Homeowner's Policy' provides in relevant part: 'This Company agrees to pay on behalf of the Insured all sums which the Insured shall become legally obligated to pay as damages because of bodily injury or property damage, to which this insurance applies, caused by an occurrence.' * * *." (10 Cal.3d at p. 99, fn. 5, 109 Cal.Rptr. 811, 514 P.2d 123.) Moreover, "[t]he applicable exclusionary clause reads: 'This policy does not apply: 1. Under Coverage E—Personal Liability * * * (a) To Bodily Injury or Property Damage Arising Out of the Ownership, Maintenance, Operation, Use, Loading or Unloading of: * * * (2) Any Motor Vehicle Owned or Operated By, or Rented or Loaned to, any Insured * * *.' " (10 Cal.3d at p. 99, fn. 6, 109 Cal.Rptr. 811, 514 P.2d 123.)

As the two provisions cited above illustrate, under the all-risk first-party property policy, because generally "all risk of physical loss" is covered, the exclusions become the limitation on loss coverage. Under the liability portion of the policy, on the other hand, the focus is, at least initially, on the insured's legal obligation to pay for injury or damage arising out of an "occurrence."

In the property insurance context, the insurer and the insured can tailor the policy according to the selection of insured and excluded risks and, in the process, determine the corresponding premium to meet the economic needs of the insured. On the other hand, if the insurer is expected to cover claims that are outside the scope of the first-party property loss policy, an "all-risk" policy would become an "all-loss" policy. (Friedman, Concurrent Causation: The Coverage Trap (1985) 86 Best's Rev.: Prop./Casualty 50, 58.) In most instances, the insured can point to some arguably covered contributing factor. As we shall discuss, if the rule in Partridge, supra, 10 Cal.3d 94, 109 Cal.Rptr. 811, 514 P.2d 123, were extended to first-party cases, the presence of such a cause, no matter how minor, would give rise to coverage.

Finally, as we explain, the reasonable expectations of the insurer and the insured in the first-party property loss portion of a homeowner's policy—as manifested in the distribution of risks, the proportionate premiums charged and the coverage for all risks except those specifically excluded—cannot reasonably include an expectation of coverage in property loss cases in which the efficient proximate cause of the loss is an activity expressly excluded under the policy. Indeed, if we were to approve of the trial court's directed verdict, we would be requiring ordinary insureds to bear the expense of increased premiums necessitated by the erroneous expansion of their insurers' potential liabilities. (See Hartford Fire Ins. Co. v. Superior Court (1983) 142 Cal.App.3d 406, 417, 191 Cal.Rptr. 37.)

C. The Court of Appeal Holding

In reversing the directed verdict, the Court of Appeal rejected defendant's argument that although third-party negligence is not specifically excluded in an all-risk policy, it is not a covered peril because it is technically not considered a "risk of physical loss" within the policy terms. We agree and find defendant's claim is not supported by authority. (See e.g., Sabella, supra, 59 Cal.2d 21, 31, 27 Cal.Rptr. 689, 377 P.2d 889.)

Next, the court recognized that recent first-party property loss cases (discussed below) have forsaken the efficient proximate cause analysis developed in Sabella, supra, 59 Cal.2d 21, 27 Cal.Rptr. 689, 377 P.2d 889, and have looked instead to the holding in Partridge, supra, 10 Cal.3d 94, 109 Cal.Rptr. 811, 514 P.2d 123, to allow coverage for property damage simply because a nonexcluded risk is an independent proximate cause of the loss. Although the Court of Appeal refused to confine the application of Partridge to liability cases, the court did attempt to limit the scope of Partridge's concurrent causation standard in both liability and property cases by requiring the included and excluded perils to be independent of origin and independent in operation. Specifically, the Court of Appeal interpreted Partridge, supra, 10 Cal.3d 94, 109 Cal.Rptr. 811, 514 P.2d 123, as holding that "because each act could have caused the loss regardless of the existence of the other act [citation], they were independent of each other." According to the Court of Appeal: "Neither [cause in Partridge] can be said to have necessarily acted upon a condition created by the other, or to have propelled the other, or to have brought to fruition the potential for damage inherent in the other." The Court of Appeal believed the "Partridge court would not have found the covered risk to be 'independent' if that risk (negligence) existed only in relation to, [or was dependent on] an excluded risk." Thus, the Court of Appeal determined that in order for coverage to be found under Partridge, the concurrent event alone must have been a "sufficient condition" of the loss—i.e., capable of producing damage itself.[39]

In its effort to interpret and apply the Partridge decision in the present case, however, the court followed the lead of other Court of Appeal decisions and assumed, without discussion, that Partridge should apply to first-party property insurance policies. In so doing, the court relied on both Partridge, and Sabella, supra, 59 Cal.2d 21, 27 Cal.Rptr. 689, 377 P.2d 889, and announced the following two-tiered rule for determining coverage: "[W]hether the covered risk and excluded risk are causes in fact should be a court's threshold inquiry in cases such as this. If (i) they both are causes in fact and if the two risks are independent of each other, Partridge analysis is triggered: the insured is covered if the covered risk was a concurring proximate cause of the loss. If (ii) the two risks are dependent on each other, Sabella analysis is triggered: the insured is covered only if the covered risk was the moving cause of the loss." The Court of Appeal determined that the jury in the present case must decide the coverage issue because it was not clear, as a matter of law, whether the two risks were dependent on or independent of each other.

The Court of Appeal's formulation was an attempt to provide trial courts with an analytical framework from which to determine property insurance coverage when a loss is arguably caused by concurrent causes. The court was on the right track in attempting to reconcile first- and

39. The term "sufficient condition" as used by the Court of Appeal missapplied the Partridge holding because it implied that negligent driving alone could have caused plaintiff's injury in that case. Although we point out the court's analytical error for purposes of clarifying any confusion the term may have caused, we leave the application of Partridge in the liability context to a future liability case that raises the concurrent causation issue.

third-party cases that use the Partridge analysis in determining coverage. We believe, however, as set forth above, that the court erroneously failed to limit at the threshold the application of Partridge to the third-party liability context.[40]

D. The Misapplication of Partridge in The First-party Property Insurance Context

In Safeco Ins. Co. of America v. Guyton, supra, 692 F.2d 551, 553, the insurer sought declaratory relief against several insureds after flooding damaged their homes. The trial court rejected the policyholders' claim that the water district's negligence in failing to provide adequate flood control facilities (a covered risk) caused the damage, and held under Sabella there was no coverage because the excluded peril—flooding—was the efficient proximate cause of the property damage. The Ninth Circuit Court of Appeals reversed on the basis that the insureds should be allowed to seek coverage under Partridge, supra, 10 Cal.3d 94, 109 Cal.Rptr. 811, 514 P.2d 123. The court determined that in order for Partridge to apply, the covered peril must have existed independently of the excluded peril. The court reasoned, however, that the requirement was met because two independently created conditions interacted to cause the flood damage. Indeed, Guyton specifically stated that "the twin causes in Partridge were independent only in the sense that each cause had an independent origin, not that they did not interact with one another to cause the loss." (692 F.2d at p. 555.)

As amici curiae for defendant point out, however, Guyton, supra, 692 F.2d 551, was actually "a classic case of dependent causation" requiring use of a Sabella analysis. Because the damage caused by the defective flood control system was necessarily dependent on flooding, the Ninth Circuit misapplied Partridge to find coverage. It should have looked to Sabella for resolution to determine whether the defectively maintained flood control system was the efficient proximate cause of the property losses even though the flood was the "immediate" cause of the losses, or whether the trial court correctly denied coverage in determining that flooding was the efficient proximate cause of the loss. The Ninth Circuit specifically ignored the effect of the express policy exclusion contained in the Safeco policy that excluded loss "caused by, resulting

40. As we explained above, Partridge, supra, 10 Cal.3d 94, 109 Cal.Rptr. 811, 514 P.2d 123, should be limited to the third-party tort liability context. In the unusual event that analysis under Sabella, supra, 59 Cal.2d 21, 27 Cal.Rptr. 689, 377 P.2d 889, would not be useful in a first-party property loss case because separate excluded and covered causes simultaneously join together to produce damage—a situation we have yet to address—we may then consider developing an appropriate doctrine of concurrent causation to apply in the property loss context. For example, if property loss were to result from the simultaneous crash of an aircraft into a structure (a covered peril in a typical all risk homeowner's policy) during an earthquake (typically excluded from coverage when it operates alone to cause a loss), it might be impossible to determine (under a Sabella analysis) which cause was the efficient proximate cause of the loss. In that "novel" case, we might consider developing a doctrine similar to the present Court of Appeal's independent concurrent causation standard in analyzing coverage under the policy. It would be imprudent to reach such a hypothetical issue here, however, and hence we leave discussion of such a doctrine to a future first-party property loss case, should one arise.

from, contributed to or aggravated by any of the following: a. Flood, surface water * * *." (Guyton, supra, 692 F.2d at pp. 552–553.)

In Premier Ins. Co. v. Welch (1983) 140 Cal.App.3d 720, 728, 189 Cal.Rptr. 657, a third party's negligence (a covered peril) damaged a subdrain. After a heavy rain, the house slid from its foundation. Water damage was an excluded peril. The trial court relied on Sabella, supra, 59 Cal.2d 21, 27 Cal.Rptr. 689, 377 P.2d 889, and determined that coverage should be denied because the efficient proximate cause of the loss was the rainfall. The same Court of Appeal division that decided the present case reversed and awarded coverage, concluding under a Sabella analysis that the efficient proximate cause of the loss was the damaged subdrain. Notwithstanding this conclusion, the court continued by stating that the insured would be covered in any event under Partridge, supra, 10 Cal.3d 94, 109 Cal.Rptr. 811, 514 P.2d 123, because "as a matter of law * * * the damage to the drain was a concurrent proximate cause of the loss." (Premier, supra, 140 Cal.App.3d at p. 728, 189 Cal.Rptr. 657.)

In its opinion in the present case, the Court of Appeal correctly acknowledged that its earlier interpretation (in Premier) of Partridge's independence requirement was wrong. Reviewing the facts of Premier, the court stated that the property loss caused by the negligently damaged subdrain was dependent on the existence of rainfall, but that nonetheless, the slide would not have occurred if the drain had not been severely damaged. Thus, the Court of Appeal recognized, "Premier was simply a Sabella situation." As the court admitted, it had reached a satisfactory result under Sabella, supra, 59 Cal.2d 21, 27 Cal.Rptr. 689, 377 P.2d 889; the Partridge analysis was simply unnecessary in Premier.

E. The Trial Court Erred in Directing the Verdict

Finally, because we believe the Partridge analysis should be limited to third-party liability cases, we cannot sustain the directed verdict in this case. Plaintiffs argue the directed verdict was proper because there was no evidence of sufficient substantiality to support a determination other than the following: the included risk of negligent construction and the excluded risk of earth movement in the form of soil creep, if any, were independent, concurrent proximate causes of the loss plaintiffs sustained to their property.

We disagree. * * *

This case presents a classic Sabella situation. Coverage should be determined by a jury under an efficient proximate cause analysis. Accordingly, bearing in mind the facts here, we conclude the question of causation is for the jury to decide. If the earth movement was the efficient proximate cause of the loss, then coverage would be denied under Sabella, supra, 59 Cal.2d 21, 27 Cal.Rptr. 689, 377 P.2d 889. On the other hand, if negligence was the efficient proximate cause of the loss, then coverage exists under Sabella. These issues were jury questions because sufficient evidence was introduced to support both possibilities.

The judgment of the Court of Appeal is affirmed with directions to remand the cause to the trial court for further proceedings consistent with the opinion of this court.

PANELLI, EAGLESON and ARGUELLES, JJ. [sitting under assignment by the Chairperson of the Judicial Council], concur.

The separate concurring opinion by KAUFMAN, J., concurred in by PANELLI, J., and the dissenting opinions by MOSK, J., and BROUSSARD, J. are omitted.

Note

Recall the *Engel* case and its hostile fire principle. Viewed through the *Garvey* lens, the issue in *Engel* is almost one of causation, that is, whether the insured's negligence in the maintenance of the machinery is at fault. Under *Garvey*, even if it is a friendly fire, the fire would be the efficient proximate cause and so the ensuing loss would be covered.

A Postscript

On balance, it appears that tort notions of proximate causation have overcome the attempted contractual restrictions on "causation" as drafted by the insurers in the policies scrutinized in the *Graham* case and the like. But basically Justice Cardozo was correct in the *Bird* decision—ultimately "causation" in insurance is a matter of contract not tort lore. In that spirit and in a counteraction to the results in the "earthquake" and "earth movement" cases when other concurrent covered causes were brought forth to effect coverage, the following redraft of the basic "Dwelling Property Form" furnished by the Insurance Services Office was made in the California version as of 1983:

GENERAL EXCLUSIONS

The first sentence:

> "We do not cover loss resulting directly or indirectly from:" [a list of exclusions follows including "water damage"]

is deleted and the following substituted:

> "We do not insure for loss directly or indirectly by any of the following. [a list of exclusions follows including "water damage"] Such loss is excluded regardless of any other cause or event contributing concurrently or in any sequence to the loss."

This redraft, a so-called anti-concurrent causation provision, will be at center stage in insurance litigation involving hurricane Katrina. Many policyholders affected by Katrina did not have coverage for losses caused by flood. Assuming such policies covered wind damage, will losses caused by "storm surge"–i.e. mini-tidal waves caused by the winds of Katrina–be covered by the insurance policy that explicitly excludes flood damage and that contains the anti-concurrent causation provision?

Courts which have considered claims involving covered causes and excluded causes have, not surprisingly, erred on the side of narrow interpretation of the exclusions where there is no anti-concurrent causation provision. Fayad v. Clarendon National Ins. Co., 899 So.2d 1082, 1087 n.3 (Fla.

2005)(citing jurisdictions in which a narrow application of the earth movement exclusion–generally excepting from the exclusion other than natural causes—is applied); State Farm Fire & Casualty Co. v. Bongen, 925 P.2d 1042, 1046 n.7 (Ak. 1996)(in accord). However, it seems that courts will give effect to the anti-concurrent cause provision reasoning that the provision unambiguously defines the scope of coverage. Fayad v. Clarendon National Ins. Co., 899 So.2d 1082, 1087 (Fla. 2005); Boteler v. State Farm Casualty Insurance Co., 876 So.2d 1067 (Miss. Ct. App. 2004); State Farm Fire & Casualty Co. v. Bongen, 925 P.2d 1042, 1044–45 (Ak. 1996). It should not be lost on the casual reader that these jurisdictions include hurricane-prone states. As *Garvey* suggests, however, California courts would not agree.

Without quarreling too much with the enforceability of the anti-concurrent cause provision, the difficulty with the provision is that it attempts to exclude covered causes even when the covered cause is the proximate cause of a loss. It is not hard to imagine a court, when faced with a loss proximately caused by a covered cause, holding an insurer liable on the basis that the loss involves a trivial degree of an excluded cause. Cox v. State Farm Fire & Casualty Co., 217 Ga.App. 796; 459 S.E.2d 446 (1995). The insured's reasonable expectations would appear to be sufficient to allow her to prevail. E.g., Murray v. State Farm Fire & Casualty Co., 203 W.Va. 477; 509 S.E.2d 1 (1998).

An Exercise in Analysis

Using the foregoing materials as a guide along the "causation" path running through the policy provisions defining coverage, how *should* these problem examples be resolved? How they *were* resolved is indicated. What should emerge from this exercise is a firm belief in the unpredictability of the outcome.

1. *Coverage provision:* "Perils NOT included: * * * loss by * * * smoke * * * caused by * * * order of any civil authority."

Sequence of events: Agricultural chemicals in warehouse vaporized and penetrated cartons of salad dressings belonging to insured and deposited residue thereon. Government agents condemned the food products. Henri's Food Products Co. v. Home Insurance Co., 474 F.Supp. 889 (E.D.Wis.1979) (held for insured finding "[t]he loss was not caused by condemnation but, instead, by the chemical residue" and further finding that "vapor" was not equivalent to "smoke").

Compare *Blaine Richards & Co. v. Marine Indemnity Ins. Co.*, 635 F.2d 1051 (2d Cir.1980) where the coverage provision excluded losses from detention by customs officials. Insured was importing beans from France and in the process a forbidden fumigant had been improperly applied by the supplier. The customs officials detained the beans for six weeks until FDA-approved clean-up measures. In consequence of the delay the insured lost sales contracts. With these facts the court held that the proximate cause was the fumigation although the immediate cause was the detention. (Notice that the Second Circuit had to modify the position taken in *Bird* and *Pan American World Airways,* supra.)

2. *Coverage provision:* direct loss by windstorm.

Sequence of events: Insured livestock exposed to cold wind in high country took shelter in lower warmer area and drowned in pond when ice broke. Lydick v. Insurance Co. of North America, 187 Neb. 97, 187 N.W.2d 602 (1971) (held for insurer).

3. *Coverage provision:* direct loss by windstorm, but excluding coverage for loss caused by, contributed to, or aggravated by, surface water or waves, wind driven or not.

Sequence of events: Wind blew a gangway onto the insured docking facility puncturing supporting pontoons which filled with water sinking the structure. Gillis v. Sun Insurance Office, Limited, 238 Cal.App.2d 408, 47 Cal.Rptr. 868, 25 A.L.R.3d 564 (1965) (held for insured).

4. *Coverage provision:* loss by windstorm

Sequence of events: Wind blew down power lines, meat in insured's cold storage plant spoiled because freezer went off. Federal Insurance Co. v. Bock, 382 S.W.2d 305 (Tex.Civ.App.1964) (held for insured).

5. *Coverage provision:* loss by windstorm

Sequence of events: Because of high wind the insured owner of a horse brought it in and stabled it next to the feed bin. Horse broke through the partition and died of overeating. Lorio v. Aetna Insurance Co., 255 La. 721, 232 So.2d 490 (1970) (held for insurer).

6. *Coverage provision:* "direct loss resulting from actual physical contact of * * * vehicle * * * with a building containing the property covered."

Sequence of events: An automobile deposited by a flood onto the sidewalk in front of the insured's shop diverted the floodwaters against the door which thereupon broke, letting in the water to cause damage to the property covered. Habaz v. Employers' Fire Insurance Co., 243 F.2d 784, 64 A.L.R.2d 1184 (8th Cir. 1957) (held for insurer).

7. *Coverage provision:* Covers damage from: "accidental discharge of water * * * from within a household appliance." Does not cover damage from: "water below the surface of the ground [which] leaks through a building [or] foundation.... "

Sequence of events: Insured put a sump pit in below the basement level the purpose being to pump out ground water before it reached basement level. Unfortunately the sump pump hose broke flooding the basement. Stone v. Royal Ins. Co., 211 N.J.Super. 246, 511 A.2d 717 (A.D. 1986) (held for insured with the finding that the sump pump was a household appliance).

8. *Coverage provision:* Federal flood policy (designed to provide insurance at affordable price) covered flood but excluded loss "by landslide or other earth movement, such as mudslide or erosion."

Sequence of events: Tropical storm Dennis hit Florida with exceptionally heavy rainfall. No water entered the insured's house, but did saturate sand fill on which house was built. The resulting soil compaction caused house to crack. Quesada v. Director, Federal Emergency Management Agency, 753 F.2d 1011 (11th Cir.1985) (held for insured).

4. The Insured Is Disqualified

a. *Breach of Warranty*

INTRODUCTORY NOTE—NO COVERAGE VS. BREACH OF WARRANTY

There is a sharp difference between the insurer's defenses that there is no contract (because a condition precedent, such as payment of the premium, has not been met) or that there is no coverage (because the condition precedent that the event insured against simply never happened) and the defense that an express term of the policy itself—e.g., a warranty made by the insured—has been broken.

The defense of "no contract" or "no coverage," once established, is fatal to the insured's claim and virtually impregnable as indicated by the repeated holdings that there can be no estoppel into coverage.

The consequences of a breach of warranty, as originally inflicted, were hardly less drastic. Vance on Insurance, 4th ed. 1952 § 71, includes the consequences of breach in his definition of "warranty" itself:

> "A warranty is a statement or promise set forth in the policy * * * the untruth or unfulfillment of which in any respect and without reference to whether the insurer was in fact prejudiced by such untruth or unfulfillment, renders the policy voidable by the insurer wholly irrespective of the materiality of such statement."

According to the California Insurance Code § 441, a warranty is defined as "[a] statement in a policy of a matter relating to the person or thing insured or to the risk, as a fact, is an express warranty thereof." California Insurance Code § 445 further provides "[a] statement in a policy which imports that there is an intention to do or not to do a thing which materially affects the risk, is a warranty that such act or omission will take place."

An implacable rule voiding purchased insurance protection for trivial or inconsequential breaches invites its own destruction. Judicial interpretation, moderating statutes, and liberal application of waiver or estoppel principles have significantly softened the effects of warranty breaches.

The problem thus becomes the usual one of categorization. Is the policy provision on which the company's defense rests a fatal "coverage" provision or the less terminal, though still dangerous, "warranty?" The problem is enhanced because of the prevalent use of the word "condition" in insurance policies. For example, what is suggested by the phrase "Conditions Restricting Insurance" or the frequent couplet "Warranties and other conditions?"

Probably intelligent laymen, who have not been exposed to a law school course in Contracts where the topic of "Conditions" is dissected at chapter length, would understand, and be comfortable with, the label "precedent condition" applied to coverage and the description "subsequent conditions'' applied to warranties (and ''similar conditions,'' to overburden the word further still) written into a contract with the understanding that a breach may bar the insured's accrued claims. Accrued, that is, in the sense that at this point the insured has proven a binding policy covering a loss which has in fact occurred. Naturally the insurer should carry the burden of proving the breach.

An Academic Analysis

Legally trained persons, however, are aware that texts on the Law of Contract confine the notion and scope of ''conditions subsequent'' to a small area. (See, e.g., Corbin on Contracts, § 739ff.) The argument is that virtually all conditions—including warranties—must be satisfied *before* the insured may recover on his policy. Hence, warranties are ''conditions precedent,'' which must be distinguished from ''conditions precedent to coverage'' in some other fashion than by label.

Prof. Edwin Patterson, late professor of law at Columbia University and an eminent authority on Contracts, Restitution and Insurance, undertook in his influential book to make the distinction in this fashion: ''the difference between warranty conditions and other conditions is that the former relate to *potential causes* of the insured event.'' Essentials of Insurance Law (2d ed. 1957), § 60. Thus the condition precedent that the loss be ''caused by windstorm'' applies to the *actual cause* of loss and is therefore a coverage clause; whereas warranties such as that the premises are protected by an automatic sprinkler system, or that the ship is ''copper clad'' are conditions (precedent likewise) dealing only with *potential* rather than the actual causes of loss.

Because Prof. Patterson was at one time Deputy Superintendent of Insurance of New York his concepts as to coverage clauses (relating to *actual* cause of loss) versus other conditional clauses, such as warranties (relating to *potential* causes of loss) were embodied in the unique New York statutory definition of a warranty:

Insurance Law § 3106

(a) In this section ''warranty'' means any provision of an insurance contract which has the effect of requiring, as a condition precedent of the taking effect of such contract or as a condition precedent of the insurer's liability thereunder, the existence of a fact which tends to diminish, or the non-existence of a fact which tends to increase, the risk of the occurrence of any loss, damage, or injury within the coverage of the contract. The term ''occurrence of loss, damage, or injury'' includes the occurrence of death, disability, injury, or any other contingency insured against, and the term ''risk'' includes both physical and moral hazards.

Question

Which definition of a ''warranty''—Vance's, the California statute, or the New York statute would be easiest to explain to an applicant for insurance?

VIOLIN v. FIREMAN'S FUND INSURANCE COMPANY

Supreme Court of Nevada, 1965.
81 Nev. 456, 406 P.2d 287.

THOMPSON, JUSTICE:

This is an action by the insureds on a policy of insurance covering a Guadagnini violin of the agreed value of $10,000. Following loss of the violin, the insurer Fireman's Fund Insurance Company canceled the policy, tendered return of the premium paid and denied liability on the ground that the insured had made a fraudulent, material misrepresentation in their application for insurance. The lower court ruled in favor of the insurer, and this appeal by the insureds followed. The sole question is whether, on the facts here disclosed, the insurer waived its right to cancel the policy or is estopped to deny liability. We have concluded that factors favoring the application of the doctrine of waiver against the insurer are here present, thus precluding avoidance of liability. Accordingly, we reverse.

The question asked on the application for insurance with which we are concerned was, "Has any company ever refused or canceled insurance?"[41] The applicants answered, "No." The answer was false. Four years earlier the same insurer, Fireman's Fund, had canceled a policy which it had issued to the same insureds covering musical instruments. The lower court found that this misrepresentation was material to the risk against which the applicants sought coverage and was not innocently made. Notwithstanding this fact the insureds insist that the insurer may not avoid liability as it was chargeable with knowledge of the prior cancellation because of information in its own records and chose to write the present policy anyway.

1. It is, of course, true that one has an obligation not to speak falsely when inducing another to make a bargain. This worthy rule is recognized both by statute and case law in Nevada. NRS 686.190: Poe v. La Metropolitana Compania Nacional De Seguros, S.A., Havana, Cuba, 76 Nev. 306, 353 P.2d 454 (1960); Smith v. North American Ins. Co., 46 Nev. 30, 205 P. 801 (1922). Thus, absent factors favoring the application of the doctrines of waiver or estoppel, an insurer is not bound by an insurance contract that he was induced to make by the fraudulent misrepresentations of the insured. The application for insurance in the instant matter contained the following language, "Signing this form does not bind the Proposer or the Company to complete the insurance, but it is agreed that this form shall be the basis of the contract, should the policy be issued. If any of the above questions have been answered falsely or fraudulently the entire insurance shall be null and void and all claims thereunder shall be forfeited." Cf. Poe v. La Metropolitana Compania Nacional De Seguros, S.A., Havana, Cuba, supra, where similar language was used in the application for insurance and noted by this court in affirming a judgment for the insurer. Relying upon the quoted clause of

41. The question is poorly phrased. However, it was not contended below, or here, that its meaning is obscure and the applicants misled.

the application for insurance, the claims superintendent of Fireman's Fund, after notice of loss, advised the insureds that the application was incorrectly filled out "resulting in a non-disclosure of information material to our acceptance of the risk," rescinded the policy and tendered return of the premium paid.

The application for insurance was not made a part of the insurance contract by incorporation by reference, i.e., a statement in the policy that the application is made a part of the policy, Phoenix Mutual Life Insurance Co. v. Raddin, 120 U.S. 183, 7 S.Ct. 500, 30 L.Ed. 644 (1887), or by endorsement on the policy itself. Smith v. North American Insurance Co., supra; cf. Universal Underwriters v. Snyder, 81 Nev. 315, 402 P.2d 483 (1965). Thus the answers in the application did not become warranties or conditions, but are representations collateral to the contract of insurance. The distinction between a warranty and a representation is sometimes of controlling significance in insurance litigation * * *. In general terms a warranty in insurance law is a term of the insurance contract which does not create an obligation on the part of the warrantor, but which creates a condition of the insurer's duty to pay the loss. The traditional view is that a warranty must be strictly complied with and, once a breach of warranty has occurred, the insurer may avoid the policy. The ancient Nevada case of Healey v. Imperial Fire Insurance Company, 5 Nev. 268 (1869), is an example of the traditional, orthodox view. On the other hand, a representation is not a term of the insurance contract and, though it may also, if false, and material to the risk, supply the basis for a rescission of the insurance contract by the insurer, courts tend to be less strict in their treatment of a representation than is the case when a warranty is involved. Here the insurer's rescission rests solely upon a false representation by the applicants which was collateral to the contract of insurance, though perhaps an inducement to its issuance, and not upon any claim that a term of the insurance contract was breached.[42] With these preliminary observations in mind we turn to discuss the question presented by this appeal.

2. The insureds do not challenge the finding below, that they fraudulently misrepresented a fact material to the risk when applying for coverage. However, they do contend that the insurer may not rely upon that misrepresentation to avoid liability, for it had in its possession full information about the prior cancellation, and elected to issue the present policy in spite of such knowledge.

The insurer's claims department, Los Angeles office, did have a record of the prior loss and subsequent cancellation. However, no agent of that department of the insurance company was in any way connected with the solicitation or issuance of the present policy, and neither the

42. The distinction between a warranty and a representation disposes of an alternative argument offered by the insurer on this appeal. The insurer seeks to sustain the judgment in its favor by the "non-waiver" provision of the insurance contract. That provision denies power to an agent or representative of the insurer to waive any condition or provision of the policy. As the representation here involved is not a term of the policy, the non-waiver clause is inapplicable.

insurer's application-taking agent nor its policy-writing agent was aware that the applicants had misrepresented a material fact in requesting coverage. It is also apparent that, because of the expense, volume and complexity of its business, the insurer in this and related situations believed itself free to rely upon the representations of fact contained in an application for insurance, and had not instituted a program for communicating information in the files of the claims department to those in the production end of the business. Pointing primarily to these circumstances the insurance company argues that it would be improper to invoke the doctrines of waiver or estoppel against it and authorize a policy liability, for we would be rewarding claimants who are not in court with clean hands.

This argument is not without persuasion. Yet it finds only meager support in case law. See Rhode v. Metropolitan Life Ins. Co., 129 Mich. 112, 88 N.W. 400 (1901); Great Northern Life Ins. Co. v. Vince, 118 F.2d 232 (6th Cir.1941), which stand for the principle that earlier records do not necessarily put the company on notice unless there is some circumstances to direct its attention to them. See also Schrader v. Prudential Ins. Co., 280 F.2d 355 (5th Cir.1960), dealing with group insurance. The overwhelming body of authority favors the insured and holds that the insurer, as a matter of law, is chargeable with knowledge of the misrepresentation, because of full information about it present in its own files. The rationale employed is not always clear. Some courts speak in terms of waiver. Others invoke estoppel. On occasion both doctrines are used interchangeably and without differentiation. Whatever the theory, a fact of overriding significance exists in every case—the insurer's ability to promptly discover the misrepresentation after the loss has occurred. We prefer that diligence to be exercised at an earlier time—when the application for insurance is taken. The Rhode Island Court in O'Rourke v. John Hancock Mutual Life Ins. Co., 23 R.I. 457, 50 A. 834, 57 L.R.A. 496, expressed the same view in the following words, "The defendant argues that it is unreasonable to hold that a company is bound to have present knowledge of all that appears on its previous files. To this suggestion at the trial the judge asked the pertinent question: 'Any more so than it was to ascertain that fact just after the boy died? They have taken the money. Now, just as soon as the boy died, and the beneficiary asks to be paid, then their records are looked up; then they saved the record.' The company had exactly the same information in its possession at the time the contract was made that it has now. If it is available at one time, it ought to be imputable at the other."

We agree that in these peculiar circumstances the insurer, as a matter of law, is chargeable with actual knowledge of the misrepresentation and may not avoid liability. Our conclusion rests upon waiver. In the law of insurance waiver is defined as the giving up of a known privilege or power. It may be express or implied from circumstances and always involves consent, express or implied, but does not necessarily rise to the level of contract. Specifically we hold that the insurer waived its power to rescind the insurance contract by issuing the policy with knowledge that the insureds had fraudulently misrepresented a material fact in their application for insurance.

The judgment below is reversed, with direction to enter judgment in favor of the appellants and against the respondent for $10,000 with interest from July 24, 1961, until paid, and taxable costs below and here.

ZENOFF, DISTRICT JUDGE (dissenting):

I respectfully dissent. There should not be a reward for a knowing and wilful misrepresentation * * *. "[T]he insured should observe the utmost good faith and deal honestly and fairly with the company in respect to all material facts inquired about, and as to which he had or should be presumed to have had knowledge, and make a full, direct, and honest answer, without evasion or fraud, and without suppression, misrepresentation, or concealment of material facts which the parties themselves deemed material to be disclosed."

* * *

In the case before this court, the information deemed by the majority to be knowledge to the insurer are facts from an inactive file. A distinction should be made between files used periodically by an insurer to record premiums paid, changes in beneficiaries and addresses, and renewals, and files containing records of rejections for coverage, claims from former policies, and cancellations.

It appears from the evidence that all current policies are on file at the head office and that inactive files are destroyed according to a specified company policy. The evidence also shows that destruction of records in various branch offices, while subject to the same policy, is not coordinated with the destruction at the head office due to different storage facilities. It seems inequitable to hold an insurance company to knowledge of what is contained in the files of one isolated outpost. Since all active files are maintained at the head office, it seems that the only workable rule is to hold an insurer cognizant of the active files.

* * * In the present case the loss of the violin occurred slightly more than two months after issuance of the policy. The trial court here found that the company did not have knowledge of the prior experience with the insured at the time of the issuance of the policy, and since there was such a short period between issuance of the policy and the loss, and only one premium had been paid, there is not sufficient evidence in the record to have alerted the insurer to search its dead files to upset the determination of the trial judge that the company should be held to be without knowledge, actual or presumed.

* * *

This was not a case where the agent of the company who had written the first policy also wrote the second. Nor was this a situation where there was another evidence file with the company that would cause it to be aware on a periodic basis that something unusual existed between the insured and the company. Nor am I satisfied that the language of the application and the policy did not sufficiently refer to each other so as to make the false inducement a part of the policy itself. And since NRS 686.190 requires that applications be attached to policies only in the life insurance and health and accident insurance classifications in order for the insured to be bound by the written statements in the application, it is clear that actual attachment of the application is not necessary in this instance. See NRS 681.030(3)(c) for the separate classification of personal property floaters. The application form itself referred to the policy and provided that, "* * * this form shall be the basis of the contract should policy be issued. If any of the above questions have been answered falsely or fraudulently the entire insurance shall be null and void and all claims thereunder shall be forfeited."

The policy as issued contained the following condition: "1. Misrepresentation and Fraud. This policy shall be void if the assured has concealed or misrepresented any material fact or circumstances concerning this insurance or the subject thereof or in case of any fraud, attempted fraud or false swearing by the assured touching any matter relating to this insurance or the subject thereof, whether before or after a loss. 'THIS POLICY IS MADE AND ACCEPTED SUBJECT TO THE FOREGOING STIPULATIONS AND CONDITIONS AND TO THE CONDITIONS PRINTED IN THE BACK HEREOF, WHICH ARE HEREBY ESPECIALLY REFERRED TO AND MADE A PART OF THIS POLICY, together with such other provisions, agreements or conditions as may be endorsed hereon or added hereto, and no officer, agent or other representative of this company shall have power to waive or be deemed to have waived any provision or condition of this policy unless such waiver, if any, shall be written upon or attached hereto, nor shall any privilege or permission affecting the insurance under this policy exist or be claimed by the assured unless so written or attached.'" (Emphasis added.)

While there is a split of authority in the state courts as to the validity of non-waiver agreements, many state courts and the Federal courts hold that these agreements are a valid limitation to the policy.

Healey v. Imperial Fire Ins. Co., 5 Nev. 268, 5–6–7 Nev. 215, seems to lend support to strictly enforcing these provisions. "There is but one safe rule, and that is to take the contract as written, subtracting nothing therefrom, adding nothing thereto. * * * The court is to enforce contracts which the parties have made, but has no power to make new contracts for them, or to alter or vary in any essential particular, those they have mutually agreed to be bound by." Id. at 220–221. Therefore, since there was no waiver written upon or attached to the policy, the insurer should not be deemed to have waived the condition requiring forfeiture for misrepresentations. * * *

Notes

1. A competitor's decision to decline a risk is generally viewed as material. E.g., Prudential Property & Casualty Ins. Co. v. Mardanlou, 607 P.2d 291, 293 (Utah S.Ct. 1980).

2. In one case, the insured claimed a loss of $1,050,000 in 1991 for a boat that he claimed was built in 1983 and that was purchased for $925,000 in 1987. Discovery revealed that the boat was built in 1980, that the purchase price was less than $500,000, and that the insured had had a prior (and undisclosed) insured loss for a vessel in 1985. Applying California law, the Ninth Circuit Court of Appeals had little difficulty in affirming the Federal District Court's grant of summary judgment for the insurer. Certain Underwriters at Lloyd's v. Montford, 52 F.3d 219 (9th Cir. 1995).

3. For the cynic who notes the coincidence of the name of the insured and the subject matter of the case, Mischa Violin was a concert violinist and conductor of world renown. He made his professional debut at age 12 with the Berlin Philharmonic and he had concert appearances with many symphony orchestras throughout the world during his career. *Music and Dance in California and the West* (Drake–Williams 1948, Richard Drake Saunders ed.).

REID v. HARDWARE MUTUAL INSURANCE CO. OF THE CAROLINAS

Supreme Court of South Carolina, 1969.
252 S.C. 339, 166 S.E.2d 317.

MOSS, CHIEF JUSTICE.

Hardware Mutual Insurance Company of the Carolinas, Inc., the appellant herein, on May 22, 1964, issued a fire insurance policy to Zelphia H. Reid and W.C. Reid, in the amount of $5,000.00, insuring against loss or damage by fire, for a five year period, a one story frame dwelling located in Conestee, South Carolina, owned by Zelphia H. Reid, the respondent herein, with a mortgagee clause payable to the Peoples National Bank of Greenville, South Carolina, as trustee for the Pickens Mill Profit Sharing Fund, which held a first mortgage on the lot on which the insured dwelling was located. The building insured was described in the policy as being one story frame constructed, approved roof, owner occupied, one family dwelling. [The building was occupied by a tenant at the time of loss.] The appellant was notified of the loss of said dwelling by fire and demand for payment by the insureds under the aforesaid policy was made and such was refused.

* * *

The final question for determination is whether the designation, at the time the policy was issued, that the insured dwelling was "owner occupied" was a continuing warranty.

A warranty, in the law of insurance, is a statement, description, or undertaking on the part of the insured, appearing in the policy of insurance or in another instrument properly incorporated in the policy, relating contractually to the risk insured against. Generically, warranties are either affirmative or promissory. An affirmative warranty is one which asserts the existence of a fact at the time the policy is entered into, and appears on the face of said policy, or is attached thereto and made a part thereof. A promissory warranty may be defined to be an absolute undertaking by the insured, contained in a policy or in a paper properly incorporated by reference, that certain facts or conditions pertaining to the risk shall continue, or that certain things with reference thereto shall be done or omitted. 29 Am.Jur., Insurance, Sections 708 and 709. While it is generally recognized that a warranty may be "promissory" or "continuing", the tendency is to construe a statement in the past or present tense as constituting an affirmative rather than a continuing warranty. Thus, a description of a house in a policy of insurance, as "occupied by" the insured, is a description merely and is not an agreement that the insured should continue in the occupation of it. Joyce v. Maine Ins. Co., 45 Me. 168. O'Niel v. Buffalo Fire Ins. Co., 3 N.Y. 122. A statement in an insurance policy that the property is occupied by the insured as a dwelling for himself and family, is not a warranty that it shall continue to be so occupied but is only a warranty of the situation at the time the insurance is effected. German Ins. Co. v. Russell, 65 Kan. 373, 69 P. 345, 58 L.R.A. 234.

There is no provision in the policy contract that the dwelling would be "owner occupied" during the term of the insurance contract nor any requirement that if the premises are otherwise occupied than by the owner, notice of such change of occupancy or use would be given to the insurer.

The insurance contract here involved contained a description of the dwelling insured as being "owner occupied". This was an affirmative warranty, not a continuing warranty, by the respondent that the dwelling was so occupied by him at the time the contract of insurance was made. The appellant argues that a breach of the warranty as to occupancy at the time the contract of insurance was made would defeat a recovery by the respondent. Even though this question is argued in the brief it is not supported by an exception and raises no issue for determination by us.

AFFIRMED.

VLASTOS v. SUMITOMO MARINE & FIRE INS. CO. (EUROPE), LTD.

United States Court of Appeals, Third Circuit, 1983.
707 F.2d 775.

ADAMS, CIRCUIT JUDGE.

Evelyn Vlastos appeals from a judgment denying her recovery on an insurance policy for a fire that occurred in a commercial building that she owned. Applying Pennsylvania law, the district court declared that Vlastos had unambiguously warranted that the third floor of her building was occupied exclusively as a janitor's residence. Based on this ruling by the court, the jury found that Vlastos had breached the warranty, and the court declined to set aside the jury verdict. Inasmuch as we hold that it was error to determine that the warranty clause in question is unambiguous, the order of the district court will be vacated and the case remanded for further proceedings.

Vlastos owned a 20′ × 80′ four-story building at 823 Pennsylvania Avenue, Pittsburgh, Pennsylvania. Prior to a fire on April 23, 1980, Vlastos and her son operated a luncheonette and a bar on the first floor of the building. The second and third floors were leased to Spartacus, Inc., which conducted a massage parlor on the second floor. Evidence was introduced at trial tending to show that the massage parlor also utilized at least a portion of the third floor. At the rear of the third floor there was a section variously described as a padlocked room or a section partitioned off from the remainder of the floor. It was in this area that Philip "Red" Pinkney, Vlastos' handyman and janitor, is alleged to have lived. Vlastos kept supplies on the fourth floor, and maintained a small office there as well. She occasionally remained overnight on the fourth floor rather than return to her residence. Vlastos was not staying there the night of the fire, but two friends of hers were residing there temporarily and were killed. A third person was also killed in the fire.

All of Vlastos' insurance matters were handled by her broker, John Mitchell. Mitchell obtained insurance for Vlastos from a group of European insurance companies through two sub-brokers. The policy in question, dated November 22, 1979, provided $345,000 of fire insurance with a $1,000 deductible provision. It contained a section, Endorsement No. 4, expressly incorporated into the policy, which stated in part: "Warranted that the 3rd floor is occupied as Janitor's residence."

After the building and its contents were destroyed by the fire, the insurers refused to pay the claim, citing an alleged breach of the warranty. * * * Vlastos has appealed, [from the adverse judgment], raising numerous points, including the contention that the jury was incorrectly instructed that the warranty was unambiguous.

Vlastos objects that "no proof was offered that the provision in Endorsement No. 4 actually was a warranty." Although her brief does not specify an alternate characterization of the provision, presumably she means to assert that it was a representation. If, as Vlastos implies, it was a representation, then the insurers would be under an obligation to show that the provision was material to the risk insured against in order for the insurers to avoid their obligations under the contract.

A representation, unlike a warranty, is not part of the insurance contract but is collateral to it. If a representation is not material to the risk, its falsity does not avoid the contract. On the other hand, the materiality of a warranty to the risk insured against is irrelevant; if the fact is not as warranted, the insurer may deny recovery. [Citations of Pennsylvania cases.] In case of doubt, courts normally construe a statement in an insurance contract as a representation rather than a warranty. * * * But no reason has been advanced for doubting that the provision in question here—which by its terms "warrant[s]" a fact and is part of the insurance contract—is a warranty. Accordingly, we cannot hold that it was improper for the trial judge to read this provision as a warranty. The district court therefore did not err in ruling that evidence of materiality would not have been relevant to the question whether Vlastos can recover on the policy.

The parties agree that the provision in question concerned a state of affairs existing at the time the contract was signed, and was not a promise that a janitor *would* occupy the third floor in the future. In other words, the provision is satisfied if a janitor occupied the floor on Nov. 22, 1979, the date the policy was issued, even if the situation had changed by the time of the fire several months later.[43] The district court erroneously instructed the jury on this issue at two points. It stated that Vlastos agreed that the floor "*would be* occupied as a janitor's residence" * * * and that the warranty was breached if "*at the time of the fire*" a massage parlor occupied any significant portion of the floor. * * * If the district court on remand decides that the case must be retried * * *, then it should instruct the jury that the relevant time for purposes of the warranty is the time at which the parties entered into the contract.

Having established that Vlastos did warrant that at the time she entered into the contract "the 3rd floor [was] occupied as Janitor's residence," it must be determined what the language of the warranty should be construed to mean. * * *

* * *

Applying Pennsylvania law to the facts of this case, we conclude that the warranty here was ambiguous. Although the view of the insurance companies—that Vlastos stated that the floor was to be the janitor's exclusive province—is a possible construction, a reasonable person could have understood Vlastos to have warranted merely that her janitor lived on the third floor.

Even if one takes the warranty clause in isolation, it is questionable that the reading proffered by the insurance companies is the only plausible one. If Pinkney resided on the third floor, then it is not simply and unambiguously false to say that he occupied that floor, even assuming the existence of a significant competing or concurrent use. In response to the query "does a janitor occupy the third floor?" a categorical "no" surely would be misleading at best, and even a qualified "no" ("no, he occupies only part of it" or "no, a massage parlor occupies it as well") is strained. It seems that the most appropriate reply, making the relevant factual assumptions, would be a qualified affirmative ("yes, although he occupies it along with a massage parlor").[44]

When the relevant language is examined in the context of the remainder of the policy, and in light of the alleged purposes for the insertion of the warranty, it becomes even more difficult to say that Vlastos unambiguously warranted that her janitor alone occupied the third floor.

43. Thus there is no contention that this provision was a so-called "promissory warranty."

44. Cf. 45 C.J.S. *Insurance* § 556 at 304 (1946) ("The mere fact that only one room in the house is actually used by the occupant does not render the building vacant or unoccupied.")

It is significant that the warranty was not made in the course of a description of the various uses to which the building was being put. The policy did not make any warranties as to any other floors of the building. Thus, it would be reasonable to infer that the warranty evinced a concern that there be a resident janitor rather than an intent that the various floors of the building, such as the third floor, be put to relatively safe uses.

Although the actual reasons for the insertion of the warranty are not clear from the record, the insurers represented at trial that one reason was that a resident janitor decreases the risk of losses due to fire. * * * This purpose of the provision would be fulfilled if Pinkney lived on the third floor, regardless of the proportion of this floor that was reserved for his sole use. Occupancy of the premises by a janitor might increase the likelihood that fire hazards would be taken care of promptly. It also might mean that there is a good chance that if a fire were to begin a responsible person would be on the scene to put it out or call the fire department, thus minimizing the damage from fires that do occur. A full-time resident janitor might also deter prowlers and vandals from entering the building. For reasons such as these, Vlastos could have assumed that the insurance companies looked kindly upon her having a resident janitor, without understanding that the insurance companies had any interest in whether the janitor occupied all or only part of the floor.

It is true that a second reason has been proposed for the insertion of the warranty. If a janitor occupied all of the third floor, then no occupant more dangerous—as a massage parlor perhaps is—would be there. Viewed in light of this possible motive, the warranty would have been intended to contemplate the occupancy of the entire third floor. Although this suggestion as to the purpose of the warranty is plausible, it is less obvious than the first suggested reason, especially when it is recalled that the insurers did not request any assurance that extremely dangerous usages were absent from the other three floors of the building.

The conclusion that the warranty is ambiguous is buttressed by the consideration that the insurers easily could have precluded doubt by the addition of one word. Had the provision read: "Warranted that the 3rd Floor is occupied solely as Janitor's residence," then the question whether there would be a breach if a massage parlor operated in some of the space would have been unlikely to arise. * * *

Because the provision is ambiguous, under Pennsylvania law it must be construed in a manner favorable to insurance coverage. We therefore hold that Vlastos warranted only that a janitor resided on the third floor, not that there was no other occupancy of the floor.

If any jury issue existed at all, it was simply whether or not a janitor resided on the third floor at the time of the contract. The district court at several points indicated that the insurers had presented no evidence that Pinkney did not live on the third floor, and that it would not let the insurers go to the jury on this question. On the other hand, the district court did instruct the jury that it could find "that nothing occupied the space at all * * *." * * *. There also is some uncertainty whether the district court, in considering the sufficiency of the evidence that Pinkney did not occupy the third floor, focused on the time of the fire as distinguished from the time that the parties entered into the contract. * * * Accordingly, on remand the district court should clarify whether, in its view, there was a jury question whether Pinkney lived on the third floor at the time the contract was made. If it determines that there was sufficient evidence to go to the jury on this issue, then a new trial on the liability issue should be held. If there is no jury question, then under the facts of this case a new trial would be unwarranted, and the district court should enter judgment for Vlastos on liability.

* * *

AMERICAN HOME ASSURANCE CO. v. HARVEY'S WAGON WHEEL, INC.

United States District Court, District of Nevada, 1975.
398 F.Supp. 379, (aff'd without opinion, 554 F.2d 1067 (9th Cir.1977)).

BRUCE R. THOMPSON, DISTRICT JUDGE.

This is a consolidated action brought by two insurers * * * against defendant, Harvey's Wagon Wheel, Inc. (Harvey's) for a declaration that the insurers are not liable for a fire loss under the business interruption policies that were issued to defendant by plaintiffs. * * *

* * *

Both policies contained automatic sprinkler warranties which provided:

"AUTOMATIC SPRINKLER WARRANTY

"THIS POLICY BEING WRITTEN AT A REDUCED RATE BASED ON THE PROTECTION OF THE PREMISES BY AN AUTOMATIC SPRINKLER SYSTEM, IT IS A CONDITION OF THIS POLICY THAT SO FAR AS THE SPRINKLER SYSTEM AND THE WATER SUPPLY THEREFOR ARE UNDER THE CONTROL OF THE INSURED, DUE DILIGENCE SHALL BE USED BY THE INSURED TO MAINTAIN THEM IN COMPLETE WORKING ORDER, AND THAT NO CHANGE SHALL BE MADE IN SAID SYSTEM OR IN THE WATER SUPPLY THEREFOR WITHOUT THE CONSENT IN WRITING OF THIS COMPANY." * * *

At the time the policies were issued, the restaurant and casino areas of Harvey's were equipped with operative automatic sprinkler systems. Prior to the issuance of the policies. Harvey's had begun to reconstruct the casino and restaurant areas. * * *

On May 15, 1973, the insured building was damaged by fire and Harvey's business was interrupted for more than sixty days. At the time of the fire, the sprinkler system in the casino was inoperative. The sprinkler system in the restaurant was operative. The casino was damaged by fire; the restaurant was not. * * *

It is a well established principle of insurance contract interpretation that if the language in a policy may be interpreted in two or more ways, it is to be construed in favor of the insured. Defendant attempts to use that principle to establish that the automatic sprinkler provisions are not warranties and therefore are not determinative of underlying coverage but rather are conditions concerned only with a reduced premium rate allowable for sprinklered building risks. Thus, defendant argues, its breach of the automatic sprinkler warranty should not affect coverage but should result only in an increase in the premium rate. * * *

Specifically, defendant argues that the phrases "written at a reduced rate based on the existence * * * of an automatic sprinkler system" and "due diligence shall be used by the insured to maintain them in complete working order" imply that the parties intended that there would always be coverage.

* * *

The instant automatic sprinkler warranty provides clearly and unequivocally that "no change shall be made in said system * * * without the consent in writing of this company." Since defendant shut off the water supply without obtaining written consent, defendant breached the warranty. See Buehler Corporation v. Home Insurance Company, 358 F.Supp. 15 (S.D.Ind.1973), aff'd, 495 F.2d 1211 (7th Cir.1974). There plaintiff's building was insured by a policy containing a provision essentially identical to the instant automatic sprinkler warranty. Because of a broken valve, the sprinkler system was shut off for a period of about four months. After a fire damaged the building, the insurers disclaimed liability. The Court held that since the plaintiff did not advise the Rating Bureau that the sprinkler system was shut off, it had violated a condition of the policy and could not recover from the insurer. * * *

It may be observed in a general way that in the area of insurance law, hardship cases produce exceptions to established contract principles. Sometimes there is plain evidence that the insurance company is taking unfair advantage of the insured by relying on technical provisions of the policy, the so-called "fine print." In such cases, the courts are naturally eager to find exceptions and doctrines of waiver and estoppel and the like are stretched to the outermost limits. This is not such a case. The automatic sprinkler endorsement was of the essence of the policy. It resulted in a premium rate approximately one-eighth the rate for non-sprinklered business premises. It was specifically bargained for by the insured and was discussed at about the time the policy was delivered. It was again called to the insured's attention when construction was underway. The unsprinklered areas were damaged by fire while the sprinklered areas were not. Law and equity require that the insurers be permitted the protection of the unambiguous policy warranty under these circumstances.

* * *

It hereby is ordered that judgment shall be entered in favor of plaintiffs and against defendant.

Statutes Which Limit the Consequences of Breach of Warranty and Similar Conditions

Missouri Annotated Statutes

379.170. Construction of warranties of fact incorporated in policy

The warranty of any fact or condition hereafter incorporated in or made a part of any fire, tornado or cyclone policy of insurance, purporting to be made or assented to by the assured which shall not materially affect the risk insured against, shall be deemed, taken and construed as representations only in all suits at law or in equity brought upon such policy in any of the courts of this state.

California Insurance Code

§ 447. Violation of material warranty

The violation of a material warranty or other material provision of a policy, on the part of either party thereto, entitles the other to rescind.

§ 448. Breach of immaterial provision

Unless the policy declares that a violation of specified provisions thereof shall avoid it, the breach of an immaterial provision does not avoid the policy.

Smith–Hurd Illinois Statutes, Chap. 215

§ 5/154. Misrepresentations and false warranties

No misrepresentation or false warranty made by the insured or in his behalf in the negotiation for a policy of insurance, or breach of a condition of such policy shall defeat or avoid the policy or prevent its attaching unless such misrepresentation, false warranty or condition shall have been stated in the policy or endorsement or rider attached thereto, or in the written application therefor. No such misrepresentation or false warranty shall defeat or avoid the policy unless it shall have been made with actual intent to deceive or materially affects either the acceptance of the risk or the hazard assumed by the company. With respect to a policy of insurance as defined in subsection (a), (b), or (c) of section 143.13, except life, accident and health, fidelity and surety, and ocean marine policies, a policy or policy renewal shall not be rescinded after the policy has been in effect for one year or one policy term, whichever is less. This Section shall not apply to policies of marine or transportation insurance.

Massachusetts General Laws, Chapter 175

§ 186. Misrepresentations by insured; effect

No oral or written misrepresentation or warranty made in the negotiation of a policy of insurance by the insured or in his behalf shall be deemed material or defeat or avoid the policy or prevent its attaching unless such misrepresentation or warranty is made with actual intent to deceive, or unless the matter misrepresented or made a warranty increased the risk of loss.

New York Insurance Law

§ 3106

(b) A breach of warranty shall not avoid an insurance contract or defeat recovery thereunder unless such breach materially increases the risk of loss, damage or injury within the coverage of the contract. If the insurance contract specified two or more distinct kinds of loss, damage or injury which are within its coverage, a breach of warranty shall not avoid such contract or defeat recovery thereunder with respect to any kind or kinds of loss, damage or injury other than the kind or kinds to which such warranty relates and the risk of which is materially increased by the breach of such warranty.

(c) This section shall not affect the express or implied warranties under a contract of marine insurance in respect to, appertaining to or in connection with any and all risks or perils of navigation, transit, or transportation, including war risks, on, over or under any seas or inland waters, nor shall it affect any provision in an insurance contract requiring notice, proof or other conduct of the insured after the occurrence of loss, damage or injury.

Michigan Compiled Laws Annotated, Chapter 28

MCL § 500.2836, § 241.2836. Breach of Warranty or Condition As Defense.

(1) An insurer shall not base a defense under the terms of a fire insurance policy permitted to be used in this state, upon a breach of warranty or condition occurring before loss, unless the breach exists at the time of the loss or contributes to the loss or to the amount of the loss.

Iowa Code Annotated

515.101 Invalidating stipulations—avoidance

Any condition or stipulation in an application, policy, or contract of insurance, making the policy void before the loss occurs, shall not prevent recovery thereon by the insured, if it shall be shown by the plaintiff that the failure to observe such provision or the violation thereof did not contribute to the loss.

Revised Statutes of Nebraska Annotated (2000)

44–358. Policies; misrepresentations; warranties; conditions; effect.

> No oral or written misrepresentation or warranty made in the negotiation for a contract or policy of insurance by the insured, or in his behalf, shall be deemed material or defeat or avoid the policy, or prevent its attaching, unless such misrepresentation or warranty deceived the company to its injury. The breach of a warranty or condition in any contract or policy of insurance shall not avoid the policy nor avail the insurer to avoid liability, unless such breach shall exist at the time of the loss and contribute to the loss, anything in the policy or contract of insurance to the contrary notwithstanding.

Notes

1. *Word Play—Disguising Warranties as "Conditions Precedent"—a ploy of variable effectiveness.* A leading case is *Fidelity–Phenix Fire Insurance Co. v. Pilot Freight Carriers*, 193 F.2d 812, 31 A.L.R.2d 829 (4th Cir. 1952), wherein the insured sought recovery on a theft policy when a truck containing 630 cartons of cigarettes was hijacked while the driver was having coffee. The insurer defended on grounds that the truck was left unattended without the alarm system on. The policy contained six paragraphs concerning the installation, maintenance, and use of anti-theft devices comprising the Babaco Alarm System. Two of the paragraphs started with the words: "It is a condition precedent to the liability of the insurer * * * "Others began with the phrase, "It is further warranted * * * "

> Paragraph 5 was one of the others: "It is further warranted by the Assured that the Babaco Alarm System on the cargo compartment of each trailer and the 'Parker' device on each trailer will be in the 'on' position when such vehicles are parked unattended * * * "

> Paragraph 6 stated: "The assured agrees, by acceptance of this policy, that the foregoing conditions precedent relate to matters material to the risk by the Insurer. Failure of the insured to comply with any of the foregoing conditions precedent in any instance shall render policy null and void as respects theft coverage for vehicles."

The insured asserted that paragraph 5 was a warranty and that a mere breach of warranty did not void the policy.

The court after noting the intertwining use of the expressions "condition precedent" and "warranties" concluded that they both involved a forfeiture and meant the same thing—in short the term "condition precedent" was here used as the equivalent of a "warranty."

Ironically, the insured lost anyway because the court held the breach of warranty to have been material. At least the insured came closer to recovery than did the plaintiff in *Blue Ridge Textile Co. v. Travelers Indemnity Co.*, 407 Pa. 463, 181 A.2d 295 (1962), where a similar Babaco alarm provision was held really to be a condition precedent to coverage rather than a warranty.

On the other hand, using the "condition precedent" technique was successful for the insurer in the Massachusetts case of *Charles, Henry & Crowley Co. v. Home Insurance Co.*, 349 Mass. 723, 212 N.E.2d 240 (1965). In its proposal form for a "Jewelers' Block Policy" against theft, the plaintiff represented that the maximum value of the jewelry displayed in the windows during business hours "would not exceed $14,500 where the window or case was protected by swinging shatterproof glass, and $500 where the window or case was not protected." The policy itself provided: "It is a condition precedent to any recovery hereunder that the values of property displayed will not exceed the amount represented in * * * the Proposal forms attached to this policy." Thieves broke a window and stole $13,620 worth of jewelry at a time when $18,512 was displayed in the protected window and $1,118.40 in the unprotected one. The appellate court reversed a lower court holding which had allowed plaintiff to invoke the mitigating Massachusetts statute relating to representations and warranties. Said the court, "A statement made in an application for a policy of insurance may become a condition of the policy rather than remain a warranty or representation if: (1) the statement made by the insured relates essentially to the insurers' intelligent decision to issue the policy: and (2) the statement is made a condition precedent to recovery under the policy, either by using the precise words 'condition precedent' or their equivalent."

2. A law firm has a policy with the following endorsement:

> "4. Protection of Valuable Papers and Records. Insurance under this policy shall apply only while valuable papers and records are contained in the premises described above, it being a condition precedent to any right of recovery that such valuable papers and record be kept in [steel cabinets] at all times when the premises are not open for business except when such valuable papers and records are in actual use."

A partner in the firm left the files on a class action bad faith insurance case (against insurers of the manufacturer of a defective drug) on his desk late Saturday night expecting to resume work on Sunday morning. A fire occurred in the firm's office at 2 a.m. Sunday morning destroying the papers. Does the insurance cover this loss? See American Indemnity Co. v. Lancer, Vandroff and Sudakoff, 452 So.2d 594, 595 (Fla.App.1984) (papers left overnight were not "in actual use" and insurance provides no coverage).

3. There is no question that the insurance industry is willing to accommodate owners whose vehicles are largely operated in areas where the accident experience is low by lowering their rates. The obvious problem is to be sure that the vehicles are indeed operating within the prescribed zone, usually defined with reference to the "place of garaging," without making the policies unmarketable or unacceptable to regulatory authority.

One "place of garaging" provision required that the insured's vehicle "be principally garaged in ... [Puenta, California].... " The insured's family moved to Oklahoma, where the insured was involved in an accident. The provision was treated as a warranty, but the insured recovered under the protection of California Insurance Code sections 447, 448. The court reasoned, "the policy contained no provision that the car insured was covered only when located and garaged at the place designated in the declaration." Republic Indemnity Co. v. Martin, 222 F.2d 438 (10th Cir. 1955). However, an insured suffered a different fate in *Purcell v. Pacific Automobile Ins. Co.*, 19 Cal.App.2d 230, 64 P.2d 1114 (1937), which involved a similar provision. Less than eight hours after the policy took effect, the insured had an accident. After a determination was made that the car was continuously used and garaged in Los Angeles, where insurance rates were higher, the court had no trouble finding for the insurer under a breach of warranty.

Courts have liberally construed provisions categorized as "endorsements" so as not to limit coverage. In *Texas Farm Bureau Mutual Ins. Co. v. Carnes*, 416 S.W.2d 863 (Tex.Civ.App.1967), the court found that a provision limiting "custom farming within a radius of 50 miles from the principal place of garagement" was an agreement and not a warranty. A later case, however, found that a provision "excluding regular or frequent use beyond 100 miles from principle place of garaging" excluded coverage in no uncertain terms, and granted summary judgment for the insurer. Carlile v. United Farm Bureau Mutual Ins. Co., 419 N.E.2d 1021 (Ind.App. 1981).

The considerations taken into account with the above cited cases include the common law and statutory constraints applicable to the type of provision it is determined actually to be. Additional factors entering into the analysis might include whether the vehicle was a commercial or private car, and whether the claim was for damage to the insured vehicle or for liability against the owner or driver.

b. Insured Fails to Meet a Condition: Increasing Hazard & Vacancy or Unoccupancy Clause

MIDWEST OFFICE TECHNOLOGY, INC. v. AMERICAN ALLIANCE INS. CO.

Supreme Court of Iowa, 1989.
437 N.W.2d 555.

SCHULTZ, J.

This appeal arises out of a dispute over the amount of insurance policy coverage provided for inventory. The insurer maintains the extent of coverage is limited by a reporting provision in the policy * * *. [T]he trial court ruled in favor of the insured, awarding the face amount of the policy. We reverse.

Midwest Office Technology, Inc. (Midwest) purchased a business protection insurance policy from the American Alliance Insurance Company (American) covering losses of inventory up to $600,000. Because its inventory fluctuated, Midwest selected a policy that provided variable coverage corresponding to the amount of inventory Midwest reported. Although the policy had a stated limit, the premiums were determined from the average inventory which the insured was required to report on a monthly basis. If a report was delinquent at the time of a loss, the coverage was limited to the amount listed in the last report filed prior to the loss.

After purchasing the policy, Midwest made inventory reports occasionally, but less often than the monthly requirement. It had not filed its monthly report when a fire destroyed Midwest's inventory. The loss was valued at over $600,000. Midwest sought the entire policy limits of $600,000. American, relying on its policy provision, paid only

$478,619.00, the amount of inventory claimed by Midwest in its most recent report prior to the fire.

* * *

* * * [Midwest] claims that a technical breach which neither contributed to the loss nor increased the risk of the insurer does not permit American to limit the inventory coverage below the actual loss sustained, subject to the policy limit.

* * * [American] insists that the reporting requirement merely sets the coverage amount, rather than serving as a forfeiture provision that voids the entire policy or portions thereof.

The clause in dispute provides: At the time of any loss, if the insured has failed to file with the Company reports of values as above required, this policy, subject otherwise to all its terms and conditions, shall cover only at the locations and *for not more than the amounts included in the last report of values filed prior to the loss* * * *. (Emphasis added.)

Midwest first contends that [Iowa Code] section 515.101 invalidates the limitation of coverage clause. This section states: Any condition or stipulation in an application, policy, or contract of insurance, making the policy void before the loss occurs, shall not prevent recovery thereon by the insured, if it shall be shown by the plaintiff that the failure to observe such provision or the violation thereof did not contribute to the loss.

The trial court found section 515.101 inapplicable to the reporting clause. The disputed clause does not abrogate the policy. It only sets the limits of coverage. We agree that the reporting clause simply does not fall within the section's terms of a "condition * * * making the policy void."

This conclusion is consistent with our previous statement that this statute becomes operative only when the breach of contract by the insured would void the insurance policy. See Carr v. Iowa Mut. Tornado Ins. Ass'n, 242 Iowa 1084, 1090, 49 N.W.2d 498, 501 (1951). "It is only when there has been sufficient proof of some act of the insured which would ordinarily abrogate the contract, that section 515.101 has any effect or meaning." Id. at 1090, 49 N.W.2d at 501. It is also consistent with the federal court conclusion that this section is "ordinarily applied to a case where the defense of 'increase of hazard' was relied upon by the insurer to avoid coverage." Hawkeye Chem. Co. v. St. Paul Fire & Marine Ins. Co., 510 F.2d 322, 326 (7th Cir.), cert. denied, 421 U.S. 965, 95 S.Ct. 1955, 44 L.Ed.2d 452 (1975). In this case, the trial court correctly concluded that section 515.101 is inapplicable.

In ruling against American, the trial court relied upon language found in Commercial Standard, which stated, "the rule is that breach of a condition must be shown to have contributed to the loss or in fact make the risk more hazardous." Commercial Standard, 282 F.Supp. at 24–25. In so doing, the trial court greatly expanded the language of Commercial Standard and erred as a matter of law.

In Commercial Standard, the federal court was interpreting Iowa law. * * * Here, the trial court correctly recognized that the rule in Commercial Standard is nothing more than a restatement of [the predecessor statute to section 515.101]. However, its ruling went on to expand the rule to also apply to a policy condition prescribing a limitation on the extent of coverage after a breach. This is inconsistent with our statement in Carr which limited the statute's application to breaches of policy conditions that abrogated or avoided coverage. Because the Commercial Standard rule is directly derived from cases grounded on this statute, we find the trial court's conclusion is faulty. Just as section 515.101 speaks to "making the policy void," the court in Commercial Standard prefaces its discussion of the rule by speaking of a condition "making the policy void." 282 F.Supp. at 24. We believe, as we did in Carr, that the application of section 515.101 and the language in Commercial Standard is limited to situations in which an insured's breach of a condition voids the policy and forfeits the insured's coverage. Such is not the case here.

Other jurisdictions have addressed the issue of whether a breach of the value reporting clause causes forfeiture or merely sets limits of coverage. These cases have evolved from the insureds' claims of waiver and estoppel. Estoppel is a defense to a forfeiture of a policy, but does not extend coverage. Northern Assurance Co. v. Stan–Ann Oil Co., 603 S.W.2d 218, 223 (Tex.Civ.App.1979). The cases uniformly reject these claims because a breach of the value reporting clause creates only a limitation of coverage rather than a forfeiture of rights. Although these cases examine the clause for a different purpose, the analysis is relevant to our inquiry of whether the breach voids coverage or merely sets its limits.

Additionally, other jurisdictions interpreting clauses similar or identical to this one have concluded they are clear and unambiguous on their faces, requiring the policy language be given full effect. Watchung Pool Supplies, Inc. v. Aetna Casualty & Sur. Co., 169 N.J.Super. 474, 486, 404 A.2d 1281, 1287 (Law Div.1979). The uniform rule is that an insured who is delinquent on its reports is limited on the amount of coverage to the amount shown on the last report filed prior to the loss. * * *

We have also considered Midwest's suggestion that the policy clause should be held invalid on public policy grounds citing Lakeside Plywood & Building Materials, Inc. v. Aetna Casualty & Surety Co., 75 Wis.2d 484, 250 N.W.2d 1 (1977). However, the Wisconsin court's holding was based on a statutory provision and determined that it was "not necessary to consider [the insured's] claim based upon general public policy." Id. at 497, 250 N.W.2d at 7. Such a provision is not against public policy. Cordeiro v. American Home Assurance Co., 409 F.2d 205, 206 (9th Cir.1969); 6 J. Appleman, Insurance Law and Practice § 3866.25 (1972). We find no merit in this contention.

In summary, we believe that neither section 515.101 nor Commercial Standard provides aid to Midwest. The rule announced in Commercial Standard applies only to policy conditions that would completely avoid coverage. The rule was directly derived from the predecessor to section 515.101 that speaks to "making the policy void." When the value reporting clause is breached, liability is not avoided, but merely limited. Value reporting clauses are standard in the insurance industry and have been often construed by litigation. The applicable case law uniformly supports our position.

The policy unambiguously provides that the insured's coverage is limited to the amount of inventory reported on the last report filed prior to any loss. The trial court erred when it concluded to the contrary.

REVERSED.

Notes

1. *Watchung Pool Supplies v. Aetna Cas. & Surety Co.*, 169 N.J.Super. 474, 404 A.2d 1281 (1979), cited in the principal case and typical of the problem, dealt with a multi-peril policy which required the insured to advise Aetna within 30 days of the value of its inventory subject to a policy limit of $100,000. The insured was consistently late in reporting and when a fire occurred in July, the latest inventory value reported was in April with a $65,000 value. After the fire, an inventory of $87,000 was reported for May and $101,000 was reported for June. The policy provided that liability was limited to the last reported value before loss.

In upholding a limit of liability to $65,000, the court noted that the purpose of the provision was both to save the insured money by not overinsuring the inventory and to protect the insurer against fraud. According to the court, the language of the limitation was clear, the provision was reasonable and material.

2. The Supreme Court of Iowa adheres to the line of reasoning set forth in the principal case. Schneider Leasing, Inc. v. United States Aviation Underwriters, Inc., 555 N.W.2d 838 (1996). In *Schneider Leasing*, an action by the owner of an airplane to recover under an aircraft insurance policy, the insurer (USAIG) argued that the loss was not covered because the pilot did not meet the qualifications required by the policy. The court held that Iowa Code § 515.101 did not apply, because the limitation on coverage being contested was not of a type that triggered the code section. "We need not reach the issue of whether use of [such] a pilot ... is a change in use that makes the risk more hazardous.... The limitation on which USAIG relies does not void any existing coverage under its policy but simply places this particular loss outside the coverages afforded from the inception of the contract."

3. In *Myers v. Merrimack Mut. Fire Ins. Co.*, 788 F.2d 468 (7th Cir. 1986), the insured owned an apartment building but the tenants had moved out. The insurance policy provided that there was no liability for loss while the building was vacant for more than 60 consecutive days. Vacancy was narrowly defined as "containing no contents pertaining to operations or activities customary to occupancy of the building, but a building in process of construction [was not to] be deemed vacant." The policy permitted "unoccupancy." Although the insured claimed the contract was ambiguous because

of the unintuitive distinction between vacancy and unoccupancy, the court was not persuaded. According to the court, unoccupancy means the lack of the habitual presence of human beings. Vacant means entirely empty. In the Seventh Circuit, the presence of minimal items is insufficient to avoid characterization as vacant. Here, the apartment building was vacant and the court sustained summary judgement for the insurer.

Note some of the larger issues. A standard fire policy makes for large bodies of law on what are seemingly arcane provisions in policies. In *Myers*, the insured is charged with knowledge of obscure meanings, possibly because standard fire insurance policy contains the vacant/unoccupied reference. Should the insured be expected to have this knowledge?

4. *When is a Commercial Rental Vacant or Unoccupied?* The court in *Knight v. United States Fidelity & Guaranty Co.*, 123 Ga.App. 833, 182 S.E.2d 693 (1971) stated:

> "It is undisputed that the property was insured as a service station and restaurant and was closed for business by the plaintiff in June, 1964. The fire occurred on November 13, 1966. Initially, we point out that a breach of these insurance contracts by reason of vacancy or unoccupancy for more than a 60 day period does not render the policies void. This provision merely suspends the insurance and the policy coverage may be revived by compliance with its terms before loss. Athens Mutual Ins. Co. v. Toney, 1 Ga.App. 492, 57 S.E. 1013. No definition of the terms 'vacant' or 'unoccupied' are contained in the policies. Our research reveals the lack of any Georgia cases construing the meaning of these terms. However, these words have been the subject of many decisions in other jurisdictions. The general definition of 'vacant' is that it means empty or deprived of contents or without inanimate objects. Couch on Insurance 2d, § 37:845, 848; Black's Law Dictionary, 4th Ed. The meaning of the term 'unoccupied' can vary depending upon the nature of the property insured, i.e., whether it is a dwelling house, a store, restaurant, school or a church. It should be construed with reference to the nature and character of the building for the use contemplated by the parties. See Annot. 158 A.L.R. 894. When these terms are used in the disjunctive, as they are here, they cannot be considered to be synonymous or complimentary. The testimony of the plaintiff shows that at the time she closed her business in 1964 all of the restaurant equipment, fixtures, booths, stools, coffee urn and stove were left in the building. In August, 1966 she decided to reopen. In connection with her intention to reopen, she testified she had purchased and installed a new refrigerator on the premises, installed a music box, electrical service was reconnected and she had the kitchen area painted. These activities according to her testimony all occurred at varying times, ranging from two weeks to not later than one month prior to the fire. From the plaintiff's testimony that there was restaurant equipment within the premises at the time of the fire, it cannot be concluded as a matter of law that the premises were vacant for the period specified by the policies so as to preclude recovery on the ground of vacancy. Notwithstanding this, if the evidence on motion for summary judgment conclusively shows that the property was unoccupied for more than 60 days prior to the fire, then the defendants are of course entitled to

summary judgment. However, as we construe the evidence, it does not conclusively show that the property was unoccupied for more than 60 days prior to the fire. Her testimony concerning installing new equipment, painting the interior, and reconnecting the electrical service are all activities consistent with making the premises ready for use for the very purpose for which it was insured. These activities are also all reasonably consistent with occupancy within the meaning of the policies. See Limbaugh v. Columbia Ins. Co. (Mo.App.), 368 S.W.2d 921; Rainwater v. Maryland Cas. Co., 252 S.C. 370, 166 S.E.2d 546. There is nothing in the policies from which it can be construed that the insured premises had to be open to the public in order to be occupied. Thus, there are issues of material fact for jury resolution. The judgments granting summary judgments were erroneous. * * * "

5. *Vacancy and Unoccupancy of House Under Construction and for Sale.* Houses under construction are always unoccupied and builders' risk insurance covering such projects stipulate that a building in the course of construction shall not be deemed vacant. After completion, however, many houses remain unsold for some time. In one case, the builder was insured against vandalism of the house in question, with an exclusion "if the described dwelling had been vacant beyond a period of 30 days." The house was a model house for a tract and the realtor had been using the building as a sales office, coming in at least four days a week. However the only furnishings were a telephone, desk, and some chairs. Vandals damaged the place after it had been on the market for more than 30 days. Was the "dwelling" vacant? Ellmex Const. Co., Inc. v. Republic Ins. Co., 202 N.J.Super. 195, 494 A.2d 339 (A.D.1985) (held no).

6. *Fire insurance in the deteriorating inner cities.* Here the "vacancy" clauses go hand in hand with the "increase of the hazard" clauses. The insured absentee owners profess lack of knowledge. For a graphic description of the situation in Chicago, see *Chicago Title & Trust Co. v. Illinois Fair Plan Association*, 90 Ill.App.3d 1061, 46 Ill.Dec. 483, 414 N.E.2d 205 (1980), wherein the court avoided the policies for breach of the above conditions. "The question was not whether the buildings would burn, but when."

7. Assume a standard fire policy with a 60 day vacancy or unoccupancy provision. The agent issuing the policy was aware that the premises were vacant and unoccupied at the time the policy took effect. The premises burned 107 days later, still vacant and unoccupied. Is the company estopped from denying liability because it knowingly issued a broken policy? See Zweygardt v. Farmers Mutual Insurance Co. of Nebraska, 195 Neb. 811, 241 N.W.2d 323 (1976) (Farmers deemed to have waived vacancy provisions where it had knowledge, through its agent, of a continuous and uninterrupted vacancy).

8. *Do any of the following constitute an increase of the hazard?*

a. Telling the fuel supplier to discontinue service in the dead of winter to a Michigan house insured against direct loss by freezing? See Smith v. Lumbermen's Mutual Insurance Co., 101 Mich.App. 78, 300 N.W.2d 457 (1980) (holding for insured, but the dissenting opinion of Bashara, P.J. cites the increase-in-hazard exclusion and would find the insurer is relieved of liability base on the insured's deliberate cancellation of fuel service which caused pipes to freeze). In *Newmont Mines Ltd. v. Hanover Ins. Co.*, 784 F.2d 127 (2d Cir.1986), the roof of a major mining complex in Canada collapsed under the weight of snow. The area received 100 feet of snow annually and the buildings and roofs were designed so that the heat of the buildings combined with the pitch of the roof would cause the snow to slide off. When operations ceased, the heat was turned off, and the collapse of the roof caused more than $6 million damage. The insurer had not been informed of the change.

b. Storing gasoline in plastic trash cans in the hall closet during gas shortage? (How many fire insurance policies may have been suspended during the 1978 gas crunch?)

c. An illegal liquor still concealed in a floor closet under the eaves of the roof? Good v. Continental Insurance Co., 277 S.C. 569, 291 S.E.2d 198 (1982) (agreeing with the insurer that the permanent, illegal still "substantially increased the hazard assumed under the policy").

d. Recall *Merchants Fire Assurance Corp. v. Lattimore*, 263 F.2d 232 (9th Cir.1959), in Chapter 3 above. Did Ms. Lattimore's failure to declare the value of her property in the floater increase the insurer's risk?

c. *The Policy Has Been Cancelled*

An insurance policy will automatically expire by its own terms if the insured fails to pay the required premium. A policy may be cancelled by agreement of the parties, independent of the terms of the policy, and the insurer may, under some circumstances, be able to cancel the policy on its own initiative. When an insurer cancels a policy, the insurer must strictly comply with the right to cancel it invokes (statutory or otherwise) and the insurer bears the burden of proving compliance. Very often, there are requirements of notice to the insured regarding cancellation of the policy, and the insurer must return any unearned premium beginning from the time of cancellation. For a comprehensive discussion of the cancellation of insurance policies, see Holmes' Appleman on Insurance 2d, § 16.7 (Termination and Cancellation of Coverage Generally), § 16.8 (Termination for Nonpayment of Premiums), and § 16.9 (Notice to Policyholder of Termination or Cancellation), Lexis Law Publishing (1998).

BAKER v. ST. PAUL FIRE & MARINE INSURANCE CO.

Supreme Court of Nebraska, 1992.
240 Neb. 14, 480 N.W.2d 192.

FAHRNBRUCH, J.

St. Paul Fire & Marine Insurance Company (St. Paul) appeals a Douglas County jury verdict awarding Victoria L. Baker $24,850 under a homeowner's insurance policy issued by St. Paul. The insurer claims that the policy had lapsed before fire damaged Baker's home, because Baker failed to pay the final installment on the policy premium.

As a matter of law and based on facts upon which reasonable minds can reach only one conclusion, Baker's homeowner's policy had lapsed before the fire damaged her home. We, therefore, reverse the jury award and direct that Baker's case be dismissed.

In November 1984, Victoria L. Kardell (now Victoria L. Baker) purchased a homeowner's insurance policy on her residence in Omaha, for the period of November 15, 1984, to November 15, 1985. The premium for the policy was to be paid in four equal installments. The first three premium installments were timely paid by Baker.

The record reflects that the fourth installment was due July 28, 1985. Baker testified that she mailed her check in the amount of $128.25 to St. Paul on July 15, 1985. She said she would typically mail her quarterly payment and the installment statement to St. Paul in the insurer's preaddressed envelope which accompanied the premium statement. Baker testified that she placed a stamp on the envelope containing her check and a portion of the statement and dropped the envelope into a mail chute in the hallway of the Livestock Exchange Building, where she worked. She stated that the mail chutes "run down to the basement where the mailroom is."

On September 26, 1985, Baker's residence was extensively damaged by fire. When Baker's mother contacted the office of Baker's insurance agent, she was told that there was no coverage for the fire. Baker was subsequently informed that there was no coverage because the policy had lapsed due to nonpayment of premium.

Thereafter, Baker filed this lawsuit in the district court for Douglas County, alleging she had not received notice from St. Paul that the insurer had not received the premium installment, nor had she received notice of St. Paul's intention to cancel her homeowner's policy. St. Paul filed a motion for summary judgment, which was denied, and the case proceeded to trial. After Baker adduced evidence and rested her case, each of the parties moved for a directed verdict. Both motions were overruled.

* * *

Because we find that the trial court erred in failing to sustain St. Paul's motion for a directed verdict at the close of all the evidence, it is necessary to discuss only that assignment of error and the award of attorney fees to Baker.

* * *

The key to resolving the issues in this case centers on the answers to two controlling questions: (1) whether Baker adduced sufficient evidence to prove that she made the final premium installment payment on her homeowner's policy and (2) whether Baker's homeowner's policy lapsed when she failed to make the final installment payment of premium.

There is no direct evidence in the record that St. Paul received the final installment of premium payment from Baker. To create a question of fact for the jury, Baker necessarily had to rely upon the presumption of receipt of mail by an addressee to prove that St. Paul received the final premium installment payment on her homeowner's policy. As a matter of law, Baker's evidence did not entitle her to the receipt-of-mail presumption, nor was the evidence sufficient to submit the issue of payment to the jury.

This court has held that the presumption of receipt of mail by the addressee does not arise unless it is shown that the letter was properly addressed, stamped, and mailed. Troy & Stalder Co. v. Continental Casualty Co., 206 Neb. 28, 290 N.W.2d 809 (1980).

In this case, the receipt-of-mail presumption in Baker's favor against St. Paul did not arise, because Baker failed to show that her claimed mailing containing her alleged installment of the premium payment was properly mailed. Baker testified that she placed the envelope containing the premium payment in a mail chute which led to a mailroom in the Livestock Exchange Building. There is no evidence that the mailroom was operated under the auspices of the U.S. Postal Service or that it was a U.S. Postal Service depository. Neither was there any evidence adduced showing that an authorized individual invariably collected and placed all outgoing mail collected from the mailroom in a regular U.S. mail depository or that such a procedure was actually followed on July 15, 1985. Baker failed to prove all the elements necessary to show that there had been a proper mailing of the premium payment, as required by Troy & Stalder Co., supra, and by Houska v. City of Wahoo, 235 Neb. 635, 641, 456 N.W.2d 750, 754 (1990), which holds:

> [A]bsent direct proof of actual deposit with an authorized U.S. Postal Service official or in an authorized depository . . . proof of a course of individual or office practice that letters which are properly addressed and stamped are placed in a certain receptacle from which an authorized individual invariably collects and places all outgoing mail in a regular U.S. mail depository and that such procedure was actually followed on the date of the alleged mailing creates an inference that a letter properly addressed with sufficient postage attached and deposited in such receptacle was regularly transmitted and presents a question for the trier of fact to decide.

Absent the presumption of receipt of mail by St. Paul, there is no relevant evidence in the record that even tends to prove St. Paul ever received Baker's alleged final premium installment payment on her homeowner's policy. Neither Baker's testimony nor her records indicate that the check she allegedly sent to St. Paul for the fourth premium installment on her homeowner's policy was ever received or cashed by St. Paul. As a matter of fact, a search of the records at Baker's bank reflects that the alleged check was never presented to Baker's bank or charged against Baker's account. There being no presumption in favor of Baker that St. Paul received mail containing Baker's final premium installment and there being no other relevant evidence that St. Paul ever received Baker's final installment of premium payment, reasonable minds can come to only one conclusion. That conclusion is that Baker failed to meet her obligation under the policy to pay St. Paul the final installment of premium payment.

Since Baker failed to show that she made the installment of premium payment, we now consider St. Paul's contention that Baker's homeowner's policy lapsed before the fire at Baker's home.

The continuance of the insurer's obligation is conditional upon the payment of premiums, so that no recovery can be had upon a lapsed policy, the contractual relation between the parties having ceased. St. Paul Mercury Ins. Co. v. Hurst, 207 Neb. 840, 301 N.W.2d 352 (1981). The burden is on an insured to keep a policy in force by the payment of premiums, rather than on the insurer to exert every effort to prevent the insured from allowing a policy to lapse through a failure to make premium payments. Id.

The burden of establishing an effective cancellation before a loss is on the insurer, and notice of cancellation must be in accord, and in substantial compliance, with the provisions of the policy relating thereto, and peremptorily explicit and unconditional. Jelsma v. Scottsdale Ins. Co., 231 Neb. 657, 437 N.W.2d 778 (1989). By the terms of the policy, St. Paul needed only to mail a notice of cancellation, which would become effective 20 days after it was mailed. The relevant statute required only that a policy contain an appropriate provision for cancellation. See Neb. Rev. Stat. § 44–379 (Reissue 1984). The parties to an insurance contract may contract for any lawful coverage, and the insurer may limit its liability and impose restrictions and conditions upon its obligation under the contract not inconsistent with public policy or statute. Allstate Ins. Co. v. Farmers Mut. Ins. Co., 233 Neb. 248, 444 N.W.2d 676 (1989). As a general rule, the proper construction of a written contract is a question of law. Spittler v. Nicola, 239 Neb. 972, 479 N.W.2d 803 (1992).

The cancellation clause contained in Baker's policy (in reality, a lapse clause) provided that "[i]f you fail to pay your premium when it's due, we'll mail cancellation notice to you that's effective 20 days from the date we mailed it." St. Paul adduced uncontroverted evidence that it mailed a provisional notice of cancellation to Baker on August 9, 1985. That provisional notice warned Baker that the final premium payment due July 28, 1985, had not been paid and that if it was not paid by September 1, 1985, her policy would be cancelled effective on that date. (In reality, the policy would lapse and Baker would have no insurance.) Reasonable minds can come to only one conclusion: The provisional notice was properly addressed to Victoria L. Kardell (Baker) at her then current address and properly deposited in the U.S. mail. A copy of the provisional notice bearing a U.S. postmark of August 9, 1985, and receipt of that provisional notice for mailing by U.S. postal authorities was received in evidence. Baker did not deny receiving the provisional notice, but testified that she did not remember whether she received the notice. She testified that her local insurance agent and First Federal of Lincoln, which held the mortgage on her home, each received a copy of the provisional notice.

By properly mailing the provisional notice of cancellation of Baker's homeowner's policy, warning her that her policy would lapse if the final premium installment was not paid, which mailing was proved to be in compliance with the rules set forth in Troy & Stalder Co. v. Continental Casualty Co., 206 Neb. 28, 290 N.W.2d 809 (1980), St. Paul became entitled to the presumption that Baker received notice of cancellation of her policy if she did not timely make the final installment premium payment. The mailing was in accord with the terms of Baker's policy.

Regarding a question of law, an appellate court has an obligation to reach a conclusion independent of that of the trial court in a judgment under review. Nebraska Builders Prod. Co. v. Industrial Erectors, 239 Neb. 744, 478 N.W.2d 257 (1992). In our independent judgment, as a matter of law, there was insufficient evidence to submit Baker's case to the jury and the contractual relationship between Baker and St. Paul ceased on September 1, 1985, leaving Baker with no coverage for the fire damage to her home on September 26, 1985. Thus, the trial court erred in overruling St. Paul's motion for a directed verdict at the close of all the evidence.

Because we are reversing the judgment entered in favor of Baker and ordering the district court to dismiss her petition, she is not entitled to attorney fees, and the district court's award of those fees is also vacated. Baker's application for attorney fees in this court is also denied, as she has not recovered under her St. Paul homeowner's policy.

REVERSED AND REMANDED WITH DIRECTIONS TO DISMISS.

Notes

1. A similar result was reached by the Nebraska Supreme Court in the earlier case of *St. Paul Mercury Ins. Co. v. Hurst*, 207 Neb. 840, 301 N.W.2d 352 (1981), cited in the principal case, in which the cancellation of an automobile insurance policy was upheld because the insured failed to pay the required premiums, after being sent first an additional premium notice and then a notice of cancellation. The insured did not even bother to respond to either the additional premium notice or the notice of cancellation.

2. One of the phenomena of the various insurance "crises" arising during the 1960s–1990s was the reliance by insurance companies on cancellation of or refusals to renew insurance policies. This is reflected by legislators' concern with the subject. Although not the only subjects, both property and automobile insurance have been the targets of legislation limiting cancellation and/or non-renewal. The present day coverage is quite extensive in those two areas and is too long to quote. Even a sampling of the California statutes would not be appropriate because its incompleteness might be misleading. Nonetheless, the reader concerned with these subjects should consult West's Ann. Cal. Insurance Code §§ 660ff (automobile policies) and 675ff (property policies). Worth remembering is the extensiveness and complexity of these statutes.

Also noteworthy is the effect of California Initiative *Proposition 103* on auto policies. The new West's Ann. Cal. Insurance Code § 1861.03(c) provides (and only in part):

(c)(1) Notwithstanding any other provision of law, a notice of cancellation or nonrenewal of a policy for automobile insurance shall be effective only if it is based on one or more of the following reasons: (A) nonpayment of premium; (B) fraud or material misrepresentation affecting the policy or insured; (C) a substantial increase in the hazard insured against.

(2) This subdivision shall not prevent a reciprocal insurer, organized prior to November 8, 1988, by a motor club holding a certificate of authority under Chapter 2 (commencing with Section 12160) of Part 5 of Division 2, and which requires membership in the motor club as a condition precedent to applying for insurance, from issuing an effective notice of nonrenewal based solely on the failure of the insured to maintain membership in the motor club. * * *

This section might well be taken to add to but not supersede West's Ann. Cal. Insurance Code § 661:

§ 661. Grounds for valid notice of cancellation

(a) A notice of cancellation of a policy shall be effective only if it is based on one or more of the following reasons:

(1) Nonpayment of premium.

(2) The driver's license or motor vehicle registration of the named insured or of any other operator who either resides in the same household or customarily operates an automobile insured under the policy has been under suspension or revocation during the policy period or, if the policy is a renewal, during its policy period or the 180 days immediately preceding its effective date.

(3) Discovery of fraud by the named insured in pursuing a claim under the policy provided the insurer does not rescind the policy.

(b) This section shall not apply to any policy or coverage which has been in effect less than 60 days at the time notice of cancellation is mailed or delivered by the insurer unless it is a renewal policy.

(c) Modification of automobile physical damage coverage by the inclusion of a deductible not exceeding one hundred dollars ($100) shall not be deemed a cancellation of the coverage or of the policy.

(d) This section shall not apply to nonrenewal.

3. The plaintiff in the *Baker* case subsequently filed a malpractice action against her lawyers. In the appeal of that case it was noted that the insurer adduced proof that the check registry reflected an erasure with the addition of St. Paul's as a payee of the check claimed to be in payment of the premium. Baker v. Fabian, Thielen & Thielen, 254 Neb. 697, 699, 578 N.W.2d 446, 449 (1998).

C. PAYING CLAIMS

1. The Amount of Recovery

TITUS v. WEST AMERICAN INSURANCE CO.

Superior Court of New Jersey, Law Division, 1976.
143 N.J.Super. 195, 362 A.2d 1236.

BEETEL, J.C.C., Temporarily Assigned.

Plaintiff is a young man who operates his own auto body repair shop and who has been an auto body mechanic all his working life. On March 16, 1972 he purchased a used 1966 Mustang convertible for a purchase price of $472.50 (including $22.50 in sales tax). About three weeks later he contacted his insurance broker, Robert Herdman, and requested that this vehicle be added to his current insurance policy underwritten by defendant. At this time he wanted only coverage for liability.

Plaintiff purchased this car with the idea of "customizing" it. He enjoys working with automobiles and wanted to make his 1966 Mustang something special. To this end he did extensive work on the automobile. During the first seven months he owned the car he repainted it, added new tires, installed a new canvas top and added several other small items to the automobile. Evidence was submitted by plaintiff showing that during these seven months he spent approximately $350 on parts alone, exclusive of his own labor.

In September 1972 he contacted his insurance broker again and requested that "comprehensive" (theft and property damage) coverage be added to his policy. The broker, Herdman, testified that when this coverage was added plaintiff never mentioned to him that the car was in the process of being extensively remodeled or customized. Herdman admitted that he knew from casual observation that plaintiff's car had been repainted and that new tires had been added, but he stated that this alone gave him no cause to suspect that the car was being customized or that these changes represented any increase in the insurable risk. The broker duly purchased this additional coverage at a cost of $9.18 a year.

Thereafter, plaintiff continued to improve and customize his vehicle. In March 1973 he rebuilt the engine at a cost of $156.10 (including labor). In May 1973 he purchased a second set of tires and a set of "mag wheels" at a total cost of $293.52 (including wheel locks). He also spent nearly $450 on other parts and equipment. During this time his automobile insurance policy was automatically renewed semi-annually. At no time did plaintiff inform the company or his broker of the extensive modification he made on the automobile.

On February 23, 1974 plaintiff's automobile was stolen. To this date it has not been returned. Shortly thereafter plaintiff filed a claim with defendant insurance company giving a description of the car and indicating that the odometer read 89,000 miles at the time of the theft. Lengthy negotiations ensued which resulted in the instant suit and the failure of the appraisers and the umpire to agree upon the standard upon which value should be determined.

At trial each side adduced expert testimony regarding the question of value and the method of evaluating auto insurance losses. Like the court-appointed umpire and defendant's appraiser, these experts were in substantial agreement regarding the market value of plaintiff's customized 1966 Mustang convertible. Among afficionados of such vehicles, plaintiff's car would have sold for $2,000 on the date of the theft. Plaintiff introduced pictures of his late beloved vehicle into evidence, and from viewing these photos this court finds that there is no question that the car was in excellent, indeed "cream puff," condition. Thus, this court finds as a fact that the market value of plaintiff's car, with the special equipment he added, was $2,000 on February 23, 1974.

The experts could not agree on the value of a 1966 Mustang convertible with full standard options in excellent condition. Defendant's expert, an appraiser with many years of experience, testified that the "book value" of such a car was $375. "Book value," he explained, refers to two publications used throughout the auto and insurance industries to evaluate used automobiles, the *Red Book* published by National Market Reports, Inc., and the *N.A.D.A. Official* Used Car Guide published by the National Automobile Dealers' Association. He testified, further, that the maximum value of such a vehicle would be double the "book" price, or $750. Plaintiff's experts testified that such a vehicle would have sold for about $1,000. They rejected the book value method of evaluation as the only guide toward the determination of actual cash value. Berezny, the umpire, agreed with plaintiff's experts and thus iterated his previous findings made during arbitration.

If this court were to make independent findings of fact on this issue, it might place the value of a fully equipped "cream puff" 1966 Mustang convertible at something closer to the double book value standard espoused by defendant's expert. However, for the reasons which follow, this court finds that $1,000 was the actual cash value of such a vehicle on the date of the theft under the terms of the insurance contract in question.

* * * The pertinent paragraph of the policy states that:

> The limit of the company's liability for loss shall not exceed the actual cash value of the property, or if the loss is a part thereof, the actual cash value of such part, at time of loss, nor what it would then cost to repair or replace the property or such part thereof with other of like kind and quality, nor, with respect to an owned automobile described in this policy, the applicable limit of liability stated in the declarations * * *.

The policy does not define actual cash value, nor is there any reported decision in this State defining the term within the context of an automobile insurance contract. N.J.A.C. 11:3–10.2 defines the term as follows:

> "Actual cash value", unless otherwise specifically defined by law or policy, means the lesser of the amounts for which the insured or the designated representative can reasonably be expected to:
>
> 1. Repair the motor vehicle to its condition immediately prior to the loss; or
>
> 2. Replace the motor vehicle with a substantially similar vehicle. Such amount shall include all monies paid or payable as sales taxes on the motor vehicle repaired or replaced. This shall not be construed to prevent an insurer from issuing a policy where the amount of damages to be paid in the event of total loss is a specified dollar amount. * * *
>
> "Substantially similar vehicle" means a vehicle of the same make, model, year and condition, including all major options of the insured vehicle. Mileage must not exceed that of the insured vehicle by more than 4,000 miles. Mileage differences of more than 4,000 miles may, at the option of the insured, be exchanged for the presence or absence of options or a cash adjustment.

Even if this section were controlling (it was made effective on May 1, 1976 and thus post-dates the controversy here), it provides little assistance in resolving the meaning of ACV.

In determining the meaning of actual cash value generally, there appears to be a split to authority. See Annotation, "Test or Criterion of 'Actual Cash Value' under Insurance Policy Insuring to Extent of Actual Cash Value at Time of Loss," 61 ALR 2d 711. Some courts adopt a market value test; others look to a formula reflecting reproduction or replacement cost; others have adopted the so-called "broad evidence rule" under which any evidence is received which logically tends to establish actual cash value, and some courts have held that actual cash value is an independent test to be applied without reference to other criteria.

* * *

Unrestrained by controlling precedent, this court is in the position to adopt what appears to be the better rule for determining the actual cash value of an automobile, and that is, its market value. See 15 Couch on Insurance 2d, § 54:232; 7 Am.Jur.2d, Automobile Insurance, § 190; Annotation: supra, 61 ALR 2d 711, § 6. As these authorities point out, there is a readily determinable market value for used automobiles, and this value adequately compensates the insured and adequately reflects his reasonable expectations. The broad evidence rule, while helpful in indemnifying owners of property which might be unique or which, when sold on the market would not bring a reasonable return (e.g., used furniture or clothing), is too uncertain a standard to be applied to the day-to-day business of adjusting automobile insurance claims.

This conclusion is buttressed by the testimony of the witnesses in this action. They all assumed that when you talk of value, you are talking about market value. They disagreed over whether the industry guidebooks were the only evidence of market value, but they agreed that market value governs.

Thus, this court holds that actual cash value means market value. * * *

The final question to be resolved is what automobile is to be evaluated. Plaintiff argues strenuously that it is his car, as he had equipped it, which should be the subject matter of the evaluation. Defendant argues with equal intensity that the subject matter of the evaluation is an automobile of the same model, year and condition, equipped with standard options. Surprisingly, research has disclosed no case directly on point, nor do the commentators provide significant enlightenment.

Defendant insurer presented uncontradicted expert testimony by an experienced insurance underwriter regarding long-established industry custom and usage. He stated that comprehensive coverage is geared to insure the ordinarily equipped automobile and that this was widely known and employed by all insurers. He further opined that the insurance buying public is aware of this custom, and that the extremely modest premiums payable for such coverage should, at a minimum, put the insured on notice that what was being insured was an ordinary risk.

Testimony was also adduced regarding the manner in which comprehensive coverage is purchased. The potential insured contacts his insurance broker or agent and is then asked to provide certain information—the make, model, year and serial number of the car; whether standard optional equipment is present or absent, e.g., automatic transmission, "power options," air conditioning, etc. The broker then consults standard industry manuals to determine the applicable premium. This is based upon the average market value of a similarly equipped motor vehicle of the same model and year.

Based on the testimony defendant argues that the subject matter of this policy was a "1966 Mustang with standard options," not a "customized 1966 Mustang with a rebuilt high-powered engine, mag wheels, racing tires, a front sloping chassis, and special paint." To point to the logical absurdity of plaintiff's position, counsel for defendant advanced a "horrible hypothetical"—a solid gold 1966 Mustang with mink seatcovers studded with precious gems. Surely, he urges, such a vehicle could not be insured at full value for the paltry sum of $9.18 a year.

Defendant's logically extreme example is compelling. It would be patently unreasonable for the owner of such a vehicle to expect full coverage in case of loss. Plaintiff's vehicle is not, however, positioned at this extreme. Surely, an owner who maintains his car in excellent condition by regular servicing and the replacement of worn parts can reasonably expect to be covered for the full value of his automobile. In fact, by providing for arbitration in its policy, the insurer recognizes that individual automobiles of the same model year do vary in value, and thus makes allowance for these legitimate expectations. This plaintiff, however, did something more than merely maintain his car in excellent condition. He added equipment which did more than make the vehicle safe and convenient, and more than was necessary to make it a running car. Shapiro v. Security Ins. Co., 256 Mass. 358, 152 N.E. 370 (Sup.Jud. Ct.1926). It is undisputed that the special improvements placed on the vehicle more than doubled its value. Thus, plaintiff could not reasonably expect to receive full value for the addition of nonessential and nonstandard equipment.

In response to this, plaintiff cites State Auto. Mut. Ins. Co. v. Cox, 309 Ky. 480, 218 S.W.2d 46 (Ct.App.1949). In that case the insured purchased a new 1946 automobile for $1,398.93. Six months later the car was stolen. His policy insured the vehicle for "actual cash value." At trial the insured presented evidence that the car had a market value of $2,100 on the date of the theft. The inflated value was produced by the post-World War II shortage of automobiles. The court found in favor of the insured despite the fact that the insurance premium was calculated upon the purchase price of the car.

Cox is not dispositive. The increased risk was caused by market conditions, not by any unanticipated alterations of the vehicle by the insured. Insurance companies are expected to absorb, either by way of profit or loss, the economic fluctuations of the market place. This is an accepted risk of doing business.

Plaintiff also urges that notwithstanding the fact that modified vehicles may not be within the ambit of the insurable risk, the insurer is in a position to protect itself by asking the potential insured whether or not his vehicle is other than an ordinary one. In essence, plaintiff argues that the insurer has a duty to ask the insured the "magic question," and failing this, the insured may safely not disclose facts relevant to the risk. Reliance is placed upon the rule of law found in Harr v. Allstate Insurance, 54 N.J. 287, 255 A.2d 208 (1969):

> Average purchasers of insurance are entitled to the broad measure of protection necessary to fulfill their reasonable expectations; * * * it is the insurer's burden to obtain * * * all information pertinent to the risk and the desired coverage before the contract is issued. * * * [at 304, 255 A.2d at 217]

This argument is not without merit. Assuming that the average purchaser of auto insurance reasonably expects that if his vehicle is customized he need not bring this to the attention of his carrier unless asked, then there might be a duty imposed on the insurer to obtain information relevant to this risk. However, defendant disputes the basic assumption upon which such a duty is premised. First, its experts asserted that the average consumer has no such justifiable and reasonable expectation; and second, that this particular plaintiff, an auto body mechanic with, at a bare minimum, peripheral involvement with claims adjustment, should have known the universal practice and custom within the insurance industry—that customized vehicles must be insured under a stated value policy.

This court need not decide whether to impose a duty on the insurance company to make inquiries in the case of an average consumer, because it is apparent that this plaintiff is not an average consumer. Given the undisputed testimony that it was clearly not the practice of the insurance industry to make inquiries regarding present or future modifications of the insured vehicle, the fact that this practice was sufficiently notorious in the trade to have put this insured plaintiff on notice and the fact that the plaintiff was in the best position to know the extent of the additional risk he was creating, plaintiff's claim for an additional $1,000 in damages must be denied. * * * It is clear that the increased value sought is attributable to parts which were not needed to make the car a working vehicle, but to parts designed to make the automobile more aesthetically pleasing. ACV coverage is not designed to insure such value.

The situation presented here may also be analogized to the long-recognized rule of law that:

> A misstatement or false declaration in the application or policy with respect to the description of the character of the insured vehicle may, if material to the risk, constitute a sufficient ground for avoidance or forfeiture of the policy, without regard to whether the misdescription was made intentionally or in good faith. [7 *Blashfield's Automobile Law and Practice* (3 ed.), § 302.1 at 331–332].

* * * Although this rule is not favored in this State, see, e.g., Merchants Indem. Corp. v. Eggleston, 37 N.J. 114, 179 A.2d 505 (1962), it does demonstrate the law's recognition of the actuarial consequences flowing from a proper or improper representation as to the identity of the risk to be insured. Here, plaintiff represented that his car was a "1966 Mustang convertible" when in fact it was (or became) a "customized 1966 Mustang convertible." Such a misstatement was certainly "material to the risk," since it both increased the potential liability of the insurer and the likelihood that the vehicle might be purloined. Had not defendant graciously admitted liability, it may well have been able to advance the argument that the policy should have been avoided on this ground.

* * *

For the reasons stated above, this court finds in favor of plaintiff in the amount of $1,000 plus taxed costs and interest. Because of the novel questions of law involved and defendant's lack of bad faith, taxed costs shall not include an award of counsel fees.

Notes

1. *The Broad Evidence Rule.* As the principal case indicates, there are various methods used to determine the amount of recovery that the insured

will receive because of a covered loss, including the use of broad evidence. While the court in *Titus* elects not to use this method for assessing the amount of recovery the insured is entitled to, in recent years, other jurisdictions have accepted this principle. See Annot. (1958), 61 A.L.R.2d 711, S 5. This method of evaluation is particularly useful when neither the market value nor replacement rate would serve as an adequate means of compensation, because the result would be overcompensation or undercompensation for the loss.

Such was the case in *McAnarney v. Newark Fire Insurance*, 247 N.Y. 176, 159 N.E. 902, 56 A.L.R. 1149 (1928), in which the insured's seven buildings designed to manufacture malt liquor burned down. The loss occurred after the passage of the National Prohibition Act (27 U.S.C.A. § 1, *et seq.*, (repealed)), so the facilities had been out of use for some time prior to the fire. Furthermore, the market value of the property was presumably nothing, as the production capabilities of the facilities were now illegal. The insured had been attempting to sell the property for $12,000, despite presenting proof at trial that the facilities were valued at $60,000. The property was insured for an aggregate sum of $42,750, and a jury trial returned a verdict for the insured in the amount of $55,000 as the value of the intrinsic or depreciated structural value of the buildings. On appeal, the court examined the insurance policy's clause addressing the method of recovery the insured would be entitled to in the event of a loss, which was:

> "The Insurance Company does insure * * * and legal representatives to the extent of the actual cash value (ascertained with proper deductions for depreciation) of the property at the time of loss or damage, but not exceeding the amount which it would cost to repair or replace the same with material of like kind and quality within a reasonable time after such loss or damage." Id. at 180.

At trial, the insurer wanted to introduce evidence of the actual market value, and the fact that the insured had received only an offer of $6,000 for the property. The insurer wanted the phrase "actual case value" to be equated with market value. The court disagreed, stating,

> If "actual cash value" were synonymous with "market value," the words in parenthesis, to have force, would require depreciation to be twice subtracted. No such anomalous result could have been intended. In order that the parenthetical words should have force, therefore, "actual cash value" must be interpreted as having a broader significance than "market value." Moreover, if market value were the rule, property, for which there was no market, would possess no insurable value, a proposition which is clearly untenable.... For methods by which actual value may be ascertained, we must look beyond the terms of the policy to general principles of the law of damages. *Id.*

The court was also unwilling to award the insured the replacement value of the property, as that would constitute a windfall, considering it was Prohibition and it is unlikely the insured would have built a replacement brewery. The court concluded that the phrase within the policy "not exceeding the amount which it would cost to repair or replace the same with material of like kind and quality within a reasonable time after such loss or damage," Id. at 183, did not mean to be a remedy for the insured, rather it was a right of the insurer to replace the destroyed facilities by hiring its own contractors and purchasing the materials, or to pay the insured the cost of reconstruction at its discretion.

After rejecting the methods to calculate recovery that would have favored each party respectively, the court interpreted the terms of the policy and made its own assessment of the determination of the rate of depreciated value of the property. The court held that the trial judge committed reversible error in not allowing the jury to take into account various extrinsic factors, including the fact that the buildings were no longer useful for the purposes for which they were initially built, to determine the amount the insured should recover and reversed the jury verdict.

Including evidence such as social context and market conditions to determine the appropriate amount of recovery is an example of the use of the broad evidence rule. Although more courts are willing to consider extrinsic factors in determining the amount of recovery the insured should receive, if legal standards of market value and replacement less deterioration are easily provable, application of the broad evidence rule will be limited, as it may unnecessarily prolong or complicate a trial.

On a related point, the language quoted from the policy above has been modified. Property insurance policies have dropped the confusing qualification that actual cash value is to be "ascertained with proper deductions for depreciation."

2. The so-called "broad evidence rule" seems to have been widely accepted in principle in recent years (see Annot. (1958) 61 A.L.R.2d 711, § 5), although the introduction of "broad" evidence when the usual legal standards of market value and replacement less deterioration are plainly provable may not be universally tolerated, perhaps because it unnecessarily complicates and prolongs a trial.

On the other hand, when there was no market for the property at the moment of loss, and replacement less deterioration is unrealistic, the admission of broad evidence is virtually compelled. The most familiar illustrations are heirlooms (which should therefore be scheduled), growing fruit trees and crops, half grown feeder livestock, minks, chinchillas, etc. Here the evidence of the potential profit, depending upon the ultimate market price less the costs of bringing the crops or animals to maturity, may be shown as the A.C.V. See Strauss Brothers Packing Co., Inc. v. American Insurance Co., 98 Wis.2d 706, 298 N.W.2d 108 (1980).

3. Does the insurer or insured benefit most from the allowance of "broad" evidence?

4. *"Valued policies."* Many American states have enacted "valued policy laws" applicable to fire insurance policies in case there has been a total loss. In such cases, the laws generally provide that the face value of the policy must be paid no matter whether the "actual cash value" is less. The state laws vary a good deal and each one has to be consulted to ascertain its precise meaning and coverage. One motivation leading legislatures to the enactment of valued policy laws was the desire to deter insurance agents from selling high face value policies on lower value premises, thus collecting higher premiums. Absent such a statute, of course, the payout in case of loss

would be based on the indemnity principle, that is, "actual cash value" lost by the insured. The suggestion that valued policy laws might also provide some temptation to arson and also to fraudulent overvaluation of property by insureds seems plausible. See Tom Baker, On the Genealogy of Moral Hazard, 75 Tex. L. Rev. 237, 270 (1996), *citing* George L. Priest, *The Current Insurance Crisis and Modern Tort Law*, 96 Yale L.J. 1521, 1547 (1987).

5. *Full Replacement Insurance.* Travelers Indemnity Co. v. Armstrong, 442 N.E.2d 349 (Ind.1982):

> Replacement cost insurance is not a pure indemnity agreement. It is an optional coverage that may be purchased and added to a basic fire policy by endorsement. It is more expensive because the rate of premiums is higher and the amount of insurance to which that rate applies is usually higher.
>
> Replacement cost coverage is available on the insurance market to meet the need which troubled the plaintiff. That need may be expressed this way:
>
> Since fire is an unwanted and unplanned for occurrence, why can't the owner of an older home buy insurance to cover the full cost of repair even if those repairs make it a better or more valuable building? Since at the time of fire the homeowner may be least able to pay for improvements, why can't that hazard be insured too? Instead of apportioning the cost of repair after a fire between the actual cash value, to be paid by the insurer, and the betterment to be paid by the insured, why can't the policyholder simply pay a higher premium each year but not have to pay anything more to have his home fully repaired in the event of fire?
>
> When the insurance industry adopted a standard extension of coverage endorsement to provide replacement cost, it took into account the one great hazard in providing this kind of coverage: the possibility for the insured to reap a substantial profit, if fire occurs. See Higgins v. Insurance Co. of North America, (1970) 256 Or. 151, 469 P.2d 766, 66 A.L.R.3d 871 and the annotation beginning at 66 A.L.R.3d 886.
>
> The cost of repair may exceed the fair market value of the building, and in the case of very old or obsolescent buildings, the difference may be very substantial. To permit recovery of the cost of repair, without also requiring the repairs to be made usually provides an even greater windfall than is provided when repairs are made. In effect the insured sells his building not at its market value but at a much higher figure and for cash.

6. *Replacement value of goods, especially inventory.* Ordinarily the value of inventory will be the cost of replacement on the appropriate market, usually wholesale in the case of inventory. Of course market value tends to fluctuate and this causes problems when the insured has to make periodic reports under a "value reporting clause" as in *Midwest Office Technology, Inc. v. American Alliance Ins. Co.*, reprinted *supra*.

For example in *FSC Paper Corp. v. Sun Ins. Co.*, 744 F.2d 1279 (7th Cir.1984) the insured maintained a huge inventory of waste paper in its warehouse. On July 8, 1979, a fire destroyed 12,827 tons of the Special Pack inventory. According to FSC's amended value report, the Special Pack had a monetary value of $611,719.63, or $47.69 per ton, as of June 30, 1979, but following the fire that occurred just eight days later, FSC claimed that it was entitled to recover $91.15 per ton, or $1,169,197.00. Sun Insurance disputed FSC's inflated valuation of recovery and FSC, in turn, filed this lawsuit.

The insurance contract in effect at the time of the fire contained two provisions concerning the reporting of the replacement value of the inventory. Endorsement 11 provided that the adjusted basis of any lost property "shall be the replacement cost at the time and place of loss" and stated that "values are to be reported on an equivalent basis" pursuant to Section 11, which read:

> "REPORTS AND PREMIUMS: Within 60 days after the end of each quarter the Assured shall report to the Company the total values of all property at risk under this policy on the last business day of that quarter. Once during each calendar year the Assured shall report to the Company the values of property at risk as of quarter September 30 by locations (as defined by Section 6 hereinabove)."

The trial judge read Endorsement 11 as the insurer's intent to "fix the value of destroyed property at a specific time and place" and read the term "equivalent basis" to mean that "values of all property * * * are to be reported on the same basis as provided in Section 11 of the policy." The trial judge therefore concluded, "Sun Insurance was required to determine 'replacement cost at time and place of loss' on the basis of the values reported by FSC under Section 11."

The Court of Appeals (2–1) rejected the District Court's conclusion and remanded for recalculation, concluding that FSC's recovery measurement should be based on the amount required to put the insured in a position it would have occupied in the absence of the fire.

Editorial Comments:

a. The replacement of over 12,000 tons of waste paper on the open market immediately after a fire would naturally drive the price up considerably. The majority recognized this and rejected the *actual* replacement cost of $1,169,197 as the appropriate measure; instead cautioning the trial court on remand to consider the commercial reasonableness of immediately replacing the depleted inventory on a thin and volatile market.

b. Should not there be an adjustment of the premium, at least to accord with the difference between the last report and the actual value? How about the previous five years during which the reports were based on the same calculations as the last one?

7. An Argentine employee of an American corporation makes off with a billion or so pesos in Buenos Aires in 1977 when the rate of exchange is 350 pesos to $1. A claim on a fidelity bond is made in 1980 when the exchange rate is 290,720 pesos to $1. In 1984 when judgment for the insured was entered the peso is really down. Which date should be used to calculate the insurer's liability in dollars? See Levi Strauss & Co. v. Aetna Cas. & Surety Co., 229 Cal.Rptr. 434 (1986) (adopting 1980 because the insurer's liability did not become fixed or certain until the insured submitted its proof of loss).

8. An insurance policy covers $5,000 property damage with $50 deductible. Damages amount to $6,000. How much is payable: $4,950, $5,000,

$5,050, or $6,000? In *Brinker v. Guiffrida*, 629 F.Supp. 130, 136 (E.D.Pa. 1985), the court held that full policy limit of $5,000 was payable where the actual loss exceeded the sum of the policy limit plus the deductible.

JEFFERSON INSURANCE CO. v. SUPERIOR COURT

Supreme Court of California, 1970.
3 Cal.3d 398, 90 Cal.Rptr. 608, 475 P.2d 880.

McComb, Justice.

By this petition for a writ of mandate, petitioners (hereinafter referred to as "the insurers") seek to compel respondent court to set aside an order vacating an appraisal award. The matter is before us on an alternative writ issued by the Court of Appeal.

Real party in interest (hereinafter referred to as "the insured") is the owner of a hotel building, which has a fair market value, excluding the value of the land, of $65,000. Prior to the fire loss which resulted in this litigation, the insured had acquired from the insurers fire insurance policies written in the California standard form prescribed by section 2071 of the Insurance Code. The policies contained an "average clause," providing for a proportionate reduction of any loss unless the building was insured to 70 percent of its "actual cash value."[46] The policies were written in the total amount of $45,000, which is approximately 70 percent of the fair market value of the building.

The parties agreed that the amount of the loss was $24,102.05 ($25,702.05, the cost of repairs, less $1,600 betterment). The insurers, however, refused to pay that amount, contending that the property was substantially underinsured according to the average clause. Their theory was that "actual cash value," as used in the policy, does not mean fair market value, but means the replacement cost of the building less depreciation. The replacement cost less a reasonable depreciation factor is approximately $170,000. The insured contended that the building was sufficiently insured, asserting that the "actual cash value" referred to in the policy means fair market value.

Upon demand by the insurers, appraisers were appointed, pursuant to the statutory appraisal clause contained in the policy, for the purpose of having them determine the actual cash value of the building.[47] The

46. The "average clause" limits the liability of the insurers, as follows: "[T]his company shall be liable for no greater proportion of such loss than the amount of insurance specified in such item bears to the percentage specified in the first page of this policy [70%] of the *actual cash value* of the property. * * * "(Italics added.)

47. The appraisal clause in the policies is in the required statutory language of section 2071 of the Insurance Code, as follows: "In case the insured and this company shall fail to agree as to the actual cash value or the amount of loss, then, on the written demand of either, each shall select a competent and disinterested appraiser and notify the other of the appraiser selected within 20 days of such demand. The appraisers shall first select a competent and disinterested umpire. * * * The appraisers shall then appraise the loss, stating separately actual cash value and loss to each item; and, failing to agree, shall submit their differences, only, to the umpire. An award in writing, so itemized, of any two when filed with this company shall determine the amount of actual cash value and loss. * * * "

appraisers, after some disagreement among themselves, accepted the insurers' contention that the term "actual cash value" means replacement cost less depreciation of the building, and determined on that basis that the actual cash value of the building was $169,547. One of the appraisers independently determined that the fair market value of the building was $65,000. From the appraisers' determination that the actual cash value was $169,547, the insurers offered to pay $10,154 as their proportion of the $24,102.05 loss sustained.[48] The insured rejected the offer and petitioned respondent court under section 1285 of the Code of Civil Procedure to vacate the appraisal award.

The evidence before respondent court established conclusively that the appraisers had determined as a matter of law that the issue before them was the "replacement cost less depreciation" of the building, and that in arriving at the value listed in their award as "cash value," they refused to consider income, location, or any other relevant factor tending to show the fair market value of the property, despite the fact that such evidence was made available for their use.

Based upon this showing, respondent court ordered that the award be vacated pursuant to section 1286.2, subdivisions (d) and (e), of the Code of Civil Procedure, thus finding by implication (1) that the appraisers had exceeded their powers by erroneously deciding a question of law (the meaning of "actual cash value"), which they had not been authorized to decide, and (2) that the insured had been substantially prejudiced by the refusal of the appraisers to consider material evidence. Respondent court, in ordering a second appraisal, directed that new appraisers "employ the standard definition of fair market value, which is synonymous with the 'actual cash value' in said insurance policy, namely, the price that a willing buyer would pay a willing seller, neither being under any compulsion to sell or buy."

Questions: First. *Did the appraisers, in determining the "actual cash value" of the insured's building, properly use "replacement cost less depreciation"?*

No. "Actual cash value," as used in section 2071 of the Insurance Code, is synonymous with "fair market value." (See Martin v. State Farm Mutual Auto. Ins. Co., 200 Cal.App.2d 459, 470, 19 Cal.Rptr. 364, 371; Hughes v. Potomac Ins. Co., 199 Cal.App.2d 239, 252–253, 18 Cal.Rptr. 650.) Thus, in *Martin,* the Court of Appeal, in construing the section, said: "The loss payable on an insurance policy is not the cost of the car to plaintiffs but its fair market value just prior to its destruction."

It is clear that the Legislature did not intend the term "actual cash value" in the standard policy form, set forth in section 2071 of the Insurance Code, to mean replacement cost less depreciation. The term appears not only in the average clause, hereinabove referred to, but also

48. The figure of $10,154 is arrived at by taking the ratio of the $45,000 policy limit to 70 percent of the actual cash value, and applying that fraction to the amount of the loss.

in the insuring clause and must be given the same meaning in both. The latter clause insures "to the extent of the actual cash value of the property at the time of loss, but not exceeding the * * * cost to repair or replace the property. * * * "Since replacement cost less depreciation can *never* exceed replacement cost, it would not be logical to interpret this clause to mean "to the extent of the replacement cost less depreciation, but not exceeding the * * * cost to repair *or replace* the property." (Italics added.) If "actual cash value" had been intended to mean replacement cost less depreciation, the Legislature would not have used "the cost to * * * replace the property" as a limiting factor, and would have specified as a limiting factor only the cost to repair the property.

Second. *Did respondent court act properly in vacating the appraisal award because the appraisers based the award on a misconception of the law?*

Yes. Although *arbitrators* are frequently, by the terms of the agreement providing for arbitration, particularly in construction contracts, given broad powers (see, e.g., Olivera v. Modiano–Schneider, Inc., 205 Cal.App.2d 9, 11, 23 Cal.Rptr. 30, where the contract provided that any controversy or claims arising out of the contract were to be settled by arbitration), *appraisers* generally have more limited powers. As stated in Hughes v. Potomac Ins. Co., supra, 199 Cal.App.2d 239, 253[9], 18 Cal.Rptr. 650, 658: "The function of appraisers is to determine the amount of damage resulting to various items submitted for their consideration. It is certainly not their function to resolve questions of coverage and interpret provisions of the policy."

Thus, in the present case the appraisers were authorized to determine only a question of fact, namely, the actual cash value of the insured building.

Since the evidence shows that the appraisers misinterpreted the meaning of "actual cash value" and therefore failed to decide the factual issue submitted to them, the insured properly invoked the jurisdiction of respondent court to vacate the award and order a rehearing. * * *

The alternative writ is discharged, and the petition for a peremptory writ is denied.

Notes

1. The term "coinsurance" (which can be used in a number of different ways) is most often used to signify a property insurance clause which provides a formula for loss-sharing between insurer and insured. The clause is widely used in policies covering commercial properties. The purpose of the clause is pretty clear. Most fires today cause less than total destruction because of fire prevention devices, fire protection services, or other reasons. Thus an insured may be inclined to insure only a relatively small portion of the value of his building at a small premium expecting enough coverage to meet any likely loss. If he insures his $100,000 building for $25,000 and his loss is $10,000, he is fully covered.

A common version of the clause illustrates how coinsurance deals with this inclination of insureds:

> The "percentage specified" is commonly enough 80%. Put in formula fashion the clause would say:
>
> $$\frac{\text{AMT of INSURANCE}}{\text{80\% of ACV}} \times \text{AMT of LOSS} = \text{AMT PAYABLE}$$
>
> Assuming that the amount of the insurance (face value of the policy) is $50,000, that the ACV is $100,000, that the amount of the loss is $8,000:
>
> $$\frac{\$50{,}000}{\$80{,}000} \text{ or } \frac{5}{8} \times \$8{,}000 = \$5{,}000$$
>
> If the amount of insurance varies, then the amount payable differs. E.g., if the amount of insurance is $90,000, then the policy would cover the entire loss.

If, however, the loss is total (that is, $100,000) then the whole amount of the policy becomes payable.

See, for some comment, Vance, Insurance (3d Ed., 1951), § 158; Keeton & Widiss, Insurance Law § 3.8 (1988).

2. The coinsurance clause applied to partial losses puts the parties into unnatural postures—the owner depreciating the worth of his property and the insurer asserting whatever appraisal formula will most inflate the value. In *Erin Rancho Motels v. United States Fidelity and Guaranty Co.*, 218 Neb. 9, 352 N.W.2d 561 (1984) a motel was insured for $247,000 with an 80 percent co-insurance clause. The owner's expert, using cost less depreciation, comparable sales, and income approaches came up with a figure of $253,700 as the value of the damaged motel, which would require no deduction from the amount of the loss. The insurer's expert "insisted that replacement cost less depreciation was the only method suitable for use in arriving at 'actual cash value' for coinsurance purposes." He arrived at the figure of $376,000 which would reduce the owner's recovery to 82 percent of the actual loss. The jury came up with $300,700 as the value of the property. How much of the partial loss should the owner be paid?

3. If A takes out a $2,500 policy on property worth $2,500 and B takes out a $2,500 policy on property worth $10,000—each policy with an 80 percent Co-insurance clause—should A and B be charged the same premium? Why not require, as a matter of law, that all property insurance policies contain a 100 percent Co-insurance clause? See Procaccia and Shafton, *Co-Insurance Clauses and Rate Equity*, Ins. L.J. #661 (February 1978) at page 69.

4. Courts have opted to use replacement cost as a measure of recovery in dealing with custom goods that have no market. Leslie Salt Co. v. St. Paul Mercury Ins. Co., 637 F.2d 657, 660 (9th Cir. 1981)(under California law replacement cost deemed appropriate for a custom made piece of equipment).

5. The standard fire insurance form includes a substantial number of clauses dealing with "appraisal." In many fire or property insurance cases, the chief issue may be the amount of payment the insured can claim. There are many people qualified as "experts" on various property issues and these people are capable of serving as appraisers to determine the insured's amount of entitlement. That amount is not always easy to determine. The policy speaks of the "actual cash value" ("ACV") of the property lost or damaged as a crucial factor. Incidentally, the language used in the form is founded on the New York standard fire form. See N.Y.Ins.Law § 3404. Many States have adopted this form in substance by statute or regulation. In California, see West's Ann.Cal.Ins.Code § 2071.

6. Most states have arbitration statutes and provisions for appraisal. The arbitration and appraisal processes withstood constitutional challenge in *Hardware Dealers' Mut. Fire Ins. Co. of Wisconsin v. Glidden Co.*, 284 U.S. 151, 52 S.Ct. 69, 76 L.Ed. 214 (1931), where the court held that a statute regulating the insurance contract remedy did not violate due process or the right to jury trial as long as it was "not unreasonable or arbitrary, and the procedure it adopts satisfies the constitutional requirements of reasonable notice and opportunity to be heard." States vary as to whether the valuation is binding on both parties or only the party invoking the provision. See 46A Corpus Juris Secundum § 1355.

7. Can appraisal or arbitration conflict with state constitutional provisions? It appears that this can happen. In *Massey v. Farmers Insurance Group*, 837 P.2d 880 (Ok.1992), the insureds purchased a fire insurance policy on their home, which contained an appraisal clause (mandated by statute) permitting the amount of loss to be determined by an appraisal of the property by appointed experts. After fire damaged their home, the Masseys placed a claim with Farmers under the policy; however, the parties disagreed as to the amount of the loss. The Masseys filed an action against Farmers, Farmers invoked the appraisal provision, and both parties appointed appraisers. Farmers later moved to appoint an umpire pursuant to the appraisal clause, and the umpire determined costs of repair at $49,146. However, the umpire was unable to contact the Masseys' appraiser and only received detailed information from Farmers' appraiser. Although the Masseys did not formally object to the award, they dismissed the initial action without prejudice and filed a new action in federal court, which went to trial and returned a jury verdict exceeding $4 million in damages. Farmers appealed the federal district court's judgment to the Tenth Circuit, claiming that the umpire's damage appraisal was preclusive as to damages.

The Tenth Circuit certified the question of preclusive effect to the Oklahoma State Supreme Court. In an opinion by Justice Simms, the Oklahoma State Supreme Court held that the umpire's damage appraisal award had no preclusive effect upon issues raised and litigated by the party who did not initially make the demand to enter into the appraisal process. The court distinguished the case at bar from previous cases on the grounds that the present appraisal clause was imposed on both the insurer and insured by statute, neither party could negotiate its inclusion or exclusion, and the appraisal process became mandatory to a party once invoked by the other party. The Oklahoma State Supreme Court followed the reasoning of the Oregon State Supreme Court in *Molodyh v. Truck Ins. Exch.*, 304 Or. 290, 744 P.2d 992 (1987), concluding, "where a statute requires mandatory compliance with the appraisal provision, the appraisal award is not binding upon the party who did not demand the appraisal, because such binding nature of the appraisal award would violate the non-demanding party's constitutional right to trial by jury." Massey, 837 P.2d at 883–84.

2. Apportionment Among Partial Interests

a. Joint Tenants

RUSSELL v. WILLIAMS

Supreme Court of California, 1962.
58 Cal.2d 487, 24 Cal.Rptr. 859, 374 P.2d 827.

THE COURT. * * *

The issue on this appeal is whether a surviving joint tenant may recover from the estate of a deceased joint tenant the proceeds of a fire insurance policy covering improvements on their joint-tenancy property, the policy having been issued to and paid for by the joint tenant who now is deceased, and the loss having occurred prior to his death.

This case was decided upon a stipulation of facts that: Dorothy Mouser, now Dorothy Russell, the plaintiff and appellant herein, and John Mouser, now deceased, whose estate is being administered by the defendant and respondent herein, while husband and wife, owned the subject property as joint tenants; in October 1957, Mrs. Mouser separated from Mr. Mouser and went to Nevada where she obtained a divorce on November 13th of that year; the divorce decree so obtained made no provision respecting any property rights of the parties and they did not enter into any property settlement agreement; the title to the subject property continued in joint tenancy and Mr. Mouser continued to live thereon until his death on June 3, 1958; in the interim, i.e., on November 29, 1957, he obtained a policy of fire insurance covering the improvements on that property, which was issued to him as the sole insured, the premiums being paid from his separate funds; no agreement existed between Mr. and Mrs. Mouser respecting the placing of any fire insurance upon the premises nor concerning the disposition of the proceeds of any such policy, and the subject policy was issued without her knowledge; about six weeks prior to Mr. Mouser's death, the improvements in question were destroyed by fire, and thereafter the proceeds of the policy, representing the full value of the destroyed premises, were paid to the administrator of his estate.

Mrs. Mouser became the sole owner of the property and brought this action to recover the proceeds in question, alleging that the defendant estate became "indebted to plaintiff for moneys had and received for the use and benefit of plaintiff."

Primarily, the plaintiff's claim is based on the contention that the moneys paid by the insurance company under the subject policy constituted proceeds of the property that was destroyed and retains the character of that property. This is a false premise.

It is a principle of long standing that a policy of fire insurance does not insure the property covered thereby, but is a personal contract indemnifying the insured against loss resulting from the destruction of or damage to his interest in that property. * * * This principle gives rise to the supplemental rule that, in the absence of a special contract, the proceeds of a fire insurance policy are not a substitute for the property the loss of which is the subject of indemnity. * * * As a consequence, the plaintiff has no claim to the proceeds of the insurance paid to Mr. Mouser's estate upon the ground that they are proceeds of the joint-tenancy property of which she now is sole owner.

There are instances where, because of contractual provisions or equitable considerations, the insured holds the proceeds of a fire insurance policy in trust for or otherwise subject to the claim of others who have an interest in the property covered by the subject policy. * * * However, unless the insured has an obligation to insure, or equitable considerations are present, the proceeds of a policy issued to and paid for by the named insured on his separate insurable interest are not subject to the claims of others who also have an interest in the property covered by the policy. * * *

There is no obligation upon the part of one cotenant to insure the other cotenant against loss of the latter's interest in their jointly owned property. * * * As to this matter there is no distinction between the various types of cotenancy. Analogously it has been held that there is no duty upon a life tenant to insure for the benefit of the remaindermen. * * * Cases to the contrary from other jurisdictions, which have been cited by the plaintiffs, are not controlling.

Following the rules heretofore stated, the right of one cotenant to recover the proceeds of a policy of insurance issued to another cotenant has been denied. [citations] The same ruling has been applied as between a life tenant and a remainderman [citations]; mortgagor and mortgagee [citations]; builder and owner; and vendor and vendee, subject to certain equitable considerations. [citations].

It has been held that where the policy of insurance purports to cover the interest of all cotenants, the question of the right of the noninsuring cotenant to a part of the proceeds, upon occurrence of a loss, is dependent upon equitable circumstances. [citations]. On the other hand, it also has been held that the mere fact that the proceeds of a fire insurance policy equal the full value of the property destroyed does not entitle the owners of noninsured interests in that property to recover a part of those proceeds. [citations]. In the instant case, even though the amount of the proceeds obtained from the policy of insurance represented the full value of the property destroyed, no equitable considerations exist which require a determination, as a matter of law, that the plaintiff was entitled to any portion thereof. She separated from Mr. Mouser and left him in full possession of the property; he obtained a policy which insured his interest therein and paid the premium thereon; and she had no knowledge or agreement with respect thereto. It may not be assumed that the policy in question covered the plaintiff's interest. Under the statutes of this state a fire insurance policy must specify the "interest of the insured in property insured, if he is not the absolute owner thereof" (Ins.Code, § 381); and, pursuant to the requirements of the standard form prescribed therefor, must recite that the amount payable thereunder, in any event, shall not be "for more than the interest of the insured" (Ins.Code, § 2071). Under the circumstances, the plaintiff's claim is wholly without foundation.

In support of her position, plaintiff cites the decisions in Hawes v. Lathrop [1869] 38 Cal. 493 and Estate of MacDonald [1955], 133 Cal. App.2d 43 [283 P.2d 271]. In the former, * * * property was transferred in trust for school purposes with a remainder reserved to the grantor; the trustees caused a policy of fire insurance covering the same to be issued to them; a fire and consequent loss resulted; the trustees decided to terminate the trust and return the property to the grantor; and the court determined that the trustees held the insurance proceeds "in their fiduciary, and not in their private capacity," were not entitled thereto, and the disposition thereof should be governed by the terms of the trust which required a return of the trust corpus to the grantor upon termination. In the latter case, i.e. Estate of MacDonald, the policy of insurance, which covered an automobile, provided that in the event of damage thereto, the insurance company might either repair the damage or purchase the automobile and pay the insured its value prior to loss; the insured was killed in an accident which resulted in damage to the subject automobile; it had been bequeathed by a will previously executed; the insurance company exercised its option to purchase the automobile and pay the value thereof rather than repair the same; and the court held that the legatee to whom the automobile had been bequeathed was entitled to the insurance proceeds in question upon the ground that she would have received the damaged automobile if the insurance company had not exercised its option to purchase, that the automobile so bequeathed was subject to the insurance contract which contained this option, and that the legatee should receive the benefits of that contract upon the exercise of that option. The decisions in the cited cases are not in conflict with the views heretofore expressed in this opinion.

It may further be noted that in Estate of MacDonald the decedent had by her will demonstrated an intent that her legatee should receive the automobile, whereas in the present case decedent Mr. Mouser by purchasing with his *separate funds* fire insurance payable *to himself alone* evidenced an intent to protect only his own interest in the property and not that his cotenant should share in any proceeds of the insurance contract to which she was not a party and for which she gave no consideration.

Plaintiff suggests that if the parties had wished to dissolve the joint tenancy by partition or other means, they could have done so; that in such event plaintiff would have been entitled to one-half of the property or its value; that to permit defendant to retain the proceeds of the fire insurance on the destroyed improvements "frustrates the parties' intent by allowing the non-survivor to receive the full value of the joint tenancy"; that "the equities" therefore require that plaintiff prevail herein. This contention is without merit either in fact or at law. In the first place the nonsurvivor here does not "receive the full value of the joint tenancy." To the contrary, plaintiff is now the sole owner, free from any claim of interest therein by Mr. Mouser's estate, of all the subject real property which was held in joint tenancy at the time such tenancy terminated. The stipulated facts show that such real property comprises 13 acres of land in the County of San Bernardino, and that the fire insurance proceeds paid to defendant administrator pursuant to decedent's contract amounted to $8,084.30. No showing has been made as to the value of the 13 acres of land received by plaintiff, and for aught that appears from the record such land may have a value in excess of the insurance money received by Mr. Mouser's estate under the personal insurance contract with him which, it is stipulated, he purchased with his separate funds. Under the circumstances plaintiff has not shown that either legal or equitable considerations support her claims.

The judgment is affirmed.

b. Mortgagor/Mortgagee

WHITNEY NATIONAL BANK OF NEW ORLEANS v. STATE FARM FIRE AND CASUALTY CO.

United States District Court, Eastern District of Louisiana, 1981.
518 F.Supp. 359.

CHARLES SCHWARTZ, JR., DISTRICT JUDGE.

* * *

On May 27, 1979 a fire damaged or destroyed property of Foreign Car Parts, Inc., 4921 Airline Highway, Metairie, Louisiana. This fire was caused by arson instigated by Robert Bradford Smith * * *. At the time of the fire Robert Bradford Smith was President, Registered Agent and General Manager and supervised all the operational activities of Foreign Car Parts, Inc. * * *

The actual value of the contents, inventory and other chattels (or movable property) located at Foreign Car Parts, Inc. as of the date and time of the fire was $264,565.00. After the fire the aforesaid property had a value of $35,000.00 and therefore the loss insofar as it pertains to contents amounted to $229,565.00.

* * *

* * * Whitney is the mortgagee as to the movable property, that is the contents, inventory and other chattels of Foreign Car Parts, Inc. as holder of a collateral mortgage note in the sum of $1,000,000.00 * * *. The mortgage indebtedness to Whitney far exceeds the fire loss and damage to the movable property, contents, inventory and other chattels

of Foreign Car Parts, Inc. Attached to and forming part of the policy are endorsements MLB–100 entitled "SMP General Property Form," * * * and MLB–101 entitled "SMP Special Building Form," * * *. It is obvious that said endorsement MLB–101 cancels and replaces any coverage on buildings provided under any other form made a part of the policy.

State Farm also issued a separate "Loss Payable Clause" Form LPC 17 (attached hereto as Appendix C) to CIT Financial Service Corporation. Both Endorsements MLB–100 and MLB–101 at Section 9 entitled "Conditions" provide in pertinent part as follows:

> "C. *Mortgage Clause:*
>
> Applicable to buildings only (this entire clause is void unless name of mortgagee (or trustee) is inserted in the Declaration): Loss, if any, under this policy shall be payable to the mortgagee (or trustee), named on the first page of this policy, as interest may appear under all present and future mortgages upon the property herein described in which the aforesaid may have an interest as mortgagee (or trustee) in order of precedence of such mortgages, and this insurance as to the interest of the mortgagee (or trustee) only therein, shall not be invalidated by any act or neglect of the mortgagor or owner of the within described property * * * "

* * *

The sole issue in this case is whether the arson of Foreign Car Parts, Inc. bars Whitney's claim as the holder of the aforesaid chattel mortgage on the contents of Foreign Car Parts, Inc.[49] In order to resolve the dispute it is necessary to determine whether Whitney is entitled to the protection of the "New York Standard" or "Union Mortgage Clauses"[50] of the policy or whether Whitney is otherwise to be treated as a party entitled to unconditional recovery. Whitney in part argues that the rights set forth in Declaration "C" are applicable to chattel mortgages and/or contents as well as to buildings, and thus claims the benefit of the standard or union mortgage clause.

Louisiana law is in accord with the law in almost all jurisdictions to the effect that where there are loss payees in a policy of insurance pursuant to an open mortgage clause, i.e. without inclusion of a standard or union mortgage clause, their right to recover is contingent upon, and purely derivative of the right of the mortgagor to recover from the insurer. [Citations.][51]

49. The parties have also stipulated that Smith's arson is imputable to Foreign Car Parts, Inc., and thus, that company is barred from recovery pursuant to the policy.

50. The distinction between the rights of a mortgagee protected by the standard or union mortgage clause and the mortgagee under the open mortgage clause is set forth in Appleman, Insurance Law and Practice, § 3401 at pp. 292–296.

51. To the same effect, although not a Louisiana case, Paskow v. Calvert Fire Insurance Co., 579 F.2d 949 (5th Cir.1978), contra J.B. Kramer Grocery Co., Inc. v. Glens Falls Ins. Co., 497 F.2d 709 (8th Cir.1974) which is distinguishable because plaintiff sought to insure contents only and building coverage was not intended to be included.

The inclusion in State Farm's policy of both endorsements MLB–100 and MLB–101 demonstrates that the parties intended MLB–101 to be the coverage afforded by the policy on the buildings, and MLB–100 to be the coverage for the contents. The language in MLB–100 which provides for application of the union or standard mortgage clause clearly states "Applicable to buildings only."[52]

* * *

* * * The mortgagees as to buildings have the benefit of the standard or union mortgage clause and others do not.

The claim of Foreign Car Parts, Inc. to recover from State Farm is barred by its arson and since Whitney is a conditional payee not entitled to protection of the standard mortgage or union clause, its claim is likewise barred. * * *

Thus, in summary, the Court concludes that Whitney only has an equitable lien on any proceeds which might become due to Foreign Car Parts, Inc. * * *

As the holder of an equitable lien on insurance proceeds payable to Foreign Car Parts, Inc., Whitney's recovery is solely contingent upon the insured's rights to recover. * * *

Accordingly, plaintiff is not entitled to any recovery herein and its suit is DISMISSED with prejudice, at plaintiff's cost.

Notes

1. Suppose a mortgagee, insured under a standard union mortgage clause, accepts a deed to the premises in satisfaction of the secured indebtedness. The insurance is still in effect. The premises are thereafter damaged by fire. May the mortgagee recover the amount of the loss? See, 495 Corp. v. New Jersey Insurance Underwriting Association, 86 N.J. 159, 160, 430 A.2d 203 (1981) ("the mortgagee may recover the full amount of loss, subject to the policy limits and the rights of superior mortgages").

2. Suppose a mortgagee, insured lender under a standard union mortgage clause, *after* a fire loss forecloses on the mortgage and bids in the property for the amount of the debt. Is the insurer now liable to the mortgagee for the damages to the property? See Farmers & Merchants Savings Bank v. Farm Bureau Mut. Ins. Co., 405 N.W.2d 834, 839 (Iowa 1987) ("Insurance is not invalidated by a post-fire foreclosure or forfeiture. What occurs is that the mortgagee's ... right to the insurance proceeds is extinguished to the extent that the underlying debt is satisfied by proceeding subsequent to the loss.").

3. Suppose premises are insured under a standard union mortgage clause. After a fire loss the mortgagor immediately effects repair of the

52. The collateral mortgage which Whitney relies upon to secure its indebtedness and which we must assume was either prepared by it and/or approved by its attorneys, with reference to insurance provides in pertinent part: "The policies of insurance to contain a clause that in the event of loss if any, payment shall be made to the mortgagee as his interest may appear." It does not provide that insurance policies shall contain the standard or union mortgage clause.

premises. The insurer now declines to pay the mortgagee on the ground that the mortgagee has sustained no loss. What result? See Talman Federal Savings & Loan Ass'n v. American States Insurance Co., 468 So.2d 868, 874–75 (Miss.1985) (loss becomes due on the happening of the event, regardless of whether the mortgagor plans to restore the damaged property).

4. Rocky Mountain Helicopters has a fleet of these machines and has bought another under a conditional sales contract from Bell Helicopters (manufacturer, seller and lienholder). The purchase agreement called upon the purchaser to insure for the benefit of the purchaser and seller as their interest may appear. The policy obtained named the purchaser as insured and the seller as loss payee, with the proviso that the interest of the lienholder "shall not be invalidated ... by any act or neglect of the insured." Because of a breach of warranty by the lienholder, the chopper crashed. The insurer paid the purchaser and seeks subrogation against the seller, who protests that there can be no subrogation against an insured under the policy. What should be the decision? See Rocky Mountain Helicopters, Inc. v. Bell Helicopters Textron, a Div. of Textron, Inc., 805 F.2d 907 (10th Cir.1986).

Hint. The court stated: "There are limits to this fiction that a mortgage clause operates as an independent contract."

5. What if the nature of one's insurable interest changes during the policy term from owner to mortgagee? A sad tale is told in *Mann v. Glens Falls Insurance Co.*, 541 F.2d 819 (9th Cir.1976). In the case, Mrs. Mann (Mann) insured her house against fire loss for $15,000 under a policy which contained a standard "mortgage clause" making insurance proceeds payable to the bank which held the mortgage to her home. During the policy term, Mann paid off her mortgage with the bank and in turn sold her home to the Bateses who used Mann as their mortgagee. Before the Bateses were able to obtain an insurance policy for themselves, the house was substantially destroyed by fire.

Mann desired to rebuild the house and keep the Bateses in possession. Glens Falls desired that she assign the mortgage debt to the company so that they could foreclose on the house and would provide Mann with $15,000 plus pro rata mortgage payments from the Bateses. In resolving the resulting dispute, the court determined that, since Mann's status with respect to her insurable interest had changed during the life of the policy (from owner to mortgagee), the policy she held was a "mortgagee-only" policy, which does not entitle the mortgagor (Bateses) to benefit from the proceeds of the policy. Therefore the Bateses had no rights under the policy, and Mann was entitled only to amounts equal to her interest in the property since she was now only the mortgagee. Further, the policy contained a subrogation clause which allowed the insurance company to require an assignment of rights of the insured which the insured may have against a third party to the extent that the loss was paid by the company. Mann refused to assign these rights against the Bateses to Glens Falls. The court found the clause valid.

Finally, during the pending litigation, the Bateses defaulted on their mortgage payments and Mann took back a deed instead of foreclosure. The court held that by choosing this course of action, the Bateses mortgage debt was discharged entirely. Since Mann discharged the Bateses debt, she concurrently violated the subrogation rights of the insurance company which, in turn, discharged the obligation of the insurance company to her. Because her claim could rise no higher than her claim against the Bateses and Mann had discharged the mortgage debt, her insurable interest and rights under the policy expired.

6. To what extent is the security interest of one who holds a deed in trust protected by a fire insurance policy? In *Kreshek v. Sperling*, 157 Cal.App.3d 279, 204 Cal.Rptr. 30 (1984), the Kresheks sold a property to the Foxes. As part of the sale, the Kresheks took back a promissory note and a second trust deed for $400,000. The deed of trust provided that the deed would be secured by an insurance policy which would insure the property against fire and the amount collected under such policy would be applied by the buyers to any debt still owed on the property, or the sellers could release the proceeds to the buyers. When the property was destroyed by fire, the buyers filed a claim, and $420,992 was paid by the insurance company. The sellers then sought declaratory relief as to how the proceeds would be distributed. The trial court found that the sellers were entitled to the full amount they were owed under the trust deed (at the time of the fire, they were still owed $319,375.60). However, the appellate court reversed, finding that, as a matter of law, the holders of a deed of trust were entitled only to the proceeds of an insurance policy to the extent that its security interest in the note is impaired. "To the extent the security was unimpaired, sellers had no right to keep the proceeds." *Id.* at 283.

c. *Vendor/Vendee*

UNIFORM VENDOR AND PURCHASER RISK ACT

§ 1. Risk of Loss.

Any contract hereafter made in this State for the purchase and sale of realty shall be interpreted as including an agreement that the parties shall have the following rights and duties, unless the contract expressly provides otherwise:

(a) If, when neither the legal title nor the possession of the subject matter of the contract has been transferred, all or a material part thereof is destroyed without fault of the purchaser or is taken by eminent domain, the vendor cannot enforce the contract, and the purchaser is entitled to recover any portion of the price that he has paid;

(b) If, when either the legal title or the possession of the subject matter of the contract has been transferred, all or any part thereof is destroyed without fault of the vendor or is taken by eminent domain, the purchaser is not thereby relieved from a duty to pay the price, nor is he entitled to recover any portion thereof that he has paid.

Notes

1. If the seller of a product ships the product to a buyer and the cargo is destroyed en route, does the seller's insurance cover the loss for the buyer, or can the seller's insurer avoid liability for the loss? In *Grain Processing*

Corp. v. Continental Insurance Co., 726 F.2d 403 (8th Cir.1984), Grain Processing Corporation (GPC) contracted to sell to Glenmore Distilleries Company (Glenmore) a quantity of grain alcohol. The product was shipped F.O.B. on the Mississippi River from Muscatine to Owensboro, Kentucky. (F.O.B. or "free on board" is shipping without shipping charge to the buyer.) When the barge on which the alcohol was traveling was destroyed, Continental, GPC's insurer, denied liability. Continental maintained that GPC no longer had an insurable interest in the cargo after it was shipped. Further, even though Glenmore had an insurable interest, it could not recover because it was not an insured party on the policy. The appellate court, affirming the trial court, found that the policy extended coverage to Glenmore for the loss. The court examined the language of the policy and found that it provided coverage for the "account of whom it may concern" and that the policy has "the same force and effect as if issued separately to each individual owner, shipper, and consignee." The court found that Glenmore was the consignee of the cargo, and so had an insurable interest in it, and therefore was covered by the policy. The court further found that it was GPC's intent to cover a consignee with an insurable interest in the cargo. Therefore, the court held Continental liable to Glenmore under the policy as the consignee of GPC.

2. *Insurable Interest and the Uniform Commercial Code.*

UCC 2–501 provides:

§ 2–501. Insurable Interest in Goods; Manner of Identification of Goods

(1) The buyer obtains a special property and an insurable interest in goods by identification of existing goods as goods to which the contract refers even though the goods so identified are non-conforming and he has an option to return or reject them. Such identification can be made at any time and in any manner explicitly agreed to by the parties. * * *

(2) The seller retains an insurable interest in goods so long as title to or any security interest in the goods remains in him and where the identification is by the seller alone he may until default or insolvency or notification to the buyer that the identification is final substitute other goods for those identified.

(3) Nothing in this section impairs any insurable interest recognized under any other statute or rule of law.

ACREE v. HANOVER INSURANCE CO.

United States Court of Appeals, Tenth Circuit, 1977.
561 F.2d 216.

BREITENSTEIN, CIRCUIT JUDGE.

In this diversity case the question is whether the seller or the buyer is entitled to the proceeds of insurance policies covering damage which occurred when the insured property was under an executory sales contract later consummated by the parties. The trial court gave summary judgment for the buyer. The seller appeals. We affirm.

On March 8, 1974, plaintiff-appellant Acree, Seller, contracted to sell his home in Chickasha, Oklahoma, to Donald R. and Joyce Martin, Buyer, for $125,000. The sale was to be completed and possession delivered to Buyer on July 8, 1974. On June 18, 1974, Seller renewed two insurance policies on the premises. On June 23, the premises were damaged by fire and vandalism.

The contract provided that if the property should be damaged to any appreciable extent by fire, Buyer could "at his option, refuse to complete said sale, and said escrow money shall be returned to him and this contract shall be null and void." The contract did not mention any obligation on the part of either party to keep the premises insured. After the fire, Buyer elected to complete the contract, paid the full purchase price, and took possession. Buyer claims, and Seller denies, that the sale was completed with the understanding that Buyer would receive the proceeds from the insurance policies.

Defendants Hanover Insurance Company and Fireman's Fund Insurance Company insured the premises. They refused to pay Seller, who then sued them in federal court. Buyer intervened. The material facts are not disputed. The district court gave judgment for Buyer against the insurors [sic] for $13,000. The insurors paid that amount into the court registry and do not participate in this appeal by Seller.

The parties agree that Oklahoma law governs the disposition of the controversy and that there is no Oklahoma decision directly in point. Seller contends that the insurance policies are personal contracts of indemnity for the benefit of the insured. He says that Buyer has not bargained for the benefit of Seller's insurance and is not entitled to the proceeds arising from the fire damage. Buyer says that the insurance is to indemnify for damage to the insured property and that, because he has paid the full purchase price, recovery of the insurance proceeds by Seller would inequitably and unjustly enrich Seller.

Two opposing lines of cases have dealt with the right to insurance proceeds when the damaged property was under an executory sales contract. One line holds in essence that insurance is a personal contract of indemnity to protect the interest of the insured. See e.g. Brownell v. Board of Education of Inside Tax District, 239 N.Y. 369, 146 N.E. 630, 632. The other line recognizes an insurable interest in both the seller and buyer and holds that when a seller has received insurance proceeds for damage to property covered by an executory sales contract and the seller has later received the full purchase price, the seller holds the proceeds in trust for the buyer. See e.g. Brady v. Welsh, 200 Iowa 44, 204 N.W. 235, 236. The existence of these two lines of authority has long been recognized. In addition to Brady v. Welsh, see Glens Falls Insurance Company v. Sterling, 219 Md. 217, 148 A.2d 453, 455–456, and Annotation in 64 A.L.R.2d 1402, 1404–1414. Oklahoma has no cases decisive of the issue.

The liability of the insurors is not before us. They have paid the loss. Our concern is whether Buyer or Seller is entitled to the amount paid.

The sale has been consummated and Seller has been paid in full. The fact that before consummation each party claimed the insurance proceeds is irrelevant. No agreement was reached. The contract provision permitting Buyer to rescind in the event of appreciable fire damage did not convert the contract into an option to purchase. Rather, it gave Buyer a choice of remedy. * * *

At the time of the fire, Buyer had equitable title to the property, and Seller, as legal title owner, held the property in trust for Buyer, see Western Assur. Co. v. Hughes, 179 Okl. 254, 66 P.2d 1056, 1058, and as security for the payment of the purchase price. It may be that Buyer was entitled to have the purchase price diminished by the amount of the fire loss. See Alabama Farm Bureau Mutual Insurance Service, Inc. v. Nixon, 268 Ala. 271, 105 So.2d 643, 646. In the case at bar, Buyer paid the full price and Seller seeks the insurance proceeds in addition thereto.

Seller asserts that Welch v. Montgomery, 201 Okl. 289, 205 P.2d 288, supports his position. That case related to a claim by a lienor to the proceeds of insurance obtained by the lienee. The claim was disallowed. The court said, Ibid. 205 P.2d at 291: "Equity will not take rights acquired by one who has been vigilant and give their benefit to one who has lost by reason of nonaction." The position of a lienor, however, is significantly different from that of a buyer. A lienor has neither equitable title to the property nor a right to demand specific performance. In the instant case Buyer held equitable title and had the right to require performance.

The effect of Welch v. Montgomery is somewhat dissipated by High Hill Rural Development Club v. Great American Ins. Co., Okl., 428 P.2d 249. There, because of annexation of school districts, a school building was no longer used for school purposes and was occupied by a club which secured insurance, naming itself as beneficiary. The building was destroyed by fire and the club claimed the insurance proceeds. The court ruled that the proceeds were held in trust for the school districts, explaining, Ibid. 428 P.2d at 251, that " * * * when the building was destroyed by fire, there was an involuntary conversion of the property and the proceeds of the insurance policy represent or stand in the place of the property destroyed." Although the case differs from that at bar because the building was public property, the quoted statement is pertinent here.

The Uniform Vendor and Purchaser Risk Act, adopted by Oklahoma in 16 O.S.A. § 202, has no applicability. The provisions of its subsection (a) apply "unless the contract expressly provides otherwise". In the instant case the sales contract has an express provision relating to the right of Buyer if the property is appreciably damaged by fire. At the time of the fire the contract was executory, but it gave Buyer the option of completion. The completion of the contract extinguished whatever risk had previously been borne by Seller. In the circumstances, the time of the fire is not determinative of the rights of the parties.

A fire insurance policy indemnifies the holder of an insurable interest against actual loss. 4 Appleman, Insurance Law and Practice, 1969 ed. § 2107, 16–17. Seller sustained no loss. He has received the full sale price. He is not entitled to a partial double payment. See Republic Insurance Company, Dallas, Texas v. French, 10 Cir., 180 F.2d 796, 799, a case arising under Oklahoma law. If the insurors had exercised their policy options of repairing and restoring the property, Buyer would have suffered no loss. Insurors paid rather than repaired. The insurance proceeds stand in place of the damages to the property.

The line of decisions which holds that in the circumstances presented here the Seller holds the legal title in trust for the equitable title of the Buyer is well reasoned. The legitimate contractual expectations of all parties are realized. Seller receives the price for which he bargained. The insurors pay the damage within the coverage of their policies. Buyer gets the property for the price which he agreed to pay and receives the benefits of the insurance as recompense for the damage to the property. * * * We are convinced that the trial judge reached the correct conclusion.

AFFIRMED.

Notes

1. The general rule is that the seller is entitled to recoup the premiums paid before crediting the proceeds against the purchase obligation. Berlier v. George, 94 N.M. 134, 607 P.2d 1152 (1980).

2. Plaintiff leased a house with option to purchase and took out property insurance in her own name on the premises. A fire destroyed the house and she exercised her option to purchase. How much can plaintiff recover under the policy? See Kelly v. Iowa Valley Mut. Ins. Ass'n, 332 N.W.2d 330, 331 (Iowa 1983) (plaintiff had an insurable interest in the house to the full extent of the loss).

3. When both the vendor and the purchaser in a contract for a land sale have procured insurance to cover the land in the contract, and that land is destroyed by fire before the final closing date, which insurer is responsible for the loss? *Paramount Fire Insurance Co. v. Aetna Casualty & Surety Co.*, 163 Tex. 250, 353 S.W.2d 841 (1962) explores this problem. In *Paramount*, a contract between the sellers and the buyers was entered into, a downpayment recited, and monthly payments stipulated for the succeeding year. The final closing date was set for exactly one year after the date of the contract, at which point the balance of the purchase price would be due. During the year, the sellers contracted for insurance, and specifically rejected a clause in the policy extending coverage to the buyers. Shortly before the fire, the purchasers also procured a fire insurance policy, and the fire occurred one day before the closing was to take place. The purchasers and the sellers both filed suit against their insurance companies, both of which contributed a pro rata share based on the amounts of their respective policies and each reserved its rights against the other. Then, the two insurance companies proceeded to litigate their liability as against each other. The trial court

awarded summary judgment to Paramount, the seller's insurer, and ordered Aetna, the buyer's insurer, to pay to Paramount the monies it had contributed in the settlement. The issue before the Texas Supreme Court was whether the sellers, who had received the full purchase price for the land from the buyers following the fire, had an insurable interest which would trigger coverage under their insurance contract, as evidenced by a " 'loss' in a legal sense." In reviewing the trial court's grant of summary judgment and the court of appeals reversal of the trial court, the court examined three different lines of cases. In the first, the liability of an insurer is fixed upon the date of the fire, and it is irrelevant that the sellers later received the full contract price because the insurance contract is unrelated to events subsequent to the fire. In the second line of cases, an insured who does not suffer any pecuniary loss, looking at the substance of the whole transaction, is not entitled to any insurance proceeds if they received the full contract price following the destruction of the property. In a third line of cases, when a buyer sustains a loss and there is no mention of insurance in the contract of sale, the proceeds of the vendor's insurance policy are held in trust for the benefit of the buyer. Although the court was prepared to combine the latter two rules, it determined that since the buyer in this case had its own insurance policy which covered the loss, it need not apply the rules. Further, the court found that the sellers had expressly rejected a provision which would have allowed the buyers to benefit from the policy. Therefore, because the sellers suffered no pecuniary loss, it was their intention to exclude coverage for the buyers, and since the buyers had procured their own insurance on the property, Paramount was not liable to the buyers or the sellers for the fire damage.

4. *Insurance of Dual Interests Under Executory Land Sale Contracts*. In order to isolate the insurance law problems in the vendor-purchaser cases, it is first necessary to determine which party bears the risk of destruction of the premises between the time of the making of the contract and the time at which the legal title is deeded to the buyer. This is a point at which the law of contracts, legal rules as to damages awardable against non-wilfully defaulting vendors, real property doctrines as to title, the equity doctrine of "equitable conversion" together with the equitable remedy of specific performance, plus the lay person's notions as to who ought to have the responsibility of protecting property from casualty loss all rub somewhat incompatibly together. The obvious result has been sharply conflicting views, much legal writing and wide divergence of authority from state to state. For present purposes, an extract from a single case summarizing the several discrepant "risk of loss" rulings, together with the Uniform Vendor–Purchaser Risk Act, will do.

Judge Hyde in *Skelly Oil Co. v. Ashmore*, 365 S.W.2d 582 (Mo.1963):

* * *

"The contract of sale here involved contained no provision as to who assumed the risk of loss occasioned by a destruction of the building, or for protecting the building by insurance or for allocating any insurance proceeds received therefor. When the parties met to close the sale on April 16, the purchaser's counsel informed vendors and their attorney he was relying on Standard Oil Co. v. Dye, 223 Mo.App. 926, 20

S.W.2d 946, for purchaser's claim to the $10,000 insurance proceeds on the building. * * * It is stated in 3 American Law of Property, § 11.30, p. 90, that in the circumstances here presented at least five different views have been advanced for allocating the burden of fortuitous loss between vendor and purchaser of real estate. We summarize those mentioned: (1) The view first enunciated in Paine v. Meller (Ch. 1801, 6 Ves.Jr. 349, 31 Eng.Reprint 1088, 1089) is said to be the most widely accepted, holding that from the time of the contract of sale of real estate the burden of fortuitous loss was on the purchaser even though the vendor retained possession. (2) The loss is on the vendor until legal title is conveyed, although the purchaser is in possession, stated to be a strong minority. (3) The burden of loss should be on the vendor until the time agreed upon for conveying the legal title, and thereafter on the purchaser unless the vendor be in such default as to preclude specific performance, not recognized in the decisions. (4) The burden of the loss should be on the party in possession, whether vendor or purchaser, so considered by some courts. (5) The burden of loss should be on the vendor unless there is something in the contract or in the relation of the parties from which the court can infer a different intention, stating "this rather vague test" has not received any avowed judicial acceptance, although it is not inconsistent with jurisdictions holding the loss is on the vendor until conveyance or jurisdictions adopting the possession test. As to the weight of the authority, see also 27 A.L.R.2d 448; Tiffany, Real Property, 3rd ed., § 309".

5. *Land sale contracts.* Most land sale contracts are simply "cash" sales or "sales through escrow" where conveyance by deed is made at the close of the transaction. If the deal is financed, the purchaser becomes the owner-mortgagor. Not infrequently the vendor, himself, will "carry the paper" and become transformed into the mortgagee. The rules as to the allocation of insurance, between mortgagee-mortgagor have been discussed in the preceding group of cases.

The principal case is an example of another type of land sale contract—the installment sale where the vendor retains title as a security device (vendor's lien) until the land installment is made. Although described as a vendor-purchaser situation its function is as a security device equivalent to a mortgage. The modern trend indeed is to treat the device as such for practical purposes. See Nelson and Whitman, *The Installment Land Contract—A National Viewpoint*, 1977 B.Y.U.L. Rev. 541. If the current attitude is to be adopted it would seem that, on the mortgagee-mortgagor analogy, the vendor's insurer in the principal case should be subrogated to the vendor's right to the unpaid purchase price. (But, of course, it wasn't.)

6. *Risk of loss on the uninsured purchaser.* Two cases have held that a land purchaser who took possession *prior* to closure of the escrow or contract cannot claim the benefit of the vendor's insurance proceeds. McGuire v. Wilson, 372 So.2d 1297 (Ala.1979); Long v. Keller, 104 Cal.App.3d 312, 163 Cal.Rptr. 532 (1980) (applying Uniform Vendor–Purchaser Risk Act); but, cf. Gilles v. Sprout, 293 Minn. 53, 196 N.W.2d 612 (1972).

7. Assume the risk of loss is on the vendor and a *material* portion of the premises have been destroyed by fire. The vendor collects on his

insurance policy. Should the purchaser seek to have the proceeds held in trust for his benefit, or sue for specific performance with abatement of the price? Cf. World Exhibit Corp. v. City Bank Farmers Trust Co., 186 Misc. 420, 59 N.Y.S.2d 648, 652 (1945), affirmed 270 App.Div. 654, 61 N.Y.S.2d 889 (1946), affirmed 296 N.Y. 586, 68 N.E.2d 876 (proper remedy is specific performance with abatement of the purchase price because insurance proceeds collected by the vendor exceeded the amount of the price abatement).

d. Bailment

The relationship between a bailor and a bailee has long been a difficult issue for courts with respect to insurance contracts. In this relationship, one party, the bailor, has entrusted another, the bailee, with its property. A typical bailor/bailee relationship is found in the warehousing business where a warehousing company has been hired to store the property of the bailor. Some policies of insurance procured by bailees cover only the property of their customers, but many of the policies cover the property of the bailee as well. The standard fire policy of one state (Illinois) contains a clause which stipulates that it covers "the personal property of others held in trust for others, or which is held on commission or consignment, in storage or for repairs, sold but not delivered or removed." A further complication may arise if both the bailor and the bailee contracted for insurance to cover their respective interests. Upon destruction of stored property held by a bailee in such a case, the question presented is which insurance company bears responsibility for coverage of the loss. Should the bailee's insurer be liable since the bailee was in control of the property? Or should the bailor's insurer be liable since the property destroyed was owned by the bailor?

Not surprisingly, the controversy over coverage centers around the wording of the policy in question. For example, policy language which holds the bailee's insurer liable for property the bailee is "liable for" as distinct from property for which the bailee is "legally liable for" has generated much litigation. Courts have held that the phrase "liable for" refers to property for which a bailee has held in trust, and that this phrase refers to property for which the bailee is responsible. This is distinct from a policy which could be written so that the bailee's insurer is liable only for the property for which the bailee is found to be legally liable. See *United States v. Globe & Rutgers Fire Ins. Co.*, 104 F.Supp. 632 (N.D.Tex.1952). Property for which the bailee is legally liable could require a showing of negligence on the part of the bailee in order for the bailor to recover. See *Folger Coffee Co. v. Great American Insurance Co.*, 333 F.Supp. 1272 (W.D.Mo.1971). Courts, barring specific language to the contrary, commonly will interpret "liability" language in such policies to refer to insurance on property, and not coverage on liability or indemnity. Cf. *Millers' Mut. Fire Ins. Ass'n v. Warroad Potato Growers Ass'n*, 94 F.2d 741 (8th Cir.1938) (holding that the policy language "if in case of loss the insured is legally liable therefor" does not insure stored property, but insures only the liability of the bailee).

D. SUBROGATION

"Subrogation," a term which occurs many times in this book, seems sometimes enigmatical. However, it is *very* important to understand the term as well as possible. The term is defined and discussed in the texts and treatises as well as in the *Welch Foods, Inc. v. Chicago Title Ins. Co.* case that follows. Nonetheless, a simple, short analysis may offer clarification.

The word "subrogation" derives from the Latin "subrogare" which could be used to mean "to put one person in the place of another." Subrogation agreed on by contract is "conventional" subrogation and is commonly included in many policies. See the Basic Standard Fire Policy, Appendix A lines 154–57. Subrogation, even absent express contractual provision, would be likely allowed in any event by operation of law. This is "legal" subrogation and really "equity" as used by the courts.

Whether legal or conventional, subrogation places an insurer in the place of the insured with respect to any claim the insured has against a third party for causing the loss. To reach this point, the insurer is required to have paid its insured under the terms of the policy. The insurer gets no greater rights than the insured had to give so far as a claim against the third party is concerned. The loss is thus charged to the negligently or wilfully acting responsible party. In a sense the principle of unjust enrichment is involved: if the insurer pays the insured and makes her whole, then the third party is in a position to extricate himself without economic loss unless the law intervenes to give an insurer a right to recover what it has paid the insured.

The definition above leaves much unanswered. Can subrogation be waived? If the insured settles independently with the third party, can the insured still make a claim against the insurer on the basis that the insurer has been adequately compensated for such payment? What if the amount recovered from the third party plus the amount payable under the policy are together insufficient to compensate the insured for her loss? Will subrogation be available where the wrong committed by the third party is "only" to breach his contract with the insured?

One or two insurance bromides can be stated that are of general application: (a) there is no subrogation against an insured, and (b) the insurer will not be recognized to have subrogation rights if it "volunteers" payment to the insured (this bears a resemblance to the maxim "equity does not aid a volunteer").[53]

53. We have not found good case examples which directly support this proposition, presumably because it is the rare insurer who will actually make payments without some reason to believe legal responsibility exists to make them, i.e., no insurer would ever truly volunteer payment. Many cases, though, invoke the principle saying it doesn't apply.

WELCH FOODS, INC. v. CHICAGO TITLE INS. CO.

Supreme Court of Arkansas, 2000.
341 Ark. 515, 17 S.W.3d 467.

LAVENSKI R. SMITH, JUSTICE.

Welch Foods, Inc. ("Welch"), appeals a summary judgment in favor of Appellee Chicago Title Insurance Company ("Chicago Title"). The Washington County Circuit Court awarded Chicago Title $23,500 for breach of warranty of title, and $6,025 in costs and fees. On appeal, Welch asserts that Chicago Title should not have been permitted to be subrogated to the rights of the buyer in a real estate transaction because it failed to adequately research the title. Welch contends that the equitable principles underlying subrogation preclude recovery. Additionally, Welch asserts that the trial court erred in assessing damages due to insufficient evidence. Finally, Welch argues that the existence of a material fact as to breach of warranty renders summary judgment inappropriate. We find no error and affirm.

FACTS

On July 12, 1995, Welch conveyed a parcel of land in an industrial area of the City of Springdale by warranty deed to Vail and Rita Paschal, husband and wife, and to William T. and Carolyn Coleman, husband and wife. On July 27, 1995, Chicago Title issued title insurance to the Paschals and the Colemans. On December 13, 1997, the Colemans conveyed their interest in the property to the Paschals. In early 1997, the Paschals discovered that a twenty-foot strip along the west side of the property actually belonged to Southwestern Electric Power Company ("SWEPCO"). This twenty-foot strip comprised a roadway and access from an adjoining street. The Paschals then made a claim against their title insurance policy to Chicago Title. Chicago Title paid the Paschal's $23,500 for the partial failure of title pursuant to the terms of the title insurance policy. They based the damage amount on an appraisal that gave that amount as the quantity of diminished value resulting from title problems. As a result of that payment, pursuant to paragraph 13 of the title policy, Chicago Title was subrogated to the rights of the Paschals in their claims against Welch. Chicago Title then brought suit against Welch, asserting Welch had breached their warranty of title to the Paschals.

On November 4, 1998, Chicago Title filed a motion for summary judgment asserting that the undisputed facts showed Welch had breached its warranty of title, that the sum paid by Chicago Title to the Paschals represented the damages suffered by the Paschals, and that under the terms of the title insurance, Chicago Title was the subrogee and rightful party to bring suit against Welch. In support of its motion, Chicago Title offered the policy of title insurance, the warranty deed showing the conveyance of the twenty-foot strip to SWEPCO in 1930, the appraisal showing diminished value, and an affidavit of Jeanine C. Ames of Chicago Title, containing a summary of the facts.

In opposition, Welch argued that Chicago Title was barred from recovery because its negligence caused the loss. In particular, Welch contended Chicago Title failed to properly research and discover the title defect when it undertook a title search in preparation for issuing the title insurance. Welch also argued that fact questions existed on the issue of damages, because it would have insisted on the same price for the property even had the lesser acreage been conveyed. Welch offered no supporting documents or affidavits in opposition to those offered by Chicago Title.

On December 16, 1998, Welch filed its own motion for summary judgment. Welch contended no issue of fact existed whether Chicago Title was negligent, and that the court should determine as a matter of law that Chicago Title's suit was barred based upon principles of equity. Again, Welch offered no supporting documents or evidence. The trial court heard both motions on January 28, 1999. At that time, Welch proffered its own appraisal to rebut the damages asserted by Chicago Title, but the trial court did not consider the appraisal because it was not provided "prior to day of the hearing" as required in Ark. R. Civ. P. 56(c). Based upon the pleadings, affidavits, and exhibits, the trial court found the undisputed facts showed Welch breached its warranty of title, and that damage to the title was $23,500 on February 11, 1999. The court awarded $23,500 in damages, $125 in costs, and $5900 in attorney's fees. The trial court thus granted Chicago Title's motion for summary judgment and denied Welch's motion. Welch timely filed its notice of appeal on March 10, 1999.

* * *

SUBROGATION

The principal issue in this case is whether Chicago Title, as subrogee to the buyers in a real estate transaction, is forbidden from enforcing the buyer's rights against the seller who breached the warranty of title contained in its deed, because Chicago Title failed to discover the defect in the title in its title investigation. This court has not previously answered this question. Welch contends that the equitable nature of subrogation makes Chicago Title subject to equitable defenses. Welch argues that this court has eliminated all distinction between conventional and equitable subrogation. We disagree and affirm.

Subrogation at its essence is the substitution of one party for another in the exercise of some legal right. BLACK'S LAW DICTIONARY, p. 1440 (7th ed. 1999). Subrogation is routinely divided into two types. They are conventional subrogation and legal subrogation. The distinction relates to the facts giving rise to the substitution of rights. "Conventional subrogation, as the term implies, is founded upon some understanding or agreement, express or implied, and without which there is no 'convention.'" Courtney v. Birdsong, 246 Ark. 162, 437 S.W.2d 238 (1969). Legal or equitable subrogation, on the other hand, is a creature of equity, and not dependent upon contract, but rather dependent upon the equities of the parties. It arises by operation of law. Courtney, 246 Ark. at 166, 437 S.W.2d 238.

Whether by agreement or by operation of law, the very concept of subrogation is of equitable origin. Southern Cotton Oil Co. v. Napoleon Hill Cotton Co., 108 Ark. 555, 158 S.W.1082 (1913). This equity arises when one not primarily bound to pay a debt, or remove an incumbrance, nevertheless does so; either from his legal obligation, as in the case of a surety, or to protect his own secondary right; or upon the request of the original debtor, and upon the faith that, as against the debtor, the person paying will have the same sureties for reimbursement as the creditor had for payment. Southern Cotton Oil Co., 108 Ark. at 559, 158 S.W. 1082. Subrogation is a doctrine steeped in equity and generally governed by equitable principles. Cooper Tire & Rubber Co. v. N.W. Nat'l Cas., 268 Ark. 334, 595 S.W.2d 938 (1980); Baker, Adm'r v. Leigh, 238 Ark. 918, 385 S.W.2d 790 (1965); Cooper v. Home Owners' Loan Corp., 197 Ark. 839, 126 S.W.2d 112 (1939); Southern Cotton Oil Co., supra; and, 73 AM.JUR. 2d, Subrogation § 16. [sic]

Welch argues that based upon subrogation's equitable origin, the equities between Welch and Chicago Title must be compared before a trial court could grant subrogation as a remedy. Welch cites Franklin v. Healthsource of Arkansas, 328 Ark. 163, 942 S.W.2d 837 (1997), for the proposition that the distinctions between conventional and legal subrogation have been entirely eliminated. However, Franklin is distinguishable from the instant case on its facts, and it does not stand for the general proposition that conventional and legal subrogation will be treated the same under all circumstances.

Franklin clearly dealt with a circumstance not present in the instant facts—the equities existing between an insured and his insurance company. In Franklin, the majority refused to enforce an express subrogation clause in favor of the insurance company where the insured had not been made fully whole. By so holding, Franklin thus reaffirmed the holding in the case of Shelter Mut. Ins. Co. v. Bough, 310 Ark. 21, 834 S.W.2d 637 (1992), and overruled Higginbotham v. Ark. Blue Cross & Blue Shield, 312 Ark. 199, 849 S.W.2d 464 (1993), which had enforced a conventional subrogation right even where the insured had not been made whole. The following explicit language in Franklin regarding its application makes it inapposite as precedent for the instant case: "[W]e take this opportunity to clarify our position on the priority given to subrogation rights of insureds versus those of insurers in instances where both parties have claims against a partial recovery from a third party." This case does not involve an insured and his insurer. Franklin is, therefore, not controlling.

Welch cites Transamerica Title Ins. Co. v. Johnson, 103 Wash.2d 409, 693 P.2d 697 (1985), and First American Title Insurance Co. v. Haggins, 1998 Ohio App. Lexis 279, 1998 WL 32776 (Ohio App. 8 Dist.1998)(an unpublished intermediate appellate decision), for the proposition that regardless of the source of the right of subrogation equities between the parties must be balanced.

However, as stated above, our court has not abolished all distinction between conventional and equitable subrogation in every circumstance. Here, where the insurer is exercising express contractual rights of subrogation in a claim against one other than its insured and against one to which it owed no legal duty, or who demonstrated no reliance, equitable defenses are unavailing. Welch acknowledges that it was not a named insured on the title policy but argues that Chicago Title owed it a legal duty and breached that duty. For support Welch relies upon Bourland v. Title Ins. Co. of Minnesota, 4 Ark.App. 68, 627 S.W.2d 567 (1982), for the establishment of the title company's duty. Clearly, our cases, and those of other jurisdictions, establish a duty on the part of title companies to make a reasonable search of the relevant records to detect clouds or defects in title. However, neither our courts, nor those of other jurisdictions, have held that that duty extends beyond those to which the company is contractually obligated, or to those shown to have reasonably relied upon the search. Welch also relies upon Lawyers Title Ins. Corp. v. Capp, 174 Ind.App. 633, 369 N.E.2d 672 (1977), but it, too, is quite different from the case at bar. In particular, the Capp court noted that the title insurance policy itself involved a tripartite agreement involving the vendor, vendee, and insurer. Moreover, Capp (the vendor) demonstrated reliance upon lawyers. In the instant case, Welch failed to show either contractual obligation or reliance.

* * *

AFFIRMED.

[Justices Corbin and Thornton would deny subrogation on the basis of the insurer's negligence.]

RICHARD D. BREW & CO. v. AUCLAIR TRANSPORTATION, INC.

Supreme Court of New Hampshire, Hillsborough, 1965.
106 N.H. 370, 211 A.2d 897.

The following reserved case was transferred by GRANT, J.

"Assumpsit to recover damages to personal property delivered by the plaintiff to the defendant for carriage by the latter to the plaintiff's consignee at Reno, Nevada. The plaintiff paid for the carriage of the goods which were delivered in a damaged condition. * * * The 'goods' in question were a high temperature electric furnace consigned to the U.S. Bureau of Mines with a value of some $15,817.00 and a so-called pyrometer of a value of some $2800.00.

* * *

"Just before the conclusion of the trial it became known to the Court that this was a subrogation case, Brew having been paid its loss by its own insurer who was seeking to recover from Auclair. The plaintiff paid an annual premium of $150.00 to Employers' Liability Assurance Corp., Ltd. and collected benefits thereunder for the loss herein described."

The contract of insurance provided in part as follows: "6. Benefit of Insurance. It is agreed by the Insured that this insurance shall not inure directly or indirectly to the benefit of any carrier, bailee, or other party, by stipulation in bill of lading or otherwise, and any breach of this agreement shall render this policy null and void."

"The Uniform Straight Bill of Lading delivered to Brew by Auclair Sec. 2, (c) reads:

" 'Any carrier or party liable on account of loss of or damage to any of said property shall have the full benefit of any insurance that may have been effected upon or on account of said property, so far as this shall not avoid the policies or contracts of insurance, provided that the carrier reimburse the claimant for the premium paid thereon.' The defendant argues that the limit of its liability is $150.00, the amount of the annual premium paid by Brew.

"Whether this portion of the Uniform Straight Bill of Lading, only whose legal effect is disputed, relieves the defendant of all damages except the $150.00 premium is reserved and transferred to the Supreme Court."

PER CURIAM.

The defendant carrier emphasizes the provisions of s. 2(c) of the bill of lading and contends according to its terms that it is liable only for the amount of the premium on the insurance policy procured by the plaintiff shipper. The insurance company, which is subrogated to the rights of the plaintiff shipper, emphasizes the provisions of the insurance policy that the insurance shall not "inure directly or indirectly to the benefit of any carrier," and contends that it is not subject to the limitation of liability contained in the bill of lading. These contentions are neither novel nor new and there is some logical support for each. The struggle between insurer and carrier as to which will bear the ultimate burden when the insured goods are damaged or lost in transit has been a protracted one. Phoenix Ins. Co. v. Erie & Western Transportation Co., 117 U.S. 312, 6 S.Ct. 750, 29 L.Ed. 873; Luckenbach v. W.J. McCahan Sugar Refining Co., 248 U.S. 139, 39 S.Ct. 53, 63 L.Ed. 170; The Turret Crown, 297 F. 766 (2d Cir.1924); Note, Subrogation of an Insurer: The Burden of the Loss of Insured Goods in Transit, 37 Harv.L.Rev. 901 (1924); Vance, Insurance 794–796 (3d ed. 1951). "In the beginning, the insurer of goods in transit was, on paying the insured, subrogated to the insured's claim, as shipper, against the carrier. Then the carrier inserted a stipulation in the bill of lading requiring the shipper to give it the benefit of any insurance that he might have, and this clause was held to cut off the insurer's right of subrogation even though the loss was due to the carrier's negligence. [Phoenix Ins. Co. v. Erie & Western Transp. Co., 117 U.S. 312 [6 S.Ct. 750, 29 L.Ed. 873] (1886)] This decision, which caused all the trouble, was an erroneous application of the perfectly sound principle that the insurer is subrogated only to the extent of the insured's claim against the third party. The carrier did not and could not by stipulation extinguish his liability to the shipper; and if the idea of subrogation is sound, the loss should ultimately fall upon the person who had the greater measure of control over it. However, the decision stood, and the insurers countered by inserting a condition, in policies on goods in transit, that the policy should be void if the insured should contract with the carrier that the latter should have the benefit of the insurance. The carrier has not been successful in counteracting the effect of these stipulations; and under most recent decisions, the ultimate loss falls upon the carrier." Patterson, Essentials of Insurance Law 150 (2d ed. 1957).

Contradictory provisions and stipulations in contracts of insurance and carriage must be resolved in spite of logical difficulties. "The apparent circularity of expression may be resolved by interpreting the provision in the bill of lading as entitling the carrier to the insurance if there is no opposing *stipulation* in the policy or contract of insurance, that is, no warranty or provision for avoidance; and not, if there is. Consequently, the insured may recover from the insurer; the insurer is effectively subrogated to his cause of action against the carrier; and the carrier is not entitled to the insurance." Campbell, Non–Consensual Suretyship, 45 Yale L.J. 69, 85 (1935). * * *

The result of the decisions was succinctly stated in Patterson, Cases and Material on Insurance 305 (1955) as follows: "The legal impasse created where the insurer of goods in transit stipulated that it should be subrogated to the shipper's right to hold the carrier liable for the loss of the goods, and the carrier in its bill of lading issued to the shipper stipulated that it should be entitled to the benefit of the shipper's insurance, seems finally to have been resolved in favor of the insurer." * * *

We conclude that the answer to the question transferred by the Trial Court without ruling is that the bill of lading does not relieve the defendant of all damages and the liability is not limited to the insurance premium. It follows, on the authorities cited above, that the insurer is effectively subrogated to the shipper's cause of action against the carrier for the damages he sustained. King, Subrogation under Contracts Insuring Property, 30 Tex.L.Rev. 62, 78–81 (1951).

* * *

Defendant's exceptions overruled.

Notes

1. Is subrogation a good idea or a windfall for insurers who are compensated to assume all or some of the insured's risk? Although subrogation clauses are generally accepted in the context of property coverage, jurisdictions are split over their enforceability in personal injury policies, with a minority disallowing subrogation. For a cogent and concise argument

urging adoption of the minority position through anti-subrogation legislation applicable to non-property damage claims, see Roger M. Baron, *Subrogation in Medical Expense Claims: The "Double Recovery" Myth and the Feasibility of Anti–Subrogation Laws*, 96 Dick. L. Rev. 581 (1992).

2. Professor Roger Baron argues that subrogation is skewed in favor of insurers. He believes that an insured's payment of premiums should allow recovery from both insurers and tortfeasors. To allow subrogation gives an insurer both the premiums paid and the possibility of suffering no loss if the tortfeasor is solvent. Roger M. Baron, *Subrogation: A Pandora's Box Awaiting Closure*, 41 S. Dak. L. Rev. 237, 242–43 (1996).

3. Subrogation is not necessarily evenly applied. In medical subrogation cases, Arkansas has followed the rule that holds absent a subrogation clause in the insurance contract, there is no right of subrogation of the insurer to a share of a settlement by its insured. American Pioneer Life Insurance Co. v. Rogers, 296 Ark. 254, 753 S.W.2d 530 (1988); see Shumpert v. Time Insurance Co., 329 S.C. 605, 496 S.E.2d 653 (1998) (in accord). This topic is addressed in greater depth in Chapter 7.

1. Limitations on Insurer's Rights of Subrogation

SUTTON v. JONDAHL

Court of Appeals of Oklahoma, 1975.
532 P.2d 478.

BRIGHTMIRE, JUDGE.

Landlord's fire insurance carrier sued a tenant and his 10–year–old son (in the name of the property owners) to recover a $2,382.57 fire loss. A jury returned a verdict favoring the insurance company against only the father. * * *

* * * Once upon a time the elder Jondahl rented from the Suttons a home for his family in Ponca City, Oklahoma. For Christmas 1968 he gave an inexpensive chemistry set to his 10–year–old son—a co-defendant—who performed experiments for about a year without mishap.

Then, on January 11, 1970, the budding scientist took an electric popcorn popper to his bedroom and while using it to heat some chemicals a flame suddenly flared upward igniting nearby curtains causing damage to the house in the amount of $2,382.57.

Central Mutual Insurance Company which covered subject premises with fire insurance, paid the loss, and then, as subrogee, brought this suit against John Jondahl and his boy, alleging, in substance, that the father contributed to the cause of the fire by breaching a duty to prohibit his son from carrying on unsupervised chemical experiments in the bedroom.

* * *

Later, at the request of defendants, the court required Central to substitute itself for the Suttons since it paid the full loss and therefore the landlords were not real parties in interest.

* * *

We hold here the instructions improperly directed the jury to return a verdict for plaintiff unless it found defendants had borne the burden of proving themselves blameless or of presenting proof otherwise sufficient to exonerate themselves from a legal presumption of negligence. Failure of the trial court on the foregoing fundamental error, we think, was prejudicial to defendant and therefore warrants a new trial.

Defendant's other proposition is that the verdict is not supported by evidence and is contrary to law. The argument is that the evidence fails to establish negligence on the part of the defending father pitched as it was on a failure to properly perform his duty to supervise his son whom the jury found innocent of negligence. While evidence bearing on the breach of such duty was indeed scarce we cannot say there was an absence. What we do say, however, is that there is no evidence to establish Central Mutual Insurance Company has been actionably damaged by such breach. The reason is that under the circumstances thus far disclosed by the record here, the insurance company has no subrogational rights against the tenant of its policyholder.

The principle of subrogation was begotten of a union between equity and her beloved—the natural justice of placing the burden of bearing a loss where it *ought to be.* Being so sired this child of justice is without the form of a rigid rule of law. On the contrary it is a fluid concept depending upon the particular facts and circumstances of a given case for its applicability. To some facts subrogation will adhere—to others it will not. Home Owners' Loan Corp. v. Parker, 181 Okl. 234, 73 P.2d 170 (1937).

Under the facts and circumstances in this record the subrogation should not be available to the insurance carrier because the law considers the tenant as a co-insured of the landlord absent an express agreement between them to the contrary, comparable to the permissive-user feature of automobile insurance. This principle is derived from a recognition of a relational reality, namely, that both landlord and tenant have an insurable interest in the rented premises—the former owns the fee and the latter has a possessory interest. Here the landlords (Suttons) purchased the fire insurance from Central Mutual Insurance Company to protect such interests in the property against loss from fire. This is not uncommon. And as a matter of sound business practice the premium paid had to be considered in establishing the rent rate on the rental unit. Such premium was chargeable against the rent as an overhead or operating expense. And of course it follows then that the tenant actually paid the premium as part of the monthly rental.

The landlords of course could have held out for an agreement that the tenant would furnish fire insurance on the premises. But they did not. They elected to themselves purchase the coverage. To suggest the fire insurance does not extend to the insurable interest of an occupying tenant is to ignore the realities of urban apartment and single-family dwelling renting. Prospective tenants ordinarily rely upon the owner of the dwelling to provide fire protection for the realty (as distinguished from personal property) absent an express agreement otherwise. Certainly it would not likely occur to a reasonably prudent tenant that the premises were without fire insurance protection or if there was such protection it did not inure to his benefit and that he would need to take out another fire policy to protect himself from any loss during his occupancy. Perhaps this comes about because the companies themselves have accepted coverage of a tenant as a natural thing. Otherwise their insurance salesmen would have long ago made such need a matter of common knowledge by promoting the sale to tenants of a second fire insurance policy to cover the real estate.

Basic equity and fundamental justice upon which the equitable doctrine of subrogation is established requires that when fire insurance is provided for a dwelling it protects the insurable interests of all joint owners including the possessory interests of a tenant absent an express agreement by the latter to the contrary. The company affording such coverage should not be allowed to shift a fire loss to an occupying tenant even if the latter negligently caused it. New Hampshire Ins. Co. v. Ballard Wade, Inc., 17 Utah 2d 86, 404 P.2d 674 (1965). A parallel effect was reached in Hardware Mut. Ins. Co. v. Dunwoody, 194 F.2d 666 (9th Cir.1952). For to conclude otherwise is to shift the insurable risk assumed by the insurance company from it to the tenant—a party occupying a substantially different position from that of a fire-causing third party not in privity with the insured landlord.

Failure of either the pleadings or the evidence to show the landlords' insurance carrier possesses a right of subrogation against the Jondahls furnishes another reason why it was fundamental error to instruct the jury that they should return a verdict for the insurance company unless "defendants prove * * * they * * * [were] not negligent."

The judgment below is therefore reversed and the cause remanded for a new trial.

DUELL v. GREATER NEW YORK MUTUAL INSURANCE CO.

Supreme Court, Appellate Division, First Department, 1991.
172 A.D.2d 270, 568 N.Y.S.2d 93.

MEMORANDUM DECISION.

* * *

Plaintiffs (collectively "Landlord") of a building known as 949 Park Avenue in Manhattan, brought this action to recover damages against defendant-attorneys arising from alleged malpractice committed by them in defense of an action brought by an art gallery tenant ("Tenant") in

Landlord's building who recovered a judgment against Landlord upon a jury verdict in the approximate sum of $77,000. That recovery was based upon Landlord's negligence in causing or permitting an infusion of water into Tenant's art gallery. Numerous acts of professional negligence in the unsuccessful defense of that lawsuit are alleged, many of which appear to raise triable issues. One of these acts consists of allegations that although the lease between Landlord and Tenant (par. 36) required Tenant to provide $100,000 of property damage insurance naming both Landlord and Tenant as the insured, Tenant never performed this obligation. Because defendants omitted to allege this breach of lease by Tenant in Landlord's answer, the trial court precluded any testimony or other reference thereto throughout the trial. Another specification of negligence is that counsel carelessly elicited misleading testimony that Landlord was insured for the loss (which it was not); because of Tenant's breach, Landlord had only excess coverage for property damage over $100,000 at the time Tenant's cause of action accrued.

The motion court recognized the principle that a plaintiff in a legal malpractice action must show that but for his attorney's negligence he would have prevailed on the underlying claim, citing Romanian American Interests, Inc. v. Scher, 94 A.D.2d 549, 464 N.Y.S.2d 821. In that connection, the motion court did not hold that this defense relating to Tenant's breach of lease could not have prevailed as a matter of law (cf. N.A. Kerson Co. Inc. v. Shayne, 45 N.Y.2d 730, 408 N.Y.S.2d 475, 380 N.E.2d 302). (Clearly a jury, if such proof were adduced before it, might have rationally concluded that the proximate cause of Tenant's loss was its own default, irrespective of Landlord's negligence). Nonetheless the court erroneously concluded that the defense, even if properly interposed, would have made no difference, inasmuch as the insurance carrier, after paying Tenant's judgment, would have had the right to recover its loss against Landlord by way of subrogation and indemnification.

This was error. "It is a well-established principle of insurance law, however, that the right of subrogation exists only with respect to the rights of the insured against third persons and that there is no right of subrogation in favor of the insurer against its own insured (16 Couch, Insurance 2d, § 61:133; 6A Appleman, Insurance Law and Practice, § 4055; 2 Richards, Insurance [5th ed.], s 185)." (New York Board of Fire Underwriters v. Trans Urban Construction Co., 91 A.D.2d 115, 120, 458 N.Y.S.2d 216, aff'd 60 N.Y.2d 912, 470 N.Y.S.2d 578, 458 N.E.2d 1255). Here, of course, had the lease been complied with, Landlord would have been a named insured under the policy, with no exposure to a subrogation action by its own carrier.

Thus plaintiffs' malpractice claim is not subject to defeat as a matter of law on the ground that the alleged negligence bears no relation to the loss sustained. The question presents a triable issue, requiring reversal of the order appealed from.

Notes

1. *Sutton v. Jondahl* has met with criticism over the years. A summary of the criticism is contained in *56 Associates v. Frieband*, 89 F.Supp.2d 189 (D.R.I.2000), which explains in detail why decisions rejecting *Sutton* represent the "better reasoned authorities on the subject." *Id.* at 193. The reasons include: (1) a court should not be free to rewrite a policy or read provisions into it to achieve a certain desired result, such as inserting names of additional insureds; (2) the fact that the tenant has an insurable interest in the property does not mean that the individual is now an insured under a policy without being named; (3) neither the tenant's expectations nor the unilateral action of the landlord giving rise to such expectations can make the tenant an insured. The Supreme Court of Iowa also criticized the *Sutton* decision in *Neubauer v. Hostetter*, 485 N.W.2d 87 (1992), citing Appelman's insurance treatise in support of their disapproval.

2. It has been suggested that "lessees should first attempt to be covered as an additional insured on the lessor's policy * * * but if for various reasons this is not permissible, the lessee should at least obtain a mutual waiver of subrogation, such as: 'Insofar as permitted under their respective policies of insurance the lessor and lessee waive all rights, each against the other, for damage caused by fire or other perils which are covered by insurance.' "What might be the reaction of the risk manager of a prospective insurer when shown such a provision in the lease? See Lindblad, *Risk Implications in Lease Agreements*, Ins. L.J. #677 (June 1979) at page 307.

3. If the tenant is by implication, or by the terms of the lease, liable for negligent harm to the demised premises, a familiar problem may then arise if the tenant repairs the premises before the insurance is paid. Is the insurer discharged because the insured landlord has sustained no loss? In this landlord-tenant area the two disparate lines of cases have been designated as the *New York rule* (holding to the principle that events subsequent to the loss do not affect the insurers' liability) exemplified in *Foley v. Manufacturers' and Builders' Fire Ins. Co.*, 152 N.Y. 131, 46 N.E. 318 (1897); and the contrary *Wisconsin rule* of *Ramsdell v. Insurance Co. of North America*, 197 Wis. 136, 221 N.W. 654 (1928). The Wisconsin rule was followed in *Mission Nat'l Ins. Co. v. Schulman*, 659 F.Supp. 270 (D.Conn.1986).

REEDER v. REEDER

Supreme Court of Nebraska, 1984.
217 Neb. 120, 348 N.W.2d 832.

PER CURIAM.

This appears to be a case of first impression in this jurisdiction and presents the question of whether one who occupies the home of another with the owner's permission, and who negligently causes damage to the home, may be sued by the owner's insurance carrier under a right of subrogation after the insurance carrier has paid the owner for the damages. The trial court concluded that the cause of action did not lie.

We believe that the trial court was correct, and, accordingly, we affirm. Theodore N. Reeder and Rosalie M. Reeder, husband and wife, were the owners of a residence located in Omaha, Nebraska. In August of 1979 they moved to Arlington, Texas, still owning the home in Omaha. Reeder's brother, Bernard Reeder, who lived in Omaha, was in the process of constructing a new home for himself and his family. The brothers agreed that Bernard Reeder and his family could occupy the Theodore Reeder home in Omaha while the Bernard Reeders were awaiting the completion of their new home. As one would anticipate in arrangements of this type, there was no formal agreement and little discussion regarding the informal agreement. Theodore Reeder testified: We didn't have a lease, he did not lease it from me, he was only living in it. He was building a house of his own in the neighborhood, and he wanted to get his children in Christ the King School as soon as possible, and my house was sitting there vacant and he asked me if he could move in while he was completing his house and be closer to it, and get his kids in the school district right away. And I said that is fine, because it is sitting there vacant, and I can sell it with furniture in it just as easy as I can without; and you move in, and that is fine. Further, Theodore Reeder testified that "there was no rent paid and no agreement. He was to just take care of it and shovel the snow, live in it. Pay the utility bills, which I wouldn't have to pay." The brothers understood that Theodore Reeder, the owner, would pay the taxes, but no rent was to be paid by Bernard to Theodore. Additionally, Theodore Reeder testified that he specifically told his brother, "that I would leave my insurance policy that I had on it on it while he was in there, and I didn't really discuss any part of his homeowner's or anything else. I just assumed he would take care of that. But we did discuss that I would leave my policy on it."

On March 4, 1980, while occupying the house, Dana Reeder, Bernard's daughter, ignited the gas fireplace in the family room of the house. Allegedly, she failed to open the damper, which caused a fire resulting in substantial destruction to the home.

Cornhusker Casualty Company, Theodore Reeder's carrier, paid the sum of $139,760 to Theodore Reeder and obtained in return a subrogation receipt. Cornhusker then filed suit against Bernard Reeder and Patricia Reeder, parents of Dana Reeder, as well as against Dana Reeder herself. The parents were dismissed from the action, and no appeal has been taken from that order. It is therefore final and binding and not at issue in this appeal. Following the order dismissing the parents, Dana Reeder filed a motion for summary judgment. On May 11, 1983, the trial court sustained the motion for summary judgment and dismissed the action as against the remaining defendant, Dana Reeder.

It is from that order, dismissing the petition against Dana Reeder, that Cornhusker appeals, assigning as error, in essence, the following claims: (1) That the granting of the summary judgment was inappropriate under the facts of the case; (2) That the trial court erred in finding that the relationship between the parties was that of landlord/tenant; (3)

That the trial court erred in finding the majority rule prohibits a landlord's insurer from subrogating against a negligent tenant.

While we believe that the order of the trial court was correct, we should at this point note that nothing in either the motion for summary judgment or in the trial court's order sustaining the motion for summary judgment indicates the basis upon which the trial court rendered its judgment. There are no findings in the trial court's order that the relationship between the parties was that of landlord/tenant, nor any finding that the trial court was adhering to any particular rule, majority or minority. The motion for summary judgment simply asks that judgment be granted "for the reason that the pleadings, including all discovery pleadings filed herein, and the depositions filed herein establish that there is no genuine issue as to any material fact, and defendant is entitled to a judgment as a matter of law." And the order of the trial court sustaining the motion for summary judgment simply recites: "Motion of defendant Dana Reeder for summary judgment is sustained."

The issue whether the relationship between Theodore Reeder and his brother, Bernard Reeder, was that of landlord/tenant, as urged by appellee, or that of licensor/licensee, as urged by appellant, is raised in part by Dana Reeder's amended answer and by the briefs of the parties to this court. It is not, however, a part of either the motion for summary judgment or the court's order. Nor do we believe that attempting to categorize this relationship is either material or helpful. One of the difficulties we too often encounter in the law is our effort to attempt to force every situation into a known and recognized relationship, hoping that by doing so the answer to our question may of necessity automatically follow.

In the instant case, we believe the facts would disclose that the relationship created between Theodore Reeder and his brother, Bernard Reeder, was neither landlord/tenant nor licensor/licensee in the full legal sense. To be sure, the relationship has characteristics of both landlord/tenant and licensor/licensee, but of a separate and unique kind, and in this instance meriting a different treatment. In Friend v. Gem International, Inc., 476 S.W.2d 134, 137–38 (Mo.App.1971), it was noted: The status of landlord and tenant is defined, generally, to arise from contract, express or implied, under the terms of which a person designated as "tenant" enters into possession of land of another, known as "landlord", with the rights of the tenant subordinate to the landlord. "The essentials of that relationship are said to be (1) a reversion in the landlord, (2) the creation of an estate in the tenant, either at will or for a term less than that for which the landlord holds, (3) the transfer of exclusive possession and control of the premises to the tenant, and (4) a contract, either express or implied, between the parties." Johnson v. Simpson Oil Company, Mo.App., 394 S.W.2d 91, 96[4] [1965]. On the other hand, the condition of licensor and licensee has also been defined, generally, to arise when one who owns or possesses land known as the "licensor" grants to another known as "licensee" the privilege of going onto land for a certain purpose without passing an estate in the land.

(Emphasis supplied.) See, also, Bentley v. Palmer House Company, 332 F.2d 107 (7th Cir.1964); Gage v. City of Topeka, 205 Kan. 143, 468 P.2d 232 (1970). As noted in 49 Am.Jur.2d Landlord and Tenant § 6 at 47 (1970), the legal status of parties in their relationships one to the other "is a question of which direction the general effect of the various tests that have been applied, after weighing opposing ones against each other, can be said to take."

An express agreement to create a landlord/tenant relationship is not necessary; nevertheless, the evidence must indicate that the parties intended to impliedly create such an arrangement, including the fact that by entering into this arrangement the tenant acquired certain rights and the landlord assumed certain obligations. See Bodie v. Epler, 132 Neb. 442, 272 N.W. 249 (1937). We believe that when one examines the relationship and discussion between the parties, it is clear that Theodore Reeder did not intend to assume any obligations, nor did Bernard Reeder obtain any "rights" other than the opportunity to occupy his brother's home for such time and under such conditions as Theodore Reeder might impose arbitrarily from day to day. It is clear, for instance, that there was no intention of any payment of rent by Bernard to Theodore, nor was Theodore precluded from occupying the house any time he might return to Omaha.

Additionally, the relationship of licensor/licensee has been thought to exist with regard to the use of land and not the occupancy of a house. See, Matter of Daben Corp., 469 F.Supp. 135 (D.Puerto Rico 1979); Moore v. Chesapeake & O. Ry. Co., 493 F.Supp. 1252 (S.D.W.Va.1980), aff'd 649 F.2d 1004 (4th Cir.1981); Wenner v. Dayton–Hudson Corp., 123 Ariz. 203, 598 P.2d 1022 (1979); Ulan v. Vend–A–Coin, Inc., 27 Ariz.App. 713, 558 P.2d 741 (1976); Union Travel Assoc. v. International Assoc., 401 A.2d 105 (D.C.App.1979).

The arrangement, for whatever difference placing titles on it may be, was really that of a host and guest. The word [guest] is descriptive of a relationship known to the common understanding. Besides its somewhat narrow technical significance in statutes, it has a broad, general meaning, implying both a social relationship and the existence of a host; and has been defined in general, as meaning a person entertained in one's house or at one's table, a visitor entertained without pay; a person received and entertained at the house of another, a visitor; * * * hence a person to whom the hospitality of a home, club, etc., is extended. 39 C.J.S. Guest at 447 (1976). In Stadelmann v. Glen Falls Ins. Co., 5 Mich.App. 536, 147 N.W.2d 460 (1967), the Michigan court said a guest is a person who is received at one's home.

The reason that we make this distinction is not to simply find our own "pigeonhole" in which to force the answer. Rather, it is to clarify the question presented by this case. This question is not whether the relationship between the brothers was that of landlord/tenant or licensor/licensee, but whether the carrier, by seeking to recover from Theodore Reeder's "guest," is, in effect, seeking to recover from the insured himself for the very risk that the carrier insured and for which it received premiums.

We should note that the question presented to us is not whether a landlord may sue his tenant for negligent destruction to the landlord's property or whether a licensor may sue a licensee for negligent destruction of the licensor's property, absent agreements to the contrary. Rather, the question is whether the relationship between the host and the guest, under the facts in this case, is such that if the carrier is permitted to sue the guest under a claim of right of subrogation, in effect the carrier is recovering from the insured himself on the very risk which the insurer agreed to take upon payment of the premium. Therefore, in this case, the issue is not whether, absent insurance, Theodore Reeder could sue his brother or his niece, but whether the relationship between the insured and his brother was such, however characterized, that by permitting the carrier to sue the brother, in effect the carrier is suing the insured. This we believe the carrier may not do.

In Cagle, Inc. v. Sammons, 198 Neb. 595, 602, 254 N.W.2d 398, 403 (1977), we noted: The doctrine of subrogation is not administered by courts of equity as a legal right, but the principle is applied to subserve the ends of justice and to do equity in the particular case under consideration.... The facts and circumstances of each case determine whether the doctrine is applicable. While it is true that the right of an insurance company to recover against a wrongdoer whose negligence has subjected the insurance company to a liability, whether the company's right be based on an equitable subrogation or an express assignment is traced through the insured, see Omaha & R.V.R. Co. v. Granite State Fire Ins. Co., 53 Neb. 514, 73 N.W. 950 (1898), it is also true that an insurer cannot recover against its own insured, see Midwest Lumber Co. v. Dwight E. Nelson Constr. Co., 188 Neb. 308, 196 N.W.2d 377 (1972).

In Stetina v. State Farm Mut. Auto. Ins. Co., 196 Neb. 441, 451, 243 N.W.2d 341, 346 (1976), we said:

> "No right of subrogation can arise in favor of an insurer against its own insured since, by definition, subrogation exists only with respect to rights of the insurer against third persons to whom the insurer owes no duty. 16 Couch on Insurance 2d, § 61:133; see also 46 C.J.S. Insurance § 1209(b); 16 Couch on Insurance 2d, § 61:136. This principle is succinctly stated in Chenoweth Motor Co. v. Cotton, 2 Ohio Misc. 123, 207 N.E.2d 412, 413 [1965]:
>
> " '* * * it is axiomatic that [an insurance company] has no subrogation rights against the negligence of its own insured.' (Bracketed material paraphrased.)
>
> "To allow subrogation under such circumstances would permit an insurer, in effect, to pass the incidence of the loss, either partially or totally, from itself to its own insured and thus avoid the coverage which its insured purchased * * *."

(Emphasis supplied.) In Alaska Ins. Co. v. RCA Alaska Commun., 623 P.2d 1216, 1218 (Alaska 1981), the court said:

> Absent an express provision in the lease establishing the tenant's liability for loss from negligently started fires, the trend has been to find that the insurance obtained was for the mutual benefit of both parties, and that the tenant "stands in the shoes of the insured landlord for the limited purpose of defeating a subrogation claim." Rizzuto v. Morris, 22 Wash.App. 951, 592 P.2d 688, 690 (1979), citing Rock Springs Realty, Inc. v. Waid, 392 S.W.2d 270, 278 (Mo.1965); Monterey Corp. v. Hart, 216 Va. 843, 224 S.E.2d 142, 146 (1976).

See, also, West American Ins. Co. v. Pic Way, 110 Mich.App. 684, 313 N.W.2d 187 (1981); Gift Box v. Scott, 272 Ark. 256, 613 S.W.2d 395 (1981); Liberty Mut. Fire Ins. Co. v. Auto Spring Supply Co., 59 Cal. App.3d 860, 131 Cal.Rptr. 211 (1976). The undisputed evidence is that Theodore Reeder testified that he told his brother, Bernard, that he would "leave my insurance policy that I had on it on it while he was in there." It is difficult to see how the insurance was not for the benefit of the Bernard Reeders to the same extent as it was for the Theodore Reeders.

In the case of Rizzuto v. Morris, 22 Wash.App. 951, 955–56, 592 P.2d 688, 690 (1979), the Washington Court of Appeals reasoned: [I]nsurance companies expect to pay their insureds for negligently caused fire, and they adjust their rates accordingly. In this context, an insurer should not be allowed to treat a tenant, who is in privity with the insured landlord, as a negligent third party when it could not collect against its own insured had the insured negligently caused the fire. In effect, a tenant stands in the shoes of the insured landlord for the limited purpose of defeating a subrogation claim. It occurs to us that if the reasoning underlying the denial of a subrogation claim applies between a landlord and a tenant, then we conclude that this reason is even more compelling when the relationship is that of host and guest, particularly when the host has assured the guest that there is insurance coverage. It may be presumed that the insured bought this policy so that he would not have to look to his guest for payment in the event of damage caused by the negligent act of the guest. We are persuaded that the relationship which existed between the brothers in this case was such that, regardless of how their relationship is characterized, a right of subrogation in the insurer against the insured's niece should not lie as a matter of law.

Having therefore concluded as a matter of law that the carrier was not entitled to maintain the right of subrogation, and, further, in view of the fact that there is no dispute as to the facts, this was a case in which there existed no genuine issue as to any material fact, the ultimate inferences to be drawn from those facts were clear, and the moving party was entitled to judgment as a matter of law. Under such circumstances the court was obligated to enter summary judgment. See Interholzinger v. Estate of Dent, 214 Neb. 264, 333 N.W.2d 895 (1983). The judgment of the trial court granting summary judgment in favor of the appellee and against the appellant was correct, and the judgment is affirmed.

AFFIRMED.

Note

Subrogation to Contract Rights and Equitable Contribution. Some years ago the court in *Patent Scaffolding Co. v. William Simpson Construction Co.*, 256 Cal.App.2d 506, 64 Cal.Rptr. 187 (1967) held that an insurance company which pays a property damage claim is not subrogated to the insured's rights against third parties (other than different insurance companies) also contractually liable to indemnify the insured unless the loss involved is *causally* related to a breach of duty by that third party. In that case a prime contractor (Simpson) agreed to procure fire insurance on the subcontractor's (Patent's) equipment at the jobsite. Patent already had insurance on its gear. When fire destroyed Patent's property it was discovered that Simpson had not procured the agreed coverage. Patent's insurer therefore paid and sought subrogation against Simpson based on Patent's claim for breach of contract. Subrogation was denied because there was no evidence that Simpson caused the fire, and therefore the loss was not causally connected with the breach of the agreement to procure insurance. The court observed however that the principle of equitable contribution (not raised in the case) might apply.

In an analogous case involving a sub-lessee's contractual liability in event of loss, *California Food Service Corp. v. Great American Ins. Co.*, 130 Cal.App.3d 892, 182 Cal.Rptr. 67 (1982), the court followed the principle of *Patent Scaffolding* and denied subrogation to the sub-lessor's insurer, but moderated the result by applying "equitable contribution" "based on the common sense notion that where two indemnitors share equal contractual responsibility for a loss, the selection of which indemnitor is to bear the loss should not be left to the sometimes arbitrary choice of the loss claimant. * * * More importantly, the indemnitor should not be given the incentive to avoid paying a just claim in hopes that the claimant will obtain payment from the co-indemnitor. * * * "130 Cal.App.3d at 901, 182 Cal.Rptr. at 72–73. Thus the insurer, although denied subrogation, recoups ½ of the loss.

WIMBERLY v. AMERICAN CASUALTY COMPANY OF READING, PENNSYLVANIA (CNA)

Supreme Court of Tennessee, 1979.
584 S.W.2d 200.

FONES, JUSTICE.

The Wimberly's restaurant was destroyed by fire, and they sustained an undisputed loss of $44,619.10. The fire was caused by Shelia McLemore's driving her automobile into the restaurant. Her insurance carrier paid the policy limits of $25,000. The Wimberlys had a total of $15,000 fire insurance coverage with defendant insurance companies.

The single question for determination is what are the subrogation rights of the two fire insurance companies when the total recovery of the insured from the tortfeasor and the fire insurance policies is less than the casualty loss.

The chancellor ruled that the insureds must be paid in full for their loss before subrogation rights arose in favor of their insurance carriers. The Court of Appeals reversed and held that the insureds and the insurers were entitled to an equal distribution of the proceeds received from the tortfeasor's insurance company. * * *

The fire insurance policies that the Wimberlys had with American Casualty and New Hampshire Casualty both contained the standard subrogation clause, which read:

> "This company may require from the insured an assignment of all rights to property against any party for loss to the extent that payment therefor is made by this company."

On February 18, 1975, the Wimberlys signed a proof of loss and subrogation receipt, by which they subrogated their insurers "to all of the rights, claims and interests which the undersigned may have against any person or corporation liable for the loss" and agreed to cooperate with their insurers in litigating or compromising their claims. On February 27, the insurers issued checks to the Wimberlys for $7,000 and $8,000, the full amount of the respective policies, for a total of $15,000. On April 16, 1975, Hartford Insurance Company, the insurer of McLemore, issued a check for $25,000, payable to Robert R. and Evelyn M. Wimberly, American Casualty Company and New Hampshire Insurance Company. In late May all of the payees of the $25,000 check executed a joint release of McLemore in consideration of the settlement with her insurer.

The American Casualty Company received $3,921.53 and the New Hampshire Insurance Company received $4,482.94, for a total of $8,404.47 as a pro rata share, and the Wimberlys received $16,595.53 of the settlement payment. Subsequently, since they had to bear an uninsured loss of $13,023.57, the Wimberlys sued to recover the $8,404.47 received by their insurers * * *.

The Court of Appeals reversed the trial court judgment in favor of the plaintiffs and held that both the insured and the insurers were entitled to a pro rata share of the sum recovered from the third-party tortfeasor. * * * The Court of Appeals appears to have bottomed its decision on its conclusion that "[b]oth the plaintiffs and defendants were legally entitled to recover all of their loss from the tortfeasor but were prevented from making a complete recovery due to the inadequacy of funds received from tortfeasor. All had an equal right to recovery, and the standing of one was not greater than the other."

Defendants contended at trial that under the stipulated facts and applicable law, they are entitled to priority because of their subrogation rights against the recovery from the third-party tortfeasor. In support of this position, defendants relied on cases from other jurisdictions which have allowed the insurer to be first indemnified out of the proceeds recovered from the third-party tortfeasor when the insured had assigned to his insurer all rights of recovery against the tortfeasor to the extent of payment, even when the insured suffered a fire loss only partially covered by his policy. *See Peterson v. Ohio Farmers Ins. Co.,* 175 Ohio St. 34, 191 N.E.2d 157 (1963); *accord, Ervin v. Garner,* 25 Ohio St.2d 231, 267 N.E.2d 769 (1971); *Travelers Indemnity Co. v. Ingebretsen,* 38 Cal.App.3d 858, 113 Cal.Rptr. 679 (1974). * * *

In *Peterson v. Ohio Farmers Ins. Co., supra,* the Ohio Supreme Court considered a factually similar case, in which the insured also executed an assignment of all of the insured's rights of recovery against the third-party tortfeasor to the extent of the insurer's payment to the insured. The Court held that the outcome of the case was determined by the subrogation provisions of the insurance policy and the subrogation receipt signed by the insured upon settlement of the claim for loss, both of which had language identical to that found in the Wimberly's policy and subrogation receipt. The Court reasoned:

> "The insured's conveyance of all right of recovery up to a certain limit, viz., the extent of the insurer's payment in settlement of the insured's claim, can mean only that the assignee is the owner of all the insured's rights of recovery until he is paid. The assignee, being the owner of all of the insured's right of recovery, must have priority in payment out of the funds recovered. Otherwise, the words 'all right of recovery' are without meaning." *Id.,* 191 N.E.2d at 159.

Although the Ohio Court gave weight to the fact that the insurer had cooperated and assisted in proceedings against the wrongdoer, the clear holding of the case was that the specific subrogation provision and the assignment of "all right of recovery" was interpreted to give the insurer priority to the proceeds received in the judgment recovery from the third party tortfeasor. In a subsequent case, *Ervin v. Garner, supra,* moreover, the Ohio Court indicated that it would not concede that cooperation and assistance are prerequisites under the *Peterson* rule. *Id.,* 267 N.E.2d at 773. Rather, as in *Peterson,* the Ohio Court found, "we fail to see how the insured can specifically assign *each and all claims and demands* to the insurer concerning the single cause of action, limited only by the monetary amount which the insured has paid, and yet still retain any part of his claim or demand."

We disagree with the position taken by the Ohio Court and find the results of these cases at odds with the principles of equitable subrogation. * * * The question for decision in this case * * * is whether the equitable operation of subrogation is modified by the terms of the underlying contract, so-called conventional subrogation.

In *Castleman Constr. Co. v. Pennington,* 222 Tenn. 82, 432 S.W.2d 669 (1968), this Court, speaking through Chief Justice Burnett, rejected the contention made by an insurance company that conventional subrogation is not governed by the same tests applied to find subrogation which arises by operation of law. The Court quoted with approval from Couch on Insurance 2d § 61:20 (1966):

> " 'The doctrine of subrogation in insurance does not arise from, nor is it dependent upon, statute or custom or any of the terms of the contract; it has its origin in general principles of equity and in the nature of the insurance contract as one of indemnity. The right of subrogation rests not upon a contract, but upon the principles of natural justice.' " * * *

The Court viewed the distinction between legal and conventional subrogation only dispositive of "whether there is a right of subrogation in the first instance, rather than in the enforcement of such right." * * * Consequently, we believe our resolution of this case must be guided by general principles of equity, to wit, that the insured must be made whole before subrogation rights arise in favor of the insurers.

The purpose of insurance subrogation is to prevent either the unjust enrichment of the insured through a double recovery or a windfall benefit to the principal tortfeasor by allowing the insurer to stand in the shoes of the insured once the insurer has fully indemnified the insured. * * * It is obvious that the insureds will not be unjustly enriched by recovering from their insurers on their fire policies as well as from the tortfeasor's insurer because the total indemnity of $40,000 will not cover the casualty loss of $44,619.10. The principal tortfeasor has not reaped a windfall, but rather has been released by the parties in consideration of a $25,000 settlement with her insurer. Finally, although defendant insurers must pay the full limits of their policies without reimbursement by way of subrogation, the insured loss was a risk that the insureds paid for them to assume. Had the tortfeasor been judgment-proof and uninsured, defendants would still have been required to bear the loss to the full extent of the policies.

In *Garrity v. Rural Mut. Ins. Co.,* 77 Wis.2d 537, 253 N.W.2d 512, 516 (1977), the Supreme Court of Wisconsin refused to follow the *Peterson* rationale and held that "we regard the differentiation between subrogation and assignment in this situation as purely procedural." The Court correctly isolated the pivotal question, not considered by the Ohio Court in *Peterson,* whether the insurance contract had changed the rule that the surety's right of subrogation does not arise ordinarily until the debt is paid in full, and held that "because the contract here contains no language to the contrary, the normal rule of subrogation applies and the subrogee has no right to share in the funds recovered from the tortfeasor until the subrogor is made whole." * * * The Court simply recognized that the assignee under the subrogation receipt is a subrogee, and nothing more. As a subrogee, the insurer does not acquire the rights of its insured until the latter is made whole. "The assignment adds nothing to the rights vested in the surety by the doctrine of subrogation." *Id.* at 516, *quoting from Couch, supra,* § 61:105.

We believe that the rule followed in *Garrity* comports with the doctrine of subrogation as applied under Tennessee law and represents the approach followed in a plurality of jurisdictions. [Citations from Montana, Utah, N. Car., Mich., Miss., Texas, and Kansas]

The judgment of the Court of Appeals is reversed and that of the trial court reinstated. Costs are adjudged against appellees.

Notes

1. The authors are grateful to Professor Robert Covington for pointing out that the *Wimberly* principle remains firmly entrenched in Tennessee. See York v. Sevier County Ambulance Authority, 8 S.W.3d 616 (Tenn.1999). In *York*, the Tennessee State Supreme Court refused to enforce an insurer's contractual "reimbursement" right where the insured's losses had not yet been fully compensated. Citing *Wimberly* with approval, the court concluded that the insured must receive its due before an insurer is entitled to reimbursement, even in the face of express policy language giving the insurer the right to reimbursement. *Id.* at 620. See also Blankenship v. Estate of Bain, 5 S.W.3d 647 (Tenn.1999) (affirming *Wimberly*).

2. The idea of equitable contribution in subrogation cases does not appear to apply among insurers. In *Maryland Casualty Co. v. W.R. Grace and Co.*, 218 F.3d 204 (2d Cir.2000), the insured entered into a settlement agreement with two insurers with each agreeing to pay 50 percent of the insured's bodily injury defense costs. Later, two other insurers were joined in the action. Both of the later added insurers refused to contribute to the costs incurred in the settlement. The Second Circuit held for the later added insurers reasoning that the contracts cannot affect the rights of a non-party. In the same way, subrogation does not apply because the first insurers were not seeking reimbursement from a third party tortfeasor. While equitable considerations are relevant in determining contribution, the settlement agreement was otherwise enforceable on its terms.

3. Professor Roger Baron neatly summarizes the underpinnings of the "make whole" doctrine. Roger M. Baron, *Subrogation: A Pandora's Box Awaiting Closure*, 41 S. Dak. L. Rev. 237, 249–52 (1996).

2. Interference with Insurer's Subrogation Rights

HOME INSURANCE CO. v. HERTZ CORP.

Supreme Court of Illinois, 1978.
71 Ill.2d 210, 16 Ill.Dec. 484, 375 N.E.2d 115.

UNDERWOOD, JUSTICE:

* * *

Plaintiff-insurer alleged that on August 2, 1974, defendant Gary L. Gardner, an employee of defendant Ingram Barge, Inc., negligently drove an automobile owned by defendant Hertz Corporation so as to injure plaintiff's insured and damage his auto. Plaintiff also alleged that it paid its insured's property damage and medical payments policy claims in the amount of $2,082.36 and that it thereby became subrogated to the interests of the insured to the extent of those payments. Ingram submitted in support of its motion to dismiss a full and final release of all personal injury and property damage claims arising from the accident, which release was executed by the insured in consideration of the payment to him of $6,000. It is not disputed that this release had been executed by the insured in connection with the settlement of his separate suit against the defendants here for personal injury damages and the $100 property damage paid by him under his deductible clause, and that no recovery had been sought in that suit for the property damage paid by the insurer. It is also undisputed that defendants had notice of plaintiff's subrogation rights prior to the settlement of the insured's suit and the signing of the release.

The precise question before us is whether an unlimited general release by an insured of all claims against a tortfeasor bars a subrogation action by an insurer-subrogee against that tortfeasor, where the tortfeasor procures the release from the insured-subrogor with knowledge of the insurer's interest.

It is true as defendants contend that the appellate court authority in this State supports their position. The appellate court here relied on Inter Insurance Exchange of Chicago Motor Club v. Andersen (1947), 331 Ill.App. 250, 73 N.E.2d 12, * * * In *Andersen,* the insurer, after paying its insured under a collision policy, brought a subrogation action against the tortfeasor for property damage to the insured's automobile; it also joined the insured as a defendant, alleging that, by executing the release, he failed to protect the insurer's subrogation rights as required by the insurance contract. The tortfeasor invoked a release, signed only by the insured, as a bar to the insurer's action. Faced with deciding whether the tortfeasor or the insured should protect the insurer's subrogation interest, the appellate court chose the insured because he had a contractual relationship with the insurer while the tortfeasor did not. The court in *Andersen* acknowledged that "[t]he general rule seems to be that where the wrongdoer procures a release from the insured with knowledge that the insurance has been paid, the release is no bar to an action by the subrogee insurer against the wrongdoer" (331 Ill.App. 250, 254, 73 N.E.2d 12, 14), but it found that "[t]he goal of prudence in one's conduct would seem to be reached more truly by making the insured duty bound to refrain from executing a release except with the approval of the insurer" (331 Ill.App. 250, 256, 73 N.E.2d 12, 15).

While our appellate court has adhered to this position, authority elsewhere is to the contrary, allowing the insurer to recover from the tortfeasor. [Citations from 21 states omitted.]

The difficulty with the *Andersen* rule, in our opinion, is that its application in the circumstances here is fundamentally unfair to both the insured and his insurer. Denied enforcement of its subrogation rights against the real wrongdoer, the insurer must instead seek recovery from its own insured, an obviously unpalatable alternative. Thus the tortfeasor and his own liability insurer, if any, escape payment for damage caused by the tortfeasor, while the tort victim is effectively denied payment from his own insurance carrier *and* from the tortfeasor. The *Andersen* rule in these circumstances constitutes a trap for the unwary insured plaintiff. While no fraud is alleged here, the rule itself encourages fraud or, at the very least, sharp practice on the part of the tortfeasor or his insurance carrier. The insured may be an unsophisticated, unrepresented party presented with a full and final release which he is told he must sign in order to effect a needed settlement. To require him to execute a release of all claims, even though the tortfeasor has knowledge of the insurer's interest and the probable existence of a standard insurance policy provision obligating the insured to protect the insurer's subrogation rights, is simply not consistent with fair dealing and ought not to be encouraged. In short, adoption of the *Andersen* rule would (1) permit the tortfeasor to escape liability for the amounts paid by the insurer, (2) require the tort victim to go uncompensated as to the amounts paid by the insurer even though he has paid insurance premiums and has also suffered loss at the hands of the tortfeasor defendant, (3) force the insurer to sue his own injured insured, and (4) place a premium on sharp practice and dishonesty. Simply put, the *Andersen* rule produces, in our judgment, an inequitable result and ought not to be applied in the circumstances before us.

* * *

REVERSED AND REMANDED.

Note

Cooperation and Subrogation.

Paxton National Ins. Co. v. Brickajlik, 513 Pa. 627, 522 A.2d 531 (1987):

"* * * Mr. William Brickajlik, [is] the owner of a truck which was stolen while in the possession of a service station. Based on a written policy insuring against theft, the insurance company reimbursed Mr. Brickajlik for his loss. The reimbursement was $3,350. The insurance company then attempted to bring a third-party action against the service station, but despite three written requests by the insurance company and similar requests by the insurance company's counsel, Mr. Brickajlik refused to sign the complaint. The insurance company then commenced an action against Mr. Brickajlik to recover the $3,350 paid on account of Mr. Brickajlik's loss, plus interest.

[Both lower courts ruled that Mr. B's refusal to sign the complaint constituted a breach of both the subrogation and co-operation clauses in the policy. The intermediate court, however, ruled for the insured on the basis that the insurer failed to show the breach was material. Finally, the Pennsylvania Supreme Court set matters straight].

"The question then remains whether Mr. Brickajlik's breach was a material one. * * *

"By the strict rules of the common law, the right to subrogation could only be enforced in the name of the creditor, 73 Am.Jur.2d, Subrogation, § 139; however, in Pennsylvania we have long recognized the right of a subrogee to sue in either his own name or the name of the subrogor to recover monies paid. Slack v. Kirk, 67 Pa. 380, 385, 5 A. 438

(1871). Thus, the insurance company could properly assess its prospects for success and, in accordance with its assessment, elect to bring the third-party action in either its name or the name of its insured.

"The general rule in Pennsylvania is that evidence of insurance is irrelevant and prejudicial and justifies grant of a mistrial. The reason is obvious: fact-finders should not be tempted to render decisions based upon the extraneous consideration that an insurance company will actually pay the bill. In view of the potential for prejudice to the insurance company if its presence were made known to the fact-finder, the insurance company properly elected to proceed against the third party in the name of its subrogor. As noted by the trial court, '[T]he insurance company's case would almost certainly be stronger if filed in the name of the insured.' We cannot, consistent with the general policy of excluding evidence of insurance coverage, conclude that Mr. Brickajlik's refusal to sign the complain, thus forcing the insurance company to proceed in its own name, was merely a technical breach. Thus we hold that Mr. Brickajlik was reasonably requested to sign the complaint in the third-party action and his refusal to do so constituted a material breach of the agreement justifying a return of the proceeds paid under the policy.

"Reversed."

EXECUTIVE JET AVIATION, INC. v. UNITED STATES

United States Court of Appeals, Sixth Circuit, 1974.
507 F.2d 508.

PHILLIPS, CHIEF JUDGE.

* * *

On July 28, 1968, one of Executive Jet's aircraft crashed on take off from the Cleveland, Ohio, airport after its engines had ingested a large number of seagulls that had been roosting on the runway. The plane was covered by a $1,300,000 policy of aircraft hull insurance issued by a group of British insurance companies. On October 17, 1968, Executive Jet received $1,300,000 from the insurers pursuant to a typical loan receipt agreement, under which Executive Jet was obligated to make repayment only out of any net recovery it might obtain from those liable for the crash. In addition, the agreement required that Executive Jet stand ready to institute suit in its own name for the purpose of effecting such a recovery. The insurers, however, were to bear the expense and to assume direction and control of any such litigation.

By letter dated May 6, 1969, Executive Jet submitted to the Federal Aviation Administration a written claim in the amount of $1,763,643.64. The letter made no reference to the insurers or to the loan receipt agreement.

On May 12, 1969, Executive Jet filed a complaint against the United States in the action out of which this appeal arises, alleging negligence on the part of the FAA air traffic controllers in not warning of the presence of seagulls on the runway and praying for $1,763,643.64 in damages. In an answer filed July 24, 1969, the Government raised several issues, including the defense that Executive Jet was not the real party in interest.

In an unreported opinion rendered on November 2, 1973, the District Court looked to the law of Ohio as stated in Cleveland Paint & Color Co. v. Bauer Manufacturing Co., 155 Ohio St. 17, 97 N.E.2d 545 (1951), and concluded that the loan receipt arrangement was a mere fiction that would not avoid subrogation. Thus the insurers, rather than Executive Jet, were held to be the real parties in interest. The court noted in passing that even if federal law were to control the effect of the loan receipt, the same result would be achieved under what the court considered the better federal rule announced in City Stores Co. v. Lerner Shops, Inc., 133 U.S.App.D.C. 311, 410 F.2d 1010 (1969). Further, the District Court held that because the insurers had not filed an administrative claim within two years of the accident as required by 28 U.S.C.A. § 2401(b), the insurers could not be joined as plaintiffs. Therefore, the court dismissed the complaint with prejudice, and Executive Jet perfected this appeal.

In the view that we take of this case, we need not decide whether the effect of the loan receipt arrangement is governed by state or federal law. It is conceded that under the law of Ohio payment pursuant to a loan receipt is considered outright payment and does not avoid subrogation of the insurer. Cleveland Paint & Color Co. v. Bauer Mfg. Co., supra, 155 Ohio St. 17, 97 N.E.2d 545 (1951). In our opinion the federal courts should follow the same rule. Thus we would reach the same result on the subrogation issue regardless of whether we apply the State law of Ohio or federal law.

Executive Jet insists that the federal practice has been to respect the form of loan receipts and to find no subrogation when this device is employed. Principal reliance is placed on Luckenbach v. W.J. McCahan Sugar Refining Co., 248 U.S. 139, 39 S.Ct. 53, 63 L.Ed. 170 (1918), an admiralty case in which the Supreme Court considered a loan receipt transaction and found "no good reason * * * either for questioning its legality or for denying it effect." Id. at 148, 39 S.Ct. at 55. *Luckenbach,* however, is distinguishable because of its unusual factual setting. In that case the insurer was liable only contingently—it would have incurred liability to the insured shipper only after it had been established that recovery against the carrier for the lost cargo was impossible. Furthermore, if the insurer had paid the shipper outright before the carrier's liability had been determined, the carrier would have become liable to no one. Therefore, the loan receipt device was used so that the insured would not be deprived of the use of the money for which either the insurer or the carrier eventually would incur liability.

Thus in *Luckenbach* there were present at least some of the indicia of a true loan. In the case at bar, not only were the insurers absolutely liable to Executive Jet, but the terms of the loan did not require repayment of a definite sum at a definite time and did not assess any interest charges. Nor is it mere coincidence that the amount loaned was precisely equal to the aircraft's agreed value in the insurance policy. Further, we note that under the loan receipt agreement the insurers assumed the expense, control, and direction of litigation against any third parties who might be liable for the plane crash. This, of course, is precisely the result that would be achieved in the ordinary case of payment and subrogation. These circumstances lead us to conclude that the transfer of $1,300,000 to Executive Jet was a loan in name only. In fact it was an outright settlement of a loss covered under the insurance policy, and we are unwilling to permit the form of the transaction to control its substance.

Executive Jet insists, however, that it does not rely solely upon *Luckenbach* and that subsequent federal cases have given literal effect to loan receipt agreements in circumstances similar to those in the case at bar. Executive Jet refers us particularly to Augusta Broadcasting Co. v. United States, 170 F.2d 199 (5th Cir.1948), a case under the Tort Claims Act in which the court held "that the giving of the loan receipt did not affect [the insured's] right to sue * * *." Id. at 200. However, the court in that case stated its conclusion without any reasoning or analysis. Moreover, it appeared to rely only on *Luckenbach* and a decision by the Georgia Court of Appeals. Obviously the Georgia case can provide no support for Executive Jet's position, and insofar as *Augusta Broadcasting* relies on *Luckenbach,* its theoretical underpinnings seem weak.

In many of the other cases cited by Executive Jet as authority for giving literal effect to loan receipts, the court looked for guidance to *Luckenbach* or to state law or to both. See, e.g., Sanders v. Liberty Mut. Ins. Co., 354 F.2d 777 (5th Cir.1965); Export Leaf Tobacco Co. v. American Ins. Co., 260 F.2d 839 (4th Cir.1958); Dixey v. Federal Compress & Warehouse Co., 132 F.2d 275 (8th Cir.1942); First Nat'l Bank v. Lloyd's of London, 116 F.2d 221 (7th Cir.1940). These cases would seem subject to the same observations we made about *Augusta Broadcasting.* In any event, we do not find the reasoning in this line of cases to be compelling in the case at bar.

On the other hand, we note that our conclusion is supported by the relatively recent case of City Stores Co. v. Lerner Shops, Inc., supra, 133 U.S.App.D.C. 311, 410 F.2d 1010 (1969). In this case the court first analyzed *Luckenbach* and found it not controlling. It could discern only one purpose for the use of a loan receipt—to avoid subrogation and thereby to circumvent the requirement of the Federal Rules that "[e]very action shall be prosecuted in the name of the real party in interest." Fed.R.Civ.P. 17(a). The court summed up its views about loan receipts as follows:

> "It does not seem sensible to say that an insured who has been paid in full by his insurer is nevertheless the real party in interest merely because of a sham 'loan agreement' which is a transparent

> subterfuge to avoid subrogation and to evade a federal rule." 410 F.2d at 1015.

We agree with the reasoning and with the decision in the *City Stores* case, and we note that it does not stand alone among federal cases in refusing to give literal effect to a loan receipt. See Potomac Elec. Power Co. v. Babcock & Wilcox Co., 54 F.R.D. 486, 489 (D.Md.1972) (concluding that a loan receipt "hardly amounts to a bona fide loan"); Condor Inv. Co. v. Pacific Coca-Cola Bottling Co., 211 F.Supp. 671 (D.Or.1962) (finding outright payment despite use of loan receipt).

We hold, then, that despite the use of the loan receipt, when the insurers in this case transferred $1,300,000 to Executive Jet, they became subrogated to Executive Jet's claims against the Government. That being so, the insurers are real parties in interest under Federal Rule 17(a) to the extent of the payment. United States v. Aetna Cas. & Sur. Co., 338 U.S. 366, 380–382, 70 S.Ct. 207, 94 L.Ed. 171 (1949).

Note

Notwithstanding the principal case, the loan receipt is commonly used in many states. The following form for a loan receipt is taken from *Pennsylvania Lumbermens Mutual Insurance Co. v. Thomason*, 178 F.Supp. 382 (D.C.N.C.1959):

> "Loan Receipt $______ [*Place*], [*Date*]
>
> "Upon receipt from ______ Insurance Company ______ Dollars as a loan and repayable only to the extent of any net recovery I/We may make from any person or persons, corporation or corporations, on account of loss by ______ to our property on or about ______ 19__.
>
> "As security for such repayment I/We hereby pledge to said ______ the said recovery and deliver to it all documents necessary to show my/our interest in said property, and we agree to enter and prosecute in my/our name, suit against such person or persons, corporation or corporations, on account of said claim for said loss, with all due diligence, at the expense and under the exclusive direction and control of said insurance company.
>
> "I/We certify that no settlement has been made by me/us with any person or persons, corporation or corporations, who may be responsible for said loss. Any money paid me/us by any other participant in loss is held in trust pending instructions by Insurance Company.
>
> "______
>
> "By ______
>
> "President"

Chapter 7

PERSONAL INSURANCE

INTRODUCTION

Much of the material in this section will be familiar. The cases contain many of the same principles discussed above in a context specific application interspersed with principles unique to personal insurance.

A. INSURANCE OF THE PERSON

PRELIMINARY NOTE

Insurance of the person provides for payment upon the occurrence of death, personal injury or sickness. Forms of coverage can include life insurance, accident insurance, and health insurance. Policies can also provide for annuities; that is, the policy may provide for the payment of a fixed monthly or annual sum after the insured has reached a certain age. Most commonly, annuities are purchased separately by people who earn very large sums during a short period of their lives, e.g. movie stars, baseball players, boxers, etc.

Life insurance policies can be organized into two main types of products: "term" insurance and "whole-life" or "ordinary life" insurance.

Term policies provide a specified amount (the "face value" of the policy) to the designated beneficiaries if the person whose life is insured dies during the coverage period which can be one, five or more years. Term policies might also depend on certain activities undertaken by an insured, e.g., while the insured is employed by a given employer, or while the insured is on a trip. "Convertible" term policies give the insured the right to change the contract to a whole-life one, often without requiring proof of insurability. Term policy premiums are calculated according to life expectancy ascertained from actuarial tables. Very often, employers provide policies to be effective during the period of employment. These policies vary, but commonly they are of the "group" insurance variety whereby an employer's work force may elect to become members of the group. Especially common among larger employers are "group health" and "accident" policies under which coverage may extend into the employee's retirement. The broad subject of health care insurance is a matter of national concern at the time this is written.

Whole-life or ordinary life policies are quite different. The intent behind these policies is that the insured will by monthly or yearly premium payments provide the insurance company with a sum of money to cover losses (that is, death benefits) and expenses, and build up equity. Insurers invest the premium such that the sum will grow. Naturally, enough money has to be produced to pay the company for its costs of doing business, and, if the insurer is a stock company, a hoped for profit.

The making of a whole-life policy is considerably different from the making of a term policy. Whole-life policies are solicited from prospective insured by salesmen. A sometimes complicated application disclosing such matters as the applicant's health and other factors has to be filed, and the insured is normally required to have a physical exam given by a physician selected by the insurer. The results of the physical and the revelations in the application are then evaluated by the company, which, if it approves, issues the policy.

A number of parties may be associated with the making of a whole-life policy, two of whom are the insured and the insurer. However, the applicant and owner of the policy may not be the person whose life is covered; among other possibilities, the latter may be the spouse, parent, child, or employer. The person whose life is covered is sometimes called the "cestui que vie." If the policy is payable to a third party, that party is called the "beneficiary." Obviously, questions of insurable interest will arise, although it is ordinarily said that a person has an unquestionable interest in his own life. Indeed, a frequently issued policy is one taken out by "John Jones" on his own life, payable to his own estate.

One of the most interesting features of the whole-life policy is the accumulation of equity, which, as time passes may amount to a considerable asset. Protection of this asset against forfeiture (by non-payment of premium, let us say, when the policy is in its twentieth year) has been a concern of lawmakers. As a result, several financial features are noteworthy. Policyholder rights include the right to obtain a loan against the policy, the right to "cash it in" by surrendering the policy in return for payment of a stipulated value, and the right to have the policy's equity applied to premiums in case the policyholder is no longer able to make payments. Certain other rights are interesting: the insured benefits by a "grace period" (for late payments, e.g. 30 days), and the policy becomes "incontestable" after a given period. "Incontestability" applies primarily to the insurer's right to rescind the policy for fraud or mistake.

There are numerous variations on the whole-life policy. For example, some allow insured directed investment strategies and others are structured to meet the insured's cash-flow profile. "Participating" policies include plans under which the insured is entitled to dividends which may be used to offset premium payments or increase the coverage by adding to the cash value. For additional information on the coverage and variations see Keeton and Widiss, *Insurance Law,* § 1.5(c) (1988), Appleman, *Insurance Law and Practice,* §§ 1–90 (1981), Couch, *Couch on Insurance 2d,* §§ 1:73–1:78 (1984).

1. Contract Formation and Conditional Receipts

As a preliminary matter, a fundamental tension in marketing life insurance products is the insurer's desire to delay coverage until after it has had an opportunity to evaluate the risk, while simultaneously emotionally binding the applicant at time of application by securing payment of part or all of the first premium. The case that follows explores the twilight zone created by the conditional receipt and the familiar complication of agency and fraud or mistake.

RINER v. ALLSTATE LIFE INSURANCE CO.

United States Court of Appeals, Fifth Circuit, 1997.
131 F.3d 530.

DEMOSS, CIRCUIT JUDGE:

Annette Riner (Riner) and Suzette Marriott (Marriott) sued Allstate Life Insurance Company (Allstate) after Allstate refused to pay benefits under a temporary insurance agreement on the life of their father, Robert Marriott (Mr. Marriott). Allstate defended on the theory that alleged misrepresentations in the insurance application absolved it of liability. The district court granted summary judgment in favor of Allstate, and Riner and Marriott appealed. We reverse the district court's judgment in favor of Allstate and render judgment in favor of Riner and Marriott on the issue of coverage. We remand the cause to the district court for further development of the remaining liability issues and for a determination of damages.

MATERIAL FACTS

Prior to 1994, Mr. Marriott had five back surgeries, which left him with chronic back pain. That back pain became aggravated and was joined by a feeling of loneliness and sadness after his wife of more than thirty years left him. Following his divorce in June 1994, Mr. Marriott wanted to replace his life insurance policy, which named his ex-wife as beneficiary, with a new policy naming his daughters as beneficiaries.

Riner referred Mr. Marriott to an Allstate agent. On June 29, 1994, Allstate sent an agent to Mr. Marriott's home to take his application information. Allstate's lengthy standardized application contained a list of medical questions. The applicant responded to those questions by checking boxes marked "yes" or "no." When a box was marked "yes," the application contained additional space for further explanation by the applicant. Mr. Marriott disclosed that he had chronic back problems and certain other medical problems. Mr. Marriott's application is marked "no," however, with respect to whether he had ever received treatment for the use of alcohol or received treatment for depression within the past three years.

Mr. Marriott explained to the agent that he was "groggy" from medication he was taking for back pain. After completing the application, the agent requested an initial premium check in the amount of $276.23. The record reflects that Mr. Marriott was too affected by the painkillers he was taking to complete the check. For that reason, the agent completed the premium check, which was then signed by Mr. Marriott.[1] In return, the agent issued a "Receipt and Temporary Insurance Agreement" to Mr. Marriott. Although the agent left a copy of the agreement, the agent did not leave a copy of Mr. Marriott's application with Mr. Marriott. The temporary insurance agreement provided that Mr. Marriott's premium was received as "payment for life insurance" in the amount of $100,000. The agreement further provided that temporary coverage would start when Mr. Marriott's medical exam was completed. Mr. Marriott completed the medical exam on July 26, 1994.

Six days after the exam, Mr. Marriott died suddenly of either an aneurism or heart disease. Thereafter, his daughters made a claim under the temporary insurance agreement. On the claim form, Suzette Marriott indicated that Mr. Marriott was seeing a doctor for "depression/chronic pain." Allstate requested Mr. Marriott's medical records and began an investigation to determine whether it would pay benefits under the temporary insurance agreement. Three months later, Allstate denied liability under the temporary insurance agreement. Allstate denied liability because it concluded that, contrary to Mr. Marriott's answers in the application, he had received treatment for his use of alcohol and for depression.

PROCEEDINGS IN THE DISTRICT COURT

Mr. Marriott's beneficiaries, Riner and Marriott, sued Allstate in Texas state court. Allstate properly removed the matter to federal court. In federal court, Riner and Marriott amended their complaint, alleging that Allstate's refusal to pay violated certain provisions of the Texas Insurance Code and the Texas Deceptive Trade Practices Act. Riner and Marriott also contended that Allstate's actions constituted a breach of contract and a breach of Allstate's duty of good faith and fair dealing. Allstate answered that Mr. Marriott's misrepresentations in the application absolved it of all liability.

Riner and Marriott moved for summary judgment on the issue of Allstate's liability, arguing that Allstate could not rely upon any misrepresentations in the application to deny coverage because Allstate failed to attach a copy of Mr. Marriott's application to the temporary insurance agreement, as required by article 21.35 of the Texas Insurance Code.

Allstate responded that it was not required to attach the application because the temporary insurance agreement was not a "contract or

1. Although the record does not conclusively establish whether the Allstate agent or Mr. Marriott completed the application form, the handwriting and tone of the answers is most consistent with the conclusion that the Allstate agent completed the application for Mr. Marriott, a fact that is clearly relevant with respect to whether Mr. Marriott's answers were intentionally deceitful.

policy of insurance" within the meaning of article 21.35. Alternatively, Allstate maintained that its delivery of the application and temporary insurance agreement to Mr. Marriott's beneficiaries after the death claim was filed satisfied the requirements of article 21.35. Allstate did not file its own motion for summary judgment.

The district court, acting sua sponte and without notice to the parties, granted summary judgment in favor of Allstate. The district court held that the temporary insurance agreement was not a "contract or policy of insurance" within the meaning of article 21.35. Instead, the district court reasoned that the temporary insurance agreement was merely a promise to provide insurance relating back to the date of application, if and when Mr. Marriott was determined to be an acceptable risk. Alternatively, the district court held that Allstate did not breach its statutory obligation to attach the application to the temporary insurance agreement because Part 2 of the application, which recorded Mr. Marriott's medical examination, was not completed until he was examined on July 26, 1994.

Riner and Marriott moved for reconsideration of the district court's denial of their motion for summary judgment and the district court's sua sponte entry of summary judgment in favor of Allstate. The motion was denied, and Riner and Marriott appealed both the final judgment and the district court's denial of their motion for reconsideration.

Discussion

I.

Allstate Issued an Enforceable Contract for Temporary Insurance

To resolve this appeal, we must first determine whether the temporary insurance agreement provided to Mr. Marriott was a "contract of insurance," as Riner and Marriott claim, or instead a conditional offer to provide coverage, as Allstate claims and the district court held.

Texas law governs our interpretation of the temporary insurance agreement. We review the district court's interpretation of Allstate's temporary insurance agreement de novo. Gladney v. Paul Revere Life Ins. Co., 895 F.2d 238, 241 (5th Cir.1990) (reviewing the district court's interpretation of Mississippi insurance law).

Allstate argues that a receipt and temporary insurance agreement is a novel creature that can never be a "contract or policy of insurance" as contemplated by article 21.35. See Tex.Ins.Code art. 21.35 (Vernon Supp.1998) (requiring that the application be attached to "every contract or policy of insurance"). We disagree. Texas law recognizes that a receipt and temporary insurance agreement can create a binding contract to provide temporary insurance. See, e.g., United Founders Life Ins. Co. v. Carey, 363 S.W.2d 236, 240–43 (Tex.1962) (receipt issued with application may create enforceable contract for temporary insurance); Life Ins. Co. of the Southwest v. Nims, 512 S.W.2d 712, 714 (Tex.Civ.App.—San Antonio 1974, no writ) (binder and receipt issued by insurance company upon payment of initial premium held to be contract of insurance); South Coast Life Ins. Co. v. Robertson, 483 S.W.2d 388, 391 (Tex.Civ. App.—Tyler 1972, writ ref'd n.r.e.) ("It has been held by the Supreme Court that conditional receipts such as the one presently before us provide for temporary life insurance."). Whether any particular agreement for temporary insurance is a "contract of insurance" depends upon the language of the particular agreement, as interpreted using ordinary rules of contract construction. Carey, 363 S.W.2d at 241 ("the wording of the particular receipt in controversy controls" whether a receipt creates an enforceable contract affording temporary coverage). When there is doubt about whether the agreement provides temporary coverage, or merely a conditional promise to consider the application, the construction that affords coverage will be adopted. See id. at 242–43; see also Blaylock v. American Guar. Bank Liab. Ins. Co., 632 S.W.2d 719, 721 (Tex.1982) (setting forth the general rule for determining whether coverage exists). "The policy of strict construction against the insurer is especially strong when the court is dealing with exceptions and words of limitation."

The temporary insurance agreement issued to Mr. Marriott provides that $276.73 has been received "as payment for life insurance," subject to certain limitations defined in the agreement. Under a heading entitled "When Temporary Insurance Starts," the agreement provides that insurance will start on the date of the agreement, provided that (1) payment is accepted, (2) Part 1 of the application (containing the medical questionnaire) is completed, and (3) Question 25 of the application does not call for a medical exam. If, as in Mr. Marriott's case, the application requires a medical exam, then the agreement specifies that insurance will start when the contemplated medical exam is complete.

Under a heading entitled "When Temporary Insurance Will Stop," the agreement provides that temporary insurance will end when the first of any of the following conditions occurs: (1) Allstate provides notice that it is no longer considering the application; (2) Allstate provides notice that further medical exams in addition to the one requested in Question 25 of the application are required; (3) Allstate agrees to provide the coverage applied for in the application; (4) Allstate agrees to provide coverage other than as applied for in the application; or (5) sixty days passes. With respect to Allstate's decision to provide the coverage applied for, the agreement states that the permanent insurance "will then be provided by the policy as of its start date and not by this Agreement."

Under a heading entitled "Amount of Insurance," the agreement provides that the temporary insurance will have the same benefits, provisions and limitations as the plan applied for, subject to a limitation of $500,000 "under this Agreement and all other Agreements issued for pending applications for each person to whom this receipt applies."

Under a heading entitled "Conditions Under Which There is No Coverage," the agreement provides, in relevant part, "[i]f in the answers in the application, there is fraud or misrepresentation material to the home office underwriter's acceptance of the risk, then no insurance starts under the Agreement."

Finally, at the very bottom of the agreement, and below the signature line, there is an "agent reminder" that states: "If there is any 'Yes' answer to questions 9, 10, 11, 12 or 13, DO NOT accept money or give this receipt. Submit a trial application."

For the reasons that follow, we conclude that Allstate is obligated to pay proceeds to Riner and Marriott under the terms of the temporary insurance agreement.

II.

Temporary Insurance Started When Mr. Marriott Completed His Medical Exam

The district court held that Mr. Marriott did not apply for "gap" coverage. Instead, the district court found that the temporary insurance agreement was nothing more than a promise to provide coverage that related back to the application date if and when Allstate determined that Mr. Marriott was an acceptable risk.

The district court's construction is negated by the plain language of the agreement. The agreement states that insurance will start when Mr. Marriott's medical exams are complete. There is no language in the agreement either implicitly or explicitly conditioning the start date for temporary insurance upon Mr. Marriott's insurability or Allstate's acceptance of the risk. To the contrary, the structure of the agreement is such that temporary insurance does not terminate when Allstate determines not to accept the risk, unless Allstate provides written notice to the applicant. Moreover, the temporary insurance does terminate when Allstate decides to accept the risk by issuing permanent coverage. Further, the terms of the agreement provide that the temporary insurance, which takes effect once the medical exam is completed, is supplanted by the permanent policy, which takes effect "as of its start date and not by" the terms of the temporary insurance agreement. Based upon the plain language of the agreement, we cannot agree with the district court's finding that the temporary insurance agreement was a relation-back policy that did not provide coverage until Allstate approved the risk. Indeed, the plain and unambiguous language of the agreement exhibits an intent to provide temporary or "gap" coverage during the period that Mr. Marriott's application was pending.

The agreement provides that "[i]f the answer to Question 25 in the application is 'Yes,' temporary insurance on each person named in Question 25 will start when all medical exams are completed for that person." Allstate keys into the use of the plural form "exams" to argue that no contract of insurance arose under the agreement because it could have required additional examinations after reviewing the initial examination required by Question 25 of the application. Although facially appealing, Allstate's argument fails when viewed in light of other contract provisions.

The provision stating when insurance will start refers to medical exams contemplated by Question 25 in the application. Similarly, the agreement provides that insurance will stop "the date we write to the Owner that a medical exam is required (other than any exams referred to in Question 25), in which event insurance will stop with respect only to the person(s) required to have a medical exam." Thus, the agreement requires that Allstate provide written notice that additional medical examinations are required. Until such notice is provided, the temporary coverage arising under the agreement continues. For that reason, Allstate's argument that it retained an unconditional right to consider asking for more medical exams, and that no insurance arose until it signaled its agreement to accept Mr. Marriott's application, must fail.

The district court also held that the agreement lacked a required element of mutuality because Allstate retained the unilateral right to terminate both the temporary insurance and the pending application for permanent coverage. We cannot agree. Both sides offered valuable consideration. Mr. Marriott paid an initial premium in exchange for Allstate's promise to provide temporary coverage when Mr. Marriott completed the medical examination. While it is true that Allstate retained the right to unilaterally terminate consideration of Mr. Marriott's application, the agreement required that Allstate provide notice that it intended to exercise that option. Texas law does not require that every right or obligation by one party be met with an identical right or obligation in the other. Howell v. Murray Mortgage. Co., 890 S.W.2d 78, 87 (Tex.App.—Amarillo 1994, writ denied) ("Generally there is mutuality in the case of mutual promises by both parties to the contract which furnish a consideration each for the other, or where both parties undertake to do something—even though every obligation of one party is not met by an equivalent counter obligation of the other."). Moreover, Allstate's right to void coverage at its option did not render the contract void or unenforceable when Allstate did not, in fact, exercise that option, but instead embarked upon performance by considering Mr. Marriott's application.

Mr. Marriott applied for binding temporary coverage that was not conditioned upon Allstate's acceptance of his application. Absent some other policy defense, the terms of the policy require the conclusion that the temporary coverage arose when Mr. Marriott completed the medical examination on July 26, 1994 as required by the application.

III.

Temporary Insurance Was Not Terminated

Moreover, none of the six conditions that could have terminated the temporary coverage occurred. Allstate did not provide notice one way or the other regarding its decision on Mr. Marriott's application for permanent insurance. Allstate did not notify Mr. Marriott that it was going to require additional medical examinations. Finally, the sixty-day time period during which the agreement could remain valid did not expire.

Thus, none of the conditions which are defined in the agreement as capable of terminating coverage occurred. Allstate's obligation under the temporary agreement arose on July 26, 1994 and, absent some other factor, was in effect at the time of Mr. Marriott's death.

IV.

ALLSTATE'S ATTEMPT TO CONDITION COVERAGE UPON TRUTHFUL APPLICATION ANSWERS WAS INEFFECTIVE AS A MATTER OF LAW

Allstate attempts to avoid the conclusion that it must pay benefits under the temporary insurance agreement by arguing that no contract was formed because truthful application answers were a condition precedent to coverage. Thus, Allstate maintains that Mr. Marriott's alleged misrepresentations preceded and avoided the formation of any contract.

Reading the agreement leaves no doubt that Allstate intended to condition coverage upon truthful answers in the separate application. The agreement specifies that "no insurance will start if the application contains fraud or misrepresentation that is material to the underwriter's acceptance of the risk." The plain language of the agreement supports Allstate's position that no contract was formed. That position is defeated, however, by Texas statutory and common law limiting the effect that untruthful answers in a life insurance application can have on coverage.

Under Texas law, the responses given in a life insurance application are mere representations, rather than warranties that would be capable of making coverage void or voidable. Short of inserting an unambiguous "good health warranty" demonstrating that the parties intended the contract to rise or fall on the literal truth of an insured's general certification of good health,[2] Texas has not allowed an insurer to change that result by contracting to make truthful application answers a condition precedent to coverage. See Mayes v. Massachusetts Mutual Life Ins. Co., 608 S.W.2d 612, 616; Cartusciello, 661 S.W.2d at 286 88; see also 48 TEX.JUR.3D Insurance Contracts and Coverage §§ 544–45 (1995). Rather, article 21.16 and article 21.35 of the Texas Insurance Code prescribe the effect that untruthful answers in an application can have on coverage. Article 21.16 provides that a provision making coverage void or voidable based upon misrepresentation in an insurance application is of no effect. Tex.Ins.Code art. 21.16 (Vernon 1981). An insured's misrepresentation in an application is, of course, a serious matter. But the insurer's remedy is limited to an affirmative policy defense, which is available only when the representation is material and the application is attached to the contract or policy of insurance. Id.; Tex.Ins.Code art. 21.35 (Vernon Supp.1998).

2. In an insurance contract, a warranty is a statement made by the insured, which is susceptible to no construction other than that the parties mutually intended that the policy should not be binding unless such statement be literally true. Lane v. Travelers Indem. Co., 391 S.W.2d 399, 402 (Tex. 1965). Warranties in insurance applications are strongly disfavored in the law, and even fairly obvious attempts to create warranties in the application process have been rejected by Texas courts. See, e.g., Cartusciello, 661 S.W.2d at 287; Allied Bankers Life Ins. Co. v. De La Cerda, 584 S.W.2d 529, 532 (Tex.Civ.App.—Amarillo 1979, writ ref'd n.r.e.).

Allstate does not cite any Texas authority to the contrary. Instead, Allstate relies primarily upon Gladney v. Paul Revere Life Ins. Co., 895 F.2d 238 (5th Cir.1990) for the premise that an insurer may place conditions precedent in a temporary insurance agreement. Our decision is not in conflict with that modest premise. We agree that a Texas insurer may impose many different types of conditions precedent upon both temporary and permanent coverage. See, e.g., Mayes, 608 S.W.2d at 616 (recognizing the enforceability of a good health warranty); Blagg, 438 S.W.2d at 907; Carey, 363 S.W.2d at 238; Harp, 577 S.W.2d at 747; Nims, 512 S.W.2d at 714; Robertson, 483 S.W.2d at 390 (all recognizing the enforceability of a condition precedent requiring insurability, acceptability, or both).

More importantly, Gladney is a diversity case applying Mississippi law. The rule limiting the effect of a provision conditioning life insurance coverage upon truthful application answers is a creature of Texas law. Regardless of what Mississippi is willing to tolerate, Texas law forbids our giving effect to a provision making truthful application answers a condition precedent to temporary life insurance coverage. Thus, the provision identified by Allstate is insufficient to defeat contract formation.

V.

Allstate is Precluded from Relying upon Representations in Mr. Marriott's Application to Avoid Coverage

Allstate may still assert an affirmative defense based upon Mr. Marriott's misrepresentations, if any, in the application process. That defense is qualified, however, by the statutory rule that statements made in a life insurance application are not admissible to establish a misrepresentation unless the application is attached to and made part of the insurance policy. See Fredonia State Bank v. General American Life Ins. Co., 881 S.W.2d 279 (1994) (applying Tex.Ins.Code art. 21.35); National Lloyds Ins. Co. v. McCasland, 566 S.W.2d 565, 566 (Tex.1978) (failure to comply with article 21.35 "renders evidence of representations made in applying for insurance inadmissible into evidence"); Johnson v. Prudential Ins. Co., 519 S.W.2d 111, 114 (Tex.1975) ("Article 21.35 . . . has been repeatedly applied to prevent the use of statements of the insured which were not attached to the policy").

Allstate maintains that article 21.35 does not apply to contracts providing temporary insurance. Having already concluded that the temporary insurance agreement issued in this case was a "contract of insurance" under Texas law, we have no difficulty finding that the Texas legislature intended to include contracts affording temporary coverage within the realm of article 21.35.

Nothing in the plain language of article 21.35 excludes an agreement to provide temporary coverage from the scope of that article. To the contrary, the article provides that it applies to "every contract or policy of life insurance." We are persuaded, both by the Texas legislature's direct command to include "every" contract, and the legislature's attempt to distinguish between a "contract" and a "policy," that there is no principled basis for excluding contracts providing insurance for a limited period of time from the scope of article 21.35. For that reason, Allstate cannot avoid liability under the contract by claiming that the temporary insurance agreement was outside the scope of article 21.35.

We are also persuaded by the fact that the purpose of the statute is well served in this context. The purpose of the requirement embodied in article 21.35 is to provide a life insurance applicant with the opportunity to review and reconsider the answers provided in the application during his or her lifetime. Fredonia, 881 S.W.2d at 283. The record establishes that Mr. Marriott was severely compromised by the painkillers in his system. The Allstate agent was informed of Mr. Marriott's condition. Indeed, the record conclusively establishes that the Allstate agent filled out Mr. Marriott's premium check and strongly suggests that the agent also completed the lengthy and fact-intensive application form. Surely, leaving Mr. Marriott a copy of the completed application responses would have afforded him an opportunity to review his responses when he was unaffected by disabling pain medication. If that opportunity were provided, it is possible that Mr. Marriott would have corrected any misstatements concerning his medical condition.

Allstate warns that including temporary insurance agreements within that group of contracts subject to article 21.35 will render insurers unable to protect themselves from uninsurable risks. We disagree. First of all, Allstate could have made insurability or acceptability a condition precedent to coverage under the temporary insurance agreement. It did not do so. Moreover, Allstate could have protected itself from the effect of any misrepresentations by simply attaching a copy of the Mr. Marriott's application to the temporary insurance agreement. Once again, Allstate did not do so. Our holding is not that Allstate cannot protect itself from uninsurable risks, but that it failed to take those precautions in this case.

Allstate contends that it could not have attached the application because Part 2 (recording the medical examination) was not completed until July 26, almost one month after the temporary insurance agreement issued. We disagree. Mr. Marriott's answers to the key medical questions could have been left with Mr. Marriott on the evening he completed the application that was submitted to Allstate. Creating the application form in multiple parts to facilitate this procedure does not seem unduly burdensome. Allstate's argument is also self-defeating. Allstate could have provided Mr. Marriott with a copy of the application and temporary insurance agreement at the time of or immediately after the medical examination was completed. Allstate chose not to pursue this course of action either. Instead, the record supports the conclusion that Allstate did not provide either Mr. Marriott or his beneficiaries with a copy of Mr. Marriott's application until more than four months after his initial application, more than three months after his medical examination and subsequent death, and almost two months after the death claim was filed with Allstate. Even then, Allstate apparently ignored several requests for the document before tendering it to Mr. Marriott's beneficiaries.

Allstate's failure to attach the application, or to provide copies of the application together with the temporary insurance agreement within a reasonable time frame, means that Allstate cannot rely upon Mr. Marriott's representations in the application to avoid coverage. For that reason, whether Mr. Marriott misrepresented his medical history, whether Mr. Marriott intended to deceive Allstate, whether Mr. Marriott's misrepresentations would have been material to the risk assumed by Allstate, and other similar issues argued by the parties are immaterial. Stated simply, Mr. Marriott's misrepresentations, if any, in the application are inadmissible to assist Allstate's efforts to defeat coverage.

A grave danger in insurance cases, particularly when we are exercising our diversity jurisdiction, is that a particular holding will be read too broadly. Both sides of this dispute have cited cases to this Court for general propositions that fall apart once the specific language of the agreement in the cited case is compared with the specific language at issue in this case. Let there be no confusion. We are not purporting to define the precise language required to create an insurance contract. Neither do we establish any new or general rule that temporary insurance agreements, conditional receipts or binders do or do not create enforceable insurance contracts under Texas law. Rather, our conclusion that the temporary insurance agreement issued to Mr. Marriott was a "contract of insurance" subject to the requirements of article 21.35 is necessarily dependent upon the facts of this case. We do nothing more than interpret the agreement between these parties.

Conclusion

The temporary insurance agreement furnished to Mr. Marriott at the time he applied for life insurance with Allstate was a binding contract for temporary insurance coverage pending approval of his application with Allstate. Coverage began when Mr. Marriott completed the medical examination required by the application and was not terminated by the occurrence of any condition specified in the contract. Allstate's attempt to make truthful application answers a condition precedent to coverage is inconsistent with Texas law defining an insurer's qualified right to avoid coverage on the basis of an applicant's untruthful representations in a life insurance application.

Article 21.35 precludes an insurer from relying upon representations in a life insurance application unless a copy of the application is attached to and made part of the contract or policy of insurance. Allstate failed to leave Mr. Marriott with a copy of his application, either at the time of application or at the time that coverage became effective. Allstate's failure to comply with the relevant statutory provision renders any evidence that Mr. Marriott made misrepresentations in his application inadmissible and precludes Allstate's misrepresentation defense as a matter of law. Having advanced no other defense to liability, Allstate is obligated to provide benefits to Mr. Marriott's beneficiaries.

For the foregoing reasons, the district court's entry of summary judgment in favor of Allstate was improper, and Riner and Marriott are entitled to summary judgment on the issue of coverage. Although Riner and Marriott moved for summary judgment on the issue of Allstate's "liability," our holding cannot sweep so broadly. Riner and Marriott's claims for violation of the Texas Insurance Code and the Texas Deceptive Trade Practices Act and for violation of the common-law duty of good faith and fair dealing all involve some conduct on the part of the insurer that is in addition to and independent of the insurer's obligation to pay proceeds under the contract of insurance. With respect to these claims, the summary judgment record is insufficiently developed to justify a rendition of summary judgment in favor of Riner and Marriott on the issue of "liability." We must therefore remand the case for further development of the issues material to a determination of Allstate's liability on these claims.

Riner and Marriott also pleaded that Allstate's failure to pay benefits under the temporary insurance agreement was a breach of contract. With respect to that claim, our conclusion that Allstate is obligated to pay Riner and Marriott at least the $100,000 proceeds of the temporary insurance agreement is sufficient to support our rendition of judgment in favor of Riner and Marriott.

Accordingly, the district court's grant of summary judgment in favor of Allstate is REVERSED.

Judgment is RENDERED in favor of appellants Riner and Marriott on the issue of Allstate's obligation to provide coverage and benefits under the temporary insurance agreement and on the issue of Allstate's liability to Riner and Marriott for breach of contract.

The cause is REMANDED for further development of additional liability issues relating to Riner and Marriott's remaining claims for breach of the duty of good faith and fair dealing and for violations of the temporary insurance agreement and the Texas Deceptive Trade Practices Act, and for a determination of damages in addition to the $100,000 face amount of the temporary insurance agreement.

Notes

1. *Termination of "Temporary" Insurance.* In jurisdictions that hold that the conditional binder receipts create a temporary contract of life insurance, it might be assumed that a rejection of the application by the insurer would terminate the temporary contract. However in one of the more debatable aspects of the case of *Smith v. Westland Life Insurance Co.*, 15 Cal.3d 111, 123 Cal.Rptr. 649, 539 P.2d 433 (1975), the majority held that a notice of rejection delivered while the insured was still alive did not alone terminate the temporary policy; rather an actual return of the premium was also essential. Does such a requirement comport with the usual mechanical practices as to rescission of contracts?

2. In *Thomas v. Thomas*, 824 P.2d 971, 250 Kan. 235 (1992), the issue before the court was whether the decedent's life insurance was effective at the time of death because of the temporary coverage provided by a conditional receipt. The conditional receipt contained a provision that if an actual policy was not issued to applicant within 45 days of issuance of the receipt, then the application for insurance should be deemed declined. The insured died 165 days after the expiration of the conditional receipt, without paying any additional premiums towards the insurance and without inquiring as to the status of the application. The insurer argued that a previous decision, *Tripp v. Reliable Life Ins. Co.*, 210 Kan. 33, 499 P.2d 1155 (1972) should be overruled. *Tripp* held that a temporary insurance contract is created as a result of submission of an application for insurance, coupled with payment of the initial premium and issuance of a receipt. Further, this contract is in effect until the insurer declines the application, notifies the insured, and returns the premium. The *Thomas* court agreed with the insurer, concluding that the conditional receipt clearly stated that coverage expired after 45 days and no insurance was issued if no policy was delivered within that time period.

3. For a complex discussion of how a condition precedent (defendant's good faith determination that the applicant meet the defendant's standard of insurability) affects a conditional receipt of insurance, see *Rohde v. Massachusetts Mutual Life Ins. Co.*, 632 F.2d 667 (6th Cir.1980) (holding that defendant's failure to honor its good faith obligation deprives defendant of any obtainable benefit from that condition). The open question here is whether Massachusetts Mutual Life Insurance Co. has devised a conditional binder receipt so explicitly a condition precedent that it cannot be transmogrified into a condition subsequent by even the linguistic ingenuity of a Pennsylvania or California Supreme Court.

4. If the conditional receipt is apt to be turned into a temporary policy anyway, the obvious solution is for the insurer to substitute a specific term insurance policy, for 60–90 days perhaps, covering the period during which the application is being reviewed (charging, of course, an appropriate premium for the particular risk). Such policies are now available.

5. Other decisions have declared the "insurability" or "satisfaction" type of receipt to be unambiguous as a list of conditions precedent, but at the same time insist that the company's determination of "insurability" be exercised objectively and in good faith. The question of whether the applicant was indeed insurable under the company's standards is one to be answered by the trial court. See e.g. Hemenway v. MFA Life Ins. Co., 211 Neb. 193, 318 N.W.2d 70 (1982); Ford v. Lamar Life Ins. Co., 449 So.2d 1204 (Miss.1984) and Hildebrand v. Franklin Life Ins. Co., 118 Ill.App.3d 861, 74 Ill.Dec. 280, 455 N.E.2d 553 (1983). The *Hildebrand* opinion clarifies the standard of proof (455 N.E.2d at 565):

> " * * * [T]he necessary standard of insurability will be supplied by the company's own underwriting rules, limits, and standards [citation]. A standard prevalent in the industry but not shared by the company in question is irrelevant to the company's defense, yet the plaintiff may introduce it if that evidence shows that the company's evidence of its own standard is improbable. (See Simpson v. Prudential Insurance Co.

of America (1962), 227 Md. 393, 177 A.2d 417 (insurability receipt implies the existence of an objective standard of insurability; beneficiary must present a *prima facie* case of insurability and may rely on general industry standards; insurer may rebut with proof of its own standards).) The company's control over its own underwriting standards and its access to instant witnesses—its underwriters—entitle the plaintiff to present evidence of general underwriting standards for this limited purpose."

6. In *Mutual of Omaha Ins. Co. v. Russell*, 402 F.2d 339 (10th Cir.1968), the insured tried to buy a life insurance policy in an airport machine. The machine issued a round-trip policy labelled "T–20" policy but the insured lacked the change to purchase the machine policy. He went to the insurer's airport booth and was unwittingly sold a "T–18" policy which was more generous in benefits but was of a shorter term. The insured died in a plane crash 12 hours after the T–18 policy expired but before the T–20 policy would have expired. The court, noting the tension between guarding against fraud (despite the lack of fraud in the case) and upholding contract law held that the contract entered into should be the one enforced. The court further declined to create an obligation by insurers to inform insureds of policy differences. Recall *Steven v. Fidelity & Cas. Co.* discussed in Chapter 3 above.

2. The Insurable Interest Requirement

MUTUAL SAVINGS LIFE INSURANCE CO. v. NOAH

Supreme Court of Alabama, 1973.
291 Ala. 444, 282 So.2d 271, 60 A.L.R.3d 81.

HEFLIN, CHIEF JUSTICE.

[William Noah drowned. His brother, Donald, had taken out insurance policies on William's life, naming himself as beneficiary. Donald filed a claim on the policies which was refused by the insurer. This case originated as a declaratory judgment action by Donald. The trial court found in his favor.]

The most divisive issue with which this court is faced is presented by appellant-respondent's contention that Donald R. Noah has no insurable interest in the life of the insured, and that each of the three policies was invalid by reason thereof. It may be well to note at the outset that this court holds the burial policy not to be subject to the insurable interest requirement. * * *

Under the evidence the two life policies were procured or "taken out" (an expression used in our cases) by the beneficiary, and thus the long-established rule that the insurance is invalid unless the beneficiary has an "insurable interest" in the life of the insured applies. This rule is to the effect that a person has an unlimited insurable interest in his own life and may designate any person as his beneficiary so long as the insurance was procured or taken out by the insured and the premiums paid by him, but one taking out a policy of insurance for his own benefit, on the life of another person, must have an insurable interest in the continuance of the life of such insured. National Life & Accident Ins. Co. v. Alexander, 226 Ala. 325, 147 So. 173; Tit. 28A, § 316, Code of Alabama, 1940 (Recomp.1958).[3]

Several reasons have been assigned as the basis for the insurable interest requirement, both of which are grounded upon public policy considerations: a policy taken out by one for his own benefit on the life of another, in whom he has no insurable interest is, in substance, a wagering contract; and such a policy may hold out a temptation to the beneficiary to hasten by improper means the death of the insured. * * *

Certain blood relationships have been held sufficient, in and of themselves to negate the supposition that the beneficiary would take out such a policy for the purpose of wagering on the insured's death, or that such a policy would entice the beneficiary to take the insured's life, and in such cases the relationship alone is said to create an insurable interest. This is true notwithstanding the fact that the beneficiary may have no reasonable expectation of pecuniary advantage through the continued life of the insured or consequent loss by reason of his death, which would otherwise be required in order to find an insurable interest.

The relationship of husband and wife has been held to be sufficiently close to give either an insurable interest in the life of the other. Jennings v. Jennings, 250 Ala. 130, 33 So.2d 251. The parent-child relationship has been accorded the same status as that given to husband and wife in *Jennings*. Warnock v. Davis, 104 U.S. 775, 26 L.Ed. 924; 44 C.J.S. Insurance § 204.

On the other hand, the following relationships have been held not to create an insurable interest on the basis of such relationship alone. Cousin and cousin, National Life & Accident Ins. Co. v. Alexander, 226 Ala. 325, 147 So. 173; beneficiary has no interest in the life of the wife of his wife's brother, National Life & Accident Ins. Co. v. Middlebrooks, 27 Ala.App. 247, 170 So. 84; aunt and niece, Commonwealth Life Ins. Co. v. George, 248 Ala. 649, 28 So.2d 910; aunt-in-law and niece, Liberty National Life Ins. Co. v. Weldon, 267 Ala. 171, 100 So.2d 696; niece and uncle, Bell v. National Life & Accident Ins. Co., 41 Ala.App. 94, 123 So.2d 598.

The specific issue presented in the case under review is whether one has an insurable interest in the life of his brother by virtue of the relationship alone. While realizing that this issue is one of first impression in Alabama, and that other jurisdictions are in conflict on this

3. Although the Insurance Code, i.e., Title 28A, became effective after all relevant times for purposes of the instant case, this court is of the opinion that the result obtained in the instant case would not be altered by the application of section 316, which provides as follows:

"§ 316. Insurable interest; personal insurance.—(1) Insurable interest with reference to personal insurance is an interest based upon a reasonable expectation of pecuniary advantage through the continued life, health or bodily safety of another person and consequent loss by reason of his death or disability, or a substantial interest engendered by love and affection in the case of individuals closely related by blood or by law."

matter, a review of the holdings of other states has convinced this court that the vast majority[4] and best reasoned holdings support the proposition that the brother-brother relationship will, in and of itself, support an insurable interest.

* * *

The reason most often assigned as the basis of a holding that such relationship will, in and of itself, support an insurable interest is that the natural love and affection prevailing between the two and the expectation that one will render the other aid in time of need is sufficient to overcome any wagering contract argument, as well as any impulse to hasten the death of the insured. This rationale was well stated in Century Life Ins. Co. v. Custer, 178 Ark. 304, 10 S.W.2d 882 (1928), as follows:

"Brothers are so closely related that they are naturally interested in the preservation of the life of each other. Generally, they will lay down their life for each other. As a rule they care for each other in illness to the extent, if necessary, of furnishing all needed comforts and medicinal aid. It would be contrary to human nature for them to speculate on the death of each other, so it may well be that their contracts for insurance on the life of each other should not be classed as wagering contracts."

* * *

Perhaps the facts of the instant case tend to contradict the closeness and mutual love and affection which the above holdings attribute to the brother-brother relationship, but this court does not write for this case alone. The holding of this court today will govern all future cases, not just the exceptional one where the natural love and affection common to the brother-brother relationship may be missing.

* * *

AFFIRMED.

JONES, JUSTICE (dissenting).

I must disagree with the majority holding that one has an insurable interest in the life of his brother (or sister) on the basis of their relationship alone.

* * * We know that the relationship of husband and wife constitutes such a relationship per se, Jennings v. Jennings, 250 Ala. 130, 33 So.2d 251; and while I do not find that this Court has been specifically called upon to decide whether in every case the relationship of parent and child, or child and parent, in and of itself, with a presumption that is not even rebuttable, gives rise to an insurable interest in either, the overwhelming weight of authority is that this relationship is sufficient to constitute an insurable interest by one in the life of the other (44 C.J.S.

4. This court's research has disclosed that of the nineteen jurisdictions which have written to this issue, fourteen have stated that one has an insurable interest in the life of his brother by virtue of the relationship alone.

Insurance § 204, at 907). But is the relationship of brothers in the same category, or does it depend upon the circumstances of the particular case?

* * *

In any case, I think that the relationship alone is not sufficient, that the rule requiring something other than the relation is the sound one and I would so hold. This is based on the rationale that there is but one test for insurable interest—that of a pecuniary interest or some reasonable expectation of monetary benefit from the continuance of the insured's life; and within certain blood or affinity relationships this pecuniary interest or benefit is conclusively presumed. Such relationships are that of husband and wife, parent and child, grandparent and grandchild, and under certain conditions loco parentis relationships. This "conclusive presumption" rule with respect to these relationships does not violate the public policy necessitating insurable interest aimed at preventing homicide and wager contracts. While an extension of this rule to the brother relationship might be permissible as to the homicide aspect, to so extend this rule would facilitate the violation of the second evil which the aforementioned public policy seeks to prevent; vis., wager contracts.

Having adopted the above view, I would hold that the line must be drawn short of the brother relationship, and that insurable interest in such cases should depend upon a pecuniary benefit, or advantage to be gained from the continued life of the insured, which cannot be conclusively presumed, but is subject to proof. * * *

Note

Another duty of life insurers; to notify the beneficiary that he or she will not be paid if he or she murders the insured. An insurance company issued to Lopez's wife (who "clearly had an insurable interest") a policy on her husband's life in the amount of $130,000 plus double the amount for accidental death. The annual premiums were $7,644 although the family's total annual income was but $9,000. Mr. Lopez signed the forms but claimed he was tricked into doing so by his wife's misrepresentation that it was health insurance. When Lopez overheard his wife and brother-in-law plotting to kill him, he notified the insurer which did nothing about it. Later the conspirators were interrupted in the process of drowning Mr. Lopez, who survived to sue the insurance company for negligence. *Life Ins. Co. of Georgia v. Lopez*, 443 So.2d 947 (Fla.1983), held that the facts stated a cause of action in tort:

> "[Insured's] notice should have triggered an investigation which would have * * * uncovered the disproportion between the insured's economic worth to the beneficiary dead and alive, the insured's lack of consent to the issuance of the policy, and the financial impossibility of the couple meeting the premium payments for any extended period of time. Such an aggregation of suspicious circumstances must surely impose on the insurance company a duty to eliminate any motive for

effecting the insured's death, if not by withdrawing the coverage as void for reasons of public policy, then at least by warning the beneficiary that no proceeds would be payable if she in fact murdered the insured."

Statutes

New York Annotated Insurance Law

§ 3205. Insurable interest in the person; consent required; exceptions

(a) In this section:

(1) The term, "insurable interest" means:

(A) in the case of persons closely related by blood or by law, a substantial interest engendered by love and affection;

(B) in the case of other persons, a lawful and substantial economic interest in the continued life, health or bodily safety of the person insured, as distinguished from an interest which would arise only by, or would be enhanced in value by, the death, disablement or injury of the insured. (2) The term "contract of insurance upon the person" includes any policy of life insurance and any policy of accident and health insurance. (3) The term "person insured" means the natural person, or persons, whose life, health or bodily safety is insured.

(b)(1) Any person of lawful age may on his own initiative procure or effect a contract of insurance upon his own person for the benefit of any person, firm, association or corporation. Nothing herein shall be deemed to prohibit the immediate transfer or assignment of a contract so procured or effectuated.

(2) No person shall procure or cause to be procured, directly or by assignment or otherwise any contract of insurance upon the person of another unless the benefits under such contract are payable to the person insured or his personal representatives, or to a person having, at the time when such contract is made, an insurable interest in the person insured.

(3) If the beneficiary, assignee or other payee under any contract made in violation of this subsection receives from the insurer any benefits thereunder accruing upon the death, disablement or injury of the person insured, the person insured or his executor or administrator may maintain an action to recover such benefits from the person receiving them.

(c) No contract of insurance upon the person, except a policy of group life insurance, group or blanket accident and health insurance, or family insurance, as defined in this chapter, shall be made or effectuated unless at or before the making of such contract the person insured, being of lawful age or competent to contract therefor, applies for or consents in writing to the making of the contract, except in the following cases:

(1) A wife or a husband may effectuate insurance upon the person of the other.

(2) Any person having an insurable interest in the life of a minor under the age of fourteen years and six months or any person upon whom such minor is dependent for support and maintenance, may effectuate a contract of insurance upon the life of such minor, in an amount which shall not exceed the limits specified in section three thousand two hundred seven of this article.

California Insurance Code

§ 10110. Insurable interest

Every person has an insurable interest in the life and health of:

(a) Himself.

(b) Any person on whom he depends wholly or in part for education or support.

(c) Any person under a legal obligation to him for the payment of money or respecting property or services, of which death or illness might delay or prevent the performance.

(d) Any person upon whose life any estate or interest vested in him depends.

§ 10110.1. Insurable interest; employers; time of requirement; charitable organizations

(a) An insurable interest, with reference to life and disability insurance, is an interest based upon a reasonable expectation of pecuniary advantage through the continued life, health, or bodily safety of another person and consequent loss by reason of that person's death or disability or a substantial interest engendered by love and affection in the case of individuals closely related by blood or law.

(b) An individual has an unlimited insurable interest in his or her own life, health, and bodily safety and may lawfully take out a policy of insurance on his or her own life, health, or bodily safety and have the policy made payable to whomsoever he or she pleases, regardless of whether the beneficiary designated has an insurable interest.

(c) An employer has an insurable interest, as referred to in subdivision (a), in the life or physical or mental ability of any of its directors, officers, or employees or the directors, officers, or employees of any of its subsidiaries or any other person whose death or physical or mental disability might cause financial loss to the employer; or, pursuant to any contractual arrangement with any shareholder concerning the reacquisition of shares owned by the shareholder at the time of his or her death or disability, on the life or physical or mental ability of that shareholder for the purpose of carrying out the contractual arrangement; or, pursuant to any contract obligating the employer as part of compensation arrangements or pursuant to a contract obligating the employer as guarantor or surety, on the life of the principal obligor. The trustee of an employer or trustee of a pension, welfare benefit plan, or trust established by an employer providing life, health, disability, retirement, or similar benefits to employees and retired employees of the employer or its affiliates and acting in a fiduciary capacity with respect to those employees, retired employees, or their dependents or beneficiaries has an insurable interest in the lives of employees and retired employees for whom those benefits are to be provided. The employer shall obtain the written consent of the individual being insured.

(d) An insurable interest shall be required to exist at the time the contract of life or disability insurance becomes effective, but need not exist at the time the loss occurs.

(e) Any contract of life or disability insurance procured or caused to be procured upon another individual is void unless the person applying for the insurance has an insurable interest in the individual insured at the time of the application.

(f) Notwithstanding subdivisions (a), (d), and (e), a charitable organization that meets the requirements of Section 214 or 23701d of the Revenue and Taxation Code may effectuate life or disability insurance on an insured who consents to the issuance of that insurance.

(g) This section shall not be interpreted to define all instances in which an insurable interest exists.

§ 10110.2. Representations of insurable interest; reliance of insurer

An insurer shall be entitled to rely upon all statements, declarations, and representations made by an applicant for insurance relative to the insurable interest that the applicant has in the insured, and no insurer shall incur any legal liability except as set forth in the policy, by virtue of any untrue statements, declarations, or representations so relied upon in good faith by the insurer.

Note

Gertrude Berg was the star of the Broadway play, "Dear Me, The Sky is Falling." The producers took out a policy which provided: "This insurance is to pay the insured in the event of inability of the insured artist to appear in the insured production, directly in consequence of her suffering any personal accident or sickness or in the event or occurrence of her death or total disability during the period of insurance." The amount of insurance payable was $1,500 per missed performance up to a certain amount. Gertrude Berg became ill and the producer sought recovery. The insurance company conceded limited liability so the following remarks by the court may be considered pure dicta:

> Plaintiff's insurable interest derived from employment of Gertrude Berg as star of the production (Ins. Law § 146 subdiv. 2, now § 3205). The economic success of the production depended on the effective appearance and performance of Gertrude Berg.

After referring to Berg as the "insured artist", the court then turned to other issues and decided in plaintiff's favor. Theatre Guild Productions v. Insurance Corp. of Ireland, 25 A.D.2d 109, 267 N.Y.S.2d 297 (1966), aff'd 9 N.Y.2d 656, 278 N.Y.S.2d 625, 225 N.E.2d 216 (1967).

3. The Insurer's Defenses

a. Payment of Premiums

FURTADO v. METROPOLITAN LIFE INSURANCE CO., INC.

District Court of Appeal of California, Fourth District, 1976.
60 Cal.App.3d 17, 131 Cal.Rptr. 250.

KAUFMAN, ASSOCIATE JUSTICE.

* * *

On February 12, 1973, Metropolitan issued a policy of life insurance with a face value of $15,000 to and on the life of plaintiff's son Vincent E. Furtado, then 18 years of age. Plaintiff was designated as beneficiary.

Premium payments of $26.45 each were to be paid on or before the 12th day of each month commencing February 12, 1973. A total of six monthly premiums were paid, the last payment being that of July 12, 1973. The payment due August 12, 1973, was not paid.

Plaintiff's son died on October 26, 1973, 75 days after August 12, 1973, the due date of the August premium. Plaintiff claimed that the insurance policy was still in effect on the date of death. Metropolitan claimed that the policy had lapsed for nonpayment of premiums. [Following a trial by the court, judgment was rendered in favor of Metropolitan. Plaintiff appeals from the judgment.]

The controversy revolves around three policy provisions. On page 6 of the policy under the large-lettered heading "PREMIUM PAYMENT AND REINSTATEMENT" and a bold-face subheading entitled "Payment of Premiums and Grace Period" the policy provides:

> "A grace period of 31 days will be granted for the payment of each premium after the first, during which period the policy will continue in force. If the Insured dies during such period, any unpaid premium will be deducted from the amount otherwise payable under this policy."

For purposes of identification we designate this provision "provision one."

On page 7 of the policy under a large-lettered heading entitled "INSURANCE OPTIONS ON NONPAYMENT OF PREMIUMS" the policy provides:

> "The insurance options provided below are available if a premium is in default beyond the grace period. The option for Extended Term insurance will be automatically effective if premiums have been paid for at least a number of years for which a period of Extended Term insurance is first shown in the Table on page 8." (Italics added.)

For purposes of identification we shall refer to this provision as "provision two."

Immediately following provision two, under the bold-face heading "Extended Term Insurance" the policy provides:

> "Under this option, the policy will be continued as nonparticipating paid-up Extended Term insurance.
>
> "For a policy without any paid-up additions, dividend accumulations, or indebtedness, the amount of such insurance will be the Face Amount of Insurance and *the term of the insurance, measured from the due date of the premium in default,* will be as specified in the Table on page 8." (Italics added.)

For purposes of identification we shall refer to this provision as "provision three."

The table on page 8 of the policy clearly specifies that for a policy in force six months the period of extended term insurance is to be 60 days.

CONTENTIONS

In a somewhat overlapping presentation plaintiff contends:

(1) The grace period of 31 days and the 60–day period of extended term insurance should run consecutively and not concurrently;

* * *

(4) Provision three constitutes an exclusion from or limitation upon coverage and is not stated in language that is conspicuous, plain and clear.

DISCUSSION AND DISPOSITION

Exclusion From or Limitation Upon Coverage

Plaintiff is correct that exclusions or limitations upon coverage must be "conspicuous, plain and clear." * * * Plaintiff is incorrect in asserting, however, that policy provision three dealing with the duration of extended term insurance constitutes an exclusion from or limitation upon coverage. Plaintiff is further mistaken in asserting that the language of provision three is not clear, plain and conspicuous.

Treating the last assertion first, the language of provision three plainly and clearly specifies that the term of the extended term insurance is "measured from the due date of the premium in default," August 12, 1973. The provision is not inconspicuous; it appears in quite readable print under the bold-face caption "Extended Term Insurance," which, in turn, appears under the large-lettered heading "INSURANCE OPTIONS ON NONPAYMENT OF PREMIUMS."

Provision three does not constitute an exclusion from or limitation upon coverage. On the contrary, provision three constitutes a nonforfeiture provision in compliance with, and indeed more liberal than, the requirements of the Standard Nonforfeiture Law (see Ins.Code, §§ 10159.1–10167).

Section 10160 of the Insurance Code mandates certain standard provisions for life insurance policies issued or delivered in California. In relevant part, that section provides:

> "Except as provided in Section 10165, no policy of life insurance shall be issued or delivered in this State unless it shall contain in substance the following provisions, or corresponding provisions which are at least as favorable to the defaulting or surrendering policyholder;
>
> "(a) Nonforfeiture benefit. That, in the event of default in any premium payment after premiums have been paid for at least one full year the insurer will grant, upon proper request not later than 60 days after *the due date of the premium in default,* a paid-up nonforfeiture benefit on a plan stipulated in the policy, *effective as of*

such due date, of such value as may be hereinafter specified." (Italics added.)

Thus, that part of provision three which provides that the term of the extended term insurance is to be "measured from the due date of the premium in default" is fully authorized by Insurance Code section 10160.

Consecutive or Concurrent Running of the Grace Period and the Term of Extended Term Insurance

In urging that the 31–day grace period and the 60–day period of extended term insurance should run consecutively and not concurrently, plaintiff correctly asserts that under policy provision two the extended term insurance option does not become operative or available unless and until "a premium is in default beyond the grace period." It does not follow, however, that the grace period and the period of extended term insurance should run consecutively and not concurrently. Policy provision three is the only provision dealing with the commencement of the term of extended term insurance, and it clearly and unmistakably specifies that, once the extended term insurance provision takes effect, the term of such insurance is to be "measured from the due date of the premium in default." Thus, the grace period and the period of extended term insurance run concurrently, not consecutively. Plaintiff's contention to the contrary is based upon the mistaken notion that policy provision one providing a grace period of 31 days affords a free month of insurance and that the concurrent running of the grace period and the period of extended term insurance would deprive him of the benefit of the prescribed grace period. To the contrary, the grace period does not afford a free period of insurance coverage. It simply allows for reinstatement of the policy by payment of the premium in default without a showing of insurability. (See Schick v. Equitable Life Assur. Soc., 15 Cal.App.2d 28, 33, 59 P.2d 163; 6 Couch, Insurance (2d ed.) § 32:133, pp. 348–349.)

Apparently the question whether the grace period and period of extended term insurance run concurrently or consecutively has not heretofore been decided in California. However, there is ample authority from other jurisdictions for the proposition that the grace period and the period of extended term insurance may both commence on the due date of the payment in default and, thus, run concurrently when the language of the policy clearly so provides [citations]. [S]ee generally, Annot., 106 A.L.R. 1276; 45 C.J.S., Insurance, § 638. As previously noted, the commencement of the period of extended term insurance at the due date of the payment in default is expressly authorized by section 10160 of the Insurance Code.

In support of his argument that the grace period and the period of extended term insurance should be construed to run consecutively, plaintiff cites Mitchell v. Southern Union Life Insurance Company (Tex.Civ.App.) 218 S.W. 586 and Prudential Insurance Company v. Devoe, 98 Md. 584, 56 A. 809, in both of which it was held that periods of extended term insurance commenced at the end of the respective grace periods. In *Mitchell,* the policy failed to prescribe the date of commencement of the period of extended term insurance. The *Mitchell* court observed that the absence of any clear provision as to the inception point of the period of extended term insurance rendered the provisions uncertain and held "* * * the policy is at least ambiguous, and * * * it admits of [plaintiff's] construction, and it being that most favorable to the insured, will be enforced." (218 S.W. at p. 590.) In *Devoe* the policy provided: " 'In the payment of any premium under this policy, except the first, a grace of one month will be allowed, during which time the policy will remain in force. If the policy, after being in force one full year, shall *lapse* for nonpayment of premium the company will continue in force the insurance under the policy for a period of sixty days *from the date of the lapse.*' "(56 A. at p. 809.) (Italics added.) The *Devoe* court, relying on the literal import of the quoted language, held that, inasmuch as the policy did not lapse until the end of the grace period, the extended term insurance would not commence until the end of the grace period. Both *Mitchell* and *Devoe* are thus distinguishable. In the case at bench policy provision three clearly and unequivocably provides that the period of extended term insurance is to be "measured from the due date of the premium in default."

* * *

AFFIRMED.

Note

Anti–Forfeiture Provisions in Life Insurance Policies

Life insurance in the form of whole life or endowment policies whereby the insured pays the premiums on a level term basis (the same periodic payments throughout) means that during their youthful years the policy holders are paying premiums that are actuarially far in excess of the risk of their deaths assumed by the insurer. In other words such policies build up sizeable "cash values", which may be advantageously used by the insured, but which at the same time might be lost in the event of termination of the policy for failure to make a premium payment. Indeed such forfeitures were once tolerated but the unfairness was so manifest—particularly with respect to the so called Industrial Life policies marketed to the low income urban working class—that legislative pressures built to mandate anti-forfeiture provisions in policies that have cash values (in contrast with term insurance policies that do not).

These statutes are usually referred to as the "Guertin" Laws and are named after a committee chaired by Alfred N. Guertin which was appointed in 1937 and which devised model legislation approved by the National Association of Insurance Commissioners. The applicable mortality tables have been periodically revised. The California statute (§ 10160 ff. West Ann.Ins.Code) cited in the principal case is typical of the legislation.

Essentially the policy forms thus mandated give the insured who stops paying the premiums, the alternative of accepting the cash surrender value, extended term insurance, or reduced paid up insurance in accordance with specified tables (see Appendix C). Absent any deliberate choice, the insured is automatically afforded paid up term insurance. For extended discussion, see Griede and Beadles, *Law and the Life Insurance Contract,* 4th ed. 1979; Meyer, *Life and Health Insurance Law,* 1972 § 10.9 ff.

b. Conditions Precedent and Misrepresentation

FRIEZ v. NATIONAL OLD LINE INSURANCE CO.

United States Court of Appeals, Ninth Circuit, 1983.
703 F.2d 1093.

SCHROEDER, CIRCUIT JUDGE:

Old Line Insurance Company appeals from the district court's judgment allowing recovery on a $12,000 life insurance policy. The policy application, completed on December 15, 1977, contained the following health question: "Do you know of any impairment, disease or disorder now existing in your health or physical condition?" The insured, Mr. Friez, answered "no." The application also contained a "good health" clause which provided: "I understand and agree that there shall be no insurance in force until the policy hereby applied for is issued and delivered to me during my lifetime and good health and the first premium is paid by me in which event the insurance shall be effective as of the Date of issue stated in the policy." The policy was issued on January 5, 1978.

When Mr. Friez died on February 21, 1978, Old Line refused to pay the death benefits specified in the policy; it returned the premiums paid by Friez and cancelled the policy. The company argues that the policy was void under Montana law on two grounds. First, Old Line argues that pursuant to the above "good health clause," the insured's good health at the time the policy was delivered was a condition precedent to coverage and that, because at the time the policy was issued the insured was suffering from an undiagnosed terminal cancer, the policy was void. Second, Old Line argues that Friez made a misrepresentation in his answer to the health question because, nine years prior to the time of application, he had been treated for ulcers. We uphold the district court's rejection, under Montana law, of both arguments.

Appellant's first argument fails because there was no fraud in connection with the "good health" clause. The insured did not know he had cancer when the policy was delivered. The relevant language of the insurance application here is similar in all material respects to the language construed in Pelican v. Mutual Life Insurance Company, 44 Mont. 277, 119 P. 778 (1911). The court in *Pelican* refused to void a policy issued to a terminally ill insured, stating that once "the premium had been paid and retained" by the insurance company, the insured was entitled to judgment "in the absence of evidence of fraud." * * *. The *Pelican* court further stressed that a warranty or condition precedent, as opposed to a representation, must be made a part of the contract by "express agreement of the parties on the face of the policy."

Here, it is not apparent on the face of the policy that the parties intended the good health clause to be a condition precedent to coverage. The district court held, and the dissent disputes, that the provision is ambiguous. In the district court's view, the policy could be construed either to require good health at the time the policy is issued, or merely to establish that no insurance coverage is provided until the policy issued. Resolving such an ambiguity in favor of the insured, the district court concluded that the provision did not create a bar to coverage under the insurance policy.

* * *

As appellee stresses, there is a more apparent ambiguity in the "good health" clause which requires upholding recovery under the policy. Whether or not the clause is a condition precedent, the term "good health" may be construed to mean "objective good health," in which case the insured's knowledge of the existence of bad health at the time of application is immaterial, or it may be construed to mean "subjective good health," in which case the clause is satisfied if the insured has no knowledge or reason to believe that he is in bad health. *See* G. Couch, *Couch On Insurance* §§ 11:7–11:8 (R. Anderson 2d ed. 1959).

This ambiguity must also be construed in favor of the insured. No Montana court has ever held that an insured who is unaware of a serious illness is not in "good health" within the meaning of a provision like this one. In both McDonald v. Northern Benefit Association, 113 Mont. 595, 131 P.2d 479 (1942), and Schroeder v. Metropolitan Life Insurance Company, 103 Mont. 547, 63 P.2d 1016 (1937), the cases upon which appellant relies, the insured knew when the policy was issued that he suffered from the illness which eventually caused his death. These cases cannot stand for the proposition, suggested by the dissent, that knowledge of bad health is "irrelevant" under Montana law. Cf. *Pelican v. Mutual Life Insurance Company,* supra (objective evidence coupled with subjective belief of ill-health allows avoidance of policy). The import of Montana case law is that if the validity of an insurance policy is to be conditioned upon the insured's objective good health, irrespective of what he knew or should have known, the condition must be clearly and conspicuously set forth. Since the "good health" clause was not so clearly expressed in this policy, we are required to hold that it cannot bar recovery.

Old Line's second argument is that the policy should have been voided because Mr. Friez's failure to reveal treatment for ulcers nine years earlier amounted to a material misrepresentation under Montana Revised Code § 33–15–403.[5] This argument also fails. Mr. Friez's mis-

5. Montana Revised Code § 33–15–403 provides:

Representations in applications—recovery precluded if fraudulent or material. (1) All statements and descriptions in any application for an insurance policy of annuity contract or in negotiations therefor by or in behalf of the insured or annuitant shall be deemed to be representations and not warranties.

statement did not affect the validity of the policy within the meaning of the Montana statute. The district court found that had the insured answered "yes," Old Line would have asked only for additional information. There is no showing that his statement was material to Old Line's acceptance of the risk or that the company would not have issued the policy had he responded otherwise. Further, the court found no intent to mislead on the part of the insured and no prejudice to the insurer, because the cause of death was not related to an ulcer. See Pelican v. Mutual Life Insurance Co., 44 Mont. at 289, 119 P. at 781; McDonald v. Northern Benefit Assoc., supra, 113 Mont. at 606, 131 P.2d at 485 (to prove fraudulent misrepresentation which will prevent recovery, party must show intention to mislead). These findings are not clearly erroneous and the district court's conclusions were therefore proper.

AFFIRMED.

WALLACE, CIRCUIT JUDGE, dissenting:

* * * We are bound to follow decisions of the highest state court in resolving diversity cases. * * *

* * *

Two Montana Supreme Court decisions dictate a finding that the good health clause is not ambiguous and that it is a condition precedent which must be strictly fulfilled. In Schroeder v. Metropolitan Life Insurance Co., 103 Mont. 547, 63 P.2d 1016 (1937) (*Schroeder*), the Montana Supreme Court held an insurance policy void because the clause "the Insured is not alive or is not in sound health" was a condition precedent. The insured had not fulfilled the condition because she had a serious heart affliction on the date the policy was issued. In McDonald v. Northern Benefit Association, 113 Mont. 595, 131 P.2d 479 (1942) (*McDonald*), the Montana Supreme Court, relying on *Schroeder*, construed a provision that "there will be no liability on the part of the Ass'n. unless and until the certificate of membership is issued and delivered to me while I am ... in good health, free from disease" as a condition precedent to liability of the insurer. The insured was not in good health on the date the insurance certificate issued. The language in the policy in the case before us is substantially identical to the language held to constitute a condition precedent by the Montana Supreme Court in *Schroeder* and *McDonald*. These decisions by the highest state court

(2) Misrepresentations, omissions, concealment of facts, and incorrect statements shall not prevent a recovery under the policy or contract unless either:

(a) fraudulent;

(b) material either to the acceptance of the risk or to the hazard assumed by the insurer; or

(c) the insurer in good faith would either not have issued the policy or contract or would not have issued a policy or contract in as large an amount or at the same premium or rate or would not have provided coverage with respect to the hazard resulting in the loss if the true facts had been made known to the insurer as required either by the application for the policy or contract or otherwise.

require us to hold that the good health clause in this case is not ambiguous. * * *

Pelican v. Mutual Life Insurance Co., 44 Mont. 277, 119 P. 778 (1911) (*Pelican*), relied on by the majority, is distinguishable. *Pelican* focused on whether the insured made a fraudulent representation to the insurer. The inquiry was relevant because the policy stated that "[a]ll statements made by the insured shall, in the absence of fraud, be deemed representations and not warranties." 44 Mont. at 287, 119 P. at 780 (summary of action). In the absence of this policy language, fraud would not have been relevant to a determination whether the good health clause was a warranty or condition precedent. In the case before us, the policy contains a statement similar to that quoted above from *Pelican*. The district court, however, correctly separated its discussion of this language from its discussion of whether the good health clause was a condition precedent.

I would reverse the judgment of the district court and hold that the "good health" clause was a condition precedent. I would remand for consideration of whether the condition precedent was met.

Note

In *Life Ins. Co. of North America v. Commonwealth of Pennsylvania Insurance Dept.*, 43 Pa.Cmwlth. 282, 402 A.2d 297 (1979) the court sustained the decision of the Insurance Commissioner who had disapproved certain policy forms for group long-term salary continuance insurance because of an objectionable provision—i.e., exclusion of "pre-existing conditions." This exclusion is "designed for individual not group policies because the chances of adverse selection in a group policy are minimal."

4. Incontestability

CRAWFORD v. EQUITABLE LIFE ASSURANCE SOCIETY OF UNITED STATES

Supreme Court of Illinois, 1973.
56 Ill.2d 41, 305 N.E.2d 144.

WARD, JUSTICE.

This appeal presents the question whether an incontestability clause contained in a group life insurance policy bars the insurer from defending against a claim on the ground that the insured was not an employee eligible for insurance under the terms of the policy. The question is one of first impression in this court.

The plaintiff, Harvey A. Crawford, brought an action in the circuit court of Rock Island County against the defendant, The Equitable Life Assurance Society of the United States, to recover the sum of $10,000 as the beneficiary of his wife under a group insurance policy issued by the defendant. * * * The circuit court granted [a] motion for summary judgment, and the appellate court affirmed. We granted the defendant's petition for leave to appeal. Leave was also granted to three other life insurance companies to file a joint brief *amici curiae.*

The undisputed facts are that effective January 1, 1965, the defendant issued a group life insurance policy to the Warm Air Heating and Air Conditioning Group Insurance Trust. The trust was established by the Warm Air Heating and Air Conditioning Association, for the purpose of providing insurance on the lives of employees of companies which were members of the association, as authorized by section 230(2)(e) of the Insurance Code Ill.Rev.Stat.1971, ch. 73, par. 842(2)(e).

One of the members of the association was the Crawford Heating and Cooling Company, Inc., whose president was the plaintiff. In December, 1964, shortly prior to the issuance of the policy, the plaintiff executed and delivered to the association an enrollment form which requested insurance for three persons, each of whom he represented to be employees of his company. Among the three were the plaintiff himself and his wife, Rose A. Crawford. A certificate of insurance was thereafter issued to Mrs. Crawford in the face amount of $10,000. The certificate also provided for certain hospital and medical expense benefits. The plaintiff was named as the beneficiary. The premiums were paid by the Crawford Heating and Cooling Company. Mrs. Crawford died in February, 1969.

The master policy contained a provision that only a "full time employee" would be eligible for insurance, subject to a proviso that any employee "whose work week calls for a schedule of less than 32 hours shall not be eligible for insurance hereunder."

The insurance certificate issued to the decedent, while stating that the insurance provided under the policy was effective "only if the Employee is eligible for insurance," did not contain the specific full-time employment requirement found in the master policy. The enrollment form executed by the plaintiff, however, did state that an employee must work at least 32 hours a week, and the plaintiff marked the form in such fashion as to indicate that each of the three persons listed did meet that requirement. The same representation was made in regular monthly statements submitted by the plaintiff to the trustee with his premium payments from February, 1965, until February, 1969.

An individual application for insurance executed by the decedent also included a representation by her that she worked 32 hours a week or more. She stated further in her application that her position with the company was that of Secretary–Treasurer, and that she earned $7500 or more a year. Information as to position and salary was significant under the policy because these factors affected the amount of death benefits payable.

In point of fact the representations made by the plaintiff and by the decedent were false. Neither at the time when the policy issued nor at any time thereafter did the decedent ever complete a week in which she worked 32 or more hours. According to the complaint the extent of her duties was to spend several hours a month in assisting the plaintiff in drawing up proposals for contracts, and in taking night telephone calls when he was on a job or out of town. She received no compensation for these functions.

It is admitted that the defendant made no inquiry into the circumstances of the decedent's employment until after her death. The facts came to light when the plaintiff submitted his claim to the trustee accompanied by a death certificate, which listed the decedent's occupation as that of housewife. The trustee notified the defendant, and requested it to verify the decedent's eligibility. An employee of the defendant then made a single call to the bookkeeper of the plaintiff's company, from whom the decedent's employment status was ascertained. The defendant thereafter wrote to the plaintiff denying the latter's claim.

The master policy contains an incontestability clause which reads as follows:

> "The validity of this policy shall not be contested, except for the non-payment of premiums, after it has been in force for two years from the date of issue; and no statement made by any employee insured under this policy relating to his insurability shall be used in contesting the validity of the insurance with respect to which such statement was made, after such insurance has been in force prior to the contest for a period of two years during such employee's lifetime nor unless it is contained in a written application signed by such employee and a copy of such application is or has been furnished to such employee or his beneficiary."

The provision quoted above incorporates portions of section 231 of the Illinois Insurance Code (Ill.Rev.Stat.1971, ch. 73, par. 843), which specifies certain provisions which must be contained in any policy of group life insurance issued or delivered in this State. Subsection (a) of section 231 requires inclusion of "A provision that the policy shall be incontestable after two years from its date of issue during the lifetime of the insured, except for nonpayment of premiums and except for violation of the conditions of the policy relating to military or naval services in time of war." Subsection (b) requires inclusion of "A provision * * * that all statements made by the employer or trustee or by the individual employees shall, in the absence of fraud, be deemed representations and not warranties, and that no such statement shall be used in defense to a claim under the policy, unless it is contained in a written application."

As presented by the parties, the basic issue in this case is whether the eligibility of an employee relates to the "coverage" of the policy and may, therefore, be challenged notwithstanding the incontestability clause. Each party apparently considers that only the first portion of the incontestability clause in the policy, reading "The validity of this policy shall not be contested, except for non-payment of premiums, after it has been in force for two years from the date of issue," is relevant in determining this issue. This view is presumably based on the assumption that the succeeding portion of the clause is intended only to deal with cases where proof of individual insurability is required. See Gregg, Group Life Insurance (2d ed.) 92.

* * *

An incontestability clause was considered in Baker v. Prudential Insurance Company of America, 279 Ill.App. 5, where recovery was sought under a group life insurance policy for the death of a former employee who had been discharged shortly prior to his death. The master policy specified that insurance should cease upon the termination of employment. Despite the incontestability clause, the appellate court held that the insurer was not liable, stating (279 Ill.App. 5, 10):

> "The incontestable provision did not prevent the defendant insurance company from showing the policy was no longer in effect because Baker had been discharged a month before death. That provision of the policy would prevent the defendant in the instant case from contending that the policy was obtained by fraud or misrepresentation or upon any other ground, going to the original validity of the policy."

Historically the incontestability clause arose in the context of individual life insurance policies, and typically involved situations where the insured, in connection with his application for insurance, made statements respecting his health. In the absence of an incontestability clause, the insurer, upon the death of the insured, would be entitled to resist payment of the claim upon a showing that there had been a material misrepresentation of fact made by the insured or on his behalf, and that the contract of insurance was therefore voidable. * * * The insurer, if he had no knowledge of the misrepresentation, was not ordinarily barred by the passage of time from making this defense, but might preserve it for use at such time as the insured died and the claim was presented for payment. The resulting situation was described by this court in Powell v. Mutual Life Insurance Company of New York, 313 Ill. 161, 164–165, 144 N.E. 825, 826, in the following language:

> "In the earlier development of insurance contracts it not infrequently occurred that, after the insured had paid premiums for a large number of years, the beneficiaries under the policy found, after the maturity thereof by the death of the insured, that they were facing a lawsuit in order to recover the insurance; that in certain answers in the application it was said by the insurer, the insured had made statements which were not true, and the beneficiaries were not entitled to recover on the policy. It is needless to call attention to the fact that this situation gave rise to a widespread suspicion in the minds of the public that an insurance contract was designed largely for the benefit of the company. Recognizing this fact and seeing the effect of it on the insurance business, numerous insurance companies inserted in their policies what is now known as an incontestable clause."

Whatever the manner of its origin, in most States, as in Illinois, the matter of incontestability is now covered by statute. (See Keeton, Basic Text on Insurance, sec. 6.5(d) (1971).) It is evident that one effect of an incontestability clause is to permit recovery in cases of false or even fraudulent representations, simply because these had not been discovered prior to the expiration of the contestable period. Balanced against this undesirable result, however, was the social desirability of assuring a beneficiary that his claim could not be put to a challenge at some remote future time when the insured was dead and when others who might have testified in the beneficiary's behalf might also be unable to do so. See Flanigan v. Federal Life Insurance Co., 231 Ill. 399, 83 N.E. 178; Williston, Contracts, sec. 745 (3d ed. 1961); Holland, The Incontestable Clause, in Krueger and Waggoner, The Life Insurance Policy Contract, 57–58 (1953).

The conventional incontestability clause contains certain exceptions, most commonly one for the nonpayment of premiums. It is clear, however, that there are other, unenumerated grounds on which an insurer may refuse to pay a claim after the period of contestability has run. The clause obviously does not preclude a refusal based on the fact that the particular event insured against has not taken place, and the insurer is thus not barred from "contesting" the claim or the interpretation of the coverage provisions advanced by the claimant. This point of distinction was described by Justice Cardozo, then the Chief Judge of the New York Court of Appeals, in the often cited case of Metropolitan Life Insurance Co. v. Conway (1930), 252 N.Y. 449, 169 N.E. 642. It was urged in that case that a rider in a policy excluding from protection death resulting from travel in an aircraft (except as a fare-paying passenger) conflicted with the incontestability provision contained in the New York insurance laws. The Court of Appeals held to the contrary, stating: "The provision that a policy shall be incontestable after it has been in force during the lifetime of the insured for a period of two years it not a mandate as to coverage, a definition of the hazard to be borne by the insurer. It means only this, that within the limits of the coverage the policy shall stand, unaffected by any defense that it was invalid in its inception, or thereafter became invalid by reason of a condition broken."

While the broad distinction drawn in *Conway* between a policy's limits of coverage and its validity has been quite generally recognized, differences of opinion have arisen as to its application, particularly with respect to group life insurance. (See, e.g., Keeton, Basic Text on Insurance, sec. 6.5(d); Young, "Incontestable—As to What?", 1964 U.Ill.L.F.) With individual life insurance the policy identifies a specific individual by name, and it is relatively easy to distinguish between a question of coverage (the death of the insured or his death from some specific cause) and a question of validity created by antecedent misrepresentations on the part of the insured. In the case of group life insurance, however, the master policy undertakes to provide insurance for a collection of unnamed persons defined only in terms of membership in a class, such as the employees of a certain company. To ascertain whether a person is insured necessitates a determination of whether he is in fact a member of the class. To the extent that that determination is based upon information furnished by the employer or by an employee or alleged employee, the question whether coverage exists tends to become intertwined with the question whether the coverage was obtained by false representations.

The courts of other States have considered a number of factual situations relating to eligibility, such as whether the insured is an employee at all, whether he was actively employed, whether he exceeded a specific maximum age, whether he was disqualified for some other reason, and whether he was incorrectly classified as to position. The decisions, which are collected in an annotation appearing in 26 A.L.R.3d 632, are not uniform in result.

[Citations.]

* * * [T]he New York view, as first expressed in a Federal decision, was that the insurer might raise the defense of ineligibility (Fisher v. United States Life Insurance Co. (4th Cir.1957), 249 F.2d 879), but a subsequent decision in 1969 by the New York Court of Appeals holds to the contrary (Simpson v. Phoenix Mutual Life Insurance Co. (1969), 24 N.Y.2d 262, 299 N.Y.S.2d 835, 247 N.E.2d 655). It is the *Simpson*[6] decision on which the appellate court principally relied in the case now before us.

We, however, consider that the question of eligibility is one which relates to the risk assumed and that a defense based on lack of eligibility is therefore not foreclosed by an incontestability clause.

It is, of course, true that eligibility may relate to circumstances existing at the inception of the contract (although it may also arise subsequently because of a change in employment status). It is also true that it may have been determined initially upon the basis of statements made by the insured or by his employer. And it may be assumed that whether a person is an employee or is a full time employee is a matter affecting the willingness of the insurer to assume the defined risk at the defined premium charge, since employment or active or full-time employment may protect the insurer against adverse selection. See Gregg, Group Life Insurance (2d ed.) 34–36.

A challenge to eligibility does not, however, involve an attack by the insurer on the validity of the master policy. The defendant is not seeking to set aside the policy because of the misrepresentations made and the only aspect of the insurance plan which is affected is the payment sought by a single beneficiary. Moreover, even as to that beneficiary, while the defendant may have relied on his representations as well as those of the

6. [Editors' Footnote.] In *Simpson,* the Phoenix Mutual Life Ins. Co. issued a master policy through the trustees of the Cemetery and Funeral Service and Supply Industry Group Insurance Fund. Simpson was an officer and attorney in the Lebanon Cemetery Association of Queens, Inc., a participating employer. He completed an enrollment card and was included in the list submitted to the insurer. However he never satisfied the eligibility provision that he work 30 hours per week at the employer's place of business. Over two years later he was killed by a robber.

decedent, the defendant's success in this litigation does not require that the defendant establish the falsity of those representations as such. Had the plaintiff alleged that the decedent had been a full-time employee, instead of admitting that she was not, the defendant would of course have been put to his proof of ineligibility. But it would be the fact of eligibility or ineligibility which would be decisive, not what prior representations had been made on the subject.

As we read *Simpson,* it represents a basic departure from the distinction announced in *Conway* between matters concerning validity, to which the incontestable clause applies, and the risk assumed, to which it does not. The court in *Simpson* takes the position that some matters which relate only to the risk assumed are nevertheless covered by the incontestable clause, namely those risks which could have been discovered at the time the contract was entered into. (See 24 N.Y.2d 262, 267, 299 N.Y.S.2d 835, 247 N.E.2d 655, 658.) We consider that conclusion both inapplicable to the policy we consider here as well as unsuitable to the group insurance situation with its constantly changing body of insured employees.

The incontestability clause of the policy, to begin with, provides only that the validity of the policy may not be contested, and, as we have seen, its validity is not disputed.

A further factor which we deem significant was expressed in Rasmussen v. Equitable Life Assurance Society of the United States, 293 Mich. 482, 487, 292 N.W. 377, 380, in connection with a group policy excluding employees over a certain age: "[A] greater social good is served by enabling employed groups to obtain the most advantageous protection that their status warrants by restricting the invitation to particular age groups. Those who deliberately misstate their age and thus tend to lower the experience record of the group should not be placed by construction within the aegis of the incontestability provision."

Similarly, in the present case we can envisage the possibility of an adverse effect upon other employers if, by virtue of the incontestability clause, claims must be paid out upon the death of persons not meeting the standards of eligibility contained in the policy, in that actuarial calculations upon which the premium rate had been determined could be distorted, with the consequence of increased rates being imposed as the result of experience rating. See Gregg, Group Life Insurance (2d ed.) 220–229.

We do not mean to intimate that the occasions in which an employer would intentionally make a misrepresentation as to the eligibility of an employee would be of frequent occurrence. In the ordinary case the employer, who is paying all or a portion of the premiums, would not appear to have any incentive to create a supply of fictitious employees. The risk does exist, however, as indicated by the facts of this case and the somewhat similar facts in such cases as Fisher v. Prudential Insurance Co. (1966), 107 N.H. 101, 218 A.2d 62.

A third consideration underlying the decision we reach lies in the possibility that an employee who is eligible at the time when the policy is issued might, at some point more than two years after the issuance date, cease to be a full-time employee, or, indeed, even terminate his employment. Were the incontestability clause to be applied in such a situation, there would appear to be no manner in which payment of a claim could be resisted if the employer or employer group had failed to notify the insurer of the change in the status of the employee. We think that the termination of employment is clearly a matter which the insurer may raise, as was held by the appellate court in Baker v. Prudential Insurance Company of America, 279 Ill.App. 5. On the same reasoning we believe that raising the question whether a person ever became an employee or became an employee of the type eligible for insurance is also not barred by an incontestability clause.

The principle of discoverability which governed the *Simpson* decision would put the insurer to an election between the risk of making payment on unwarranted claims or conducting an investigation, in some manner not dependent upon information provided by the employer or employee, into the employment status of every person purportedly insured. The contention is made here that the latter course of action would cause substantial expense and the unnecessary duplication of records. It would undermine group life insurance which is customarily conducted on a "self administrative" fashion with the employer or employer group maintaining the record of individual employees, thus reducing the cost of premiums. (Cf. General American Life Insurance Co. v. Charleville (Mo.1971), 471 S.W.2d 231, 236.) The record made in this case does not supply us with evidence as to what overall method of administration was followed under the insurance plan involved or as to what the costs of some alternative method might be, and we therefore do not consider this contention in reaching our decision.

* * *

Reversed and remanded, with directions.

GOLDENHERSH, JUSTICE (dissenting).

I dissent. The incontestability clause provides:

> "[A]nd no statement made by any employee insured under this policy relating to his insurability shall be used in contesting the validity of the insurance with respect to which such statement was made, after such insurance has been in force prior to the contest for a period of two years during such employee's lifetime * * *."

As used in this policy the term "insurability" does not refer solely to the condition of the employee's health; it means "capable of being insured" or the "quality or condition of being insurable" (Kahn v. Continental Casualty Co., 391 Ill. 445, 63 N.E.2d 468), and the only contention made by defendant of her ineligibility or lack of insurability is her failure to be regularly employed. Defendant accepted premiums covering Mrs. Crawford for 52 months, and admittedly, if she had been afflicted with some incurable malady at the time the policy was issued, her "insurability" could not, after two years, have been contested. Neither logic nor the authorities cited support the drawing of a distinction between noninsurability based on illness and noninsurability based on failure to be employed for a minimum number of hours during each week. Indeed, if any distinction were to be drawn it should serve to more rigidly apply the incontestability clause to the latter situation for the reason that it is so easily discoverable.

The reason for the inclusion of the incontestability clause in policies of this type is obvious, and the fixing of the two-year period is clearly for the purpose of providing ample time for the insurer to investigate the veracity of the representations made. It is naive to believe that group insurers are trusting souls who accept, without question, the representations of the groups whom they insure, and the fact is that the policies provide for, and the insurers make, periodic inspections and audits. I cannot share the majority's apprehension with regard to the hypothetical case of the terminated employee. If the insurer failed to learn of the termination, and accepted premiums for a period of two years after its occurrence, that too should be governed by the incontestability clause. Under the terms of this policy the defendant was entitled to inspect and audit payroll records, and its failure to discover within the two-year period that Mrs. Crawford was not employed should not permit it to invoke a defense in clear violation of the express provisions of its policy. The rationale of Simpson v. Phoenix Mutual Life Insurance Co., 24 N.Y.2d 262, 299 N.Y.S.2d 835, 247 N.E.2d 655, which the appellate court followed, is preferable to the grounds upon which the majority rests its decision, and I would affirm the judgment.

Notes

1. A group life policy covered "Employee's legal spouse residing with the employee." In 1973, the employee listed Beulah as his spouse on the enrollment card. Premiums were deducted from his paycheck. In 1979 Beulah died. In fact she was not his wife but had lived with him for 35 years as his common law wife. May the insurer refuse payment despite the incontestability clause? See Jackson v. Continental Casualty Co., 402 So.2d 175 (La.App.1981) (held yes).

2. Besides employer sponsored group disability insurance, one can buy individual private disability insurance. In *Galanty v. Paul Revere Life Ins. Co.*, 23 Cal.4th 368, 97 Cal.Rptr.2d 67, 1 P.3d 658 (2000), the California Supreme Court unanimously held that statutorily required incontestability clauses in private disability insurance policies bar insurers from denying coverage for an insured's disability, regardless of whether the causative sickness manifested itself before the date the policy was issued.

In Galanty, the insured applied for a private disability insurance policy at a time that he was HIV positive but he did not have AIDS. The insured did not volunteer information regarding his condition and the application contained no question dealing with either HIV or AIDS. The insurer asked for the insured's medical records but did nothing else during the two-year statutory incontestability period to investigate the insured's medical condition. The insured developed AIDS, became disabled, and filed a claim after the incontestability period had run. After initially paying benefits, the insurer denied the claim after it discovered the insured's condition. The insurer claimed that, based on the policy's definitional provision, the insured's illness had manifested itself prior to the issuance of the policy. The court held that the statutory incontestability clause trumped the policy's definitions. The court noted that of the two statutorily authorized disability policies, the insurer chose the one that did not offer insurers explicit protection from fraud, ostensibly to make the policy more palatable to customers.

3. For an excellent review and analysis of the problem, see *Words, Coverage Clauses and Incontestable Statutes: The Regulation of Post Claim Underwriting*, 1979 Ill. L. Forum 809.

4. *Group Insurance and Conflicts of Law*. It is the nature of the group policies that the beneficiaries, and even the insureds, are apt to be scattered over a number of jurisdictions, each possibly different from the corporate domicile of the insurer. § 192, comment h of the Restatement (Second) of Conflicts of Law provides that, "the rights against the insurer are usually governed by the law which governs the master policy."

Krauss v. Manhattan Life Insurance Co. of New York, 643 F.2d 98 (2d Cir.1981), however, indicates that the choice of law problem may not be that easily resolved. In that case a New York insurer issued and delivered in New York a group policy covering the employees of an Illinois concern. As in the *Crawford* case the plaintiff (a lawyer) was included in the plan, although "ineligible" because he was only a part-time employee. His death occurred after the expiration of the "incontestable" period. Illinois law under the *Crawford* decision would not allow the Illinois beneficiary to recover, whereas New York under the *Simpson* rule would. The 2d Circuit using New York choice of law doctrine held that Illinois law applied in this situation.

> "Because certificate holders in other states under the same master policy are apt to be governed by other states' laws, we recognize that the rule formulated by the Second Restatement might offer greater uniformity than the interest-analysis and center of gravity approach used by New York courts. This does not, however, compel a different result. Uniformity and predictability were undeniably compromised when the classical territorial approach to choice of law problems was abandoned [in New York] * * *. Moreover, this outcome retains substantial uniformity as to the [employer] all of whose employees are in Illinois."

Query: What if the certificate holders were not all in Illinois?

5. Accidents

Life insurance policies commonly contain provisions for "double indemnity" if the insured dies as a result of accidental bodily injury. The double indemnity simply means that if death is accidental, the policy will pay double the amount of the policy. The next cases illustrate the elusiveness of the term "accidental."

VALLEY DENTAL ASS'N, P.C. v. THE GREAT-WEST LIFE ASSURANCE CO.

Court of Appeals of Arizona, 1992.
173 Ariz. 327, 842 P.2d 1340.

EHRLICH, JUDGE.

The issue presented in this case is whether Gregory S. Christensen's death was "accidental" for purposes of his beneficiaries' recovery under the double indemnity portion of a life insurance policy. We hold that his death was not an accident and therefore reverse the summary judgment granted to the beneficiaries.

I. FACTS AND PROCEDURAL HISTORY

A. The Insurance Policy

The Great-West Life Assurance Company ("Great-West") issued a group insurance policy to the American Dental Society, of which Christensen was a member. Named as the beneficiaries of the policy issued on Christensen's life were Valley Dental Association and Amalgamated Investment Resources ("the beneficiaries"). The policy amount was $350,000, with a provision for double indemnity in case of accidental death. The accidental death provision read: If a Member sustains bodily injury which: (1) is caused solely by accidental means; and (2) is sustained while he is insured under the Group Policy; and (3) results in his death; then the Company will pay an additional amount of insurance. Payment will be made only if death: (a) occurs within 90 days after the accident; (b) is a direct result of an accident; and (c) is unrelated to any other cause. The word "accident" is undefined.

B. Christensen's Death

The material facts are undisputed for purposes of this appeal. On September 27, 1987, Christensen picked up a 15-year-old female hitchhiker. After starting to take the girl in her intended direction, Christensen drove the car off the road in a remote area. He forced the girl at knife-point to perform oral sex on him and sexually assaulted her. He then grabbed her throat, announced "I have to kill you" and began choking her. The girl resisted and, in the struggle, they both fell out of the car, onto the ground. She grabbed the knife, but Christensen knocked it from her hand. He then got on top of her and placed both hands around her throat, choking her as he banged her head against the ground. She managed to kick Christensen in the face, knocking off his glasses. As he turned to get his glasses, the girl again picked up the knife. Christensen, having retrieved his glasses, approached the girl. She stabbed him in the leg. He backed away and the girl escaped. Christensen, whose left femoral artery had been severed, bled to death at the scene.

C. The Insurance Claim

Following Christensen's death, the beneficiaries filed a claim with Great-West, seeking the death benefit of $350,000 plus the additional

$350,000 accidental death benefit. Great–West paid the death benefit but denied the accidental death benefit, asserting that the death was not an accident. The beneficiaries then filed this suit under breach of contract and bad faith theories. On cross-motions for summary judgment, the trial court awarded the beneficiaries judgment on the breach of contract claim and awarded Great–West summary judgment on the bad-faith claim.

Great–West appealed. The interpretation of the insurance contract is a question of law for this court to decide independently of the conclusions of the trial court. Thomas v. Liberty Mutual Insurance Co., 173 Ariz. 322, 334, 842 P.2d 1335, 1337 (App.1992).

II. Discussion

The insurance policy states that extra benefits will be paid if the insured dies of "accidental means." In Landress v. Phoenix Mutual Life Insurance Co., 291 U.S. 491, 497, 54 S.Ct. 461, 463, 78 L.Ed. 934 (1934), the Supreme Court held that, in such a policy, the mechanism or action causing the injury or death must have been accidental; it is not enough that the result was accidental or unintended.

Justice Cardozo dissented in Landress, decrying the court's distinction between means and results. 291 U.S. at 498–501, 54 S.Ct. at 463–464. In Knight v. Metropolitan Life Insurance Co., 103 Ariz. 100, 103–04, 437 P.2d 416, 419–20 (1968), our supreme court adopted the dissent:

> In an oft-quoted dissent which has now become the majority rule throughout the states, Justice Cardozo said: "The attempted distinction between accidental results and accidental means will plunge this branch of the law into a Serbonian Bog. Probably it is true to say that in the strictest sense and dealing with the region of physical nature there is no such thing as an accident. On the other hand, the average man is convinced that there is, and so certainly is the man who takes out a policy of accident insurance * * *. When a man has died in such a way that his death is spoken of as an accident, he has died because of an accident, and hence by accidental means. If there was no accident in the means, there was none in the result, for the two were inseparable. There was an accident throughout, or there was no accident at all." [Citation omitted.]
>
> * * *
>
> [W]e are going to clarify our position and determine along with the growing majority rule that an accident is an accident whether it be in the "means" or the "result." [Footnote omitted.]

Knight died following a dive from the top of Coolidge Dam. An experienced diver, who indeed had jumped from this dam before, he nonetheless seemingly misjudged the distance and rolled onto his back from a swan dive before hitting the water. The court, after discussing the "average man" approach taken by Justice Cardozo in Landress, held that this was an accident, stating:

> One paying the premium for a policy which insures against "death by accidental means" * * * *intends to insure against the*

fortuitous, the unintentional, and the unexpected, that which happens through mishap, mischance or misjudgment. When he pays that premium month after month he does not intend that any act committed by him, no matter how daring, reckless or foolhardy, be adjudged by a court under "reasonable man tests" or "natural and probable consequence" standards to deprive his beneficiary of contractual rights arising out of his unintended and unexpected and, therefore, accidental death. [Emphasis added.] The term "accidental means" as used in this policy should not be construed in a technical sense but should be given its ordinary and popular meaning according to common speech and usage and the understanding of the average man. [Citation omitted.] 103 Ariz. at 104, 437 P.2d at 420.

In urging that the "ordinary and popular meaning" be applied to the term "accident" in determining whether a death is covered by the accidental death provision of a policy, the court in Knight again acted in consonance with the then-growing majority of jurisdictions in applying the common understanding of "accident" as an event that is at least unexpected. As applied to an insured such as Christensen, [t]he general rule to be gleaned from the cases is that if the insured threatens to kill, or inflict serious bodily injury on, another person or assaults another person under circumstances making it likely the other person will respond with deadly force, and does so and kills the insured, the insured's death is not accidental. Hoffman, 669 P.2d at 417. See e.g., Howard, 474 So.2d at 1111; Cockrell v. Life Ins. Co., 692 F.2d 1164, 1168 (8th Cir.1982); James v. Aetna Life Ins. Co., 161 Ga.App. 64, 289 S.E.2d 290, 291 (1982); Butcher, 290 S.E.2d at 375–76; Byrd v. Life Ins. Co., 219 Va. 824, 252 S.E.2d 307, 310 (1979); Rodolph v. New York Life Ins. Co., 412 P.2d 610, 611–12 (Wyo.1966); Henry, 217 N.E.2d at 486; Perringer, 244 S.W.2d at 617; Meister, 179 P. at 916; Annot., 26 A.L.R.2d at 402; Couch on Insurance, § 41:204 at 300 ("essential" to coverage that insured not have provoked act). When there have been differing interpretations, the division "seems to arise from the courts' varying ideas regarding the degree of foresight which should be required of the insured. Cf. R. Keeton, Insurance Law § 5.4(f) (1971)." Carlyle, 551 P.2d at 666. The court in Knight, by referring to "the understanding of the average man," sought to strike a balance between focusing exclusively on the insured and the subjective state of mind that cannot comprehend death and the artificial "reasonable man" who would declare not an accident any "daring, reckless or foolhardy" act. 103 Ariz. at 104, 437 P.2d at 420.

Here, by any definition, Christensen's death was not an accident.[7] He created a situation in which another person had to fight for her life in order to survive. It was he who was armed with a knife and the intent

7. We are not in this opinion creating a criminal act exclusion in Christensen's insurance policy. It is for the insurance company, and not the court, to write its policy and the fact that an insured was engaged in criminal conduct does not in every case preclude a finding that a death or injury was accidental. Roque, 467 A.2d at 1129; Hoffman, 669 P.2d at 417.

to kill and, as was certain, the victim struggled against death and seized the weapon to defend herself. Christensen's resulting death cannot be classified as "fortuitous" or "unexpected," or as having occurred through "mishap, mischance or misjudgment." Knight, 103 Ariz. at 104, 437 P.2d at 420.

If there was no accident in the means, there was none in the result, for the two were inseparable. There was an accident throughout, or there was no accident at all. Id. at 103, 437 P.2d at 419 (quoting Landress, 291 U.S. at 501, 54 S.Ct. at 464 (Cardozo, J., dissenting)).

Accordingly, Great–West need not pay accidental death benefits under the policy.

* * *

The judgment in favor of the beneficiaries is reversed. The case is remanded to the trial court for further proceedings.

Notes

1. In *Knight v. Metropolitan Life Ins. Co.*, 103 Ariz. 100, 437 P.2d 416 (1968), cited in the principal case, the insured's death after swan dive off Coolidge Dam on Gila River was held covered given evidence that the insured was experienced at such dives. Is *Knight* consistent with *Valley Dental*?

2. Some life insurance policies provide that the accidental death benefits are not payable if death is contributed to by disease or bodily infirmity. In *Arata v. California–Western States Life Insurance Co.*, 50 Cal.App.3d 821, 123 Cal.Rptr. 631 (1975), the insured accidently slipped and fell causing himself injury. Because he had suffered from hemophilia throughout his life, he sustained abnormal bleeding which eventually led to his death. Despite the fact that it was uncontroverted that a person without hemophilia would have recovered from the injury, the court held that the proximate cause of the insured's death was the fall. Accordingly, the court allowed the insured's beneficiary to collect the accidental death benefit.

3. In an attempt to counter cases like *Arata*, an express exclusion has been drafted to forestall recovery where a pre-existing disease is connected with the insured's accident. The exclusion reads:

> "no payment shall be made for any loss resulting from any injury caused or contributed to by, or as a consequence of, any of the following excluded risks, *even though the proximate or precipitating cause of loss is accidental bodily injury* (emphasis added):
>
> (a) bodily or mental infirmity; or
>
> (b) disease * * *."

This provision was held to preclude recovery in the common situation where the insured with cardiovascular disease passes out and hits his or her head on floor, the blow being the immediate cause of death. See Sekel v. Aetna Life Ins. Co., 704 F.2d 1335, 1336–1337 (5th Cir.1983) (applying Texas law).

4. Should there be a criminal act exclusion in the policies discussed?
5. Is the identity or plight of the beneficiaries relevant?

WETZEL v. WESTINGHOUSE ELECTRIC CORP.

Superior Court of Pennsylvania, 1978.
258 Pa.Super. 500, 393 A.2d 470.

CERCONE, JUDGE:

Willy C.J. Wetzel died on March 16, 1975 at the hand of his son, Roy Wetzel. Roy Wetzel was tried by a jury for murder and voluntary manslaughter in the Court of Common Pleas of Beaver County and was found not guilty. Mary Margaret Wetzel, appellant and widow of Willy Wetzel, then brought this suit to recover the insurance proceeds from an accidental death policy issued on her husband's life. * * * The lower court found that Willy Wetzel's death did not occur through accidental means and therefore there could be no recovery under the insurance policy. The court granted defendant's motion for summary judgment and it is from that order this appeal comes to us. We reverse the decision of the lower court.

Willy Wetzel and his son, Roy Wetzel, were experts in the martial arts, including karate, and operated a school in Beaver County. On the day of Willy Wetzel's death, Roy had been working on his father's income tax return. Willy visited his son and began reading the completed tax forms. The testimony of Roy, admitted through an excerpt from the transcript in the criminal proceedings in Beaver County, describes the events that ensued. As Willy Wetzel started to sign the tax forms, he threw the pen against the drapes and began to scream obscenities. He walked toward the front door mumbling that he was going to lose his house, car and everything. Grabbing a Hawaiian sword, Willy Wetzel turned and let out a battle cry called a "kewah." The fight began.

Willy began to remove the sword from its case when Roy attempted to grab the case. Willy kicked Roy and the sword was bent in half. The hand-to-hand fight continued for approximately twenty-five minutes. Roy made several attempts to reach the telephone to call for help, but was stopped each time by his father's tactics. Finally, Roy placed nanchukas sticks, used in karate, around his father's head to try to render him unconscious. Shortly after that Roy realized his father was dead.

Based on these facts, we are faced with deciding whether the death of Willy Wetzel occurred through accidental means under the insurance policy in question. The Benefit Provisions of the Certificate of Insurance in this case read in part:

> "If, while insured under the Group Policy for Personal Accident Insurance, the Employe sustains bodily injuries solely through violent, external and accidental means, and within ninety days thereafter suffers any of the losses specified in Section C hereof as a direct result of such bodily injuries independently of all other causes, the

Insurance Company shall pay the amount of the insurance specified for such loss * * * provided, however, that in no case shall any payment be made for death or any other loss which is:

* * *

(D) caused by or resulting from intentional self-destruction or intentionally self-inflicted injury, while sane or insane."

* * * The lower court opinion correctly stated that subsection (D) of the benefit provisions of the insurance contract in this case does not apply where the death was due to the acts of another. The difficult question arises when the policy does not contain a violation of law clause "or the commission of a crime exception and the injury is as a result of the insured's culpable conduct." Mohn v. American Casualty Co., 458 Pa. at 579, 326 A.2d at 348.

In Mohn v. American Casualty Co., supra, a father sued for expenses incurred when his son was fatally wounded by a police bullet while he was fleeing from a burglary. The insurance policy did not contain a violation of law clause, just as is the case with the policy before us. The *Mohn* case aptly discusses the split of authorities in this kind of case. One view is to preclude recovery when the insured's injury is the direct result of his own criminal conduct. However, even these jurisdictions that base the view on public policy involved grant an exception where the suit for recovery is brought by an innocent beneficiary.[8] Other jurisdictions refuse relief on the grounds that the occurrence was the foreseeable consequence of the acts of the insured and therefore not accidental.[9] This was the reasoning given in the opinion of the lower court and argued by appellee in the case before us. However, the Pennsylvania cases have expressly rejected the public policy reasoning as well as the use of the reasonably foreseeable test in denying recovery where the insured was involved in culpable conduct. Eisenman v. Hornberger, 438 Pa. 46, 264 A.2d 673 (1970); Beckham v. Travelers Ins. Co., 424 Pa. 107, 225 A.2d 532 (1967). Thus the *Mohn* court permitted recovery by the father.

In justifying its decision, the court in *Mohn,* supra, cited with approval Eisenman v. Hornberger, supra. There, two persons broke into a home and stole liquor. In the course of their crime, they lit matches in order to see their way. One of the matches lodged in a chair and caused a fire that destroyed the home. The insurance contract involved did not contain a "violation of law" clause and therefore recovery could not be denied. The court further explained that it was not convinced of any overriding public policy which would deny recovery.

"There is no evidence whatsoever that the policy was procured *in contemplation* of the crime. Nor can the insurance policy be said to have *promoted* the unlawful act. Moreover, it seems equally implausible that denying coverage would serve as a crime *deterrent.* Finally,

8. See 43 A.L.R.3d 1125 et seq. (1972).

9. See Id. at 1132–34.

the insurance policy in no way saves the insured from the consequences of his criminal act." 438 Pa. at 50, 264 A.2d at 675.

When applying the factors used by the *Eisenman* court to the case before us, we reach the same result. Although stealing liquor is distinguishable from the criminal assault Willy Wetzel committed upon his son, Roy, both involved criminal conduct not covered by a violation of law clause in the policy. The facts of the case before us show Willy's rage was due to his income tax return and was in no way related to the procurement of the accidental insurance policy. Nor would denying recovery to an innocent beneficiary in this case deter this type of culpable conduct on the part of the insured.

The *Mohn* case explains that recovery must be placed on the actions of the insured and not on the acts of a third party. From this view it may be argued that it was reasonably foreseeable to Willy Wetzel that his son could have killed him due to his skill in the martial arts. However, "the modern legal trend is to abandon the former 'reasonably foreseeable' rule and treat the occurrence as accidental even though it resulted from the insured's criminal conduct." Mohn v. American Casualty Co., 458 Pa. at 585, 326 A.2d at 351. Our Supreme Court adhered to the modern trend in allowing recovery on an insurance policy in the *Mohn* case and in *Eisenman*.[10] In following this reasoning, we find that the death of Willy Wetzel was due to "violent, external and accidental means" within the meaning of the policy, and appellant, as an innocent beneficiary, must recover.

Order of the lower court reversed.

* * *

VAN DER VOORT and HESTER, JJ., dissent. * * *

Notes

1. The *Wetzel* case finds no overriding public policy which would *imply* the felony exclusion clause in all accident policies. But, what about an insured arsonist for hire who is burned to death by the premature explosion of his gasoline cans because a pilot light was on in the targeted house? See, Taylor v. John Hancock Mutual Life Insurance Co., 11 Ill.2d 227, 142 N.E.2d 5 (1957). Should professional criminals be allowed to provide this sort of family protection against the hazards of their trade?

Compare a later decision by the Pennsylvania Supreme Court, *Roque v. Nationwide Mut. Ins. Co.*, 502 Pa. 615, 467 A.2d 1128 (1983), involving the same type of policy as in *Wetzel*. The insured, trapped by police when he was

10. See also Beckham v. Travelers Ins. Co., 424 Pa. 107, 225 A.2d 532 (1967). In *Beckham,* the mother of the insured sued to collect the insurance proceeds under the policy issued on the life of her son who died due to a self-administered overdose of narcotics. The court expressly abandoned the artificial distinction between accidental means and accidental results, as well as stating that the determination of what was "foreseeable" would be just as troublesome for the courts. Recovery under the policy was allowed.

burglarizing a home, called out a warning to the policeman to get out or he would kill him. The insured emerged from a bedroom carrying a gun and was shot dead. The lower courts relying on *Wetzel* granted summary judgment for the insured's beneficiary. The Supreme Court reversed: "In *Mohn* [discussed at length in the Wetzel opinion] * * * there was nothing * * * to indicate that the insured had threatened or otherwise provoked the officer who fired the fatal shot * * *. In this case, unlike *Mohn,* the insured repeatedly told police officers that he had a gun and intended to shoot to kill * * *. In these circumstances, it must be concluded that insured's conduct provoked the shooting and that the insured's death was thus not accidental." *Wetzel* was not even cited.

2. Justice Udall admonished in *Knight v. Met. Life* (see *Valley Dental*) that, if the accident insurers desire to exclude "reckless and foolhardy acts," they may do so with "simplicity and clarity of expression." It is an invitation which has been accepted (with limitations) by the industry. Still, achieving simplicity and clarity of expression is not easy when attempting to limit bizarre human behavior. It is doubtful that any court would accept a blanket exclusion of the results of "reckless and foolhardy (or stupid) acts" from coverage under an accident policy. At the same time, the attempt to extend by specific exclusion the catalogue of foolhardy behavior begun by Justice Udall would produce a policy of such length as to invite judicial derision.

3. Current policies (see Rider below) do seek to exclude some of the forms of aberrant behavior which have been particularly troublesome. Consider how some of these exclusions (such as "intentional self inflicted injury;" "medicine, drug or sedative * * * except when prescribed;" and the absorption or inhalation of toxic matter under any circumstances) might affect the decisions in the example cases set forth in the next note.

RIDER

ACCIDENTAL DEATH BENEFIT (ADB)

[*Reprinted with permission of Provident Mutual Life Insurance Company of Philadelphia*]

BENEFIT. The Company will pay this benefit upon receipt of due proof that the Insured's death was the direct and independent result of accidental bodily injury. Such death must have occurred:

1. within one year after the injury was sustained; and
2. while this rider was in force.

The amount of this benefit, shown on page 3, will be paid as a part of the proceeds of this policy.

EXCLUSIONS FROM COVERAGE. This benefit will not be payable if the Insured's death was the result of:

1. a physical or mental disease or ailment;
2. suicide while sane or insane;
3. intentional, self-inflicted injury while sane or insane;
4. medicine, drug or sedative voluntarily taken or administered, except those prescribed by a duly licensed physician;

5. poison, chemical, chemical compound, gas or fumes voluntarily taken, administered, absorbed or inhaled;
6. committing or attempting to commit assault or a felony;
7. travel in or descent from an aircraft of any kind if the Insured;
   a. was a pilot, officer or member of its crew;
   b. was giving or receiving any training or instruction;
   c. had any duty aboard; or
   d. had any duty requiring descent from the aircraft;
8. war, declared or not, or any act incident to a war or to a conflict involving the armed forces of any country.

AUTOPSY. The Company at its own expense will have the right to examine the Insured's body and to perform an autopsy unless prohibited by law.

INCONTESTABILITY. The Company will not contest this rider after it has been in force during the Insured's lifetime for 2 years from the issue date of this policy, except for nonpayment of premiums.

TERMINATION. This rider will terminate:

1. upon written request;
2. 31 days after the due date of any unpaid premium for either this rider or the policy to which it is attached;
3. at attained age 70; or
4. upon the surrender, maturity, expiry or other termination of this policy.

Attached by PROVIDENT MUTUAL LIFE INSURANCE COMPANY OF PHILADELPHIA on the issue date of this policy.

The exclusion from coverage of accidents incurred while committing or attempting to commit a felony certainly operates to deny recovery for many instances of foolhardy behavior. Note its potential applicability to the situation in the *Wetzel* case.

4. The expressions "accident," "accidental result" and "accidental means" must certainly be considered among the most intractable in the legal lexicon. Synonyms are hard to come by; impossible, indeed, for a straight "accident" policy, and seemingly useless in property or liability insurance where the substitution of "occurrence" for the word "accident" has led only to the redefinition of occurrence as an accident. Justice Cardozo's simplistic (as critics describe it) attempt to take "accidental means" out of the Serbonian Bog by equating it with "accidental result" may not have accomplished much more than to have moved the problem to another, albeit shallower, part of the Bog. The continuing inability to obtain a judicial consensus on the meaning of these expressions invites litigation which in turn affords numerous recent examples of situations which have reoccurred so often as to make possible rough categorizations.

I. *Provocation cases.* In *Floyd v. Equitable Life Assurance Society*, 164 W.Va. 661, 264 S.E.2d 648 (1980), the husband, a 240 lb. ex-Marine, was killed in a marital fight by his wife (the beneficiary, who weighed 80 lbs).

She stabbed him with a knife, at which point he said, "You can't hurt me. Stab me again." She did. The court reversed the summary judgment grant for insurer, explaining, "We do not believe (Floyd's) statement at the time of stabbing compels the conclusion as a matter of law that the deceased could have reasonably foreseen his conduct would result in his death." Compare Davis v. Continental Cas. Co., 560 F.Supp. 723 (N.D.Miss.1983) (in a family quarrel the inclination is to find death is the result of accident).

II. *Aberrant behavior of a risky nature—flirting with death.* Autoerotica is a phenomenon that involves the participant "hanging himself by the neck creating an asphyxial state in an attempt to stimulate nerve centers in the brain and heighten the masturbation experience." The insured was found dead in the noose he had placed on his neck. The court found for the insurer, reasoning, "* * * a reasonable person would foresee that placing a noose about his neck for the purpose of inducing asphyxia could result in his death. * * * [H]e should have expected that his actions could be fatal." But see: Connecticut General Life Ins. Co. v. Tommie, 619 S.W.2d 199, 203 (Tex.Civ.App.1981) (accidental death where decedent (1) "did not intentionally inflict upon himself bodily injury in the normal and usual meaning of that term" and (2) autoerotica is not a disease).

III. *Pre-existing disease cases.* In *Gottfried v. Prudential Ins. Co. of America*, 82 N.J. 478, 414 A.2d 544 (1980), the insurance contract contained an accidental result clause that excluded "loss which results ... directly or indirectly from bodily infirmity." The insured, 44 years old with known arterio-sclerotic condition, died of a heart attack playing basketball. (No autopsy was requested by the insurer. The beneficiary testified that her rabbi informed her that an autopsy was forbidden by her religion.) By divided vote, the New Jersey Supreme Court reversed two lower court decisions and held for the beneficiary. A Minnesota case, decided the same year and involving the same insurance company, also sided with the beneficiary when the insured had a cerebral aneurism (classified as a disease) which burst, causing him to topple into a bathtub to his death. Orman v. Prudential Ins. Co. of America, 296 N.W.2d 380 (Minn.1980).

6. Rights to Proceeds

a. Beneficiary Rights

IN RE THE MARRIAGE OF O'CONNELL

Court of Appeal of California, Sixth District, 1992.
8 Cal.App.4th 565, 10 Cal.Rptr.2d 334.

COTTLE, ACTING PRESIDING J.

INTRODUCTION

John O'Connell died on December 25, 1990, leaving two life insurance policies sponsored by his employer totaling $212,000, according to his widow, Nona O'Connell. At issue is whether John's ex-wife, Raytha O'Connell, and their son, Richard, are entitled to two-thirds of the insurance proceeds because of a court order requiring they be designated as beneficiaries of the policies. Nona, as an individual and as executrix of

John's estate, appeals from an order denying her motion to vacate the order that John designate Raytha and Richard as joint life insurance beneficiaries with Nona. Nona contends the court lacked jurisdiction to make the original order because it was beyond the court's power, the life insurance was not properly before the court, and Nona received no prior notice of the request to modify the life insurance. Facts are stated where relevant. For the reasons stated below, we will affirm the order.

Facts

On July 15, 1985, John, a design specialist for Lockheed Missiles and Space Co., filed for dissolution of his 16–year marriage to Raytha. In July 1986 the parties stipulated to bifurcate the proceedings as to the issue of status. On November 12, 1986, their marriage was dissolved with the court reserving jurisdiction over "all other issues in this proceeding, including, but not limited to, division of property and debts, spousal support, child support and injunctive orders."

According to Nona, John married her on November 14, 1986, and designated her the beneficiary of life insurance provided through Lockheed.

On December 30, 1987, after trial of remaining issues, the court ordered John to pay monthly spousal support of $651 and child support of $912 for two minor children. This amended judgment also divided the parties' property and reserved jurisdiction over other issues. There was no disposition of John's life insurance.

By stipulation and order filed April 18, 1990, the parties agreed that child support would be reduced to $450 and spousal support to $200 monthly as of September 1, 1989.

On June 4, 1990, John filed a motion seeking a reduction in child and spousal support due to his disability. Raytha offered, by letter and telephone call but without a formal responsive pleading, to agree to reduction if she alone or she and their children were named beneficiaries of John's life insurance. According to Nona, John did not appear at the hearing on July 27, 1990, due to illness. At the hearing John's counsel objected to the request to modify the insurance because it was not made through formal pleadings, it would be unfair to Nona, John had no obligation to support his adult son, and both children would be entitled to social security benefits on John's death if he survived to the age of 62 on October 17, 1990. The court ordered reductions in monthly spousal support to nothing and child support to $125 during John's disability and, as child and spousal support, that John name Raytha and Richard, his minor son, as beneficiaries of his life insurance along with Nona. This order was served on John on September 20, 1990.

John died on December 25, 1990, without providing for his children in his will. According to Nona, John was covered by two life insurance policies purchased through his employer, a $112,000 basic policy and a $100,000 optional policy, the latter purchased by John's earnings without his employer's contribution.

On January 15, 1991, Raytha filed a motion seeking enforcement of the life insurance modification order and alleging John did not change beneficiaries before he died. On January 31, 1991, the court granted Nona's request to intervene in this action. Nona was appointed the executrix of John's estate on March 4, 1991.

On March 15, 1991, Nona filed a motion to vacate the order modifying the life insurance. The motion was denied at a hearing on May 10, 1991, for reasons partly quoted below.

Discussion

1. Was the Marital Dissolution Court Empowered to Order the Designation of Life Insurance Beneficiaries as a Support Substitute?

In a dissolution action the court can order a spouse as a form of support to maintain life insurance to benefit either the other spouse or a minor child. Section 4801.4 of the Family Law Act (§ 4000 et seq.), cited in the trial court's statement of decision, provides in pertinent part: "For the purposes of Section 4801, where it is just and reasonable in view of the circumstances of the respective parties, the court, in determining the needs of a supported spouse, may include an amount sufficient to purchase an annuity for the supported spouse or to maintain insurance for the benefit of the supported spouse on the life of the spouse required to make the payment of support, * * * so that the supported spouse will not be left without means for support in the event that the order for support is terminated by the death of the party required to make the payment of support. Except as otherwise agreed to by the parties in writing, an order made under this section may be modified or terminated at the discretion of the court at any time prior to the death of the party required to make the payment of support."

As explained in In re Marriage of Ziegler (1989) 207 Cal.App.3d 788, 255 Cal.Rptr. 100: "[T]he Law Revision Commission comments to section 4801.4 * * * state: 'If insurance is already in force on the life of the support obligor, this section authorizes the court to order that the support obligor maintain some or all of the insurance in force and name the supported spouse as the beneficiary of the insurance.' " (Id. at p. 791, 255 Cal.Rptr. 100.) The statute authorized a court to require an ex-husband to maintain a military survivor benefit plan as a form of annuity for his ex-wife. (Ibid.)

* * *

Nona also contends this order violates the rule that a spousal support obligation ordinarily ends on the obligor's death. (§ 4801, subd. (b).) Ziegler, supra, 207 Cal.App.3d 788, 255 Cal.Rptr. 100, also rejected this contention. "Section 4801.4 does not change this rule. (Cal.Law Revision Com. com., 12A West's Ann.Civ.Code, supra, § 4801.4 * * *.)" (Id. at p. 792, 255 Cal.Rptr. 100.) The obligor's death still ends the obligor's support obligation, specifically to maintain the insurance or annuity, and creates a new obligation in the insurer or annuity provider to the supported spouse. (Ibid.)

On the same reasoning, provision of insurance for a minor does not extend the obligor's child support obligation beyond the obligor's death. Even if it did, a child support obligation survives the obligor's death and becomes the obligation of the obligor's estate. (Franklin Life Ins. Co., supra, 249 Cal.App.2d 623, 631, 57 Cal.Rptr. 652; In re Marriage of Gregory (1991) 230 Cal.App.3d 112, 115–116, 281 Cal.Rptr. 188.)

Thus, courts have the power in marital dissolutions to order maintenance of life insurance for the benefit of children and former spouses as a support substitute.

2. Was the Issue of Modifying John's Life Insurance Before the Court?

Nona contends this particular dissolution court had no jurisdiction to order modification of John's life insurance because Raytha did not formally bring the issue before the court by either a motion or a pleading responding to John's request to reduce support * * *.

* * *

We agree with the trial court that John's motion to reduce support put his life insurance in issue. When a support obligor pleads inability to maintain an existing level of spousal and child support from current income, it is reasonable to expect that the court will consider available support alternatives including modification of life insurance. The trial court found that local practice also justified this expectation. At the hearing John did not claim to be so surprised as to be unable to respond to the merits, nor could he in light of Raytha's informal requests to modify his life insurance. John in fact did respond to the merits, arguing that his children had other support alternatives, such as social security benefits. Under these circumstances, the trial court in ruling on John's motion to reduce support had jurisdiction over his life insurance.

3. Must an Order to Change Life Insurance Beneficiaries Be Preceded by Notice to the Current Beneficiary?

Nona contends that the dissolution court could not order her husband to add beneficiaries to his life insurance without notice to her as the existing beneficiary. This contention requires consideration of the nature of Nona's interests in John's life insurance as both the designated beneficiary and his surviving spouse.

It remains surprisingly unsettled whether the community interest in an insurance policy limits an insured spouse's ability to change beneficiaries. We will attempt to define this community interest after analyzing related interests. It helps to distinguish among four related interests: (1) the insured's contractual or statutory right to change beneficiaries (Ins.Code, § 10170)[11], (2) any community interest in that right, (3) the

11. Insurance Code section 10170, subdivision (e) provides that an agreement to

beneficiary's interest in remaining designated, and (4) the community interest in the policy proceeds.

A. The Insured's Right to Designate Beneficiaries and the Beneficiary's Interest in Remaining Designated

To an insured, the right to designate and change insurance beneficiaries may be a vested contractual right worthy of constitutional protection against impairment. (Frazier v. Tulare County Bd. of Retirement (1974) 42 Cal.App.3d 1046, 1051–1052, 117 Cal.Rptr. 386—beneficiary designation could not be overridden by Gov.Code amendment.) To the designated beneficiary, however, the insured's unfettered right to change beneficiaries trivializes the beneficiary's interest into a mere unvested expectancy unworthy of constitutional protection. (Wissner v. Wissner (1950) 338 U.S. 655, 661, 70 S.Ct. 398, 401, 94 L.Ed. 424—California community property law neither prevents federal insured from changing insurance beneficiary nor controls distribution of proceeds.) It has long been established, when the insured retains the right to change beneficiaries, the designated beneficiary's interest is a mere revocable expectancy vesting only on the insured's death, though the policy is acquired with community funds.

The insured can waive any right to change beneficiaries by appropriate agreement, such as by making an irrevocable beneficiary designation. An irrevocably designated beneficiary obtains a vested contractual right not dependent on any community interest. When an insured ignores a court order or contractual obligation to retain an irrevocable beneficiary, that beneficiary is entitled to recover the insurance proceeds.

B. The Community Interest in Life Insurance Proceeds

Acquisition by community funds does affect life insurance. Both spouses ordinarily have a community interest in the proceeds of an insurance policy to the extent it was acquired with community funds. Life insurance proceeds are subject to the general rule that a spouse cannot dispose of community personal property without either the other spouse's written consent or consideration. (§ 5125, subd. (b).) Thus, it is established that after the insured's death the surviving spouse can bring an action to set aside any unauthorized gift of insurance proceeds to the extent of his or her community interest, if this right has not been waived or released.

C. The Community Interest, If Any, in an Insured's Right to Change Beneficiaries

What remains unsettled is whether there is a community interest in the insured's right to change beneficiaries. Is this interest more like the community interest in the insurance proceeds or the designated beneficiary's mere expectancy?

pay life insurance "may be rescinded or amended by the parties thereto without the consent of any beneficiary therein designated unless the rights of any such beneficiary have been expressly declared to be irrevocable."

On the one hand we find dictum stating a spouse can completely set aside an insurance beneficiary change during the insured's life if it amounts to an unauthorized gift of community property. None of those cases involved any challenge to a beneficiary change during the insured's life. Tyre, supra, and Polk, supra, actually applied the rule that after the insured's death the surviving spouse can set aside a beneficiary change to the extent of her community interest in the insurance proceeds. (54 Cal.2d at pp. 404–406, 6 Cal.Rptr. 13, 353 P.2d 725; 228 Cal.App.2d at pp. 782, 785, 39 Cal.Rptr. 824.) Benson, supra, merely discussed the community interest in life insurance in order to contrast it with public employee pension benefits. (60 Cal.2d at p. 363, 33 Cal.Rptr. 257, 384 P.2d 649.) None of these cases considered the effect of the provision in Insurance Code section 10170 that a beneficiary's consent to change life insurance is only necessary when the beneficiary is irrevocable. Polk, supra, expressly held this statute inapplicable because it post-dated the insurance policies in issue. (228 Cal.App.2d at p. 787, 39 Cal.Rptr. 824.)

On the other hand, in addition to the unsettled scope of Insurance Code section 10170, we find dictum stating a spouse has no cause of action arising from an insurance beneficiary change until the insured's death, though meanwhile the spouse can notify the insurer of the community interest in a policy. (See Estate of Mendenhall (1960) 182 Cal.App.2d 441, 445–446, 6 Cal.Rptr. 45.) That opinion was filed four days after Tyre, supra, and does not discuss it. That case also involved no challenge to a beneficiary change during the insured's life. It involved the taxability to the surviving spouse's estate of insurance proceeds.

Thus, there is nonbinding, inconclusive support for concluding a spouse by virtue of his or her community interest in a life insurance policy has a somewhat greater interest in the insured spouse's right to change beneficiaries than the designated beneficiary's mere unvested expectancy.

D. Nona's Entitlement to Notice of a Potential Court Order to Change her Husband's Life Insurance Beneficiary

Applying the rules above to the facts of this case, we conclude, absent any evidence that Nona was an irrevocable life insurance beneficiary, her status as a designated beneficiary conferred no protection against John changing life insurance beneficiaries. However, her status as his spouse arguably enhanced her interest in his right to change beneficiaries to the extent the insurance was acquired by community funds of her marriage to John.

As Raytha points out, Nona's claim on appeal that the life insurance was purchased with her community funds is unwarranted. Nona merely declared, "The premiums on the optional life policy were paid entirely from John's earnings * * *." Based on this declaration, she asked the trial court to find "all premiums on the life insurance policies * * * were paid with the community property of John O'Connell and Nona O'Connell." The trial court made no finding on this issue, perhaps due to the following conflicting evidence. John's original declaration of income and expenses, filed May 30, 1986, reflected a deduction from income during his marriage to Raytha for life insurance. Later declarations filed June 9, 1987, April 12, 1989, and June 20, 1990, showed unspecified tax and insurance expenses but no life insurance deduction. We cannot assume the trial court implicitly resolved this factual dispute against Nona. (Code Civ.Proc., § 634.)

Even if we accept for the sake of discussion the questionable factual premise that the insurance policies were acquired with Nona's community funds and we apply the questionable legal premise that she therefore had a right during John's life to set aside his change of life insurance beneficiaries, Nona was not entitled to prior notice of the dissolution court's potential order to change John's life insurance beneficiaries. Any community interest in an insured's right to change beneficiaries is limited to avoiding gifts of community personal property. As Raytha contends and Nona disputes, there was no actual or potential unauthorized gift in this case.

John's remarriage created new community and separate property, both of which were subject to his existing spousal and child support obligations. A change in life insurance beneficiaries to fulfill existing support obligations is not a gift, particularly when ordered by a court. Thus, even if the life insurance policies were acquired with Nona's community funds, it was no gift for the court to order John to add Raytha and Richard as beneficiaries. (Cf. Burgart, supra, 5 Cal.App.3d at pp. 412–413, 85 Cal.Rptr. 122.)

Whatever the exact nature of Nona's interest as John's spouse in his right to change life insurance beneficiaries, it did not extend beyond the prevention of an unauthorized gift of community property. Raytha's request to designate herself and her child as additional beneficiaries of John's life insurance was made and considered by the dissolution court as a support substitute. This request did not propose a potential gift of Nona's community property and the resulting order did not effectuate such a gift. Therefore, Nona had no interest at stake justifying advance notice to her of the possibility of an order to change John's life insurance beneficiaries.[12]

DISPOSITION

THE ORDER IS AFFIRMED.

Notes

1. As noted, life insurers may have special administrative problems in community property states. In *Prudential Ins. Co. of America v. Burke*, 614 S.W.2d 847 (Tex.Civ.App. 1981), the insurer declined to effectuate a change

12. A different conclusion might result if the court had attempted to adjudicate without notice to Nona the extent of her community interest in the life insurance proceeds or her right to reimbursement, if any (§ 5120.150; e.g., In re Marriage of Williams (1989) 213 Cal.App.3d 1239, 262 Cal.Rptr. 317), but these issues were not presented.

of beneficiary from an ex-wife to the new wife of the insured on the grounds that the ex-wife had a community property right which could not be divested by the act of the insured. The Texas appellate court, however, held that the insurer was obliged to make the change although it would only apply to the insured's community property interest. Prudential Ins. Co. of America v. Burke, 614 S.W.2d 847 (Tex.Civ.App.1981).

2. In *Leonard v. Occidental Life Insurance Co.*, 31 Cal.App.3d 117, 106 Cal.Rptr. 899 (1973), the widow Leonard claimed a community property interest in the life insurance policies held by her husband nearly one month after the insurer had paid the benefits on the policies. The first policy named the children of the deceased from a prior marriage, and the second policy named the children and the widow Leonard as beneficiaries. In affirming summary judgment for the insurer, the California Court of Appeal found that the insurer had discharged its obligation under the policies, pursuant to California Insurance Code § 10172, when it paid the beneficiaries of the policy prior to receiving notice from the widow of her claim. The court found that the statute was aimed at promoting the "free writing" of insurance. Without the statute, the insurer would be forced to determine the amount and proportion of community property funds which had been used to pay the premiums. The court also dismissed the widow's claim that a 72 day waiting period would allow her reasonable time to make a claim on the policy. The court reasoned that the purpose of life insurance is to place money at the disposal of the beneficiaries as soon as possible after the death of the insured. The court found that the balance of interests controlled by § 10172 favors prompt payment of life insurance proceeds. The text of § 10172 follows.

California Insurance Code

§ 10172. Discharge of insurer by payment

Notwithstanding Sections 751 and 1100 of the Family Code, when the proceeds of, or payments under, a life insurance policy become payable and the insurer makes payment thereof in accordance with the terms of the policy, or in accordance with the terms of any written assignment thereof if the policy has been assigned, such payment shall fully discharge the insurer from all claims under such policy unless, before such payment is made, the insurer has received, at its home office, written notice by or on behalf of some other person that such other person claims to be entitled to such payment or some interest in the policy.

§ 10172.5. Failure to pay within 30 days of death of insured; interest; notice to beneficiaries

(a) Notwithstanding any other provision of law, each insurer admitted to transact life insurance in this state which fails or refuses to pay the proceeds of, or payments under, any policy of life insurance issued by it within 30 days after the date of death of the insured shall pay interest, at a rate not less than the then current rate of interest on death proceeds left on deposit with the insurer computed from the date of the insured's death, on any moneys payable and unpaid after the expiration of such 30–day period. This section shall apply only to deaths of insureds which occur on or after January 1, 1976.

(b) Nothing in this section shall be construed to allow any insurer admitted to transact life insurance in this state to withhold payment of money payable under a life insurance policy to any beneficiary for a period longer than reasonably necessary to transmit such payment. Whenever possible payment shall be made within 30 days after the date of death of the insured.

(c) In any case in which interest on the proceeds of, or payments under, any policy of life insurance becomes payable pursuant to subdivision (a), the insurer shall notify the named beneficiary or beneficiaries at their last known address that interest will be paid on the proceeds of, or payments under, such policy from the date of death of the named insured. Such notice shall specify the rate of interest to be paid.

(d) This section shall not require the payment of interest in any case in which the beneficiary elects in writing delivered to the insurer to receive the proceeds of, or payments under, the policy by any means other than a lump sum payment thereof.

3. *Pay now and regret later—when to interplead.* According to both California Insurance Code § 10172 and *Leonard v. Occidental Life Insurance Co.*, 31 Cal.App.3d 117, 106 Cal.Rptr. 899 (1973), the insurer is reasonably secure in paying immediately to the beneficiary of record. But, if the company receives notice of a claim adverse to that of the named beneficiary before disbursement of the proceeds, should it invariably interplead (a litigational process quite detrimental to the named beneficiary in any event)? Or, in the interest of prompt distribution of the monies, should it be given considerable discretion, leaving it to the intervening claimant to proceed directly against the beneficiary in doubtful cases?

In *Butler v. Metropolitan Life Ins. Co.*, 500 F.Supp. 661 (D.C.D.C.1980). The insurer issued a policy on Kitrell pursuant to the Federal Employees Group Life Insurance Act (FEGLIA). FEGLIA mandates that, when an insured fails to name a beneficiary and is not married, the proceeds be paid to the "parents" of the insured. Because Kitrell was unmarried, the insurer paid one half of the proceeds to his mother and the other one-half to the "biological" father. However, the "biological" father had never married his mother, and had deserted Kitrell before birth. Holding that under the D.C.Code a biological father is not treated as a "parent" for all purposes, the court held that the insurer had paid at its peril and should have interpleaded. Metropolitan's assertion that this conclusion will work an administrative nightmare in the processing of FEGLIA claims was brushed aside as "without merit".

b. Changing the Beneficiary

MANHATTAN LIFE INSURANCE CO. v. BARNES

United States Court of Appeals, Ninth Circuit, 1972.
462 F.2d 629.

PREGERSON, DISTRICT JUDGE:

The Manhattan Life Insurance Company [hereinafter "Manhattan"] brought this action in interpleader on March 11, 1968, pursuant to 28 U.S.C.A. § 1335, to determine the beneficiary of group life insurance policy #1878 GL. Manhattan had issued the policy on April 14, 1960, on the life of one Victor H. Barnes. Barnes had died on December 22, 1967. In its complaint Manhattan admitted liability in the amount of $55,000 plus interest at the rate of 3.5% from the time of the insured's death. It paid that sum into the registry of the court below and asked that court to restrain defendants from instituting other actions to recover any part of the proceeds of the policy, to require defendants to interplead so that the beneficiary could be determined, and to discharge it from any additional liability in connection with the policy.

The complaint named five defendants: Margaret Ann Barnes, Mr. Barnes's former wife, who was named as beneficiary on Manhattan's records at the time of Mr. Barnes's death; Mr. Barnes's three daughters, Margaret Ann Smith, Victoria L. Bakke, and Barbara J. Thompson; and Mr. Barnes's estate, the administratrix of which was Mrs. Smith. On May 27, 1968, after the defendants had answered Manhattan's complaint, the court below dismissed Manhattan, discharging it from any additional liability in connection with the policy and restraining the defendants from instituting other suits against it in order to collect proceeds of the policy. On August 2, 1968, Mr. Barnes's estate was voluntarily dismissed. Mrs. Barnes filed a motion for summary judgment on October 9, 1969, and the court below granted the motion on January 22, 1970. Mrs. Smith and Mrs. Bakke have appealed from the judgment entered below.

Section VI of the policy provided, in part,

> "The Beneficiary for the Individual shall be the person or persons designated on the insurance records maintained in accordance with the Group Policy and the Beneficiary shall be in accordance with the Individual's selection. The Individual may change his Beneficiary at any time upon satisfactory written request."

Mrs. Smith and Mrs. Bakke concede that at the time of Mr. Barnes's death, Mrs. Barnes was the beneficiary designated on Manhattan's records in accordance with Section VI of the policy. They contend, however, that on February 21, 1966, twenty-two months before his death, Mr. Barnes executed a form in which he requested a change of beneficiary and named his three daughters as the new beneficiaries of the policy in question. Mrs. Smith allegedly found the change of beneficiary request card among some of her father's papers thirty-two days after his death. Along with the request card she also allegedly found a note, written in the hand of one of her father's employees, which read, "Change Manhattan, beneficiary of Manhattan policy." The daughters also submitted depositions that indicated that their father had believed that he had changed the beneficiary of the policy. This evidence was contradicted, however, by evidence offered by Mrs. Barnes.

The parties agree that California law governs this case; they disagree as to what that law is. Mrs. Smith and Mrs. Bakke argue that the formal requirements for changing a beneficiary that are specified in the insurance policy—i.e., written notice on a prescribed form—serve only to protect the insurer. They contend, therefore, that if the insurer institutes an action in interpleader, it waives its right to insist on compliance with these formalities, because after the insurer pays the funds that are the subject of the dispute into the registry of the court, the court will shield it from any additional liability. Since no other party has a right to invoke these formalities, the daughters conclude, a court of equity must determine whether or not the insured intended to change the beneficiary, and it must give effect to that intent. In this case, of course, there is considerable dispute over what Mr. Barnes's intent actually was. It is clear, therefore, that if Mrs. Smith and Mrs. Bakke accurately state the applicable law, material issues of fact remain unresolved, the summary judgment entered below was inappropriate, and the case should go to trial.

The California case law is not entirely free from ambiguity. Nevertheless, the Supreme Court of California has laid down the applicable rules of law in Pimentel v. Conselho Supremo, 6 Cal.2d 182, 57 P.2d 131 (1936). The Supreme Court stated in its decision,

> "While there is a division of authority on the question of whether interpleader and payment into court operates as a waiver of the insured's failure to comply with the policy provisions concerning change of beneficiary, *it is settled in this jurisdiction that it does not.* * * * Appellant concedes this to be the present rule in this state, but argues that it is against the weight of authority and asks that the cases so holding be overruled. We are satisfied that the better reasoning supports the rule adopted by our courts * * *. Nor are we convinced that the rules requiring certain formalities for the change of beneficiaries are solely for the benefit of the insurer and are not in any degree intended to protect the insured and the original beneficiary." 57 P.2d 132–133. [Emphasis added.]

The Supreme Court pointed out that the earlier decisions had recognized three exceptions to the general rule requiring strict compliance with the prescribed procedures. Two of those exceptions are not relevant to this case, but the third one is relevant: if an insured has pursued the prescribed course of action and has done all in his power to change the beneficiary, but has died before the formal procedures could be complied with in their entirety, a court of equity will treat the change of beneficiary as having been made.[13] See, e.g., McLaughlin v. McLaughlin, 104 Cal. 171, 37 P. 865 (1894); Supreme Lodge v. Price, 27 Cal.App. 607, 150 P. 803 (1915); Barboza v. Conselho Supremo, 43 Cal.App. 775, 185 P. 1028 (1919); Johnston v. Kearns, 107 Cal.App. 557, 290 P. 640 (1930). The Supreme Court pointed out, however, that this exception

13. The other two exceptions are as follows: (1) If the insurer has waived strict compliance with its own rules by issuing a new certificate pursuant to a request by the insured, a court of equity will treat the change of beneficiary as complete; (2) if it was beyond the power of the insured to comply literally with the requirements—if, for example, he was unable to gain access to the policy itself or to prescribed forms—a court of equity will also treat the change as having been made. See, e.g., Pimentel v. Conselho Supremo, supra, 57 P.2d at 133.

> "has been variously interpreted as meaning all that is required of the insured, leaving only ministerial duties to be performed by the insurer * * * or as all that it was possible for the insured to do under the circumstances under which he attempted to make the change." 57 P.2d at 134.

The Supreme Court resolved this conflict by concluding,

> "We think that where the insurer is not contesting the change the rule is not to be applied rigorously and where the insured makes every reasonable effort under the circumstances, complying as far as he is able with the rules, and there is a clear manifestation of intent to make the change, which the insured has put into execution as best he can, equity should regard the change as effected." 57 P.2d at 134.

Institution of an action in interpleader, in short, does not waive compliance with the prescribed procedures. It merely relaxes the requirements, and a court of equity may give effect to an intended change if "the insured [made] every reasonable effort under the circumstances, complying as far as he [was] able with the rules," and if there has been "a clear manifestation of intent to make the change."

Mrs. Smith and Mrs. Bakke cite a more recent decision by the California District Court of Appeal in support of their contention that California law regards the institution of an action in interpleader as a waiver of strict compliance with contractual requirements. In Saunders v. Stevers, 221 Cal.App.2d 539, 34 Cal.Rptr. 579 (1963), the court stated,

> "Where, as here, the company makes no contest but interpleads the contesting beneficiaries and pays the proceeds of the policy into court, a liberal rule obtains and courts of equity seek to do that which the insured intended to have done and to award the funds to the claimant who has the strongest claim under the facts of the case." 34 Cal.Rptr. at 581.

The only authority for this statement cited by the court was *Pimentel* and two cases decided by the District Court of Appeal prior to *Pimentel.* Examined in the light of this authority, the statement is ambiguous and may be read in two ways: it either does no more than loosely paraphrase the rule established in *Pimentel,* or it contradicts that rule and, as a result, finds no support in the California Supreme Court decision that purportedly stands as its authority.

The details of the *Saunders* case support the former interpretation. The relevant contractual provision stated,

> "The insured shall have the right at any time, and from time to time, to change the beneficiary, by written notice in form acceptable to the Company, which will be furnished on request."

The insured wrote to the insurer, notifying it of her intention to change beneficiaries. The insurer sent her its forms, the insured executed them, at least in part, but they were inadvertently destroyed before she could send them back to the insurer. She requested new forms, and they were sent. The insured died one month later, however, and never executed the second set of forms. The District Court of Appeal held that the beneficiary had been changed. The court did not hold that by instituting an action in interpleader the insurer had waived compliance with the contract. It emphasized, instead, the ambiguity of the contractual provision and reasoned that the institution of the action in interpleader constituted acceptance by the insurer of the insured's initial letter to it as "written notice in form acceptable to the Company." The court also stressed the fact that there was additional evidence of the insured's desire to change the beneficiary, while there was no evidence of any desire not to change the beneficiary. The decision, in short, was not necessarily inconsistent with *Pimentel.* The institution of an action in interpleader relaxed the ordinary rule requiring strict compliance. * * *

* * *

* * * California requires at least substantial compliance with the provisions of the insurance contract, even if the insurer has brought an action in interpleader. That requirement protects both the original beneficiary and the expressed intent of the insured from interference based on modest bits of evidence. * * * The evidence submitted by the daughters shows, at most, that during February 1966 Mr. Barnes executed a change of beneficiary request card and that on one occasion during the next twenty-two months he instructed an employee to change the beneficiary of the policy. There is no evidence that Mr. Barnes was incapacitated in any way during these twenty-two months; all the evidence shows that he continued to conduct his business. Under these circumstances, he could certainly have done more to insure that the contractual requirements were complied with. It cannot be said that he made "every reasonable effort" to change the beneficiary. The insured in *Saunders* twice wrote to the insurer in regard to her desire to change beneficiaries. The insured in *Pimentel* gave instructions for changing beneficiaries from his deathbed, repeatedly asked whether his wishes had been followed, but received mistaken assurances. In Johnston v. Kearns, supra, the insured wrote a letter to the insurer while on his deathbed, gave instructions that the letter be mailed, but died before it could be deposited in the mail. The efforts allegedly made by Mr. Barnes do not approach what was done in these cases.[14] Summary judgment for Mrs. Barnes was appropriate, and the district court's decision will be affirmed.

Notes

1. *"Every Reasonable Effort"—Suppose beneficiary has the policy?* Evelyn Jenkins was named beneficiary of a policy on the life of her husband, Hercules Jenkins. The policy permitted a change of beneficiary which "shall be effective only if written notice thereof is received by the company at its

14. Our decision is based on the inadequacy of Mr. Barnes's efforts to change the beneficiary; we have not considered whether or not there has been a "clear manifestation of intent to make the change," within the meaning of *Pimentel.*

Home Office and if such designation is accepted by the Company; * * * except that the Company may at its discretion, waive this requirement." After 19 years of marriage the Jenkins' in April 1976, separated unamicably and an annulment action was begun. On June 23, 1976, Hercules, using forms supplied by the insurance company, requested that the beneficiary of his policy be changed from Evelyn to his nephew. Included was a "declaration of lost policy" form with the explanation that Evelyn had removed it without authorization and had it in a bank vault. (The testimony was in conflict as to whether Hercules had actually requested its return). On July 8, 1976, the Company wrote Evelyn that Hercules desired to change the beneficiary of the policy which was not available to him, and stated: "we must consider waiving presentation of the policy to the company. Therefore, unless within 30 days of the date of this letter we receive a claim of sufficient interest in the policy that would stand in the way of the insured's request, we must proceed in waiving presentation of the policy and grant the insured's request."

Hercules died on August 5, 1976. Evelyn called the company with the somewhat ambiguous explanation for not responding, "because I was going to bury my husband."

Was every reasonable effort made? See Haynes v. Metropolitan Life Insurance Co., 166 N.J.Super. 308, 399 A.2d 1010 (1979) (held for the nephew).

2. In *Horne v. Gulf Life Ins. Co.*, 277 S.C. 336, 287 S.E.2d 144 (1982) the insured desired to change the beneficiary (his ex-wife) of a policy apparently in the beneficiary's possession. He certified (falsely) that the original was lost, stolen or destroyed. He then obtained duplicates from the insurer and formally changed the beneficiary by endorsement with the company's consent. The ex-wife sued on the policy when the insured died but was denied recovery. Two dissenting justices objected that the agent of the company knew all along that the policy was not lost.

3. *More beneficiary problems for the insurer. Inadequate records and computer foul-ups.* Dr. Collins joined the Exxon Travel Club. One of the side benefits was an accidental death policy issued by Travelers Ins. Co. payable to his estate in the absence of a specific beneficiary designation. Some years later the Collins' divorced and Mrs. Collins remarried three days later. Dr. Collins changed or attempted to change the beneficiaries of a number of other policies to his two children. Although the Travel Club's records indicated a beneficiary had been named, the beneficiary's name was not identified and could not be retrieved: "They [Travelers], through mistake, pushed a button on a computer that destroyed the evidence that Dr. Collins had made to name the beneficiary." The court held that since "a beneficiary" had been named, the estate of Dr. Collins was excluded. As to the ex-wife and children the court held that *both* should be paid the *full* amount of the policy—for breach of the insurer's duty to maintain proper records. Travelers Insurance Co. v. Collins, 484 F.Supp. 196 (E.D.Va.1980).

Query: Why not give *each* child the full amount of the policy? How many potential beneficiaries did Dr. Collins have to whom the Company owes a duty to maintain proper records?

4. *Change of Life Insurance Beneficiaries—Its Role in Family Wealth Transference.* Every generation succeeds to the accumulated personal wealth of its predecessors. As to that portion of such wealth as passes by intestate succession or by will the transfer has been supervised through tight legal controls. Intestate succession follows rigid statutory guidelines obviously drafted to confine the disposition as far as possible within the nuclear family. Testate succession requires formalities amounting almost to ritual.

The methods of transferring the legal right of access to life insurance proceeds (always in negotiable cash), which represent a very large proportion of the wealth passing from one generation to the next,[15] are casual. The matter of formulating the ground rules for designating the recipients and changing them back and forth has been left to the life insurance companies in drafting their policy forms. Even such formal requirements as are laid down (and these vary widely from insurance company to insurance company) may be casually waived by the insurers, since the judicial attitude is that the change of beneficiary provision is primarily for the convenience of the party which drafted it. The only other controls provided by the judicial system to this wealth transferral process is the loose and variable case by case review of the equally loose and variable practices of the insurance companies in switching beneficiaries around. In analyzing the opinions it is proper to ask if the same court would allow the interest of a specific legatee of $10,000 to be cancelled in as informal a fashion as allowed in the case of the named beneficiary of the same amount of insurance.

In *Lemke v. Schwarz*, 286 N.W.2d 693 (Minn.1979) the insured had been married three times. He had been married to his named beneficiary for a little more than a year and the last six months had been rocky. The insured's wife indicated intent to leave, whereupon the insured executed a letter, describing it as his "will" addressed to his daughter "bequeathing" the proceeds of his insurance under a company plan to them and admonishing "share nothing with Bernie [the wife-beneficiary] because she has not been willing to share her life with me." He died the next day, the letter being postmarked the day of his death. No copy was sent to the employer or the insurance company. Although it was conceded the document was not a will, the daughters were nevertheless awarded the insurance proceeds. "We hold that where an insured has clearly and unambiguously demonstrated an intent to change the beneficiary of a life insurance policy, this intent should be given effect unless prejudice to the insurer would result."

5. Can a beneficiary be changed by a will? See Burkett v. Mott, 152 Ariz. 476, 733 P.2d 673 (App.1986) (change of beneficiary provisions are for the benefit of the insurer which can waive compliance by interpleader, thus the insured may change the beneficiary by valid will inasmuch as beneficiary cannot question the manner of effecting a change of beneficiary).

6. *A Statutory Rule.* A Wisconsin statute (§ 632.48(1)(b) Stats.) provides that: "as between beneficiaries, any act that indicates an intention to make the change is sufficient to effect it." Suppose insured gives oral

15. The American Council of Life Insurance states that in 1989 the total amount of life insurance in force in the United States amounted to $8,694,015,000,000.

instruction to his attorney to change the beneficiary (his business) on his life policy, and "for the proceeds to go for the benefit of my family." The change of beneficiary forms were not completed before his death. Under the statute who gets the proceeds? See Empire General Life Ins. Co. v. Silverman, 135 Wis.2d 143, 399 N.W.2d 910 (1987) (Doucas Olds car dealership designated as beneficiary where deceased, president and sold shareholder of Doucas Olds car dealership, clearly intended to remove plaintiff Silverman as beneficiary but it was unclear who the new beneficiary would be).

7. Will the intention of a deceased be honored if he manifests intent to change the beneficiaries named on the policy by contacting his insurer despite the fact that the insurer does not make the change? In *Occidental Life Insurance Co. of California v. Row*, 271 F.Supp. 920 (S.D.W.Va.1967), the insured advised the insurer of his desire to change the beneficiary, he completed and mailed to the insurer to effect the change, he had done all within his power to effect the change and he had acted in good faith. Accordingly, the court gave effect to his "unequivocal attempt" to change the beneficiary of his policy. What are some of the policy reasons behind this "substantial compliance" rule?

c. *Murder of the Insured*

PRUDENTIAL INSURANCE CO. OF AMERICA v. ATHMER

United States Court of Appeals, Seventh Circuit, 1999.
178 F.3d 473.

POSNER, CHIEF JUDGE.

A pair of insurance companies brought this interpleader action to determine who should receive the proceeds of two life insurance policies owned by a man who was murdered by his wife. The contenders are the victim's natural daughter, and the murderess's natural son and sister. Upon stipulated facts, the district judge rendered judgment for the latter two, and the daughter appeals.

Kevin Spann, a soldier in the U.S. Army, was the insured. Prudential had issued him a life insurance policy pursuant to the Servicemen's Group Life Insurance Act of 1965 (SGLI), 38 U.S.C. §§ 1965 et seq., for $200,000 in 1992 when he was stationed in Germany. The policy named Spann's wife, Gina Spann, as primary beneficiary and Gina's natural son, Steven Hill, as contingent or secondary beneficiary. Steven was 13 and had been living with Kevin and Gina throughout the eleven years of their marriage. The other policy, which was for $100,000, had been issued in 1994, also in Germany, by Boston Mutual. This policy also named Gina as primary beneficiary, but it named her sister, Betty Jo Pierce, rather than Steven, as the contingent beneficiary, and it was not issued under SGLI. Neither policy mentioned Chrystal Athmer, Kevin Spann's natural daughter. He had never lived with her or even acknowledged the relationship, which was established by DNA testing after his death. In his will Spann devised his estate to Steven, describing him as "my son."

At the time of his death in 1997, Spann was a permanent resident of Illinois but was stationed in Georgia. His wife had him murdered there by her 18–year-old lover and three of his 16–year old pals. She pleaded guilty to the murder and was sentenced to life in prison without parole plus five additional years (as the district judge judiciously put it, "the State of Georgia even tacked an additional five years onto that already lengthy sentence"). * * * Gina is conceded to be disqualified from taking anything under the life insurance policies. The question is whether Steven and his aunt are also disqualified. The district judge held not.

[The discussion adopting federal common law as the applicable law in soldier's life insurance policies is omitted.]

The principle that no person shall be permitted to benefit from the consequences of his or her wrongdoing has long been applied to disqualify murderers from inheriting from their victims, whether the route of inheritance is a will, an intestacy statute, or a life insurance policy. E.g., Mutual Life Ins. Co. v. Armstrong, 117 U.S. 591, 600, 6 S.Ct. 877, 29 L.Ed. 997 (1886); Riggs v. Palmer, 115 N.Y. 506, 22 N.E. 188 (N.Y.1889); Swietlik v. United States, 779 F.2d 1306 (7th Cir.1985); see annotations at 25 A.L.R.4th 787 (1981 & 1998 Supp.), 27 A.L.R.3d 794 (1970 & 1997 Supp.). It is undoubtedly an implicit provision of the Servicemen's Group Life Insurance Act of 1965, Prudential Ins. Co. v. Tull, supra, and it disqualifies Gina Spann from receiving any of the proceeds of Kevin's SGLI policy, even though she is the primary beneficiary named in it.

The usual consequence when a primary beneficiary disclaims or is forced to disclaim an interest under an insurance policy, will, pension plan, or other such instrument is that the contingent beneficiary takes in the place of the primary one. And this is the approach that a majority of courts take when the beneficiary is disqualified by reason of having murdered his benefactor. E.g., Lee v. Aylward, 790 S.W.2d 462 (Mo. 1990); Spencer v. Floyd, 30 Ark.App. 230, 785 S.W.2d 60 (Ark.App.1990); Seidlitz v. Eames, 753 P.2d 775 (Colo.App.1987); National Home Life Assurance Co. v. Patterson, 746 P.2d 696 (Okl.App.1987). (There is a slew of minority rules, see Annot., 26 A.L.R.2d 987 (1952 & 1998 Supp.); Lee R. Russ & Thomas F. Segalla, Couch on Insurance, § 62:19 (3d ed.1997)—which is a good reason for having a uniform federal rule for SGLI policies.) We take it, although the case law is sparse, that if the contingent beneficiary is himself a wrongdoer and his wrongdoing contributed to the death of his benefactor, as where the contingent beneficiary is the accomplice of the primary beneficiary in the benefactor's murder, the same rule that disqualifies the primary beneficiary disqualifies the contingent beneficiary. In re Estate of Vallerius, 259 Ill.App.3d 350, 196 Ill.Dec. 341, 629 N.E.2d 1185, 1188 (Ill.App.1994). We are surprised that Reynolds v. American–Amicable Life Ins. Co., 591 F.2d 343 (5th Cir.1979) (per curiam), allowed an accessory after the fact to inherit.

But this leaves the case in which the primary beneficiary may derive an indirect benefit if the contingent beneficiary (assumed to be completely innocent) is allowed to obtain the benefits. Estate of Vallerius is the plainest illustration: the grandchildren murdered their grandmother, who had left her estate to their (innocent) mother, who died, having devised her estate, now including the grandmother's money, to her children—the murderers. They were, of course, barred from taking under their mother's will. Subtler cases of indirect benefit can be imagined. Suppose that Steven Hill (the murderess's son and victim's stepson) were an adult and he promised that he would use the life insurance proceeds to pay for his mother's lawyer or to buy her books or other goods that the prison would allow her to receive. Or suppose that Steven needed an expensive operation that Kevin could not or would not pay for and Gina killed Kevin so that the proceeds of his life insurance could be used to pay for the operation; or that Gina had been given a short prison sentence and Kevin had promised to support her in style out of the life insurance proceeds when she was released. The lawyer for Steven and Betty Jo argued to us that the fulfillment of such a promise would be barred by the "murdering heir" rule itself, but that is not correct. The rule forbids the murderer to take under the will or other instrument; it does not impress on the benefits a kind of reverse constructive trust placing them forever beyond the murderer's reach.

These cases can be multiplied indefinitely. Some states have decided that the best way to deal with them and make utterly certain that the murderer does not profit from his crime is to disqualify all the murderer's relatives, except his or her children if they are also the victim's children. E.g., Ga. Stat. 53–4–64(c); Crawford v. Coleman, 726 S.W.2d 9 (Tex.1987). Under that rule, Steven and Betty Jo would be disqualified. We need not decide whether that is or should be the federal common law rule governing murders by beneficiaries of Servicemen's Group Life Insurance policies, because Chrystal, the daughter, the party who would benefit from such a rule, does not advocate a uniform federal rule. She argues for the rule of the insured's domicile, here Illinois. Steven and Betty Jo argue for a uniform federal rule, not a borrowed state rule—a uniform rule that does not cut out the murderer's bloodline, that instead requires proof that the murderer will in fact benefit if the contingent beneficiary is allowed to take in the murderer's place. We could turn the tables on Steven and Betty Jo and say, yes, we agree with you that a uniform federal rule is desirable, but we don't like your rule; we like the rule that would entitle the natural daughter to a victory in this suit. But we do not reverse judgments in civil cases on the basis of grounds not argued by the appellant at any stage of the litigation—grounds, therefore, that the appellee had no opportunity to meet. See, for the general principle, Cosgrove v. Bartolotta, 150 F.3d 729, 735 (7th Cir.1998), and for its application to murdering-heir cases, Reynolds v. American–Amicable Life Ins. Co., supra, 591 F.2d at 344.

[The discussion adopting Illinois law as the applicable law in the case of the Boston Mutual policy is omitted.]

Neither side argues for the application of German law. Although that is where the contracts were made, the parties to the contracts had only the most adventitious connection to Germany and it is highly doubtful that they contemplated the application of German law to any dispute under the policy that might arise. Spinozzi v. ITT Sheraton Corp., supra, 174 F.3d at 845–46. The choice is thus between Illinois and Georgia.

Both states have "slayer statutes," but they are not the same. The Illinois statute forbids the murderer to "receive any property, benefit or other interest by reason of the death [of the murderer's victim], whether as heir, legatee, beneficiary . . . or in any other capacity," and provides that if the murderer is disqualified, the property, etc. shall "pass as if the person causing the death died before the decedent." 755 ILCS 5/2–6. Judicial interpretation has established that the statute is applicable to life insurance. State Farm Life Ins. Co. v. Davidson, 144 Ill.App.3d 1049, 99 Ill.Dec. 139, 495 N.E.2d 520 (Ill.App.1986); Eskridge v. Farmers New World Life Ins. Co., 250 Ill.App.3d 603, 190 Ill.Dec. 295, 621 N.E.2d 164, 169 (Ill.App.1993). Georgia has a statute that deals expressly with murder by the beneficiary of a life insurance policy, and provides that in such a case the property goes to the secondary beneficiary if one is named in the policy. Ga.Code Ann. § 33–25–13. So the Illinois statute defines "benefit" broadly enough to encompass cases of indirect benefit such as we posited earlier, while the Georgia statute, read literally, allows no room for such consideration. This creates a tension with Georgia's will statute, which, as noted earlier, absolutely excludes the murderer's family, provided there is no blood relationship between them and the victim.

Kevin Spann's daughter pitches her appeal with regard to both policies on cases interpreting the Illinois statute, and since those cases do not carry the day for her, we have no need to delve into Georgia case law, and anyway we cannot find any relevant cases. The daughter relies primarily on a case in which an Illinois court refused to allow the children of a convicted murderess to take under the victim's will. In re Estate of Mueller, 275 Ill.App.3d 128, 211 Ill.Dec. 657, 655 N.E.2d 1040 (Ill.App.1995). As in this case, the victim was the murderess's husband and the children were hers, not his. But Chrystal has missed the real significance of Estate of Mueller. What it shows is that Illinois does not cut off the murderess's bloodline regardless of circumstances. The court thought it important that the murderess had already been released from prison and had custody of one of her children (the other was an adult) and that the marriage had been a sham and the children had not lived with her husband. Id. at 1043, 1046. It was quite likely in these circumstances that the murderess would benefit if her husband's bequest went to the children; indeed, it was almost certain so far as the bequest to the younger child was concerned, since she was living with her murderous mom.

Estate of Mueller suggests that Illinois "murdering heir" case law requires the trial court to make a factual determination whether allowing a relative of the murderer to take in the place of the murderer is likely to confer a significant benefit on him. Estate of Vallerius, discussed earlier, is consistent with that approach (see also State Farm Life Ins. Co. v. Pearce, supra, 286 Cal.Rptr. at 273), and we cannot find any contrary precedent in Illinois. Which is not to say that it is necessarily the best approach. Rejected by many states, see, e.g., Lee v. Aylward, supra, 790 S.W.2d at 463; Neff v. Massachusetts Mutual Life Ins. Co., 158 Ohio St. 45, 107 N.E.2d 100 (Ohio 1952); In re Estate of Benson, 548 So.2d 775, 777 (Fla.App.1989), it requires an inherently speculative judgment about the future and an investigation of family relations quite likely to be of Faulknerian opacity, but it is Illinois's approach and we are bound by it. It is the approach followed by the district judge, and, as should be apparent from the stipulated facts sketched at the outset of this opinion, the conclusion he reached cannot be adjudged clearly erroneous. It is exceedingly unlikely that Gina Spann will ever benefit significantly from the proceeds of her husband's life insurance policies in the hands of her son and her sister.

But we do not think the judge was right to place any weight on the tenuousness of Chrystal's claim to any place in her father's affections. The question of indirect benefit to the murderer is the focus of inquiry under Illinois law as we understand it and it is unaffected by the victim's affection for the person who will take under the will or the insurance policy if the named beneficiary is disqualified. Compare Bennett v. Allstate Ins. Co., 317 N.J.Super. 324, 722 A.2d 115, 117–18 (N.J.Super.1998). The "person" could be the state under an escheat statute, so far as anything to do with the policy behind Illinois's murdering-heir rule is concerned. But we do not think the judge's decision would have been different had he ignored the affective dimensions of Chrystal's relationship with her father; his emphasis was quite properly on the remoteness of Gina's prospects of ever deriving any benefit from the life insurance policies.

AFFIRMED.

Notes

1. As the cases cited in *Athmer* indicate, the sad scenario above is all too frequently repeated. Is the assumption that a spouse has an insurable interest sufficient to negate the possibility of murder open to question?

2. When the insurer is made aware that the named beneficiary may have been involved in the murder of the insured an obligation of good faith requires a reasonable and prudent prepayment investigation. Otherwise the insurer also will have to pay the contingent beneficiary. Harper v. Prudential Ins. Co. of America, 233 Kan. 358, 662 P.2d 1264 (1983). The potential of dual exposure to bad faith claims suggests interpleader in such cases.

d. Subrogation

SHUMPERT v. TIME INSURANCE CO.

Court of Appeals of South Carolina, 1998.
329 S.C. 605, 496 S.E.2d 653. Rehearing Denied Mar. 19, 1998.

ANDERSON, JUDGE:

* * *

FACTUAL/PROCEDURAL BACKGROUND

Appellant Richard Shumpert purchased a health insurance policy from Respondent, Time Insurance Company, in 1976. In July of 1991, he was seriously injured in an automobile wreck caused by another driver. Pursuant to the policy, Time paid Shumpert a total of $18,818.76 for medical bills incurred due to the accident.

The Shumperts initiated a civil action against the at-fault driver. By letter dated November 30, 1992, Time advised the Shumperts, through their attorney, that it had a right of subrogation. A legal assistant from the firm representing the Shumperts responded to Time on December 8, 1992 that "[w]e will honor your right of subrogation on the above referenced insured." In February of 1993, the Shumperts' attorney asked for documentation supporting Time's claim for subrogation. Time asserted it was basing its "equitable right of subrogation on South Carolina law." Time continued periodically to send letters to the Shumperts' attorney asserting its subrogation lien. However, the attorney stated that once he took control of the case, he never responded to any of these letters.

On February 16, 1996, the Shumperts' attorney informed Time the at-fault driver had agreed to a settlement. The attorney advised Time that he did not believe equitable subrogation applied in a health insurance context, and if Time did not inform him within one week that it would not assert a subrogation lien, he would "take all steps necessary to have this matter judicially resolved." The Shumperts' case against the driver was settled for $75,000.

The Shumperts thereafter brought an action against Time seeking a declaration that Time had no subrogation interest in the settlement proceeds because there was no provision in the contract for subrogation. The Shumperts alleged a claim for bad faith for Time's assertion of a subrogation interest when it had failed to include a subrogation clause in the policy. Time answered and counterclaimed, maintaining it had an equitable subrogation interest and alleging a claim for bad faith based on Richard Shumpert's "assuring [T]ime that he would honor [Time's] subrogation claim against [the Shumperts'] settlement with a third-party tortfeasor [and by] stringing [Time] along and leading it to believe that" he was going to honor his "recognized obligation."

The Shumperts and Time both filed motions for summary judgment. In its supporting memorandum, the Shumperts' attorney stated the

December 8, 1992 letter acknowledging Time's assertion of a subrogation lien was merely a "professional courtesy," and that counsel did not address the validity of the claim because he did not have a copy of the policy at that time.

In an order dated December 19, 1996, the circuit court granted Time's motion for summary judgment and denied the motion made by the Shumperts. The court ruled Time was entitled to equitable subrogation in the absence of a contractual provision in the health insurance policy allowing subrogation, and determined Time was entitled to subrogation in the amount of $18,818.76. The order did not mention the bad faith claims. The Shumperts served a notice of appeal on December 31, 1996.

On January 6, 1997, Time's counsel wrote a letter to the court informing it of a typographical error in the order. By letter dated January 7, 1997, the Shumperts' attorney informed the court that the December 19th order made no mention of the bad faith claims. The Shumperts' counsel did not mention an offset for attorney's fees in this letter.

In an amended order dated January 21, 1997, the court corrected the typographical error and denied both parties' claims for bad faith. The court denied any demand for contribution to litigation expenses by Time, but did not address offset for the Shumperts' litigation expenses from the subrogation award. The Shumperts appeal.

* * *

LAW/ANALYSIS

1. RIGHT TO EQUITABLE SUBROGATION

The Shumperts contend the circuit court erred in concluding Time was entitled to equitable subrogation after it failed to contractually include the right to subrogation in the health insurance policy as provided by section 38–71–190. They argue the doctrine of equitable subrogation, although invoked in the areas of property and casualty insurance, is not universally applied to health insurance policies and should not be permitted. We agree.

"Subrogation may be broadly defined as the substitution of one person in the place of another with reference to a lawful claim or right." 73 Am.Jur.2d Subrogation § 1 (1974). The general rule is that when an insurer pays its insured for a loss resulting from the tortious conduct of a third party, the insurer is subrogated to the rights of its insured against the third party. Frank B. Hall & Co. v. Bailey Lincoln–Mercury, Inc., 298 S.C. 282, 379 S.E.2d 892 (1989). Subrogation enables the insurer to recover the amount paid to its insured out of any judgment or settlement proceeds received by the insured from the third party.

Subrogation can arise by statute, by contract, or through equity. Dailey v. Secura Ins. Co., 164 Wis.2d 624, 476 N.W.2d 299 (App.1991). Conventional subrogation arises by contract and is specifically bargained for by the parties. In contrast, equitable (or legal) subrogation is implied subrogation that arises under the common law.

> Legal subrogation is not dependent upon contract. The doctrine is an equitable one, founded not upon any fixed law, but upon principles of natural justice; its purpose is to require the ultimate discharge of a debt by the person who in equity and good conscience ought to pay it; and it is to be applied according to the dictates of equity and good conscience in the light of the actions and relationship of the parties. Calvert Fire Ins. Co. v. James, 236 S.C. 431, 435, 114 S.E.2d 832, 834 (1960).

The elements of the doctrine of equitable subrogation are (1) the party claiming subrogation has paid the debt; (2) the party was not a volunteer, but had a direct interest in the discharge of the debt or lien; (3) the party was secondarily liable for the debt or for the discharge of the lien; and (4) no injustice will be done to the other party by the allowance of the equity. United Carolina Bank v. Caroprop, Ltd., 316 S.C. 1, 446 S.E.2d 415 (1994).

Time argues the enactment of section 38–71–190 permitting subrogation clauses to be included in contracts for health insurance did not abolish the availability of equitable subrogation arising under the common law. Time contends this Court has stated equitable subrogation is permissible in health insurance policies in Provident Life and Accident Insurance Co. v. Driver, 317 S.C. 471, 451 S.E.2d 924 (Ct.App.1994).

In Provident, we held an insurer did not waive, and was not estopped from asserting, its right to subrogation due to the insurer's failure to respond to three letters from the insured's attorney and, further, laches did not bar the subrogation claim. Unlike the case now before us, the health insurance policy in Provident did contain a subrogation clause. In reviewing the equitable defenses of waiver, estoppel, and laches, we stated the general principle that subrogation is an equitable procedure arising independently of the contract. Contrary to Time's assertion, we do not consider Provident dispositive because the question directly before the Court did not concern the application of subrogation in the absence of a subrogation clause in the health insurance contract and we were not asked to rule on that issue.

Other jurisdictions specifically considering the question now before us have determined the principle of equitable subrogation should not be applied to health insurance policies. E.g., Schultz v. Gotlund, 138 Ill.2d 171, 149 Ill.Dec. 282, 561 N.E.2d 652 (1990) (group health insurer had no common law or equitable right to subrogation in personal injury settlement between insured and tortfeasor; absent express subrogation clause in policy, insurer had no right to share in proceeds of settlement); McCain Foods, Inc. v. Gerard, 489 A.2d 503 (Me.1985) (insurer was not entitled to subrogation because it was primary obligor and required under its own contract to pay insured's medical expenses); Frost v. Porter Leasing Corp., 386 Mass. 425, 436 N.E.2d 387 (1982) (group insurer which provided medical and hospital expense benefits to an insured did not have a right of subrogation in a recovery by the insured against a tortfeasor for personal injuries where the group policy contained no express provision entitling the insurer to subrogation rights); Cunningham v. Metropolitan Life Ins. Co., 121 Wis.2d 437, 360 N.W.2d 33 (1985) (hospitalization and physician's services coverage was in nature of investment insurance and absent express subrogation clause, insurer who paid benefits thereunder was not equitably subrogated to insured's claims). See also Allen E. Korpela, Annotation, Right of "Blue Cross" or "Blue Shield," or Similar Hospital or Medical Service Organization, to be Subrogated to Certificate Holder's Claims Against Tortfeasor, 73 A.L.R.3d 1140 (1976).

In Frost, 386 Mass. 425, 436 N.E.2d 387, the insured was injured in an automobile accident. Frost had medical expenses totaling $26,566.04, which were paid under his group health insurance. Frost filed a tort action against the at-fault driver alleging damages for medical expenses, pain and suffering, impaired earning capacity, and future medical expenses. His wife claimed damages for loss of consortium. The Frosts settled their claims for a lump-sum of $250,000, the limits of the driver's insurance policy. The group health insurer intervened, seeking a share of the settlement proceeds up to the amount of medical expenses it had paid.

The Supreme Judicial Court of Massachusetts noted that the reason for implied subrogation in insurance contracts is to prevent an unwarranted windfall to the insured. Subrogation returns any excess to the insurer, which can then recycle it in the form of lower insurance costs. However, the court stated the right of implied subrogation does not arise automatically upon the payment of benefits under any contract of insurance; rather, the availability of subrogation generally depends on the type of coverage involved. Courts have readily implied the right to subrogation in policies covering property and casualty damage, but not the area of personal insurance. In the former, the insured's loss is generally liquidated and the tort recovery is usually comparable, if not identical, to the insurance coverage. Therefore, the actual loss, and the amount of any excess compensation from the combination of insurance proceeds and the tort recovery, can be determined with certainty. The court observed:

> If medical expenses are isolated from the other consequences of an accident, excess compensation of an insured accident victim may appear definite and quantifiable. However, when subrogation is based on broad principles of equity and efficiency, rather than on the contract of the parties, isolation of medical expenses is artificial, and the accident victim's position should be viewed as a whole. Subrogation played no part in the bargain between insurer and insured, and in this circumstance, the courts should not intervene to adjust the rights of the parties unless all the adverse consequences of the accident have been offset. Id., 436 N.E.2d at 390–91 (citations and footnotes omitted).

In American Pioneer Life Insurance Co. v. Rogers, 296 Ark. 254, 753 S.W.2d 530 (1988), the Arkansas Supreme Court found the reasoning of Frost persuasive and held that in the absence of a specific subrogation clause, a medical expense insurer has no right to share in the proceeds of an insured's settlement or recovery from a third-part tortfeasor. The court noted that many jurisdictions have readily implied the doctrine of equitable subrogation in cases concerning property insurance.

> However, recovery for medical insurance benefits and tort damages does not necessarily produce a windfall or duplicative recovery. Most always when there is tort recovery the consideration for payment by the tortfeasor includes loss of wages, loss of earning capacity, pain and suffering, permanent or temporary physical impairment, medical expenses, property damages and intangible losses which are not susceptible to exact measurement. The principles which cause us to recognize equitable subrogation in property disputes are not present in the field of medical expense payments for personal injuries. Id. at 258–59, 753 S.W.2d 530.

Courts have distinguished cases involving subrogation in workers' compensation settings, where there is a statutory provision for it. E.g., Schultz, 138 Ill.2d 171, 149 Ill.Dec. 282, 561 N.E.2d 652. In Schultz, the Illinois Supreme Court noted that courts generally have not recognized implied rights of subrogation in the area of personal insurance, which includes policies for medical expense benefits as well as accident insurance. Id., 149 Ill.Dec. at 283–84, 561 N.E.2d at 653–54.

Finally, some authorities have noted health insurers are primarily liable for the medical expenses they contract to provide to their insureds. See McCain Foods, 489 A.2d 503 (holding a group medical insurer was not entitled to equitable subrogation because it was the primary obligor and required under its own contract to pay the insured's medical expenses). See also Michigan Hosp. Serv. v. Sharpe, 339 Mich. 357, 63 N.W.2d 638 (1954) (holding the doctrine of equitable subrogation arises only in favor of those who pay the debt of another, and not in favor of one who pays the debt in performance of his own covenants; where hospital service organization furnished services to members injured in automobile accident and each received a settlement from the tortfeasor which included the hospital bill, hospital organization was not entitled under the common law and equitable principles of subrogation to recover from the members the sums received in settlement for hospital services).

We find the reasoning of these cases persuasive and conclude a health insurer which does not include a provision for subrogation in the insurance policy is not entitled to obtain subrogation through the alternative means of equitable subrogation.

2. AMOUNT OF SUBROGATION INTEREST

The Shumperts contend the trial judge erred in determining the amount of Time's subrogation interest. Our finding that Time was not entitled to equitable subrogation is dispositive of this issue. Therefore, we need not address it.

3. GRANTING OF SUMMARY JUDGMENT ON BAD FAITH CLAIM

The Shumperts contend the trial judge erred in granting summary judgment on their claim against Time for bad faith for its assertion of a claim for equitable subrogation. We disagree.

In the initial order dated December 19, 1996, the circuit court granted the motion for summary judgment by Time and denied the motion by the Shumperts. The court found Time was entitled to equitable subrogation in the amount of $18,818.76. The court did not specifically mention the bad faith claims of either party.

Ordinarily, an issue not ruled upon must be brought to the attention of the trial judge by a timely motion to alter or amend the judgment. However, since the circuit court found Time was entitled to equitable subrogation, as a necessary consequence, and implicit in the court's ruling, was the additional finding that Time did not exhibit bad faith in asserting its claim. Cf. In the Interest of Dave G., 324 S.C. 347, 477 S.E.2d 470 (Ct.App.1996) (affirming implicit finding in judge's order). Counsel for the parties likewise acknowledged at the hearing on the summary judgment motions that the court's decision as to whether Time was entitled to equitable subrogation would effectively decide the case.

Although we reverse the court's finding that Time was entitled to equitable subrogation, we hold the Shumperts' claim for bad faith is without merit. The issue of equitable subrogation was a matter Time was justified in litigating. Therefore, we cannot say Time was without just cause in asserting its claim or that it acted in bad faith. See Strickland v. Prudential Ins. Co., 278 S.C. 82, 292 S.E.2d 301 (1982) (where insurance company was justified in litigating issue, it did not act in bad faith).

CONCLUSION

For the foregoing reasons, we hold a health insurer which does not include a provision for subrogation in the accident and health policy is not entitled to subrogation. Accordingly, we reverse the circuit court's determination that Time was entitled to equitable subrogation, and we affirm its ruling that the Shumperts were not entitled to recover on their claim for bad faith.

AFFIRMED IN PART, REVERSED IN PART.

CONNOR AND HUFF, JJ., CONCUR.

Notes

1. The recovery issues in this context are well set forth in Roger M. Baron, *Subrogation in Medical Expense Claims: The "Double Recovery" Myth and the Feasibility of Anti-Subrogation Laws*, 96 Dick. L. Rev. 581 (1992).

2. Subrogation issues raised in the Shumpert case arise in relation to medical claims and HMO's rights to receive a share of personal injury

settlements. Allan E. Korpela, *Right of Blue Cross or Blue Shield, or Similaly Hospital or Medical Service Organization, to be Subrogated to Certificate Holder's Claims Against Tortfeasors*, 73 A.L.R.3d 1140 (2000). These issues also are found in the state claims to a right of subrogation for judgments and settlements awarded to indigents due to harm caused by smoking. Cliff Sherrill, *Tobacco Litigation: Medicaid Third Party Liability and Claims for Restitution*, 19 U. Ark. Little Rock L.J. 497 (1997).

PERREIRA v. REDIGER

Supreme Court of New Jersey, 2001.
169 N.J. 399, 778 A.2d 429.

The opinion of the court was delivered by LONG, J.

The question presented in these consolidated appeals is whether the collateral source rule embodied in *N.J.S.A.* 2A:97–15 allows a health insurer, who expends funds on behalf of an insured, to recoup those payments through subrogation or contract reimbursement when the insured recovers a judgment against a tortfeasor. The answer is no.

The purpose underlying *N.J.S.A.* 2A:15–97 is twofold: to eliminate the double recovery to plaintiffs that flowed from the common-law collateral source rule and to allocate the benefit of that change to liability carriers. Allowing health insurers to recover funds expended pursuant to an insurance contract either by way of subrogation or contract reimbursement would reallocate the benefit accorded by *N.J.S.A. 2A:15–97* in contravention of the underlying legislative intent Accordingly, we hold such recovery to be interdicted by the statutory scheme.

I

[The two cases consolidated in the opinion both involve insured victims (Beninato and Perreira) whose health insurer, Oxford Health Plans, Inc. ("Oxford"), expended sums paid for medical expenses. The insureds then sued the tortfeasors.

In each case, while the underlying case against the tortfeasors was pending, the insureds filed an action against Oxford, seeking a declaration that Oxford was barred by the collateral source statute, *N.J.S.A.* 2A:15–97, from asserting a subrogation or reimbursement remedy.

Each case involved a summary judgment motion in which Oxford argued that if medical expenses were included in any recovery or settlement by the insured, it had a right to be reimbursed for what it had expended. If those expenses were not included in the settlement, then Oxford claimed a right to bring a subrogation action against the insureds. For their part, the insureds argued that "the collateral source rule and the subrogation provision within [Oxford's] insurance contract conflict with each other." In each case the trial court entered judgment for the insureds, concluding that Oxford's claim was barred by the collateral source statute. Oxford appealed.]

The Appellate Division consolidated Oxford's appeals and reversed the judgments for the insureds, holding that the collateral source rule does not bar the health insurer of a plaintiff in a non-PIP personal injury negligence action from asserting a claim for reimbursement from the plaintiff or subrogation against the tortfeasor. In so doing, the court observed that its ruling "places the ultimate burden on the tortfeasor, where in fairness it belongs.... " *Perreira v. Rediger, 330 N.J. Super. 455, 466, 750 A.2d 126 (2000).*

* * *

We now reverse.

[PART II OF THE OPINION IS OMITTED]

III

The collateral source rule, with deep roots in English common law, is firmly embedded in American common law as well. It was first cited in an American judicial decision in 1854 and has had continued currency in the centuries to follow. Michael F. Flynn, *Private Medical Insurance and the Collateral Source Rule: A Good Bet?, 22 U. Tol. L. Rev. 39, 40 (1990)* (citing *The Propeller Monticello v. Mollison, 58 U.S. (17 How.) 152, 15 L. Ed. 68 (1854)).* The common law collateral source rule "allows an injured party to recover the value of medical treatment from a culpable party, irrespective of payment of actual medical expenses by the injured party's insurance carrier. The purpose of the collateral source rule is to preserve an injured party's right to seek tort recovery from a tortfeasor without jeopardizing his or her right to receive insurance payments for medical care." *Ibid.* The rule "prohibits the tortfeasor from reducing payment of a tort judgment by the amount of money received by an injured party from other sources" and "bars the submission of evidence that the injured plaintiff received payment for any part of his damages, including medical expenses, from other sources." *Id.* at 42. It is thus a rule of damages as well as a rule of evidence. *Ibid.*

According to the *Restatement (Second) of Torts § 920A(2)* (1977), under the collateral source rule, payments made to an injured party by a source other than the tortfeasor are "not credited against the tortfeasor's liability, although they cover all or a part of the harm for which the tortfeasor is liable." The policy advanced by the rule is that "a benefit that is directed to the injured party should not be shifted so as to become a windfall for the tortfeasor." *Id.* § 920A comment b. Thus, if an injured party has the foresight to provide that his or her medical expenses will be paid by maintaining an insurance policy, the common law collateral source rule allows him or her to benefit from that foresight by recovering not only the insurance proceeds but also the full tort judgment. *Ibid.*

However, in the early to mid–1980's, state legislatures began to revisit the collateral source rule based on the notion, advanced by insurance industry analysts, that the rule contributed "to the liability insurance availability and affordability crisis in this country.... " Christian D. Saine, *Note, Preserving the Collateral Source Rule: Modern Theories of Tort Law and a Proposal for Practical Application, 47 Case W. Res. L. Rev. 1075, 1080 (1997).* Indeed, in 1986, a report commissioned by the Attorney General of the United States and prepared by a governmental inter-agency working group and the White House recommended a series of initiatives to address "the rapidly expanding crisis in liability insurance availability and affordability." *Report of the Tort Policy Working Group on the Causes, Extent and Policy Implications of the Current Crisis in Insurance Availability and Affordability* 1 (Feb. 1986). Included among those initiatives was the suggestion that tort judgments be reduced by collateral sources of compensation for the same injury. *Id.* at 70.

In response, many state legislatures passed comprehensive tort reform legislation in the latter half of the 1980's. Statutory modification of the collateral source rule in one form or another was a common factor among those different legislative initiatives. Christian D. Saine, *supra*, 47 *Case W. Res. L. Rev.* at 1075. No universal approach was adopted in all jurisdictions. One common legislative reform to avoid double recovery to plaintiffs requires a tort judgment to be reduced by the amount of collateral source payments but specifies that such reduction will not occur if a subrogation or reimbursement right exists. *Alaska Stat. § 09.17.070(a)*(Michie 1998); *Colo. Rev. Stat. Ann. § 13–21–111.6* (West 2001); *Conn. Gen. Stat. Ann. § 52–225a* (West 1991); *Fla. Stat. Ann. § 768.76(1)* (West Supp. 2000); Haw. Rev. Stat. § 633–10 (1986), *Idaho Code § 6–1606* (1998); *735 Ill. Comp. Stat. 5/2–1205.1* (West 1992); *Me. Rev. Stat. Ann. tit. 24, § 2906* (West 2000); *Mich. Comp. Laws Ann. § 600.6303* (West 2000); *Minn. Stat. Ann. § 548.36* (West 2000); *Mont. Code Ann. § 27–1–308* (West 2000), *Utah Code Ann. § 78–14–4.5* (1953).

Reimbursement, a contractual undertaking, allows the insurer to recover payments directly from its own insured upon its insured's recovery of the loss from a third party. *Couch on Insurance* 3d § 222:81.

A second approach permits a plaintiff to introduce evidence at trial of collateral source benefits received, presumably to reduce the amount of the tort judgment and benefit liability carriers. *Cal. Civil Code. Ann.* § 3333.1 (West 2001); *Ga. Code Ann. § 51–12–1* (West 2000). Within that category, contractual reimbursement is allowed and subrogation denied to the health insurers in some states. *Ga. Code. Ann.* § 33–24–56.1 (West 2000). In other states, contract reimbursement and subrogation are specifically prohibited. *Cal. Civil Code. Ann.* § 3333.1(b) (West 2001).

A third approach does not purport to tinker with the common-law collateral source rule at all, but simply creates a statutory right to subrogation for health insurers, thus eliminating double recovery to plaintiffs and benefitting the health insurance industry. *S.C. Code Ann. § 38–71–190* (Law. Co-op. 2000).

Each of the aforementioned initiatives has the effect of avoiding double recovery to plaintiffs and thus altering the effect of the common-law collateral source rule. However, they differ dramatically regarding which segment of the insurance community will benefit from the change. Where subrogation or contract reimbursement rights are granted to health insurers, that industry is the beneficiary of the legislative modification. Where subrogation and reimbursement are prohibited, the liability carriers benefit.

Like other jurisdictions, New Jersey responded to the call for modification of the collateral source rule by enacting *N.J.S.A. 2A:15–97* in 1987. Although, like the modifications enacted in other jurisdictions, its primary effect was to eliminate double recovery to plaintiffs, it was not modeled exactly on any of the other statutes. It provides:

> In any civil action brought for personal injury or death, except actions brought pursuant to the provisions of P.L. 1972, c. 70 (C. 39:6A–1 et. seq.), if a plaintiff receives or is entitled to receive benefits for the injuries allegedly incurred from any other source other than a joint tortfeasor, the benefits, other than workers' compensation benefits or the proceeds from a life insurance policy, shall be disclosed to the court and the amount thereof which duplicates any benefit contained in the award shall be deducted from any award recovered by the plaintiff, less any premium paid to an insurer directly by the plaintiff or by any member of the plaintiff's family on behalf of the plaintiff of the policy period during which the benefits are payable. Any party to the action shall be permitted to introduce evidence regarding any of the matters described in this act.
>
> [*N.J.S.A. 2A:15–97.*]

On its face, *N.J.S.A. 2A:15–97* eliminates double recovery by directing the court to deduct from any tort judgment the amount received by plaintiff from collateral sources (other than workers' compensation and life insurance) less any insurance premiums plaintiff has paid. Unlike the out-of-state enactments, the statute is silent regarding any right to subrogation or reimbursement on the part of the health insurers.

The legislative history of the statute is instructive. The Senate Judiciary's Committee statement to the bill, then S. 2708, declared:

> The traditional 'collateral source rule' holds that damages awarded in a suit for personal injury or wrongful death should not be reduced because the insured claimant has received insurance proceeds or other compensation covering the same injuries. In effect a claimant is paid twice for the same injury.
>
> [*Statement by Senate Judiciary Committee* (October 30, 1986).]

The Committee's comments made clear that S. 2708 "would eliminate the collateral source rule and require that *awards* for personal injury *be reduced* by any compensating benefits which the plaintiff has received from other sources." *Ibid.* (emphasis added).

The Assembly Insurance Committee statement to S. 2708 reiterated the Senate statement and noted a separate goal to be achieved by the amendment:

> Generally, awards in civil suits are intended to compensate injured persons for such things as loss of wages, medical costs, and other costs which are attendant to the injury. To the extent that the injured party is being compensated for the same things from different sources there is double recovery on the part of the plaintiff. *This bill, by requiring that the benefits received from the other sources be offset against the award, is intended to effect cost containment.*
>
> [*Statement by Assembly Insurance Committee* (Sept. 1, 1987)(emphasis added).]

Significantly, the Passed Bill memo prepared by Governor's counsel stated:

> *This bill attempts to reduce the cost of liability insurance* by reducing the likelihood of a 'double recovery' in a liability award for items which were already compensated by insurance or by other 'collateral' sources, other than a tortfeasor.
>
> [*Passed Bill Memo to Governor Thomas H. Kean* (Dec. 7, 1987)(emphasis added).]

That legislative history reaffirms the plain language of *N.J.S.A.* 2A:15–97 and underscores that it had more than one purpose. To be sure, its primary purpose was to disallow double recovery to plaintiffs, but a secondary goal was clearly the containment of spiraling insurance costs. The effectuation of no-double-recovery therefore required a separate legislative decision regarding which segment of the insurance industry would be the beneficiary of that disallowance. The Legislature had two choices: to benefit health insurers by allowing repayment of costs expended on a tort plaintiff, or to benefit liability carriers by reducing the tort judgment by the amount of health care benefits received.

As the legislative history reveals, the choice was made to favor liability carriers. *See Kiss v. Jacob, 138 N.J. 278, 282, 650 A.2d 336 (1994)* (stating that intent of the legislature was to control spiraling automobile-insurance costs); *Fayer v. Keene Corp., 311 N.J. Super. 200, 208, 709 A.2d 808 (App. Div. 1998)* (agreeing that purpose of statute is to shift burden to health industry); *Parker v. Esposito, 291 N.J. Super. 560, 565, 677 A.2d 1159 (1996)*(stating that purpose of collateral source statute is to prevent double recovery thereby giving relief from increasing costs of liability insurance); *Lusby v. Hitchner, 273 N.J. Super. 578, 591, 642 A.2d 1055 (App. Div. 1994)*(stating that legislative determination "was apparently not only to prevent plaintiffs from obtaining a double recovery but also, except where PIP payments are involved, to shift the burden, at least to some extent, from the liability and casualty insurance industry to health and disability third-party payers"). That legislative determination took the form of a reduction from the tort judgment of the amount received from collateral sources. By that action, the Legislature eliminated double recovery to plaintiffs, reduced the burden on the tortfeasors' liability carriers and left health insurers in the same position as they were prior to the enactment of *N.J.S.A. 2A:15–97.*

IV

One of Oxford's core claims is that health insurers had a common-law equitable right to subrogation that pre-dated *N.J.S.A. 2A:15–97* and that that right has to be taken into account in interpreting the collateral source statute. The Appellate Division agreed, and held that the statutory silence on the subject of subrogation should be viewed as essentially importing the prior legal landscape into the scheme. The vexing question about the meaning of legislative silence may be avoided here because we find no evidence of a common-law equitable right to subrogation that pre-dated *N.J.S.A. 2A:15–97*.

Although courts have identified an implied right of subrogation under certain contracts of insurance, such an implied equitable right has not been recognized with respect to all forms of insurance. Thus, for example, policies covering property damage such as fire insurance have regularly been held to include an implied right of subrogation. *Couch on Insurance* 3d § 222:25; *Feaster v. Old Sec. Life Ins. Co., 87 N.J. Super. 339, 349–50, 209 A.2d 354 (Law. Div. 1965), aff'd, 91 N.J. Super. 120, 219 A.2d 340 (1966); Williams v. Erie Ins. Group, 86 Ohio App. 3d 660, 621 N.E.2d 770, 773 (1993); Gatzweiler v. Milwaukee Elec. Ry. & Light Co., 136 Wis. 34, 116 N.W. 633, 634 (1908).* But the same has not been true in the area of personal insurance, a category that includes health and medical insurance. *Couch on Insurance* 3d § 222:25; *Feaster, supra, 87 N.J.Super. at 349–50, 209 A.2d 354.*

Among the courts that have addressed the question of the existence of a common-law equitable right of subrogation, the weight of authority concludes that no such right exists in the health insurance field. *Couch on Insurance* 3d § 222:25, § 222:26; *American Pioneer Life Ins. v. Rogers, 296 Ark. 254, 753 S.W.2d 530, 532–33 (1988)* (stating that absent specific subrogation clause medical insurer has no right to share in proceeds of insured's settlement or recover from tortfeasor); *Schultz v. Gotlund, 138 Ill. 2d 171, 149 Ill. Dec. 282, 561 N.E.2d 652, 653–54 (1990)*(holding that because no common law or equitable right to subrogation is recognized in group health policies, absent express subrogation clause in policy, group health insurer had no right to share in proceeds of personal injury settlement between insured and tortfeasor); *Frost v. Porter Leasing Corp., 386 Mass. 425, 436 N.E.2d 387, 389–90 (1982)*(stating that insurer providing medical and hospital expense benefits had no right of subrogation in insured's recovery against tortfeasor or personal injuries when group policy contained no express provision entitling insurer to subrogation rights); *Michigan Hosp. Serv. v. Sharpe, 339 Mich. 357, 63 N.W.2d 638, 641–42 (1954)*(holding that equitable subrogation not allowed for health insurance contract); *Ridge Tool Co. v. Silva, 33 Ohio App. 3d 260, 515 N.E.2d 945, 946–47 (1986)*(denying reimbursement because health insurer's contract did not expressly provide for reimbursement in event of insured's recovery from tortfeasor); *Shumpert v. Time Ins. Co., 329 S.C. 605, 496 S.E.2d 653, 656–58 (Ct. App. 1998)*(holding that health insurance provider cannot obtain equitable subrogation of insured's recovery against third-party tortfeasor when it fails to include subrogation provision in health insurance policy); *Cunningham v. Met Life Ins. Co., 121 Wis. 2d 437, 360 N.W.2d 33, 38 (1985)*(stating that group hospitalization and physician's services coverage contained in same contract with indemnity coverage is in nature of investment insurance and, absent subrogation clause, insurer who paid benefits under such policy was not equitably subrogated to insured's claims). *Compare Nossoughi v. Federated Dep't Stores, Inc., 175 Misc. 2d 585, 669 N.Y.S.2d 479 (N.Y. County 1998)*(collateral source rule did not prevent insured's health insurer from asserting equitable right to subrogation) *with* Vincent C. Alexander, *New York Civil Practice Law and Rules*, supplementary practice commentary on *N.Y.C.P.L.R. 4545* (1999)(stating that "[t]he effect of CPLR 4545 on the subrogation rights of a health insurer who has reimbursed its insured remains unsettled").

The rationale behind the rule against finding equitable subrogation in personal insurance contracts is set forth in one treatise as follows:

> Subrogation rights are common under policies of property or casualty insurance, wherein the insured sustains a fixed financial loss, and the purpose is to place that loss ultimately on the wrongdoer. To permit the insured in such instances to recover from both the insurer and the wrongdoer would permit him to profit unduly thereby.
>
> In personal insurance contracts, however, the exact loss is never capable of ascertainment. Life and death, health, physical well being, and such matters are incapable of exact financial estimation. There are, accordingly, not the same reasons militating against a double recovery. The general rule is, therefore, that the insurer is not subrogated to the insured's rights or to the beneficiary's rights under contracts of personal insurance, at least in the absence of a policy provision so providing. Nor would a settlement by the insured with the wrongdoer bar his cause of action against the insurer. However, if a subrogation provision were expressly contained in such contracts, it probably would be enforced quite uniformly. Such a provision cannot be read into a policy by calling it an indemnity contract, however.
>
> [3 J.A. Applebaum & J. Appelbaum, *Insurance Law & Practice*, § 1675 at 495–97.]

Thus, courts typically have not implied a non-contractual or non-statutory right to subrogation in health insurance.

We are satisfied that no equitable remedy of subrogation was available to health insurers in 1987, at the time *N.J.S.A.* 2A:15–97 was enacted. We reach that conclusion based on learned treatises and the weight of cited out-of-state authority to that effect, and on the complete lack of evidence that such a right was ever exercised. *See* William A. Krais & Michael C. Weiss, *Exploring the Ruins of the Collateral Source Rule After Perreira v. Rediger, 160 N.J.L.J. 29, 33* (June 19, 2000)(indicating that attorneys and health insurers have never asserted any alleged equitable right to subrogation in personal injury litigation). Most significant to us, however, is that one of the core purposes of *N.J.S.A.* 2A:15–97, as conceded by all parties, was to avoid "double recovery" by plaintiffs. If, under the law existing prior to 1987 when the collateral source rule was amended, health insurers could equitably obtain repayment from tortfeasors for the health care costs they advanced to plaintiffs, then plaintiffs, in fact, would not have experienced double recovery and there would have been no point to *N.J.S.A. 2A:15–97*. In a word, double recovery occurs only when a plaintiff recovers not only the health insurance proceeds but also the full tort judgment. If health insurers had a common-law equitable right to be repaid out of a tort judgment for the health care costs they advanced to plaintiff, the entire notion of double recovery would not have existed. *Report of the Tort Policy Working Group on the Causes, Extent and Policy Implications of the Current Crisis in Insurance Availability and Affordability*, *supra* at 70. Thus, we have found no support for the proposition that health insurers had an equitable right of subrogation available under the common law.

V

We turn next to contract reimbursement. Oxford's policies contained a reimbursement provision allowing it to recover expended health care costs "when payment is made directly to the member in third-party settlements or satisfied judgments." That contract provision was not authorized by law at the time the collateral source rule was amended in 1987. The Commissioner of Insurance refused to allow such provisions in health insurance contracts pursuant to his regulatory authority. 28 N.J. Reg. 2003(a)(April 15, 1996)(stating that prior to 1996 "all subrogation and third party liability provisions in [group health, blanket, and group life insurance] policy forms would have been disapproved"). Presumably, that decision mirrored the lack of a statutory or equitable right on the part of a health insurer to recover costs against a tortfeasor by way of subrogation.

In 1993, after years of declining to approve such provisions, the Department of Insurance allowed the inclusion of subrogation and reimbursement provisions in health insurance policies provided through the Small Employer Health Benefits Program and the Individual Health Coverage Program. *N.J.A.C.* 11:20 App. Exhibit F; *N.J.A.C.* 11:21 App. Exhibit F. Later, the Commissioner promulgated regulations that for the first time permitted such provisions in large group health insurance policies. *N.J.A.C. 11:4–42.10*.

Each of those rules set forth the requirements for contract provisions for subrogation and repayment of benefits. In the case of large group policies, for example, *N.J. Admin. Code tit.* 11:4–42.10 reads as follows:

> (a) Group policies and certificates providing health insurance may contain subrogation provisions or provisions that require the return to the insurer by a covered person of benefits paid for illness or injury up to the amount a covered person *receives* from a third party

> through settlement, a satisfied judgment or other means, as compensation for the medical costs of such illness or injury . . .
>
> [*N.J.A.C.* 11:4–42.10 (emphasis added).]

It is pursuant to that authority that the Oxford reimbursement provision was included in its contract. The question presented is whether, in light of *N.J.S.A.* 2A:15–97, the Commissioner's regulations exceeded his authority.

We generally accord a high degree of deference to administrative agency regulations that are consistent with the statutes and public policy of the state. *Parkway Ins. Co. v. New Jersey Neck & Back, 330 N.J. Super. 172, 182, 748 A.2d 1221 (Law Div. 1998).* However, "[n]o administrative agency has inherent power, and none may arrogate to itself the authority to accomplish ends not envisioned by the legislative grant or to employ means not fairly within the powers that have been bestowed." *Knight v. City of Hoboken Rent Leveling & Stabilization Bd., 332 N.J. Super. 547, 552, 753 A.2d 1231 (App. Div. 2000).* In short, an administrative code provision must give way if it is inconsistent with a state statute. *State v. Auringer, 335 N.J. Super. 94, 102, 761 A.2d 102 (App. Div. 2000).*

The Commissioner's authorization of subrogation and reimbursement provisions in health insurance contracts must be tested against *N.J.S.A. 2A:15–97.* As we have indicated, in that statute the legislature eliminated double recovery to plaintiffs and allocated the benefit of what had previously been double recovery to the liability insurance industry. The Commissioner was not free to alter that scheme. Accordingly, the regulations authorizing the inclusion of subrogation and reimbursement provisions in health insurance contracts must be interpreted narrowly as limited to cases in which the collateral source rule does not apply, for example, a case in which choice of law principles require application of the law of a jurisdiction with a collateral source rule at variance from our own. The health insurance benefits at issue in this case clearly do not fall into that category. Such an interpretation, that narrowly limits the application of the regulations, fairly accords with their very language that earmarks for reimbursement health care sums "received" by the insured. Where the collateral source rule applies, those amounts are subtracted from the judgment, and the insured has no entitlement to "receive" them. Oxford therefore cannot invoke the contract provision as a basis for reimbursement.

VI

Our ruling makes it unnecessary for us to address the public policy argument advanced by Oxford that it is only fair to make the tortfeasor's liability carrier reimburse the health insurer. However, we choose to do so. Our conclusion is informed by the nature of insurance:

> Insurance is a plan of risk management or risk sharing. For a price or premium, an insured is offered an opportunity to share the costs of a defined possible economic loss. The economic loss insured

> against may include a variety of subjects defined by the contract or policy, such as personal loss associated with loss of life, health or income due to death, illness, disability, unemployment or old age; property loss due to direct or indirect damage to personal or real property as a result of a variety of causes; or liability loss, resulting from negligence that caused bodily harm or property damage to others.
>
> The risk management or risk sharing commonly occurs through an insurer. However, persons may choose to self-insure, or spread or 'pool' the effects of a risk through group plans. The economic loss being shared with the insurer or group is defined by a contract or policy offered by the insurer for a price or premium. The premium includes an assessment of initial and continuing expenses, actual and contingent, creation of a 'pool' from which to pay claims, and contribution to the insurer's investment income from which the insurer pays the cost of operation and development of business. Since the risk or loss covered by the insurance is in the future, the exact risk or loss is not known when the insurance contract or policy is issued. All who are sharing the risk, both insurers and insureds, view the risk as the probable amount of loss, and the amount of coverage and the premium for the insurance actually purchased are calculated on this unknown.
>
> [Joseph DuBray, *A Response to the Anti–Subrogation Argument: What Really Emerged From Pandora's Box, 41 S.D. L. Rev. 264, 272 (1996).]*

That bargain, struck between an insurer and its insured guarantees payments, in exchange for a premium, regardless of whether an injury was caused by the insured or a third party. *Ibid.*; *see also* Roger Baron, *Subrogation: A Pandora's Box Awaiting Closure, 41 S.D. L. Rev. 237, 241–43(1996)*(stating that insured is not getting double recovery but is simply recovering on contract for which premiums have been paid, and insurer should not benefit from plaintiff's foresight to purchase insurance); *Youngblood v. American States Ins. Co., 262 Mont. 391, 866 P.2d 203, 208 (Mont.1993)*(holding that subrogation provision invalid due to public policy considerations including fact that insured had paid premium for medical payment coverage).

In light of the nature of the insurance gamble, we are unwilling to accept the suggestion that placing the burden of reimbursing the health insurers' rate-payers on the liability carriers' premium-payers is ineluctably the only fair outcome. Although the Legislature could certainly have made such a judgment, where it clearly chose a different course we see no compelling public policy argument requiring us to interpret the statute to achieve a different end. Our judgment is not on the wisdom of the legislative enactment, but only on its meaning. *Burt v. West Jersey Health Systems, 339 N.J. Super. 296, 309, 771 A.2d 683 (App. Div. 2001).*

VII

Health insurers have no common law equitable right to subrogation. Under the common-law collateral source rule, plaintiffs had the right to keep their health insurance proceeds and their full tort judgments. In amending the common-law collateral source rule, *N.J.S.A. 2A:15–97* eliminated double recovery to plaintiffs, allocated the benefit of that elimination to liability carriers, and left health insurers in the same position they had been in before its enactment—with no right to recover paid benefits from the insured or from the tortfeasor. In allocating the benefit of no-double-recovery to liability carriers, *N.J.S.A. 2A:15–97*, in turn, barred the Commissioner of Insurance from enacting a different allocation scheme. Thus, the Commissioner's regulations empowering health insurers to include reimbursement and subrogation provisions in their contracts only apply to cases that do not involve the collateral source rule.

VIII

The judgment of the Appellate Division is reversed. The judgments of the trial court are reinstated.

CHIEF JUSTICE PORITZ and JUSTICES STEIN, COLEMAN, VERNIERO, LaVECCHIA, and ZAZZALI join in JUSTICE LONG's opinion.

Notes

1. The term "collateral source" (see California Civil Code § 3333.1(b) which appears below after the *Scott* case) deserves emphasis. A classic discussion of it in California is found in *Helfend v. Southern California Rapid Transit District*, 2 Cal.3d 1, 84 Cal.Rptr. 173, 465 P.2d 61 (1970) in which the collateral source doctrine was employed to deny the tortfeasor defendant the right to offset the plaintiff's hospitalization benefits against the plaintiff's claim. The court noted that the collateral source rule which was applied in the case "embodies the venerable concept that a person who has invested years of insurance premiums to assure his medical care (in the case Blue Cross) should receive the benefit of his thrift." 2 Cal.3d 1, 9–10. The court observed that the policy concerned provided for a "refund of benefits" to the insurer out of any recovery made by the plaintiff. Subrogation and "collateral source" are opposite sides of the same coin. This makes the provision of Sec. 3333.1 doubly interesting.

2. The United States Supreme Court has held that ERISA does not authorize "reimbursement" (a term that the court in *Perriera* distinguishes from subrogation) of costs expended on behalf of an injured employee health plan participant who recovers damages from a tortfeasor. Great–West Life & Annuity Ins. Co. v. Knudson, 534 U.S. 204, 122 S.Ct. 708, 151 L.Ed.2d 635 (2002). Professor Roger Baron, no fan of subrogation, has written a comprehensive piece that discusses the *Great–West* case in which he persuasively lays out the case against subrogation. Roger M. Baron, *Public Policy Considerations Warranting Denial of Reimbursement to ERISA Plans: It's Time to Recognize the Elephant in the Courtroom*, 55 Mercer L. Rev. 595 (2004).

Professor Baron questions the basic equitable underpinning of subrogation (reimbursement in this context) on the basis that payment of premiums has given the health insurer its due and that personal injury is fundamentally different than property losses. Id. at 620–627.

3. A rejoinder to Professor Baron is contained in Joseph DuBray, *A Response to the Anti–Subrogation Argument: What Really Emerged From Pandora's Box*, 41 S.D. L. REV. 264 (1996). At the time his article was published, Mr. DuBray was the Chief Executive Officer of Blue Cross Blue Shield of South Dakota.

4. Another term used in this arena is from "coordination of benefits." "Coordination of benefits occurs where a reduction of benefits takes place up front as an insurance company limits the benefits it pays on the basis of an insured's additional or third-party coverage." Arana v. Ochsner Health Plan, 352 F.3d 973, 978 (5th Cir. 2003).

IN RE ESTATE OF SCOTT

Appellate Court of Illinois, Second District, 1991.
208 Ill.App.3d 846, 153 Ill.Dec. 647, 567 N.E.2d 605.

JUSTICE GEIGER delivered the opinion of the court:

The respondent estate (the estate) of William W. Scott, Jr. (Billy), appeals from the trial court's order awarding the claimant Sundstrand–Sauer (Sundstrand or the company) judgment on the subrogation provision of its Health and Disability Group Insurance Plan (the Plan). We affirm.

In March 1988, Billy, who was age 18, was seriously injured while riding as a passenger on a motorcycle. He was later declared a disabled adult and his estate brought suit based upon the accident. Sundstrand, Billy's father's employer, paid approximately $200,000 for Billy's injuries pursuant to the terms of the Sundstrand health plan. The Plan includes a subrogation clause which states: "*Subrogation, Assignment and Lien.* On payments of benefits hereunder as a result of Injury or Illness, the Fund shall be subrogated, to the extent of benefits made or to be made under This Plan, to all the rights of a Covered Individual against any person, firm or organization arising out of such Injury or Illness and the Covered Individual shall execute and deliver instruments and documents and do whatever is necessary to secure such rights to the Fund. The Covered Individual shall do nothing to prejudice such rights. Each Covered Employee hereby assigns to the Trustees of the Fund out of any amounts received or to be received by the Covered Individual as a result of Injury or Illness for which the Covered Individual has a claim against any person, firm or organization to the extent of benefits made or to be made under This Plan. In addition, the Covered Individual hereby grants a lien to the Trustees of the Fund out of any amounts received or to be received by the Covered Individual as a result of Injury or Illness for which the Covered Individual has a claim against any person, firm or organization to the extent of benefits made or to be made under This Plan."

In January 1989, the court signed an order approving the estate's settlement with the motorist who had struck Billy's motorcycle. That settlement was for the motorist's $121,000 insurance policy limit. After the payment of court-approved fees, there remained approximately $82,000 in estate assets. In February 1990, after a hearing and receipt of written arguments regarding Sundstrand's claim for subrogation, the court entered its order finding that under the Plan's subrogation clause, the company was entitled to the remainder of the estate's assets from the settlement. The estate brought this appeal.

The estate's first argument on appeal is that either Sundstrand's claim should be denied or it should be allowed only on a pro rata basis because Billy did not receive full compensation for his injuries. It notes that the trial court observed that Billy's damages could be worth $3 to $5 million and that the settlement did not make him whole. The argument's focus is that the subrogation award, by depleting the estate's assets, is inequitable.

Sundstrand responds to this argument by asserting that the estate, through Billy, is an intended third-party beneficiary of the Plan and that Sundstrand's clear contractual rights should not be overridden by inapplicable equitable analysis.

Rights to subrogation originated in equity, and they may now arise in common-law, or through statute or contract. (See Dworak v. Tempel (1959), 17 Ill.2d 181, 190–92, 161 N.E.2d 258.) Medical subrogation clauses in insurance contracts are generally enforceable; furthermore, if such a clause is enforceable, it is not common-law concepts of subrogation but the contract terms that control. See Spirek v. State Farm Mutual Automobile Insurance Co. (1978), 65 Ill.App.3d 440, 449, 21 Ill.Dec. 817, 382 N.E.2d 111.

In this case, it is clear that, in the fashion that Billy was named as a covered dependant under his father's health plan with Sundstrand, the parties manifested their intent to confer third-party beneficiary status upon him so that he was a direct contract beneficiary. (See Altevogt v. Brinkoetter (1981), 85 Ill.2d 44, 54–55, 51 Ill.Dec. 674, 421 N.E.2d 182.) It is also clear that based on that coverage, Sundstrand extended some $200,000 in payments on account of Billy's accident and the resulting disability. The insurance contract that obligated Sundstrand to cover Billy's expenses also included a clear right to subrogation. It provided that the company's insurance fund would be subrogated, to the extent of benefits extended, to all amounts received by or due a covered individual because of an injury creating a claim under the Plan. Billy's insurance settlement following the injury was for a lesser amount than the benefits already extended by Sundstrand on account of that same injury.

We find that the trial court's careful analysis was correct and that the company was entitled to the full subrogation ordered. This is not a case based in equity, but rather on contractual terms. Furthermore, courts have recognized the equity of subrogating insurers to their insureds' rights against tortfeasors who had caused an insurance claim.

(See Dworak v. Tempel (1959), 17 Ill.2d 181, 190–92, 161 N.E.2d 258.) Further, we note that it is not determinative that the subrogation order depletes the estate's assets. To the extent, if any, that the estate's settlement did not accurately compensate the estate, Sundstrand is not at fault. We note, also, that, to the extent that the estate's resources are less than the claim payments made by Sundstrand, the company is also disadvantaged by the estate's small settlement.

We are not persuaded by the estate's foreign authority (see Rimes v. State Farm Mutual Automobile Insurance Co. (1982), 106 Wis.2d 263, 275, 316 N.W.2d 348, 353), where the court held that an insurer may not be subrogated unless the insured has been made whole for his loss. In Illinois, also, the doctrine of subrogation will be applied or not applied, according to the dictates of equity, good conscience, and public policy considerations. (Reich v. Tharp (1987), 167 Ill.App.3d 496, 501, 118 Ill.Dec. 248, 521 N.E.2d 530.) However, its use is encouraged in appropriate circumstances. (See In re Estate of Schmidt (1979), 79 Ill.App.3d 456, 458, 34 Ill.Dec. 766, 398 N.E.2d 589.) We are not aware that Illinois has ever made a statement analogous to that of the Rimes court.

As Sundstrand points out, this case is distinct from the wrongful death cases upon which the estate partially relies. There, courts noted a public policy against subrogation in the case of wrongful death. (See In re Estate of Schmidt (1979), 79 Ill.App.3d 456, 458, 34 Ill.Dec. 766, 398 N.E.2d 589; National Bank v. Podgorski (1978), 57 Ill.App.3d 265, 14 Ill.Dec. 951, 373 N.E.2d 82.) In Hardware Dealers Mutual Fire Insurance Co. v. Ross (1970), 129 Ill.App.2d 217, 262 N.E.2d 618, also a wrongful death case, the court found no full recovery by the injured insured and no right to subrogation by the plaintiff insurer. The absence of full recovery by the injured insured, however, was not determinative in Ross. There, importantly, the insurer had sought to avoid liability for the insured's claim, and only after the insured had received a third-party insurance settlement had it stipulated to its coverage.

Here, where Sundstrand's insurance contract with Billy through his father included an unambiguous applicable subrogation clause, and where Sundstrand apparently has made all payments which it was obligated to make under that contract, we find no reason to deny subrogation. Furthermore, we find no Illinois authority to support the estate's alternative argument that Sundstrand should receive only a pro rata share of settlement proceeds.

The estate also argues that Sundstrand's subrogation interest amounts to an assignment of a personal tort, which is void as against public policy. According to the estate, the enforcement of the subrogation to Sundstrand, when Billy had not been made whole by the settlement, would operate as an assignment of all Billy's rights. As a consequence, Billy would not be compensated for his injuries, disability, pain and suffering, and lost earnings.

We agree with Sundstrand that the estate has improperly characterized the subrogation claim as an "assignment." Sundstrand neither sought nor received Billy's rights to make full claims for his injury. Rather, it merely sought and was awarded the right to recoup payments advanced to the estate which had been recovered from a third-party source. (See Remsen v. Midway Liquors, Inc. (1961), 30 Ill.App.2d 132, 144, 174 N.E.2d 7.) Contrary to the estate's assertion, the language of the Plan's subrogation provision does not call for the full assignment of the insured's rights but, rather, mere reimbursement of amounts forwarded by the Plan.

The estate's concluding argument is that allowance of Sundstrand's claim would violate article 1, section 12, of the Illinois Constitution (Ill. Const.1970, art. I, § 12), or be a denial of due process under the United States Constitution. Article 1, section 12, provides that "[e]very person shall find a certain remedy in the laws for all injuries and wrongs which he receives to his person * * *. He shall obtain justice by law, freely, completely, and promptly." Ill. Const.1970, art. I, § 12.

We agree with Sundstrand's response that there is no merit to this argument. Sundstrand was awarded subrogation only after a full hearing in which the estate fully participated. We find no basis for a due process claim. (See Mathews v. Eldridge (1976), 424 U.S. 319, 96 S.Ct. 893, 47 L.Ed.2d 18.) Also, we reiterate that, to the extent that Billy was not fully compensated for damages beyond his medical expenses, that is a result of the limited settlement to which the estate agreed; Sundstrand, which has a valid claim to recovery of its insurance expenses in Billy's behalf, is not responsible for that agreement.

Based upon our conclusions above, we need not consider Sundstrand's argument that ERISA (Federal Employee Retirement Income Security Act) provisions preempt any Illinois limitations upon Sundstrand's right to subrogation.

Accordingly, we affirm the judgment of the circuit court of Stephenson County.

Affirmed.

McLaren, J., concurs.

Presiding Justice Reinhard, specially concurring:

I would affirm the trial court, but I do not agree with the entire analysis of the majority opinion.

In its principal contention the estate asks us, under principles of equity and public policy, to either deny or restrict Sundstrand's contractual right to recoup up to the full amount of its medical expense payments from the settlement. Sundstrand responds that the Employee Retirement Income Security Act of 1974 (ERISA) (29 U.S.C. § 1001 et seq. (1988)) preempts State judicial or statutory limitations on subrogation provisions in self-insured employee benefit plans. Although the estate acknowledges that there is authority for Sundstrand's position (see, e.g., Reilly v. Blue Cross & Blue Shield United (7th Cir.1988), 846 F.2d 416), the estate asks us to rely on contrary authority (see, e.g., FMC Corp. v. Holliday (3d Cir.1989), 885 F.2d 79).

The Supreme Court recently addressed these conflicting decisions on this issue and ruled that States may not restrict contractual subrogation provisions contained in self-insured employee benefit plans. (FMC Corp. v. Holliday (1990), 498 U.S. 52, 111 S.Ct. 403, 112 L.Ed.2d 356.) The estate concedes in its reply brief that, if ERISA's preemption provisions are applied, "then all state laws including Illinois common law of subrogation and equity are preempted." Thus, the Supreme Court's decision in Holliday preempts judicial modification of the contractual subrogation provision. The majority's analysis of the validity of the subrogation provision under Illinois law is unnecessary, and I do not partake in it. I concur in the balance of the majority opinion regarding the other issues raised.

Notes

1. *Public policy and subrogation to medical claims.* When an auto insurer makes first party medical payments and then claims subrogation "to all of the insured's rights of recovery" (up to the amount of the payments) against the tortfeasor, objections continue to be made. E.g. Maxwell v. Allstate Ins. Cos., 102 Nev. 502, 505, 728 P.2d 812 (1986):

> "Assuming, without deciding, that a medical payments subrogation clause would now be statutorily permissible, we consider whether the subrogation clause violates public policy" [The court held that it does]. "Precluding subrogation does not result in double recovery, the insured is merely receiving the benefits for which he has already paid. * * * Further, the injured party may be unable to fully recover his actual damages * * *. [He] must often compromise because of liability problems or limited coverage carried by the tort feasor * * *. The injured party suffers 'out of pocket' losses such as loss of income or earning power and costs of asserting the claim and non-economic losses such as pain and mental anguish * * *. Yet under a subrogation for its medical expense payments, the insurer is assured full reimbursement for its medical expense payments regardless of whether the injured person's tort recovery fully covers his actual damages."

Does this make sense? What if premiums reflected anticipated subrogation recovery?

2. *Subrogation and settlements.* In *Westendorf by Westendorf v. Stasson*, 330 N.W.2d 699 (Minn.1983) a Health Maintenance Organization (HMO) paid the medical expenses of an enrollee who had been injured in an auto accident and sought "reimbursement" from a settlement effected between the enrollee and the tortfeasor. The court held that the clause in question applied only to payments specifically collected by the enrollee for those medical expenses. It further held that although the word used was "reimbursement" the equitable principles that govern "subrogation" would apply. Therefore reimbursement "will not be allowed where the insured's total recovery is less than the insured's actual loss." [Note that this is the same rule laid down in *Wimberly v. American Casualty Co. of Reading, Pa. (CNA),* 584 S.W.2d 200 (Tenn.1979) reprinted as a main case *supra.*]

Questions remain:

a) is the "insured's actual loss" the medical expenses incurred by the enrollee in the HMO in the *Westendorf* case; or the more expansive concept of loss developed in the *Maxwell* case in note 1?

b) the settlement reached between the enrollee in the HMO and the tortfeasor in the *Westendorf* case was for $100,000. How do we know how much went for actual medical expenses? Suppose the parties (as in the actual case) do not say? Could they be trusted if they did say?

3. The X insurance company issued an auto policy to D providing both personal injury protection (P.I.P.) up to $10,000 and uninsured motorist protection up to $35,000. A separate premium was paid for each coverage. The P.I.P. portion read: "If we (the insurer) make a payment under this coverage and the person to whom payment is made recovers damages from another, that person shall reimburse us to the extent of our payment."

D was badly injured in a collision with an uninsured motorist and the X insurance company immediately paid $10,000 in P.I.P. benefits. D settled her claim against the uninsured motorist for $25,000. The amount of her damages has been fixed at $45,000. D now claims an additional $35,000 under the uninsured motorist provision, asserting that the reimbursement provision is unenforceable. At least she claims it was contrary to her reasonable expectations. What decision? Suppose the amount of her personal injury damages was determined to be $60,000. Would that affect the decision? Cf. Keenan v. Industrial Indemnity Ins. Co., 108 Wash.2d 314, 738 P.2d 270 (1987) (setoff against uninsured motorist coverage was permissible to the extent that it prevented the insured's receipt of double recovery for her damages).

4. By 1975, when the numbers of medical malpractice lawsuits in California had swollen to what many thought were unbearable numbers, the Legislature, in extraordinary sessions, enacted a number of Code sections [known collectively as the Medical Injury Compensation Reform Act or "MICRA"] which it was hoped would alleviate the "crisis." Extracts follow (for brevity definitions and certain other materials are omitted):

Business and Professions Code

§ 6146. Limitations; periodic payments

(a) An attorney shall not contract for or collect a contingency fee for representing any person seeking damages in connection with an action for injury or damage against a health care provider based upon such person's alleged professional negligence in excess of the following limits:

(1) Forty percent of the first fifty thousand dollars ($50,000) recovered.

(2) Thirty-three and one-third percent of the next fifty thousand dollars ($50,000) recovered.

(3) Twenty-five percent of the next five hundred thousand dollars ($500,-000) recovered.

(4) Fifteen percent of any amount on which the recovery exceeds six hundred thousand dollars ($600,000).

The limitations shall apply regardless of whether the recovery is by settlement, arbitration, or judgment, or whether the person for whom the recovery is made is a responsible adult, an infant, or a person of unsound mind.

(b) If periodic payments are awarded to the plaintiff pursuant to Section 667.7 of the Code of Civil Procedure, the court shall place a total value on these payments based upon the projected life expectancy of the plaintiff and include this amount in computing the total award from which attorney's fees are calculated under this section.

(c) * * *.

Code of Civil Procedure

§ 667.7. Action against health care provider; periodic payments of future damages; contempt; legislative intent

(a) In any action for injury or damages against a provider of health care services, a superior court shall, at the request of either party, enter a judgment ordering that money damages or its equivalent for future damages of the judgment creditor be paid in whole or in part by periodic payments rather than by a lump-sum payment if the award equals or exceeds fifty thousand dollars ($50,000) in future damages. In entering a judgment ordering the payment of future damages by periodic payments, the court shall make a specific finding as to the dollar amount of periodic payments which will compensate the judgment creditor for such future damages. As a condition to authorizing periodic payments of future damages, the court shall require the judgment debtor who is not adequately insured to post security adequate to assure full payment of such damages awarded by the judgment. Upon termination of periodic payments of future damages, the court shall order the return of this security, or so much as remains, to the judgment debtor.

(b)(1) The judgment ordering the payment of future damages by periodic payments shall specify the recipient or recipients of the payments, the dollar amount of the payments, the interval between payments, and the number of payments or the period of time over which payments shall be made. Such payments shall only be subject to modification in the event of the death of the judgment creditor.

(2) In the event that the court finds that the judgment debtor has exhibited a continuing pattern of failing to make the payments, as specified in paragraph (1), the court shall find the judgment debtor in contempt of court and, in addition to the required periodic payments, shall order the judgment debtor to pay the judgment creditor all damages caused by the failure to make such periodic payments, including court costs and attorney's fees.

(c) However, money damages awarded for loss of future earnings shall not be reduced or payments terminated by reason of the death of the judgment creditor, but shall be paid to persons to whom the judgment creditor owed a duty of support, as provided by law, immediately prior to his death. In such cases the court which rendered the original judgment, may, upon petition of any party in interest, modify the judgment to award and apportion the unpaid future damages in accordance with this subdivision.

(d) Following the occurrence or expiration of all obligations specified in the periodic payment judgment, any obligation of the judgment debtor to make further payments shall cease and any security given, pursuant to subdivision (a) shall revert to the judgment debtor.

(e) * * *.

§ 1295. Contract for medical services; mandatory provision; waiver of right to sue; form of notice; nature of contract

(a) Any contract for medical services which contains a provision for arbitration of any dispute as to professional negligence of a health care provider shall have such provision as the first article of the contract and shall be expressed in the following language: "It is understood that any dispute as to medical malpractice, that is as to whether any medical services rendered under this contract were unnecessary or unauthorized or were improperly, negligently or incompetently rendered, will be determined by submission to arbitration as provided by California law, and not by a lawsuit or resort to court process except as California law provides for judicial review of arbitration proceedings. Both parties to this contract, by entering into it, are giving up their constitutional right to have any such dispute decided in a court of law before a jury, and instead are accepting the use of arbitration."

(b) Immediately before the signature line provided for the individual contracting for the medical services must appear the following in at least 10–point bold red type:

"NOTICE: BY SIGNING THIS CONTRACT YOU ARE AGREEING TO HAVE ANY ISSUE OF MEDICAL MALPRACTICE DECIDED BY NEUTRAL ARBITRATION AND YOU ARE GIVING UP YOUR RIGHT TO A JURY OR COURT TRIAL. SEE ARTICLE 1 OF THIS CONTRACT."

(c) Once signed, such a contract governs all subsequent open-book account transactions for medical services for which the contract was signed until or unless rescinded by written notice within 30 days of signature. Written notice of such rescission may be given by a guardian or conservator of the patient if the patient is incapacitated or a minor.

(d) Where the contract is one for medical services to a minor, it shall not be subject to disaffirmance if signed by the minor's parent or legal guardian.

(e) Such a contract is not a contract of adhesion, nor unconscionable nor otherwise improper, where it complies with subdivisions (a), (b) and (c) of this section.

(f) * * *

(g) * * *

Civil Code

§ 3333.1. Negligence of health care provider; evidence of benefits and premiums paid; subrogation

(a) In the event the defendant so elects, in an action for personal injury against a health care provider based upon professional negligence, he may introduce evidence of any amount payable as a benefit to the plaintiff as a result of the personal injury pursuant to the United States Social Security Act, any state or federal income disability or worker's compensation act, any health, sickness or income-disability insurance, accident insurance that provides health benefits or income-disability coverage, and any contract or agreement of any group, organization, partnership, or corporation to provide, pay for, or reimburse the cost of medical, hospital, dental, or other health care services. Where the defendant elects to introduce such evidence, the plaintiff may introduce evidence of any amount which the plaintiff has paid or contributed to secure his right to any insurance benefits concerning which the defendant has introduced evidence.

(b) No source of collateral benefits introduced pursuant to subdivision (a) shall recover any amount against the plaintiff nor shall it be subrogated to the rights of the plaintiff against a defendant.

(c) * * *

§ 3333.2. Negligence of health care provider; noneconomic losses; limitation

(a) In any action for injury against a health care provider based on professional negligence, the injured plaintiff shall be entitled to recover noneconomic losses to compensate for pain, suffering, inconvenience, physical impairment, disfigurement and other nonpecuniary damage.

(b) In no action shall the amount of damages for noneconomic losses exceed two hundred fifty thousand dollars ($250,000).

(c) * * *.

2. For purposes of the above sections, the definition in Civil Code Sec. 3333.1(c)(2) will suffice as illustrative:

"Professional negligence" means a negligent act or omission to act by a health care provider in the rendering of professional services, which act or omission is the proximate cause of a personal injury or wrongful death, provided that such services are within the scope of services for which the provider is licensed and which are not within any restriction imposed by the licensing agency or licensed hospital.

e. "Other Insurance" and Multiple Insurance

BLUE CROSS AND BLUE SHIELD OF KANSAS, INC. v. RIVERSIDE HOSPITAL

Supreme Court of Kansas, 1985.
237 Kan. 829, 703 P.2d 1384.

McFarland, Justice:

* * *

The facts are not in dispute and may be summarized as follows. Leslie Stadalman is an employee of defendant Riverside Hospital and, as such, is a "covered person" under that institution's employee health care plan. Leslie Stadalman is the wife of Gregory Stadalman. Mr. Stadalman is employed by the City of Wichita and is covered under his employer's Blue Cross–Blue Shield group health plan. The Blue Cross–Blue Shield plan provides coverage for Mr. Stadalman's dependents. In the Fall of 1982, Leslie Stadalman incurred medical expenses in the amount of $1,963.19. The Riverside plan refused to pay the claims on the basis it provided only secondary coverage. Blue Cross–Blue Shield (plaintiff) initially refused to pay the claims for the same reason—that its plan provided only secondary coverage. Ultimately, Blue Cross–Blue Shield paid the claims, expressly reserving the right to seek contribution and indemnity from Riverside. This action resulted.

Blue Cross–Blue Shield Plan

The Blue Cross–Blue Shield plan contains the following provisions:

Non–Duplication of Benefits.

"M.1 *The Plans will not duplicate benefits for covered health care services for which You are eligible under any of the following Programs:*

Group, blanket, or franchise insurance.

* * *

"Individual health insurance contracts are not included as Programs.

"M.2 To avoid duplicate benefit payments, one Program will be 'Primary' and others will be 'Secondary'.

"a. *When the Plans are Primary, benefits will be paid without regard to other coverage.*

"b. *When the Plans are Secondary, the benefits under this Certificate may be reduced. The benefits for Covered Services will be no more than the balance of charges remaining after the benefits of other Programs are applied to Covered Services.** * *

"M.3 Under this Certificate, the *Plans are Secondary when:*

"a. *You are covered as a dependent under this Certificate but are covered as an employee, union, or association member under another Program;* or

* * *

"c. The other Program does not have a non-duplication of benefits provision; or

* * *

"In all other instances, the Plans are Primary under this Certificate." (Emphasis supplied.)

Riverside Plan

The Riverside Plan contains the following provisions:

"1. ELIGIBILITY FOR COVERED PERSONS: The following persons will be eligible for coverage under the Plan;

(a) All permanent full-time employees in Active Service at their customary place of employment who work a minimum of 30 hours per week for the Employer.

(b) All other persons are excluded."

The Riverside plan contains the further provision:

Non–Duplication of Benefits

"This *Plan* has been *designed* by specific action of the Board of Directors of Osteopathic Hospital *to coordinate payment of benefits with other plans so as to avoid overpayments. This Plan requires that if any person covered hereunder is also covered under any other plan* (as defined below), *the other plan shall be primary and this Plan shall pay the balance of expenses up to the total eligible charges.* In no event shall the combined payments exceed 100%.

"However, it is the intent of the Plan to be primary as regard to any participant who is not covered under any other Plan as defined below.

"*Plan means any plan providing benefits or services for any health or dental care under any group, franchise, blanket insurance,* health maintenance plan, union welfare, governmental plan, or any coverage required by statute." (Emphasis supplied.)

The district court held the non-duplication of benefits provisions of the two plans to be conflicting and mutually repugnant and directed that the Stadalman claim be paid 50% by each plan. Both Blue Cross–Blue Shield and Riverside were aggrieved by this determination and duly appealed therefrom.

* * *

As applicable to the narrow issue raised herein, both plans have quite similar purposes. They are group health care plans provided by employers to their employees without cost to the employees where only the employee is covered (single coverage). If the employee desires family coverage, he or she must contribute to the cost of the coverage. These plans seek to provide adequate financially responsible coverage at the lowest cost. In keeping with this goal, benefits should not be duplicated where an individual has coverage under more than one such plan—hence the need for non-duplication of benefits clauses, or as sometimes referred to, "coordination of benefits" clauses.

* * *

If both plans are studied side by side, as equals, it would appear Leslie Stadalman has two secondary coverages and no primary coverage. This is an untenable position to maintain, and this led the district court to hold the plans to be mutually repugnant. This approach was followed (relative to automobile liability policies) in *Western Cas. & Surety Co. v.*

Universal Underwriters Ins. Co., 232 Kan. 606, 657 P.2d 576, wherein we held:

* * *

> " '[W]here two or more policies provide coverage for the particular event and all the policies in question contain 'excess insurance' clauses—it is generally held that such clauses are mutually repugnant and must be disregarded, rendering each company liable for a pro rata share of the judgment or settlement, since, if literal effect were given to both 'excess insurance' clauses of the applicable policies, neither policy would cover the loss and such a result would produce an unintended absurdity.' 7A Am.Jur.2d, Automobile Insurance § 434, pp. 87–88 . . . ."

* * *

The difficulties of such a proration procedure when applied to employee health care group plans has been pointed out by Blue Cross–Blue Shield—the two plans have different deductibles, covered services, and coinsurance provisions.

Leslie Stadalman is an employee of Riverside and coverage was provided to her as a "covered person" as defined by the plan. Mrs. Stadalman, as a "covered person" (as opposed to a covered dependent), received the coverage as a part of her employment, and, as required by ERISA, was fully advised of the plan in writing. The Riverside plan was intended to provide her coverage but would not pay duplicate benefits with those she would have under another group employee plan. We believe the logical approach is to look to her own plan first in determining the effect of non-duplication of benefits provisions. The Riverside plan (repeated for convenience) provides:

> "This Plan has been designed by specific action of the Board of Directors of Osteopathic Hospital to *coordinate payment of benefits with other plans so as to avoid overpayments.* This Plan requires that if any person covered hereunder is also covered under any other plan (as defined below), the other plan shall be primary and this Plan shall pay the balance of expenses up to the total eligible charges. In no event shall the combined payments exceed 100%." (Emphasis supplied.)

If Mrs. Stadalman had held two jobs with primary coverage provided by the two respective employers, the Riverside plan would intend to avoid duplication of benefits by becoming secondary. As a dependent of Gregory Stadalman under his Blue Cross–Blue Shield family plan, Leslie Stadalman has Blue Cross–Blue Shield coverage that is only excess (secondary) in nature. Her own group plan is primary unless another group plan provides primary coverage. The Blue Cross–Blue Shield plan does not provide primary coverage to Mrs. Stadalman by virtue of the fact she is a covered employee in her own group plan. Therefore, there is no potentiality for duplication of benefits or overpayment. In such circumstances, generally, the primary coverage of Riverside should pay all benefits due thereunder on the claims, and the excess claims should be submitted to Blue Cross–Blue Shield for determination of benefits due under its secondary coverage. On the specific claims involved herein, the parties do not directly address the matter of whether the Riverside plan, as the provider with primary coverage, would provide full coverage therefor. There are inferences that such is the case, but we are not satisfied that the parties have agreed such is true. Therefore, we decline to reverse and enter judgment against Riverside for the entire amount of the claims paid by Blue Cross–Blue Shield. This aspect of the case must be determined by the district court.

The judgment of the district court is reversed and the case is remanded with directions to enter judgment against defendant consistent with this opinion.

O'BAR v. MFA MUTUAL INSURANCE COMPANY

Supreme Court of Arkansas, 1982.
275 Ark. 247, 628 S.W.2d 561.

HICKMAN, JUSTICE.

The only issue on appeal is whether a reduction clause in an automobile insurance policy that provides for $5,000 in accidental death benefits is void because it violates public policy. The trial court held that the clause which reduced payment by any amounts paid under worker's compensation law was valid. We disagree and find such a provision void as against public policy.

The appellant's husband, Jeweral Wayne O'Bar, was killed in a vehicle accident while driving his employer's truck. His widow, Reba Faye O'Bar, the appellant, and his child received over $5,000 for his death from worker's compensation. O'Bar had an automobile insurance policy with the appellee, MFA Mutual Insurance Company, and it provided $5,000 in benefits for accidental death. MFA refused to pay, relying on a clause in the policy which reads:

> REDUCTION OF AMOUNT PAYABLE—Any amount payable under the terms of this coverage on account of death of an insured shall be reduced by the amount paid and the present value of all amounts payable on account of such death under any workmen's compensation law, disability benefits law or any other similar law.

The case was submitted to the trial court for summary judgment and the court ruled for MFA. Both parties relied to an extent on our decision in Aetna Ins. Co. v. Smith, 263 Ark. 849, 568 S.W.2d 11 (1978), which held such a reduction clause for medical and disability benefits was not void. *Aetna* interpreted Arkansas's no fault insurance law, enacted in 1973. Ark.Stat.Ann. §§ 66–4014—66–4021 * * *. The no fault law was enacted " * * * to make an insured whole on relatively minor automobile injury damage claims without regard to fault * * * " * * *. It provided that policies must give an insured the right to certain minimum medical and hospital benefits, income disability benefits and accidental death benefits. * * * But the insured has the right to reject in writing any one or all of such benefits. * * *.

More importantly, an insurance company has the *right* to reduce, or claim reimbursement for any medical hospital benefits or income disability benefits paid out. Ark.Stat.Ann. § 66–4019. No such right was granted in regard to accidental death benefits. Therein lies the crux of this case. While requiring automobile insurance policies to provide for three different types of benefits, the General Assembly granted the insurer the right to reduce only medical and income disability benefits by any amount recovered by the insured from another source. Obviously medical or income disability benefits if not so reduced would allow double recovery to certain beneficiaries. Accidental death benefits are like life insurance and life insurance is treated differently from medical and income disability benefits so far as double coverage is concerned. Life insurance is more in the nature of an investment and is actually a contract to pay a sum certain upon the death of the insured. 43 Am.Jur.2d *Insurance* §§ 3, 1594 (1969).

There is no convincing reason such a benefit should be reduced simply because an insured also receives worker's compensation and since the General Assembly made no such provision, we hold such a clause to be in violation of public policy.

REVERSED.

Notes

1. *Coordination of Private Medical Coverage with Medicare.* A common provision in private medical insurance policies is called the Medicare Care "carve out" provision of which the following is a sample:

INTEGRATION WITH MEDICARE

> 1. Any benefits payable under the medical expense insurance provisions of this policy will be reduced by the amount of any benefit to which the insured is entitled under Medicare. The reduction will apply whether or not the individual has received, or made application for, such other benefits.

2. *An insured is deemed "entitled" to all Medicare benefits for which he or she is or has become eligible.* Hanton was insured under a medical policy containing that provision. He became 65 years of age on Aug. 11, 1982. He was hospitalized on Aug. 13 and on Aug. 18 called the Social Security Administration to apply for Medicare, but was unable to complete the processing of his application before his death on Aug. 20. His estate got around to filing the application in June 1983, but it was rejected by the Social Security Administration because it violated its rule that written application had to be filed within 6 months of the original contact with the office to be entitled to retirement insurance benefits. Therefore no benefits were payable. In the meantime Hanton's private insurer has refused to pay anything on the ground that he was "entitled" to Medicare under the Integration provision.

Who should pay, if anyone? See Jeczala v. Lincoln Nat. Life Ins. Co., 146 Ill.App.3d 1043, 100 Ill.Dec. 536, 497 N.E.2d 514 (1986) (because of unambiguous integration with Medicare clause, the insurer did not have to pay for the portion of the insured's hospital bill that would have been covered by Medicate if insured had timely applied for Medicare).

3. Because health care and workers' compensation insurance costs continue to outpace other expenses, employers and insurers have sought to ensure that "double recovery" be prevented through increasing coordination of all benefits. One proposal is "24–Hour Care", a plan which would combine workers' compensation coverage with health care coverage in a single package. It is likely that thorough coordination of benefits will be included in any changes adopted in state or national healthcare reform.

7. Personal Insurance and Business

WELLS v. JOHN HANCOCK MUTUAL LIFE INSURANCE CO.

Court of Appeal of California, Second District, 1978.
85 Cal.App.3d 66, 149 Cal.Rptr. 171.

KAUS, PRESIDING JUSTICE.

Plaintiff, Ruth Wells, appeals from judgment in favor of defendant John Hancock Mutual Life Insurance Company (John Hancock) after John Hancock's demurrer to her first amended complaint was sustained with leave to amend, but she failed to do so.

FACTS

The various causes of action which plaintiff has attempted to allege against John Hancock, arise out of these basic facts:

One Robert S. Parker, who died on March 11, 1975, had been plaintiff's accountant and financial adviser for over twenty years. Between May 1, 1973 and August 1, 1974, plaintiff loaned Parker a total of $31,000.[16] On September 1, 1974—one month after the last loan had been made to him—Parker assigned to plaintiff as security for these loans a life insurance policy which John Hancock had issued to him on January 20, 1972. The policy in question was a ten-year decreasing term policy, which at no time had any surrender or nonforfeiture value. The initial sum insured was $100,000. At the time of the assignment to plaintiff it was $85,900. At the time of issue, Parker had been 46 years old.

The assignment was executed on a printed form furnished by John Hancock. It recites the amount of the loan which the policy purportedly secures—$31,000. A duplicate of the assignment was filed at John

16. The loans were evidenced by three promissory notes. The first, in the amount of $15,000, was executed on May 1, 1973 and payable on May 1, 1976; the second in the amount of $6,000 was executed on December 6, 1973 and repayable in installments; the third note in the sum of $10,000 was dated August 1, 1974 and payable in full on August 1, 1977.

Hancock's home office on October 3, 1974. On that date John Hancock in fact acknowledged receipt of the assignment as follows: "The John Hancock Mutual Life Insurance Company, without assuming any responsibility for the validity or the sufficiency of the foregoing assignment, has, on this date, filed a duplicate thereof at its Home Office." This acknowledgment is itself part of John Hancock's printed form.[17]

On May 22, 1974, however, Parker had assigned the same policy to First Los Angeles Bank to secure a loan of $35,000. This assignment had also been filed with John Hancock's home office on June 14, 1974, but John Hancock at no time advised plaintiff of its existence.

Another blemish of the assignment was that at the time John Hancock received and acknowledged the assignment, the policy did not really exist—it had in fact lapsed for nonpayment of premiums and the passage of the grace period.[18] John Hancock at no time advised plaintiff of the fact that the policy had lapsed.

The First Amended Complaint

The first amended complaint contains five causes of action, only four of which concern John Hancock, the first being directed against the administrator of Parker's estate. The second cause of action, labeled "FRAUD AND DECEIT," alleges that John Hancock fraudulently represented to plaintiff that there had been no prior assignment of the policy and that it was in full force and effect and that John Hancock made these misrepresentations intending to defraud plaintiff in various respects.[19] Had plaintiff been advised of the true condition of the policy she would have taken "necessary action to obtain other, more adequate, security for the * * * three notes." In addition, John Hancock's nondisclosure of the lapse of the policy prevented plaintiff from attempting to revive it by paying the overdue premiums and submitting proof of insurability.[20]

The third cause of action, labeled "NEGLIGENCE," omits the allegations of intentional fraud and pleads more benignly that John

17. Right below the John Hancock signature line appears a 6–part "notice," the first part of which reads as follows: "The company furnishes this form of assignment for the convenience of the parties, and it assumes no responsibility for its sufficiency or validity."

18. The policy could, however, have been reinstated on evidence of insurability satisfactory to John Hancock and payment of overdue premiums with interest.

19. "* * * with the intent to defraud and deceive plaintiff, to lull her into an unwarranted sense of security, to induce her not to pay premiums due or require ROBERT S. PARKER to submit evidence of insurability, to induce her to forbear making an investigation into ROBERT S. PARKER's financial condition or to otherwise take any action calculated to obtain other, more adequate, security for the aforementioned three notes."

20. See footnote 59, supra. Plaintiff does not allege that proof of Parker's insurability could have been furnished. We note again that Parker died only six months later; we are not told, however, whether his death was accidental or the result of an illness which made him uninsurable in October 1974. One can, of course, speculate that his proven ability to borrow large sums of money on a term policy suggests that he did not look well.

Hancock negligently failed to inform plaintiff that there had been a prior assignment and that the policy had lapsed.

Plaintiff's fourth cause of action repeats the gist of the second and third counts and adds the conclusion that by reason of the pleaded facts John Hancock "is estopped to claim that the subject policy was not in full force and effect" at the time of Parker's death.

The fifth cause of action seeks declaratory relief against all defendants. It adds no relevant allegations, but does contain the intriguing news that on January 20, 1975, Parker had once more assigned the policy to one Phyllis Bracker as security for a loan of $15,000.

Discussion

Of course, if anybody connected with the litigation had taken seriously plaintiff's allegations of actual, intentionally misleading fraud, we would not be here, for no court would have sustained defendant's general demurrer to the entire complaint. In truth, plaintiff has always made it clear that in spite of the liberal use of pejoratives in her pleadings, her grievance is not any hardcore lie by John Hancock, but its failure to advise her, in connection with its acknowledgment of having received a copy of the assignment, that the policy had lapsed and that there had been a previous assignment to another creditor of Parker.

What it boils down to is simply this: When a life insurance company is advised that a policy issued by it has been assigned as security for a loan and acknowledges in writing that it has received a duplicate of such assignment, is it under a duty to inform the assignee that it has been advised of other assignments of the same policy, that the policy has lapsed for nonpayment of premiums, or both?

The Previous Assignment: Plaintiff gives us neither authority nor persuasive reason for holding that John Hancock was under any obligation to advise her of the previous assignment of which it had notice.[21] John Hancock had no way of knowing whether the debt secured by that assignment had been paid off in whole or in part or whether the Los Angeles Bank had accepted different security for the loan due to it. John Hancock's books are not like the records of a county recorder, where satisfaction of mortgages and reconveyances of deeds of trust are recorded. To advise plaintiff that Parker had made a previous loan on the strength of the policy could have been an officious betrayal of confidential information, serving possibly no useful purpose.

In brief, we are satisfied that John Hancock was under no duty to reveal previous assignments known to it.

The Lapse of the Policy. The fact that at the time John Hancock acknowledged receiving a copy of the assignment the policy had actually lapsed, presents an entirely different problem. Unlike a previous assign-

21. It so happens that under the facts of this case the previous assignment was the least of plaintiff's worries. As noted, the sum insured at the time of Parker's death was $85,900 and the previous assignment secured a loan of $35,000, leaving plenty to satisfy plaintiff's three notes.

ment—which may or may not be still in effect as far as the insurer knows—the fact that a policy has lapsed and that, therefore, the insurer is under no legal obligation if the insured dies, is, of course, a fact of which the insurer must be fully aware.

The simple question to be decided by us is, therefore, whether under all of the circumstances John Hancock was under a duty to advise plaintiff that the policy which she had accepted as security for a $31,000 loan was, in fact, worthless?

Several considerations are relevant to a correct answer:

First: this is not a case of a former obligor who has casually learned that a former obligee has purported to assign the extinguished obligation for value and who would have to go out of his way to tell the assignee that he has bought the Brooklyn Bridge. Since John Hancock was returning the duplicate assignment form to plaintiff anyway—precisely as was contemplated by its own procedures—it would not even have had to buy an extra stamp to advise plaintiff that the assignment was worthless.

Second: John Hancock is not entirely a disinterested third party in connection with assignments of the policies it sells. Life insurance companies conduct business of a "quasi-public nature." (Barrera v. State Farm Mut. Automobile Ins. Co. (1969) 71 Cal.2d 659, 673, 79 Cal.Rptr. 106, 456 P.2d 674). The life insurance industry as a whole and—according to the allegations of the complaint—John Hancock in particular, have quite properly emphasized the role of life insurance policies as convenient security devices. In order to regularize assignment procedures with respect to its own policies and to keep itself advised, John Hancock has devised a useful form on which such assignments for security purposes can be made and which does double-duty as a means of notifying John Hancock of the assignment and, in turn, of notifying the parties that John Hancock has been so notified. By thus involving itself in the transaction, John Hancock acts in part in its own interest: it not only promotes the efficiency of life insurance policies as a security device, but also keeps itself informed concerning the changing interests of owners and creditors of owners in the policies which it has issued.[22]

Third and most vitally: As between the creditor who accepts a life insurance policy as security for a debt and the life insurance company itself, knowledge concerning the legal status of the policy is peculiarly that of the insurer. A long unbroken line of California decisions recognizes that such disparity of knowledge may result in an imperative of disclosure. (Massei v. Lettunich (1967) 248 Cal.App.2d 68, 73, 56 Cal. Rptr. 232 [duty to disclose that lots were on filled land]; Rothstein v. Janss Inv. Corp. (1941) 45 Cal.App.2d 64, 68, 113 P.2d 465 [ditto]; Curran v. Heslop (1953) 115 Cal.App.2d 476, 480, 252 P.2d 378 [failure

22. The policy provides: "The Company will not be on notice of any assignment unless it is in writing, nor until a duplicate of the original assignment has been filed at the Home Office of the Company. The company assumes no responsibility for the validity or sufficiency of any assignment."

to disclose violation of State Housing Act, not discoverable on casual inspection]; Barder v. McClung (1949) 93 Cal.App.2d 692, 697, 209 P.2d 808 [failure to disclose violation of zoning ordinances]; Witkin, Summary of Cal.Law (8th ed. 1974) Torts, § 462.) We think the present situation easily falls within the principle of these decisions.

In sum since the processing of assignments of policies was part of John Hancock's regular business, since its involvement served a business purpose of its own and, finally, since it was fully aware of a vital fact—the lapse of the policy—unknown to the plaintiff, we hold that it was under a duty to disclose that fact.[23]

John Hancock makes much of the disclaimer of responsibility which appeared just above the signature on the printed form and the "notice" just below that signature. It argues in its brief that these caveats indicate that it was not warranting the "*validity or sufficiency* of the policy as collateral." (Emphasis ours.) This argument rests, with all respect, on a total misunderstanding or misreading of the two provisions. In one John Hancock declares that it assumes no responsibility for the validity or the sufficiency of "the foregoing assignment. * * * " In the "notice" it again assumes no responsibility "for *its* sufficiency or validity." (Emphasis ours.) In context, the "it" may be the form of assignment or the assignment itself. (See fn. 58, supra.) Certainly, neither disclaimer has anything to do with the validity or sufficiency of the policy itself. The point has no merit.

To support its claim that it had no duty to notify plaintiff of the lapse of the policy, John Hancock relies on a series of cases which stand for the proposition that the insurer is under no obligation to notify an assignee that premiums are coming due and that the policy is about to lapse.[24] (See 2A Appleman, Insurance Law & Practice, § 1315, 5 Couch, Insurance 2d, p. 677, § 30.143.) The validity and good sense of these authorities need not be questioned. They are, however, not in point. Plaintiff does not contend that she would have been entitled to continuous nudges from John Hancock concerning matters that had to be done in order to keep the policy alive. All that she claims is that if the company is notified in writing that the insured has purported to assign the policy and the company acknowledges that it has received such notification and knows that the policy has, in fact, lapsed, it should advise the assignee of that fact. We think that simple fairness demands nothing less.

23. Actually a layman may think that it would have been so natural for John Hancock to note that the assignment of which it was notified and which it formally acknowledged was, in fact, worthless, that a jury might reasonably infer that the failure to do so amounted to more than mere nondisclosure: that it was an implied representation that the policy was valid. We need not and do not go that far in our holding. We merely cite the reasonableness of such a conclusion in support of what we do hold: that there was a duty to speak.

24. This apparently general rule of law was changed by the 1975 enactment of section 10173.2 of the Insurance Code, obligating the insurer to give the assignee not less than ten days notice before "the final lapse of the policy, * * * " It permits the insured to charge $2.50 for each such notice.

If we are correct so far, and John Hancock was under an obligation to advise plaintiff what it knew for a fact—that the policy had lapsed—our holding really swallows up plaintiff's purported cause of action for negligence: there is no point in asking whether John Hancock was negligent in failing to inform plaintiff about the true status of Parker's policy when it was under a positive obligation to do so.

Estoppel: In plaintiff's fourth cause of action she claims that by reason of all of the facts previously pleaded, John Hancock is "estopped to claim that the subject policy was not in full force and effect at the time of Robert S. Parker's death." If that pleading was intended as nothing but another way of asserting that John Hancock should have revealed that the policy had lapsed, it presumably does no harm. If, as seems more likely, the claim of estoppel is intended to dispense with the proof of damages, some remarks are in order.

All that we have held so far is that John Hancock should have informed plaintiff that the policy had lapsed. Although plaintiff sanguinely pleads that, had she been so informed, she would have taken "necessary action to obtain other, more adequate security," the general impression one gets from the few facts pleaded in the complaint is that no such security would have been available, that Parker was barely one step ahead of his creditors and that John Hancock's failure to inform plaintiff that her security was worthless probably caused no damage. If, on the other hand, it were the law that John Hancock is estopped to claim that the policy was not in full force and effect, plaintiff would find herself in a creditor's paradise: there would be $85,900 in insurance, plenty to satisfy her and all the other assignees who have surfaced so far. Yet, at least as far as this plaintiff is concerned an estoppel to deny full coverage would be an undeserved windfall: it should be recalled that plaintiff had parted with her $31,000 long before there were any communications from John Hancock. By no stretch of the facts, therefore, can she claim that whatever John Hancock did or did not do caused her to relinquish $31,000. Her loss is measured by the "other, more adequate, security" she was led not to demand and obtain. The burden of proving the exact amount of such loss cannot be swept under the rug by a glib slogan: that John Hancock is estopped to deny full coverage.

The judgment is reversed.

Note

In *Kotler v. Life Insurance Company of California (Estate of Coate)*, 98 Cal.App.3d 982, 159 Cal.Rptr. 794 (1979), the court extended the obligation to notify an assignee of policy lapses to include prospective lapses.

RYAN v. TICKLE

Supreme Court of Nebraska, 1982.
210 Neb. 630, 316 N.W.2d 580.

BRODKEY, RETIRED JUSTICE.

Lois M. Ryan, the plaintiff and appellant herein, is the widow of Eugene Ryan and the executrix of his estate. She commenced this action to recover the proceeds of a life insurance policy which were paid to the decedent's former business partner, appellee Gerald L. Tickle. After a trial in the District Court of Lincoln County, Nebraska, the appellee demurred to the evidence presented by the appellant and moved to dismiss appellant's petition. In its judgment entered on June 4, 1980, the trial court sustained the appellee's motions and dismissed the appellant's petition with prejudice. We affirm.

The facts as revealed in the record disclose that the decedent, Eugene Ryan, was a licensed mortician doing business in North Platte as the manager and president of Ryan Funeral Home, Inc. Tickle was licensed as a mortician doing business in Arnold, Nebraska, as owner of the Quig–Tickle Funeral Home. It appears that the two men had known each other since 1964, and in October 1971 they went into business together. The Ryan Funeral Home, Inc., had 477 outstanding shares of stock distributed among 12 shareholders. Ryan owned 50 shares of the company and Tickle purchased 25 shares. The two men also obtained an option to purchase the remaining outstanding stock in the Ryan Funeral Home from the other shareholders. The 5–year option was to expire on September 2, 1976, and granted Ryan and Tickle, or the survivor of them, the right to exercise the option.

In March 1972 Ryan and Tickle were offered an opportunity to purchase the Mullen Funeral Home located in nearby Mullen, Nebraska. They purchased the funeral home together for $20,000, as equal partners. They borrowed $7,000 for the downpayment and arranged to finance the balance over a period of 5 to 6 years.

Shortly after the purchase of the Mullen Funeral Home, Ryan and Tickle decided to purchase life insurance policies on each other's lives, their ultimate business goal being to acquire ownership of the Ryan and Mullen funeral homes and to provide a fund by which the survivor could purchase the homes upon the death of one of the partners. It was their estimate that if one died, the survivor would need $20,000 to $25,000 to purchase the other's interest in the Mullen Funeral Home and an additional $75,000 to purchase the outstanding stock of the Ryan Funeral Home from the owners thereof under the option agreement.

Ryan and Tickle thereupon purchased decreasing term life insurance policies on their joint lives in the total amount of $100,000. Tickle was designated the owner of one policy which had a face value of $50,000, and Ryan was designated the owner of a second policy, also valued at $50,000. Both policies insured the joint lives of Ryan and Tickle so that the entire proceeds were payable to the survivor of them. The premiums for the insurance were paid by an automatic bank withdrawal arrangement through a partnership bank account maintained for the Mullen Funeral Home.

In early 1973 it was discovered that Ryan had cancer from which he subsequently died on October 25, 1975. Following Ryan's death, Tickle collected a total of $88,000 as the beneficiary of the two life insurance policies. On September 22, 1976, Tickle and the appellant entered into a settlement agreement in which Tickle purchased the decedent's interest in the Mullen Funeral Home for the sum of $15,000. In addition, Tickle agreed to pay an additional $3,000 to the appellant in full and complete distribution of any sum of money claimed to be distributable to the decedent as undistributed earnings from the Mullen partnership. Tickle also agreed to assume and pay the unpaid balance due on the Mullen Funeral Home in the amount of $9,000. He also purchased all the assets of the Ryan Funeral Home from the board of directors and shareholders of the corporation for the sum of $147,000.

On November 7, 1977, the appellant, as executrix of the estate of Eugene Ryan, instituted this action alleging that the estate was entitled to all insurance proceeds paid upon the death of the decedent. In her brief on appeal to this court, appellant makes two principal arguments, to wit: That Tickle did not have an insurable interest in the life of the deceased, Eugene Ryan, and hence was not entitled to receive the proceeds of the insurance policies as the surviving partner of the deceased; and that the proceeds paid under the insurance agreement on decedent's life exceeded by $73,000 the amount of decedent's insurable interest in the Mullen Funeral Home, thus creating a wagering contract which is void as against public policy.

We note at the outset that the evidence in the record clearly indicates that the agreement between the partners had a dual purpose: not only to acquire for the survivor the Mullen Funeral Home but also to acquire the outstanding shares of stock in Ryan Funeral Home, Inc. The trial court found, and we conclude that the record sustains such finding, that the parties made a good faith estimate that the amount of money necessary to accomplish both such purposes would be approximately $100,000. That being so, appellee argues that the insurance contract was not a "wagering" contract but, rather, was a valid and enforceable contract of insurance. Also, with regard to appellant's contention that appellee did not have an insurable interest in the life of the decedent, appellee points out that the term "insurable interest" is defined in Neb.Rev.Stat. § 44–103(13) (Reissue 1978) as follows: "Insurable interest, in the matter of life and health insurance, exists when the beneficiary because of relationship, either pecuniary or from ties of blood or marriage, has reason to expect some benefit from the continuance of the life of the insured." In view of their avowed purpose in obtaining the insurance in question, in addition to the fact that evidence in the record discloses income tax returns showing increased profits from the operation of the funeral homes since the association of the parties as partners, appellee argues that there was clearly an expectation of benefit from the continuance of the life of the insured, and that therefore Tickle had an "insurable interest" in the life of the decedent Ryan.

We conclude, however, that we need not, and indeed may not, decide these issues, for the reason that the appellant herein has no standing or right to bring this lawsuit.

The law is well established throughout the country that only the insurer can raise the objection of want of an insurable interest. "The question of the lack of insurable interest in a life insurance policy may be raised only by the insurance company, and, where the company recognizes the validity of the policy, as by paying the amount thereof to the person named therein or into court, ordinarily adverse claimants to the fund may not raise the objection of lack of insurable interest." 44 C.J.S. Insurance § 212 at 915 (1945). See, also, Poland v. Fisher's Estate, 329 S.W.2d 768 (Mo.1959); Ryan v. Andrewski, 206 Okla. 199, 242 P.2d 448 (1952); Edgington v. Equitable L. Assur. Soc., 236 Iowa 903, 20 N.W.2d 411 (1945). "The heirs of the insured have no cause of action against the insurer upon a policy the proceeds of which have been paid by the insurer to a third person who was the beneficiary designated in the policy, on the ground that the insurer could have refused to make the payment for want of an insurable interest on the part of the beneficiary." 3 Couch on Insurance 2d, Insurable Interest, § 24:6 at 76 (1960).

The above-cited authorities make it clear that only an insurer has standing to complain of a lack of insurable interest and that the heirs of the insured may not proceed on such cause of action against the designated beneficiary. This position was recently discussed in an excellent opinion by the Michigan Court of Appeals in Secor v. Pioneer Foundry, 20 Mich.App. 30, 173 N.W.2d 780 (1969). In that case Pioneer Foundry obtained a $50,000 life insurance policy on Secor, who was a 9–year employee of the company. Three years later Secor terminated his employment; however, the company paid the 1964 policy premium 8 months after Secor had terminated his employment. Secor died a month later, and the company collected the proceeds of the insurance. Secor's widow filed suit, alleging that Pioneer Foundry had no insurable interest in Secor's life and sought a constructive trust to be imposed in favor of Secor's estate. The trial court dismissed Mrs. Secor's suit.

On appeal, the Michigan court, citing Hicks v. Cary, 332 Mich. 606, 52 N.W.2d 351 (1952), held: " 'We hold to the rule that lack in the beneficiary of an insurable interest equal to the full amount of the insurance policy, to the extent that it thereby renders the policy a wagering contract, constitutes a barrier to the beneficiary's right to receive and retain the full amount of the insurance proceeds, but that it is one which may be raised by and for the benefit of the insurer alone.' "Id. 20 Mich.App. at 33, 173 N.W.2d at 781. The court concluded that it was the insurer alone who had standing to complain of a lack of insurable interest and noted that the insurance company had paid the proceeds of the policy to Pioneer Foundry without raising the issue. The court affirmed the dismissal of the plaintiff's action based on a lack of standing to complain.

In Secor the court at 33, 173 N.W.2d at 782, stated: "The rule that only the insurer can raise the question of lack of insurable interest appears to be well supported in other jurisdictions," and cites in support thereof, 3 Couch on Insurance, supra; 2 Appleman, Insurance Law &

Practice, § 765 (1966); Vance on Insurance, § 31 at 199 (3d ed. 1951). In the opinion, the court at 34, 173 N.W.2d at 782, states: "In recognition of these considerations the almost universal rule of law in this country is that if the insurable interest requirement is satisfied at the time the policy is issued, the proceeds of the policy must be paid upon the death of the life insured without regard to whether the beneficiary has an insurable interest at the time of death." The court in Secor also recognized that there are cases that hold that a creditor who acquires insurance on his debtor's life may not recover more than the amount of the debt and the premiums he paid. In this connection, however, the court at 37, 173 N.W.2d at 784, stated: "This analysis has been rejected in the better-reasoned cases; it is contrary to the principle that the termination of an insurable interest does not affect the rights of an owner-beneficiary in a life policy." The court also noted at 35, 173 N.W.2d at 783: "Life insurance is not meant to assuage grief; its primary function is monetary. It serves fundamentally the same purpose whether the beneficiary is a widow or a business; it seeks to replace with a sum of money the earning capacity of the life insured." The court concluded at 36, 173 N.W.2d at 783: "We also decline to limit Pioneer Foundry's recovery to the amount of its investment in the policy and its financial loss (probably nil) upon Secor's death. Pioneer Foundry's investment in the policy was large both quantitatively and relatively."

The holding and reasoning of the Michigan Court of Appeals is persuasive in the instant case, and we conclude that appellant is without standing to object that no insurable interest existed between the decedent and the appellee, or that the parties had entered into an illegal wagering agreement. The judgment of the District Court dismissing appellant's cause of action must be, and hereby is, affirmed.

AFFIRMED.

Note

In *American Casualty Co. v. Rose*, 340 F.2d 469 (10th Cir.1964), Rose had a $50,000 accidental death policy for a thirty day term. The named beneficiary was Rose's employer, King. Upon Rose's death, the insurer initially denied liability but ultimately settled for $24,000 in return for King's release. Rose's widow brought action on theory that King held the policy in trust for benefit of the insured's family largely on evidence of letters from Rose to his wife. In holding for the insurer, the court noted that the rights of the family had to flow from King. Other than the letters, nothing in the record supported the idea that Rose intended to deny the effect of naming King as beneficiary. There also existed reasonable grounds to believe that naming King as beneficiary was appropriate because of Rose's form of employment and existing employee loans.

California Insurance Code

§ 286. When insurable interest required

An interest in property insured must exist when the insurance takes effect, and when the loss occurs, but need not exist in the meantime; and interest in the life or health of a person insured must exist when the insurance takes effect, but need not exist thereafter or when the loss occurs.

Problems

1. A agreed to let B in on a sort of partnership-franchise of a highly dubious enterprise to publish a "TV Journal." The whole affair was woefully underfinanced and neither of the parties, B in particular, had much in the way of qualifications. B nevertheless was expected to do the work while A was to provide the capital. In a sanguine mood B, whose annual income at the moment was $7,800, agreed to pay A $1000 per month for the next 20 years for this golden privilege. B could however terminate the deal on 60 days notice.

A then took out a $240,000 life insurance policy on B, naming himself as beneficiary. The policy was delivered in October although the first payment on B's debt to A was not due until the following April. In November B was killed while on a hunting party with A and a group of A's relatives. A brings an action to recover on the policy. One of the defenses is lack of insurable interest. See Rubenstein v. Mutual Life Ins. Co. of New York, 584 F.Supp. 272 (E.D.La.1984) (beneficiary lacks an insurable interest in the life of the decedent debtor where the face value of the life insurance policy is grossly disproportionate to the amount of the debt).

2. X (designated owner) was a farmer who named his wife as the beneficiary of a $200,000 life policy X had taken out on his life. X also had borrowed $200,000 from Bank to finance his farming operations and assigned the life policy as collateral security. X had also by will named various devisees and legatees other than his wife to share in his rather large estate. When X died, the Bank applied the proceeds of the policy to the satisfaction of the debt. The wife now seeks subrogation to the claim the Bank would have had against X's estate if there had been no insurance policy. See Matter of Estate of Winstead, 144 Ill.App.3d 502, 98 Ill.Dec. 162, 493 N.E.2d 1183 (1986) (named beneficiary is entitled to subrogation claim the bank would have had against the decedent's estate absent the availability to the bank of the life insurance proceeds).

Buy–Sell Agreements—Insurance Aspects

Buy-sell agreements are contractual arrangements made by partners or by the shareholders in closely held corporations regarding the disposition to be made of the ownership interest of the partner or shareholder in the business entity upon such person's death (or withdrawal, which does not here concern us). There is a voluminous specialized body of literature dealing with these agreements mostly with regard to the tax and corporate law considerations. However, because life insurance is frequently the source of funding for the carrying out of the agreements, a brief outline of some of the insurance aspects is warranted. (For a full bibliography see O'NEAL, Close Corporations § 7.25). The main reasons for such agreements are to prevent the deceased's proprietary interest from going to unwelcome outsiders, thereby destroying the essential personalized nature of the small business entity; and, secondly, to provide an agreeable and predetermined formula for compensating the spouse or other next of kin of the decedent, who has by the agreement been bound to yield the business interest which would have passed to him or her. This means a sizeable cash sum will be needed at an undetermined time. Life insurance whose maturation will correspond precisely with this business need obviously offers a most convenient method of funding such agreements. Since there are different ways of setting up the insurance plan, some awareness of the existence of insurance law problems is essential. Let us consider a business partnership of A, B and C, or a closely held corporation of three equal shareholders, also A, B and C. Their buy-sell arrangements are motivated as stated above. Consider the problems (and how to avoid them) with these possible alternatives of insurance funding.

I

	)	B
A insures the life of	)	
	)	C
	)	A
B insures the life of	)	
	)	C
	)	A
C insures the life of	)	
	)	B

Each pays the premiums on the policies held on the others' lives. In case of death (say of A), B and C collect and pay off the spouse of A according to the compensation formula set forth in the agreement and keep the balance of the proceeds.

Questions: Are we safe in assuming that a partner has an insurable interest in the life of another partner; or that a shareholder has an insurable interest in the life of another shareholder? (Is this question really likely to be raised?)

Suppose A is a young person and B and C are elderly, would this not be a costly arrangement for junior partners? Would this arrangement be suitable if there are 50 partners?

II

	)	B
A insures own life and names	)	as beneficiaries.
	)	C
	)	A
B insures own life and names	)	as beneficiaries.
	)	C
	)	A
C insures own life and names	)	as beneficiaries.
	)	B

Here, if A dies then B and C receive proceeds and pay off A's spouse according to the plan formula and keep the balance of the proceeds. There is no problem as to insurable interest. Nor is there quite the bulk of policies needed as in I.

Questions: Suppose A, B or C is uninsurable or elderly? Suppose A failed to pay premiums?

III

The closely held corporation or partnership insures each individual A, B and C, deducting the premiums as a business expense.

Here if A dies the business entity collects the proceeds and pays off A's estate according to the agreed valuation formula and keeps any surplus.

Questions: Is there an insurable interest issue here? (Why should a *corporation* have an insurable interest in the life of a shareholder?) In most states a corporation cannot purchase its own shares except from retained earnings or earned surplus. Do the insurance proceeds qualify as corporate earnings for this purpose?

IV

A insures own life and names corporation or partnership as beneficiary or assignee of the policy.

B does same.

C does same.

Here A (say a shareholder) dies. The corporation will collect and use the proceeds to buy A's stock from his or her estate. This is commonly done through a trustee.

Question: Suppose the insurance proceeds exceed the amount needed to purchase the stock, who would be entitled to the surplus? See Hamilton National Bank v. Graning Paint Co., 59 Tenn.App. 37, 436 S.W.2d 883 (1968) (policies transferred to the corporation remain its property).

STATE FARM LIFE INSURANCE CO. v. FORT WAYNE NATIONAL BANK

Court of Appeals of Indiana, Third District, 1985.
474 N.E.2d 524.

HOFFMAN, JUDGE.

Fort Wayne National Bank, in the capacity of personal representative, filed suit against State Farm Life Insurance Company and Robert Houser, for failure to properly effect insurance on the life of its decedent, James Zimmerman. Following trial to the court, judgment was rendered in favor of the estate for $34,373.97, plus pre-judgment interest. State Farm and Houser appeal.

The record discloses that James owned 95% of Zimmerman Excavating Service, Inc., while his son, Steven, owned the remaining 5%. In 1975, James purchased insurance on his life from Robert Houser of State Farm Insurance. Steven was named beneficiary, and the undisputed purpose of this policy was to fund Steven's purchase of stock in the event of James' death. On April 1, 1980, James died. The insurance proceeds were paid to Steven, but because the policy named James as owner, the proceeds passed through his estate causing a $34,373.97 tax consequence.

The dispute between the parties centers around James' ownership of the policy. The trial court concluded that State Farm and Houser were negligent in that they knew the purpose of this policy, but failed to advise James of the consequences. Had Steven been named as owner, the estate would have saved $34,373.97 in state and federal taxes.

[Affirmed. There is no indication that an attorney had a role in this buy-sell arrangement.]

B. DISABILITY INSURANCE

1. Payment of Premiums

MEGEE v. UNITED STATES FIDELITY AND GUARANTY CO.

Supreme Court of Delaware, 1978.
391 A.2d 189.

HERRMANN, CHIEF JUSTICE:

* * *

On May 14, the plaintiff, a self-employed contractor, filed an application for disability income insurance with the defendant United States Fidelity and Guaranty Company (USF & G). The agent through whom the plaintiff filed the application was the defendant Chandler T. McEvilly, an agent of the defendant Vertex Insurance Agency, Inc. of Newark, Delaware (Vertex). The plaintiff did not choose to remit the premium at the time because Vertex could not assure the plaintiff that he would qualify for coverage at the desired level under USF & G's standard of eligibility. The plaintiff preferred to withhold the first premium until he knew the specific amount of benefits provided by the policy.

The application was received in the Philadelphia office of USF & G on May 20 and forwarded to its home office in Baltimore where it was received May 21. A credit investigation of the plaintiff was completed May 25 and a physical examination of the plaintiff was conducted on June 1 at plaintiff's convenience. Thereupon, a policy was issued, dated June 1. The policy was sent from the Baltimore office to the Philadelphia office of USF & G on June 2, and received there on June 4. It was received by Vertex in Newark on Saturday, June 5.

On that same day, June 5, the plaintiff was accidentally injured and has been unable to work ever since. Upon learning on Monday, June 7, that the plaintiff was injured, McEvilly asked USF & G for instructions. USF & G directed McEvilly not to deliver the policy and not to accept the first premium. On June 10, the plaintiff mailed a check for the first premium, but it was returned uncashed on June 30, with a letter declining coverage.

The plaintiff brought an action against USF & G for breach of contract and negligent failure to deliver the policy, and an action against Vertex and McEvilly for negligent failure to forward the application to USF & G and negligent failure to deliver the policy to the plaintiff. The Superior Court granted the defendants' motion for summary judgment. * * *

The plaintiff contends that the Trial Court erred in granting summary judgment for the defendants upon the ground that there was no contract for insurance in existence at the time of the accident.

Under the plaintiff's theory, the policy was in effect at the time of the injury because it had been constructively delivered to him on the morning of June 5th in that it had been delivered to the agent McEvilly, at that time, with no condition precedent to delivery, the advance payment of the premium having been waived, and the first premium having been tendered later in accordance with the terms of the application.

We find no error in the Trial Court's conclusion that no contract was in existence at the time of the accident. Immediately above the plaintiff's signature on the application, the following appeared:

> "It is agreed that USF & G's liability shall only be as specified in the policy, A & H 1381, applied for, beginning (a) when the policy is issued and full first policy premium paid during the lifetime of and while the health of the person(s) proposed for insurance is as here described on the policy date, or (b) if the premium is paid with this application, as specified in the conditional receipt."

Manifestly, neither condition set forth for the commencement of USF & G's liability was met in the instant case: no premium was paid with the application; nor was the first full premium proffered while the health of the plaintiff was the same as on June 1, 1977.

* * *

The plaintiff further contends that the contract for insurance should have been interpreted in accordance with his reasonable expectations, citing State Farm Mutual Automobile Insurance Co. v. Johnson, Del. Sup., 320 A.2d 345 (1974). Such reasonable expectations, according to the plaintiff, were that the policy became effective when the credit check and physical examination were completed and approved, and not when the premium was paid. Assuming, *arguendo,* the applicability of *State Farm* to the instant facts, in view of the clear language of the application which he signed and presumably read, regarding payment of premium, we are of the opinion that the plaintiff's asserted expectations were unreasonable.

* * *

For these reasons, we find no reversible error in the Trial Court's decision on the contract facet of the summary judgment.

On the negligence facet of the case, the plaintiff contends that the defendants were negligent in not processing the application within a reasonable time.

The cases allowing recovery for violation of the duty to act upon an application for insurance within a reasonable time generally involve payment of the first premium with the application. See Anno., "Insurance Application—Delay", 32 A.L.R.2d 487 at 511. The rationale is that the insurance company has received consideration and has a duty to act promptly; that acting otherwise would prejudice the defendant because he would believe he is insured and not seek insurance elsewhere. E.g., Pohorily v. Kennedy, Del.Super., 269 A.2d 240 (1969). Such is not the situation here. Because no premium had been paid by the plaintiff under the explicit terms of the application, neither USF & G nor Vertex had a duty to act within a time certain. Moreover, delay created by compiling information as to an applicant's health and other material facts cannot be considered unreasonable delay, 43 Am.Jur.2d Insurance § 215, especially where, as here, the physical examination was scheduled to suit the convenience of the plaintiff.

Thus, it is clear that the Trial Court was correct in finding no negligence as a matter of law on the part of the defendants.

Affirmed.

2. Implied Terms—"The Process of Nature"

WILLDEN v. WASHINGTON NATIONAL INSURANCE CO.

Supreme Court of California, 1976.
18 Cal.3d 631, 135 Cal.Rptr. 69, 557 P.2d 501.

TOBRINER, JUSTICE.

This case involves the interpretation of an accident and disability policy. As a result of injuries caused by an automobile accident in 1966, the record indicates that plaintiff began to suffer debilitory effects of multiple sclerosis, finally becoming totally disabled in February of 1969. After receiving special verdicts, the trial court denied plaintiff's claim for accident disability benefits. * * * We affirm the judgment.

Defendant issued plaintiff a "Disability Income Policy for Realtors and Real Estate Salesmen" in 1965. Part 2 of the policy provides 60 months' coverage for injuries which "totally and continuously disable the Insured within thirty days of the date of the accident so as to prevent him from performing each and every duty pertaining to his occupation."[25] If, after payment of disability benefits for 60 months, the

25. The portion of part 2 providing occupational disability benefits reads as follows: "If injury shall totally and continuously disable the Insured within thirty days from the date of the accident so as to prevent him from performing each and every

insured is unable to perform "each and every duty pertaining to any gainful occupation," the policy provides additional benefits for as long as the disability continues. The policy also extends one year of benefits for total disability caused by sickness.

Plaintiff, a real estate salesman, was injured in an automobile accident on February 11, 1966. He experienced tremors in his leg the following day; numbness in the leg by April of 1966; and on October 10, 1966, his condition was diagnosed as multiple sclerosis. Unemployed from April of 1966 to April of 1967, he obtained a business license and worked as a real estate and business opportunity broker until 1972. His condition continued to deteriorate, and he was unable to resume any gainful employment until May 1, 1973. The duration of plaintiff's total disability was disputed at trial, but partially resolved by a special verdict that plaintiff was not totally disabled between April 21, 1967, and February 25, 1969, but was totally disabled thereafter.

Defendant paid plaintiff one year of sickness benefits, terminating on April 21, 1967. Plaintiff then sued for accident benefits accruing after that date. At trial, plaintiff, appearing in propria persona, presented expert testimony that his multiple sclerosis was precipitated by the trauma of the automobile accident. The jury returned a special verdict finding plaintiff's "disability resulted directly and independently of all other causes from the accident of February 11, 1966." * * * The trial court then requested additional special verdicts, and the jury rendered a finding that plaintiff was not totally and continuously disabled within 30 days of the accident. * * * On the basis of these special verdicts the trial court entered judgment for defendant, and plaintiff appealed.

As we have observed, part 2 of the policy (see fn. 27) provides occupational disability benefits if the injury "shall totally and continuously disable the Insured *within thirty days from the date of the accident* so as to prevent him from performing each and every duty pertaining to his occupation." (Italics added.) Consequently the special verdict that plaintiff was *not* totally and continuously disabled within 30 days of the accident appears to bar his claim for accident disability benefits.

Plaintiff contends, however, that the special verdict rests upon a construction of the policy which is inconsistent with the judicially recognized "process of nature" rule. The "process of nature" rule holds that, within the meaning of policy provisions requiring disability within a specified time after the accident, the onset of disability relates back to the time of the accident itself whenever the disability arises directly from the accident "within such time as the process of nature consumes in bringing the person affected to a state of total [disability]." (Schilk v. Benefit Trust Life Ins. Co. (1969) 273 Cal.App.2d 302, 307, 78 Cal.Rptr. 60, 39 A.L.R.3d 1019.)

duty pertaining to his occupation, the Company will pay at the rate of the Monthly Accident Indemnity for the period of such total disability beginning with the day of total disability specified in the Policy Schedule, but not exceeding sixty months during any one period of disability."

The process of nature rule, created by judicial decision in other states in response to the efforts of insurers to enforce arbitrary limitations on coverage, was first established in California in Frenzer v. Mutual Ben. H. & A. Assn. (1938) 27 Cal.App.2d 406, 81 P.2d 197. In *Frenzer,* the insured became disabled from blood poisoning and later died; medical testimony opined that the blood poisoning resulted from a minor injury incurred several hours before any symptoms became evident. Rejecting the insurer's contention that recovery was barred by a provision limiting benefits to injuries which are "immediately and totally disabling," *Frenzer* stated that "While courts are not altogether in accord in the interpretation of the meaning of the words 'immediately and totally disabling' as used in the policy, the weight of authority is toward the so-called process of nature rule; that is, that when a disability follows from an accidental injury within such time as the processes of nature consume in bringing the affected person to the state of total incapacity to prosecute every kind of business pertaining to his occupation such disability is immediate under the terms of the policy." (27 Cal.App.2d at p. 413, 81 P.2d at p. 201.)

The Court of Appeal decision in Schilk v. Benefit Trust Life Ins. Co., supra, 273 Cal.App.2d 302, 78 Cal.Rptr. 60, confirmed the process of nature rule and applied that rule to interpret a policy essentially identical to the policy at issue here. Schilk sustained a whiplash injury on September 27, 1961, and became totally disabled as of February 2, 1962. In denying benefits, the insurer relied on a provision limiting coverage to injuries which "within twenty days of the date of the accident, totally and continuously disable the Insured." The Court of Appeal, however, upheld the trial court's conclusion that under the process of nature rule *Schilk* was deemed disabled within the policy's 20–day period. Rejecting the insurer's attempt to distinguish *Frenzer,* the court stated that "The reasoning applied to the word 'immediately' in *Frenzer* has equal force when the language of a policy provides a specific number of days, as here." (273 Cal.App.2d 302, 307, 78 Cal.Rptr. 60, 64.)

On the facts of this case the jury should have been instructed concerning the process of nature rule. Plaintiff, however, bears the fault for the court's failure to so instruct the jury. * * * Plaintiff proposed no instruction concerning the process of nature rule, and consequently cannot complain of the court's failure to instruct on that subject. (Barrera v. De La Torre (1957) 48 Cal.2d 166, 170, 308 P.2d 724.)

Plaintiff further contends that the 30–day provision of the policy is unconscionable and hence, invalid as a matter of law. No authority supports this contention; the cases clearly indicate that similar provisions, *if* interpreted in accord with the process of nature rule, are not unconscionable. (See Schmidt v. Pacific Mut. Life Ins. Co. (1969) 268 Cal.App.2d 735, 740, 74 Cal.Rptr. 367; Schilk v. Benefit Trust Life Ins. Co., supra, 273 Cal.App.2d 302, 307–308, 78 Cal.Rptr. 60.) The harsh and arguably unconscionable application of the 30–day provision[26] to bar plaintiff's claim in the present case is the result of plaintiff's failure to seek a jury instruction based upon the more liberal process of nature rule.

* * *

The judgment is affirmed.

3. The Scope of Coverage

EMOND v. STATE FARM MUTUAL AUTOMOBILE INSURANCE CO.

Court of Appeals of Georgia, 1985.
175 Ga.App. 548, 333 S.E.2d 656.

CARLEY, JUDGE.

The facts relevant to this appeal are as follows: Appellant-plaintiff was injured in an automobile collision in 1979. Appellant was insured by appellee-defendant. Although the policy specifically purported to provide only basic PIP coverage, appellant had "the right to demand and receive the benefit of $50,000 [optional PIP] coverage upon [her] tender * * * of such additional premium as may be due and filing of proof of loss * * *." Flewellen v. Atlanta Cas. Co., 250 Ga. 709, 712, 300 S.E.2d 673 (1983). However, since Jones v. State Farm Mut. Auto. Ins. Co., 156 Ga.App. 230, 274 S.E.2d 623 (1980) and Flewellen v. Atlanta Cas. Co., supra, had yet to be decided at the time, appellant received only her $5,000 basic PIP benefits. Appellant's policy with appellee also provided $5,000 medical payment coverage for the "payment of medical expenses incurred for services furnished within one year from the date of the accident." The policy also provided that medical payment coverage "shall be excess insurance over any Personal Injury Protection benefits paid or payable under this or any other automobile insurance policy because of bodily injury sustained by an eligible injured person." After appellant was paid $5,000 in basic PIP benefits, she was paid the full $5,000 of her excess medical payment benefits.

Subsequent to the decision in Flewellen v. Atlanta Cas. Co., supra, appellant paid a premium for $50,000 optional PIP coverage. Appellee agreed that appellant was entitled to that coverage. Appellee, having

26. As Justice Taylor pointed out in Schilk v. Benefit Trust Life Ins. Co., supra, 273 Cal.App.2d 302, 78 Cal.Rptr. 60, in discussing a similar limitation "* * * [S]erious internal injuries often do not manifest themselves until long after the accident happened and the injured person may be completely oblivious of his condition, although the process of nature may be actively engaged in developing the latent hurt into a severe or even fatal injury. The fact that respondent, under such circumstances, pursued his usual occupation * * * ought not, in all fairness, militate against him when the more serious but hidden injury subsequently manifests itself." (pp. 307–308, 78 Cal.Rptr. p. 64.) "The strict interpretation of the clause here," Justice Taylor concluded, "would lead to an unjust result * * *. Such a very limited and highly technical construction of an insurance contract cannot be foisted onto a layman nor does it make any sense in terms of the risks insured against." (p. 308, 78 Cal.Rptr. p. 64.)

already paid $10,000 of appellant's claims in the form of $5,000 basic PIP and $5,000 excess medical payments, paid $40,000 more, bringing its total payments to $50,000. Appellant then submitted a claim for medical expenses, all of which she had incurred more than one year after the collision. Appellee refused to pay this claim.

Appellant then instituted the instant civil action against appellee. Under the allegations of the complaint, appellant asserted that she had been paid only $45,000 in PIP benefits and that she was entitled to an additional $5,000 in such benefits. Appellee answered, and among its other defenses, asserted that appellant "has been paid all benefits available under [the] terms of the applicable policy."

Cross motions for summary judgment were filed. The trial court concluded that the $5,000 that had originally been paid to appellant under the excess medical payment coverage of the policy should, as the result of appellant's subsequent invocation of Flewellen v. Atlanta Cas. Co., supra, be reallocated so as to be considered as payment under her optional PIP coverage. Thus, rather than $45,000 in PIP benefits and $5,000 in excess medical payment benefits, the trial court determined that $50,000 in PIP benefits had already been paid to appellant. The trial court further concluded that appellant would not be afforded excess medical payment coverage under the terms of the policy until her full $50,000 in PIP benefits had first been exhausted. The trial court's final conclusion was that appellant was not entitled to any additional benefits for her medical expenses under the policy. According to the trial court's analysis, appellant was not entitled to recover pursuant to the PIP coverage, which had already been exhausted at $50,000, or pursuant to her excess medical payment coverage, which required that medical expenses be incurred within one year of the collision. Summary judgment was granted in favor of appellee. Appellant's motion for summary judgment was denied. Appellant appeals, asserting that appellee was erroneously granted summary judgment and that she was erroneously denied partial summary judgment as to liability for the $5,000 in additional benefits.

1. The trial court was correct in holding that appellant was not entitled to excess medical payment benefits under the terms of her policy until her full $50,000 in PIP benefits had first been exhausted. Hall v. State Farm Mut. Auto. Ins. Co., 254 Ga. 633, 331 S.E.2d 530 (1985.)

2. The issue thus becomes whether the trial court erred in determining that the $5,000 which was originally paid as excess medical payment benefits should now be deemed reallocated so as to have constituted payment under appellant's PIP coverage.

OCGA § 13–1–13 provides, in relevant part, as follows: "Payments of claims made through ignorance of the law or where all the facts are known and there is no misplaced confidence and no artifice, deception, or fraudulent practice used by the other party are deemed voluntary and cannot be recovered unless made under an urgent and immediate necessity therefor or to release person or property from detention or to prevent an immediate seizure of person or property." Although appellee does not seek a $5,000 judgment against appellant, it does seek to have the $5,000 that it originally paid as excess medical payment benefits now applied against its liability to appellant for optional PIP benefits. Under these circumstances, we believe that OCGA § 13–1–13 is applicable. Cf. Mitchell v. Holden, 58 Ga.App. 712, 713(3), 199 S.E. 835 (1938). "An insurer cannot recover the payment of a claim made by mistake without showing a valid reason for failing to ascertain the truth." 658 Barker v. Federated Life Ins. Co., 111 Ga.App. 171, 141 S.E.2d 206 (1965).

"While money voluntarily paid may not ordinarily be recovered, this rule is not without exception. [Cits.]" Greene v. McIntyre, 119 Ga.App. 296, 298, 167 S.E.2d 203 (1969). "If [payment] was made in ignorance of law, recovery is barred; if in mistake of law, recovery is permitted. [Cits.]" American Surety Co. v. Groover, 64 Ga.App. 865, 870, 14 S.E.2d 149 (1941) (On Motion For Rehearing). As noted above, appellant in the instant case was paid the $5,000 in excess medical payment benefits after she had exhausted her basic PIP benefits but prior to the determination that she was entitled to an additional $45,000 in optional PIP benefits. Compare Hawkins v. Travelers Ins. Co., 162 Ga.App. 231, 235, 290 S.E.2d 348 (1982). Appellee contends that, but for its mistaken interpretation of the no-fault law prior to the Jones and Flewellen decisions, appellant would not have been paid any excess medical payment benefits until such time as her full $50,000 in optional PIP benefits had been exhausted. In our opinion, this would constitute payment under a mistake of law rather than through ignorance of the law. "While it is true that we held in Flewellen that 'the mandate of the law was clear' * * *, its interpretation by the bench, bar, insurers and insureds were obviously less so." Cotton States Mut. Ins. Co. v. McFather, 251 Ga. 739, 743, 309 S.E.2d 799 (1983). Where one acts "under a mistake of what the law was as applicable to [the] state of facts, or was requiring of it, we think that the mistake, though a product of ignorance, would be such a mistake of law * * * as would come within the rule." (Emphasis in original.) American Surety Co. v. Groover, supra 64 Ga.App. at 871, 14 S.E.2d 149 (On Motion For Rehearing).

Moreover, it does not appear that, in good conscience, appellee should not be allowed to reallocate the $5,000 towards its payment of PIP benefits to appellant. Appellant is not thereby deprived of any benefits to which she would otherwise be entitled. The payment of benefits already received is merely being redesignated to conform strictly with the terms of the contract, the enforcement of the terms of which appellant herself initiated by invoking Jones and Flewellen.

Accordingly, we find that the trial court did not err in holding that appellee was not a "volunteer" as to the original $5,000 payment and is now entitled to have that payment reallocated as payment of PIP benefits. Appellant has thus received her full $50,000 in PIP benefits.

3. It is undisputed that the medical expenses for which appellant seeks coverage were incurred more than one year after the collision.

Citing Strickland v. Gulf Life Ins. Co., 240 Ga. 723, 242 S.E.2d 148 (1978), appellant contends that that provision of the policy which limits excess medical payment coverage to those expenses incurred within one year is unconscionable and unenforceable.

In Strickland, the policy provided coverage for loss of a limb only in the event that the loss occurred within 90 days of the injury to the limb. Our Supreme Court held that "[w]here loss of a limb is involved at an arbitrary point in time, here 90 days, the insured under these cases is confronted with the ugly choice whether to continue treatment and retain hope of regaining the use of his leg or to amputate his leg in order to be eligible for insurance benefits which he would forego if amputation became necessary at a later time. We find an insurance limitation forcing such a gruesome choice may be unreasonable and thus may be void as against public policy." Strickland v. Gulf Life Ins. Co., supra at 725, 242 S.E.2d 148.

Unlike Strickland, the policy provision in the instant case does not provide for a short-term period after the occurrence of a potentially insured event, within which period the insured faces a gruesome choice determinative of whether coverage will or will not be afforded. Under the instant policy, it is clear that appellant was being afforded coverage for excess medical payments, the only limitations on eligibility being the exhaustion of her PIP coverage and the consequent incurring of payments within one year of her injury. In our opinion, this provision specifically defines the coverage being afforded (see Hawkins v. Travelers Ins. Co., supra 162 Ga.App. at 236(2), 290 S.E.2d 348) and is not analogous to the provision under consideration in Strickland, supra. Nothing in the record would authorize a finding that appellee has waived enforcement of the one-year limitation on coverage, or that such provisions are so unreasonable as to violate public policy. Cf. Porter v. Allstate Ins. Co., 172 Ga.App. 657, 658, 324 S.E.2d 515 (1984).

Judgment affirmed.

Notes

1. With *Emond* in mind, consider the following coverage limitations: (1) accidental loss of limb provided there is dismemberment within 90 days, and (2) life insurance with double indemnity if death occurs within 90 days. The *Strickland* case cited in *Emond* is a variation of the first type wherein the victim's dilemma is so obviously acute as to tempt an emotional resolution. However, the *Strickland* opinion relies upon a case from Pennsylvania and one from New Jersey, which are based on the second type and are stated to represent the minority view. In *National Life and Accident Insurance Co. v. Edwards*, 119 Cal.App.3d 326, 174 Cal.Rptr. 31 (1981), the insured had an $8,000 life insurance policy with double indemnity ($16,000) in case death ensued within 90 days after an auto accident. The insured was rendered a quadriplegic in an auto crash but lived for two years before dying of complications. The insurer tendered the face amount of the policy but resisted the double indemnity claim. The majority opinion frankly stated:

> "Although there is a substantial and growing body of law applying the process of nature rule to disability policies the courts have shown reluctance in extending this concept to time limitations in double indemnity provisions in life insurance policies."

Nevertheless the majority held the insurer liable for double indemnity citing the same two cases from Pennsylvania and New Jersey as in *Strickland.* The dissenting justice asserted that it is inappropriate to classify such policies as "adhesive." The insured could have procured $16,000 ordinary life coverage from a variety of competing policies and a variety of competing companies, but chose a cheaper one with $8000 coverage in any event and double indemnity only under exceptional and well understood circumstances.

2. In *Alvarado v. Pilot Life Ins. Co.*, 663 S.W.2d 108 (Tex.App.1983) the insurer was granted summary judgment on insured's claim for accidental loss of a foot badly mangled by a gunshot but not amputated until 59 days after the "90 day" period specified in the policy. The court found no violation of public policy in the provision nor any ambiguity in the word "severance." See Annot. (1971) 39 A.L.R.3d 1311.

3. As a result of the AIDS epidemic, a number of insurance companies and other entities are buying life insurance policies to make cash available to terminally ill persons. West's Ann. California Insurance Code § 10113.1, for example, authorizes these types of "viatical" settlement. With these accelerated death benefits, the terminally ill insured can receive anywhere between 25% and 95% of the value of the policy during their lifetimes. Rather than simply purchasing the policy from the insured, some insurance companies are offering riders or separate policies to guarantee accelerated payment of a portion of the policy upon diagnosis of a terminal illness. These riders tend to come at a substantial extra charge, although the nation's largest insurance company has established a program that pays full benefits minus only the interest the company would have earned by holding the money an extra six months. These types of arrangements, however, may have tax consequences and California Insurance Code § 10113.2(d)(2) requires disclosure of possible tax consequences. See Samuel Goldreich, *Battle to the Death? Viatical Firms Fight Insurers Over Rules on Settlements*, Wash. Times, November 5, 1996, at B6; Jo–Ann Johnston, *For the Terminally Ill, a Path to Financial Peace; New Options Allow Sick to Pay Bills and Live Rest of Lives More Completely*, Boston Globe, October 13, 1997, at A10; Kathryn Sullivan and Joann Canning, *Life Benefits from Insurance May Be Taxable*, 49 Taxation for Accountants 1, July, 1992; Wayne M. Gazur, *Death and Taxes: The Taxation of Accelerated Death Benefits for the Terminally Ill*, 11 Va. Tax Rev. 263, Fall 1991; Tamar Lewin, *Terminally Ill Can Collect Death Payout While Alive*, N.Y. Times, January 27, 1990, at A1.

4. The growing use of accelerated death benefits currently poses a federal income tax problem; while the Internal Revenue Code excludes from gross income insurance benefits paid by reason of death of the insured, accelerated benefits are treated separately. In 1996 Congress enacted I.R.C. § 101(g) as part of the Health Insurance Portability and Accountability Act. Briefly, the Internal Revenue Code treats payment of proceeds to a terminally ill (a person is deemed terminally ill if death can be reasonable expected within 24 months after certification by a physician) individual as paid by

reason of the death of an insured. Thus, under I.R.C. § 101(a)(1), payment of accelerated death benefits are excluded from gross income.

5. A group accidental death and dismemberment policy provides for payment of $100,000 for loss of "life," "two hands," "two feet," etc. but specifically provided that "with regard to hands and feet, loss shall mean dismemberment by severance at or above wrist or ankle joints respectively * * *." An insured under the policy sustained a severe spinal cord injury which has resulted in total loss of control and sensation in his legs. Could it be reasonably argued that functional loss of use of legs by severance of the spinal cord was within the policy coverage? See Cunninghame v. Equitable Life Assurance Society of United States, 652 F.2d 306, 309 (2d Cir.1981) ("dismemberment" implies actual separation and "it could not refer to any thing [sic] other that actual, physical separation of the feet from the rest of the body").

CHALMERS v. METROPOLITAN LIFE INSURANCE CO.

Court of Appeals of Michigan, 1978.
86 Mich.App. 25, 272 N.W.2d 188.

BEASLEY, JUDGE.

After long service as an airplane pilot for General Motors Corporation, plaintiff suffered a severe heart attack on January 17, 1971. Although he recovered, his pilot's license was permanently suspended as a result of the heart attack. Plaintiff claimed benefits under an extended disability benefit section of a group insurance policy issued by defendant Metropolitan Life Insurance Company for the reason that he is totally disabled to perform his job as an airplane pilot. Defendant denied extended disability benefits on the basis that, although plaintiff is no longer able to get a pilot's license, there are many jobs that he is physically qualified to do. * * * The trial court granted plaintiff a partial summary judgment for benefits payable as of that time based on a finding that plaintiff was totally disabled within the meaning of the language of the insurance policy. Defendant appeals as of right.

* * *

Essentially, the question here involves interpretation of the disability provisions of the group life insurance policy issued by defendant. The key provision in the policy reads:

> "If, while insured * * * the Employee is both under age 65 and *totally disabled so as to be unable to engage in any gainful occupation or employment for which he is reasonably qualified by education, training or experience,* the amount of Extended Disability Benefit Insurance (Monthly Benefits) then in force on account of the Employee shall be paid to the Employee each month during the period the Employee is so disabled, as set forth herein." (Emphasis added.)

Generally, two aspects or elements are involved in defining "total disability". First, there is the element of *quality,* which involves the question of whether the insured must be unable to work in his particular occupation, or whether he must be unable to work in other occupations as well. Then, there is the element of *quantity,* which is concerned with the amount of work an insured can be capable of performing and still be considered "totally disabled", that is, whether the insured need be absolutely helpless, or whether he may be able to perform minor acts only, or whether he may be able to perform substantial acts.[27]

It should be noted that since plaintiff in the instant case is one hundred percent disabled from performing within his former occupation of airplane pilot, the question of what quantity of work he is capable of performing within his given occupation is not at issue. The question is: Does the fact that plaintiff could possibly pursue some occupations other than that of licensed airplane pilot preclude a conclusion that he is totally disabled as the term is used in the insurance policy?

* * *

There is an ambiguity in the provision * * * The policy provides that a person is totally disabled if he is unable to engage in any gainful occupation or employment for which he is *reasonably qualified* by education, training or experience. Careful reading indicates the policy language covers "any gainful occupation or employment" but that the words "any gainful occupation or employment" are modified by the clause, and limited to those, "for which he is reasonably qualified by education, training or experience". Thus, the ambiguity arises from and the question then is as to the meaning, under the policy, of "reasonably" qualified.

In general, there are three views relating to the interpretation of "total disability" provisions in insurance policies. They are:

> 1) the *extreme view in favor of the insured* that total disability exists whenever the insured is unable to perform the duties of his particular occupation;
>
> 2) the *extreme view in favor of the insurer* that total disability exists only when there is incapacity to pursue any occupation whatever, and
>
> 3) the *intermediate view,* which regards total disability as a relative term, which rejects both of the two extreme views and which employs differing language to explain the degree of incapacity required to constitute total disability.[28]

We interpret the Michigan cases to follow the so-called intermediate view.

In Ebert v. Prudential Ins. Co. of America,[29] the Michigan Supreme Court utilized the above terminology and affirmed a judgment in favor of plaintiff who was an undertaker. The evidence indicated that plaintiff injured his back in an automobile accident suffering what was described

27. 21 A.L.R.3d 1155, 1158–1159.

28. Id. at 1161; See also, 21 A.L.R.3d 1383, 1393–1394.

29. 338 Mich. 320, 330, 61 N.W.2d 164 (1953).

as hypertrophic arthritis. The Court said that while he could do some light work he could not perform the embalming and lifting required of an undertaker. The Court concluded that he was permanently and totally disabled so as to be entitled to benefits under a provision contained in his life insurance policies. The *Ebert* Court made it clear that where there is ambiguity, insurance policies are to be liberally construed in favor of the insured. Technical construction to defeat claims is not favored.

We recognize that the language of the insurance policies involved in the Michigan cases tends to vary, but within those varying provisions, the Michigan Court has indicated a strong commitment to a liberal construction of such insurance policies that does not permit defeat of a reasonable expectation of payment of benefits. See Crowell v. Federal Life & Casualty Co.[30]

Applying that view to the facts of the instant case, we note that the record reveals beyond dispute that plaintiff is totally disabled from pursuing his former occupation of airplane pilot. There is considerable evidence of record to indicate that all significant education, training and experience accumulated by plaintiff was geared to his preparation for the specialized occupation of airplane pilot. It is this particular occupation for which plaintiff is reasonably qualified.

Defendant argues that prior to his heart attack plaintiff had experience in sales and aviation-related jobs such as maintenance, scheduling and flight operations. Defendant says this experience compels the conclusion that plaintiff is reasonably qualified for such jobs and that, therefore, since plaintiff is now physically capable of doing that kind of work, he is *not* totally disabled within the meaning of the term as delineated in the insurance policy. In support of this argument, defendant cites Przbylinski v. Standard Pressed Steel Co.[31]

In *Przbylinski,* this Court affirmed a directed verdict for defendant where plaintiff failed to offer evidence that "he suffered a disability which prevented him from engaging in any occupation for which he was reasonably fitted" and also failed to offer evidence that he was being treated by a physician for the disability as required under that insurance policy. In fact, the evidence showed that plaintiff, a supervisor, believed he was still physically able to do the work and did similar work for another employer for 4½ months subsequent to his alleged disablement. We conclude, *Przbylinski* is, on its facts, readily distinguishable from this case and is not controlling precedent here.

In the within case, the trial judge said:

> "Now it would seem to me that to say that this man now is reasonably qualified by education, training, or experience to do anything but fly is stretching it a little bit far. Clearly his whole adult life for all practical purposes has been devoted to flying, and to

30. 397 Mich. 614, 247 N.W.2d 503 (1976).

31. 62 Mich.App. 461, 233 N.W.2d 614 (1975).

say now that at age 51 he is reasonably qualified by education, training, or experience to undertake something else, real estate or some other type of employment, seems to me stretching the language a little bit."

We do not believe his finding was clearly erroneous.

To hold as defendant contends would be to interpret the policy as extending very limited coverage. We believe the coverage afforded under this group policy looked to the work performed by the employee for this employer. We also note that the work experience relied upon by defendant as a basis to attempt to defeat liability occurred many years ago. The trial judge's ruling is consistent with the Michigan cases.

AFFIRMED.

Notes

1. One of the more troublesome provisions in accident policies has concerned the loss of sight. "With respect to eyes", reads this provision, " 'loss' means the entire and irrecoverable loss of sight." Suppose the insured who had 20/20 vision in both eyes accidentally sustains an injury to one eye reducing vision to 2/200. The other eye is unaffected. By the use of a contact lens the visual acuity of 20/25 can be obtained in the injured eye. Should the insured recover? This question split the Missouri Supreme Court 4–3 in *Crim v. National Life and Accident Insurance Co.*, 605 S.W.2d 73 (Mo.1980). Holding for the insurer, the majority stated:

> The logic of the holdings that vision which has been restored by the use of artificial lenses has not been irrevocably lost is compelling. It is common knowledge that such devices are frequently employed in order to avoid loss of sight. To say that one whose sight has been so restored has lost his sight ignores reality. The fact that vision might be recovered through medical treatment or naturally does not exclude the fact that it may also be recovered by mechanical or artificial means. The determinative term in the language here in question is the word "irrecoverable." That recovery may come about by more than one means does not make that term ambiguous. The fact that a word or phrase may be accorded a flexible meaning does not make it ambiguous. *Id.* at 76.

2. Would a lawyer who sustained an injury rendering one hand useless be considered as totally disabled? See Laidlaw v. Commercial Insurance Co., 255 N.W.2d 807 (Minn.1977) (lawyer was disabled because disability does not mean a "state of absolute helplessness": but rather the "inability to perform the substantial and material parts of one's occupation in the customary and usual manner and with substantial continuity").

C. AUTOMOBILE INSURANCE

A few words of caution are appropriate with respect to automobile insurance. First, the coverage of the subject that follows is cursory because many of the core concepts relating to liability insurance and property insurance are treated in more detail above. Second, automobile insurance is heavily regulated by statute in all of the states. The latter phenomenon is owed to the fact that automobile insurance involves a large number of relatively small claims so that the most efficient mechanism for dealing with them is a systematic statutory resolution of the issues. Thus the cases and materials that follow reflect the preceding words of caution.

1. "Use, Maintenance or Operation" of a Car

AMERICAN STATES INSURANCE COMPANY v. ALLSTATE INSURANCE COMPANY

District Court of Appeal of Florida, Fifth District, 1986.
484 So.2d 1363.

ORFINGER, JUDGE.

When a dog which is riding in the back of a pickup truck bites a passenger who has just exited from it, does the injury to the passenger arise "out of the use, operation or maintenance" of the truck? The trial court held that under the facts of this case it did not. We affirm.

William C. Connor drove his mother's pickup truck to a store to make a purchase. Accompanying him in the truck was a friend, William J. Sullivan. In the back of the pickup, which was equipped with a camper, was William Connor's pit bull dog, Lila, just along for the ride. When they reached the store, Connor stopped the truck and both men got out. As Sullivan passed the open rear window of the camper, Lila bit him, causing serious injury.

Sullivan made a claim against William's mother, June V. Connor, who referred the claim to American States Insurance Company, her homeowner's insurance carrier. American States settled the claim with Sullivan, took an assignment of June Connor's rights, then in turn filed this action for reimbursement against Allstate Insurance Company, June Connor's automobile insurance carrier. Allstate denied liability, asserting lack of coverage because the incident did not arise "out of the ownership, maintenance or use" of the motor vehicle, as required by the policy of insurance.

This court has previously held that where a motor vehicle is merely the *situs* of an injury that could have happened anywhere, the injuries do not arise out of the "ownership, maintenance or use" of the motor vehicle. *Reynolds v. Allstate Insurance Company,* 400 So.2d 496 (Fla. 5th DCA 1981). Other courts have applied the same principle in various factual situations. *See Doyle v. State Farm Mutual Automobile Insurance Company,* 464 So.2d 1277 (Fla. 3d DCA 1985) (injuries suffered at the hands of a robber who shot the insured as he exited his automobile, held not to have arisen out of ownership or use of automobile); *Allstate Insurance Company v. Famigletti,* 459 So.2d 1149 (Fla. 4th DCA 1984) (injury to insureds who were shot by a neighbor when they passed by in their automobile, did not arise out of the ownership or use of the automobile); *Hutchins v. Mills,* 363 So.2d 818 (Fla. 1st DCA 1978), *cert. denied,* 368 So.2d 1368 (Fla.1979) (accidental shooting of decedent by insured while using the flatbed of his truck as a deer stand, held not "arising out of the use" of the truck); *Watson v. Watson,* 326 So.2d 48 (Fla. 2d DCA 1976) (death of the son who was killed when the pistol discharged as he was removing it from his father's car at the scene of an accident so that the car could be taken to a garage for repairs, held not to have arisen out of the ownership, maintenance or use of the car).

The appellant relies primarily on *Government Employees Insurance Company v. Novak,* 453 So.2d 1116 (Fla.1984) and *National Indemnity Company v. Corbo,* 248 So.2d 238 (Fla. 3d DCA 1971), but these cases are clearly distinguishable on their facts. In *Novak,* while noting that the phrase "arising out of the use of a motor vehicle" is a comprehensive term which should be liberally construed to extend coverage broadly, the supreme court held that there must be some nexus between the motor vehicle and the injury. In *Novak,* the majority of the court found the nexus in the fact that the person who attacked and injured the insured wanted to use the vehicle because he shot the insured, pulled her out of the car and drove off in it after he had been refused a ride. Thus, the use of the car was the reason for the attack, and a sufficient nexus. While *Corbo* is closer, the dog which bit the plaintiff in that case was a guard dog owned by the insured and being transported to the insured's place of business at the time of the incident. Thus, the transportation of the dog was the sole reason for the vehicle's use at that time, thereby providing the nexus between the use of the automobile and the injury.

Here, the only purpose of the trip was to go to the store, and the dog was merely along for the ride, as was the passenger. The accident occurred at the vehicle, but it did not arise out of the use of the vehicle.

AFFIRMED.

Note

Surprisingly enough the facts of the principal case have been replicated. See Duvigneaud v. Government Employees Insurance Co., 363 So.2d 1292 (La.App.1978).

Arising out of "use, maintenance or operation" of car

Issues of fact, issues of causation, and imaginative interpretation tinged with a bit of the "reasonable expectation" approach, characterize the surprisingly large number of cases which turn upon this bit of phraseology. Consistency is not to be expected although it may be safely pointed out that the average owner's or permittee's expectancy would envision the automobile's use as limited to its use as a vehicle. (Indeed policies may be so worded). Parents with even a limited recall of their own escapades might well cringe at the implications of full liability for all that may take place in the family auto. A sampling of cases may give a sense of things.

The vehicle as a helpful appliance or tool

1. The insured, under first party insurance (no fault) saw ripe plums along a highway. Because he was unable to reach the plums from the bed of the truck, he stood with both feet on top of the side panel, and fell off. Leverette v. Aetna Casualty and Surety Co., 157 Ga.App. 175, 276 S.E.2d 859 (1981) (held for the insurer). The court noted that "the injury need not be the proximate result of 'use' in the strict sense, but it cannot be extended to something distinctly remote. Each case turns on its precise individual facts. The question to be answered is whether the injury 'originated from' or 'had its origin in' or 'grew out of' or 'flowed from' the use of the motor vehicle as a vehicle." The injury in this case resulted "neither from an accident peculiar to the motor vehicle nor was it intrinsically related to the vehicle itself."

Would your answer be different if the plum picking activity of the pick-up was as a moving carrier for pickers along orchard rows?

Suppose X is sleeping in the bed of a recreational vehicle and falls out when it is moving. Is there coverage under the insured's homeowners policy or auto no fault policy? Would your answer be different if the vehicle was parked for the night?

2. Insured (auto liability policy) also owned an airplane (not covered) with a dead battery. He was charging the plane's battery with jumper wires from the car when the plane took off down the runway damaging other aircraft. Associated Indemnity Corp. v. Warner, 143 Ariz. 567, 694 P.2d 1181 (1985) (held for the insurer); but cf. Hedlund v. Milwaukee Mutual Ins. Co., 373 N.W.2d 823 (Minn.App.1985) (held for insured injured in trying to jump start his tractor).

3. Individuals were sitting in the car loading rifles in preparation for target shooting. One of the rifles accidentally discharged injuring a member of party. Aetna Casualty & Surety Co. v. Safeco Insurance Co., 103 Cal. App.3d 694, 163 Cal.Rptr. 219 (1980) (held for insurer because no action by driver related to the accident). Note this action was between insurance companies. Very frequently the car owner also has general liability protection under his H.O. policy for the consequences of actions taking place in or around autos but not arising from their use.

If the movement of the car caused the firearm to discharge would the result change? Yes, according to *State Farm Mutual Auto. Insurance Co. v. Partridge*, 10 Cal.3d 94, 109 Cal.Rptr. 811, 514 P.2d 123 (1973), wherein a pistol had been modified to a hair trigger condition so that it went off when the car turned off the paved highway onto rough trail. Southeastern Fidelity Insurance Co. v. Stevens, 142 Ga.App. 562, 236 S.E.2d 550 (1977) (in accord).

A towing case

4. Perry and his two sons had an antique Model A Ford which was inoperable, without license plates, and uninsured. To move it the trio hooked it to a van which was insured under a "no fault" plan. The sons drove the van and Perry was steering the Model A when the procession was stopped by a police officer. When Perry was getting out of the Model A, he was fatally shot by the officer. Did his death arise out of the use of the van? Perry v. State Farm Mutual Automobile Insurance Co., 506 F.Supp. 130 (D.Minn. 1980) (held for the beneficiary inasmuch as there was a causal connection between the death and the use of the van).

A most common occurrence

5. Road rage. The enraged participants engage in a fist fight injuring each other. Do their auto policies apply? Cf. Day v. State Farm Mutual Insurance Co., 261 Pa.Super. 216, 396 A.2d 3 (1978) (held no in case arising out of uninsured motorist provision).

Projectile cases

6. A boy threw an egg from moving car thereby putting out the eye of a pedestrian. National American Insurance Co. v. Insurance Co. of North America, 74 Cal.App.3d 565, 140 Cal.Rptr. 828 (1977) (held covered by auto policy: "Only minimal causal connection is necessary." "Need not be proximate cause."). There is little uniformity here. The throwing of bottles was considered as connected with the use of car in *Wyoming Farm Bureau Mutual Insurance Co. v. State Farm Mutual Auto. Insurance Co.*, 467 F.2d 990 (10th Cir.1972), and *Government Employees Insurance Co. v. Melton*, 357 F.Supp. 416 (D.C.S.C.1972), affirmed 473 F.2d 909 (4th Cir.1973). Coverage was denied, however, in some cases involving cherry bombs. McDonald v. Great American Insurance Co., 224 F.Supp. 369 (D.R.I.1963), and Wirth v. Maryland Casualty Co., 368 F.Supp. 789 (D.Ky.1973), affirmed 497 F.2d 925 (6th Cir.1974); see also, Farm Bureau Mutual Insurance Co., Inc. v. Evans, 7 Kan.App.2d 60, 637 P.2d 491 (1981) (car was not in motion).

Does visualizing the auto as a launching pad help in the analysis?

"Maintenance" cases

7. Insured (under no fault policy) could not get his truck started in cold weather. He decided to heat the oil pan by putting charcoal in an old tire rim, lighting it and shoving the whole thing under the pan. He seeks P.I.P. benefits. Wagner v. Michigan Mut. Liab. Ins. Co., 135 Mich.App. 767, 356 N.W.2d 262 (1984) (held for the insured because the procedure constituted "maintenance").

Suppose the insured has a no fault policy covering injuries arising out of use, etc. of an automobile. He steps on the starter of his car and is killed by an explosive device attached to the ignition. Does the policy cover?

"Operating" cases

8. A seven year old child left in car disengages the brakes. The car runs over his mother. Tucker v. State Farm Mutual Automobile Insurance Co., 154 So.2d 226 (La.App.1963) (held for the insurer because no purposeful use or operation of car).

Concurrent Contributing Causes

9. Insured (both auto liability and HO's) shoveled some hot ashes into uncovered barrels, put the barrels into a pick-up truck and headed for the dump at 35 miles per hour. The breeze fanned the embers into flame and set the countryside afire. Waseca Mut. Ins. Co. v. Noska, 331 N.W.2d 917 (Minn.1983). Held that the H.O.'s policy covered the negligent act of putting hot ashes into barrels as non automobile related; the auto policy also applied as its use was a contributing cause. Reliance was placed on *State Farm Mut. Auto. Ins. Co. v. Partridge*, 10 Cal.3d 94, 109 Cal.Rptr. 811, 514 P.2d 123 (1973) cited in note 3 above.

Assume the insured has a H.O.'s policy with the use or operation of an auto exclusion. Her daughter, driving with permission but with only rudimentary instruction, causes an accident. Can the exclusion be overridden by alleging that the insured "negligently entrusted" the car to the daughter as a contributing cause of the accident? Numerous decisions have dealt with this ploy. An exhaustive list may be found in *Southeastern Fire Ins. Co. v. Heard*, 626 F.Supp. 476 (N.D.Ga.1985) together with *Huggins v. Tri–County Bonding Co.*, 175 W.Va. 643, 337 S.E.2d 12 (W.Va.1985).

Suppose a terrorist borrows a car from an innocent insured, turns it into a dynamite chamber and explodes it in a crowded market place? Does an omnibus provision cover? See Kraus v. Allstate Insurance Co., 258 F.Supp. 407 (W.D.Pa.1966), affirmed 379 F.2d 443 (3d Cir.1967) (holding no, because the harm inflicted was due to a criminal act, not the ownership, maintenance, and use of an automobile, an further that it would be against public policy to insure against financial responsibility the perpetrator of a murder). Would the owner be liable under provisions such as § 17150 and § 17151 of the California Vehicle Code?

Loading and Unloading Provisions

Closely associated with the policy clauses covering liability arising out of the "use" of a vehicle are provisions extending the coverage to include accidents during the loading and unloading period. A typical fact situation which triggers the wealth of litigation interpreting such clauses is presented in *Estes Co. of Bettendorf v. Employers Mutual Casualty Co.*, 79 Ill.2d 228, 37 Ill.Dec. 611, 402 N.E.2d 613, 6 A.L.R.4th 679 (1980). Here Ready–Mix concrete was being delivered to a building construction site where the contractor had the forms ready. The concrete was poured by the Ready–Mix driver into a bucket connected to an overhead crane which lifted the concrete into the forms. This operation was performed by the contractor's workmen. As one filled bucket was being swung from the concrete truck over to the forms, the crane hit a high tension wire injuring the contractor's employees. The basic issue becomes whether the insurance policy of the concrete supplier covered. The court stated:

> "Loading and unloading clauses have been a feature of insurance policies for many years. A substantial body of case law has developed to assist in the construction of these clauses in particular situations. As the appellate court has noted, the decisions construing unloading clauses have utilized one of two theories to determine when unloading is complete, the 'coming to rest' doctrine or the 'complete operations' doctrine. Under the 'coming to rest' approach, the unloading process includes only the actual moving of the article from the motor vehicle until it first comes to rest. When the article has begun to move toward its final destination, independent of the motor vehicle, the vehicle is no longer connected with the process of unloading. (See American Automobile Insurance Co. v. American Fidelity & Casualty Co. (1951), 106 Cal.App.2d 630, 235 P.2d 645.) Unloading under the 'complete operations' doctrine, however, includes all the operations necessary to effect a completed delivery. (See Entz v. Fidelity & Casualty Co. of New York (1966), 64 Cal.2d 379, 412 P.2d 382, 50 Cal.Rptr. 190.) We agree with the appellate court that the 'complete operations' doctrine, which embraces all of the operations necessary to effect a completed delivery of the article, is the preferred view. See Magarick, Loading and Unloading Under the Standard Automobile Policy, 67 Dick.L.Rev. 257, 258–59

(1963); Risjord, Loading and Unloading, 13 Vand.L.Rev. 903, 904 (1960); Annot., 95 A.L.R.2d 1122, 1129 (1964).

"The mere assertion of the 'complete operations' doctrine, however, will not serve to resolve this case. Those courts which have adopted this doctrine have arrived at inconsistent conclusions in resolving substantially similar controversies. Some courts following this rule have held that 'unloading' is not completed until the material has been delivered to its ultimate destination, in the present case, the concrete forms. (See St. Paul Mercury Insurance Co. v. Huitt (6th Cir.1964), 336 F.2d 37, 42; Employers' Liability Assurance Corp. v. Travelers Insurance Co. (D.Conn.1968), 293 F.Supp. 604, 607.) Other courts, applying the same doctrine, have held that loading is completed when commercial delivery has been accomplished. See Galloway Crane & Trucking Co. v. Truck Insurance Exchange (1977), 67 Cal.App.3d 386, 391, 136 Cal.Rptr. 645, 648; Liberty Mutual Insurance Co. v. Johnson, Drake & Piper, Inc. (8th Cir.1968), 390 F.2d 410, 416.

"Although it is true that the loading and unloading clause expands the scope of activities included within the use of the vehicle, we do not believe that the parties intended to extend coverage to an accident occurring after the concrete has been placed in a receptacle furnished by or on behalf of the purchaser. (Galloway Crane & Trucking Co. v. Truck Insurance Exchange (1977), 67 Cal.App.3d 386, 390, 136 Cal.Rptr. 645, 646.) We believe it more reasonable to hold that 'unloading' has been completed when, subsequent to removal of the material from the vehicle, the deliverer has finished his handling of it, and the material has been placed in the hands of the receiver at the designated reception point, despite the fact that it is necessary to transport the material thereafter to another point. * * *

"In the present case, it is unrebutted that the custom in the industry is that delivery of the premixed concrete to the purchaser is complete when placed in the first receptacle provided at the construction site. The injuries to Cosper and Jones occurred subsequent to delivery of the cement to Anderson Construction Company. The truck was unloaded so far as the concrete deposited in the bucket was concerned. At that point the concrete had been placed in the hands of the receiver at the designated reception point. Ready Mixed exercised no control over the cement, the bucket, or the crane. We therefore hold that the injuries to Cosper and Jones did not arise out of the unloading of the vehicle. " * * * The fact that there remained additional material to be delivered will not serve to bring these subsequent injuries within the scope of the unloading clauses."

2. Insurer's Defenses

a. The Policy Has Been Rescinded or Cancelled

BARRERA v. STATE FARM MUTUAL AUTOMOBILE INSURANCE CO.

Supreme Court of California, 1969.
71 Cal.2d 659, 79 Cal.Rptr. 106, 456 P.2d 674.

TOBRINER, JUSTICE.

Plaintiff sued State Farm Mutual Automobile Insurance Company (hereinafter "State Farm") to compel payment of a judgment obtained against Anthony and Sandra Alves. Plaintiff obtained the judgment against the Alveses on the ground that plaintiff, while a pedestrian, was injured by Mrs. Alves's negligent driving. Plaintiff alleged and urged the enforceability at the time of the accident of an automobile liability policy issued by State Farm to the Alveses. State Farm denied the validity of the policy, and filed a cross-complaint seeking a declaration that the policy was void *ab initio* because issued in reliance on a material misrepresentation by Mr. Alves. In opposition, plaintiff contended that State Farm was estopped to rescind the policy six months after the accident because State Farm led Mr. Alves to believe that he was insured and because State Farm negligently failed to discover within a reasonable time the misrepresentation in the application tendered 1½ years prior to the accident.

The trial court found that State Farm issued the automobile liability policy in reliance on a material misrepresentation, that rescission was therefore justified, and that State Farm acted promptly *upon discovery* of the misrepresentation. Accordingly, the court entered judgment for State Farm on both the complaint and the cross-complaint. Plaintiff moved for a new trial, urging that the public policy expressed in California's Financial Responsibility Law impelled a finding of laches by State Farm in its belated discovery of the misrepresentations; that its failure to act promptly worked to the detriment of an innocent member of the public, who should therefore recover against the carrier. The trial court denied the motion. Plaintiff appeals.[32]

We conclude that an automobile liability insurer must undertake a reasonable investigation of the insured's insurability within a reasonable period of time from the acceptance of the application and the issuance of a policy. This duty directly inures to the benefit of third persons injured by the insured. Such an injured party, who has obtained an unsatisfied judgment against the insured, may properly proceed against the insurer; the insurer cannot then successfully defend upon the ground of its own failure reasonably to investigate the application. On retrial, therefore, plaintiff, upon showing that State Farm did not, within a reasonable time, reasonably investigate the insured's insurability, may recover from State Farm, within the policy limits, the amount of the judgment she obtained against the Alveses.[33]

32. The Alveses are not a party to this appeal.

33. In addition to arguing that State Farm was estopped to rescind the policy because of negligent failure to discover the misrepresentation within a reasonable time, plaintiff also argued that section 651 of the Insurance Code applied to rescission as well as to prospective cancellation of automobile insurance policies, and that therefore the attempted rescission did not take effect until 10 days after notice of the rescission was sent to Mr. Alves. If termination of the policy did not occur until after notice, the policy remained in effect at the time of the accident.

Plaintiff's contention regarding section 651 runs counter to the statutory scheme for termination of insurance contracts and blurs the clear statutory distinction between "rescission" (retroactive termination) and "cancellation" (prospective termination) of insurance policies. Section 651

The parties stipulated to the following facts: On April 29, 1958, Mr. Alves signed an application for automobile insurance prepared by Mr. Pucci, State Farm's agent, and on that same date, State Farm issued a policy insuring Alves against public liability for $10,000, for any one person's injury. Alves paid premiums on the policy in April 1958, October 1958, and April 1959. On November 28, 1959, Mrs. Alves, while driving a Lincoln automobile, struck plaintiff. On December 4, 1959, plaintiff's attorneys notified State Farm of plaintiff's claim. On December 8, 1959, State Farm sent a reply letter to plaintiff's attorneys. On April 22, 1960, State Farm rescinded the insurance policy and returned all premiums paid. On July 26, 1960, plaintiff sued the Alveses, and Alves forwarded a copy of the summons and complaint to State Farm. On August 2, 1960, State Farm advised the Alveses that it would not defend the action. On November 3, 1960, judgment was entered in favor of plaintiff against the Alveses.

The parties further stipulated that plaintiff did not consent to, or concur in, any rescission or attempted rescission between State Farm and the Alveses. They further agreed that on September 6, 1958, five months after the issuance of the original policy, State Farm paid to, or on behalf of, Mr. Alves a claim arising out of the comprehensive coverage provisions of the policy in effect at that time.

provides: "Notwithstanding any other provision of this code, no cancellation by an insurer of an auto liability insurance policy shall be effective prior to the mailing or delivery to the named insured at the address shown in the policy, of a written notice of the cancellation stating when, not less than ten (10) days after the date of such mailing or delivery, the date the cancellation shall become effective."

The Legislature added section 651 in 1957. (Stats.1957, ch. 723, § 1, p. 1931.) In 1957, the Insurance Code did not contain a separate chapter on "Cancellation" (present ch. 10). Section 651 was incorporated into the "Rescission" chapter (ch. 9). The Legislature did not insert the section in the "Cancellation" chapter when that chapter was added by 1965 Statutes, chapter 1716, section 1, page 3850. The Insurance Code specifically provides, however, that "Division, part, chapter, article, and section headings contained herein shall not be deemed to govern, limit, modify or in any manner affect the scope, meaning, or intent of the provisions of any division, part, chapter, article or section hereof." (§ 6.)

The statutory scheme reflects a deliberate distinction between "rescission" and "cancellation." Sections 331, 338, and 359, which prescribe the grounds for rescission, all involve false statements or material omissions in the procurement of the policy. Section 660 (Stats.1965, ch. 1716, § 1, p. 3850), on the other hand, provided: "The commissioner, by regulation, shall prescribe the grounds upon which an insurer may cancel a policy of automobile insurance. No insurer shall cancel a policy of automobile insurance except upon such ground or grounds as have been prescribed by the commissioner." (Repealed, Stats.1968, ch. 137, p. 352, § 1, effective Jan. 1, 1969).

Unless we say that automobile liability insurance policies cannot be rescinded at all and that section 660 completely abrogated the rescission section for automobile liability insurance, we must hold that section 651, which specifically refers to "cancellation", does not control the procedure for "rescission" of automobile liability insurance. Instead, the general section governing rescission of insurance policies, section 650, applies. Section 650 provides: "Whenever a right to rescind a contract of insurance is given to the insurer by any provision of this part such right may be exercised at any time previous to the commencement of an action on the contract." The issue, then, turns on the validity of plaintiff's contention that the public policy of this state requires that an automobile liability insurer reasonably investigate within a reasonable time after issuance of the policy or otherwise be estopped to rescind the policy, at least in an action by an injured person who has obtained judgment from the insured.

The record discloses the following facts as to the application for insurance and the misrepresentations. In April 1958 Mr. Alves purchased a Chevrolet from one Roberti, a used-car salesman. Roberti arranged with Pucci, State Farm's agent, that he come to the agency in order to obtain insurance for Alves's car. Both Alves, who was 24 years old at the time, and Pucci testified that Alves did not read the application, and that Pucci filled in the answers to the questions.

Question 18 on the application stated: "Has your license to drive or registration been suspended, revoked or refused, to the applicant or any member of his household in the last five years?" Contrary to the Department of Motor Vehicles (hereinafter "DMV") report on Mr. Alves which evidenced one suspension and two probation orders within the five years preceding April 1958, a "No" answer appeared on the application in response to question 18.

* * * [W]e must therefore accept the trial court's finding of misrepresentation.[34]

* * *

Maurice Hammer, an insurance broker for the previous two years, and prior thereto an agent for Allstate Insurance for three years, testified that the general custom and practice of the insurance industry was to obtain DMV reports in connection with applications, either as a basis for determining rates or insurability of the risk.

With respect to State Farm's policy on initial applications, Pucci testified that State Farm always issued a policy when he gave a binding receipt to the applicant. The binding receipt provided for insurance coverage for 30 days from the date of the receipt, even if the company subsequently refused to approve the risk. Pucci handed Alves a binding receipt on April 28, 1958.

Daniel Priest, an underwriting superintendent of State Farm, testifying as to State Farm's investigative policies, stated that State Farm orders DMV reports and makes other inspections "on a judgment basis." In some cases State Farm does check on statements made by its applicants; but "in other cases the underwriting people just passed on the risk based on the statement on the application as submitted." In response to the question whether State Farm customarily checks the driving record of an insured when a claim is presented against him,

34. Alves's response to question 18 on the application constitutes "concealment" sufficient to justify rescission under Insurance Code, section 331. That section explicitly states, and the cases construing it so hold, that the misrepresentation involved need not be intentional in order to justify rescission. Furthermore, whether the insured misstated or concealed certain facts with the intention to deceive the insurer is irrelevant to the right to rescind. (See, Telford v. New York Life Ins. Co. (1937) 9 Cal.2d 103, 105, 69 P.2d 835.)

Indeed, the trial court in the present case found only that Alves materially misrepresented facts within his knowledge; there was no finding of *scienter,* that Alves fraudulently misrepresented the facts. Thus, under the present interpretation of the Insurance Code, an insurer may rescind the contract of insurance *ab initio* for a material misrepresentation—even though the insured's misstatements were the result of negligence, or, indeed, the product of innocence.

Priest stated: "Again, it depends upon the nature of the claim, the type of claim situation, circumstances involved, things of this nature. * * * We don't have any fixed custom or practice." He further stated that once a claim has occurred the claims, rather than the underwriting, department, determines whether the claim is sufficiently "significant" to warrant an investigation. Before any claim has been made against the insured, the underwriter handling the file exercises the discretion to decide whether to obtain a DMV report. Priest further testified that the cost of an entire investigation in 1958 was $3.35, and that the cost of a DMV check was only 25 cents.

Although at the time of his application in April 1958 Alves, then being under 25 years of age, fell within the class of applicants who received the greatest number of spot checks, State Farm did not begin its investigation until February 4, 1960, more than two months after plaintiff was injured, and almost two years after the initial application. After discovering that Alves's file did not contain a DMV report, the underwriting department requested one. On February 12, 1960, it received a reply from the department; on March 2, 1960, it obtained the report. Prior to obtaining the report, and in response to an underwriter's question whether to cancel Alves's policy, the claims department on February 16 responded that it was in the process of developing evidence for rescission. On April 22, State Farm notified Alves of the rescission of his policy.

The evidence suggests that State Farm, in failing to investigate Alves's insurability and to obtain a DMV report, pursued a policy of saving minor costs on its part at the expense and sacrifice of the interests of its insured and those of the general public who were the potential victims of the insured's negligence. If, at the time of an initial or transfer application, the underwriter handling the risk relies on the application and fails to order a DMV report, the claims department thereafter determines whether a claim by or against an insured is sufficiently "significant" to warrant investigation. Here, State Farm must have considered Mr. Alves's September 6, 1958, claim under the comprehensive provisions of his policy "insignificant," since State Farm apparently did not investigate but paid the claim. Not until plaintiff's attorneys notified State Farm of a $10,000 claim under the personal liability provision of the policy did State Farm attempt to check Alves's driving record.

State Farm's investigative practices may fail to conform to the standard of service which the public may reasonably expect of an insurance company and, more importantly here, may violate the public policy underlying California's Financial Responsibility Law. [T]he "quasi-public" nature of the insurance business and the public policy underlying the Financial Responsibility Law impose upon the automobile liability insurer a duty both to the insured and to the public to conduct a reasonable investigation of insurability within a reasonable time after issuance of an automobile liability policy. We may characterize this duty as one sounding either in tort or quasi-contract. The label is not important. We hold, however, that in order to avoid liability to an innocent victim of the insured an insurer cannot take advantage of a breach of its duty reasonably to check an application for automobile liability insurance within a reasonable time after acceptance of that application.

The requirement that the carrier act promptly to determine insurability after issuance of an automobile liability insurance policy inures primarily to the benefit of those members of the public who suffer injury from negligent motorists and seek recovery against the responsible tortfeasors. The duty arises from the public policy that protects the innocent victim of the careless use of automobiles from an inability to sue a financially responsible defendant. This duty, which the insurer incurs with the issuance of an automobile liability policy, therefore runs directly to the class of potential victims of the insured. Consequently, when the insurer breaches that duty, it may not defeat recovery by the injured person, who has recovered a judgment against the insured, by relying on an untimely attempt to rescind.

* * *

* * * After the injured person has obtained a judgment against the insured, therefore, he may compel the insurer to pay the judgment to the extent of the monetary limits set forth in the Financial Responsibility Law. (Veh.Code, § 16430.)

That the automobile liability insurer that fails to make such an investigation loses its right to rescind does not, however, necessarily mean that it forfeits all remedies *against the insured* for his misrepresentations. The insurer may still prosecute a cause of action against the insured for damages for wrongful misrepresentation, after satisfying the injured person's claim, or, in an action brought by the insured, after he has satisfied a judgment against him by the injured person, defend on the ground of misrepresentations in the application. (Cf., e.g., De Campos v. State Comp. Ins. Fund (1954) 122 Cal.App.2d 519, 528–529, 265 P.2d 617.) This recognition of the right of the insurer to rely on the insured's misrepresentations either as a basis for a damages suit against the insured or as a defense in an action by the insured does not conflict with the purpose of the Financial Responsibility Law, the assurance of a solvent defendant for those innocently injured by the use of automobiles.

The question whether State Farm negligently breached a duty owed to plaintiff in the present action is a question of fact to be determined on remand

* * * The trial court in the present case awarded judgment for State Farm without reference to this duty. Accordingly, the judgment must be reversed. On remand, the trial court will determine whether or not the insurer conducted such a reasonable investigation. If the court finds that State Farm acted reasonably in light of its duty to undertake a reasonable investigation of insurability, it may allow State Farm once again to assert the invalidity of its contract of insurance with the Alveses as a

defense to the plaintiff's action. On the other hand, if the trial court concludes that State Farm breached its duty, as defined in this opinion, the defense of the rescission *ab initio* will no longer be available to State Farm.

Factors to be taken into account by the trial court in assessing the reasonableness of State Farm's course of conduct in failing to investigate Alves's driving record are, inter alia: the cost of obtaining the information from the Department of Motor Vehicles, the availability of this information from the department or elsewhere (e.g., Alves claimed that his license suspensions appeared on the back of his driver's license), and the general administrative burden of making such an investigation. These factors must be weighed against the importance of the protection of innocent members of the public against the consequences of automobile owners driving with voidable liability policies.

The judgment on plaintiff Barrera's complaint and defendant State Farm's cross-complaint is reversed. The cause is remanded for proceedings consistent with this opinion.

Notes

1. Below is a statutory modification of the general California requirement of disclosure in insurance applications (see West's Ann. Insurance Code § 332) with regard to auto liability insurance:

§ 11580.08 Motor vehicle insurance: Arrest record

> With respect to disclosure of the fact of an arrest for any violation of the Vehicle Code or of a city or county ordinance or resolution relating to vehicles or their operators or owner which did not result in a conviction, the issuer, or his agency or employee, of any policy of automobile liability insurance (as described in Section 16056 of the Vehicle Code), any motor vehicle liability policy (as described in Section 16450 of the Vehicle Code), or any policy or coverage described in Section 660, shall not inquire of an applicant whether he has been arrested under such circumstances or to condition the issuance of any such policy on the applicant's making such disclosure.

2. Are incidents of arrest which do not result in convictions material facts within the meaning of West's Ann. California Insurance Code § 334?

3. Is West's Ann. California Insurance Code § 11580.08 consistent with the public policy rationale of *Barrera?*

4. Subsection F, Arizona Revised Statutes § 28–1170 reads:

> Every motor vehicle liability policy shall be subject to the following provisions which need not be contained therein:
>
> 1. The liability of the insurance carrier with respect to the insurance required by this chapter shall become absolute when injury or damage covered by th e motor vehicle liability policy occurs. The policy may not be cancelled or annulled as to such liability by an agreement between the insurance carrier and the insured after the

occurrence of the injury or damage, and no statement made by the insured or on his behalf and no violation of the policy shall defeat or void the policy.

The constitutionality of the above statute was challenged in *Allstate Insurance Co. v. Dorr*, 411 F.2d 198 (9th Cir.1969), wherein the insurer's practices followed the pattern revealed in the *Barrera* decision. In upholding the statute the Court observed:

> "We think that the economic burden placed by the Arizona statute upon companies which sell liability insurance of paying an occasional claim which they would not, but for the statute, have had to pay, falls easily within the power of a legislature to legislate. Insurance companies can alleviate their situation by exercising more care in selling their policies, by exerting more diligence in earlier discovery of their mistakes, and, of course, by increasing their insurance rates to spread the cost over larger numbers of the motoring public."

5. *An Important Addendum*. The above Arizona statute reads in part that "no statement made by the insured * * * *and no violation of the policy* shall defeat or void the policy" after an auto accident occurs. Does the italicized language mean that breaches of policy conditions by the insured as well as misrepresentations by him cannot be asserted by the insurer when suit is brought by the victim upon the judgment obtained by the latter against the insured? An example would be the insureds' duty to co-operate with the insurer in the defense of the tort action, which is taken up in the next section. In *Tibbs v. Johnson*, 30 Wn.App. 107, 632 P.2d 904 (1981), the precise issue was raised under the Washington Financial Responsibility Law (R.C.W. 46.29.490) which uses the same language as the Arizona statute. The court held that the insurer could not assert the non-cooperation of the insured as a defense to the 3rd person's action on the policy, except to the extent the policy limits exceed the minimum established by the Financial Responsibility Law.

Statutory Limitations on Cancellation of Automobile Liability Policies

California Insurance Code

§ 661. Grounds for valid notice of cancellation

(a) A notice of cancellation of a policy shall be effective only if it is based on one or more of the following reasons:

(1) Nonpayment of premium.

(2) The driver's license or motor vehicle registration of the named insured or of any other operator who either resides in the same household or customarily operates an automobile insured under the policy has been under suspension or revocation during the policy period or, if the policy is a renewal, during its policy period or the 180 days immediately preceding its effective date.

(3) Discovery of fraud by the named insured in pursuing a claim under the policy provided the insurer does not rescind the policy.

(b) This section shall not apply to any policy or coverage which has been in effect less than 60 days at the time notice of cancellation is mailed or delivered by the insurer unless it is a renewal policy.

(c) Modification of automobile physical damage coverage by the inclusion of a deductible not exceeding one hundred dollars ($100) shall not be deemed a cancellation of the coverage or of the policy.

(d) This section shall not apply to nonrenewal.

[§§ 662 et seq. address other limitations on cancellation including notice requirements, special renewal notice provisions, and proof of mailing. Violation of certain of the provisions is a misdemeanor.]

§ 1861.03. Unfair insurance practices; prohibition

* * *

(c)(1) Notwithstanding any other provision of law, a notice of cancellation or nonrenewal of a policy for automobile insurance shall be effective only if it is based on one or more of the following reasons: (A) nonpayment of premium; (B) fraud or material misrepresentation affecting the policy or insured; (C) a substantial increase in the hazard insured against. (2) This subdivision shall not prevent a reciprocal insurer, organized prior to November 8, 1988, by a motor club holding a certificate of authority under Chapter 2 (commencing with Section 12160) of Part 5 of Division 2, and which requires membership in the motor club as a condition precedent to applying for insurance, from issuing an effective notice of nonrenewal based solely on the failure of the insured to maintain membership in the motor club.

* * *

Financial Responsibility Laws

Many states require vehicle owners or operators to show the ability to satisfy a minimum financial liability arising from ownership or use of the vehicle. As an example, a portion of the California Financial Responsibility Law, West's Ann.California Vehicle Code §§ 16000ff, is reproduced below with some of the basic provisions relating to civil liability found in West's Ann.California Vehicle Code §§ 17000ff. However, the "total public policy" of the State is set forth in the West's Ann.California Insurance Code, see § 11580.05, quoted at p. 669.

California Vehicle Code

§ 16020. Evidence of financial responsibility

(a) Every driver and every owner of a motor vehicle shall at all times be able to establish financial responsibility pursuant to Section 16021, and shall at all times carry in the vehicle evidence of the form of financial responsibility in effect for the vehicle.

(b) "Evidence of financial responsibility" means any of the following:

(1) The name of the insurance or surety company that issued a policy or bond for the vehicle that meets the requirements of Section 16056 and is currently in effect, and the number of the insurance policy or surety bond.

(2) If the owner is a self-insurer, as provided in Section 16052 or a depositor, as provided in Section 16054.2, the certificate or deposit number issued by the department.

(3) An insurance covering note, as specified in Section 382 of the INSURANCE CODE.

(4) A showing that the vehicle is owned or leased by, or under the direction of, the United States or any public entity, as defined in Section 811.2 of the Government Code.

(c) For purposes of this section, "evidence of financial responsibility" also includes the identifying symbol issued to a highway carrier by the Public Utilities Commission pursuant to Section 3543 of the Public Utilities Code and displayed on the motor vehicle.

(d) For purposes of this section, "evidence of financial responsibility" shall be in writing, and established by writing the name of the insurance company or surety company and the policy number on the vehicle registration card issued by the department.

§ 16021. Establishing financial responsibility

Financial responsibility of the driver or owner is established if the driver or owner of the vehicle involved in an accident described in Section 16000 is:

(a) A self-insurer under the provisions of this division.

(b) An insured or obligee under a form of insurance or bond which complies with the requirements of this division and which covers the driver for the vehicle involved in the accident.

(c) The United States of America, this state, any municipality or subdivision thereof, or the lawful agent thereof.

(d) A depositor in compliance with subdivision (a) of Section 16054.2.

(e) In compliance with the requirements authorized by the department by any other manner which effectuates the purposes of this chapter.

§ 16025. Accidents; exchange of information; fines and penalties

(a) Every driver involved in the accident shall, unless rendered incapable, exchange with any other driver or property owner involved in the accident and present at the scene, all of the following information:

(1) Driver's name and current residence address, driver's license number, vehicle identification number, and current residence address of registered owner.

(2) Evidence of financial responsibility, as specified in Section 16020. If the financial responsibility of a person is a form of insurance, then that person shall supply the name and address of the insurance company.

(b) Any person failing to comply with all of the requirements of this section is guilty of an infraction punishable by a fine not to exceed two hundred fifty dollars ($250).

§ 17150. Liability of private owners

Every owner of a motor vehicle is liable and responsible for death or injury to person or property resulting from a negligent or wrongful act or omission in the operation of the motor vehicle, in the business of the owner or otherwise, by any person using or operating the same with the permission, express or implied, of the owner.

§ 17151. Limitation of liability

(a) The liability of an owner, bailee of an owner, or personal representative of a decedent imposed by this chapter and not arising through the relationship of principal and agent or master and servant is limited to the amount of fifteen thousand dollars ($15,000) for the death of or injury to one person in any one accident and, subject to the limit as to one person, is limited to the amount of thirty thousand dollars ($30,000) for the death of or injury to more than one person in any one accident and is limited to the amount of five thousand dollars ($5,000) for damage to property of others in any one accident.

(b) An owner, bailee of an owner, or personal representative of a decedent is not liable under this chapter for damages imposed for the sake of example and by way of punishing the operator of the vehicle. Nothing in this subdivision makes an owner, bailee, or personal representative immune from liability for damages imposed for the sake of example and by way of punishing him for his own wrongful conduct.

§ 17152. Liability of operator

In any action against an owner, bailee of an owner, or personal representative of a decedent on account of liability imposed by Sections 17150, 17154, or 17159 for the negligent or wrongful act or omission of the operator of a vehicle, the operator shall be made a part defendant if service of process can be made in a manner sufficient to secure personal jurisdiction over the operator. Upon recovery of judgment, recourse shall first be had against the property of the operator so served.

§ 17153. Subrogation of owner

If there is recovery under this chapter against an owner, bailee of an owner, or personal representative of a decedent, the owner, bailee of an owner, or personal representative of a decedent is subrogated to all the rights of the person injured or whose property has been injured and may recover from the operator the total amount of any judgment and costs recovered against the owner, bailee of an owner, or personal representative of a decedent.

§ 17154. Bailee as operator

If the bailee of an owner with the permission, express or implied, of the owner permits another to operate the motor vehicle of the owner, then the bailee and the driver shall both be deemed operators of the vehicle of the owner within the meaning of Sections 17152 and 17153.

Every bailee of a motor vehicle is liable and responsible for death or injury to person or property resulting from a negligent or wrongful act or omission in the operation of the motor vehicle, in the business of the bailee or otherwise, by any person using or operating the same with the permission, express or implied, of the bailee.

§ 17155. Settlement of claims

Where two or more persons are injured or killed in one accident, the owner, bailee of an owner, or personal representative of a decedent may settle and pay any bona fide claims for damages arising out of personal injuries or death, whether reduced to judgment or not, and the payments shall diminish to the extent thereof such person's total liability on account of the accident. Payments aggregating the full sum of thirty thousand dollars ($30,000) shall extinguish all liability of the owner, bailee of an owner, or personal representative of a decedent for death or personal injury arising out of the accident which exists pursuant to this chapter, and did not arise through the negligent or wrongful act or omission of the owner, bailee of an owner, or personal representative of a decedent nor through the relationship of principal and agent or master and servant.

§ 17158. Owner as passenger; liability

No person riding in or occupying a vehicle owned by him and driven by another person with his permission has any right of action for civil damages against the driver of the vehicle or against any other person legally liable for the conduct of the driver on account of personal injury to or the death of the owner during the ride, unless the plaintiff in any such action establishes that the injury or death proximately resulted from the intoxication or willful misconduct of the driver.

b. Permissive Users and the Omnibus Clause

CURTIS v. STATE FARM MUTUAL AUTOMOBILE INSURANCE CO.

United States Court of Appeals, Tenth Circuit, 1979.
591 F.2d 572.

HOLLOWAY, CIRCUIT JUDGE.

Defendant State Farm Mutual Automobile Insurance Company appeals from a declaratory judgment, entered on a jury verdict, declaring that a liability insurance policy issued by State Farm to Robert E. Ahrens and JoAnn Ahrens extended coverage to one Joseph Wallace, the driver of the Ahrens vehicle at the time of the accident involved herein. Jurisdiction is founded upon diversity. The primary question before us is whether Wallace comes within the definition of "insured" contained in the policy's omnibus clause, as "any * * * *person* while using the *owned motor vehicle,* PROVIDED THE OPERATION AND THE ACTUAL USE OF SUCH VEHICLE ARE WITH THE PERMISSION OF THE NAMED INSURED * * * AND ARE WITHIN THE SCOPE OF SUCH PERMISSION * * *."[35]

35. The omnibus clause constitutes only one part of the five-part definition of "insured" contained in the policy. The definition as a whole states that the unqualified word "insured" includes:

(1) the named insured, and

The Ahrens family had three cars—an Oldsmobile, a Volkswagen owned by Mr. and Mrs. Ahrens, and a pickup. The older Ahrens girls, Beth and Shawnna, mainly used the Oldsmobile and Volkswagen, and Mr. Ahrens used the pickup to drive to work.

The accident in question occurred in the early morning of July 5, 1973, outside of Cheyenne, Wyoming. During the previous afternoon, Deborah Ahrens, the 14–year-old daughter of Robert and JoAnn Ahrens, had made arrangements with her friend Helen Curtis and with Brian Tottenhoff and Joseph Wallace to meet at the local ballpark between 1:00 and 2:00 a.m. to shoot off some fireworks. * * * Helen was spending the night of July 4 with Deborah at her home. Sometime between 1:30 and 2:00 a.m., Deborah and Helen left the Ahrens home—after Deborah's parents had gone to bed—and proceeded to drive the family Volkswagen to the chosen meeting place.

Deborah was not licensed to drive. She had taken the car keys from their customary location on top of the television set without her parents' knowledge. * * * On their way out of the Ahrens' neighborhood, the girls encountered Deborah's older sister, Beth, driving home in the family Oldsmobile. The two sisters stopped and talked for five or ten minutes, but Deborah's use of the Volkswagen was never discussed. * * * Before she left home, Deborah had also told Shawnna what they were going to do that night; Shawnna knew the girls were going out and made no comment either to forbid or consent to their going. However, Deborah did not tell Beth or Shawnna that she and Helen were going to pick up the boys.

Deborah and Helen picked up the boys and went to shoot off the fireworks. The four then started home around 3:30 a.m. Deborah had been driving all along, but at this point Joe Wallace asked if he could drive, and she agreed. * * * Wallace, like Deborah, was unlicensed. According to Deborah, the accident occurred about five minutes after Wallace took the wheel: "He was going too fast, and he went airbound with the car, and it went over on to the embankment."

Helen Curtis suffered extensive injuries in the accident, and her father incurred about $15,000 in medical expenses for her treatment. When State Farm disclaimed coverage as to Wallace, Helen's father brought this suit on her behalf for a determination that the defendant

(2) if the named insured is a *person* or *persons,* also includes his or their spouse(s), if a *resident* of the same household, and

(3) if *residents* of the same household, the relatives of the first *person* named in the declarations, or of his spouse, and

(4) any other *person* while using the *owned motor vehicle,* PROVIDED THE OPERATION AND THE ACTUAL USE OF SUCH VEHICLE ARE WITH THE PERMISSION OF THE NAMED INSURED OR SUCH SPOUSE AND ARE WITHIN THE SCOPE OF SUCH PERMISSION, and

(5) under coverages A and B any other *person* or organization, but only with respect to his or its liability for the use of such *owned motor vehicle* by an *insured* as defined in the four subsections above.

(Plaintiff's Ex. No. 1). It is evident that Wallace can fit—if at all—only within the omnibus clause (4), since he is unrelated to the named insureds, Robert E. Ahrens and JoAnn Ahrens.

State Farm was obligated to defend and indemnify Wallace under the company's policy issued to Mr. and Mrs. Ahrens. As noted, a verdict and declaratory judgment adverse to the company resulted. This appeal followed.

I

The company's primary contention on appeal is that the evidence is clear that Wallace did not have permission to drive the vehicle under the terms of the omnibus clause of the policy, so that coverage did not extend to him. The company says that the district court therefore erred in its denial of a motion for a directed verdict made at the conclusion of plaintiff's case and again at the end of defendant's case, as well as in its denial of a motion for judgment n.o.v.

Wallace was not covered by the policy unless his operation and actual use of the Volkswagen were with the permission of a named insured. The district court instructed the jury that Robert Ahrens and his wife JoAnn were the named insureds under the policy and that neither named insured gave Wallace actual permission to drive the car. * * * Thus, the controlling question is whether Wallace had implied permission for use of the car so as to bring him within the coverage of the policy.

In United Services Automobile Association v. Preferred Accident Insurance Co., 190 F.2d 404, 406 (10th Cir.), we stated that:

> The necessary permission may be in the form of implied affirmative consent. It may result by implication from the relationship of the parties and their course of conduct in which they mutually acquiesced. And it may arise from a course of conduct pursued with knowledge of the facts for such time and in such manner as to signify clearly and convincingly an understanding consent which amounts in law to a grant of the privilege involved.

The question of implied permission is thus one of fact. Phoenix Assurance Co. v. Latta, 373 P.2d 146, 149 (Wyo.). Plaintiff points to much in the record which, it is said, supports the jury's implicit finding of implied permission. In view of such evidence, plaintiff argues that it would have been improper for the trial court to direct a verdict or grant judgment n.o.v. for defendant, because the evidence did not point "all one way" in favor of the moving party. Bertot v. School District No. 1, 522 F.2d 1171, 1178 (10th Cir.).

The foundation for a finding of implied permission, plaintiff argues, is the fact that JoAnn Ahrens, Deborah's mother and one of the named insureds, has been blind due to the effects of diabetes since before 1973. Because of this tragic fact, Mrs. Ahrens has had to rely on her three daughters to "take care of everything" around the house. * * * In July 1973, the two older daughters, Beth (then age 17) and Shawnna (age 16), were licensed drivers and had free use of the family cars, both for carrying out family-related responsibilities such as grocery shopping and for going to and from their part-time jobs. * * * As noted, the family custom was to keep the car keys on top of the television set; anyone who had used the car would lay the keys down on the set and anyone who wanted to use the car would take the keys off the set.

Around that time Beth also often took one of the cars out of town on recreational trips to Steamboat Springs and similar places, staying two or three days. Mrs. Ahrens knew that on such trips friends of Beth's went with her and drove the car. There was testimony that Beth's friends McCue and Fleming would sometimes drive the car on such trips and that, while neither JoAnn nor Robert Ahrens gave express permission to them to drive, both parents knew about such driving and neither objected to it. * * * Also, Shawnna was allowed to take the family cars around town frequently and drove one of the cars to work sometimes.

Thus, Beth and Shawnna were allowed to drive the cars "as they needed or liked"

—except when their father was using them. They bought gas "when they had money and they were out and they needed it"—though customarily their father would maintain the automobiles in working condition. * * * And with Beth at least, there was precedent for allowing other persons to drive the family automobiles without express permission from either parent.

With respect to Deborah, there was testimony that Mr. Ahrens had signed a statement that he had never given Deborah any restrictions as to her use of the car and that there had been no express prohibition to its use. The statement also said, however, that "Debbie was not supposed to drive this vehicle." * * * Mr. Ahrens testified that he thought his wife had been asked during the taking of earlier statements whether the parents had ever specifically told Deborah she could not take the car, that he had said they never specified she could not take it, but that it was "understood on down the line, that I think it probably started with Beth and then Shawnna and then Debbie." * * *. Both Mr. and Mrs. Ahrens testified that they had not given Deborah permission to use the car on the night of the accident and did not know that she had taken the car until they were notified about the accident.

Deborah testified that one time she had driven a family car with her father to a friend's house. She also said that once about a month before the accident she had driven the car without her father. * * * However, her parents both testified they had not known that Deborah had taken the Volkswagen out on any occasion before the accident. * * *

Plaintiff argues that because of the unusual circumstances relating to the blindness of Mrs. Ahrens, the mother and father had permitted the two older daughters to operate the family vehicles as if they had actually been owners, and that when the older daughters were aware of Deborah's going for the ride in the Volkswagen on the night of July 4, they had unqualified permission to allow Deborah to operate the car. * * * From Beth and Shawnna's implied consent that Deborah drive the car, and from Deborah's actual consent for Wallace to drive, plaintiff says there was implied consent by Mr. and Mrs. Ahrens that Wallace drive the Volkswagen at the time of the accident.[36]

We must hold that, on this record, the judgment in favor of coverage cannot stand. Plaintiff had the burden of proof to establish coverage. See Chronister v. State Farm Mutual Automobile Insurance Co., 72 N.M. 159, 381 P.2d 673, 675; 46 C.J.S. Insurance § 1641. Under the terms of the omnibus clause, permission of the named insureds, Mr. and Mrs. Ahrens, to the operation and actual use of the Volkswagen was required for coverage to apply. The only plausible theory in this case is that permission flowed from the parents to Beth and Shawnna, from them to Deborah, and from Deborah then to Wallace, the driver at the time of the accident. As noted, however, Beth and Shawnna were not told by Deborah that Wallace would even be accompanying Deborah and Helen the night of the accident and, of course, the parents did not even know that Deborah was going to use the car.

In view of the broad permission given by the parents to Beth and Shawnna for use of the family cars, an inference might be drawn that the older daughters as first permittees could permit Deborah to use the Volkswagen. See Gillen v. Globe Indemnity Co., 377 F.2d 328, 331 (8th Cir.); Krebsbach v. Miller, 22 Wis.2d 171, 125 N.W.2d 408, 411; Baesler v. Globe Indemnity Co., 33 N.J. 148, 162 A.2d 854, 857; Government Employees Insurance Co. v. Lammert, 483 S.W.2d 652 (Mo.Ct.App.). The trial judge apparently accepted such a view as valid under Wyoming law since he charged the jury that "the named insured's permission to a second permittee need not be express, *but may be implied from the broad nature of scope of the initial permission,* or from the conduct of the parties and from the attendant facts and circumstances."

The difficulty, however, is that here it is not the driving of Deborah as a second permittee which is in question, but that of Wallace as a *third* permittee. We note again that neither of the first permittees, Beth and Shawnna, were told by Deborah that Wallace was to be in the car with Deborah and Helen. We are convinced that implied permission cannot be stretched so far as to include the driving of Wallace on the night of the accident. See West v. McNamara, 159 Ohio St. 187, 111 N.E.2d 909; Bailey v. General Insurance Co., 265 N.C. 675, 144 S.E.2d 898; Novo v. Employers' Liability Assurance Corp., 295 Mass. 232, 3 N.E.2d 737, denying coverage as to third permittees.[37] A scintilla of evidence, such as

36. There is no evidence which would support an inference that Deborah had direct permission to drive the Volkswagen from her parents. For this reason it cannot be said that Wallace had implied permission from Mr. and Mrs. Ahrens as the named insureds merely because he had Deborah's actual permission to drive. See Travelers Insurance Co. v. Weatherford, 520 S.W.2d 726 (Tenn.); State Farm Mutual Automobile Insurance Co. v. Strang, 27 Utah 2d 362, 496 P.2d 707; Bilsten v. Porter, 547 P.2d 255 (Colo.Ct.App.).

37. We find only one case holding that a third permittee was covered under an omnibus clause and it is easily distinguished from this case, as well as from *West, Bailey* and *Novo.* In Boyer v. Massachusetts Bonding & Insurance Co., 277 Mass. 359, 178 N.E. 523, the named insured lent the vehicle to his son (the first permittee) who in turn permitted one Chester Carter (the second permittee) to take the car to Massachusetts and have use of it, and then leave it with his family to be sold. Chester Carter left the car with his father, who permitted the remote permission of the parents given to Beth and Shawnna to drive the family cars, was not enough to raise a jury question of implied permission for Wallace to drive the Volkswagen. We are convinced that the evidence points only one way and is not susceptible of a reasonable inference that Wallace had any implied permission of the parents to drive their car. Bertot v. School District No. 1, supra, 522 F.2d 1171, 1175–76.

* * *

Plaintiff Curtis further contends that if the company were to prevail here, then an undesirable situation would result, contrary to the public's understanding about insurance coverage. The argument is that if any children were riding in a vehicle driven and operated by a child of the owner, and that child were to permit another child to drive, then according to the company there would be no coverage, contrary to the public's expectation. This policy argument does not persuade us. We cannot impose liability contrary to the terms of the agreement and without justification in the facts of record. As the Supreme Court of Wyoming stated in Wyoming Farm Bureau Mutual Insurance Co. v. May, supra, 434 P.2d at 511–12, in rejecting a similar public policy argument:

> Granting that the need for better regulation of use of highways is a meritorious and even a necessary objective, to argue that liability coverage of one person should be extended to cover another simply because it is desirable that all drivers of motor vehicles should be covered, is whimsical and unsupported either in reason or by law. This contention is without merit.

For these reasons we conclude that the verdict and judgment cannot stand and that the defendant was entitled to judgment notwithstanding the verdict. Accordingly, the judgment is reversed and the cause is remanded for entry of judgment in accordance with this opinion.

Notes

1. The requirement of *permission* as an integral part of the omnibus clause has been variously rephrased in the newer, "simplified," language policies. One version reads: "*with permission or reasonably believed to be with the permission of the owner.*" Is the scope of coverage broader under the italicized language than that used in *Curtis,* supra? *Government Employees Ins. Co. v. Kinyon*, 119 Cal.App.3d 213, 173 Cal.Rptr. 805 (1981) reviews the decisions on this point. Are not insurers inviting litigation by making coverage depend upon the subjective perception of the potential insured?

Chester's brother Lloyd to use the car, and Lloyd's use resulted in the accident. It was found that the insured's son (the first permittee) had been given full use and custody of the car and that his acts were within his authority.

On appeal, the Massachusetts Court referred to the fact that the insured "knew what his son had done, and [that] it could be found that he assented to the use of the vehicle by the Carters, although the details of that use were not specifically authorized." Thus, *Boyer* is unlike the instant case where the named insureds had no knowledge that either Deborah or Wallace would use the car.

Another version (see Appendix D) states that: "we do not provide Liability Coverage for any person using a vehicle without a reasonable belief that that person is entitled to do so." (Note that such a provision applies not only to the omnibus clause but also to the coverage of an insured who is driving someone else's automobile.) Could an unlicensed 14 year old, like Deborah in the *Curtis* case, supra, reasonably believe that she was "entitled" to drive the car? See Safeco Insurance Co. of America v. Davis, 44 Wash.App. 161, 721 P.2d 550 (1986) (word "entitled" was ambiguous, and therefore coverage was apt). Is the scope of the supposed permission an issue when such language is used? See United Pacific Ins. Co. v. Larsen, 44 Wash.App. 529, 723 P.2d 8 (1986) (insurer's use of "reasonable belief" language allowed auto owner's permission to comport with the policy though the driver used the car beyond the scope of permission).

2. In *Universal Underwriters Insurance Co. v. Taylor*, 185 W.Va. 606, 408 S.E.2d 358 (1991), a prospective automobile buyer, Taylor, took keys from an automobile dealer to test drive a car. When he didn't return three hours later, the car was reported stolen. Sixteen days later, Taylor, in the borrowed car, injured Beafore. The question was whether the car dealer's insurer was required to indemnify Taylor. The case turned on the scope of permission. The court considered two possibilities: first, an initial permission rule with a broad reading as to scope under which anything short of conversion or theft is permissive; second, a minor deviation rule under which only slight deviations are within the scope of permission. The court opted to use the initial permission rule as the better approach—this approach is followed by most jurisdictions because it harmonizes with the policy of providing recovery for injured persons.

3. The holding here has applied to negate the effect of a Budget Rent–A–Car System's rental agreement-restricting the driving of the car to the renter (unless otherwise stipulated). The omnibus clause in the lessor's policy has been held to cover the renter's unauthorized permittee regardless of the language in the rental agreement. State Farm Mut. Auto Ins. Co. v. Budget Rent–A–Car Systems, 359 N.W. 2d 673 (Minn. App. 1984).

4. On the evening of May 6, 1960, Summers and Straus were present at a party at Snowcrest Inn outside of Hanover, New Hampshire, where both were attending Dartmouth College. Summers gave permission to one Haynesworth to borrow his automobile to drive to Hanover, and when he failed to return as expected, Summers and Miss Brandt went out into the parking lot where they discovered Straus' automobile with the keys in it. They took the car to drive to Hanover in search of Haynesworth and enroute met with an accident. Straus testified by deposition that if Summers had asked permission to use his car he would probably have granted it. There was evidence of a general custom at Dartmouth whereby students loaned their cars to one another, but Summers had neither driven Straus' car before nor asked permission to do so.

The policy contained a provision extending coverage to persons using the automobile provided "the actual use thereof is with the permission of the named insured." Concededly, there was no express permission given so the question becomes whether permission may be implied from the circumstances and the relationship of the parties.

While Summers and Straus were classmates and acquainted with one another, they were not fraternity brothers, had no classes together, and did not participate in any common college activities.

Is the Insurance Company obliged to provide a defense for Summers in a personal injury action brought by Brandt? See Fireman's Fund Insurance Co. v. Brandt, 217 F.Supp. 893 (D.C.N.H.1962) (Straus did not give Summers either express or implied permission to use the car; thus Summers is not covered and insurer has no duty to defend Summers).

Regulation of the Contents of the "Omnibus Clause" by Statute

WEST'S Annotated California Insurance Code

§ 11580. Required policy provisions

A policy insuring against losses set forth in subdivision (a) shall not be issued or delivered to any person in this state unless it contains the provisions set forth in subdivision (b). Such policy, whether or not actually containing such provisions, shall be construed as if such provisions were embodied therein.

(a) Unless it contains such provisions, the following policies of insurance shall not be thus issued or delivered:

(1) Against loss or damage resulting from liability for injury suffered by another person other than (i) a policy of workers' compensation insurance, or (ii) a policy issued by a nonadmitted Mexican insurer solely for use in the Republic of Mexico.

(2) Against loss of or damage to property caused by draught animals or any vehicle, and for which the insured is liable, other than a policy which provides insurance in the Republic of Mexico, issued or delivered in this state by a nonadmitted Mexican insurer.

(b) Such policy shall not be thus issued or delivered to any person in this state unless it contains all the following provisions:

(1) A provision that the insolvency or bankruptcy of the insured will not release the insurer from the payment of damages for injury sustained or loss occasioned during the life of such policy.

(2) A provision that whenever judgment is secured against the insured or the executor or administrator of a deceased insured in an action based upon bodily injury, death, or property damage, then an action may be brought against the insurer on the policy and subject to its terms and limitations, by such judgment creditor to recover on the judgment.

§ 11580.05. Legislative declaration

The Legislature declares that the public policy of this state in regard to provisions authorized or required to be included in policies affording automobile liability insurance or motor vehicle liability insurance issued or delivered in this state shall be as stated in this article, that this article expresses the total public policy of this state respecting the content of such policies, and that no provision of this article or of the Vehicle Code shall apply to policies affording automobile liability insurance or motor vehicle liability insurance in the Republic of Mexico issued or delivered in this state by a nonadmitted Mexican insurer. The Legislature further declares that it is the intent of the Legislature that the requirements set forth in Article 2 (commencing with Section 16450) of Chapter 3 of Division 7 of the Vehicle Code shall apply only to an owner's policy or operator's policy of liability insurance certified as provided in Section 16431 of the Vehicle Code as proof of ability to respond in damages, and that the requirements set forth in Article 4 (commencing with Section 11620) of Chapter 1 of Part 3 of Division 2 of the Insurance Code shall apply only to automobile liability insurance policies issued under the California Assigned Risk Plan. Except as provided above, any other policy issued or delivered in this state affording liability insurance with respect to ownership, maintenance, or use of a motor vehicle shall comply with the requirements set forth in Sections 11580, 11580.1, and 11580.2.

§ 11580.1. Automobile liability insurance; required and optional provisions

(a) No policy of automobile liability insurance described in Section 16054 of the Vehicle Code covering liability arising out of the ownership, maintenance, or use of any motor vehicle shall be issued or delivered in this state on or after the effective date of this section unless it contains the provisions set forth in subdivision (b). However, none of the requirements of subdivision (b) shall apply to the insurance afforded under any such policy (1) to the extent that such insurance exceeds the limits specified in subdivision (a) of Section 16056 of the Vehicle Code, or (2) if such policy contains an underlying insurance requirement, or provides for a retained limit of self-insurance, equal to or greater than the limits specified in subdivision (a) of Section 16056 of the Vehicle Code.

(b) Every policy of automobile liability insurance to which subdivision (a) applies shall contain all of the following provisions:

(1) Coverage limits not less than the limits specified in subdivision (a) of Section 16056 of the Vehicle Code.

(2) Designation by explicit description of, or appropriate reference to, the motor vehicles or class of motor vehicles to which coverage is specifically granted.

(3) Designation by explicit description of the purposes for which coverage for such motor vehicles is specifically excluded.

(4) Provision affording insurance to the named insured with respect to any motor vehicle covered by such policy, and to the same extent that insurance is afforded to the named insured, to any other person using, or legally responsible for the use of, such motor vehicle, provided such use is by the named insured or with his or her permission, express or implied, and within the scope of such permission, except that: (i) with regard to insurance afforded for the loading or unloading of any such motor vehicle, the insurance may be limited to apply only to the named insured, a relative of the named insured who is a resident of the named insured's household, a lessee or bailee of the motor vehicle, or an employee of any such person; and (ii) the insurance afforded to any person other than the named insured need not apply to: (A) any employee with respect to bodily injury sustained by a fellow employee injured in the scope and course of his or her employment, or (B) any person, or to any agent or employee thereof, employed or otherwise

engaged in the business of selling, repairing, servicing, delivering, testing, road-testing, parking, or storing automobiles with respect to any accident arising out of the maintenance or use of a motor vehicle in connection therewith.

(c) In addition to any exclusion as provided in paragraph (3) of subdivision (b), the insurance afforded by any such policy of automobile liability insurance to which subdivision (a) applies, including the insurer's obligation to defend, may, by appropriate policy provision, be made inapplicable to any or all of the following:

(1) Liability assumed by the insured under contract.

(2) Liability for bodily injury or property damage caused intentionally by or at the direction of the insured.

(3) Liability imposed upon or assumed by the insured under any workers' compensation law.

(4) Liability for bodily injury to any employee of the insured arising out of and in the course of his employment.

(5) Liability for bodily injury to an insured or liability for bodily injury to an insured whenever the ultimate benefits of that indemnification accrue directly or indirectly to an insured.

(6) Liability for damage to property owned, rented to, transported by, or in the charge of, an insured. A motor vehicle operated by an insured shall be considered to be property in the charge of an insured.

(7) Liability for any bodily injury or property damage with respect to which insurance is or can be afforded under a nuclear energy liability policy.

(8) Any motor vehicle or class of motor vehicles, as described or designated in the policy, with respect to which coverage is explicitly excluded, in whole or in part.

The term "the insured" as used in paragraphs (1), (2), (3), and (4) shall mean only that insured under the policy against whom the particular claim is made or suit brought. The term "an insured" as used in paragraphs (5) and (6) shall mean any insured under the policy including those persons who would have otherwise been included within the policy's definition of an insured but, by agreement, are subject to the limitations of paragraph (1) of subdivision (d).

(d) Notwithstanding the provisions of paragraph (4) of subdivision (b), or the provisions of Article 2 (commencing with Section 16450) of Chapter 3 of Division 7, or Article 2 (commencing with Section 17150) of Chapter 1 of Division 9, of the Vehicle Code, the insurer and any named insured may, by the terms of any policy of automobile liability insurance to which subdivision (a) applies, or by a separate writing relating thereto, agree as to either or both of the following limitations, such agreement to be binding upon every insured to whom such policy applies and upon every third party claimant:

(1) That coverage and the insurer's obligation to defend under such policy shall not apply nor accrue to the benefit of any insured or any third party claimant while any motor vehicle is being used or operated by a natural person or persons designated by name. These limitations shall apply to any use or operation of a motor vehicle including the negligent or alleged

negligent entrustment of a motor vehicle to such designated person or persons. The insurer shall have an obligation to defend the named insured when all of the following apply to such designated natural person:

1. He or she is a resident of the same household as the named insured.

2. As a result of operating the insured motor vehicle of the named insured, he or she is jointly sued with the named insured.

3. He or she is an insured under a separate automobile liability insurance policy issued to him or her as a named insured, which policy does not provide a defense to the named insured.

* * *

(2) That with regard to any such policy issued to a named insured engaged in the business of leasing vehicles for those vehicles which are leased for a term in excess of six months, or selling, repairing, servicing, delivering, testing, road-testing, parking, or storing automobiles, coverage shall not apply to any person other than the named insured or his or her agent or employee, except to the extent that the limits of liability of any other valid and collectible insurance available to such person are not equal to the limits of liability specified in subdivision (a) of Section 16056 of the Vehicle Code. If the policy is issued to a named insured engaged in the business of leasing vehicles, which business includes the lease of vehicles for a term in excess of six months, and the lessor includes in the lease automobile liability insurance, the terms and limits of which are not otherwise specified in the lease, the named insured shall incorporate a provision in each vehicle lease contract advising the lessee of the provisions of this subdivision and the fact that this limitation is applicable except as otherwise provided for by statute or federal law.

* * *

§ 11580.2. Uninsured motorist endorsement or coverage; underinsured motorist coverage

(a)(1) No policy of bodily injury liability insurance covering liability arising out of the ownership, maintenance, or use of any motor vehicle, except for policies which provide insurance in the Republic of Mexico issued or delivered in this state by nonadmitted Mexican insurers, shall be issued or delivered in this state to the owner or operator of a motor vehicle, or shall be issued or delivered by any insurer licensed in this state upon any motor vehicle then principally used or principally garaged in this state, unless the policy contains, or has added to it by endorsement, a provision with coverage limits at least equal to the limits specified in subdivision (m) and in no case less than the financial responsibility requirements specified in Section 16056 of the Vehicle Code insuring the insured, the insured's heirs or legal representative for all sums within the limits which he, she, or they, as the case may be, shall be legally entitled to recover as damages for bodily injury or wrongful death from the owner or operator of an uninsured motor vehicle. The insurer and any named insured, prior to or subsequent to the issuance or renewal of a policy, may, by agreement in writing, in the form specified in paragraph (2) or paragraph (3), (1) delete the provision covering damage caused by an uninsured motor vehicle completely, or (2) delete the coverage when a motor vehicle is operated by a natural person or persons designated by name, or (3) agree to provide the coverage in an amount less than that required by subdivision (m) but not less than the financial responsibility requirements specified in Section 16056 of the Vehicle Code. Any of these agreements by any named insured or agreement for the amount of coverage shall be binding upon every insured to whom the policy or endorsement provisions apply while the policy is in force, and shall continue to be so binding with respect to any continuation or renewal of the policy or with respect to any other policy which extends, changes, supersedes, or replaces the policy issued to the named insured by the same insurer, or with respect to reinstatement of the policy within 30 days of any lapse thereof.

* * *

(c) The insurance coverage provided for in this section does not apply either as primary or as excess coverage:

(1) To property damage sustained by the insured.

(2) To bodily injury of the insured while in or upon or while entering into or alighting from a motor vehicle other than the described motor vehicle if the owner thereof has insurance similar to that provided in this section.

(3) To bodily injury of the insured with respect to which the insured or his or her representative shall, without the written consent of the insurer, make any settlement with or prosecute to judgment any action against any person who may be legally liable therefor.

(4) In any instance where it would inure directly or indirectly to the benefit of any workers' compensation carrier or to any person qualified as a self-insurer under any workers' compensation law, or directly to the benefit of the United States, or any state or any political subdivision thereof.

(5) To establish proof of financial responsibility as provided in subdivisions (a), (b), and (c) of Section 16054 of the Vehicle Code.

(6) To bodily injury of the insured while occupying a motor vehicle owned by an insured or leased to an insured under a written contract for a period of six months or longer, unless the occupied vehicle is an insured motor vehicle. "Motor vehicle" as used in this paragraph means any self-propelled vehicle.

(7) To bodily injury of the insured when struck by a vehicle owned by an insured.

(8) To bodily injury of the insured while occupying a motor vehicle rented or leased to the insured for public or livery purposes.

(d) Subject to paragraph (2) of subdivision (c), the policy or endorsement may provide that if the insured has insurance available to the insured under more than one uninsured motorist coverage provision, any damages shall not be deemed to exceed the higher of the applicable limits of the respective coverages, and the damages shall be prorated between the applicable coverages as the limits of each coverage bear to the total of the limits.

(e) The policy or endorsement added thereto may provide that if the insured has valid and collectible automobile medical payment insurance available to him or her, the damages which the insured shall be entitled to recover from the owner or operator of an uninsured motor vehicle shall be reduced for purposes of uninsured motorist coverage by the amounts paid or due to be paid under the automobile medical payment insurance.

(f) The policy or an endorsement added thereto shall provide that the determination as to whether the insured shall be legally entitled to recover damages, and if so entitled, the amount thereof, shall be made by agreement between the insured and the insurer or, in the event of disagreement, by arbitration. The arbitration shall be conducted by a single neutral arbitrator. An award or a judgment confirming an award shall not be conclusive on any party in any action or proceeding between (i) the insured, his or her insurer, his or her legal representative, or his or her heirs and (ii) the uninsured motorist to recover damages arising out of the accident upon which the award is based.

* * *

(g) The insurer paying a claim under an uninsured motorist endorsement or coverage shall be entitled to be subrogated to the rights of the insured to whom the claim was paid against any person legally liable for the injury or death to the extent that payment was made. The action may be brought within three years from the date that payment was made hereunder.

(h) An insured entitled to recovery under the uninsured motorist endorsement or coverage shall be reimbursed within the conditions stated herein without being required to sign any release or waiver of rights to which he or she may be entitled under any other insurance coverage applicable; nor shall payment under this section to the insured be delayed or made contingent upon the decisions as to liability or distribution of loss costs under other bodily injury liability insurance or any bond applicable to the accident. Any loss payable under the terms of the uninsured motorist endorsement or coverage to or for any person may be reduced:

(1) By the amount paid and the present value of all amounts payable to him or her, his or her executor, administrator, heirs, or legal representative under any workers' compensation law, exclusive of nonoccupational disability benefits.

(2) By the amount the insured is entitled to recover from any other person insured under the underlying liability insurance policy of which the uninsured motorist endorsement or coverage is a part, including any amounts tendered to the insured as advance payment on behalf of the other person by the insurer providing the underlying liability insurance.

(i) No cause of action shall accrue to the insured under any policy or endorsement provision issued pursuant to this section unless one of the following actions have been taken within one year from the date of the accident:

(1) Suit for bodily injury has been filed against the uninsured motorist, in a court of competent jurisdiction.

(2) Agreement as to the amount due under the policy has been concluded.

(3) The insured has formally instituted arbitration proceedings.

(j) Notwithstanding subdivisions (b) and (i), in the event the accident occurs in any other state or foreign jurisdiction to which coverage is extended under the policy and the insurer of the tortfeasor becomes insolvent, any action authorized pursuant to this section may be maintained within three months of the insolvency of the tortfeasor's insurer, but in no event later than the pertinent period of limitation of the jurisdiction in which the accident occurred.

(k) Notwithstanding subdivision (i), any insurer whose insured has made a claim under his or her uninsured motorist coverage, and the claim is pending, shall, at least 30 days before the expiration of the applicable statute of limitation, notify its insured in writing of the statute of limitation applicable to the injury or death. Failure of the insurer to provide the written notice shall operate to toll any applicable statute of limitation or other time limitation for a period of 30 days from the date the written notice is actually given. The notice shall not be required if the insurer has received notice that the insured is represented by an attorney.

* * *

(m) Coverage provided under an uninsured motorist endorsement or coverage shall be offered with coverage limits equal to the limits of liability for bodily injury in the underlying policy of insurance, but shall not be required to be offered with limits in excess of the following amounts:

(1) A limit of thirty thousand dollars ($30,000) because of bodily injury to or death of one person in any one accident.

(2) Subject to the limit for one person set forth in paragraph (1), a limit of sixty thousand dollars ($60,000) because of bodily injury to or death of two or more persons in any one accident.

(n) Underinsured motorist coverage shall be offered with limits equal to the limits of liability for the insured's uninsured motorist limits in the underlying policy, and may be offered with limits in excess of the uninsured motorist coverage. For the purposes of this section, uninsured and underinsured motorist coverage shall be offered as a single coverage. However, an insurer may offer coverage for damages for bodily injury or wrongful death from the owner or operator of an underinsured motor vehicle at greater limits than an uninsured motor vehicle.

* * *

c. The Family Exclusion

Before 1973 California Vehicle Code § 17158 was the "automobile guest" statute. It not only prohibited liability of the driver to "guests" (unless they paid compensation or unless the driver was intoxicated or guilty of wilful misconduct) but also prohibited liability of the driver to the owner of the car "riding in or occupying the vehicle" when it was driven by another person with his permission, unless the driver was intoxicated or guilty of wilful misconduct. In 1973, *Brown v. Merlo*, 8 Cal.3d 855, 106 Cal.Rptr. 388, 506 P.2d 212 (1973), held the section unconstitutional so far as the "guest" was concerned. The Legislature amended the section thereafter to drop the reference to the "guest" so that the bar against liability of the driver extended only to the owner. The constitutionality of this bar was upheld in *Schwalbe v. Jones*, 16 Cal.3d 514, 128 Cal.Rptr. 321, 546 P.2d 1033 (1976). Within a short time after *Schwalbe v. Jones*, the California Supreme Court reversed itself in *Cooper v. Bray* and struck down the bar (against the owner holding the driver liable) on Federal and State constitutional grounds, 21 Cal.3d 841, 148 Cal.Rptr. 148, 582 P.2d 604 (1978). This had the potential of serious implications for a common policy provision sometimes called the "family exclusion" which excluded from the policy coverage liability of an insured driver to the insured named in the policy or his relatives resident in the same household.

What should be the result when the named insured drives his own car with his wife as passenger and she is injured? Thus far, California courts have upheld the right of insurers to exclude rights of recovery for members of the insured's household. The ostensible reason is that insurers are placed at a disadvantage in situations that lack a true adversarial basis. Farmers Insurance Exchange v. Cocking, 29 Cal.3d 383, 173 Cal.Rptr. 846, 628 P.2d 1 (1981).

STATE FARM MUTUAL INSURANCE CO. v. SCHWARTZ

United States Court of Appeals, Tenth Circuit, 1991.
933 F.2d 848.

MOORE, CIRCUIT JUDGE.

State Farm filed this action in district court seeking a declaratory judgment that it is not obligated to defend or indemnify Glenda Schwartz in an Oklahoma state court action filed against her by her children. The children brought suit against their mother alleging that her negligent driving resulted in their injury. The district court granted summary judgment in favor of the Schwartz children, holding that the "household exclusion" in their parents' State Farm insurance policy, denying coverage for bodily injury to any insured or member of the insured's household, violated the public policy of Oklahoma under the state's compulsory automobile liability insurance law. The court held that State Farm is therefore liable to defend and indemnify Glenda Schwartz against her children's lawsuit. We affirm.

I. BACKGROUND

The parties stipulated: 1) the insurance policy covering the automobile involved in the accident was in full force; 2) the policy excludes from coverage damages "[f]or any bodily injury to: ... c. any insured or any member of the insured's family residing in the insured's household" [the household exclusion at issue here]; 3) the policy defines "insured" as: "1. you [Charles Schwartz, in this case]; 2. your spouse; 3. the relatives of the first person named in the declarations [Charles Schwartz is the only named insured]; 4) the policy defines 'relative' as: 'a person related to you or your spouse by blood, marriage, or adoption who lives with you. It includes your unmarried and unemancipated child away at school;' and 5) the Schwartz children are relatives for the purposes of this policy. We review a summary judgment order de novo and apply the same legal standard used by the district court under Fed.R.Civ.P. 56(c)." Osgood v. State Farm Mut. Auto. Ins. Co., 848 F.2d 141, 143 (10th Cir.1988).

The issue in this case is straightforward: whether the district court erred in determining that the household exclusion in the Schwartz' insurance policy with State Farm contravenes the public policy established by Oklahoma's compulsory liability insurance law. In reviewing the district court's decision, we are faced with the difficult task of divining a coherent state policy from an ambiguous statute, directly conflicting positions announced in dicta in several state court opinions, and the persuasive authority of the public policies of other states with compulsory liability insurance laws.

II. Conceptual Analysis

Conceptually, there are two ways to analyze this issue: 1) whether the policy definition of the children as "insureds" precludes recovery, or 2) whether the household exclusion in the policy offends Oklahoma public policy. First, taking notice of the fact that the Schwartz children are defined as "insureds" in the policy, and the fact that according to the policy "insureds" may not recover for bodily injury under the liability provisions, one could argue that under Looney v. Farmers Ins. Group, 616 P.2d 1138, 1141 (Okla.1980), the children, as "insureds," are not covered by the insurance policy. This resolution would avoid reaching the difficult public policy question of the validity of the household exclusion.

However, there are flaws in this rationale. First, the claimant in Looney, as the spouse of the policyholder, was defined in the policy as a "named insured." In the present case the children are defined within the class of the "insured." Id. at 1139 n. 2. While the linguistic distinction between a "named insured" and an "insured" may not be significant, it does point to a more serious problem. The spouse of the policyholder is much more likely than the children of the policyholder to be a true, consenting party to the contract. It is highly unlikely that household members such as minor, unemancipated children will have consented, or are legally able to consent, to the terms of the insurance contract.[38] In Young v. Mid–Continent Casualty Co., 743 P.2d 1084, 1088 (Okla.1987), the court distinguished parties to the contract from those "innocent

38. See Mutual of Enumclaw Ins. Co. v. Wiscomb, 97 Wash.2d 203, 643 P.2d 441, 446 (1982) (citations omitted), distinguishing "named insureds" from children excluded from coverage by a household exclusion, reasoning that: [t]hose named insureds could then intelligently choose to add the exclusion, with an adjustment in their premiums reflecting any decreased risks, or retain the coverage at the higher premium rate. Under any circumstances, exclusion clauses which purport to deny coverage to children of the insured or any person not a party to the insurance contract are violative of this state's public policy * * *. The family or household exclusion clause violates this state's public policy of assuring compensation to the victims of negligent and careless drivers.

victims" the Act intended to protect. Id. at 1087–88. The Young court noted that this conclusion was consistent with Looney because, in essence, a "named insured" is simply another name for a party to the contract.

In the present case, the district court properly pointed out that under Oklahoma law, Okla.Stat.Ann. tit. 15, § 11 (West 1983), children are incapable of contracting, and, in addition, simply because they are third party beneficiaries does not make them contracting parties. Okla. Stat.Ann. tit. 15, § 29 (West 1983). Logic supports this conclusion as well.

Adopting Young's division of the world into two populations: innocent victims and parties to the contract, and remembering that parental immunity has been abrogated in automobile injury cases in Oklahoma, Unah By and Through Unah v. Martin, 676 P.2d 1366 (Okla.1984), it would undermine Unah for parents and their insurance company to be able to prevent suits against the parents by their children by simply defining the children as "insureds."

Also, assuming for the moment that the household exclusion does contravene Oklahoma public policy, the contracting parties should not be able to accomplish the same results as would a household exclusion by simply defining all parties they would like to exclude from coverage as "insureds." For these reasons, we follow the second conceptual path. Our quest will therefore be to analyze whether the household exclusion violates Oklahoma public policy.

III. Public Policy

Oklahoma's compulsory liability insurance law states in relevant part: "On and after January 1, 1983, every owner of a motor vehicle registered in this state, other than a licensed used motor vehicle dealer, shall, at all times, maintain in force with respect to such vehicle security for the payment of loss resulting from the liability imposed by law for bodily injury, death and property damage *sustained by any person* arising out of the ownership, maintenance, operation or use of the vehicle." Okla.Stat.Ann. tit. 47, § 7–601(B) (West 1988) (emphasis added). Also, as mentioned above, Oklahoma has abrogated parental immunity from suit to allow a child's action for negligence arising from an automobile accident to the extent of the parent's automobile insurance. Unah, 676 P.2d at 1369–70.

Since passage of the Compulsory Liability Insurance Act (the Act) in 1976, Oklahoma courts have invalidated several insurance policy exclusions as contrary to the public policy established by the Act. In Young, 743 P.2d at 1087–88, the Oklahoma supreme court held an age exclusion (no liability coverage if the operator was under age twenty-five and not a relative of the insured) violated the public policy. The Young court reached this result by concluding the legislative intent underlying the Act was to mandate that "any vehicle operated on the highways of Oklahoma be secured against liability to innocent victims of the negligent operation or use of the insured vehicle." Id. at 1088. Young also cited that portion of the Act requiring coverage for loss "sustained by any person" as further support for its conclusion. Id. at 1087, 1088.

In Equity Mut. Ins. Co. v. Spring Valley Wholesale Nursery, Inc., 747 P.2d 947, 952 (Okla.1987), the Oklahoma supreme court held that a geographical exclusion (policy did not cover travel outside a two hundred mile radius) also contravened the public policy of the Act, holding that "when liability insurance is issued in compliance with compulsory insurance laws, statutory policy *at the very minimum* requires coverage for all actionable claims which may arise within the state." Id. (emphasis in original). The Equity court noted in dictum, mischaracterizing the holding of Looney, that, unlike the geographical exclusion, the household exclusion would comply with Oklahoma public policy under the Act because "[t]he purpose of the law is to shield the public, not members of the named insured's household." Id. 747 P.2d at 953.

The Young and Equity discussions of the household exclusion are at best persuasive dicta because they dealt with other types of exclusions. Looney is closer to the facts of the present case because it indirectly involved a household exclusion as well as an exclusion prohibiting recovery by one of the insured parties. Id. at 1139 n. 2. The Equity court stated that Looney determined the household exclusion did not violate public policy in Oklahoma. This is a questionable characterization of Looney because the court there based its decision in favor of the insurance company upon the fact that the claimant was a named insured. The court simply did not base its decision on the validity of the household exclusion; indeed, the court stated, "[t]he appellant was more than a mere member of the family of the *insured;* she was the *insured.* Her relationship with the defendant Looney surpasses mere household member status." Id. at 1141 (emphasis in original). However, the Looney court unfortunately obscured the exact basis for its holding by expressing agreement with this court's treatment of household exclusions in Farmers Ins. Co. v. McClain, 603 F.2d 821 (10th Cir.1979).

McClain was a declaratory judgment action filed to determine whether the insurance company was obligated to defend and indemnify the policyholder for torts committed in his automobile against a member of his family. The policy in question contained a household exclusion. The McClain court held that the explicit terms of the policy (i.e., the household exclusion) relieved the insurance company from its duty to defend and indemnify the policyholder. Id. at 823.

The court's reference to McClain is not helpful, however, because the McClain court did not consider the validity of the household exclusion in the context of the compulsory liability insurance law. This consideration undermines Looney as precedent for the question before us. We are constrained to conclude that the discussion of the household exclusion in Looney is also nonbinding dictum.

Finally, the Oklahoma supreme court in Unah, in the context of partially abrogating parental immunity, stated, "[w]e can no longer countenance the legal anomaly where two minor children, negligently injured in the operation of a motor vehicle, one of them a stranger, could recover compensation for his injuries and the other one, a minor child of the operator of the vehicle, could not. Today, where all other passengers in a car are mandatorily protected by liability coverage it is unfair and against public interest to deprive an unemancipated minor the benefit of recovery." Id. at 1370. As dictum, this discussion is also of scarce precedential value in determining the validity of the household exclusion in Oklahoma, but it nonetheless demonstrates clear public policy preferences that assist us in determining the scope of the comprehensive liability insurance law.

To summarize, Oklahoma courts have presented us with four opinions adopting contradictory positions in dicta bearing on the validity of the household exclusion. The Young and Unah opinions make a strong argument for affirming the district court in this case. The Equity and Looney opinions, however, appear to urge an opposite conclusion. Since Oklahoma case law is contradictory, we must look elsewhere for guidance.

Many states have addressed the issue of whether household exclusions are valid in the context of a compulsory liability insurance law. These states have almost uniformly held that the household exclusion is contrary to the public policy created by compulsory liability insurance laws.[39] Most state courts that have addressed this issue but which have not explicitly ruled that the household exclusion violates public policy, are states without compulsory liability insurance laws.[40] Thus, our re-

39. See Beacon Ins. Co. of Am. v. State Farm Mut. Ins. Co., 795 S.W.2d 62, 64 (Ky.1990); Stepho v. Allstate Ins. Co., 259 Ga. 475, 383 S.E.2d 887, 888 (1989) (household exclusion invalid if broader than common law tort immunity); Government Employees Ins. Co. v. Ropka, 74 Md.App. 249, 536 A.2d 1214, 1218, cert. denied, 312 Md. 601, 541 A.2d 964 (1988) (household exclusion invalid only to extent of statutorily required minimum insurance amount); State Farm Mut. Auto. Ins. Co. v. Mastbaum, 748 P.2d 1042, 1044 (Utah 1987) (household exclusion invalid only to extent of statutorily required minimum insurance amount); Farmers Ins. Group v. Reed, 109 Idaho 849, 712 P.2d 550, 552 (1985); Meyer v. State Farm Mut. Auto. Ins. Co., 689 P.2d 585, 589–90 (Colo.1984); Dowdy v. Allstate Ins. Co., 68 Or.App. 709, 685 P.2d 444, 449 (1984); Transamerica Ins. Co. v. Royle, 202 Mont. 173, 656 P.2d 820, 824 (1983); Allstate Ins. Co. v. Wyoming Ins. Dept., 672 P.2d 810, 813–16 (Wyo.1983); DeWitt v. Young, 229 Kan. 474, 625 P.2d 478, 482 (1981); Bishop v. Allstate Ins. Co., 623 S.W.2d 865, 866 (Ky.1981); State Farm Mut. Auto. Ins. Co. v. Traycik, 86 Mich. App. 285, 272 N.W.2d 629, 631 (1978); Estate of Neal v. Farmers Ins. Exchange, 93 Nev. 348, 566 P.2d 81, 83 (1977); Hughes v. State Farm Mut. Auto. Ins. Co., 236 N.W.2d 870, 885–86 (N.D.1975); Jordan v. Aetna Casualty and Sur. Co., 264 S.C. 294, 214 S.E.2d 818, 820 (1975).

40. See, e.g., Faraj v. Allstate Ins. Co., 486 A.2d 582, 585–86 (R.I.1984); State Farm Mut. Auto. Ins. Co. v. Suarez, 104 Ill.App.3d 556, 60 Ill.Dec. 305, 309, 432 N.E.2d 1204, 1208 (1982). Appellant cites Southern Guaranty Ins. Co. v. Preferred Risk Mut. Ins. Co., 257 Ga. 355, 359 S.E.2d 665 (1987), and various other cases in support of its assertion that the household exclusion has "long enjoyed judicial support." Appellant's Brief in Chief, at 15. However, each of these decisions have been either overturned or limited to their facts by subsequent decisions. See cases cited in footnote 4. Arizona and Indiana appear to be the only states which have upheld the household exclusion in the face of a compulsory liability insurance law. State Farm Mut. Auto. Ins. Co. v. Transport Indem. Co., 109 Ariz. 56, 505 P.2d 227, 230 (1973); Transamerica Ins. Co. v. Henry, 563 N.E.2d 1265 (Ind.1990). California has adopted a somewhat qualified acceptance of the household exclusion by allowing an insurer

view leads us to conclude the overwhelming majority of states that have addressed this issue have determined, under various lines of reasoning, that the household exclusion violates public policy created by compulsory liability insurance laws.

One of the most common lines of reasoning in these cases leading to invalidation of the household exclusion, and the logic used by the Young and Unah courts in Oklahoma, holds that: "[compulsory liability insurance] legislation embodies a public policy that innocent victims of the negligent operation of motor vehicles should be compensated for their injuries. The perspective which this public policy adopts is that of the innocent victim rather than that of the insurer or the insured tort-feasor." Young, 743 P.2d at 1087 (footnotes omitted). Young noted that this interpretation of legislative intent is also consistent with the explicit statutory requirement of the Act that every driver have security to cover losses sustained by "any person." Id.

We believe that this position, combined with the passage we have quoted from Unah, best harmonizes the language of the Act, the legislative intent expressed by the Oklahoma courts, and the overwhelming trend among other jurisdictions in finding the household exclusion contrary to public policy in compulsory liability insurance states. Therefore, we hold the district court did not err in granting summary judgment in favor of the Schwartz children because the household exclusion in their parents' insurance policy contravened the public policy of Oklahoma under the Act.

AFFIRMED.

Notes

1. There is little practical purpose in going through the laborious process of abolishing intra-family tort immunity, unless there are familial sources of funds to pay for the consequences. Such a pragmatic consideration no doubt contributes to the hostility toward the "household exclusion." Representative decisions are cited in the last two notes of the principal case.

Kansas demonstrates that shifts in public policy and in the bodies making the policy are difficult to follow. In 1980 the Kansas Supreme Court abolished parental immunity in auto accident cases. The following year it declared the "household exclusion" void. In 1982 the Kansas legislature expressly authorized the clauses, but in 1984 repealed that validation. However the Supreme Court declined to give the repeal retroactive effect. See Hilyard v. Estate of Clearwater, 240 Kan. 362, 729 P.2d 1195 (1986).

2. *What is given by statute may be taken away by contract interpretation (who is "family" anyway?).* The family exclusion in the omnibus clause may be (oftentimes grudgingly) sanctioned, but as an exclusion it is, of course, subject to the close scrutiny for ambiguity given to insurance policies (Part A, Chap. 2A and a dozen other places in this book). Would the ordinary

to exclude from coverage any person insured under the policy. Farmers Ins. Exch. v. Cocking, 29 Cal.3d 383, 173 Cal.Rptr. 846, 847–48, 628 P.2d 1, 2–3 (1981).

layman say that a young man living with his mother, brother, and his stepfather (the insured) who treated him as a natural son and fully supported him, was a member of the family? The California Supreme Court in *Reserve Ins. Co. v. Pisciotta*, 30 Cal.3d 800, 180 Cal.Rptr. 628, 640 P.2d 764 (1982), said he was not, thus allowing the young man, who was injured by his stepfather's boat the benefit of the stepfather's liability policy.

3. *The "family exclusion" clauses and uninsured motorist coverage.* Assume a jurisdiction which sustains the validity of the "family exclusion," but has discarded the intra-family immunity doctrine as to tort liability. Father, insured under liability policy containing the "family exclusion" clause, negligently runs over an offspring. The child sues Father. Can the child collect judgment under the uninsured motorist's provisions of Father's policy? See Severs v. Country Mutual Insurance Co., 89 Ill.2d 515, 61 Ill.Dec. 137, 434 N.E.2d 290 (1982) (minor child excluded under family exclusion policy but allowed recovery under uninsured motorist provisions because the car was driven by an unrelated uninsured driver); Faraj v. Allstate Ins. Co., 486 A.2d 582 (R.I.1984) (to the same effect even though the uninsured driver was the mother); but cf. Harrison v. Metropolitan Property and Liability Ins. Co., 475 So.2d 1370 (Fla.App.1985) (to allow recovery where the uninsured driver was the mother would render the family exclusion meaningless).

4. *The Named Driver Exclusion.* Statutory provisions such as West's Ann. Cal. Ins. Code § 11580(d)(1) allowing named drivers (or sometimes drivers under a certain age) to be excluded from coverage have also been challenged usually without success on public policy grounds. Garza v. Glen Falls Ins. Co., 105 N.M. 220, 731 P.2d 363 (1986). Some jurisdictions, however, have held the exclusion to have no force or effect up to the limits of the Financial Responsibility Law. Jones v. Motorists Mut. Ins. Co., 177 W.Va. 763, 356 S.E.2d 634 (1987).

APPENDIX

Glossary of Insurance Terms.
Basic Standard Form Fire Insurance Policy.
Commercial General Liability Coverage Form Policy.
Employment–Related Practices Liability Coverage Form Policy.
Personal Auto Policy.

GLOSSARY OF INSURANCE TERMS

Those wishing a more extensive list than that provided below can consult some of the major texts and treatises, for example: Couch, Cyclopedia of Insurance Law 2d (see the "words and phrases" entries in the Index volumes); Appleman, Insurance Law and Practice; Keeton and Widiss, Insurance Law–Basic Text; Robert H. Jerry II, Understanding Insurance Law, 3d ed. (2001). Additionally, the statutes of the student's own state may also offer definitions of some of these terms. Although there are other words to be defined, the following will be a start on gaining a grasp of "insurance law". The authors thank Douglas Richmond, a Senior Vice President, AON Professional Services Group, for the compilation of the glossary.

Accidental Death and Dismemberment. A policy or provision in a disability income policy which pays either a specified amount or a multiple of the weekly disability benefit if the insured dies, loses his or her sight, or loses two limbs as the result of an accident. A lesser amount is payable for the loss of one eye, one arm, one leg, one hand, or one foot.

Accidental Death Benefit. An extra benefit which generally equals the face amount of the policy or principal sum, payable in addition to other benefits in the event of death, as a result of an accident. Generally refers to a life insurance policy provision resulting in "double indemnity."

Actuarial. Having to do with insurance mathematics. An actuary is a specialist trained in mathematics, statistics, and accounting who is responsible for rate, reserve and dividend calculations, and other insurance statistical studies.

Additional Insured. A person other than the named insured who is protected under the terms of the policy. Usually, additional insureds are added to the policy by endorsement. Additional insureds differ from automatic insureds, who are categorically referred to in the wording of the definition of "insured" in the policy itself.

Adjuster. A representative of the insurer who seeks to determine the extent of the insurer's liability for a loss when a claim is submitted. Also referred to as a "claims adjuster" or "claims representative."

Adverse Selection. The tendency of poorer than average risks to buy and maintain insurance. Adverse selection occurs when insureds select only those coverages that are most likely to have losses.

Aggregate Limit. Usually refers to liability insurance and indicates the amount of coverage that the insured has under the policy for a specific period of time, no matter how many separate accidents may occur during the policy period.

All-Risk Insurance. Used to mean insurance against loss of or damage to property arising from any fortuitous cause except those that are specifically excluded.

Application. A form on which the prospective insured states facts requested by the insurer from which, together with information from other sources, the insurer decides whether to accept the risk, modify the coverage offered, or decline the risk.

Assignment. Transfer by the policy holder of legal rights or interest in the policy to a third party. Most policies cannot be assigned without the insurer's permission.

Assignment of Benefits. A method where the person receiving the medical benefits assigns the payment of those benefits to a physician or hospital.

Beneficiary. A person who may become eligible to receive benefits under an insurance policy. *E.g.*, a beneficiary under a life insurance policy.

Binder. A temporary or preliminary contract of insurance that protects the insured until the insurer actually issues the policy.

Bond. A three-party contract guaranteeing that if one person (the principal) fails to perform as specified (in the case of the typical "performance and maintenance bond" used in construction) or proves to be dishonest (*e.g.*, a "fidelity bond" for an employee who handles large amounts of cash or valuables), the person to whom the duty is owed (the obligee) will be made whole by the issuer of the bond (the surety). Sureties typically are insurance companies.

Carrier. Sometimes used to designate the insurer. The term "insurer" is preferred because of the possible confusion of "carrier" with an entity in the transportation business.

Certificate of Insurance. (1) A statement of the coverage and general provisions of a master contract and group insurance that is issued to individuals covered in the group; or (2) a form which verifies that a policy has been written and states the coverage in general, often used as proof of insurance in any number of commercial transactions.

Claim. A demand made by the insured, or the insured's beneficiary, for payment of the benefits provided for by the insurance policy at issue.

Coinsurance. An agreement whereby the insured and the insurer share all losses covered by the policy in a proportion agreed upon in advance. For example, an 80–20 "coinsurance" clause would mean that the insurer would pay 80% of a covered loss and the insured would be liable for 20% of the covered loss.

Collateral Source Rule. The rule of law which allows a plaintiff to recover damages from a tortfeasor even if the plaintiff has already recovered for his or her damages from a source other than the defendant. For example, a plaintiff that has all of her medical care or treatment paid for by her health insurer can still recover for her medical expenses from the tortfeasor or, more probably, from the tortfeasor's liability insurer.

Commercial General Liability (CGL) Policy. General liability coverage which may be written as a monoline policy or a part of a commercial insurance package. CGL policies are the primary form of insurance coverage for most businesses.

Comprehensive Policy. In automobile and liability insurance, this is all-risk coverage with certain specified exclusions.

Compulsory Insurance. Any form of insurance required by law. For example, most states have compulsory automobile insurance laws, which require all drivers to have a minimum amount of liability coverage.

Concurrent Causation. A term referring to two or more perils acting concurrently (or in sequence) to cause a loss. This creates special problems for property insurers when one of the perils is covered and the other is not.

Coverage. The scope of the protection afforded under an insurance policy.

Coverage Trigger. A mechanism that determines whether a policy covers a particular claim for loss. For example, the difference between the coverage triggers of liability "occurrence" policies and "claims made" policies is that loss must occur during the policy period in the first instance, and the claim must be made during the policy period in the second.

Covered Loss. Any illness, injury, death, property loss, legal liability, or any other situation or loss for which an insurance company will pay benefits under a policy when such event occurs.

Declaration. A term used in insurance other than for life or health insurance to denote that portion of the policy in which it is stated such information as the insured's name, the insured's address, the property insured, its location and description, the policy period, the amount of coverage provided, applicable premiums, and similar information. This is usually a single page, hence the term "declaration page."

Deductible. The portion of an insured loss to be borne by the insured before he is entitled to recover benefits under the policy.

Earth Movement. A peril including landslide, mudflow, earth sinking, rising or shifting, and earthquake. Damages caused by earth movement are usually excluded from coverage under homeowners and commercial property insurance policies.

Endorsement. A written or printed form attached to an insurance policy which alters the policy provisions.

Excess Insurance. An insurance policy providing coverage in excess over one or more scheduled underlying or primary policies which does not pay a loss until the loss amount exceeds the limits of the primary or underlying policy. For example, a commercial insured may have a CGL policy with liability limits of $1,000,000, and an excess insurance policy with limits of $5,000,000, both in force and effect during the same policy period. If the insured suffers a covered $800,000 loss, only the primary policy would pay. If the insured suffers a $1,500,000 covered loss, the primary liability policy would pay $1,000,000 and the excess insurer would pay the remaining $500,000.

Exclusion. An insurance policy provision that denies coverage for certain perils, persons, property, or locations.

Experience. The insured's loss record.

Exposure. The state of being subject to the possibility of loss.

Face Amount. The amount of insurance provided by the terms of an insurance policy, usually found on the face of the policy. In a life insurance policy, the face amount is the death benefit.

Financed Premium. The payment of insurance premiums with funds borrowed outside the policy itself. By way of explanation, there are companies (called premium financing companies) that loan money to pay insurance premiums.

Financial Responsibility Law. State law which requires the insured to furnish evidence of ability to pay for losses. Evidence of ability to pay most often takes the form of an insurance policy with a certain minimum limit of liability coverage.

First-Party Insurance. Insurance covering the insured's own property or person.

Floater. A form of insurance that applies to movable property, whatever its location, if it is within the policy's stated territorial limits. The coverage "floats" with the property.

Homeowners Policy. A property and liability insurance policy that insures against any of the property or liability perils to which a homeowner is typically exposed.

Incontestability Clause. A provision in an insurance policy (usually a life insurance policy) setting forth the conditions under which or the period of time during which the insurer may contest or void the policy. After that time has lapsed—normally two years—the policy cannot be contested.

Indemnify. To restore the victim of a loss to the same position the victim enjoyed before the loss occurred.

Independent Adjuster. An adjuster who works as an independent contractor, hiring himself out to insurance companies or other organizations for the investigation and settlement of claims. Independent adjusters represent the interests of the insurance companies employing them.

Insurable Interest. Any interest a person has in a possible subject of insurance, such as a car or home, of such a nature that certain happenings might cause him financial loss. For example, if a brother and sister jointly own an office building, each has an "insurable interest" in that building.

Insurance Services Office (ISO). An insurance trade organization made up of liability and property insurers. ISO develops standard insurance policies, gathers statistics and disseminates industry information, and so on. ISO's development of standard policy forms is no doubt its greatest contribution.

Insuring Agreement. That portion of an insurance policy which states the perils insured against, the persons and/or property covered, and the policy period.

Lapse. Termination of a policy because of a failure to pay the premium.

Law of Large Numbers. This law states that the larger the number of exposures considered, the more closely the losses reported will match the underlying probability of loss. Perhaps the simplest example of the law of large numbers is the flipping of a coin. The more times a coin is flipped, the closer it will come to actually reaching the underlying probability of 50% heads and 50% tails.

Limit of Liability. The maximum amount for which an insurer is liable as set forth in the policy.

Loss. Generally refers to (1) the amount of reduction in the property value of an insured's property caused by an insured peril; (2) the amount sought in an insured's claim; or (3) the amount paid on the insured's behalf under the insurance policy.

Manuscript Policy. A policy written to include specific coverages or conditions not provided in a standard policy.

Master Policy. In group insurance, the insurer issues the master policy to the employer. Individuals insured under the group plan receive certificates evidencing their coverage.

Named Insured. Any person, or entity (or member or employee thereof) specifically designated by name as being insured under the subject policy. For example, if you purchase an automobile insurance policy, you are the "named insured." Of course, other persons may be covered under your policy even though they are not the "named insured." For example, your policy also covers other drivers who use your car with your permission.

National Association of Insurance Commissioners (NAIC). An association of state insurance commissioners formed for the purpose of exchanging information and developing uniformity in the regulatory practices through model legislation and regulations. The NAIC has no official power to enforce compliance with its recommendations.

No-Fault Insurance. Many states have passed laws permitting individual automobile accident victims to collect directly from their own insurance companies for medical and hospital expenses regardless of who was at fault in the accident giving rise to the injury.

Notice of Loss. Notice to an insurer that a loss has occurred. Notice of loss is a condition of most policies, and it is frequently required to be given within the specified time and in a particular manner.

Omnibus Clause. Agreements in automobile liability insurance policies and some other policies that, by their definition of who is an insured, extend coverage to others within the definition without the necessity of specifically naming them in the policy.

Personal Injury Protection (PIP). The formal name usually given to no-fault benefits in states that have enacted mandatory no-fault automobile insurance coverages. PIP usually includes benefits for medical expenses, lost income, essential services, accident death and funeral expenses.

Personal Lines. This terms is used to refer to insurance for individuals and families, such as private passenger automobile insurance and homeowners insurance policies.

Policyholder. Often used loosely to refer to the insured.

Preferred Risk. Any risk considered to be better than the standard risk on which the premium rate was calculated.

Premium. The price of insurance protection for a specified risk for a specified period of time. Basically, the price the insurer receives for its policy providing coverage.

Premium Notice. A form notice sent by an insurer to the insured specifying the premium that will be due on a given date in order to confer coverage.

Primary Coverage. This is the coverage which pays any loss first, without consideration as to whether or not there are any other coverages for the same loss. A primary policy may provide "first dollar coverage," as distinguished from an excess policy, which pays only after the primary coverage has been exhausted.

Proof of Loss. A formal statement made by an insured and given to an insurer regarding a loss. It is intended to give the insurer information sufficient to enable it to determine the extent of its liability.

Public Adjuster. An insurance adjuster who represents an insured on a fee basis in claims resolution.

Red-lining. Discriminating unfairly against a risk solely because of its location. For example, insurers have been sued for refusing to insure African–American homeowners because they lived in depressed areas or high crime locations.

Reinsurance. A type of insurance that involves acceptance by an insurer, called the reinsurer, of all or part of a risk of a loss covered by another insurer, called the ceding company. It is a way for an insurer to avoid having to pay for larger catastrophic losses. In other words, the ceding insurer "reinsures" its own risks.

Reserve. An amount representing actual or potential liabilities kept by the insurer to cover debts to policyholders or losses. For example, any time a third-party sues an insured who is covered under a liability policy for an alleged tort, a liability insurer establishes a "reserve" to pay that claim or to pay any judgment. When looking at potential losses or claims in the aggregate, one typically refers to an insurers' "reserves," referring to the total or aggregate monies set aside to pay claims or losses.

Risk. A person or thing insured.

Schedule. A list of items covered by an insurance policy, such as various buildings and their contents, sometimes including their specific descriptions and valuations. Also, an excess insurance policy is normally excess to "scheduled" primary policies. In other words, the declaration page of the excess policy specifies that it is excess to specifically identified primary policies. Those primary policies specifically identified are referred to as "scheduled" policies.

Standard Policy. A policy which has identical coverage provisions and exclusions regardless of the issuing insurers. Many common policies are standardized. Most standardized policies are drafted by ISO.

Tail. This term describes both the exposure that exists after expiration of a policy, and the coverage that may be purchased to cover that exposure. Under "occurrence" policies a claimant's tail may extend for years after the policy's expiration. On "claims made" policies, "tail coverage" may be purchased to extend the period for reporting covered claims beyond the policy period.

Third-Party Administrator (TPA). A firm providing administrative services related to insurance for insurers and insureds. For example, a TPA might adjust claims for an insurer or for a large commercial insured. Or, a TPA might administer a company's group health plan acting as a liaison with the insurer, certifying eligibility, preparing reports, *etc.*

Third-Party Insurance. Liability insurance. So called because the loss or damage for which payment is sought is suffered by a third-party as a result of the insured's conduct.

Umbrella Policy. Like an excess policy, an umbrella policy insures against catastrophic liability, *i.e.*, liability exceeding the insured's primary coverage. Unlike true excess policies, however, many umbrella policies provide primary coverage for risks that the underlying policies do not cover.

Underinsured. A condition in which not enough insurance is carried to cover the insurable value.

Underinsured Motorists Coverage. A coverage in an automobile insurance policy under which the automobile insurer will pay damages up to specified limits for bodily injury if the limits of liability under the liable motorist's policy are exhausted and he cannot pay the full amount for which he is liable.

Underwriting. The process of selecting risks and classifying them according to their degrees of insurability so that the appropriate rates may be assigned. The process also includes rejection of those risks that do not qualify. An "underwriter" is a person trained in evaluating risks and determining rates and coverages for them. The term derives from the practice at Lloyd's of London begun years ago, whereby each person willing to accept a portion of the risk being shopped wrote his name under the description of the risk signifying his acceptance.

Unearned Premium. That portion of the written premium applicable to the unexpired or unused part of the policy for which the premium has been paid. Thus, in the case of an annual premium, at the end of the first month of the policy year eleven-twelfths of the premium is "unearned."

Uninsured Motorists Coverage. Coverage in an automobile insurance policy under which the insurer will pay damages to the insured for which another motorists is liable if that motorist is unable to pay because he is uninsured. This coverage usually applies to bodily injury damages only. Injuries to the insured caused by a hit-and-run driver are also covered.

Valuation Clause. A clause stating the value of items for insurance purposes, making the policy containing the clause a "valued policy." In the event of a total loss, then, the policy pays a specific amount provided in the valuation clause. The effect is to eliminate the need for determining the actual cash value of an item of property in the event of a total loss.

Valued Policy Law. A law passed by a state legislature which requires that in the event of a total loss to a building, the insurer must pay the face amount of a valued policy, regardless of the actual cash value of the property which was destroyed. It can have the effect of allowing the insured to recover an amount much greater than the actual cash value of the property. The intent of such laws is to guard against unscrupulous insurers purposely writing policies exceeding the value of the subject property in order to collect inflated premiums.

Write. To insure, to underwrite, or to accept an application.

BASIC STANDARD FORM FIRE INSURANCE POLICY

West's California Annotated Insurance Code Section 2071

(a) The following is adopted as the standard form of fire insurance policy for this state:

California Standard Form Fire Insurance Policy

No.

[Space for insertion of name of company or companies issuing the policy and other matter permitted to be stated at the head of the policy.]

[Space for listing amounts of insurance, rates and premiums for the basic coverages insured under the standard form of policy and for additional coverages or perils insured under endorsements attached.]

In consideration of the provisions and stipulations herein or added hereto and of ______ dollars premium this company, for the term of ______

from the ____ day of _______, 20___) At 12:01 a.m.,

to the ____ day of _______, 20___) standard time,

at location of property involved, to an amount not exceeding _______ dollars, does insure _______ and legal representatives, to the extent of the actual cash value of the property at the time of loss, but not exceeding the amount which it would cost to repair or replace the property with material of like kind and quality within a reasonable time after the loss, without allowance for any increased cost of repair or reconstruction by reason of any ordinance or law regulating construction or repair, and without compensation for loss resulting from interruption of business or manufacture, nor in any event for more than the interest of the insured, against all LOSS BY FIRE, LIGHTNING AND BY REMOVAL FROM PREMISES ENDANGERED BY THE PERILS INSURED AGAINST IN THIS POLICY, EXCEPT AS HEREINAFTER PROVIDED, to the property described hereinafter while located or contained as described in this policy, or pro rata for five days at each proper place to which any of the property shall necessarily be removed for preservation from the perils insured against in this policy, but not elsewhere.

Assignment of this policy shall not be valid except with the written consent of this company.

This policy is made and accepted subject to the foregoing provisions and stipulations and those hereinafter stated, which are hereby made a part of this policy, together with any other provisions, stipulations and agreements as may be added hereto, as provided in this policy.

IN WITNESS WHEREOF, this company has executed and attested these presents; but this policy shall not be valid unless countersigned by the duly authorized agent of this company at

Secretary. President.

Countersigned this ______ day of ______, 20______

______ Agent

Concealment, fraud

This entire policy shall be void if, whether before or after a loss, the insured has willfully concealed or misrepresented any material fact or circumstance concerning this insurance or the subject thereof, or the interest of the insured therein, or in case of any fraud or false swearing by the insured relating thereto.

Uninsurable and excepted property

This policy shall not cover accounts, bills, currency, deeds, evidences of debt, money or securities; nor, unless specifically named hereon in writing, bullion or manuscripts.

Perils not included

This company shall not be liable for loss by fire or other perils insured against in this policy caused, directly or indirectly, by: (a) enemy attack by armed forces, including action taken by military, naval or air forces in resisting an actual or an immediately impending enemy attack; (b) invasion; (c) insurrection; (d) rebellion; (e) revolution; (f) civil war; (g) usurped power; (h) order of any civil authority except acts of destruction at the time of and for the purpose of preventing the spread of fire, provided that the fire did not originate from any of the perils excluded by this policy; (i) neglect of the insured to use all reasonable means to save and preserve the property at and after a loss, or when the property is endangered by fire in neighboring premises; (j) nor shall this company be liable for loss by theft.

Other insurance

Other insurance may be prohibited or the amount of insurance may be limited by endorsement attached hereto.

Conditions suspending or restricting insurance

Unless otherwise provided in writing added hereto this company shall not be liable for loss occurring (a) while the hazard is increased by any means within the control or knowledge of the insured; or (b) while a described building, whether intended for occupancy by owner or tenant, is vacant or unoccupied beyond a period of 60 consecutive days; or (c) as a result of explosion or riot, unless fire ensues, and in that event for loss by fire only.

Other perils or subjects

Any other peril to be insured against or subject of insurance to be covered in this policy shall be by endorsement in writing hereon or added hereto.

Added provisions

The extent of the application of insurance under this policy and of the contribution to be made by this company in case of loss, and any other provision or agreement not inconsistent with the provisions of this policy, may be provided for in writing added hereto, but no provision may be waived except such as by the terms of this policy or by statute is subject to change.

Waiver provisions

No permission affecting this insurance shall exist, or waiver of any provision be valid, unless granted herein or expressed in writing added hereto. No provision, stipulation or forfeiture shall be held to be waived by any requirement or proceeding on the part of this company relating to appraisal or to any examination provided for herein.

Cancellation of policy

This policy shall be canceled at any time at the request of the insured, in which case this company shall, upon demand and surrender of this policy, refund the excess of paid premium above the customary short rates for the expired time. This policy may be canceled at any time by this company by giving to the insured a 20 days' written notice of cancellation with or without tender of the excess of paid premium above the pro rata premium for the expired time, which excess, if not tendered, shall be refunded on demand. Notice of cancellation shall state that said excess premium (if not tendered) will be refunded on demand. If the reason for cancellation is nonpayment of premium, this policy may be canceled by this company by giving to the insured a 10 days' written notice of cancellation.

Mortgagee interests and obligations

If loss hereunder is made payable, in whole or in part, to a designated mortgagee not named herein as the insured, the interest in this policy may be canceled by giving to the mortgagee a 10 days' written notice of cancellation.

If the insured fails to render proof of loss the mortgagee, upon notice, shall render proof of loss in the form herein specified within 60 days thereafter and shall be subject to the provisions hereof relating to appraisal and time of payment and of bringing suit. If this company shall claim that no liability existed as to the mortgagor or owner, it shall, to the extent of payment of loss to the mortgagee, be subrogated to all the mortgagee's rights of recovery, but without impairing mortgagee's right to sue; or it may pay off the mortgage debt and require an assignment thereof and of the mortgage. Other provisions relating to the interests and obligations of the mortgagee may be added hereto by agreement in writing.

Pro rata liability

This company shall not be liable for a greater proportion of any loss than the amount hereby insured shall bear to the whole insurance covering the property against the peril involved, whether collectible or not.

Requirements in case loss occurs

The insured shall give written notice to this company of any loss without unnecessary delay, protect the property from further damage, forthwith separate the damaged and undamaged personal property, put it in the best possible order, furnish a complete inventory of the destroyed, damaged and undamaged property, showing in detail quantities, costs, actual cash value and amount of loss claimed; and within 60 days after the loss, unless the time is extended in writing by this company, the insured shall render to this company a proof of loss, signed and sworn to by the insured, stating the knowledge and belief of the insured as to the following: the time and origin of the loss, the interest of the insured and of all others in the property, the actual cash value of each item thereof and the amount of loss thereto, all encumbrances thereon, all other contracts of insurance, whether valid or not, covering any of said property, any changes in the title, use, occupation, location, possession or exposures of said property since the issuing of this policy, by whom and for what purpose any building herein described and the several parts thereof were occupied at the time of loss and whether or not it then stood on leased ground, and shall furnish a copy of all the descriptions and schedules in all policies and, if required and obtainable, verified plans and specifications of any building, fixtures or machinery destroyed or damaged.

The insured, as often as may be reasonably required and subject to the provisions of Section 2071.1, shall exhibit to any person designated by this company all that remains of any property herein described, and submit to examinations under oath by any person named by this company, and subscribe the same; and, as often as may be reasonably required, shall produce for examinations all books of account, bills, invoices, and other vouchers, or certified copies thereof if the originals be lost, at any reasonable time and place as may be designated by this company or its representative, and shall permit extracts and copies thereof to be made. The insurer shall inform the insured that tax returns are privileged against disclosure under applicable law but may be necessary to process or determine the claim.

The insurer shall notify every claimant that they may obtain, upon request, copies of claim-related documents. For purposes of this section, "claim-related documents" means all documents that relate to the evaluation of damages, including, but not limited to, repair and replacement estimates and bids, appraisals, scopes of loss, drawings, plans, reports, third-party findings on the amount of loss, covered damages, and cost of repairs, and all other valuation, measurement, and loss adjustment calculations of the amount of loss, covered damage, and cost of repairs. However, attorney work product and attorney-client privileged documents, and documents that indicate fraud by the insured or that contain medically privileged information, are excluded from the documents an insurer is required to provide pursuant to this section to a claimant. Within 15 calendar days after receiving a request from an insured for claim-related documents, the insurer shall provide the insured with copies of all claim-related documents, except those excluded by this section. Nothing in this section shall be construed to affect existing litigation discovery rights.

After a covered loss, the insurer shall provide, free of charge, a complete, current copy of this policy within 30 calendar days of receipt of a request from the insured. The time period for providing this policy may be extended by the Insurance Commissioner.

An insured who does not experience a covered loss shall, upon request, be entitled to one free copy of this policy annually. The policy provided to the insured shall include, where applicable, the policy declarations page.

Appraisal

In case the insured and this company shall fail to agree as to the actual cash value or the amount of loss, then, on the written request of either, each shall select a competent and disinterested appraiser and notify the other of the appraiser selected within 20 days of the request. Where the request is accepted, the appraisers shall first select a competent and disinterested umpire; and failing for 15 days to agree upon the umpire, then, on request of the insured or this company, the umpire shall be selected by a judge of a court of record in the state in which the property covered is located. Appraisal proceedings are informal unless the insured and this company mutually agree otherwise. For purposes of this section, "informal" means that no formal discovery shall be conducted, including depositions, interrogatories, requests for admission, or other forms of formal civil discovery, no formal rules of evidence shall be applied, and no court reporter shall be used for the proceedings. The appraisers shall then appraise the loss, stating separately actual cash value and loss to each item; and, failing to agree, shall submit their differences, only, to the umpire. An award in writing, so itemized, of any two when filed with this company shall determine the amount of actual cash value and loss. Each appraiser shall be paid by the party selecting him or her and the expenses of appraisal and umpire shall be paid by the parties equally. In the event of a government-declared disaster, as defined in the Government Code, appraisal may be requested by either the insured or this company but shall not be compelled.

Adjusters

If, within a six-month period, the company assigns a third or subsequent adjuster to be primarily responsible for a claim, the insurer, in a timely manner, shall provide the insured with a written status report. For purposes of this section, a written status report shall include a summary of any decisions or actions that are substantially related to the disposition of a claim, including, but not limited to, the amount of losses to structures or contents, the retention or consultation of design or construction professionals, the amount of coverage for losses to structures or contents and all items of dispute.

Company's options

It shall be optional with this company to take all, or any part, of the property at the agreed or appraised value, and also to repair, rebuild or replace the property destroyed or damaged with other of like kind and quality within a reasonable time, on giving notice of its intention so to do within 30 days after the receipt of the proof of loss herein required.

Abandonment

There can be no abandonment to this company of any property.

When loss payable

The amount of loss for which this company may be liable shall be payable 60 days after proof of loss, as herein provided, is received by this company and ascertainment of the loss is made either by agreement between the insured and this company expressed in writing or by the filing with this company of an award as herein provided.

Suit

No suit or action on this policy for the recovery of any claim shall be sustainable in any court of law or equity unless all the requirements of this policy shall have been complied with, and unless commenced within 12 months next after inception of the loss.

Subrogation

This company may require from the insured an assignment of all right of recovery against any party for loss to the extent that payment therefor is made by this company.

COMMERCIAL GENERAL LIABILITY COVERAGE FORM

COMMERCIAL GENERAL LIABILITY
CG 00 01 12 04

COMMERCIAL GENERAL LIABILITY COVERAGE FORM

Various provisions in this policy restrict coverage. Read the entire policy carefully to determine rights, duties and what is and is not covered.

Throughout this policy the words "you" and "your" refer to the Named Insured shown in the Declarations, and any other person or organization qualifying as a Named Insured under this policy. The words "we", "us" and "our" refer to the company providing this insurance.

The word "insured" means any person or organization qualifying as such under Section II – Who Is An Insured.

Other words and phrases that appear in quotation marks have special meaning. Refer to Section V – Definitions.

SECTION I – COVERAGES

COVERAGE A BODILY INJURY AND PROPERTY DAMAGE LIABILITY

1. Insuring Agreement

a. We will pay those sums that the insured becomes legally obligated to pay as damages because of "bodily injury" or "property damage" to which this insurance applies. We will have the right and duty to defend the insured against any "suit" seeking those damages. However, we will have no duty to defend the insured against any "suit" seeking damages for "bodily injury" or "property damage" to which this insurance does not apply. We may, at our discretion, investigate any "occurrence" and settle any claim or "suit" that may result. But:

(1) The amount we will pay for damages is limited as described in Section III – Limits Of Insurance; and

(2) Our right and duty to defend ends when we have used up the applicable limit of insurance in the payment of judgments or settlements under Coverages **A** or **B** or medical expenses under Coverage **C.**

No other obligation or liability to pay sums or perform acts or services is covered unless explicitly provided for under Supplementary Payments – Coverages **A** and **B.**

b. This insurance applies to "bodily injury" and "property damage" only if:

(1) The "bodily injury" or "property damage" is caused by an "occurrence" that takes place in the "coverage territory";

(2) The "bodily injury" or "property damage" occurs during the policy period; and

(3) Prior to the policy period, no insured listed under Paragraph **1.** of Section II – Who Is An Insured and no "employee" authorized by you to give or receive notice of an "occurrence" or claim, knew that the "bodily injury" or "property damage" had occurred, in whole or in part. If such a listed insured or authorized "employee" knew, prior to the policy period, that the "bodily injury" or "property damage" occurred, then any continuation, change or resumption of such "bodily injury" or "property damage" during or after the policy period will be deemed to have been known prior to the policy period.

c. "Bodily injury" or "property damage" which occurs during the policy period and was not, prior to the policy period, known to have occurred by any insured listed under Paragraph **1.** of Section II – Who Is An Insured or any "employee" authorized by you to give or receive notice of an "occurrence" or claim, includes any continuation, change or resumption of that "bodily injury" or "property damage" after the end of the policy period.

d. "Bodily injury" or "property damage" will be deemed to have been known to have occurred at the earliest time when any insured listed under Paragraph **1.** of Section II – Who Is An Insured or any "employee" authorized by you to give or receive notice of an "occurrence" or claim:

(1) Reports all, or any part, of the "bodily injury" or "property damage" to us or any other insurer;

(2) Receives a written or verbal demand or claim for damages because of the "bodily injury" or "property damage"; or

(3) Becomes aware by any other means that "bodily injury" or "property damage" has occurred or has begun to occur.

e. Damages because of "bodily injury" include damages claimed by any person or organization for care, loss of services or death resulting at any time from the "bodily injury".

2. **Exclusions**

This insurance does not apply to:

a. **Expected Or Intended Injury**

"Bodily injury" or "property damage" expected or intended from the standpoint of the insured. This exclusion does not apply to "bodily injury" resulting from the use of reasonable force to protect persons or property.

b. **Contractual Liability**

"Bodily injury" or "property damage" for which the insured is obligated to pay damages by reason of the assumption of liability in a contract or agreement. This exclusion does not apply to liability for damages:

(1) That the insured would have in the absence of the contract or agreement; or

(2) Assumed in a contract or agreement that is an "insured contract", provided the "bodily injury" or "property damage" occurs subsequent to the execution of the contract or agreement. Solely for the purposes of liability assumed in an "insured contract", reasonable attorney fees and necessary litigation expenses incurred by or for a party other than an insured are deemed to be damages because of "bodily injury" or "property damage", provided:

(a) Liability to such party for, or for the cost of, that party's defense has also been assumed in the same "insured contract"; and

(b) Such attorney fees and litigation expenses are for defense of that party against a civil or alternative dispute resolution proceeding in which damages to which this insurance applies are alleged.

c. **Liquor Liability**

"Bodily injury" or "property damage" for which any insured may be held liable by reason of:

(1) Causing or contributing to the intoxication of any person;

(2) The furnishing of alcoholic beverages to a person under the legal drinking age or under the influence of alcohol; or

(3) Any statute, ordinance or regulation relating to the sale, gift, distribution or use of alcoholic beverages.

This exclusion applies only if you are in the business of manufacturing, distributing, selling, serving or furnishing alcoholic beverages.

d. **Workers' Compensation And Similar Laws**

Any obligation of the insured under a workers' compensation, disability benefits or unemployment compensation law or any similar law.

e. **Employer's Liability**

"Bodily injury" to:

(1) An "employee" of the insured arising out of and in the course of:

(a) Employment by the insured; or

(b) Performing duties related to the conduct of the insured's business; or

(2) The spouse, child, parent, brother or sister of that "employee" as a consequence of Paragraph (1) above.

This exclusion applies:

(1) Whether the insured may be liable as an employer or in any other capacity; and

(2) To any obligation to share damages with or repay someone else who must pay damages because of the injury.

This exclusion does not apply to liability assumed by the insured under an "insured contract".

f. Pollution

(1) "Bodily injury" or "property damage" arising out of the actual, alleged or threatened discharge, dispersal, seepage, migration, release or escape of "pollutants":

(a) At or from any premises, site or location which is or was at any time owned or occupied by, or rented or loaned to, any insured. However, this subparagraph does not apply to:

(i) "Bodily injury" if sustained within a building and caused by smoke, fumes, vapor or soot produced by or originating from equipment that is used to heat, cool or dehumidify the building, or equipment that is used to heat water for personal use, by the building's occupants or their guests;

(ii) "Bodily injury" or "property damage" for which you may be held liable, if you are a contractor and the owner or lessee of such premises, site or location has been added to your policy as an additional insured with respect to your ongoing operations performed for that additional insured at that premises, site or location and such premises, site or location is not and never was owned or occupied by, or rented or loaned to, any insured, other than that additional insured; or

(iii) "Bodily injury" or "property damage" arising out of heat, smoke or fumes from a "hostile fire";

(b) At or from any premises, site or location which is or was at any time used by or for any insured or others for the handling, storage, disposal, processing or treatment of waste;

(c) Which are or were at any time transported, handled, stored, treated, disposed of, or processed as waste by or for:

(i) Any insured; or

(ii) Any person or organization for whom you may be legally responsible; or

(d) At or from any premises, site or location on which any insured or any contractors or subcontractors working directly or indirectly on any insured's behalf are performing operations if the "pollutants" are brought on or to the premises, site or location in connection with such operations by such insured, contractor or subcontractor. However, this subparagraph does not apply to:

(i) "Bodily injury" or "property damage" arising out of the escape of fuels, lubricants or other operating fluids which are needed to perform the normal electrical, hydraulic or mechanical functions necessary for the operation of "mobile equipment" or its parts, if such fuels, lubricants or other operating fluids escape from a vehicle part designed to hold, store or receive them. This exception does not apply if the "bodily injury" or "property damage" arises out of the intentional discharge, dispersal or release of the fuels, lubricants or other operating fluids, or if such fuels, lubricants or other operating fluids are brought on or to the premises, site or location with the intent that they be discharged, dispersed or released as part of the operations being performed by such insured, contractor or subcontractor;

(ii) "Bodily injury" or "property damage" sustained within a building and caused by the release of gases, fumes or vapors from materials brought into that building in connection with operations being performed by you or on your behalf by a contractor or subcontractor; or

(iii) "Bodily injury" or "property damage" arising out of heat, smoke or fumes from a "hostile fire".

(e) At or from any premises, site or location on which any insured or any contractors or subcontractors working directly or indirectly on any insured's behalf are performing operations if the operations are to test for, monitor, clean up, remove, contain, treat, detoxify or neutralize, or in any way respond to, or assess the effects of, "pollutants".

(2) Any loss, cost or expense arising out of any:

(a) Request, demand, order or statutory or regulatory requirement that any insured or others test for, monitor, clean up, remove, contain, treat, detoxify or neutralize, or in any way respond to, or assess the effects of, "pollutants"; or

(b) Claim or "suit" by or on behalf of a governmental authority for damages because of testing for, monitoring, cleaning up, removing, containing, treating, detoxifying or neutralizing, or in any way responding to, or assessing the effects of, "pollutants".

However, this paragraph does not apply to liability for damages because of "property damage" that the insured would have in the absence of such request, demand, order or statutory or regulatory requirement, or such claim or "suit" by or on behalf of a governmental authority.

g. Aircraft, Auto Or Watercraft

"Bodily injury" or "property damage" arising out of the ownership, maintenance, use or entrustment to others of any aircraft, "auto" or watercraft owned or operated by or rented or loaned to any insured. Use includes operation and "loading or unloading".

This exclusion applies even if the claims against any insured allege negligence or other wrongdoing in the supervision, hiring, employment, training or monitoring of others by that insured, if the "occurrence" which caused the "bodily injury" or "property damage" involved the ownership, maintenance, use or entrustment to others of any aircraft, "auto" or watercraft that is owned or operated by or rented or loaned to any insured.

This exclusion does not apply to:

(1) A watercraft while ashore on premises you own or rent;

(2) A watercraft you do not own that is:

(a) Less than 26 feet long; and

(b) Not being used to carry persons or property for a charge;

(3) Parking an "auto" on, or on the ways next to, premises you own or rent, provided the "auto" is not owned by or rented or loaned to you or the insured;

(4) Liability assumed under any "insured contract" for the ownership, maintenance or use of aircraft or watercraft; or

(5) "Bodily injury" or "property damage" arising out of:

(a) The operation of machinery or equipment that is attached to, or part of, a land vehicle that would qualify under the definition of "mobile equipment" if it were not subject to a compulsory or financial responsibility law or other motor vehicle insurance law in the state where it is licensed or principally garaged; or

(b) the operation of any of the machinery or equipment listed in Paragraph **f.(2)** or **f.(3)** of the definition of "mobile equipment".

h. Mobile Equipment

"Bodily injury" or "property damage" arising out of:

(1) The transportation of "mobile equipment" by an "auto" owned or operated by or rented or loaned to any insured; or

(2) The use of "mobile equipment" in, or while in practice for, or while being prepared for, any prearranged racing, speed, demolition, or stunting activity.

i. War

"Bodily injury" or "property damage", however caused, arising, directly or indirectly, out of:

(1) War, including undeclared or civil war;

(2) Warlike action by a military force, including action in hindering or defending against an actual or expected attack, by any government, sovereign or other authority using military personnel or other agents; or

(3) Insurrection, rebellion, revolution, usurped power, or action taken by governmental authority in hindering or defending against any of these.

j. Damage To Property

"Property damage" to:

(1) Property you own, rent, or occupy, including any costs or expenses incurred by you, or any other person, organization or entity, for repair, replacement, enhancement, restoration or maintenance of such property for any reason, including prevention of injury to a person or damage to another's property;

(2) Premises you sell, give away or abandon, if the "property damage" arises out of any part of those premises;

(3) Property loaned to you;

(4) Personal property in the care, custody or control of the insured;

(5) That particular part of real property on which you or any contractors or subcontractors working directly or indirectly on your behalf are performing operations, if the "property damage" arises out of those operations; or

(6) That particular part of any property that must be restored, repaired or replaced because "your work" was incorrectly performed on it.

Paragraphs **(1)**, **(3)** and **(4)** of this exclusion do not apply to "property damage" (other than damage by fire) to premises, including the contents of such premises, rented to you for a period of 7 or fewer consecutive days. A separate limit of insurance applies to Damage To Premises Rented To You as described in Section III – Limits Of Insurance.

Paragraph **(2)** of this exclusion does not apply if the premises are "your work" and were never occupied, rented or held for rental by you.

Paragraphs **(3)**, **(4)**, **(5)** and **(6)** of this exclusion do not apply to liability assumed under a sidetrack agreement.

Paragraph **(6)** of this exclusion does not apply to "property damage" included in the "products-completed operations hazard".

k. Damage To Your Product

"Property damage" to "your product" arising out of it or any part of it.

l. Damage To Your Work

"Property damage" to "your work" arising out of it or any part of it and included in the "products-completed operations hazard".

This exclusion does not apply if the damaged work or the work out of which the damage arises was performed on your behalf by a subcontractor.

m. Damage To Impaired Property Or Property Not Physically Injured

"Property damage" to "impaired property" or property that has not been physically injured, arising out of:

(1) A defect, deficiency, inadequacy or dangerous condition in "your product" or "your work"; or

(2) A delay or failure by you or anyone acting on your behalf to perform a contract or agreement in accordance with its terms.

This exclusion does not apply to the loss of use of other property arising out of sudden and accidental physical injury to "your product" or "your work" after it has been put to its intended use.

n. Recall Of Products, Work Or Impaired Property

Damages claimed for any loss, cost or expense incurred by you or others for the loss of use, withdrawal, recall, inspection, repair, replacement, adjustment, removal or disposal of:

(1) "Your product";

(2) "Your work"; or

(3) "Impaired property";

if such product, work, or property is withdrawn or recalled from the market or from use by any person or organization because of a known or suspected defect, deficiency, inadequacy or dangerous condition in it.

o. Personal And Advertising Injury

"Bodily injury" arising out of "personal and advertising injury".

p. Electronic Data

Damages arising out of the loss of, loss of use of, damage to, corruption of, inability to access, or inability to manipulate electronic data.

As used in this exclusion, electronic data means information, facts or programs stored as or on, created or used on, or transmitted to or from computer software, including systems and applications software, hard or floppy disks, CD-ROMS, tapes, drives, cells, data processing devices or any other media which are used with electronically controlled equipment.

Exclusions **c.** through **n.** do not apply to damage by fire to premises while rented to you or temporarily occupied by you with permission of the owner. A separate limit of insurance applies to this coverage as described in Section III – Limits Of Insurance.

COVERAGE B PERSONAL AND ADVERTISING INJURY LIABILITY

1. Insuring Agreement

a. We will pay those sums that the insured becomes legally obligated to pay as damages because of "personal and advertising injury" to which this insurance applies. We will have the right and duty to defend the insured against any "suit" seeking those damages. However, we will have no duty to defend the insured against any "suit" seeking damages for "personal and advertising injury" to which this insurance does not apply. We may, at our discretion, investigate any offense and settle any claim or "suit" that may result. But:

(1) The amount we will pay for damages is limited as described in Section III – Limits Of Insurance; and

(2) Our right and duty to defend end when we have used up the applicable limit of insurance in the payment of judgments or settlements under Coverages **A** or **B** or medical expenses under Coverage **C.**

No other obligation or liability to pay sums or perform acts or services is covered unless explicitly provided for under Supplementary Payments – Coverages **A** and **B.**

b. This insurance applies to "personal and advertising injury" caused by an offense arising out of your business but only if the offense was committed in the "coverage territory" during the policy period.

2. Exclusions

This insurance does not apply to:

a. Knowing Violation Of Rights Of Another

"Personal and advertising injury" caused by or at the direction of the insured with the knowledge that the act would violate the rights of another and would inflict "personal and advertising injury".

b. Material Published With Knowledge Of Falsity

"Personal and advertising injury" arising out of oral or written publication of material, if done by or at the direction of the insured with knowledge of its falsity.

c. Material Published Prior To Policy Period

"Personal and advertising injury" arising out of oral or written publication of material whose first publication took place before the beginning of the policy period.

d. Criminal Acts

"Personal and advertising injury" arising out of a criminal act committed by or at the direction of the insured.

e. Contractual Liability

"Personal and advertising injury" for which the insured has assumed liability in a contract or agreement. This exclusion does not apply to liability for damages that the insured would have in the absence of the contract or agreement.

f. Breach Of Contract

"Personal and advertising injury" arising out of a breach of contract, except an implied contract to use another's advertising idea in your "advertisement".

g. Quality Or Performance Of Goods – Failure To Conform To Statements

"Personal and advertising injury" arising out of the failure of goods, products or services to conform with any statement of quality or performance made in your "advertisement".

h. Wrong Description Of Prices

"Personal and advertising injury" arising out of the wrong description of the price of goods, products or services stated in your "advertisement".

i. Infringement Of Copyright, Patent, Trademark Or Trade Secret

"Personal and advertising injury" arising out of the infringement of copyright, patent, trademark, trade secret or other intellectual property rights.

However, this exclusion does not apply to infringement, in your "advertisement", of copyright, trade dress or slogan.

j. Insureds In Media And Internet Type Businesses

"Personal and advertising injury" committed by an insured whose business is:

(1) Advertising, broadcasting, publishing or telecasting;

(2) Designing or determining content of web-sites for others; or

(3) An Internet search, access, content or service provider.

However, this exclusion does not apply to Paragraphs **14.a., b.** and **c.** of "personal and advertising injury" under the Definitions Section.

For the purposes of this exclusion, the placing of frames, borders or links, or advertising, for you or others anywhere on the Internet, is not by itself, considered the business of advertising, broadcasting, publishing or telecasting.

k. Electronic Chatrooms Or Bulletin Boards

"Personal and advertising injury" arising out of an electronic chatroom or bulletin board the insured hosts, owns, or over which the insured exercises control.

l. Unauthorized Use Of Another's Name Or Product

"Personal and advertising injury" arising out of the unauthorized use of another's name or product in your e-mail address, domain name or metatag, or any other similar tactics to mislead another's potential customers.

m. **Pollution**

"Personal and advertising injury" arising out of the actual, alleged or threatened discharge, dispersal, seepage, migration, release or escape of "pollutants" at any time.

n. **Pollution-Related**

Any loss, cost or expense arising out of any:

(1) Request, demand, order or statutory or regulatory requirement that any insured or others test for, monitor, clean up, remove, contain, treat, detoxify or neutralize, or in any way respond to, or assess the effects of, "pollutants"; or

(2) Claim or suit by or on behalf of a governmental authority for damages because of testing for, monitoring, cleaning up, removing, containing, treating, detoxifying or neutralizing, or in any way responding to, or assessing the effects of, "pollutants".

o. **War**

"Personal and advertising injury", however caused, arising, directly or indirectly, out of:

(1) War, including undeclared or civil war;

(2) Warlike action by a military force, including action in hindering or defending against an actual or expected attack, by any government, sovereign or other authority using military personnel or other agents; or

(3) Insurrection, rebellion, revolution, usurped power, or action taken by governmental authority in hindering or defending against any of these.

COVERAGE C MEDICAL PAYMENTS

1. **Insuring Agreement**

a. We will pay medical expenses as described below for "bodily injury" caused by an accident:

(1) On premises you own or rent;

(2) On ways next to premises you own or rent; or

(3) Because of your operations;

provided that:

(1) The accident takes place in the "coverage territory" and during the policy period;

(2) The expenses are incurred and reported to us within one year of the date of the accident; and

(3) The injured person submits to examination, at our expense, by physicians of our choice as often as we reasonably require.

b. We will make these payments regardless of fault. These payments will not exceed the applicable limit of insurance. We will pay reasonable expenses for:

(1) First aid administered at the time of an accident;

(2) Necessary medical, surgical, x-ray and dental services, including prosthetic devices; and

(3) Necessary ambulance, hospital, professional nursing and funeral services.

2. **Exclusions**

We will not pay expenses for "bodily injury":

a. **Any Insured**

To any insured, except "volunteer workers".

b. **Hired Person**

To a person hired to do work for or on behalf of any insured or a tenant of any insured.

c. **Injury On Normally Occupied Premises**

To a person injured on that part of premises you own or rent that the person normally occupies.

d. **Workers Compensation And Similar Laws**

To a person, whether or not an "employee" of any insured, if benefits for the "bodily injury" are payable or must be provided under a workers' compensation or disability benefits law or a similar law.

e. **Athletics Activities**

To a person injured while practicing, instructing or participating in any physical exercises or games, sports, or athletic contests.

f. **Products-Completed Operations Hazard**

Included within the "products-completed operations hazard".

g. **Coverage A Exclusions**

Excluded under Coverage A.

SUPPLEMENTARY PAYMENTS – COVERAGES A AND B

1. We will pay, with respect to any claim we investigate or settle, or any "suit" against an insured we defend:

a. All expenses we incur.

b. Up to $250 for cost of bail bonds required because of accidents or traffic law violations arising out of the use of any vehicle to which the Bodily Injury Liability Coverage applies. We do not have to furnish these bonds.

c. The cost of bonds to release attachments, but only for bond amounts within the applicable limit of insurance. We do not have to furnish these bonds.

d. All reasonable expenses incurred by the insured at our request to assist us in the investigation or defense of the claim or "suit", including actual loss of earnings up to $250 a day because of time off from work.

e. All costs taxed against the insured in the "suit".

f. Prejudgment interest awarded against the insured on that part of the judgment we pay. If we make an offer to pay the applicable limit of insurance, we will not pay any prejudgment interest based on that period of time after the offer.

g. All interest on the full amount of any judgment that accrues after entry of the judgment and before we have paid, offered to pay, or deposited in court the part of the judgment that is within the applicable limit of insurance.

These payments will not reduce the limits of insurance.

2. If we defend an insured against a "suit" and an indemnitee of the insured is also named as a party to the "suit", we will defend that indemnitee if all of the following conditions are met:

a. The "suit" against the indemnitee seeks damages for which the insured has assumed the liability of the indemnitee in a contract or agreement that is an "insured contract";

b. This insurance applies to such liability assumed by the insured;

c. The obligation to defend, or the cost of the defense of, that indemnitee, has also been assumed by the insured in the same "insured contract";

d. The allegations in the "suit" and the information we know about the "occurrence" are such that no conflict appears to exist between the interests of the insured and the interests of the indemnitee;

e. The indemnitee and the insured ask us to conduct and control the defense of that indemnitee against such "suit" and agree that we can assign the same counsel to defend the insured and the indemnitee; and

f. The indemnitee:

(1) Agrees in writing to:

(a) Cooperate with us in the investigation, settlement or defense of the "suit";

(b) Immediately send us copies of any demands, notices, summonses or legal papers received in connection with the "suit";

(c) Notify any other insurer whose coverage is available to the indemnitee; and

(d) Cooperate with us with respect to coordinating other applicable insurance available to the indemnitee; and

(2) Provides us with written authorization to:

(a) Obtain records and other information related to the "suit"; and

(b) Conduct and control the defense of the indemnitee in such "suit".

So long as the above conditions are met, attorneys' fees incurred by us in the defense of that indemnitee, necessary litigation expenses incurred by us and necessary litigation expenses incurred by the indemnitee at our request will be paid as Supplementary Payments. Notwithstanding the provisions of Paragraph **2.b.(2)** of Section I – Coverage A – Bodily Injury And Property Damage Liability, such payments will not be deemed to be damages for "bodily injury" and "property damage" and will not reduce the limits of insurance.

Our obligation to defend an insured's indemnitee and to pay for attorneys' fees and necessary litigation expenses as Supplementary Payments ends when:

a. We have used up the applicable limit of insurance in the payment of judgments or settlements; or

b. The conditions set forth above, or the terms of the agreement described in Paragraph f. above, are no longer met.

SECTION II – WHO IS AN INSURED

1. If you are designated in the Declarations as:

a. An individual, you and your spouse are insureds, but only with respect to the conduct of a business of which you are the sole owner.

b. A partnership or joint venture, you are an insured. Your members, your partners, and their spouses are also insureds, but only with respect to the conduct of your business.

c. A limited liability company, you are an insured. Your members are also insureds, but only with respect to the conduct of your business. Your managers are insureds, but only with respect to their duties as your managers.

d. An organization other than a partnership, joint venture or limited liability company, you are an insured. Your "executive officers" and directors are insureds, but only with respect to their duties as your officers or directors. Your stockholders are also insureds, but only with respect to their liability as stockholders.

e. A trust, you are an insured. Your trustees are also insureds, but only with respect to their duties as trustees.

2. Each of the following is also an insured:

a. Your "volunteer workers" only while performing duties related to the conduct of your business, or your "employees", other than either your "executive officers" (if you are an organization other than a partnership, joint venture or limited liability company) or your managers (if you are a limited liability company), but only for acts within the scope of their employment by you or while performing duties related to the conduct of your business. However, none of these "employees" or "volunteer workers" are insureds for:

(1) "Bodily injury" or "personal and advertising injury":

(a) To you, to your partners or members (if you are a partnership or joint venture), to your members (if you are a limited liability company), to a co-"employee" while in the course of his or her employment or performing duties related to the conduct of your business, or to your other "volunteer workers" while performing duties related to the conduct of your business;

(b) To the spouse, child, parent, brother or sister of that co-"employee" or "volunteer worker" as a consequence of Paragraph (1)(a) above;

(c) For which there is any obligation to share damages with or repay someone else who must pay damages because of the injury described in Paragraphs (1)(a) or (b) above; or

(d) Arising out of his or her providing or failing to provide professional health care services.

(2) "Property damage" to property:

(a) Owned, occupied or used by,

(b) Rented to, in the care, custody or control of, or over which physical control is being exercised for any purpose by

you, any of your "employees", "volunteer workers", any partner or member (if you are a partnership or joint venture), or any member (if you are a limited liability company).

b. Any person (other than your "employee" or "volunteer worker"), or any organization while acting as your real estate manager.

c. Any person or organization having proper temporary custody of your property if you die, but only:

(1) With respect to liability arising out of the maintenance or use of that property; and

(2) Until your legal representative has been appointed.

d. Your legal representative if you die, but only with respect to duties as such. That representative will have all your rights and duties under this Coverage Part.

3. Any organization you newly acquire or form, other than a partnership, joint venture or limited liability company, and over which you maintain ownership or majority interest, will qualify as a Named Insured if there is no other similar insurance available to that organization. However:

a. Coverage under this provision is afforded only until the 90th day after you acquire or form the organization or the end of the policy period, whichever is earlier;

b. Coverage A does not apply to "bodily injury" or "property damage" that occurred before you acquired or formed the organization; and

c. Coverage B does not apply to "personal and advertising injury" arising out of an offense committed before you acquired or formed the organization.

No person or organization is an insured with respect to the conduct of any current or past partnership, joint venture or limited liability company that is not shown as a Named Insured in the Declarations.

SECTION III – LIMITS OF INSURANCE

1. The Limits of Insurance shown in the Declarations and the rules below fix the most we will pay regardless of the number of:

a. Insureds;

b. Claims made or "suits" brought; or

c. Persons or organizations making claims or bringing "suits".

2. The General Aggregate Limit is the most we will pay for the sum of:
   a. Medical expenses under Coverage C;
   b. Damages under Coverage A, except damages because of "bodily injury" or "property damage" included in the "products-completed operations hazard"; and
   c. Damages under Coverage B.
3. The Products-Completed Operations Aggregate Limit is the most we will pay under Coverage A for damages because of "bodily injury" and "property damage" included in the "products-completed operations hazard".
4. Subject to 2. above, the Personal and Advertising Injury Limit is the most we will pay under Coverage B for the sum of all damages because of all "personal and advertising injury" sustained by any one person or organization.
5. Subject to 2. or 3. above, whichever applies, the Each Occurrence Limit is the most we will pay for the sum of:
   a. Damages under Coverage A; and
   b. Medical expenses under Coverage C

   because of all "bodily injury" and "property damage" arising out of any one "occurrence".
6. Subject to 5. above, the Damage To Premises Rented To You Limit is the most we will pay under Coverage A for damages because of "property damage" to any one premises, while rented to you, or in the case of damage by fire, while rented to you or temporarily occupied by you with permission of the owner.
7. Subject to 5. above, the Medical Expense Limit is the most we will pay under Coverage C for all medical expenses because of "bodily injury" sustained by any one person.

The Limits of Insurance of this Coverage Part apply separately to each consecutive annual period and to any remaining period of less than 12 months, starting with the beginning of the policy period shown in the Declarations, unless the policy period is extended after issuance for an additional period of less than 12 months. In that case, the additional period will be deemed part of the last preceding period for purposes of determining the Limits of Insurance.

SECTION IV – COMMERCIAL GENERAL LIABILITY CONDITIONS

1. **Bankruptcy**

   Bankruptcy or insolvency of the insured or of the insured's estate will not relieve us of our obligations under this Coverage Part.

2. **Duties In The Event Of Occurrence, Offense, Claim Or Suit**
   a. You must see to it that we are notified as soon as practicable of an "occurrence" or an offense which may result in a claim. To the extent possible, notice should include:
      (1) How, when and where the "occurrence" or offense took place;
      (2) The names and addresses of any injured persons and witnesses; and
      (3) The nature and location of any injury or damage arising out of the "occurrence" or offense.
   b. If a claim is made or "suit" is brought against any insured, you must:
      (1) Immediately record the specifics of the claim or "suit" and the date received; and
      (2) Notify us as soon as practicable.

      You must see to it that we receive written notice of the claim or "suit" as soon as practicable.
   c. You and any other involved insured must:
      (1) Immediately send us copies of any demands, notices, summonses or legal papers received in connection with the claim or "suit";
      (2) Authorize us to obtain records and other information;
      (3) Cooperate with us in the investigation or settlement of the claim or defense against the "suit"; and
      (4) Assist us, upon our request, in the enforcement of any right against any person or organization which may be liable to the insured because of injury or damage to which this insurance may also apply.
   d. No insured will, except at that insured's own cost, voluntarily make a payment, assume any obligation, or incur any expense, other than for first aid, without our consent.
3. **Legal Action Against Us**

   No person or organization has a right under this Coverage Part:
   a. To join us as a party or otherwise bring us into a "suit" asking for damages from an insured; or

b. To sue us on this Coverage Part unless all of its terms have been fully complied with.

A person or organization may sue us to recover on an agreed settlement or on a final judgment against an insured; but we will not be liable for damages that are not payable under the terms of this Coverage Part or that are in excess of the applicable limit of insurance. An agreed settlement means a settlement and release of liability signed by us, the insured and the claimant or the claimant's legal representative.

4. Other Insurance

If other valid and collectible insurance is available to the insured for a loss we cover under Coverages **A** or **B** of this Coverage Part, our obligations are limited as follows:

a. Primary Insurance

This insurance is primary except when **b.** below applies. If this insurance is primary, our obligations are not affected unless any of the other insurance is also primary. Then, we will share with all that other insurance by the method described in **c.** below.

b. Excess Insurance

This insurance is excess over:

(1) Any of the other insurance, whether primary, excess, contingent or on any other basis:

(a) That is Fire, Extended Coverage, Builder's Risk, Installation Risk or similar coverage for "your work";

(b) That is Fire insurance for premises rented to you or temporarily occupied by you with permission of the owner;

(c) That is insurance purchased by you to cover your liability as a tenant for "property damage" to premises rented to you or temporarily occupied by you with permission of the owner; or

(d) If the loss arises out of the maintenance or use of aircraft, "autos" or watercraft to the extent not subject to Exclusion g. of Section I – Coverage A – Bodily Injury And Property Damage Liability.

(2) Any other primary insurance available to you covering liability for damages arising out of the premises or operations, or the products and completed operations, for which you have been added as an additional insured by attachment of an endorsement.

When this insurance is excess, we will have no duty under Coverages **A** or **B** to defend the insured against any "suit" if any other insurer has a duty to defend the insured against that "suit". If no other insurer defends, we will undertake to do so, but we will be entitled to the insured's rights against all those other insurers.

When this insurance is excess over other insurance, we will pay only our share of the amount of the loss, if any, that exceeds the sum of:

(1) The total amount that all such other insurance would pay for the loss in the absence of this insurance; and

(2) The total of all deductible and self-insured amounts under all that other insurance.

We will share the remaining loss, if any, with any other insurance that is not described in this Excess Insurance provision and was not bought specifically to apply in excess of the Limits of Insurance shown in the Declarations of this Coverage Part.

c. Method Of Sharing

If all of the other insurance permits contribution by equal shares, we will follow this method also. Under this approach each insurer contributes equal amounts until it has paid its applicable limit of insurance or none of the loss remains, whichever comes first.

If any of the other insurance does not permit contribution by equal shares, we will contribute by limits. Under this method, each insurer's share is based on the ratio of its applicable limit of insurance to the total applicable limits of insurance of all insurers.

5. Premium Audit

a. We will compute all premiums for this Coverage Part in accordance with our rules and rates.

b. Premium shown in this Coverage Part as advance premium is a deposit premium only. At the close of each audit period we will compute the earned premium for that period and send notice to the first Named Insured. The due date for audit and retrospective premiums is the date shown as the due date on the bill. If the sum of the advance and audit premiums paid for the policy period is greater than the earned premium, we will return the excess to the first Named Insured.

c. The first Named Insured must keep records of the information we need for premium computation, and send us copies at such times as we may request.

6. Representations

By accepting this policy, you agree:

a. The statements in the Declarations are accurate and complete;

b. Those statements are based upon representations you made to us; and

c. We have issued this policy in reliance upon your representations.

7. Separation Of Insureds

Except with respect to the Limits of Insurance, and any rights or duties specifically assigned in this Coverage Part to the first Named Insured, this insurance applies:

a. As if each Named Insured were the only Named Insured; and

b. Separately to each insured against whom claim is made or "suit" is brought.

8. Transfer Of Rights Of Recovery Against Others To Us

If the insured has rights to recover all or part of any payment we have made under this Coverage Part, those rights are transferred to us. The insured must do nothing after loss to impair them. At our request, the insured will bring "suit" or transfer those rights to us and help us enforce them.

9. When We Do Not Renew

If we decide not to renew this Coverage Part, we will mail or deliver to the first Named Insured shown in the Declarations written notice of the nonrenewal not less than 30 days before the expiration date.

If notice is mailed, proof of mailing will be sufficient proof of notice.

SECTION V – DEFINITIONS

1. "Advertisement" means a notice that is broadcast or published to the general public or specific market segments about your goods, products or services for the purpose of attracting customers or supporters. For the purposes of this definition:

a. Notices that are published include material placed on the Internet or on similar electronic means of communication; and

b. Regarding web-sites, only that part of a web-site that is about your goods, products or services for the purposes of attracting customers or supporters is considered an advertisement.

2. "Auto" means:

a. A land motor vehicle, trailer or semitrailer designed for travel on public roads, including any attached machinery or equipment; or

b. Any other land vehicle that is subject to a compulsory or financial responsibility law or other motor vehicle insurance law in the state where it is licensed or principally garaged.

However, "auto" does not include "mobile equipment".

3. "Bodily injury" means bodily injury, sickness or disease sustained by a person, including death resulting from any of these at any time.

4. "Coverage territory" means:

a. The United States of America (including its territories and possessions), Puerto Rico and Canada;

b. International waters or airspace, but only if the injury or damage occurs in the course of travel or transportation between any places included in **a.** above; or

c. All other parts of the world if the injury or damage arises out of:

(1) Goods or products made or sold by you in the territory described in **a.** above;

(2) The activities of a person whose home is in the territory described in **a.** above, but is away for a short time on your business; or

(3) "Personal and advertising injury" offenses that take place through the Internet or similar electronic means of communication

provided the insured's responsibility to pay damages is determined in a "suit" on the merits, in the territory described in **a.** above or in a settlement we agree to.

5. "Employee" includes a "leased worker". "Employee" does not include a "temporary worker".

6. "Executive officer" means a person holding any of the officer positions created by your charter, constitution, by-laws or any other similar governing document.

7. "Hostile fire" means one which becomes uncontrollable or breaks out from where it was intended to be.

8. "Impaired property" means tangible property, other than "your product" or "your work", that cannot be used or is less useful because:

a. It incorporates "your product" or "your work" that is known or thought to be defective, deficient, inadequate or dangerous; or

b. You have failed to fulfill the terms of a contract or agreement;

if such property can be restored to use by:

a. The repair, replacement, adjustment or removal of "your product" or "your work"; or

b. Your fulfilling the terms of the contract or agreement.

9. "Insured contract" means:

a. A contract for a lease of premises. However, that portion of the contract for a lease of premises that indemnifies any person or organization for damage by fire to premises while rented to you or temporarily occupied by you with permission of the owner is not an "insured contract";

b. A sidetrack agreement;

c. Any easement or license agreement, except in connection with construction or demolition operations on or within 50 feet of a railroad;

d. An obligation, as required by ordinance, to indemnify a municipality, except in connection with work for a municipality;

e. An elevator maintenance agreement;

f. That part of any other contract or agreement pertaining to your business (including an indemnification of a municipality in connection with work performed for a municipality) under which you assume the tort liability of another party to pay for "bodily injury" or "property damage" to a third person or organization. Tort liability means a liability that would be imposed by law in the absence of any contract or agreement.

Paragraph f. does not include that part of any contract or agreement:

(1) That indemnifies a railroad for "bodily injury" or "property damage" arising out of construction or demolition operations, within 50 feet of any railroad property and affecting any railroad bridge or trestle, tracks, road-beds, tunnel, underpass or crossing;

(2) That indemnifies an architect, engineer or surveyor for injury or damage arising out of:

(a) Preparing, approving, or failing to prepare or approve, maps, shop drawings, opinions, reports, surveys, field orders, change orders or drawings and specifications; or

(b) Giving directions or instructions, or failing to give them, if that is the primary cause of the injury or damage; or

(3) Under which the insured, if an architect, engineer or surveyor, assumes liability for an injury or damage arising out of the insured's rendering or failure to render professional services, including those listed in **(2)** above and supervisory, inspection, architectural or engineering activities.

10. "Leased worker" means a person leased to you by a labor leasing firm under an agreement between you and the labor leasing firm, to perform duties related to the conduct of your business. "Leased worker" does not include a "temporary worker".

11. "Loading or unloading" means the handling of property:

a. After it is moved from the place where it is accepted for movement into or onto an aircraft, watercraft or "auto";

b. While it is in or on an aircraft, watercraft or "auto"; or

c. While it is being moved from an aircraft, watercraft or "auto" to the place where it is finally delivered;

but "loading or unloading" does not include the movement of property by means of a mechanical device, other than a hand truck, that is not attached to the aircraft, watercraft or "auto".

12. "Mobile equipment" means any of the following types of land vehicles, including any attached machinery or equipment:

a. Bulldozers, farm machinery, forklifts and other vehicles designed for use principally off public roads;

b. Vehicles maintained for use solely on or next to premises you own or rent;

c. Vehicles that travel on crawler treads;

d. Vehicles, whether self-propelled or not, maintained primarily to provide mobility to permanently mounted:

(1) Power cranes, shovels, loaders, diggers or drills; or

(2) Road construction or resurfacing equipment such as graders, scrapers or rollers;

e. Vehicles not described in **a., b., c.** or **d.** above that are not self-propelled and are maintained primarily to provide mobility to permanently attached equipment of the following types:

(1) Air compressors, pumps and generators, including spraying, welding, building cleaning, geophysical exploration, lighting and well servicing equipment; or

(2) Cherry pickers and similar devices used to raise or lower workers;

f. Vehicles not described in **a., b., c.** or **d.** above maintained primarily for purposes other than the transportation of persons or cargo.

However, self-propelled vehicles with the following types of permanently attached equipment are not "mobile equipment" but will be considered "autos":

(1) Equipment designed primarily for:

(a) Snow removal;

(b) Road maintenance, but not construction or resurfacing; or

(c) Street cleaning;

(2) Cherry pickers and similar devices mounted on automobile or truck chassis and used to raise or lower workers; and

(3) Air compressors, pumps and generators, including spraying, welding, building cleaning, geophysical exploration, lighting and well servicing equipment.

However, "mobile equipment" does not include any land vehicles that are subject to a compulsory or financial responsibility law or other motor vehicle insurance law in the state where it is licensed or principally garaged. Land vehicles subject to a compulsory or financial responsibility law or other motor vehicle insurance law are considered "autos".

13. "Occurrence" means an accident, including continuous or repeated exposure to substantially the same general harmful conditions.

14. "Personal and advertising injury" means injury, including consequential "bodily injury", arising out of one or more of the following offenses:

a. False arrest, detention or imprisonment;

b. Malicious prosecution;

c. The wrongful eviction from, wrongful entry into, or invasion of the right of private occupancy of a room, dwelling or premises that a person occupies, committed by or on behalf of its owner, landlord or lessor;

d. Oral or written publication, in any manner, of material that slanders or libels a person or organization or disparages a person's or organization's goods, products or services;

e. Oral or written publication, in any manner, of material that violates a person's right of privacy;

f. The use of another's advertising idea in your "advertisement"; or

g. Infringing upon another's copyright, trade dress or slogan in your "advertisement".

15. "Pollutants" mean any solid, liquid, gaseous or thermal irritant or contaminant, including smoke, vapor, soot, fumes, acids, alkalis, chemicals and waste. Waste includes materials to be recycled, reconditioned or reclaimed.

16. "Products-completed operations hazard":

a. Includes all "bodily injury" and "property damage" occurring away from premises you own or rent and arising out of "your product" or "your work" except:

(1) Products that are still in your physical possession; or

(2) Work that has not yet been completed or abandoned. However, "your work" will be deemed completed at the earliest of the following times:

(a) When all of the work called for in your contract has been completed.

(b) When all of the work to be done at the job site has been completed if your contract calls for work at more than one job site.

(c) When that part of the work done at a job site has been put to its intended use by any person or organization other than another contractor or subcontractor working on the same project.

Work that may need service, maintenance, correction, repair or replacement, but which is otherwise complete, will be treated as completed.

b. Does not include "bodily injury" or "property damage" arising out of:

(1) The transportation of property, unless the injury or damage arises out of a condition in or on a vehicle not owned or operated by you, and that condition was created by the "loading or unloading" of that vehicle by any insured;

(2) The existence of tools, uninstalled equipment or abandoned or unused materials; or

(3) Products or operations for which the classification, listed in the Declarations or in a policy schedule, states that products-completed operations are subject to the General Aggregate Limit.

17. "Property damage" means:

a. Physical injury to tangible property, including all resulting loss of use of that property. All such loss of use shall be deemed to occur at the time of the physical injury that caused it; or

b. Loss of use of tangible property that is not physically injured. All such loss of use shall be deemed to occur at the time of the "occurrence" that caused it.

For the purposes of this insurance, electronic data is not tangible property.

As used in this definition, electronic data means information, facts or programs stored as or on, created or used on, or transmitted to or from computer software, including systems and applications software, hard or floppy disks, CD-ROMS, tapes, drives, cells, data processing devices or any other media which are used with electronically controlled equipment.

18. "Suit" means a civil proceeding in which damages because of "bodily injury", "property damage" or "personal and advertising injury" to which this insurance applies are alleged. "Suit" includes:

a. An arbitration proceeding in which such damages are claimed and to which the insured must submit or does submit with our consent; or

b. Any other alternative dispute resolution proceeding in which such damages are claimed and to which the insured submits with our consent.

19. "Temporary worker" means a person who is furnished to you to substitute for a permanent "employee" on leave or to meet seasonal or short-term workload conditions.

20. "Volunteer worker" means a person who is not your "employee", and who donates his or her work and acts at the direction of and within the scope of duties determined by you, and is not paid a fee, salary or other compensation by you or anyone else for their work performed for you.

21. "Your product":

a. Means:

(1) Any goods or products, other than real property, manufactured, sold, handled, distributed or disposed of by:

(a) You;

(b) Others trading under your name; or

(c) A person or organization whose business or assets you have acquired; and

(2) Containers (other than vehicles), materials, parts or equipment furnished in connection with such goods or products.

b. Includes

(1) Warranties or representations made at any time with respect to the fitness, quality, durability, performance or use of "your product"; and

(2) The providing of or failure to provide warnings or instructions.

c. Does not include vending machines or other property rented to or located for the use of others but not sold.

22. "Your work":

a. Means:

(1) Work or operations performed by you or on your behalf; and

(2) Materials, parts or equipment furnished in connection with such work or operations.

b. Includes

(1) Warranties or representations made at any time with respect to the fitness, quality, durability, performance or use of "your work", and

(2) The providing of or failure to provide warnings or instructions.

EMPLOYMENT-RELATED PRACTICES LIABILITY COVERAGE FORM

EMPLOYMENT-RELATED PRACTICES LIABILITY COVERAGE FORM

Various provisions in this policy restrict coverage. Read the entire policy carefully to determine rights, duties and what is and is not covered.

Throughout this policy the words "you" and "your" refer to the Named Insured shown in the Declarations, and any other person or organization qualifying as a Named Insured under this policy. The words "we", "us" and "our" refer to the company providing this insurance.

The word "insured" means any person or organization qualifying as such under Section II – Who Is An Insured.

Other words and phrases that appear in quotation marks have special meaning. Refer to Section VII – Definitions.

SECTION I – EMPLOYMENT-RELATED PRACTICES LIABILITY COVERAGE

A. Insuring Agreement

1. We will pay those sums the insured becomes legally obligated to pay as damages resulting from an "injury" to which this insurance applies. We will have the right and duty to defend the insured against any "suit" seeking those damages. However, we will have no duty to defend the insured against any "suit" seeking damages because of an "injury" to which this insurance does not apply. We may, at our discretion, investigate any incident that may result in "injury". We may, with your written consent, settle any "claim" that may result. But:
   a. The amount we will pay for damages and "defense expenses" is limited as described in Section III – Limit Of Insurance and in Section IV – Deductible;
   b. The coverage and duty to defend provided by this policy will end when we have used up the applicable limit of insurance for "defense expenses" or the payment of judgments or settlements.

   No other obligation or liability to pay sums, such as civil or criminal fines, imposed on you or any other insured, or to perform acts or services is covered unless explicitly provided for under Supplementary Payments.

2. This insurance applies to "injury" only if:
   a. The "injury" arises out of an offense that takes place in the "coverage territory";
   b. The offense out of which the "injury" arose did not commence before the Retroactive Date, if any, shown in the Declarations or after the end of the policy period; and
   c. A "claim" because of the "injury" is first made against any insured, in accordance with Paragraph 3. below, during the policy period or the Section VI – Extended Reporting Period, if provided.

3. A "claim" will be deemed to have been made at the earlier of the following times:
   a. When notice of such "claim" is received by any insured and reported to us in writing; or
   b. When a "claim" against an insured is made directly to us in writing.

   A "claim" received by the insured during the policy period and reported to us within 30 days after the end of the policy period will be considered to have been reported within the policy period. However, this 30 day grace period does not apply to "claims" that are covered under any subsequent insurance you purchase, or that would be covered but for exhaustion of the amount of insurance applicable to such "claims".

4. All "claims" arising out of an "injury" to the same person, including damages claimed by any person for care, loss of services or death resulting at any time from the "injury", will be deemed to have been made at the time the first of such "claims" is made, regardless of the number of "claims" subsequently made.

B. Exclusions

This insurance does not apply to:

1. **Criminal, Fraudulent Or Malicious Acts**

   An insured's liability arising out of criminal, fraudulent or malicious acts or omissions by that insured.

This exclusion does not affect our duty to defend, in accordance with Paragraph **A.1.** above, an insured prior to determining, through the appropriate legal processes, that that insured is responsible for a criminal, fraudulent or malicious act or omission.

2. Contractual Liability

"Injury" for which the insured is obligated to pay damages by reason of the assumption of liability in a contract or agreement. This exclusion does not apply to liability for damages that the insured would have in the absence of the contract or agreement.

3. Workers Compensation And Similar Laws

Any obligation of the insured under a workers compensation, disability benefits or unemployment compensation law or any similar law.

4. Violation Of Laws Applicable To Employers

A violation of your responsibilities or duties required by any other federal, state or local statutes, rules or regulations, and any rules or regulations promulgated therefor or amendments thereto, except for the following: Title VII of the Civil Rights Act of 1964 and amendments thereto, the Americans With Disabilities Act, the Age Discrimination in Employment Act, the Equal Pay Act, the Pregnancy Discrimination Act of 1978, the Immigration Reform Control Act of 1986 and the Family and Medical Leave Act of 1993 or any other similar state or local statutes, rules or regulations to the extent that they prescribe responsibilities or duties concerning the same acts or omissions.

However, this insurance does not apply to "injury" arising out of your failure to comply with any of the accommodations for the disabled required of you by, or any expenses incurred as the result of physical modifications made to accommodate any person pursuant to, the Americans With Disabilities Act, or any amendments thereto, or any similar state or local statutes, rules or regulations to the extent that they prescribe responsibilities or duties concerning the same acts or omissions.

This Exclusion **4.** does not apply to any "claim" for retaliatory treatment by an insured against any person making a "claim" pursuant to such person's rights under any statutes, rules or regulations.

5. Strikes And Lockouts

"Injury" to any striking or locked-out "employee", or to an "employee" who has been temporarily or permanently replaced due to any labor dispute.

C. Supplementary Payments

We will pay, with respect to any "claim" we investigate or settle, or any "suit" against an insured we defend:

1. Prejudgment interest awarded against the insured on that part of the judgment we pay. If we make an offer to pay the applicable limit of insurance, we will not pay any prejudgment interest based on that period of time after the offer.
2. All interest on the full amount of any judgment that accrues after entry of the judgment and before we have paid, offered to pay, or deposited in court the part of the judgment that is within the applicable limit of insurance.

These payments will not reduce the limit of insurance nor be subject to Section IV – Deductible.

SECTION II – WHO IS AN INSURED

A. If you are designated in the Declarations as:

1. An individual, you and your spouse are insureds.
2. A partnership or joint venture, you are an insured. Your partners or members are also insureds.
3. A limited liability company, you are an insured. Your members and managers are also insureds.
4. An organization other than a partnership, joint venture or limited liability company, you are an insured. Your "executive officers" and directors are also insureds.

B. Your "employees" are also insureds, unless otherwise excluded in this policy.

C. Your former "employees" are also insureds, unless otherwise excluded in this policy, but only with respect to offenses committed while in your employ.

D. Any organization you newly acquire or form, other than a partnership, joint venture or limited liability company, and over which you maintain ownership or majority interest, will qualify as a Named Insured if no other similar insurance applies to that organization. You must notify us of such acquisition or formation as soon as practicable. However, coverage under this provision:

1. Is afforded only until the 90th day after you acquire or form the organization, or until the end of the policy period, whichever is earlier; and

2. Does not apply to an offense committed before you acquired or formed the organization.

No person or organization is an insured with respect to the conduct of any current or past partnership, joint venture or limited liability company that is not shown as a Named Insured in the Declarations.

SECTION III – LIMIT OF INSURANCE

A. The Limit of Insurance shown in the Declarations and the rules below fix the most we will pay regardless of the number of:
   1. Insureds;
   2. "Claims" made or "suits" brought; or
   3. Persons, organizations or government agencies making "claims" or bringing "suits".

B. The Limit of Insurance is the most we will pay for the sum of:
   1. All damages; and
   2. All "defense expenses"

   because of the total of all "claims" first made against an insured during the policy period.

The Limit of Insurance of this Coverage Part applies separately to each consecutive annual period and to any remaining period of less than 12 months, starting with the beginning of the policy period shown in the Declarations, unless the policy period is extended after issuance for an additional period of less than 12 months. In that case, the additional period will be deemed part of the last preceding period for purposes of determining the Limit of Insurance.

SECTION IV – DEDUCTIBLE

A. We will not pay for our share of damages and "defense expenses" until the amount of damages and "defense expenses" exceeds the Deductible shown in the Declarations. We will then pay the amount of damages and "defense expenses" in excess of the Deductible, up to the limit of insurance.

   Example No. 1

   Deductible: $5,000

   Limit of Insurance: $100,000

   Damages and "Defense Expenses": $75,000

   The Deductible will be subtracted from the amount of damages and "defense expenses" in calculating the amount payable:

   $75,000 - $5,000 = $70,000 Amount Payable

   Example No. 2

   Deductible: $5,000

   Limit of Insurance: $100,000

   Damages and "Defense Expenses": $120,000

   The Deductible will be subtracted from the amount of damages and "defense expenses" ($120,000 - $5,000 = $115,000). Since the amount of the damages and "defense expenses" minus the Deductible exceeds the Limit of Insurance, the policy will pay the full Limit of Insurance ($100,000).

B. The Deductible amount shown in the Declarations applies to all "claims" arising out of:
   1. The same "injury"; or
   2. A series of incidents, circumstances or behaviors which arise from a common cause

   regardless of the number of persons, organizations or government agencies making such "claims".

C. We may pay any part or all of the deductible amount to effect settlement of any "claim" and, upon notification of the action taken, you shall promptly reimburse us for such part of the deductible amount as has been paid by us.

SECTION V – CONDITIONS

A. Bankruptcy

Bankruptcy or insolvency of the insured or of the insured's estate will not relieve us of our obligations under this policy.

B. Consent To Settle

If we recommend a settlement to you which is acceptable to the claimant, but to which you do not consent, the most we will pay as damages in the event of any later settlement or judgment is the amount for which the "claim" could have been settled, to which you did not give consent, less any deductible

C. Duties In The Event Of A "Claim" Or An Incident That May Result In "Injury"

1. If a "claim" is received by any insured, you must:
   a. Immediately record the specifics of the "claim" and the date received; and
   b. Notify us, in writing, as soon as practicable.
2. You and any other involved insured must:
   a. Immediately send us copies of any demands, notices, summonses or legal papers received in connection with the "claim";

b. Authorize us to obtain records and other information; and

c. Cooperate with us in the investigation or settlement of the "claim" or defense against the "suit".

d. Assist us, upon our request, in the enforcement of any right against any person or organization which may be liable to the insured because of "injury" or damage to which this insurance may also apply.

3. No insured will, except at that insured's own cost, voluntarily make a payment, assume any obligation, or incur any expense without our written consent.

4. If you have knowledge of an incident which may result in "injury" and for which a "claim" has not yet been received, you must notify us, in writing, as soon as practicable. Notice of an incident is not notice of a "claim".

D. Legal Action Against Us

No person or organization has a right under this policy:

1. To join us as a party or otherwise bring us into a "suit" asking for damages from an insured; or
2. To sue us on this policy unless all of its terms have been fully complied with.

A person or organization may sue us to recover on an agreed settlement or on a final judgment against an insured obtained after an actual trial; but we will not be liable for damages that are not payable under the terms of this policy or that are in excess of the applicable limit of insurance. An agreed settlement means a settlement and release of liability signed by us, the insured and the claimant or the claimant's legal representative.

We will also not be liable for the insured's share of any payment due because of a settlement or judgment for which the insured is responsible under Section IV – Deductible.

E. Other Insurance

If other valid and collectible insurance is available to the insured, our obligations are limited as follows:

1. **Primary Insurance**

This insurance is primary. We will not seek contribution from any other insurance available to you or the involved insured unless the other insurance is specifically designed to provide coverage because of liability arising out of an "injury". Then we will share with that other insurance by the method described below.

2. **Method Of Sharing**

If all of the other insurance permits contribution by equal shares, we will follow this method also. Under this approach each insurer contributes equal amounts until it has paid its applicable limit of insurance or none of the loss remains, whichever comes first.

If any of the other insurance does not permit contribution by equal shares, we will contribute by limits. Under this method, each insurer's share is based on the ratio of its applicable limit of insurance to the total applicable limits of insurance of all insurers.

The method chosen for the handling of other valid insurance will not affect your responsibility to share with us as specified under Section IV – Deductible.

F. Premium Audit

1. We will compute all premiums for this policy in accordance with our rules and rates.
2. Premium shown in this policy as advance premium is a deposit premium only. At the close of each audit period we will compute the earned premium for that period and send notice to the first Named Insured. The due date for audit and retrospective premiums is the date shown as the due date on the bill. If the sum of the advance and audit premiums paid for the policy period is greater than the earned premium, we will return the excess to the first Named Insured.
3. The first Named Insured must keep records of the information we need for premium computation, and send us copies at such times as we may request.
4. We will waive the premium audit only with your consent.

G. Representations

By accepting this policy, you agree that:

1. The statements in the Declarations are accurate and complete;
2. Those statements are based upon representations you made to us; and
3. We have issued this policy in reliance upon your representations.

H. Separation Of Insureds

Except with respect to the Limit of Insurance, and any rights or duties specifically assigned in this policy to the first Named Insured, this insurance applies:

1. As if each Named Insured were the only Named Insured; and
2. Separately to each insured against whom "claim" is made.

I. Transfer Of Rights Of Recovery Against Others To Us

If the insured has rights to recover all or part of any payment we have made under this policy, those rights are transferred to us. The insured must do nothing after loss to impair them. At our request, the insured will bring "suit" or transfer those rights to us and help us enforce them.

J. If You Are Permitted To Select Defense Counsel

If, by mutual agreement or court order, the insured is given the right to select defense counsel and the Limit of Insurance has not been used up, the following provisions apply:

1. We retain the right, at our discretion, to:
   a. Settle, approve or disapprove the settlement of any "claim"; and
   b. Appeal any judgment, award or ruling at our expense.
2. You and any other involved insured must:
   a. Continue to comply with Section V – Paragraph **C.**, Duties In The Event Of A "Claim" Or An Incident That May Result In "Injury" Condition as well as the other provisions of this policy; and
   b. Direct defense counsel of the insured to:
      (1) Furnish us with the information we may request to evaluate those "suits" for coverage under this policy; and
      (2) Cooperate with any counsel we may select to monitor or associate in the defense of those "suits".
3. If we defend you under a reservation of rights, both your and our counsel will be required to maintain records pertinent to your "defense expenses". These records will be used to determine the allocation of any "defense expenses" for which you may be solely responsible, including defense of an allegation not covered by this insurance.

K. Transfer Of Duties When Limit Of Insurance Is Used Up

1. If we conclude that, based on "claims" which have been reported to us and to which this insurance may apply, the limit of insurance is likely to be used up in the payment of judgments or settlements for damages or the payment of "defense expenses", we will notify the first Named Insured, in writing, to that effect.
2. When the limit of insurance has actually been used up in the payment of judgments or settlements for damages or the payment of "defense expenses", we will:
   a. Notify the first Named Insured in writing, as soon as practicable, that such a limit has actually been used up and that our duty to defend the insured against "suits" seeking damages subject to that limit has also ended;
   b. Initiate, and cooperate in, the transfer of control, to any appropriate insured, of all "suits" for which the duty to defend has ended for the reason described in Paragraph **2.a.** above and which are reported to us before that duty to defend ended; and
   c. Take such steps, as we deem appropriate, to avoid a default in, or continue the defense of, such "suits" until such transfer is completed, provided the appropriate insured is cooperating in completing such transfer.
3. When **2.a.** above has occurred, the first Named Insured, and any other insured involved in a "suit" seeking damages subject to that limit, must:
   a. Cooperate in the transfer of control of "suits"; and
   b. Arrange for the defense of such "suit" within such time period as agreed to between the appropriate insured and us. Absent any such agreement, arrangements for the defense of such "suit" must be made as soon as practicable.
4. We will take no action with respect to defense for any "claim" if such "claim" is reported to us after the applicable limit of insurance has been used up. It becomes the responsibility of the first Named Insured, and any other insured involved in such a "claim", to arrange defense for such "claim".
5. The first Named Insured will reimburse us as soon as practicable for expenses we incur in taking those steps we deem appropriate in accordance with Paragraph **2.** above.
6. The exhaustion of the applicable limit of insurance and the resulting end of our duty to defend will not be affected by our failure to comply with any of the provisions of this Condition.

L. When We Do Not Renew

If we decide not to renew this policy, we will mail or deliver to the first Named Insured shown in the Declarations written notice of the nonrenewal at least 30 days before the end of the policy period, or earlier if required by the state law or regulation controlling the application of this Coverage Part.

If notice is mailed, proof of mailing will be sufficient proof of notice.

SECTION VI – EXTENDED REPORTING PERIOD

A. You will have the right to purchase an Extended Reporting Period from us if:

1. This Coverage Part is cancelled or not renewed for any reason; or
2. We renew or replace this Coverage Part with insurance that:
   a. Has a Retroactive Date later than the date shown in the Declarations of this Coverage Part; or
   b. Does not apply to "injury" on a claims-made basis.

B. An Extended Reporting Period, as specified in Paragraph **A.** above, lasts three years and is available only by endorsement and for an additional charge.

C. The Extended Reporting Period starts with the end of the policy period. It does not extend the policy period or change the scope of coverage provided. It applies only to "claims" to which the following applies:

1. The "claim" is first made during the Extended Reporting Period;
2. The "injury" occurs before the end of the policy period; and
3. The offense out of which the "injury" arose did not commence before the Retroactive Date, if any.

D. You must give us a written request for the Extended Reporting Period Endorsement within thirty (30) days after the end of the policy period or the effective date of cancellation, whichever comes first.

E. The Extended Reporting Period will not go into effect unless you pay the additional premium promptly when due and any premium or deductible you owe us for coverage provided under this policy. Once in effect, the Extended Reporting Period may not be cancelled.

F. We will determine the additional premium in accordance with our rules and rates. In doing so, we may take into account the following:

1. The exposures insured;
2. Previous types and amounts of insurance;
3. Limit of Insurance available under this policy for future payment of damages; and
4. Other related factors.

The additional premium will not exceed 200% of the annual premium for this policy.

G. When the Extended Reporting Period Endorsement is in effect, we will provide a Supplemental Limit of Insurance for any "claim" first made during the Extended Reporting Period.

The Supplemental Limit of Insurance will be equal to the dollar amount shown in the Declarations in effect at the end of the policy period.

Paragraph **B.** of Section **III** – Limit Of Insurance will be amended accordingly.

SECTION VII – DEFINITIONS

A. "Claim" means a "suit" or demand made by or for the injured person for damages because of alleged "injury".

B. "Coverage territory" means:

1. The United States of America (including its territories or possessions) and Puerto Rico; or
2. All parts of the world if the insured's responsibility to pay damages is determined in a "suit" on the merits brought in the territory described in Paragraph **1.** above or in a settlement we agree to.

C. "Defense expenses" means payments allocated to a specific "claim" we investigate, settle or defend, for its investigation, settlement or defense, including:

1. Fees and salaries of attorneys and paralegals we retain, including attorneys and paralegals who are our "employees".
2. Fees of attorneys the insured retains when, by our mutual agreement or court order (or when required by administrative hearing or proceeding), the insured is given the right to retain defense counsel to defend against a "claim".
3. All other litigation or administrative hearing expenses, including fees or expenses of expert witnesses hired either by us or by the defense attorney retained by an insured.

4. Reasonable expenses incurred by the insured at our request to assist us in the investigation or defense of the "claim", including actual loss of earnings up to $250 a day because of time off from work.

5. Costs taxed against the insured in the "suit".

"Defense expenses" does not include salaries and expenses of our "employees" or the insured's "employees" (other than those described in Paragraphs 1. and 4. above).

D. "Discrimination" means violation of a person's civil rights with respect to such person's race, color, national origin, religion, gender, marital status, age, sexual orientation or preference, physical or mental condition, or any other protected class or characteristic established by any federal, state or local statutes, rules or regulations.

E. "Employee" includes a "leased worker" and a "temporary worker" but does not include an independent contractor.

F. "Executive officer" means a person holding any of the officer positions created by your charter, constitution, by-laws or any other similar governing document.

G. "Injury" means injury to your "employee" arising out of one or more of the following offenses:

1. Demotion or failure to promote, negative evaluation, reassignment or discipline of your current "employee" or wrongful refusal to employ;

2. Wrongful termination, meaning the actual or constructive termination of an "employee":

   a. In violation or breach of applicable law or public policy; or

   b. Which is determined to be in violation of a contract or agreement, other than any employment contract or agreement, whether written, oral or implied, which stipulates financial consideration if such financial consideration is due as the result of a breach of the contract;

3. Wrongful denial of training, wrongful deprivation of career opportunity, or breach of employment contract;

4. Negligent hiring or supervision which results in any of the other offenses listed in this definition;

5. Retaliatory action against an "employee" because the "employee" has:

   a. Declined to perform an illegal or unethical act;

   b. Filed a complaint with a governmental authority or a "suit" against you or any other insured in which damages are claimed;

   c. Testified against you or any other insured at a legal proceeding; or

   d. Notified a proper authority of any aspect of your business operation which is illegal;

6. Coercing an "employee" to commit an unlawful act or omission within the scope of that person's employment;

7. Work-related harassment;

8. Employment-related libel, slander, invasion of privacy, defamation or humiliation; or

9. Other work-related verbal, physical, mental or emotional abuse arising from "discrimination".

H. "Leased worker" means a person leased to you by a labor leasing firm under an agreement between you and the labor leasing firm, to perform duties related to the conduct of your business. "Leased worker" does not include a "temporary worker".

I. "Suit" means a civil proceeding in which damages because of "injury" to which this insurance applies are alleged, including:

1. An arbitration proceeding in which such damages are claimed and to which the insured must submit or does submit with our consent;

2. Any other alternative dispute resolution proceeding in which such damages are claimed and to which the insured submits with our consent; or

3. Any administrative proceeding or hearing conducted by a governmental agency (federal, state or local) having the proper legal authority over the matter in which such damages are claimed.

J. "Temporary worker" means a person who is furnished to you to substitute for a permanent "employee" on leave or to meet seasonal or short-term workload conditions.

PERSONAL AUTO POLICY

PERSONAL AUTO POLICY

AGREEMENT

In return for payment of the premium and subject to all the terms of this policy, we agree with you as follows:

DEFINITIONS

A. Throughout this policy, "you" and "your" refer to:

1. The "named insured" shown in the Declarations; and

2. The spouse if a resident of the same household.

If the spouse ceases to be a resident of the same household during the policy period or prior to the inception of this policy, the spouse will be considered "you" and "your" under this policy but only until the earlier of:

1. The end of 90 days following the spouse's change of residency;

2. The effective date of another policy listing the spouse as a named insured; or

3. The end of the policy period.

B. "We", "us" and "our" refer to the Company providing this insurance.

C. For purposes of this policy, a private passenger type auto, pickup or van shall be deemed to be owned by a person if leased:

1. Under a written agreement to that person; and

2. For a continuous period of at least 6 months.

Other words and phrases are defined. They are in quotation marks when used.

D. "Bodily injury" means bodily harm, sickness or disease, including death that results.

E. "Business" includes trade, profession or occupation.

F. "Family member" means a person related to you by blood, marriage or adoption who is a resident of your household. This includes a ward or foster child.

G. "Occupying" means:

1. In;

2. Upon; or

3. Getting in, on, out or off.

H. "Property damage" means physical injury to, destruction of or loss of use of tangible property.

I. "Trailer" means a vehicle designed to be pulled by a:

1. Private passenger auto; or

2. Pickup or van.

It also means a farm wagon or farm implement while towed by a vehicle listed in **1.** or **2.** above.

J. "Your covered auto" means:

1. Any vehicle shown in the Declarations.

2. A "newly acquired auto".

3. Any "trailer" you own.

4. Any auto or "trailer" you do not own while used as a temporary substitute for any other vehicle described in this definition which is out of normal use because of its:

a. Breakdown;

b. Repair;

c. Servicing;

d. Loss; or

e. Destruction.

This Provision (**J.4.**) does not apply to Coverage For Damage To Your Auto.

K. "Newly acquired auto":

1. "Newly acquired auto" means any of the following types of vehicles you become the owner of during the policy period:

a. A private passenger auto; or

b. A pickup or van, for which no other insurance policy provides coverage, that:

(1) Has a Gross Vehicle Weight Rating of 10,000 lbs. or less; and

(2) Is not used for the delivery or transportation of goods and materials unless such use is:

(a) Incidental to your "business" of installing, maintaining or repairing furnishings or equipment; or

(b) For farming or ranching.

2. Coverage for a "newly acquired auto" is provided as described below. If you ask us to insure a "newly acquired auto" after a specified time period described below has elapsed, any coverage we provide for a "newly acquired auto" will begin at the time you request the coverage.

a. For any coverage provided in this policy except Coverage For Damage To Your Auto, a "newly acquired auto" will have the broadest coverage we now provide for any vehicle shown in the Declarations. Coverage begins on the date you become the owner. However, for this coverage to apply to a "newly acquired auto" which is in addition to any vehicle shown in the Declarations, you must ask us to insure it within 14 days after you become the owner.

If a "newly acquired auto" replaces a vehicle shown in the Declarations, coverage is provided for this vehicle without your having to ask us to insure it.

b. Collision Coverage for a "newly acquired auto" begins on the date you become the owner. However, for this coverage to apply, you must ask us to insure it within:

(1) 14 days after you become the owner if the Declarations indicate that Collision Coverage applies to at least one auto. In this case, the "newly acquired auto" will have the broadest coverage we now provide for any auto shown in the Declarations.

(2) Four days after you become the owner if the Declarations do not indicate that Collision Coverage applies to at least one auto. If you comply with the 4 day requirement and a loss occurred before you asked us to insure the "newly acquired auto", a Collision deductible of $500 will apply.

c. Other Than Collision Coverage for a "newly acquired auto" begins on the date you become the owner. However, for this coverage to apply, you must ask us to insure it within:

(1) 14 days after you become the owner if the Declarations indicate that Other Than Collision Coverage applies to at least one auto. In this case, the "newly acquired auto" will have the broadest coverage we now provide for any auto shown in the Declarations.

(2) Four days after you become the owner if the Declarations do not indicate that Other Than Collision Coverage applies to at least one auto. If you comply with the 4 day requirement and a loss occurred before you asked us to insure the "newly acquired auto", an Other Than Collision deductible of $500 will apply.

PART A – LIABILITY COVERAGE

INSURING AGREEMENT

A. We will pay damages for "bodily injury" or "property damage" for which any "insured" becomes legally responsible because of an auto accident. Damages include prejudgment interest awarded against the "insured". We will settle or defend, as we consider appropriate, any claim or suit asking for these damages. In addition to our limit of liability, we will pay all defense costs we incur. Our duty to settle or defend ends when our limit of liability for this coverage has been exhausted by payment of judgments or settlements. We have no duty to defend any suit or settle any claim for "bodily injury" or "property damage" not covered under this policy.

B. "Insured" as used in this Part means:

1. You or any "family member" for the ownership, maintenance or use of any auto or "trailer".
2. Any person using "your covered auto".
3. For "your covered auto", any person or organization but only with respect to legal responsibility for acts or omissions of a person for whom coverage is afforded under this Part.
4. For any auto or "trailer", other than "your covered auto", any other person or organization but only with respect to legal responsibility for acts or omissions of you or any "family member" for whom coverage is afforded under this Part. This Provision (**B.4.**) applies only if the person or organization does not own or hire the auto or "trailer".

SUPPLEMENTARY PAYMENTS

We will pay on behalf of an "insured":

1. Up to $250 for the cost of bail bonds required because of an accident, including related traffic law violations. The accident must result in "bodily injury" or "property damage" covered under this policy.
2. Premiums on appeal bonds and bonds to release attachments in any suit we defend.
3. Interest accruing after a judgment is entered in any suit we defend. Our duty to pay interest ends when we offer to pay that part of the judgment which does not exceed our limit of liability for this coverage.

4. Up to $200 a day for loss of earnings, but not other income, because of attendance at hearings or trials at our request.
5. Other reasonable expenses incurred at our request.

These payments will not reduce the limit of liability.

EXCLUSIONS

A. We do not provide Liability Coverage for any "insured":

1. Who intentionally causes "bodily injury" or "property damage".
2. For "property damage" to property owned or being transported by that "insured".
3. For "property damage" to property:
   a. Rented to;
   b. Used by; or
   c. In the care of;

   that "insured".

   This Exclusion (A.3.) does not apply to "property damage" to a residence or private garage.
4. For "bodily injury" to an employee of that "insured" during the course of employment. This Exclusion (A.4.) does not apply to "bodily injury" to a domestic employee unless workers' compensation benefits are required or available for that domestic employee.
5. For that "insured's" liability arising out of the ownership or operation of a vehicle while it is being used as a public or livery conveyance. This Exclusion (A.5.) does not apply to a share-the-expense car pool.
6. While employed or otherwise engaged in the "business" of:
   a. Selling;
   b. Repairing;
   c. Servicing;
   d. Storing; or
   e. Parking;

   vehicles designed for use mainly on public highways. This includes road testing and delivery. This Exclusion (A.6.) does not apply to the ownership, maintenance or use of "your covered auto" by:
   a. You;
   b. Any "family member"; or
   c. Any partner, agent or employee of you or any "family member".
7. Maintaining or using any vehicle while that "insured" is employed or otherwise engaged in any "business" (other than farming or ranching) not described in Exclusion A.6.

   This Exclusion (A.7.) does not apply to the maintenance or use of a:
   a. Private passenger auto;
   b. Pickup or van; or
   c. "Trailer" used with a vehicle described in a. or b. above.
8. Using a vehicle without a reasonable belief that that "insured" is entitled to do so. This Exclusion (A.8.) does not apply to a "family member" using "your covered auto" which is owned by you.
9. For "bodily injury" or "property damage" for which that "insured":
   a. Is an insured under a nuclear energy liability policy; or
   b. Would be an insured under a nuclear energy liability policy but for its termination upon exhaustion of its limit of liability.

   A nuclear energy liability policy is a policy issued by any of the following or their successors:
   a. Nuclear Energy Liability Insurance Association;
   b. Mutual Atomic Energy Liability Underwriters; or
   c. Nuclear Insurance Association of Canada.

B. We do not provide Liability Coverage for the ownership, maintenance or use of:

1. Any vehicle which:
   a. Has fewer than four wheels; or
   b. Is designed mainly for use off public roads.

   This Exclusion (B.1.) does not apply:
   a. While such vehicle is being used by an "insured" in a medical emergency;
   b. To any "trailer"; or
   c. To any non-owned golf cart.
2. Any vehicle, other than "your covered auto", which is:
   a. Owned by you; or
   b. Furnished or available for your regular use.
3. Any vehicle, other than "your covered auto", which is:
   a. Owned by any "family member"; or
   b. Furnished or available for the regular use of any "family member".

However, this Exclusion (**B.3.**) does not apply to you while you are maintaining or "occupying" any vehicle which is:

a. Owned by a "family member"; or

b. Furnished or available for the regular use of a "family member".

4. Any vehicle, located inside a facility designed for racing, for the purpose of:

a. Competing in; or

b. Practicing or preparing for;

any prearranged or organized racing or speed contest.

LIMIT OF LIABILITY

A. The limit of liability shown in the Declarations for each person for Bodily Injury Liability is our maximum limit of liability for all damages, including damages for care, loss of services or death, arising out of "bodily injury" sustained by any one person in any one auto accident. Subject to this limit for each person, the limit of liability shown in the Declarations for each accident for Bodily Injury Liability is our maximum limit of liability for all damages for "bodily injury" resulting from any one auto accident.

The limit of liability shown in the Declarations for each accident for Property Damage Liability is our maximum limit of liability for all "property damage" resulting from any one auto accident.

This is the most we will pay regardless of the number of:

1. "Insureds";

2. Claims made;

3. Vehicles or premiums shown in the Declarations; or

4. Vehicles involved in the auto accident.

B. No one will be entitled to receive duplicate payments for the same elements of loss under this coverage and:

1. Part B or Part C of this policy; or

2. Any Underinsured Motorists Coverage provided by this policy.

OUT OF STATE COVERAGE

If an auto accident to which this policy applies occurs in any state or province other than the one in which "your covered auto" is principally garaged, we will interpret your policy for that accident as follows:

A. If the state or province has:

1. A financial responsibility or similar law specifying limits of liability for "bodily injury" or "property damage" higher than the limit shown in the Declarations, your policy will provide the higher specified limit.

2. A compulsory insurance or similar law requiring a nonresident to maintain insurance whenever the nonresident uses a vehicle in that state or province, your policy will provide at least the required minimum amounts and types of coverage.

B. No one will be entitled to duplicate payments for the same elements of loss.

FINANCIAL RESPONSIBILITY

When this policy is certified as future proof of financial responsibility, this policy shall comply with the law to the extent required.

OTHER INSURANCE

If there is other applicable liability insurance we will pay only our share of the loss. Our share is the proportion that our limit of liability bears to the total of all applicable limits. However, any insurance we provide for a vehicle you do not own, including any vehicle while used as a temporary substitute for "your covered auto", shall be excess over any other collectible insurance.

PART B – MEDICAL PAYMENTS COVERAGE

INSURING AGREEMENT

A. We will pay reasonable expenses incurred for necessary medical and funeral services because of "bodily injury":

1. Caused by accident; and

2. Sustained by an "insured".

We will pay only those expenses incurred for services rendered within 3 years from the date of the accident.

B. "Insured" as used in this Part means:

1. You or any "family member":

a. While "occupying"; or

b. As a pedestrian when struck by;

a motor vehicle designed for use mainly on public roads or a trailer of any type.

2. Any other person while "occupying" "your covered auto".

EXCLUSIONS

We do not provide Medical Payments Coverage for any "insured" for "bodily injury":

1. Sustained while "occupying" any motorized vehicle having fewer than four wheels.
2. Sustained while "occupying" "your covered auto" when it is being used as a public or livery conveyance. This Exclusion (**2.**) does not apply to a share-the-expense car pool.
3. Sustained while "occupying" any vehicle located for use as a residence or premises.
4. Occurring during the course of employment if workers' compensation benefits are required or available for the "bodily injury".
5. Sustained while "occupying", or when struck by, any vehicle (other than "your covered auto") which is:
   a. Owned by you; or
   b. Furnished or available for your regular use.
6. Sustained while "occupying", or when struck by, any vehicle (other than "your covered auto") which is:
   a. Owned by any "family member"; or
   b. Furnished or available for the regular use of any "family member".

   However, this Exclusion (**6.**) does not apply to you.
7. Sustained while "occupying" a vehicle without a reasonable belief that that "insured" is entitled to do so. This Exclusion (**7.**) does not apply to a "family member" using "your covered auto" which is owned by you.
8. Sustained while "occupying" a vehicle when it is being used in the "business" of an "insured". This Exclusion (**8.**) does not apply to "bodily injury" sustained while "occupying" a:
   a. Private passenger auto;
   b. Pickup or van; or
   c. "Trailer" used with a vehicle described in **a.** or **b.** above.
9. Caused by or as a consequence of:
   a. Discharge of a nuclear weapon (even if accidental);
   b. War (declared or undeclared);
   c. Civil war;
   d. Insurrection; or
   e. Rebellion or revolution.
10. From or as a consequence of the following, whether controlled or uncontrolled or however caused:
    a. Nuclear reaction;
    b. Radiation; or
    c. Radioactive contamination.
11. Sustained while "occupying" any vehicle located inside a facility designed for racing, for the purpose of:
    a. Competing in; or
    b. Practicing or preparing for;

    any prearranged or organized racing or speed contest.

LIMIT OF LIABILITY

A. The limit of liability shown in the Declarations for this coverage is our maximum limit of liability for each person injured in any one accident. This is the most we will pay regardless of the number of:
   1. "Insureds";
   2. Claims made;
   3. Vehicles or premiums shown in the Declarations; or
   4. Vehicles involved in the accident.

B. No one will be entitled to receive duplicate payments for the same elements of loss under this coverage and:
   1. Part **A** or Part **C** of this policy; or
   2. Any Underinsured Motorists Coverage provided by this policy.

OTHER INSURANCE

If there is other applicable auto medical payments insurance we will pay only our share of the loss. Our share is the proportion that our limit of liability bears to the total of all applicable limits. However, any insurance we provide with respect to a vehicle you do not own, including any vehicle while used as a temporary substitute for "your covered auto", shall be excess over any other collectible auto insurance providing payments for medical or funeral expenses.

PART C – UNINSURED MOTORISTS COVERAGE

INSURING AGREEMENT

A. We will pay compensatory damages which an "insured" is legally entitled to recover from the owner or operator of an "uninsured motor vehicle" because of "bodily injury":

1. Sustained by an "insured"; and

2. Caused by an accident.

The owner's or operator's liability for these damages must arise out of the ownership, maintenance or use of the "uninsured motor vehicle".

Any judgment for damages arising out of a suit brought without our written consent is not binding on us.

B. "Insured" as used in this Part means:

1. You or any "family member".

2. Any other person "occupying" "your covered auto".

3. Any person for damages that person is entitled to recover because of "bodily injury" to which this coverage applies sustained by a person described in **1.** or **2.** above.

C. "Uninsured motor vehicle" means a land motor vehicle or trailer of any type:

1. To which no bodily injury liability bond or policy applies at the time of the accident.

2. To which a bodily injury liability bond or policy applies at the time of the accident. In this case its limit for bodily injury liability must be less than the minimum limit for bodily injury liability specified by the financial responsibility law of the state in which "your covered auto" is principally garaged.

3. Which is a hit-and-run vehicle whose operator or owner cannot be identified and which hits:

a. You or any "family member";

b. A vehicle which you or any "family member" are "occupying"; or

c. "Your covered auto".

4. To which a bodily injury liability bond or policy applies at the time of the accident but the bonding or insuring company:

a. Denies coverage; or

b. Is or becomes insolvent.

However, "uninsured motor vehicle" does not include any vehicle or equipment:

1. Owned by or furnished or available for the regular use of you or any "family member".

2. Owned or operated by a self-insurer under any applicable motor vehicle law, except a self-insurer which is or becomes insolvent.

3. Owned by any governmental unit or agency.

4. Operated on rails or crawler treads.

5. Designed mainly for use off public roads while not on public roads.

6. While located for use as a residence or premises.

EXCLUSIONS

A. We do not provide Uninsured Motorists Coverage for "bodily injury" sustained:

1. By an "insured" while "occupying", or when struck by, any motor vehicle owned by that "insured" which is not insured for this coverage under this policy. This includes a trailer of any type used with that vehicle.

2. By any "family member" while "occupying", or when struck by, any motor vehicle you own which is insured for this coverage on a primary basis under any other policy.

B. We do not provide Uninsured Motorists Coverage for "bodily injury" sustained by any "insured":

1. If that "insured" or the legal representative settles the "bodily injury" claim and such settlement prejudices our right to recover payment.

2. While "occupying" "your covered auto" when it is being used as a public or livery conveyance. This Exclusion (**B.2.**) does not apply to a share-the-expense car pool.

3. Using a vehicle without a reasonable belief that that "insured" is entitled to do so. This Exclusion (**B.3.**) does not apply to a "family member" using "your covered auto" which is owned by you.

C. This coverage shall not apply directly or indirectly to benefit any insurer or self-insurer under any of the following or similar law:

1. Workers' compensation law; or

2. Disability benefits law.

D. We do not provide Uninsured Motorists Coverage for punitive or exemplary damages.

LIMIT OF LIABILITY

A. The limit of liability shown in the Declarations for each person for Uninsured Motorists Coverage is our maximum limit of liability for all damages, including damages for care, loss of services or death, arising out of "bodily injury" sustained by any one person in any one accident. Subject to this limit for each person, the limit of liability shown in the Declarations for each accident for Uninsured Motorists Coverage is our maximum limit of liability for all damages for "bodily injury" resulting from any one accident.

This is the most we will pay regardless of the number of:

1. "Insureds";
2. Claims made;
3. Vehicles or premiums shown in the Declarations; or
4. Vehicles involved in the accident.

B. No one will be entitled to receive duplicate payments for the same elements of loss under this coverage and:

1. Part A or Part B of this policy; or
2. Any Underinsured Motorists Coverage provided by this policy.

C. We will not make a duplicate payment under this coverage for any element of loss for which payment has been made by or on behalf of persons or organizations who may be legally responsible.

D. We will not pay for any element of loss if a person is entitled to receive payment for the same element of loss under any of the following or similar law:

1. Workers' compensation law; or
2. Disability benefits law.

OTHER INSURANCE

If there is other applicable insurance available under one or more policies or provisions of coverage that is similar to the insurance provided under this Part of the policy:

1. Any recovery for damages under all such policies or provisions of coverage may equal but not exceed the highest applicable limit for any one vehicle under any insurance providing coverage on either a primary or excess basis.
2. Any insurance we provide with respect to a vehicle you do not own, including any vehicle while used as a temporary substitute for "your covered auto", shall be excess over any collectible insurance providing such coverage on a primary basis.
3. If the coverage under this policy is provided:
   a. On a primary basis, we will pay only our share of the loss that must be paid under insurance providing coverage on a primary basis. Our share is the proportion that our limit of liability bears to the total of all applicable limits of liability for coverage provided on a primary basis.
   b. On an excess basis, we will pay only our share of the loss that must be paid under insurance providing coverage on an excess basis. Our share is the proportion that our limit of liability bears to the total of all applicable limits of liability for coverage provided on an excess basis.

ARBITRATION

A. If we and an "insured" do not agree:

1. Whether that "insured" is legally entitled to recover damages; or
2. As to the amount of damages which are recoverable by that "insured";

from the owner or operator of an "uninsured motor vehicle", then the matter may be arbitrated. However, disputes concerning coverage under this Part may not be arbitrated.

Both parties must agree to arbitration. If so agreed, each party will select an arbitrator. The two arbitrators will select a third. If they cannot agree within 30 days, either may request that selection be made by a judge of a court having jurisdiction.

B. Each party will:

1. Pay the expenses it incurs; and
2. Bear the expenses of the third arbitrator equally.

C. Unless both parties agree otherwise, arbitration will take place in the county in which the "insured" lives. Local rules of law as to procedure and evidence will apply. A decision agreed to by at least two of the arbitrators will be binding as to:

1. Whether the "insured" is legally entitled to recover damages; and
2. The amount of damages. This applies only if the amount does not exceed the minimum limit for bodily injury liability specified by the financial responsibility law of the state in which "your covered auto" is principally garaged. If the amount exceeds that limit, either party may demand the right to a trial. This demand must be made within 60 days of the arbitrators' decision. If this demand is not made, the amount of damages agreed to by the arbitrators will be binding.

PART D – COVERAGE FOR DAMAGE TO YOUR AUTO

INSURING AGREEMENT

A. We will pay for direct and accidental loss to "your covered auto" or any "non-owned auto", including their equipment, minus any applicable deductible shown in the Declarations. If loss to more than one "your covered auto" or "non-owned auto" results from the same "collision", only the highest applicable deductible will apply. We will pay for loss to "your covered auto" caused by:

1. Other than "collision" only if the Declarations indicate that Other Than Collision Coverage is provided for that auto.
2. "Collision" only if the Declarations indicate that Collision Coverage is provided for that auto.

If there is a loss to a "non-owned auto", we will provide the broadest coverage applicable to any "your covered auto" shown in the Declarations.

B. "Collision" means the upset of "your covered auto" or a "non-owned auto" or their impact with another vehicle or object.

Loss caused by the following is considered other than "collision":

1. Missiles or falling objects;
2. Fire;
3. Theft or larceny;
4. Explosion or earthquake;
5. Windstorm;
6. Hail, water or flood;
7. Malicious mischief or vandalism;
8. Riot or civil commotion;
9. Contact with bird or animal; or
10. Breakage of glass.

If breakage of glass is caused by a "collision", you may elect to have it considered a loss caused by "collision".

C. "Non-owned auto" means:

1. Any private passenger auto, pickup, van or "trailer" not owned by or furnished or available for the regular use of you or any "family member" while in the custody of or being operated by you or any "family member"; or
2. Any auto or "trailer" you do not own while used as a temporary substitute for "your covered auto" which is out of normal use because of its:
   a. Breakdown;
   b. Repair;
   c. Servicing;
   d. Loss; or
   e. Destruction.

TRANSPORTATION EXPENSES

A. In addition, we will pay, without application of a deductible, up to a maximum of $600 for:

1. Temporary transportation expenses not exceeding $20 per day incurred by you in the event of a loss to "your covered auto". We will pay for such expenses if the loss is caused by:
   a. Other than "collision" only if the Declarations indicate that Other Than Collision Coverage is provided for that auto.
   b. "Collision" only if the Declarations indicate that Collision Coverage is provided for that auto.
2. Expenses for which you become legally responsible in the event of loss to a "non-owned auto". We will pay for such expenses if the loss is caused by:
   a. Other than "collision" only if the Declarations indicate that Other Than Collision Coverage is provided for any "your covered auto".
   b. "Collision" only if the Declarations indicate that Collision Coverage is provided for any "your covered auto".

However, the most we will pay for any expenses for loss of use is $20 per day.

B. Subject to the provisions of Paragraph A., if the loss is caused by:

1. A total theft of "your covered auto" or a "non-owned auto", we will pay only expenses incurred during the period:
   a. Beginning 48 hours after the theft; and
   b. Ending when "your covered auto" or the "non-owned auto" is returned to use or we pay for its loss.
2. Other than theft of a "your covered auto" or a "non-owned auto", we will pay only expenses beginning when the auto is withdrawn from use for more than 24 hours.

Our payment will be limited to that period of time reasonably required to repair or replace the "your covered auto" or the "non-owned auto".

EXCLUSIONS

We will not pay for:

1. Loss to "your covered auto" or any "non-owned auto" which occurs while it is being used as a public or livery conveyance. This Exclusion (1.) does not apply to a share-the-expense car pool.
2. Damage due and confined to:
   a. Wear and tear;
   b. Freezing;
   c. Mechanical or electrical breakdown or failure; or
   d. Road damage to tires.

   This Exclusion (2.) does not apply if the damage results from the total theft of "your covered auto" or any "non-owned auto".
3. Loss due to or as a consequence of:
   a. Radioactive contamination;
   b. Discharge of any nuclear weapon (even if accidental);
   c. War (declared or undeclared);
   d. Civil war;
   e. Insurrection; or
   f. Rebellion or revolution.
4. Loss to any electronic equipment that reproduces, receives or transmits audio, visual or data signals. This includes but is not limited to:
   a. Radios and stereos;
   b. Tape decks;
   c. Compact disk systems;
   d. Navigation systems;
   e. Internet access systems;
   f. Personal computers;
   g. Video entertainment systems;
   h. Telephones;
   i. Televisions;
   j. Two-way mobile radios;
   k. Scanners; or
   l. Citizens band radios.

   This Exclusion (4.) does not apply to electronic equipment that is permanently installed in "your covered auto" or any "non-owned auto".
5. Loss to tapes, records, disks or other media used with equipment described in Exclusion 4.
6. A total loss to "your covered auto" or any "non-owned auto" due to destruction or confiscation by governmental or civil authorities.

   This Exclusion (6.) does not apply to the interests of Loss Payees in "your covered auto".
7. Loss to:
   a. A "trailer", camper body, or motor home, which is not shown in the Declarations; or
   b. Facilities or equipment used with such "trailer", camper body or motor home. Facilities or equipment include but are not limited to:
      (1) Cooking, dining, plumbing or refrigeration facilities;
      (2) Awnings or cabanas; or
      (3) Any other facilities or equipment used with a "trailer", camper body, or motor home.

   This Exclusion (7.) does not apply to a:
   a. "Trailer", and its facilities or equipment, which you do not own; or
   b. "Trailer", camper body, or the facilities or equipment in or attached to the "trailer" or camper body, which you:
      (1) Acquire during the policy period; and
      (2) Ask us to insure within 14 days after you become the owner.
8. Loss to any "non-owned auto" when used by you or any "family member" without a reasonable belief that you or that "family member" are entitled to do so.
9. Loss to equipment designed or used for the detection or location of radar or laser.
10. Loss to any custom furnishings or equipment in or upon any pickup or van. Custom furnishings or equipment include but are not limited to:
    a. Special carpeting or insulation;
    b. Furniture or bars;
    c. Height-extending roofs; or
    d. Custom murals, paintings or other decals or graphics.

    This Exclusion (10.) does not apply to a cap, cover or bedliner in or upon any "your covered auto" which is a pickup.
11. Loss to any "non-owned auto" being maintained or used by any person while employed or otherwise engaged in the "business" of:
    a. Selling;
    b. Repairing;

c. Servicing;

d. Storing; or

e. Parking;

vehicles designed for use on public highways. This includes road testing and delivery.

12. Loss to "your covered auto" or any "non-owned auto", located inside a facility designed for racing, for the purpose of:

a. Competing in; or

b. Practicing or preparing for;

any prearranged or organized racing or speed contest.

13. Loss to, or loss of use of, a "non-owned auto" rented by:

a. You; or

b. Any "family member";

if a rental vehicle company is precluded from recovering such loss or loss of use, from you or that "family member", pursuant to the provisions of any applicable rental agreement or state law.

LIMIT OF LIABILITY

A. Our limit of liability for loss will be the lesser of the:

1. Actual cash value of the stolen or damaged property; or

2. Amount necessary to repair or replace the property with other property of like kind and quality.

However, the most we will pay for loss to:

1. Any "non-owned auto" which is a trailer is $1500.

2. Electronic equipment that reproduces, receives or transmits audio, visual or data signals, which is permanently installed in the auto in locations not used by the auto manufacturer for installation of such equipment, is $1,000.

B. An adjustment for depreciation and physical condition will be made in determining actual cash value in the event of a total loss.

C. If a repair or replacement results in better than like kind or quality, we will not pay for the amount of the betterment.

PAYMENT OF LOSS

We may pay for loss in money or repair or replace the damaged or stolen property. We may, at our expense, return any stolen property to:

1. You; or

2. The address shown in this policy.

If we return stolen property we will pay for any damage resulting from the theft. We may keep all or part of the property at an agreed or appraised value.

If we pay for loss in money, our payment will include the applicable sales tax for the damaged or stolen property.

NO BENEFIT TO BAILEE

This insurance shall not directly or indirectly benefit any carrier or other bailee for hire.

OTHER SOURCES OF RECOVERY

If other sources of recovery also cover the loss, we will pay only our share of the loss. Our share is the proportion that our limit of liability bears to the total of all applicable limits. However, any insurance we provide with respect to a "non-owned auto" shall be excess over any other collectible source of recovery including, but not limited to:

1. Any coverage provided by the owner of the "non-owned auto";

2. Any other applicable physical damage insurance;

3. Any other source of recovery applicable to the loss.

APPRAISAL

A. If we and you do not agree on the amount of loss, either may demand an appraisal of the loss. In this event, each party will select a competent and impartial appraiser. The two appraisers will select an umpire. The appraisers will state separately the actual cash value and the amount of loss. If they fail to agree, they will submit their differences to the umpire. A decision agreed to by any two will be binding. Each party will:

1. Pay its chosen appraiser; and

2. Bear the expenses of the appraisal and umpire equally.

B. We do not waive any of our rights under this policy by agreeing to an appraisal.

PART E – DUTIES AFTER AN ACCIDENT OR LOSS

We have no duty to provide coverage under this policy if the failure to comply with the following duties is prejudicial to us:

A. We must be notified promptly of how, when and where the accident or loss happened. Notice should also include the names and addresses of any injured persons and of any witnesses.

B. A person seeking any coverage must:

1. Cooperate with us in the investigation, settlement or defense of any claim or suit.
2. Promptly send us copies of any notices or legal papers received in connection with the accident or loss.
3. Submit, as often as we reasonably require:
   a. To physical exams by physicians we select. We will pay for these exams.
   b. To examination under oath and subscribe the same.
4. Authorize us to obtain:
   a. Medical reports; and
   b. Other pertinent records.
5. Submit a proof of loss when required by us.

C. A person seeking Uninsured Motorists Coverage must also:

1. Promptly notify the police if a hit-and-run driver is involved.
2. Promptly send us copies of the legal papers if a suit is brought.

D. A person seeking Coverage For Damage To Your Auto must also:

1. Take reasonable steps after loss to protect "your covered auto" or any "non-owned auto" and their equipment from further loss. We will pay reasonable expenses incurred to do this.
2. Promptly notify the police if "your covered auto" or any "non-owned auto" is stolen.
3. Permit us to inspect and appraise the damaged property before its repair or disposal.

PART F – GENERAL PROVISIONS

BANKRUPTCY

Bankruptcy or insolvency of the "insured" shall not relieve us of any obligations under this policy.

CHANGES

A. This policy contains all the agreements between you and us. Its terms may not be changed or waived except by endorsement issued by us.

B. If there is a change to the information used to develop the policy premium, we may adjust your premium. Changes during the policy term that may result in a premium increase or decrease include, but are not limited to, changes in:

1. The number, type or use classification of insured vehicles;
2. Operators using insured vehicles;
3. The place of principal garaging of insured vehicles;
4. Coverage, deductible or limits.

If a change resulting from **A.** or **B.** requires a premium adjustment, we will make the premium adjustment in accordance with our manual rules.

C. If we make a change which broadens coverage under this edition of your policy without additional premium charge, that change will automatically apply to your policy as of the date we implement the change in your state. This Paragraph **(C.)** does not apply to changes implemented with a general program revision that includes both broadenings and restrictions in coverage, whether that general program revision is implemented through introduction of:

1. A subsequent edition of your policy; or
2. An Amendatory Endorsement.

FRAUD

We do not provide coverage for any "insured" who has made fraudulent statements or engaged in fraudulent conduct in connection with any accident or loss for which coverage is sought under this policy.

LEGAL ACTION AGAINST US

A. No legal action may be brought against us until there has been full compliance with all the terms of this policy. In addition, under Part **A**, no legal action may be brought against us until:

1. We agree in writing that the "insured" has an obligation to pay; or
2. The amount of that obligation has been finally determined by judgment after trial.

B. No person or organization has any right under this policy to bring us into any action to determine the liability of an "insured".

OUR RIGHT TO RECOVER PAYMENT

A. If we make a payment under this policy and the person to or for whom payment was made has a right to recover damages from another we shall be subrogated to that right. That person shall do:

1. Whatever is necessary to enable us to exercise our rights; and
2. Nothing after loss to prejudice them.

However, our rights in this Paragraph (**A.**) do not apply under Part **D**, against any person using "your covered auto" with a reasonable belief that that person is entitled to do so.

B. If we make a payment under this policy and the person to or for whom payment is made recovers damages from another, that person shall:

1. Hold in trust for us the proceeds of the recovery; and
2. Reimburse us to the extent of our payment.

POLICY PERIOD AND TERRITORY

A. This policy applies only to accidents and losses which occur:

1. During the policy period as shown in the Declarations; and
2. Within the policy territory.

B. The policy territory is:

1. The United States of America, its territories or possessions;
2. Puerto Rico; or
3. Canada.

This policy also applies to loss to, or accidents involving, "your covered auto" while being transported between their ports.

TERMINATION

A. Cancellation

This policy may be cancelled during the policy period as follows:

1. The named insured shown in the Declarations may cancel by:
   a. Returning this policy to us; or
   b. Giving us advance written notice of the date cancellation is to take effect.
2. We may cancel by mailing to the named insured shown in the Declarations at the address shown in this policy:
   a. At least 10 days notice:
      (1) If cancellation is for nonpayment of premium; or
      (2) If notice is mailed during the first 60 days this policy is in effect and this is not a renewal or continuation policy; or
   b. At least 20 days notice in all other cases.
3. After this policy is in effect for 60 days, or if this is a renewal or continuation policy, we will cancel only:
   a. For nonpayment of premium; or
   b. If your driver's license or that of:
      (1) Any driver who lives with you; or
      (2) Any driver who customarily uses "your covered auto";

      has been suspended or revoked. This must have occurred:

      (1) During the policy period; or
      (2) Since the last anniversary of the original effective date if the policy period is other than 1 year; or
   c. If the policy was obtained through material misrepresentation.

B. Nonrenewal

If we decide not to renew or continue this policy, we will mail notice to the named insured shown in the Declarations at the address shown in this policy. Notice will be mailed at least 20 days before the end of the policy period. Subject to this notice requirement, if the policy period is:

1. Less than 6 months, we will have the right not to renew or continue this policy every 6 months, beginning 6 months after its original effective date.
2. 6 months or longer, but less than one year, we will have the right not to renew or continue this policy at the end of the policy period.
3. 1 year or longer, we will have the right not to renew or continue this policy at each anniversary of its original effective date.

C. Automatic Termination

If we offer to renew or continue and you or your representative do not accept, this policy will automatically terminate at the end of the current policy period. Failure to pay the required renewal or continuation premium when due shall mean that you have not accepted our offer.

If you obtain other insurance on "your covered auto", any similar insurance provided by this policy will terminate as to that auto on the effective date of the other insurance.

D. Other Termination Provisions

1. We may deliver any notice instead of mailing it. Proof of mailing of any notice shall be sufficient proof of notice.
2. If this policy is cancelled, you may be entitled to a premium refund. If so, we will send you the refund. The premium refund, if any, will be computed according to our manuals. However, making or offering to make the refund is not a condition of cancellation.
3. The effective date of cancellation stated in the notice shall become the end of the policy period.

TRANSFER OF YOUR INTEREST IN THIS POLICY

A. Your rights and duties under this policy may not be assigned without our written consent. However, if a named insured shown in the Declarations dies, coverage will be provided for:

1. The surviving spouse if resident in the same household at the time of death. Coverage applies to the spouse as if a named insured shown in the Declarations; and
2. The legal representative of the deceased person as if a named insured shown in the Declarations. This applies only with respect to the representative's legal responsibility to maintain or use "your covered auto".

B. Coverage will only be provided until the end of the policy period.

TWO OR MORE AUTO POLICIES

If this policy and any other auto insurance policy issued to you by us apply to the same accident, the maximum limit of our liability under all the policies shall not exceed the highest applicable limit of liability under any one policy.

*

Index

References are to Pages

References are to Pages

References are to Pages

References are to Pages

References are to Pages

References are to Pages

References are to Pages

References are to Pages

†